THE MOST
TRUSTED NAME
IN TRAVEL

Arthur Frommer's

# EUROPE

By Arthur Frommer, Stephen Brewer, Jason Cochran, Teresa Fisher, Lucy Gillmore, Patricia Harris, David Lyon, John Newcomb, Margie Rynn, and Donald Strachan

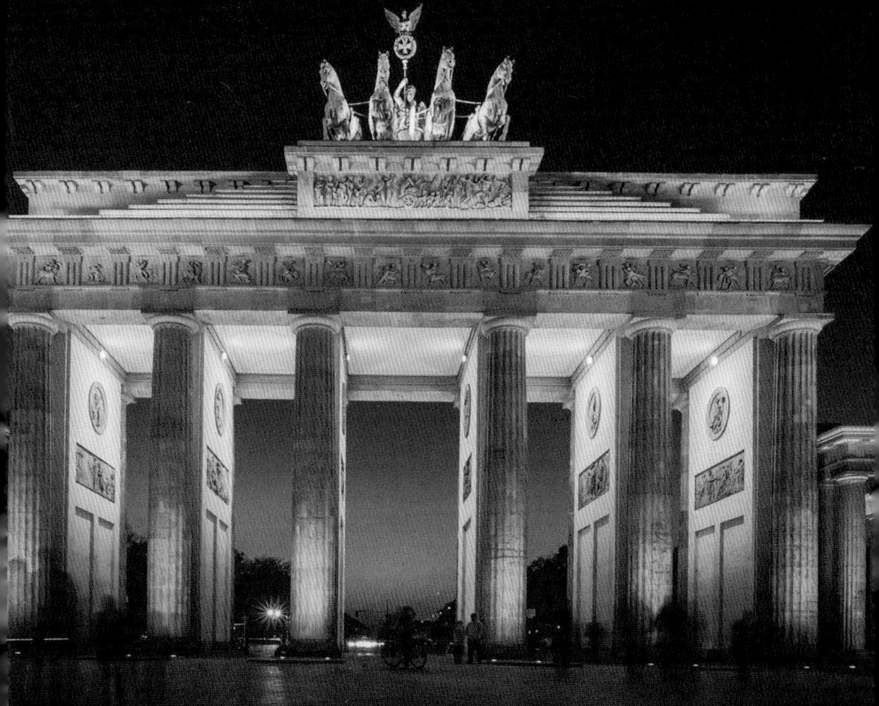

FrommerMedia LLC

Published by
**Frommer Media LLC**

Copyright © 2015 by Frommer Media LLC, New York City, New York. All rights reserved. No part of this publication may be reproduced, stored in a retrieval system, or transmitted in any form or by any means, electronic, mechanical, photocopying, recording, scanning or otherwise, except as permitted under Sections 107 or 108 of the 1976 United States Copyright Act, without the prior written permission of the Publisher. Requests to the Publisher for permission should be addressed to Support@FrommerMedia.com.

Frommer's is a registered trademark of Arthur Frommer. Frommer Media LLC is not associated with any product or vendor mentioned in this book.

ISBN 978-1-62887-208-8 (paper), 978-1-62887-209-5 (e-book)

Editorial Director: Pauline Frommer
Editor: Elizabeth Heath
Production Editor: Erin Geile
Cartographer: Liz Puhl
Photo Editor: Meghan Lamb
Editorial Assistant: Ross F. Walker
For information on our other products or services, see www.frommers.com.

Frommer Media LLC also publishes its books in a variety of electronic formats. Some content that appears in print may not be available in electronic formats.

Manufactured in China

5 4

## HOW TO CONTACT US

In researching this book, we discovered many wonderful places—hotels, restaurants, shops, and more. We're sure you'll find others. Please tell us about them, so we can share the information with your fellow travelers in upcoming editions. If you were disappointed with a recommendation, we'd love to know that, too. Please write to: Support@FrommerMedia.com

## FROMMER'S STAR RATINGS SYSTEM

Every hotel, restaurant and attraction listed in this guide has been ranked for quality and value. Here's what the stars mean:

★ Recommended
★★ Highly Recommended
★★★ A must! Don't miss!

## AN IMPORTANT NOTE

The world is a dynamic place. Hotels change ownership, restaurants hike their prices, museums alter their opening hours, and busses and trains change their routings. And all of this can occur in the several months after our authors have visited, inspected, and written about, these hotels, restaurants, museums and transportation services. Though we have made valiant efforts to keep all our information fresh and up-to-date, some few changes can inevitably occur in the periods before a revised edition of this guidebook is published. So please bear with us if a tiny number of the details in this book have changed. Please also note that we have no responsibility or liability for any inaccuracy or errors or omissions, or for inconvenience, loss, damage, or expenses suffered by anyone as a result of assertions in this guide.

# CONTENTS

# LIST OF MAPS



*Some map data © OpenStreetMap contributors (openstreetmap.org).*

## ABOUT THE AUTHORS

**Stephen Brewer** has been writing travel articles and guides for almost three decades. He frequently writes about England, Germany, and Italy for Frommer's.

**Jason Cochran** is a two-time winner of Guide Book of the Year by the Society of American Travel Writers' Lowell Thomas Travel Journalism Competition. He is the author of *Frommer's EasyGuide to London* and *Frommer's EasyGuide to Disney World, Universal, and Orlando.* His writing appears in publications including *Travel + Leisure, the New York Post, USA Today, Entertainment Weekly,* and *Budget Travel,* and he has been a regular commentator on, among others, *CBS This Morning, The Early Show (CBS), BBC World, Good Morning America,* and CNN. He is the former Executive Editor of AOL Travel and the current editor-in-chief of Frommers.com.

**Teresa Fisher** is an author, photographer, and travel writer who has had a life-long love affair with Switzerland. She has written extensively for a variety of publishers including Frommer's, National Geographic, and Thomas Cook. She has also penned more than 30 guidebooks and children's travel reference books on a wide variety of destinations worldwide, and features periodically on BBC local radio as a travel advisor. Her travel features have appeared in such British publications as *The Daily Telegraph, The Sunday Telegraph* and *The Sunday Times.* She specialises in European cities, adventure travel, and all things Alpine, dividing her time between photojournalism and her family-oriented website, www.familyskinews.com.

**Lucy Gillmore** was the deputy travel editor at *The Independent* newspaper but, after 8 years on the travel desk, left London to move to Scotland. She specializes in travel and food and writes for newspapers such as *The Guardian, The Independent* and *The Times* and magazines including *Food and Travel, Olive, House & Garden* and *Conde Nast Traveller.* After a couple of years in Edinburgh, she headed even farther north and now lives in the hills above Loch Ness in the Highlands.

**Patricia Harris** and **David Lyon** have journeyed the world for American, British, Swiss, and Asian publishers to write about food, culture, art, and design. Wherever they go, they are repeatedly drawn back to Spain for the flamenco nightlife, the Moorish architecture of Andalucía, the world-weary and lust-ridden saints of Zurbarán, and the design-obsessed streets of Barcelona. They can usually be found conversing with the locals in neighborhood bars while drinking the house wine and eating *patatas bravas* and grilled shrimp with garlic. They are the proprietors of HungryTravelers.com and authors of *Frommer's Spain* and *Frommer's EasyGuide to Barcelona and Madrid.*

**John Newcomb** is an experienced travel writer who enjoys nothing more than hitting the road.

**Margie Rynn** has been living in and writing about France for over 15 years. The author of *Pauline Frommer's Paris,* she has also written features for several travel magazines, including *Time Out New York* and *Budget Travel.* In a previous New York life, she acted in a Broadway play and performed her own one-woman show. Margie is married to a kind and understanding Frenchman, and they have a lovely 13-year-old son. She lives in Paris, France.

**Donald Strachan** is a travel and technology journalist who has written about Italy for publications worldwide, including *National Geographic Traveller, The Guardian, Sydney Morning Herald,* and CNN.com.

## ABOUT THE FROMMER TRAVEL GUIDES

For most of the past 50 years, Frommer's has been the leading series of travel guides in North America, accounting for as many as 24% of all guidebooks sold. I think I know why.

Though we hope our books are entertaining, we nevertheless deal with travel in a serious fashion. Our guidebooks have never looked on such journeys as a mere recreation, but as a far more important human function, a time of learning and introspection, an essential part of a civilized life. We stress the culture, lifestyle, history, and beliefs of the destinations we cover, and urge our readers to seek out people and new ideas as the chief rewards of travel.

We have never shied from controversy. We have, from the beginning, encouraged our authors to be intensely judgmental, critical—both pro and con—in their comments, and wholly independent. Our only clients are our readers, and we have triggered the ire of countless prominent sorts, from a tourist newspaper we called "practically worthless" (it unsuccessfully sued us) to the many rip-offs we've condemned.

And because we believe that travel should be available to everyone regardless of their incomes, we have always been cost-conscious at every level of expenditure. Though we have broadened our recommendations beyond the budget category, we insist that every lodging we include be sensibly priced. We use every form of media to assist our readers, and are particularly proud of our feisty daily website, the award-winning Frommers.com.

I have high hopes for the future of Frommer's. May these guidebooks, in all the years ahead, continue to reflect the joy of travel and the freedom that travel represents. May they always pursue a cost-conscious path, so that people of all incomes can enjoy the rewards of travel. And may they create, for both the traveler and the persons among whom we travel, a community of friends, where all human beings live in harmony and peace.

Arthur Frommer

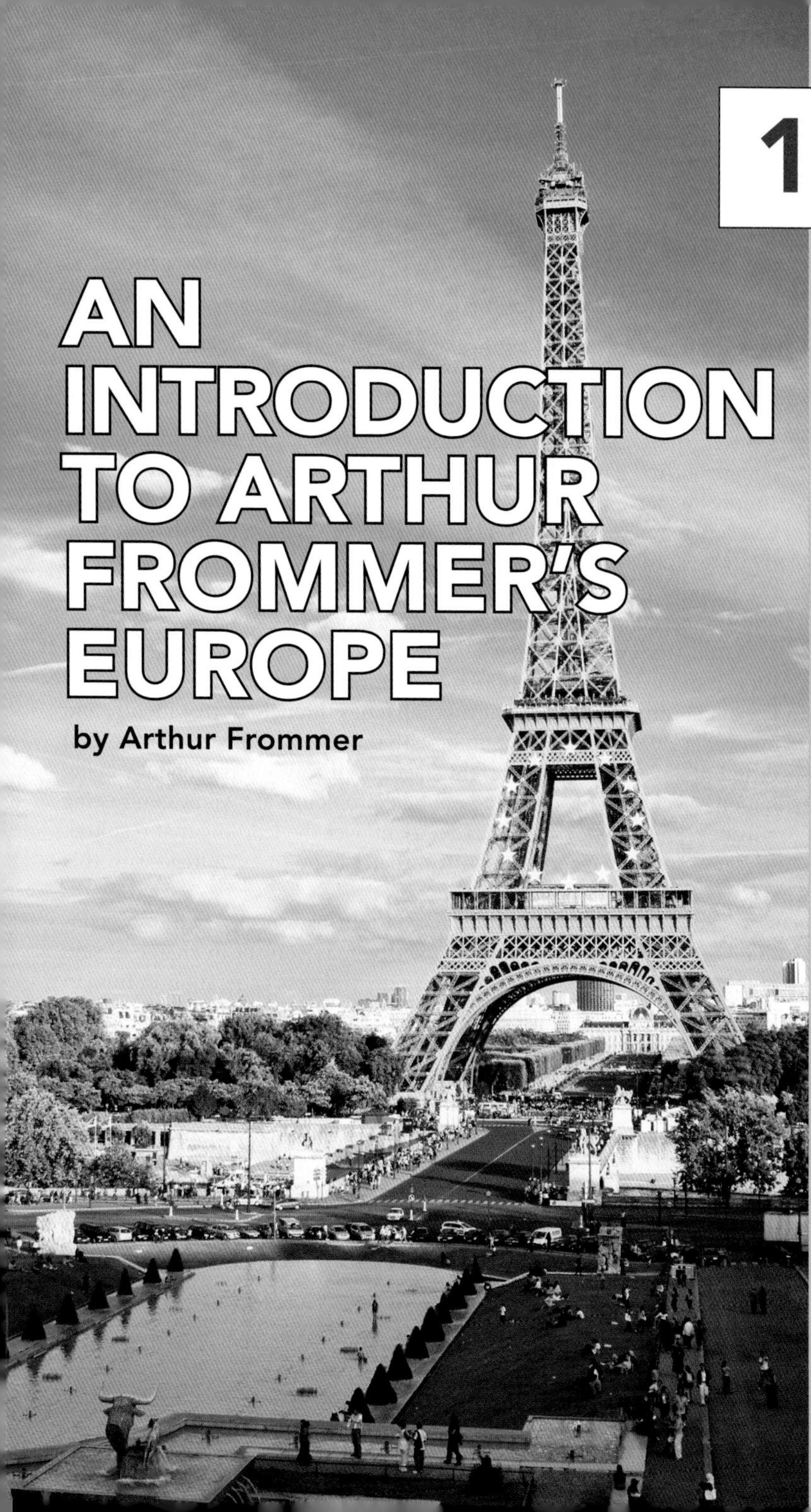

# AN INTRODUCTION TO ARTHUR FROMMER'S EUROPE

by Arthur Frommer

In the immediate post-war years, when only a small number of Americans flew trans-Atlantic to Europe, the airlines decided to grow that business by offering an enticing "multi-stopover" plan. On it, you bought a ticket to a remote European city, and simultaneously won the right, for not a penny more, to stop by air at several other European locations en route to the destination city and at several more on your way home.

---

I waxed rhapsodic about those stopover privileges in the transportation chapter of my earlier book, *Europe on $5 a Day.* I pointed out that by simply buying a moderately priced round-trip fare to Rome, for instance, you could stop for free, and via air, at Glasgow, Belfast, Manchester, London, Amsterdam, Brussels, Paris, Zurich, Geneva and Nice en route to the Italian capital, and at Milan, Stuttgart, Munich, Frankfurt, Hanover, and Bremen on your way home. It was a stupefying bonanza.

And that's the plan that I—and numerous other Americans—used for a grand European vacation in that faraway time. We flew there for at least a month's stay, went to nine or ten cities throughout that month, and enjoyed a kaleidoscopic encounter with the Old World. We heard several different languages, saw different stages of history, learned about varying national reactions to social and political problems, ate wildly contrasting cuisines, and grew dizzy with excitement over the learning that resulted.

And it's that several-nation trip that I hope to encourage with this guidebook to most of Western Europe.

The ability to make a multi-nation tour of Europe used to be confined to young aristocrats traveling with a man-servant in charge of several large trunks of clothing. We are now the first generation in human history to enjoy the same experiences without the advantage of great wealth, but simply on ordinary incomes. That gift—and it is a gift—should not be wasted on superficial travel arrangements designed by commercial hucksters; it should be accompanied by advance reading, an open mind, a sincere desire to understand the lifestyles and beliefs of other people, an urge to witness some of the greatest accomplishments of earlier generations—and also their many mistakes. Such an approach—dare I say?—can be greatly aided by the right kind of guidebook, one that enables its readers to learn from the European experience.

## Culture Comes First

Europe provides these lessons to an extraordinary extent. It is like a vast open-air museum—a treasure house, first, of art, music, drama, dance,

PREVIOUS PAGE: **The Eiffel Tower, Paris.**

Western Europe
0 200 mi
0 200 km
ICELAND
Norwegian Sea
FAROE ISLANDS (Denmark)
SHETLAND ISLANDS (U.K.)
ATLANTIC OCEAN
North Sea
SCOTLAND
Glasgow
Edinburgh
NORTHERN IRELAND
Belfast
UNITED KINGDOM
Newcastle
REPUBLIC OF IRELAND
Dublin
Limerick
Cork
Liverpool
Manchester
Leeds
WALES
Birmingham
ENGLAND
Cardiff
Bath
London
English Channel
Trondheim
NORWAY
Lillehammer
Bergen
Oslo
Skien
Stavanger
Kristiansand
SWEDEN
Umeå
Vaasa
FINLAND
Gulf of Bothnia
Turku
Uppsala
Stockholm
Gothenburg
Gotland
Baltic Sea
Copenhagen
Malmö
DENMARK
Kaliningrad
Bornholm (Denmark)
Gdansk
POLAND
Łódź
Hamburg
Elbe
Bremen
Berlin
NETHERLANDS
The Hague
Amsterdam
Rotterdam
GERMANY
Oder
Dresden
Bruges
Antwerp
Cologne
Brussels
BELGIUM
Rhine
Frankfurt am Main
Prague
CZECH REPUBLIC
SLOVAKIA
Le Havre
Seine
Heidelberg
Nürnberg
Danube
Bratislava
LUXEMBOURG
Stuttgart
Vienna
Paris
Strasbourg
Rennes
Munich
Salzburg
Loire
Zürich
LIECHTENSTEIN
AUSTRIA
HUNGARY
Lucerne
Bern
FRANCE
SWITZERLAND
La Rochelle
Limoges
Geneva
Zermatt
Ljubljana
SLOVENIA
Zagreb
CROATIA
Lyon
Milan
Venice
Bay of Biscay
Bordeaux
Po
Turin
SAN MARINO
BOSNIA & HERZEGOVINA
Genoa
Bologna
A Coruña
Florence
Toulouse
Nice
Bilbao
PROVENCE
MONACO
Siena
Côte d'Azur
Vigo
Ourense
Pamplona
Marseille
ITALY
Adriatic Sea
PYRENEES
ANDORRA
Porto
Valladolid
Duero
CORSICA (France)
Rome
Ebro
PORTUGAL
Zaragoza
Barcelona
Naples
Madrid
Sassari
Tajo
BALEARIC ISLANDS
Menorca
SARDINIA (Italy)
SPAIN
Tyrrhenian Sea
Lisbon
Valencia
Palma
Mallorca
Ibiza
Córdoba
Murcia
Palermo
Sevilla
Catania
SICILY
Granada
MEDITERRANEAN SEA
Málaga
Cadiz
Annaba
Algiers
Tunis
Gibraltar (U.K.)
Tangier
Ceuta (Spain)
Constantine
Oran
Setif
Sousse
MALTA
Melilla (Spain)
Batna
ALGERIA
Rabat
Sfax
Fez
Oujda
Djelfa
Biskra
Casablanca
MOROCCO
Laghouat
TUNISIA
Touggourt
Zuwarah
Tripoli
LIBYA

literature, science, philosophy and architecture—whose many museums and theatres, historic homes, structures, schools and more, are alone a reason to visit. If you should doubt the importance of those cultural treasures, you need only review in your mind the European greats who surely outnumber their past or present counterparts in other parts of the world, and have shaped our own outlooks and tastes. Again, if you should doubt the above assertion, simply review in your mind such Europeans as Beethoven, Mozart, and Verdi, Rembrandt, Rubens and Picasso, Madame Curie and Louis Pasteur, Rousseau, Immanuel Kant and Voltaire, Dante and Cervantes, Augustine and Luther, Wittgenstein and Bertrand Russell, Albert Einstein and Sigmund Freud. We go to Europe, among other reasons, to reflect on its extraordinary history of cultural and intellectual achievement, and to steep ourselves in the masterpieces they created.

## But Politics Are Also Important

We also go to Europe for a reason that many will cite as important, but other die-hards will angrily reject. We go to Europe to observe, judge, and learn from the many social and political policies that Europeans as a whole have almost universally adopted, and that should be considered—even by enemies of the European approach—in order to choose smart social and political policies at home. I'm not saying that life in Europe is better than elsewhere, but there are areas in which it can be legitimately claimed or denied that the Europeans have achieved the world's highest quality of life. Studying those claims through first-hand contact with Europe, perhaps discussing them with Europeans, is another major opportunity in a multi-nation tour of that continent. In what areas of life would most Europeans claim that they have reached a better place than the rest of us? For one, longevity in Europe is among the highest in the world, reaching an average lifespan of 82 and 83 years in at least a dozen major European nations, as compared with 79 years in the United States. (Nearly every European nation extends universal, free healthcare to all its citizens, perhaps the basis for its longevity record.) Europe has a larger and healthier segment of small businesses than we have in the United States, a far smaller percentage of teenage pregnancies (and an almost universal right to abortion), less HIV and AIDS, far less economic inequality than in the U.S., greater social and economic mobility from one class to another, a far greater percentage of workers belonging to unions (enjoying the right to collective bargaining), and most Europeans—as I have endlessly pointed out in Frommers.com—enjoy one full month of paid vacation per year, in addition to many more holidays with pay.

In a recent article in the electronic magazine Salon, analyst Alex Henderson pointed to numerous other areas in which Europeans enjoy a higher quality of life than in virtually every other continent, including North America, in addition to citing the advantages I have listed above. Among those benefits are lengthy and paid maternity leave, free

The Coliseum, Rome.

university tuition, and far too many other humane programs to list.

I'm not asserting that you should agree with my own opinions about the quality of life in Europe, but the citizens of every other country (including the United States) owe it to themselves to witness and judge the relatively uniform social and political policies in nearly every nation of Western Europe. And this you can do by undertaking a wholly independent tour of Europe in which you can interact with and speak with Europeans as only an independent tourist can do. And it's to support such a productive method of travel that this guidebook has been compiled.

## And Now, a Word About Expenses

But enough of the heavy lifting. It's also important in this introduction to deal with the far more prosaic topic of stretching your travel dollars in a trip to Europe. While that topic is already heavily emphasized in our guidebook series, let me briefly summarize some of the points we stress.

**Selecting hotels:** It's vital, first, to keep in mind that in Europe, the difference between a budget-priced hotel and a deluxe one is often psychological only; the budget hotels supply you with the same comfortable bed, the same freshly laundered sheets and pillow cases, the same freedom from outside noise, as the deluxe ones. When you have turned out the lights, slipped into bed, and closed your eyes, you do not know that you are in a budget hotel rather than a pricier one. What is important is simply to fall asleep. And what you are paying for in an expensive deluxe hotel are such inessentials as the uniformed porter on the sidewalk outside, the beauty parlor and gift shop in the lobby, the several attendants at the front desk, who are all the last thing you need. Consider saving the expense of a pretentious, upscale European lodging. And if you are truly adventurous, think about using a low-cost European hostel of the sort found in all its major cities; they no longer impose a maximum age limit on the guests they accept. In many months of the year, when young people are in school, the predominant clientele of European hostels are people of mature age enjoying a spectacular bargain for their lodging needs.

**Skipping hotels altogether:** It's no secret that across the globe nowadays, locals are opening their homes to guests in B&B-like situations, or renting out entire apartments or villas for the cost of a hotel room. Such lodgings are nearly always in real residential neighborhoods, where you'll get a far better feel for the local life than in the areas occupied by standard hotels. And they'll have kitchens, which can be a huge money-saver, as well as a joy in Europe, since they cause you to explore the local markets, buying farm-fresh foods at moderate costs. You can find rentals and B&B situations through such online sites as AirBnB.com, Wimdu.com, HomeAway.com, VRBO.com, Rentalo.com, EVrentals.com, and FlipKey.com.

In addition to offering apartment rentals, major and minor European cities present such value-conscious alternatives as college dorm rooms (in summer months when the students are away); rooms at monasteries and convents (a fascinating means for witnessing another way of life); and in some cities, guest-accepting houseboats and campgrounds. So get creative with your lodgings, to save money for more important needs.

**Dining where the locals do:** Know that the best, most authentic, and cheapest European meals are in restaurants found alongside vegetable and fruit markets, their mealtime ingredients obtained from the inexpensive victuals found across the street. Smart Europeans patronize such market locations, whose whereabouts will be known to the proprietor of your budget hotel.

**Picnicking in the out-of-doors:** Don't fail to make an occasional meal out of fresh ingredients purchased in a grocery, *boulangerie,* or deli and eaten picnic-style from a park bench or alongside a river. European cheeses, pâtés, and breads are legendary, and as good as many restaurant meals.

**Learn to use the low-cost air carriers:** Though getting around Europe isn't quite as cheap as it once was, an eruption of budget airlines can drastically cut that cost. The key to obtaining rock-bottom rates on the cheap carriers is to book your flights well in advance (aggressive lines like Ryanair, easyJet, Norwegian, Air Berlin, and more will often offer 10€–30€ promotional fares to fill their first few seats, with prices rising as dates get closer to departure. You'll find pricing for these carriers at such websites as DoHop.com, WhichAirline.com, and Momondo.com. Rather than creating a multi-stop itinerary that includes your flight across the Atlantic, book your round-trip flight to Europe separately. Then book your intra-European airfares with one or more of the low-cost carriers.

**Hop on a bus:** A number of bus lines have emerged in recent years to serve cost-conscious travelers, with extensive networks and excellent prices (especially when compared to hefty car-rental rates). A good source for inexpensive bus fares in Europe is www.buseurope.eu.

**Explore on your own:** For sightseeing, the best way to do that in Europe is on your own two feet, walking at random into the center of town and enjoying contacts with the local people you ask for directions or information. That confrontation with Europe is far more satisfying and instructive than the escorted variety, and many of your most memorable moments will occur when you walk on your own, carefree and open to people. Taking public transportation is also a "best way" to get around, enabling a more direct look at the life around you.

**The local cash:** As for money, avoid changing large sums into euros or other currencies before you leave home; the exchange rate you'll get at home is insulting, and you will also risk losing cash to pickpockets at the arrival airports or in the opening hours of your stay. Rather, get your European cash at the ATMs found here in exactly the same quantities as at home; the ATMs found at banks will usually deliver a good rate for your exchange. But to avoid a big loss to pickpockets, take out no more than the amount of cash you'll need for a day or so at a time.

**Pack light:** Doing so will allow you to come to peace with the probability that you will not be invited to a cocktail party or to meet royalty, making it unnecessary to have an outfit for every conceivable social occasion. Dress modestly. And enjoy the pleasant feeling of being unencumbered by multiple or heavy suitcases of unnecessary clothing. (Packing light is especially important for those planning to make use of budget airlines in Europe, as they charge hefty baggage fees.)

**Be smart about your smart phone:** If you need to keep in touch with loved ones or business associates back home, be sure to research your options before you start phoning and texting. If they don't take precautions before they leave, many travelers arrive home to a phone bill that's half the cost of their airfare. These can range from unlocking your phone so that you can insert a local chip when abroad; to renting a phone just for use in Europe; to picking a phone plan that goes light on the international roaming charges (like T-Mobile, currently). Research and determine what the best solution will be for you.

**Advance preparation:** Most importantly, precede your departure for Europe with a few nights of reading about the history, culture, lifestyle, and politics of the countries or cities you plan to visit. That advance preparation will be the single most effective method for turning the trip into an exciting, productive, and memorable activity.

A canal in Amsterdam.

### *Some special tips for readers seeking luxury in Europe*

Although the more glamorous parts of Europe aren't my own cup of tea, we do have readers attracted to that lifestyle, but anxious to achieve their dreams for very little money. For them, the following tactics might prove useful:

**Seek out the oddball room in the old deluxe hotels:** No

matter how grand or luxurious, if the European hotel was built more than a hundred years ago, chances are it possesses some rooms of diminutive size, convoluted shape, or without a tub and shower (and thereby priced below a normally sky-high level). As hard as it may be to believe, some of the most famous European hotels house a few budget-priced rooms with those characteristics, particularly the lack of a private bath.

**Bargain for the best in the off-season:** Though it's confined to a mere 5 months—from November 1 to March 31—there is an off-season in Europe, when prices plummet in the resort hotels (namely, those alongside lakes or the sea) and in cities almost exclusively devoted to tourism (Venice, Florence, Bruges, and the like). But even off-season rates are high at the more famous resorts, and the smart tourist bargains for further off-season discounts at such celebrated properties. If they have a vacancy off-season, they'll accede to your request to pay less.

**Devote your evenings to high-grade concerts and recitals:** You imbibe the finest champagne, figuratively speaking, but at a cost more suited to beer, when you spend your evenings in Europe at the most exalted of the performing arts. Avoid like the plague the "nightclubs"—the loud cabarets, the "themed" shows and girlie spectacles catering to tourists. With the exception perhaps of the Lido in Paris or the flamenco bars of Spain, there's not a single European nightspot worth crossing the street for. Travelers who devote their precious evenings to the Moulin Rouges or the Crazy Horse Saloons, have only themselves to blame.

**At top quality restaurants, share, split, and order by halves.** As a couple dining at a pricey place, order an appetizer apiece and then one main course, which you divide. Split the dessert. You'll have reduced the bill by almost half, and still have far too much to eat. And if the pâté de *foie gras* at $18 is irresistible but budget-breaking, ask for a half plate (*"une demi portion, s'il vous plait"*). It will still prove more than you need, but for only $9.

There's much more of this advice in the chapters that follow, and many valuable suggestions of where to stay, eat, and experience the best of Europe. We very much appreciate your support of our Frommer travel guides, and we earnestly hope that this carefully written book will serve your needs and bring you all the vaunted pleasures and lessons of Europe. And as for me, a longtime fan of travel to Europe, I wish you the very best of trips.

*Bon Voyage!*

***–Arthur Frommer***

2

# ENGLAND & SCOTLAND

by Jason Cochran & Lucy Gillmore

Though it is technically possible to fly non-stop between the U.S. and an uncrowded airport in Manchester, hardly any large percentage of travelers does so; we fly to London, instead. It is London, that immense and sprawling metropolis, which kicks off our experience of Great Britain—and does so, as I have frequently seen, in wondrous fashion. It confronts you in the very opening moments, as you present your passport, not with an impassive or even scowling immigration officer (as in other countries), but with the nearest equivalent to a host welcoming you to a country estate.

"Good morning," he (or she) says, in the orotund tones of a Shakespearean actor. "May I know the purpose of your visit?" "Thank you very much," handing back the passport, as if you are a valued guest. And whether it is your first visit or your fiftieth, you are made sharply aware through such courtesies that you have arrived at the center of a remarkable civilization.

If, during your stay in Great Britain, you show the same regard and politeness to the residents you meet, you will find Great Britain to be a refreshing change of pace from the harsher life we sometimes know at home.

***London kicks things off.*** Your stay will also be an immersion into an intense world of learning and new ideas. Though London is not the only city to possess scores of theatres, concert and lecture halls, bookstores, great museums, universities and schools of every sort, it nevertheless possesses more of these than any tourist could hope to visit. If you have even a smidgeon of interest in recent and ancient history, in parliamentary debates, in gatherings called to discuss public policies, you will find all of these on every day and in every section of the city.

Theatre is the major highlight of your stay—more playhouses and theatre auditoriums than in any other city, more provocative plays presented at any one time than in any other city, more of an effort to introduce new—and sometimes outlandish—ideas through the mechanism of dramatic plays, more skilled productions of classical works, more outstanding actors than in any other place, Some people I know are so enamored of the London theatre that they attend three plays a day—a normal matinee, a 5pm matinee, and then an evening performance. Except for a very few super hits,

PREVIOUS PAGE: **The Houses of Parliament and Big Ben.**

tickets are always available, and the avid theatregoer is constantly aglow at the ideas and talents they encounter here.

Be sure, as well, to attend a production of Shakespeare at the recreated Globe Theatre near the Thames, and make the trip there even if you don't have a reservation. Tell the ticket seller that you are willing to be a "groundling," standing in front of the stage (and sometimes leaning on it) as Londoners of the 1600s did.

There's more than theatre to attract you. Unlike in most other capital cities, the great national museums of London are almost always free of admission charges. From the British Museum to the British Library, from the National Gallery to the V&A, you pay not a single cent—not even a "suggested contribution"—to while away the days amid many of the most fascinating collections on earth.

As you do that, you will recall the famous comment of Samuel Johnson: "When a man is tired of London, he is tired of life, for there is in London all that life can afford."

***And then you go to Edinburgh.*** Where to after London? Our choice is Edinburgh. It's not the second largest city in Britain—such less-than-enchanting places as Birmingham, Manchester, Liverpool, Leeds, and Sheffield are each much bigger. But Edinburgh is clearly the second richest in castles and palaces, in museums and galleries, in cathedrals and historic homes, in parliament buildings, memorials—and whisky distilleries.

It's where you'll best hear tales of the rich and bloody history of Scotland, from residents who recently threw a scare into the British establishment by nearly voting to secede from Britain. It's where you'll learn about Robert Burns ("Scots wha hae . . .") and Sir Walter Scott, about William Wallace and Robert the Bruce, who gave the present-day population of Scotland such pride in themselves as a nation.

And if you're in Edinburgh in August, you'll witness the world's greatest array of month-long festivals, attracting dynamic people in giant numbers to attend the most provocative plays and presentations—literally hundreds of them—in all the world of theatre. Seek out a theatre expert—someone whose judgment you respect—to advise you which of them to see.

London followed by Edinburgh. I can't imagine a more delightful way to enjoy the rewards of travel, and I'm proud to introduce you to a chapter on them prepared by our Frommer experts. Have a jolly good time!

***–Arthur Frommer***

Oxford Circus.

# LONDON

Whether you realize it or not, London shaped your destiny. There's hardly a quarter of the globe that it hasn't changed. The United States was founded in reaction to London's edicts. Australia was first colonized with London's criminals. Modern Canada, South Africa, and New Zealand were cultivated from London. India's course was irrevocably changed by the aspirations of London businessmen, as were the lives of millions of Africans who were shipped around the world while Londoners lined their pockets with profits. You're holding proof in your hands of London's pull: that you bought this book, written in English somewhere other than in England, is evidence of London's reach across time and distance. And its dominion continues to this day: London is the world's most popular destination for foreign tourists.

London is inexhaustible. You could tour it for months and barely get to know it. Few cities support such a variety of people living in remarkable harmony. That diversity makes London like a cut diamond; approach it from a different angle each day, and it presents an entirely fresh shape and color. From famous stories to high style, London is many things in every moment.

## Essentials

**ARRIVING** Transatlantic flights almost always land at Heathrow, Europe's busiest international airport (LHR; 17 miles west), or Gatwick, perhaps the most disliked (LGW; 31 miles south). With a few minor exceptions, the other four airports, Stansted (STN; 37 miles northeast), Luton (LTN;

34 miles northwest), London City (LCY; in London's Docklands area), and Southend (SEN; 42 miles east) serve flights from Europe, and they're where cut-rate flyers and executive jets tend to go. Every airport offers some kind of rail connection to the central city, and that's the smart way to go. Tickets can be bought at windows in the arrivals halls, at machines, or online, where you get a discount. You'll rarely have to wait more than 20 minutes for the next train.

**Heathrow Express** (www.heathrowexpress.com; © **08456/00-15-15;** Express Saver £22 single, £35 return; kids 5 to 15 £11 single, £18 return; 15 min.) zooms to Paddington every quarter hour. First Class is a waste of money; Express Saver, the cheapest option for purchase online or at vending machines, is plenty plush. **Heathrow Connect** (www.heathrowconnect.com; © **084/5678-6975;** £11 single; 30–45 min.) is designed to give access to local stations, so it takes twice as long (still not long at all). It uses commuter-style carriages and leaves half-hourly. Both trains arrive at Paddington, where you can hop the Tube system or a taxi (above Platform 12). The cheapest way into town is by **London Underground** (£5.70 cash or £5.10 Oyster; 75 min.) using the Piccadilly Line.

**Gatwick Express** (www.gatwickexpress.com; © **084/5850-530;** £20 single, £35 return; kids £10/£18, discounts online; 30 min.) runs to and from Victoria. On **Thameslink & Great Northern** (www.thameslinkrailway.com; © **0345/026-4700;** £11 single; 30–50 min.), you can get to Gatwick via Blackfriars, Farringdon, St Pancras, or London Bridge stations four times an hour—service ends around 11:45pm.

**Stansted Express** (www.stanstedexpress.com; © **0845/600-7245;** from £19 single, £32 return; 47 min.) runs from Liverpool Street station. **Luton** has rail service from St Pancras station, Blackfriars, London Bridge stations by **Thameslink & Great Northern** (www.thameslinkrailway.com; © **0345/026-4700;** £14 single including 5-min. shuttle bus; 45 minutes; four times hourly). The correct stop is Luton Airport Parkway Station, linked by a 10-minute shuttle (5am–midnight) to the terminals.

**City Airport** is linked so expediently and affordably by the Docklands Light Railway (£4.80 cash, £3.30 Oyster; 25 min. from Tower Gateway or Bank) that it doesn't support commuter rail or coach service. **London Southend** (www.southendairport.com), too, is so well-connected to a shiny new station by **Greater Anglia** rail from Liverpool Street that buses don't bother to go there, so the train (£17 single; 53 min.) is the sole option.

**National Express** (www.nationalexpress.com; © **08717/818-8178**) buses will also go to airports (except City and Southend) for less than £10, although given traffic we don't recommend that. It's also the least expensive way to get from city to city in Britain (but not the fastest—that's usually the train), and because the country's not very big, it rarely takes more than a few hours to reach anywhere. Even Scotland is only 5 hours away. A major carrier with scads of departures, **Megabus**

(www.megabus.com; ✆ **090/0160-0900** or +44-141/352-4444) serves more than 100 cities across Europe, and charges as little as £1.50 for early bookings, although £19 to £45 for Edinburgh is a more typical rate. It accepts bookings 2 months ahead; book online to avoid phone fees. Both coach services depart from the miserable Victoria Coach Station, located behind Victoria railway station.

What's the best place to hear about inexpensive ground tours? Hostels. Drop into one; most of their lobbies are papered with brochures. Don't neglect their bulletin boards, either, since you may catch wind of a shared-ride situation that'll often cost you no more than your share of the gasoline (in Britain, *petrol*).

A few coach companies also travel to Europe, usually crossing the Channel with a ferry. Because of the pressure put on the market by mushrooming no-frills airlines, rates are extremely low. You'll pay as little as £21 one-way to Paris via **Eurolines** (www.eurolines.co.uk; ✆ **08717/81-81-78;** 8–10 hr. each way). Brussels or Amsterdam are £25 with a 7-day advance purchase. The trade-off: It can take all day, sunrise to sunset, to reach Paris by this method.

The original railway builders plowed their stations to every town of size, making it easy to see the highlights of the United Kingdom without getting near a car. The British whine about the declining quality of the service, but Americans, Canadians, and Australians will be blown away by the speed (and the cost, if they don't book ahead) of the system. Find tickets to all destinations through **National Rail** (www.nationalrail.co.uk/cheapestfare; ✆ **08457/48-49-50**) or the indispensable **TheTrainLine.com**. Seats are sold 12 weeks ahead, and early-bird bookings can yield some marvelous deals, such as £26 for a 4-hour trip to Scotland (£125 last-minute is common). When hunting for tickets, always search for "off-peak" (non–rush hour) trips going or coming from London in general, not a specific London station, because each London terminal serves various cities. Unfortunately, not every train company website accepts international credit cards; TheTrainLine does.

For trips from northwestern Europe, the train is more dignified. Unlike taking a flight, you won't need to set aside extra hours and pounds to get to and from airports; train stations are in the middle of town. We're living in marvelous times: The Channel Tunnel opened 2 decades ago (although they *still* seem to be working out the kinks), so

### Thinking of Driving in London? Don't!

Roads are clogged. In bad traffic, a trip from Heathrow to the western fringe of London can take 2 hours. And once you're in the city, just about every technology is deployed against you. There's a hefty fee just to drive to the city center. Roads are confusingly one-way. Cameras catch and ticket your honest driving errors. Parking is a fantasy. Many North Americans think of cars as the default transportation mode, but in London, trains are the thing. The only time to *maybe* drive a car is if you're on a cross-country tour—but in cities, it won't be easy for you.

you can reach the heart of Paris in an incredible 2 hours and 15 minutes from London. You can literally ride both the Tube and the Métro before lunch. In fact, you can ride both a black taxi and Space Mountain before lunch, since the Eurostar train alights in the middle of Disneyland Resort. Eurostar links London's St Pancras station with Paris, Brussels, Lille, and Calais, and from there, you can go just about anywhere using other trains.

Book via **Eurostar** (www.eurostar.co.uk; ✆ **08432/186-186** in the U.K. or +44 1233/61-75-75; phone bookings are US$7 more) itself or the U.S.-based **Rail Europe** (www.raileurope.com; ✆ **800/361-7245** in North America), which also sells European rail passes. Check both sites, because prices can differ, but do it early, because rates boom as availability decreases. Pay attention to the special offers on Eurostar's site; deals go as low as £69 round-trip in summer.

Ferry travel is obsolete, mostly used by people who need to transfer cars. No ferry to Europe sails directly to London. You'll have to get down to the Southern coastal towns of Folkestone and Dover (for France), or Portsmouth (for Spain). Unless you have your own car, it's hard to get to the ports of the France-destined lines. Advance purchase can be from £35 each way with a car and including taxes (150 min.) on **P&O Ferries** (www.poferries.com; ✆ **08716/64-64-64**). The aggregator **DirectFerries.co.uk** sells European routes from a rapidly diminishing roster of companies. One ocean liner still makes the storied 7-day trip between New York City and Southampton, which connects by rail to London in an hour. That's the ***Queen Mary* 2** (www.cunard.com; ✆ **800/728-6273**), which isn't scheduled often enough to work as return transportation for most people. Fares start around $1,000 per person, including all your food.

**CITY LAYOUT** London's neighborhoods were laid out during a period of wagon and foot traffic, when districts were defined in narrower terms than we define them today; indeed, for centuries people often lived complete lives without seeing the other side of town. Ironically, in our times, the Tube has done much to divide these districts from each other. Visitors are likely to hop a train between them and don't often realize how remarkably close together they really are. As a vestige of the old times, when the southern banks of the River Thames were swampy and undesirable, most of the major attractions in the city center lie on the north side of the water and are within a short walk of it. One major difference? Today, more than 8 million people reside in or within a few miles of the city.

**GETTING AROUND** Londoners call their 249-mile metro system the Underground, its official name, or just as commonly, "the Tube." Its elegant, distinctive logo—a red roundel bisected by a blue bar—debuted in 1913 as one of the world's first corporate symbols, and it remains one of the city's most ubiquitous sights. There's no older subway system on earth—the first section opened in 1863 while America was fighting it Civil War—and it often acts its age, with frequent delays and shutdowns. Check in the ticket hall to see what "engineering works" are scheduled.

## LONDON'S major EVENTS

England observes **eight public holidays** (also known as "bank holidays"): New Year's Day (Jan 1); Good Friday and Easter Monday (usually Apr); May Bank Holiday (first Mon in May); Spring Bank Holiday (usually last Mon in May, but occasionally the first in June); August Bank Holiday (last Mon in Aug); Christmas Day (Dec 25); and Boxing Day (Dec 26). If a date falls on a weekend, the holiday rolls over to the following Monday.

Hotel room rates may spike during these major tourist events:

**New Year's Eve Fireworks.** As Big Ben strikes midnight, London rings in the New Year with fireworks over the Thames and the Eye. It's so crowded that in 2015, the city began limiting attendance to 100,000 and requiring tickets. They cost £10 and can be booked via www.london.gov.uk/nye starting in late September.

**London Fashion Week.** Collections are unveiled for press and buyers at a biannual fashion festival also held in September. It's tough to get a runway show ticket, but there's a raft of slick events and parties across the city. www.londonfashionweek.co.uk. Mid-February and mid-September.

**London Marathon.** Although it draws some 35,000 runners, the marathon is also a kick for spectators, so hotels tend to fill up ahead of it. The starter pistol fires in Greenwich, and the home stretch is along Birdcage Walk near Buckingham Palace. If you want to run, apply by the previous October. www.virginmoneylondonmarathon.com. Sunday in mid-April.

**Chelsea Flower Show.** The Royal Horticultural Society, which calls itself a "leading gardening charity dedicated to advancing horticulture and promoting good gardening" (don't you just love the English?), mounts this esteemed show for 5 days in late May on the grounds of the Royal Hospital in Chelsea. The plants, all raised by champion green thumbs, are sold to attendees on the final day, but sadly, foreigners aren't usually able to get their plants past Customs. Tickets go on sale in November for this lilypalooza, and they're snapped up quickly. The event is so celebrated that it is covered on nightly prime-time TV. Really. www.rhs.org.uk. **✆ 0845/260-5000.**

**Trooping the Colour.** Never mind that the Queen was born in April. This is her birthday party, and as a present, she gets the same thing every year: soldiers with big hats. A sea of redcoats and cavalry swarm over Horse Guards Parade, 41 guns salute, and a flight of Royal Air Force jets slam through the sky overhead. The Queen herself leads the charge, waving politely to her subjects before they lose themselves in a hearty display of marching band prowess. Held in mid-June, it starts at 10am. If you want grandstand seats instead of standing in the free-for-all along the route, where you'll only get a fast glimpse of passing royalty, send a request in

There are 13 named lines, plus the Docklands Light Railway (DLR) serving East London and a tram line in South London, which together serve nearly 300 stations. Lines are color-coded: The Piccadilly is a peacock purple, the Bakerloo could be considered Sherlock Holmes brown, and so on. Navigating is mostly foolproof. Look for signs pointing to the color and name of the line you want. Pretty soon, more signs separate you according to the direction you want to go in, based on the Tube map.

January or February only to Brigade Major, Headquarters Household Division, Horse Guards, Whitehall, London, SW1A 2AX, United Kingdom. SASEs are required, so include an International Reply Coupon from your post office so that your return postage is paid. Otherwise, check out the Beating Retreat for a similar, if less elaborate, experience. www.householddivision.org.uk/trooping-the-colour. ✆ **020/7414-2479.**

**Wimbledon Championships.** Why watch on television yet again? Late June to early July. www.wimbledon.org. ✆ **020/8971-2473.**

**The Mayor's Thames Festival.** In conjunction with the Great River Race, nearly half a million souls attend London's largest free open-air arts festival, which includes more than 250 stalls selling food and crafts (Southwark Bridge is closed for a giant feast), a flotilla of working river boats, circus performers, and antique fireboats, tugs, and sailboats. The climax is the Night Carnival, a lavish procession of thousands of lantern-bearing musicians and dancers crawling along the water. Everything is topped off with barge-launched fireworks. September. www.thamesfestival.org. ✆ **020/7928-8998.**

**Guy Fawkes Night.** In 1605, silly old Guy Fawkes tried to assassinate James I and the entire Parliament by blowing them to smithereens in the Gunpowder Plot. Joke's on him: To this day, the Brits celebrate his failure by blowing up *him*. His effigy is thrown on bonfires across the country, fireworks displays rage in the autumn night sky, and more than a few tykes light their first sparklers in honor of the would-be assassin's gruesome execution. Although displays are scattered around town, including at Battersea Park and Alexandra Palace, get out of the city for the weekend nearest November 5, also called Bonfire Night, because the countryside is perfumed with the woody aroma of burning leaves on this holiday. Head to Mount Primrose Hill or Hampstead Heath for a view of the fireworks going off around the city.

**Lord Mayor's Show.** What sounds like the world's dullest public access program is actually a delightfully pompous procession, about 800 years old, involving some 140 charity floats and 6,000 participants to ostensibly show off the newly elected Lord Mayor to the Queen or her representatives. The centerpiece is the preposterously carved and gilt Lord Mayor's Coach, built in 1757—a carriage so extravagant it makes Cinderella's ride look like a Toyota Corolla. That's a lot of hubbub for a city official whose role is essentially ceremonial; the Mayor of London (currently Boris Johnson) wields the true power. All that highfalutin strutting is followed by a good old-fashioned fireworks show over the Thames between the Blackfriars and Waterloo bridges. It's held on the second Saturday in November. www.lordmayorsshow.org.

If you know the name/color of the line you want, as well as the direction of your destination, the signs will march you to the platform you need. Nearly every station is combed with staircases. You'll shuffle through warrens of cylindrical tunnels, many of them faced in custard-yellow tiles and overly full of commuters, and you'll scale alpine escalators lined with ads. Stand to the right so "climbers" can pass you.

### About British Money

The British pound (£1), a small, chunky, gold-colored coin, is usually accepted in vending machines, so you can never have too many in your pocket. It's commonly called a "quid." Like money in America, Canada, and Australia, it's divided into 100 pennies (p)—the plural, "pence," is used to modify amounts over 1p. Pence come in 1p, 2p, 5p, 10p, 20p, and 50p coins. You'll see large bull's-eye £2 coins, too. Bills come in £5, £10, £20, and £50. Now and then, you'll receive notes printed by the Bank of Scotland; they're perfectly valid, but an increase in forgeries means some shops refuse them. Banks will exchange them.

Be quick when using ATMs. Retrieve your card immediately from ATM slots; many machines suck them in within 10 to 15 seconds, for security. Should that happen, you'll have to petition the bank to have it returned to you.

The Tube shuts down nightly from Sunday to Thursday. Exact times for first and final trains are posted in each station (using the 24-hr. clock), but the Tube generally operates from 5:30am (0530) to just after midnight (0000), and Sundays 7am (0700) to 11:30pm (2330). On Friday and Saturday nights, many lines in Central London run every 10 minutes all night long: "Night Tube" trains are the Piccadilly, Victoria, Central, and Jubilee lines, plus the Charing Cross branch of the Northern line. Still, if you plan to take the train after midnight, always check the Night Tube map and schedule beforehand.

One of the groovier things about the Underground is the electronic displays on platforms that tell you how long it'll be until the next train. A 24-hour information service is also available at ✆ **0343/222-1234.** The best resource is the TfL Journey Planner, online at **www.tfl.gov.uk/journeyplanner**. The best resource is the free app **Citymapper,** which tells you which Tube, bus, or train to use, how long it takes, and includes mapped walking directions to the nearest stop.

There are three ways to pay for your Tube ride:

- **In cash, per ride.** It doesn't make sense to buy at vending machines per ride. Why? The math. It costs about $7,920 in winter to fly 3,500 miles from London to New York City in first class on British Airways—about $2.28 per mile. To travel a mile in zone 1 on the Underground, the cash fare is £4.80 (about $7.40). So it costs 3½ times more to go a mile on the Tube than to go a mile in transatlantic First Class. Bus drivers don't take cash, so buy multiple rides ahead of time via cards (the next options).
- **Via Travelcard.** Aimed at tourists, it's an unlimited pass for 1 or 7 days on the Tube, rail, and bus. "Day Anytime" Travelcards for zones 1 through 3 with no timing restrictions are £12. If you find you have to pop into a zone that isn't covered by your card, buy an extension from the ticket window before starting your journey; it's usually £1.50 to £2 more. Seven-Day Travelcards cost adults £32 for travel anytime

in zones 1 and 2. For Travelcard prices that include more zones, visit **www.tfl.gov.uk/tickets**.

- **Via Oyster Pay As You Go (PAYG).** This is the best option, and it's what locals use. Rub this credit card–size pass on yellow dots at the turnstiles and you get the lowest fares. You load it with cash and it debits as you go, no tickets required, on all forms of in-city public transit. No matter how many times you ride the Tube (debited at £2.30 in zone 1—that's a lot better than the £4.80 cash fare!) and bus (debited as £1.50—you can't pay cash on a bus), the maximum taken off your card in a single day will **always be less** than what an equivalent Day Travelcard would cost. Non-stop Oyster use will always peak at £6.40 for anytime travel in zones 1 and 2, versus the flat rate of £12 you'd have paid if you'd bought an equivalent Travelcard. Getting an Oyster usually requires a £5 deposit, but you can get that back before you skip town at any Tube ticket office (there's also a desk at Heathrow; ID may be requested). It won't get erased if you keep it beside your mobile phone. And if you don't use up all the money you put on it, you can get a refund as long as there's less than £10 value left on your card. (Travelcards offer no refunds for unused monies.)

It's most economical to get an Oyster PAYG and then do everything you can to plan days during which you don't take transport at all. A significant aspect of that strategy is choosing a hotel that's within walking distance of lots of the things you want to do. Fortunately, the city's extremely walkable. Trains go shockingly slowly (34kmph/21 mph is the *average* and has been for over 100 years); and in the center of town, stops are remarkably close together and the stairs can wear you out. In fact, if your journey is only two or three stations, you'll often find it less strenuous to simply walk.

## The Neighborhoods in Brief

**SOHO, COVENT GARDEN & CENTRAL WEST END** London's undisputed center of nightlife, restaurants, and theater, the West End seethes with tourists and merry-makers. Oxford Street is the city's premier shopping corridor; the western half between Oxford Circus and Marble Arch is the classier end, with marquee department stores such as Selfridges and Marks & Spencer. Prim Trafalgar Square, dominated by the peerless National Gallery, has often been called London's focal point.

**THE CITY** The City is where most of London's history happened. It's where Romans cheered gladiators. It's where the Great Fire raged. And, more recently, it's where the Deutsche Luftwaffe focused many of its nocturnal bombing raids, which is why you'll find so little evidence of the aforementioned events. Outside of working hours, the main thing you'll see in The City is your own reflection in the facade of corporate fortresses. Although this is where you'll find such priceless relics as the

Tower of London, St Paul's Cathedral, the Tower Bridge, the Bank of England, and the Monument to the Great Fire, many remnants are underfoot, since much of the spider web of lanes and streets dates back to the Roman period.

**WESTMINSTER, INCLUDING ST JAMES'S** It's a district tourists mostly see by day. South of Trafalgar Square, you'll find regiments of robust government buildings but little in the way of hotels or food. Whitehall's severity doesn't spread far. Just a block east, its impenetrable character gives way to the proud riverside promenade of Victoria Embankment, overlooking the London Eye, and just a block west, to the greenery of St James's Park, which is, in effect, Buckingham Palace's front yard. North of the park, the staid streets of St James's are even more exclusive than Mayfair's, if that's possible.

**SOUTH BANK & SOUTHWARK** During Southwark's recent rehabilitation from a crumbling industrial district, a blighted power station became one of the world's greatest museums (the Tate Modern), a master playwright's theater was re-created (the Globe), and a sublime riverfront path replaced the coal lightermen's rotting piers. A dramatic showpiece (the National Theatre) anchors them. Now, the South Bank, which stretches from the London Eye east to Tower Bridge, has reclaimed its status as a pleasure garden, and its once-dank railway viaducts are filled with cafes, reasonable restaurants, and foodie heaven Borough Market.

**KENSINGTON, KNIGHTSBRIDGE & EARL'S COURT** Here, one expensive neighborhood bleeds into another. South Kensington draws the most visitors to its grand museums, the V&A, the Natural History Museum, and the Science Museum; and Knightsbridge is where moneyed foreigners spend and brag—London now has the most billionaires in the world, nearly twice as many as New York or Moscow. Privilege has long had an address here—Kensington Palace, at the Gardens' western end, is where Diana lived and it's the official London home of Prince William and Kate and their royal offspring.

### Pass on the London Pass

The heavily promoted **London Pass** (www.londonpass.com) gets you into a bevy of attractions for a fixed price (such as £52 a day or £71 for 2 days), but is unlikely to pay off in the small amount of time you're given to use it. Only the version that lasts 6 days (£116 adult, £80 child) would potentially pay off, but still only marginally and only if you don't take much time for meals.

**Historic Royal Palaces** operates The Banqueting House, Hampton Court, Kensington Palace, Kew Palace, and the Tower of London. An annual membership pass will possibly save you money if you plan to see several of them; do the math (www.hrp.org.uk; ✆ **0844/482-7788;** £47 one adult, £71 two adults, £59 for one adult plus up to six children, £90 two adults plus up to six children).

The British Library.



## Exploring London

England has been a top dog for 500 years, and London is where it keeps its bark. Many of the world's finest treasures came here during the Empire and never left. Most cities store their best goodies in one or two brand-name museums. In London, riches hide everywhere. The major attractions could by themselves occupy months of contemplation. But the sheer abundance of history and wealth—layer upon layer of it—means that London boasts dozens of exciting smaller sights, too. You could spend a lifetime seeing it all, so you'd better get started.

### SOHO, COVENT GARDEN & NEARBY

**The British Library ★★★** MUSEUM  One of the planet's most precious collections of books, maps, and manuscripts, the **Treasures of the British Library** at the Sir John Ritblat Gallery, is displayed in a cool, climate-controlled suite of black cases and rich purple carpeting. The display changes, but it has included:

- Two of the four known copies of the **Magna Carta,** 800 years old in 2015
- The Beatles' first lyric doodles: "A Hard Day's Night" on Julian Lennon's first birthday card (with a choo-choo on it) and "Strawberry Fields Forever," sketched on Lufthansa airline notepaper
- The **Diamond Sutra,** the oldest known printed book, which was found in a Chinese cave in 1907 and was probably made by woodblock nearly 600 years before Europeans developed similar technology
- Jane Austen's diary and writing desk

London Attractions
0
1/2 mi
0
0.5 km
PRIMROSE HILL
Regent's Park Road
PRIMROSE HILL
CAMDEN TOWN
Camden Town
Camden High St.
Pratt St.
Camden St.
Regent's Canal
Parkway
Delancey St.
CAMDEN
Rd.
Albert
Avenue Rd.
London Zoo
Prince
Wellington Rd.
REGENT'S PARK
Albany St.
NW1
Eversholt St.
Abercorn Pl.
NW8
Maida Vale
Lord's Cricket Ground
Boating Lake
QUEEN MARY'S GARDENS
Euston Station
Euston
Hampstead Rd.
Albany St.
EUSTON
Euston Rd.
Euston Sq.
Maida Vale Rd.
St. John's Wood Rd.
Park Rd.
MAIDA VALE
LISSON GROVE
W9
Lisson Grove
Church St.
Rossmore Rd.
Euston Rd.
Gower St.
Great Portland St.
Tottenham Court Rd.
Warwick Avenue
Marylebone Station
Baker St.
Marylebone Rd.
Regent's Park
Marylebone
ST. MARY'S CHURCHYARD
Edgware Rd.
Marylebone Rd.
MARYLEBONE
Portland Pl.
Gt. Portland St.
BLOOMSBURY
Goodge St.
Harrow Rd.
Harrow Rd.
Edgware Rd.
Gloucester Pl.
Baker St.
FITZROVIA
Goodge St.
Paddington
Mortimer St.
Tottenham Court Rd.
Bishop's Bridge Rd.
Paddington Station
PADDINGTON
WESTMINSTER
W1
Cavendish Square
Westbourne Terr.
Paddington
Sussex Gardens
Edgware Rd.
George St.
Portman Square
Wigmore St.
Oxford St.
Oxford Circus
Soho Square
Seymour St.
Oxford St.
Oxford St.
Bond St.
Hanover Sqare
W2
Marble Arch
SOHO
BAYSWATER
Sussex Square
Bayswater Rd.
Regent St.
Bayswater
Lancaster Gate
Speakers Corner
Grosvenor Square
Shaftesbury
Queensway
Piccadilly Circus
Berkeley Square
Piccadilly
Regent St.
The Long Water
HYDE PARK
MAYFAIR
Park Ln.
KENSINGTON GARDENS
Green Park
St. James's Square
Round Pond
Piccadilly
ST. JAMES'S
Pall Mall
The Serpentine
The Mall
Kensington Palace
GREEN PARK
St. James's Palace
Hyde Park Corner
ST. JAMES'S PARK
Albert Memorial
Constitution Hill
Queen Victoria Memorial
Kensington Rd.
Kensington Gore
Kensington Rd.
Knightsbridge
Buckingham Palace
Birdcage Walk
Knightsbridge
Royal Albert Hall
KNIGHTSBRIDGE
Grosvenor Pl.
PALACE GARDENS
St. James's Park
Buckingham Gate
KENSINGTON
Queen's Gate
SW7
Exhibition Rd.
Harrods
Sloane St.
Belgrave Square
Victoria & Albert Museum
Brompton Rd.
Belgrave Pl.
Grosvenor Gardens
Victoria
WESTMINSTER
Gloucester Rd.
Natural History Museum
Eaton Square
Victoria
Westminster Cathedral
Cromwell Rd.
South Kensington
Thurloe Square
BROMPTON
Cadogan Square
BELGRAVIA
Eccleston St.
Palace St.
Victoria Station
Wilton Rd.
SW1
Gloucester Rd.
Pelham St.
Sloane St.
Ebury St.
Vauxhall Bridge Rd.
Vincent Square
Sloane Ave.
Sloane Square
Sloane Sq.
Victoria Coach Station
Buckingham
Eccleston Square
VICTORIA
SOUTH KENSINGTON
Onslow Square
Old Brompton Rd.
Fulham Rd.
Warwick Way
Belgrave Rd.
Rd.
Lower Sloane St.
Pimlico Rd.
Warwick Square
Pimlico
KENSINGTON & CHELSEA
SW3
King's Rd.
Ebury Bridge Rd.
Sutherland St.
PIMLICO
The Boltons
Chelsea Square
Sydney St.
CHELSEA
Chelsea Bridge Rd.
Lupus St.
Royal Hospital Rd.
Fulham Rd.
King's Rd.
SW10
Chelsea Embankment
Chelsea Bridge
Thames
Grosvenor Rd.
Albert Bridge
Nine Elms

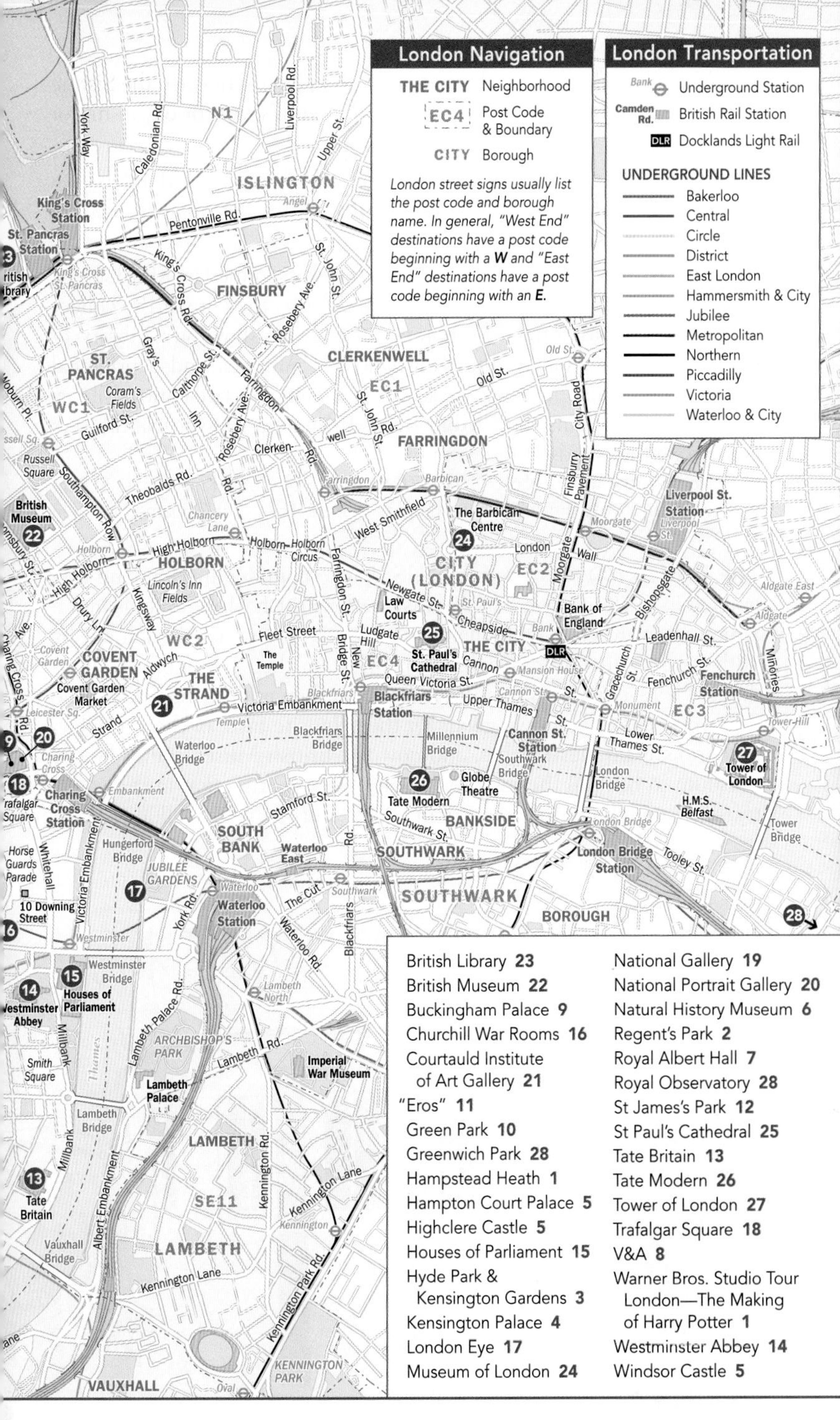
London Navigation
THE CITY Neighborhood
EC4 Post Code & Boundary
CITY Borough
London street signs usually list the post code and borough name. In general, "West End" destinations have a post code beginning with a W and "East End" destinations have a post code beginning with an E.
London Transportation
Bank Underground Station
Camden Rd. British Rail Station
DLR Docklands Light Rail
UNDERGROUND LINES
Bakerloo
Central
Circle
District
East London
Hammersmith & City
Jubilee
Metropolitan
Northern
Piccadilly
Victoria
Waterloo & City
British Library 23
British Museum 22
Buckingham Palace 9
Churchill War Rooms 16
Courtauld Institute of Art Gallery 21
"Eros" 11
Green Park 10
Greenwich Park 28
Hampstead Heath 1
Hampton Court Palace 5
Highclere Castle 5
Houses of Parliament 15
Hyde Park & Kensington Gardens 3
Kensington Palace 4
London Eye 17
Museum of London 24
National Gallery 19
National Portrait Gallery 20
Natural History Museum 6
Regent's Park 2
Royal Albert Hall 7
Royal Observatory 28
St James's Park 12
St Paul's Cathedral 25
Tate Britain 13
Tate Modern 26
Tower of London 27
Trafalgar Square 18
V&A 8
Warner Bros. Studio Tour London—The Making of Harry Potter 1
Westminster Abbey 14
Windsor Castle 5
ISLINGTON
N1
FINSBURY
CLERKENWELL
EC1
FARRINGDON
ST. PANCRAS
WC1
HOLBORN
WC2
COVENT GARDEN
THE STRAND
CITY (LONDON)
EC2
THE CITY
EC4
EC3
SOUTH BANK
BANKSIDE
SOUTHWARK
BOROUGH
LAMBETH
SE11
VAUXHALL
King's Cross Station
St. Pancras Station
Liverpool St. Station
Fenchurch Station
Blackfriars Station
Cannon St. Station
London Bridge Station
Charing Cross Station
Waterloo Station
Waterloo East
The Barbican Centre
Bank of England
Law Courts
The Temple
St. Paul's Cathedral
Tate Modern
Globe Theatre
Tower of London
H.M.S. Belfast
Tower Bridge
British Museum
Covent Garden Market
Trafalgar Square
Horse Guards Parade
10 Downing Street
Houses of Parliament
Westminster Abbey
Lambeth Palace
Imperial War Museum
Tate Britain
JUBILEE GARDENS
ARCHBISHOP'S PARK
KENNINGTON PARK
Thames

- Michelangelo's letter to his dad telling him he had finished the Sistine Chapel and pages from **Leonardo da Vinci's notebook,** in mirror writing
- Music in the hand of Mozart, Handel, Beethoven, and Mendelssohn (*The Wedding March*)—you can listen to the final works on headphones



**The King's Library,** some 85,000 tomes assembled by King George III, floats in a glassed-in central tower and forms the core of the collection, like Thomas Jefferson's library does for Washington's Library of Congress—which means the King who lost America and a principal engineer of the loss provided the seeds for their respective nations' libraries. The hall contains the **Philatelic Exhibition,** 500 vertical drawers containing thousands of rare stamps.

96 Euston Rd. NW1. www.bl.uk. ✆ **01937/546-060.** Free. Tube: King's Cross St Pancras. Mon and Wed–Fri 9:30am–6pm, Tues 9:30am–8pm, Sat 9:30am–5pm, Sun 11am–5pm.

**The British Museum ★★★** MUSEUM Founded in 1753 and first opened in 1759 in a converted mansion, the British Museum is as much a monument to great craftsmanship as it is to the piracy carried out by 18th- and 19th-century Englishmen, who, on their trips abroad, plundered whatever goodies they could find and then told the bereft that the thievery was for their own good. Yet the exquisite taste of these English patriarchs is unquestionable, and now the British Museum may be the museum to beat all the rest. In fact, it's the top attraction in the country—6.7 million people visited in 2013. Put on your walking shoes, because it's huge.

The British Museum.

Holdings are grouped in numbered rooms by geography, with an emphasis on the Greek and Roman Empires, Europe, and Britain. Dominating the center of the glass-roofed **Great Court** like a drum in a box, the cream-and-gold, round **Reading Room,** completed in 1857, was once part of the British Library. Patrons had to apply for tickets, and they included Lenin and Karl Marx, who developed their political theories here; other habitués included Bram Stoker, Sir Arthur Conan Doyle, and Virginia Woolf, who wrote upon entering, "one stood under the vast dome, as if one were a thought in the huge bald forehead which is so splendidly encircled by a band of famous names." The Reading Room still houses some 25,000 books, but is usually closed to the public.

Consider renting a hand-held audio/video tablet (£5, both adult and kids' versions) that spotlights 200 of the best objects. From 10:30am to 3pm on weekends, it lends free kids' backpacks including discovery maps. The website also has themed tour plans that cost nothing—useful because maps range from £2 to £6 depending on the level of information you want. But don't miss:

- The museum's most famous, and most controversial, possessions are the so-called **Elgin Marbles,** gingerly referred to as **The Sculptures of the Parthenon** (rooms 18 and 19) to disguise imperialist provenance. These slab sculptures (called friezes and metopes), plus some life-size weathered statuary, once lined the pediment of the famous Parthenon atop Athens's Acropolis. They're laid out in the gallery in the approximate position in which they appeared on the Parthenon, only facing inward so you can admire them.
- Fragments of **sculptures from The Mausoleum at Halikarnassos,** one of the lost Seven Wonders of the Ancient World, loom in room 21.
- The pivotal **Rosetta Stone** (196 B.C.), in room 4, is what helped linguists crack hieroglyphics, and its importance to anthropology can't be exaggerated. Napoléon's soldiers found it in Egypt in 1799, but the British nabbed it in 1801.
- The array of **Egyptian Mummies** in rooms 62, 63, and 64 petrify living children, and on your visit, they'll probably be thronged as usual. In addition to the wizened, raisin-like corpses, there are painted coffins, and the hair and lung of the scribe Sutimose, dating from 1100 B.C.
- Kids also stare moon-eyed at crumpled, leather-faced **Lindow Man** in room 50; he was discovered, throat slit, in a Cheshire bog nearly 2,000 years after his brutal demise.

The **Great Court Restaurant** above the Reading Room serves a full afternoon tea from 3pm for just £20—a bargain (✆ **020/7323-8990**).

Great Russell St., WC1. www.thebritishmuseum.org. ✆ **020/7323-8299.** Free. Tube: Tottenham Court Road or Holborn or Russell Square. Sat–Thurs 10am–5:30pm and Fri 10am–8:30pm, closed New Year's Day, Good Friday, and Dec 24–26.

**The Courtauld Institute of Art Gallery ★★★** MUSEUM Art historians consider the Courtauld one of the most prestigious collections on earth. Its two-level selection is small but supreme, with several masterpieces you will instantly recognize. Among the winners are Manet's *A Bar at the Folies-Bergère,* showing a melancholy barmaid standing in front of her disproportionate reflection. There are multiple Cézannes, Toulouse-Lautrecs, and Tahitian Gauguins. Degas's *Two Dancers on the Stage* is popular, as is Van Gogh's *Self-Portrait with Bandaged Ear.* Especially rare is a completed Seurat, *Young Woman Powdering Herself,* which depicts his mistress in the act of dressing and initially included his own face in the frame on the wall—he painted over it with a vase of flowers to avoid ridicule. **Somerset House,** the museum's home, was once a naval center and later was where Londoners came to settle taxes and research family history. The central courtyard, beneath which lie the foundations of a Tudor palace, has a grove of 55 ground-level fountains that delight small children, and it's the scene of both popular summer concerts and a winter ice rink, plus a cafe by the popular charcuterie/bakery Fernandez & Wells. The terrace overlooking the Thames (from across the street) can be enjoyed for free.

Somerset House, Strand, WC2. www.courtauld.ac.uk. ✆ **020/7848-2526.** £6 adults, £5 children/seniors/students; posted prices are higher and include a "voluntary donation." Tube: Temple. Daily 10am–6pm, until 9pm one Thurs/month.

**National Gallery ★★★** MUSEUM Few museums can compete with the strongest, widest collection of paintings in the world—one of every important style is on display, and it's almost always the best in that genre. There are 2,300 Western European works, which is plenty to divert you for as long as you can manage, and 6 million visitors are drawn here every year. As you enter via the main Portico Entrance, galleries imperceptibly surge through time in a clockwise arrangement. The best course is to start in the Sainsbury Wing (through room 9 or from Pall Mall East) and backtrack, which will order viewings more or less chronologically. Rooms jumble together, so grab a £1 map—but drop a coin in the slot or a sentry will bark at you. At the basement Espresso Bar, use the ArtStart computers to locate up to six works and to print out a free map to them. Among the many noteworthy holdings:

- Sandro Botticelli fell under the spell of the reformer Savonarola. He burned many of his finest paintings in the Bonfire of the Vanities and changed to an inferior style, so his best works are rare; ***Venus and Mars*** (1485, room 58), depicting the lovers reclining, is one of them.
- Michelangelo's ***The Entombment*** (around 1500, room C) is unfinished but powerful. The feminine figure in the red gown is now thought to be St John, but it's hard to know, because the artist favored masculine traits.
- Kids love Holbein's ***The Ambassadors*** (1533, room 4), full of symbolic riddles that refer to the guy on the left, and famous for a stretched

image of a skull that can only be viewed in proper perspective from the side. Get close; the delicate brushwork includes feathers on the shoes.

- Kids also love Quinten Massys's grotesque, porcine ***An Old Woman*** (*"The Ugly Duchess"*; 1513, room 65), thought to be a satire on ladies who try to look younger than they are, but possibly a woman suffering from a disease. Not so funny if it's the latter, hilarious if it's the former.
- George Stubbs's life-size portrait of rearing stallion ***Whistlejacket*** (room 34) stops everyone in their tracks; it was painted for its proud owner.

There's much more: George Seurat's almost-pointillist ***Bathers at Asnières*** (1884, room 44), Van Gogh's ***Sunflowers*** (room 45, another in 46), Jan van Eyck's ***The Arnolfini Portrait*** (Sainsbury Wing, room 56), a mysterious but fabulously skillful depiction of light that dates to 1434, years ahead of its time. **Brueghels. Cézannes. Uccellos.** There's so much art here that you may want to go twice during your visit, and the Gallery is centrally located, so you can.

Trafalgar Sq., WC2. www.nationalgallery.org.uk. ✆ **020/7747-2885.** Free. Tube: Charing Cross or Leicester Square. Sat–Thurs 10am–6pm and Fri 10am–9pm.

**The National Portrait Gallery ★★★** MUSEUM Here, the names from your high school textbook flower into flesh-and-blood people, and the accompanying biographies are so sublimely evocative (Samuel Johnson is described as "massive, ungainly, plagued with nervous tics") that subjects come alive. Take the escalator to the top and work your way down over about 2 hours. The oldest works (Tudors, Jacobeans, Elizabethans) come first, and you'll progress forward in time—adding photography when canvas fatigue sets in. One of the most instantly recognizable paintings is the **Ditchley portrait of Elizabeth I** (room 2), in which the queen's jeweled gown spreads like wings and Her Majesty firmly glares at the viewer under stormy skies. Right away, it becomes clear that many artists are slyly commenting on the disposition of their sitters. The troublesome **Henry VIII** is shown in several likenesses. One is a delicate 1537 paper cartoon by Hans Holbein the Younger (for a mural at Whitehall—a rare survivor from that palace), in which the king suspiciously peers with flinty grey eyes—hinting at a shiftiness that His Majesty probably couldn't recognize in his own likeness, but that all who knew him feared (room 1). One painting of **King Edward VI,** painted when he was 9, is executed in a distorted perspective (called anamorphosis) that requires it to

### London's Treasures for Free

The following attractions named in this guide charge no admission fees for their permanent collections. Not a shabby lineup!

The British Library; The British Museum; Museum of London; Museum of London Docklands; The National Gallery; National Maritime Museum; The National Portrait Gallery; The Natural History Museum; The Royal Observatory; The Science Museum; The Tate Britain; The Tate Modern; The V&A.

be viewed from a hole on the right side of its case (room 1). You'll also find **George Washington** (he was born an Englishman, after all, room 14). In room 18, there's the sketch of **Jane Austen** by her sister Cassandra—friends said it stank. The **Brontë Sisters** appear together in an 1834 portrait found folded atop a cupboard in 1914; their brother Patrick, the artist, was painted out, but his ghostly image is eerily re-appearing (room 24). Fortunately, the portraits don't stop when cameras were invented. The image of **Margaret Thatcher,** demure in a chair, makes the Iron Lady look as sweet as your granny (room 32); she is faced down by Paul Emsley's warm oil-on-canvas of **Catherine, HRH The Duchess of Cambridge** (2012). Late shift evenings (Thurs, Fri 6–9pm), programmed with DJs, talks, live music, and drawing sessions, are fun. Also consider the pre-theater menu (£19 for two courses, £23 for three) served from 5:30 to 6:30pm in the rooftop Portrait Restaurant, which has a breathtaking view taking in Nelson's Column and Big Ben's tower (✆ **020/7312-2490**).

St Martin's Place, WC2. www.npg.org.uk ✆ **020/7312-2463.** Free. Tube: Leicester Square. Sat–Wed 10am–6pm, Thurs–Fri 10am–9pm, last admission 45 min. before closing.

**Trafalgar Square ★★** PARK/SQUARE Once a stable, Trafalgar Square has evolved to become the setting for demonstrations, such as infamous riots over poll taxes and unemployment. The English gather here for happy things, too, as they did for the announcement of V-E Day (May 8, 1945), and as they still do for free summer performances. The statue of Lord Nelson (1843), who sacrificed his life in 1805 to defeat Napoléon Bonaparte's naval aspirations, looks down Whitehall from 167

**Trafalgar Square.**

Buckingham Palace and the Victoria Memorial.



feet up; climb the portico of the **National Gallery ★★★** (p. 26), and you'll see the same heart-stirring view of Big Ben's tower. The northwestern plinth of Trafalgar Square was designed for an equestrian statue of its own, but money ran out and it stood empty from 1841. More than 150 years later, the naked spot was named The Fourth Plinth and filled by works commissioned by a subversive panel of top artists. And what of Trafalgar's Square's famous pigeons? Where are they? Until the early 1990s, the square swarmed with them—the fluttering flock was estimated to peak at 35,000. But with the help of captive hawks, they were banished for overactive excretion.

Free. Tube: Charing Cross or Leicester Square. Open 24 hrs.

### "Eros"

When he finished his legendary fountain in the middle of Piccadilly Circus in 1893, sculptor Alfred Gilbert thought the playful maritime-themed sculptures on its base would be celebrated. Audiences have minds of their own. They responded to the archer god on top. But they even got that bit of admiration wrong—they thought he represented Eros, god of erotic love, when Gilbert had actually intended Anteros, god of requited love. Today, even Piccadilly Circus isn't a circus (roundabout) anymore—it's an interchange—but the ceaseless tourist crowd photographing Gilbert's misunderstood masterpiece at least puts the circus back into Piccadilly. Gilbert's fabulous fountain is now dry and full of McDonald's wrappers, but his misidentified god, ironically the one who punishes mortals for failing to return love, nevertheless blesses the city as an icon.

## WESTMINSTER & NEARBY

**Buckingham Palace ★★** HISTORIC SITE If you were to fall asleep tonight and wake up inside one of the **State Rooms,** you'd never guess where you were. Is it opulent? No question. But if ever gilding, teardrop chandeliers, 18th-century portraits, and ceremonial halls could be considered standard-issue, Buckingham Palace is your basic palace. Queen Elizabeth's mild tastes—call it "respectable decadence," of yellows and creams and pleasant floral arrangements, thank you very much—are partly the reason. Remember, too, that much of this palace was built or remodeled in the 1800s—not so long ago in the scheme of things—and that the Queen considers Windsor to be her real home. All tickets are timed and include an audio tour that rushes you around too quickly. The route threads through the public and ceremonial rooms (nowhere that the Royal Family spends personal time, and besides, the Palace is open only a few months a year, when they're in Scotland) at the back of the palace. Highlights include the 50m-long (164-ft.) **Picture Gallery** filled mostly with works amassed by George IV, an obsessive collector; the 14m-tall (46-ft.) **Ballroom,** where the Queen confers knighthoods; the parquet-floored **Music Room,** unaltered since John Nash decorated it in 1831, where the Queen's three eldest children were baptized in water brought from the River Jordan; and a stroll through the thick **Garden** in the back yard. (If you want to see highlights of the formal gardens, that's another £8.10.) It's definitely worth seeing—how often can you toodle around the spare rooms in a Queen's house, inspecting artwork given as gifts by some of history's most prominent names? But it's no Versailles. If you're in London and spot her standard of red, gold, and blue flying above, you'll at least know the Queen is home. (If it's the Union Jack, she's gone.) So near, yet so far.

Buckingham Palace Rd., SW1. www.royalcollection.org.uk. ✆ **020/7766-7300.** £21 adults, £12 children 5–16, £19 seniors/students. Tube: Victoria or Green Park. April, Late July to late Aug daily 9:30am–7:30pm, Sept 9:30am–6:30pm, last admission 2 hr. 15 min. before closing.

**Churchill War Rooms ★★★** MUSEUM/HISTORIC SITE One of London's most fascinating museums is the secret command center used by Winston Churchill and his staff during the most harrowing moments of World War II, when it looked like England might become German. Here, in the cellar of the Treasury building, practically next door to 10 Downing Street, the core of the British government hunkered down where one errant bomb could have incinerated the lot of them. When the war ended, the bunker was abandoned, but everything was left just as it was in August 1945, and when it was time to make it a museum, everything was intact—from pushpins tracing convoy movements on yellowed world maps to rationed sugar cubes hidden in the back of a clerk's desk drawer. Midway through, you disappear into the **Churchill Museum,** surely the most cutting-edge biographical museum open at this moment. Exhaustively displaying every conceivable facet of his life (his bowtie, his bowler hat, and even the original front door to 10 Downing Street), it covers the exalted statesman's life from entitled birth through his antics as a journalist in South Africa (where he escaped a kidnapping and became a national hero) to, of course, his years as prime minister. You even learn his favorite cigar (Romeo y Julieta) and brandy (Hine). The entire museum is atwitter with multimedia displays, movies, and archival sounds, but the centerpiece will blow you away: a 15m-long (50-ft.) Lifeline Interactive table, illuminated by projections, that looks like a long file cabinet and covers every month of Churchill's life. Touch a date, and the file "opens" with 4,600 pages of rare documents, photos, or, for critical dates in history, animated Easter eggs that temporarily consume the entire table (select the original Armistice Day or the *Titanic* sinking to see what we mean). You could play for hours, dipping into his life day by day.

Clive Steps, King Charles St., SW1. www.iwm.org.uk. ✆ **020/7930-6961.** £16 adults, £9 kids 5–15, £13 seniors/students; posted prices are higher and include a "voluntary donation." Tube: Westminster. Daily 9:30am–6pm, last admission 5pm.

**Houses of Parliament ★★** LANDMARK Luckily, the nation allows you to tour a dozen stately halls and even to wander through its vaunted House of Lords and House of Commons when they're not in session. There are now two ways to see it: Choose a 100-minute guided group tour, which presents the usual issues of audibility and pace, or take it easy with the new 2-hour audio guide (and eavesdrop on groups whenever you want). The historical highlights: Massive Westminster Hall, one of the world's most precious spaces and a UNESCO World Heritage Site, was built in 1097 by William Rufus, son of William the Conqueror. Richard II commissioned its cherished oak hammer-beam ceiling before he was deposed in the 1390s. Charles I, William Wallace, Sir Thomas More, and Guy Fawkes were all condemned in it; monarchs lie in state in it. The rest of the Palace is roughly divided into three areas: those for the House of Lords (whose members inherit seats, done in rose with an unbelievable gilt sitting area where Queen Victoria would preside on designated occasions); the House of Commons (by far the most powerful, elected by the people, but plainer, with seats of blue-green under a hanging forest of microphones); and some flabbergasting lobbies, sitting rooms, and the "Robing Room" (golds, browns, burgundies), which the Sovereign flits through when she shows up once a year to kick off sessions. You walk right onto the floor of both Houses. Many delicious details are elucidated, from the knock-marks on the Commons door made by the Crown's emissary, the Black Rod, to the line in the carpet members may not cross when in the throes of vigorous debates. Frustratingly, the Elizabeth Tower (1859) beside the Houses—it contains the 13½-ton bell known as Big Ben plus four smaller bells—is only open to U.K. residents. If the green Ayrton Light atop it burns, Parliament is

### Ritual Abuse

I'm only telling you this because I love you: **Changing of the Guard** (Buckingham Palace; www.royal.gov.uk; free; 11:30am daily in May–July, and every other day in other months, cancelled in heavy rain; Tube: St James's Park, Victoria, or Green Park), sometimes called Guard Mounting, is an underwhelming use of 40 minutes of your time. Arrive at Buckingham Palace at least 45 minutes ahead if you don't want to face the backs of other tourists—Buckingham Palace sells a $1 smartphone app that will help decode the ritual. A marching band advances from Birdcage Walk (often playing themes from *Star Wars, West Side Story,* or ABBA songs—so much for traditional English customs!), then members of the Queen's Life Guard—two if the Queen's away, three or four if she's in—do a change around their sentry boxes. And that's it, give or take additional prancing.

Guards patrol all day, without crowds, at both Buckingham Palace and at Horse Guards Arch on Whitehall (which does its own, un-crowded change at 11am, 10am Sun). Or park yourself at **Wellington Barracks,** just east of the Palace along Birdcage Walk, by 11am, and catch the Inspection of the Guard that happens before the same guards march over to the Palace for the main event. Then use the day's golden hours for something less touristy.

sitting after dark. Booking House tours ahead is advisable, but you can try your luck for openings at the ticket office next to the Jewel Tower, across the street. It also puts on afternoon tea in a room abutting the river, if that interests you (book ahead, of course).

Bridge St. and Parliament Sq., SW1. www.parliament.uk/visiting. ✆ **020/7219-4114.** Tube: Westminster. Most Saturdays and Mon–Sat in Aug: 9am–4:15pm, but always check ahead. Admission £25 adults, £20 seniors/students, £10 children 5–15, children under 5 free. Reservations recommended.

**London Eye ★★★** OBSERVATIONAL WHEEL After the Eye was erected in 1999 as the Millennium Wheel, it set off a modern trend for observational wheels. It rises above everything in this part of the city—at 443 ft. high, it's 1½ times taller than the Statue of Liberty. The 30-minute ride above the Thames affords an unmatched and unobstructed perspective on the prime tourist territory. On a clear day, you can see to Windsor, but even on an average day, the entire West End bows down before you. The whirl is adulterated by a lame "4D Experience" movie (the camera moves through London while a fan blows in your face—Orlando-fied twaddle) but that's included in the price. Each of the 32 enclosed capsules, which accommodate up to 28 people at once, is climate-controlled and rotates so gradually that it's easy to forget you're moving—which means it will upset only the desperately height-averse. By the time you reach the top, you'll have true 360-degree views unobstructed by the support frame. The ticket queue often looks positively wicked, but it moves quickly, chewing through 15,000 riders a day, 800 per revolution. ***Tip:*** Booking on the Web saves waiting in the ticketing queues, and it gives other advantages: You can pick your time ahead and

View from the London Eye.



you'll save 10% off the price listed below. There's a host of ticket options—basically, you can pay more to go anytime you want rather than stick to a reservation, but a standard ticket satisfies most needs.
Riverside Building, County Hall, SE1. www.londoneye.com. ✆ **0871/781-3000.** £22 adults, £16 children 4–15, free under 4, £19 seniors; save 10% online at least 4 days ahead. Tube: Waterloo or Westminster. Jan–Mar and Sept–Dec 10am–8:30pm, April–June 10am–9pm, July–August 10am–9:30pm.

**Tate Britain** ★ MUSEUM Tourists often wonder about the difference between the Tate Modern and this, its sister upstream on the Thames. Well, the Modern is for contemporary art of any origin, and the Britain, besides its calmer and more civilized affect, is mostly for British-made art made after 1500. Shifting objectives consistently rotate beloved paintings into storage, a frustrating habit with Tate, but some masterpieces can be relied upon. J. M. W. Turner's trenchant ***The Field of Waterloo*** (room 1810) was painted in 1818, 3 years after the battle; its shadowy piles of corpses, and of bereaved family members searching them, made viewers question his patriotism. The oil-on-canvas ***Carnation, Lily, Lily, Rose*** (1840) is by another American who settled in London, John Singer Sargent, and it depicts children holding paper lanterns so luminous that when it was first exhibited in 1887, its worth was instantly recognized and it was purchased for the nation. John Everett Millais's depiction of a drowning ***Ophelia*** (1840) is also considered a treasure for its phenomenally tricky depiction of water; the artist painted the plants in the summer so he'd get them right and waited until winter to paint his model, a hat-shop girl, in a tub of water. Naturally, she caught a severe cold (he paid for her doctor's bill after her father threatened to

sue). Check out the sculptures, too, including forms by **Henry Moore,** who gets two rooms, and Barbara Hepworth. But the crowning attraction here is the **Turner Galleries,** with their expansive collection of J. M. W. Turners. Turner (1775–1851), the son of a Covent Garden barber, was a master of landscapes lit by misty, perpetual sunrise, and the dozens of paintings testify to both his undying popularity and his doggedly British tendency to convey information purely by implication. Maps are £1.
Millbank, SW1. www.tate.org.uk/britain. ✆ **020/7887-8888.** Free. Tube: Pimlico. Daily 10am–6pm.




**Westminster Abbey ★★★** HISTORIC SITE If you have to pick just one church to see in London—nay, one church in the entire *world*—this is the one. The echoes of history are mind-blowing: The current building dates from the 1200s, but it was part of a monastery dating to at least 960. Every English monarch since 1066 has been crowned here (with three minor exceptions: Edward V, Edward VIII, and possibly Mary I). Seventeen monarchs are interred here (their deaths date from 1066–1760), as are dozens of great writers and artists. Kate and William married here, and he will be crowned here. A visit should take about 3 hours and should begin early, because entry lines are excruciating. Unlike St Paul's Cathedral, which has an airy, stately beauty, the smaller Westminster is more like time's attic, packed with artifacts, memorials, tombs, and virtuosic shrines. Take your time and don't get swept along in the current of visitors. Let them pass. There are stories to be told in every square meter of this place.

Inside the sanctuary, tourists are corralled clockwise from the North Transept. The royal tombs are clustered in the first half of the route, in the region of the High Altar, where coronations and funerals are conducted. The most famous rulers of all time are truly *here*—not in story, but in body, a few inches away behind marble slabs. Some are stashed in cozy side chapels (which once held medieval shrines before Cromwellians bashed them to pieces during the Reformation; some vandalism is still visible), but the oldest are on the sanctuary side of the ambulatory (aisle). The executed **Mary Queen of Scots** was belatedly given a crypt of equal stature to her rival, **Elizabeth I,** by Mary's son **James I,** who gave himself only a marker for his own tomb beneath **Henry VII**'s elaborate resting place. James I's infant daughter Sophia, who died aged 3 days, was given a creepy bassinet sarcophagus in the Lady Chapel.

The South Transept is **Poet's Corner,** where Britain's great writers are honored. You'll see many plaques, but most (Shakespeare, Austen, Carroll, Wilde, the Brontës) are merely memorials. The biggest names who truly lie underfoot are Geoffrey Chaucer (he was placed here first, starting the trend), Robert Browning, Charles Dickens, Thomas Hardy (buried without his heart), John Gay, Rudyard Kipling, Dr. Samuel Johnson, Laurence Olivier, Edmund Spenser, and Alfred Lord Tennyson. Ben

Westminster Abbey.



Jonson is commemorated here, but is actually buried in the nave near Isaac Newton and Charles Darwin.

Now for a few Abbey secrets:

- That oak seat between the Sanctuary and the Confessors' Chapel, near the tomb of Henry V, is the **Coronation Chair.** Unbelievably, every English monarch since 1308 has been crowned on this excruciating-looking throne. The slot under the seat is for the 152kg (336-lb.) Stone of Scone, a central part of Irish, Scottish, and English coronations since at least 700 B.C. After spending 7 centuries in the Abbey (except for when Scottish nationalists stole it for 4 months in late 1950), the Stone was returned to Scotland in 1996, where it's on view at Edinburgh Castle. It will return for every future coronation.
- **Oliver Cromwell,** who overthrew the monarchy and ran England as a republic, was buried with honors behind the High Altar in 1658. Three years later, after the monarchy was restored, his corpse was dug up, hanged, decapitated, the body tossed into a common grave, and its head put on display outside the Abbey. (Didn't they realize he was already dead?) Cromwell's daughter, who died young, was mercifully allowed to remain buried in the Abbey.
- The **Quire** is where the choir sings; it comprises about 12 men and 30 or so boys who are educated at the adjoining Westminster Choir School, the last of its type in the world. The wooden stalls are so delicate they're dusted using vacuum cleaners.

The door to the **Chapter House** was made between 924 and 1030 and is Britain's oldest-known door. The Abbey's oft-overlooked **Museum,** in a vaulted undercroft, contains some astounding treasures, including **Edward III's death mask** (thought to be the oldest of its kind in Europe; it's made of walnut and doesn't ignore his facial droop, which resulted from a stroke), **ancient jewelry** "found in graves" (we know what that means—pried from skeletons), the **fake Crown Jewels** used for coronation rehearsals, 14th-century leather shoes and Roman tiles unearthed on the grounds, and the fateful **Essex Ring,** which Elizabeth I gave to her brilliant confidant Robert Devereux, telling him to send it if he needed her. He tried to, but his enemies intercepted it, and he was beheaded at the Tower of London in 1601. Oops.

Next door, pop into **St Margaret's Chapel** (free), which the monks built in 1523 so they'd be left alone in peace. The Germans didn't comply: Some southern windows were destroyed by a bomb and were replaced by plain glass, and in addition to damage to the north wall, Pew 3 remains charred.

Broad Sanctuary, SW1. www.westminster-abbey.org. ✆ **020/7222-5152.** £18 adults, £8 children 11–18, £15 seniors/students, free for children under 11. Tube: Westminster. Generally open Mon–Tues and Thurs–Fri 9:30am–4:30pm, Wed 9:30am–7pm, Sat 9:30am–2:30pm, last admission 1 hr. before closing; closed Sun. for worship. Check ahead for closures.

### KENSINGTON

**Kensington Palace** ★ HISTORIC SITE Most people know it as the place where Lady Diana raised Princes William and Harry with Prince Charles from 1984 to 1996, but now it's where Prince William, Kate, and their little royals live when in London. (Sorry. You won't run into them in the bathroom.) It has been a royal domicile since 1689, when William and Mary took control of an existing home (then in the country, far from town, which inflamed William's asthma) and made it theirs. Handsome and haughty, with none of the symmetry that defined later English tastes, the redbrick palace is not as ostentatious as you might expect. The venerable palace was stripped of a sense of import by a recent renovation, and now it's a spook house for art snobs. In 2014, the newly reopened King's Apartments, pegged to King George III and Queen Caroline, was explained to visitors not with a detailed historical dossier but with a scratch-and-sniff guide to odors that might have filled the palace once—kids love such sensationalism and the costumed characters wandering about, but anyone who can reach the pedals knows it's all style over substance. Queen Victoria has her own section, but she's given the trashy treatment, too; rather than teaching visitors how a girl of 18 rose to successfully control the most powerful empire in the world, she is shown, misogynistically, in terms of gender roles: as a good girl, a loving wife, and a grieving widow. One room draped in black leads you to believe Prince Albert died in it, but no, he died at Windsor. Thankfully, the

Kensington Palace.



walk-through still includes the magnificent King's Staircase, lined with delicate canvas panels whose perimeters are rigged with tissue paper slivers designed to tear as a warning of shifting or swelling. The staircase is considered so precious that it was only opened to the public in 2004, 105 years after the rest of the palace first accepted sightseers. Also, in the Gallery there's a working Anemoscope, which has told the outside wind direction since 1694, and a map of the world as known in that year. You'll also get a chance to see gowns worn by HM the Queen, Diana, and Princess Margaret, who also lived here. Overall though, if you're short on time, the Palace is no longer a must-see.

Kensington Gardens, W8. www.hrp.org.uk. ✆ **084/4482-7777.** Admission £15 adults, children under 16 free, £12 seniors/students including audio tour; posted prices are higher and include "voluntary donation." Tube: High Street Kensington or Queensway. Mar–Oct daily 10am–6pm, Nov–Feb daily 10am–5pm, last admission 1 hr. before closing.

**Natural History Museum ★★** MUSEUM The commodious NHM, which attracts 5.3 million visitors a year (mostly families, and by far the most of the three big South Ken museums), is a true blockbuster museum, and it's good for several hours' wander, but you'll have plenty of company. In all ways, it's a zoo. You get a hall of dinosaur bones, a taxidermist's menagerie, and case after case of stuffed goners. Mostly, you'll encounter the wildest creatures of all: lurching, wailing, scampering children in all their varieties. On weekends and school holidays, the outdoor queue can be an hour long, so go at opening and enter through Exhibition Road for lighter crowds. The trove is rich: At the top of the stairs, the **Treasures** gallery holds such historically meaningful stuff as a dodo skeleton and Britain's only moon rock. The pretend kitchen full of hiding

The Natural History Museum.

places for insects and **Creepy Crawlies** (the **Green Zone**) is a longtime visitor favorite, as is the **Red Zone** (the Earth Galleries), anchored by a toned-down, ride-along mock-up of a Japanese supermarket jolted by the 1995 Kobe earthquake. Even the dinosaurs (in the Blue Zone) are supplemented by scary robotic estimations of how they sounded and moved. The **Darwin Centre's** Cocoon looks like a seven-story egg laid in the back atrium; hidden inside are some 20 million bottled specimens (including those that came back on the *Beagle*) on 27km of shelves. Most of the discussion here, and throughout the museum, is aimed at a child's mind, with signs answering such riveting questions such as why we study nature, but now and then you'll see an expert through a window of the Darwin Centre, who can use a microphone to respond to more intelligent concerns. Even if you don't give a hooey about remedial ecology, the cathedral-like 1880 Victorian building is an unforgettable landmark. Its columns crawl with carved monkeys whimsically clinging to the terra-cotta and plants creeping across ceiling panels. All that and the requisite ceiling whale.

Cromwell Rd., SW7. www.nhm.ac.uk. ✆ **020/7942-5000.** Free. Tube: South Kensington. Daily 10am–5:50pm.

**Royal Albert Hall ★★** LANDMARK In addition to being a great concert venue, the Royal Albert is also one of London's great landmarks, and you don't need a seat to enjoy it. The halls was conceived by Queen Victoria's husband Albert and opened in 1871, a decade after his death from typhoid (Vicky was so distraught that she didn't speak at the opening ceremonies). You can take a 1-hour tour. The hall contains such oddities as Britain's longest single-weave carpet (in the corridors), the Queen's Box (still leased to the monarchy), and a spectacular glass dome (135 ft. high and supported only at its rim). Be warned: You don't get to go backstage. Some 320 performances a year are presented, many with less than 24 hours' set-up time, and a flow of sightseers would be in the way.

Kensington Gore, SW7. www.royalalberthall.com. © **0845/401-5045.** Admission to lobby free, tours £12 adults, £10 seniors/students. Tube: South Kensington. Tours available most days, times vary; generally 9:30am–4:30pm.

**V&A ★★★** MUSEUM If it was pretty, well-made, or valuable, the British Empire wanted to have it. As a decorative arts repository, the Victoria & Albert, occupying a haughty High Victorian edifice (it was endowed by the proceeds from the first world's fair, the Great Exhibition of 1851), is all about the eye candy of everyday objects. And if you're paying attention, it tells the story of humankind through the development of style and technique. The ground floor, a jumbled grid of rooms, has lots of good stuff, but lots more bric-a-brac (Korean pots, 1,000-year-old rock crystal jugs from Egypt) that you'll probably walk past with polite but hasty appreciation. The second, third, and fourth levels have less space and therefore are more manageable. Rooms are arranged by country of origin or by medium (ironwork, tapestries, and the like). Not to miss:

- The seven **Raphael Cartoons** (room 48a), 500 years old in 2015, are probably the most priceless items. These giant paper paintings—yes, paper—were created by the hand of Raphael as templates for the weavers of his ten tapestries for the Sistine Chapel. The colors are fugitive, meaning they're fading: Christ's red robe, painted with plant-based madder lake, has turned white—his reflection in the water, painted with a different pigment, is still red.
- In the just-renovated, sky-lit **Cast Court** (rooms 46 and 46a), find casts of the greatest hits in Renaissance art. They were jumbled here like a yard sale of antiquity in 1873 for the poor, who could never hope to see the real articles for themselves. Find Ghiberti's doors to the baptistery at Florence's San Giovanni, whose design kicked off the artistic frenzy of the Renaissance. See Michelangelo's *David,* floppy puppy feet and all; he was fitted with a fig leaf for royal visits. Depressingly, many of these replicas are now in better shape than the originals.
- Tipu Sultan of India hated imperialists. So, in the 1790s he commissioned an automaton of a tiger devouring one. A crank on **Tippoo's Tiger** (room 41) activates a clockwork that makes an Englishman's hand flail and an organ makes his gaping mouth moan. In the end, Tipu was killed by Europeans and the English got his Tiger after all. It

The V&A.

has been a crowd favorite since 1808, when it was part of the East India Company's trophy museum.

- The **Ardabil carpet** (room 42), the world's oldest dated carpet (copies lay on the floors of 10 Downing Street and Hitler's Berlin office alike), is from 1539. It's illuminated 10 minutes at a time on every half hour.
- The **Hereford Screen** (1862, Ironworks balcony) is a liturgical riot by Gilbert Scott, the architect of the *Eros* (p. 29). It took 38 conservators 13 months to restore the 8-ton choir screen to its full golden, brassy, painted, Gothic glory.
- The **Gilbert Collection** (rooms 70–73) of impossibly fine jewel boxes, cameos, silver, and mosaics amassed by a rich enthusiast is so impressive that it once had its own museum at Somerset House.

Also visit the V&A's western exterior. Scarred during the Blitz, the stonework was left unrepaired as a memorial.

Cromwell Road, SW7. www.vam.ac.uk. ✆ **020/7942-2000.** Free. Tube: South Kensington. Daily 10am–5:45pm, Fri until 10pm.

## THE CITY & SOUTHWARK

**Museum of London** ★★★ MUSEUM The tale of London is the tale of the Western world, so this repository's miraculous cache of rarities from everyday life wouldn't be out of place in the greatest national museums of any land. This huge storehouse contains so many forehead-smackingly rare items that by the time you're two-thirds through it, you'll start to lose track of all the goodies you've seen. When it comes to the history of London, no stone has been left unturned—literally—because exhibits start with local archaeological finds (including elephant vertebrae and a lion skull) before continuing to 3,500-year-old spearheads and swords found in the muck of the Thames. Voices from the past come alive again in chronological order: There's a 1st-century oak ladder that was discovered preserved in a well, Norman chain mail, loaded gambling dice made of bone in the 1400s, a leather bucket used in vain to fight the Great Fire of 1666, a walk-in wooden prison cell from 1750, Selfridge's original bronze Art Deco elevators, and far, far more. The biggest drawback is that you need to budget a few hours, otherwise you'll end up in a mad rush through the entire lower floor covering the Great Fire to now—and it'd be such a shame to miss Tom Daley's tiny Stella McCartney swim trunks from the Olympics. You also don't want to miss the Victorian Walk, a kid-friendly re-creation of city streets, shops and all, from the 1800s (grab a card at its entrance to know what you're seeing). You also can't miss the Lord Mayor's state coach, carved in 1757, which garages here all year awaiting its annual airing at the Lord Mayor's Show in November. The museum, which overlooks a Roman wall fragment outside, is easy to combine with a visit to St Paul's, and it sells one of the best selections of books on city history. It also runs an excellent second museum in East London about Docklands and how London became such a trading power.

150 London Wall, EC2. www.museumoflondon.org.uk. ✆ **020/7001-9844.** Free. Tube: Barbican or St Paul's. Daily 10am–6pm.

**St Paul's Cathedral ★★★** HISTORIC SITE St Paul's cost £750,000 to build, an astronomical sum in 1697 when the first section opened for worship, and now, it costs £3 million a year to run. Its architect, Christopher Wren, overspent so badly that decoration was curtailed; the mosaics weren't added until Queen Victoria thought the place needed spiffing up. Stained glass is still missing, which allows the sweep and arch of Wren's design to shine cleanly through. Many foreigners were introduced to the sanctuary during the wedding of Prince Charles and Lady Diana Spencer in 1981, but the cathedral also saw a sermon by Martin Luther King, Jr., in 1964 and Churchill's funeral the next year. The **High Altar** has a canopy supported by single tree trunks that were hollowed out and carved, and its 15th-century crucifix and candlesticks require two men to lift. (They're nailed down, anyway. As one docent, a half-century veteran of Cathedral tours, lamented, "You'd be surprised what people try to steal.") Behind it is the **American Memorial Chapel** to the 28,000 American soldiers who died while based in England in World War II. In a glass case, one leaf of a 500-page book containing their names is turned each day. The **organ,** with 7,000 pipes, was regularly played by Mendelssohn and Handel, and the lectern is original. The **Great West Doors** are 27m high (90 ft.) and on their original hinges; they're so well-hung that even a weakling can swing them open. In 2005, the Cathedral completed a £10.8-million cleaning program; a stone panel beside the doors was left filthy to show just how bad things were.

## going green: LONDON'S ICONIC PARKS AND GARDENS

Parks are central to London life, and the city does them right. Many were once the vast hunting grounds or private retreats of the Royals; today these gorgeous green spaces offer, for jaded locals and tourists alike, peaceful respite from the nearby hubbub. They're all free of charge, with fees for concessions such as boat rentals. Here are a few of our favorites:

**The Green Park ★★** The area south of Mayfair between Hyde Park and St James's Park was once a burial ground for lepers, but now is a simple expanse of meadows and light copses of trees. It doesn't have much to offer except pastoral views, and most visitors find themselves crossing it instead of dawdling in it, although its springtime flower beds (which bloom brightest in Mar and Apr) are marvelous. Don't sit in one of those picturesque striped deck chairs unless you've got a few bob to pay as rent.

Piccadilly, SW1. ✆ **030/0061-2350.** Tube: Green Park. Open 24 hours.

**Greenwich Park ★★**
Decently sized (183 acres), it was once a deer preserve maintained for royal amusement; a herd of them still have 13 acres at their disposal. It's been a Royal Park since the 15th century, although the boundary wasn't formally defined until James I erected a brick wall around it in the early 1600s, much of which still survives. On top of its clean-swept main hill are found marvelous views of the Canary Wharf district, and the world-famous **Royal Observatory ★★** (p. 48). Most people combine a visit with the many other museums of Greenwich (www.rmg.co.uk).

Greenwich Park, SE10. www.royalparks.org.uk. ✆ **030/0061-2380.** National Rail: Greenwich or Maze Hill, or Cutty Sark. DLR or Greenwich ferry. Daily 6am–dusk.

**Hampstead Heath ★★★**
Some 7 million visitors a year come to the 320-hectare (791-acre) Heath, in northwest London, to walk on the grass, get enveloped by thick woods, and take in the view from the magnificent Pergola, a beguiling, overgrown Edwardian garden, and a true London secret. The Heath is a perennial locale for aimless strolls and (it must be confessed, George Michael) furtive trysts. The Heath has several sublime places to rest, including **Kenwood House,** a sumptuous neoclassical home from 1640 adorned with miles of gold leaf and important paintings by Reynolds, Turner, and Vermeer (*The Guitar Player*); and the inviting and woody **Spaniards Inn** (Spaniards Rd. at Spaniards End, NW3; www.thespaniardshampstead.co.uk; ✆ **020/8731-8406;** Tube: Hampstead). The Heath's hilltop is another favored lookout point. The Heath isn't considered a park by locals, but a green space. The difference is irrelevant. It's transporting.

www.cityoflondon.gov.uk/hampsteadheath. ✆ **020/7606-3030.** Tube: Hampstead or Hampstead Heath Overground. 7:30am–dusk.

**Hyde Park & Kensington Gardens ★★★** Bordered by Mayfair, Bayswater, and Kensington, together the two conjoined are the largest park in the middle of the city. Hyde Park is home to the famous **Speakers' Corner** (Tube: Marble Arch), a meandering lake called the Serpentine, and the Diana, Princess of Wales Memorial Fountain (Tube: South Kensington) The most famous promenade is Rotten Row, probably a corruption of "Route de Roi," or

King's Way, which was laid out by William III as his private road to town; it runs along the southern edge of the park from Hyde Park Corner. Kensington Gardens, which flows seamlessly from Hyde Park, only opened to plebes like us in 1851, and it hasn't yet shed its country-manor quality. You'll also find the **Serpentine Gallery** (west of West Carriage Dr. and north of Alexandra Gate; www.serpentinegalleries.org; ✆ **020/7402-6075;** Tues–Sun 10am–6pm; free; Tube: South Kensington), a popular venue for its modern art exhibitions and an art bookshop. Each summer, a leading architect creates a fanciful pavilion there. Volunteers sometimes run guided tours of the park's quirks; check the bulletin boards at each park entrance to see if one's upcoming. Borrow a Boris Bike and cruise around this giant green playground, and don't forget to look for Sir George Frampton's marvelous bronze statue of Peter Pan (1912) near the west shore of the Long Water.

Hyde Park, W2. www.royalparks.org.uk. ✆ **030/0061-2100.** Tube: Hyde Park Corner, Marble Arch, or Lancaster Gate. Hyde Park open daily 5am–midnight, Kensington Gardens open daily 6am–dusk.

**Regent's Park ★★★** It's the people's park (195 hectares/487 acres), best for sunning, strolling long expanses—it can take a half-hour to cross it—and darting into the bohemian neighborhoods that fringe it. Once a hunting ground, it was very nearly turned into a development for the buddies of Prince Regent (later King George IV), but only a few of the private terrace homes were built; Winfield House, on 5 hectares (12 acres) near the western border of the park, has the largest garden in London, after the Queen. The American ambassador lives there—surprised? The most breathtaking entrance is from the south through John Nash's elegant Park Crescent development, by the Regent's Park and Great Portland Street Tube stations. North of the park, just over the Regent's Canal and Prince Albert Road, **Primrose Hill Park** (Tube: Chalk Farm or Camden Town) affords a panorama of the city from 62m (203-ft.) high.

Regent's Park, NW1. www.royalparks.gov.uk. ✆ **030/0061-2300.** Tube: Baker St., Great Portland St., or Regent's Park. Daily 5am–dusk.

**St James's Park ★★** The easternmost segment of the quartet of parks that run east from Kensington Gardens is bounded by Whitehall to the east and Piccadilly to the north. James I laid it out in 1603, and Buckingham Palace redeveloped it a century later. Its little pond, St James's Park Lake, hosts ducks and other waterfowl. The Russian ambassador made a gift of pelicans to the park in 1667, and the Brits would rather pour the milk after the tea than give up tradition, so six (three of them a 2013 gift from the city of Prague) still call it home; they're fed their 13kg (28 lb.) of whiting daily at 2:30pm at the Duck Island Cottage. The park has a fine view of Buckingham Palace's front facade, where royal couples smooch on balconies. The real draw is people-watching, because a cross-section of all London passes through here. Not a place for picnics or ball throwing, there's little in the way of amenities or activities, unless you count voyeurism, and why wouldn't you?

The Mall, SW1. www.royalparks.org.uk. ✆ **020/7930-1793.** Tube: St James's Park. Open 5am–midnight.

St Paul's Cathedral.

If you're fit, you can mount the 259 steps (each an awkward 5 in. tall, with benches on many landings) to the **Whispering Gallery,** 98 feet above the floor. Famously, its acoustics are so fine you can turn your head and mutter something that can be understood on the opposite side. That's in theory; so many tourists are usually blabbing to each other that you won't hear a thing, although it is a transcendent place to listen to choir rehearsal on a mid-afternoon. Climb higher (you've gone 378 steps now) to the **Stone Gallery,** an outdoor terrace just beneath the Dome, then catch your breath for the final 152-step push to the **Golden Gallery,** which requires you to scale the inner skin of the Dome, past ancient oriel windows and along tight metal stairs. It's safe, but it's not for those with vertigo or claustrophobia. The spectacular 360-degree city view from the top (85m/279 ft. up), at the base of the Ball and Lantern, is so beautiful that it defies full appreciation. For more than 250 years, this was the tallest structure in London, and therefore the top of the world.

If you miss the **Crypt,** you'll have missed a lot. In addition to memorials to the famous dead (such as Florence Nightingale and plenty of obscure war heroes), you'll find the tombs of two of Britain's greatest military demigods: **Admiral Horatio Nelson** (whose body was preserved for the trip from the battlefield by soaking in brandy and wine; the 72,000-ton weight of the Dome is borne by the walls of this small chamber), and **Arthur Duke of Wellington** (flanked by flags captured on the field of battle; they will hang there until they disintegrate). To the right of the OBE Chapel, in **Artists Corner,** there's a monument to poet **John Donne** that still bears the scorch marks it suffered in Old St Paul's during the Great Fire (they're on its urn, and it was the only thing that survived the conflagration), and you'll find the graves of the artists

**J. M. W. Turner** and **Henry Moore,** plus **Christopher Wren** himself, who rests beneath his masterpiece. "I build for eternity," he once said, and so far, so good. Lest you forgot it's actually a cathedral, you can also worship here outside of sightseeing hours—for free.

St Paul's Churchyard, EC4. www.stpauls.co.uk. ✆ **020/7246-8357.** £17 adults, £7.50 children 7–16, free children under 6, £15 seniors/students, including guided tour (cheaper online). Tube: St Paul's. Mon–Sat 8:30am–4:30pm, for worship only on Sun, Whispering Gallery and Dome open at 9:30am and are cleared at 4pm.

**Tate Modern ★★★** MUSEUM In 2000, Bankside's chief eyesore, a goliath power station—steely and cavernous, a cathedral to soulless industry—was ingeniously converted into the national contemporary art collection and is now as integral to London as the Quire of Westminster Abbey or the Dome of St Paul's. With 5.3 million annual visitors, it's now Britain's number-two attraction. The mammoth Turbine Hall, cleared of machinery to form a meadowlike expanse of concrete, hosts works created by major-league artists. Holdings focus on art made since 1900 and are divided into four loose areas of thought: On Level 2, there's Poetry and Dream (about surrealism) plus a changing exhibition (usually £10); on Level 3, you'll see Transformed Visions (post-war works) and another paid exhibition; on Level 4, Structure and Clarity (abstract art) and Energy and Process (arte povera, a radical movement). In room 6 of Transformed Visions, seven of the nine mono-tonal series created by Mark Rothko for New York City's Four Seasons restaurant never fail to put visitors in a meditative mood. A 10-story southern expansion is set to be completed in 2016. The Tate website is updated with what's on display either here or in the **Tate Britain ★** (p. 33). The sit-down Tate Modern Restaurant on Level 6 can be inhospitable due to crowds (make a reservation: ✆ **020/7401-5103**)—but there are 30 first-come bar seats facing floor-to-ceiling glass and the indelible panorama of St Paul's and the Thames. Afternoon tea is just £15, and the fish and chips platter with mushy peas has our approval for flavor if not price (£17). You can get the same dish for £5.50 less in the cafe on the second floor, but without that stirring view. At lunch, kids under 12 eat free if a grown-up buys a main course.

Bankside, SE1. www.tate.org.uk/modern. ✆ **020/7887-8888.** Free. Tube: Southwark. Sun–Thurs 10am–6pm, Fri–Sat 10am–10pm.

**The Tower of London ★★★** MUSEUM/HISTORIC SITE It's the most famous castle in the world, a UNESCO World Heritage Site, and a symbol of not just London, but also of a millennium of English history. Less a tower than a fortified minitown of stone and timber, its history could fill this book. Suffice it to say that its oldest building, the four-cornered White Tower, went up in 1078, and the compound that grew around it has served as a palace, prison, treasury, mint, armory, zoo, and now, a lovingly maintained tourist attraction that no visitor should neglect. It's at the very heart of English history, and exploring its sprawl should take

The White Tower at the Tower of London.



between 3 and 5 hours. Grab a copy of the free "Daily Programme," which runs down the times and places of all the free talks, temporary exhibitions, and mini performances. The prime excursion is the **Yeoman Warder's Tour,** led with theatrical aplomb by one of the Beefeaters who live in the Tower (there are about 100 residents, including families, but only one Beefeater, Moira Cameron, is female) and preserve it. Those leave every 30 minutes from just inside the portcullis in the Middle Tower.

The key to touring the Tower is to arrive close to opening. At 9am, there's a short ceremony during which guards unlock the gates for the day. As you enter the **Crown Jewels** exhibition (see it first), you'll glide via people-movers past cases of glittering, downlit crowns, scepters, and orbs worn (awkwardly—they're 2.3kg/5 lb. each) by generations of British monarchs. Check out the legendary 105-carat Koh-i-Noor diamond, once the largest in the world, which is fixed to the temple of the **Queen Mother's Crown** (1937), along with 2,000 other diamonds; the Indian government has been begging to get the stone back. The 530-carat Cullinan I, the world's largest cut diamond, tops the Sovereign's **Sceptre with the Cross** (1661). The **Imperial State Crown,** ringed with emeralds, sapphires, and diamonds aplenty, is the one used in the annual State Opening of Parliament. After those come candlesticks that could support the roof of your house, trumpets, swords, and the inevitable traffic jam around the **Grand Punch Bowl** (1829), an elaborate riot of lions, cherubs, and unicorns that shows what it would look like if punch bowls could go insane. Because Oliver Cromwell liquidated every royal artifact he could get his hands on, everything dates to after the Restoration (the 1660s or later). Clearly, the monarchy has more than made up for the loss. Touring the four levels of the cavernous **White Tower** requires much stair-climbing but takes in a wide span of history, including a fine stone chapel, Norman-era fireplaces and toilets, and the gleaming **Line of Kings**

### The Ravens, Forevermore

**Ravens** probably first visited the Tower in the 1200s to feast on the dripping corpses of the executed, who were taken from Tower Hill (the public execution ground, near the present-day Tube stop) and affixed to the battlements as a warning. You've probably heard the legend that if the ravens ever leave the Tower, England will fall—so seven of the carnivorous birds are kept in cages north of Wakefield Tower, where they are fed raw meat, blood-soaked cookies, and the occasional finger from a tourist dumb enough to stick one between the bars.



collection of the Royal Armoury. Once you've got those two areas under your belt, take your time exploring the rest. On Tower Green is the circular glass memorial designating the **Scaffold Site,** where the unlucky few (including queens Anne Boleyn and Lady Jane Grey) are said to have lost their heads. In reality, we don't know exactly where they were killed, but Queen Victoria wanted a commemorative site set, and because of the evident perils of displeasing the queen, this spot was chosen.
Tower Hill, EC3. www.hrp.org.uk. ✆ **084/4482-7777.** £22 adults, £10 children 5–15, £17 students/seniors, £55 family of up to five, posted prices are higher and include a "voluntary donation." Tube: Tower Hill or Tower Gateway DLR. Nov–Feb Tues–Sat 9am–4:30pm and Sun–Mon 10am–4:30pm, Mar–Oct Tues–Sat 9am–5:30pm and Sun–Mon 10am–5:30pm, last admission 30 min. before closing.

## ATTRACTIONS OUTSIDE CENTRAL LONDON

**Hampton Court Palace ★★★** MUSEUM/HISTORIC SITE If you have to pick just one palace to visit in London, select this one, because there's so much more to do than look at golden furniture. A 35-minute commuter train ride from London Waterloo (they go every half-hour), Hampton Court looks like the ideal palace because it defined the ideal: The redbrick mansion was a center for royal life from 1525 to 1737, and its forest of chimneys stands regally in 24 hectares (59 acres)

Hampton Court Palace and Gardens.

of achingly pretty riverside gardens, painstakingly restored to their 1702 appearance. Guides pander to Tudor scandals to make history more interesting, and days are full of events, which may include re-enactments of gossipy events by costumed actors, Tudor-style cook-offs in the old kitchens, Shakespeare plays in the hammer-beamed Great Hall, or ghost tours. Whatever you do, don't neglect the 24-hectare (59-acre) **gardens** and make time to lose yourself in the Northern Gardens' shrubbery **Maze,** installed by William III; kids giggle their way through to the middle of this leafy labyrinth.

East Molesey, Surrey. www.hrp.org.uk. ✆ **084/4482-7777.** £18 adults, £8.25 children 5–15, £15 seniors/students, posted prices are higher and include a "voluntary donation." National Rail: Hampton Court from Waterloo Station. March to late Oct daily 10am–6pm and late Oct to Mar daily 10am–4:30pm, last admission 1 hr. before closing.

**Highclere Castle ★★★** MUSEUM/HISTORIC SITE The 8th Earl and Countess of Carnarvon still dwell under the sandstone turrets that are known to TV viewers as the idyllic and stately *Downton Abbey.* Time and spendthrift earls took their toll on this historic home, and as recently as 2009, more than 50 rooms were uninhabitable due to mold and leaks. The current Earl faced repair bills of around £12 million, so he welcomes visitors to admire his home and spend the day exploring the 1,000 acres of private rolling Berkshire countryside. At Highclere, the basement is filled not with servants but with mummy stuff. The 5th Earl is the guy who bankrolled Howard Carter's 1923 discovery and emptying of King Tut's tomb in Luxor, so unseen beneath Lord Grantham's feet lay items taken from the tombs of Egypt. Highclere is only open for 60 to 70 days a year but they're scattered all over the calendar. The castle is typically open Easter Week, bank holiday weekends, and from mid-August to mid-September. Taking a group tour guarantees you a ticket, but those sell out months ahead and herd you along. If you show up independently at either 10am or 2:30pm, you can get a walk-up ticket even though advance tickets are sold out, but that involves taking a 52-minute train from Paddington (from £23) or a National Express bus (£13) to the adorable town of Newbury and then a £15 taxi (try www.newburytaxi.co.uk; ✆ **078/2734-3332**) from there.

Highclere Park, Newbury. www.highclerecastle.co.uk. ✆ **01635/253-204.** £20 adults, £18 students/seniors, £13 children 4–16.

**The Royal Observatory ★★** HISTORIC SITE Commanding a terrific view from the hill in Greenwich Park, with the towers of Canary Wharf spread out in its lap, the Observatory is yet another creation of Christopher Wren (from 1675), and the place from which time zones emanate. Historically the Empire's most important house for celestial observation, it houses significant relics of star-peeping. But since it began charging in 2011, the paid areas became a tourist trap. Most of the good stuff—marked on the map in red—is free, including a small Astronomy Centre and an exhibition on time. The only things admission get you are an unremarkable ceiling-projection planetarium and the bulk of the Flamsteed House by Wren, which includes a collection of clocks that cracked the mystery of measuring longitude, ushering the English Empire to worldwide dominance. Most people plunk down admission not because they care about those but to get access to the Meridian Courtyard. The Prime Meridian, located at precisely 0° longitude (the equator is 0° latitude), crosses through the grounds, and interminable queues of coach tourists pay at least £7 to wait an hour for a silly Instagram moment of straddling the line with a foot in two hemispheres at once—but the dirty secret is they don't have to. The line continues on the walkway north of the courtyard, where it's free and there's never a wait. In the old days, the red Time Ball fell precisely at 1pm daily so that the city could synchronize their clocks; it still rises at 12:55pm and drops 5 minutes later. You could set your watch by it, but technically, you already do. Down the hill is the superb (and free) National Maritime Museum, which is especially strong in kids' activities.

Greenwich Park, Greenwich, SE10. www.rmg.co.uk. ✆ **020/8312-6565.** Free admission for most of grounds. Flamsteed House and Meridian Courtyard £6.35 adults, £4.50 seniors/students, £2.25 kids under 16; planetarium £6.50 adults, £4.50 kids 5–15, £5.50 seniors/students; combination ticket £12 adults, £6 kids under 16, £10 seniors/students. Tube: Cutty Sark DLR, Greenwich river ferry, or Greenwich National Rail. Daily 10am–6pm, last admission 5:30pm.

**Warner Bros. Studio Tour London—The Making of Harry Potter ★★★** MUSEUM London's most popular new family outing is like a DVD of extra features that comes to life, and it's as gripping as the fine museums can be. On the very lot where the eight movies of history's most successful film franchise were shot, it seems that every set, prop, prosthetic, wig, and wand was lovingly saved for this exhaustive

**Hogwart's Great Hall, Warner Bros. Studio Tour London.**

walk-though feast. You could spend hours grazing the bounty, from the students' Great Hall to Dumbledore's roost to Dolores Umbridge's den to the actual Diagon Alley and Hogwarts Express steam engine. There's little filler, so book your entry time for early in the day so you'll have time to wander. The finale, an astounding 1:24 scale model of Hogwarts Castle embedded with 2,500 fiber optic lights, is 50 feet across and takes up an arena-size room lit to simulate day and night. And you won't *believe* the gift shop. Easy 15-minute trains go three times an hour from Euston Station—but not, fans sigh, from Platform 9¾ at King's Cross. (Although there, an enterprising Potter souvenir stall affixed a sign and takes pictures for £9.)

Warner Bros. Studios Leavesden, Aerodrome Way, Leavesden, Hertfordshire. www.wbstudiotour.co.uk. ✆ **08450/840-900.** £33 adults, £26 kids 5–15, under 5 free, £101 family of 4, return train ticket £10. National Rail: Watford Junction, then a £2 shuttle bus that meets trains. Reservations required. First tours 9–10am, last tours 4–6:30pm, closes 3 hrs. after last tour time.

**Windsor Castle ★★★** MUSEUM/HISTORIC SITE A fortress and a royal home for more than 900 years, it was expanded by each successive monarch who dwelled in it—more battlements for the warlike ones, more finery for the aesthetes. The resulting sprawl, which dominates the town from nearly every angle, is the Queen's favorite residence—she spends lots of time here—and its history is richer than that of Buckingham Palace. The castle's **State Apartments** are sumptuous enough to be daunting, and a tour through them, available unless there's a state visit, includes entrance to some mind-bogglingly historic rooms. Around a million people file through every year, so sharpen your elbows, and there are no cafes, so eat in town first. The palace has a cache of priceless furniture (some of it solid silver), paintings, ephemera (look for the bullet that killed Lord Nelson, sealed in a locket) and weaponry, all of which, frustratingly, the audio guide, signage, and £5 souvenir book do little to describe, so the only recourse is to pepper staff with questions. **St George's Chapel** (closed Sun), a delicately vaulted Gothic spectacle opened by Henry VIII, is his final resting place and that of nine more monarchs, including Elizabeth II's father (George VI). EII's mother (the Queen Mum) and sister (Princess Margaret) are with him in a side chapel, and it's safe to assume that this is where she will wind up one day, too. There's a **Changing the Guard** ceremony at 11am (Mon–Sat, but alternate days Aug–Mar; check the website). **Trains** (www.nationalrail.co.uk; ✆ **08457/48-49-50;** 38–56 min.; £9.70) go directly from Waterloo station to Windsor & Eton Riverside or from Paddington to Windsor & Eton Central with a change at Slough. Trains requiring no changes leave twice an hour, and trains requiring a change leave a little more frequently.

Castle Hill. www.royalcollection.org.uk. ✆ **020/7766-7304.** £19 adults, £18 students and seniors, £11 children 5–16, free 4 and under, £50 family of 5 (2 adults and 3 children 16 and under). National rail: Windsor Central or Windsor & Eton Riverside.

Daily Mar–Oct 9:45am–5:15pm, last admission 4pm; Nov–Feb 9:45am–4:15pm, last admission 3pm. Closed for periods in Apr, June, and Dec, when the royal family is in residence.

## Organized Tours & Excursions

There are so many guides to choose from—the best ones are led by government-accredited "Blue Badge" professionals, so always look for the Blue Badge—that you could fill a week with walking tours alone. Plenty of qualified operators cater to custom business (many only cater to groups), but many others will let you join individually: **City of London Guided Walks** (www.cityoflondonguides.com; £7), run by the government—so its facts are unimpeachable—and light on theatrics; **Eating London Tours** (www.eatinglondontours.co.uk; £65), a recommended 3½-hour, stuff-yourself-silly walking romp though some of the greatest victuals in the East End; **Greenwich Guided Walks** (www.greenwichtours.co.uk; ✆ **020/8858-6169;** £8), which is run by the local council in Greenwich and specializes in its distinct stories; **Muggle Tours** (www.muggletours.co.uk; ✆ **07917/411-374;** £12 adults, £10 children 11 and under) for Harry Potter fans; and the indomitable **London Walks** (www.walks.com; ✆ **020/7624-3978;** most tours £9). This long-running and extremely popular outfit offers more than a dozen topics across the city and is both reliable and entertaining. Also check *Time Out* (www.timeout.com/london), where museums and organizations announce one-off tours.

Narrated bus tours often make you wait 15 to 30 minutes for the next bus each time you get off, which can add up to hours wasted, and although your ticket will be good for 24 hours, don't expect to catch anything between 6pm or so until after 9am the next morning. Day tickets may come with a free walking tour (Changing the Guard, Jack the Ripper) and a hop-on, hop-off pass for the river shuttle boat. Both of those perks must often be used during the same 24 hours as the bus ticket's validity. The three major players in town, which cost £25 to £33 for adults, are **Big Bus Tours** (www.bigbustours.com; ✆ **020/7808-6753**), **Golden Tours Open Top Bus Tours** (11a Charing Cross Rd., WC2, 156 Cromwell Rd., SW7, and 4 Fountain Sq., 123-151 Buckingham Palace Rd., SW1; www.goldentours.com; ✆ **020/7630-2028** [U.K.] and **800/509-2507** [North America]), and **The Original Tour London Sightseeing** (17-19 Cockspur St., SW1. www.theoriginaltour.com; ✆ **020/8877-1722**). You might have a more enjoyable time seeing the city's waterfront landmarks and Greenwich from the Thames using **City Cruises** (www.citycruises.com; ✆ **020/774-0400;** £8.30 single, £12 return). The most economical way to see the town if you have limited time is from the top level of a red double-decker city bus: The **15 bus,** which crosses the city northwest to southeast, takes in Paddington, Oxford Street, Piccadilly Circus, Trafalgar Square, Fleet Street, St Paul's, and the Tower of London.

## Especially for Kids

There's no bad neighborhood to stay in if you've got kids, because London is low-rise and manageable. But make sure they're ready to climb stairs if you're taking the Tube. On paper, some of London's museums sound as if they'd be too dry, but in reality, they bend over backward to cater to children—sometimes even at the expense of adult minds. Every major museum, no exceptions, has an on-site cafe for lunch, and nearly all of them offer activity packs to helps kids engage with the exhibitions. Make your way to Covent Garden's **London Transport Museum ★** (Covent Garden, WC2; www.ltmuseum.co.uk; ✆ **020/7565-7298;** £15 adults, £12 seniors/students, free for kids under 18; Sat–Thurs 10am–6pm, Fri 11am–6pm, last admission 45 min. before closing; Tube: Covent Garden) where kids can pretend to drive a bus and explore other eye-level exhibits. Then bring your brood a 15-minute walk north to the **British Museum ★★★** (p. 24) and hook them up with crayons and pads, exploration backpacks, and the special 12-object collections tour geared to young minds. If they're the daring types, the mummies never fail to impress. Just east you'll find a city park just for children: The 7-acre **Coram's Fields ★** (www.coramsfields.org) was set aside in 1739 for an orphanage at a time when 75% of London kids died before the age of 5. Its southern stone gate is where mothers once abandoned their babies in desperation. Today, no adult may enter without a child, and it's the scene of daily joy between parents and children; there's a petting zoo, two playgrounds for all ages, sand pits, and a paddling pool.

Take the Piccadilly Line to South Kensington, where the **V&A ★★★** (p. 39) has hundreds of hands-on exhibits for kids (look for the hand symbol on the maps), such as trying on Victorian costumes to trying on armor gauntlets. Next door, the plain-speaking signs and robotic dinosaurs of the **Natural History Museum ★★** (p. 37) impress kids as much as the airplanes and space capsules over their heads at the world-class **Science Museum ★** (Exhibition Rd., SW7; www.sciencemuseum.org.uk; ✆ **087/0870-4868;** Free; Daily 10am–6pm; Tube: South Kensington)—both institutions furnish even more kids' trails and activities for free.

## Where to Stay

Accommodations are subject to a Value Added Tax (VAT) of 20%. Happily, almost all small B&Bs include taxes in their rates, although you may be charged 3% to 5% to use a credit card. More expensive hotels (those around £150 or more) tend to leave taxes off their tariffs, which can result in a nasty surprise at checkout. It never hurts to ask if the rate "excludes VAT."

### SOHO, COVENT GARDEN & NEARBY

#### Expensive

**Hazlitt's ★★★** A stay here is like a slumber in a time machine. Each room is its own individual historic universe, the centerpiece of which is a deep oak or carved four-poster bed. Around you is a bathroom with antique

fixtures and heavy silk curtains that, when pulled closed after a long day, make you feel as if you are the master of your own Georgian townhouse—plus, of course, modern expectations such as air-conditioning, flatscreen TV, and safes. When you step out your front door, you can retreat to the library or step into the thick of Soho, completing the opulent fantasy. "Dandyism is a variety of genius," wrote William Hazlitt, a great writer of his age. That statement may not be true, but it sounds good. He died here when it was a rooming house, in a small bedroom at the back of the third floor, in 1830 at age 52.
6 Frith St., W1. www.hazlittshotel.com. ✆ **020/7434-1771.** 30 units. Doubles £215–£354. Tube: Tottenham Court Rd. **Amenities:** Room service; free Wi-Fi.

**The Langham ★★** In 1863, while Americans were shooting each other in farmyards, London was assembling the first and most celebrated grande dame hotel in Europe. She survives, but it was touch and go during the 20th century. The polished lobby is perfumed, the lifts swathed in leather, the rooms each a private cocoon of ordered wainscoting, enveloping beds, and bathrooms with toiletries in pink paper cartons kept in a box by the sink. Its Palm Court has been serving high tea (£40) since 1865. For its brag-worthy reputation, the Langham is favored by moneyed tourists from the Far East, and for service and discretion, along with that long history, there are few peers. The tariff is also something for the record books, but that's the price you pay to be in the company of Lady Di, Wallis Simpson, and Winston Churchill, who rightly favored it, and Arthur Conan Doyle, who sent Sherlock Holmes here in several stories. It's a few short blocks from Oxford Street's best shopping.
1c Portland Place, Regent St., W1. www.langhamhotels.com. ✆ **020/7636-1000.** 380 units. Doubles £312–£444. Tube: Oxford Circus. **Amenities:** 2 restaurants; 2 bars; spa; business center; swimming pool; free Wi-Fi.

**The Langham.**

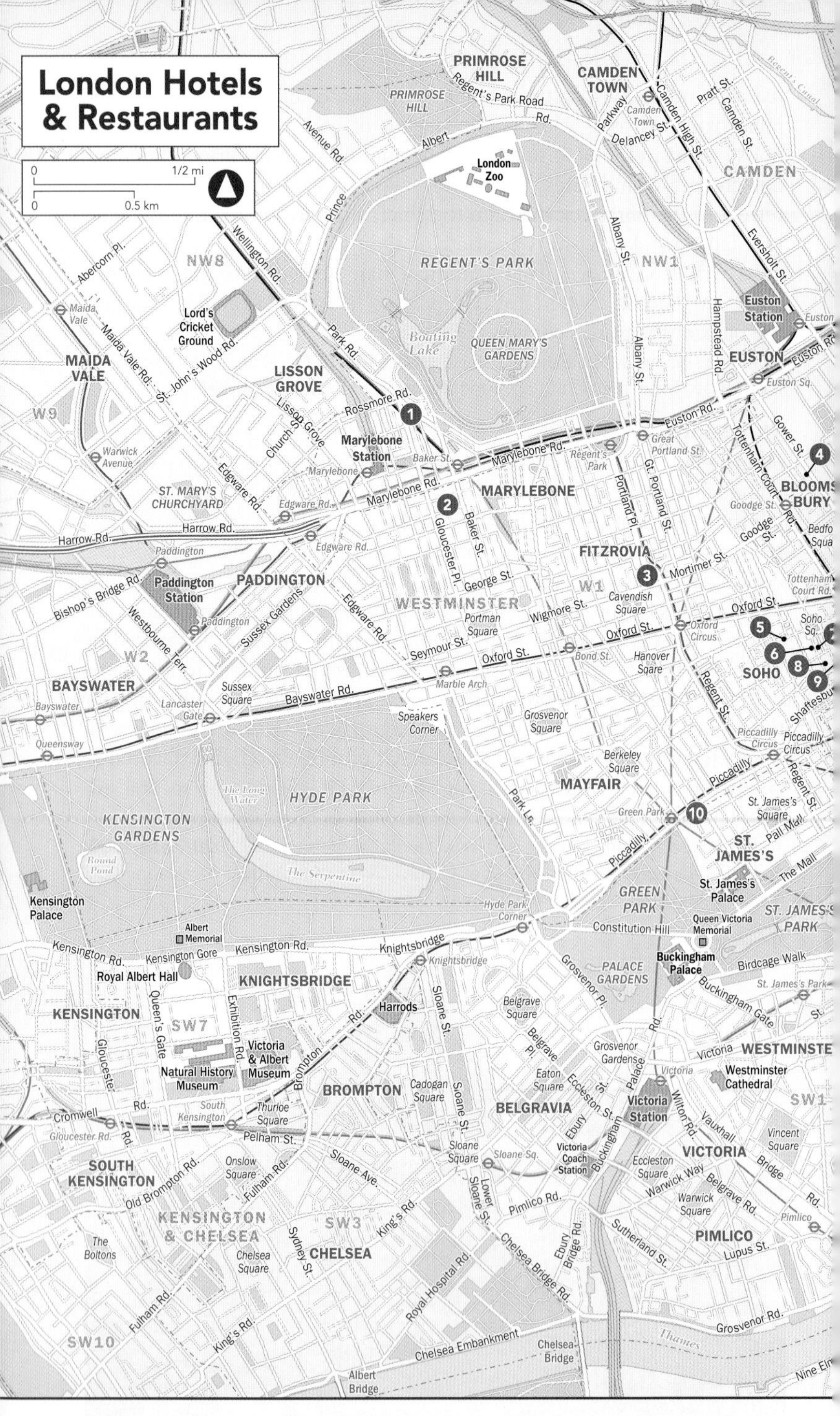

London Hotels & Restaurants
0 1/2 mi
0 0.5 km
PRIMROSE HILL
CAMDEN TOWN
CAMDEN
REGENT'S PARK
London Zoo
QUEEN MARY'S GARDENS
Boating Lake
NW8
NW1
Lord's Cricket Ground
MAIDA VALE
LISSON GROVE
EUSTON
Euston Station
Marylebone Station
MARYLEBONE
FITZROVIA
BLOOMSBURY
ST. MARY'S CHURCHYARD
Paddington Station
PADDINGTON
WESTMINSTER
W1
W2
W9
BAYSWATER
SOHO
Oxford Circus
Marble Arch
Speakers Corner
Grosvenor Square
Berkeley Square
MAYFAIR
HYDE PARK
KENSINGTON GARDENS
The Long Water
The Serpentine
Round Pond
Kensington Palace
Albert Memorial
Royal Albert Hall
KNIGHTSBRIDGE
KENSINGTON
Harrods
SW7
Natural History Museum
Victoria & Albert Museum
BROMPTON
BELGRAVIA
GREEN PARK
ST. JAMES'S
St. James's Palace
ST. JAMES'S PARK
Buckingham Palace
PALACE GARDENS
Victoria Station
VICTORIA
WESTMINSTER
Westminster Cathedral
SW1
SOUTH KENSINGTON
KENSINGTON & CHELSEA
SW3
CHELSEA
PIMLICO
SW10
Thames
Chelsea Bridge
Albert Bridge

HOTELS
22 York Street 2
Alhambra Hotel 24
Captain Bligh House 28
Charing Cross Hotel 15
CitizenM London Bankside 29
Hazlitt's 7
Hotel Americano 1
Jesmond Hotel 4
The Langham 3
The Nadler Soho 5
One Aldwych 18
Qbic London City 37
Rosewood London 22
Shangri-La Hotel at the Shard 32
South Place Hotel 34
Z Hotel Soho 11
RESTAURANTS
Arbutus 6
Beigel Bake 36
Bill's 21
The Black Friar 27
Borough Market 30
Browns 13
Café in the Crypt 14
Ceviche 8
The Fryer's Delight 23
The George Inn 31
Gordon's Wine Bar 16
Great Queen Street 19
J. Sheekey 12
The Princess Louise 20
Restaurant Story 33
Rochelle Canteen 35
Rules 17
The Stockpot 9
The Wolseley 10
Ye Olde Cheshire Cheese 26
Ye Olde Mitre 25
ISLINGTON
FINSBURY
CLERKENWELL
SHOREDITCH
ST. PANCRAS
FARRINGDON
HOLBORN
COVENT GARDEN
THE STRAND
CITY (LONDON)
THE CITY
SOUTH BANK
BANKSIDE
SOUTHWARK
BOROUGH
NEWINGTON
ELEPHANT & CASTLE
LAMBETH
VAUXHALL

**One Aldwych ★★★** The pie-shaped, onetime headquarters of the *Morning Post,* built in 1907, contains a consistently high-quality boutique with two restaurants; a double-tall, sculpture-filled lobby lounge; and a theatrically lit, chlorine-free underground swimming pool where the printing presses used to be. Rooms are contemporary and designed with environmentalism in mind, have beds to sink into, and some even sneak a view of the Thames. The staff is truly five-star in that it tries to meet needs without being asked, and the location feels impossibly considerate, too: steps from Covent Garden and Trafalgar, a walk down the Strand to St Paul's, and a quick and gorgeous stroll over the Waterloo Bridge to the glories of Southbank.

1 Aldwych, WC2. www.onealdwych.com. ✆ **020/7300-1000.** 105 units. Doubles from £264–£312. Tube: Covent Garden or Temple. **Amenities:** 2 restaurants; cocktail bar; pool; gym; free Wi-Fi.

**Rosewood London ★★★** On the hot list of London hotels since its 2013 opening after an £85-million refit, this chic retreat is entered through a stone courtyard arch of a gloriously elaborate edifice (constructed with pomp as the Pearl Assurance citadel). It's the *ne plus ultra* of London's modern luxury properties. A foyer sheathed entirely in brass! Songbirds by the lifts! Toilet paper as indulgently soft as puppies' ears! Rooms are so quiet you could hear a champagne bubble pop. They're also lush: Giant 46" LCD TVs are standard, as is Italian bedding you sink into like a swimming pool. Push a button to bring down your window blinds and sip homemade sloe gin from the minibar. If it weren't for the hard reality of the tariff, you might lament that the rest of the planet can't be executed with such theatricality. The neighborhood seems at first to be too dry, but the British Museum and Covent Garden are both 5 minutes away.

252 High Holborn, WC1. www.rosewoodhotels.com/london. ✆ **020/7781-8888.** 262 units. Doubles £320–£510. Tube: Holborn. **Amenities:** Bar; restaurant; lounge; gym; spa; free Wi-Fi.

### Moderate

**Charing Cross Hotel ★★** The railway terminal hotel above Charing Cross Station was opened in 1865 and underwent many lives (and Blitz damage) before coming under the recent control of Guoman Hotels, a capable British hospitality company that's rising in global stature. Now the Charing Cross is a well-run, upper-moderate hotel that dips its toes into luxury trimmings (heated bathroom floors, illuminated wardrobes, walk-in showers, and so forth) without going over-the-top on price. The location is spectacular and could command higher rates: steps from Trafalgar Square in one direction, and morning strolls on the Thames in the other. Breakfast (not included in room rate) is taken with a view toward St Martin-in-the-Fields, and at night, some 350 candles are placed throughout the hallways and up the sweeping grand staircase that once signified the privilege of a more genteel age.

The Strand, WC2. www.guoman.com/charingcross. ✆ **0871/376-9012.** 200 units. Doubles £169–£322. Tube: Charing Cross or Embankment. **Amenities:** Restaurant; bar; business center; free Wi-Fi.

**The Nadler Soho ★★★** Announced by an Art Nouveau sculpture of the Greek goddess of the moon, this newer custom-built hotel gets moderate lodging right by providing style without pretension or henpecking guests with extra fees. Quiet, high-design rooms are compact but kitted-out with twists such as wide beds, mini-kitchens with filtered water, a microwave, big glassy bathrooms with rain showers, plenty of power points plus a loaner plug adapter, a half-hour of free national calls a day, and HD TVs that double as music players. Deluxe rooms, at the top of the middle-rate scale, sleep up to four. There's no restaurant (breakfast can be delivered from the nearby Princi Bakery at prices that aren't marked up), but all of Soho is heaving right outside your door—reason alone to book here.

10 Carlisle St., W1. www.thenadler.com. ✆ **020/3697-3697.** 78 units. Doubles £135–£255. Tube: Tottenham Court Road or Piccadilly Circus. **Amenities:** Free Wi-Fi.

### Inexpensive

**Alhambra Hotel ★★★** A well-kept, family-run spot, the comforting Alhambra is an inn with heart, and a top value. Its proprietors, whose family has owned the land for decades and isn't at risk of being elbowed out, take pride in the family business, and they keep the prices low. Picture simple but dignified rooms (always spotless, with LCD TVs but no phones) squeezed into old spaces and freshened up with bright bedspreads, cream pinstripe wallpaper, inviting royal-blue carpeting, and built-in desks with chairs. Frank Valoti, the patriarch, does the cooking, and he dabbles in art, too; in the basement breakfast area, check out the pastel still life he drew to show Europeans what's included in his generous full English breakfast. Bruno Cabral, his attentive son-in-law, handles the hotel's modernization, such as the addition of free Wi-Fi and in-room safes, a rarity for this price point. If you share a bathroom, there are plenty to go around. The same family runs an annex across the street that has the same high standards. In winter, it's easy to negotiate rates down by as much as 30%.

17-19 Argyle St., WC1. www.alhambrahotel.com. ✆ **020/7837-9575.** 52 units. Doubles £80–£111, includes breakfast. Tube: King's Cross St Pancras. **Amenities:** Lobby computer; free Wi-Fi.

**Jesmond Hotel ★★★** Glyn Beynon does a solid job of running the family B&B where he grew up, in a historic Georgian townhouse (ask to read the history he wrote of it). The Jesmond is far beyond the expectations of its tariff range. Bathrooms are of recent vintage, with larger-than-average showers. Soundproofed front windows keep out the roar of Gower Street's bus traffic. The house's 18th-century coal chute has been converted into a kitchen where full English breakfasts are served in a cellar breakfast room that doubles as a day lounge. The back garden

provides welcome respite and is cultivated with flowers and wooden chairs. Beynon also converted the former parlor, with its antique (non-working) fireplace, into room 2, a spacious double. It's simple, it's friendly, and it's still one of London's last "they're charging *how* much?" values. Don't confuse this place with the Jesmond Dene, a B&B on Argyle Square in King's Cross—it's very good, too, but not as central as the Jesmond.
63 Gower St., WC1. www.jesmondhotel.org.uk. ✆ **020/7636-3199.** 15 units. Doubles £85–£110, includes breakfast. Tube: Goodge Street. **Amenities:** Free Wi-Fi.





**The Z Hotel Soho ★★★** Here's the formula: extremely compact rooms, glassy sleek style, thrilling location, and because extras such as breakfast are pre-paid when you book, there's a skeleton staff, keeping costs down. The formula, devised by career hotel professionals, works because it's done with design smarts: they poured a lot of cash into the bedding and the 40-inch TVs (the better to drown out Soho noise with streaming music from your phone) but did without closets and drawers. Quarters are close (around 9 sq. m/90 sq. ft.), but quirky, with a zig-zaggy courtyard and a roof deck with a nifty view of the Palace Theatre. If you share a room with a platonic friend, note that bathrooms, though stocked with Thierry Mugler toiletries, are enclosed by panels of fogged glass. Lowest rates are for singles; add £20 for a double bed and another £10 for a queen; doubles without windows cost the same as a single room. Just be sure to pronounce it "zed." Rhymes with bed—what it's good for. There is a second location in much-less-desirable Victoria, a block west of the station (5 Lower Belgrave St., SW1; ✆ **020/3589-3990;** 106 units, 60% windowless) and another just south of Piccadilly Circus.
17 Moor St., W1. www.thezhotels.com. ✆ **020/3551-3701.** 85 units. Rooms start at £75 but are usually £145–£195. Tube: Leicester Square. **Amenities:** Cafe; free Wi-Fi.

### SOUTHWARK & WESTMINSTER

#### Expensive

**Shangri-La Hotel at the Shard ★★** Be warned that if you decide to book at the Shangri-La, you must be prepared to never leave it. Staying here, on the 36th to 52nd floors of this glass-sheathed skyscraper, means that your room will be encased with floor-to-ceiling windows overlooking the entire city. No structure in London will be higher than you. When you take a bath (in your marble-coated washroom with heated floors), you may feel as if you're flying over the Thames and the Tower of London, and when you swim in the horizon pool in the sky above St Paul's, the vista is so surreal that you may wonder if it's all dream. Such glassy heaven comes with decor and amenities that are clean-lined, simple, and inflected by the Asian culture from which the Shangri-La brand hails (for example, in-room amenities might be stored in a bento-style box). The Thames and the famous Borough Market are right at its base. Rates are higher than other luxury hotels in town but, well, so are the rooms, and that seems to justify it to nearly everyone's satisfaction.

31 St Thomas St., SE1. www.shangri-la.com/london/shangrila. ✆ **020/7234-8000.** 202 units. Doubles from £375. Tube: London Bridge. **Amenities:** Restaurant; bar; gym; pool; free Wi-Fi.

### Moderate

**CitizenM London Bankside ★★★** This affordable Dutch hotel chain is blossoming, deservedly so, and its welcome concept of smart-and-stylish quarters without added fees or interference from groveling staff makes it the best casual choice in Southwark. The glassy open-plan lobby, a playpen of designer coffee table books and orange-and-white Penguin classic paperbacks, seems to hum day and night with people sipping coffees and telecommuting. Check-in is self-guided by kiosk, and rooms are compact—almost podlike—but arranged with genius. Platform beds are massive and piled with body pillows, curvy bathrooms slotted into the space with calculated aplomb, and you control everything from motorized blinds to the color of the room's mood lighting with a bedside tablet. There's even a hefty library of free movies (including porn of all persuasions—it's a Dutch company, and it's sassy). With new properties opening in Holborn, Tower Hill, and Shoreditch, odds are on CitizenM to become a major in the mid-range market.

20 Lavington St., SE1. www.citizenm.com/london-bankside. ✆ **020/3519-1680.** 192 units. Doubles £109–£189. Tube: Southwark or London Bridge. **Amenities:** Free movies; free Wi-Fi.

### Inexpensive

**Captain Bligh House ★★★** For a delicious taste of local London life without venturing far from the center of town, the Bligh, where Captain William Bligh lived after that sordid mutiny affair, is a transporting choice. Artists Gayna and Simon approach their wee guesthouse, built in the 1780s (before the invention of the lift), as a quiet home away from home: Units have little kitchens for cooking up market ingredients, but you also get a starter pack of breakfast supplies. Although the excellent Imperial War Museum is across the street, it's not a neighborhood crawling with tourists, so you'll kick back at the local pub and jump the many bus lines that go past. The value is over-the-top.

100 Lambeth Rd., SE1. www.captainblighhouse.co.uk. ✆ **020/7928-2735.** 5 units. Doubles with kitchen from £88–£114. Tube: Lambeth North. **Amenities:** Free Wi-Fi.

## OTHER TOP HOTELS

### Expensive

**South Place Hotel ★★★** Plugged-in, stylish, and sexy: That's the crowd this hotel goes for, and you'll feel that way, too. The first hotel to be built from the ground up in the city for a century, every inch was run through the design filter, and much of the art was commissioned by celebrated contemporary artists. Rooms, charcoal-grey with wool carpets, are large, hushed, and fully up-to-date with luxury expectations, so you'll find plenty of outlets, AV connections, blackout blinds closed from a bedside panel, and a big bed you can flop around in. The two restaurants,

Angler and 3 South Place Bar & Grill, have lured both name chefs and some of the liveliest professionals from the city, who nosh before they head just east to the party grounds at Spitalfields. Despite the hot scene, it never ignores the relaxation of its guests. On weekends, rates can dip to £170.

3 South Place, EC2. www.southplacehotel.com. ✆ **020/3503-0000.** 80 units. Doubles from £213. Tube: Moorgate or Liverpool Street. **Amenities:** 2 restaurants; 3 bars; lounge; gym; spa; business center; free Wi-Fi.

### Moderate

**22 York Street ★★** You might wonder at first if you have knocked on the door of a private home of some bohemian doctor or lawyer. Inside, Michael and Liz Callis are going for a farmhouse feel, with warm wooden floorboards, plenty of antiques and oriental rugs, and large bathrooms, almost all of which have tub/shower combinations. Guests get their own keys and are let loose to treat the five-level premises as their own, which includes plenty of tea, coffee, and biscuits for munching. Adding to the home-away-from-home feel, breakfasts are served in the kitchen at a communal country table where you meet your fellow guests. The food includes some fantastic pain au chocolate. Although they're not explicitly banned, kids may not feel comfortable.

22 York St., W1. www.22yorkstreet.co.uk. ✆ **020/7224-2990.** 10 units. Doubles from £150, includes breakfast. Tube: Baker Street. **Amenities:** Free Wi-Fi.

### Inexpensive

**Hotel Americana ★** Beige-simple, without unnecessary flourish, but extremely well-maintained, the Americana is a strong value in a neighborhood besieged by rising rates. Robert, the chatty and opinionated longtime manager, is exactly the kind of authority on London (and on everything, really) that you wish to encounter behind a B&B desk. Room 124, a twin, is slightly larger than the others, but all have showers, tiny TVs, a safe, and plenty of light. Although it's composed of two conjoined townhouses, there's a wee lift, and it's also very near Regent's Park and, unusually, steps away from a launderette. Rates can go even lower in winter or if you agree to stay for longer than 3 nights.

172 Gloucester Place, NW1. www.americanahotel.co.uk. ✆ **020/7723-1452.** 29 units. Doubles £99–£156, includes breakfast. Tube: Baker Street or Marylebone. **Amenities:** Free Wi-Fi.

**Qbic London City ★★** From a growing, affordable design hotel chain in Holland, Qbic is a wacky antidote to the formula budget hotels. Everything you need—bed, outlets, bathroom with a rain shower, TV—is a part of a prefabricated unit that dominates the middle of the room. It's not a capsule hotel, just a hotel that figured out a way to build everything into a single multi-purpose unit, with plenty of room to walk around it and stash your suitcase, without making you uncomfortable in the least. Your lamp is made out of a coiled and immobilized garden hose, your clothing rack a strange ladder/planter of some sort—it's just fun. There are free coffee/tea machines on every floor, and a preposterously funky lobby where organic continental breakfast is served daily (extra charge). You'll be within walking distance to Brick Lane (5 min.), the Tower of London (15 min.), and the scene of Spitalfields (15 min.), and you'll be amused to learn that the United States's Liberty Bell was made on the very same block at the Whitechapel Bell Foundry, which you can see from courtyard-facing rooms. It's a kick, the managers are sensitive to local culture, and it's worth every penny.

42 Adler St. E1. www.london.qbichotels.com. ✆ **020/3021-3300.** 171 units. Windowless ("Smart") rooms from £69, windowed doubles ("Cosy" and "Fun") from £79. Tube: Aldgate East. **Amenities:** Free coffee; lounge; free Wi-Fi.

## THE MODERATE HOTEL CHAINS

A few reliable hotel chains specialize in moderately priced rooms and have locations across the city, including in prime locations no family-owned B&B can afford. Be warned—so many Europeans habitually turn to these that their prices frequently rise past the point of value, particularly close to the dates of stay, so these are best when booked far in advance. In addition to these names, look into **Motel One** (www.motel-one.com), a stylish German newcomer, which has rates from £89 at a Tower Hill property.

**easyHotel ★** This is how you do London super-cheaply while avoiding hostels. Reservations typically cost £25 for double rooms if you book 6 months ahead, and £35 to £90 if you procrastinate. Its revelation is, to others, a curse: prefabricated room units that differ only in how little floor space you're given (the smallest are 6 sq. m./65 sq. ft.). Beds are double-size with white duvets, with rarely an inch of space between mattress and wall. No phone, no hair dryer, no frills at all. You may find a long ledge on which to pop a travel alarm clock, but bathrooms aren't more than plastic cubicles combining a shower, toilet, and sink in one water-splashed closet. The cheapest rooms don't even have windows. Want to watch TV? You'll pay £5 for 24 hours. Want housekeeping? £10. Wi-Fi is pay-as-you-use. This is no-nonsense sleep.

www.easyhotel.com. No phone reservations. 5 locations in central London. Rooms from £25–£90.

**Ibis Hotels ★★** This 600-strong French chain by the Accor hotel giant is distinguished by its trademark 3-foot-square windows, its just-off-the-margins locations, and its simple but cheerful decor. You'll get a double bed, bathroom with shower, climate control, a 24-hour kitchen, TV, phone, free Wi-Fi, at least one outlet, and a built-in desk. The breakfast charge varies by property (£7.50 is typical), but food is usually served from 4am, making this a smart choice if you need to catch an early flight or train. The fresh-baked breakfast baguettes are delicious—hey, it's French. But let's be frank: You'd have to be mad to think these rooms are worth the price once they go above £170, so book as far ahead as possible. There's also **Ibis Styles,** the "all-inclusive" brand that is slightly more upscale and includes breakfast and Wi-Fi, and **Ibis Budget,** a bare-bones, shower-only crash pad once known as Etap or Formule 1; rooms there have style but are very simple, sleep up to three people, and have free Wi-Fi and TV, but practically nothing else frilly.



www.ibishotel.com. No English-reservations hotline. 6 locations around the city. Rooms £60–£209, varying by season and location.



**Premier Inn ★★★** This is many British travelers' favorite hotel brand. At 50,000 bedrooms and growing, it's the largest hotel chain in the United Kingdom, and rooms (maximum of two adults) offer a king-size bed, bathtub and shower with all-purpose shower gel, tea- and coffee-making facilities, TV, phone, iron, air-conditioning (sometimes), at least three outlets, and a desk. Increasingly, it requires you to check in at a kiosk, eliminating local interaction. Many locations include a mass-appeal bar/cafe, Thyme. Unlike Travelodge, there are in-room phones and hair dryers. Its prices start at £19 nearly a year ahead, but final prices can rival a much nicer hotel's. Like airline tickets, prices rise as availability dwindles, and in busy times, prices soar far higher than where they should be, so book ahead or look elsewhere. These are the best central locations—if you choose a different property, you may save £25 but you might also waste time and money on the Tube. The brand opened a cheaper and tinier concept, **Hub by Premier Inn** (www.hubhotels.co.uk) in 2014; locations are near Covent Garden, King's Cross, Spitalfields, and the Tower of London. Hub rooms are just 11.4 sq. m. (123 sq. ft.), and functions such as air-conditioning and TV are controlled by app.

www.premierinn.com. ✆ **0845/099-0095.** 10 locations around the city. Rooms from £80–£126, depending on season and location. **Amenities:** Bar/cafe; 30 min. free Wi-Fi daily, then £3 for 24 hr.

**Travelodge ★** Rates start at a head-slapping £19 for a non-flexible reservation if you book 11 months ahead. That more than makes up for the thinnest amenities of the economy brands, which has some two dozen properties in Greater London. It's nicer than the American Travelodge brand, which isn't related to it. Expect king-size beds, bathtub and shower, TV (but no phone, hair dryer, or toiletries), paid in-room movies, a wardrobe, at least one power point, and a desk. Breakfast, if your property offers it, is about £8 more. "Family rooms" have a pullout couch for two kids but cost the same as a double. Search its site for a grid of available London hotels. These prices are typical, but they go down to £25 if you're first to book and skyrocket for peak periods.

www.travelodge.co.uk. ✆ **08719/848484.** 8 locations around the city. Rooms £65–£116, depending on season and neighborhood. **Amenities:** Wi-Fi £3 a day.

**Tune Hotels ★★** This Malaysian import provides everything you need in a modern crash pad but nothing else: en-suite power shower, round-the-clock reception, air-conditioning, but not even a closet—you get hangers. If you want more, you pay a few pounds more at a time: towel rental, TV, Wi-Fi, safe, hair dryer, and even windows come at a price. The a la carte model keeps costs down but isn't a path to luxury, yet the facilities are clean and designed with minimalist zip. Don't write off a windowless room's power to mediate jet lag. Prices are as low as £35 months in advance and go to £125 or so last-minute.

www.tunehotels.com/london. No phone. 5 locations in the city. Rates can range from £35–£125.



## Where to Eat

The English palette has caught up with the rest of the world. Cabbage is no longer the national affliction, and let's be honest: English teeth are now better than in America, where people can't afford dentists. If London's stomachs suffer from anything today, it's from a trend toward overpriced places that appeal more to vanity and conspicuous consumption than value and authentic hospitality.

### SOHO, COVENT GARDEN & NEARBY

#### Expensive

**Arbutus** ★★★ CONTEMPORARY EUROPEAN A pair of celebrated city chefs, Anthony Demetre and Will Smith, opened an exquisite restaurant with the intention of serving magnificent modern food at reasonable prices, and they have triumphed, winning a Michelin star for their efforts (and you can buy Demetre's cookbook on bistro food). The menu changes according to what ingredients are in season and top-quality, but might include Welsh Elwy Valley lamb, English pea soup, Dorset crab, Scottish organic salmon, or braised pig's head. Some of these may sound dauntingly adventurous, but deliciousness is assured. Service is also impeccable, and as another budget bonus, wines are available in carafes equal to a third of a bottle. Between 5 and 6:30pm, you'll find great deals such as £10 for the plat du jour plus a carafe of wine.

63-64 Frith St., W1. www.arbutusrestaurant.co.uk. ✆ **020/7734-4545.** Mains £16–£21; £19 two-course/£21 three-course pre-theatre set menu 5–6:30pm. Tube: Tottenham Court Road. Mon–Thurs noon–2:30pm and 5–11pm, Fri–Sat noon–2:30pm and 5–11:30pm, Sun noon–3pm and 5:30–10:30pm. Reservations recommended.

**J. Sheekey** ★★ SEAFOOD Smartly turned out waiters prep you with so many strange fish-eating implements that your place setting starts to look like a workstation at Santa's workshop. Such presentational flourishes are appropriate to theatreland, where this has been a bistro-style classic for years, and although prices aren't generous, portions and quality are. The least expensive main dish option, fish pie, is fortunately its trademark, but there are plenty of other choices, from shrimp-and-scallop burgers to a delectable lemon sole, plus a changing slate of game and meats for the fish-averse. For all the folderol, children are welcomed. The adjoining horseshoe-shaped Oyster Bar (same hours without a mid-afternoon break) does a limited menu that includes a velvety rich crab bisque with cognac.

28–32 St Martin's Court, WC2. www.j-sheekey.co.uk. ✆ **020/7240-2565.** Main courses £16–£42; weekend set-lunch menu, 3 courses £27. Tube: Leicester Square. Mon–Fri noon–3pm and 5:30pm–midnight, Sat noon-3:30pm and 5:30pm–midnight, Sun noon–3:30pm and 5:30–11pm. Reservations recommended.



**Rules ★★** TRADITIONAL BRITISH For a high-end kitchen that takes British cuisine seriously, go with an icon. In fact, Rules is London's oldest restaurant, cooking since 1798, and its patrons have included Graham Greene, Charles Dickens, Evelyn Waugh, and Edward VII, who regularly dined here with his paramour Lillie Langtry. (The management is less than discreet about it; the nook they used is named for him.) Being a major stop on the tourist trail has gone slightly to its head, and its view of a dining experience is steeped in its own hype; beer comes in a "silver tankard," for example, and the landmarked dining rooms are an overdressed mélange of yellowing etchings, antlers, and rich red fabrics. But what's on the table is indisputably high-class London: English-reared meat like roast loin of roe deer, whole roast squab or grouse (it serves 18,000 game birds annually), and cocktails like that famous one made of tonic, juniper, and quinine. Its nearest rival, Simpsons-in-the-Strand at the Savoy hotel, has been going since 1828, but that has become overly touristy. This is the heartier choice.

35 Maiden Lane, WC1. www.rules.co.uk. ✆ **020/7836-5314.** Mains £18–£29. Tube: Covent Garden. Mon–Sat noon–11:45pm, Sun noon–10:45pm.

**The Wolseley ★★★** CONTEMPORARY EUROPEAN "No Flash or Intrusive Photography please," chastises a footnote on the menu. That's because this opulent bistro in the Grand European style, posing with every polished surface to appear like something Renoir would want to paint, is home base for celebrities and power lunchers. Built as a luxury car dealership for a doomed manufacturer, then used as a bank, a decade ago it became the caviar-scooping, oyster-shucking, tea-pouring hotspot that fools nearly everyone who sips its pea-and-lettuce soup into thinking that it's always been this way. Waiters are unattainably attractive and look down their noses as they gingerly place salad Niçoise and Swiss soufflé, enacting the calculated Continental crispness we crave.

160 Piccadilly, W1. www.thewolseley.com. ✆ **020/7499-6996.** Sandwiches £11, mains £15–£20. Tube: Green Park. Mon–Fri 7am–midnight, Sat 8am–midnight, Sun 8am–11pm.

### Moderate

**Bill's ★★** INTERNATIONAL A 5-minute walk from the British Museum and handy for many uses—big breakfasts, lunches, dinner, tea with scones and clotted cream, feeding kids, or downing cheap cocktails—this casual and affordable group of restaurants started as a green grocer and is rigorous about quality ingredients. In few other London establishments will you find mac and cheese, burgers, pecan pie, and

Caesar salad together on the same menu. It's a lifesaver when you're indecisive or in need of drama-free grub served briskly, which is why you'll be glad to hear there are also locations near Piccadilly Circus (36–44 Brewer St., W1), off the Long Acre shopping street (St Martin's Courtyard, WC2; Tube: Covent Garden), and off Strand (21 Wellington St., WC2; Tube: Temple).

41 Kingsway, WC2. www.bills-website.co.uk. ✆ **020/7836-8368.** Mains £8.50–£13. Tube: Holborn. Mon–Fri 7am–11pm, Sat 8am–11pm, Sun 8am–10:30pm.

**Browns** ★ TRADITIONAL BRITISH In London, there's a Browns for fashion, and a Brown's Hotel, but Browns the spacious brasserie is the Browns you can afford. Installed in the former Westminster County Courts, this high-quality, Brighton-based chain serves updated English food and imported beer. The globe lanterns, enormous mirrors, and staff buttoned into crisp white oxford shirts impart the sense of a Gilded Age chophouse. Expect lots of indulgently hearty dishes such as fish pie in cream and white wine sauce; steak, mushroom, and Guinness pie; a house salad with beets, quinoa, pumpkin seeds, artichoke hearts, and more; or a nice fat wild boar and chorizo burger. British tradition—starchy but welcoming to casual tourists—is the main product here: Come for the £9 two-course lunch or for Sunday roast served with meat, Yorkshire pudding, cauliflower cheese, and vegetables. There's another Browns at 47 Maddox St. in Mayfair (Tube: Oxford Circus), a riverside one southeast of Tower Bridge (Butlers Wharf; Tube: London Bridge or Tower Hill), and one at 2 Cardinal Walk (Tube: Victoria).

82-84 St Martins Lane, WC2. www.browns-restaurants.com. ✆ **020/7497-5050.** Mains £8.50–£15, Sunday roast £11–£15. Tube: Leicester Square. Mon–Thurs 8am–10:30pm, Fri 8am–11pm, Sat 10am–11pm, Sun 10am–10:30pm.

**Ceviche** ★★★ PERUVIAN This relative newcomer is my firm favorite in Soho. Owner Martin Morales quit his job at Disney's European music division to pursue his true passion: food. Now he has a cookbook and runs this hopping, no-attitude Peruvian hangout that re-creates the look of one of his favorite hangouts in Lima and pours the best pisco sour in town. Flavors are indescribably punchy. Favorite small plates include Amor Amar scallops dish with lúcuma fruit puree, the don ceviche made with Amarillo chili tiger's milk, and the succulent corazón mío of beef skewers marinated in panca chili anticuchera. Once your tongue tastes its first citrusy zip, you'll feel compelled to come back. If you want to understand the vibrancy of London's newfound passion for cuisine exploration, this is the place.

17 Frith St., W1. www.cevicheuk.com. ✆ **020/7292-2040.** Small plates £7–£12. Tube: Piccadilly Circus or Tottenham Court Road. Mon–Sat noon–11:30pm, Sun noon–10:15pm. Reservations suggested.

**Great Queen Street** ★★★ TRADITIONAL BRITISH Here, the essence of gastropub cuisine is served in the convenient environs of Covent Garden. There's a pub feel—scuffed wood floors, burgundy walls, sconces capped with fringed mini-shades. The slow-cooked dishes are clean and reassuringly ingredient-proud. Samples (they change) include Old Spot (a breed of pig) pork chops with sticky shallots; griddled quail with celery salt; and lamb's shoulder cooked for 7 hours and accompanied by gratin dauphinoise—that one feeds four, which hints at the social atmosphere encouraged here. The Cellar Bar, open until midnight, serves the cold dishes from the same menu.

32 Green Queen St., WC2. www.greatqueenstreetrestaurant.co.uk. ✆ **020/7242-0622.** Mains £12–£25. Tube: Covent Garden or Holborn. Mon–Sat noon–2:30pm and Sun 1–4pm; Mon–Sat 6–10:30pm.



### Inexpensive

**Café in the Crypt ★** INTERNATIONAL This is the most delicious graveyard in town, and a perennial savior of budget travelers. Under the sanctuary of the historic St Martin-in-the-Fields church at Trafalgar Square, atop the gravestones of 18th-century Londoners, one of the West End's sharpest bargains is served. The menu at this dependable cafeteria changes daily, but the satisfying options always include a few hot meat mains, a vegetarian choice, soups, salads topped with meats, and a traditional English dessert such as plum fruit cobbler with warm custard, all homemade—even the strawberries are topped with rich, fresh whipped cream. The soup-and-pudding deal is £6.50 and afternoon tea is but £6. April to September, it also serves al fresco on the plaza at street level.

Trafalgar Sq., WC2. www.stmartin-in-the-fields.org. ✆ **020/7766-1158.** Mains £6–£8. Tube: Charing Cross. Mon–Tues 8am–8pm, Wed 8am–10:30pm with jazz for ticket holders after 6:30pm, Thurs–Sat 8am–9pm, Sun 11am–6:30pm.

**Gordon's Wine Bar ★** INTERNATIONAL The atmosphere is matchless at London's most vaunted and vaulted wine bar. It was established in 1890 (when Rudyard Kipling lived upstairs) and, thank goodness, hasn't been refurbished since—look in the front display window and you'll see some untouched champagne bottles that have intentionally grown furry with dust. These tight, craggy cellars beneath Villiers Street are wallpapered with important newspaper front pages from the 20th century—Thatcher's resignation, the death of King George VI—while ceiling fans threaten to come loose from their screws. Everything is suffused in a mustardy ochre from more than 42,000 past evenings of indoor tobacco smoke (no longer legal). Tables are candlelit, music is not played—not that you could hear it over the din of conversation. Dozens of wines and sherries are offered by the glass, and you can select from a marble display of English and French cheeses or a steam table of hot food. In good weather, the event expands outside along Embankment Gardens with casual al fresco meals such as stuffed peppers and marinated pork loin (the stone arch at the middle was built around 1625 as a palace gate on the Thames, but its mansion is long gone and the river

moved 46m/150 ft. south). Come down well before offices let out to secure seating; it won't accept bookings.
47 Villiers St., WC2. www.gordonswinebar.com. ✆ **020/7930-1408.** Meals £7–£10. Tube: Charing Cross or Embankment. Mon–Sat 11am–11pm, Sun noon–10pm.

**The Stockpot** ★ INTERNATIONAL High on function and low on glitz, this budget eatery has been indispensable to scrimping visitors and families for years. It got me through many a lean day of backpacking. No dish, be it spaghetti Bolognese, pork steak, or coq au vin, will set you back more than £7, though everything's good and all portions overflow their plates, and even dessert is £2.50—and that's the essence of its appeal. Staff waits around with dishrags at the ready on their shoulders, and the wall is hung with old drawings of gentlemen, just to class things up. On one memorable visit, a brief power outage interrupted dinner. "Just like the food," my neighbor inveighed, "it has a certain Eastern Bloc flavor." For those who can barely afford to visit London, the Stockpot is salvation. Forget the ravens at the Tower. When the Stockpot goes, London is over.
18 Old Compton St., W1. ✆ **020/7287-1066.** Mains £6–£7, 2-course set menu £8. Tube: Leicester Square or Tottenham Court Road. Mon–Tues 11:30am–11:30pm, Wed–Sat 11:30am–midnight, Sun noon–11:30pm.

## THE CITY & SOUTHWARK

### Expensive

**Restaurant Story** ★★★ MODERN BRITISH The moment you sit, your server lights a white taper and you slide your menu from the leafs of *Sketches by Boz* by Dickens, who started his life penniless nearby. By the time a fusillade of about six *amuse bouche* "snacks" hits you (paper-thin cod skin studded with emulsified cod roe, a sweet black eel mousse

### London Food Chains We Recommend:

London, like so many other cities, is experiencing an economic shift that is squeezing out mom-and-pop establishments in favor of better-heeled chains, so you'll often see these mid-priced, kid-friendly names cropping up on storefronts wherever you go. They're reliable and taste good, so consider them, too:

- **Busaba Eathai:** Peppy noodles and Asian dishes at communal tables.
- **Carluccio's:** New York–style Italian. Tile walls, pasta, fish, meats, coffees.
- **Giraffe:** Every kind of comfort food, extremely family-friendly.
- **Ping Pong:** Chinese dim sum in a vibrant, hip environment, plus cocktails.
- **Pizza Express:** Artisan-style pie. No one pays full price; see www.pizza-express.com/latest-offers for consistent discounts such as 25% off.
- **Simply Food:** Marks & Spencer's standalone shops for sandwiches, truly delicious ready-made dishes, and well-selected, inexpensive wines.
- **Wagamama:** Hearty noodle bowls eaten at shared long tables.
- **Wahaca:** Substantial Mexican done well with British-grown ingredients.

"Storeo"), your candle has quickly melted, you're told that the wax was actually edible beef fat, and you're handed a leather pouch of fresh-baked bread to sop up the rich drippings. And there are 10 more frivolously surprising small-plate courses to go. The dramatic and whimsical delights are by hot young talent Tom Sellers, and his prix-fixe menu, which never stops amusing and dazzling with flavor duets, speaks of London cooking both old and new: scallop carpaccio with cucumber balls rolled in dill ash; Jensen's gin (Sellers loves gin) and apple consommé topped with garlic blossoms; and "Three Bears" porridge—one sweet, one salty, one just right. It's food you'll be talking about. Reserve ahead.
201 Tooley St., SE1. www.restaurantstory.co.uk. ✆ **020/7183-2117.** Six courses £60, ten courses £80. Tube: London Bridge or Bermondsey. Tues–Sat noon–2:30pm, 6:30–9:30pm.





### Moderate

**Rochelle Canteen ★★** BRITISH A sublime secret is hidden away, discovered only if you ring a doorbell beside a green door in a brick wall. You'll pass through the grassy yard of an 1880s school, and in the old bike shed, join a daytime garden party. The changing menu is rigorously British: without flourish, high-quality, and fresh. Think green pea soup, roast sirloin, cuttlefish ink stew, leek and wigmore tart, fish and chips, loose-leaf tea. Your companions will be high-functioning artists, designers, and professionals, many of whom now lease space in the former school, plus the occasional kid, if they behave as well as a Victorian child. In fine weather, it's easier to find a seat because dining spills outdoors, the better to enjoy jugs of rhubarb and ginger fizz.
Rochelle School, Arnold Circus, E2. www.rochelleschool.org. ✆ **020/7729-5677.** Mains £13–£15. Tube: Shoreditch High Street. Mon–Fri 9am–2:30pm.

### Inexpensive

**Beigel Bake ★★** BAKERY This is the city's most famous bakery, Jewish or otherwise. The queue moves quickly here even if time doesn't—signs still post an area code that hasn't been active since 2000. Patrons are a microcosm of London, ranging from bikers to hipsters to arrogant yuppies to the homeless. Its beigels (*BI*-gulls) are not as puffy or as salty as the New York bagel variety, but they even come filled for under £1.50. Pastries are gorgeous, too: The chocolate fudge brownie could be nursed for hours. Watching the clerks slice juicy chunks of pink salt beef in the window, then slather it onto a beigel with nostril-clearing mustard from a crusty jar, is an attraction unto itself. Londoners complain it's touristy, but if it's a tourist trap, why does it still serve coffee for only 60p?
159 Brick Lane, E1. ✆ **020/7729-0616.** Tube: Shoreditch High Street. Daily 24 hr.

**Borough Market ★★★** INTERNATIONAL/TAKE-AWAY A chronicle of overstimulation, it combines Victorian commercial hubbub with glorious, farm-fresh flavors, rendered as finger food for visitors. About a dozen greenmarket vendors sell their countryside meats, cheeses, and vegetables all week long, but the market blooms beneath its metal-and-glass canopy Thursdays through Saturdays, when more than 100 additional vendors unpack and the awe-inspiring, touristy scene hits overcrowded swing. The least crowded time is Thursdays between 11am and noon; Saturdays are plain nuts.

If there's any country that has farming down, it's England, and this market is its showplace. Follow the crowd to the west end of the fence by the cathedral to **Kappacasein** dairy (www.kappacasein.com), which places great wheels of cheese under burners and sloughs bubbling swaths of it onto plates of boiled new potatoes (it's called *raclette,* and the only thing to rival it for decadence is the same booth's goopy grilled cheese, which you'll taste all day after eating). **Roast Hog** (www.roasthog.com) slices pig off a turning spit. You can't export either melt-in-your-mouth **Bath soft cheese** (www.parkfarm.co.uk) or aromatic unpasteurized **Gorwydd Caerphilly** cheese (www.trethowansdairy.co.uk). The **Brindisa** booth (www.brindisa.com) feeds a steady line of punters its grilled chorizo sandwich with oil-drizzled piquillo peppers from Spain (£3.75); and **Shellseekers,** the fishmonger in the center, is known for hand-dived Devon scallop, served in its own shell and topped with a bacon and sprout stir-fry. **Roast** (www.roast-restaurant.com), which runs an expensive restaurant upstairs, has a stall for rich meats such as roast pork belly with crackling and Bramley apple sauce and beef with horseradish cream. Outside on Stone Street, opposite the well-stocked **Market Porter** pub, are three more finds: **Monmouth Coffee** (www.monmmouthcoffee.co.uk) is one of London's most revered roasters; **Gelateria 3bis** has an ultra-creamy *fior di latte* flavor made from rich English milk, plus a warm chocolate fountain for pre-filling cones; and **Neal's Yard Dairy** (www.nealsyarddairy.co.uk), stacked high and tended by clerks in caps and aprons, is the gold standard for English cheese.

8 Southwark St., SE1. www.boroughmarket.org.uk. ✆ **020/7407-1002.** Tube: London Bridge. Mon–Wed 10am–3pm, Thurs 11am–5pm, Fri noon–6pm, Sat 8am–5pm.

**Gourmet goods at Borough Market.**

## 5 pubs YOU'LL LOVE

The following pubs, all centrally located, should do you right. Be they truly ancient, stunningly beautiful, happily situated, or simply charming, they all provide that authentic British pub experience. All of them serve food of some kind (burgers, meat pies, and the like) for at least part of the day.

**The Black Friar ★★** Deservedly protected by landmark status, this 1904 Art Nouveau masterpiece, a short walk from St Paul's near the Thames, is as jolly as the fat friars that bedeck it in bronze, wood, and glass. 174 Queen Victoria St., EC4. www.nicholsonspubs.co.uk. ✆ **020/7236-5474.** Tube: Blackfriars. Mon–Sat 10am–11pm, Sun noon–10:30pm.

The Black Friar pub.

**The George Inn ★★★** Unquestionably one of the most important ancient pubs still standing, this one-time coaching inn traces its lineage to at least 1542. Shakespeare knew it, and now it's protected by the government. 77 Borough High St., SE1. www.nationaltrust.org.uk/george-inn. ✆ **020/7407-2056.** Tube: London Bridge. Mon–Sat 11am–11pm, Sun noon–10:30pm.

**The Princess Louise ★** Your most elaborate fantasies of Victorian-era decor come true here, near the British Museum. Etched glass, bar lamps, marble urinals—even the beers are authentically (and lovingly) old-school. 208 High Holborn, WC1. www.princesslouisepub.co.uk. ✆ **020/7405-8816.** Tube: London Bridge. Mon–Fri 11am–11pm, Sat noon–11pm, Sun noon–6:45pm.

**Ye Olde Cheshire Cheese ★★★** It played host to Dr. Samuel Johnson (who lived behind it), Charles Dickens, Yeats, Wilde, and Thackeray. There are six drinking rooms, but the front bar—of pallid light, antique paintings of fish, and the stuffed carcass of Polly the Parrot—is the most magical. Wine Office Court, off 145 Fleet St. ✆ **020/7353-6170.** Tube: Blackfriars, Temple, or Chancery Lane. Mon–Sat 11am–11pm.

**Ye Olde Mitre ★★** Suspended in a hidden courtyard and seemingly between centuries, this extremely tiny enchanter—no TVs, no music—was once part of a great palace. The entrance on the left grants you access to "the Closet," a fine example of a semi-private sitting area called a "snug." 1 Ely Court, off Ely Place, EC1. www.yeoldemitreholborn.co.uk. ✆ **020/7405-4751.** Tube: Farringdon or Chancery Lane. Mon–Fri 11am–11pm, closed weekends.

**The Fryer's Delight ★★** TRADITIONAL BRITISH/TAKE-AWAY In this age, no one would dare name their joint something as hydrogenated as The Fryer's Delight. Fortunately, this joint is not of this age. It's a true old-world chippy, where the fry fat is from beef drippings, chips come in paper wrappings, the wooden booths and checkered floor date to the lean postwar years, and the men behind the counter gruffly demand to have your order. Prices are anachronistic, too: Nothing's more expensive than £6.20. Seamy? Not at all—it's just a last hanger-on from the dying fish-and-chips tradition, so get a taste while you still can. Order yours with mushy peas. It's a 10-minute walk east of the British Museum. 19 Theobald's Rd., WC1. ✆ **020/7405-4114.** Meals £5–£6.20. Tube: Holborn or Chancery Lane. Mon–Sat noon–10:30pm.



## Shopping

Appropriately for a city obsessed with class, London's prime shopping streets aren't usually defined so much by what they sell as by how much you'll spend to bring home their booty. **Oxford Street** (www.oxfordstreet.co.uk), the king of London shopping streets, supports the biggest mass-appeal names, including Topshop, H&M, the ever-mobbed Primark, and a few lollapalooza department stores like John Lewis, and Marks & Spencer. Boy, are weekends crowded! The ultimate high-end purchasing pantheon is **New Bond Street,** which runs from Oxford Street to Piccadilly, partly as Old Bond Street. Every account-draining trinket-maker has a presence, including Van Cleef & Arpels, Harry Winston, Chopard, and Boucheron. Asprey's, at 165-169, sells adornments few can afford, but its Victorian facade is a visual treat for all incomes. **Jermyn Street,** the quintessential street for the natty man, is home to several multi-named haberdashers that have been in business for more than a century (Harvie & Hudson, Hilditch & Key, Hawes & Curtis, and Turnbull & Asser—dresser of Chaplin, Churchill, Prince Charles, and James Bond) as well as specialists such as Tyrwhitt for shirts, Daks, and

**Shopping on Oxford Street.**

## LONDON'S shopping PALACES

**Fortnum & Mason** (181 Piccadilly, W1; www.fortnumandmason.london; ✆ **020/7734-8040;** Tube: Green Park or Piccadilly Circus) So venerable is this vendor, which began life in 1707 as the candle maker to Queen Anne, that in 1922 archaeologist Howard Carter used empty F&M boxes to tote home the treasures of King Tut's tomb. The veddy British, modestly sized department store, which has a focus on gourmet delectables, is renowned for its glamorous hampers, but its glorious Food Hall is where dreams are made and fortunes spent.

**Harrods** (87-135 Brompton Rd., SW1; www.harrods.com; ✆ **020/7730-1234;** Tube: Knightsbridge) Now owned by the Qatari royal family's financiers, a miraculous holdover from the golden age of shopping has been retooled into a bombastic mall appealing largely to moneyed foreigners. Few London-born people bother with it. Tourists beeline for the souvenir "emporium" on the 2nd floor (£17 for sandwich-sized gusset bags; £15 mugs; teddy bears aplenty).

**Liberty** (210-220 Regent St., W1; www.liberty.co.uk; ✆ **020/7734-1234;** Tube: Oxford Circus) Founded in 1875, it made its name as an importer of Asian art and as a major proponent of Art Nouveau style. Now its focus is distinctly British. The store's stationery and scarf selections are celebrated, as are its fabrics (many of which are designed in-house), and the beauty hall is one of the best.

**Selfridges** (400 Oxford St., W1; www.selfridges.com; ✆ **0800/123-400** [U.K.] or 113/369-8040 [from overseas]; Tube: Bond Street or Marble Arch) Big as a city block, Selfridges fills the real-life role in London life that many tourists think Harrods does, and aside from Harrods's olive drab sacks, no shopping bag speaks louder about your shopping preferences than a canary yellow screamer from Selfridges. Since its 1909 opening by Harry Gordon Selfridge, an immoderate American marketing genius from Marshall Field's in Chicago, Selfridges pioneered many department-store practices; some 17 million visits are recorded each year.

T. M. Lewin. It connects to Piccadilly by **Princes Arcade**, strong on shoes. Every lane around the north side of Covent Garden (among them Long Acre, Henrietta Street, Floral Street) is an obvious shopping drag, full of the usual brands but increasingly some one-off names. A half century ago, Soho's **Carnaby Street** was for the mod crowd, but today its legendary hyper-alternative looks are mostly found on Memory Lane. Instead, expect mainstream sporty choices such as North Face and Vans. Better for browsing is **Kingly Court,** a former timber warehouse converted into a mini-mall for 30-odd upcoming designers (carnaby.co.uk). **Redchurch Street,** once a down-at-heel lane in Shoreditch, is now at the forefront for hipsters and stylists.

## Entertainment & Nightlife

With hundreds of theaters, nightclubs, cinemas, and music halls, London has more to offer on a single night than many cities can muster in an entire year, and its output influences the whole world.

Enjoying a pint in a pub.

If you are desperate to see a specific theatre piece, book tickets before you leave home to ensure you won't be left out. Check with **The Society of London Theatre** (www.officiallondontheatre.co.uk) for a rundown of what's playing and soon to play, as well as discount offers. Given a lead-time of a few weeks, the established **LastMinute.com** sells tickets for half price, as does **LoveTheatre.com** (click "Special Offers"). BroadwayBox.com's **www.theatre.co.uk** posts the known discount codes for the West End shows. Unless you buy discounted seats

## Getting the Scoop on Nightlife

Complete listings information for entertainment is published Saturdays in the London papers, but you don't have to wait until you arrive. Excellent online sources for things to do include **Londonist.com, LondonCalling.com, TimeOut.com/London, Townfish.com**, and the Twitter accounts Everything London (**@LDN**), **@LeCool_London** (nightlife), and **@SkintLondon** (for cheap or free activities). These are good, too:

- **Visit London:** The "Tickets & Offers" section of its website is assiduously updated and, even better, it's free (www.visitlondon.com).
- ***Metro:*** Free in racks at Tube stations, most copies are gone by mid-morning, but commuters leave copies behind on the trains; it's considered green to recycle a pre-read newspaper (www.metro.co.uk).
- ***The Evening Standard:*** Free at Tube stop entrances in mid-afternoon—some days, there's an accompanying lifestyle magazine in a nearby stack. ES is also available online for free (www.standard.london).

**Bars and pubs** are a huge part of London's cultural identity, and the thickest choice of those lie in Soho and around Shoreditch, Hoxton, and Dalston, all the East End, where the venues can afford to be more cutting-edge. The king of dance clubs remains **Fabric** (77a Charterhouse St., EC1; www.fabriclondon.com; ✆ **020/7336-8898;** Tube: Farringdon or Barbican), a former butchery that for more than a decade has had lines around the block. The **Ministry of Sound** (103 Gaunt St., SE1; www.ministryofsound.com; ✆ **020/7740-8600;** Tube: Elephant & Castle) is known around the planet for its top-notch sound system and upper-crust DJs.

## GLBT London

London has the most varied and vibrant gay and lesbian scene in the world. The city claims more than 100 pubs, clubs, and club nights, and a dozen saunas—beat that, San Francisco or New York! The music seems to crank a few notches louder when the jolly and outrageous Pride London (www.pridelondon.ca) season rolls along, in late June or early July. Daily gay-oriented pursuits have traditionally centered around Soho, where the bars take on a festive, anyone-is-welcome flair; after work, guys spill into the streets. But nearly every neighborhood now has its own gay pubs or gay nights. **Boyz** (www.boyz.co.uk) and **QX Magazine** (www.qxmagazine.com) post schedules that favor club events. The Sapphically inclined should turn to **Gingerbeer** (www.gingerbeer.co.uk) and www.planet-london.com for listings.

directly from the box office of the theater, there's only one intelligent place to get same-day tickets: **TKTS** (south side of Leicester Square; tkts.co.uk; Mon–Sat 10am–7pm, Sun noon–3pm; Tube: Leicester Square), operated by the Society of London Theatre. It sells same-day seats for as much as half off—the best stuff is sold in the first hour of opening.

The **English National Opera** (www.eno.org) and **Royal Opera House** (www.roh.org.uk), both in Covent Garden, are world-famous, and the latter is also home to the **Royal Ballet.** You'll find eclectic musical performances on the slate at the famous **Royal Albert Hall** (www.royalalberthall.com), the progressively programmed **King's Place** (www.kingsplace.co.uk), and the more traditional **St Martin-in-the-Fields** church on Trafalgar Square (www.stmartin-in-the-fields.org), as well as the home of the Royal Philharmonic Orchestra, **Cadogan Hall** (www.cadoganhall.com).

# EDINBURGH

Edinburgh is a classic, cultured beauty. It is a very civilized city with a disarmingly understated air. The Scottish Parliament, tucked in the shadow of an extinct volcano, Arthur's Seat, might be strikingly modern, but the Scottish capital feels more like an historical film set than a contemporary political powerhouse—even after the 2014 referendum for Scottish independence. Edinburgh was a staunch no vote for the record. It's also conservative with a small "c".

Don't be confused by talk of the Old Town, New Town split. The medieval Old Town—with its tumble of tenements, dim alleyways, and brooding castle on top of a craggy cliff—sits huddled across the verdant sweep of Princes Street Gardens from the young upstart: the Georgian New Town, all elegant crescents, leafy squares and terraces. Dubbed the Athens of the North when it was built to ease the overcrowding in "Auld Reekie" in the 18th century, this vision of neoclassical town planning

The Royal Mile.



feels calmly ordered in contrast to the Old Town's more chaotic, organic evolution. However, parts of the Old Town are newer than the New Town, built on top of demolished tenements in the 1800s. In fact, there's an architectural unity to this sandstone city—one recognized by UNESCO, which bracketed the Old Town and New Town into one World Heritage Site in 1995—although the two sides of the divide do have very different vibes.

This is not just a Tale of Two Cities, however, it is also a tale of small villages. Surprisingly compact and built around a series of hills, Edinburgh is peppered with tiny neighborhoods, each with its own distinct character and charm. Dipping in and out of these is one of the best ways

### Scotland's Summer Festivals

In an Edinburgh summer, there are more festivals than you can shake a porridge spurtle at. Edinburgh is host to one of the biggest cultural shindigs in the world. Come summer, that famous reserve melts away and the low-key capital cranks it up a gear. Thousands of visitors from all over the world flock to the Edinburgh Festival. The Royal Mile becomes a rippling river of ticket scalpers, street performers, and face-painters, and the whole city turns into a vast open-air arena.

Underneath the **Edinburgh Festival** (www.edinburghfestivalcity.com) banner, you'll find the **Fringe** (www.edfringe.com; ✆ **0131/226-0026**), **International Festival** (www.eif.co.uk; ✆ **0131/473-2000**), **Book Festival** (www.edbookfest.co.uk; ✆ **0845/373-5888**), and **Jazz & Blues Festival** (www.edinburghjazzfestival.com; ✆ **0131/467-5200**).

And don't forget the **Royal Edinburgh Military Tattoo** (www.edintattoo.co.uk; ✆ **0131/225-1188**): thousands of visitors flock here to join the party and dip into the cultural medley of comedy, dance, drama, and music.

to explore the city, and to shake off the crowds. Away from the main arteries there are pockets of peace where the strangled squeal of bagpipes fades away, and it feels almost sleepily provincial. All you can hear is the rumble of cars on cobbles as you breathe in the heady scent of hops and soak up the history seeping out of the stonework.



## Essentials

For trip planning, **Visit Scotland** (www.visitscotland.com) offers a comprehensive website.

**ARRIVING** **Edinburgh Airport** (www.edinburghairport.com; ✆ **0844/448-8833**) is 7½ miles west of the city center. Double-decker Airlink buses make the round-trip from the airport to Edinburgh city center every 10 minutes, letting you on and off at Haymarket or Waverley train stations. The journey takes around 25 minutes and costs £4 one-way or £7 round-trip. For more information, call ✆ **0131/555-6363** or visit www.lothianbuses.com. You can also take the swanky new tram into town. They run every 8 to 12 minutes from the airport to York Place via Haymarket train station and Princes Street and the fare is £5 one-way, £8 return. You buy your ticket from the machine at the stop. There's a busy taxi rank at the airport and a ride into town costs around £25, depending on traffic.

Edinburgh has two **train stations**—Haymarket in the West End and Waverley, the main station in the city center at the east end of Princes Street. The **East Coast** (www.eastcoast.co.uk; ✆ **03457/225-111**) trains that link London's King's Cross with Waverley station depart London every hour or so, take about 4½ hours and cost from £134 return. Savings can be made if you reserve in advance and commit to traveling on specific trains. **Scotrail** (www.scotrail.co.uk; ✆ **0330/303-0111**) operates the Caledonian Sleeper service—overnight trains from London with sleeper berths. One-way fares cost from £66. There's a taxi rank in Waverley station and Edinburgh's bus station (see below) is only a short walk away.

The least expensive way to travel between London and Edinburgh is by **bus,** but it's a 9½ hour journey. **MegaBus** (www.megabus.com; ✆ **0900/1600-900**) is the cheapest option, with one-way fares costing from £13. **National Express** (www.nationalexpress.com; ✆ **0208/458-3096**) also runs a regular service, and one-way fares cost anywhere between £17 and £68. Coaches depart from London's Victoria Coach Station to Edinburgh's **St Andrews Square Bus Station.**

Edinburgh is 46 miles east of Glasgow and 105 miles north of Newcastle-upon-Tyne in England. No express **motorway** links Edinburgh with London, which lies 393 miles to the south. The M1 from London takes you part of the way north, and then becomes the A1—otherwise known as the "Great North Road"—leading drivers along the coast to enter Edinburgh from the east. Allow 8 hours or more if you're driving from London. A city bypass, the A720, circles Edinburgh and routes from all other directions meet this road, making it easy to enter the city from whichever point suits you. The M8 links Edinburgh with Glasgow and connects with the city on the west side of the bypass, while the M90/A90 travels down from the north over the Forth Road Bridge.

**CITY LAYOUT** The hills might be calf-burning and the cobbles capable of twisting an ankle, but Edinburgh is a city to wander on foot. You can hike from one side to the other in a couple of hours, discovering hidden pockets and veering off down tiny alleyways. The **Old Town** lies at the heart, with Edinburgh Castle at the top of the **Royal Mile,** which snakes downhill to the Palace of Holyroodhouse. For many visitors, this *is* Edinburgh, with its mews, closes, and wynds. But across the valley to the north, now filled by the grassy sweep of Princes Street Gardens, is the city's **New Town,** which dates back to the 1770s. Here you'll find elegant crescents, leafy squares, and broad avenues peppered with gourmet restaurants, buzzing bars, smart shops, and attractions such as the **National Portrait Gallery.** The New Town rolls down to the village-like setting of **Stockbridge** with its cafes, delis, and boutiques. From here, you can walk along the city's narrow meandering river, the Water of Leith to **Dean Village** (another rural pocket) and the **National Gallery of Modern Art.** Or head in the other direction and you'll emerge in the revamped docklands of Leith, with its Michelin-starred restaurants and gastropubs.

Between the city center and Haymarket is the **West End** where there are a cluster of performance spaces such as **Usher Hall** and the **Traverse Theatre.**

Edinburgh's **Southside** is mostly residential, but offers the sprawling park known as the **Meadows,** the precincts of Edinburgh University, as well as suburbs such as Marchmont.

### World Heritage Edinburgh

Edinburgh's Old and New Towns have been designated a UNESCO World Heritage site, in recognition of their historical and architectural importance. Edinburgh World Heritage (www.ewht.org.uk; ✆ **0131/220-7720**) provides a wealth of information to help visitors make the most of their time here. You can follow a range of themed trails, such as Walk in the Footsteps of Robert Louis Stevenson, around the Heritage Site; download them from Edinburgh World Heritage's website, along with a series of accompanying podcasts.

**GETTING AROUND** Many of Edinburgh's attractions are scattered around a small area along or near the Royal Mile, Princes Street, or one of the major streets in New Town. As such, it's easy to explore on foot and, because of its narrow lanes, wynds, and closes, you can only explore Old Town in any depth by walking.

Edinburgh's **bus** system is operated by **Lothian Buses** (www.lothianbuses.com; ✆ **0131/555-6363**), whose frequent, inexpensive service covers every corner of the city. The fare for a one-way journey of any distance is £1.50 for adults, 70p for children aged 5 to 15, free for children under 4. A **Day Saver Ticket** allows 1 day of unlimited travel on city buses at a cost of £3.50 for adults and £2 for children. You need to have the exact change to buy tickets. Route maps and timetables can be downloaded from Lothian Buses's website, or call into one of their travel shops on either Waverley Bridge or Hanover Street for more information. Both offices are open Monday through Friday 9am to 6pm and Saturday 9am to 5.30pm. The Waverley Bridge Travel shop also opens on Sunday from 10am to 5:30pm and is open until 7pm Monday and Thursday.

You can hail a **taxi** or pick one up at any of Edinburgh's numerous taxi stands. Meters begin at £2.10 and increase £2 every ⅔ mile. Taxi ranks are at Hanover Street, North St Andrews Street, Waverley Station, Haymarket Station, Lothian Road, and Lauriston Place. Fares are displayed in the front of the taxi, including extra charges for night drivers or destinations outside the city limits. You can also call a taxi: Try **City Cabs** (✆ **0131/228-1211**) or **Central Radio Taxis** (✆ **0131/229-2468**).

Most residents don't **drive** around the center of Edinburgh; public transport is very good, the city's traffic system is tricky, and parking is expensive and difficult to find. Metered parking is available (exact change required) but some zones are only for permit holders; vehicles with no permit are towed away, and Edinburgh's traffic wardens are notoriously active in handing out tickets. A yellow line along the curb indicates no parking. Major car parks (parking lots) are at Castle Terrace, convenient for Edinburgh Castle, Lothian Road, and the West End; and St John Hill, convenient for the Royal Mile and St James Centre (entrance from York Place), close to the east end of Princes Street.

Edinburgh is relatively **bicycle**-friendly; however, the cobbled streets in the New and Old Towns can make cycling a challenge, as does the fact that the city is built around a series of hills. That said, there's a network of bike paths round the city. Bike rental companies include **Leith Cycles** (www.leithcycleco.com; ✆ **0131/467-7775**) rentals start at £12 for a half-day and include a helmet, lock, map, and puncture repair kit. Children's bikes, trailers, and tag-alongs can also be rented.

## The Neighborhoods in Brief

**OLD TOWN** The **Royal Mile** is the backbone of the Old Town, a medieval thoroughfare snaking along the spine of the volcanic crag that supports Edinburgh Castle to the flat land of Holyrood Park—a wild landscape in the heart of the city and home to the Palace of Holyroodhouse and the imposing Arthur's Seat. English author Daniel Defoe described the Royal Mile as "the largest, longest, and finest street for buildings and number of inhabitants in the world." Many argue that little has changed today, and you haven't really experienced Edinburgh until you've explored the Old Town's dark, cobbled, history-soaked streets.

**NEW TOWN** North of the Old Town, Edinburgh's New Town is one of the largest Georgian developments in the world, a network of elegant squares, terraces, and circuses. It stretches from Haymarket in the west to Abbeyhill in the east and from Canonmills at its northern perimeter uphill to Princes Street, its main artery, along the southern tier. The **West End Village,** an area north of Shandwick Place, is peppered with chic boutiques and gastropubs. While technically outside New Town, Edinburgh's **West End** leads along Lothian Road, where you'll find many of the city's theatres, cinemas, and nightclubs.

**BRUNTSFIELD** This suburb to the southwest of the Old Town is fringed by Bruntsfield Links, the park where James IV gathered his Scottish army before marching to their devastating defeat at Flodden in 1513. It's also the site of the mass graves of the city's plague victims. Today, the main thoroughfare, Bruntsfield Place, is lined with quirky boutiques and bustling cafes.

**STOCKBRIDGE** Northwest of New Town, Stockbridge is one of Edinburgh's hidden gems. Once a village on the outskirts of the city, it was incorporated into Edinburgh in the 19th century, yet still retains a village feel. This is an upmarket area with a bohemian edge and is known for its delis, cafes, and galleries, as well as its proximity to the Water of Leith and Edinburgh's Botanic Gardens.

**LEITH** Once a down-at-heel area, the revamped Port of Leith, the city's major harbor, opens onto the Firth of Forth. The port might not flex the maritime muscle it used to, but the regeneration has given it a new lease on life, the waterfront now lined with fish restaurants and lively pubs. Today, cruise ships dock at Leith's Ocean Terminal, and although this isn't an area in which many visitors stay, it's one of the best places in the city to eat and a must-see for anyone wanting to glimpse the often overlooked maritime side of Edinburgh past and present.

## Exploring Edinburgh

### ALONG THE ROYAL MILE

The Old Town's **Royal Mile ★★★** is, in fact, 1 mile and 107 yards long and stretches from Edinburgh Castle all the way down to the Palace of Holyroodhouse. It's made up of a chain of linked streets: Castlehill, Lawnmarket, High Street, and Canongate and is lined with a mix of museums, churches, and shops selling cashmere, tweed, and whisky—and a fair bit of tartan tat—to the tourists who flock here. Walking its length, you'll see some of the most fascinating parts of the old city, including a section of the **Flodden Wall** if you veer off along St Mary Street. Built in the 16th century, this 1.2m-thick (3 ft. 11 in.) structure used to mark the city limits. The point where a fortified gateway once stood as it crossed the Royal Mile was known as the World's End. A pub of the same name now stands near the spot.

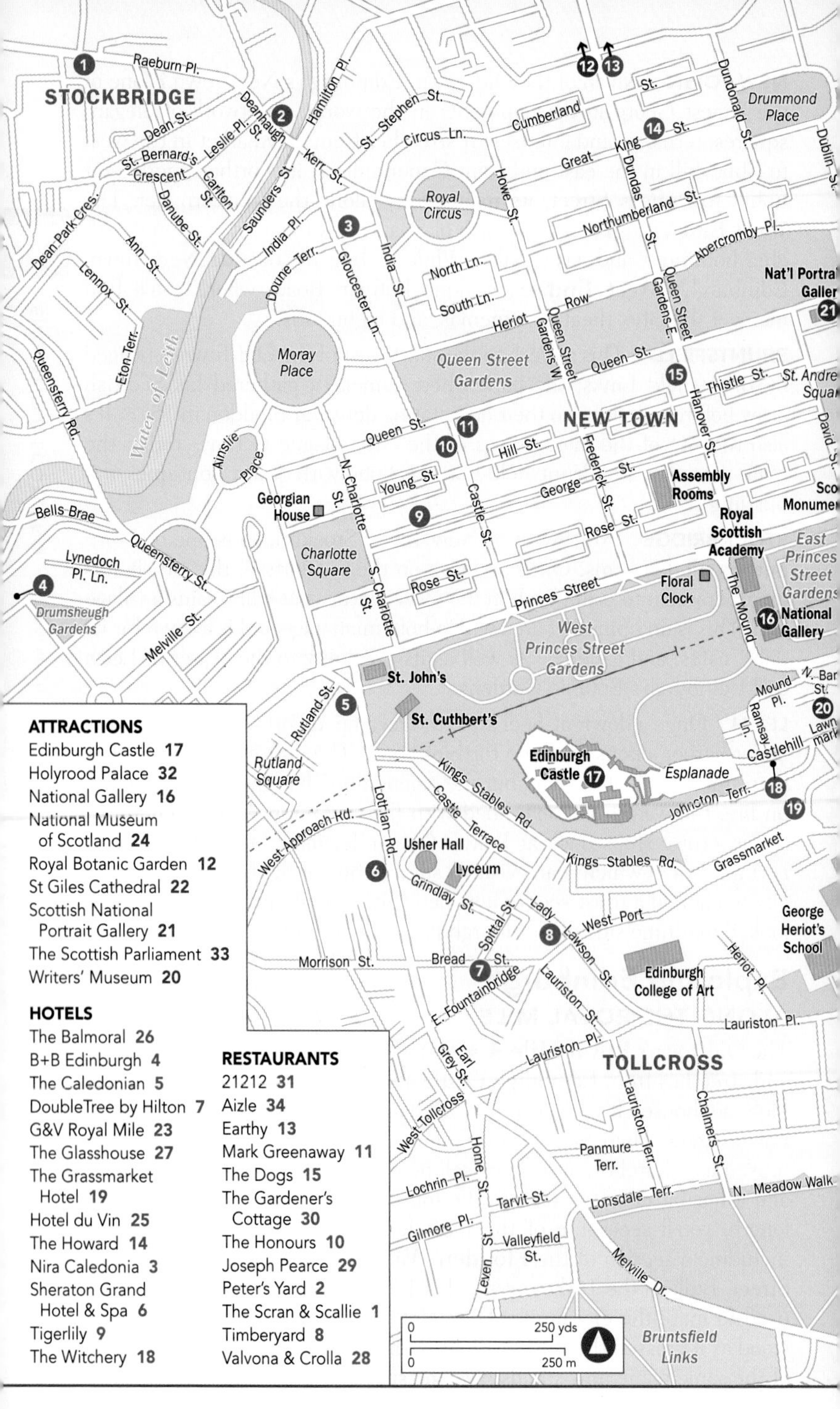
STOCKBRIDGE
NEW TOWN
TOLLCROSS
Raeburn Pl.
Dean St.
St. Bernard's Crescent
Leslie Pl.
Deanhaugh St.
Carlton St.
Danube St.
Dean Park Cres.
Ann St.
Lennox St.
Eton Terr.
Queensferry Rd.
Water of Leith
Hamilton Pl.
Kerr St.
Saunders St.
India Pl.
Doune Terr.
St. Stephen St.
Circus Ln.
Royal Circus
Gloucester Ln.
India St.
Howe St.
Cumberland St.
Great King St.
Dundas St.
Dundonald St.
Drummond Place
Dublin St.
Northumberland St.
Abercromby Pl.
North Ln.
South Ln.
Heriot Row
Queen Street Gardens W.
Queen Street Gardens E.
Queen Street Gardens
Queen St.
Moray Place
Ainslie Place
Nat'l Portrait Gallery
Thistle St.
St. Andrew Square
Hanover St.
David St.
Hill St.
Young St.
George St.
Rose St.
Frederick St.
Castle St.
N. Charlotte St.
S. Charlotte St.
Georgian House
Charlotte Square
Assembly Rooms
Royal Scottish Academy
Scott Monument
East Princes Street Gardens
Bells Brae
Lynedoch Pl. Ln.
Drumsheugh Gardens
Queensferry St.
Melville St.
Princes Street
Floral Clock
The Mound
National Gallery
West Princes Street Gardens
St. John's
St. Cuthbert's
Rutland St.
Rutland Square
Mound Pl.
N. Bank St.
Ramsay Ln.
Castlehill
Lawnmarket
Edinburgh Castle
Esplanade
Johnston Terr.
Kings Stables Rd
Castle Terrace
West Approach Rd.
Lothian Rd.
Usher Hall
Lyceum
Grindlay St.
Kings Stables Rd.
Grassmarket
Spittal St.
Lady Lawson St.
West Port
George Heriot's School
Heriot Pl.
Morrison St.
Bread St.
E. Fountainbridge
Lauriston St.
Edinburgh College of Art
Lauriston Pl.
Earl Grey St.
West Tollcross
Lauriston Terr.
Chalmers St.
Panmure Terr.
Home St.
Lochrin Pl.
Tarvit St.
Lonsdale Terr.
N. Meadow Walk
Gilmore Pl.
Leven St.
Valleyfield St.
Melville Dr.
Bruntsfield Links
0 250 yds
0 250 m
ATTRACTIONS
Edinburgh Castle 17
Holyrood Palace 32
National Gallery 16
National Museum of Scotland 24
Royal Botanic Garden 12
St Giles Cathedral 22
Scottish National Portrait Gallery 21
The Scottish Parliament 33
Writers' Museum 20
HOTELS
The Balmoral 26
B+B Edinburgh 4
The Caledonian 5
DoubleTree by Hilton 7
G&V Royal Mile 23
The Glasshouse 27
The Grassmarket Hotel 19
Hotel du Vin 25
The Howard 14
Nira Caledonia 3
Sheraton Grand Hotel & Spa 6
Tigerlily 9
The Witchery 18
RESTAURANTS
21212 31
Aizle 34
Earthy 13
Mark Greenaway 11
The Dogs 15
The Gardener's Cottage 30
The Honours 10
Joseph Pearce 29
Peter's Yard 2
The Scran & Scallie 1
Timberyard 8
Valvona & Crolla 28

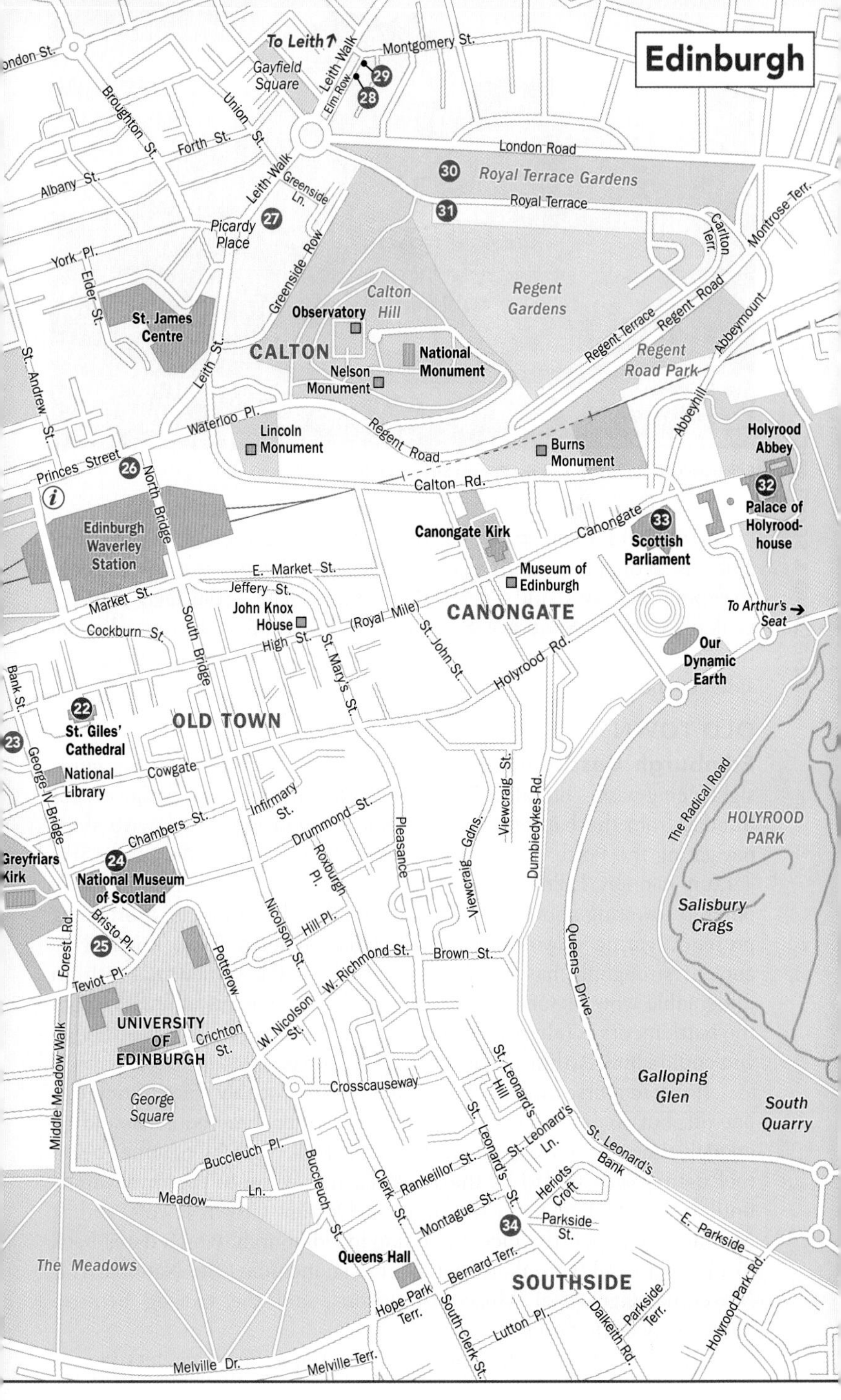
Edinburgh
To Leith
Montgomery St.
London St.
Gayfield Square
Leith Walk
Elm Row
29
28
Broughton St.
Union St.
Forth St.
London Road
30
Royal Terrace Gardens
Albany St.
Leith Walk
Greenside Ln.
31
Royal Terrace
Picardy Place
27
Carlton Terr.
Montrose Terr.
York Pl.
Elder St.
Greenside Row
Calton Hill
Regent Gardens
Regent Road
Regent Terrace
St. James Centre
Observatory
Abbeymount
CALTON
National Monument
Regent Road Park
St. Andrew St.
Leith St.
Nelson Monument
Abbeyhill
Waterloo Pl.
Lincoln Monument
Regent Road
Burns Monument
Holyrood Abbey
Princes Street
26
North Bridge
Calton Rd.
32
Palace of Holyrood-house
Edinburgh Waverley Station
Canongate Kirk
Canongate
33
Scottish Parliament
E. Market St.
Museum of Edinburgh
Jeffery St.
Market St.
John Knox House
(Royal Mile)
CANONGATE
To Arthur's Seat
Cockburn St.
High St.
South Bridge
St. John St.
Our Dynamic Earth
Holyrood Rd.
Bank St.
St. Mary's St.
22
St. Giles' Cathedral
OLD TOWN
23
George IV Bridge
National Library
Cowgate
The Radical Road
Infirmary St.
Viewcraig St.
Dumbiedykes Rd.
HOLYROOD PARK
Chambers St.
Drummond St.
Pleasance
Viewcraig Gdns.
Greyfriars Kirk
24
National Museum of Scotland
Roxburgh Pl.
Salisbury Crags
Nicolson St.
Hill Pl.
Queens Drive
Bristo Pl.
Forrest Rd.
25
W. Richmond St.
Brown St.
Teviot Pl.
Potterow
UNIVERSITY OF EDINBURGH
Crichton St.
W. Nicolson St.
Middle Meadow Walk
St. Leonard's Hill
Galloping Glen
Crosscauseway
George Square
South Quarry
St. Leonard's Ln.
St. Leonard's St.
St. Leonard's Bank
Buccleuch Pl.
Buccleuch St.
Rankeillor St.
Meadow Ln.
Clerk St.
Heriots Croft
Montague St.
Parkside St.
34
E. Parkside
The Meadows
Queens Hall
Bernard Terr.
SOUTHSIDE
Holyrood Park Rd.
Hope Park Terr.
Parkside Terr.
South Clerk St.
Dalkeith Rd.
Lutton Pl.
Melville Dr.
Melville Terr.

Edinburgh Castle looms over the Princes Street Gardens.

**Holyrood Park ★,** which opens out at the bottom of the Royal Mile, is a dramatic landscape, characterized by rocky crags, a loch, sweeping meadows, and a tiny ruined chapel. The 250m-high (820-ft.) peak of **Arthur's Seat ★★★** is the park's crowning glory, rewarding all who climb with heart-stopping views over Edinburgh and the countryside beyond.

## OLD TOWN

**Edinburgh Castle ★★★** HISTORIC SITE This is the big guns, sightseeing-wise—literally. The one o'clock gun is fired every day except Sunday from the battlements, a tradition begun in 1861 to give ships navigating the Forth a time check. Then there's Mons Meg, the 15th-century cannon. Edinburgh castle dominates the skyline from its rocky outcrop towering above the jumble of medieval tenements, a brooding presence gazing down over the gracious Georgian New Town. This ancient stronghold has history seeping out of the stonework, with an undeniable wow factor. It's big, it's bold, it's bolshie, and the view from the battlements is (almost) worth the hefty price tag in itself—although you could climb Arthur's Seat for free, of course.

If you're a first-timer to Edinburgh, you'll probably want to tick this one off, but go early to avoid the crowds. Two or three hours should be enough time to traipse through the Great Hall (with its hammer-beam roof dating back to 1511); the Royal Palace, home to the royal family until 1603; and check out the Stone of Destiny, Crown Jewels, and St Margaret's Chapel (the oldest building in Edinburgh, which dates back to 1130); and all the military paraphernalia, including the National War Museum, Regimental Museums, prisons, and the moving Scottish National War Memorial.

You'll want to get your money's worth. And at the price, let's face it, you probably won't be coming back in a hurry. It's not the easiest attraction

A view from Edinburgh Castle.

to navigate if you have a disability—there are all those cobbles for a start, and steep hills. But there is a mobility vehicle and a number of wheelchairs—although the chapel and prisons have narrow entrances. Castlehill. www.edinburghcastle.gov.uk. ✆ **0131/225-9846.** £16 adults, £13 seniors (60+), £9.60 children (5-15), free for children under 5. Apr–Sept 9.30am–6pm, Oct–Mar 9.30am–5pm last admission 1hr. before closing.



**Holyrood Palace ★★★** HISTORIC SITE The Royal Mile is topped and tailed by a castle and a palace. While the former is a fortress drenched in military history and housing an arsenal of weapons, Holyrood, by comparison, is all lightness, grace, and charm. Its official title, the Palace of Holyroodhouse, is a bit of a mouthful, so it's generally referred to as Holyrood Palace. The Queen's official residence in Scotland, Holyrood started life as an Augustinian abbey built by King David I of Scotland in 1128. You can wander around the ruins after visiting the palace. It morphed over the centuries into the elegant building you see today. Highlights include the grand Royal Apartments, the Throne Room still used today for state occasions, and the oak-paneled chambers where Mary Queen of Scots once lived at the top of a steep spiral staircase. Following the audio tour, the grizzly tale of the night her jealous husband, Lord Darnley, murdered her Italian secretary, Rizzio, believing him her lover, takes you spiraling back in time.
Canongate. www.royalcollection.org.uk. ✆ **0131/556-5100.** £12 adults, £11 seniors/students, £7 children under 17, free under 5, £30 family (2 adult, 3 under 17) with

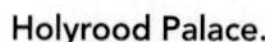

Holyrood Palace.

The National Museum of Scotland.

complimentary audio tour. Nov–Mar 9:30am–4:30pm, last admission 5:15pm; Apr–Oct 9:30am–6pm, last admission 4:30pm.

**National Museum of Scotland** ★★ MUSEUM Trumpeted as the largest museum in the U.K. outside London, with 20,000 exhibits displayed in 36 galleries, expect a whirlwind tour of Scotland's geological origins to the present day. A recent £46-million project restored the museum's glorious glass-roofed atrium, giving its Victorian section a wow factor to match that of the contemporary extension added in 1998. The Grand Gallery is now a light, bright, four-story-high galleried space, with halls—loosely named Living Lands, Imagine, and Patterns of Life—branching away from it. With a subject matter as broad as "Scotland" (although before any accusations of insularity are made, keep in mind that the Window on the World installation showcases items from around the globe), the resulting collection was always going to be a bit of a mish-mash. There are dinosaurs, meteorites, the jaws of a sperm whale, and frocks. It's worth dipping into, however, for the Grand Gallery alone, plus there's a cafe, shop, regular events, and, up on the roof, The Tower Restaurant, a fine dining spot from restaurateur royalty James Thomson, with stunning views of the Castle.
Chambers Street. www.nms.ac.uk. ✆ **0300/123-6789.** Free. Daily 10am–5pm, closed Dec 25, Dec 26 noon–5pm, Jan 1 noon–5:30pm.

**St Giles' Cathedral** ★★ CATHEDRAL This moodily magnificent cathedral standing sentinel on the Royal Mile is also known as the High Kirk of Edinburgh, and is one of the most important churches in Scotland. The oldest parts date back to 1124, but after a fire in 1385, many sections were rebuilt and altered during its restoration in the 19th century. The brooding stone exterior features a distinctive crowned spire and graceful flying buttresses. One of the outstanding features of the dimly lit, vaulted interior is the Thistle Chapel. Built in 1911 and dedicated to the Knights of the Thistle, Scotland's order of chivalry, this intricate space houses beautiful stalls and detailed heraldic stained-glass windows.
High St. www.stgilescathedral.org.uk. ✆ **0131/225-9442.** Free (£3 donation suggested). May–Sept Mon–Fri 9am–7pm, Sat 9am–5pm and Sun 1–5pm; Oct–April Mon–Sat 9am–5pm and Sun 1–5pm.

**The Scottish Parliament** ★★ ARCHITECTURE Like it or loathe it, this bold and controversial modern building stands opposite and in contrast to the Palace of Holyroodhouse at the east end of the Royal Mile and embodies a strong statement of Scotland's past, present, and future. Designed by the late Spanish architect Enric Miralles, who died before his vision was completed, this unique building cost a cool US$893 million. The facade is amazing enough in itself, but to truly understand the philosophy behind the architecture and to enter the hallowed debating chamber, a guided tour is a must.

Canongate. www.scottish.parliament.uk. ✆ **0131/348-5200.** Free. Mon, Fri and Sat 10am–5pm; Tues–Thurs 9am–6.30pm.

**Writers' Museum ★★** MUSEUM You might need to hunt for the entrance to this hidden gem between the gift shops on the Royal Mile. Up a flight of worn stone steps is an alleyway leading to Lady Stairs House, which dates back to the early 17th century and now houses this atmospheric little museum. Dedicated to three of Scotland's finest writers: Robert Burns, Sir Walter Scott, and Robert Louis Stevenson, their personal items (leather boots, pipes, and even locks of their hair) are dotted along with a number of first editions, portraits, and the press used to print Sir Walter Scott's Waverley novels. We are so used to all-singing, all-dancing state-of-the-art visitor attractions these days, but this little place has real old-world charm.

Lady Stairs House, Lady Stairs Close, Lawnmarket. www.edinburghmuseums.org.uk. ✆ **0131/529-4901.** Free. Mon–Sat 10am–5pm, Sun noon–5pm (Aug only).

### Greyfriars Bobby

Think Lassie—only shorter, scruffier and more terrier-shaped. There's nothing like a tragic tale of doggy devotion to bring a lump to your throat—even if it does stretch the truth a little. Greyfriars Bobby was a Skye terrier whose master, police constable John Gray, died of tuberculosis in 1858. Bobby, faithful to the last, guarded his grave in 17th-century Greyfriars Kirk (www.greyfriarskirk.com), until he too died in 1872. Bobby almost came to a sticky end earlier however, after it was discovered that he had no owner he had no license, and so could be destroyed as a stray. The Lord Provost of Edinburgh was so moved by the tale that he stepped in, bought Bobby a license himself and granted him the highest honor, the Freedom of the City. There's a statue of Bobby near the entrance to the kirkyard (opposite the National Museum of Scotland) and there have been a number of books and films made about his story. Granted the Freedom of the City, you can see his collar and bowl in the Museum of Edinburgh on the Royal Mile.

Greyfriars Bobby, Edinburgh's most loyal dog.

## NEW TOWN

**National Gallery Complex** ★ GALLERY The grand columned buildings of this imposing museum complex, slap bang in the middle of Princes Street Gardens, have real stage presence—and are a fitting home for Scotland's national collection of fine art from the early Renaissance to the end of the 19th century, including works from artists such as Raphael, Rubens, Van Gogh, and Cézanne, as well as a dedicated Scottish collection. The traditional gallery space feels rather staid; however, at the Royal Scottish Academy linked to the National Gallery via the Weston Link, there is a world-class program of temporary exhibitions.
The Mound. www.nationalgalleries.org. ✆ **0131/624-6200.** Free (fees for some temporary exhibitions). Fri–Wed 10am–5pm; Thurs 10am–7pm.

**Royal Botanic Garden Edinburgh** ★★ PARK/GARDEN Edinburgh is a green city pricked with parks, but the jewel in the crown is the Botanic Gardens. Established in the 17th century as a physic garden, today the 70-acre site is a haven of tranquility. Highlights include the Chinese Hillside, its slopes bushy with the largest collection of wild-origin plants outside of China; the rock garden (5,000 plants at any one time); and the steamy Victorian Palm House. The state-of-the-art visitor center, with its striking design, is a vertical vision of wood-cladding. The cutting-edge, low-carbon building houses a cafe upstairs that spills out onto the decking, plus exhibition space, a shop, and a nursery. Inverleith House, an 18th-century mansion on the grounds, showcases temporary art exhibitions. There are guided garden tours at 11am and 2pm during the summer, or just while away an hour or two beneath the magnificent trees, lying on the grass with a picnic.
Arboretum Place. www.rbge.org.uk. ✆ **0131/248-2909.** Gardens admission free, glasshouses £5 adults, £4 seniors, under 15 free. Daily (except for Dec 25 and Jan 1), Nov–Jan 10am–4pm, Feb-Oct 10am–5pm, Mar–Sept 10am–6pm.

**Scottish National Gallery of Modern Art** ★★ MUSEUM A head emerges from the pavement at the entrance of Modern One, a grand Neoclassical building dating back to 1825. Across the road is Modern Two, originally a 19th-century orphanage. You get two museums for the price of one here, although both are free. Slightly off the beaten tourist track—not that anywhere in Edinburgh is much of a schlep—the Scottish National Gallery of Modern Art is just above the Water of Leith, the little river that tumbles through the city to the docklands at Leith. The head in front of Modern One is one of Antony Gormley's 6 Times sculptures, a series of cast-iron, life-size figures rising out of the river—and out of the pavement. The galleries in both buildings showcase an impressive permanent collection, from works by Picasso and Matisse to Damien Hirst and Tracey Emin, along with a series of changing exhibitions. It's the sculpture park that's the biggest draw, however, featuring works by Henry Moore and Barbara Hepworth. On the grounds of

Modern One, the garden features a giant grassy undulation with stepped serpentine mounds and crescent-shaped pools.

73-75 Belford Road. www.nationalgalleries.org. ✆ **0131/624–6200.** Free. Daily 10am–5pm.

**Scottish National Portrait Gallery ★★** GALLERY In a grand, red-sandstone Arts and Crafts building dating back to 1889, this is the first purpose-built portrait gallery in the world. Its mix of intimate rooms and light-filled contemporary spaces are strung with images, from paintings to photographs, of famous and not so famous Scots. It's a wonderful place to dip in and out of: marveling at the ornate Great Hall, the detailed frieze of famous Scots in chronological order, and external decorative statues of Scottish poets and monarchs.

1 Queen St. www.nationalgalleries.org. ✆ **0131/624-6200.** Free. Daily 10am–5pm, Aug until 6pm.

### LEITH

Leith is the hub of Edinburgh's long maritime history. Archaeological excavations discovered medieval wharfs dating back to the 12th century, while today cruise ships dock at Ocean Terminal. For years a dilapidated area, over the last couple of decades the Shore has been revamped and is now a chic spot sprinkled with gastropubs, Michelin-starred restaurants, and even a boutique hotel, the cobbled waterfront scattered with interpretive boards depicting old harbor life.

The biggest tourist draw is the **Royal Yacht Britannia ★** (www.royalyachtbritannia.co.uk; ✆ **0131/555-5566**), moored at Ocean Terminal. Launched on April 16, 1953, this 125m (410-ft.) luxury yacht sailed more than a million miles before she was decommissioned in 1997. Onboard, an audio tour takes you around the five levels, including the decks where Prince Charles and Princess Diana strolled on their honeymoon, the Royal Apartments, engine room, and captain's cabin. It costs £14 for adults, £13 for seniors and £8.50 for children and is open daily in November to March 10am to 3:30pm; April to September 9:30am to 4:30pm and October 9:30am to 4pm.

## Organized Tours

Every city seems to have a hop on, hop off open-top **bus tour** these days, and they can be a fun introduction to the main sights. **Edinburgh Bus Tours** (www.edinburghtour.com; ✆ **0131/220-0770**) has a range of routes and themes, starting on Waverley Bridge and lasting around an hour. Tickets cost £14 for adults, £13 for seniors and students, and £6 for children aged 5 to 15.

There's no shortage of literary and ghost tours nowadays, but back in 1985, when a group of history teachers set up **Mercat Tours** (www.mercattours.com; ✆ **0131/225-5445**), they were ground-breaking. Thirty years on and a clutch of awards later, they're still going strong—as are two of the original tours: "Secrets of the Royal Mile" and "Ghosts and Ghouls." Tickets start at £11 for adults and £6 for children 5 to 15 (no children under age 5).

## Especially for Kids

There are dungeons, a castle, *and* giant pandas, what more could kids want? And, when they need to let off steam, there are plenty of parks and beaches nearby.

Giant Pandas Tian Tian (Sweetie) and Yang Guang (Sunshine) arrived at **Edinburgh Zoo ★★** (134 Corstorphine Rd.; www.edinburghzoo.org.uk; ✆ **0131/334-9171**) in 2011. On loan from China, they're so popular that you have to book a timed viewing slot to see them—at no extra cost. The penguins—splashing about in the largest outdoor penguin pool in Europe, with a waterfall feature and water shoot—are also a big hit with kids. Tickets for the zoo cost £17 for adults, seniors £15, children £13. At the **Botanic Gardens ★★** (see p. 86), you can picnic on the lawns and try to spot red squirrels scampering around, while in neighboring Inverleith Park there are swans and ducks to feed on the pond. For a view of Edinburgh, tramp to the top of Calton Hill or scramble up Arthur's Seat, or for a breath of salty air, head to the town beach at Portobello for fish and chips on the seafront or an ice cream on the beach.

For the appliance of science, **Camera Obscura ★** (549 Castlehill; www.camera-obscura.co.uk; ✆ **0131/226-3709**) at the top of the Royal Mile is a must, to see live images of Edinburgh projected into the rooftop chamber via a giant periscope, along with floor upon floor of holograms. Adults £14, seniors £12, children £9.95. There are also plenty of hands-on activities for kids at the **National Museum of Scotland ★★** (see p. 84). A tour with a costumed guide of the **Real Mary King's Close ★★** (2, Warriston's Close, High St.; www.realmarykingsclose.com; ✆ **0845/070-6244**), a warren of underground streets with the odd ghost story thrown in for good measure, is a spooky experience (no under 5s are allowed): adults £13, seniors and students £12, children £7.75. Meanwhile, **Edinburgh Dungeons ★** (31 Market St.; www.thedungeons.com; ✆ **0871/423-2250**) is an 80-minute rollercoaster of a journey through 1,000 years of Scottish history with a cast of costumed actors. Funny, scary, and a real thrill a minute—it's not for the very young. Tickets cost £17 for adults, £16 for students and seniors, £13 for children. There are discounts if you book online and get a pre-booked time slot.

## Where to Stay

Edinburgh has a vibrant accommodation scene, and one that continues to raise its game. At the top end, a host of five-star properties have undergone multi-million pound revamps over the past few years, including the once faded "Caley" **(The Caledonian)** now rebranded as a smart

Waldorf Astoria (see below) and the **Sheraton Grand Hotel & Spa** at 1 Festival Square (www.sheratonedinburgh.co.uk; ✆ **0131/229–9131**) whose spa and open-air rooftop hydrotherapy pool have definite sybaritic appeal. In the lower price bracket, the grand old St Cuthbert's Co-operative building houses the sleek **DoubleTree by Hilton** (34 Bread St.; www.doubletree.com; ✆ **0131/221-5555**).

One of the most noteworthy trends is the arrival of a new breed of design-led budget chains. Now, along with the traditional no-frills options such as **Ibis** (www.accorhotels.com; ✆ **0131/240-7000**) and **Premier Inn** (www.premierinn.com; ✆ **0871/527-8368**), you can find two outposts of German budget design chain, **Motel One** (www.motel-one.com; ✆ **0844/693-1077**), both just a sporran's throw from Waverley Station and with rooms from £69. Then there is the budget airline equivalent of the hotel chain: **Tune Hotel Haymarket.** On the right side of town for the airport, directly opposite the train station and tram stop, it's the perfect crash pad if you've an early or late flight. Using the low-cost airline model, rooms start at £25 and you just pay for any extras you need, such as the TV and Wi-Fi . . . and towels (www.tunehotels.com; ✆ **0131/347-9700**).

Hostels are no longer the bare-bones option. Many are now spruced up, sleek alternatives to the traditional guesthouse, with private rooms as well as dorms. **Edinburgh Central,** a five-star hostel and part of the Scottish Youth Hostel Association, at 9 Haddington Place, along Leith Walk (www.syha.org.uk; ✆ **0845/293-7373**), has single en-suite rooms from £37 and double and twins from £54.

If you have an early flight and want a more characterful option than the airport Hilton, **The Bridge Inn** in the tiny village of Ratho (27 Baird Rd, EH28 8RA; www.bridgeinn.com; ✆ **0131/333-1320**) is a gourmet bolthole on the side of the Union Canal. It feels a million miles away from the city but is actually just 20 minutes by car from the center of Edinburgh and 10 minutes from the airport. The four charming double rooms start at £80 including breakfast.

## NEW TOWN

### Expensive

**The Balmoral ★★★** For sheer class, this grande dame still has the edge. Yes there are other luxury hotels in the Scottish capital, but they haven't got the pizzazz wrought by Olga Polizzi, Rocco Forte's sister and the hotel's design director. Taste, style, and luxury seep out of the walls. As soon as the doorman ushers you from frenetic Princes Street into the elegant marble foyer, dripping in fresh flowers, you're enveloped in a chic cocoon that's smattered with eclectic artwork. The Victorian railway hotel, next to Waverley Station with its distinctive clock tower, opened in 1902, becoming part of the Rocco Forte portfolio in 1997. Today, it boasts a Michelin-starred restaurant, Number One, as well as a relaxed brasserie; a light, airy Palm Court where harp music soothes away city cares over afternoon tea; and a sleek spa. Rooms, many with panoramic castle views, reflect the soft heathery tones of the Scottish landscape while Scotch, the whisky bar, is daubed in the earthy amber tones of the 400 or so drams you can nose on a cowskin barstool.

1 Princes St. www.roccofortehotels.com. ✆ **0131/556-2414.** 188 units. Doubles £180–£565 double, suites £665–£2,350. **Amenities:** 2 restaurants; 2 bars; spa; sauna; steam room; gym; indoor pool; free Wi-Fi.





**The Caledonian ★★** Affectionately nicknamed the Caley by locals, this grand Victorian sandstone railway hotel (past guests include Charlie Chaplin, Elizabeth Taylor, and Bing Crosby) was, to put it bluntly, more than a little tired before the multi-million pound refurbishment in 2012. Re-branded a Waldorf Astoria, it mirrors The Balmoral at the opposite end of Princes Street. Gastronomic restaurant (with whisky trolley) and brasserie: check. Peacock Alley, the buzzing lounge and bar area: check. Spa (the U.K.'s first by Guerlain): check. There's also the Caley Bar, of course, for cocktails, and sleekly chic bedrooms in a cool color palette of smoky grey, silver and blue, some with castle views. The Balmoral, however, just has the edge.

Princes Street. www.thecaledonianedinburgh.com. ✆ **0131/222-8888.** 241 units Doubles £175–£689, suites £255–£2,249. **Amenities:** 2 restaurants; bar; lounge; spa; swimming pool; sauna; steam room; Jacuzzi; gym; salon; room service; free Wi-Fi.

### Moderate

**The Glasshouse ★★** Curiouser and curiouser: The entrance to this boutique hotel is through the facade of a grand, 19th-century stone church attached to a modern cinema complex. Inside, it's a slightly disjointed affair, a warren of dimly lit corridors, the walls peppered with paintings by local artists, surreal white featureless statues dotted around. The hotel is part of the Marriot Autograph stable—and every Autograph hotel has a theme: Here it's art. Other slight oddities: The elegant restaurant (sunny and sleek, overlooking lush, green Calton Hill) only serves breakfast. But once you enter the rooms, any reservations fall away. The floor to ceiling windows look out over the city's skyline to the front or open onto the neatly trimmed two-acre rooftop garden, which is a peaceful sanctuary far from the dusty streets down below. Out of sight, out of mind.

2 Greenside Place. www.theglasshousehotel.co.uk. ✆ **0131/525-8200.** 65 units, Doubles £110–£475 double, suites £270–£575. **Amenities:** Breakfast room; lounge bar; room service; free Wi-Fi.

**The Howard ★★** If you've been nursing a secret "Downton" fantasy, this discreet Georgian townhouse could be the answer. Butler service comes standard. Your butler will unpack your suitcase, whisk away any crumpled clothing for pressing, or organize a private whisky tasting. There's no tea tray in the room—ring for your butler and he'll make you a fresh pot. It's more of a small luxury property than a boutique hotel, spread throughout three Georgian townhouses. Bedrooms are on the traditional side (read: slightly old-fashioned), or book a terraced suite for your own entrance and to feel like a resident of one of the grandest cobbled streets in Edinburgh's New Town.

34 Great King St. www.thehoward.com. ✆ **0131/557-3500.** 18 units. Doubles £125–£265, suites £215–£425. **Amenities:** Restaurant; drawing room; bar service; butler; room service; free Wi-Fi.

**Nira Caledonia ★★** An elegant Georgian facade can hide a multitude of sins—or styles. From the outside, the Nira Caledonia looks like a traditionally understated townhouse on a broad cobbled street. Inside, the dark arts are at work. This 28-room boutique hotel eschews traditional tartan in favor of a dramatic black-and-gold color scheme, bold stripes, and a smattering of Oriental objects. In the restaurant, Blackwood's Bar & Grill, the chandelier is draped in black silk, while large Venetian mirrors add a touch of glamour—as do the three Jacuzzi suites. It was once the home of John Wilson, an important 19th-century literary figure, magazine founder, and friend of Wordsworth, Coleridge, and Sir Walter Scott (his statue is in East Princes Street Gardens). Fabrics and furnishings might be modern, but original features, from the sash windows to the cornicing and plasterwork, are still intact.

10 Gloucester Place. www.niracaledonia.com. ✆ **0131/225-2720.** 28 units, Doubles £120–£260, suites £175–£350. **Amenities:** Restaurant; bar; room service; free Wi-Fi.

**Tigerlily ★★** From the outside, the only hint to the glitter balls and glitz—the mirrored mosaic wall, giant cumulous cloud light, shocking pink bar stools, and smoky grey velvet sofas secreted within this Grade A-listed Georgian townhouse on George Street, the New Town's beating party heart—is the fake flowers cascading around the doorway. Tigerlily is not for shrinking violets. The 33 rooms and suites ooze sex appeal, seductively draped in bright Designers Guild fabrics, bespoke four-posters, Perspex chairs, and statement wallpapers. There are pre-loaded iPods, plasma screen TVs, and GHD hair straighteners. You might feel like you're out on ladies' night—and in the bar and basement nightclub, Lulu's, you may well be—but if it's all a little too pink, check into the Black Room in the eaves, with its wicker egg chair and black toilet paper. It's fabulously over-the-top; however, breakfast in the dimly lit restaurant booths does feel a little "morning after the night before."

125 George St. www.tigerlilyedinburgh.co.uk. ✆ **0131/225-5005.** 33 units. Doubles £105–£275, suites £150–£470. **Amenities:** Restaurant; bar; nightclub; free gym and swimming pool access nearby; room service; free Wi-Fi.

### Inexpensive

**B+B Edinburgh ★★** There's a lot to recommend at this cross between a bed-and-breakfast and boutique hotel (essentially, they've ditched the restaurant and focused on the rooms, no hardship in Scotland's culinary capital). The grand, Grade II–listed 19th-century building, designed for newspaper owner John Ritchie Findlay, is one thing. The rooms, another. Each floor has a different color scheme (heather, bracken—you get the gist), beds are comfy, furniture funky (think Perspex chairs), and some have freestanding bathtubs. The only disappointment is the dentist's waiting room–style scratchy carpets. At the front, rooms face the castle, but views at the back—of pretty Dean Village to the Forth and hills of Fife—are equally good. The first-floor library, with two-story-high bookshelves stacked with an eclectic collection of tomes, is the wow factor. The bar, walls lined with framed front pages of *The Scotsman,* is a cozy spot for a dram. The Belong + Benefit reward scheme is also a nice touch: For every 6 nights you stay, you get 1 free.

3 Rothesay Terrace. www.bb-edinburgh.com. ✆ **0131/225-5084.** 27 units. Doubles £75–£140. **Amenities:** Breakfast room; bar; library; lounge with free tea, coffee, and newspapers; loaner bikes; free Wi-Fi.

## OLD TOWN

### Expensive

**The Witchery ★★★** This flamboyant and fabulously gothic bolthole is all your historical fantasies rolled into one. If it doesn't make your pulse race, quite frankly you haven't got one. James Thomson opened this restaurant with rooms in 1979 in a clutch of 16th-century buildings tucked away beneath the castle. More than three decades later, it's still the ultimate romantic retreat. There are nine suites scattered through a higgledy-piggledy warren of buildings. Peppered with antiques and ornately carved four-posters and strewn with rich brocades and velvets, hedonistic tubs for two, and the odd suit of armor, it's the antidote to years of mealy-mouthed minimalism. Breakfast can be taken in the equally theatrical restaurant (all wood-paneling and candlelight at night), but why struggle out of bed when they'll bring a gourmet breakfast hamper to your suite? If it's fully booked, try Prestonfield (www.prestonfield.com; ✆ **0131/225-7800**) James Thomson's second hotel and mini country estate on the outskirts of the city. This 17th-century baroque pad is a lavishly opulent five-star boutique hotel with 18 rooms and 5 suites in his signature overblown style. Surrounded by 20 acres of gardens and parkland, yet only 5 minutes by taxi from the Royal Mile, it is the best of both worlds.

Castlehill, The Royal Mile. www.thewitchery.com. ✆ **0131/225-5613.** 9 units. Doubles £325–£360. **Amenities:** Restaurant; breakfast hamper and a bottle of champagne; free Wi-Fi.

### Moderate

**G&V Royal Mile Hotel ★★★** The Carlson Rezidor Hotel Group took over this modern five-star design hotel from the Missoni fashion label. The G&V stands for George & Victoria, with a nod to the area's royal heritage. Fashion designer Judy R Clark and 21st-century kilt legend Howie Nicholsby redesigned the uniforms, while Glasgow-based Timorous Beasties was put in charge of the crockery and linen. The renaming of the rooms *Brave*–style (wee, bonnie, braw, and muckle) might have been a step too far however, and much of the redesign does seem

superficial. Colors are still bright, patterns bold. Blink and you could be forgiven for thinking you were still in the Missoni. One Italian fixture thankfully not erased was Cucina, the fabulous restaurant set up by Giorgio Locatelli—and the Prosecco on tap also got a stay of execution.
1 George IV Bridge. www.gandvhotel.com. ✆ **0131/220-6666.** 136 units. Doubles £115–£500, suites £450–£1,000. **Amenities:** Restaurant; lobby bar; spa; room service; free Wi-Fi.



**Hotel du Vin ★★** This boutique chain revolving around, and reveling in, wine is as inspired an idea today as it was when the first property opened in Winchester in 1994. With rooms named after wines and champagnes, an encyclopedic wine list, monthly Saturday wine tastings, and a giant wine glass chandelier in reception, there's no getting away from the grape. The other trademark features are all here: the contemporary conversion of an historic building (in this case a mental asylum); a relaxed French bistro (with affordable prix-fixe menu); a bar, and, with a nod to Scotland, a whisky snug, with leather wingback chairs and a smattering of tasteful tartan. The building is a warren, and rooms vary. Many have luxurious freestanding tubs; those in the older part have sloping ceilings and beams; some look inward over the inner courtyard. For a view of Arthur's Seat, splash out on a luxury suite with private terrace.
11 Bristo Place. www.hotelduvin.com. ✆ **0844/736-4255.** 47 units. Doubles £99–£180, suites £150–£350. **Amenities:** Restaurant; bar; whisky snug; tasting room; room service; free Wi-Fi.

### Inexpensive

**The Grassmarket Hotel ★★** If you think hotel websites can be a little dull, check out The Grassmarket's. The distance to the city's major attractions, for instance, is noted in footsteps. That sense of fun is echoed in the hotel itself. Designer Jim Hamilton has been willfully playful. Walls around the reception desk are hung with old keys, and there are high silver banquettes and bookshelves stacked with games and comic books. You can grab a cappuccino here, but for breakfast you need to stumble next door to Biddy Mulligans pub. Rooms are divided into cosy (single), snug (double), and comfy categories—double, triple, and quad. All the amenities the hotel-savvy guest expects are here (rainfall showers and iPod docking stations), along with a few they probably don't, including comic strip Dandy wallpaper, a magnetic city map across one wall, and complimentary Tunnocks teacakes, for the big kid in you.
94–96 Grassmarket. www.thegrassmarkethotel.co.uk. ✆ **0131/220-2299.** 42 units. Doubles £68–£345. **Amenities:** Free Wi-Fi.

## LEITH

### Moderate

**Malmaison ★★** This grand 19th-century building in the Scottish baronial style opened in 1885 as a Seaman's mission, housing up to 56 sailors—with room for 50 more, after a shipwreck, in the attic. It was also a "house of ill-repute" at one time, apparently. Now a design hotel, it's a respectable part of the spruced-up waterfront, its brasserie and bar buzzing, with guests spilling out onto the cobbled street. Opt for a room at the front that overlooks the port, if possible, as rooms at the back are darker, and with no view to speak of. The hotel might lack a city center location, but transport links are quick and easy, and this vibrant area is now a destination in itself.

1 Tower Place. www.malmaison.com. ✆ **0131/468-5000.** 100 units. Doubles £175–£205, suites £245–£295. Bus 16 or 22. **Amenities:** Restaurant; bar; gym; room service; free Wi-Fi.

## Where to Eat

Edinburgh is the gourmet as well as political capital of the country, with no fewer than five Michelin-starred restaurants to its name along with a burgeoning scene of rustic-chic, field-to-plate eateries. Gone are the days when jokes about deep-friend Mars Bars and Irn Bru were bandied about whenever Scottish cuisine was mentioned. The country's natural larder is stocked with wild venison from ancient Highland estates, heather-fed lamb, Aberdeen Angus beef, and salmon from its rushing rivers. Add shellfish from the chilly waters off the Scottish coast—langoustines (aka Dublin Bay Prawns), oysters, mussels, and plump hand-dived scallops along with fish such as halibut, bream, and sea bass—and chefs have all the ingredients they need to create a gastronomic extravaganza. Fresh vegetables include asparagus, kale, and, of course, potatoes—the spuds grown in Ayrshire's sandy soils are said to be unparalleled for their fluffy texture and rich taste.

A good guide to grab for more dining ideas is ***The List*** magazine's comprehensive ***Eating & Drinking Guide,*** updated annually and featuring reviews of hundreds of restaurants, bars, and cafes in Edinburgh. It is available to buy, or check out the reviews online (food.list.co.uk).

### NEW TOWN

#### Expensive

**21212** ★★★ CONTEMPORARY FRENCH The concept is simple: a choice of two starters, a set soup course, a choice of two mains, a set cheese course, and so on. The works of art presented to awed diners at 21212, however, are anything but simple. Michelin-starred chef Paul Kitching takes the wow factor and lets it spiral into outer space. Along with his open-kitchen theater, the dramatic restaurant design features a giant moth-themed carpet, crystal chandelier, and cool gray color scheme. The four-story Georgian townhouse also has four luxury rooms and a private dining "pod" with a pink marble table, circular cream leather banquette, and cherub-laced Caravaggio print wallpaper. But the food is the star. Each course is a multi-layered, multi-faceted explosion of flavors: a cauliflower cheese starter for instance, was an invention of

Gruyere risotto, black pudding, apple, walnuts and sultanas, roasted onion, cauliflower, and Branston pickle—with foam. What are you waiting for? Book a table.

3 Royal Terrace. www.21212restaurant.co.uk. ✆ **0131/523-1030.** Five-course dinner £69, two-course lunch £22 on weekdays. Tues–Sat noon–1:45pm; Tues–Thurs 7–9pm; Fri–Sat 6:45–9:30pm.



**Mark Greenaway ★★★** PROGRESSIVE BRITISH The pudding man cometh. When Mark Greenaway opened his eponymous restaurant in the New Town, waistbands groaned at the prospect. Deconstructed desserts—such as the Knot Chocolate tart, composed of custard jelly, frozen cookies, crème fraiche parfait, salted caramel, and kumquat puree—spelled disaster for will power. Of course, there are also some savory options worth mentioning. The signature Loch Fyne crab cannelloni with smoked cauliflower custard, lemon pearls, herb butter, and baby coriander is a theatrical (smoke swirls under a glass top)—and delicious—tour de force. A good lunchtime option is the three-course Market Menu, while for a real splurge opt for the eight-course tour menu. The surroundings are subtly dramatic: Think dark teal walls and crisp white tablecloths with a statement brass cluster chandelier. For a less formal option, head down the hill to his second eatery, Bistro Moderne by Mark Greenaway (www.bistromoderne.co.uk; ✆ **0131/225-4431**), which serves French brasserie classics with a Scottish twist.

69 North Castle St. www.markgreenaway.com. ✆ **0131/226-1155.** Mains £21–£29, three-course market menu £22, eight-course tasting menu £65. Tues–Sat noon–2:30pm, 5:30–10pm.

### Moderate

**The Honours ★★** BRITISH BRASSERIE Martin Wishart's Michelin-starred eponymous restaurant down in Leith's revamped docklands might be on the formal side, but at his city center brasserie everything loosens up a bit. Designer Ian Smith's interiors jump from Las Vegas to Dubai via Paris: bold and gold geometric brasserie bling with a dash of razzle dazzle (think bright turquoise banquettes, a broad black-and-white striped tiled floor, and honey-hued walls) in the bar. The name, incidentally, is a nod to Sir Walter Scott, who lived nearby and rediscovered the Scottish Crown Jewels known as the Honours of Scotland, which had gone missing for a century. (They had been hidden, it turns out, from the pesky English in an old oak chest in Edinburgh Castle.) The menu features a traditional lunchtime prix-fixe menu, with oysters and scallops and a lengthy grill section. Along with Donald Russell grass-fed and dry-aged beef, there's a select-breeds option that includes Black Angus cattle from Creekstone Farm and Shorthorn cattle from the Glenarm Estate. The chateaubriand served with duck fat chips, fried onion rings, green salad, and sauce béarnaise comes with an eye-watering price tag. But whatever you do, don't miss the sublime crab cappuccino (served, thankfully, in a large bowl instead of a coffee cup), with chunks of succulent crab submerged in a creamy bisque and topped, of course, with foam.

58A North Castle St. www.thehonours.co.uk. ✆ **0131/220-2513.** Mains £17–£33. Tues–Sat noon–2:30pm, 6–10pm.



### Inexpensive

**The Dogs ★★★** BRITISH REVIVAL David Ramsden's shabby-chic little joint (old wooden pews and an eclectic collection of tongue-in-cheek dog memorabilia) on the first floor of a grand Georgian townhouse keeps pulling them in with its off-beat menu—think devilled ox liver, offal toast, and Arbroath smokie fishcakes with vanilla sauce—and prices that won't mug your wallet. For dessert, don't miss the legendary lemon posset with an oat and ginger biscuit.

110 Hanover St. www.thedogsonline.co.uk. ✆ **0131/220-1208.** £9.95–£17. Daily noon–4pm, 5–10pm.

## OLD TOWN

### Moderate

**Timberyard ★★★** MODERN BRITISH The foodie Radford family's latest venture, Timberyard is housed in a sprawling 19th-century costume and props warehouse. Tucked behind a giant red doorway, the space opens out into the Warehouse, an industrial-scale dining area with metal columns, rough-hewn floor, and tartan rugs flung over chairs. There's a butchery, smokehouse, private dining in the Shed, and open-air seating in the south-facing Yard. The imaginative menu features dishes such as raw venison, burnt oak oil, shallot, mustard, and buckwheat alongside smoked beef loin, shallot, burnt ramson, cauliflower, kohlrabi, and mustard. Andrew and Lisa Radford's son Ben heads up the kitchen, while his brother Jo performs bartender alchemy, conjuring seasonal cordials and infusions along with herbal tonic for the gin and homemade cola, and ginger beer from herbs grown in the kitchen garden.

10 Lady Lawson St. www.timberyard.co. ✆ **0131/221-1222.** Mains £16–£22; eight-course set menu £55, paired drinks an extra £35. Tues–Sat noon–2pm, 5:30–9:30pm.

## SOUTHSIDE

### Moderate

**Aizle ★★** SCOTTISH BISTRO Aizle rhymes with hazel (and is the old Scots word for spark or ember). At first glance, the new-fangled culinary style—Scottish Neo-Bistro—might set your teeth on edge, but go with it. You haven't seen the menu yet. In fact, there isn't one, just a list of ingredients from which your four-course tasting menu will be conjured. Yes, it's gimmicky, but it's fun and adds a sense of adventure to your dining experience. It can feel a bit like the Concentration Game trying to remember what's in each dish as it's reeled off. Our list featured foraged wildflowers sea aster, sea plantain, and pink purslane, and mead, miso, feuilletine (sweet patisserie flakes), and bee pollen. The *boudin blanc* with purslane, celeriac, and slithers of pear was exquisite. The

husband and wife team behind Aizle is Stuart Ralston, a Scottish chef who's worked with Gordon Ramsay in New York, and Krystal Goff, a mixologist from Seattle. The decor is a little more shabby than chic—or possibly done up in a hurry—but the culinary mystery tour is magical.
107-109 St Leonard's St. www.aizle.co.uk. ✆ **0131/662-9349.** 4-course tasting menu £35. Wed–Sun 6–10pm.



## STOCKBRIDGE

### Moderate

**The Scran & Scallie ★★** GASTROPUB The rise of the gastropub might be old news (although Scotland could still do with a few more), but when two Michelin-starred chefs (Tom Kitchin and Dominic Jack) start playing with the concept, they take it to a new level. This is gastropub with attitude. (*Scran* means grub and *Scallie* is scallywag). Alongside the traditional fish and chips, you'll find forgotten classics such as sheep's heid (old Scots spelling) Scotch broth and hearty dishes such as braised *hogget* shoulder (a young sheep—older than a lamb, but not as old as mutton). Design-wise, it's also up a notch, with a nod to Scandinavia (Tom's wife Michaela is Swedish) mixed in with Scottish tweeds, mismatched chairs, exposed brickwork, rough wooden floors, a wood-burner, and a scattering of sheepskin rugs.
1 Comely Bank Road. www.scranandscallie.com. ✆ **0131/332-6281**. Mains £9.50–£19. Mon–Fri noon–3pm, 6–10pm; Sat, Sun noon–10pm.



### Inexpensive

**Peter's Yard ★★** SWEDISH BAKERY Swede Peter Ljunquist established his first artisanal bakery and cafe in the city's Southside Quartermile conversion, a hard-angled vision of glass and pale wood, softened by the mounds of freshly baked bread. In 2012, he opened a second spot in village-y Stockbridge, adding signature sourdough pizzas, traditional open-topped sandwiches (think herring with oat crumble, potato, crème fraiche, and boiled egg on Swedish rye bread), and cardamom buns and hot chocolate, which patrons consume at communal wooden tables or wrapped in cozy blankets at the tables outside. The place exudes a clean-lined Swedish chic.
3 Deanhaugh St. www.petersyard.com. ✆ **0131/332-2901.** Pizza £10, sandwiches £4.90–£5.80. Mon–Fri 8am–9pm; Sat, Sun 9am–9pm.

## CANONMILLS

### Inexpensive

**Earthy ★★** CAFE DELI/NEW BRITISH "Forage. Nourish. Share" is the tagline at Earthy. The staff are called Earthlings, the word "mission" is bandied about, and the cheerily painted distressed furniture is made from reclaimed timber and wind-damaged trees. The cafe is open for breakfast, lunch, dinner, all-day grazing, and takeaways. Whether you're slurping organic sweet potato soup with coconut and cardamom; munching carrot cake; or savoring a plate of seared East Lothian venison fillet with salsify, figs, buttered spinach, and a dark chocolate and chili sauce (£17), share the love and share the food.

1-6 Canonmills Bridge. ✆ **0131/556-9696.** Mains £5.50–£17. Mon–Sat 9am–5pm, Sun 9am–5pm, Tues–Sat 6–9pm.



## EAST END

### Moderate

**The Gardener's Cottage ★★** BRITISH Chefs Edward Murray and Dale Mailley's communal dining hotspot is in a 19th-century stone cottage in the wooded Royal Terrace Gardens. The country flavor of this old bothy (rustic shelter) is enhanced by the old wooden tables, jars of wildflowers, mismatched china, church chairs, and an old record player churning out jazz. The daily changing menu, scrawled on a blackboard outside, features seasonal and local ingredients—so local in fact, that some of the herbs and vegetables are plucked from the restaurant's own patch, for delicious dishes such as mackerel tartare with rhubarb and sea vegetables.

1 Royal Terrace Gardens. www.thegardenerscottage.co. ✆ **0131/558-1221.** Six-course set dinner menu £30, lunch a la carte mains £15–£17. Sat–Sun 10am–2:30pm, 5–10pm; Mon, Thurs, Fri noon–2:30pm, 5–10pm.

### Inexpensive

**Joseph Pearce ★★** SWEDISH GASTROPUB It all started with Bar Boda, a tiny hole-in-the-wall joint down Leith Walk. Now, at the last count, entrepreneurial Swedish couple Anna and Mike Christopherson have five bohemian bars and eateries: Boda, Victoria, Sofi, Hemma, and Joseph Pearce. Decor is eclectic: Think retro chic with junk shop chairs and frilly lampshades. The place is fashionably cool but with a homey vibe, and regular events include knitting nights and a language cafe as well as cult film and music nights. There's a family-friendly ethos—in the back of Joseph Pearce, with its soaring ceilings, potted plants, checked curtains, and comfy sofas, there's a stack of high chairs, toys, and games. Food-wise it's a step up from your traditional gastropub grub, with a menu that includes Swedish meatballs with feta, mint and green bean salad, or a catfish fillet marinated in lemongrass and ginger with polenta fritters and caper salad. In August, swing by for traditional Swedish crayfish parties.

23 Elm Row. www.bodabar.com. ✆ **0131/556-4140.** Mains £9.90–£13. Sun–Thurs 11am–midnight, Fri–Sat 11am–1am.

**Valvona & Crolla ★★** ITALIAN The Contini family are Edinburgh deli royalty—and this local institution, established in 1934, is reassuringly old school. It feels like stepping back in time, with hams dangling from the high ceiling, old wooden shelves crammed with Scottish and Italian delicacies that include the family specialty, a spicy fonteluna sausage, the recipe created in their Italian mountain village a thousand years ago. At the back of the long, narrow shop, the space opens out into a cafe where you can tuck into traditional rustic fare, made from recipes handed down over the years and washed down with a fine vintage plucked from the shelves for the shop price plus £6 corkage. There's a wine recommendation next to each dish in case you're daunted by the staggering array to choose from.

19 Elm Row. www.valvonacrolla.co.uk. ✆ **0131/556-6066.** Mains £9.95–£16. Mon–Thurs 8:30am–6pm; Sat, Sun 8am–6:30pm; Sun 10:30am-4pm.



### LEITH

#### Expensive

**The Kitchin** ★★★ MODERN BRITISH After stints in a clutch of three-Michelin-starred restaurants in London, Paris, and Monte Carlo, Tom Kitchin came home and opened his own restaurant in an old whisky warehouse in the rejuvenated Leith docklands in 2006. Just seven months later, at the age of 29, he became the youngest chef-proprietor to be awarded a Michelin star. Other notches on his belt include a string of TV appearances, from *The Great British Menu* to *Master Chef* judging. His philosophy, From Nature to Plate (also the name of his first book), focuses on Scotland's abundant natural larder. Don't miss the signature surf and turf starter, pig's head and langoustine. Main courses of note include Ox (boudin of Inverurie ox tongue with braised ox shin, bone marrow potato, Parisienne carrots, and Perthshire girolles) and Lamb (a selection of Highland lamb with raw vegetable salad and black olive jus). The restaurant is intimate and understated, despite the chef-y window onto the kitchen. Some people find Michelin-starred dining intimidating—this isn't.

78 Commercial St. www.thekitchin.com. ✆ **0131/555-1755.** Mains £28–£36, three-course set lunch £29. Tues–Sat 12:15–2.30pm; Tues–Thurs 6:30–10pm; Fri, Sat 6:30–10:30pm.

## Shopping

The best places to mooch around the shops are Edinburgh's "village" neighborhoods. In the New Town, **Princes Street** is the glorious setting for an uninspiring shopping experience. The castle looms over the long, wide thoroughfare lined with the usual big-name chain stores on one side and Princes St Gardens and the Old Town's rollercoaster skyline on the other. It is worth popping into Edinburgh's stately department store, **Jenners,** a lavish landmark at the east end since 1838, to pick up some posh shortbread. However, it's no longer an independent shop after being bought by House of Fraser a decade ago. A block north, George Street is a higher-end high shopping area, crowned at its eastern edge off St. Andrews Square with a large branch of **Harvey Nichols** and a cluster of stylish shops within teetering distance along Multrees Walk.

In the Old Town, the **Royal Mile** is strung with shops selling cashmere, tweed, and specialty whisky as well as tartan tat, but swing down **Cockburn Street** and **Victoria Street** and you'll stumble upon one-of-a-kind shops and quirky boutiques. Wind down to the **Grassmarket** for vintage clothes, **Bruntsfield** for chic boutiques and cafe culture. Or mosey along to the **West End Village,** a string of Georgian streets between the Caledonian hotel and Haymarket which even has its own website, www.westendedinburgh.org, promoting its independent boutiques and bustling bars and restaurants. **Stockbridge,** meanwhile, is peppered with delis and specialist food stores—a real hub for food lovers. It's also home to an increasingly popular farmers market every Sunday, giving the jauntily striped stalls of the original Saturday **farmers market** (www.edinburghfarmersmarket.co.uk; on Castle Terrace every Saturday morning) a run for its money.

## Entertainment & Nightlife

Summer festival season isn't the only time Edinburgh comes alive; there is plenty to do at other times of the year too. The West End is the cradle of theater and music, with the innovative **Traverse Theatre** (www.traverse.co.uk; ✆ **0131/228-1404**) as well as the grand Victorian **Royal Lyceum Theatre** (lyceum.org.uk; ✆ **0131/248-4848**), and, for concerts, the classic and acoustically excellent **Usher Hall** (www.usherhall.co.uk; ✆ **0131/228-1155**). Nearby, the **Filmhouse** (www.filmhousecinema.com; ✆ **0131/228-6382**) offers the best in independent and art-house cinema. For comedy, **The Stand ★★** is an Edinburgh stalwart showcasing local talent as well as big name acts (www.thestand.co.uk; ✆ **0131/558-7272**). For a non-stop, eclectic program of funk, fusion, soul, blues, acoustic sessions—and jazz, **The Jazz Bar ★★** is a cool, dimly lit, late-night hangout at 1A Chambers St. in the Old Town (www.thejazzbar.co.uk; ✆ **0131/220-4298**).

Pick up a copy of ***The List*** magazine from newsstands and bookshops, or visit www.list.co.uk for previews, reviews, and details of arts events around the city.

When it comes to **bars and pubs,** the **Grassmarket** in Old Town and **Broughton Street** in New Town are buzzing, as is the waterfront in the port of **Leith.** The cocktail is king in Edinburgh, and one of the best places to sip one in the New Town is **Bramble ★★** (16A Queen St.; www.bramblebar.co.uk; ✆ **0131/226-6343**). This tiny boho basement bar is all exposed brickwork, dimly lit nooks and crannies, alcoves for lounging, and bartenders conjuring up margaritas in teacups and delicate lavender martinis. The **Voodoo Rooms ★★** offer live music, cabaret, and cocktails sprinkled throughout a string of bars and ballrooms in a historic building down a little alley just off Princes Street. The main first-floor bar and restaurant is a glamorous affair with booths, banquettes, huge arched windows, and soaring ceilings ornately decorated with gold leaf. It's also home to around 60 specialty tequilas (19A W. Register St.; www.thevoodoorooms.com; ✆ **0131/556-7060**).

# EDINBURGH specialties

For the finest Scottish cashmere, head down to **Hawico** at 71 Grassmarket (www.hawickcashmere.com; ✆ **0131/225-8634**), which has been producing cashmere in its Scottish Borders mills for over a century. Or trek over to New Town and splash out on beanies and wrist-warmers, wraps and cropped cardigans from luxury brand **Brora** at 48 Frederick St. (www.brora.co.uk; ✆ **0131/220-6404**).

For stylish Scottish tweed, **Walker Slater** on quaint and colorful Victoria St, which curves downhill to the Grassmarket, feels reassuringly old-school yet is far from stuffy, offering contemporary tailoring alongside rugged knitwear and linens in its two stores on Victoria Street: menswear is at number 20, womenswear is at 46 (www.walkerslater.com; ✆ **0131/220-2636**). Another bastion of Scottish style and tasteful tartan, **Anta,** has its sleek flagship store on George Street over in the New Town. Provenance is key for this brand, and everything from the cushions to the capsule clothing collection is made in Scotland: the yarn for the tweeds, carpets and tartan cabin bags comes from the Western Isles and is woven in the Borders, the furniture is made from Scottish oak, while the signature ceramics are hand-decorated in the Highlands (www.anta.co.uk; ✆ **0131/225-9096**).

For another contemporary take on traditional Scottish design, traipse down narrow, cobbled Thistle Street to 21st Century Kilts. For camouflage to Harris Tweed, PVC to denim, **Howie Nicholsby's** tiny shop can be found at 48 Thistle St. (www.21stcenturykilts.com; ✆ **0131/220-9450**). For a more traditional kilt and all the trimmings (sporrans, kilt pins, and big buckles) his father is Geoffrey the Tailor (57–59 High St; www.geoffreykilts.co.uk; ✆ **0131/557-0256**), who includes Sean Connery and Mel Gibson among past clients. The traditional 8-yard worsted wool kilts are hand-sewn and made to measure—and will set you back around £500.

Whisky, of course, is the traditional Scottish tipple, and there's no shortage of specialist stores to browse, such as **The Whisky Shop,** a small chain with a branch at 28 Victoria St. (www.whisky-shop.com; ✆ **0131/225-4666**). A few doors down you can also decant a Bladnoch 13-year-old single malt into your own glass bottle at **Demijohn** (32 Victoria St.; www.demijohn.co.uk; ✆ **0131/225-3265**). Here, you are encouraged to try before you buy from the array of fragrant oils, vinegars, liqueurs, artisan wines, and meads which are decanted into an Italian glass bottle of your choice. Perthshire rapeseed oil or elderflower vinegar, sloe gin or Bramble Scotch whisky liqueur?

It's not all about whisky these days, however. Gin is now basking in the spotlight. **Edinburgh Gin** is created in copper stills under the city's pavements at 1 Rutland Place (www.edinburghgindistillery.co.uk; ✆ **0131/656-2810**). You can take a tour, opt for a tutored tasting, or go for the full works and create your own gin with a range of botanicals. There's also a small shop where you can buy a bottle or two. At night the place turns into a buzzing cocktail bar.

Choices, choices.

## Gay & Lesbian Edinburgh

Edinburgh's "Pink Triangle" is around the top end of Leith Walk and Broughton Street, incorporating **Calton Hill.** That said, the LGBT scene is not on the same scale as London's, and there's no distinct gay quarter to match districts such as Manhattan's Christopher Street or San Francisco's Castro.

The city's oldest gay bar is **CC Blooms** (22-24 Greenside Place; www.ccbloomsedinburgh.com; ✆ **0131/556-9331**), while **The Regent** (2 Montrose Terrace; www.theregentbar.co.uk; ✆ **0131/661-8198**) is a cozy, traditional pub.

For details on **Pride Edinburgh,** the city's Gay Pride festival and march held each year in June, check out www.prideedinburgh.org.

And for a nightcap? A dram of course. There's no shortage of whisky bars and olde-worlde pubs with an eye-watering range of malts. Rustic **Whiski Rooms ★★** has exposed stone walls, with a mural of a stag and a contemporary brasserie vibe. It has a shop stocking around 500 whiskies, a bar, bistro, and tasting room—where along with traditional tastings, whisky is matched with cheese and chocolate. You can take a whisky flight in the bar or try a whisky cocktail—Whiski Martini or a Monkey Mojito anyone?—or just relax with the perfect dram (4–7 North Bank St.; www.whiskirooms.com; ✆ **0131/225-7224**).

# [FastFACTS] UNITED KINGDOM

### Business Hours

Banks are usually open Monday through Friday 9am to 5pm; some also open on Saturdays from 10am to 3pm. Stores generally open Monday through Saturday 9 or 10am to 6pm; on Thursday, some stores stay open until 8pm. Offices generally open Monday through Friday 9am to 5pm.

### Currency

Although the United Kingdom is a member of the European Union, it has retained the pound sterling (£) as its currency. See p. 860 for information on money and costs.

### Doctors & Dentists

For a medical or dental emergency, ask at your hotel first. Then try the GP (general practitioner) finder at **www.nhs.uk**. ***Note:*** U.S. and Canadian visitors who become ill while they're in the U.K. are eligible only for free *emergency* care. For other treatment, including follow-up care, you'll pay £60–£150 just to see a physician or dentist. In Edinburgh, the city's 24-hour Accident and Emergency Department is located at the **Royal Infirmary of Edinburgh,** 51 Little France Crescent, Old Dalkeith Rd. (✆ **0131/536-1000;** www.nhslothian.scot.nhs.uk).

### Embassies & Consulates:

**Australia:** Australia House Strand London WC2B 4LA (www.uk.embassy.gov.au; ✆ **020/7379 4334**).

**Canada:** Macdonald House 1 Grosvenor Square London W1K 4AB (www.UnitedKingdom.gc.ca; ✆ **020/7258-6600**).

**New Zealand:** New Zealand House 80 Haymarket London SW1Y 4TQ (www.nzembassy.com/uk; ✆ **020/7930-8422**).

**United States:** 24 Grosvenor Square London W1A 6AE (http://london.usembassy.gov; ✆ **020/7499-9000**).

### Emergencies

The one-stop number for the U.K. is ✆ **999**—that's for fire, police, and ambulances. It's free from any phone, even mobiles. Less urgent? Call 111.

### Internet

If your hotel insists on charging for Wi-Fi (and oddly many of the more expensive hotels still do), it's provided free at pubs, cafes, museums, and in London, on some Tube routes.

### Pharmacies

Every police station keeps a list of pharmacies (chemists) that are open 24 hours. Also try **Zafash,** a rare chemist that is open 24 hours, 233-235 Old Brompton Rd., SW5 (✆ **020/7373-2798;** Tube: Earl's Court); and **Bliss,** open daily 9am to midnight, 5-6 Marble Arch, W1 (✆ **020/7723-6116;** Tube: Marble Arch). For non-emergency health advice, as well as information about the nearest late-night pharmacy, call the NHS at ✆ **111.**

# 3

# FRANCE

by Margie Rynn

Though it's nearly 500 miles from Paris to the French Riviera, a great many tourists combine the two on a first trip to France. And they're right to do so! While the world may have other, more compelling travel destinations, I can't imagine what they might be, or how anyone could claim they are rivals to Paris and its Mediterranean counterpart. Paris is nothing short of magical. And so is the Riviera and its adjacent Provence. That's why we've combined these areas in this chapter on France.

***The City of Light.*** I can never get enough of it. To me, Paris is on the frontier, the leading edge, of every touristic activity. It rules the roost in cuisine—who could deny that?—but also in art and museums, in concerts, dance and opera, in political discourse and intellectual debate (scan the newspaper headlines if you doubt that), in monuments and history (from the Panthéon to the Tomb of Napoléon), in fashion and shopping, in its cafes and bars (where you can sit the entire afternoon over a single glass of wine and not be asked to move on), in the availability of its civic services (get sick and a roaming ambulance with a doctor on board will almost instantly be at your side), in its luscious-looking open-air markets, in the excitement of its student life, in literature and economics (its resident novelists, philosophers. scientists and scholars are legendary)—and in every other field and endeavor I can name. Return to it for the second time or even the fiftieth—and it still seems new.

Although the chapter that follows this introduction devotes more-than-sufficient space to organized commercial tours of Paris (including the fabled Bateaux-Mouches river cruises), it's clear from our text that we primarily regard Paris as a walking city, to be explored on your own, often wandering at random. Here, after all, is a metropolis so built to human scale, so lovely in its architectural design, so lined with small shops with their dynamic proprietors, that there is never an uninteresting block in it. Let me repeat: You can walk its ancient streets for hours and you will never be uninterested.

***And now to the south of France.*** Provence . . . The Riviera. Simply to utter those words is to imagine pleasure, sheer pleasure. It's to visualize a world of resplendent casinos (in Nice and Cannes); of broad, graceful boulevards flanking the sea; of beaches with light blue umbrellas; of stunning vacationers in bikinis or the like; and of the French on vacation.

FACING PAGE: **Montmartre hill, with the Basilique du Sacré-Coeur.**

It's often been said that no one knows better than the French how to enjoy themselves. I witnessed that condition once, most indelibly, at a giant Mediterranean Club Med where a planeload of French vacationers had just arrived. Within three minutes of alighting from the airport buses, the entire planeload was gyrating on the dance floor and dashing to the bar for bouts of wine and worse. Within three minutes.

You'll have another experience of the French enjoying themselves at the exquisite lunchtime buffets on the beach in front of grand hotels like the Negresco in Nice or the Martinez in Cannes. Never in your life will you ever have such a buffet lunch, a repast to rival the gourmet meals in many famed restaurants.

And you'll encounter such pleasures not simply in Nice, which you should definitely visit (the railroad station hotels there are unusually cheap), but also to the west of Nice in St-Tropez and Juan les Pins, and to the east of Nice in Eze-Village. There's no need for a car. Trains go along the sea, and it's usually about half an hour by rail to reach whatever you're seeking.

From the Riviera north through Provence is another sort of pleasure, one of the most visually awesome areas of France, so beautifully depicted by 19th-century postimpressionists from Cezanne to van Gogh. When I think of it, I think of fields of lavender stretching on into the distance, of university towns like Aix en Provence, of Roman ruins near Avignon, of ancient Arles on the River Rhone where van Gogh painted his famous *Night Café* and numerous Provençal landscapes.

But enough enthusiasm, which these massively popular destinations really don't need. It's time to reach specifics, and to wish you, *chers amis,* a hearty *bon voyage! Bon plaisir!*

***–Arthur Frommer***

# PARIS

Just saying word "Paris" conjures up a spate of images and an orchestral soundtrack: historic monuments, mansard-roofed buildings, Belle Epoque curlicues, glistening pavements, and perhaps a baguette or two. But beyond the clichés lies a city that is not only elegant, graceful, and beautiful to look at, but also the pulsing heart of the French nation. The metropolitan area encompasses the country's capital, 20% of its population, and the source of most of its jobs. For the best in art, culture, and business, all roads lead to Paris.

The Eiffel Tower and the Bateaux Mouches.

There are so many wonderful thing things to see and do in the City of Light, it's hard to know where to begin. You can eat your way to nirvana in the city's restaurants, gourmet food stores, and bakeries. You can admire dazzling architecture that ranges from the opulence of **Place de la Concorde ★★★** (p. 126) to the contemporary madness of **Musée du Quai Branly ★★★** (p. 131). You can lose yourself at the **Louvre ★★★** (p. 121), one of the world's greatest museums, or amble though dozens of other smaller, more specialized receptacles of art and culture. Relax in a royal garden like the **Jardin du Luxembourg ★★★,** take in a concert, dance in a club, or just watch the world go by in a classic Parisian cafe. Even if you have time to see only a fraction of what you'd like to see, don't worry—just noodling around a neighborhood may be the stuff of great travel memories. What counts is that you'll have been to Paris, sampled its wonders, and savored the experience—and that counts for a lot.

## Essentials

The municipal tourist office, the **Office du Tourisme et des Congrès** (www.parisinfo.com; ✆ **01-49-52-42-63**) has an excellent website and offices throughout the city.

**ARRIVING** Paris has two international airports: **Aéroport d'Orly,** 18km (11 miles) south of the city (mostly European flights), and **Aéroport Roissy-Charles-de-Gaulle** (mostly long haul carriers, also known as CDG), 30km (19 miles) northeast (for both airports: www.aeroportsdeparis.fr; ✆ **00-33-1-70-36-39-50** from abroad, or **39-50** from

France). If you are taking Ryanair or another discount airline that arrives at **Beauvais Airport** (www.aeroportbeauvais.com; ✆ **08-92-68-20-66,** 0.34€ per min.), be advised that the airport is located about 80km (50 miles) from Paris.

**From Roissy-Charles-de-Gaulle Airport,** the quickest way into central Paris is the **RER B** (www.ratp.fr), a suburban train that leaves every 10 to 15 minutes between 5am and 10pm (midnight on weekends). It takes about 40 minutes to get to Paris, stopping at several central Métro stations. A single ticket costs 9.75€.

There are also two bus options for getting in to the city center. **Les Cars Air France** (www.lescarsairfrance.com; ✆ **08-92-35-08-20**) offers two routes stopping at major Métro connections. Depending on the route, a one-way trip costs 17€ to 18€ for adults; there are reductions for young adults, children, and groups of four or more. Buses leave every 30 minutes between 6am and 11pm; both trips take about an hour, depending on traffic. The **Roissybus** (www.ratp.fr; ✆ **32-46** from France only) departs every 20 minutes from the airport daily from 6am to 12:30am and costs 11€ for the 60-minute ride. The bus leaves you at the corner of rue Scribe and rue Auber, near the Opéra.

A **taxi** from Roissy into the city will cost at least 50€, not including 1€ per item of luggage, and the fare is 15% higher from 5pm to 10am, as well as on Sundays and bank holidays.

**From Orly Airport,** you can take the 8-minute monorail **OrlyVal** to the RER station "Anthony," where you catch the **RER B** into the center. Combined travel time is about 40 minutes. Trains run between 6am and 11pm, and the one-way combined fare is 12.05€ for adults.

The **Air France bus** (**Les Cars Air France;** www.cars-airfrance.com; ✆ **08-92-35-08-20**) leaves Orly every 20 minutes between 6am and 11:40pm, stopping at Gare Montparnasse, Invalides, and Charles de Gaulle-Etoile. The fare is 12.50€ one-way. Depending on the traffic, the journey takes about an hour. Alternatively, the **Orlybus** (www.ratp.fr) runs every 15 minutes between 5am and midnight, linking the airport with Place Denfert-Rochereau in the city center. The 30-minute trip costs 7.70€.

A **taxi** from Orly to central Paris will cost at least 50€, not including 1€ per item of luggage, and the fare is 20% higher from 5pm to 10am, as well as on Sundays and Bank Holidays.

**From Beauvais Airport,** buses leave about 20 minutes after each flight has landed, and, depending on the traffic, takes about 1 hour and 15 minutes to get to Porte Maillot, on the western edge of Paris. To return to Beauvais, you need to be at the bus station at least 3 hours before the departure of your flight. A one-way ticket costs 17€.

Paris has six major train stations: **Gare d'Austerlitz** (13th arrond), **Gare de Lyon** (12th arrond.), **Gare Montparnasse** (14th arrond.), **Gare St-Lazare** (8th arrond.), **Gare de l'Est** (10th arrond.), and **Gare du Nord** (10th arrond.). Stations can be reached by bus or Métro; for details on a specific station visit the national railway **(SNCF)** station site (www.gares-connexions.com/en). ***Warning:*** As in many cities, passengers arriving at stations from foreign countries are targets for pickpockets. Be alert, especially at night.

The **SNCF** connects Paris with other major cities and quite a few smaller towns; for reservations and information visit the SNCF website (www.voyages-sncf.com). The **Eurostar** (www.eurostar.com) will get you from Paris's Gare du Nord to St Pancras Station, London in just 2½ hours. Visit the **Thalys** site (www.thalys.com) for high-speed trains from Paris to Brussels, Amsterdam, and Cologne. For rail passes that you can use throughout Europe, visit **Rail Europe** (www.raileurope.com).

Long-haul **bus** travel is handled by **Eurolines** (www.eurolines.com; from France ✆ **08-92-89-90-91;** 0.34€ per min.; international ✆ 33-1-41-86-24-21), a consortium of dozens of different bus lines with routes that span the continent. International arrivals stop at the **Eurolines France** station on the eastern edge of the city, 23 ave. du Général-de-Gaulle, Bagnolet, Métro: Gallieni.

**CITY LAYOUT** Compared to cities like London or New York, Paris is relatively small. Inside the long-gone city walls, it measures about 87 sq. km (34 sq. miles) and counts a mere 2.2 million habitants. The suburbs, on the other hand, are sprawling.

The city is vaguely egg shaped, with the Seine cutting a wide upside-down "U" shaped arc through the middle. The northern half is known as the **Right Bank** (*Rive Droite,* "reeve dwaht") and the southern, the **Left Bank** (*Rive Gauche,* "reeve gohsh").

The city is neatly split up into 20 official ***arrondissements,*** or districts, which spiral out from the center of the city. The lower the number of the arrondissement, the closer you'll be to the center. Note that the arrondissements don't always correspond to historical neighborhoods.

If you are staying for more than a couple of days, and still believe in maps, invest in a *Paris Par Arrondissement,* a small book of maps showing streets, Métro lines, bus routes, and Velib' stations that costs around 8€.

**GETTING AROUND** Paris is delightfully walkable. With a good pair of shoes, you can enjoyably get around the center of town on foot. However, there are so many things to see, it's also easy to wear yourself out.

Fortunately, Paris has an excellent **public transit network** (RATP; www.ratp.fr) composed of Métro (subway), bus, RER (suburban trains that cross Paris), and a streetcar that runs around the city limits. Transit maps can be picked up at any tourist office or Métro station, or downloaded from the RATP website. During the week, try to avoid rush hour, which is generally between 7:30am and 10am and 6pm to 8pm.

**Transit tickets** are valid on the Métro, bus, and RER (the suburban train system that also runs through the city). Paris and its suburbs are divided into six zones, but you'll probably only travel in zones 1 and 2, the city center. Tickets can be purchased at the window or from machines at most Métro entrances, and from cafes that have a tabac sign outside. A **single ticket** costs 1.80€ and a *carnet* of 10 tickets costs 14.10€. Children 4 to 10 years old pay half price; under 4 rides free. The **Paris Visite** pass offers unlimited travel on the bus, Métro, and RER, and discounts on some attractions. Before you buy one, however, remember that you'll probably end up walking a lot, and a cheaper *carnet* of 10 tickets might suffice. A 1-day adult pass for zones 1 to 3 costs 11.15€, a 2-day pass 18.15€, a 3-day pass 24.80€, and a 5-day pass 35.70€. More expensive passes for zones 1 to 5 will also get you to both Versailles and the airport. A bit cheaper is the 1-day **Mobilis** ticket, which offers unlimited travel in zones 1 up to 5; a pass for zones 1 and 2 costs 7€. Travelers under 26 can buy a **Ticket Jeunes,** a 1-day ticket that provides unlimited travel on Saturday, Sunday, or bank holidays; zones 1 to 3 cost 3.85€, and zones 1 to 5 cost 8.35€.



Fast and frequent, the **Métro** starts up around 5:30am and runs until 1am Sunday to Thursday; Friday and Saturday it closes at 2am. The Métro is quite safe at night in the city center, though as in any large city, you should be careful late at night in the outer districts. Lines are color-coded; simply follow the direction indicated by the line's final destination.

The **RER** (pronounced *ehr-euh-ehr*) are suburban trains that dash through the city making limited stops. Métro and RER are often accessed from the same station. Although the RER gets you quickly across the city, the system is harder to decipher, because the same lines can have multiple final destinations. ***Important:*** Make sure to hold on to your

## velib'—A GREAT WAY TO CYCLE AROUND PARIS

The **Velib'** (vel-*leeb*) low-cost bicycle rental system is transforming Paris into a bike-friendly city. Although vehicular traffic is still crazy enough to make you periodically scream for mercy, the Velib' system makes it hard to resist the temptation to pedal.

You can buy a 1- or 7-day subscription (1.70€ or 8€, respectively) from the machine at any Velib' bike stand, which gives you the right to as many half-hour rides as you'd like. You'll pay 1€ for the first extra half-hour, 2€ for the half-hour after that one, and 4€ for the third half-hour on. Everything is meticulously explained in English on the website, **www.velib.fr**, and there's even a number you can call for English-speaking assistance (✆ **01-30-79-79-30**). However—to use the machines you must have a credit or debit card with a chip in it. If you don't have one, get a TravelEx "cash passport" with money on it (www.travelex.com) or just **buy your subscription online ahead of time** (make sure you have your secret code to punch in on the stand). Helmets are not provided, so bring one along. ***One more tip:*** Before you ride, download the app or get a city map that indicates Velib' stands so you can find one when you need it.

## Personal Safety in Paris

In general, Paris is a safe city and it is safe to use the Métro at any time, though it's best to avoid the RER late at night. **Beware of pickpockets,** especially in tourist areas and the Louvre; organized gangs will even use children as decoys. Avoid walking around the less safe neighborhoods (Barbès-Rochechouart, Strasbourg St-Denis) alone at night, and never get into an unmarked taxi.

ticket as you'll need it to exit the turnstile on the way out. ***Also important:*** Avoid taking the RER to certain suburbs late at night.

Slower but more scenic, **buses** crisscross the city from 6:30am to anywhere between 9:30pm and midnight, depending on the line. During the day, buses arrive every 10 minutes or so; service is reduced on Sundays and holidays. You can use Métro tickets on the buses (which give you a free transfer to another bus or tram if used within 1½ hr.) or you can buy tickets directly from the driver (2€, no transfer included). You must validate your ticket in the machine next to the driver's cabin.

After the bus and Métro services stop running, head for the **Noctilien** night bus (www.transilien.com/static/noctilien). The 47 lines crisscross the city and head out to the suburbs every half-hour or so from 12:30 to 5:30am. Tickets cost the same as for the regular bus (see above).

When you get into a **taxi,** the meter should read 2.60€. On top of that, you'll be charged 1.04€ to 1.54€ per kilometer, depending on the day of the week and the hour. There's a minimum fare of 6.86€; for more than three people, you'll also be charged 3€ for each additional passenger, as well as 1€ for each suitcase you put in the trunk. Tipping is not obligatory, but a 1€ tip is customary for short trips; for longer hauls tip 5% to 10%. It's often easier to call a cab than to hail one on the street: Contact **Les Taxis Bleus** (www.taxis-bleus.com; ✆ **36-09;** 0.15€ per min.) or **Taxi G7** (www.taxisg7.fr; ✆ **36-07;** 0.15€ per min.). Avoid minicabs or unlicensed taxis.

Unless there is some pressing reason why you must, do not **drive** in Paris. It's a harrowing experience and will not get you to where you want to go in a hurry. If driving is imperative, consider the new **Autolib'** electric car rental scheme (www.autolib.eu; ✆ **08-00-94-20-00**) which functions very much like Velib' (see box p. 110). At least you'll be spared the ordeal of finding a parking place.

## The Neighborhoods in Brief

**THE RIGHT BANK** Although the *Rive Droite* has a reputation for being the posh part of town, in fact it is quite a mix. Most of the high rent district is to the west, in the 16th, 17th, and 8th arrondissements, where you will find the **Champs Elysées,** the **Arc de Triomphe,** and breathtakingly expensive shops on Avenue Montaigne and rue du Faubourg St-Honoré. There are also a passel of delightful museums, like the **Musée**

**Marmottan Monet** and the **Musée Jacquemart-André.** The 1st arrondissement and the **Ile de la Cité** (an island in the Seine River) hold the most famous historic and cultural sites, like the **Louvre,** the **Sainte-Chapelle,** and **Notre-Dame Cathedral.** Just north of the center lies the **Opéra Garnier;** the surrounding area bustles with shopping and business people. Farther north in the 18th, at the top of the hill, is the village-y atmosphere of **Montmartre,** presided over by the **Basilica of Sacré-Coeur.** East and back toward the river, the 3rd and 4th arrondissement make up the **Marais,** famed for its 17th-century mansions, home to splendid museums like the **Carnavalet** and the **Musée Picasso.** It's also known for its oodles of cool shops and restaurants, a phenomenon that spreads east into the younger, earthier, and less elegant 10th, 11th, and 19th arrondissements. Monuments are minimal in the eastern reaches of the Right Bank (excepting the **Place de la Bastille**), but for nightlife and youth culture, this is the place to be.



**THE LEFT BANK** The *Rive Gauche* was once known for artists and intellectuals, but real estate prices have turned Paris's creative juices to the north and east. University life, however lives on in the **Latin Quarter** (5th arrondissement), whose life line is the **Boulevard St-Michel,** which flows past Roman baths at the **Musée de Cluny** and the **Sorbonne** to the stunning gardens of the **Jardin du Luxembourg.** South of the gardens are the legendary cafes and shops of the **St-Germain** neighborhood (6th arrondissement), which is clustered around the ancient church of **St-Germain-des-Prés.** Down by the river is the magnificent **Musée d'Orsay.** As you continue west into the 7th, the atmosphere becomes increasingly stately and ministerial (many government offices here). The esplanade and gilded dome of **Les Invalides** finally gives way to the **Champ de Mars** and the **Eiffel Tower.**

### Paris Museum Pass

In recent years, many of the city's major museums, including the **Louvre,** the **Pompidou Center,** and the **Musée d'Orsay,** have joined the many attractions covered by this pass, making it a good deal if you are planning on seeing several museums and/or castles like **Versailles** (also on the list) during a short stay. Take a look at the list of museums included on the website and see if the price is right (42€ for a 2-day pass, 56€ for a 4-day pass, and 69€ for a 6-day pass) for the number of days you are staying. Keep in mind that average adult museum entry fee ranges around 10€ to 14€, and castles like Versailles and Fontainebleau run anywhere from 11€ to 25€. For more information and a list of attractions, visit www.parismuseumpass.com.

There are two massive parks on either side of the city limits: to the east, the **Bois de Vincennes,** and to the west the **Bois de Boulogne.**

## Exploring Paris

If you are only in Paris for a few days, you'll have enough time to visit some star attractions, a few lesser-known wonders, and make a list of what you'd like to see next time you come to town. Just remember to leave enough time for at least one or two aimless rambles through Paris's legendary streets and gardens after you've tracked down a few choice monuments and museums.

## ILE DE LA CITÉ

**Cathédrale de Notre-Dame ★★★** CATHEDRAL This remarkably harmonious ensemble of carved portals, huge towers, and flying buttresses has survived close to a millennium's worth of French history and served as a setting for some of the country's most solemn moments. Napoléon crowned himself Emperor here, Napoléon III was married here, and the funerals of some of France's greatest generals (Foch, Joffre, Leclerc) were held here. In August 1944, the liberation of Paris from the Nazis was commemorated in the cathedral, as was the death of General de Gaulle in 1970.

Construction on the cathedral began in 1163 and lasted more than 200 years. Time and the French Revolution took their toll however, and what you see today is the result of a major restoration in the mid-19th century by Viollet-le Duc.

The glorious facade includes three enormous **carved portals** depicting (from left to right) the Coronation of the Virgin, the Last Judgment, and scenes from the lives of the Virgin and St-Anne. Above is the **Gallery of the Kings of Judah and Israel**—thought to be portraits of the kings of France, the original statues were chopped out of the facade during the Revolution.

Cathédrale de Notre-Dame at dusk.

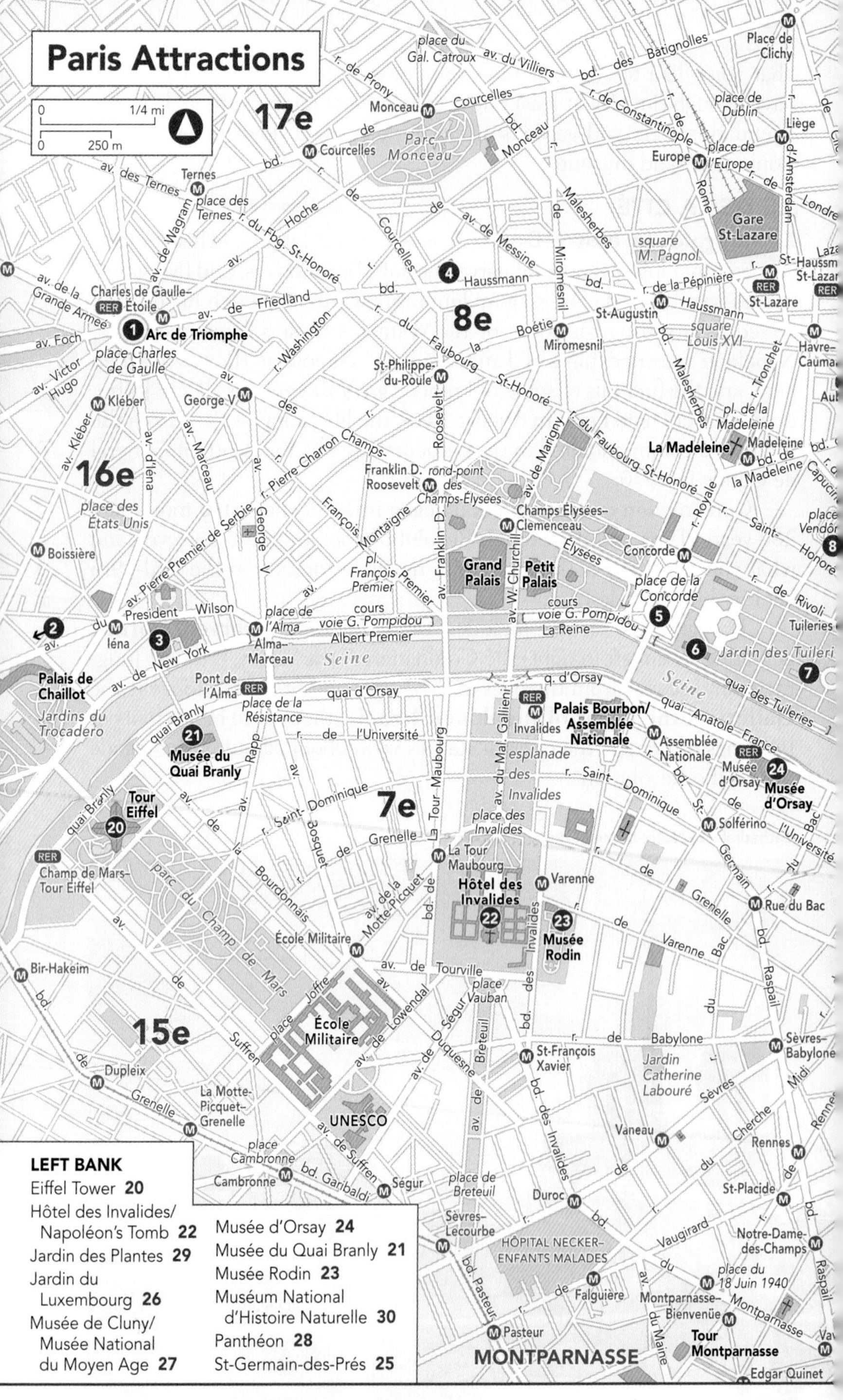

Paris Attractions
0 1/4 mi
0 250 m
17e
8e
16e
7e
15e
1 Arc de Triomphe
Charles de Gaulle–Étoile
place Charles de Gaulle
Parc Monceau
Gare St-Lazare
La Madeleine
Grand Palais
Petit Palais
place de la Concorde
Jardin des Tuileries
Seine
Palais de Chaillot
Jardins du Trocadero
Musée du Quai Branly
Tour Eiffel
Champ de Mars–Tour Eiffel
parc du Champ de Mars
Palais Bourbon/ Assemblée Nationale
esplanade des Invalides
Musée d'Orsay
Hôtel des Invalides
Musée Rodin
École Militaire
UNESCO
Jardin Catherine Labouré
HÔPITAL NECKER–ENFANTS MALADES
Tour Montparnasse
MONTPARNASSE
LEFT BANK
Eiffel Tower 20
Hôtel des Invalides/ Napoléon's Tomb 22
Jardin des Plantes 29
Jardin du Luxembourg 26
Musée de Cluny/ Musée National du Moyen Age 27
Musée d'Orsay 24
Musée du Quai Branly 21
Musée Rodin 23
Muséum National d'Histoire Naturelle 30
Panthéon 28
St-Germain-des-Prés 25

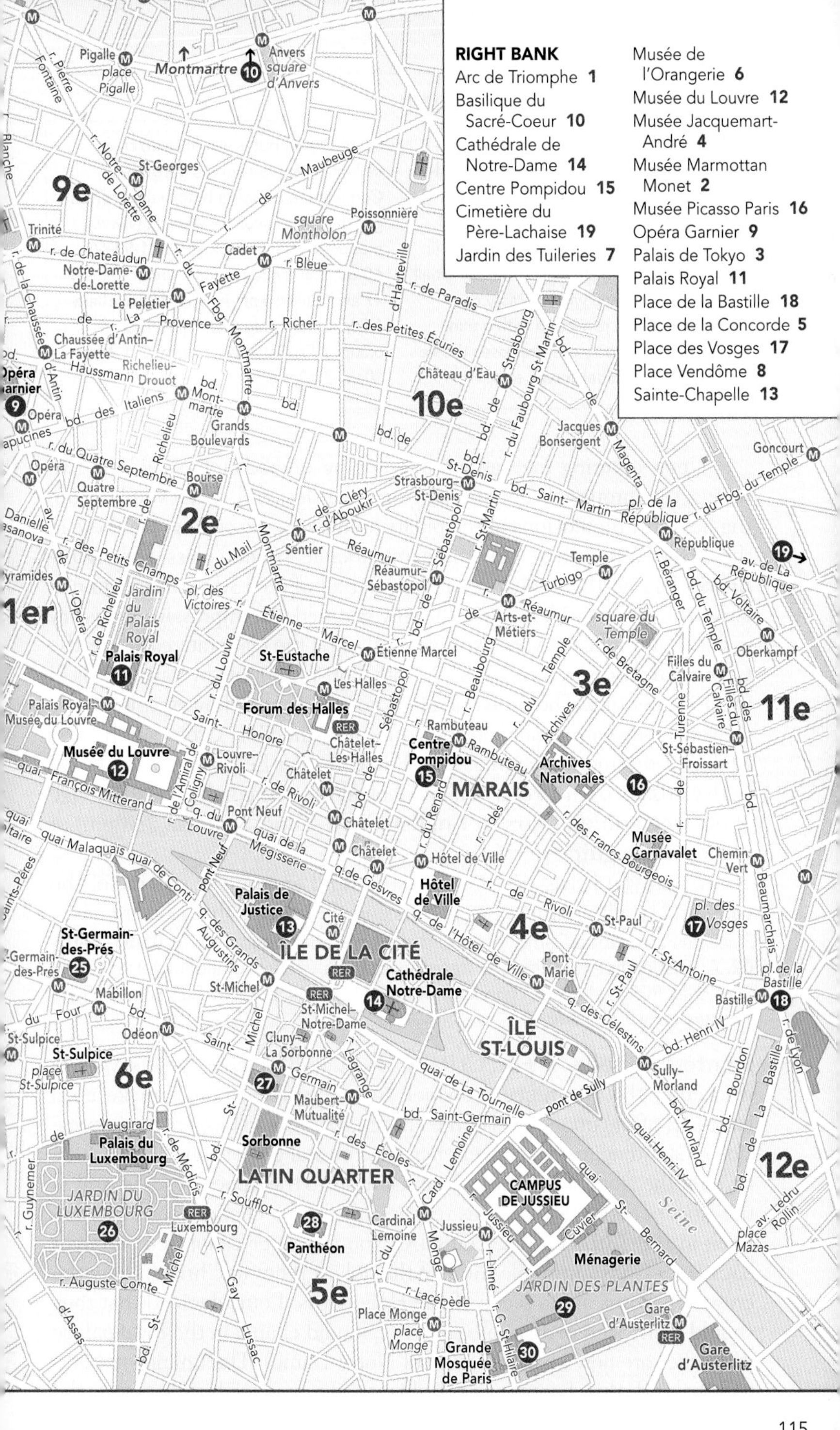
RIGHT BANK
Arc de Triomphe 1
Basilique du Sacré-Coeur 10
Cathédrale de Notre-Dame 14
Centre Pompidou 15
Cimetière du Père-Lachaise 19
Jardin des Tuileries 7
Musée de l'Orangerie 6
Musée du Louvre 12
Musée Jacquemart-André 4
Musée Marmottan Monet 2
Musée Picasso Paris 16
Opéra Garnier 9
Palais de Tokyo 3
Palais Royal 11
Place de la Bastille 18
Place de la Concorde 5
Place des Vosges 17
Place Vendôme 8
Sainte-Chapelle 13
Montmartre
Pigalle
place Pigalle
Anvers
square d'Anvers
r. Pierre Fontaine
r. Notre-Dame de Lorette
St-Georges
9e
Trinité
r. de Chateâudun
Notre-Dame-de-Lorette
Le Peletier
Cadet
r. Bleue
Poissonnière
square Montholon
r. de Maubeuge
r. La Fayette
r. du Fbg. Montmartre
r. de Provence
Chaussée d'Antin-La Fayette
r. de la Chaussée d'Antin
bd. Haussmann
Richelieu-Drouot
Opéra Garnier
Opéra
bd. des Italiens
bd. Montmartre
Grands Boulevards
r. du Quatre Septembre
Quatre Septembre
Bourse
Richelieu
2e
r. Richer
r. des Petites Écuries
r. de Paradis
r. d'Hauteville
Château d'Eau
10e
bd. de Strasbourg
r. du Faubourg St Martin
bd. de Magenta
Jacques Bonsergent
Goncourt
r. du Fbg. du Temple
bd. St-Denis
Strasbourg-St-Denis
bd. Saint-Martin
pl. de la République
République
19
av. de La République
bd. Voltaire
r. de Cléry
r. d'Aboukir
Sentier
r. Montmartre
r. du Mail
r. des Petits Champs
Pyramides
av. de l'Opéra
r. de Richelieu
1er
Jardin du Palais Royal
pl. des Victoires
Réaumur
Réaumur-Sébastopol
bd. de Sébastopol
r. St-Martin
Temple
r. de Turbigo
Réaumur Arts-et-Métiers
square du Temple
r. Béranger
bd. du Temple
Oberkampf
Palais Royal
11
r. Étienne Marcel
Étienne Marcel
St-Eustache
Les Halles
Forum des Halles
RER
r. Beaubourg
r. du Temple
r. de Bretagne
3e
Filles du Calvaire
bd. des Filles du Calvaire
11e
Palais Royal-Musée du Louvre
r. Saint-Honoré
r. du Louvre
Châtelet-Les Halles
r. Rambuteau
Rambuteau
Centre Pompidou
15
r. des Archives
Archives Nationales
16
r. de Turenne
St-Sébastien-Froissart
Musée du Louvre
12
quai François Mitterand
r. de l'Amiral de Coligny
Louvre-Rivoli
Châtelet
r. de Rivoli
r. du Renard
MARAIS
quai Voltaire
quai Malaquais
quai de Conti
Pont Neuf
q. du Louvre
pont Neuf
quai de la Mégisserie
Hôtel de Ville
r. des Francs Bourgeois
Musée Carnavalet
Chemin Vert
bd. Beaumarchais
r. des Saints-Pères
Palais de Justice
13
q. de Gesvres
Hôtel de Ville
r. de Rivoli
pl. des Vosges
17
St-Germain-des-Prés
25
q. des Grands Augustins
Cité
ÎLE DE LA CITÉ
q. de l'Hôtel de Ville
4e
St-Paul
Pont Marie
r. St-Paul
r. St-Antoine
pl. de la Bastille
Bastille
18
Mabillon
St-Michel
St-Michel-Notre-Dame
Cathédrale Notre-Dame
14
q. des Célestins
r. de Lyon
r. du Four
Odéon
bd. Saint-Germain
bd. St-Michel
Cluny-La Sorbonne
ÎLE ST-LOUIS
bd. Henri IV
St-Sulpice
place St-Sulpice
6e
27
r. Lagrange
quai de La Tournelle
pont de Sully
Sully-Morland
bd. Bourdon
bd. de La Bastille
Vaugirard
Maubert-Mutualité
bd. Saint-Germain
bd. Morland
quai Henri IV
Palais du Luxembourg
r. de Médicis
Sorbonne
r. des Écoles
r. du Card. Lemoine
CAMPUS DE JUSSIEU
quai St-Bernard
12e
r. Guynemer
LATIN QUARTER
JARDIN DU LUXEMBOURG
26
r. Soufflot
Luxembourg
28
Panthéon
Cardinal Lemoine
Jussieu
r. Jussieu
r. Cuvier
Seine
av. Ledru Rollin
place Mazas
r. Monge
r. Linné
Ménagerie
r. Auguste Comte
r. Gay Lussac
5e
r. Lacépède
JARDIN DES PLANTES
29
Place Monge
place Monge
r. G. St-Hilaire
Gare d'Austerlitz
d'Assas
bd. St-Michel
Grande Mosquée de Paris
30
Gare d'Austerlitz

### Views from the Two Towers

The lines are long and the climb is longer, but the view from the **rooftop balcony** at the base of the cathedral's towers is possibly the most Parisian of all. After trudging up some 255 steps (in a narrow winding staircase—not for small children or anyone with mobility concerns), you'll be rewarded with a panorama that not only encompasses the Île de la Cité, the Eiffel Tower, and Sacré-Coeur, but is also framed by a collection of photogenic **gargoyles.** Come in the morning before the crowds get thick, and avoid weekends (www.monuments-nationaux.fr; ✆ **01-53-40-60-80;** 8.50€ adults, 5.50€ under 26, free 17 and under; Apr–June and Sept 10am–6:30pm; July–Aug Sun–Thurs 10am–6:30pm, Fri–Sat 10am–11pm; Oct–Mar 10am–5:30pm).



Upon entering the cathedral, you'll be immediately struck by two things: the throngs of tourists clogging the aisles, and, when you look up, the heavenly dimensions of the pillars holding up the ceiling. Up there in the upper atmosphere are three remarkable stained-glass **rose windows.** The north window retains almost all of its 13th-century stained glass; the other two have been heavily restored. An impressive **treasury** is filled with relics of various saints including the elaborate cases for the **Crown of Thorns,** brought back from Constantinople by Saint Louis in the 13th century. The crown itself is not on display; however, it can be viewed, along with a nail and some pieces of the Holy Cross, on the first Friday of the month (3pm), every Friday during Lent (3pm) and Good Friday (10am–5pm). For a detailed look at the cathedral, take advantage of the **free guided tours in English** (Wed–Thurs 2pm, Sat 2:30pm) or rent an **audioguide** for 5€.

When you leave, be sure to take a stroll around the outside of the cathedral to admire the other portals and the famous flying buttresses.

Place du Parvis Notre-Dame, 4th arrond. www.notredamedeparis.fr. ✆ **01-53-10-07-02.** Admission free to cathedral. Treasury 4€ adults, 2€ 25 and under. Métro: Cité or St-Michel. RER: St-Michel. Cathedral Mon–Fri 8am–6:45pm, Sat–Sun 8am–7:15pm. Treasury daily 9:30am–6pm.

**Sainte-Chapelle ★★★** CHURCH A wall of color greets visitors who enter this magnificent chapel. Stained-glass windows make up a large part of the upper level of the church, giving worshippers the impression of standing inside a jewel-encrusted crystal goblet. The 15 windows recount the story of the Bible, from Genesis to the Apocalypse, as well as the story of St-Louis, who was responsible for the chapel's construction. Back in the 13th century, Louis IX (who was later canonized) brought back from Constantinople some of the holiest relics in Christendom: the crown of thorns and a piece of the Holy Cross. Louis decided that they should be housed in an appropriately splendid chapel in the royal palace (the relics are now in the treasury of Notre-Dame). The unknown architect behind this beauty was brilliant: He managed to support the

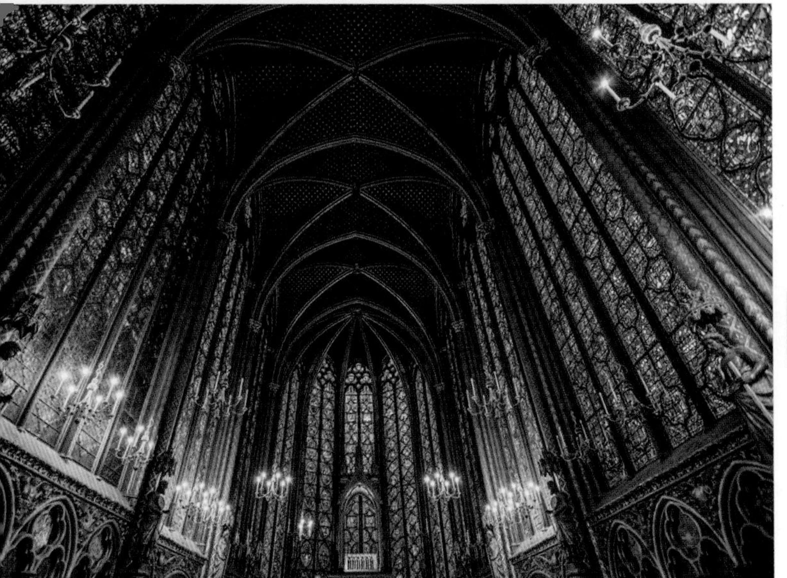
Interior, Sainte-Chapelle.



structure with arches and buttresses in such a way that the walls of the upper chapel are almost entirely glass.

The **lower chapel,** which was meant for the servants, has a low, vaulted ceiling painted in blue and red and gold and covered with fleur-de-lys motifs. Up a small staircase is the **upper chapel,** clearly meant for the royals. This masterpiece suffered both fire and floods in the 17th century and was pillaged by zealous revolutionaries in the 18th. By the mid-19th century, the chapel was being used to store archives—2m (6½ ft.) of the bottom of each window was removed to install shelves. Fortunately, renewed interest in medieval art eventually led to a conscientious restoration by a team that was advised by master restorer Viollet-le-Duc. The quality of the work on the windows is such that it is almost impossible to detect the difference between the original and the reconstructed stained glass (which makes up about one-third of what you see).

Palais de Justice, 4 bd. du Palais, 1st arrond. www.monuments-nationaux.fr. ✆ **01-53-40-60-80.** 8.50€ adults, 5.50€ ages 18–25, free 17 and younger. Métro: Cité, St-Michel, or Châtelet-Les Halles. RER: St-Michel. Mar–Oct daily 9:30am–6pm; Nov–Feb daily 9am–5pm.

## THE RIGHT BANK

**Arc de Triomphe ★★★** MONUMENT Crowning the Champs-Elysées, this mighty archway both celebrates the military victories of the French army and memorializes the sacrifices of its soldiers. Over time, it has become an icon of the Republic and a setting for some if its most

Arc de Triomphe at dusk.

emotional moments: the laying in state of the coffin of Victor Hugo in 1885, the burial in 1921 of the ashes of an unknown soldier who fought in World War I, and General de Gaulle's pregnant pause under the arch before striding down the Champs-Elysées before the cheering crowds after the liberation in 1944.

It took chutzpah to erect such a shrine, and sure enough, it was Napoléon who instigated it. In 1806, the Emperor decided to erect a monument to the Imperial Army along the lines of a Roman triumphal arch. Construction soon began on the largest triumphal arch on the planet. The Empire came to an end before the arch was finished, and it was completed by Louis-Philippe in 1836.

The arch is covered with bas-reliefs and sculptures, the most famous of which is the enormous "Depart of the Volunteers" of 1792, better known as the Marseillaise, by François Rude. At the base of the arch is the Tomb of the Unknown Soldier, over which a flame is relit every evening. The inscription reads ici repose un soldat français mort pour la patrie, 1914–1918 ("Here lies a French soldier who died for his country").

Don't try to cross the vast traffic circle to get to the arch; instead take the underpass near the Métro entrances. You'll need to climb 284 steps to get to the rooftop panorama; the elevator is only for the very young, the very old, and the disabled. The view is impressive: Below, you will see the 12 boulevards that radiate from the star-shaped intersection; out front is the long sweep of the Champs-Elysées, ending at the obelisk of the place de la Concorde, behind which lurks the pyramid of the Louvre. The rooftop is closed in bad weather.

Place Charles de Gaulle-Etoile, 8th arrond. www.monum.fr. ✆ **01-55-37-73-77.** 9.50€ adults, 6€ ages 18–24, free 17 and under. Métro: Charles-de-Gaulle-Etoile. Apr–Sept daily 10am–11pm; Oct–Mar daily 10am–10:30pm.

**Basilique du Sacré-Coeur ★★** CHURCH Poised at the apex of the *butte* (hill) of Montmartre, like a *grande dame* in crinolines, this odd-looking 19th-century basilica has become one of the city's most famous landmarks. After France's defeat in the Franco-Prussian War, prominent Catholics vowed to build a church consecrated to the Sacred Heart of Christ as a way of making up for whatever sins the French may have committed that had made God so angry at them. Since 1885, prayers for humanity have been continually chanted here (the church is a pilgrimage site, so dress and behave accordingly). Inspired by the Byzantine churches of Turkey and Italy, this multi-domed confection was begun in 1875 and completed in 1914, though it wasn't consecrated until 1919 because of World War I. The white stone was chosen for its self-cleaning capabilities: When it rains, it secretes a chalky substance that acts as a fresh coat of paint. Most visitors climb the 300 stairs to the **dome,** where the splendid city views extend over 48km (30 miles).

Parvis de la Basilique, 18th arrond. ✆ **01-53-41-89-00.** www.sacre-coeur-montmartre.com. Free admission to basilica, joint ticket to dome and crypt 8€ adults, 5€ ages 4–16, free under 4. Métro: Abbesses; take elevator to surface and follow signs to funicular. Basilica daily 6am–10:30pm; dome and crypt daily 8:30am–8pm May–Sept, 9am–5pm Oct–Apr.

**Centre Pompidou ★★** MUSEUM The bizarre architecture of this odd building provokes such strong emotions, it's easy to forget that there is something inside. It was designed in 1971 by Italo-British architects Renzo Piano and Richard Rogers, whose concept was to put the support structure on the outside of the building, thereby liberating space on the inside for a museum and cultural center. To some, it's a milestone in contemporary architecture; to others, it's simply a horror. Either way, it's one of the most visited structures in France. The actual museum, the **Musée National d'Art Moderne,** is on the fourth and fifth floors.

The permanent collection is in constant rotation, so it's impossible to say what you're likely to see on your visit, but the emphasis is generally on works from the second half of the 20th century, with a good dose of surrealism, Dada, and other modern movements from the first half. It includes relatively tame abstracts by **Picasso** and **Kandinsky, Andy Warhol**'s multi-headed portrait of Elizabeth Taylor, and a felt-wrapped piano by **Joseph Beuys.**

Take note of the monumental sculpture/mobile by Alexander Calder on the vast esplanade that slopes down toward the building, and don't miss the delightful **Stravinsky Fountain** around the side; kids are

**Centre Pompidou.**

mesmerized by its colorful mobile sculptures by Niki de Saint Phalle and Jean Tinguely.

Place Georges-Pompidou, 4th arrond. www.centrepompidou.fr. ✆ **01-44-78-12-33.** 11€–13€ adults, 9€–10€ ages 18–25, free children 17 and younger; admission varies depending on exhibits. Métro: Rambuteau, Hôtel de Ville, or Châtelet-Les Halles. Wed–Mon 11am–10pm.

**Cimetière du Père-Lachaise** ★★ CEMETERY This is no ordinary cemetery. As romantic and rambling as a 19th-century English garden, this hillside resting place is wonderfully green, with huge leafy trees and narrow paths winding around the graves, which include just about every French literary or artistic giant you can imagine, plus several international stars. Proust, Moliére, La Fontaine, Colette, Delacroix, Seurat, Modigliani, Bizet, Rossini are all here, as well as Sarah Bernhardt, Isadora Duncan, Simone Signoret and Yves Montand (buried side by side, of course), not to mention Oscar Wilde, whose huge stone monument is usually covered with lipstick kisses. Even the Lizard King, Jim Morrison, is here.

Celebrity graves can be hard to find, so a map is essential. You can find one at the newsstand across from the main entrance; on the website; or on the Paris municipal site (www.paris.fr; search for "Père Lachaise"). 16 rue de Repos, 20th arrond. www.pere-lachaise.com. No phone. Free. Métro: Père-Lachaise or Philippe Auguste. Mon–Fri 8am–6pm; Sat–Sun 8:30am–6pm (closes at 5pm Nov to early Mar).

**Jardin des Tuileries ★★★** GARDENS This exquisite park spreads from the Louvre to the place de la Concorde. Along with 17th- and 18th-century sculptures of various gods and goddesses among the greenery, you'll notice works by modern masters such as Alberto Giocometti, Jean Dubuffet, and Henry Moore.

Pulling up a metal chair and sunning yourself on the edge of the large **fountain** in the center of the gardens (the **Grande Carrée**) is a delightful respite for tired tourists after a day in the Louvre; tots will enjoy playing with one of the wooden **toy sailboats** that you can rent from a stand (2.50€/half-hour).

Near place de la Concorde, 1st arrond. http://equipement.paris.fr/jardin-des-tuileries-1795. ✆ **01-40-20-90-43.** Free. Métro: Tuileries or Concorde. Daily Apr–May 7am–9pm; June–Aug 7am–11pm; Sept 7am–9pm; Oct–Mar 7:30am–7:30pm.



**Musée de l'Orangerie ★★** MUSEUM Since 1927, this former royal greenhouse has been the home of Monet's stunning *Nymphéas,* or **water lilies,** which he conceived as a "haven of peaceful meditation." Two large oval rooms are dedicated to these masterpieces, in which Monet tried to replicate the feeling and atmosphere of his garden at Giverny. He worked on these enormous canvases for 12 years, with the idea of creating an environment that would soothe the "overworked nerves" of modern men and women—in what could be called one of the world's first art installations.

The other highlight here is the Guillaume collection, an impressive assortment of late-19th- and early-20th-century paintings, including lesser-known works by Renoir, Cezanne, Rousseau, Picasso, and Modigliani.

Jardin des Tuileries, 1st arrond. www.musee-orangerie.fr. ✆ **01-44-77-80-07.** 9€ adults, 6.50€ ages 18–25, free ages 17 and younger. Métro: Concorde. Wed–Mon 9am–6pm.

**Musée du Louvre ★★★** MUSEUM The best way to thoroughly visit the Louvre would be to move in for a month. Not only is it one of the largest museums in the world, with more than 35,000 works of art displayed over 60,000 sq. m (645,835 sq. ft.), but it's packed with enough artistic masterpieces to make the Mona Lisa weep. Rembrandt, Rubens, Botticelli, Ingres, and Michelangelo are all represented here; you can gape at a diamond the size of a golf ball in the royal treasury, or marvel over exquisite bronze figurines in the vast Egyptian section.

The building is divided into three wings, Sully, Denon, and Richelieu, each one with its own clearly marked entrance, found under I. M. Pei's glass pyramid. Get your hands on a museum map (there's an excellent interactive map on the museum's website), choose your personal "must-sees," and plan ahead. There's no way to see it all, and you'll be an instant candidate for early retirement if you try. If you're really in a rush or you just want to get an overall sense of the place, you can take the

The Louvre, with I. M. Pei's pyramid.

introductory guided tour in English (1½ hr.; 11:15am, 2pm; Wed–Sun except the first Sunday of the month; 12€).

The museum's three biggest stars are all located in the Denon wing. Da Vinci's La Joconde, otherwise known as the ***Mona Lisa,*** now has an entire wall to herself, making it easier to contemplate her enigmatic smile. Another inscrutable female in this wing is the ***Venus de Milo,*** who was found on a Greek island in 1820. Possibly the most photographed woman in the world, this armless marble goddess gives no hint of the original position of her limbs or her exact identity.

Recently restored and lovelier than ever, the ***Winged Victory of Samothrace,*** is the easiest to locate. Standing at the top of a majestic flight of stairs, her powerful body pushing forward as if about to take flight, this headless, yet magnificent, Greek sculpture once guarded the Sanctuary of the Great Gods on the island of Samothrace.

Because a complete listing of the Louvre's highlights would fill a book, below is a decidedly biased selection of my favorite areas:

**13TH- TO 18TH-CENTURY ITALIAN PAINTING** A few standouts in the immense Italian collection include the delicate fresco by Botticelli called *Venus and the Three Graces Presenting Gifts to a Young Woman,* Veronese's enormous *Wedding Feast at Cana,* and of course the *Mona Lisa.*

**GREEK & ROMAN SCULPTURE** The Salle des Caryatides (the room itself is a work of art) boasts marble masterworks like *Artemis* hunting with her stag and the troubling *Sleeping Hermaphrodite,* an alluring female figure from behind—and something entirely different from the front.

**THE GALERIE D'APOLLON** Commissioned by Louis XIV, aka "The Sun King," every inch of this gallery is covered with gilt stucco sculptures and flamboyant murals evoking the journey of the Roman sun god Apollo. The main draw here is the collection of crown jewels.

**THE EGYPTIANS** Sculptures, figurines, papyrus documents, steles, musical instruments, and of course mummies fill numerous rooms in the Sully Wing, including the colossal statue of Ramses II and the strangely moving Seated Scribe.

**LARGE-FORMAT FRENCH PAINTINGS** Enormous floor-to-ceiling (and these are high ceilings!) paintings of monumental moments in history cover the walls in these three rooms. The *Coronation of Napoléon* by Jacques-Louis David depicts the newly minted Emperor crowning Josephine, while the disconcerted pope and a host of notables look on.

***Note:*** When visiting the museum, **watch your wallets and purses**—there has been an unfortunate increase in pickpockets; organized groups even use children to prey on unsuspecting art lovers.

quai du Louvre, 1st arrond. Main entrance in the glass pyramid, cour Napoléon. www.louvre.fr. ✆ **01-40-20-50-50.** 12€ adults, children 17 and younger free. Métro: Palais-Royal-Musée du Louvre. Sat–Mon and Thurs 9am–6pm; Wed and Fri 9am–9:30pm.

**Musée Jacquemart-André ★★★** MUSEUM The love-child of a couple of passionate art collectors, this terrific museum takes the form of a 19th-century mansion filled with primarily 18th-century French art and furniture. The paintings of Fragonard, Boucher, and Chardin are in evidence, as is an impressive assortment of Louis XV– and Louis XVI–era decorative objects. There are many superb portraits, including that of an officious-looking *Comte Français de Nantes* by David. The couple also amassed a number of 17th-century Dutch paintings, including a jaunty *Portrait of a Man* by Frans Hals, and Rembrandt's evocative *Pilgrims at Emmaus.*

However, their collection of Renaissance Italian art is, for me, the highlight of the museum. In a small, darkened room, Quattrocento masterpieces like Botticelli's *Virgin and Child* and works by

### Leaping over the Louvre Line

The best way to avoid long lines is by ordering tickets in advance online (in English) at **www.fnactickets.com** or by calling ✆ **08-92-68-36-22,** 0.34€/min. If you prefer to pick up tickets at the entrance, here are a few ways to avoid the lines that often snake around the pyramid entryway: 1) Enter directly from the Palais Royal-Musée du Louvre Métro stop; 2) Take one of the two staircases on either side of the Arc du Carrousel in the Tuileries Gardens that lead directly down to the ticketing area; or 3) Enter at the Porte des Lions (in the Denon Wing).

masters like Bellini, Uccello, and Mantegna are beautifully lit; you feel like you are walking into a felt-lined jewel box. Leave time to have tea in the Jacquemart-André's lovely dining room.

158 bd. Haussmann, 8th arrond. www.musee-jacquemart-andre.com. ✆ **01-45-62-11-59.** 12€ adults, 10€ students and children 7–17, free for children 6 and younger. Métro: Miromesnil or St-Philippe-du-Roule. Daily 10am–6pm.

**Musée Marmottan Monet ★★** MUSEUM Boasting the world's largest collection of Monets, this museum offers an in-depth look at this prolific genius and some of his talented contemporaries. Among the dozens of Monet canvases is one that provided the name of an entire artistic movement: *Impression, Sunrise*. Pressed to give a name to this misty play of light on the water for the catalog for an 1874 exposition that included Cézanne, Pissarro, Renoir, and Degas, Monet apparently said, "put 'impression.'" Thereafter, the group was referred to as the Impressionists. Fans of the artist's endless water lily series will not be disappointed; the collection includes dozens of paintings of his beloved garden in Giverny.

2 rue Louis-Boilly, 16th arrond. www.marmottan.fr. ✆ **01-44-96-50-33.** 11€ adults, 6.50€ ages 8–24, free for children 7 and younger. Métro: La Muette. RER: Boulainvilliers. Tues–Wed and Fri–Sun 10am–6pm; Thurs 10am–9pm.

**Musée Picasso Paris ★★★** MUSEUM After extensive renovations, this shrine to all things Picasso has at last reopened with double the exposition space and a more comfortable visit for the millions of visitors that tramp through its doors. Housed in the stunning Hôtel Salé, a 17th-century mansion, this unique institution valiantly strives to make sense of the incredibly diverse output of this prolific genius. Some 400 carefully selected paintings, sculptures, collages, and drawings are presented in a more or less chronological and thematic order, which is no small task when dealing with an artist who experimented with every style, from neoclassicism to surrealism to his own flamboyantly abstract inventions. Impressionist portraits (*Portrait of Gustave Coquiot, 1901*), cubist explorations (*Man with Guitar, 1911*), mannerist allegories (*The Race, 1922*), and deconstructionist forms (*Reclining Nude, 1932*), are just a few of the treasures on display from this massive collection of 5,000 works. There is also a sampling of the highly abstract and somewhat disturbing portraits of the many women in his life, including portraits of Dora Maar and Marie-Thérèse, both painted in 1937. On the top floor is Picasso's private collection, which includes works by artists he admired like Courbet and Cézanne, as well as paintings by his friends, who included masters like Braque and Matisse. ***Note:*** Unless you enjoy waiting in long lines exposed to the elements, **buy your ticket in advance online;** you'll usually walk right in with your e-ticket.

5 rue de Thorigny, 3rd arrond. www.museepicassoparis.fr. ✆ **01-85-56-00-36.** 11€ adults, free 17 and younger. Métro: St-Paul or Chemin Vert. Tues–Fri 11:30am–6pm, Sat–Sun 9:30am–6pm.

**Opéra Garnier ★★** OPERA HOUSE Flamboyant, extravagant, and baroque, this opulent opera house is a splendid example of Second Empire architectural excess. Corinthian columns, loggias, busts, and friezes cover the **facade** of the building, which is topped by a gold dome. Inside, a vast **lobby** holds a spectacular double staircase that sweeps up to the different levels of the auditorium, as well as an array of glamorous antechambers, galleries, and ballrooms that make you wonder how the opera scenery could possibly compete. The relatively small **auditorium,** which holds fewer than 2,000 seats, has a beautiful **ceiling** painted by Marc Chagall in 1964.

You can visit the building on your own (for a fee; see ticket prices below), but you might want to take advantage of the **guided visits in English** (14€ adults, 13€ children under 10; Wed, Sat and Sun at 11:30am and 2:30pm; July–Aug and French school vacations daily 11:30am and 2:30pm). Or simply **buy tickets to a show;** consult the Opéra website to see what's on at the Palais Garnier.

Corner of rue Scribe and rue Auber, 9th arrond. www.operadeparis.fr. ✆ **08-92-89-90-90** (.34€ per min). 10€ adults, 6€ students and ages 10–25, free children under 10. Métro: Opéra. Oct to mid-July daily 10am–4:30pm, mid-July to Sept 10am–5:30pm.

**Palais de Tokyo ★★** MUSEUM/PERFORMANCE SPACE If you're traveling with cranky teenagers who've had enough of La Vieille France, or if you're also sick of endless rendezvous with history, this is the place to come for a blast of contemporary madness. This vast space, one of the largest sites devoted to contemporary art in Europe, not only offers a rotating bundle of expositions, events, and other happenings, but it's also one of the only museums in Paris that stays open until midnight. There's no permanent collection, just continuous temporary exhibits, installations, and events, which include live performances and film screenings. In warm weather, you can eat on the splendid terrace or repair to its arty restaurant, **Tokyo Eat.**

13 av. du Président-Wilson, 16th arrond. www.palaisdetokyo.com. ✆ **01-81-97-35-88.** 10€ adults, 8€ ages 18–25, free for ages 17 and younger. Métro: Iéna. Wed–Mon noon–midnight.

**Palais Royal ★★** HISTORIC SITE/GARDEN The gardens and long arcades of the Palais Royal are not only a delight to stroll through, they were also witness to one of the most important moments in French history. On July 12, 1789, Camille Desmoulins stood up on a table in front of one of the cafes in the galleries and called the people to arms—2 days later, the mob would storm the Bastille, igniting the French Revolution. Today, the shops in the arcades are very subdued, and very expensive—mostly antique toy and stamp dealers, and a smattering of high-end designer clothes.

Rue St-Honoré, 1st arrond. Free admission to gardens and arcades, buildings closed to public. Métro: Palais Royal-Musée du Louvre. Gardens daily 7:30am–dusk.

**Place de la Bastille ★** Now an enormous traffic circle where cars careen around at warp speed, this was once the site of the Bastille prison, an ancient stone fortress that became a symbol for all that was wrong with the French monarchy. Over the centuries, kings condemned rebellious citizens to stay inside these cold walls, sometimes with good reason, other times on a mere whim. By the time the Revolution started to boil, though, the prison was barely in use; when the angry mobs stormed the walls on July 14, 1789, there were only seven prisoners left to set free. Be that as it may, the destruction of the Bastille came to be seen as the ultimate revolutionary moment; July 14 is still celebrated as the birth of the Republic. Surprisingly, the giant bronze column in the center honors the victims of a different revolution, that of 1830.
12th arrond. Métro: Bastille.



**Place de la Concorde ★★★** PLAZA Like an exclamation point at the end of the Champs-Elysées, the Place de la Concorde is a magnificent arrangement of fountains and statues, held together in the center by a 3,000-year-old Egyptian obelisk (a gift to France from Egypt in 1829). Looking at it today, it is hard to believe that this magnificent square was once bathed in blood, but during the Revolution, it was a grisly stage for public executions. King Louis XVI and his wife, Marie-Antoinette, both bowed down to the guillotine here, as did many prominent figures of the Revolution.

On the north side of the square are two palatial buildings that date from the 18th century: On the east side is the **Hôtel de la Marine,** and on the west side is the **Hôtel Crillon,** where on February 6, 1778, a treaty was signed by Louis XVI and Benjamin Franklin, among others, wherein France officially recognized the United States as an independent country and became its ally.
8th arrond. Métro: Concorde.

**Place des Vosges ★★★** SQUARE Possibly the prettiest square in the city, this beautiful spot combines elegance, greenery, and quiet. Nowhere in Paris will you find such a unity of Renaissance-style architecture; the entire square is bordered by 17th-century brick townhouses, each conforming to rules set down by Henri IV himself, under which run arched arcades. Over the centuries, a number of celebrities lived in the 36 houses, including Mme de Sévigne and Victor Hugo. Today the homes are for the rich, as are the chic boutiques under the arcades, but the lush lawns, trees, fountains, and children's playground are for everyone.
4th arrond. Métro: St-Paul.

**Place Vendôme ★★** SQUARE Constructed in 1686 by Louis XIV, this über-elegant octagonal ensemble of 17th-century buildings today is the home of the original Ritz Hôtel, as well as the world's most glitzy

Place Vendôme.



jewelry makers, including Cartier, Van Cleef & Arpels, and Boucheron. The huge Roman-style column in the center was commissioned by Napoléon to honor his glorious army's victory at Austerlitz. A long spiral of bas-reliefs recounting the campaign of 1805 march up the Colonne de la Grande Armée, which is crowned by a statue of the Emperor himself. Enter by rue de Castiglione, 1st arrond. Métro: Tuileries or Concorde.

## THE LEFT BANK

**Eiffel Tower ★★★** MONUMENT In his wildest dreams, Gustave Eiffel probably never imagined that the tower he built for the 1889 World's Fair would become the ultimate symbol of Paris and, for many, of France. Originally slated for demolition after its first 20 years, the Eiffel Tower has survived more than a century and is one of the most visited sites in the nation. No fewer than 50 engineers and designers worked on the plans, which resulted in a remarkably solid structure that despite its height (324m/1,063 ft., including the antenna) does not sway in the wind.

But while the engineers rejoiced, others howled. When the project for the tower was announced, a group of artists and writers published a manifesto that referred to it as an "odious column of bolted metal." Others were less diplomatic: Novelist Joris-Karl Huysmans called it a "hole-riddled suppository." Construction dragged on for 2 years, but finally, on

March 31, 1889, Gustave Eiffel proudly led a group of dignitaries up the 1,710 steps to the top, where he unfurled the French flag for the inauguration.

Over 100 years later, the tower has become such an integral piece of the Parisian landscape that it's impossible to think of the city without it. Over time, even the artists came around—the tower's silhouette can be found in the paintings of Seurat, Bonnard, Duffy, Chagall, and especially those of Robert Delaunay, who devoted an entire series of canvases to the subject. It has also inspired a whole range of stunts, from Pierre Labric riding a bicycle down the stairs from the first level in 1923 to Philippe Petit walking a 700m-long (2,296-ft.) tightrope from the Palais de Chaillot to the tower during the centennial celebration in 1989. Eiffel performed his own "stunts" toward the end of his career, using the tower as a laboratory for scientific experiments. By convincing the authorities of the tower's usefulness in studying meteorology, aerodynamics, and other subjects, Eiffel saved it from being torn down.



Though several tower elevators whisk visitors skyward, they do take time to come back down, so be prepared for a wait. The first floor has a restaurant, displays, and a bit of glass floor, so you can pretend you are walking on air. Personally, I think the view from the second level is the best; you're far enough up to see the entire city, yet close enough to clearly pick out the various monuments. But if you are aching to get to the top (and unlike me, don't have vertigo), an airplane-like view awaits. Champ de Mars, 7th arrond. www.tour-eiffel.fr. ✆ **01-44-11-23-23.** Lift to 1st and 2nd floor 9€ adults, 7€ ages 12–24, 4.50€ ages 4–11; Lift to all three floors 16€ adults, 14€ ages 12–24, 11€ ages 4–11; stairs to 1st and 2nd floors 5€ adults, 4€ ages 12–24, 3.50€ ages 4–11; free admission for children 3 and under. Métro: Trocadéro or Bir Hakeim. RER: Champ de Mars-Tour Eiffel. Mid-June to Aug daily 9am–midnight, Sept to mid-June daily 9:30am–11pm; Sept to mid-June stairs open only to 6pm.

**Hôtel des Invalides/Napoléon's Tomb ★★** MUSEUM This grandiose complex was commissioned by Louis XIV, who wanted to construct a home for soldiers wounded in the line of duty. An on-site hospital was constructed for the severely wounded, which is still in service today.

As you cross the main gate, you'll find yourself in a huge courtyard (102×207m, 335×207 ft.), the *cour d'honneur,* once the site of military parades. The surrounding buildings house military administration offices and the **Musée de l'Armée,** one of the world's largest military museums, with a vast collection of objects testifying to man's capacity for self-destruction. The most impressive section is **Arms and Armor,** a panoply of 13th- to 17th-century weaponry. There is also a huge wing covering the exploits of everyone from **Louis XIV** to **Napoléon III,** and another wing for the two **World Wars,** where the centennial of World War I (1914–1918) is honored in a series of galleries dedicated to the *Grand Guerre.*

The back half of the **Eglise du Dôme** harbors the **Tomb of Napoléon,** which lies under one of the most splendid domes in France. The interior soars 107m (351 ft.) up to a skylight, which illuminates a brilliantly colored cupola. Below is an opening where you can look down upon the huge porphyry sarcophagus, which holds the emperor's remains, encased in five successive coffins (one tin, one mahogany, two lead, and one ebony). Don't blame the over-the-top setting on Napoléon; the decision to transfer his remains to Paris was made in 1840, almost 20 years after his death.

Place des Invalides, 7th arrond. www.musee-armee.fr. ✆ **01-44-42-38-77.** Admission to the museums, church, and Napoléon's Tomb: 9.50€ adults, free 17 and younger. Métro: Latour-Maubourg, Varenne, Invalides; RER: Invalides. Apr–Oct 10am–6pm, Nov–Mar 10am–5pm.

**Jardin du Luxembourg ★★★** GARDENS Rolling out like an exotic Oriental carpet before the Italianate Palais du Luxembourg (the seat of the French Senate since 1958, not open to the public), this vast expanse of fountains, flowers, lush lawns, and shaded glens is the perfect setting for a leisurely stroll, a relaxed picnic, or a serious make-out session, depending on whom you're with. At the center of everything is a fountain with a huge basin, where kids can sail toy wooden sailboats (2.50€ for a half-hour) and adults can sun themselves in the green metal chairs at the pond's edge. Sculptures abound: At every turn there is a god, goddess, artist, or monarch peering down at you from their pedestal. The most splendid waterworks is probably the Medici Fountain (reached

**Jardin du Luxembourg.**

via the entrance at place Paul Claudel behind the Odéon), draped with lithe Roman gods sculptured by Auguste Ottin, and topped with the Medici coat of arms, in honor of the palace's first resident, Marie de Medici.

Entry at Place Edmond Rostand, place André Honnorat, rue Guynemer, or rue de Vaugirard, 6th arrond. www.senat.fr/visite/jardin. Métro: Odéon; RER: Luxembourg. 8am–dusk.





**Musée de Cluny/Musée National du Moyen Age ★★** MUSEUM Ancient Roman baths and a 15th-century mansion set the stage for a terrific collection of medieval art and objects at this museum. Built somewhere between the 1st and 3rd centuries, the baths (visible from bd. St-Michel) are some of the best existing examples of Gallo-Roman architecture. They are attached to the former home of a 15th-century abbot, whose last owner amassed a vast array of medieval masterworks. Sculptures, textiles, furniture, and ceramics are shown, as well as gold, ivory, and enamel work. There are several magnificent tapestries, but the biggest draw is the late-15th-century ***Lady and the Unicorn*** series, one of only two sets of complete unicorn tapestries in the world (the other is in New York City).

6 place Paul Painlevé, 5th arrond. www.musee-moyenage.fr. ✆ **01-53-73-78-00.** 8€ adults, 6€ ages 18–26, free 17 and under. Métro/RER: Cluny-La Sorbonne or St-Michel. Wed–Mon 9:15am–5:45pm.

**Musée d'Orsay ★★★** MUSEUM In 1986, the magnificent Gare d'Orsay train station, built to coincide with the 1900 World's Fair, was brilliantly transformed into an exposition space devoted to 19th-century

Central hall, Musée d'Orsay.

artists, and in particular, the Impressionists. The huge, airy central hall lets in lots of natural light, which is artfully combined with artificial lighting to illuminate a collection of treasures.

The collection spans the years 1848 to 1914, a period that saw the birth of many artistic movements, such as the Barbizon school and Symbolism, but today it is best known for the emergence of Impressionism. All the superstars of the epoch are here, including Manet, Degas, and Renoir, not to mention Cézanne, Monet, and van Gogh. The most famous canvases, like Edouard Manet's masterpiece, *Le Déjeuner sur l'Herbe,* are on the top floor. Though Manet's composition of bathers and friends picnicking on the grass draws from those of Italian Renaissance masters, the painting shocked its 19th-century audience, which was horrified to see a naked lady lunching with two fully clothed men.

The middle level is devoted to the post-Impressionists, with works by artists like Gauguin, Seurat, Rousseau, and van Gogh, like the latter's *Church at Auvers-sur-Oise,* an ominous version of the church in a small town north of Paris where he moved after spending time in an asylum in Provence. This was 1 of some 70 paintings he produced in the 2 months leading up to his suicide.

A few other standouts:

**RENOIR'S DANCE AT LE MOULIN DE LA GALETTE, MONTMARTRE:** The dappled light and the movement of the crowd in this joyous painting are such that you wonder if it's not going to suddenly waltz out of its frame. The blurred brushstrokes that created this effect rankled contemporary critics.

**MONET'S LA GARE ST-LAZARE:** The metallic roof of the station frames an almost abstract mix of clouds and smoke; rather than a description of machines and mechanics, this painting is a modern study of light and color.

**GAUGUIN'S THE WHITE HORSE:** Not everyone was charmed by the vibrant colors in Gauguin's Tahitian version of paradise: The pharmacist who commissioned the painting refused it because the horse was too green.

1 rue de la Légion d'Honneur, 7th arrond. www.musee-orsay.fr. ✆ **01-40-49-48-14.** 11€ adults, 8.50€ ages 18–25, free ages 17 and younger. Métro: Solférino. RER: Musée d'Orsay. Tues–Wed and Fri–Sun 9:30am–6pm; Thurs 9:30am–9:45pm.

**Musée du quai Branly** ★★★ MUSEUM This museum's wildly contemporary design includes an enormous central structure that floats on a series of pillars, under which lies a lush garden, separated from the noisy boulevard by a huge glass wall. However you feel about the outside, the inside will win you over: The vast space is filled with exquisite examples of the traditional arts of Africa, the Pacific Islands, Asia, and the Americas.

## A DAY TRIP TO versailles

A trip to the **Chateau of Versailles ★★★** (Place d'Armes; www.chateauversailles.fr; ✆ **01-30-83-78-00**) will give you a glimpse of the most grandiose epoch of the French monarchy, and the excesses that led to its downfall. One of the world's largest castles, this 17th-century mammoth was the brainchild of Louis XIV, who wanted a palace big enough to house his entire court, so he could nip any conspiracies in the bud. This required a new abode that could not only host anywhere from 3,000 to 10,000 people, but would also be grand enough to let the world know who was in charge. Louis brought in a flotilla of architects and artists, as well as thousands of workers to take on the challenge. Meanwhile, legendary garden designer André Le Nôtre carved out formal gardens and a huge park out of what had been marshy countryside.

In 1682, after years of construction, the King and his court finally moved in, but construction went on right through the rest of his reign and into that of Louis XV. Louis XVI and his wife, Marie Antoinette, made few changes, but history made a gigantic one for them: On October 6, 1789, an angry mob of hungry Parisians marched on the palace, and the royal couple was eventually forced to return to Paris. Versailles would never again be a royal residence.

Give yourself most of the day to visit, as not only is the castle enormous, but the **gardens and grounds** are almost worth the visit on their own. Indoor must-sees include the splendiferous **Grand Apartments,** used primarily for ceremonial events (a daily occurrence), the **Queen's Apartments,** and the **Galerie des Glaces.** First runners up include the **King's Apartments** and the **Chapel.** If you have time and fortitude, you can take a **guided visit** to the royal family's private apartments (check website for schedule) to see a more intimate look at castle life. If time is of the essence, consider visiting just the castle, or just **Marie Antoinette's Estate,** which includes the **Petit Trianon** and other lovely sites in the ill-fated queen's private playground.

A comprehensive ticket to all palace attractions is 25€ for adults (free for under 18s and persons with disabilities). From April through October, the **Grands**



Magnificent samples of each culture's artwork are carefully exposed and lit in uncrowded displays such that you to admire the skill and artistry that went into their creation. Delicately carved headrests from Papua New Guinea in the form of birds and crocodiles, intricately painted masks from Indonesia, and abstract "magic stones" resembling Brancusi sculptures from the island nation of Vanuatu are just a few of the treasures of this vast collection. Other highlights include Australian aboriginal paintings, Moroccan embroidery, and Malian marriage cloths. The Americas section includes rare Nazca pottery and Inca textiles, as well as Haitian voodoo objects and Sioux beaded tunics.

37 quai Branly and 206 and 218 rue de Université, 7th arrond. www.quaibranly.fr. ✆ **01-56-61-70-00.** 9€ adults, free children 17 and younger. Métro: Alma-Marceau. RER: Pont d'Alma. Tues–Wed and Sun 11am–7pm; Thurs–Sat 11am–9pm.

**Eaux Musicales** (musical fountain displays; included with admission) and other events run mostly on the weekends.

To get there, take the **RER C** (www.transilien.fr; 30 min. from the Champs de Mars station) to **Versailles Rive Gauche-Château de Versailles,** then walk 5 minutes to the château. **Make sure** the final destination for your train is Versailles Rive Gauche-Château de Versailles and *not* Versailles Chantier, which will send you in the opposite direction and add an hour to your trip. You can also take the **SNCF** Transilien suburban train (www.transilien.fr; 45 min.) from the Gare St-Lazare station to **Versailles-Rive Droite,** and then walk 10 minutes to the palace.

Chateau of Versailles.

**Musée Rodin** ★★★ MUSEUM Considered by many to be the father of modern sculpture, August Rodin left behind a massive legacy of marble and bronze works, over 6,000 of which are in this lovely museum's collection. Only a carefully chosen portion is on display at any given time in the newly restored main building (renovations are scheduled to be finished in early 2016). The gorgeous gardens harbor some of the sculptor's most famous works. Large bronzes, including ***The Thinker,*** the ***Burghers of Calais, Balzac,*** and the ***Gates of Hell*** are tucked into the greenery between flowers and fountains and benches. Indoors, marble compositions prevail, though works in terracotta, plaster, and bronze, as well as sketches and paintings are also on display. The most famous of the marble works is ***The Kiss,*** which was inspired by the tragic story of Paolo and Francesca, in which a young woman falls in love with her husband's brother. Upon their first kiss, the husband discovers them and

stabs them both. There are hundreds of works here, many of them legendary, so don't be surprised if after a while your vision starts to blur. That'll be your cue to head outside and enjoy the garden.
79 rue de Varenne, 7th arrond. www.musee-rodin.fr. ✆ **01-44-18-61-10.** 7€ adults, 5€ ages 18–25, free children 17 and younger. Métro: Varenne or St-Francois-Xavier. Tues, Thurs–Sun 10am–5:30pm, Wed 10am–8:30pm.

**Panthéon** ★ MAUSOLEUM High atop the "montagne" (actually a medium-sized hill) of St-Geneviève, the dome of the Panthéon is one of the city's most visible landmarks. This erstwhile royal church has been transformed into a sort of national mausoleum—the final resting place of luminaries such as Voltaire, Rousseau, Hugo, and Zola. Initially dedicated to St-Geneviève, the church was commissioned by a grateful Louis XV, who attributed his recovery from a serious illness to the saint. However, during the Revolution, it was converted into a memorial and burial ground for Great Men of the Republic. The enormous empty space, lined with huge paintings of great moments in French history, resembles a cavernous tomb. Though the building is of architectural interest, unless you're a fan of one of the men (or women) who are buried under the building, it's probably best admired from the outside.
Place du Panthéon, 5th arrond. www.monuments-nationaux.fr. ✆ **01-44-32-18-00.** 7.50€ adults, 6€ ages 18–25, free children 17 and younger. Métro: Cardinal Lemoine, RER: Luxembourg. Apr–Sept daily 10am–6:30pm; Oct–Mar daily 10am–6pm.

**St-Germain-des-Prés** ★ CHURCH The origins of this church stretch back over a millennium. First established by King Childebert in 543, who constructed a basilica and monastery on the site, it was built, destroyed, and rebuilt several times over the centuries. Nothing remains of the original buildings, but the bell tower dates from the 10th century and is one of the oldest in France. The church and its abbey became a major center of learning and power during the Middle Ages, remaining a force to be reckoned with up until the eve of the French Revolution. Once the monarchy toppled, however, all hell broke loose: The abbey was destroyed, the famous library burned, and the church vandalized. Restored in the 19th century, the buildings have regained some of their former glory, though the complex is a fraction of its original size.

Much of the interior is painted in a range of greens and golds—one of the few Parisian churches to retain a sense of its original decor.
3 place St-Germain-des-Prés, 6th arrond. www.eglise-sgp.org. ✆ **01-55-42-81-10.** Free. Métro: St-Germain-des-Prés. Daily 8am–7:45pm.

## Organized Tours

The famed **Bateaux-Mouches** (www.bateaux-mouches.fr; ✆ **01-42-25-96-10;** Métro: Alma-Marceau) **river cruises** leave from Pont de l'Alma on the Right Bank and cruise down the Seine past major sites for a little over 1 hour. Tickets cost 14€ for adults, 5.50€ for kids 4 to 11, free

3 and under; the recorded commentary is in French, English, and up to 3 other languages.

There are two **hop-on, hop off bus lines** for seeing the city in a hurry. **L'Open Tour** (www.paris.opentour.com; ✆ **01-42-66-56-56**) offers four routes; 1-day adult pass costs 32€, and a 2-day pass 36€; either pass is 16€ for children 4 to 11. **Big Bus Paris** (www.bigbustours.com/paris; ✆ **01-53-95-39-53**) stops at nine top sites and offers a multilingual recorded commentary. A 1-day adult tickets costs 29€, and a 2-day adult ticket costs 33€, either pass is 16€ for children 4 to 12.

The best **guided walks** in English are by **Paris Walks** (www.paris-walks.com; ✆ **01-48-09-21-40**), which organizes 2-hour walks of the city, based on either a theme or a neighborhood. Most of the walks cost 12€ for adults and do not require reservations. **Paris Greeters** (www.parisgreeters.fr) arranges free tours for one to six people with local volunteers. You register online and request a specific day and language; you'll then be contacted with the details of your tour.

## Especially for Kids

At first glance, Paris is a big city with a grown-up air that does not seem to be much fun for small children. But looks can be deceiving. For tiny tots, the city has **playgrounds** tucked into just about any garden or square, and **merry-go-rounds** are planted at strategic points like the **Hôtel de Ville** (29 rue de Rivoli, 4th arrond.; Métro: Hôtel-de-Ville) and Paris's city hall, where there is also an **ice-skating rink** set up in the winter months. You can rent **wooden toy sailboats** (2.50€ per half-hour) to float in the main fountain at the kid-friendly **Luxembourg Gardens,** where you can let your offspring run wild in the an **extra-large playground** (1.20 adults, 2.50€ under 12), or watch kids scream at Guignol (the French version of Punch) in a variety of **puppet shows** (www.marionnettesduluxembourg.fr). Guignol also stars at the **Marrionettes des Champs Elysées** (www.theatreguignol.fr; Promenade des Champs Elysées; Métro: Franklin D. Roosevelt). Show times are usually afternoons on Wednesdays, weekends, and school vacations; check the websites for exact hours.

The **Muséum National d'Histoire Naturelle ★★** (36 rue Geoffrey, 5th arrond; www.mnhn.fr; ✆ **01-40-79-54-79;** Métro: Jussieu or Gare d'Austerlitz), is actually a series of natural history museums enclosing the **Jardin des Plantes** and its small **zoo** (see below). The biggest draw is the **Grande Galerie de l'Evolution,** where a Noah's ark of animals snakes its way around a huge hall filled with displays that trace the evolution of life and man's relationship to nature. The **Galerie des Enfants** has hands-on interactive displays for tykes. Admission to each galerie is 5€ to 9€ adults; 4€ to 7€ students, seniors 60 and older, and children 4 to 13; the Muséum is open Wednesday to Monday from 10am to 6pm.

There is a small but well-kept **zoo** tucked into the **Jardin des Plants** (www.mnhn.fr; ✆ **01-40-79-56-01;** 11€ adults, 9€ students 18–26 and children 4–16, free under 4; daily 9am–6pm). Created in 1794, the **Ménagerie** is the oldest zoo in the world. It showcases mostly smaller species, in particular birds and reptiles, but you'll also find a healthy selection of mammals, including rare species like red pandas, Przewalski horses, and even Florida panthers.

## Where to Stay

Hotels are sprinkled all over the city center. Don't feel that you have to stay near the Eiffel Tower; although there are some nice hotels over there, it is not in the center of town and you will pay for the pleasure. The best deals are in neighborhoods with few sightseeing options, but with a good transit connection you'll be at the Louvre in no time.

High season is hard to pin down in Paris; it comes and goes with trade shows and other annual events. Everyone seems to agree that August is the low season. To be safe, and to find the best rates, always book well ahead. If you are stuck, try the **Paris Tourist Office** (p. 107) or their website (www.paris-info.com); they can steer you in the right direction.

### THE RIGHT BANK

#### Expensive

**Hotel Brighton ★★** Stunning views of the Louvre and the Tuileries gardens await those who opt for "deluxe" and "executive" categories at this gracious hotel, where all the rooms feature elegant fabrics draping the windows and tasteful decorative touches. This classy establishment under the arcades of the rue de Rivoli may not be not quite as grand as the Meurice, just down the block, but it is also about one-third the price. Rooms with views book up early, so plan ahead.

218 rue de Rivoli, 1st arrond. www.paris-hotel-brighton.com. ✆ **01-47-03-61-61.** 61 units. Doubles 199€–391€, suites 310€–422€. Métro: Tuileries. **Amenities:** Bar; concierge; room service; tea room; free Wi-Fi.

**Pavillon de la Reine ★★★** Just off the place des Vosges, the "Queen's Pavilion" harkens back to the days when the magnificent square was home to royalty. Set back from the hustle and bustle of the Marais, this heavenly hideaway feels intimate, like a lord's private hunting lodge in the country. The decor is a suave combination of subtle modern and antique: The dark period furniture blends with rich colors on the walls and beds; choice objects and historic details abound. Several deluxe duplexes have staircases leading to cozy sleeping lofts.

28 place des Vosges, 3rd arrond. www.pavillon-de-la-reine.com. ✆ **01-40-29-19-19.** 54 units. Doubles 385€–550€, suites 600€–1,200€. Métro: Bastille. **Amenities:** Bar; concierge; gym; room service, sauna, spa, free Wi-Fi.

### Moderate

**Hôtel Arvor Saint Georges ★★** Located just south of Montmartre, these spiffy lodgings offer an arty yet relaxed atmosphere, where fresh white walls show off modern photography and Daniel Buren graphics. Rooms are a little small, but simple and chic, with white walls, a splash of color, and a distinctive table or armchair. The airy lobby area, with large windows and bookshelves, is an invitation to kick back and read or sip a cup of tea.

8 rue Laferrière, 9th arrond. www.hotelarvor.com. ✆ **01-48-78-60-92.** 30 units. Doubles 120€–200€, suites 200€–280€. Métro: St-Georges. **Amenities:** Bar; free Wi-Fi.

**Hôtel Caron de Beaumarchais ★★★** In the 18th century, the author of *The Barber of Seville* lived near here, and this small hotel celebrates both the playwright and the century he lived in. A pianoforte that dates from 1792 stands in the lobby, next to an antique card table set up for a game. Walls are covered in high-quality reproductions of period fabrics; rooms are furnished with antique writing tables and chandeliers; and period paintings and first-edition pages of *The Barber of Seville* hang on the walls. Rooms are not huge here, but the charm factor is high.

12 rue Vieille-du-Temple, 4th arrond. www.carondebeaumarchais.com. ✆ **01-42-72-34-12.** 19 units. Doubles 120€–200€. Métro: St-Paul or Hôtel de Ville. **Amenities:** Free Wi-Fi.

**Hôtel Thérèse ★★** Just a few steps from the Palais Royal and the Louvre, these lodgings combine old-fashioned Parisian charm with modern Parisian chic. Soft grey/teal blues highlight a creative decor that complements the building's age instead of fighting it. Comfy sofas invite you to relax in the lobby, whose stylish look includes mirrors, bookcases, and unique lighting fixtures. The comfort factor extends to the rooms, which include high ceilings, lush fabrics, and upholstered headboards.

5-7 rue Thérèse, 1st arrond. www.hoteltherese.com. ✆ **01-42-96-10-01.** 40 units. Doubles 180€–390€. Métro: Palais-Royal or Pyramides. **Amenities:** Concierge; library/bar; free Wi-Fi.

### Inexpensive

**Hôtel Chopin ★★** Nestled at the back of the delightful Passage Jouffroy, this budget hotel has remarkably quiet rooms considering its location in the middle of the rush and bustle of the Grands Boulevards. The staircase is a little creaky, but the recently refreshed rooms are clean and colorful and the new bathrooms are spotless. Rooms on the upper floors get more light; many have nice views of Parisian rooftops.

10 bd. Montmartre or 46 passage Jouffroy, 9th arrond. www.hotel-chopin.com. ✆ **01-47-70-58-10**. 36 units. Doubles 106€–124€. Métro: Grands Boulevards or Richelieu-Drouot. **Amenities:** Free Wi-Fi.

**Hôtel Jeanne d'Arc le Marais ★★★** With a prime location, comfortable rooms, and great prices, it's no wonder this hotel books up

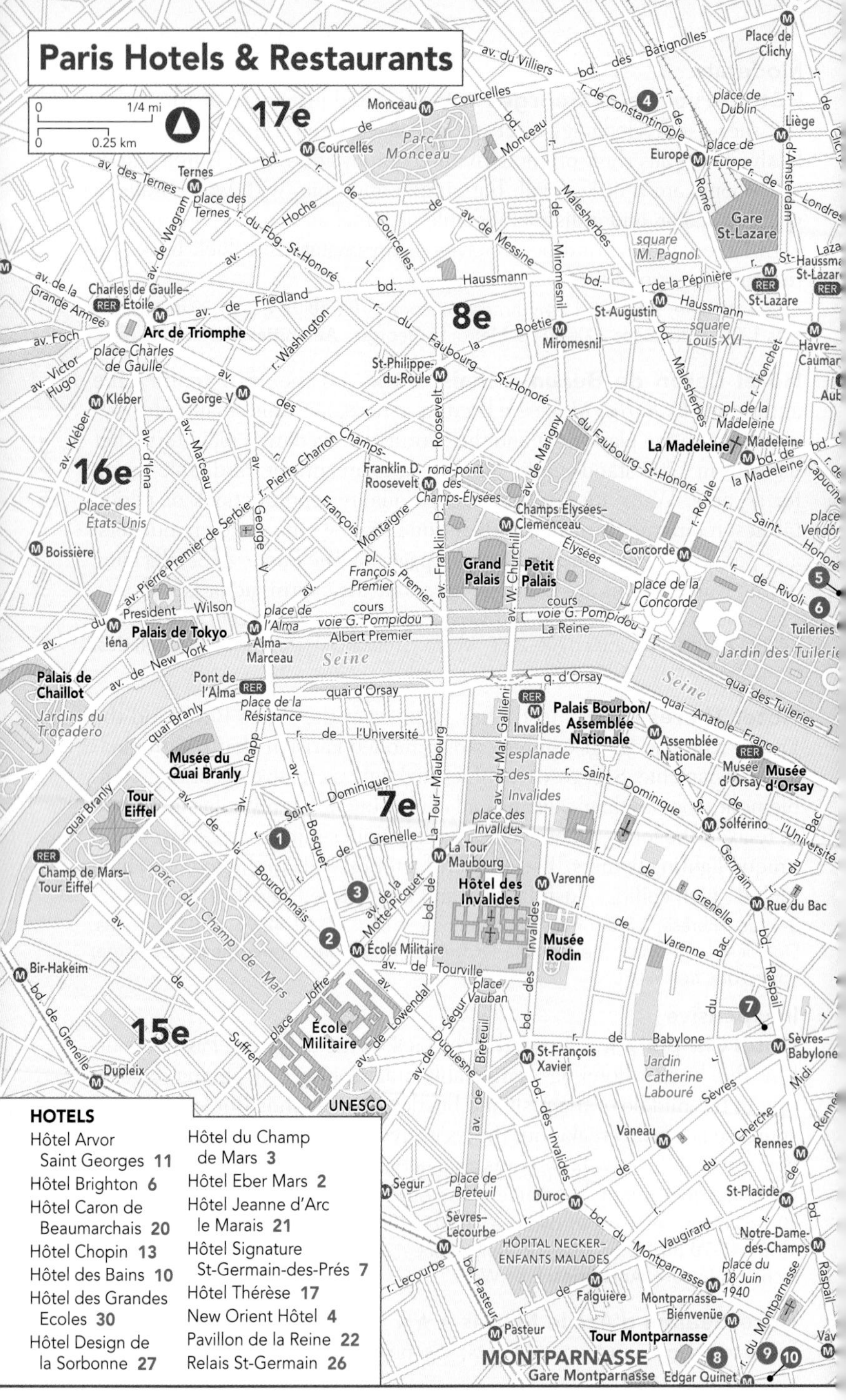
Paris Hotels & Restaurants
0
1/4 mi
0
0.25 km
17e
8e
16e
7e
15e
Monceau
Courcelles
Parc Monceau
Ternes
place des Ternes
av. des Ternes
av. de Wagram
r. du Fbg. St-Honoré
av. Hoche
r. de Courcelles
bd. de Courcelles
av. de Messine
bd. Malesherbes
r. de Miromesnil
bd. Haussmann
av. de Friedland
Charles de Gaulle–Étoile
RER
Arc de Triomphe
place Charles de Gaulle
av. de la Grande Armée
av. Foch
av. Victor Hugo
Kléber
av. Kléber
George V
av. d'Iéna
av. Marceau
av. George V
r. Pierre Charron
av. des Champs-Élysées
r. Washington
St-Philippe-du-Roule
r. du Faubourg St-Honoré
r. La Boétie
Miromesnil
St-Augustin
Franklin D. Roosevelt
rond-point des Champs-Élysées
r. François Premier
av. Montaigne
pl. François Premier
av. Franklin D. Roosevelt
av. W. Churchill
Grand Palais
Petit Palais
Champs Élysées–Clemenceau
av. de Marigny
Concorde
place de la Concorde
cours La Reine
voie G. Pompidou
cours Albert Premier
av. Pierre Premier de Serbie
place des États-Unis
Boissière
av. du President Wilson
Iéna
Palais de Tokyo
place de l'Alma
Alma–Marceau
av. de New York
Seine
Palais de Chaillot
Jardins du Trocadéro
Pont de l'Alma
RER
place de la Résistance
quai d'Orsay
quai Branly
r. de l'Université
Musée du Quai Branly
av. Rapp
av. Bosquet
r. Saint-Dominique
r. de Grenelle
Tour Eiffel
Champ de Mars–Tour Eiffel
parc du Champ de Mars
av. de la Bourdonnais
av. de la Motte-Picquet
bd. de La Tour-Maubourg
La Tour Maubourg
Hôtel des Invalides
esplanade des Invalides
place des Invalides
av. du Mal. Gallieni
Invalides
Palais Bourbon/Assemblée Nationale
Assemblée Nationale
Musée d'Orsay
bd. St-Germain
Solférino
r. de l'Université
r. du Bac
Rue du Bac
Varenne
r. de Varenne
Musée Rodin
bd. des Invalides
École Militaire
av. de Tourville
place Vauban
av. de Ségur
av. de Lowendal
av. Duquesne
av. de Breteuil
av. de Suffren
place Joffre
École Militaire
UNESCO
Bir-Hakeim
bd. de Grenelle
Dupleix
St-François Xavier
r. de Babylone
Jardin Catherine Labouré
r. de Sèvres
Vaneau
Sèvres–Babylone
bd. Raspail
r. du Cherche Midi
Rennes
St-Placide
Ségur
place de Breteuil
Duroc
Sèvres–Lecourbe
r. Lecourbe
bd. Pasteur
HÔPITAL NECKER–ENFANTS MALADES
bd. du Montparnasse
r. de Vaugirard
Falguière
Montparnasse–Bienvenüe
Notre-Dame-des-Champs
place du 18 Juin 1940
Pasteur
Tour Montparnasse
MONTPARNASSE
Gare Montparnasse
Edgar Quinet
av. du Villiers
bd. des Batignolles
r. de Constantinople
Place de Clichy
place de Dublin
Liège
Europe
place de l'Europe
r. de Rome
r. d'Amsterdam
r. de Londres
Gare St-Lazare
square M. Pagnol
r. de la Pépinière
St-Lazare
Havre–Caumartin
square Louis XVI
r. Tronchet
pl. de la Madeleine
La Madeleine
Madeleine
bd. de la Madeleine
bd. des Capucines
r. Royale
r. Saint-Honoré
place Vendôme
r. de Rivoli
Tuileries
Jardin des Tuileries
quai des Tuileries
quai Anatole France
1
2
3
4
5
6
7
8
9
10
HOTELS
Hôtel Arvor Saint Georges 11
Hôtel Brighton 6
Hôtel Caron de Beaumarchais 20
Hôtel Chopin 13
Hôtel des Bains 10
Hôtel des Grandes Ecoles 30
Hôtel Design de la Sorbonne 27
Hôtel du Champ de Mars 3
Hôtel Eber Mars 2
Hôtel Jeanne d'Arc le Marais 21
Hôtel Signature St-Germain-des-Prés 7
Hôtel Thérèse 17
New Orient Hôtel 4
Pavillon de la Reine 22
Relais St-Germain 26

RESTAURANTS
Chartier 14
Chez Gladines 28
Chez Nenesse 19
Crêperie de Saint Malo 9
Itinéraires 29
La Cerisaie 8
La Fresque 18
Le Grand Véfour 16
Le Relais de l'Entrecôte 23
Le Relais Louis XIII 25
Le Violon d'Ingres 1
Mangetout 24
Nansouty 12
Pinxo 5
Saturne 15
Montmartre
9e
10e
2e
1er
3e
11e
4e
6e
5e
12e
Opéra Garnier
HÔPITAL ST-LOUIS
Canal Saint-Martin
Palais Royal
St-Eustache
Forum des Halles
Musée du Louvre
Centre Pompidou
Archives Nationales
MARAIS
Musée Carnavalet
Palais de Justice
ÎLE DE LA CITÉ
Hôtel de Ville
Cathédrale Notre-Dame
ÎLE ST-LOUIS
St-Germain-des-Prés
St-Sulpice
Palais du Luxembourg
JARDIN DU LUXEMBOURG
Sorbonne
LATIN QUARTER
Panthéon
CAMPUS DE JUSSIEU
Ménagerie
JARDIN DES PLANTES
Grande Mosquée de Paris
Gare d'Austerlitz
Seine

months in advance. It's located in the lower Marais, right next to the leafy place du Marché St-Catherine. Although definitely not luxurious, the rooms are in excellent shape, decked out in warm colors and old-fashioned prints; several have been given a more modern makeover and new bathrooms.

3 rue de Jarente, 4th arrond. www.hoteljeannedarc.com. ✆ **01-48-87-62-11.** 35 units. Doubles 120€–150€. Métro: St-Paul. **Amenities:** Free Wi-Fi.

**New Orient Hôtel ★★★** A quick trot to the Saint Lazare train station and not far from the Champs Elysées, this lovely hotel offers simple, comfortable rooms with high ceilings, 19th-century moldings, and antique headboards and armoires. The friendly owners, inveterate flea market browsers, have refinished and restored the antique furniture themselves. Rooms are in tip-top shape, and bathrooms sparkle. There's an elevator, but you'll have to negotiate stairs to get to it.

16 rue de Constantinople, 8th arrond. www.hotelneworient.com. ✆ **01-45-22-21-64.** 30 units. Doubles 110€–190€ double. Métro: Villiers, Europe, or St-Lazare. **Amenities:** Free Wi-Fi.



## THE LEFT BANK

### Expensive

**Hôtel Signature St-Germain-des-Près ★★★** Bright colors on the walls blend harmoniously with subdued bedsteads and linens at this stylish hotel; smart mid-century reproduction furniture and faux antique phones take the edge off of sleek modern lines. The "Prestige" rooms cost more, but are especially roomy (30 sq. m, 323 sq. ft.), a rarity even in upscale Parisian hotels. This hotel is also blessed with an excellent location for shopping addicts: It's just down the street from Bon Marché.

5 rue Chomel, 7th arrond. www.signature-saintgermain.com. ✆ **01-45-48-35-53.** 26 units. Doubles 190€–380€; 2-room family suite 440€–540€. Métro: Sèvres-Bablylone or St-Sulpice. **Amenities:** Concierge service; free Wi-Fi.

**Relais St-Germain ★★★** Exposed beams abound in this 17th-century townhouse, where spacious rooms mix old-world charm and jazzy modernity. The decor artfully blends period furniture with modern prints, like the Louis XV armchair covered in zigzagged leather, or the 18th-century painting hung in the middle of a wall of mirrors. There are some extra stairs between floors when you get out of the elevator. Guests have priority at the hotel restaurant, **Le Comptoir,** where you might otherwise have a 6-month wait for a reservation. Book your room at least a month in advance.

9 carrefour de l'Odéon, 6th arrond. www.hotelrsg.com. ✆ **01-44-27-07-97.** 22 units. Doubles 295€, suites 460€, rates include breakfast. Métro: Odéon. **Amenities:** Restaurant; free Wi-Fi.

### Moderate

**Hôtel Design de la Sorbonne ★★** In the thick of the student quarter, this cozy boutique hotel combines comfort with an unusual but classy decor. Period furniture is covered in lively green, blue, and dark-brown stripes; colorful wall fabrics put a modern spin on Victorian patterns; and excerpts from French literary classics are woven into the carpets. Each room has a desk with an iMac for guest's use. As pretty as they are, the rooms are small, and some have bathrooms that are downright tiny. If you need space, opt for a deluxe with a bathtub or the large room on the top floor with a view of the Sorbonne and the Panthéon.

6 rue Victor Cousin, 5th arrond. www.hotelsorbonne.com. ✆ **01-43-54-58-08.** 38 units. Doubles 120€–380€. Métro: Cluny-La Sorbonne. RER: Luxembourg. **Amenities:** Free Wi-Fi.

**Hôtel Eber Mars ★★** The reception desk here is often helmed by Monsieur Eber, who has spent the last decade lovingly renovating his hotel, giving it a low-key 1930s-era decor. Walls in the spacious rooms are papered in period patterns in neutral colors, lit by authentic Art Deco hanging fixtures found at antiques fairs. Old-fashioned radiators have been scraped and lacquered; prints dating from the Universal Exposition of 1889 are hung on the walls. Rooms in this hotel are unusually large for Paris; the triples and connecting suites are ideal for families.

117 av. de la Bourdonnais, 7th arrond. www.hotelebermars.com. ✆ **01-47-05-42-30.** 25 units. Doubles 120€–280€. Métro: Ecole Militaire. **Amenities:** Bar; free Wi-Fi.

### Inexpensive

**Hôtel des Bains ★★** With cute, comfortable rooms and excellent rates, this friendly hotel is one of the best deals on the Left Bank, especially for families. In a city where large rooms are rare, it offers several good-size, two-room suites for up to four people. Doubles are amply sized as well, with high ceilings; the largest ones face the pretty courtyard. The elevator stops at a landing between floors, which have a few stairs.

33 rue Delambre, 14th arrond. www.hotel-des-bains-montparnasse.com. ✆ **01-43-20-85-27.** 42 units. Doubles 105€, 2–4 person suites 140€–175€. Métro: Vavin, Edgar Quinet or Montparnasse. **Amenities:** Free Wi-Fi.

**Hôtel des Grandes Ecoles ★★★** Tucked into a private garden, this hotel makes you feel as if you have just walked out of Paris and into the countryside. A path leads to a flower-bedecked interior courtyard; the reception area adjoins an inviting breakfast room with potted plants and an upright piano. The spotless rooms are filled with country-style furniture and papered in old-fashioned prints. Families will appreciate the six large suites that can sleep four. There are no TVs in the rooms.

75 rue de Cardinal-Lemoine, 5th arrond. www.hotel-grandes-ecoles.com. ✆ **01-43-26-79-23.** 51 units. Doubles 135€–165€, family rooms 185€. Métro: Cardinal Lemoine or Place Monge. **Amenities:** Free Wi-Fi.

Hôtel des Grandes Ecoles.

**Hôtel du Champ de Mars ★★** An adorable and affordable little inn right around the corner from the food shops of rue Cler—what more could you ask for? The impeccable rooms are decorated with the kind of care people generally reserve for their own homes: thick cotton bedspreads, framed etchings, and printed fabrics in warm colors on the walls and windows. Two rooms have a tiny courtyard, while those on the upper floors get lots of light.

7 rue du Champ de Mars, 7th arrond. www.hotelduchampdemars.com. ✆ **01-45-51-52-30.** 25 units. Doubles 130€–170€. Métro: Ecole Militaire. **Amenities:** Laptop loan for guests; free Wi-Fi.

## Where to Eat

Everywhere you look in Paris, someone is doing their best to ruin your waistline. *Boulangeries* (bakeries) with buttery croissants and decadent pastries lurk on every street corner, open-air markets tempt the senses, and terrific restaurants with intriguing menus sprout up on every block. Below is just a sampling of Paris's gourmet delights.

As you sally forth on your culinary adventure, remember the following: unless you see a sign that says service nonstop, meals are usually severely restricted to set hours. As dining rooms tend to be small, it a good idea to **reserve, if you can.** Lunch is generally served between noon and 2pm, and dinner is served from 7:30 to 10:30pm. Cafes and restaurants with a bar stay open between mealtimes serving drinks and coffee; if you are starving, you can usually order a light sandwich, or a *croque-monsieur* (a French take on a grilled ham and cheese sandwich). ***Tip:*** If you didn't reserve and you don't want to wait in line, try to arrive

A Paris cheese shop.



at the beginning of the service, noon or around 7:30pm. Most French people eat later than that, so you'll avoid the rush.

## THE RIGHT BANK

### Expensive

**Le Grand Véfour** ★★★ CLASSIC FRENCH Channel centuries of history at this illustrious restaurant, where Napoléon, Danton, Hugo, Colette, and Cocteau all once dined. Thanks to Guy Martin, chef and owner, the food is as memorable as the magnificently preserved 18th-century salon: Signature dishes like Prince Rainier III pigeon and truffled oxtail *parmentier* share the menu with new creations with contemporary flavors like sumac and sancho pepper. Reserve at least 2 weeks in advance.

17 rue de Beaujolais, 1st arrond. www.grand-vefour.com. ✆ **01-42-96-56-27.** Mains 98€–114€; fixed-price lunch 98€, fixed-price dinner 298€. Métro: Louvre-Palais-Royal or Pyramides. Mon–Fri 12:30–1:45pm and 8–9:45pm. Closed August.

**Saturne** ★★★ MODERN FRENCH The chef's Scandinavian roots are evident in the decor of this chic restaurant, with its sleek blonde wood and white walls. But it's what's on the plate that makes it difficult to get a reservation here: exquisitely refined combinations of flavors and textures, resembling works of contemporary art. At lunch you can choose between a menu of three or six dishes; and dinner, there's a set fixed-price menu for one and all.

17 rue Notre-Dame-des-Victoires, 2nd arrond. www.saturne-paris.fr. ✆ **01-42-60-31-90.** Fixed-price lunch 40€–70€, fixed-price dinner 70€, with wines 135€. Métro: Bourse. Mon–Fri noon–2pm and 8–10:30pm. Closed 3 weeks in Aug.

Sidewalk dining in lively Montmarte.

## Moderate

**Nansouty ★★** MODERN FRENCH Just north of the Butte de Montmartre, this popular wine bar appeals to both gourmets and wine enthusiasts. Choose from over 100 bottles on the massive blackboard and order a plate of nibbles, or sit down and savor a delicious meal fixed with the freshest ingredients and a dash of contemporary *je ne sais quoi.* 35 rue Ramey, 18th arrond. ✆ **01-42-52-58-87.** Mains 18€; fixed-price lunch 17€, fixed-price dinner 30€. Métro: Lamarck-Caulincourt or Château Rouge. Tues–Fri noon–2:30pm and 8–11pm; Sat and Mon 8–11pm.

**Pinxo ★★** MODERN FRENCH/TAPAS Sample exquisite cooking in a relaxed atmosphere at this modern tapas restaurant, where food is made to be shared. Everyone grazes on small plates with magnificent mouthfuls (each dish is priced per person on the menu) such as baby squid with fried ginger; terrine of goat cheese with eggplant; or sliced Chalosse beef a la plancha. Wash it all down is with a glass of wine—choose from 120 bottles, many of which are available by the glass. 9 rue d'Alger, 1st arrond. www.alaindutournier.com. ✆ **01-40-20-72-00.** Portions per person 6€–9€,

### Let's Do Lunch

Many restaurants in Paris serve a set-price menu at lunch that is considerably cheaper than the same food served at dinnertime. It is not at all unusual to find a two- or three-course lunch prix-fixe, called alternately a *formule* or a menu for 16€ to 25€. The only downside is that your choice of dishes will usually be limited on the *formule.* **Note:** Set lunches are usually only served Monday through Friday.

meal per person 35€–40€. Métro: Tuileries. Mon–Fri 12:30–2:15pm and 7–10:30pm, Sat 7–10:30pm. Closed part of Aug.

### Inexpensive

**Chartier** ★ TRADITIONAL FRENCH This gargantuan establishment is one of the last of the *bouillons,* or workers' restaurants, that used to be found all over Paris back in the 19th century. You come here for the experience more than for the food, which is tasty, but certainly won't win any Michelin stars. The menu covers a wide variety of traditional dishes like roast chicken with fries, or rump steak with pepper sauce. Service is fast and furious (how could it not be with this many tables?), but it's all part of the atmosphere, which is something that belongs to another time and place. There are no reservations, so be prepared to wait.

7 rue du Faubourg Montmartre, 9th arrond. www.restaurant-chartier.com. ✆ **01-47-70-86-29.** Mains 9€–13€. Métro: Grands-Boulevards. Daily 11:30am–10pm.

**Chez Nenesse** ★★★ TRADITIONAL BISTRO This neighborhood haunt has stayed true to its proletarian roots in a frighteningly hip part of the northern Marais. At lunchtime, the chef sends out traditional bistro fare (such as blanquette de veau, or rump steak) into the busy dining room, while dinner comes with a change in menus and ambience—the checked plastic tablecloths are traded for white linen. Thursday is steak-frites day, when regulars crowd in at lunch for their weekly dose of the yummy house fries.

17 rue Saintonge, 3rd arrond. ✆ **01-42-78-46-49.** Mains: lunch 11€–12€, dinner 16€–22€. Métro: Filles de Calvaire or Oberkampf. Mon–Fri noon–2:15pm and 8–10:15pm. Closed Aug and from Christmas to New Years.

**19th-century Chartier.**

**La Fresque ★★** MODERN FRENCH Named for its frescoed walls, this cozy, centrally located favorite serves modern bistro cooking with plenty of vegetables and vegetarian choices. Located across the street from Les Halles, this is a tasty, fresh, and affordable option in a neighborhood filled with fast food and uninspired tourist fare.

100 rue Rambuteau, 1st arrond. www.restaurant-la-fresque-paris.fr. ✆ **01-42-33-17-56.** Mains 12€–17€, fixed-price lunch 15€. Métro: Les Halles. RER: Châtelet-Les Halles. Mon–Sat noon–3:30pm and 7pm–midnight, Sun noon–3:30pm. Closed 1 week in Aug.



## THE LEFT BANK

### Expensive

**Itinéraires ★★** FRENCH FUSION This elegant enterprise is devoted to finding the meeting point between French and more far-flung cuisines. The seasonal menu, which features lots of organic ingredients, might include a griddled sea bass with kabocha, capers, and olives and a chocolate crumble with banana–passion fruit ice cream for dessert. If everyone in your party is of a like mind, you can order a tasting menu either at lunch (49€) or at dinner (89€).

5 rue de Pontoise, 5th arrond. www.restaurant-itineraires.com. ✆ **01-46-33-60-11.** Mains 34€–38€, fixed-price dinner 65€–69€. Métro: Maubert-Mutualité. Tues–Fri noon–2pm and 7–10:30pm, Sat 7–10:30pm. Closed Aug.

**Le Relais Louis XIII ★★★** TRADITIONAL FRENCH This acclaimed restaurant pays homage to traditional French cuisine at its most illustrious. No tonka beans or reduced licorice sauce here—the chef turns his formidable talents on classic sauces and time-honored dishes like seabass *quenelles* and roast duck, though he's not opposed to topping off the meal with a mango-avocado tart with gin jelly. The atmospheric dining room, crisscrossed with exposed beams and ancient stonework, makes you wonder if the Three Musketeers might not tumble through the doorway bearing your *mille-feuille* with Bourbon vanilla cream.

8 rue des Grands-Augustins, 6th arrond. www.relaislouis13.fr. ✆ **01-43-26-75-96.** Mains 59€; fixed-price lunch 55€; fixed-price dinner 85€–135€. Métro: Odéon or St-Michel. Tues–Sat 12:15–2:30pm, 7:30–10:30pm. Closed Aug.

**Le Violon d'Ingres ★★★** TRADITIONAL FRENCH Decked out in shades of cream and chocolate, this is the most elegant and refined of the three Christian Constant restaurants on rue Saint-Dominque. The menu treats classic dishes with kindness and care, giving each a dash of delicious originality. Menu choices might include roast sea bass in a sliced almond crust with capers and lemon, free-range squab with fava beans, and the chef's own *cassoulet*. Top it all off with a Grand Marnier soufflée with salted caramel sauce.

135 rue St-Dominique, 7th arrond. www.leviolondingres.com. ✆ **01-45-55-15-05.** Mains 37€–42€; tasting menu 95€. Métro: Invalides or Ecole-Militaire. Daily noon–3pm and 6:30–11:30pm.

### Moderate

**La Cerisaie** ★★ SOUTHWESTERN FRENCH/BISTRO This shoebox-size dining room near the Tour Montparnasse serves a classy version of the soul-warming cuisine of southwestern France. In autumn and winter, the chef does amazing things with wild game, and his menu features every animal in the forest, from hare to partridge to boar. Finish with the incredible Armagnac (as opposed to rum) baba, which comes with a scoop of luscious vanilla *crème fouettée.* It's best to reserve ahead, but if you can't, you can line up for one of the two seatings, at 7pm and 9pm.

70 bd. Edgar-Quinet, 14th arrond. www.restaurantlacerisaie.com. ✆ **01-43-20-98-98.** Mains 16€–21€. Métro: Montparnasse-Bienvenüe or Edgar Quinet. Mon–Fri noon–2pm and 7–10pm. Closed mid-July to mid-Aug.

**Le Relais de l'Entrecôte** ★★ TRADITIONAL FRENCH/STEAK You won't have to trouble yourself with deciding what to eat here: There is one set menu for one and all. First comes a fresh green salad, and then a giant silver platter of steak arrives, doused in an addictive "secret sauce" and served with crispy golden fries. What's more, you'll be offered a second helping. If you have room, the deserts are delicious. Get here early, because you can't reserve and there is often a line out the door. There are two other locations: 101 bd. Montparnasse in the 6th, or 15 rue Marbeuf in the 8th. This is a great option for families.

20 rue St-Benoît, 6th arrond. www.relaisentrecote.fr. ✆ **01-45-49-16-00.** Fixed-price lunch and dinner 27€. Métro: St-Germain-des-Prés. Daily noon–2:30pm and 7–11:30pm.

**Mangetout** ★★★ MODERN FRENCH This affordable taste treat comes courtesy of Michelin-starred chef Alain Dutournier, the force behind **Pinxo** ★★ (p. 144). Considering the quality of the goods, the price is most definitely right. You could start with mushroom-infused scallops in herbs, proceed to milk-fed lamb with spring vegetables, and finish with a decadent chestnut cream *Mont Blanc* and still get out for under 50€. Because the dining room is tiny, dinner reservations are essential.

82 rue Mazarine, 6th arrond. www.alaindutournier.com/wp/mangetout. ✆ **01-43-54-02-11.** Mains 13€–29€. Métro: Mabillon or Odéon. Tues–Sat noon–2pm and 7–10:30pm. Closed in Aug.

### Inexpensive

**Chez Gladines** ★ SOUTHWESTERN Hungry? Come here for enormous and tasty portions of rib-sticking French southwestern specialties, like duck confit with sautéed potatoes, Basque-style chicken (with tomatoes and bell peppers), and the like. Even the salads are gargantuan, filled with things like bacon, goat cheese, smoked ham, and *foie gras.* There are four other locations: the original Gladines, 30 rue des Cinq

Diamants, 13th arrond.); 11 bis rue des Halles, 1st arrond.; 74 bd. des Batignolles, 17th arrond.; and 64-66 rue de Charonne, 11th arrond.
44 bd. St-Germain, 5th arrond. www.gladines.com. ✆ **01-46-33-93-88.** Mains 10€–15€. Métro: Maubert-Mutualité. Mon–Thurs noon–11pm; Fri–Sat noon–midnight, Sun noon–11:30pm.

**Crêperie de Saint Malo ★★** CREPERIE Of the dozens of crêperies concentrated near the Montparnasse train station, this is one of the best. The *galettes* and crêpes are perfectly cooked with lacy, crispy edges, and what's more, they use organic flour. The friendly service and easy-going atmosphere makes this a good choice for families with kids.
53 rue du Montparnasse, 14th arrond. ✆ **01-43-20-87-19.** Mains 7€–12€; fixed-price menu 14€. Métro: Edgar Quinet. Daily 11:30am–2:30pm and 6:30–11:30pm.



## Shopping in Paris

Like us, most Parisians can't actually afford to buy the French luxury brands so revered around the world—and yet they manage to look terrifically put together. What's their secret? Read on as I attempt to shed some light on this puzzling mystery; the shops and services listed below will give you a good point of departure for your Parisian shopping adventure.

### GREAT SHOPPING AREAS

You can find clothes and knickknacks at significantly reduced prices at discount shops, which tend to conglomerate on certain streets. **Rue d'Alésia** (14th, Métro: Alésia) is lined with outlet stores *(déstock)* selling discounted wares, including designer labels; and **Rue St-Placide** (6th, Métro: Sèvres-Babylone) has both outlet stores and discount shops.

Chain and other midrange stores concentrate on and near **Rue de Rennes** (6th arrond.); **Les Halles** (1st arrond.); **Rue de Rivoli** (1st arrond., btw. rue du Pont Neuf and Hotel de Ville); and the **Grands Magasins** (9th arrond.)—be sure look in the little streets that weave around the Printemps and Galeries Lafayette department stores.

If boutiques are what you are after, Paris has oodles of them, ranging from funky to fantastic. A few of the best streets for boutique shopping are: **Rue des Abbesses** (18th arrond.; Métro: Abbesses), for affordable chic and the shops of hip, young startup designers; **Rue de Charonne** (11th arrond.; Métro: Bastille), a youth-oriented street; **Rue des Francs Bourgeois** (4th arrond.; Métro: St-Paul), for a cornucopia of fashionable/cool/hip stores, most of which are open on Sunday; and **Rue Etienne Marcel** (2nd arrond.; Métro: Etienne Marcel), next to the hip Montorgueil pedestrian zone, with stylish boutiques galore.

If you don't look at price tags and are always searching for the ultimate everything, you'll find it on or near **Avenue Montaigne** (8th arrond.; Métro: Franklin D. Roosevelt), with flagships like Dior and Chanel; the **Place Vendôme** (1st arrond.; Métro: Concorde or Tuileries),

## WHAT TO bring home

Since the days when royalty paraded around in silks and satins, Paris has been known for luxury goods, so if your budget allows, enjoy. But what about the rest of us? Less perishable foodstuffs make great, if ephemeral gifts, like chocolates from **Via Chocolat** (5 rue Jean Baptiste Pigalle, 9th arrond.; www.viachocolat.com; ✆ **01-45-26-12-73**), which specializes in "chocolate d'auteur," featuring the works of several local masters. You'll find **artisanal jams and honey** along with other intriguing goodies at any of the city's many **covered markets** (for locations and hours, visit www.paris.fr/marches). One of the best is the **Marché d'Aligre** (place Aligre, 12th arrond.), which is open Monday through Saturday from 9am to 1pm and 4 to 7:30pm as well as Sunday from 9am to 1pm. Excellent and relatively inexpensive **wines** can be had at Les **Domaines Qui Montent** (22 rue Cardinet, 17th arrond.; www.lesdomainesquimontent.com; ✆ **01-42-27-63-96;** Métro: Courcelles or Wagram), an association of some 150 wine producers that offers a vast selection of wines from small, independent vineyards. There is a second location at 136 bd. Voltaire in the 11th arrondissement and a third on the corner of rue Ballu and rue Vintimille in the 9th.

You'll have no trouble finding famous **perfumes,** but for something a little different, try the appropriately named **The Different Company** (10 rue Ferdinand Duval, 4th arrond.; www.thedifferentcompany.com; ✆ **01-42-78-19-34;** Métro: St-Paul), an independent perfume house that makes its own unique fragrances with mostly natural materials.

Offbeat and original items can be found **L'Objet qui Parle** (86 rue des Martyrs, 18th arrond.; ✆ **06-09-67-05-30;** Métro: Abbesses), a quirky shop that sells a jumble of vintage finds, from framed butterflies to teapots to trophies. If you still need ideas, try one of the city's hip concept stores, the most famous of which is **Colette** (213 rue St-Honoré, 1st arrond.; www.colette.fr; ✆ **01-55-35-33-90;** Métro: Tuileries) a shopping phenomenon that offers both high style and high concept—everything from heart-shaped sunglasses to psychedelic nail polish to designer toilet brushes.

with eye-popping jewelry shops (Cartier, Boucheron, and so on); and **Rue du Faubourg St-Honoré** (8th arrond.; Métro: St-Philippe du Roule), where deeply elegant boutiques are filled with choice morsels of designer goods.

## Entertainment & Nightlife

While simply walking around town and gaping at the beautifully illuminated monuments can be an excellent night out, Paris is also a treasure trove of rich evening offerings: bars and clubs from chic to shaggy, sublime theater and dance performances, top-class orchestras, and scores of cinemas and art-film houses.

With few exceptions, the city's major concert halls and theaters are in action between September and June, taking off during the summer months during the annual vacation exodus. Summer is the season for wonderful music festivals, including the **Festival Chopin** and **Jazz à**

## Finding Out What's On

For dates and schedules for what's happening in music, theater, dance, and film, pick up the **weekly listing magazines *Pariscope*** or ***l'Officiel des Spectacles*** (both 0.50€), the Parisian bibles for weekly events. Both come out on Wednesdays and are available at any newsstand.

**La Villette,** many of which take place in Paris's lovely parks and gardens.

For the best in opera and ballet, head for the **Opéra de Paris** ★★★ (www.operadeparis.fr; ✆ **08-92-89-90-90** [.34€ per min.]; from outside of France: ✆ **01-71-25-24-23**) which includes both the gorgeous **Palais Garnier** and its less-inspired modern sister, the **Opéra Bastille** (2 place de la Bastille, 12th arrond.; Métro: Bastille) For classical concerts, head directly for the spectacular new **Philharmonie de Paris,** 221 avenue Jean-Jaurès, 19th arrond (www.philharmoniedeparis.fr; ✆ **01-44-84-44-84;** Métro: Porte de Pantin).

**Jazz** fiends should head for rue des Lombards, where there are several legendary clubs including **Le Sunset/Le Sunside ★★,** 60 rue des Lombards, 1st arrond. (www.sunset-sunside.com; ✆ **01-40-26-46-60;** Métro: Châtelet), an intimate space headlining top names. A roomier space with an even more impressive line-up is **New Morning ★★★**, 7 rue des Petites Ecuries, 10th arrond. (www.newmorning.com; ✆ **01-45-23-51-41;** Métro: Château d'Eau), where international stars abound.

There are over 100 **theatres** in Paris, and terrific performances to be seen, but all in French. If your French is up to it, a night at the splendiferous **Comédie Française ★★**, Place Colette, 1st arrond. (www.comedie-francaise.fr; ✆ **08-25-10-16-80** [.15€ per min.]; Métro:

Palais Garnier, home of Opéra de Paris.

Palais-Royal), will be one to remember. Language will not be a problem at one of the city's **dance** performances, the best of which usually end up at the **Théâtre National de Chaillot ★★** 1 place du Trocadéro, 16th arrond. (www.theatre-chaillot.fr; ✆ **01-53-65-30-00;** Métro: Trocadéro). For laughs in English, ***How to Become a Parisian in One Hour*** (Théâtre des Nouveautés; Métro: Grands Boulevards; details at www.oliviergiraud.com), is a terrific one-person show written by a Frenchman who spent several years in the U.S.

Some people think they just haven't been to Paris if they haven't forked out a wad of money to see sequins-studded women dancing and (more often than not) lip-synching at a **cabaret** like the **Moulin Rouge ★,** 82 bd. Clichy, place Blanche, 18th arrond. (www.moulinrouge.fr; ✆ **01-53-09-82-82;** Métro Blanche) or the **Lido,** 116 ave. des Champs-Élysées, 8th arrond. (www.lido.fr; ✆ **01-40-76-56-10;** Métro: George V).

For a more authentic outing, spend a lot less on an original concoction at the **Experimental Cocktail Club** (37 rue St-Sauveur, 2nd arrond.; www.experimentalcocktailclub.com; ✆ **01-45-08-88-09;** Métro: Sentier), an ultra-hip bar serving the best cocktails in town; or nibble on tapas at **La Rotonde** (6-8 place de la Bataille de Stalingrad, 19th arrond.; www.larotonde.com; ✆ **01-80-48-33-40;** Métro: Stalingrad or Jaurès), a relaxed hangout in an 18th century pavilion on the southern end of the Bassin de la Villette. Just to the south, cool cafes and bars line the **Canal St-Martin;** at the far end of the canal you can wander over east to more bars and clubs on **Rue Oberkampf** and **Rue Ménilmontant.** Rejoice in the fruit of the vine at one of Paris's many **wine bars,** where experts will help you choose the right glass of nectar to suit your mood. A couple of favorites: **Le Baron Rouge,** 1 rue Théophile Roussel, 12th arrond. (✆ **01-43-43-14-32;** Metro: Ledru-Rollin), a rollicking, boisterous place with affordable prices, and the **5e Cru,**

## Gay & Lesbian Paris

Paris has a vibrant gay nightlife scene, primarily centered around the Marais. Gay dance clubs come and go so fast that even the magazines devoted to them, like ***Qweek*** (www.qweek.fr)—distributed free in gay bars and bookstores—have a hard time keeping up. ***Têtu*** magazine, sold at most newsstands, has special nightlife inserts for gay bars and clubs.

Two of the most popular (and longest-lived) bars for boys in the Marais are **Le Cox ★,** 15 rue des Archives, 4th arrond. (www.cox.fr; ✆ **01-42-72-08-00;** Métro: Hôtel de Ville), and **Open Café ★★,** 17 rue des Archives, 4th arrond. (www.opencafe.fr; ✆ **01-42-72-26-18;** Métro: Hôtel-de-Ville). Girls who like girls cluster at **Le 3w Kafe ★★,** 8 rue des Ecouffes, 4th arrond. (✆ **01-48-87-39-26;** Métro: St-Paul), where there's a DJ downstairs on the weekends.

7 rue du Cardinal Lemoine, 5th arrond. (www.5ecru.com; ✆ **01-40-46-86-34;** Métro: Jussieu), a serious *caviste* with some 300 bottles to choose from.

# PROVENCE

The ancient Greeks left their vines, the Romans their monuments, but it was the 19th-century Impressionists who most shaped the romantic notion of Provence today. Cezanne, Gauguin, Chagall, and countless others were drawn to the unique light and vibrant spectrum brought forth by what van Gogh called "the transparency of the air." Modern-day visitors will delight in the region's culture, colors, and world-class museums. And they will certainly dine well too.

Provence blends past and present with an impassioned pride. It has its own language and customs, and some of its festivals go back to medieval times. The region is bounded on the north by the Drôme River, on the west by the Rhône, on the east by the Alps, and on the south by the Mediterranean. Costal Provence is known as the Côte d'Azur, or the French Riviera.

## Avignon ★★

In the 14th century, Avignon was the capital of Christendom. What started as a temporary stay by Pope Clement V in 1309, when Rome was deemed too dangerous even for clergymen, became a 67-year golden age. The cultural and architectural legacy left by the seven popes who served during this period makes Avignon one of Europe's most alluring medieval destinations.

**Lavender fields, Provence.**

Provence
RHÔNE-ALPES
DRÔME
ARDÈCHE
HAUTES-ALPES
Mt. Ventoux
ALPES-DE-HAUTE-PROVENCE
ALPES-MARITIMES
LANGUEDOC-ROUSSILLON
GARD
HERAULT
VAUCLUSE
BOUCHES-DU-RHÔNE
VAR
PROVENCE-ALPES-CÔTE D'AZUR
PARC NATUREL RÉGIONAL DU LUBERON
MASSIF DU LUBERON
Grand Canyon du Verdon
Pont-St-Esprit
Vaison-la-Romaine
Sisteron
Bagnols-sur-Cèze
Orange
Volonne
Digne
Alès
Châteauneuf-du-Pape
Carpentras
Peyruis
Uzès
Pont du Gard
Sauve
Avignon
Forcalquier
Barrême
Gordes
Roussillon
Apt
Oraison
Nîmes
Cavaillon
Bonnieux
Manosque
Riez
Castellane
Beaucaire
Tarascon
St-Rémy-de-Provence
Les Baux-de-Provence
Cadenet
Fontvieille
Vauvert
St-Gilles
Arles
Castries
Salon-de-Provence
Grasse
Montpellier
Rians
Camargue
Aix-en-Provence
Barjols
Aigues-Mortes
Istres
Draguignan
Étang de Vaccarès
Étang de Berre
St-Maximin-la-St-Baume
Le Muy
Fréjus
St-Raphaël
Stes-Maries-de-la-Mer
Fos-sur-Mer
Beauduc
Pt-St-Louis
Martigues
Pierrefeu
Brignoles
Marseille
Aubagne
Château d'If
Îles du Frioul
Cassis
Cap Croisette
Le Beausset
Cuers
Ste-Maxime
St-Tropez
Île de Riou
La Ciotat
Bandol
Sanary
Toulon
Hyères
Golfe du Lion
Golfe de Fos
MEDITERRANEAN SEA
Îles d'Hyères
Île du Levant
Île de Porquerolles
Île de Port-Cros
PORT-CROS NATIONAL PARK
Rhône
Petit Rhône
Grand Rhône
Durance
Gard
A7
A9
A51
A54
A8
A52
A50
A55
A57
D6
D938
D900
D999
N110
N106
N572
D570
D99
D973
N568
N85
D952
D562
D98
D559
Paris
FRANCE
Area of detail
0
20 mi
20 km

Today this walled city is a major stop on the route from Paris to the Mediterranean. In recent years, it has become known as a cultural center, thanks to its annual international performing-arts festivals and wealth of experimental theaters and art galleries.

## ESSENTIALS

Avignon's **Office de Tourisme** website is www.avignon-tourisme.com.

**ARRIVING** Frequent TGV **trains** depart from Paris's Gare de Lyon (trip time: 2 hr. 40 min.; 57€–95€) and arrives at Avignon's TGV station, located 6 minutes from town by a speedy rail link. TGVs also arrive from Marseille (trip time: 35 min.; 30€ one-way), and Aix-en-Provence (trip time: 20 min.; 25€ one-way). Regular trains leaving from the Avignon Centre station depart for Arles every hour or so (trip time: 20min, 7.70€ one way) For schedules: www.voyages-sncf.com or ✆ **36-35.**

**Buses** (✆ **08-21-20-22-03;** www.info-ler.fr) link Avignon to Aix-en Provence (trip time: 1 hr., 15 min.; 17.40€ one-way). The bus station is at 5 av. Monclar (✆ **04-90-82-07-35**).

If you're **driving** from Paris, take A6 south to Lyon, and then A7 to Avignon.

**GETTING AROUND** All of Avignon inside the ramparts is easily accessible **on foot,** but you'll need one of the free maps from the tourist office if you don't want to get lost in its labyrinth of back streets. **Driving** is not recommended; the one-way streets are very narrow and parking is a nightmare. Park in one of the lots outside the city walls. When you get tired of walking, hop on a **Cityzen,** or a **Baladine,** eco-friendly shuttle buses that will drop you at the major sites for a mere 0.50€ per ride (www.tcra.fr).

## EXPLORING AVIGNON

Crowned by the crenellated majesty of the Palais des Papes, Avignon is a gorgeous maze of cobbled streets, medieval chapels, and ancient

### Events in Avignon

One of the world's most prestigious theater festivals, the **Festival d'Avignon** (www.festival-avignon.com; ✆ **04-90-14-14-14**), is held for 3 weeks in July. Companies from around the world come here to strut their latest stuff in the "On," or official, festival. Tickets, which range from 17€ to 47€, are snapped up quickly; visit the website for info on advanced sales. Prices for hotel rooms skyrocket during this period. An edgier (and cheaper) alternative festival, the **Avignon OFF** (www.avignonleoff.com; ✆ **04-90-85-13-08**), takes place at the same time, with hundreds of theater companies performing short pieces in various improbable venues. From morning to midnight, the streets are packed with theater lovers and actors hawking their shows; be sure to pick up a program to see what's on.

Palais des Papes, Avignon.



dwellings. While the large central square, the **Place de l'Horloge,** is delightful, getting lost in the back streets is also a treat. At every turn is a historic architectural gem dating from when the city was the center of the Christian universe.

And then there's that bridge they all sing about. The star of "Sur le Pont d'Avignon" is actually a bridge called the **Pont St-Bénézet ★★** (www.avignon-pont.com; ✆ **04-32-74-32-74**). Constructed between 1177 and 1185, it once spanned the Rhône, connecting Avignon with Villeneuve-lèz-Avignon. Today it is a ruin, with only 4 of its original 22 arches remaining (half of it fell into the river back in 1669). The remains of the bridge have the same opening hours as those of the Palais des Papes (see below). Admission is 5€ adults, 4€ ages 8 to 17, and free for children 7 and under.

**Collection Lambert ★★** MUSEUM This contemporary art space is housed in an 18th-century mansion that once belonged to collector and gallery owner Yvon Lambert. Works range from video and photography to conceptual installations, organized in three annual exhibitions that feature major artists such as Anselm Kiefer, Jenny Holzer, and Cy Twombly.

5 rue Violette. www.collectionlambert.fr. ✆ **04-90-16-56-20.** Admission changes according to exhibition, free for children 5 and under. July–Aug daily 11am–7pm; Sept–June Tues–Sun 11am–6pm.

**Musée du Petit-Palais ★** MUSEUM Set in what was once the archbishop's palace, this museum's collection focuses on paintings from the Italian and Provençal schools of the 13th to 16th century, in particular the "Avignon School" an artistic movement that was a product of the city's golden age, when the Pope lived in the palace next door. The collection's star attraction is Botticelli's *Madonna with Child.*

Palais des Archevêques, place du Palais des Papes. www.petit-palais.org. ✆ **04-90-86-44-58.** 6€ adults, 3€ students, seniors and ages 12–18, free for children 11 and under. Wed–Mon 10am–1pm and 2–6pm.





**Palais des Papes ★★★** PALACE Dominating Avignon from a hilltop, this vast fortified castle was once as powerful and awesome as the Vatican. Back in 1305, after a vehement power struggle, a French pope, Clement V, was elected in Rome. However, the struggle was far from over, and Clement decided to park in Avignon until things calmed down. They didn't, and the popes stayed there for the next 67 years. This gargantuan palace, one of the largest Gothic buildings in Europe, was home to seven popes, a huge library, and the administrative offices of all Christendom. It was a mighty period of great cultural growth, but it eventually came to an end when it became politically necessary to move the papacy back to Rome.

After the popes left, the palace went through hard times, and by the time Napoléon came to power, it was in such a sorry state that it was used as a military barracks and a prison. As a consequence, what you see today is impressive, but bare. The dimensions alone are awe-inspiring; the **Grand Tinel (Banquet Hall)** is 41m (134 ft.) long and 9m (30 ft.) wide. One of the few rooms that retains some of its original artwork is the **Chapelle St-Jean,** known for its frescoes of John the Baptist and John the Evangelist painted between 1345 and 1348. The walls of the **Pope's Bedroom,** on the first floor of the Tour des Anges, are also painted with foliage, birds, and squirrels. The **Grande Audience (Great Receiving Hall)** contains frescoes of the prophets, painted in 1352.

Place du Palais des Papes. www.palais-des-papes.com. ✆ **04-32-74-32-74.** 11€ adults, 9€ seniors, students, and ages 8-17, free for children 7 and under; includes audioguide. Daily Nov–Feb 9:30am–5:45pm; Mar 9am–6:30pm; Apr–June and Sept–Nov 9am–7pm; July 9am–8pm; Aug 9am–8:30pm.

## ORGANIZED TOURS

Avignon's Office de Tourisme (www.avignon-tourisme.com) organizes a range of themed tours around the city, in particular the **"Secret Palace" tour,** an access-all-areas ramble around the Palais de Papes (35€, in English Apr–May and Sept–Oct).

## ESPECIALLY FOR KIDS

The history and beauty of Avignon might be lost on the little ones, but they will appreciate the pretty park and playground at the **Rocher des**

## A Stroll Through Avignon

Most tourists head straight up the rue de la République to the Palais des Papes, but some of the nicest corners of Avignon are the smaller streets and squares in the labyrinth of alleyways to the east and south of the palace. From the Place de l'Horloge, take the rue Favart to pretty place Carnot and on to Place Pie, where there is a terrific **covered market,** one of the best in the region (Les Halles d'Avignon, Place Pie; www.avignon-leshalles.com; Tues–Sun 6am–1:30pm). Turn down rue d'Amphoux and left on rue de la Bonneterie, which leads into **rue des Tenturiers,** a lovely cobbled lane that runs along a small stream and is lined with restaurants and cafes. Another nice spot for an evening *apéro* (light cocktail), is the nearby **Place des Corps Saints,** a small square shaded by plantain trees that is covered with cafe tables in the warmer months.



**Doms,** where there is also a pond with a fountain harboring ducks and the occasional swan. They will also enjoy a short ride on the **ferry** (leaves from the foot of the Pont St-Bénézet; hours at www.avignon-tourisme.com) that crosses the Rhône to the Ile de la Barthelasse, where there is a promenade and lots of green space for picnicking and running around. The island is also a great place to ride bikes; rent them from **Provence Bike,** 7 av. St-Ruf (www.provence-bike.com; ✆ **04-90-27-92-61;** 12€–15€ per day).

### WHERE TO STAY

**Hôtel Le Colbert ★★** An excellent choice for travelers on a budget, these cozy lodgings are located right in the historic town center, just a short trot from the (non-TGV) train station. The small but tidy rooms are decked out in that particularly Provençal shade of gold, and the walls are hung with offbeat prints and posters. Breakfast is on the tiny, flower-bedecked patio.

7 rue Agricol Perdiguier. www.avignon-hotel-colbert.com. ✆ **04-90-86-20-20.** 12 units. Doubles 64€–108€, 98€–140€ during festival. Closed Nov to Mar. **Amenities:** Free Wi-Fi.

**La Mirande ★★★** Once upon a time, this was a 14th-century cardinal's palace. It now boasts an additional 7 centuries of fixtures and features in one gloriously palatial package. Guest rooms are no-expense-spared collections of antique furniture, Carrera marble, period prints, and Murano chandeliers. La Mirande's gourmet restaurant and Le Marmiton, a classic French cooking school, are headed by Chef Jean-Claude Altmayer. All-organic afternoon tea—featuring homemade madeleines, thick hot chocolate, and Kombucha—is served daily on the patio.

4 place de l'Amirande. www.la-mirande.fr. ✆ **04-90-14-20-20.** 27 units. Doubles 370€–690€, suites 810€–1,715€. Restaurant closed in January. **Amenities:** Restaurant; bar; boutique; concierge; room service; free Wi-Fi.

## WHERE TO EAT

**La Fourchette** ★★ PROVENÇAL Set a block back from the bustling place de l'Horloge, this upscale bistro has been a local favorite since it opened its doors in 1982. The cuisine is sophisticated yet hearty: Think saffron-infused salt cod *brandade* served with crusty bread, or seared scallops atop fennel puree. The wine list features lots of local stars, like nearby Châteauneuf-du-Pape. Reserve ahead or be prepared to wait.
17 rue Racine. www.la-fourchette.net. ✆ **04-90-85-20-93.** Mains 20€; fixed-price menu 35€. Mon–Fri 12:15–1:45pm and 7:15–9:45pm. Closed 3 weeks in Aug.

**Restaurant Christian Etienne** ★★★ PROVENÇAL This temple of gastronomy is perched atop a 12th-century stone edifice—complete with 15th-century frescoes—just next door to the Palais des Papes. Avignon-born Chef Etienne is wildly innovative, and many of his dishes have a more than a hint of molecular influence. Fixed-price menus are themed around single ingredients such as duck, lobster, truffles, or (summertime only) heavenly heirloom tomatoes. Reservations required.
10 rue de Mons. www.christian-etienne.fr. ✆ **04-90-86-16-50.** Fixed-price lunch 35€, dinner 80€–150€. Tues–Sat noon–1:15pm and 7:30–9pm. Closed 2 weeks in Nov.

## SHOPPING

The chain boutique **Souleiado,** 19 rue Joseph-Vernet (✆ **04-90-86-32-05**), sells reproductions of 18th- and 19th-century Provençal fabrics

### VISITING roman ruins IN PROVENCE

Surprisingly, some of best existing examples of Roman architecture are not in Italy, but Provence. A number of extraordinary temples, arenas, and aqueducts have been carefully preserved from the ravages of time in southern France. Here are a few that make great day trips from Avignon:

- **Pont du Gard** is a magnificent three-tiered chunk of an aqueduct that once stretched 50 kilometers across the landscape to the city of Nîmes. The splendid arches cross the Gardon River at a point about 25 kilometers (15 miles) west of Avignon. There is an on-site museum and restaurant. (La Bégude, 400 Route du Pont du Gard, Vers-Pont-du-Gard; www.pontdugard.fr; ✆ **04-66-37-50-99**).
- One of the world's best conserved Roman temples, extraordinary **Maison Carrée** is no ruin; it has walls and a roof and you can even go inside. It's located in the historic center of Nîmes, which also boasts its own mini-Coliseum, the **Arènes de Nîmes,** still in use today for bullfights and other events. (Nîmes; www.arenes-nimes.com; ✆ **04-66-21-82-56**).
- **Théâtre Antique & Musée d'Orange** is a provincial town 32km (20 miles) from Avignon that boasts a beautifully preserved Roman theater, complete with its stage wall—a rarity of rarities. The acoustics have also been preserved, making this a prime venue for dance and musical events. (rue Madeleine Roch, Orange; www.theatre-antique.com; ✆: **04-90-51-17-60**).

by the meter or made into clothing and linens. **Pâtisserie Mallard,** 32 rue des Marchands (www.patisseriemallard.fr; ✆ **04-90-82-42-38**), makes the hard-to-find local specialty *les papalines d'Avignon*. Dark chocolate is coated in a pink chocolate, then filled with local Origan du Comat liquor. In addition to the **covered market** in Place Pie (see box p. 157), there is a **flower market** on place des Carmes on Saturday (8am–1pm), and the **flea market** occupies the same place each Sunday morning (6am–1pm).

### ENTERTAINMENT & NIGHTLIFE

Start your evening at **Avitus Bar à Vin,** 11 rue du Vieux Sextier (www.avituslacave.com; ✆ **09-84-27-57-97**), a cozy wine bar offering a wide range of local wines by the glass. Avignon's beautiful people continue on to **Les Ambassadeurs,** 27 rue Bancasse (www.clublesambassadeurs.fr; ✆ **04-90-86-31-55**), an upscale dance club. Behind the Hôtel d'Europe, disco-bar **L'Esclave,** 12 rue du Limas (www.esclavebar.com; ✆ **04-90-85-14-91**), is a focal point of the city's gay scene.

## St-Rémy-de-Provence ★

St-Rémy is most frequently associated with Vincent van Gogh, who committed himself to a local asylum in 1889 after cutting off part of his left ear. *Starry Night* was painted during this period, as were many versions of *Olive Trees* and *Cypresses.*

Wednesday morning is market day, when stalls bursting with the region's bounty, from wild-boar sausages to olives, elegant antiques to bolts of French country fabric, huddle between the sidewalk cafes beneath the plane trees.

### ESSENTIALS

St-Rémy's **Office de Tourisme** website is www.saintremy-de-provence.com.

**ARRIVING** A regional **bus** (line 57) runs frequently between Avignon and St-Rémy (trip time: 45 min.; 3.60€ one-way). For bus information, see www.lepilote.com or call ✆ **08-10-00-13-26.** The St-Rémy Tourist Office also provides links to bus schedules on their website (see above). If **driving,** head south from Avignon along D571.

### EXPLORING SAINT-RÉMY-DE-PROVENCE

Scattered among Saint-Rémy's charming streets are 18th-century private mansions, art galleries, medieval church towers, and bubbling fountains.

**Le Site Archéologique de Glanum ★★** RUINS Kids will love a scramble around this bucolically sited Gallo-Roman settlement, which thrived here during the final days of the Roman Empire. Its monuments include a triumphal arch from the time of Julius Caesar, garlanded with sculptured fruits and flowers. Visitors can see streets and foundations of private residences from the 1st-century town, plus the remains of a pre-Roman, Gallo-Greek town of the 2nd century B.C.

Route des Baux-de-Provence. www.glanum.monuments-nationaux.fr. ✆ **04-90-92-23-79.** 7.50€ adults, 4.50€ ages 18–25, free ages 17 and under. Apr–Aug daily 10am–6:30pm; Sept Tues–Sun 10am–6:30pm; Oct–Mar Tues–Sun 10am–5pm.

**Saint Paul de Mausole ★** MONASTERY This former monastery and clinic is where Vincent van Gogh was confined from 1889 to 1890. It's now a psychiatric hospital for women, which specializes in art therapy. You can't see the artist's actual cell, but there is a reconstruction of his room. The Romanesque chapel and cloisters are worth a visit, as van Gogh depicted their circular arches and beautifully carved capitals in some of his paintings.

Chemin Saint-Paul. www.saintpauldemausole.fr. ✆ **04-90-92-77-00.** 4.65€ adults, 3.30€ students, free for children 12 and under. Apr–Sept daily 9:30am–6:30pm; mid-Feb to Mar, Oct–Dec daily 10:15am–5:15pm. Closed Jan–Feb.

## WHERE TO STAY

**Château des Alpilles ★★★** A former castle situated at the heart of magnolia-studded parkland, Château des Alpilles was constructed by the Pichot family in 1827. Luxurious rooms can be found inside the castle itself, with additional private accommodation in the property's former chapel, farm, and washhouse. Decor throughout encompasses a mix of antiques (plush upholstery, local artworks) and cool amenities (deep travertine-trimmed bathtubs, iPod docks). It's 2km (1¼ miles) from the center of St-Rémy.

Route de Rougadou. www.chateaudesalpilles.com. ✆ **04-90-92-03-33.** 21 units. Doubles 215€–350€, suites and apartments 320€–480€. Closed Jan to mid-Mar. **Amenities:** Restaurant; bar; gym; outdoor pool; room service; sauna; 2 tennis courts; free Wi-Fi.

**L'Amandière ★** Tucked into the Provençal countryside about 1.5km (1 mile) north of town, these budget lodgings are justly favored by visitors who would rather splurge on the region's gourmet restaurants. Rooms are spacious, all boast their own balcony or private patio, and there's a large outdoor pool. Breakfast is served in the lavender-trimmed gardens.

Av. Théodore Aubanel. www.hotel-amandiere.com. ✆ **04-90-92-41-00.** 26 units. Doubles 80€–99€. **Amenities:** Outdoor pool; free Wi-Fi in common areas.

## WHERE TO EAT

**La Maison Jaune ★★** FRENCH/PROVENÇAL This 18th-century townhouse features two chic dining rooms, as well as a terrace overlooking the neighboring Hôtel de Sade's lush gardens. Creative chef François Perraud concocts upscale Provençal cuisine, relying almost exclusively on local ingredients. Mediterranean anchovies may be doused in a parsley pesto, Provençal lamb seared with smoky eggplant, or the darkest chocolate cake paired with frozen lemon parfait. Be sure to reserve ahead.

15 rue Carnot. www.lamaisonjaune.info. ✆ **04-90-92-56-14.** Mains 38€–44€; fixed-price lunch 32€; fixed-price dinner 42€–72€. Wed–Sat noon–1:30pm, Tues–Sat 7:30–9pm; Closed Nov to Feb.

**L'Estagnol ★★** MEDITERRANEAN This popular eatery offers hearty local cuisine, ranging from Camargue bull hamburger topped with goat cheese and eggplant to Provençal gazpacho with basil sorbet. Dining takes place either in the ancient *orangerie* (private greenhouse) or in the sun-dappled courtyard adjacent.

16 bd. Victor Hugo. www.restaurant-lestagnol.com. ✆ **04-90-92-05-95.** Mains 14€–28€; fixed-price lunch 14€, fixed-price dinner 30€. Tues–Sun noon–2:30pm and 7:15–10pm; closed Sunday evenings Oct–Jan and Mar–Apr. Closed Feb.

## LES BAUX DE PROVENCE ★★★

Les Baux de Provence's location and geology are extraordinary. This eagle's nest outcropping consists of a vast plateau and the remains of a mighty fortress, with boxy stone houses stacked like cards on the rock's east side. The combination is so cinematic that it seems like a living movie set.

The power-thirsty lords who ruled the settlement in the 11th century were so successful that they eventual controlled 79 other nearby fiefdoms. After they were overthrown, Les Baux was annexed to France with the rest of Provence, but Louis XI ordered the fortress demolished. The settlement experienced a rebirth during the Renaissance, when structures where restored and lavish residences built, only to fall again in

Les Baux de Provence.

1642 when, wary of rebellion, Louis XIII ordered his armies to destroy it once and for all. Today the fortress compound is a collection of fascinating ruins—so fascinating that Les Baux is often overrun with visitors at peak times, so time your visit wisely.

### ESSENTIALS

Le Baux's **Office de Tourisme** website is www.lesbauxdeprovence.com.

**ARRIVING** Les Baux is best reached by car. From St-Rémy, take D27 south; from Arles, D17 east. Alternatively, on weekends in June and September, and every day during July and August, the Cartreize **bus** no. 57 (35 min.; 2.40€ one-way) runs between Arles and St-Rémy, stopping at Les Baux en route. For information, see www.lepilote.com or call ✆ **08-10-00-13-26.**

### EXPLORING LES BAUX DE PROVENCE

Les Baux's windswept ruins, **Château des Baux** ★★★ (www.chateau-baux-provence.com; ✆ **04-90-54-55-56**), cover an area of 7 hectares (17 acres), much larger than the petite hilltop village itself. Consider visiting them early in the morning before the sun gets too strong.

The medieval compound is accessed via the 15th-century **Hôtel de la Tour du Brau.** Beyond are replicas of medieval military equipment that will thrill kids fond of knights in shining armor. Built to scale—that is to say, enormous—are a battering ram and various catapults capable of firing huge boulders. From April to August, these are fired every weekend and daily during school holidays at 11am and 1:30pm, 3:30pm, and 5:30pm, with an extra show during July and August at 6:30pm. Medieval jousting demonstrations (noon, 2:30, and 4:30pm) are held in summer.

Other stopping points include the **Chapel of St-Blaise**, the **Tour Sarrazin,** a windmill, the skeleton of a 16th century hospital, and a cemetery. There is a sweeping 360-degree **panorama** of the entire region from the plateau.

Admission to the Château (including audioguide) is 8€ adults, 6€ children 7 to 17 from September to March. The rest of the year, it costs 10€ adults, 8€ children 7 to 17 and students (daily Apr–June and Sept 9am–7:15pm; July and Aug 9am–8:15pm; Mar and Oct 9:30am–6:30pm; Nov–Feb 10am–5pm).

**Carrières de Lumières** ★ LIGHT SHOW A 10-minute stroll downhill from Les Baux, this high-tech light show shines its stuff on the massive walls and pillars of a former limestone quarry. Dazzling images of modern artworks are projected against the 7m to 9m (23- to 30-ft.) walls.

Route de Maillane. www.carrieres-lumieres.com. ✆ **04-90-54-47-37.** 11€ adults, 8.50€ children 7–17 and students, free children 6 and under. Daily Apr–Sept 9:30am–7pm; Oct–Jan and Mar 10am–6pm. Closed Jan–Feb.

### WHERE TO STAY & EAT

**Baumanière, Les Baux de Provence ★★★** A combination luxury hotel and gourmet palace, this is the most magical resort in all of Provence. First there is the hotel complex, composed of five stunning Provençal manors, the most grand being **l'Oustal de la Baumanière,** which has hosted the likes of Queen Elizabeth and Johnny Depp. The complex is surrounded by enchanting grounds and features an organic garden and three swimming pools. Then there are the two restaurants, notably the Michelin-starred **Cabro d'Or,** which proposes high-end Provençal cuisine on a gorgeous outdoor terrace. Diners revel in dishes featuring Mediterranean langoustines, roasted red mullet, fresh pea velouté, and slow-cooked suckling pig.

Chemin départemental 27. www.oustaudebaumaniere.com. ✆ **04-90-54-33-07.** 56 units. Doubles 200€–630€, suites 380€–990€. Breakfast/half-board available. Cabro d'Or closed Jan–Feb. **Amenities:** Concierge; outdoor pools; 2 restaurants; tennis courts; free Wi-Fi.

**Le Mas d'Aigret ★★** Surrounded by olive trees and shady pines, this hotel is a 5-minute stroll from Les Baux. Guest rooms are simple yet elegant, and almost all of them have their own private terrace or balcony. Two rooms are built into Les Baux's rock face itself. An outdoor swimming pool is nestled into the hotel's rustic grounds. In winter, meals are served in the dining room/grotto with open fireplace; in summertime, the outdoor terrace overlooks Les Baux's valley and Château.

D27A. www.masdaigret.com. ✆ **04-90-54-20-00.** 16 units. Doubles 100€–215€, family room 180€–250€. Breakfast/half-board available. **Amenities:** Outdoor pool; restaurant; free Wi-Fi.

#### The Legendary Luberon

Made up of three massifs, long sloping mountains that make perfect backdrops for Impressionist paintings, the **Parc Naturel Régional du Luberon ★★★** (www.parcduluberon.fr), is the area that put Provence on the tourist map, especially after Peter Mayle let the world know about it in his book, *A Year In Provence.* Golden valleys, cobbled villages, and epic fields of lavender lay under a vivid blue sky and are bathed in brilliant light that no sunglasses can contend with. Mayles's hilltop hamlet, **Ménerbes ★,** became so famous that the author was forced to move away, but there are many other gem-like villages, like **Oppède le Vieux ★★, Bonnieux ★,** and **Gordes ★★,** not to mention the red and orange canyons of the "Little Colorado," near the town of **Roussillon ★★,** where ochre pigments are mined and celebrated. This is an ideal area for **hiking:** There are 7 major hiking paths (marked GR for *Grand Randonée*) that wind their way past craggy hills, tiny hamlets, and natural wonders. For more details, visit www.luberon-apt.fr and click on "on foot" on the "sports" pull-down menu. If **cycling** is your game, visit Vélo Loisir Provence and click on "Luberon" (www.veloloisirprovence.com; ✆ **04-90-76-48-05**); you'll find bike rentals, route maps, bike-friendly hotels, farm stays and much more.

## Arles ★★

On the banks of the Rhône River, Arles (pop. 53,000) is a heady mix of Provence and ancient Rome. Smack in the middle of its golden-toned historic center is a spectacular Roman amphitheater that is still used for bullfights, concerts, and other events. It was Julius Caesar who established a colony here in the 1st century, and the town evolved into the second Roman capital under Constantine the Great, when it was known as "the little Rome of the Gauls." In a later century, Arles was a favorite subject of painters, in particular Vincent van Gogh, who painted dozens of canvases during his 1-year stay. This is also where he famously chopped off part of his ear, the result of a psychotic episode.



### ESSENTIALS

Arles's **Office de Tourisme** website is www.arlestourisme.com.

**ARRIVING** There are direct **trains** from Avignon Centre train station (just outside the ramparts, not the TGV station) once every hour or two (trip time: 20 min.; 7.70€ one-way). For information and tickets, visit www.sncf-voyages.com or call **36-35** (.34€ per minute). If **driving,** head south from Avignon along D570.

### EXPLORING ARLES

The **Place du Forum ★,** shaded by plane trees, stands around the old Roman forum. The cafe that was immortalized by van Gogh has taken his name and is now the Café Van Gogh. Visitors keen to follow on in the

Place de la République, Arles.

### Les Taureaux

Bulls are a big part of Arlesien culture. It's not unusual to see bull steak on local menus, and *saucisson de taureau* (bull sausage) is a local specialty. The first bullfight, or *corrida,* took place in the amphitheater in 1853. Appropriately, Arles is home to a bullfighting school (the **Ecole Taurine d'Arles**). Like it or loathe it, *corridas* are still held during the two *ferias,* huge street festivals with a Spanish accent. At Easter, it's called the *Feria de Pâques* and in September, it's the *Feria du Riz.* The bull is killed only during the Easter *corrida;* expect a few protestors. A seat on the stone benches of the amphitheater costs 19€ to 97€. Tickets are usually available a few hours beforehand at the ticket office on **Les Arenes d'Arles** (1 rond-pont des Arènes). For information or advance tickets, go to www.arenes-arles.com or contact ✆ **08-91-70-03-70.**



footsteps of the artist may pick up a **van Gogh walking map** (1€) from the tourist office. Three blocks south, the **Place de la République** is dominated by a 15m-tall (49-ft.) Roman obelisk that once towered above a nearby stadium.

Emperor Augustus started work on the Roman **Théâtre Antique ★**, rue du Cloître (✆ **04-90-18-41-20**) in the 1st century; only two Corinthian columns remain. The theater is open May through September daily from 9am to 7pm; April and October daily from 9am to 6pm; and November through February daily from 10am to 5pm. Admission is 8€ adults, 6€ students, and free for children 17 and under. The same ticket admits you to the nearby **Amphitheater (Les Arènes) ★★**, rond-pont des Arènes (same phone number and opening hours), also built in the 1st century. Still in use, it seats almost 25,000. For a good view, climb the three towers that remain from medieval times, when the amphitheater was turned into a fortress.

**Fondation Vincent van Gogh Arles ★★** EXHIBITION SPACE This much-anticipated permanent home for the Van Gogh Foundation (founded more than 3 decades ago) opened at long last in 2014 in a 15th-century private mansion. Highlighting the connection between Arles and van Gogh, it stages a variety of temporary exhibitions, seminars, and interactive debates. Check the website for the current program.

35 ter rue du Docteur Fanton. www.fondation-vincentvangogh-arles.org. ✆ **04-90-93-08-08.** 9€ adults, 7€ seniors, 4€ students and children 12–18, free children 11 and under. Admission may vary depending on temporary exhibition. Daily 11am–7pm.

**Le Cloître et l'Église St-Trophime ★** CHURCH This church is noted for its 12th-century portal, one of the finest achievements of the southern Romanesque style. Frederick Barbarossa was crowned king of Arles here in 1178. In the pediment, Christ is surrounded by the symbols of the Evangelists. The pretty cloister, in Gothic and Romanesque styles, possesses noteworthy medieval carvings. During July's Les

Rencontres d'Arles festival, contemporary photographs are also exhibited here.

East side of place de la République. ✆ **04-90-18-41-20.** Free admission to church; cloister 4.50€ adults, 3.60€ students, free for children 17 and under. Church daily 10am–noon and 2–5pm; cloister May–Sept daily 9am–7pm; Mar, Apr, and Oct daily 9am–6pm; Nov–Feb daily 10am–5pm.

**Les Alyscamps** ★ RUINS This once-Roman necropolis became a Christian burial ground in the 4th century. Mentioned in Dante's *Inferno,* it has been painted by both van Gogh and Gauguin. Today it is lined with poplars and studded with ancient sarcophagi. Arlesiens escape here with a cold drink to enjoy a respite from the summer heat.

Avenue des Alyscamps. ✆ **04-90-18-41-20.** 3.50€ adults, 2.60€ students, free children 17 and under. May–Sept daily 9am–7pm; Mar, Apr, and Oct daily 9am–noon and 2–6pm; Nov–Feb daily 10am–noon and 2–5pm.



**Musée Départemental Arles Antiques** ★★ MUSEUM Set within a sleek compound about 1km (½ mile) south of Arles's town center, this archaeological museum hosts finds uncovered throughout the region's rich territories. Vast, airy rooms present Roman sarcophagi, sculptures, mosaics, and inscriptions from ancient times through the 6th century A.D. Temporary exhibitions highlight the inspiration the local landscape has had on the city through the ages. A special wing showcases the 31m (102-ft.) flat-bottomed Roman barge (*chaland*) that was unearthed from the Rhône River in 2010.

Avenue 1ere Division France Libre, presqu'île du Cirque Romain. www.arles-antique.cg13.fr. ✆ **04-13-31-51-03.** 8€ adults, 5€ seniors, free ages 17 and under. Wed–Mon 10am–6pm.

## A day out IN THE CAMARGUE

A marshy delta south of Arles, the Camargue is located between the Mediterranean and two arms of the Rhône. With the most fragile ecosystem in France, it has been a nature reserve since 1970. You cannot drive into the protected parts, and some areas are accessible only to the Gardians, the local cowboys.

Flora and fauna abound. Black bulls are bred in the Camargue both for their meat and for the regional bullfighting arenas. The region is also known for its wild horses, an ancient breed with a pale, often white coat that is the preferred mount of the gardians. The birdlife here is among the most luxuriant in Europe. Don't be surprised to see colonies of pink flamingos *(flamants roses),* which share living quarters with some 400 other bird species, including ibises, egrets, kingfishers, owls, wild ducks, swans, and ferocious birds of prey. The best place to see flamingo colonies is at the **Parc Ornithologique de Pont de Gau,** route d'Arles (www.parcornithologique.com; ✆ **04-90-97-82-62**).

For information on guided visits by boat, bike, jeep, or horse, visit Arles's tourist office or head to the one in Stes-Maries-de-la-Mer, at 5 av. Van Gogh (www.saintesmaries.com; ✆ **04-90-97-82-55**).

### WHERE TO STAY

**Hôtel Jules César ★★** A local landmark, this former 17th-century convent was recently entirely renovated, a project undertaken in collaboration with Arles born-and-bred designer Christian Lacroix. The hotel's rooms and suites have been thoroughly refreshed, with Lacroix focusing on rustic decor inspired by the nearby Camargue region. There's a pool on the grounds, as well as a spa and the top-notch Lou Marqués restaurant, which serves classic Provençal cuisine.

9 boulevard des Lices. www.hotel-julescesar.fr. ✆ **04-90-52-52-52.** 52 units. Doubles 179€–399€, suites 545€–749€. **Amenities:** Bar; concierge; gym; outdoor pool; restaurant; room service; spa; free Wi-Fi.

**Le Cloitre ★★** Perfectly positioned in Arles's Old Town, midway between Les Arènes and place de la République, Le Cloître is a unique medley of ancient stone features and funky 1950s furnishings. Each room is individually decorated in bright tones, with wooden ceiling beams, mosaic floors, and designer knickknacks. Free bikes are available for guest use. Organic breakfast is served up on the rooftop terrace.

18 rue du Cloître. www.hotel-cloitre.com. ✆ **04-88-09-10-00.** 19 units. Doubles 96€–185€. **Amenities:** Bar; laundry service; free Wi-Fi.

### WHERE TO EAT

**Cuisine de Comptoir ★** FRENCH This superb little lunch spot is tucked just off Place du Forum in an ancient boulangerie. Each day, the owners dish up a dozen different *tartines,* or open-faced sandwiches, created using toasted Poilâne bread. Both smoked duck breast with Cantal cheese and the *brandade* (creamy cod and potato) *tartines* are highly recommended.

10 rue de la Liberté. www.cuisinedecomptoir.com. ✆ **04-90-96-86-28.** Mains 11€–13€; fixed-price lunch 15€. Mon–Sat 8:30am–2pm and 7–9pm.

**L'Atelier Jean-Luc Rabanel ★★★** MODERN PROVENÇAL One of the best restaurants in southern France. Mega-chef Rabanel pairs organic ingredients from his own garden with locally reared bull, pork, and game (and even herbs, mushrooms, and flowers). Asia meets Paris on the elegant plates that are set before you; the wine list offers a passionate oenophile's tour of France. The chef also oversees two adjoining restaurants. The **Bistro Acote** (www.bistro-acote.com; ✆ **04-90-47-61-13**) is softer on the wallet and serves Provençal classics on a 29€ set menu; and **Iode** (www.iode-rabanel.com; ✆ **04-90-91-07-69**) specializes in "hyper-fresh" crustaceans and shellfish.

7 rue des Carmes. www.rabanel.com. ✆ **04-90-91-07-69.** Fixed-price lunch 65€; fixed-price dinner 125€. Wed–Sun noon–1:30pm and 8pm–9pm.

## Aix-en-Provence ★★

You may have heard that Aix is a sleepy provincial burg filled with flowers and fountains, but it also a bustling university town of nearly 143,000 inhabitants (the Université d'Aix dates from 1413). It is this combination of laid back southern style and youthful energy that gives Aix its unique charm.

Founded in 122 B.C. by Roman general Caius Sextius Calvinus, Aix started life as a military outpost, but by the Middle Ages it was the capital of Provence. Aix's most celebrated son, Paul Cézanne, immortalized the surrounding countryside in his paintings, in particular the Montagne Ste-Victoire, which still provides the town a glorious backdrop.

As its hip boutiques attest to, Aix has taken on a decidedly more bourgeois air since Cézanne's time, but there are still plenty of decades-old, family-run shops on its narrow streets. A lazy summer lunch or early evening aperitif at one of the cafes on the cours Mirabeau is an experience not to be missed.

## ESSENTIALS

Aix's **Office de Tourisme** website is www.aixenprovencetourism.com.

**ARRIVING** Direct **trains** arrive frequently from Marseille (trip time: 40 min.; 8€ one-way). High-speed trains—from Paris as well as Marseille and Nice—arrive at the TGV station, 18km (11 miles) west of Aix. Bus transfers to the center of Aix cost 4.10€ one-way. There are **buses** from Marseille, Avignon, and Nice; for information, see www.lepilote.com or call ✆ **08-10-00-13-26.** If you're **driving** to Aix from Avignon or other points north, take A7 south to A8 and follow the signs into town. From Marseille, take A51 north.

A market in Aix-en-Provence.

**SPECIAL EVENTS** The renowned **Festival d'Aix** (www.festival-aix.com; ✆ **08-20-92-29-23**, 0.12€ per min.), held the first 3 weeks of July, offers music and opera from all over the world. Held 2 weeks over the Easter holidays, **Festival de Pâques** (www.festivalpaques.com; ✆ **08-20-13-20-13**) is a classical music extravaganza featuring international stars.

## EXPLORING AIX-EN-PROVENCE

The magnificent **cours Mirabeau ★,** Aix's main street, is lined with a double row of plane trees shading it from the Provençal sun. Shops and sidewalk cafes line one side; 17th- and 18th-century *hôtels particuliers* (private mansions) take up the other. Stop into the grand old **Brasserie Les Deux Garçons,** 53 cours Mirabeau, for a coffee or a glass of rosé.

Boulevard Carnot and cours Sextius circle the heart of the **old quarter**, which is mostly a pedestrian zone. The city was built atop thermal springs, and 40 fountains still bubble away in picturesque squares around town.

If you're not up for walking, flag down a **Diabline** (www.la-diabline.fr; Mon–Sat 8:30am–7:30pm; 0.50€/ride), an electric shuttle bus that operate three routes along cours Mirabeau and through most of the Old Town.

**Atelier de Cézanne ★★** MUSEUM A 10-minute (uphill) stroll north from the town center brings you to Cézanne's studio, where visitors enjoy a glimpse into his daily life. Virtually untouched since the artist's death in 1906, the studio has remained perfectly preserved for close to a century. Note the furnishings, vases, and small figurines on display, all of which feature in Cézanne's drawings and canvases. From April to September, there are guided tours in English at 5pm, and from October to March at 4pm.

9 av. Paul-Cézanne. www.atelier-cezanne.com. ✆ **04-42-21-06-53.** 6€ adults, 2.50€ students and children 13–25, free for children 12 and under. July–Aug daily 10am–6pm; Apr–June and Sept daily 10am–noon and 2–6pm; Oct–Feb Mon–Sat 10am–noon and 2–5pm; Mar daily 10am–noon and 2–5pm.

**Musée Granet ★★** MUSEUM One of the South of France's top art venues, this popular museum displays a permanent collection of paintings and sculpture ranging from 15th-century French canvases to 20th-century Giacometti sculptures. However, it's the large-scale temporary exhibitions that truly impress, such as 2015's "American Icons."

Place Saint Jean de Malte. www.museegranet-aixenprovence.fr. ✆ **04-42-52-88-32.** Permanent collection: 5€ adults, free students under 26 and all under 18. Additional fee for temporary exhibitions. Tues–Sun mid-July to mid-Oct 10am–7pm; mid-Oct to mid-July noon–6pm.

## ORGANIZED TOURS

Aix's Tourist Office organizes a bilingual **tour of the historic city center** (✆ **04-42-16-11-61**; Jan–Mar Sat 10am, Apr–Oct Tues and Sat

10am; 2 hr.; 9€ adults; 5€ seniors, students, and ages 7–25; free under 7), and **"In the Steps of Cézanne"** (Apr–Oct Thurs 10am; 2 hr.; 9€ adults, free under 7).

## WHERE TO STAY

**Hôtel Cézanne ★★** This super-chic—and friendly—boutique hotel is for guests seeking an unusual spot to snooze. Conceived by one of the designers of the sophisticated *hotel particulier* **28 à Aix** (www.28-a-aix.com), the Cézanne is a mélange of colorful decor and hip designer touches. Baroque furnishings, unique artworks, and a beautiful terrace all add to the atmosphere. The hotel's location—midway between the train station and Aix's Old Town—makes it ideal for visitors planning day trips farther afield.

40 av. Victor Hugo. www.hotelaix.com. ✆ **04-42-91-11-11.** 55 units. Doubles 150€–260€, suites 170€–460€. **Amenities:** Bar; concierge, gym, massage; free Wi-Fi.

**Hôtel du Globe ★★** A terrific location enhances this budget option, where clean, comfy (if small) rooms are complemented by a lovely rooftop terrace. The rooms were recently renovated in crisp shades of white and grey. Light sleepers should ask for a room that does not face the busy street.

74 cours Sextius. www.hotelduglobe.com. ✆ **04-42-26-03-58.** 46 units. Doubles 69€–93€. Closed mid-Dec to mid-Jan. **Amenities:** Free Wi-Fi.

## WHERE TO EAT

**La Fromagerie du Passage ★★** FRENCH Duck through the tiny entrance to Passage Agard and then follow the sounds of bells and farm animals. It's here that the cheery La Fromagerie—part wine and cheese shop, part restaurant—is dedicated to all things cheese-related. Order from the menu or just enjoy a mixed cheese platter paired with local wines (18€–25€) on the rooftop terrace. At night there is a tapas menu (8€–28€); during the day you can also grab a sandwich.

Passage Agard, 55 cours Mirabeau. www.lafromageriedupassage.fr. ✆ **04-42-22-90-00.** Mains 16€–21€. Fixed-price lunch 20€–25€. Mon–Sat noon–3pm and 6–11pm, Sun brunch 10am–3pm.

**Le Mille Feuille ★★** PROVENÇAL Nestled into a quiet corner of Aix's Old Town, this excellent eatery stands out against the often-average local dining scene. The market-fresh menu changes daily but may include yellow and green zucchini crumble with cœur de bœuf tomatoes, Sisteron lamb atop wild mushrooms and sautéed potatoes, or a delectable vanilla bourbon millefeuille pastry. You can dine either on the small outdoor terrace or indoors, but you should reserve ahead, especially for dinner.

8 rue Rifle-Rafle. www.le-millefeuille.fr. ✆ **04-42-96-55-17.** Mains 15€; fixed-price lunch 26€–31€, dinner 37€–43€. Wed–Sat noon–2pm and 8–9:30pm. Closed last week of Aug.

## SHOPPING

Opened more than a century ago, **Béchard** (12 cours Mirabeau; **✆ 04-42-26-06-78**), specializes in the famous *Calissons d'Aix,* a candy made from ground almonds, preserved melon, and fruit syrup. **Chocolaterie de Puryicard,** 7 rue Rifle-Rafle (www.puyricard.fr; **✆ 04-42-21-13-26**), creates sensational chocolates filled with candied figs, walnuts, or local lavender honey. **Santons Fouque,** 65 cours Gambetta (www.santons-fouque.com; **✆ 04-42-26-33-38**), stocks close to 2,000 traditional *santons* (crèche figurines). Copper pots and pocket knives by famous French forgers such as Laguiole are on offer at **Quincaillerie Centrale,** 21 rue de Monclar (**✆ 04-42-23-33-18**), a hardware/housewares store that's been offering a little bit of everything since 1959.

## ENTERTAINMENT & NIGHTLIFE

**Au P'tit Quart d'Heure,** a wine bar at 21 place Forum de Cardeurs (www.auptitquartdheure.fr), and the bar next door **La Curieuse,** 23 place Forum des Cardeurs (**✆ 06-06-66-77-01**), are two of the city's liveliest spots to stop for an evening aperitif. **La Rotonde,** 2A place Jeanne d'Arc (www.larotonde-aix.com; **✆ 04-28-31-06-62**), is a bar, cafe, and hangout.

# Marseille ★★

Founded by the Greeks in the 6th century B.C., Marseille is France's oldest metropolis. Today it's the second-largest city in France, as well as one of its most ethnically diverse, with nearly 1.5 million inhabitants. Many associate Marseille with a seedy scruffiness, but its racy reputation is quickly becoming a thing of the past, especially since 2013, when Marseille was crowned **European Capital of Culture**. The city used the opportunity to show off its vivid southern soul, opened a flurry of new cultural venues and museums, and finished up projects like the renovation of the old docklands west of the Vieux Port. From the cafes and vintage shops that pepper Le Panier's backstreets to the new boutiques that are flinging open their doors, it's evident that France's second city has come of age.

## ESSENTIALS

Marseille's **Office de Tourisme** website is www.marseille-tourisme.com.

**ARRIVING** **Marseille-Provence Airport** (www.marseille-airport.com; **✆ 08-20-81-14-14;** 0.12€ per min.), is 27km (17 miles) northwest of the city center. Shuttle buses from the airport (www.navettemarseilleaeroport.com; **✆ 08-92-70-08-40**, 0.34€ min.) arrive at Marseille's St-Charles rail station, near the Vieux-Port (8.20€; daily every 20 min. from 5am–midnight; the trip takes 25 min.).

There is regular **train** service to and from major European cities; dozens of TGV high-speed trains link the city with Paris every day (trip time: 3 hr., 20 min.; 40€–125€ one-way). **Buses** leave from the main station (**Gare Routière,** rue Honnorat; www.rtm.fr; ✆ **04-91-08-16-40**); there are several daily runs between Aix-en-Provence and Marseille (trip time: 40 min.; 5.70€ one-way, for schedule visit www.navetteaixmarseille.com). If you're **driving** from Paris, follow A6 south to Lyon, and then continue south along A7 to Marseille. The drive takes about 8 hours. From Provence, take A7 south.



**CITY LAYOUT** Marseille is a large, sprawling metropolis. If you're keen to explore different parts of the city, you'll probably need to take advantage of its public transport.



**SPECIAL EVENTS** The **Festival de Marseille** (www.festivaldemarseille.com), a citywide celebration of music, dance, and arts, is held from mid-June to mid-July. But Marseille's most popular music festival since its inception in 1992 is **Fiesta des Suds** (www.dock-des-suds.org). Held annually in late October, it features prominent South American and African bands.

## GETTING AROUND

Each of Marseille's neighborhoods is easily navigable **on foot.** However, unless you're an avid walker, you may want to rely on either the Métro or the tramway to zip you around town. **Parking and car safety** are so problematic that it's best to park in a garage and rely on public transport. Visit **www.parking-public.fr** for public parking lots and fees.

There are two **Métro** lines, as well as a tram that services the Canabière and the refurbished Joliette Docks district before continuing out to the suburbs. Individual tickets are 1.50€; they're valid on Métro, tram, and bus lines for up to 60 minutes after purchase. If you plan to use a lot of public transport, buy a **Pass XL,** valid for 1 day for 5.20€ or 3 days for 10.80€ (or consider the Marseille City Pass, see box below). For more information, visit the city transit authority site: www.rtm.fr.

Finally, if you need a taxi, contact **Taxis Radio Marseille** (www.taximarseille.com; ✆ **04-91-02-20-20**).

**THE NEIGHBORHOODS IN BRIEF** The major arteries divide Marseille into 16 *arrondissements.* Visitors tend to spend most of their time in four main neighborhoods. The first is the **Vieux Port,** the atmospheric natural harbor

### Marseille City Pass

The **Marseille City Pass** covers all public transport, including the round-trip ferry trip to **Château d'If** ★★ (p. 174) as well as entrance to more than a dozen of the city's museums and a ride on the ***petit-train*** (p. 175) up to the **Basilique Notre-Dame-de-la-Garde** ★ (p. 174). A 1-day pass is 24€; 2-day, 31€; and 3-day, 39€). Passes can be purchased at the tourist office or via their website (www.rtm.fr).

point for the city center. From here, the wide La Canebière Boulevard runs eastward, bisected by Marseille's most popular shopping avenues. To the north lies **Le Panier,** the oldest part of the city, crisscrossed by a pastel network of undulating alleyways. This neighborhood's western edge is trimmed by former docklands ("Les Docks"), which have been completely redeveloped over the past few years. Southeast of the Vieux Port, the alternative neighborhood around **cours Julien** is home to convivial restaurants and one-off boutiques aplenty. And come summertime, action shifts to the **Plages du Prado,** a strip of beaches due south of the city center.



## EXPLORING MARSEILLE

Immerse yourself in local life with a wander through Marseille's busy streets, including along the famous **La Canebière.** Lined with hotels, shops, and restaurants, it used to be a very seedy street, but with Marseille's ongoing urban regeneration it has become the heart and soul of the city.

La Canebière joins the **Vieux Port ★★,** dominated at its western end by the massive neoclassical forts of St-Jean and St-Nicolas. The harbor is filled with fishing craft and yachts and ringed by seafood restaurants. For a panoramic view, head to the **Jardin du Pharo,** a promontory facing the entrance to the Vieux-Port. From the terrace of the Château du Pharo, built by Napoléon III, you can clearly see the city's old and new cathedrals, as well as the recently redeveloped docklands, now the **Cité de la Méditerranée,** which includes **Fort Saint-Jean** and the stunning new **MuCEM (Museum of European and Mediterranean Civilizations ★★;** facing page).

Vieux Port with Notre-Dame-de-la-Garde in the distance, Marseilles.

North of the old port is **Le Panier,** Marseille's Old Town. Small boutiques and designer ateliers now populate these once-sketchy streets. To the south, the **corniche Président-J.-F.-Kennedy** is a 4km (2½-mile) promenade. You'll pass villas and gardens facing the Mediterranean, before reaching the popular **Plages du Prado.** These spacious, sandy beaches have children's playgrounds, sun-loungers, and waterside cafes. Serious hikers can continue south of here into the **Parc National des Calanques** ★★★ (www.calanques-parcnational.fr), France's newest national park. This series of stunning limestone cliffs, fjords, and rocky promontories stretches along the coast for 20km (12 miles) southeast of Marseille; the **Calanque d'En Vau** in particular is well worth seeking out.

**Basilique Notre-Dame-de-la-Garde** ★ CHURCH This landmark church crowns a limestone rock overlooking the southern side of the Vieux-Port. It was built in the Romanesque-Byzantine style popular in the 19th century and topped by a 9.7m (32-ft.) gilded statue of the Virgin. Visitors come for the views (best at sunset) from its terrace. Spread out before you are the city, the islands, and the shimmering sea.
Rue Fort-du-Sanctuaire. www.notredamedelagarde.com. ✆ **04-91-13-40-80.** Free. Métro: Estrangin-Préfecture. Bus: 60. Daily Apr–Sept 7am–7:15pm, Oct–Mar to 6:15pm.

**MuCEM (Museum of European and Mediterranean Civilizations)** ★★ MUSEUM Opened in 2013, this museum's outside, encased in a unique concrete lace, has created almost as much of a stir as what's inside. More than 250,000 objects from throughout the Mediterranean region are exhibited here, along with local prints, photographs, and historical postcards. The permanent collection is superbly displayed, mixing objects and artworks with video diaries, commissioned cartoons, and enchanting photographs from around the Mediterranean. The premises are linked to the 17th-century **Fort Saint-Jean** and its suspended gardens via a panoramic elevated walkway.
1 esplanade du J4. www.mucem.org. ✆ **04-84-35-13-13.** 8€ adults, 5€ ages 18–25 and over 65, free children 17 and under. Additional fee for temporary exhibitions. Métro: Vieux-Port. Bus: 49 or 82. May–June and Sept–Oct daily 11am–7pm (Fri to 10pm); Nov–Apr Wed–Mon 11am–6pm, July–Aug daily 9am–8pm (Fri to 10pm).

**Musée Cantini** ★ ART MUSEUM This 17th-century *hôtel particulier* (private mansion) is the home of one of the largest collections of early-20th-century art in France. Surrealism is one of the major themes here, along with art produced in the city of Marseille. The works of artists like André Breton, Max Ernst, and Joan Miró are complimented by the art of Picasso, Dufy, Matisse, Giacometti, and others, as well as a strong photography section.
19 rue Grignan. www.marseille.fr. ✆ **04-91-54-77-75.** 5€ adults, 3€ students and seniors, free for children 17 and under. Métro: Estrangin/Préfecture. Bus: 18, 21, 41S, 54, or 221. Tues–Sun 10am–6pm.

## OUTLYING ATTRACTIONS

A 25-minute ferry ride takes you to the **Château d'If** ★★ (www.if.monuments-nationaux.fr), a fortress built by King François I to defend Marseille. Alexandre Dumas used it as a setting for the fictional adventures of *The Count of Monte Cristo*. The château is open daily May 16 to September 16 9:30am to 6:10pm; September 17 to March 31 Tuesday to Sunday 9:30am to 4:45pm; and April 1 to May 31 daily 9:30am to 4:45pm. Entrance to the island is 5.50€ adults, free for children 17 and under. Boats leave approximately every 45 to 60 minutes, depending on the season; the round-trip transfer is 10.50€. For information, contact the **Frioul If Express** (www.frioul-if-express.com; ✆ **04-96-11-03-50;** Métro: Vieux-Port).

## ORGANIZED TOURS

One of the easiest ways to see Marseille's centrally located monuments is aboard the fleet of open-top **L'Open Tour Buses** (www.marseille.opentour.com; ✆ **04-91-91-05-82;** Métro: Vieux-Port). You can hop off or on at any of 13 different stops on the route. A 1-day pass costs 19€ adults; the fare for children ages 4 to 11 is 8€. Two-day passes are also available for just a few euros more.

The motorized **Trains Touristiques de Marseille** (www.petit-train-marseille.com; ✆ **04-91-25-24-69;** Métro: Vieux-Port), or *petit-trains,* make circuits around town. Year-round, train no. 1 makes a 75-minute grand tour of the city center; from April to mid-November, train no. 2 makes a 65-minute round-trip of old Marseille. The fare for train no. 1 is 8€ adults and 4€ children; train no. 2 is 1€ less for both.

There are boat tours to the **Parc National des Calanques;** tour operators with various packages (example, six Calanques in 2 hr./23€; www.croisieres-marseille-calanques.com) cluster at quai des Belges at the Vieux-Port.

## WHERE TO STAY

**C2 Hotel ★★★** Twenty luxurious, light-filled rooms spill over a 19th-century merchant family mansion, each one decked out in exposed brick walls and designer furnishings. Some have a private hammam steam bath. There's a spa with indoor pool and Jacuzzi, as well as a cocktail bar. But the real thrill is the hotel's beach, located on a private island, Île Degaby.

48 rue Roux de Brignoles. www.c2-hotel.com. ✆ **04-95-05-13-13.** 20 units. Doubles 189€–469€. Métro: Estrangin-Préfecture. **Amenities:** Bar; private beach; concierge; spa; free Wi-Fi.

**Casa Honoré ★** Interior designer Annick Lestrohan has transformed this former print shop into an ultra-stylish bed-and-breakfast. Guest rooms are decorated with Lestrohan's exquisite creations, from sleek designer furnishings to quality linens (and all are for sale too). An oasis of tranquility just south of Marseille's Vieux Port, the four rooms all center on a courtyard with a small swimming pool. Book far in advance.

123 rue Sainte. www.casahonore.com. ✆ **04-96-11-01-62.** 4 units. Doubles 150€–200€, includes breakfast. Minimum 2-night stay. No credit cards. Métro: Vieux-Port. **Amenities:** Outdoor pool; free Wi-Fi.

### WHERE TO EAT

**La Table du Môle ★★★** MODERN MEDITERRANEAN This chic bistro lies atop the **MuCEM ★★** (p. 174). Stellar dishes herald from across the Mediterranean, including seafood tart served with a creamy ginger jus, crab paired with spicy harissa, or grilled turbot with truffled potatoes. All are served against a sweeping backdrop of Marseille's port and the Mediterranean Sea. Note the lower-key (and cheaper) sister restaurant, **La Cuisine ★★★** (lunch only), located in the adjacent dining room—no sea views however. The fabulous two-course buffet here is a steal at just 22€.

MuCEM, 1 esplanade du J4. www.passedat.fr. No phone. Reservations required, via internet only. Mains 38€; fixed-price lunch 52€; fixed-price dinner 73€. Métro: Vieux-Port. Bus: 49, 60, or 82. Wed–Mon 12:30–3pm; Wed–Sat and Mon 7:30–10:30pm.

**Le Grain du Sel ★★** MODERN MEDITERRANEAN Marseille-born chef Pierre Giannetti concocts the city's most creative bistro cuisine. Following morning market finds, the daily menu may include Sardinian gnocchi with clams, mussel *escabèche,* or Spanish rice with shellfish harvested from the Camargue seaside town of Saintes-Maries-de-la-Mer. You can dine outside on sunny days in the petite courtyard.

39 rue de la Paix Marcel Paul. ✆ **04-91-54-47-30**. Mains 13€–28€; fixed-price lunch 22€–26€. Métro: Vieux-Port. Tues–Sat noon–2pm, Fri–Sat 8–10pm. Closed Aug.

**L'Epuisette ★★** SEAFOOD/MEDITERRANEAN This is *the* place to sample **bouillabaisse** stew. Pack your appetite: Fresh fish is poached in saffron-infused soup; the final product is served as two separate courses, accompanied by *rouille,* a mayonnaise-like sauce flavored with garlic, cayenne pepper, and saffron. L'Epuisette's setting is as sublime as the cuisine: The seaside dining room overlooks Château d'If from the picturesque fishing port of Vallon des Auffes, 2.5km (1½ miles) south of Marseille's Vieux Port. Reserve ahead.

Vallon des Auffes. www.l-epuisette.fr. ✆ **04-91-52-17-82.** Mains 45€–58€; fixed-price dinner 70€–145€. Bus: 83. Tues–Sat noon–1:30pm and 7:30–9:30pm. Closed Aug.

### SHOPPING

The streets just southeast of the **Vieux-Port** are crowded with stores of all kinds; **Rue Paradis** and **rue Saint Ferréol** have many of the same upscale fashion boutiques found in Paris. For more bohemian wear, try **cours Julien** and **rue de la Tour** for richly brocaded and beaded items on offer in North African boutiques. **Le Panier** is now home to a vibrant range of unique boutiques. Try **5.7.2,** 23 rue du Panier (www.5-7-2.com; ✆ **06-07-14-62-92**) for 1930s to 1970s homewares, or **Les Baigneuses,** 3 rue de l'Eveche (www.lesbaigneuses.com; ✆ **09-52-68-67-64**), which sells a gorgeous range of designer swimwear.

*Navettes,* small cookies that resemble boats, are a Marseillaise specialty; the best are at **Le Four des Navettes,** 136 rue Sainte (www.fourdesnavettes.com; ✆ **04-91-33-32-12**) and **Navettes des Accoules,** 68 rue Caisserie (✆ **04-91-90-99-42**).

One of the region's most authentic fish markets at **Quai de la Fraternité** (daily 8am–1pm), on the old port. On **cours Julien,** you'll find a market with fruits, vegetables, and other foods (Mon, Tues, Fri, Sat 8am–1pm); exclusively organic produce (Wed 8am–1pm); stamps (Sun 8am–1pm); and secondhand goods (third Sun of the month 8am–1pm).

### ENTERTAINMENT & NIGHTLIFE

For an amusing and relatively harmless exposure to the town's saltiness, walk around the **Vieux-Port,** where cafes and restaurants angle their sightlines for the best view of the harbor.

**L'Escale Borély,** avenue Pierre Mendès France, is 20 minutes south of the town center (take bus no. 83). With a dozen animated bars and cafes, plus restaurants of every possible ethnicity, you'll be spoiled for choice.

Marseille's dance clubs are habitually packed out, especially **Trolley Bus,** 24 quai de Rive-Neuve (✆ **04-91-54-30-45**; Métro: Vieux-Port), known for techno, house, hip-hop, jazz, and salsa. Equally buzzing is **l'Exit,** 12 quai de Rive-Neuve (✆ **06-42-59-96-24;** Métro: Vieux-Port), a bar/disco with a terrace that profits from Marseille's sultry nights and two floors of seething nocturnal energy (happy hour starts at 5pm and runs all night on Thurs). The **New Can Can,** 3-7 rue Sénac (www.newcancan.com; ✆ **04-91-48-59-76;** Métro: Noailles), is a lively, sprawling bar and disco that identifies itself as a gay venue but attracts many straight folks, too. It's open Friday through Sunday midnight until 7am.

## THE FRENCH RIVIERA

The fabled real estate known as the French Riviera, also called the Côte d'Azur (Azure Coast), ribbons for 200km (125 miles) along the sun-kissed Mediterranean. The region has long attracted artists and jetsetters alike with its clear skies, blue waters, and carefree cafe culture. Chic, sassy, and incredibly sexy, the Riviera can be explored by bus, train, boat, bikes, Segway, electric car, or in a dozen novel ways.

Modern artists captivated by the region's light and setting have left a rich heritage: Matisse at Vence, Cocteau at Villefranche, Léger at Biot, Renoir at Cagnes, and Picasso at Antibes and seemingly everywhere else.

A century ago, winter and spring were considered high season on the Riviera. In recent decades, July and August have become the most crowded months, and reservations are imperative. The region basks in more than 300 days of sun per year, and even December and January are often clement and bright.

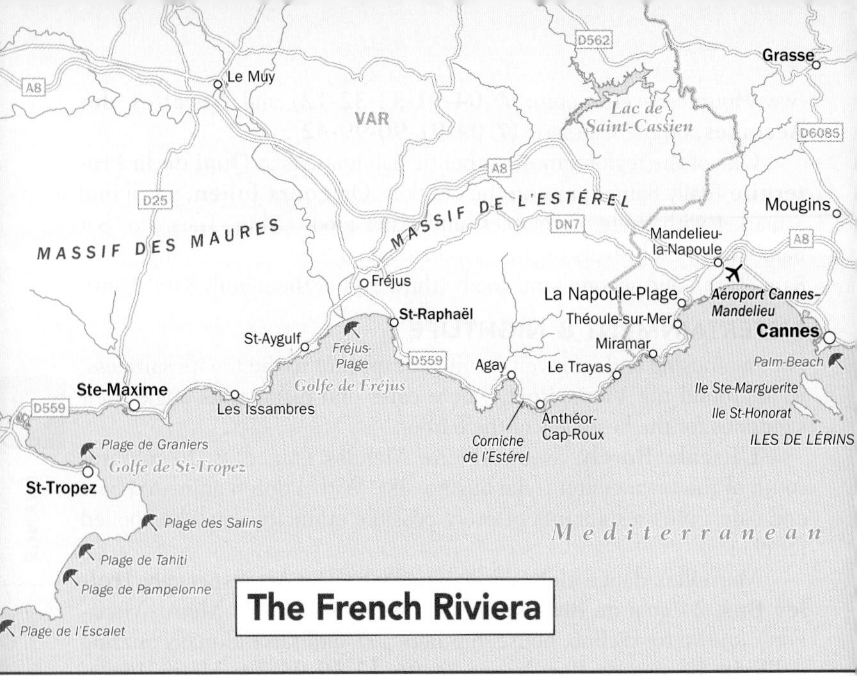


The ribbonlike corniche roads stretch across the western Riviera from Nice to Menton. The lower road, the 32km (20-mile) Corniche Inférieure, rolls past Villefranche, Cap-Ferrat, Beaulieu, Monaco, and Cap-Martin. The 31km (19-mile) Moyenne Corniche (Middle Road) winds in and out of mountain tunnels and past the cliff top village of Eze. La Turbie is the principal town along the 32km (20-mile) stretch, which reaches more than 480m (1,574 ft.) high at Col d'Eze.

## St-Tropez ★★★

Known for sun, glamour, and Brigitte Bardot, this golden-hued Shangri-La can actually be blissfully understated off-season. In the summer, St-Tropez attracts artists, musicians, models, writers, and movie stars, trailing a flamboyant parade of humanity in its wake. But in winter it morphs back into a boho fishing village, albeit one with modern art galleries and terrific restaurants.

### ESSENTIALS

St-Tropez's **Office de Tourisme** website is www.ot-saint-tropez.com.

**ARRIVING** The nearest rail station is in St-Raphaël, a neighboring coastal resort. From its Vieux Port, you can take a **boat** (www.bateaux-saintraphael.com; ✆ **04-94-95-17-46**) for St-Tropez (trip time: 1 hr.). The one-way fare is 15€. Year-round, 10 to 15 Varlib **buses** per day leave from the Gare Routière in St-Raphaël (www.varlib.fr; ✆ **04-94-24-60-00**) for St-Tropez. The trip takes 1½ to 2 hours, depending on the bus and the traffic, which during midsummer is usually horrendous. A

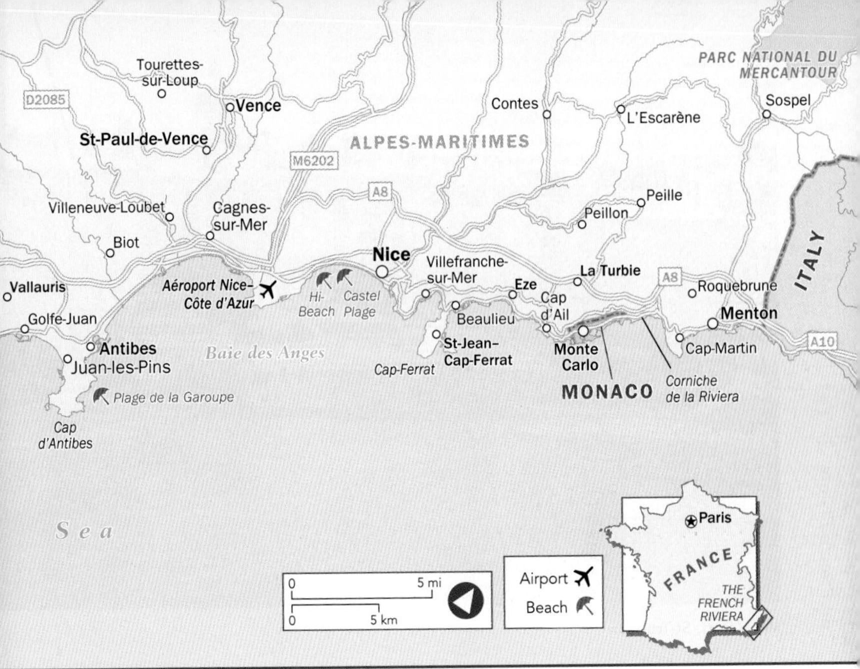


one-way ticket is 3€. Buses also run from Toulon train station 56km (35 miles) away.

If you **drive,** note that parking in St-Tropez is tricky, especially in summer. For parking, follow the signs for **Parking des Lices** beneath place des Lices, or **Parking du Nouveau Port,** on waterfront avenue Charles de Gaulle. To get here from **Cannes,** drive southwest along the coastal highway (D559), turning east when you see signs to St-Tropez.

## EXPLORING ST-TROPEZ

In the summer, and especially in the evenings, the port is filled with superyachts berthing after a day of hedonistic excess at nearby Plage de Pampelonne. Yacht owners, their lucky guests, spectators, and celebrity-seekers intermingle along the town's chic quays.

In the Old Town, one of the most interesting streets is **rue de la Miséricorde.** It's lined with stone houses that hold boutiques and evoke medieval St-Tropez. At the corner of rue Gambetta is **Chapelle de la Miséricorde,** with a blue, green, and gold tile roof. Towering above town is the **Citadelle** (✆ **04-94-97-59-43**), a fortified castle complete with drawbridges and stunning views across the Bay of St-Tropez. Inside, the **Maritime Museum** ★ charts famous local historical figures and their travels around the world, including Admiral Suffren, who whupped the British several times during the War of American Independence. From April to September, the entire complex is open daily from 10am to 6:30pm; October through March from 10am to 5:30pm. Admission is 3€; entrance is free for those 11 and under.

Vieux Port, St-Tropez.

**Musée de l'Annonciade** ★★★ MUSEUM Set in a 16th-century chapel just off the harbor, this small museum showcases a collection of superb post-Impressionist paintings (1890–1950). Many of the artists, including St-Tropez's adopted son, Paul Signac, painted the port of St-Tropez, a backdrop that lies right outside the building. The museum includes such masterpieces as Bonnard's *Nu devant la Cheminée* as well as artworks by Matisse, Braque, Dufy, Marquet, and Derain.
2 rue de l'Annonciade, place Grammont. www.saint-tropez.fr. ✆ **04-94-17-84-10.** 6€ adults, 4€ children 11 and under. Wed–Mon 10am–1pm and 2–6pm. Closed Nov.

## OUTDOOR ACTIVITIES

**BEACHES** The hottest Riviera beaches are at St-Tropez. The best for families are closest to the center, including **Plage de la Bouillabaisse, Plage des Graniers,** and **Plage des Salins.** More daring is the 5km (3-mile) crescent of **Plage de Pampelonne,** about 10km (6¼ miles) from St-Tropez. Here, about 35 hedonistic beach clubs dot the sand. Overtly decadent is **Club 55** (www.club55.fr; ✆ **04-94-55-55-55**), a former Brigitte Bardot hangout, while the American-run **Nikki Beach** (www.nikkibeach.com; ✆ **04-94-79-82-04**) is younger and more understated, if painfully chic. Gay-friendly **Aqua Club** (✆ **04-94-79-84-35**) and bare-all **Plage de Tahiti** (www.tahiti-beach.com; ✆ **04-94-97-18-02**) are extremely welcoming.

You'll need a car, bike, or scooter to get from town to Plage de Pampelonne. Parking is around 10€ for the day. More than anywhere else on the Riviera, topless bathing is the norm.

## WHERE TO STAY

**Hôtel Byblos ★★★** Opened in 1967 on a hill above the harbor, this hamlet of pastel-hued, Provençal-style houses is opulence personified. Favored by visiting celebrities, rock stars, aristocrats, and the über-rich, its patios and private spaces are splashed with antiques, rare objects, bubbling fountains, and ancient olive trees. Rooms range in size from medium to mega; views take in the pool, the garden, or the village. Other perks include a boat-shuttle to Pampelonne and yacht rental. **Rivea** (✆ **04-94-56-68-20**), the hotel's superb restaurant, offers tapas-style sharing dishes, with ingredients sourced exclusively from the French and Italian Rivieras.

20 av. Paul Signac. www.byblos.com. ✆ **04-94-56-68-00.** 96 units. Doubles 440€–1,225€, suites 875€–3,070€. Closed Nov to mid-Apr. **Amenities:** 2 restaurants; 1 bar; nightclub; babysitting; concierge; gym; massage; outdoor pool; room service; sauna; spa; free Wi-Fi.

**Hôtel Les Palmiers ★** In a town packed with pricey accommodation options, this friendly, family-run hotel is a real find. Apart from its fantastic location—on the place des Lices in the center of St-Tropez—the hotel boasts compact Provençal-style rooms and a sun-dappled courtyard garden.

34 bd. Vasserot (place des Lices). www.hotel-les-palmiers.com. ✆ **04-94-97-01-61.** 25 units. Doubles 87€–280€. **Amenities:** Bar; free Wi-Fi.

**Pastis Hôtel-St-Tropez ★★** This portside Provençal house feels more like a sophisticated, eclectic home than a hotel—albeit one decorated with a phenomenal eye for design. The owners have arranged their private collection of Matisse prints, vintage photographs, 1970s framed album artwork, and Provençal antiques in and around the guest-only lounge and inspired guest rooms surrounding the courtyard swimming pool.

75 av. du Général Leclerc. www.pastis-st-tropez.com. ✆ **04-98-12-56-50.** 10 units. Doubles 225€–750€. Closed Dec–Jan. **Amenities:** Bar; outdoor pool; free Wi-Fi.

## WHERE TO EAT

St-Tropez's dining scene is both expensive and exclusive—particularly during the summer season. Reserve well in advance; alternatively, be prepared to dine very early or very late.

**L'Aventure ★** MODERN PROVENÇAL A backstreet St-Tropez eatery beloved of locals and visitors alike, L'Aventure serves globally inspired market-fresh cuisine: Think snails, Provençal lamb, and harbor-fresh fish alternately laced with pesto, honey, and ginger. It's blessedly unpretentious, right down to the authentically battered tables on the petite terrace.

4 rue du Portail-Neuf. ✆ **04-94-97-44-01.** Mains 21€–34€. Tues–Sun 7:30–10pm. Closed Dec–Easter.

**Pizzeria Bruno** ★ ITALIAN Proving that not all good meals in St-Tropez have to break the bank, this casual joint has been turning out thin, crispy, wood-fired pizzas since 1959. The menu includes a handful of creative salads, pasta dishes, and grilled meats. Note that the restaurant's copious wood-paneled and overly snug seating isn't the comfiest—but the atmosphere is among the liveliest in town.

2 rue de l'Eglise. ✆ **04-94-97-05-18.** Mains 12€–20€. Daily noon–2pm and 7–11pm. Closed Oct–Apr.

### SHOPPING

Dotted throughout the town's *triangle d'or,* the rough triangle formed by place de la Garonne, rue François Sibilli, and place des Lices, are shops bearing chic labels like Hermès, Sonia Rykiel, and Louis Vuitton. There are also scores of unique boutiques around the Vieille Ville (Old Town), including **K. Jacques,** 39 bis rue Allard (www.lestropeziennes.com; ✆ **04-94-97-41-50**), with its iconic *tropéziennes* sandals and neighboring **Kiwi Saint Tropez,** 34, rue du general Allard (www.kiwi.fr; ✆ **04-94-97-42-26**), where you can give your bikini wardrobe an overhaul. Place des Lices hosts an excellent **outdoor market,** Marché Provençal, with food, clothes, and *brocante* (vintage items), on Tuesday and Saturday mornings.

### ENTERTAINMENT & NIGHTLIFE

On a lower level of the Hôtel Byblos's grounds, **Les Caves du Roy,** 20 avenue Paul-Signac (www.lescavesduroy.com; ✆ **04-94-56-68-00**), is the most self-consciously chic nightclub in St-Tropez. It's open nightly from Easter to early October from 11:30pm until dawn. Relatively fresh on the scene is **White 1921,** place des Lices (www.white1921.com; ✆ **04-94-45-50-50**), a champagne and cocktail bar set within a jasmine-cloaked courtyard garden. **Le Papagayo,** port de St-Tropez (www.papagayo-st-tropez.com; ✆ **04-94-97-95-95**), is one of the largest nightclubs in town. Adjacent to Le Papagayo is **Le VIP Room,** in the Résidence du Nouveau-Port (www.st-tropez.viproom.fr; ✆ **06-38-83-83-83**), a younger yet similarly chic version of Les Caves du Roy.

On the port, **Café de Paris** (www.cafedeparis.fr; ✆ **04-94-97-00-56**), is one of the most popular—and friendly—hangouts in town. It has 1900s-style globe lights, masses of artificial flowers, and a long zinc bar.

## Cannes ★★

When Coco Chanel came here and got a suntan, returning to Paris bronzed, she shocked the milk-white society ladies—who quickly began to copy her. Today the bronzed bodies, clad in nearly nonexistent swimsuits, line the beaches of this chic resort and continue the late fashion designer's example. A block back from the famed promenade de la Croisette are the boutiques, bars, and bistros that make Cannes the Riviera's capital of cool.

Le Suquet, the Old Town and Le Vieux Port in Cannes.



Cannes's **Office de Tourisme** website is www.cannes-destination.fr.

**ARRIVING** By **train,** Cannes is 10 minutes from Antibes, 30 minutes from Nice, and 45 minutes from Monaco. The TGV from Paris reaches Cannes in 5 hours. The one-way fare from Paris is 66€ to 158€. For rail information and schedules, visit www.voyages-sncf.com or call ✆ **36-35. Lignes d'Azur** (www.cg06.fr; ✆ **08-00-06-01-06**) line 200 provides bus service from Cannes's Gare Routière (place Bernard Cornut Gentille) to Antibes every 20 minutes during the day (trip time: 25 min.). The one-way fare is 1.50€.

The **Nice International Airport** (www.nice.aeroport.fr; ✆ **08-20-42-33-33**) is a 30-minute drive east. **Bus no. 210** picks up passengers at the airport every 30 minutes during the day (hourly at other times) and drop them at Cannes's Gare Routière. The one-way fare is 20€, round-trip is 30€.

By **car** from Marseille, take A51 north to Aix-en-Provence, continuing on A8 east to Cannes. From Nice, follow A8 or the coastal D6007 southwest to Cannes.

**SPECIAL EVENTS** Cannes is at its most frenzied in mid-May during the **International Film Festival** (www.festival-cannes.com) at the Palais des Festivals, on promenade de la Croisette. You have a better chance of being named prime minister of France than you do attending one of the major screenings (hotel rooms and tables at restaurants are equally scarce during the festival), but the people-watching is absolutely fabulous!

## GETTING AROUND

Cannes's small town center is a labyrinth of one-ways and serious traffic—which makes it best explored **on foot.** Despite the summertime commotion, the flat landscapes in and around Cannes are well suited for **bikes and motor scooters**. At **Daniel Location,** 7 rue de Suffern (www.daniel-location-cannes.com; ✆ **04-93-99-90-30**), city or mountain bikes cost 15€ a day. Motorized bikes and scooters cost from 30€ per day. For larger motorbikes, you must present a valid driver's license. **Driving** is difficult, to say the least; visit the tourist office website (see above) for a listing of **public parking lots** and their hourly fees. If you need a taxi, call **Allô Taxi Cannes** (www.allo-taxis-cannes.com; ✆ **08-90-71-22-27**).

**Buses** and other public transport is operated by **Palm Bus** (www.palmbus.fr; ✆ **08-25-82-55-99**). There's little need for public transport in the city center—although the open-top no. 8, which runs along the seafront from the port in the west to the Palm Beach peninsula in the east, makes for a fun and scenic ride. Tickets cost 1.50€ and can be purchased directly aboard any bus.

## EXPLORING CANNES

Far and away, Cannes's most famous street is the **promenade de la Croisette**—or simply La Croisette—which curves along the coast. It's lined by grand hotels (some dating from the 19th c.), boutiques, and exclusive beach clubs. It's also home to temporary-exhibition space **La Malmaison,** 47 La Croisette (www.cannes.com; ✆ **04-97-06-44-90**), which holds major modern art shows—featuring artists ranging from Miró to Picasso—each year. It's open daily July to August 11am to 8pm (Fri until 9pm), September 10am to 7pm, and October to April Tuesday to Sunday 10am to 1pm and 2 to 6pm. Admission varies with exhibits. Above the harbor, the **Old Town** of Cannes sits on Suquet Hill, where visitors can climb the 14th-century **Tour de Suquet.**

**Musée Bonnard ★★** ART MUSEUM The only museum in the world dedicated to the Impressionist painter Pierre Bonnard is located 3km (1¾ miles) north of Cannes, in the suburb of Le Cannet. Portraits, sculptures, and sketches on display in this small museum were created primarily between 1922 and 1947, the period during which the artist was a local resident.

16 bd. Sadi Carnot, Le Cannet. www.museebonnard.fr. ✆ **04-93-94-06-06.** 5€ adults, 3.50€ ages 12–18 and over 65, free for children 11 and under. Bus 1 from Cannes city center. Sept–June daily 10am–6pm; July–Aug daily 10am–8pm (Thurs to 9pm).

## ORGANIZED TOURS

One of the best ways to get your bearings in Cannes is to climb aboard the **Petit Train touristique de Cannes** (www.cannes-petit-train.com;

**✆ 06-22-61-25-76**). The vehicles operate two different itineraries every day, one that focuses on the Croisette, the other on the Suquet neighborhood. All trains depart from outside the Palais des Festivals every 30 to 60 minutes. Both 35-min. tours cost 7€ for adults and 3€ for children aged 3 to 10.

## OUTDOOR ACTIVITIES

**Beachgoing** in Cannes has more to do with exhibitionism than actual swimming. **Plage de la Croisette** extends between the Vieux Port and the Port Canto. The beaches along this billion-dollar stretch of sand are *payante,* meaning entrance costs between 15€ to 30€. Why should you pay an entry fee? Well, the price includes a full day's use of a chaise longue (the seafront is more pebbly than sandy), and a parasol, as well as easy access to freshwater showers. There are also outdoor restaurants and bars where no one minds if you dine in your swimsuit. Every beach allows topless bathing. For a free public beach without chaises or parasols, head for **Plage du Midi,** just west of the Vieux Port, or **Plage Gazagnaire,** just east of the Port Canto.

## WHERE TO STAY

**Five Seas Hôtel ★★** The newest, coolest hotel in Cannes harks back to a Gatsby era of Art Deco furnishings and no-limits lavishness. The style is Louis Vuitton meets vintage ocean liner. Popular with both guests and non-residents is the hotel's **Cinq Mondes & Carita Spa.** The top-floor terrace features a small infinity pool, a cocktail bar, and linen-shaded sun loungers. It's also the location of the acclaimed **Sea Sens** modern Mediterranean restaurant (main dishes 18€–49€) under the direction of head chef Arnaud Tabarec. And boy, what a view it has. Desserts come courtesy of World Pastry Champion Jérôme de Oliveira, who also maintains **Intuitions by J,** a tea and pastry shop on the ground floor.

1 rue Notre Dame. www.five-seas-hotel-cannes.com. ✆ **04-63-36-05-05.** 45 units. Doubles 200€–1,000€, suites from 700€. **Amenities:** Restaurant; bar; concierge; outdoor pool; room service; spa; free Wi-Fi.

**Hôtel Pruly ★★** Recently renovated, this century-old townhouse harbors charming rooms decorated in bright colors and Provençal textiles; some boast traditional terra-cotta *tomette* floors or private balconies. An afternoon nap on a sun lounger in the hotel's palm-splashed private garden is a welcome respite from Cannes's summertime crowds. It's located just behind the train station. ***Note:*** Rates double during conventions and the film festival.

32 bd. d'Alsace. www.hotel-pruly.com. ✆ **04-93-38-41-28.** 14 units. Doubles 65€–115€. Closed Jan–Feb. **Amenities:** Garden; free Wi-Fi.

## WHERE TO EAT

Restaurants are scattered across the city center, with a particularly heavy concentration around Le Suquet, Cannes's Old Town.

**Aux Bons Enfants ★★** PROVENÇAL You could easily miss this old-fashioned eatery, tucked among a crowd of mediocre tourist-targeted restaurants. But what an oversight that would be. Family-run for three generations, the authentic menu includes traditional dishes such as *daube de canard;* slow-cooked *duck a la niçoise;* and zucchini flower fritters. Seasonal ingredients come from the Marché Forville, just around the corner. The restaurant has no telephone and does not accept reservations or credit cards.

80 rue Meynadier. www.aux-bons-enfants.com. No telephone. No reservations. Mains 16€–23€; fixed-price menus 28€. No credit cards. Tues–Sat noon–2pm and 7–10pm. Closed Dec.

**La Palme d'Or ★★★** MODERN FRENCH Double-Michelin-starred chef Christian Sinicropi has presided over this theater of fine dining for more than a decade, yet his level of innovation knows no bounds. Think algae lollipops, flavored smoke, herb perfume. Guests are greeted at the table by the man himself. Diners are then taken on an intensely seasonal 5- to 10-course gastronomic journey in a dining room so rococo that even Liberace would feel at home. Unforgettable.

In the Grand Hyatt Hotel Martinez, 73 bd. de la Croisette. cannesmartinez.grand.hyatt.com. ✆ **04-92-98-74-14.** Reservations required, jacket and tie. Mains 75€–144€; fixed-price lunch 72€, fixed-price dinner 78€–205€. Wed–Sat 12:30–2pm and 8–10pm. Closed Jan–Feb.

**Le Park 45 ★★★** MEDITERRANEAN This is one of the most inventive—and least expensive—of the Riviera's top restaurants. Locally grown vegetables and Atlantic seafood sparkle with additions of yuzu condiment, ponzu cream, Parmesan bouillon, and zingy Granny Smith apple *jus.* Surrounding Le Park 45 is the modernist splendor of **Le Grand Hotel** (✆ **04-93-38-15-45**).

In Le Grand Hotel, 45 bd. de la Croisette. www.grand-hotel-cannes.com. ✆ **04-93-38-15-45.** Reservations recommended. Mains 35€–40€; fixed-price lunch 55€, dinner 55€–120€. Daily midday–2pm and 7:30–10pm.

## SHOPPING

You'll see every big-name designer you can think of (Saint Laurent, Rykiel, and Hermès) here, plus a legion of one-off designer boutiques and shoe stores. There are also real-people shops; resale shops for star-studded castoffs; flea markets for fun junk; and a fruit, flower, and vegetable market.

Most of the big names in fashion line promenade de la Croisette, the main drag running along the sea. Among the most prestigious are

**Dior,** 38 La Croisette (✆ **04-92-98-98-00**), and **Hermès,** 17 La Croisette (✆ **04-93-39-08-90**). Young hipsters should try **Bathroom Graffiti,** 52 rue d'Antibes (✆ **04-93-39-02-32**), for sexy luggage, bikinis, and designer homeware. The rue d'Antibes is also brilliant for big-brand bargains (Zara and MaxMara), as well as one-off boutiques.

The **Marché Forville,** in place Marché Forville just north of the Vieux Port, is the fruit, vegetable, and flower market that supplies the dozens of restaurants in the area (Tues–Sun, 7am–1pm). Monday (8am–6pm) is *brocante* day, when the market fills with antiques and flea-market finds.

## ENTERTAINMENT & NIGHTLIFE

A strip of sundowner bars stretches along rue Félix Faure. Most are chic, some have happy hour cocktails, and several have DJs after dinner. For an aperitif with history, the **Bar l'Amiral,** in the Hôtel Martinez, 73 La Croisette (www.cannesmartinez.grand.hyatt.fr; ✆ **04-93-90-12-34**), is where deals have always gone down during the film festival. Alternatively, head to **Le 360,** Radisson Blu 1835 Hotel & Thalasso, 2 bd. Jean Hibert (www.radissonblu.com; ✆ **04-92-99-73-20**), a panoramic rooftop terrace overlooking the port that's idyllic for a cocktail as the sun sets. At **Le Bâoli,** Port Pierre Canto, La Croisette (www.lebaoli.com; ✆ **04-93-43-03-43**), Europe's partying elite, from Prince Albert of Monaco to Jude Law, dance until dawn.

Cannes has world-class **casinos** loaded with high rollers, voyeurs, and everyone in between. The better established is the **Casino Croisette,** in the Palais des Festivals, 1 espace Lucien Barrière (www.lucienbarriere.com; ✆ **04-92-98-78-00**). Its main competitor is the newer **Palm Beach Casino,** place F-D-Roosevelt, Pointe Croisette (www.casinolepalmbeach.com; ✆ **04-97-06-36-90**), on the southeast edge of La Croisette. It attracts a younger crowd with a summer-only beachside poker room, a beach club with pool, a restaurant, and a disco that runs until dawn.

## DAY TRIPS FROM CANNES

### Grasse ★

18km (11 miles) N of Cannes

Grasse, a 20-minute drive from Cannes, has been renowned as the capital of the world's perfume industry since the Renaissance. Today some three-quarters of the world's essences are produced here from thousands of tons of petals, including violets, daffodils, wild lavender, and jasmine. The quaint medieval town, which formed the backdrop for the 2006 movie *Perfume,* has several free perfume museums where visitors can enroll in workshops to create their own scent.

The comprehensive **Musée International de la Parfumerie ★** (2 bd. du Jeu-de-Ballon; www.museesdegrasse.com; ✆ **04-97-05-58-00;** 4€–6€ adults, 2€–3€ students, free for children under 18) chronicles both Grasse's fragrant history, as well as worldwide perfume development over the past 4,000 years. Wander among raw materials, ancient flasks (including Marie Antoinette's 18th-c. toiletry set) and scented soaps, all set against a backdrop of contemporary artworks. Kids age 7 and older have their own dedicated pathway, lined with interactive exhibits to touch—and, of course, smell.

Both **Parfumerie Molinard,** 60 bd. Victor Hugo (www.molinard.com; ✆ **04-93-36-01-62**), and **Parfumerie Fragonard,** 20 bd. Fragonard (www.fragonard.com; ✆ **04-93-36-44-65**), offer factory tours, where you'll get a firsthand peek into scent extraction and perfume and essential oil production. You can also purchase their products on-site.

For light lunch or an afternoon snack, pop into **Le Péché Gourmand,** 8 rue de l'Oratoire (✆ **06-62-69-61-57**), a combination mini-restaurant, tearoom, and ice cream parlor. Try the goat cheese and candied tomato crumble, or order up a bowl of the decadent chocolate sorbet.

**Trains** run to Grasse from Cannes, depositing passengers a 10-minute walk south of town. From here, a walking trail or shuttle bus leads visitors into the center. One-way train tickets cost 4.40€ from Cannes. **Buses** pull into town every 10 to 60 minutes daily from Cannes (trip time: 50 min.), arriving at the Gare Routière, place de la Buanderie (✆ **04-93-36-37-37**), a 5-minute walk north of the town center. The one-way fare is 1.50€. Visitors arriving by **car** may follow RN85 from Cannes. The **Office de Tourisme** is at place de la Buanderie (www.grasse.fr; ✆ **04-93-36-66-66**).

### Vallauris ★

7km (4½ miles) NE of Cannes

Once simply a stopover along the Riviera, Vallauris's ceramics industry was in terminal decline until it was "discovered" by Picasso just after World War II. The artist's legacy lives on both in snapshots of the master in local galleries and in his awesome *La Paix et La Guerre* fresco. His ***l'Homme au Mouton*** *(Man and Sheep)* is the outdoor statue at place Paul Isnard, in front of which Prince Aly Kahn and screen goddess Rita Hayworth were married. The local council had intended to enclose this statue in a museum, but Picasso insisted that it remain on the square, "where the children could climb over it and dogs piss against it." Closed for years, you can now enjoy art at the newly renovated **Galerie Madoura ★,** rue Georges et Suzanne Ramié, Picasso's former ceramics studio. It is open 10:30am to 1pm and 2 to 5pm Monday to Friday.

Three museums in one, **Musée Magnelli, Musée de la Céramique & Musée National Picasso La Guerre et La Paix ★★** (Place de la Libération; www.musees-nationaux-alpesmaritimes.fr; ✆ **04-93-64-71-83;** 4€ adults, free for children 15 and under) is a small cultural center developed from a 12th-century chapel where Picasso painted *La Paix* ("Peace") and *La Guerre* ("War") in 1952. Visitors can physically immerse themselves in this tribute to pacifism. Images of love and peace adorn one wall, scenes of violence and conflict the other. Also on site is a permanent exposition of works by Florentine-born abstract artist Alberto Magnelli, as well as a floor dedicated to traditional and innovative ceramics from potters throughout the region.

Join the locals for lunch at **Le Café du Coin,** 16 place Jules Lisnard (www.cafe-du-coin.com; ✆ **04-92-90-27-79**), where a small selection of market-fresh specials are scribbled on the chalkboard daily. For souvenirs, head around the corner to avenue Georges Clemenceau, lined with small shops selling brightly glazed, locally made ceramics.

Envibus **bus** (www.envibus.fr; ✆ **04-89-87-72-00**) connects Cannes's train station with Vallauris every 30 minutes (journey time: 20 min.). Tickets cost 1€ each way. There's an **Office de Tourisme** (www.vallauris-golfe-juan.fr) at 67 ave. George Clemenceau (✆ **04-93-63-82-58**).

## Antibes ★★

Antibes has a quiet charm unique to the Côte d'Azur. Its harbor is filled with fishing boats and pleasure yachts. The likes of Picasso and Monet painted its oh-so-pretty streets, today thronged with promenading locals and well-dressed visitors. A pedestrianized town center makes it a family-friendly destination as well, and a perfect place for an evening stroll. An excellent covered market is also located near the harbor, open every morning except Mondays.

### ESSENTIALS

Antibes's **Office de Tourisme** website is www.antibesjuanlespins.com.

**ARRIVING** **Trains** from Cannes arrive at the rail station, place Pierre-Semard, every 20 minutes (trip time: 12 min.); the one-way fare is 3€. Around 25 trains arrive from Nice daily (trip time: 20 min.); the one-way fare is 3.70€. The **bus** station, or Gare Routière, place Guynemer (www.cg06.fr or www.envibus.fr; ✆ **04-89-87-72-00**), offers bus service throughout Provence. Bus fares to Nice, Cannes, or anywhere en route cost 1.50€ one-way. To **drive** to Antibes from Nice, travel along coastal D6007 south; from Cannes, follow the D6007 north.

### EXPLORING ANTIBES

Antibes's largely pedestrianized Old Town—all pale stone homes, weaving lanes, and window boxes of colorful flowers—is easily explored on

Old Town, Antibes.

foot. A dip into Picasso's former home, now a museum, and a stroll along the pleasure port, where artist Jaume Plensa's giant *Nomad* sculpture shimmers against the night sky, are undoubtedly its highlights.

From June to September, Antibes's Tourist Office offers **guided tours** of the historic old town in English every Thursday at 10am. Prices are 7€ for adults, 3.50€ for children under 16, and free for childen aged 8 and under. The rest of the year, visits in English are by request only.

**Musée Picasso ★★** ART MUSEUM Perched on the Old Town's ramparts, the 14th-century Château Grimaldi was home to Picasso in 1946, when the Spanish artist lived and worked here at the invitation of the municipality. Upon his departure, he gifted all the work he'd completed to the château museum: 44 drawings and 23 paintings, including the famous *La Joie de Vivre*. In addition to this permanent collection, contemporary artworks by Nicolas de Staël, Arman, and Modigliani, among many others, are also on display.

Château Grimaldi, Place Mariejol. www.antibes-juanlespins.com. ✆ **04-92-90-54-20.** 6€ adults, 3€ students and seniors, free for children 17 and under. Mid-June to mid-Sept Tues–Sun 10am–6pm (July–Aug Wed and Fri until 8pm); mid-Sept to mid-June Tues–Sun 10am–noon and 2–6pm.

## WHERE TO STAY

**Hôtel du Cap-Eden-Roc ★★★** This legendary hotel was first launched in 1887, serving as a Mediterranean getaway for visitors seeking winter sunshine. Over the intervening years, it has played host to the world's most famous clientele, from the Duke and Duchess of Windsor to Hollywood superstars. Surrounded by a maze of manicured gardens, accommodation is among the most sumptuous on the Riviera. Guests lounge by the swimming pool, carved from natural basalt rock, while evenings are spent at the panoramic **Restaurant Eden-Roc** or the **Bellini Bar.**

Bd. J.F. Kennedy. www.hotel-du-cap-eden-roc.com. ✆ **04-93-61-39-01.** 117 units. Doubles 850€–1,500€, suites 1,750€–6,300€. Closed mid-Oct to mid-Apr. **Amenities:** 2 restaurants; 2 bars; babysitting; gym; massage; outdoor pool; room service; spa; tennis courts, free Wi-Fi.

**Le Relais du Postillon ★★** If your budget doesn't allow splurges like the Cap-Eden-Roc, you can still enjoy a night in Antibes at this homey hotel. Located on the town's principal square, the interior bar—with a cozy fireplace in winter—has toasted a century of local color. Guest rooms aren't exactly the Ritz, but they are tidy and spotlessly clean. Le Relais also rents a 40-sq.-m holiday apartment next door from 600€ to 900€ per week, or 120€ to 160€ per night.

8 rue Championnet. www.relaisdupostillon.com. ✆ **04-93-34-20-77.** 16 units. Doubles 69€–149€. **Amenities:** Bar; free Wi-Fi.

## WHERE TO EAT

For light bites and unusual local wines, stop into **Entre 2 Vins,** 2 rue James Close (✆ **04-93-34-46-93**). Antibes's **Marché Provençal** produce market is a top spot for picnic items. Purchase olives, cheese, or a whole-roast chicken and simply dine on the beach.

**Bistro Le Rustic ★** FRENCH/PIZZA For hearty local dishes on a budget, it's hard to beat family-run Le Rustic. The menu here focuses on wood-fired pizzas and rich pots of fondue, with plenty of Riviera classics (fish soup, a fresh shrimp platter, slow-roasted duck) thrown in, too. The restaurant is located at the heart of Antibes's Old Town, with spacious (and kid-friendly) outdoor seating in the square.

33 place Nationale. ✆ **04-93-34-10-81.** Mains 10€–18€; fixed-price menu 19€. Daily noon–2pm and 6–11pm. Closed Wed in Oct–Feb.

**Restaurant de Bacon ★★** FISH This legendary family-run establishment has been wowing the crowds for 60 years. Watch as your server skillfully dissects lobster, sea bream, sea bass, and other Mediterranean fish, bathes it in soup and concocts a bouillabaisse before your very eyes. If your needs are simpler, choose a grilled, steamed, or sautéed fish

### kid stuff ON THE RIVIERA

If you'd like to reward your kids for patiently marching around cute towns and art museums, consider taking them to the massive theme-park complex just south of Biot, all run by **Marineland** (www.marineland.fr). The main park, Marineland, offers the chance to get personal with penguins, polar bears, and sharks. **Aqualand** (www.aqualand.fr) boasts more than 2km (1¼ miles) of waterslides, including toboggan-style Le Draguéro and the Rainbow Cannon. **Adventure Golf** is criss-crossed by two dinosaur-dotted miniature golf courses. And **Kid's Island** caters to animal-loving little ones, with pony rides and a petting zoo, plus plenty of jungle gyms and a Magic River. Admission is as follows: Marineland 40€, 32€ children between 3 and 12; Aquasplash 27€, 21€ children between 3 and 12; Adventure Golf 12€, 10€ children between 3 and 12; and Kid's Island 14€, 11€ children between 3 and 12. All are free for children 2 and under; combination entrance tickets are also available. Marineland is open daily July and August 10am to 11pm, mid-April to June and September 10am to 7pm, and mid-March to mid-April 10am to 6pm. Aquasplash, Adventure Golf, and Kid's Island all have varying opening hours; visit Marineland website for details.

dish from the menu, which includes one or two non-seafood options as well.

Boulevard de Bacon, Cap d'Antibes. www.restaurantdebacon.com. ✆ **04-93-61-50-02.** Mains 50€–80€; fixed-price menu lunch 55€, fixed price menu dinner (not available July–Aug) 55€–85€. Tues 7:30–11pm, Wed–Sun 12:30–2pm and 7:30–11pm; closes a half to one hour earlier in winter. Closed Nov–Feb.

## St-Paul-de-Vence ★★

Of all the hilltop villages of the Riviera, St-Paul-de-Vence is by far the most famous. It gained popularity in the 1940 and '50s, when artists including Picasso, Chagall, and Matisse frequented the town, trading their paintings for hospitality at the Colombe d'Or inn. Art and tourism are now the town's principal activities, and the winding streets are studded with contemporary galleries. Circling the town are magnificent old ramparts (allow about 30 min. to walk the full loop) that overlook flowers and olive and orange trees.

### ESSENTIALS

St-Paul's **Office de Tourisme** website is www.saint-pauldevence.com.

**ARRIVING** Some 20 **buses** per day (no. 400) leave from central Nice, dropping passengers off in St-Paul-de-Vence (1.50€ one-way, journey time: 1 hr.), then in Vence 10 minutes later. For information, contact Ligne d'Azur (www.lignesdazur.com; ✆ **08-10-06-10-06**). If you're **driving** from Nice, take either the A8 highway or the coastal route, turn inland at Cagnes-sur-Mer, and follow signs north to St-Paul-de-Vence.

## EXPLORING ST-PAUL

The entire village can be easily explored **on foot,** and in fact, driving is prohibited. Perched at the top of the village is the **Collégiale de la Conversion de St-Paul ★,** constructed in the 12th and 13th centuries and much altered over the years. On your left as you enter is the painting *Ste-Cathérine d'Alexandrie,* which has been attributed to Tintoretto. The **Trésor de l'Eglise** is one of the most beautiful in the region, with a spectacular ciborium. The church is open daily 9am to 6pm (to 7pm July–Aug). Admission is free.

Just around the corner is the light-flooded **Chapelle des Pénitents Blanc** (www.saint-pauldevence.com; ✆ **04-93-32-41-13**). The artist Jean-Michel Folon, who worked on this unmissable masterpiece until his death in 2005, decorated the church with stained-glass windows, shimmering mosaics, and rainbow-hued frescos. It's open May to September daily 10am to 12:30pm and 2 to 6pm, and October to April daily from 10:30am to 12:30pm to 2 to 4pm. Admission is 4€ adults, 3€ students and children 6 to 15, and free for children 5 and under.

**Fondation Maeght ★★★** ART MUSEUM Established in 1964, this building houses one of the most impressive modern-art collections in Europe. In the gardens, colorful Alexander Calder installations are clustered with skinny bronze sculptures by Alberto Giacometti. A rotating selection of artworks is displayed over the various levels inside, showcasing key pieces by artists like Matisse, Chagall, Bonnard, and Léger. There's also a library, a cinema, a cafeteria, and a magnificent museum store.

623 chemin des Gardettes, outside the town walls. www.fondation-maeght.com. ✆ **04-93-32-81-63.** 15€ adults, 10€ students and ages 10–18, free for children 9 and under, 5€ fee for photographs. July–Sept daily 10am–7pm; Oct–June daily 10am–6pm.

## WHERE TO STAY

**La Vague de Saint-Paul ★★★** Here is an affordable hotel for art lovers seeking country tranquility and wow-factor design. The wavelike main hotel building was originally conceived by far-out architect André Minangoy in the 1960s. Color-coded guest rooms now look out onto a vast garden complete with *pétanque* run, tennis court, bar, and a pool. The attached restaurant delivers three locally sourced set menus at 18€, 24€, and 29€. The complex sits a short walk from the Fondation Maeght contemporary art museum—and a longer stroll through the forest to St-Paul-de-Vence village via a secret trail. Highly recommended.

Chemin des Salettes. www.vaguesaintpaul.com. ✆ **04-92-11-20-00.** 37 units. Doubles 85€–208€, suites 246€–328€. Closed Nov. **Amenities:** Restaurant; bar; concierge; outdoor pool; room service; spa; tennis; free Wi-Fi.

## WHERE TO EAT

**La Colombe d'Or ★★** PROVENÇAL This celebrated restaurant opened its doors in 1920. It was Paul Roux, the restaurant's art-adoring owner, who encouraged the era's struggling artists, such as Raoul Dufy, Paul Signac, and Chaime Soutine, to swap a canvas or two for generous room and board. Picasso, Braque, and Miró followed—and today La Colombe d'Or's boasts a stellar art collection. For a peek at these masterpieces, you'll need to dine here, either indoors or outdoors on the fig-trimmed terrace. The menu features fresh, Provençal dishes, including its famous *anchoïade,* a scrumptious anchovy dip accompanied by a vast array of vegetables. If you'd like to sleep here, the restaurant offers 25 luxurious doubles and suites. Prices are 250€ for a double, 430€ for a suite.

1 place du Général-de-Gaulle. www.la-colombe-dor.com. ✆ **04-93-32-80-02.** Reservations required. Mains 25€–45€. Daily noon–1:45pm and 7:30–10pm. Closed Nov to mid-Dec.

**Les Terrasses ★** PROVENÇAL A few minutes' stroll downhill from the Fondation Maeght, this laidback eatery offers classic regional cuisine and superb views over St-Paul's Old Town. Opt for *aïoli,* steamed vegetables, and cod served alongside a garlic-spiked mayonnaise dip; *secca d' Entrevaux,* a locally cured beef dished up with grilled goat cheese; or one of a dozen different pizzas.

20 chemin des Trious. www.laterrassesursaintpaul.com. ✆ **04-93-32-85-60.** Mains 11€–30€; fixed-price menu 29€. Thurs–Tues 9am–10pm. Closed 2 weeks in Nov.

## SHOPPING

**Galerie Capricorne,** 64 rue Grande (www.galeriecapricorne.com; ✆ **04-93-58-34-42**), offers a colorful array of prints, including a selection by Marc Chagall. Stock up on olive oils, fruit vinegars, and olive-wood chopping boards at **Premier Pression Provence,** 68 rue Grande (www.ppp-olive.com; ✆ **04-93-58-07-69**). It's worth plunging into the town's winding streets, too: **Saint Georges Editions,** 5 montée de l'Eglise (✆ **09-71-57-68-21**), stocks superb, unique handbags, each one created from lengths of unusual antique textiles.

## DAY TRIP FROM ST-PAUL DE VENCE

### Vence ★

Often bypassed in favor of nearby St-Paul-de-Vence, the pretty village of Vence is well worth a detour. Its pale stone Old Town is atmospheric yet untouristy, splashed with shady squares and pavement cafes. The highlight is undoubtedly Matisse's Chapelle du Rosaire, set among a countryside studded with cypresses, olive trees, and oleanders.

Vence's medieval Old Town is compact, making it easy to explore on foot. A poke around its picturesque squares reveals place du Peyra's bubbling **Vieille Fontaine (Old Fountain),** while nearby the **Chateau de**

**Villeneuve/Fondation Émile Hugues,** 2 place du Frêne (www.museedevence.com; ✆ **04-93-58-15-78**), is a temporary-exhibition space dedicated to 20th-century art. At **place Godeau,** the **mosaic** *Moses saved from the Nile* by Marc Chagall adorns the 11th-century **cathedral**'s baptistery (free).

When he was 47, Henri Matisse decided to make Nice his home. Thirty years later, when he discovered that the local order of nuns was planning the construction of a new chapel, he offered not only to design it, but fund the project as well. Now, his **Chapelle du Rosaire ★★** (466 av. Henri-Matisse; www.vence.fr; ✆ **04-93-58-03-26;** 6€ adults) is Vence's biggest attraction. The front of the chapel is unremarkable, with the notable exception of a 12m (39-ft.) crescent-adorned cross rising from a blue-tile roof. But when you walk into this beautifully bright space, you feel as though you have walked into a three-dimensional artwork. Dozens of stained-glass windows shimmer cobalt blue (symbolizing the sea), sapphire green (the landscape), and golden yellow (the sun). Most remarkable are the 14 black-and-white-tile Stations of the Cross, featuring Matisse's self-styled "tormented and passionate" figures.

Vence's unpretentious attitude is also evident in the local cuisine. For good regional cooking and friendly service, try **Le Pigeonnier,** 3 place du Peyra (✆ **04-93-58-03-00**). Creative Provençal cusine is on offer at **Les Bacchanales,** 247 av. de Provence (www.lesbacchanales.com; ✆ **04-93-24-19-19**). For homemade hot chocolate or artisanal sweets, **Entre Mes Chocolats,** 12 av. Marcellin Maurel (www.entre-mes-chocolats.com; ✆ **09-81-82-34-59**), is highly recommended.

Frequent **buses** (no. 94 or 400) originating in Nice take 65 to 80 minutes to reach Vence. The one-way fare is 1.50€. For schedules, contact **Ligne d'Azur** (www.lignesdazur.com; ✆ **08-10-06-10-06**). To **drive** to Vence from Nice, take D6007 west to Cagnes-sur-Mer, and then D36 north. The **Office de Tourisme** is on place du Grand-Jardin (www.vence-tourisme.com; ✆ **04-93-58-06-38**).

## Nice ★★★

Known as the "Queen of the Riviera," Nice is also one of the region's most ancient cities, founded by the Greeks, who called it Nike (Victory). By the 19th century, Russian aristocrats and the British upper class—led by Queen Victoria herself—were sojourning here. These days, however, Nice is not as chi-chi as Cannes or St-Tropez. In fact, of all the major French resorts, Nice is the most down-to-earth, with more museums than any other French city outside Paris.

Nice is also the best place to base yourself on the Riviera, especially if you're dependent on public transportation. From Nice airport, the second largest in France, you can travel by train or bus along the entire coast to resorts such as Antibes, Juan-les-Pins, and Monaco.

Because of its brilliant sunshine and liberal attitude, Nice has long attracted artists and writers, among them Dumas, Nietzsche, Flaubert, Hugo, Sand, and Stendhal. Henri Matisse, who made his home in Nice, said, "Though the light is intense, it's also soft and tender." The city averages 300 sunny days a year.

## ESSENTIALS

A comprehensive website for planning your visit to Nice is www.nicetourisme.com.

**ARRIVING** **Trains** arrive at the city's main station, Gare Nice-Ville, with connections to Cannes for 5.90€, Monaco for 3.30€, and Antibes for 3.70€, as well as Paris and Marseille. For schedules and tickets, visit www.voyages-sncf.com or call ✆ **36-35. Buses** (www.lignesdazur.com; ✆ **08-10-06-10-06**) to towns east depart from place Garibaldi; to towns west, from Jardin Albert I.

Transatlantic and intercontinental flights land at **Aéroport Nice-Côte d'Azur** (www.nice.aeroport.fr; ✆ **08-20-42-33-33**). From there, municipal bus nos. 98 and 99 depart at 20-minute intervals for the port and Gare Nice-Ville, respectively; the one-way fare is 6€. A **taxi** from the airport to the city center costs between 35€ and 40€ each way. Trip time is about 20 minutes.

**CITY LAYOUT** There are five main neighborhoods: the Italianate Old Town; the vintage port; the commercial city center between place Masséna and the main train station; the affluent residential quarter known as the Carré d'Or, just inland from the promenade des Anglais; and hilltop Cimiez. All are easy to navigate on foot, with the exception of Cimiez.

**SPECIAL EVENTS** The **Nice Carnaval** (www.nicecarnaval.com), runs from mid-February to early March, celebrating the return of spring with 3 weeks of parades, *corsi* (floats), *veglioni* (masked balls), confetti, and battles in which young women toss flowers at spectators. The **Nice Festival du Jazz** (www.nicejazzfestival.fr) runs for a week in mid-July, when jazz, funk, and reggae artists perform in the Jardins Albert I near the seafront.

## GETTING AROUND

Nice is very easy to manage **on foot,** and no point of interest downtown is more than a 10-minute walk from place Massena, including the seafront promenade des Anglais, Old Town, and harbor. Like many French cities, Nice has its own bike-sharing scheme, **Vélo Bleu** (www.velobleu.org). You can register directly at one of Nice's 175 bike stands (difficult) or online (much easier); fees range from 1€ for 1 day to 5€ for a week. Alternatively, you can rent bikes (from 14€ per day) and scooters (from 26€ per day) from **Holiday Bikes,** 23 rue de Belgique (www.loca-bike.fr;

✆ **04-93-16-01-62**). If you need a **taxi,** call **Taxis Niçois Indépendants** (www.taxis-nicois-independants.fr; ✆ **04-93-88-25-82**); they will pick up within 5 minutes across town.

Most local buses leave from the streets around place Masséna. Municipal buses charge 1.50€ for rides within the entire Alpes-Maritime province, even as far as Monaco or Cannes. The same ticket can also be used on Nice's tramway, which connects the Old Town with Gare Nice-Ville and northern Nice. Tickets, day passes (5€), and week passes (15€) can be bought directly onboard buses (although not trams) or at electronic kiosks around the city. For further information, see www.lignesdazur.com.



## EXPLORING NICE

In 1822, Nice's orange crop had an awful year. The workers faced a lean time, so the English residents employed them to build the **promenade des Anglais ★★,** today a wide boulevard fronting the bay that stretches for 7km (4¼ miles), all the way to the airport. Along the beach are rows of grand cafes, the Musée Masséna, and the city's most glamorous hotels.

Crossing this boulevard in the tiniest bikinis are some of the world's most attractive bronzed bodies. They're all heading for the **beach.** Tough

Promenade des Anglais and Bay of Angels in Nice.

on tender feet, *le plage* is made not of sand, but of pebbles (and not small ones, either).

Rising sharply on a rock at the eastern end of the promenade is the **Colline du Château.** Once a fortified bastion, the hill has since been turned into a wonderful public park complete with a waterfall, cafes, and a giant children's play area, as well as an incredibly ornate cemetery. Head up aboard an elevator from the quai des Etats-Unis; athletic visitors can walk up one of five sets of steep steps. The park is open daily from 8am to dusk.

Continuing east of the Colline, you reach the **Vieux Port,** or harbor, where the restaurants are filled with locals. While lingering over a drink at a sidewalk cafe, you can watch the ferries depart for Corsica and the yachts for St-Tropez. Just inland, the neighborhood around rue Bonaparte and place Garibaldi has become one of the hippest in town: Head here for authentic eateries, hip bars, and the superb **MAMAC Museum of Contemporary Art ★★★,** place Yves Klein (www.mamac-nice.org; ✆ **04-97-13-42-01;** closed Mon). Your 10€ MAMAC ticket will get you into four other museums (and under 18s get in free).

### Museum Tickets & Passes in Nice

Nice's municipal museums are part of a ticket/pass system, which works like this: your 10€ ticket, will get you into one, or a themed group of museums for a 48-hour period. For example, you could opt for just the Palais Lascaris or just the Matisse Museum, or you could use your ticket to visit the "Contemporary Art Group" of five museums, including the MAMAC (see above). If you have time and want access to all the municipal museums, invest 20€ in the 7-day museum pass. Students, children under 18, and residents get into all city museums for free.

The **Vieille Ville ★★,** or Old Town, begins at the foot of the Colline and stretches to place Masséna. Sheltered by red-tiled roofs, many of the Italianate facades suggest Genoese palaces, including the **Palais Lascaris,** 15 rue Droite (www.palais-lascaris-nice.org; ✆ **04-93-62-72-40;** 10€ adults, 17 and under free; closed Tues). This splendid 17th-century mansion, which once belonged to a prominent noble family, also harbors an excellent collection of musical instruments. The Old Town is a maze of narrow streets filled with local life, flower-strewn squares, and traditional *boulangeries:* Sample a Niçois-style onion pizza (*pissaladière*) here.

From Tuesday through Sunday (8am–1pm), the Old Town's main pedestrianized thoroughfare, the **cours Saleya,** is crowded with local producers selling seasonal fruits and vegetables, cured meats, and artisanal cheeses. At the market's western end is the **Marché aux Fleurs.** A rainbow of violets, lilies, and roses, the market operates Tuesday to Sunday from 8am to 5:30pm. On Monday (7am–6pm) the cours Saleya is occupied by a superb **antiques market,** with vendors carting wares in from across France and Italy.

Nice's centerpiece is **place Masséna,** with rococo buildings and bubbling fountains, as well as the new **Promenade du Paillon** parkway that stretches from the **MAMAC** art museum down to the **Jardin Albert-1er.** With palms and exotic flowers, this pedestrian-only zone is one of the prettiest places in town.

**Musée Masséna ★★★** MUSEUM Riviera aficionados will adore this terrific history museum. Set inside an imposing Belle Epoque villa, it exhibits a quirky range of objects charting local life in Nice and its surrounds, from the first Victorian visitors through the roaring 1920s. Elegantly printed menus, train tickets from London to Nice, period maps, and snapshots of the promenading rich on vacation bring the past to life.

65 rue de France or 35 promenade des Anglais. www.nice.fr. ✆ **04-93-91-19-10.** 10€ adults; ticket includes entrance to the Prieuré du Vieux-Logis. Wed–Mon 10am–6pm.

**Théâtre de la Photographie et de l'Image ★** PHOTOGRAPHY MUSEUM Nice's most overlooked exhibition space houses world-beating photography displays. Shows are displayed over its six Belle Epoque salons. Recent exhibitions have included homages to Riviera photographer Jean Gilletta and Paris chronicler Brassaï, as well as images from Nice in the roaring 1920s. The most famous collection is that of Charles Nègre, who photographed the city in its pre-tourism splendor in the 1860s.

27 bd. Dubouchage. www.tpi-nice.org. ✆ **04-97-13-42-20.** 10€ adults; ticket includes entrance to MAMAC and three other museums. Tues–Sun 10am–6pm.

## OUTLYING ATTRACTIONS IN CIMIEZ

In the once-aristocratic hilltop quarter of Cimiez, 5km (3 miles) north of Nice, Queen Victoria wintered at the Hôtel Excelsior. Be sure to stroll over to the adjacent **Monastère de Cimiez** (Cimiez Convent), which offers panoramic views over Nice and the Baie des Anges; artists Matisse and Dufy are buried in the cemetery nearby. To reach this suburb and its attractions, take bus no. 15 from boulevard Dubouchage.

**Musée Matisse ★★** ART MUSEUM In 1963, this beautiful old Italian villa was transformed into a museum honoring Henri Matisse. The painter came to Nice for the light and made the city his home until his death in Cimiez in 1954. Most of the pieces in the museum's permanent collection—including *Nude in an Armchair with a Green Plant* (1937) and *Blue Nude IV* (1952)—were created in Nice. Artworks are interspersed with Matisse's personal possessions, such as ceramic vases and antique furniture, as well as scale models of his masterpiece, Vence's **Chapelle du Rosaire ★★** (p. 195).

164 av. des Arènes de Cimiez. www.musee-matisse-nice.org. ✆ **04-93-81-08-08.** 10€ adults. Wed–Mon 10am–6pm.

**Musée National Message Biblique Marc Chagall ★★** ART MUSEUM Surrounded by pools and a garden, this handsome museum is devoted to Marc Chagall's brilliant treatment of biblical themes. This museum's focal set of artworks—12 large paintings, illustrating the first two books of the Old Testament—was originally created to adorn the central cathedral in Vence. The church's high humidity nixed the artist's original plans, and Chagall assisted in planning this purpose-built space instead. The 200 additional artworks include gouaches, a mosaic, sculptures, and prints.

Av. du Dr. Ménard. www.musee-chagall.fr. ✆ **04-93-53-87-20.** 8€ adults, 6€ students. May–Oct Wed–Mon 10am–6pm; Nov–Apr Wed–Mon 10am–5pm.







## ORGANIZED TOURS

One of the most enjoyable ways to quickly get an overview of Nice is aboard a **Nice-L'Open Tour** (www.nice.opentour.com; ✆ **04-92-29-17-00**) double-decker bus. Between 10am and 6pm year-round, one of a flotilla of this company's buses departs from a position adjacent to the Jardin Albert I. The 90-minute hop-on, hop-off tour takes in the harbor, the museums of Cimiez, the Russian church, and the promenade. Per-person rates for one day are 22€ adults, 18€ students, and 8€ children 4 to 11.

Another easy way to see the city is by the small **Train Touristique de Nice** (www.trainstouristiquesdenice.com; ✆ **06-08-55-08-30**), which also departs from the promenade des Anglais, opposite Jardin Albert I. The 45-minute ride passes many of Nice's must-sees, including place Masséna, the Old Town, and the Colline du Château. Departing every 30 minutes, the train operates daily 10am to 5pm (until 6pm Apr–May and Sept, until 7pm June–Aug). The round-trip price is 8€ adults and 4€ children 4 to 12.

## OUTDOOR ACTIVITIES

Along Nice's seafront, **beaches** extend uninterrupted for more than 7km (4¼ miles), going from the edge of Vieux-Port to the international airport. Tucked between the public areas are several rather chic private beaches, which provide chaise lounges and parasols for 12€ to 22€.

## WHERE TO STAY

**Hôtel Negresco ★★** For more than a century, the Negresco has been Nice's most iconic hotel. Its flamingo-pink dome crowns the promenade des Anglais, its Belle Epoque facade turned toward the sea. Guest rooms—a luxurious mix of period antiques and flashy colors—have hosted each era's most noted celebrities, from the Beatles and Salvador Dali to Michael Jackson. Public areas are decorated with works from an exceptional collection of private art, which kicks off with the shimmering Nikki de St-Phalle jazz musician welcoming guests at the hotel's entrance.

37 promenade des Anglais. www.hotel-negresco-nice.com. ✆ **04-93-16-64-00.** 117 units. Doubles 185€–600€, suites 530€–2,700€. **Amenities:** 2 restaurants; bar; babysitting; concierge service, gym; massage; private beach; room service; free Wi-Fi.

**Hôtel Windsor** ★★★ The coolest, funkiest, and friendliest hotel in Nice is also one of its best-value lodgings. Thirty of their rooms have been decorated by acclaimed artists, like Ben, whose colorful words drip down the walls, or Claudio Parmigiani, who painted the walls and ceiling with gold. Other, less expensive rooms are decked with frescos by Antoine Baudoin. There's a tiny pool in the tropical garden where breakfast is served in good weather. Back indoors, **WiLounge** serves dinner and chilled rosé. **WiZen** is the fifth-floor spa, hammam, sauna, and meditation zone.

11 rue Dalpozzo. www.hotelwindsornice.com. ✆ **04-93-88-59-35.** 57 units. Doubles 81€–260€. **Amenities:** Restaurant; bar; spa; outdoor pool; room service; sauna; free Wi-Fi.

**Villa Saint Exupéry Beach** ★ Just outside Nice's Old Town, this upscale hostel makes an ideal base for budget travelers of all ages. Accommodation ranges from dormitories that sleep 4 to 14, to private single or twins. Also onsite is a communal kitchen, gym with sauna, daily happy hour, and quality meals at backpacker prices.

6 rue Sacha Guitry. www.villahostels.com. ✆ **04-93-16-13-45.** 10 rooms, 16 dormitories. 25€–80€ per person in a single or twin-bedded room; 16€–40€ per person for dormitory bed. **Amenities:** Bar; kitchen; computers; TV lounge; free WiFi.

### Alternate Accommodations

**Nice Pebbles** ★★★ A short-term rental of one of these holiday apartments allows you time to truly immerse yourself in local life, from cooking up a morning-market bounty to sipping sunset aperitifs on your private terrace. More than 100 carefully selected properties (from studios to 10-bed homes) are dotted throughout the city's central neighborhoods, including the Old Town and harbor and along the promenade des Anglais. Apartments boast first-class amenities (iPod docks, HD TVs, and designer bathrooms are common), yet weigh in at just a fraction of the price of a hotel room. Demand is high, so book well in advance.

20 rue Gioffredo. www.nicepebbles.com. ✆ **04-97-20-27-30.** 70€–450€ per apartment per night; 700€–6,000€ per week in high season.

## WHERE TO EAT

The regional capital of Nice teems with exquisite restaurants, from the high end to the downright local. In addition to the suggestions below, the portside **Le Bistrot du Port,** 28 quai Lunel (www.lebistrotduportdenice.fr; ✆ **04-93-55-21-70**), is where the Orsini family has been dishing up top-quality fish and creative seafood concoctions for more than 30 years.

**Flaveur ★★** MODERN FRENCH Brothers Gaël and Mickaël Tourteaux are a pair of very talented chefs. A childhood growing up on the tropical islands of Réunion and Guadeloupe means their modern French cuisine is laced with exotic flavors: Plump scallops are seasoned with Japanese *gomasio;* artistically displayed lemongrass and bubbles of lemon caviar sit atop risotto. Note that meals are variations on fixed-price menus only; there's no ordering a la carte, although lunchtime menus allow for gourmet bites on a relative budget. Reserve ahead.
25 rue Gubernatis. www.flaveur.net. ✆ **04-93-62-53-95.** Fixed-price lunch 46€–95€; fixed-price dinner 60€–95€. Tues–Fri noon–2pm and 7:30–10pm; Sat 7:30–10pm. Closed last 2 weeks of Aug.

**La Merenda ★★★** NIÇOIS Top chef Dominique Le Stanc left the world of *haute cuisine* far behind to take over this tiny, traditional, family-run bistro. La Merenda is now one of most authentic and unpretentious eateries along the French Riviera. Market-fresh specials are scribbled on a small chalkboard; depending on the season, they may include stuffed sardines, tagliatelle drenched in delicious basil pesto, or a delectable *tarte au citron.* The restaurant has no phone, so you must reserve in person.
4 rue Raoul Bosio. www.lamerenda.net. No phone. Mains 13€–21€. No credit cards. Mon–Fri noon–2pm and 7:30–10pm.

**Vinivore ★★** MODERN FRENCH This vibrant eatery, located just behind the port, mixes fresh Provençal ingredients with Cantonese flair. Each day, Hong Kong–born chef Chun Wong's changing menu features just four appetizers, four main courses, and four desserts. Recent highlights include beef *tataki* with garlic flowers, wild rice risotto with grilled scallops, and vanilla-infused candied pineapple. Some 200 vintages are carefully noted on the large chalkboards, many from organic wineries across southern France. Next door, you can focus on wine at the **Vinivore wine bar.**
10 rue Lascaris. www.vinivore.fr. ✆ **04-93-14-68-09.** Mains 12€–34€; fixed-price lunch or dinner 39€–41€. Tues–Fri noon–2pm, Tues–Sat 7:30–10pm.

## SHOPPING

Nice's densest concentrations of fashionable French labels are clustered around **rue Masséna** and **avenue Jean-Médecin.** For more high-end couture, the streets around **place Magenta,** including **rue de Verdun, rue Paradis,** and **rue Alphonse Karr** are a credit card's worst nightmare. **Lucien Chausseur,** 6 rue Bonaparte (✆ **04-93-55-52-14**), is the city's coolest spot for Italian-designed shoes, scarves, and soft leather satchels. If you're thinking of indulging in a Provençale *pique-nique,* **Nicola Alziari,** 14 rue St-François de Paule (www.alziari.com.fr; ✆ **04-93-62-94-03**), will provide everything from olives, anchovies, and pistous to aiolis and tapenades. In the port, **Confiserie Florian,** 14 quai Papacino (www.confiserieflorian.com; ✆ **04-93-55-43-50**), has been candying fruit, chocolate-dipping roasted nuts, and crystalizing edible flowers since 1949.

The best selection of Provençal fabrics is at **Le Chandelier,** 7 rue de la Boucherie (✆ **04-93-85-85-19**), which features Valdrôme brands. Nearby at **Atelier des Cigales,** 13 rue du Collet (✆ **04-93-85-70-62**), expect top-class, hand-painted pottery and ceramics from across the province. For offbeat gifts, **Chambre Cinquante-Sept,** 16 rue Emmanuel Philibert (✆ **04-92-04-02-81**), stocks beautifully unique Art Deco *objets d'art.*

## ENTERTAINMENT & NIGHTLIFE

Big evenings out in Nice usually begin at a cafe or bar, take in a restaurant, opera, or film, and finish in a club. The website **riviera.angloinfo.com** lists all the week's English-language movies in *version originale.*

A chic gaming spot is the **Casino in the Palais de Mediterranée,** 15 promenade des Anglais (www.casinomediterranee.com; ✆ **04-92-14-68-00**), which is open daily from 10am for slot machines, 8pm for gaming tables.

Within the cool-kitsch decor of a former garage, **Rosalina,** 16 rue Lascaris (✆ **04-93-89-34-96**) serves up fruity cocktails and great wines. Around the corner, gay-friendly **Comptoir Central Électrique,** 10 rue Bonaparte (✆ **04-93-14-09-62**), is the place Garibaldi neighborhood's epicenter of cool. If you are ready to move your body, head 1 block inland to **Wayne's Bar,** 15 rue de la Préfecture (www.waynes.fr; ✆ **04-93-13-46-99**), where dancing on the tables to raucous cover bands is the norm.

## DAY TRIPS FROM NICE

### Eze & La Turbie ★★

The hamlets of Eze and La Turbie, 6.5km (4 miles) apart, are picture-perfect hill villages that literally cling to the mountains. Both have fortified medieval cores overlooking the coast, and both were built during the early Middle Ages to stave off raids from Saracen pirates. In Eze's case, it's now tour buses, not coastal raiders, which make daily invasions into town. Impossibly cute streets contain galleries, boutiques, and artisans' shops. La Turbie is much quieter, offering a welcome respite from the coast's summertime heat.

Aside from its pretty lanes and stunning views, the leading attraction in Eze is the **Jardin d'Eze ★,** 20 rue du Château (www.eze-tourisme.com; ✆ **04-93-41-10-30**). Here exotic plants are interspersed with feminine sculptures by Jean Philippe Richard, all perched atop the town at 1,400 feet. Admission is 6€ adults, 2.50€ students and ages 12 to 25, and free for children 11 and under. In July and August, it's open daily 9am to 8:30pm; the rest of the year it closes between 4 and 7pm, depending on the time of sunset.

La Turbie boasts an impressive monument erected by Roman emperor Augustus in 6 B.C., the **Trophée des Alps (Trophy of the Alps)** ★. Still partially intact today, it was created to celebrate the subjugation of the French Alpine tribes by the Roman armies. The nearby **Musée du Trophée d'Auguste,** avenue Albert-1er (www.ville-la-turbie.fr; ✆ **04-93-41-20-84**), is an interactive mini-museum containing finds from digs nearby, a historical 3D film, and details about the monument's restoration. Both the ruins and the museum are open Tuesday to Sunday mid-May to mid-September from 9:30am to 1pm and 2:30 to 6:30pm, and mid-September to mid-May from 10am to 1:30pm and 2:30 to 5pm. Admission to both sites is 5.50€ adults, free for children 17 and under.

If you work up an appetite on your excursion, **Gascogne Café** ★ (151 av. de Verdun, place de la Collette, Eze; www.gascogne-hotel-restaurant.fr; ✆ **04-93-41-18-50**), on the main road just outside of Eze's fortified Old Town, is a friendly spot to sample authentic local fare. The menu ranges from traditional flavors (homemade lasagna, sea bass on a bed of ratatouille) to more creative offerings (Asian-style rolls stuffed with snails and garlic cream). Tasty pizzas are also available. Ambience is decidedly casual.

**Trains** (www.voyages-sncf.com; ✆ **36-35**) connect Eze-sur-Mer with Nice, Monaco, and the rest of the Côte d'Azur every 30 minutes. You may take a taxi from here up (1,400 ft.) to Eze; alternatively, bus no. 83 connects the rail station with the hilltop village. **Bus** line no. 82 runs between Nice and Eze around every 90 minutes, while five to seven daily buses (no. 116) connect Nice and La Turbie (www.lignesdazur.com; ✆ **08-10-06-10-06**). By **car** from Nice, take the spellbindingly pretty D6007 (the *moyenne corniche*) east. Eze's **Office de Tourisme** is on place du Général-de-Gaulle, Eze-Village (www.eze-tourisme.com; ✆ **04-93-41-26-00**). La Turbie's small **tourist information point** is at 2 place Detras, La Turbie (www.ville-la-turbie.fr; ✆ **04-93-41-21-15**).

## [Fast FACTS] FRANCE

### Business Hours

**Stores** in the big cities are generally open from around 10am to 6 or 7pm. In the provinces, most **smaller stores** close from noon to at least 2pm for lunch. Except for some tourist areas in Paris, most shops and restaurants are closed on Sunday and many close Monday as well. Businesses are often closed in August, especially in the provinces.

### Currency

France is a member of the European Union and uses the E.U. common currency, the euro (€). See p. 860 for information on money and costs.

### Dentists & Doctors

For a list of English-speaking dentists and doctors in Paris and other French cities, visit the Citizens Services page on the US Embassy website: http://france.usembassy.gov/living_in_france.html, or call Citizens Services at ✆ **01-43-12-22-22**.

## Embassies & Consulates:

**Australia:** 4 Rue Jean Rey, Paris; www.france.embassy.gov.au; ✆ **01-40-59-33-00.**

**Canada:** 35 Montaigne Avenue, Paris; www.france.gc.ca.; ✆ **01-44-43-29-00.**

**New Zealand:** 7 ter, rue Leonard de Vinci, Paris; www.nzembassy.com; ✆ **01-45-01-43-43.**

**United Kingdom:** 35 rue du Faubourg St-Honore, Paris; www.gov.uk/government/world/france; ✆ **01-44-51-31-00.**

**United States:** 2 avenue Gabriel, Paris; http://france.usembassy.gov; ✆ **01-43-12-22-22.**

**Emergencies** Emergency services: ✆ **112.** You can also call the fire brigade (*Sapeurs-Pompiers;* ✆ **18**). For an ambulance, call ✆ **15.** For the police, call ✆ **17.**

**Mail & Postage** Post offices (**La Poste;** www.laposte.fr; ✆ **36-31**) can be found in every French town. Most are open Monday to Friday 8:30am to 7pm, Saturday 8am to 1pm, but hours may be reduced in small villages. Stamps are also sold in *tabacs* (tobacconists).

**Pharmacies** Pharmacies are plentiful in France; look for the green neon cross above the door. Most are closed Sun, but they always post the whereabouts of the closest one that is open (the "Pharmacie de Garde") at night or on the weekend on the door. Pharmacists also offer some medical advice and take blood pressure.

# BELGIUM

by John Newcomb

4

It never fails to amaze. You round the corner of a perfectly ordinary street—in Ghent, in Brussels, in Bruges—and there rushes toward you a mammoth medieval square. Soaring belfry towers of the 1200s, flying red-and-yellow heraldic flags, giant Gothic cathedrals surging with vertical lines into the sky above. Turreted town halls adorned with streaming pennants. Intricately sculpted cloth halls and guild houses of the 1300s, the 1400s. Again and again, on every visit, in an experience that never grows stale, you react with physical thrill to the most radiantly beautiful city squares in all the world—in Belgium.

In a country of frequent grey skies, the predominant impression is nevertheless one of color. It is color that best recalls a Belgian vacation: the bright, vibrant reds and greens of Flemish masterworks of the late Middle Ages, the Memlings and van Eycks, the Brueghels and Rubenses, found in no fewer than 16 major museums; the warm, orange-yellow glow glimpsed through the casement windows of more restaurants per capita than anywhere else on earth, their interiors brightened by dancing firelight from open hearths, their entrances stacked with displays of red lobsters and black mussels; the festive rose-and-lavender stripes of the canvas bathing huts along the 70-kilometer beach of the Belgian coast.

Yet Belgium is not always an easy nation to admire and understand. Although it has attractions that overwhelm even the untrained eye—the Grand-Place of Brussels is the supreme example—its sights are often cerebral, its culture profound and complex, its history unfamiliar. Belgium requires an effort—but what rewards that effort brings!

Belgium can be puzzling for outsiders because it is the most broadly European of all the nations of the Old World. Its people display none of the uniform characteristics of most other Europeans (the elegant French, the effusively warm Italians). As well, the sense of class divide that is still felt in many European cities is missing here. Walk into even the haughtiest of Belgian restaurants and you are treated as a welcome visitor.

Belgium also requires an effort because its main sights are associated with a little-understood era of history: the High Middle Ages. When you have walked, open-mouthed, through the splendors of Bruges, you will suddenly realize that all your prior notions

FACING PAGE: **Brussels's Grand-Place with flower carpet.**

of human history were possibly mistaken, and that humankind may have declined, in some respects, since the days when the Belgian cities reached the height of their importance. And you may never again look at the world in the same way.

All this takes an effort, as I said—but what rewards that effort brings!

***–Arthur Frommer***

# BRUSSELS



Brussels is all of Europe in one city. Not simply one style or era, but all styles and eras. The medieval and the Renaissance. The Austrian neoclassic and the Spanish flamboyant. The French 19th century and the modern skyscraper. The accents and tones, in the very sounds you hear, of both the Latin-influenced languages of Europe (here, the French) and the Germanic strains (here, the Flemish)—a rare, bilingual city. And not only do you see all of Europe here, and hear much of Europe here, but the very people that you meet—in a metropolis where a full quarter of the population is foreign—are from every corner of Europe, mixing and mingling in a setting that was always a crossroads for both invasions and trade. Brussels is not simply the nominal capital of Europe, it is fast becoming the true capital of Europe and shows that status in a hundred intriguing ways.

Of course, Brussels is also the capital of Belgium, which means that here you will see the grandest of all the great city squares. And restaurants so numerous as to make you dizzy. And subways decorated with modern art. And great museums of ancient art. And open-air markets of antiques and food, of secondhand fashions and leather bound books. And chocolatiers. And beery cafes. Brussels is all of these . . . and it is more.

It is Bruges. And it is Ghent. And it is Antwerp. Because Brussels is also a hub, a base for short day excursions, a geographical phenomenon unequalled on earth, a metropolis so centrally located that the lures and attractions of a dozen other great cities are also the attractions of remarkable Brussels.

## Essentials

The city tourist organization, **Visit Brussels** (www.visitbrussels.be) has an excellent website that is handy for advance planning.

**ARRIVING** **Brussels Airport** (www.brusselsairport.be; ✆ **0900/70000** for general and flight info, ✆ **322/753-7753** from outside Belgium; airport code BRU) is 15km (9 miles) northwest of Brussels city center. This one-terminal airport handles most of Belgium's air traffic. Moving walkways connect passengers with the Arrivals Hall and Passport Control, Baggage Reclaim, and Customs.

The **Brussels Airport Express train service** to Brussels's three main rail stations (Bruxelles-Nord, Bruxelles-Central, and Bruxelles-Midi) has up to four departures hourly daily between 5:30am and 11:30pm, for a one-way fare of 8.50€. The ride to Bruxelles-Central takes 17 minutes, and trains leave from the basement level of the airport. Most airport trains have wide corridors and extra space for baggage.

Every half-hour from the airport's bus platform C outside Arrivals, **Airport Line** no. 12 (Mon–Fri 8am–8pm) and no. 21 (Mon–Fri 8–11pm and Sat–Sun 5am–11pm) depart to the European District in the city. The fare is 8€ for a round-trip ticket purchased from a ticket machine before boarding the bus and 12€ for one purchased onboard. For more info: www.stib-mivb.be; ✆ **32/70-232-000.**

**Taxis** that display an orange sticker depicting a white airplane offer reduced fares (around 45€) from the airport to the center city.

**Brussels-South-Charleroi-Airport** (www.charleroi-airport.com; ✆ **0902/02490** for general and flight info, ✆ **322/7815-2722** from outside Belgium; airport code CRL) is 55km (35 miles) south of Brussels. It is the domain of European budget flights rather than transatlantic services; there are Brussels City Shuttle (www.brussels-city-shuttle.com) connections every 30 minutes between the airport and Brussels-Midi/Zuid rail station. Round-trip fare is 28€.

If you are arriving by **car,** major expressways to Brussels are E19/A16 from Amsterdam (driving time: 2 hr. 20 min. on a good day) and the E19/E17 from Paris (driving time 3½ hr.). Take the E40/A10 from Bruges and Cologne. If possible, avoid driving on the hell on wheels that has become the R0 Brussels ring road; if you miss your turn off, expect to go all the way around again. Once you're installed in your hotel, leave the car at a parking garage. Brussels is choked with traffic even in the middle of the day, parking is scarce, and one-way streets are baffling.

The Brussels metropolitan area has three main **rail** stations: **Bruxelles-Central,** Carrefour de l'Europe; **Bruxelles-Midi,** rue de France (the Eurostar, Thalys, TGV, and ICE terminal); and **Bruxelles-Nord,** rue du Progrès. All three are served by Métro, tram, or bus lines, and have taxi stands outside. For train information and reservations, call ✆ **02/528-2828** or visit www.sncb.be.

From London, Brussels is served by **Eurostar** (www.eurostar.com; ✆ **08432/186-186** in Britain; ✆ **44/1233-617-575** from outside the U.K.); from Paris, Amsterdam, and Cologne by **Thalys** (www.thalys.com; ✆ **320/7079-7979**); from everywhere in France apart from Paris by **TGV** (www.voyages-sncf.com; ✆ **3635** in France;

### Passport to Brussels

One of the best discounts is the **Brussels Card** (www.brusselscard.be), available from all Brussels tourist offices (see p. 208). Valid for 1, 2, or 3 days, and costing 24€, 36€, and 43€, respectively, it allows free use of public transportation, free and discounted admission to about 30 of the city's museums and attractions, and discounts at some restaurants and other venues, as well as on some guided tours.

✆ **33/892-353-535** from outside France;); and from Frankfurt by **ICE** (www.nsinternational.nl; ✆ **0900/9296;** 0.35€ per minute).

**Buses** from London, Paris, Amsterdam, and other cities arrive at the bus station below Bruxelles-Nord train station via **Eurolines** (www.eurolines.com; ✆ **08717/818-178** in Britain or ✆ 32/02-274-1350).

**CITY LAYOUT** Brussels is divided into **19** ***communes*** **(districts)**—"Brussels" being both the name of the central commune and of the city as a whole (which comprises Belgium's autonomous Brussels Capital Region, often called Urbizone). The city center was once ringed by fortified ramparts but is now encircled by the broad boulevards known collectively as the Petite Ceinture (Little Belt). Most of the city's premier sightseeing sights are in this zone. Around 14% of the zone's total area of 160 sq. km (63 sq. miles) is occupied by parks, woods, and forest, making Brussels one of Europe's greenest urban centers.

You'll hear both French and Dutch (well, Flemish) along with a babel of other tongues spoken on the streets of Brussels. The city is bilingual: Bruxelles in French and Brussels in Dutch/Flemish, and (confusingly for many a map-reader) street names and places are in both languages. Grand-Place is Grote Markt in Dutch; Théâtre Royal de la Monnaie is Koninklijke Munttheater. ***Note:*** Rather than translate place names into three languages in this chapter, the French place names are utilized.

Brussels is flat in its center and western reaches, where the now-vanished River Senne once flowed (p. 216). To the east, a range of low hills rises to the upper city, which is crowned by the Royal Palace and has some of the city's most affluent residential and prestigious business and shopping districts. The **Grand-Place** stands at the heart of the city and is both a starting point and reference point for most visitors.

**GETTING AROUND** Brussels's center city is small enough that **walking** is a viable option. In fact, there's no better way to explore the historical core, especially the myriad tiny streets around Grand-Place. It's also a pleasant stroll uptown through the pedestrianized Mont des Arts to place Royale. Outside these areas, city traffic is both heavy and frantic. To see the best of the city, divide your time into walking tours and utilize the excellent public transportation to get to your destination. For example, take the Métro out to Merode to explore the museums of Parc du Cinquantenaire (p. 224).

Be careful when crossing roads at black-and-white pedestrian crossings that do not have signals; pedestrians do not have legal priority over cars on these crossings. Likewise watch out for vehicles turning right or left at traffic lights, even when the green flashing lights indicates you are allowed to cross; this is quite legal and catches many visitors off guard.

Brussels's excellent, fully integrated **transit network**—Métro (subway), tram (streetcar), and bus—operates daily 5am to midnight, after which a limited NOCTIS night-bus network takes over until 3am, heading out to the suburbs every 30 minutes. It is run by **STIB** (www.stib-mivb.be; ✆ **070/232-000**).

Both **trams and urban buses** are painted in gray-and-brown. Their stops are marked with red-and-white signs. You stop a tram or bus by extending your arm as it approaches; if you don't signal, the bus or tram won't stop.

The **Métro** is quick and efficient, and covers many important center-city locations, as well as the suburbs, the Bruparck recreation park (p. 228), and the Heysel congress center. Stations are identified by signs with a white m on a blue background. A trip underground takes you into an art center: Métro stations are decorated with commissioned paintings, installations, and other artworks by contemporary Belgian artists.

Maps of the transport system are available free from the city tourist office on Grand-Place, and transit maps are posted at all Métro stations as well as bus and tram stops. Timetables are posted at all tram and bus stops.

Up to four children ages 5 and under can ride for free along with a fare-paying adult. Fares for a single-ride **JUMP ticket** on public transport are 2.10€ when purchased onboard and 2€ when purchased before boarding. Whatever ticket you need, you must purchase it before boarding Métro trains; you may purchase bus and tram tickets onboard. Single and multi-day tickets can be purchased from the GO vending machines in Métro stations and KIOSK sales points.

Validate your ticket by inserting it into the orange electronic machines inside buses and trams and at the access to Métro platforms. Although the one-ride JUMP ticket must be revalidated on each leg of your journey, you're allowed multiple transfers within a 1-hour period of the initial validation.

If possible, plan your journey to avoid the crush at morning and evening rush hours. And again, watch out for pickpockets, especially at busy times.

**Taxi** fares start at 2.40€ between 6am and 10pm and at 4.40€ between 10pm and 6am, increasing by 1.80€ per kilometer inside the city (tariff 1) and 2.70€ per kilometer outside Brussels (tariff 2)—so make sure the meter is set to the correct tariff. Tip and taxes are included, and you need not add an extra tip unless there has been extra service, such as help with heavy luggage. Taxis cannot be hailed on the street, but there are taxi stands on many principal streets, particularly in the center city, and at rail stations. To request a cab by phone, call **Taxis Verts** (www.taxisverts.be; ✆ **02/349-4949**).

I can't think of a good reason for casual visitors to **drive** a car in Brussels. Driving is fast, except at rush hour, and always aggressive. At rush hour (which lasts about 2 hrs. either side of 9am and 5pm), it is almost impossible to move on main roads inside the city and on the notorious R0 outer ring road (beltway).

## The Neighborhoods in Brief

**THE LOWER TOWN** The **Bas de la Ville,** the core area of the Old Center, has at its heart the **Grand-Place** (p. 213) and its environs. Two of the most traveled lanes nearby are restaurant-lined **rue des Bouchers** and **Petite rue des Bouchers,** part of an area known as the **Ilot Sacré (Sacred Isle).** A block from the Grand-Place is the classical, colonnaded **Bourse (Stock Exchange).** A few blocks north, on **place de la Monnaie,** is the Monnaie opera house and ballet theater (p. 237), named after the coin mint that once stood here. Brussels's busiest shopping street, pedestrianized **rue Neuve,** starts from place de la Monnaie and runs north for several blocks. Just north of the center lies **Gare du Nord** and nearby place Rogier. Central Brussels also includes the **Marché-aux-Poissons (Fish Market)** district.

**THE UPPER TOWN** The **Haut de la Ville** lies east of and uphill from the Grand-Place, along rue Royale and rue de la Régence and abutting the unpretentious, working-class **Marolles** district. Lying between the Palais de Justice and Gare du Midi, the Marolles has cozy cafes, drinking-man's bars, and inexpensive restaurants; its denizens even speak their own dialect. The Upper Town is spread along an escarpment east of the center, where you find **place du Grand-Sablon** (p. 237) as well as the Royal Museums of Fine Arts (p. 222) and the museums of the place Royale (p. 221). If you head southwest and cross the broad **boulevard de Waterloo,** where you find the most exclusive designer stores, you come to **place Louise.**

**AVENUE LOUISE** From place Louise, Brussels's most fashionable thoroughfare, **Avenue Louise** runs south all the way to a large wooded park called the **Bois de la Cambre.** On either side of **Avenue Louise** are the classy districts of **Ixelles** and **Uccle;** they're both good areas for casual, inexpensive restaurants, bars, cafes, and shopping, and both border the wide green spaces of the Bois de la Cambre and the Forêt de Soignes.

**EUROPEAN DISTRICT** East of the city center lies the **European Union district** (see box p. 227). It's centered around place Schuman, where the European Commission, Parliament, and Council of Ministers buildings jostle for space in a warren of offices (the area is also home to a wealth of restaurants and cafes that cater to Euro appetites). North of Ixelles, the modern European Union district surrounds **place Schuman.** The **Cinquantenaire,** a park crisscrossed with tree-lined avenues, extends from just east of the European District to the Porte de Tervuren and is bisected east to west by avenue John F. Kennedy. At the park's eastern end are the museums of the monumental Palais du Cinquantenaire (p. 224) and the Arc du Cinquantenaire.

**BRUPARCK** In the north of the city (and something of a leap of the imagination) is the **Bruparck.** Inside this recreation complex, you'll find the Mini-Europe theme park (p. 228); and the Océade water park. Beside this stands the Atomium (p. 228), Brussels Planetarium, Roi Baudoin Soccer Stadium, and the Parc des Expositions congress center.

## Exploring Brussels

Brussels offers so much to the visitor that the city can feel overwhelming; there are more than 75 museums alone, as well as the glorious architecture of King Léopold I's purpose-built city, and one of the best art galleries in the world. Most of the sights are clustered around the Grand-Place in the lower town, and the rue Royale in the upper town; these areas are within easy walking distance of each other, connected by the landscaped Mont des Arts, which leads up to Place Royale from Place de l'Albertine. If you head out into the suburbs, there's a comprehensive public transport system that will get you around easily.



### THE CITY'S PRINCIPAL SQUARES

#### Grand-Place ★★★

If I was asked to name the top two or three sights in all of Europe, I would include the **Grand-Place.** You cannot see it from afar; you must first walk through a narrow, cobblestoned street that gives no hint of what awaits, but suddenly opens onto this great enclosed plaza, flanked on all four sides by the gilded, ornamented, flag-bedecked houses of the

Grand-Place.

**ATTRACTIONS**

Atomium **28**
Autoworld **36**
BELvue Museum & Coudenberg **35**
Cathédrale des Sts-Michel-et-Gudule **30**
Centre Belge de la Bande-Dessinée **27**
eB! experience Brussels **31**
European District **36**
Fondation Jacques Brel **14**
Grand-Place **21**
Hôtel de Ville (Town Hall) **18**
Manneken-Pis **15**
Mini-Europe **28**
Musée Bruxellois de la Gueuze **2**
Musée David et Alice van Buuren **5**
Musée de la Ville de Bruxelles **20**
Musée du Cinquantenaire **36**
Musée du Costume et de la Dentelle **17**
Musée Horta **5**
Musée Magritte **32**
Musée René Magritte **1**
Musée Royal de l'Armée et d'Histoire Militaire **36**
Musées Royaux des Beaux-Arts de Belgique **33**
Notre-Dame du Sablon **10**
Parc du Cinquantenaire **36**
place du Grand Sablon **11**
place du Petit Sablon **9**
place Royale **34**

**HOTELS**

Apart-Hotel **23**
Auberge de Jeunesse Jacques Brel **29**
Espérance **26**
The Hotel **8**
Hotel Amigo **19**
Made in Louise **6**
Métropole **25**

**RESTAURANTS**

Belga Queen **24**
Cecilia **16**
Coin de Mer **22**
Comme Chez Soi **3**
La Quincaillerie **4**
Le Wine Bar Sablon des Marolles **7**
Lola **12**
Pistolet Original **13**
Restaurant Bon-Bon **37**

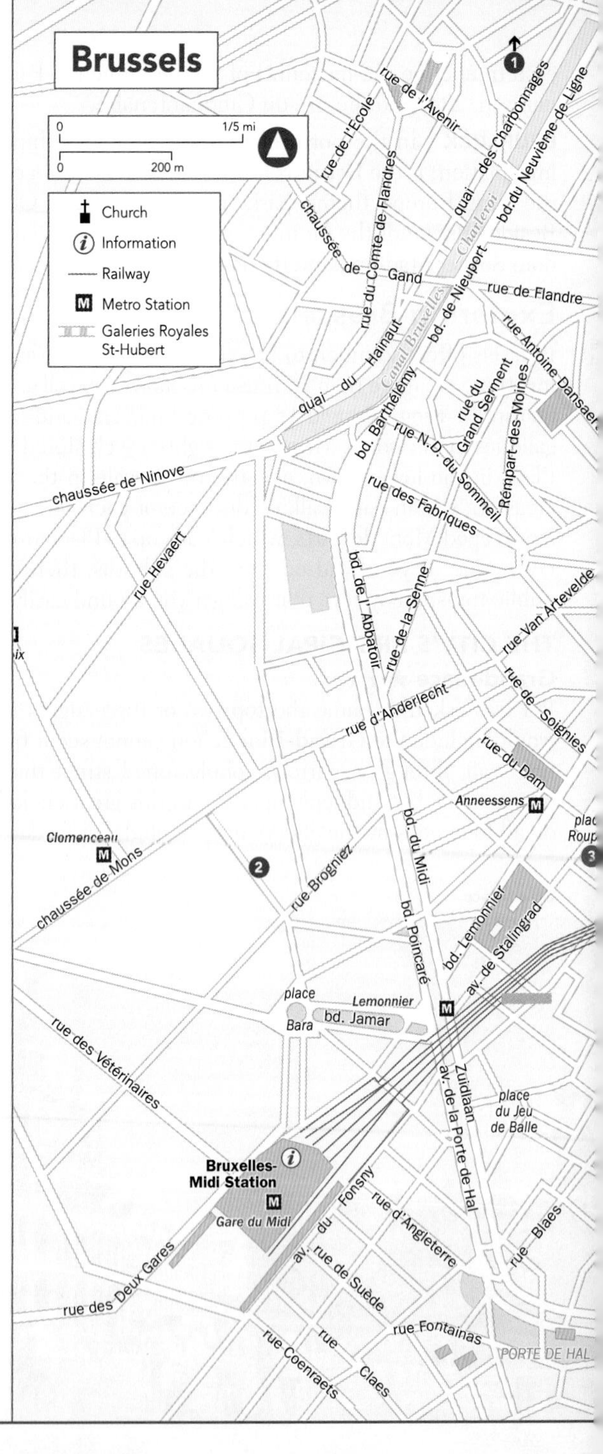

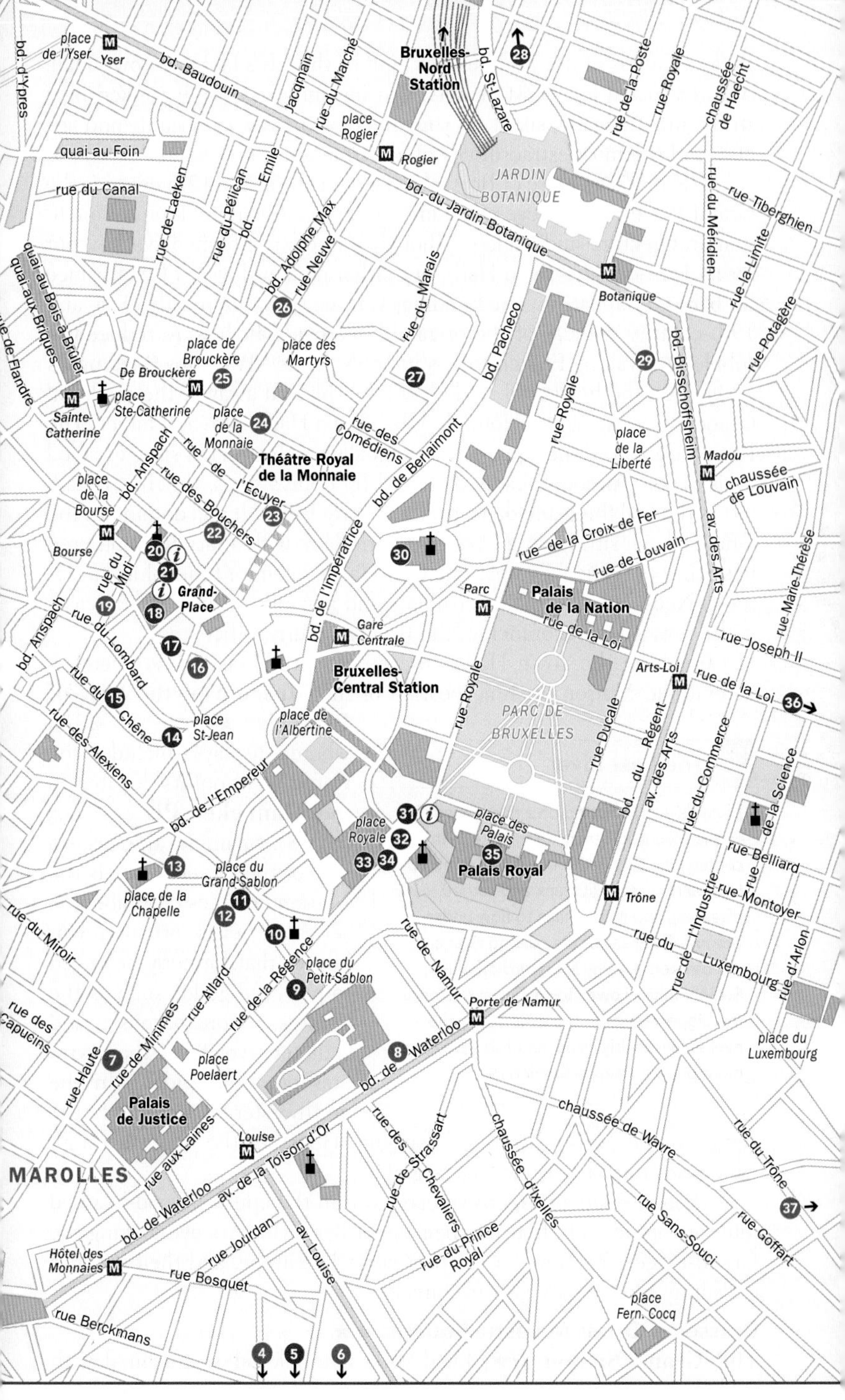

place de l'Yser
Yser
bd. d'Ypres
bd. Baudouin
Jacqmain
rue du Marché
Bruxelles-Nord Station
bd. St-Lazare
28
rue de la Poste
rue Royale
chaussée de Haecht
place Rogier
Rogier
quai au Foin
rue du Canal
rue de Laeken
rue du Pélican
bd. Emile
bd. Adolphe Max
rue Neuve
bd. du Jardin Botanique
JARDIN BOTANIQUE
rue du Méridien
rue Tiberghien
rue la Limite
Botanique
rue du Marais
bd. Pacheco
quai au Bois à Brûler
quai aux Briques
rue de Flandre
26
place de Brouckère
place des Martyrs
29
rue Potagère
De Brouckère
25
27
place Ste-Catherine
Sainte-Catherine
place de la Monnaie
24
rue Royale
bd. Bisschoffsheim
place de la Liberté
rue des Comédiens
bd. Anspach
rue de l'Ecuyer
Théâtre Royal de la Monnaie
bd. de Berlaimont
Madou
chaussée de Louvain
place de la Bourse
rue des Bouchers
23
22
bd. de l'Impératrice
rue de la Croix de Fer
Bourse
20
21
30
rue de Louvain
av. des Arts
rue du Midi
Grand-Place
Parc
Palais de la Nation
rue Marie-Thérèse
19
18
rue de la Loi
bd. Anspach
rue du Lombard
Gare Centrale
17
16
rue Joseph II
Bruxelles-Central Station
Arts-Loi
rue de la Loi
36
rue du Chêne
15
rue Royale
PARC DE BRUXELLES
place St-Jean
14
place de l'Albertine
rue Ducale
bd. du Régent
av. des Arts
rue du Commerce
rue des Alexiens
rue de la Science
bd. de l'Empereur
31
place des Palais
place Royale
32
rue Belliard
35
13
place du Grand-Sablon
33
34
Palais Royal
rue Montoyer
place de la Chapelle
11
12
Trône
rue de l'Industrie
10
rue du Luxembourg
rue du Miroir
rue de Namur
rue d'Arlon
place du Petit-Sablon
rue de la Régence
rue Allard
9
Porte de Namur
rue des Capucins
rue de Minimes
bd. de Waterloo
place du Luxembourg
7
8
rue Haute
place Poelaert
Palais de Justice
chaussée de Wavre
rue aux Laines
Louise
rue des Chevaliers
rue de Strassart
chaussée d'Ixelles
rue du Trône
MAROLLES
av. de la Toison d'Or
bd. de Waterloo
37
rue Sans-Souci
rue Jourdan
av. Louise
rue du Prince Royal
rue Goffart
Hôtel des Monnaies
rue Bosquet
place Fern. Cocq
rue Berckmans
4
5
6

ancient Guilds of the Middle Ages, and by the city's fairytale Town Hall. And if you are like most visitors, you instantly stop, as if yanked by a string, mouth agape, silent, as you are consumed by the beauty and age of one of the most extraordinary of all attractions.

The market square of Brussels since as early as the 12th century, the Grand-Place is today revered as among the greatest summations of medieval architecture and society—though it's not strictly medieval (except for its 15th-century Town Hall), but rather medieval with a Renaissance (or baroque) updating. The buildings you see today are mostly 18th- and 19th-century replicas of the original buildings, which were reduced to rubble by invading French troops in 1695. Louis XIV's army lined up its artillery on the heights of Anderlecht and blasted away at the medieval Grand-Place, using the Hôtel de Ville (Town Hall) spire as a target. The French destroyed the square, but ironically the Town Hall spire escaped undamaged. Although badly damaged by Louis's guns, the Town Hall, too, is the real thing and dates from the early 1400s. It still dominates the Grand-Place, sitting on its southwestern flank with a facade smothered in statues of biblical figures. The City Hall is open for tours of its sumptuous Neo-Gothic public apartments and magnificent marble staircase; it also now houses a branch of the Brussels tourist office.

Opposite the Town Hall is the ornate facade of the 19th-century neo-Gothic Maison du Roi, location of the **Museum of the City of Brussels** ★ (see p. 221), where displays include the wardrobe of outfits donated to the **Manneken-Pis** (see box p. 218). Spanning the eastern side of the Grand-Place is the Maison de Ducs de Brabent, a series of seven ornate townhouses that formerly belonged to powerful guilds such as the tanners, stonemasons, and sculptors (you'll see their symbols on the facades). In the northwestern corner of the square is the Maison de Roi d'Espagne (House of the Spanish King), which was the base of the bakers' guild.

### The Lost River

Brussels is constructed on a river called the Senne (Zenne in Dutch). In the late 19th century, the City Fathers had it covered up for health reasons (it stank and carried many diseases), and it continues to flow underground. Glimpses of the missing river can still be seen in a tiny courtyard off place St-Géry in the Lower Town, which was once the biggest island in the river. Today the river is reasonably clean, and fish have once more been sighted swimming in it.

There are lots of expensive cafes within the opulent wood-beamed interiors of old guild houses; their upper-floor windows overlooking the Grand-Place offer some of the best views in Europe, and their terraces are sunny spots for an early evening beer.

### Brussels's Other Majestic Squares ★★

**The Grand Sablon** ★★, filled with sidewalk cafes and lined with gabled mansions, is antiques territory; many of its mansions have been

Notre-Dame du Sablon at Grand Sablon.

turned into stores or art galleries. On Saturday and Sunday mornings, an excellent antiques market sets up its stalls in front of **Notre-Dame du Sablon.** This flamboyantly Gothic church has five naves and glorious, slender stained-glass windows; it was built with money donated by the city's wealthy Guild of Crossbowmen in the 15th century.

Just across busy rue de la Régence is the Grand Sablon's little sister, the **Place du Petit Sablon ★.** It contains an ornamental garden with a fountain and pool, a tranquil retreat from the city bustle. The 48 bronze statuettes adorning the wrought-iron fence surrounding the garden symbolize Brussels's medieval guilds. The two statues at the head of the pond commemorate the Catholic counts of Egmont and Hornes, who were beheaded in 1568 for rebelling against Spain's Holy Inquisition in the Low Countries.

Brussels's royal square, **The Place Royale ★,** is at the meeting point of rue de la Régence and rue Royale, the two thoroughfares that hold many of the city's premier museums. This 18th-century square was laid out in neoclassical style and is graced by a heroic **equestrian statue** of the leader of the First Crusade, Duke Godefroid de Bouillon. Archaeologists have excavated the foundations of the Royal Palace of Emperor Charles V on the square, and the site has been covered over again to form the Coudenberg museum (see p. 221).

## dressing THE MANNEKEN-PIS

The celebrated **Manneken-Pis** statue features a tiny, chubby boy peeing into a fountain. Located on the corner of rue du Chêne and rue de l'Etuve, 2 blocks from the Grand-Place, the minute bronze statue is only 60cm high, which is a shock to most people who seek him out expecting something on a grander scale. It's known that the miniscule effigy has graced the city since at least the time of Philip the Good, who was Count of Flanders in 1419. Among the speculation about the boy's origins are that he was the son of a Brussels nobleman who got lost and was found while answering nature's call; another is that he was a patriotic Belgian kid who sprinkled a hated Spanish sentry passing beneath his window. Perhaps the best theory is that he saved the Town Hall from a sputtering bomb by extinguishing it—like Gulliver—with the first thing handy.

Most of the time the Manneken-Pis goes about his business stark naked, although always surrounded by a throng of picture-takers. On high days and holidays, he is dressed in a range of outfits dedicated to the city over the centuries. Louis XV of France began the tradition of presenting colorful costumes for the lad to make amends for the French abduction of the statue in 1747. His 800 or so outfits can be seen in the Musée de la Ville on the Grand-Place (see p. 221). ***Note:*** This is not the original statue, which was prone to theft and anatomical maltreatment; the original was removed for safekeeping.

The diminutive Manneken-Pis

### THE LOWER TOWN

**Cathédrale des Sts-Michel-et-Gudule** ★ CHURCH Rising above the hectic chaos of the Lower Town on Treurenberg, this magnificent twin-towered Roman Catholic church is the purest flowering of the Gothic style; its choir is Belgium's earliest Brabantine Gothic work. Begun in 1226, it wasn't officially consecrated as a cathedral until 1962. The 16th-century Habsburg Emperor Charles V donated the superb stained-glass windows in the Chapelle du St-Sacrément. Apart from these, the spare interior decoration focuses attention on the soaring columns and arches as well as the extravagantly carved wooden pulpit, which depicts Adam and Eve being expelled from Eden, and the statues of the Apostles lined up along the columns supporting the central aisle. It's the official wedding and funeral church of the Belgian Royal Family.

In the **crypt** lie the foundations of the earlier Romanesque church dating from the 11th century. The **Trésor (Treasury)** is also worth visiting for its glowing ecclesiastical vessels in gold, silver, and precious stones.

Parvis Ste-Gudule. www.cathedralisbruxellensis.be. ✆ **02/217-8345.** Cathedral free, crypt and archaeological zone 2.50€, treasury 1€. Mon–Fri 7am–6pm, Sat 8am–3:30pm, Sun 2–6pm.

**Centre Belge de la Bande-Dessinée (Belgian Center for Comic-Strip Art) ★★★** MUSEUM In Belgium, comics are taken as seriously as any other art form, and they are everywhere: on the walls of buildings, occupying their own special sections in book shops, and in this excellent museum, which is inside an Art Nouveau landmark building designed by Victor Horta. "From the early beginnings man told his own story in pictures," states a sign near the entrance, and the hallway welcomes you with a life-size rocket from one of Tintin's adventures. Then you're off on a whirlwind tour, learning about the history of comics, which goes far back. Monks may have invented the language of cartoons: they illustrated sacred texts, divided the story into panels, described movement, painted backgrounds, and even wrote dialogues in bubbles. Texts in the museum are written in French and Dutch, but only partly in English. A short guidebook, however, is available in English, and included in the entrance fee.

Rue des Sables 20. www.comicscenter.net. ✆ **02/219-1980.** 8€ adults; 6€ seniors, students, children 12–18; 3€ children 11 and under. Tues–Sun 10am–6pm.

**Fondation Jacques Brel ★** MUSEUM Dedicated to Belgium's most famous singer and actor, Jacques Brel, this museum offers an overview of his life and work from his birth in 1929 to his death in 1978. Born into an affluent family, Brel composed songs on the piano as a child and made his first record in 1953; he then hotfooted it to Paris, touring almost incessantly for the next 15 years. Along the way, he became one of Europe's foremost singer-songwriters, famously morose and sentimental by turn. He died in Tahiti and is buried close to artist Paul Gauguin. This place offers Brel memorabilia, tracks from his albums, snippets from his movies, and an in-depth examination of his life.

Place de Vieille Halle aux Blés 11. www.jacquesbrel.be. ✆ **02/511-1020.** 5€ adults, 3.50€ seniors/students. Sept–June Tues–Sun noon–6pm, July–Aug daily noon–6pm.

**Hôtel de Ville (Town Hall) ★★** HISTORIC BUILDING Easily the most extravagant in a square full of extravagant buildings, the dazzling Town Hall dates from 1402 and is a masterpiece of Gothic design, with a lacy facade ornamented with dozens of arched windows and sculptures displaying drunken monks, a sleeping Moor and his harem, and St. Michael slaying a female devil. The enormous central tower rears 66m (215 ft.) high and is visible for miles around.

Hôtel de Ville.



The interior is a mélange of the best and most lavish styles from Gothic to Louis XIV and can be toured only by appointment. The mirrored Gothic Hall is a spectacular highlight of the visit to this ultimate monument to urban power, as are the 16th- to 18th-century Flemish tapestries depicting the trades of the guildsmen who commissioned them to hang in the series of embellished council chambers.

Grand-Place. www.brussels.be. ✆ **02/548-0447.** Guided tours only 5€ adults; 3€ seniors, students, and children 6-12; free for children 5 and under. Tickets sold at tourist office in Grand-Place. Tours in English, French, or Dutch Apr–Sept Tues 10am–5pm, Wed 10am–noon, Thurs 2–5pm.

**Musée du Costume et de la Dentelle (Costume and Lace Museum) ★★** MUSEUM Set up in 1977 to celebrate the long tradition of making textiles and lace in Flanders, this collection is surprisingly engaging. As well as ecclesiastical vestments and fine samples of delicate handmade lace, you'll find cabinets full of Panama hats (an obsession in Brussels; scores of stores sell them), Barbie dolls with their many costume changes, and plenty of carefully conserved and elaborately embroidered gowns from the 18th and 19th centuries. Best of all are the cheery displays of 1960s fashion, including tiny miniskirts and bright-red raincoats.

Rue de la Violette 12. www.museeducostumeetdeladentelle.be. ✆ **02/213-4450.** 4€ adults, 3€ seniors/students, 2€ children 5 to 18, free for children 4 and under; free first Sun each month, free for children 17 and under Sat–Sun. Tues–Sun 10am–5pm.

**Musée de la Ville de Bruxelles (Museum of the City of Brussels)** ★ MUSEUM In the opulent neo-Gothic Maison du Roi (King's House), which—despite its name—never housed any kings, the museum documents the history of Brussels. Founded in 1860, showpieces among this broad collection include original Gothic statuary that once adorned the Town Hall, fine tapestries from Brussels's textile workshops, and plans showing how the city developed. But most people visit out of curiosity (or disbelief) to see the nigh-on 800 costumes acquired by the diminutive Manneken-Pis statue around the corner (see box p. 218); it seems that every time an overseas VIP visits Brussels (which is quite often these days, it being the E.U: HQ), they bring yet another outfit for the little guy.

Grand-Place. www.brussels.be. ✆ **02/279-4350.** 4€ adults, 3€ seniors/students, 2€ children 6–15, free for children 5 and under. Tues–Sun 10am–5pm.



## THE UPPER TOWN

**BELvue Museum & Coudenberg** ★ MUSEUM Housed in the former Coudenberg Palace, these two museums are uneasy bedfellows, both very interesting in their own right but not working together to form a cohesive picture of Brussels history. The BELvue relates the story of Belgium through the struggles for independence from The Netherlands and the final breakaway in 1830 to its present (almost) unified political state. Displays include black–and-white film, heaps of old weapons, and some graphic images of Flanders trenches in World War I. The Coudenberg dives down underneath the palace to explore the vast maze of tunnels that were at street level in the 17th century; the tentacles of the museum spread right under the Place Royale, taking in former kitchens,

**The Coudenberg.**

chapels, a few Roman remains, and whole streets that were covered over when King Léopold I constructed his palatial new city in the 1860s.

Place des Palais 7. www.belvue.be. ✆ **070/220-492.** 5€ adults, 4€ seniors, 3€ students 18–25, free for children 17 and under. Mon–Fri 10am–5pm, Sat–Sun 10am–6pm.

**Musée Magritte ★★** MUSEUM Do not confuse this spectacular collection with the museum in artist René Magritte's Brussels home. Located in the Hôtel Altenloh, a neoclassical mansion dating from 1779, the collection holds more than 150 works of Magritte's eccentric, surreal works and covers all periods of his oeuvre, exhibiting musical scores and photos of his private life as well as signature works such as his series *The Dominion of Light* and *The Domain of Arnheim.*

Place Royale. www.musee-magritte-museum.be. ✆ **02/508-3211.** 8€ adults, 6€ seniors/students, 2€ ages 6–26; combination ticket with all 4 museums 13€ adults, 9€ seniors/students, 3€ ages 6–26; free for all 1st Wed afternoon each month.

**Musées Royaux des Beaux-Arts de Belgique (Royal Fine Arts Museums of Belgium) ★★★** MUSEUM A feast for the senses, the Royal Museums of Fine Arts of Belgium are in effect four separate museums: the **Musée d'Art Ancien** (Museum of Old Masters), which covers the 15th to the 17th centuries; the **Musée d'Art Moderne,** with works from the 19th century onward; the **Musée de la Fin de Siècle,** which opened in late 2013 and covers works around the turn of the 20th century; and the **Magritte Museum,** devoted to the Surrealist genius René Magritte.

As you'd expect, this is a huge complex, with over 20,000 works. So how to tackle it? I would recommend first visiting the Old Master Museum, and then coming back another day for the next two. (Because the Magritte Museum is devoted to a single artist, its focus and feel is very different; it's covered under a separate entry, above.) The Museum of Old Masters is a blockbuster, with masterpieces by most of the founders of European art. It's centered around the Southern Netherlands, with many paintings from there worth lingering on, including the *Portrait of Anthony of Burgundy* by Rogier van der Weyden. The "Great Bastard of Burgundy," as its noble subject was known, was one of the illegitimate children of Philip the Good, who ruled over an empire covering most of Belgium in the 15th century. Another standout is Brueghel the Elder's *Census at Bethlehem,* showing Mary riding a donkey through a snowy Brabant village. Don't miss the significant collection of works by Peter Paul Rubens, including *The Ascent to Calvary,* plus art by Anthony van Dyck and Jacques Jordaens in the galleries devoted to Flemish art in the 17th and 18th centuries. The rich collection comes courtesy of Napoléon, who in 1801 founded the museum from works seized during the French Revolution. A visit to *Marat Assassiné,* Jacques Louis David's dramatic and iconic portrayal of the French Revolutionary stabbed to death in his bath in 1793, makes a fitting end to a visit.

The **Museum of Modern Art** is also spectacular, filled with work by symbolists like Constant Montald and Victor Rousseau, and realists such as Jef Lambeaux and Constantin Meunier, alongside contemporary works, including Thierry De Cordier's *Emerald Vision* (2009). The **Fin-de-Siècle Museum** displays works created between 1868, when the Société libre des Beaux-Arts was founded, and 1914, when World War I began. Brussels was at the heart of the flowering of Art Nouveau, and this museum's four floors cover all the major artistic disciplines it influenced, including painting, sculpture, photography, film, architecture, furniture, jewelry, and glassware. Some names (van Gogh, Burne-Jones, Bonnard, Sisley) are likely to be familiar, but many others will be happy discoveries, particularly to non-Belgians (Hippolyte Boulenger and Léon Spilliaert are among them). It's a stunning collection showing the wonderful exuberance and explosion of arts and crafts during the Belle Epoque.

Place Royale 1-3. www.fine-arts-museum.be. ✆ **02/508-3211.** Admission per museum 8€ adults, 6€ seniors/students, 2€ ages 6–26; combination ticket with all 4 museums 13€ adults, 9€ seniors/students, 3€ ages 6–26; free for all 1st Wed afternoon each month. Tues–Sun 10am–5pm.



## PARC DU CINQUANTENAIRE

Designed to celebrate the half-centenary of Belgium's 1830 independence, the **Cinquantenaire (Golden Jubilee) Park** was a work in progress from the 1870s until well into the 20th century. Extensive gardens surround the triumphal Arc du Cinquantenaire, topped by a bronze chariot representing "Brabant Raising the National Flag" and flanked by colonnaded pavilions housing three fine museums; plan to spend the day here to really do all three justice. **Autoworld** and the **Royal Museum of the Armed Forces and Military History** face each other across the gardens; the **Musée du Cinquantenaire** is tucked away around the back of Autoworld.

### Understanding Brussels Today

**eB! experience Brussels ★★★** is the latest attraction to join the museums clustered together around the place Royale (see p. 217). It concentrates on providing a lively and informative snapshot of the city today—warts and all—and gets its message across loud and clear about contentious issues such as multicultural tensions; the Flemish/Dutch/French language dichotomy; urban development; and the need for greater green measures to conserve the city's limited energy resources. If all this sounds dull, it's not. The exhibitions come alive through interactive media, big screens and film, impressive color photography, and plenty of personal accounts. For a précis of where Brussels is today, this exhibition is a great place to start. You'll find it at BIP, place Royale 2-4 (www.biponline.be; ✆ **02/563-6399**). It's open daily 10am to 6pm, and best of all, it's free.

Parc du Cinquantenaire.



**Autoworld** ★★ MUSEUM This massive museum's holdings are drawn primarily from the motor enthusiast Ghislain Mahy's collection of 800 vehicles, which were acquired over a period of 40 years; more than 250 of those are on display here. The cars include outstanding models from familiar brands like Bentley and Daimler, Formula 1 monsters, and many obscurities, such as a motorized tricycle from 1899, a Delahaye fire engine from 1907 and a Leon Bollee Voiturette from 1886.

Parc du Cinquantenaire 11. www.autoworld.be. ✆ **02/736-4165.** 9€ adults, 7€ seniors/students, 3€ children 6–12, free for children 5 and under. Apr–Sept daily 10am–6pm; Oct–Mar Tues–Fri 10am–5pm, Sat–Sun 10am–6pm.

**Musée du Cinquantenaire** ★★★ MUSEUM The magnificent collection at this museum takes you on a journey through five continents with four main themes: Belgian archaeology, antiquities, European decorative art, and non-European civilizations (the Indonesian works, from ivory shadow puppets to wooden models of traditional stilt houses, are particularly fascinating). The rotation of the huge permanent collection, as well as special exhibits, means that what's on display changes regularly. Founded in 1835, the museum has holdings that were initially drawn from the treasures owned by the dukes of Brabant and the archdukes of Hapsburg, who ruled Belgium for centuries. Today there are over 650,000 items from all over the world.

Parc du Cinquantenaire 10. www.kmkg-mrah.be. ✆ **02/741-7211.** 5€ adults, 4€ seniors/students, 1.50€ children 5–17, free for children 4 and under. Tues–Fri 9:30am–5pm, Sat–Sun 10am–5pm.

**Musée Royal de l'Armée et d'Histoire Militaire (Royal Museum of the Armed Forces and Military History)** ★★ MUSEUM The Royal Museum of the Army and of Military History was first created for

## A new ART

A new design style appeared toward the end of the 19th century and flourished for a few decades across Europe. It was called Art Nouveau and its prime materials were glass and iron, which were worked with decorative curved lines and floral and geometric motifs. Belgium produced one of its greatest exponents in **Victor Horta** (1861–1947); his work can be seen all over Brussels and especially at the **Tassel House** (1893; rue Paul Emile Janson 6) and the **Hôtel Solvay** (1895; avenue Louise 224). His own house is open to the public: the **Musée Horta ★ (Horta Museum;** see below) in St-Gilles, a southern suburb of Brussels.

Fans of the city's superb legacy of Art Nouveau architecture should check out the works of **Gustave Strauven** (1878–1919), the Brussels-born student of Horta. Strauven's signature is his use of blue and yellow bricks. He designed around 100 private houses in Brussels, including the slender **Maison Saint-Cyr** (1903) at square Ambiorix 11. This flamboyant, almost sensuous Gaudíesque masterpiece of curling wrought-iron, curved windows, and swirling brick was built for the artist Georges Léonard de Saint-Cyr by Strauven when he was a 22-year-old student.



the World Exhibition in 1910. Its extensive holdings trace changes in military techniques from medieval times onward. The most impressive section of the museum is the massive, glass-walled hangar-style atrium containing more than 100 military planes and helicopters from Spitfires, Hurricanes, and Junkers to Soviet MiGs and French Mirages.

Parc du Cinquantenaire 3. www.klm-mra.be. ✆ **02/737-7811.** Free. Tues–Sun 9am–5pm.

### SUBURBS

**Musée Bruxellois de la Gueuze (Museum of Gueuze Brewing)** ★★ BREWERY/MUSEUM The last Lambic brewery still operating in Brussels is a family-run affair where organic Lambic beers have been produced since 1900. This boutique brewery has built a thriving business in its quaintly old-fashioned premises, running self-guided tours of the traditional cooperage and brewing rooms and offering a bistro menu in the **Carillon restaurant.** Highly prized by beer buffs among these are Rosé de Gambrinus, flavored with raspberries, and the Grand Cru Bruocsella, which is matured for 3 years in oak casks. A visit here is both informative and entertaining. The location in Anderlecht is not great, however—be prepared for some of the rougher elements of Brussels life to be on show.

Rue Gheude 56. www.cantillon.be. ✆ **02/521-4928.** 7€. Mon–Fri 9am–5pm, Sat 10am–5pm.

**Musée Horta (Horta Museum)** ★ MUSEUM Visiting the Horta Museum takes you straight back to the golden age of Art Nouveau. Victor

Horta (1861–1947), was the most important architect of Art Nouveau buildings in the capital. The Horta Museum, which was both his private house and studio, was built between 1898 and 1901 and extended and changed over the following decade. The museum has been pretty well left as it was during Horta's day, a small Art Nouveau masterpiece in which, in true Horta fashion, every detail was planned to fit into the overall design. There are mosaics, enameled bricks, stained glass, and metal arches throughout, and the original furniture and details are what help make it all fit together in glorious harmony. It gives you a very real feel of the era, something that the Fin-de-Siècle Museum (which you'll still want to visit if you're an Art Nouveau fan) fails to achieve. ***Tip:*** Get there 30 minutes before the doors open to make sure you get in.

Rue Américaine 25. www.hortamuseum.be. ✆ **02/543-0490.** 8€ adults, 4€ seniors/students, 2.50€ children 5–18, free for children 4 and under. Tues–Sun 2–5:30pm.

**Musée René Magritte** ★ MUSEUM The famous Belgian surrealist artist René Magritte lived and worked in a meager townhouse in suburban Jette in northwest Brussels between 1930 to 1954. Maintained in its original state as a private museum, the house provides a rather slight glimpse at Magritte's career. You have to knock to gain entrance, and of the 19 rooms on view, most are protected with glass screens so you can only peer myopically into his life, although you do get to see the dining room–cum–studio where he painted many of his fantastical masterpieces. Definitely one only for the ardent lover of Surrealism; everybody else is better off at the **Musée Magritte** ★★ in place Royale (p. 222).

Rue Esseghem 135 (Métro 6 to Belgica). www.magrittemuseum.be. ✆ **02/428-2626.** 7.50€ adults, 6€ ages 9–22, free for children 8 and under. Wed–Sun 10am–6pm.

**Musée David et Alice van Buuren** ★★ MUSEUM The collection of the banker David van Buuren and his wife, Alice, is well worth the journey out to the southern suburbs of Brussels. The cultured and wealthy couple designed the house and garden as a harmonious whole, and from 1928 began to fill it with five centuries of art, including rare pieces of furniture, carpets, sculptures, and stained-glass windows. Alice turned it into a museum in 1975. The exterior gives little hint of the beautiful Art Deco interior, which makes much use of exotic woods and precious materials. Inside are paintings by Peter Brueghel the Elder, the school of Rembrandt, van Gogh, and James Ensor. Many people come here just for the extensive gardens, which include a symbolist garden and an Art Deco rose garden.

Avenue Léo Errera 41. www.museumvanbuuren.be. ✆ **02/343-4851.** Garden and museum 10€ adults, 8€ seniors, 5€ students, free for children 11 and under; garden only 5€ adults, 4€ seniors, 2.50€ students. Wed–Mon 2–5:30pm.

## THE european DISTRICT

Home to the European Commission, European Parliament, Council of Ministers, and related institutions, Brussels has no less than 1.2 million sq. m (12.7 million sq. ft.) of office space packed with 25,000-plus Eurocrats to back up its "Capital of Europe" tag.

To tour the heartland of European Union governance, take the Métro to Schuman station. If you wish to view that exotic species, the European civil servant, in its native habitat, take the tour Monday to Friday, because the district is dead on the weekend.

Your first sight is the X-shaped **Palais de Berlaymont,** the commission's former headquarters at Rond-Point Schuman. Across rue de la Loi, the Council of Ministers headquarters, the **Consilium** is instantly recognizable for its facade's lavish complement of rose-colored granite blocks. On its far side, take a soothing stroll through **Parc Léopold,** an island of green tranquility. This little park is laid out above an ornamental lake and was originally conceived as a zoo and science park. The zoo didn't fly for long, but a cluster of scientific institutes dating from the late 19th and early 20th centuries still occupies part of the terrain.

A walk through Parc Léopold brings you to the postmodern **European Parliament and International Conference Center,** an architectural odyssey in white marble and tinted glass. Take the passageway through the building's middle to **place Luxembourg,** an old square that looks lost and forlorn in comparison to its powerful new neighbors.



## Organized Tours

Guided **bus tours** of Brussels last 2½ hours, operate throughout the year, and are available from **Brussels City Tours** (www.brussels-city-tours.com; ✆ **02/513-7744**). The tours start at 30€ for adults, 28€ for seniors, and 15€ for children 17 and under. Reservations can be made through most hotels, and hotel pickup is often available.

**CitySightseeing Brussels** (www.city-sightseeing.com) offers the now-ubiquitous hop-on, hop-off circular tour of the city; with two lines servicing 22 stops at all major attractions. Prices start at 24€; departures vary from every 45 minutes in winter to every 15 minutes in July and August.

**Brussels Walking Tours** (www.bravodiscovery.com; ✆ **02/495-320-362**) operates a series of nine themed walking tours, from Art Nouveau spotting to beer or chocolate tasting, discovering Jewish Brussels to exploring the Marolles. They last about two hours and prices start at 8€. Meeting points vary according to tour, so check online for further details.

## Especially for Kids

Brussels is fast-paced and chaotic, and not always conducive to visits by families. However, it is the home of a peeing statue (p. 218) and also to Tintin and his little white dog, Snowy. Kids have great fun spotting the

The Atomium.

murals of the intrepid pair in the streets and will appreciate the cartoons and comic strips on display in the **Centre Belge de la Bande-Dessinée ★★★** (p. 219). And let's not forget that Brussels is also the home of chocolate; most children will jump at the chance of a guided tour around the **Musée du Cacao et du Chocolat** (Rue de la Tête d'Or; www.mucc.be; ✆ **02/514-2048**) as much as they will adore gazing longingly through the windows of the classy confectioners (see p. 236).

But to really give the kids a good time, head out to **Bruparck**, north of the city center, to visit the **Atomium ★.** There's nothing quite like this cluster of giant silvery orbs representing the atomic structure of an iron crystal enlarged 165 billion times, rising 102m (335 ft.) like a giant plaything of the gods that's fallen to earth. Constructed for the 1958 World's Fair, the Atomium is visible from pretty much all over Brussels, and it's a fair bet that when you stand underneath this vast construction, you'll be suitably impressed. An elevator shoots up the central column to the five spheres currently open to the public; three provide a permanent record of Expo '58 and the other two host temporary art and science exhibitions. The highest sphere has a glass roof, permitting 360-degree views toward Brussels, and on a clear day Antwerp's cathedral spire can be spotted on the horizon. The Atomium is located at Square de l'Atomium, Bruparck, Heysel (www.atomium.be; ✆ **02/475-4775**). Admission is 11€ adults; 8€ seniors, students, and children 12 to 18; 6€ children 6 to 11; free for children 5 and under. Combined tickets with Mini-Europe are available at 24€ for adults, 21€ seniors, 16€ for children 11 and under, free for children under 1.2m (4 ft.) tall when accompanied by parents. It's open daily 10am until 6pm.

Almost next door is **Mini-Europe ★,** which will intrigue kids and adults alike as they stroll around iconic landmarks from member states of the European Union, including London's Big Ben, Berlin's Brandenburg Gate, the Leaning Tower of Pisa, and Montmartre in Paris. As the E.U. expands, new models appear at Mini-Europe; the latest arrivals are St. Mark's Church from Croatia, and a diorama celebrating the succession of King Philippe to the Belgian throne on July 23, 2013. *Son et lumière* and firework spectaculars are held on Saturday evenings in July and August. Mini-Europe is adjacent to the Atomium (www.minieurope.com; ✆ **02/478-0550**). Admission is 14€ adults, and seniors, 11€

children 11 and under, free for children under 1.2m (4 ft.) tall when accompanied by parents. Combined tickets with the Atomium are available. Opening hours are mid-March to June and September daily 9:30am to 6pm, July and August daily 9:30am to 8pm, October through mid-January daily 10am until 6pm, with an annual closure between mid-January and mid-March.

## Where to Stay

The most popular Brussels districts in which to stay are in the extended zone around the **Grand-Place;** in the upper town district around place Stéphanie and boulevard de Waterloo; and along upmarket **avenue Louise.** These range from large, glittering, and pricey establishments, to decent medium-priced and even budget hotels (mostly in the streets around the Grand-Place and in the Ixelles district to the south of avenue Louise). The **European District** hotels are convenient for visiting Eurocrats, politicians, lobbyists, and media people, but that doesn't make them a good choice for travelers.

At every level, hotels fill up during the week with E.U.–related business travelers, and they empty out on weekends as well as during July and August. In these off-peak periods, rates can drop as much as 50%, making Brussels the perfect destination for weekend breaks.

Obviously the best way of securing rooms in your hotel of choice is to book online well in advance, but if you find yourself stuck, staff at **Brussels tourist offices** can make reservations for the same day if you go to their offices in person and pay a small fee, which is deducted by the hotel from its room rate.

### LOWER TOWN

#### Expensive

**Hotel Amigo ★★★** If you have the money to stay here, then the Amigo is definitely the number-one place to stay in Brussels. It's got it all: the best location in the heart of the city, beautifully decorated rooms (bold colors and stylized furniture, some antiques) that look out onto the rooftops of the Hotel de Ville, great service from a well-trained and charming staff, and superb Italian food at the Ristorante Bocconi. It also has an intriguing history dating back to the 16th century (at one stage it was the city prison; "amigo" was the ironic nickname for the prison when Belgium belonged to the Spanish Low Countries). ***Note:*** There are often good weekend offers in the off-season.

Rue de l'Amigo 1-3. www.hotelamigo.com. ✆ **02/547-4747.** 173 units. Doubles 265€–467€, suites 1,272€–4,500€. **Amenities:** Restaurant; bar; concierge; gym; Wi-Fi (fee).

**Métropole ★★** The Metropole is one of the historic grande dames of Brussels, a glorious evocation of the Belle Epoque era with an echoing central lobby, high ceilings, stained-glass windows, and ornate touches everywhere. It was built by the Wielemans brothers in 1890 to sell beer and was so successful that the family then bought the neighboring building and constructed a hotel to welcome the great and the famous. Today it's still here, though the gracious boulevards of yore have become rivers of traffic, and the fashionable shops have been supplanted by scruffy kebab houses and downmarket clothing stores. It's not the best area of Brussels, which means good rates. Rooms are large; the decor ranges from smart comfort to regal Louis XVI style, with half-tester beds, large sofas to sink into, and desks worthy of signing megadeals at.

Place de Brouckère 31. www.metropolehotel.com. ✆ **02/217-2300.** 305 units. Doubles 88€–215€, suites 325€–675€. **Amenities:** Restaurant; lounge; cafe; business center; boutique; concierge; gym; spa; free Wi-Fi.

### Moderate



**Apart-Hotel ★** With 5 blocks of self-catering apartments scattered through central Brussels, Apart-Hotels offer top-level accommodations with all conveniences, including well-equipped kitchens, comfy beds with quality linen bedding, DVDs, and daily cleaning service. Just be careful which address you go for; the apartments in rue des Dominicains are on a pretty alleyway just steps away from the Grand-Place and all the restaurants around rue des Bouchers, but the noise level ratchets up to an unbearable level come weekend nights. The newer alternatives at boulevard du Regent 58 make better, quieter options, and they are a brief Métro ride away from the action in the Grand-Place.



Rue des Dominicains 25. www.b-aparthotels.com. ✆ **02/743-5111.** 200 units. Doubles 107€–179€. **Amenities:** Wi-Fi (fee).

**Espérance ★** In a small alleyway off the boulevard Anspach, this former *maison de passé,* where rooms were once rented out by the hour to women of the night, is now a small hotel with compact rooms decorated in primary colors; their bathrooms are pristine but also on the tiny side. The **Taverne bar** downstairs remains a perfect Art Deco specimen, with stained-glass windows and aged wooden furniture; it doubles as the breakfast room as well as a restaurant. If you are thinking of staying here, bear in mind that there's no elevator and the staircase is steep.

Rue du Finistère 1-3. www.hotel-esperance.be. ✆ **02/219-1028.** 13 units. Doubles 89€–160€. **Amenities:** Free Wi-Fi.

### Inexpensive

**Auberge de Jeunesse Jacques Brel ★★** This amiable, rather ramshackle hostel is the best budget choice in Brussels. It's on a small road leading up to the delightful place des Barricades. Because the hostel has been shoehorned into an old house, rooms are of odd shapes and sizes, with a total bed capacity of 170, spread over 40 rooms (they hold from two to eight beds and can be sold either on a bed basis or as entire private rooms). The decor is basic, but there's an exceptional, mostly organic buffet breakfast included.

Rue de la Sablonnière 28. www.lesaubergesdejeunesse.be. ✆ **02/219-5676.** 40 units. 97€ private room, rates include breakfast. **Amenities:** Free Wi-Fi.

### UPPER TOWN

#### Expensive

**The Hotel ★** You can't miss The Hotel. It's the 24-story white building on the chic shopping district boulevard de Waterloo. Once a Hilton, The Hotel is now owned by the Swedish group Pandox AB and was completely renovated at the end of 2013. The decor is classy, with lots of blacks, deep browns, white, and beige. Every room has a massive bed, a built-in desk, a large sofa in front of the window with a circular table, and throws on the bed. Unless you suffer from vertigo, book one of the rooms on the top floors and go for a corner room with panoramic views on two sides.

Boulevard de Waterloo 38. www.thehotel-brussels.be. ✆ **02/504-3335.** 421 units. Doubles 110€–210€, suites 360€, rates include buffet breakfast. **Amenities:** Spa; gym; free Wi-Fi.

**Made in Louise ★** When Made in Louise burst on to the Brussels scene in 2012, this chic family-run boutique hotel quickly became a force to be reckoned with. Located in a residential neighborhood, the former townhouse is a historic, protected building; its owners have cleverly used what could have been a major restriction to enhance the feel of a private family home. The vast central staircase leads to the elegantly furnished guest rooms, each of which has a unique style. A room with striped wallpaper feels masculine and bold; another, with vivid, blue-flowered wallpaper, is much more feminine. All rooms have generously sized bathrooms. The separate cottage has 10 rooms overlooking the internal courtyard; these are good for stays of a week or longer, as they come with well-equipped kitchenettes.

Rue Veydt 40. www.madeinlouise.com. ✆ **02/537-4030.** 48 units. Doubles 79€–325€, includes buffet breakfast. **Amenities:** Bar, cafe, pool room, free Wi-Fi.

## Where to Eat

Food is a passion in Brussels, which boasts more Michelin-star restaurants per capita than Paris. It's just about impossible to eat badly, no matter what your price range.

The Brussels restaurant scene covers the entire city, but there are a couple of culinary pockets you should know about. It has been said that you haven't truly visited this city unless you've dined along **rue des Bouchers** and its offshoot, **Petite rue des Bouchers,** both of which are near the Grand-Place. Both are lined with an extraordinary array of ethnic eateries, most with a proudly proclaimed specialty, and all with modest prices. Reservations are not usually necessary in these colorful

# QUICK bites IN BRUSSELS

In business since 1873, the snack bar **Au Suisse,** boulevard Anspach 73-75 (www.ausuisse.be; ✆ **02/512-9589**), serves great sandwiches with fresh ingredients and homemade sauces. This is the place to try a raw-herring sandwich (the seafood in general is ace), and you can sip an iced *frappé* on the sidewalk terrace at lunchtime.

For a tasty breakfast, lunch, or snack, head for the convivial **Roi des Belges ★,** rue Jules Van Praet 34 (✆ **02/513-5116**), on the corner of trendy place St-Géry. The soup of the day or a decent salad won't set you back more than a few euros.

Another seductive invitation is the aroma of **fresh Brussels waffles,** sold from street stands around the city. Thicker than American waffles, they cost about 3€ and are smothered in sugar icing. The stands are all pretty decent, so there's not much reason to try one over another. Should you want to sample an impressive range of toppings and accompaniments, head to **Aux Gaufres de Bruxelles,** rue du Marché aux Herbes 113 (www.belgiumwaffle.com; ✆ **02/514-0171**).

And don't forget those *frites* (fries). Belgians usually eat their favorite snack with mayonnaise rather than ketchup. Prices run from around 2.50€ to 4€ for a *cornet* (cone); sauces, such as peanut, tartare, samurai (hot!), or curry, cost extra. Brussels is dotted with dozens of fast-food stands serving *frites* in paper cones. One of the best, **Maison Antoine ★,** place Jourdan 1 (www.maisonantoine.be; ✆ **02/230-5456**), in the European District, has been in situ since the 1940s. You'll have to join the line at peak times, but it's worth it. ***Vegetarians take note:*** Unless otherwise specified or requested, those tasty *frites* are fried in beef tallow—that's what gives them their distinct flavor.

**Decadent Belgian waffles.**

and crowded restaurants; if you cannot be seated at one, simply stroll to the next.

There's also the cluster of fine restaurants at the **Marché aux Poissons (Fish Market),** a short walk from the Grand-Place around place Ste-Catherine, where fishermen once unloaded their daily catches. Take an afternoon stroll through the area to examine the menus exhibited in windows and make your reservation for the evening.

## LOWER TOWN

### Expensive

**Belga Queen ★★** CONTEMPORARY BELGIAN Housed in a former bank, Belga Queen has pomp and circumstance to spare, with a

huge marble entrance, columns and pillars, and a curved roof with frescoes and stained glass. This brasserie is huge, and the menu is long, which could be a recipe for disaster. But the cooking is spot-on; not three-star worthy, perhaps, but reliable (try dishes like a simple sole meunière with pan-fried vegetables, €37, or crusted rack of lamb with beans and rosemary-infused cream €38). There's an oyster bar to one side of the entrance. Don't listen to those who sniff at Belga Queen as passé; it's a great place to eat.
Rue du Fossée aux Loups 32. www.belgaqueen.be. ✆ **02/217-2187.** Reservations recommended on weekends. Lunch 18€, dinner mains 23€–47€. Daily noon–2:30pm and 7pm–midnight.

**Comme Chez Soi ★★★** FRENCH Classic French cuisine at its most refined. Dinner is served in an opulent Art Nouveau dining room resplendent with swirling woodwork and delicate garlands of wrought iron, and under the influence of Chef Lionel Rigolet, service is attentive but delightfully unstuffy. With menus changing seasonally, most of the ingredients are organic and all are prepared with loving care and attention to the most minute of details; menus might encompass cod with Mechelen asparagus or quail stuffed with sweet pepper and artichoke. Book for dinner as far ahead as possible; getting a table at short notice is more likely at lunchtime. You can also choose to eat in the kitchen to spy on the chefs at work.
Place Rouppe 23. www.commechezsoi.be. ✆ **02/512-2921.** Reservations required. Lunch 55€, dinner mains 43€–173€, fixed-price menus 94€–199€. Tues–Sat noon–1:30pm and 7–9:30pm.

### Moderate

**Cecila ★★** BELGIAN This small restaurant has been a hit since it opened in 2013. Chef Melanie Englebin has a sure touch, using the freshest of seasonal ingredients and making sure the dishes look beautiful on the plate, with herbs and edible flowers adding color. On the regularly changing set menu (there's no a la carte), you might get a winter butternut squash soup with a bacon emulsion or sea bass served with something unusual, such as lamb cheek. The open kitchen shows a happy crew doing what they love. Be sure to book in advance.
Rue de Chapeliers 16. www.resaurantcecila.com. ✆ **02/503-4474.** Mains 14€–28€. Mon–Fri noon–3pm and 6–11:30pm, Sat–Sun noon–11:30pm.

**Coin de Mer ★** BELGIAN One of scores of seafood restaurants tucked away around the Grand-Place, Coin de Mer has a buzzing atmosphere in bright-white, simple surroundings, and a fast turnover of people grabbing at the chance to sample their vast seafood platters. These great piles of delectability come with crab, lobster, oysters, cockles, and razor clams, all fresher than fresh. Other top choices include the classic *moule-frîtes* combo and dishes of delicious Spanish paella. Service is

> **Lunchtime Bargains in Brussels**
>
> Most restaurants serve lunch between noon and 2pm, and reopen for dinner from 7 to 10pm, with brasseries staying open all day. Almost every eatery in Brussels offers a *menu du jour* at lunchtime, consisting of a fixed menu with a couple of two- or three-course options—often with a glass of table wine thrown in—that are often markedly good values in this expensive city. If you are yearning to try one of the fancier restaurants but can't face the bill, try them out for lunch.

surprisingly cordial and relaxed, which is why this place stands out from its neighbors.

Rue de la Fourche 31-35. ✆ **02/503-0703.** Mains lunch 14€, dinner 18€–28€. Mon–Fri noon–3pm and 6–11:30pm, Sat–Sun noon–midnight.



## UPPER TOWN

### Expensive

**La Quincaillerie ★★★** BELGIAN/FRENCH Inside a former ironmonger shop built in 1903, La Quincaillerie has a beautiful Art Nouveau exterior and an interior of wrought-iron balconies, polished brass, and a huge clock. It's always buzzing as waiters deliver dishes with style to a chic clientele. The restaurant takes the environmental route with ingredients, using sustainable fish sources; lamb from its own farm in Bresse, France; locally procured vegetables; and organic and biodynamic wines. This is combined with an intriguing menu, which may include grilled bone marrow, pig's trotters, and toasted sourdough bread for a starter; and Challans duck with leeks and dauphinoise potatoes as a main.

Rue de Page 45. www.quincaillerie.be. ✆ **02/533-9833.** Reservations recommended. Lunch menu 14€, fixed-price menu 29€, dinner mains 19€–34€. Tues–Sat noon–2:30pm, 7pm–midnight.

**Lola ★★** BRASSERIE Genteel elderly couples and smart young things, tourists as well as suits clearly working for the E.U.—all are cheerfully welcomed in this savvy contemporary brasserie. The long, narrow, canteen-style room is decked in cheery colors and industrial-style piping. The pan-European menu includes Scottish smoked salmon with horseradish cream as well as good Belgian shrimp croquettes. For mains, items like duck breast with caramelized apples, cider, and mashed potatoes hit the spot. The wine list is moderately priced, and the older waiters are some of the most professional—and friendliest—in town. Lola deserves her success.

Place du Grand Sablon 33. www.restolola.be. ✆ **02/514-2460.** Mains 12€–34€. Daily noon–3pm and 6:30–11:30pm, Sat–Sun noon–11:30pm.

### Moderate

**Le Wine Bar Sablon des Marolles ★★** TRADITIONAL BELGIAN A glass of wine from the short but good list, and a selection of plates from the menu, is just the thing after a morning shopping at the famous *brocante* market in the place du Jeu de Balle (p. 236) or in the antiques shops of the Marolles. This wine bar is located in a 17th-century house with wooden floors, chairs, and tables; the simple surroundings are elevated by the vast paintings and prints on the walls. The short menu is cleverly put together, with plates ideal for sharing from 8€ to 10€. Try the chicken liver pâté, geese rillettes, or sardines with olive oil. More substantial dishes could include smoked sausage with Puy lentils or beef braised in red wine. There's also a fish dish that changes daily, and a good selection of cheese for dessert.

Rue Haute 198. www.winebarsablon.be. ✆ **02/496-0105.** Mains 10€–20€. Wed–Sat 6–11pm, Sat–Sun noon–3pm.

### Inexpensive

**Pistolet Original ★** BELGIAN A *pistolet* is a filled, crusty bread roll—something that every Belgian child grows up on—so Valérie Lepla struck a rich, nostalgic vein with this deli/cafe in the smart Sablon district. (Pistolet Original makes a perfect spot for lunch after rummaging around the weekend antiques markets.) A few of the available fillings: Ardenne ham, shrimp, sharp-tasting pickles, *rollmops* (pickled herring filets), roast beef, celery root, braised chicory, blood pudding, *potjesvlees* (Flemish terrine), and butter or chocolate.

Rue Joseph Steven 24-26. www.pistolet-original.be. ✆ **02/880-8098.** Mains 4€–8€. Daily 8am–6pm.

## SUBURBS

### Expensive

**Restaurant Bon-Bon ★★★** HAUTE CUISINE Chef Christophe Hardiquest is one of Belgium's top young chefs, a name to watch as he collects Michelin stars (he's up to two; you must now book dinner months in advance). Billed as a *salon d'artisan cuisinier* (the salon of an artisan chef), this is serious dining. Chef believes strongly in the connection between the region and the taste of a product—only ingredients that have the location-specific *appellation d'origine contrôlée* designation are used here, and to very tasty effect.

Avenue de Tervueren 453, Woluwe-Satin-Pierre. www.bon-bon.be. ✆ **02/346-6615.** Reservations required. Fixed-price menus 80€–175€. Tues–Fri noon–1:30pm, Mon–Fri 7:30–9pm.

# Shopping

Brussels is not a city where you'll find shopping bargains. It's expensive—certainly as expensive as Paris, and more so than Amsterdam. As a general rule, the upper city around avenue Louise and Porte de Namur is more expensive than the lower city around rue Neuve and the center-city shopping galleries around La Monnaie and place de Brouckère. But that's not hard and fast; rue Haute in the upper city is currently

## BRUSSELS specialties

The Bruxellois know a thing or two about chocolate. Just ask anyone who has ever bitten into one of those devilish little handmade pralines made by Wittamer at Place du Grand Sablon 12-13 (www.wittamer.com; ✆ **02/512-3742**)—and that includes today's Royal Family of Belgium. Operating since 1910, its hot pink wrapping paper is as well known in Belgium as the duck-egg blue of Tiffany. A worthy competitor is the store **Mary** (Rue Royal 73; www.marychoc.com; ✆ **02/217-4500**), established in 1919 by one of the very few female chocolatiers in Belgium; and the beloved **Nihoul,** at chaussée de Vleurgat 111 (www.nihoul.be; ✆ **02/648-3796**). And for a different type of sweet treat, head to **Maison Dandoy** (Rue au Beurre 31; www.biscuiteriedandoy.be; ✆ **02/511-0326**). Founded in 1829, Dandoy is still the place for the sweet treat of spicy cinnamon and brown-sugar speculoos cookies, still baked traditionally in wooden molds.

Lace is another favorite that's widely available in the city, particularly around the Grand-Place. Purchase from **Maison Antoine** (Grand-Place 26; ✆ **02/512-4859**) or at the oh-so-traditional **Manufacture Belge de Dentelle** (www.mbd.be) which is based in the Galeries Royal St-Hubert and has been there since 1847, selling only the finest, handmade lace.

For local beers such as gueuze, kriek, and faro—among the 450 or so different Belgian beers—head for the **Musée Bruxellois de la Gueuze** (p. 225) or **Beer Mania** (Chaussée de Wavre 174; www.beermania.be; ✆ **02/512-1788**). Both can ship beer overseas. Also check out the aisles in local supermarkets, where you'll find a great choice of beers at decent prices, too. And if you're serious about your brew go for the local specialty, a Lambic beer. These use naturally occurring yeast for fermentation, are often flavored with fruit, and come in bottles with champagne-type corks. They're almost akin to sweet sparkling wine. Try raspberry-flavored framboise or cherry-flavored kriek. If you prefer something less sweet, order Gueuze, a blend of young and aged Lambic beers.

And if you're not sure what you want, head to the **Vieux Marché** (Place du Jeu de Balle), Brussel's best flea market. Set on a large piazza, it's a joy to rummage around here; it has an eccentric bunch of stallholders selling an equally eccentric range of items from vintage clothes to knock-off watches. Those in the know go on Thursday, when there may be a sprinkling of antiques to be unearthed. Bargaining is sometimes acceptable, but play it by ear before diving in with insulting offers. The market's open daily 7am until 2pm (until 3pm weekends).

**A Brussels chocolate shop.**

inexpensive, although as more and more design and antiques stores open, this will cease to be the case. The Galeries Royales St-Hubert, in the lower city, are wildly expensive.

**Rue Neuve,** which starts at place de la Monnaie and extends north to place Rogier in the lower city, is a busy and popular area that's home to many boutiques and department stores, including the City 2 shopping

### Brussels's Oldest Shopping Mall

One of Europe's oldest shopping malls consists of the three interconnected, glass-roofed arcades of the **Galeries Royales St-Hubert** (www.galeries-saint-hubert.com). Constructed in Italian neo-Renaissance style and opened in 1847, architect Pierre Cluysenaer's elegant galleries are light and airy, hosting top-end boutiques Delvaux, Oriande, Manufacture Belge de Dentelles, Longchamp, numerous chocolate shops (Godiva, Neuhaus, Léonidas), sidewalk cafes, and musicians playing classical music. The Galerie du Roi, Galerie de la Reine, and Galerie des Princes were the forerunners of city malls like Burlington Arcade in London, and lie just north of the Grand-Place, between rue du Marché aux Herbes and rue d'Arenberg.

complex. **Boulevard Anspach,** which runs from the Stock Exchange up to place de Brouckère, offers mid-range fashion boutiques and electronic-appliance stores, plus the **Anspach Center** mall.

**Avenue Louise** and **boulevard de Waterloo** in the upper city attract those in search of world-renowned, high-quality goods from Cartier, Burberry's, Louis Vuitton, and Valentino. The **place du Grand Sablon** is home of snooty antiques shops and expensive galleries, while trendsters hit edgy **rue Antoine Dansaert** for small, independent boutiques and contemporary designers.

## Entertainment & Nightlife

An **opera** house in flamboyant baroque style, the **Théâtre Royal de la Monnaie ★★,** place de la Monnaie (www.lamonnaie.be; ✆ **02/229-1211**), is home to drama performances and chamber-music concerts as well as the **Opéra Royal de la Monnaie**—regarded as the best in the French-speaking world—and the **Orchestre Symphonique de la Monnaie.** The resident modern **dance** company, renowned Belgian choreographer Anne Teresa de Keersmaeker's group **Rosas ★★** (www.rosas.be), is noted for its innovative performances. The box office is at rue Léopold 4 and is open Tuesday to Friday noon to 6pm, Saturday 10am until 6pm. Ticket prices vary from 20€ to 350€ according to the event.

**BOZAR ★,** rue Ravenstein 23 (www.bozar.be; ✆ **02/507-8200**), aka the Palais des Beaux-Arts, is a lovely building designed by Victor Horta and now home to a mixed bag of cultural offerings from classical concerts by Belgium's National Orchestra to jazz and world music, movies, and a full program of plays. The box office is open Tuesday to Friday 11am to 7pm, with tickets running from 15€ to 100€, depending on the event.

Brussels offers more than 30 **theatres** presenting performances in French, Dutch, and (occasionally) English. Foremost among these is the **Théâtre Royal du Parc ★★,** rue de la Loi 3 (www.theatreduparc.be;

> **Brussels Gay & Lesbian Life**
>
> The Brussels LGBT scene is somewhat subdued, but there are several gay and lesbian bars along rue des Riches-Claires and rue du Marché au Charbon.
>
> **Brussels Gay Pride** (www.pride.be) takes place in May each year, a vibrant street party taking over the center of the city.
>
> For the inside slant on gay life in Brussels, stop by the gay and lesbian community center, **Tels Quels,** rue du Marché au Charbon 81 (www.telsquels.be; ✆ **02/512-4587**), open Monday to Friday 8:30am to 12:30pm and 2 to 7pm. On the same street there is a gay meeting room and cafe at **Rainbow House,** rue du Marché au Charbon 42 (www.rainbowhouse.be; ✆ **02/503-5990**). Both venues are run by volunteers.

✆ **02/505-3040**), a magnificent edifice occupying a corner of the Parc de Bruxelles, where classic and contemporary drama and comedies are performed. The **Théâtre National de la Communauté Française,** boulevard Emile Jacqmain 111-115 (www.theatrenational.be; ✆ **02/203-4145**), offers avant-garde drama; and the **Théâtre Royal des Galeries,** Galerie du Roi 32 (www.trg.be; ✆ **02/512-0407**), is known for comedy and musicals. Bringing theater to the city in Flemish is the **Koninklijke Vlaamse Schouwburg,** quai aux Pierres de Taille 9 (www.kvs.be; ✆ **02/210-1112**), in a restored neo-Renaissance-style building dating from 1887.

Bars and pubs are where Brussels lives. It's hard to be disappointed, whether you pop into a neighborhood watering hole where a *chope* or *pintje* (a glass of beer) will set you back a mere 2.50€, or fork out several times as much in sleek, designer bars. In fact, even the expensive bars around Grand-Place are worth a visit for the scenery and grandeur of both architecture and service. Of the hundreds of bars in Brussels, I enjoy the style and ambiance at A la Mort Subite (Rue Montagne aux Herbes Potageres 7; www.alamortsubite.com; ✆ **02/513-1318**), an old-fashioned drinking hall with hundreds of bottled and tap beers; the swankiest cafe in the city, La Chaloupe d'Or ★ (Grand-Place 24-25; ✆ **02/511-4161**); **La Fleur en Papier Doré** ★★ (Rue des Alexiens 55; www.lafleurenpapierdore.be; ✆ **02/511-1659**), an artist's haunt since 1846; and at the Belle Epoque beauty (love that long brass bar) **Le Cirio** ★★ (Rue de la Bourse 18; ✆ **02/512-1395**).

# BRUGES

A city arrested in time. A Pompeii or a Brigadoon. An urban portrait caught as if by stop-frame photography, of a community that died while it was still young. The most heavily visited touristic destination in all of Belgium, it is the victim of one of the strangest events of history—the "silting of the Zwin"—which snuffed out its commercial life in the late

Twilight along the canals of Bruges.

Middle Ages, caused it to miss the Industrial Revolution, and thus paradoxically saved its medieval legacy from the wrecker's ball. If only more medieval cities had suffered such a misfortune.

Bruges in medieval times was the greatest trading center in Northern Europe, a multi-national marketplace for importing and exporting cloth and spices, herring and wine, and every variety of goods. The city's vital access road was the Zwin, an estuary that connected Bruges to the North Sea. In the mid-1300s, for reasons still not fully understood, the Zwin began to "silt up"—to fill with sand—denying passage to deep draft ships. And when commerce died, Bruges died. Large portions of the population—some estimate as many as half—left to seek employment in Antwerp and other cities, abandoning their stunning homes, their commercial palaces, their magnificent squares.

Of course, not all ended. With the onset of the religious wars in the late 1500s, Catholic priests, nuns, monks and friars fled to Bruges for safety, building additional churches and accommodations which survive to this day. In the 16th century, various wealthy philanthropists dotted the city with almshouses ("godshuizen") built for the poor; they too, remain. In the 17th century, there occurred a weak revival of sorts, and gabled structures in fair number survive from that era. But Bruges remained a backwater, dozing through the 18th and 19th centuries until an author named Georges Rodenbach inadvertently broadcast its charms to the world in a novel called *Bruges-la-Morte* (Dead Bruges) and set off a wave of tourism that continues today.

## Essentials

**Visit Bruges** (www.visitbruges.be) is the official, multilingual website of the city.

**ARRIVING** Two **trains** arrive in Bruges every hour from Brussels, four or five from Ghent, two from Antwerp, and up to three every hour from the ferry ports of Zeebrugge and Ostend (Oostende). The travel time is around 1 hour from Brussels, 25 minutes from Ghent, 1 hour and 20 minutes from Antwerp, and 15 minutes from both Ostend and Zeebrugge. Train information is available from **SNCB** (**Belgian Railways;** www.belgianrail.be; ✆ **02/528-28-28**).

Although the city is called Bruges in both English and French, look for its Flemish name, brugge, written on the station name boards. The station is on Stationsplein, 1.5km (1 mile) south of the center of town, a 20-minute walk or a short taxi or bus ride—choose any bus labeled centrum and get out at the Markt to be in the center of the action.

**Buses** are less useful than trains for getting to Bruges, although there is frequent service from Zeebrugge, Ostend, and other Belgian seacoast resorts. The Bruges bus station adjoins the rail station. Schedule and fare information is available from **De Lijn** (www.delijn.be/en; ✆ **070/220-200**).

**Eurolines** (www.eurolines.co.uk) operates a cheap daily bus service to Bruges from London, Amsterdam, Paris, Cologne, and other cities around Europe.

If you're **driving**, Bruges is 96km (60 miles) northwest of Brussels on the E40/A10; 50km (30 miles) northwest of Ghent on the E40/A10; 107km (66 miles) west of Antwerp on either the E17/A14 and E40/A10, or the E34, which bypasses Ghent; 18km (11 miles) south of the ferry port of Zeebrugge on E403 and N371; and 30km (19 miles) southeast of Ostend on E40/A10. From the Eurotunnel and Calais in France, take E40/A16 east to Bruges.

**CITY LAYOUT** Bruges is a circular tangle of streets surrounded by canals and moats; the monumental squares of the Markt and the Burg are fairly central, adjoined by a labyrinth of alleyways and dramatic,

### Brugge City Card

For the avid museum-goer, the money-saving **Brugge City Card** is available from all the tourist offices, with the most convenient being at the **Historium Brugge ★★** in Markt (see p. 245). You get free entry to 27 museums, plus discounted entrance to several others; a free canal trip (p. 251); a trip up the Belfort (p. 261); discounts on theater tickets (p. 237) and bike hire (p. 242); and the chance to buy 3 days of transport on DeLijn buses (see p. 241) for 6€. All this is priced at 40€ for a 48-hour pass, and 45€ for 72 hours. You can also order the Brugge City Card ahead of time at **www.bruggecitycard.be**.

## events IN BRUGES

One of the most popular and colorful folklore events in Belgium is Bruges's **Heilig-Bloedprocessie (Procession of the Holy Blood) ★,** which dates back to at least 1291 and takes place every year on Ascension Day (fifth Thurs after Easter). During the procession, the bishop of Bruges proceeds through the city streets carrying the golden shrine containing the Relic of the Holy Blood (p. 245). Residents wearing Burgundian-era and biblical costumes follow the relic, acting out biblical and historical scenes along the way.

Every 5 years, the canals of Bruges are the subject and location of the **Reiefeest (Canal Festival) ★★.** This multi-day evening event takes place on 6 nonconsecutive days in August and is a combination of historical tableaux, dancing, open-air concerts, and lots of eating and drinking. The next Reiefeest is in 2018. (www.brugge.be; ✆ **050/444-646**).

The **Praalstoet van de Gouden Boom (Pageant of the Golden Tree) ★★★** celebrates the 1468 marriage of Charles the Bold, Duke of Burgundy, to Margaret of York with street processions in medieval costume, jousts, and a ceremonial recreation of the entry of Margaret into Bruges. It takes place every 5 years in the second half of August; the next one will be in 2017. (www.goudenboomstoet.be).



imposing buildings. The city's major attractions fan out from there, with many lying to the southwest and another pocket to the northwest.

Outside the canals are the suburban residential neighborhoods where most residents have their homes, although of the 120,000 people who live in the city, around 20,000 actually live and work in the ancient center.

**GETTING AROUND** The center of Bruges is compact and filled with cobbled pedestrians-only streets, which makes walking the best way to get around. Wear comfortable shoes: those charming cobblestones can be really hard on your feet.

Most city and regional **buses** are operated by **De Lijn** (www.delijn.be/en; ✆ **070/22-02-00**) and depart from the bus station next to the train station on Stationsplein, or from a secondary station at 't Zand near the Concertgebouw (p. 258), and many buses stop at the Markt in the Old Town. Purchase your ticket from a De Lijn sales point or automatic ticket machine before boarding and you'll pay less than buying tickets on the bus. An *enkele rit* (one-way) ticket costs 1.30€ in advance, or 2€ on the bus for two zones, and 2€ to 3€ for three or more zones. A *dagkaart* (day pass), valid for the entire city network, costs 5€/7€ for 1 day; 10€/12€ for 3 days; and 15€/18€ for 5 days. A 1-day pass for children 6 to 11 is 3€/4.50€, and children 5 and under ride free.

**Cycling** is a terrific way to get around Bruges. Unlike most Belgian cities, it has made cyclists privileged road users so they can travel in both directions on some—but not all—of the narrow, one-way streets in the center city. Others are one-way only, and you'll be fined if you're caught riding against the traffic flow, so keep a close eye on the street signs. Ride with caution, because the streets are filled with throngs of tourists, but apart from that, the streets are gloriously traffic-free and safe for families with older children to navigate by bicycle.

There are eight bike-rental points in the city, from **Fietspunt Station** on Stationsplein (✆ **050/396-826**) to **B-Bike Concertgebouw** (✆ **0479/971-280**) near the tourist office on 't Zand. Prices start at around 4€ per hour, or 12€ for a full day. There's a discount with the Brugge City Card at some rental outfits. An electric bike from **Electric Scooters** (Gentpoortstraat 62; www.electric-scooters.be; ✆ **050/000-000**) costs 30€ for 8 hours.

You don't need to **drive** in Bruges. There's no point. Leave your car in your hotel parking garage; one of six **underground parking garages** in the center (expect to pay 9€ per day); one of four cheap **park-and-ride lots** next to the train station, which charge around 3.50€ per day; or a **free parking zone** outside the city center. It's a short walk into the heart of the Old Town from any of the parking lots. Parking rules are firmly enforced, and unlawfully parked cars will be ticketed, booted, or towed.

There are **taxi** stands at the Markt (✆ **050/334-444**) and outside the rail station on Stationsplein (✆ **050/384-660**).

## Exploring Bruges

A fairy-tale confection of gabled houses, meandering canals, magnificent squares, and narrow cobblestone streets is catnip for travelers. What is most astonishing is the consistently warm welcome its residents provide to the swarms of visitors who swallow the place up every summer. The basis for this goes way beyond economics—the good burghers of Bruges have a deep love for their show-stopping city and are only too delighted that others share their enthusiasm.

### THE MARKT

The gigantic open space of Markt is lined with venerable facades swathed in heraldic banners; together with the adjacent Burg (p. 245), these two great squares formed the commercial and administrative heart of Bruges and are today the focal point of its sightseeing. Most of what you'll want to see is less than 10 minutes' walk away from these two squares.

**Bruggemuseum-Belfort (Belfry) ★★** HISTORIC BUILDING
The Belfry of Bruges was built in the 1200s in one of those perfectly proportioned shapes that makes a breath-catching masterpiece out of a simple tower (the tower of the Palazzo della Signoria in Florence comes to mind as another example). This one is mammoth in width and depth, yet "as delicate as a vase," its summit being the tallest in Belgium at 83m

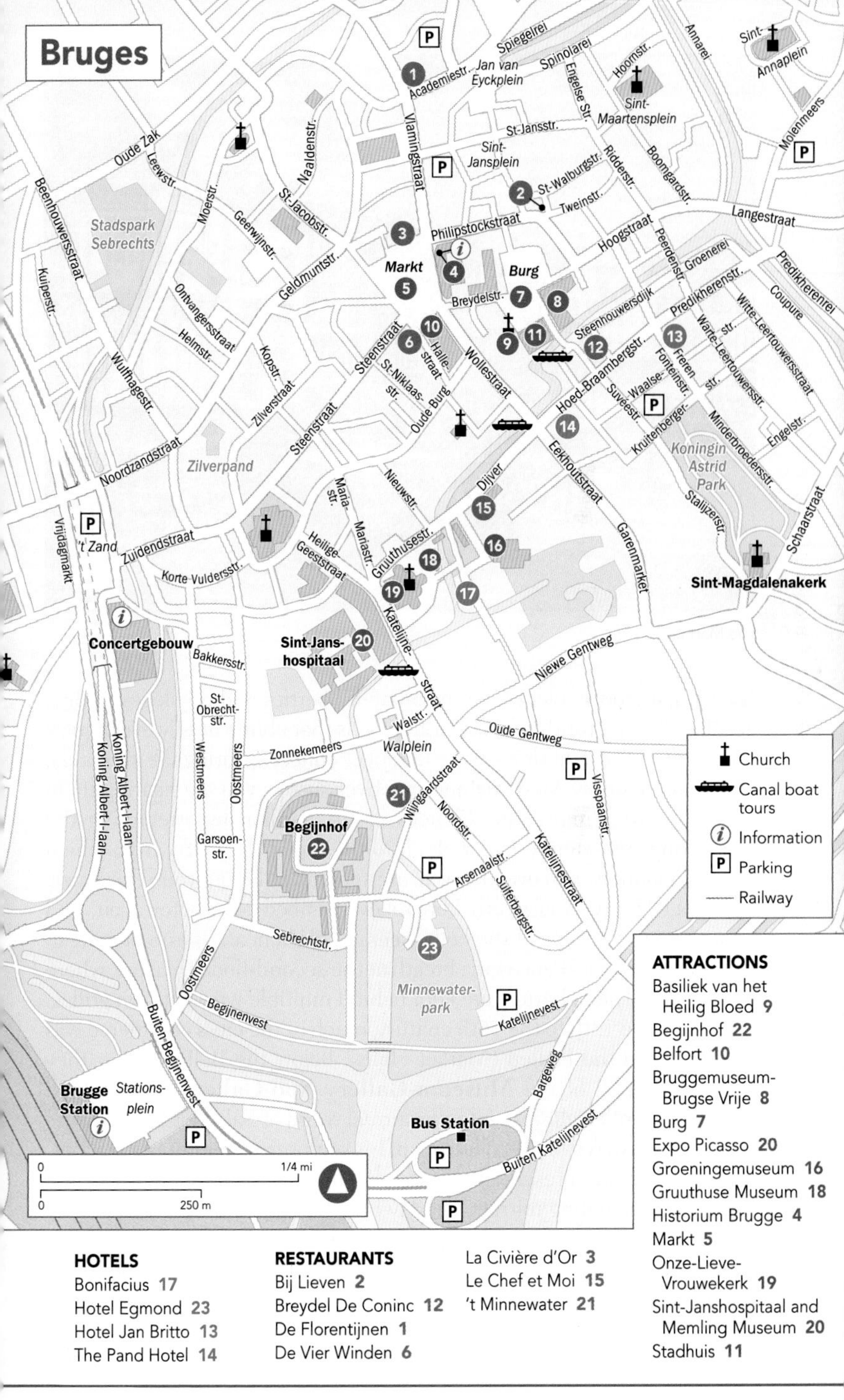


**ATTRACTIONS**

Basiliek van het Heilig Bloed **9**
Begijnhof **22**
Belfort **10**
Bruggemuseum-Brugse Vrije **8**
Burg **7**
Expo Picasso **20**
Groeningemuseum **16**
Gruuthuse Museum **18**
Historium Brugge **4**
Markt **5**
Onze-Lieve-Vrouwekerk **19**
Sint-Janshospitaal and Memling Museum **20**
Stadhuis **11**

**HOTELS**

Bonifacius **17**
Hotel Egmond **23**
Hotel Jan Britto **13**
The Pand Hotel **14**

**RESTAURANTS**

Bij Lieven **2**
Breydel De Coninc **12**
De Florentijnen **1**
De Vier Winden **6**
La Civière d'Or **3**
Le Chef et Moi **15**
't Minnewater **21**

The Markt, Bruges.

(272 ft.), a crown celebrating the ancient liberties and privileges of Bruges. Inside: the world-famous carillon bells that chime briefly every quarter hour (and several times a day in longer concerts during the summer), and were heard by Memling and van Eyck just as you are hearing them now. You can glimpse the 47 bells of the carillon by attempting the exhausting, 366-step, circular climb to the top of the belfry from which most of Flanders, and even the sea, are spread out before you. The American poet Henry Wadsworth Longfellow climbed here before you, and wrote that the pealing of the bells "seemed like a heart of iron beating in the ancient tower." Pause for a breath at the second-floor Treasury, where the town seal and charters are kept behind multiple wrought-iron grilles.

From the 13th to the 16th century, much of the city's commerce was conducted in the Hallen (Market Halls), below the Belfort. Now they are the location of the **Museum-Gallery Xpo-Gallery Dalí,** which allows a fun-filled glimpse into the surreal world of Salvador Dalí, Spain's strangest artist. A vibrant collection of his sculptures, paintings, sketches, and glassware are presented in a suitably bizarre but beautifully curated display incorporating mirrors, sparkly blue lighting, and splashes of gold against a backdrop of bright blues and crimsons. Half the charm of this exhibition is its unexpected contrast to the medieval beauty of the building housing it.

Markt 7. https://bezoekers.brugge.be/musea-2. ✆ **050/448-711.** 8€ adults, 6€ seniors, 4€ children 6–25, free for children 5 and under. Daily 9:30am–5pm.

The Belfort, seen from the Dijver Canal.



**Historium Brugge ★★** MUSEUM Housed in an intricate balcony-and-tower adorned Gothic Revivalist building next to the Provinciaal Hof (Provincial Palace), the Historium aims to explain all the twists and turns of the city's turbulent history in an approachable and entertaining manner. The exhibit romps through 15th-century Bruges with a series of interactive experiences utilizing film, music, holograms, sounds, smells, and multilingual headphones. Afterward, catch your breath with a complementary tasting at the **Duvelorium Grand Beer Café**—which has incomparable views over Markt—in the same building.

Markt 1. www.historium.be. ✆ **050/270-311**. 1€ adults, 9€ students, 5.50€ children 2–14, 30€ families. Daily 10am–6pm.

### THE BURG

The Burg is the second of Bruges's vast squares, just steps away from the Markt. It parades a similar array of handsome medieval buildings, which together add up to a time-traveler's trip through the history of European architecture. On this site, Baldwin Iron Arm, Count of Flanders, built a fortified castle (or *burg*) in the late 9th century, around which a village developed into Bruges. The rest, as they say, is history.

**Basiliek van het Heilig Bloed (Basilica of the Holy Blood) ★★★** CHURCH When knights returned from the Crusades, they often returned with relics—a fragment of the True Cross, a tiny branch from the Crown of Thorns. But when Derek of Alsace, Count of Flanders,

Interior, the Basilica of the Holy Blood.

returned to Bruges in 1150 from the Second Crusade, he brought back the relic that staggered all of Europe: a cloth allegedly soaked with the blood of Christ. It was immediately placed in the Burg, in the Chapel of St. Basel, now the Basilica of the Holy Blood, where it is displayed to the public daily between 11:30am and noon, and 2 to 4pm.

The awesome artifact is kept today in a small rock crystal vial, in an open container of gold, that is placed (during viewing hours) on an elevated side altar in the Upper Chapel, behind which sits a priest flanked by an armed city policeman and a member of the 40-person, centuries old "Cofraternity of the Holy Blood," the ultimate guardian of the relic. Solemnly, the faithful line up to view and kiss the vial, after first offering up a few euros in a coin collection nearby. After each kiss, the priest carefully wipes dry the vial. But even non-Catholics are welcome to head up and see the vial (though you will be expected to make a donation).

The Basilica, built in the 1100s, was once a thoroughly Romanesque structure, and its downtown interior still is—probably the purest example of Romanesque architecture you'll see in Belgium, with its distinctive rounded arches and heavy pillars, its squat and horizontal lines, its gloomy, stone interior with poignant statues of crucified Jesus. Upstairs everything changes! Now the Basilica becomes a green-and-yellow fairyland of emeralds and gilt, of rich paneling, paintings, striped ornaments of every sort, a dazzling display of both Gothic and Renaissance elements that, in later centuries, completely transformed the formerly Romanesque facade and upper story of the building into a Venetian-like palace of a church. A wide stone staircase worn by the feet of millions of pilgrims leads both to the upper story and adjoining museum housing the ornately figured reliquaries—golden containers or casques—associated with the relic. Its top treasure, by Bruges goldsmith Jan Crabbe, is a gem-encrusted case styled as a medieval castle and topped with a golden statue of the Virgin. This houses the relic on its annual pilgrimage around the streets of Bruges in the colorful **Procession of the Holy Blood ★** (p. 241) on Ascension Day.

Burg 13. www.holyblood.com. ✆ **050/336-792.** Basilica free; museum 2€. Nov–Mar 24 Thurs–Tues 9:30am–noon and 2–5pm; Mar 25–Oct daily 9:30am–noon and 2–5pm. Mass Fri–Wed 11am.

**Bruggemuseum-Brugse Vrije (Liberty of Bruges) ★** HISTORIC BUILDING The center of the city's judiciary until 1984, the Landhuis (Palace) of the Liberty of Bruges also served as the administrative HQ of the region of Flanders around Bruges from the Middle Ages onward. Much of it was rebuilt between 1722 and 1727; the palace now houses the city archives. It's chiefly visited for the exceptional **Renaissancezaal (Renaissance Chamber) ★★,** which has been restored to its original 16th-century condition, and a monumental black marble fireplace decorated with a carved alabaster frieze and topped by an oak chimneypiece carved with statues of Emperor Charles V, who visited Bruges in 1515, and his grandparents: Emperor Maximilian of Austria, Duchess Mary of Burgundy, King Ferdinand II of Aragon, and Queen Isabella I of Castile. That's quite memorable in itself for the size of some of the wooden codpieces. The gloomy oil painting by Gillis van Tilborgh was executed in 1659 and clearly shows the Charles V fireplace on its right-hand side, behind all the aldermen in black robes.

Burg 11a. https://bezoekers.brugge.be/musea-2. ✆ **050/448-711.** Courtyard free; Renaissance Hall 4€. Daily 9:30am–12:30pm and 1:30–5pm.

**Bruggemuseum-Stadhuis (Town Hall) ★** HISTORIC BUILDING This lacy Gothic structure was built in 1376, making it one of the oldest town halls in Belgium. The statues in the niches of the facade are 1980s replacements of the originals by Jan van Eyck, which were destroyed by pro-French rebels in the 1790s. Go in to check out the glowing, ostentatious beauty of the **Gotische Zaal (Gothic Room) ★★** upstairs; it is adorned with 19th-century wall murals depicting highlights from Bruges's history amid intricate gilded patterning all topped by a spectacular, vaulted and gilded oak ceiling.

Burg 12. https://bezoekers.brugge.be/en/stadhuis-city-hall. ✆ **050/448-711.** 4€. Daily 9:30am–5pm.

## OTHER TOP SIGHTS

Please note that along with the attractions listed below are a brewery tour (at the Browerj De Halve Maan—I think the beer at this family-owned factory is better than the tour); an attraction devoted to the art of diamond cutting (a longtime Bruges specialty, and only interesting at 12:15 and 3:15 when the actual polishing takes place); the Kantcentrum (a lace shop with demonstrations of the ancient art); and a Folklore Museum, devoted to life in Bruges at the turn of the 20th century. It's only worthwhile seeing these attractions if you have a *lot* of time to kill in Bruges (or antsy children along).

**Bruggemuseum-Gruuthuse ★★** MUSEUM In the brilliant Belgian era of the Dukes of Burgundy (1388–1477), then the richest sovereigns of Europe, more wealthy than the kings of France, the most powerful of the Flemish nobles serving those Dukes were the residents of this house, the Gruuthuse clan. You'll learn the story of Lodewijk van Gruuthuse here: he was a counselor to the dukes of Burgundy in the 1400s, and lived in appropriately splendid style in this ornate, Gothic, brick mansion. The vast courtyard and equine statue above the intricate entrance set the standard of opulence for the interior, which is crammed with extravagantly carved stone fireplaces, oak balconies, and gilded wooden ceilings. Among all this luxurious detailing is a superb collection of silverware, ceramics, glassware, tapestries, and ecclesiastical robes, all representing the very best of 15th-century Flemish craft. And if you'd care to glimpse the gulf that separated such as man as Louis de Gruuthuse from the ordinary citizens of Bruges, walk immediately to Room 17 upstairs. This was the Gruuthuse private chapel, its windows cut into the

### The Old Walls of Bruges

Medieval Bruges was heavily fortified, totally encircled by its circular walls and further protected by a moat and defense towers. The walls were largely knocked down in the 19th century and today only the moat and four of the nine powerfully fortified gates from the 14th century have survived. Of these, the **Kruispoort** is the most monumental, looking like a mini-castle complete with drawbridge and defending the city's eastern approach routes. The others are (clockwise from the railway station in the southwest) the imposing **Smedenpoort; Ezelpoort,** which is known for the many swans that grace the moat beside it; **Kruispoort;** and **Gentpoort.**

The Kruispoort.

walls of the immense adjoining Church of Our Lady, so that Louis and the Gruuthuses could attend services from their own home, unsullied by the presence of common folk.

Dijver 17. https://bezoekers.brugge.be/en/gruuthusemuseum. ✆ **050/448-711.** 8€. Tues–Sun 9:30am–5pm.

**Expo Picasso** ★★ ART GALLERY This collection starts with the early Impressionists and works its way to Picasso, stopping along the way with paintings and drawings by Monet, Renoir, Degas, and Rodin. Along with drawings by Magritte, Chagall, Matisse, and Cocteau, Miró has a corridor full of fluid lithographs to himself, but the standout pieces belong to Picasso. Chances are you'll probably have this little treasure to yourself, so make the most of it.

Mariastraat 38. www.expo-brugge.be. ✆ **050/476-100.** 8€ adults, 6.50€ seniors and children 7–18, free 6 and under. Daily 9am–5pm. Closed Jan.

**Groeningemuseum** ★★★ MUSEUM One of the two sublime museums experiences in Bruges (the other is the **Sint-Janshospitaal ★★★,** see p. 250), this is the home, the shrine, the ark of the Flemish Primitives. Though all of the artists known as the "Primitives" are displayed in museums and churches all over Belgium, nowhere else are so many major 15th-century works clustered together. Everyone except Dirk Bouts is represented: van Eyck and Memling, Rogier van der Weyden, Hugo van der Goes, Petrus Christus, Gerard David, Hieronymous Bosch and the various anonymous "Masters" of various schools and subjects. Here are the bright and luminous tones resulting from the world's first use of pigments mixed with oil, the photographic realism and exquisite precision, the magnificent groupings of figures, the pure and unquestioning religious belief of the "Age of Faith," the painstaking devotion of long months and indeed years to a single painting, with which the Flemish greats of the 1400s stunned the artistic world of that time.

Standout pieces among all this glory include Bosch's surreal triptych *The Last Judgment* (ca. 1486) with its suffering sinners; Gerard David's horrific *Judgment of Cambyses* (1498), which depicts an errant judge being sentenced and flayed alive (so brutal it's hard to look at, it hung for centuries in the Town Hall of Bruges as an admonition to the politicians who worked there); and van Eyck's unstintingly honest, blemishes-and-all portrait of his wife Margareta (1439). We'd also urge you to spend some time pondering Hugo van der Goes's *Death of the Virgin,* which is infused with an unusual and unforgettable bluish-white light. This was van der Goes's last picture, painted shortly before he died of melancholia. Important later works in the galleries encompass paintings by James Ensor and the Belgian surrealists René Magritte and Paul Delvaux.

Entrance to the Groeninge museum also includes access to the adjacent **Arenthuis,** which shows temporary exhibitions and a permanent collection of lithographs and sketches by Anglo-Welsh artist Sir Frank Brangwyn—well worth a visit if time permits.

Dijver 12. https://bezoekers.brugge.be/nl/groeningemuseum. ✆ **050/448-711.** Combined ticket with neighboring Arentshuis 8€. Tues–Sun 9:30am–5pm.

**Onze-Lieve-Vrouwekerk (Church of Our Lady) ★★** CHURCH It took 2 centuries (13th–15th) to build this landmark church, which is renowned for its soaring 122m (400-ft.) spire, tallest in Flanders; and also because it serves as a display case for the only statue by Michelangelo—*Madonna and Child* in Carrera white marble—to have permanently departed Italian soil. Purchased from the Italian genius by a wealthy Flemish merchant, the statue juxtaposes a delightfully human, cherubic and slightly pudgy 5-year-old Jesus, touchingly clinging to his mother's thumb for security, with a more abstract and other-worldly Mary, obviously troubled by the eventual fate of her son. A minor work for Michelangelo, but a masterpiece nonetheless. Other impressive artworks include a *Crucifixion* by Anthony van Dyck and the imposing bronze tombs of Charles the Bold, Duke of Burgundy, and his daughter Mary. The church is currently under long-term restoration until sometime in 2016, and although it is still open, the tombs are not accessible.

Onze-Lieve-Vrouwekerkhof Zuid. https://bezoekers.brugge.be/en/onze-lieve-vrouwekerk-church-of-our-lady. ✆ **050/448-711.** 6€. Mon–Sat 9am–5pm, Sun 1:30–5pm.

**Sint-Janshospitaal (St. John's Hospital and Memling Museum) ★★★** MUSEUM Built in the 12th century and magnificently preserved (it was a working hospital until 1976), this started as a charitable hospital of the Middle Ages, one of whose wards is depicted in an ancient painting hung near the main entrance: There you see the very same large room of arches and brick walls that now stands before you, but lined in those days with compact, wooden sleeping cubicles in which two or more patients would be crammed for warmth. The medieval hospital wards are filled with antique beds, sedan chairs, and rather macabre surgical instruments that will probably enthrall the kids. To the side of the main entrance is the picturesque Apothecary Room of those ancient days, which should also be seen.

But the primary reason you are here is the Museum of Hans Memling (ca. 1440–94), the painter who belongs as much to Bruges as El Greco does to Toledo, Spain. He moved to Bruges in 1465 and became one of the city's most famous residents. Commissioned in 1479 to produce six paintings for the hospital, his delightful, radiant works are now found in the barnlike, timber-roofed chapel. They include Memling's *Shrine of St. Ursula*, which experts have named one of the seven wonders of Belgium. A small box, less than 3 feet in length, the shrine is shaped like a Gothic cathedral, gilded throughout, its major illustrations appearing in the arched spaces on both ends. And in the scant space afforded

## A Quiet Corner of Bruges

Since it was founded in 1245 by the Countess Margaret of Constantinople, the **Prinselijk Begijnhof ten Wijngaarde (Princely Beguinage of the Vineyard) ★**, Wijngaardstraat (www.monasteria.org; ✆ **050/330-011**), at the Minnewater (Lake of Love), has been one of the most tranquil spots in Bruges, and so it remains today. *Begijns* were religious women, similar to nuns, who accepted vows of chastity and obedience but drew the line at poverty, preferring to earn a living by looking after the sick and making lace.

Begijnhuisje, Bruges.

This beautiful little cluster of 17th-century houses surrounds a lawn shaded by poplar trees and makes a marvelous escape from the din of the outside world. One of the houses, the **Begijnhuisje (Beguine's House),** is now a museum. The Begijnhof courtyard is always open, and admission is free. The Beguine's House is open Monday to Saturday 10am to 5pm, Sunday 2:30 to 5pm. Admission is 2€ for adults, 1.50€ for seniors, 1€ for students and children 8 to 11.



him, Memling wrought an exquisite miracle. In each of the work's six tiny panels, he has portrayed multiple scenes that unfold in time sequence within each panel; drawn faces, bodies, and buildings of haunting loveliness within the space of a few millimeters; and recreated an entire medieval world of commerce, religion, and war in miniature. In the room, you'll also find Memling's exquisite *tondos* and the sublime three-paneled altarpiece of St. John the Baptist and St. John the Evangelist.

Mariastraat 38. https://bezoekers.brugge.be/en/sint-janshospitaal-saint-johns-hospital. ✆ **050/448-711.** 8€. Tues–Sun 9:30am–5pm.

## Organized Tours

It's practically law that every visitor to Bruges should take a **boat cruise ★★** around the city canals. There are five landing stages, the most convenient for tourists being the two along Dijver, but all are marked with an anchor icon on maps available at the tourist office. These open-top canal boats can be scorching in hot weather and bracing in cold, but they only last 30 minutes, they are free with the **Brugge City Card** (p. 240), the commentary is multi-lingual, *and* they reveal a uniquely satisfying view of the city. They operate March to November daily 10am to 6pm, with weather-dependent departures between December and February. A half-hour cruise is 7.60€ for adults, and 3.40€ for children 4 to 11 when accompanied by an adult.

Canal boats in Bruges, near the Church of Our Lady.



Wherever you are in Bruges, you'll hear the clip-clop of horses' hooves, so if you fancy a tour of the city by **horse-drawn carriage** (*caleche* in Flemish), the departure point is on the Markt between March and November; carriages are stationed on the Markt (in the Burg on Wed mornings) between 9am and 6pm. The 35-minute ride is 39€ per carriage for up to five people; there's a jumping off point for you and a resting point for the horses at the Beguinage (see box p. 251); see if you can spot the fountain nearby that's adorned with two horses' heads.

If you'd appreciate a little help uncovering the secrets of Bruges, take a **walking tour.** The tourist office (**www.visitbruges.be**) runs such tours from April through September costing 9€ (free for kids 11 and under) for a 2½-hour stroll through the pretty streets to all the main sights. Tours depart at 2:30pm daily from the Concertgebouw (see p. 258), with Sunday kick off at 10:30pm in July and August. During October, the tours only run on the weekend, leaving at 2:30pm.

## Especially for Kids

In spite of its concentration of art museums, churches, and lace shops, Bruges is absolute heaven for kids. They can explore the city by **canal boat** or **pony-and-trap,** and also navigate the pedestrianized streets safely by **bike.** In fact, the city itself is the attraction for some children, who love the notion that around every corner there's a 1,000-year-old building or some hidden courtyard.

St. Bonifacius Bridge.



And nowhere else will you find museums with such child-appeal factor as the **Friet Museum** (Vlamingstraat 33; www.frietmuseum.be; ✆ **050/340-150;** admission 7€ adults, 6€ seniors/students, 4€ children 6–12, free for children 5 and under; open daily 10am–5pm, closed Jan 1, 2nd and 3rd week of Jan, Dec 24–25, and Dec 31.), which tells the story of the humble potato, or **Choco-Story** (Wijnzakstraat 2; ✆ **050/612-237;** www.choco-story-brugge.be; admission 7€ adults, 6€ seniors/students, 4€ children 6–12, free for children 5 and under; open daily 10am–5pm, closed Jan 1, 2nd and 3rd week of Jan, Dec 24-25, and Dec 31), a chocolate museum where they can learn about the process of making the world's favorite sweet treat. The **Historium Brugge ★★** (p. 245) offers the city's most child-appropriate introduction to Bruges, with a dynamic and entertaining walk-through exhibition encompassing film, multi-media, and interactive exhibits. The **Archeologiemuseum (Archaeological Museum)** at Mariastraat 36a (https://bezoekers.brugge.be/en/archeologiemuseum-archeological-museum; ✆ **050/448-711**), is also designed with kids in mind, with lots of interactive displays, the occasional skeleton, and medieval costumes to dress up in.

The cuisine of Belgium, with its waffles, fries, omelets, and toasted sandwiches, lends itself to junior appetites—try the ***frietkoten* (fries stands)** in the Markt—as do the numerous yummy **chocolate stores**. And winter visits to Bruges turn up Christmas fairs and an ice rink in the Markt, plus wacky installations on Stationesplein during the **Snow &**

## Bruges's Windmills

Where once 25 windmills graced the outskirts of Bruges, now only 4 survive. They are found in the park that abuts the old city walls on their eastern flank between Kruispoort and Dampoort; of these, two are open to the public in summer, and both are grain mills coming under the banner of Musea Brugge, which also runs the city's main museums. The **Koeleweimolen** was built in 1765 and was moved to its present spot from the Dampoort in 1996, while the **Sint-Janshuismolen** has been in situ since 1770. Both windmills are found along Kruisvest and share the same opening times and admission: May to August Tuesday through Sunday 9:30am to 12:30pm and 1:30 to 5pm; admission 3€ adults, 2€ seniors and ages 6 to 25, free for children 5 and under.

The Sint-Janshuismolen windmill.



**Ice Sculpture Festival,** which lasts from mid-November to early January.

## Where to Stay

Bruges is Belgium's premier tourist destination, and even though many visitors are day-trippers from Brussels, it's essential to make your hotel reservations at least 2 weeks in advance, especially at the height of summer.

### EXPENSIVE

**Bonifacius ★★** An exclusive guesthouse tucked away behind the gabled facade of a glorious 16th-century mansion, in the backstreets a step away from the **Groeningemuseum ★★★** (p. 249); staying at this little piece of heaven is like stepping back in time into a world brightened with classy antiques and stylish decoration. A decent breakfast is served in a suitably Gothic, tiled room overlooking the canal, and there's a sunny roof terrace to bask with a beer in the early evening. Need another reason to stay? The Michelin-starred **De Gouden Harynck** (www.goudenharynck.be; ✆ **050/337-637**) is just across the lane.

Groeninge 4, 8000 Bruges. www.bonifacius.be. ✆ **050/490-049.** 3 units. Doubles 300€–380€, includes breakfast. **Amenities:** Concierge; free Wi-Fi.

**The Pand Hotel ★★★** The Pand is frequently called the most romantic hotel in a very romantic city, an accolade that seems totally deserved when you walk into what was a carriage house in the 18th century and is now a delightful country-house-style refuge. The location is ideal: on one of Bruges's most famous canals and just south of the Burg

and the Markt squares. New owners, who took over in 2013, have done a subtle renovation that retains the elegance of the place while sprucing up the fabrics and furniture. Each of the charming bedrooms is different, but all are decorated with small antiques, the odd Louis Vuitton trunk, perhaps a small four-poster bed, and prints or paintings on the walls.
Pandreitje 16, 8000 Bruges. www.pandhotel.com. ✆ **050/340-666.** 26 units. Doubles 199€–265€, suites 249€–390€. **Amenities:** Bar; concierge; room service; free Wi-Fi.

### MODERATE

**Hotel Jan Britto ★★** A fine example of the type of classy hotel that Bruges does so well, the Jan Britto has elegant period accommodations tucked behind an historic facade; in this case a historic 16th-century townhouse on a backwater side street. Many rooms have vaulted ceilings, and all are individually kitted out, perhaps with four-poster beds or gilded walls in heraldic style. While the suites are humongous—even by U.S. standards—this is also a good family-friendly option as several duplex rooms can accommodate up to four, and if you're traveling with a small wallet but you like your hotels big on charm, the Jan Britto has several budget rooms on offer, shoehorned into the old maids' quarters. Secreted away at the back of the hotel is a delightfully ornate Renaissance knot garden; it's a charming spot to catch your breath after a day attacking the sights of Bruges.
Freren Fonteinstraat 1, 8000 Bruges. www.janbrito.com. ✆ **050/330-601.** 20 units. Doubles 99€–220€, suites 199€–380€, rates include breakfast. **Amenities:** Bar; concierge; free Wi-Fi.

### INEXPENSIVE

**Hotel Egmond ★** The Egmond is located in a rambling mansion next to the romantic **'t Minnewater ★** (p. 257) and has just eight rooms, but the lucky few who stay here will find ample space, plenty of family-run attention to detail, and—best of all in this dynamic, crowded little city—peace and tranquility. Despite its quiet location, the Egmond is just a 5-minute walk from the **Groeningemuseum ★★★** (p. 249) and 10 minutes from Bruges's twin central squares of Burg and Markt. Looking like something that has just stepped out of a Vermeer painting, the interiors are all tiled floors, stone fireplaces, and wooden ceilings, and all of the simply furnished, traditional rooms feature views of the garden and the lake where swans float serenely about. There's an honesty bar where you help yourself to a drink and leave payment in the evening.
Minnewater 15, 8000 Bruges. www.egmond.be. ✆ **050/341-445.** 8 units. Doubles 90€–140€, includes breakfast. **Amenities:** Free Wi-Fi.

## Where to Eat

The foodie choices in Bruges range from gourmet temples to mobile stands in the Markt selling *frites* in paper cones, with just about everything between. There's no need to be snobbish by eschewing the "tourist" restaurants in the central squares; service is (almost) universally slick and charming, prices can be reasonable if you follow the "menu du jour," and all menus feature local specialties.

Before you commit to sitting down in a restaurant, check the prices on the menus that must—by law—be displayed outside. This will put a stop to any nasty surprises over the cost of the dishes on offer, but drinks are often a budget-buster—unfortunately Bruges is an expensive city. Beer and wine are cheaper options than cocktails, and everyone drinks bottled water in restaurants. If you ask for tap water, you'll be refused.

## EXPENSIVE

**Breydel De Coninc ★★** SEAFOOD With a reputation as one of the best seafood restaurants in Bruges, De Coninc is just off the Markt, with a surprisingly pared-down interior, simple wooden tables, and stripped pine floors. Don't come for the ambience but instead for the platters of shellfish, eels, and lobsters prepared in countless different ways. Non-fish eaters can choose from steak or steak, so this is not the pick for vegetarians.

Breidelstraat 24. www.restaurant-breydel.be. ✆ **050/339-746.** Mains 24€–46€. Thurs–Tues noon–3pm and 6–9:30pm.

**De Floreintijinen ★★★** BELGIAN Housed in a former merchant's house, de Floreintijinen is the place for a special meal. The two-story restaurant has huge windows that let light flood into the dining room, where smart and savvy locals sit at tables covered with crisp white linen. It could all seem stuffy, but the quirky modern art on the walls helps head that off. The service is impeccable, and the kitchen delivers dishes that mix classic tradition with contemporary spicing. Top ingredients appear in starters like terrine of goose liver with pear compote (€27) or a foaming "cappuccino" of crab with Armagnac cream (€24). Fish get royal treatment here, from a simple sole meunière to the superb crab from the Barents sea. Meat makes an appearance with classic dishes like leg of lamb with green beans, a potato dauphinois, and a thyme jus (€29). The wine list ranges throughout the world.

Academiestraat 1, West of Jan van Eyckplein. www.deflorentijnen.be/en. ✆ **050/677-533.** Mains €34–€74, lunch menus €29, dinner menus €45–€65.

**Le Chef et Moi ★★** BELGIAN This classic little gem is creeping up the foodie destination charts in Bruges and is definitely one for booking ahead of time, partly due to the high quality of the cuisine and partly due to the fact that it's tiny. Oil paintings cover the walls, chandeliers drip crystal, and the intimate dining room is lit by candlelight at night. Menu choice is limited to what is available seasonally and what Chef Stefan Cardinael (a rising star) feels like cooking, but the results are always sublime; dishes might include scallops, skate wing, or milk-fed roast lamb.

Dijver 13. www.lechefetmoi.be. ✆ **050/396-011.** Fixed-price lunch 22€, dinner 35€. Tues–Sat noon–2pm and 6:30–10pm.

### MODERATE

**Bij Lieven** ★★★ BELGIAN Bij Lieven quickly became a Bruges institution after opening a few years ago. Although it's inside a historic house (with beamed ceilings and elegant fireplaces still intact), the interior strikes the right contemporary note. There are pale wood floors and fashionably dark walls in the front room; in the next dining room, tall tables and bar-style chairs face the open kitchen. This set-up works well for single diners, who can chat to the cooks and the waitstaff as they work. The cooking is as stylish as the decor; here's another Flemish chef who is transforming Belgian cooking from homey to modern. Dishes might include a Thai-inspired salad with tiger shrimp, chicken, and peanut sauce (€20), bouillabaisse (€28), or pigeon with rösti potatoes, peas, and garlic (€32), all beautifully presented.

Philipstockstraat 45. www.etenbijlieven.be. ✆ **050/680-975.** Mains €28–€36, lunch menu €14, three-course dinner menu €35, four courses €47. Tues–Sat noon–2:30pm and 6–9:30pm.

### INEXPENSIVE

**De Vier Winden** ★ FLEMISH Honest, straightforward food at a very cheap price, especially considering De Vier Winden's location right at the foot of the **Belfort** ★★ (p. 242) on the Markt—that's the lure here. Order a liter of rosé wine, tuck into brasserie staples such as *coq au vin,* mussels, seafood platters, and pasta, and finish off your feast with a crème brûlée. Simple and good.

Markt 9. ✆ **050/331-933.** Mains 7€–18€, fixed-price menu 20€. Daily 10am–10:30pm.

**La Civière d'Or** ★★ BELGIAN One of the best options in the sometimes hit-or-miss row of restaurants on the Markt (in terms of price, ambience, and level of waiting-staff charm) La Civiere d'Or is actually three family-owned venues rolled into one, offering brasserie, cafe, and fine-dining menus. Grab a table outside, order a bucket full of mussels, a plate of frites, a Belgian beer, and sit back to watch the action on the dramatic stage that is the Markt. After all, this place just celebrated its 67th anniversary, so it must be doing something right.

Markt 33. www.lacivieredor.be. ✆ **050/343-036.** Mains 10€–18€, fixed-price lunch 18€. Daily 10am–midnight.

**'t Minnewater** ★ CREPERIE The perfect respite from the surging crowds in Bruges's swarming museum district, this easygoing crêperie won't break the bank. Bribe fractious youngsters with a chocolate-smothered pancake, or tuck into mussels and tasty carbonnade on the exceptionally reasonable fixed-price menu. In winter there's a welcoming log fire inside, and in summer there are lakeside views from the al fresco terrace out front.

Wijngaardstraat 28. ✆ **050/341-300.** Mains 5€–15€, fixed-price lunch menu 15€. Daily 4:30pm–12:30am.

## Shopping

Bruges is too tiny to keep pace with Brussels or Antwerp when it comes to shopping, but it certainly has its moments. This little city is a monument to the skills of lace-makers, chocolatiers, and brewers. You'll find souvenir shops selling machine-made lace concentrated around Mark and Burg, but the best, and far more expensive, handmade types of lace are bobbin, ribbon, princess, or needlepoint. If you're after a handcrafted chemise or tablecloth, check out **Rococo** at Wollestraat 18 and **Point de Rose** on the same street at Wollestraat 27. Souvenirs of a more perishable nature include Oud-Brugge cheese from **Diksmuids Boterhuis** at Geldmuntstraat 23; and marzipan from **Brown Sugar** at Mariastraat 1; but best of all chocolate, which Bruges is simply mad for. Pick up delicious arrays of calorie-laden confectionary from **Mary** at Katelijnestraat 21, or the four branches of **ChocOHolic** on Katelijnestraat and Wollestraat.

Local **beers** such as Straffe Hendrik, Brugs Tarwebier, and Brugge Tripel can be tracked down at **2be** on Wollestraat 53 (see facing page), or **Bacchus Cornelius** at Academiestraat 17 (www.bacchuscornelius.com), where you'll also find a selection of stone-bottled, ginlike liqueur ***jenever.***

If you're looking for unusual gifts for back home, try **De Witter Pelikaan** at Vlamingstraat 23 for festive Christmas baubles and handmade wooden toys.

Most stores are open Monday to Saturday 9am to 6pm, with hours extended to 9pm on Friday. Many open on Sunday as well, especially in summer.

If you're after a piece of silverware or pre-loved diamond rings, the weekend **Antiques and Flea Market** on Dijver puts on a fine show alongside the canal from March to October, Saturday and Sunday from noon to 5pm.

## Entertainment & Nightlife

For information on what to do in the evening, pick up the free monthly newsletter **"events@brugge"** from the tourist office, hotels, and performance venues or check online at www.brugge.be for details of what's on where.

The ultramodern **Concertgebouw** ★★ ('t Zand 34; www.concertgebouw.be; ✆ **070/223-302**), the home base of the **Symfonieorkest van Vlaanderen** (**Flanders Symphony Orchestra;** www.symfonieorkest.be; ✆ **050/840-587**), is the city's main venue for opera, classical music, theater, and dance. This has left the former principal venue for these events in Bruges, the circa-1869 **Stadsschouwburg** (**City Theater;** Vlamingstraat 29; www.ccbrugge.be; ✆ **050/443-060**), to back up the mother ship by mounting smaller-scale performances. Theater at both venues is likely to be in Dutch or French and rarely, if ever, in English.

Contemporary dance, drama by rising artists, rock and pop concerts, festivals, and lots of children's activities are held in the futuristic **Magdalena Concert Hall** (**MaZ** for short; Magdalenastraat 27; www.ccbrugge.be; ✆ **050/443-060**).

One for **jazz fans:** Between October and May there are free jam sessions in the foyer of **Kunstencentrum (Arts Center) De Werf** (Werfstraat 108; www.dewerf.be; ✆ **050/330-529**) every second Monday of the month at 8pm. Also on the agenda here are productions for children, contemporary drama, and dance.

The summer months between April and October see high drama of a different sort each Friday and Saturday night with fire-eating, falconry, juggling, and feasting at a **mock medieval banquet** in the hallowed setting of the neo-Gothic former **Heilige-Hartkerk (Sacred Heart Church).** Tickets for this historical extravaganza range from 45€ to 74€ (half price for children 11–14; children 10 and under not permitted) from Celebrations Entertainment (Vlamingstraat 86; www.celebrations-entertainment.be; ✆ **050/347-572**). Shows start at 7:30pm.

For rowdier nightlife, head to Bruges's boisterous **beer halls**. Try **2be ★★★** (Wollestraat 53; www.2-be.biz; ✆ **050/611-222;** daily 9:30am–7:30pm.), which usually offers seven draft beers (they change with the seasons but might include fruit beers, *trippels,* and white beer). The beer is fresh and the views over the canal from the little terrace just gorgeous. There's little in the way of nourishment to soak up the alcohol, so things can get a little rowdy on weekend evenings. Or choose **Staminet De Garre ★★★** (De Garre 1; ✆ **050/34-10-29;** Mon–Fri and Sun noon–midnight, Sat 11am–1am), which is tucked into a 16th-century house with just the right kind of atmosphere (old wooden beams, exposed redbrick walls, and closely packed tables). It's great for beer-lovers: De Garre is known for its Trappist beers and its kriek lambics. The brave might want to try a Tripel van De Garre, at a whopping 11.5% alcohol.

# DAY TRIPS FROM BRUSSELS & BRUGES

Brussels and Bruges are close and convenient to many historic towns and scenic regions in Belgium. Here are a few I recommend.

## Ghent ★★

48km (30 miles) NW of Brussels

Ghent's monuments and townscapes might not be as picture perfect as those of Gothic Bruges, but then few places are. Yet Ghent is a city with attitude, forward thinking and cosmopolitan but with a number of important historic sights, left from the days when this was one of the largest and most important cities in medieval Northern Europe. Tourists are welcomed here with open arms, but they don't make the city tick as they do in Bruges, because Ghent is also an important university city, an inland port, and an industrial center. Largely thanks to its 60,000-strong student population, Ghent compensates for its less precious appearance with a vigorous, gritty social and cultural scene, with bars, restaurants, and clubbing options aplenty.

## ESSENTIALS

Try the **Visit Ghent** tourism portal (www.visitgent.be) for trip-planning information.

**ARRIVING** Ghent is a 35-minute **train ride** from Brussels, and there are at least five direct trains every hour between the two, with a round-trip fare of 18€. The main station of **Gent-Sint-Pieters** is on Koningin Maria-Hendrikaplein, 2km (1½ miles) south of the center city. Tram No. 1 runs into the Korenmarkt.

By **car,** take A10/E40 from Brussels; the journey takes 45 minutes when the traffic is clear.

**GETTING AROUND** Ghent has an excellent, integrated **tram and bus network** plus a single **electric trolley-bus** line, all operated by **De Lijn** (www.delijn.be; ✆ **070/220-200**). The four tramlines (1, 4, 21, and 22) stop at **Gent-Sint-Pieters station** and at multiple points throughout the city center. Purchase your travel ticket from the De Lijn sales point in the station before boarding and you'll pay 20% less. The most useful ticket for sightseers is the ***dagkaart* (day card)** valid for the entire network; it costs 5€ in advance, 7€ from the driver once on the tram.

There are plenty of regulated **taxis** with ranks in the streets; you'll find them outside **Gent-Sint-Pieters** and **Ghent Dampoort stations** as well as on Korenmarkt. Otherwise call **Vtax** (www.v-tax.be; ✆ **09/222-2222**).

### Party Time in Ghent

If you hit the town in July, you've crashed in on party heaven. For 10 days around July 21, Belgium's greatest extended street party, the **Gentse Feesten** (**Ghent Festivities;** www.gentsefeesten.be; ✆ **09/210-1010**) swirl through the city with concerts from classical to indie and dance, street theater, performance art, puppet shows, a street fair, special museum exhibits, and riotous fun and games.

## EXPLORING GHENT

This is a city best seen by walking its streets, gazing at its gabled guild houses and private mansions, and stopping on its bridges to take in the waterside views. Ghent's historical monuments have not all been prettified; some of them look downright gray and forbidding, which, oddly enough, gives them a more authentic feel. The city's heart surrounds the funnel-shaped piazza of **Korenmarkt,** and this is where local big wheels had their residences in times past. Most of the city's major

A building facing the busy Korenmarkt, Ghent.

sights—including **St. Bavo's Cathedral ★★★** (p. 264), and the **Belfort ★** (below)—are close by. To the north lies the foreboding **Gravensteen Castle ★,** and beyond that is the revamped medieval enclave of **Patershol,** today something of a hot drinking and dining spot. The River Leie winds through the city center on its way to join the River Schelde and a network of canals leading to the port. Citadelpark, location of the **Museum voor Schone Kunsten Gent ★★** (p. 264) is in the south of the city near Gent-Sint-Pieters station, and is one to avoid at night thanks to recent muggings.

**Belfort en Lakenhalle (Belfry and Cloth Hall) ★** HISTORIC SITE
The Belfry tower and Cloth Hall stand across the sweeping square of Botermarkt from Sint-Baafskathedraal (St. Bavo's Cathedral, p. 264) and form a glorious medieval ensemble. The 14th-century **Belfry** holds the great bells that have rung out Ghent's civic pride down the centuries; the most beloved was a giant bell known as Roland (1315), which was used as the city's alarm bell to advise of invading armies, to

### Your Sightseeing Passport to Ghent

Save money as you sightsee with the **CityCard Gent,** available from **Visit Gent** (see above) in time allotments of 48 hours for 30€ or 72 hours costing a bargain 35€. The pass includes free use of the city's public transportation and admission to key museums and monuments, a city map, and a 50-minute boat trip from either **Rederij De Gentenaer** or **Gent Watertoerist** (p. 267 for both).

call out the town militia, and to inspire uprisings and defiance. It was destroyed by Emperor Charles V in 1540 as punishment for Ghent's insubordination against the Spanish. No fewer than 28 of the 54 bells that now make up the tower's huge carillon were cast from Roland's broken pieces. The massive Triomfanten bell, cast in 1660, now rests in a small park at the foot of the Belfry, still bearing the crack it sustained when it broke in 1914. Take the elevator up 66m (217 ft.) to the Belfry's upper gallery, to see the bells and take in fantastic **panoramic views of the city.** The other key item here was the great iron chest that was kept in the Belfry's *Secreet* (strongroom) to hold the all-important charters, extracted over the centuries from the Counts of Flanders, granting privileges to the guilds and the burghers of medieval Ghent. People then believed that if these papers were lost, the privileges would be lost; on several noted occasions, rowdy crowds forced guardians of the Belfry to open the chest and extract other less admired papers—such as papers reducing the privileges—which they tore into shreds or ate!

The **Cloth Hall** at the foot of the Belfry dates from 1425 and was the gathering place of wool and cloth merchants. A baroque extension from 1741 on Goudenleeuwplein was used until 1902 as a prison, dubbed De Mammelokker (the Suckler). The name comes from a relief above the doorway that depicts the Roman legend of Cimon, starving to death in prison, being suckled by his daughter Pero.

Sint-Baafsplein. www.belfortgent.be. ✆ **09/233-3954.** 6€ adults, 4.50€ seniors, 2€ students 19–26, free for ages 18 and under. Daily 10am–6pm.

**Design museum Gent ★★** MUSEUM Located in the Hotel de Coninck (ca. 1755), a baroque mansion with a modern extension grafted on to the rear, this decorative arts museum showcases the very best in world design. In the old wing, the exhibits range through period salons decked out with swagged curtains, frescoed ceilings, elaborate chandeliers, fine French furniture, and Chinese porcelain in typically aristocratic 18th- and 19th-century Flemish style. In marked contrast to all that ornate period luxury, the light-filled new wing sings a contemporary tune and features examples of Art Nouveau furniture by Henry van de Velde and Paul Hankar, and even the Belgian master of the genre, Victor Horta. Seminal works from the 20th and early 21st centuries include Alessi silverware, stools in recycled plastic by Bar und Knell Design, and chairs by Richard Gehry. Temporary exhibitions take on controversial subjects such as the use of plastic and pollution.

Jan Breydelstraat 5. www.design.museum.gent.be. ✆ **09/267-9999.** 8€ adults, 6.50€ seniors, 2€ ages 19–26, free for 18 and under. Tram: 1 or 4 to Korenmarkt. Tues–Sun 10am–6pm.

## Landmarks in Ghent

Ghent's main square is **Vrijdagmarkt**—huge, tree shaded, ever bustling, and surrounded by old guild houses hosting stores selling Ghent noses (a syrupy confection like an overgrown jelly baby in fruity flavors) and restaurants that spill onto sidewalks when the sun shines. There are markets here most weekends, but historically this square has been the scene of much turbulence, a fact marked by the central bronze statue of 14th-century rebel leader Jacob van Artevelde, who fought the English ban on Flemish wool exports in the 14th century. The statue was erected in 1863 to commemorate van Artevelde's assassination in 1345.

Few traditional sights clutter the small yet beguiling **Patershol** neighborhood along the west bank of the Leie River and north of the Lieve Canal, but it provides a charming taste of Old Ghent. The nest of narrow, pedestrianized streets and tightly packed brick cottages were built in the 17th century for the city's weavers, craftsmen, and tradesmen; about 100 of these buildings are protected monuments and have been delightfully restored. Restaurants and bars have now flooded in to the area, making it a popular late-night drinking and clubbing spot.



**Gravensteen (Castle of the Counts)** ★ HISTORIC SITE MCLXXX.1180. The Roman numerals carved into stone at the gateway entrance of this castle, marking the year it was built, are as grey and foreboding as the 12th-century bulk that looms before you. It was designed to intimidate and impress by Philip of Alsace, Count of Flanders, who had returned to Ghent from the Crusades and built it to resemble a Crusader's castle he had seen in Syria. Imagine the subliminal fear that burghers of Ghent carried with them as they passed this symbol of power on their daily rounds; imagine the courage it took to storm the castle, as the people of Ghent did repeatedly in the 1300s. Endowed with six-foot-think walls, drawbridges and encircling moats, battlements, turrets, firing holes and towers, it was nearly impregnable. Inside were deep water wells (which you can view); "oubliettes" (sinister holes in cellar floors) for disposing of the recalcitrant; armories and penal chambers; and a labyrinth of damp stone passages and stairwells through which, today, you can clamber and climb in a structure far more complex, and larger, than it first appears. It is important to ascend the ramparts of the high central building for a panoramic view of the ancient rooftops of Ghent. On the way, you'll pass torture rooms and a chilling torture museum displaying instruments of coercion and punishment.

Sint-Veerleplein 11. www.gravensteengent.be. ✆ **09/225-9306.** 10€ adults, 7.50€ seniors, 6€ ages 19–25, free for 18 and under. Apr–Oct daily 10am–6pm, Nov–Mar daily 9am–5pm.

**Het Huis van Alijn (House of Alijn)** ★★ MUSEUM Ghent's intriguing folklife museum takes visitors on a journey through 20th-century life. Inside the clutch of whitewashed, gabled, and restored cottages are replicas of Ghent weaving and metalwork workshops as well as shop interiors of a sweet shop and a baker, but the most fascinating rooms are those dating from the 1950s and 1980s. One long corridor features flickering home movies, mundane in subject but rich in vicarious detail of every-day Belgian folk going about their lives. The museum is set in only medieval *godshuis* (almshouse) still standing in the city, the House of Alijn (built in the 12th century).

Kraanlei 65. www.huisvanalijn.be. ✆ **09/269-2350.** 6€ adults, 4.50€ seniors, 2€ ages 19–26, free for 18 and under. Museum and tavern Tues–Sat 11am–5:30pm, Sun 10am–5:30pm.

**Museum voor Schone Kunsten Gent (Ghent Fine Arts Museum)** ★★ MUSEUM Tucked behind a pillared, neoclassical facade on the edge of Citadelpark, the fine arts museum traces the story of Belgian art from the glowing, almost Byzantine religious art of the Middle Ages to the modern day. Although it has its fair share of work by the Flemish Primitives—including the dark, gaunt *Bearing of the Cross* (ca. 1500) by Bosch, plus Rubens and Van Dyck—where this museum really excels is in its later offerings. The late 19th century was a period of great artistic flowering in Ghent, and this is reflected in the works by *fin de siècle* artists such as James Ensor and Theo van Rysselberghe, whose work bears an uncanny resemblance to the paintings of his American contemporary John Singer Sargent. If contemporary artwork is your thing, there's an offshoot of MSK close by in Citadelpark at **SMAK** ★★ (see p. 267).

Fernand Scribedreef 1, Citadelpark. www.mskgent.be. ✆ **09/240-0700.** 8€ adults, 6€ seniors, 2€ ages 19–26, free for 18 and under. Tues–Sun 10am–6pm.

**Sint-Baafskathedraal (St. Bavo's Cathedral)** ★★★ CHURCH Viewed from afar, its white stone turned brown by the passage of tie, St. Bavo's is not among the more impressive cathedrals of Belgium, and its towers of four spires placed in a square is in fact rather unimaginative. But inside! Inside it is breathtaking, perhaps the most lavishly decorated of Belgium, flinging black and white marble in intricate baroque patterns and shapes against the often unadorned facades of the Gothic era, covering every inch of its two dozen chapels with priceless paintings and statuary, tomb carvings and screens, inscriptions, memorials, and remembrances.

St. Bavo's was largely built in the 14th and 15th century atop the site of the 12th-century Church of St. John, a part of which still survives in the central section of the Cathedral's remarkable crypt. Ravaged by Protestant iconoclasts in the 16th century who destroyed noted stained glass windows and artworks (the famed *Mystic Lamb,* see below, was

St. Bavo's Cathedral.

successfully hidden from them in an attic), it was largely redecorated in the 17th century by Bishop Anthony Triest. It is therefore appropriate that one of the sculptural masterworks of the Cathedral is Bishop Triest's tomb, done by the son of the great Jerome de Quesnoy, who sculpted the delightful Manneken-Pis in Brussels. Other important works in the church include Rubens's *The Conversion of St. Bavo* (1623) in the Rubens Chapel behind the elaborate high altar, and the ornate rococo oak pulpit entwined with white marble statuary.

But St. Bavo's showpiece, indeed the major artistic masterpiece of Ghent, is altarpiece ***The Adoration of the Mystic Lamb*** ★★ in the Villa Chapel, commissioned by a wealthy city alderman and completed by Flemish Primitive artist Jan van Eyck and his brother Hubert in 1432. A dazzling 24 panels requiring, it is believed, at least 12 years to complete, its monumental theme is nothing less than the summarized State of Mankind following the sacrifice of Christ. And when you have stared at it for a time, in awe at its naturalism and exacting details, you will suddenly realize that although the painting deals with religion, it is also occupied with people and proudly so. For the first time, ordinary mortals mix on an equal basis with saints and angels, are portrayed to the same dramatic extent, are magnificently garbed, are creatures worthy of respect. The ultimate redemption of man is now in progress, the painting seems to say, and a great, beautiful world has emerged, wondrous to

### Ghent Light Plan

In 2010, Ghent city fathers hatched a plan to light the city after dark. This had dual purposes: to increase safety at night and to show off the city's phenomenal architecture to its best advantage. Now you can follow the route through the streets on a 2-hour circular walk from Kouter in the south to Vrijdagmarkt in the north, but by far the most spectacular sights are the medieval guild houses in Korenlei and Graslei. But don't get too sidetracked in Ghent's enticing bars, because the illuminations, like Cinderella, disappear at midnight. You can download the walk for free from www.visitgent.be/en/node/9407.

behold, a model to be served with high ideals and fervor. ***Note:*** The work is currently being restored, but at least two-thirds of the panels are present at any one time for viewing; the others are replaced by black and white images. Work will finish in 2017.

Sint-Baafsplein. www.sintbaafskathedraal.be. ✆ **09/269-2045.** Cathedral free; *Mystic Lamb* chapel 4€ adults (includes audio guide in English), 1.50€ school children. Cathedral: Apr–Oct Mon–Sat 8:30am–6pm, Sun 9:30am–6pm; Nov–Mar Mon–Sat 8:30am–5pm, Sun 1–5pm; *Mystic Lamb* chapel: Apr–Oct daily 9:30am–5pm, Sun 1–5pm; Nov–Mar Mon–Sat 10:30am–4pm, Sun 1–4pm.

**Sint-Niklaaskerk (St. Nicholas's Church)** CHURCH The first to be constructed of the triumvirate of church spires that dominate central Ghent, St. Nicholas displays a mixture of Romanesque elements and the Flemish Schelde Gothic architectural style. An impressive 13th- to 15th-century church, it is a veritable mountain of Tournai bluestone and was paid for by Ghent's wealthy medieval merchants as an ostentatious signal of their wealth to other Flemish cities. A baroque high altar and other rich decorations embellish the interior; these date from after the Protestant *Beeldenstorm* (Iconoclastic Fury) of 1566, during which Catholic churches across the Low Countries were ransacked. An extensive restoration is ongoing, so currently the best ways to appreciate the Gothic detailing of St. Nicholas's flying buttresses and slender stained-glass windows is from the viewing platform of the Belfort (see p. 261).

Korenmarkt. ✆ **09/234-2869.** Free. Tues–Sun 10–5pm, Mon 2–5pm.

**Stadsmuseum van Gent (Ghent City Museum)/STAM ★★★** MUSEUM STAM offers the perfect introduction to Ghent, as it details the development of the city from its medieval beginnings to the cultured city we meet today. It's housed in an eccentric space that flows from the 14th-century Bijloke Abbey, through its neat knot of gardens, and into a contemporary block of airy exhibition space with exterior walls made of glass, mirroring the historical progress of the city as it moves from medieval to modern. A chronological trail meanders through multimedia exhibits, images, archaeological finds, artwork, and "listening benches" to bring Ghent's rich history to life in a museum that's stylishly curated, educational, and entertaining.

Godshuizenlaan 2. www.stamgent.be. ✆ **09/267-1400.** 8€ adults, 6€ seniors, 2€ ages 19–26, free for ages 18 and under. Tues–Sun 10am–6pm.

**Stedelijk Museum voor Actuele Kunst Gent (Museum of Contemporary Art)/SMAK ★★** MUSEUM Better known by yet another acronym, SMAK is Ghent's primary attraction for contemporary art fans, located in a 1930s building in Citadelpark near the Fine Arts Museum (see p. 264). The collection contains primo works by Karel Appel of CoBrA fame and big international names like Andy Warhol and Christo, but they're not always on display. You're more likely to find wacky, weird, and sometimes wonderful temporary exhibitions (such as the rainbow-hued paintings and installations of American colorist Richard Jackson) that showcase the work of Europe's leading contemporary artists; standards can be hit or miss so check what's on before a visit.

Citadelpark. www.smak.be. ✆ **09/240-7601.** 8€ adults, 6€ seniors, 2€ ages 19–26, free for children 18 and under. Tues–Sun 10am–6pm.

## CRUISING GHENT

A 50-minute **cruise ★** on the canals with either **Rederij De Gentenaer** (www.rederijdegentenaer.be; ✆ **09/269-0869**) or **Gent Watertoerist** (www.gent-watertoerist.be; ✆ **09/269-0869**) is included in the **CityCard Ghent** package (p. 261) and is well worth it to see the historic buildings lining the medieval waterways. Tour boats sail from Graslei and Korenlei, and opening hours and costs are the same for both cruise companies: April to mid-October daily 10am to 5pm, mid-October through March daily 11am to 4pm. Without the card, cruises cost 6.50€ for adults; 6€ for seniors, students, and ages 13 to 25; 3€ for children 3 to 11.

## ESPECIALLY FOR KIDS

As well as canal tours to explore the medieval canals (see above) and views from the top of the **Belfort** (p. 261), several of Ghent's major museums, including the **House of Alijn** (p. 264), **Design museum Gent** (p. 262), and **Ghent City Museum** (above), have tours specially designed to appeal to kids. The torture chamber at **Gravensteen Castle** (p. 261), is guaranteed to enthrall gloomy, emo-inclined teenagers. As much of the city center is pedestrianized, it's safe to explore by bike; rent from **Max Mobiel vzw** (www.max-mobiel.be); prices start at 7€ per day. If all else fails, bribe the kids with must-have treats including fruity, pyramid-shaped *neuzekes* (Ghent noses) from the shops around the Vrijdagmarkt or Temmerman (Kraanlei 79).

## THE medieval HARBOR

Undoubtedly the most beautiful parts of Ghent are the medieval quays of **Graslei** and **Korenlei** just west of Korenmarkt. Facing each other across the Leie waterway, they were the site of Tusschen Brugghen, the city's medieval harbor. Both embankments are lined with rows of intricately gabled former guild houses, warehouses, and elegant townhouses built in a variety of architectural styles between the 1200s and 1600s. It is fair to say that if all Ghent was as lovely as these two streets, it would give Bruges a run for its money. To see them all lit up at night under the **Ghent Light Plan** (see box p. 266) is a genuinely breathtaking experience. By day, both quays are lined with tour-boat docks (see p. 267).

**Graslei** Graslei today is one of the city's most picturesque meeting points, awash with **bars and restaurants** backlit by graceful gabled guild houses. At no. 8, the Brabantine Gothic **Gildehuis van de Metselaars (Stonemasons' Guild House)** has graceful pinnacles and is decorated with a medallion of an angel and reliefs of the "Quatuor Coronati," four Roman martyrs who were the guild's patrons. It dates from 1527, but what you see is actually a 1912 reconstruction of a 16th-century guild house originally located on Cataloniëstraat.

No. 9, dating from 1435, was the first **Korenmetershuis (House of the Grain Measurers),** where officials weighed imported grain before it was transported to the Korenmarkt. Next door, at no. 10, is the solidly constructed **Het Spijker (Stockpile House),** dating from around 1200, where corn was stored. The front of its forward-leaning Romanesque facade reaches up to the world's oldest step gable. Inside is the chic restaurant and club **Belga Queen** (www.belgaqueen.be).

The tiny building squished in at no. 11 is the **Tolhuisje (Little Customs House),** which was constructed in 1682 in the Flemish Renaissance style as the office of the city's corn revenue agent. It now houses a great little cafe, **Het Tolhuisje.** Next door, nos. 12 to 13 were an annex to the **Korenmetershuis (House of the Grain Measurers)** and date from 1540; the patterned red-and-white brickwork was added in 1698.

No. 14, with a facade dating from 1531 covering the 14th-century building underneath, was the ornate Brabantine Gothic **Gildehuis van de Vrije Schippers (Guild House of the Free Boatmen) ★.** This is one of the finest sights on Graslei, decorated with symbols of sailing ships and sailors on its sandstone facade.

**Korenlei** Across the water from Graslei by the Sint-Michielsbrug (St.



### WHERE TO EAT

A night out in Ghent is never going to be a problem, with a proliferation of dining options from traditional grand cafes to contemporary restaurants. For lovely nighttime views over gracious guild houses, choose **De Graslei** (Graslei 7; www.restaurantdegraslei.be; ✆ **09/225-5147**); the place buzzes in many languages and offers a typically Flemish menu of teeming seafood platters or *waterzooi* served with piles of fries. An on-trend lunchtime spot with a sunny terrace bang in the middle of Ghent's tourist heartland, **Restaurant Picardie** (Hooiaard 7; ✆ **09/233-8444**) overflows with bonhomie and a menu of well-priced bistro staples.

Michael's Bridge), Korenlei is a fine vantage point from which to appreciate the architectural wonders on the opposite bank. However, this street has many treasures of its own, most built later than the historic facades along Graslei.

The step-gabled 16th-century house constructed of red brick at no. 23 on the corner by the bridge was the **Brewers' Guild House.** The redbrick, step-gabled building called **De Swaene (the Swans),** at no. 9 Korenlei, dates from 1609; it has a pair of gilded swan medallions on the facade, and in its time has been a brewery and a bordello.

At no. 7 is the pink-and-white-shaded **Gildehuis van de Onvrije Schippers (Guild House of the Tied Boatmen) ★.** Dating from 1739 and dubbed Den Ancker (the Anchor), it is a masterpiece of Flemish baroque architecture, with a graceful bell gable and carved dolphins and lions on the facade; that's all topped with a gilded weathervane of a sailing ship at full mast on the roof.

**Graslei.**

## Antwerp ★★

48km (30 miles) N of Brussels

Until a few years ago, Antwerp was one of Western Europe's secret places, known only to a lucky few, but now it's been discovered big time. Owing its historical wealth to its location on the Schelde (Scheldt) River, the city's reputation as a thriving port and diamond-trade center is well deserved, but that's far from all there is to say about this booming, highbrow, and—in some small parts—seedy city. The capital town of the province of Antwerpen boasts monuments from its wealthy medieval,

Renaissance, and baroque periods; a magnificent cathedral; a fine-arts museum full of Old Flemish masterpieces (closed, alas, until 2017); a maze of medieval streets; and a thriving nightlife and cool cultural scene. Given all this, it's no surprise that international visitors to Belgium have been remedying their former neglect of the city: Antwerp is on the rise.

## ESSENTIALS

The **Antwerp Tourism & Convention** website is www.visitantwerpen.be.

**ARRIVING** **SNCB trains** run in approximately 50 minutes between Brussels-Midi and Antwerp Centraal Station, which is 1.5km (1 mile) east of the Grote Markt. Trains leave every 15 minutes, and fares are 15€ round-trip. For more details, go to www.belgianrail.be.

By **car**, two main arteries connect Antwerp and Brussels: the A1/E19 via Mechelen and the A12. Journey time is 1 hour and 15 minutes.

**GETTING AROUND** The integrated public-transportation system of **bus, tram,** and **Premetro trams** in Antwerp is run by **De Lijn** (www.delijn.be; ✆ **070/22-0200**). Other than pounding the pavement of this pocket-size metropolis, tram is the best way to get around. The most useful services for tourists are lines 2, 3, 5, and 15, which run between Centraal Station and Groenplaats near the cathedral; and lines 10 and 11, which run past the Grote Markt. Purchase your ticket from the De Lijn sales point in the station and tourist office before boarding and you'll pay 20% less. The most useful ticket for sightseers is the ***dagkaart* (day card),** valid for the entire network; it costs 5€ in advance, 7€ once on the tram.

### Antwerp's Port

When you come down to it, if there were no River Schelde, there would be no Antwerp. The city's location close to the point where the river meets the tidal Westerchelde estuary made it a strategic port as far back as the 2nd century B.C. Antwerp was a trading station within the powerful medieval Hanseatic League but, unlike Bruges, it did not have the status of a full-fledged *Kontor,* with its own separate district and mercantile installations. In the early days, ships moored along the city's wharves, where the Steen now stands; nowadays the port has moved 13km (8 miles) downstream to docks that jam up against the Dutch border. After Rotterdam, Antwerp is Europe's second biggest port for goods handled, and the third biggest (after Rotterdam and Hamburg) for containers.

On the waterfront in the center of town, Antwerp's oldest building, **De Steen (The Castle),** Steenplein 1, is a glowering stone-built 13th-century fortress that once overlooked Antwerp's port. It is currently closed to the public, but it's worth a glance for its mighty proportions and the bizarre statue of what appears to be a giant peeing on two small boys at the foot of the left-hand steps.

## Antwerp Touristram

Save your feet on all those cobbled streets and take a **circular tour** of Antwerp's attractions in a **mini electric tram;** you'll start off in the Groenplaats, trundle around the cobbled lanes of the Old Town, pass the Gothic facades in Grote Markt, venture through the main shopping thoroughfares, and potter along the Schelde riverfront to MAS (see p. 272). There are seven departures a day during summer, on the hour from 11am until 5pm; tickets cost 6€ for adults, 4€ for children ages 4 to 12. See **www.touristram.be** for details.

Regulated **taxis** wait outside Centraal Station and in Groenplaats; otherwise call **Antwerp Tax** (www.antwerp-tax.be; ✆ **03/238-3838**). After 10pm, an extra 10€ is added to the fare.

### EXPLORING ANTWERP

Most visitors to Antwerp head straight for the warren of winding streets in the medieval Old Town, which fan out from the **Grote Markt**. South of there, the old shipping warehouses along Vlaamsekaai and Waalsekaai have burst back into life as edgy bars, restaurants, and art galleries. The area around Centraal Station, east of De Keyserlei and Koningin Astridplein, is more than a little seedy and has problems with drug dealing and prostitution; best leave that area well alone at night.

**Grote Markt** ★★ HISTORIC SQUARE A lovely 16th-century square lined with buzzing sidewalk cafes and restaurants filled with Antwerp's

**Antwerp's Grote-Markt and City Hall.**

sleek residents, the Grote Markt is the city's social and cultural epicenter. Dominated by the neoclassical Brabo Fountain, it is surrounded by majestic buildings like the many-gabled **Huis den Spieghel** at Grote Markt 9. This was a meeting place for great Renaissance thinkers such as Erasmus and Sir Thomas More, who was in Antwerp when he began to write *Utopia* in 1515.

The Renaissance **Stadhius (City Hall)** takes up the entire west side of the Grote Markt and was designed by Cornelius Floris de Vriendt; it is an outstanding example of the Flemish mannerism that replaced Antwerp's early Gothic architectural style in the 16th century; it has a splendid central tower and a pleasing, symmetrical frontage. The hall was burned during the city's sack by invading troops in the "Spanish Fury" of 1576 and rebuilt in 1579. If you are lucky enough to get inside, look out for the frescoes by Hendrik Leys, a 19th-century Antwerp painter.

Grote Markt. ✆ **03/221-1333.** Guided tours Mon–Wed and Fri–Sat 2 and 3pm (council business permitting). Tickets 1€.

**Koninklijk Museum voor Schone Kunsten Antwerpen (Antwerp Royal Museum of Fine Arts) ★★★** MUSEUM In the number of its masterworks, the depth of its collections of various Flemish schools, its representative sampling from every Flemish period, Antwerp's Museum of Fine Arts ranks with Brussels's Musee de l'Art Ancien as one of the two outstanding museums of Belgium. It is a fit witness to the power of Antwerp, because only a rich and confident city could have gathered such an array. The museum contains world's biggest and best collection of paintings and frescoes by Peter Paul Rubens. Other artists displayed here include the Flemish Primitives Jan van Eyck, Rogier van der Weyden, Hans Memling, and Pieter Brueghel, as well as more recent Belgian favorites James Ensor and Paul Delvaux. Alas, the closed for restoration until the end of 2017, although a few works from KMSKA are on display in the **Golden Cabinet at Museum Rockoxhuis** (Keizerstraat 10-12; ✆ **03/201-9250;** www.rockoxhuis.be).

Leopold de Waelplaats 2. www.kmska.be. ✆ **03/238-7809.** Closed until 2017.

**Museum aan de Stroom (MAS) ★★★** MUSEUM Located in Antwerp's blooming Willemdok harbor area, sandwiched between the traditional city center and the brutal sprawl of the port, MAS is a multifloored homage to Antwerp, its people, and its culture today. Sitting on a dock commissioned by Napoléon, the museum was designed by Dutch architects Neutelings and Riedijk and looks like a pile of untidy Lego bricks clamped loosely together with teeth of glass. It opened in May 2011; the five themed floors of interactive and entertaining artworks, photos, newspaper cuttings, video, newsreel, and nearly half a million other artifacts offer an insightful explanation of how much the city owes

Museum aan de Stroom.



to its riverside position on the River Schelde, to its immigrants, and to its diamond industry (see box p. 275). There's a panorama across the city from the 9th-floor roof, and a couple of decent watering holes too; in fact **Restaurant 'Zilte** is so decent it has garnered two Michelin stars.
Hanzestedenplaats 1. www.mas.be. ✆ **03/338-4400.** 5€ adults, 3€ seniors and ages 12–25, free for children 11 and under. Tues–Fri 10am–5pm, Sat–Sun 10am–6pm.

**Museum Plantin-Moretus ★★** MUSEUM The patrician 16th-century residence of Christoffel Plantin, inventor of one of the world's most popular printing fonts, has been awarded UNESCO World Heritage status for its period rooms, gardens, and collection of original printing presses dating as far back as the 16th century. In 1555, Plantin established a workshop in his stately mansion, and its output contributed greatly to Antwerp's reputation as a center of printing excellence; today it is laid out as if the compositors and printers had just put down their tools for the day. Rubens, that local-boy-made-good, illustrated many of the books published by the Plantin-Moretus workshop and painted some of the family portraits displayed in the museum; a further incitement to visit is the rare chance to see a Gutenberg Bible dating from 1455.
Vrijdagmarkt 22-23. www.museumplantinmoretus.be. ✆ **03/221-1450.** 8€ adults, 6€ seniors/students ages 19–26, 1€ free for children 18 and under. Tues–Sun 10am–5pm.

**Onze-Lieve-Vrouwekathedraal (Cathedral of Our Lady) ★★** CHURCH Antwerp's iconic landmark is a masterpiece of Brabantine

## Antwerp City Card

Save much money as you see the sights with the Antwerp City Card, which is valid in three chunks of time, costing 19€ for 24 hours, 25€ for 48 hours, and 29€ for 72 hours. This permits free entrance to 17 museums and three churches as well as free use of the public transport system, a city map, and discounts at **ZOO Antwerpen ★★** (see facing page) as well as on various stores and restaurants. The card is also available as an app; check **www.visitantwerpen.be** for more details.

Gothic architecture—and in fact the largest Gothic structure in Belgium. And the cathedral breaks more records too—it also boasts the tallest church spire in the country, an ornate affair looming 123m (404 ft.) over the city's ancient heart. Looking from the main entrance to the cathedral, you'll see that a second tower, intended to be of similar size, was never completed, giving the facade an oddly lopsided aspect. Begun in 1352 to a design by Jean Appelmans, whose statue stands outside, the cathedral was finally completed in 1521; its backstory includes a destructive fire in 1533, devastation by Protestant rebels during the religious wars of the 16th century, de-consecration by anticlerical French revolutionaries in 1794, and a slow rebirth after Napoléon's final defeat in 1815.

Its interior is a gleaming, white affair with seven aisles supported by 125 pillars, its embellishment a heady mix of baroque and neoclassical stained glass windows, carved wood pulpits and lecterns, and tombs of the Bourbon royal family, but pole position goes to the four exquisite Rubens altarpieces: The two standout pieces are his *The Raising of the Cross* (1610) and *The Descent from the Cross* (1614). During July and August, the cathedral bells peal out in a 49-bell carillon concert on Sunday from 3 to 4pm and on Monday from 8 to 9pm.

Groenplaats 21. www.dekathedraal.be. ✆ **03/213-9951.** 6€. Mon–Fri 10am–5pm, Sat 10am–3pm, Sun 1–4pm. Closed to tourist visits during services.

**Rubenshuis (Rubens House) ★★★** HISTORIC SITE Far from being the stereotypical starving artist in a garret, the artist Peter Paul Rubens (1577–1640) amassed a tidy fortune from his light-kissed paintings, which allowed him to build an impressive mansion in 1610 when he was just 33. Today you have to beat off the tourist hordes to file through one glorious period apartment after another, all richly decorated with fine furniture, marble Roman sculptures, and examples of Rubens's exquisite portraiture, including one of Anthony van Dyck, who was his pupil. When you've fought your way through the house, take a breather in the Renaissance courtyard and reflect on the sumptuous lifestyle of a patrician Flemish gentleman in the 17th century.

Wapper 9-11. www.rubenshuis.be. ✆ **03/201-1555.** 8€ adults, 6€ seniors/students ages 12–25, free for children 11 and under. Tues–Sun 10am–5pm.

**Sint-Pauluskerk (St. Paul's Church)** ★★ CHURCH Although there was a monastery on this site as early as 1256, the present St. Paul's Church dates from the late 17th century and exhibits a cheerful clash of spindly Gothic exterior and a calm, white interior with hints of gilded baroque flourish. It is chiefly notable for the unsung collection of paintings by Rubens and his pupil Anthony van Dyck that line the outer aisles. The works of Rubens are *The Flagellation* (painting number 7 of the *Stations of the Cross* sequence in the left-hand aisle) and *The Adoration of the Shepherds* just in front of the choir on the same side. Van Dyck's contribution was *The Bearing of the Cross* (number 9 in the *Stations of the Cross*). If you get lucky, the choir may perform a 13th-century plainsong during Mass on Sunday morning.

Veemarkt 14. www.sint-paulusparochie.be. ✆ **03/221-3321.** Free. Apr–Oct daily 2–5pm. Mass Sun 10:30am.

## ESPECIALLY FOR KIDS

Antwerp offers enough diversions to keep kids happy for a couple of days. Try **harbor cruises** with Rederij Flandria (www.flandria.nu; ✆ **03/231-3100**), rides in the **electric tram** (p. 271), and dazzling them with diamonds (see box below). If that fails, then abandon all ideas of discovering the secrets of the **Rubenshuis** and the **MAS** (see above for both) and head straight for **ZOO Antwerpen** ★★ (Koningin

### diamonds ARE ANTWERP'S BEST FRIEND

Antwerp remains the world's leading market for cut diamonds and is second only to London as an outlet for raw and industrial diamonds, despite intense competition from India, Dubai, and Israel. The raw facts are sparkling enough: 84% of all the world's diamonds pass through Antwerp at some point on their journey from rough stone to polished, set gem. There are four diamond-trading houses in Antwerp, and together they comprise an industry that turns over 147 million euros for the city each year. The trade, with its diamond cutters and polishers, workshops, brokers, and merchants, is centered on the few heavily guarded streets that form the city's **Diamantkwartier (Diamond Quarter),** a surprisingly down-at-the-heels area steps away from Centraal Station. It is regulated by the Antwerp World Diamond Center (www.awdc.be) and mostly run by members of the city's Hasidic Jewish community, who found a niche market when they arrived in Antwerp in the 15th century.

To buy diamonds or watch them being cut, visit the glittering jewelry stores in the Diamond Quarter. **Diamondland,** Appelmansstraat 33a (www.diamondland.be; ✆ **03/229-2990**), is the city's biggest diamond salesroom and offers guided tours of its workshops as well as trustworthy, personalized, and knowledgeable service for serious buyers (all tax-free for non-E.U. visitors).

Astridplein 20-26; www.zooantwerpen.be; ✆ **03/224-8910**), which has an enviable reputation for animal conservation and success in breeding rare animals. The 10-hectare (25-acre) zoo is housed in something of an Art Nouveau masterpiece, although whether the 5,000 animals appreciate this is doubtful. The 950 species include endangered okapi and red pandas, rare Siberian tigers and Arabian oryx, aviaries, polar bears, gorillas, panthers, and cuddly koalas. Right across the road is **Aquatopia** (Koningin Astridplein 7; www.aquatopia.be; ✆ **03/205-0750**), with 40 aquariums filled with marine creatures from sea horses to sharks; kids can explore underneath the sea by submarine.

### WHERE TO EAT

To experience Flemish hospitality at its best, head for **Grand Café De Rooden Hoed ★★** (Oude Koornmarkt 25; www.deroodenhoed.be; ✆ **03/289-0909**), a smart, traditional brasserie serving up pails of mussels Antwerp-style with leeks, garlic, and cream; plus a wait staff that funnier than most comedy routines. For slick service in Art Nouveau surroundings after visiting the Rubenshuis, grab a table on the terrace at **Grand Café Horta ★★** (Hopland 2; www.grandcafehorta.be; ✆ **03/203-5660**) for scrumptious Thai beef salads and multi-decker club sandwiches.

### SHOPPING

The long shopping street of Meir has mid-range international chains and department stores, while the upmarket stores and boutiques have colonized the area south of the Grote Markt between Steenhouwersvest and Komedieplaats; here you'll find Diane von Furstenberg, Gucci, Ralph Lauren, Petite Filou, and many others. For lace, scour the streets surrounding the cathedra,l and for diamonds, head for Appelmansstraat and nearby streets around Centraal Station.

## [Fast FACTS] BELGIUM

**Business Hours** Stores open Monday to Saturday from 9 or 10am to 6pm. On Friday evening, many center-city stores stay open until 8 or 9pm. Most stores close on Sunday, except the tourist-oriented ones. The majority of museums open Tuesday through Sunday from 10am until 5pm, and most close on Monday.

**Currency** Belgium is a member of the European Union and uses the E.U. common currency, the euro (€). See p. 860 for information on money and costs.

**Doctors & Dentists** For doctors, call **Médi Garde** (✆ **02/479-1818**) or **SOS Médecins** (✆ **02/513-0202**) and ask for an English-speaking doctor. For emergency dental care, call ✆ **02/426-1026.**

**Embassies & Consulates:** **Australia:** Rue Guimard/Guimardstraat, 6-8, Brussels; www.eu.mission.gov.au; ✆ **02/286-0500.**

**Canada:** Avenue de Tervuren 2, Brussels; www.belgium.gc.ca; ✆ **02/741-0611.**

**New Zealand:** Avenue des Nerviens 9/31, Brussels; E-mail: nzemb.skm@mft.net.nz; ✆ **02/512-1040.**

**United Kingdom:** Avenue d'Auderghem 10, Brussels; www.gov.uk/government/world/organisations/british-embassy-brussels; ✆ **02/287-6211.**

**United States:** Regentlaan 27 Boulevard du Regent, Brussels; www.belgium.usembassy.gov; ✆ **02/811-4000.**

### Emergencies

Dial ✆ **112** for police, ambulance, paramedics, and the fire department.

### Pharmacies

In Belgium, a pharmacy is called either an ***apotheek*** or a ***pharmacie*** and sells both prescription and nonprescription medicines. Regular hours are Monday to Saturday from around 9am to 6pm. Pharmacies post details of nearby **all-night and Sunday pharmacies** on their doors, or you can call ✆ **09/001-0500** or go to the website www.servicedegarde.be and type in your postal code to find the nearest 24-hour pharmacy.

### Post Offices

The national mail company is known as **bpost** (www.depostlaposte.be; ✆ **02/201-2345**); most post offices are open Monday to Friday 9am to 5pm.

5

# THE NETHERLANDS

By John Newcomb

Most of it lies below sea level, which is why they named the country "the Netherlands"—"nether" meaning "low" and the name meaning "The Low Country." (An earlier, medieval reference to "Holland" is no longer officially used.) And much of the land in the "Low Country" (Netherlands) was wrested from the sea by the Dutch themselves. "God made the world," goes a proverb, "but the Dutch made the Netherlands."

That effort has continued as recently as the late 1920s. In an astonishing act of self-improvement, which should be a model for the rest of us, the Dutch decided in recent times to increase their land area by building a 20-mile-long dike across a salt-water inlet of the North Sea. They (including ordinary citizens and not simply professional construction crews) dumped sand, mud, and stones into the very waters of a raging ocean, and thus walled off a large portion of the North Sea, creating an immense fresh-water lake. Later, they pumped water from that lake to create hundreds of thousands of acres of new land for towns, villages, and farming.

Today, the visitor can drive atop the 20-mile length of the Enclosure Dike ("Afsluitdijk"), and gaze out at the ocean it held back on one side.

I think of that immense, cooperative national effort whenever I visit the Netherlands (where I once operated a hotel), and of its hardy, resolute, determined people who don't permit opponents to keep them from taking the steps they believe their nation needs, including the legalization of euthanasia, abortion, prostitution, and (in part) drugs. The center of these efforts is **Amsterdam,** from which today's visitor can easily make side trips to Rotterdam (with the world's largest sea port), The Hague (with multiple international courts), Leiden (a charming university city) and Haarlem (the Frans Hals Museum). But Amsterdam commands most of the attention of visitors to the Netherlands.

In a long-ago time when Amsterdam was thought to be "quaint," a place of tulips and wooden shoes, I wrote a travel guide called *Surprising Amsterdam,* whose point was that Amsterdam wasn't quaint or superannuated at all. In it, and in associated lectures I delivered, I argued that far from being quaint, Amsterdam was a devilish, in-your-face, unexpected center of red light



FACING PAGE: **Canal and St. Nicolas Church in Amsterdam.**

districts, pot-smoking coffee houses, and outlandish but exciting social experimentation. As a city, I claimed, it had taken over the role once played by Stockholm, and was now a place of advanced social conventions, controversial economic policies, and novel civic institutions. It was not the place you expected it to be, and it certainly didn't make a point of wooden shoes and tulips.

Amsterdam was the first city I had ever encountered that openly tolerated socializing by gays. It—and the country of which it was the economic capital—was the first I had ever seen that prohibited the firing of employees for anything other than the most egregious misdeeds. Its social security and unemployment benefits were among the highest in Europe, and its people were constantly marching and agitating for international social causes. It was one of the most progressive cities on earth,

Want another example? In my *Surprising Amsterdam* travel guide, I confessed to be shocked but yet intrigued by the decisions of the city and the church to each sponsor the operation of two teenager nightclubs (called "Fantasio" and "Paradiso"), in which the sale of drugs was openly permitted. The theory was that by eliminating the thrill and challenge of breaking the law, youngsters would find the atmosphere of these clubs to be boring and subdued, without sexual tension, without exciting danger; and having had their fill of these prohibited practices, the youngsters would gladly return to the traditional dancehalls and enjoy themselves without drugs.

Is it still an outlandish and outrageous city? Well, yes. The ambitious effort to close the marijuana-dispensing coffee houses has failed (Amsterdam's merchants were aghast at the thought), and the vast red-light district is as active as ever. And though the city has a checkered record in terms of its recent treatment of Muslim immigrants, even those questions seem on the brink of resolution—from a liberal standpoint.

So when you visit Amsterdam, you'll be viewing institutions both modern and ancient. You'll gaze to your delight at the 17th-century masterworks in the Rijksmuseum (Rembrandt and Vermeer the top highlights), you'll stroll a vast area of totally untouched 17th-century canal houses arrayed picturesquely along semi-circular canals dug in those long-ago days, and yet you'll be aware of super-modern institutions and attitudes that continue to reflect the viewpoints of most of its citizens.

Here it is, in the pages that follow, along with passing glances at side trips nearby.

***–Arthur Frommer***

# AMSTERDAM

Open-hearted, welcoming, and prosperous, Amsterdam is a good-time city that merrily opens its arms to all comers. It embraces its tourists, its cyclists, its boat-folk, and its multi-cultural community. It's a long-outdated cliché to regard Amsterdam as some sort of latter-day Sodom and Gomorrah. Some of the coffee houses where patrons smoke marijuana have closed down (due to bans on the indoor smoking of tobacco, which is often mixed with weed in Holland), as have some of the prostitutes' infamous windows, and smart restaurants, bars, and upmarket independent stores are starting to move in to the pretty side streets of the Rosse Buurt (Red Light District), which ironically hides some of the most unspoiled architecture in Amsterdam. The truth is Amsterdam is an open-hearted, welcoming, prosperous, and highly cultured place, so be sure to give yourself time to absorb the freewheeling spirit of this vibrant burg.

## Essentials

Amsterdam's main tourism portal is **www.iamsterdam.com**, offering everything from hotel and restaurant reservations to special events tickets to LGBT info and more.

**ARRIVING** **Amsterdam Airport Schiphol** (www.schiphol.nl; airport code AMS), 14km (9 miles) southwest of Amsterdam is pronounced *Skhip*-ol and is universally regarded as one of the best airports in the world for its ease of use, its massive duty-free shopping center, and its outpost of the Rijksmuseum (p. 297). Located southwest of the city center, it handles the country's international arrivals and departures.

Beyond the Customs check is Schiphol Plaza, a one-stop destination that combines a tourist office (open daily 7am–10pm), transport ticket office, rail station access, a shopping mall, bars and restaurants, baggage lockers, and car-rental and hotel-reservation desks all in the one location. Bus and shuttle stops plus a taxi stand are just outside the terminal.

For those coming by **car,** a network of major **international highways** crisscrosses the Netherlands. European expressways E19, E35, and E231 converge on Amsterdam from France and Belgium to the south and from Germany to the north and east. These roads also have Dutch designations; as you approach the city they are, respectively: A4, A2, and A1. Amsterdam's ring road is A10. Distances between destinations are relatively short. Traffic is invariably heavy and delays are frequent, but road conditions are otherwise pretty good, service stations are plentiful, and highways are plainly signposted.

**DFDS Seaways** (www.dfdsseaways.co.uk; ✆ **0871/522-9955** in the U.K., 44/330-333-0245 outside the U.K.) has daily **car-ferry**

Centraal Station.





services between Newcastle in northeast England and Ijmuiden, west of Amsterdam. **P&O Ferries** (www.poferries.com; ✆ **0871/664-2121** U.K., 020/200-8333 in Holland) has daily car-ferry service between Hull in northeast England and Rotterdam. **Stena Line** (www.stenaline.co.uk; ✆ **08447/707-070** U.K.) has a twice-daily car ferry service between Harwich in southeast England and Hoek van Holland near Rotterdam.

**Rail services** to Amsterdam from other cities in the Netherlands and elsewhere in Europe are frequent and fast. **International trains** arrive at Centraal Station. **Nederlandse Spoorwegen (Netherlands Railways)** trains arrive in Amsterdam from gateways across the Netherlands. Schedule and fare info is available at www.ns.nl.

The burgundy-colored **Thalys high-speed train,** with a top speed of 300kmph (186 mph), connects Paris, Brussels, Amsterdam, and (via Brussels) Cologne. Travel time from Paris to Amsterdam is 3 hours, 20 minutes, and from Brussels 1 hour, 50 minutes. For Thalys info and reservations, visit www.thalys.com. Tickets are also available from railway stations and travel agents.

International buses arrive at the **bus terminal** opposite the Amstel rail station (Metro: Amstel) in the south of the city. Eurolines operates coach services between London Victoria Bus Station and Amstel Station (via ferry), with up to five departures daily in the summer. Travel time is 12 hours. For reservations, contact **Eurolines** (www.eurolines.com; ✆ **08717/818-178** in Britain or 31/88-076-1700 in Holland). From here, you can go by train or Metro to Centraal Station, or by tram no. 12 to the Museumplein area and to connecting points for trams to the center city. For the Leidseplein, take the Metro toward Centraal Station,

## Bag a Bike Taxi

If you're keen on your green credentials, use a bike taxi or rickshaw to get around the city. They're clean, relatively comfortable, and can nip along the cobbled streets, giving Amsterdam's lethal cyclists a run for their money. The rickshaws are easy to spot all over the city, but especially around Centraal Station, Leidseplein, Museumplein, and Waterlooplein, or you can order your eco-taxi in advance. Contact **Amsterdam Bike Taxi** (www.amsterdambiketaxi.info; ✆ **645/412-725**). Charges are 30€ per half hour per rickshaw.

get out at Weesperplein, and take tram 7 or 10.

**CITY LAYOUT** Amsterdam is not a huge city, and its central district, where most of the tourist attractions are concentrated, can be walked easily. The canals and streets fan out in a series of concentric circles from the historic city center. However, despite its size, this city is very diverse in mood and style, changing in feel almost from one street to another.

**GETTING AROUND** Public transportation in Amsterdam uses an electronic card called the **OV-chipkaart.** The cards are valid for 5 years, cost 7.50€, and can be loaded and reloaded with up to 50€. They can only be used by one rider at a time. Reduced-rate cards are available for seniors and children. Electronic readers on Metro and train station platforms and onboard trams and buses deduct the correct fare—just hold your card up against the reader at both the start and the end of the ride. These cards are valid throughout the Netherlands.

Another option for short-term visitors who plan to use public transportation a lot is a **1-day or a multiday card** from GVB: 24 hours (7.50€), 48 hours (12€), 72 hours (17€), 96 hours (21€), 120 hours (26€), 144 hours (30€), and 68 hours (32€).

The central ticket sales point for GVB Amsterdam, the city's public transportation company, is **GVB Tickets & Info,** Stationsplein (open

Relaxing in a cafe along one of Amsterdam's 165 canals.

Mon–Fri 7am–6pm and Sat–Sun 10am–6pm; www.gvb.nl), in front of Centraal Station. In addition, cards are available from GVB and Netherlands Railways ticket booths in Metro and train stations, ticket machines (automats) at Metro and train stations, and ticket machines onboard some trams.

Half the fun of Amsterdam is walking along the canals. The other half is riding the blue-and-gray **trams** that roll through most major streets. There are 16 tram routes, 10 of which (lines 1, 2, 4, 5, 9, 13, 16, 17, 24, and 26) begin and end at Centraal Station, so you know you can always get back to that central point if you get lost and have to start over. Lines 3, 5, 12, and 24 are useful for visiting the sights south of the city around Museumplein, while 4, 9, 14, 16, and 24 serve the city center.

Trams have one access door that opens automatically, normally toward the rear; arrowed indicators point the way to the door. Always remember to hold your card against the reader as you get on and off the tram. ***Note:*** If you don't "check out" as you get off, your card will carry on being charged and will run out of credit.

An extensive **bus** network complements the trams, with many bus routes beginning and ending at Centraal Station, but it's generally much faster to go by tram. Some areas of the city are served only by bus.

Amsterdam does have its own **Metro,** with four lines that run partly over ground and transport commuters in and out from the suburbs, running between 6am and midnight. From Centraal Station, you can use Metro trains to reach both Nieuwmarkt and Waterlooplein in the old city center.

It used to be that you couldn't simply hail a **taxi** from the street in Amsterdam, but nowadays they often stop if you do. Otherwise, find one of the taxi stands sprinkled around the city, generally near luxury hotels, at major squares such as the Dam, Spui, Rembrandtplein, Westermarkt, and Leidseplein, and of course at Centraal Station. Taxis have rooftop signs and blue license plates, and are metered. Hotel staff can order cabs, too.

There's no point whatsoever in **renting a car** if you are intending to stay in Amsterdam and not venture out of the city, as the public transport system works efficiently and most attractions are within walking distance of each other. In addition, the streets are narrow, many are one-way, some are pedestrianized, and all are crowded with bonkers cyclists; in short, driving in the city is a nightmare. However, if you are traveling outside Amsterdam, it's usually cheapest to book a rental car online before you leave home from one of the major, multi-national firms.

## The Neighborhoods in Brief

**THE OLD CENTER** The oldest, most central district of Amsterdam centers on the rackety Dam Square, **Oude Kerk,** and the Nieuwmarkt and is probably best known for containing the infamous **Red Light District,** which lies between the two canals Oudezijds Voorburgwaal and Oudezijds Achterburgwaal. Despite its seedy reputation, it is safe and well policed. A recent gentrification policy has seen more restaurants and design stores moving in.

**CANAL RING** The concentric band of three canals that surround the Old Center was built in the 17th century as the cramped, disease-ridden old city drastically needed to expand. Herengracht, Keizersgracht, and Prinsengracht today form an aristocratic enclave of grand townhouses overlooking the three canals. Some of the city's smartest hotels and many major attractions lie within this belt, including the **Westerkerk,** the **Anne Frank Huis,** the Canal House Museum, and the **Willet-Holthuysen Museum.**

**JORDAAN** This area of formerly artisanal housing lining narrow canals interspersed with hump-backed ridges is now the favored residential area of Amsterdam's intelligentsia. There are lots of bars and traditional brown cafes to discover as well as innovative art galleries. Jordaan also has scores of canal-house hotels tucked into its pretty lanes.

**MUSEUM QUARTER** Housing Amsterdam's triumvirate of heavyweight art museums, the **Rijksmuseum,** Stedelijk Museum (p. 298), and the Van Gogh Museum (p. 298), this quarter is also home to the Concertgebouw concert hall (p. 317), embassies, and upmarket stores, as well as one of the city's most glorious public spaces, the **Museumplein.** The **Heineken Brewery** is close by.

**OUD ZUID** Adjoining the Museum Quarter and the Vondelpark, Amsterdam's poshest residential area is also its most exclusive shopping district and home to several exclusive hotels.

**DE PLANTAGE** Incorporating the **Artis Royal Zoo,** the **Hortus Botanicus,** and Amsterdam's Jewish Quarter, Plantage is an area of wide boulevards surrounded by residential streets. **The Jewish Museum** and **Portuguese Synagogue** mark the district's western limits.

## Exploring Amsterdam

Where to start in this city of 165 canals, 1,250 bridges, countless cobbled streets, the UNESCO World Heritage–listed Canal Ring (p. 294), and more than 40 beckoning museums? The answer to that question is easy. Your first adventure in Amsterdam should be a canal cruise (p. 302), both to get your bearings and acquire a feel for the city's carefree vibe. For other adventures, read on.

### OLD CENTER

**Amsterdam Museum** ★★ MUSEUM Amsterdam's history museum recounts the tale of Amsterdam's progression from simple fishing village to world power (in the 17th century) with a superbly interactive, initial exhibition called "Amsterdam DNA." Included in this whirlwind tour (the best part of the museum) are reproductions of Old Dutch Master paintings, maps, tools, armor, and religious sculpture. You

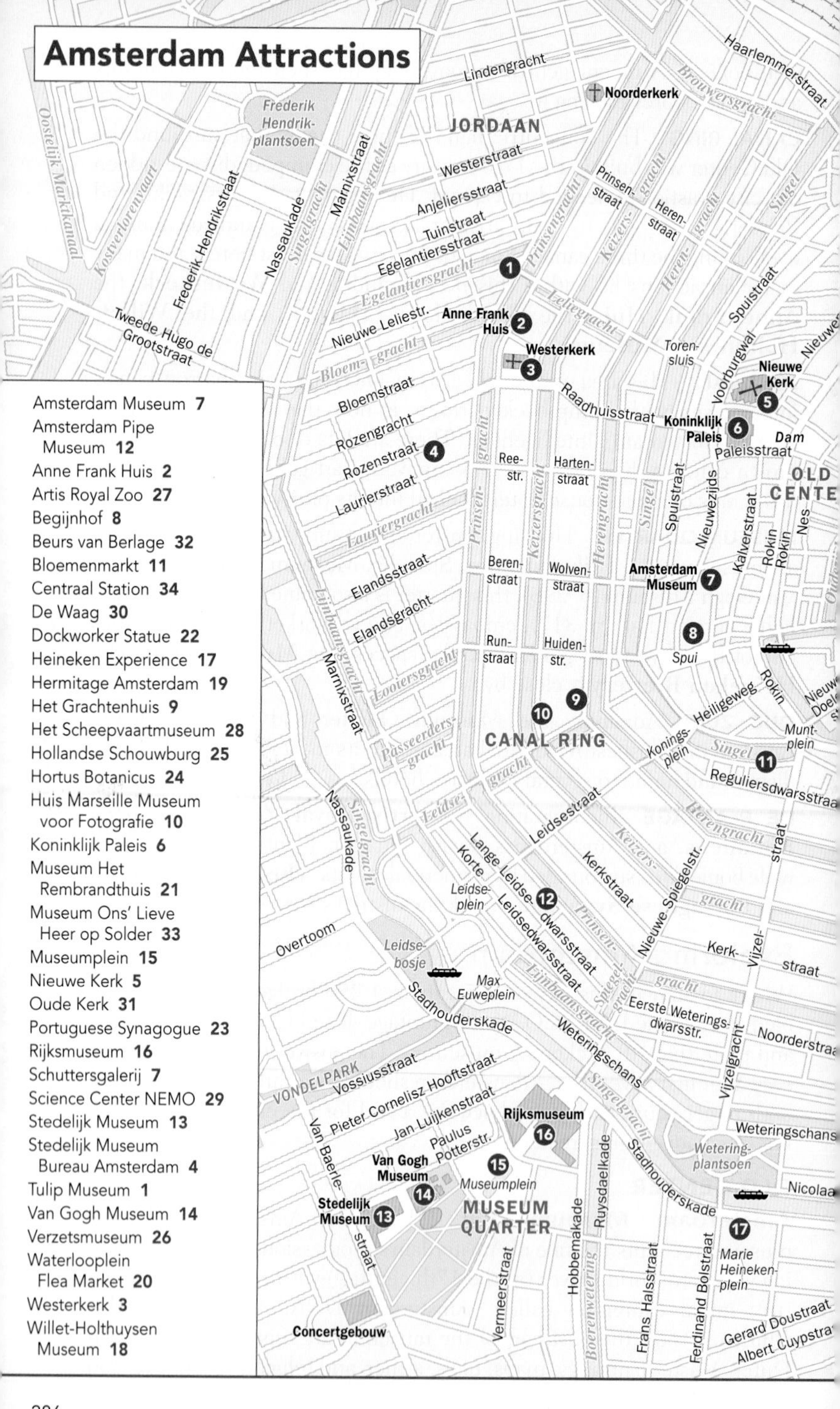
Amsterdam Attractions
Amsterdam Museum 7
Amsterdam Pipe Museum 12
Anne Frank Huis 2
Artis Royal Zoo 27
Begijnhof 8
Beurs van Berlage 32
Bloemenmarkt 11
Centraal Station 34
De Waag 30
Dockworker Statue 22
Heineken Experience 17
Hermitage Amsterdam 19
Het Grachtenhuis 9
Het Scheepvaartmuseum 28
Hollandse Schouwburg 25
Hortus Botanicus 24
Huis Marseille Museum voor Fotografie 10
Koninklijk Paleis 6
Museum Het Rembrandthuis 21
Museum Ons' Lieve Heer op Solder 33
Museumplein 15
Nieuwe Kerk 5
Oude Kerk 31
Portuguese Synagogue 23
Rijksmuseum 16
Schuttersgalerij 7
Science Center NEMO 29
Stedelijk Museum 13
Stedelijk Museum Bureau Amsterdam 4
Tulip Museum 1
Van Gogh Museum 14
Verzetsmuseum 26
Waterlooplein Flea Market 20
Westerkerk 3
Willet-Holthuysen Museum 18
JORDAAN
CANAL RING
MUSEUM QUARTER
OLD CENTE
Noorderkerk
Anne Frank Huis
Westerkerk
Nieuwe Kerk
Koninklijk Paleis
Dam
Amsterdam Museum
Rijksmuseum
Van Gogh Museum
Stedelijk Museum
Concertgebouw
Frederik Hendrik-plantsoen
VONDELPARK
Leidse-bosje
Leidseplein
Max Euweplein
Museumplein
Muntplein
Koningsplein
Spui
Torensluis
Weteringplantsoen
Marie Heinekenplein
Haarlemmerstraat
Brouwersgracht
Lindengracht
Westerstraat
Anjeliersstraat
Tuinstraat
Egelantiersstraat
Egelantiersgracht
Nieuwe Leliestr.
Leliegracht
Bloemgracht
Bloemstraat
Rozengracht
Rozenstraat
Laurierstraat
Lauriergracht
Elandsstraat
Elandsgracht
Looiersgracht
Passeerdersgracht
Leidsegracht
Raadhuisstraat
Paleisstraat
Reestr.
Hartenstraat
Berenstraat
Wolvenstraat
Runstraat
Huidenstr.
Prinsengracht
Keizersgracht
Herengracht
Singel
Prinsenstraat
Herenstraat
Spuistraat
Voorburgwal
Nieuwezijds
Kalverstraat
Rokin
Nes
Heiligeweg
Reguliersdwarsstraat
Leidsestraat
Kerkstraat
Nieuwe Spiegelstr.
Spiegelgracht
Lange Leidsedwarsstraat
Korte Leidsedwarsstraat
Lijnbaansgracht
Eerste Weteringsdwarsstr.
Vijzelstraat
Vijzelgracht
Noorderstraat
Weteringschans
Stadhouderskade
Singelgracht
Overtoom
Vossiusstraat
Pieter Cornelisz Hooftstraat
Jan Luijkenstraat
Paulus Potterstr.
Van Baerlestraat
Vermeerstraat
Hobbemakade
Ruysdaelkade
Boerenwetering
Frans Halsstraat
Ferdinand Bolstraat
Gerard Doustraat
Albert Cuypstraat
Nicolaa
Marnixstraat
Nassaukade
Lijnbaansgracht
Singelgracht
Frederik Hendrikstraat
Tweede Hugo de Grootstraat
Kostverlorenvaart
Oostelijk Marktkanaal

Het IJ
De Ruijterkade
Centraal Station
34
Prins Hendrikkade
Stationsplein
Centraal Station
Muziekgebouw aan 't IJ/ Bimhuis
Passenger Terminal Amsterdam
IJ-Tunnel
JAVA-EILAND
IJhaven
OOSTERDOK
Piet Heinkade
Oosterdokskade
Dijksgracht
Damrak
Zeedijk
33
32
Oude Kerk
31
RED LIGHT DISTRICT
Geldersekade
Kromme Waal
Scheepvaarthuis
Oosterdok
Science Center NEMO
29
MARINETERREIN
(Former naval complex, under development)
Binnenkant
Oude Waal
Eilandsgracht
Prins Hendrikkade
30
Nieuwmarkt
Het Scheepvaartmuseum
28
Kattenburgerstraat
Rechtboomssloot
Rapenburg
Sint-Antoniesbreestraat
Kromboomssloot
Oudeschans
Nieuwe Uilenburgerstraat
Uilenburgergracht
Valkenburgerstraat
Kattenburgergracht
Wittenburgergracht
Kattenburgervaart
Hoogte Kadijk
Laagte Kadijk
Nieuwe Vaart
Raamgracht
Kloveniersburgwal
Groenburgwal
Zwanenburgwal
21
Jodenbreestr.
20
Waterlooplein
Rapenburgerstr.
Entrepotdok
Mr. Visserplein
Muiderstr.
National Opera & Ballet
22
23
J.D. Meierplein
Wertheimpark
26
Plantage Doklaan
Planetarium
Binnenamstel
Amstel
Waterlooplein
Hortus Botanicus
24
Blauwbrug
Nieuwe Herengracht
25
Plantage Kerklaan
ARTIS ZOO
27
Rembrandtplein
18
Plantage Middenlaan
Hermitage Amsterdam
19
Aquarium
Herengracht
Nieuwe Keizersgracht
Plantage Muidergracht
Utrechtsestraat
Amstel
Nieuwe Kerkstraat
Roetersstraat
Keizersgracht
Magere Brug
Weesperstraat
Nieuwe Prinsengracht
Kerkstraat
Nieuwe Achtergracht
Sarphatistraat
Tropenmuseum
Amstelveld
Prinsengracht
Amstelsluizen
Valckenierstraat
Singelgracht
Mauritskade
Reguliersgracht
dwarsstraat
Weesperplein
Utrechtsedwarsstraat
Achtergracht
Falckstraat
Frederiksplein
Hoge sluis
Sarphatistraat
Sajetplein
Boerhaaveplein
OOSTERPARK
Huidekoperstr.
Oosteinde
Mauritskade
'S-Gravesandeplein
Westeinde
Toronto Brug
Wibautstraat
Singelgracht
Witsenkade
Stadhouderskade
Weesperzijde
Amsteldijk
Ruyschstraat
Blasiusstraat
Eerste Oosterparkstr.
Van Woustraat
DE PIJP
Nieuwe Amstelbrug
Ceintuurbaan
To Wibautstraat
SARPHATIPARK
Canal-boat cruises
Metro station
Information
Ferry route
0
1/4 mi
0
0.25 km

Begijnhof.

can breeze quickly through the rest of the galleries of poorly organized artifacts; a highlight is the 1677 scale model of the Koninklijk Paleis (p. 291).

Kalverstraat 92. www.amsterdammuseum.nl. ✆ **020/523-1822.** 12€ adults, 6€ children 5–18. Daily 10am–5pm.

**Begijnhof ★★** HISTORIC SITE Entered through an ornate gate off Spui, this cluster of gabled houses is the perfect place to feel the ambience of old Amsterdam. Built as a *hofje* (almshouse; see box p. 294) intended to offer *beguines* (devout women) the option to live independently without becoming nuns (back when Holland was still Catholic), the 47 houses of the Begijnhof today are homes for the elderly. In the southwest corner of the cloister, at no. 34, stands Het Houten Huys, one of Amsterdam's two surviving timber houses, built around 1425. The Engelse Kerk (English Church) dates to 1607 and is used today by British expats. Opposite the church, at no. 30, is the Begijnhofkapel, a secret Catholic chapel dating from 1671.

Spui and Gedempte Begijnensloot. Free. Daily 9am–5pm.

**Beurs van Berlage ★★** HISTORIC BUILDING Amsterdam's former stock exchange was built in 1903 by Hendrik Berlage and is now an occasional concert venue. This monumental building is exceptional for

## Iamsterdam City Card: Get It!

This euro-saving sightseeing card provides free entry into most of Amsterdam's museums and free travel on public transport. It also entitles cardholders to a free canal cruise (p. 302), discounts in certain stores and restaurants, admission to attractions outside Amsterdam, and the museums in Haarlem (p. 321), a free city map, and 2.50€ off admission to the Rijksmuseum (p. 297). Prices in 2015: 24 hours 49€, 36 hours 59€, 72 hours 69€. You can buy the passes at Iamsterdam at Stationsplein 10, right outside Centraal Station (www.iamsterdam.com; ✆ **020/702-6000**), open daily 9am to 5pm (Sun until 4pm), or at the branch in Schiphol Plaza at the airport (same phone number), open daily 7am to 10pm.

its use of patterned brickwork and clean lines, which broke away from the fancy Dutch Revivalist styles of the time (as seen at the Stedelijk Museum and Centraal Station). A frieze on the facade shows man's (questionable) evolution from Adam to 20th-century stockbroker. It's rarely open, so you'll have to content yourself with the outside view.
Beursplein 1. www.beursvanberlage.nl. ✆ **020/530-4141.**

**Bloemenmarkt (Flower Market) ★★** HISTORIC MARKET Amsterdam's last remaining floating market is also the world's only floating flower market; this explosion of color is now a permanent fixture on a row of moored barges along the Singel canal. Yes, these days the market is touristy, but the seasonal displays are always a pleasure to view, especially over Christmas and during the spring when the stalls abound with bright tulips and daffodils.
Singel between Koningsplein and Muntplein. Free. Mon–Sat 9am–5:30pm, Sun 11am–5:30pm.

**The Bloemenmarkt.**

## A Party Fit for a King

Put simply, Amsterdam loves a good party, and the celebration that brings Amsterdammers out on to the streets like no other is **Koningsdag (King's Day)** celebrated on April 27 in honor of their monarch, King Willem-Alexander. The whole city grinds to a halt, parties spring up on every corner, and the canals are chock full of barges blaring music. The crowds wear orange and float orange balloons, the bars overflow, and everybody gets happily drunk and dances and sings their hearts out.

**Centraal Station ★★** HISTORIC BUILDING Amsterdam's humongous main railway station is an architectural masterpiece. Designed by Dutch architect P. J. H. Cuypers, it was built between 1884 and 1889 on three artificial islands in the IJ waterway (it's the starting point for canal cruises). The air of crazy chaos is augmented by the station being in a fairly constant state of renovation.
Stationsplein, off Prins Hendrikkade. Free. Open 24/7.

**De Waag ★★** HISTORIC BUILDING Amsterdam's only surviving medieval fortified gate sits on the fringe of Chinatown. The many-towered, squat Waag was constructed in 1498 of red-and-white brick and is now the oldest secular building in the city. De Waag had many functions over the centuries; it was the site of public executions before later becoming a guild house, most notably for the Surgeon's Guild (a fact that is immortalized in Rembrandt's graphic painting *The Anatomy Lesson,* which depicts the dissection of a cadaver). Today, its outdoor bar, part of

De Waag.

the historic **Restaurant-Café In de Waag ★** (p. 312), is a prime people-watching spot.

Nieuwmarkt 4. Free. Daily 10am–10:30pm (when restaurant is open).

**Koninklijk Paleis ★★** HISTORIC BUILDING The behemoth building in the middle of Amsterdam's focal Dam Square is the official residence of the reigning Dutch House of Orange, although these days the Royal Family prefers to reside in The Hague. Originally designed in 1655 as the City Hall, it has a solid, neoclassical facade. It was repurposed into a royal palace by Louis Bonaparte, brother of Napoléon, when he was crowned king of Holland in 1806, and its public rooms are now open to view. The interior is crammed with early-19th-century furniture, chandeliers, sculptures, and vast oil paintings reflecting Amsterdam's wealth during the Golden Age of the 17th century. Highlights include the highly ornate Council Chamber and the high-ceilinged Burgerzaal (Council Chamber), where maps inlaid on the marble floors place Amsterdam at the center of the world. The palace is closed to visitors during periods of royal residence and state receptions.

Dam, off Damrak. www.paleisamsterdam.nl. ✆ **020/620-4060.** 10€ adults, 9€ seniors/students, free 17 and under. Daily 11am–5pm (check website before visiting, because there are frequent changes and closures).

**Museum Het Rembrandthuis ★★★** MUSEUM The former home of Rembrandt van Rijn proved a money-pit for the "Old Master." He bought this elegant townhouse in 1639 when his career was flying, but overstretched himself with a massive mortgage that led to his bankruptcy in 1656. He moved to a smaller house on Rozengracht, where he died in 1669. Still, the museum (opened in 1911) is a wonder because it was furnished faithfully in period style, thanks to a notary's inventory of the artist's possessions. Rembrandt's hallway served as his gallery, and the family's living quarters are hung with his masterful oil paintings. Upstairs you'll find the airy studio where he painted *The Night Watch.*

Jodenbreestraat 4. www.rembrandthuis.nl. ✆ **020/520-0400.** 13€ adults, 10€ students, 4€ children 6–17. Daily 10am–6pm.

**Museum Ons' Lieve Heer op Solder (Our Lord in the Attic) ★★** MUSEUM Following the sacking of all Catholic churches in 1578, practicing Roman Catholicism was banned, so the devout had to find ways to worship in secret. Between 1661 and 1663, the wealthy Catholic merchant Jan Hartman bought this stately townhouse and two others behind it, converting all three attics into a clandestine but lushly decorated Catholic chapel. Worshipers entered from a side street and climbed the narrow stairs to the hidden third-floor chapel, which could hold a congregation of 150. Renovated in 2012, the secret chapel is once again resplendent with its baroque flourishes, organ, and marble columns.

Oudezijds Voorburgwal 40. www.opsolder.nl. ✆ **020/624-6604.** 9€ adults, 4.50€ students and children 5–18. Mon–Sat 10am–5pm, Sun and holidays 1–5pm.

Dam Square and Nieuwe Kerk.

**Nieuwe Kerk (New Church) ★★** CHURCH This handsome church is the most important in the Netherlands. It was built in the last years of the 14th century, and in 1814, King William I was inaugurated here (Dutch royalty are not crowned). It still retains its relevance today: His Majesty King of the Netherlands Willem-Alexander married Argentinian Princess Máxima here in 2002. Although many of its original priceless treasures were removed or painted over in 1578 when it passed into Protestant hands, much of its original grandeur has since been recaptured. The church has a stately arched nave, an elaborately carved altar, a great pipe organ from 1645, several noteworthy stained-glass windows, and sepulchral monuments for many of Holland's most revered poets and naval heroes.

Dam, off Damrak. www.nieuwekerk.nl. ✆ **020/626-8168.** Admission varies with events; free when there's no exhibit. Daily 10am–5pm.

**Oude Kerk (Old Church) ★★** CHURCH This late-Gothic, triple-nave church has its origins in 1250 but was only completed with the extension of the bell tower in 1566. Its exterior is encrusted with 17th- and 18th-century houses; the barnlike interior was stripped of all its adornment in the Alteration of 1578. Rembrandt's beloved first wife lies in vault 28K, which bears the simple inscription "Saskia Juni 1642." The magnificent 1728 organ is regularly used for recitals. Take a guided tour up the church tower (Thurs–Sat 1–5pm, Apr–Sept only) for fantastic views across the rooftops, canals, and spires of Amsterdam.

Oudekerksplein 23. Church: www.oudekerk.nl. ✆ **020/625-8284;** tower: 020/689-2565. Church and tower 10€ adults; 7.50€ seniors, students, and children 13–18; Mon–Sat 10am–6pm, Sun 1–5:30pm.

**Rosse Buurt (Red Light District)** ★★ HISTORIC AREA A few steps away from the Oude Kerk and De Waag and you're immersed in the sleazy underbelly of Amsterdam's infamous Red Light District. Here barely clad prostitutes advertise themselves behind illuminated glass windows along medieval canals and alleyways; if the curtains are closed, you know that a deal has been struck. But if they are open, sometimes you can glimpse the stark beds upon which the deed is done. Needless to say, throngs of testosterone-driven men circle these tiny alleyways, egging each other on either to visit a prostitute or one of the live, hard-core sex shows.

Despite all this, the Red Light District is seedy rather than dangerous (though pickpockets can be a problem). ***Important tip:*** Don't photograph the prostitutes. Thuggish bouncers parade the area, and you may well find your camera in the canal. Dusk is the best time to visit, before the drunken/stoned hordes of Euro-trash youth arrive to ogle the women.

Along Oudezijds Achterburgwal and surrounding alleyways.

**Schuttersgalerij (Civic Guards Gallery)** ★ MUSEUM Outside the entrance to the Amsterdam Museum, this narrow, glass-roofed walkway links Kalverstraat to the Begijnhof and has been transformed into a public art gallery currently displaying 17th-century portraits of the city's heroic musketeers, the Civic Guards. These militia once played an important role in the city's defense but eventually degenerated into decadent banqueting societies. Their portraits are accompanied by photographs of Amsterdam's contemporary elite side by side with the Barbara Broekman carpet representing the 179 nationalities of Amsterdam.

Kalverstraat 92. www.amsterdammuseum.nl. ✆ **020/523-1822.** Free. Daily 10am–5pm.

**Waterlooplein Flea Market** ★★ MARKET Amsterdam's best-known and biggest flea market occupies the Waterlooplein, the market square that was created when two canals were covered over in 1882. Before World War II, this daily market was central to Jewish life (it lay in the heart of the Jewish Quarter), but as Amsterdam's Jews were deported it fell into disrepair. During the 1960s the market was reborn when dazed hippies floated in from all over Europe. Today the market has around 300 stalls flogging everything from knock-off DVDs to piles of vintage clothes, plastic jewelry, and (ironically) Nazi pilot leather jackets.

Waterlooplein 2. www.waterloopleinmarkt.nl. ✆ **020/552-4074.** Mon–Fri 9am–5:30pm, Sat 8:30am–5:30pm.

## CANAL RING

**Amsterdam Pipe Museum ★** MUSEUM Yes, it's a niche museum, but a surprisingly charming one, thanks in part to the gregarious owner/curator who personally leads guests around. What you'll see: the world's largest collection of Dutch clay pipes, intricately carved and bejeweled Meerschaum pipes, and bronze cast pipes from Cameroon in Africa. You'll also get to drink in the atmosphere of the traditional 17th-century house renovated in 19th-century fashion.

Prinsengracht 488. www.pijpenkabinet.nl. ✆ **020/421-1779.** 8€ adults, 4€ children 18 and under. Wed–Sat 12–6pm.

**Anne Frank Huis ★★★** MUSEUM For more than two years the talented young writer Anne Frank (and her family, another Jewish family, and a single man) hid in this modest canal house. The diary she left behind when the Nazis finally captured them all (tragically close to the end of World War II) captured the world's imagination and put a face to the horrific loss of life and human potential that was the Holocaust. Climbing the steep staircase, walking through the hidden annex rooms, and learning anew about the life of the house's occupants (and their untimely deaths at Auschwitz) is by far and away the most moving experience you'll likely have in Amsterdam. The annex looks almost exactly as it did at the time of Frank's departure. In addition to the historic rooms, the museum hosts compelling temporary exhibits on the topic of genocide and human rights abuses. ***Tip:*** To avoid the lines, buy tickets online well in advance of your visit.

Prinsengracht 263-267. www.annefrank.org. ✆ **020/556-7100.** 9€ adults, 4.50€ children 10–17. Nov–Mar Sun–Fri 9am–7pm, Sat 9am–9pm; Apr–June and Sept–Oct Sun–Fri 9am–9pm, Sat 9am–10pm; July–Aug daily 9am–10pm. Closed Yom Kippur.

**Het Grachtenhuis (Canal Museum) ★★★** MUSEUM This brilliant museum recounts the tale of Amsterdam's historic expansion

### AMSTERDAM'S hofjes

Amsterdam has many secret courtyards surrounded by almshouses—they could be considered an early form of care in the community where the poor or disadvantaged of the parish could be housed and supported. The best known is the **Begijnhof ★★** (p. 288), where a community of pious women lived for several centuries. The **Hermitage Amsterdam ★★** (p. 300) is also housed in a former *hofje*, where homes were provided for elderly women of slender means. **Zon's Hofje** at Prinsengracht 159-171 is an example of a tranquil *hofje* with courtyard garden; the outer door is open Monday through Saturday between 10am and 5pm, and you can walk quietly through the passageway to the serene courtyard. A walk around the pretty streets of the Jordaan will reveal several *hofjes*, including the **Raepenhofje** at Palmgracht 28-38, and the **Suyckerhofje** at Lindengracht 149-163.

through a cleverly curated series of interactive displays. First off, a sound-and-light show centers on a model of the city in medieval times when it was grim, overcrowded, and a breeding ground for disease. By the 17th century, expansion became imperative. The planning and construction of the ring of three canals around the city is dealt with in lively films, models, interactive displays, and holograms; the final exhibit is an all-singing, all-dancing celebration of multi-cultural Amsterdam today. You couldn't wish for a more instructive or entertaining intro to the city. To get to the museum take the tram to Herengracht on the Grachtengordel (Canal Ring).

Herengracht 386. www.hetgrachtenhuis.nl. ✆ **020/421-1656.** 12€ adults, 6€ children 6–17. Tues–Sun 10am–5pm.

**Huis Marseille Museum voor Fotografie ★★** MUSEUM At this distinguished photo museum, six galleries alternate images from the museum's permanent collection with worthy exhibitions of contemporary photos that change every 3 months. Like so many Amsterdam galleries and museums in the Canal Ring, the building is part of the attraction; this one dates from the 17th century and takes its name from the plaque on the front of the house that depicts a map of Marseille harbor in France. The interior maintains many original features, including fireplaces and plaster moldings, as well as a ceiling fresco by Jacob van Campen.

Keizersgracht 401. www.huismarseille.nl. ✆ **020/531-8989.** 8€ adults, 4€ seniors/students, free children 17 and under. Tues–Sun 11am–6pm.

**Tulip Museum ★★** MUSEUM The revamped Tulip Museum is just across Prinsengracht from the Anne Frank Huis; head there if you need cheering up. It gives a jaunty and informative slant on the story of Amsterdam's obsession with tulips, which were imported from the Himalayas and nearly brought the country's economy down when trade in the bulbs collapsed in 1637. On the ground level is a top-quality souvenir store selling bulbs, pretty plant holders, and other classy, tulip-related ephemera.

Prinsengracht 116. www.amsterdamtulipmuseum.com. ✆ **020/421-0095.** 5€ adults, 3€ students. Daily 10am–6pm.

**Westerkerk ★★** CHURCH Just around the corner from the Anne Frank Huis, the Protestant Westerkerk is yet another ecclesiastical masterpiece by the Dutch celebrity architect of the 17th century, Hendrick de Keyser (who also designed the Noorderkerk and the Zuiderkerk). The foundation stone was laid in 1620 (de Keyser died a year later), and the tower finally completed in 1638; it is more than 85m (270 ft.) tall and is topped with the gilded Crown of Maximilian. The church itself is austere inside; in accord with the Calvinist beliefs of the time there is no altar, but the gold and silver pipes and baroque sculpture adorning the organ make up for the lack of ornamentation. It's the burial place of Rembrandt—although no one knows where his grave is on the unmarked stone floor—as well as his wife Saskia and son Titus.

Prinsengracht 281. www.westererkerk.nl. ✆ **020/624-7766.** Free (4€ for Westerpass guide). Mon–Sat 10am–3pm; Sun services only.

**Willet-Holthuysen Museum ★★★** MUSEUM This delightful museum, with a pristine interior dating from the 19th century in a perfectly restored canal house, is redolent of the sybaritic lifestyle of Amsterdam's prosperous merchant classes. Every curtain, piece of furniture, and scrap of wallpaper is in keeping with the period. Displays include a history of the aristocratic owners and a collection of painstakingly detailed silver figurines. There's an exquisite formal knot garden at the rear of the house.

Herengracht 605. www.willetholthuysen.nl. ✆ **020/523-1822.** 8.50€ adults, 6.50€ students, 4.25€ children 5–18. Mon–Fri 10am–5pm, Sat–Sun 11am–5pm.

## JORDAAN

**Stedelijk Museum Bureau Amsterdam ★★** ART GALLERY This micro-outpost of the Stedelijk Museum (p. 298) showcases promising Amsterdam artists. Regarded in the Netherlands as *the* place to watch for new young talent, the gallery has hosted exhibits of photography, videos, abstract works, bizarre installations, and, occasionally, intense performance art.

Rozenstraat 59. www.smba.nl. ✆ **020/422-0471.** Free. Wed–Sun 11am–5pm.

## MUSEUM QUARTER

**Heineken Experience ★★** BREWERY One of Amsterdam's most popular attractions, the Heineken Experience is housed inside the redbrick former brewery, which functioned from 1867 until 1988 (production is now in The Hague and Den Bosch). As you might expect, this corporate history tour is a fun one, incorporating holograms, interactive exhibits, and simulated rides alongside the original copper brewing vats,

### Art Galleries in the Jordaan

Bohemian Jordaan is an area of narrow cobbled streets-and even narrower canals-crammed with around 40 art galleries. Check out Diana Stigter's gallery **Stigter van Doesburg** (Elandsstraat 90; www.stigtervandoesburg.com; ✆ **020/624-2361**); she has her finger on the pulse of what's hot and what's not. **GO Gallery** (Prinsengracht 64; www.gogallery.nl; ✆ **020/422-9581**) promotes street art. And the **Edouard Planting Gallery** (Eerste Bloemdwarsstraat 2 L; www.eduardplanting.com; ✆ **020/320-6705**) exhibits the best of contemporary photography.

Heineken Experience.

malt silos, and vintage brewing equipment. (You'll also visit a stable full of Shire horses used to pull the promotional drays.) The ultimate goal for most visitors is to glug back Heineken beer, so expect a wait at the bar. Stadhouderskade 78. www.heinekenexperience.com. ✆ **020/523-9435.** 18€ adults (includes 2 beers), 13€ children 12–17, free children 10 and under. Sept–June Mon–Thurs 11am–7:30pm, Fri–Sun 10:30am–9pm; July–Aug daily 10:30am–9pm.

**Rijksmuseum** ★★ MUSEUM The Rijksmuseum is the world's biggest repository of Dutch Golden Age treasures, stacked over four sprawling floors in the redbrick P. J. H. Cuypers monolith opened in 1855. A 10-year refurbishment that finished in 2014 has spruced up the elegant Cuypers decorations in the central Voorhal (Great Hall) but the layout of the museum remains confusing. It's almost sacrilegious to criticize this venerable institution, but to my mind the biggest mistake made in laying out the displays is crowding all the famous **Dutch Old Masters** ★★★ together in the Gallery of Honour on the second floor. Over 2 million people visit this museum annually, and they all want to see Rembrandt's *The Night Watch* from 1642 and the wonderful works by Jan Steen, Jan Vermeer, and Frans Hals, so be prepared for impenetrable throngs in that part of the museum. *The Milkmaid* and *The Merry Drinker* are truly mesmerizing close up, so you'll have to bear with the crowds.

The Rijksmuseum.





Lines are always long, so either reserve a ticket online before your visit or turn up on the dot of opening time. ***Tip:*** Watch out for the bikers who zoom through the museum's underpass with little regard for pedestrians.
Museumstraat 1. www.rijksmuseum.nl. ✆ **020/674-7000.** 18€ adults, 9€ students, free 18 and under. Daily 9am–7pm.

**Stedelijk Museum ★★★** MUSEUM The second of the triumvirate of great art museums in Amsterdam, the Stedelijk houses the largest collection outside Russia of Kasimir Malevich's abstract paintings, but centers its exhibits around the De Stijl, CoBrA, post-CoBrA, nouveau réalisme, Pop Art, color-field painting, zero, minimalist, and conceptual schools of art. Things get off to an excellent start with the sparkly mural by Dutch artist Karel Appel in the first gallery, followed by iconic works by such major names as Mondrian, Chagall, Van Gogh, Pollock, Warhol, and Liechtenstein. The museum's design collection contains many stand-out pieces, including De Stijl designer Gerrit Rietveld's famous painted chair and Jeff Koons's kitsch *Ushering in Banality* (1988).
Museumplein 10. www.stedelijk.nl. ✆ **020/573-2911.** 15€ adults, 7.50€ students, free 17 and under. Daily 10am–6pm (Thurs until 10pm).

**Van Gogh Museum ★★★** MUSEUM The third of Amsterdam's heavyweight art museums was opened in 1973 and designed by Gerrit Rietveld, the leading exponent of the Dutch De Stijl movement; it has three floors of white space in which to show off the tortured artist's

> ### Nazis in the Netherlands
>
> When the Germans arrived in Amsterdam on May 16, 1940 after a day of intense bombing that all but destroyed Rotterdam (p. 322), they were cautiously welcomed into the Netherlands. But slowly the Nazis clamped down on the city and its open-minded people; brutal new laws took away individual freedoms, and underground resistance to the Nazis mounted. The 10% of the population that was Jewish were persecuted, forced to wear yellow Stars of David, and stripped of their jobs. In 1942, the roundup of Jewish families began; thousands of people were taken to the Hollandse Schouwburg (p. 301) before being deported to labor camps, Bergen-Belsen in Germany, or Auschwitz in Poland. Of the 140,000 Sephardic and Ashkenazi Jews who lived in Amsterdam before World War II, fewer than 30,000 survived until Liberation on May 5, 1945. The most famous Dutch victim of the Holocaust was Anne Frank, whose tragic story is told at the Anne Frank Huis (p. 294). To learn about opposition to the German occupation, visit the Resistance Museum (p. 302).

ethereal works to their best advantage. Vincent van Gogh was born in 1853 in Groot-Zundert in the south of Holland and during his short life he produced over 800 paintings. More than 200 of his portraits, landscapes, and still lifes, plus more than 500 drawings, are held in the collections here, forming the biggest cache of Van Gogh in the world. Some of these works are hung alongside contemporary work by Pissarro, Gauguin, and Monet to provide useful historical context.

Paulus Potterstraat 7. www.vangoghmuseum.nl. ✆ **020/570-5200.** 15€ adults, free children 17 and under. Daily 9am to 5 or 6pm, Fri to 10pm, July–Aug Sat to 10pm.



### PLANTAGE/OOST

**Artis Royal Zoo ★★** ZOO Amsterdam's wonderfully family-friendly zoo was established in 1838 and covers more than 35 acres of tree-lined pathways and landscaped gardens. It has more than 900 species of animals, successfully combining 19th-century layout and buildings with a 21st-century commitment to conservation and breeding.

Plantage Kerklaan 38-40. www.artis.nl. ✆ **0900/278-4796.** 20€ adults, 17€ children 3–9. Nov–Feb daily 9am–5pm, Mar–Oct daily 9am–6pm.

**Dockworker Statue ★★** MONUMENT Just to the left of the Portuguese Synagogue is Jonas Daniël Meijerplein, where many Dutch Jews were held, awaiting deportation to concentration camps. The bronze figure is always surrounded by wreaths of flowers; it was created by Mari Andriessen and erected in 1952 in commemoration of the February 1941 strike by workers protesting Jewish deportations, which was violently suppressed by Amsterdam's Nazi occupiers and ended in a bloodbath.

Jonas Daniël Meijerplein. Free. Daily 24/7.

**Hermitage Amsterdam** ★★ MUSEUM The Amsterdam branch of St. Petersburg's Hermitage (housed in a handsome, 17th-century former almshouse) is a delight, a state-of-the art gallery displaying the rich pickings from the Russian state collection. Two exhibitions run simultaneously for about 6 months, so check online before you visit, but with the Hermitage's holding more than 3 million works of art, chances are the current exhibition will be spectacular.

Amstel 31. www.hermitage.nl. ✆ **020/530-7488.** 15€ adults, 12€ seniors/students, 5€ children 6–16. Daily 10am–5pm.

**Het Scheepvaartmuseum (National Maritime Museum)** ★★ MUSEUM A bonanza for anyone who loves ships and the sea, the Maritime Museum overlooks the busy harbor and is housed in a former Amsterdam Admiralty arsenal from 1656. All the exhibits chronicle the country's abiding ties to the sea through commerce, fishing, yachting, exploration, and war. Room after room is filled with boats and ship models, seascapes and ship paintings, prints, navigational instruments, cannons and other weaponry, and old maps and charts. Among the cartographic highlights are a 15th-century Ptolemaic atlas. The best exhibits detail the growth of the Dutch East India Company and sensitively address the slave trade and today's whaling issues. But the main point of a trip to this museum is for youngsters to get on board the gaily painted, full-size replica of the merchant ship Amsterdam, moored on the quay outside. Everything on board is as it was in 1749 when the original boat foundered on its maiden voyage to the East Indies (present-day Indonesia). Actors playing the part of sailors fire cannons, sing sea

**The Scheepvaartmuseum maritime museum.**

shanties, mop the deck, hoist cargo on board, and attend a solemn burial at sea.

Kattenburgerplein 1. www.scheepvaartmuseum.nl. ✆ **020/523-2222.** 15€ adults, 7.50€ students and children 5–17. Daily 9am–5pm.

**Hollandse Schouwburg ★★** MUSEUM/MEMORIAL The imposing white Hollandse Schouwburg was originally a theater, but in World War II hundreds of Dutch Jewish families were forcibly detained here before deportation to the concentration camps. Today, this is the official memorial to the Nazi Holocaust in Amsterdam, with a deeply moving documentary on the persecution of the Jews through a series harrowing interviews with victims. The small museum on the upper floor is mainly notable for its pictures of the ingenious hiding places used to conceal Jews from the Nazis. However, it's the monument out back that grabs attention—a simple cast column scattered with flowers.

Plantage Middenlaan 24. www.hollandscheschouwburg.nl. ✆ **020/531-0310.** Combined ticket includes the Jewish Historical Museum and the Portuguese Synagogue. 15€ adults 7.50€ students and children 13–17, 3.75€ children 6–12. Daily 11am–5pm.

**Portuguese Synagogue ★★** SYNOGOGUE Europe's largest synagogue was built in 1675 by Sephardic Jews who moved to Amsterdam from Spain and Portugal. The building was restored in the 1950s and today looks pretty much as it did 3 centuries ago. The women's gallery on the upper floor of the synagogue is supported by 12 stone columns representing the Twelve Tribes of Israel, and the large, low-hanging brass chandeliers together hold 1,000 candles. In the courtyard complex that surrounds the synagogue are the mikvah ritual baths; the mourning room complete with a coffin stand; and the synagogue's treasure chambers containing precious menorahs, torahs, and ornate clerical robes.

Mr. Visserplein 3. www.portugesesynagoge.nl. ✆ **020/531-0380.** Combined ticket includes the Jewish Historical Museum and the Hollandse Schouwburg. 15€ adults, 7.50€ students and children 13–17, 4€ children 6–12. Apr–Oct Sun–Thurs 10am–5pm, Fri 10am–4pm; Nov–Mar Sun–Thurs 10am–4pm, Fri 10am–2pm.

**Science Center NEMO ★★★** MUSEUM More children's play station than museum, NEMO is the number-one place to hit with kids if it's a rainy day. This accessible, hands-on, interactive science center is housed in a magnificent, pale green, ship-shaped building designed by Renzo Piano in 1997. Its aim is to introduce science and technology to kids in an understandable and interesting form. Through games, experiments, and demonstrations, kids learn how chain reactions work, search for ETs, blow a soap bubble large enough to stand inside, and much more fun stuff. NEMO's broad, stepped, and sloping roof is an attraction in itself; a place to hang out, have a beer or catch the sun in summer, and take in the views.

Oosterdok 2. www.e-nemo.nl. ✆ **020/531-3233.** 15€, free for children 4 and under. Tues–Sun 10am–5pm.

**Verzetsmuseum (Dutch Resistance Museum)** ★★★ MUSEUM Holland's dark World War II days, during the Nazi occupation (1940–45), are the subject of the Verzetsmuseum which exhibits authentic photographs, documents, weapons, communications equipment, spy gadgets, and other materials actually used by the Dutch Resistance. The displays show the ingenuity (pedal-powered printing presses!)—along with courage—the freedom-fighters brought to bear. The fate of Amsterdam's Jewish community, herded into a ghetto, then rounded up for deportation to concentration camps, has a prominent place, as do the actions of workers who in 1941 went on strike to protest the first deportation of 400 Jewish Amsterdammers. Yet the museum doesn't shrink from less palatable aspects of Holland's wartime record, like the actions of collaborators. The museum, which has a cafe, is in the 1876 neoclassical Plancius Building, which once housed a Jewish social club. A changing program of exhibits takes the story beyond Holland's foreign occupation to feature resistance struggles of recent times.
Plantage Kerklaan 61. www.verzetsmuseum.org. ✆ **020/620-2535.** 10€ adults, 5€ children 7–15. Tues–Fri 10am–5pm, Sat–Sun 11am–5pm.

## Organized Tours

There's no better way to discover Amsterdam than with a **canal cruise** on its waterways. **Holland International** (www.canal.nl/en/holland-international-canal-cruises; ✆ **020/217-0501**) canal cruises leave from the pier to the left of Centraal Station and are free with the Iamsterdam City Card (p. 289). During the summer season (Mar 20–Nov 2), tours leave daily every 15 minutes from 9am to 6pm, and every 30 minutes from 6 to 10pm. In winter, departures are every 45 minutes from 10am to 4pm. There's a rather lackluster commentary in English, but it is still an entertaining way to learn about Amsterdam in a short time.

Other canal tour-boat lines are: **Amsterdam Canal Cruises** (www.amsterdamcanalcruises.nl; ✆ 020/679-1370), **Gray Line** (www.graylineamsterdam.com; ✆ 303/394-6920), **Reederij P Kooij** (www.rederijkooij.nl; ✆ 020/623-4186), **Rederij Lovers** (www.lovers.nl; ✆ 020/530-1090), **Rederij Plas** (www.rederijplas.nl; ✆ 020/624-5406), and **Blue Boat Company** (www.blueboat.nl; ✆ 020/679-1370). Prices vary from company to company, but a basic hour-long tour is around 15€ for adults, 8€ for children 4 to 12, and free for children 3 and under. Evening tours are available through most of these companies; 3-hour candlelit dinner cruises are among the most popular.

Still other canal cruising options include the hop-on, hop-off **Canal Bus** (www.canal.nl; ✆ **20/217-0500**), which stops at (or near) all the major attractions and allows you to build your own sightseeing itinerary. After a lunchtime treat for the kids? Try the **Pannenkoekenboot** (**Pancake Boat;** www.pannenkoekenboot.nl; ✆ **020/638-88170**) for unlimited servings of pancakes with sweet or savory fillings with your boat trip.

**Cycling** in flat Amsterdam is a classic way to get around the city. Such outlets as **Yellow Bike** (www.yellowbike.nl; ✆ **020/620-6940**) and **Viator** (www.viator.com; ✆ **888/651-9785** in the U.S.) both offer multiple options, from 2-hour canal jaunts to all-day rides out into the country past windmills. Prices start at around 25€.

Romantic, family-friendly **horse-and-carriage tours** run by **Karos Citytours** (www.karos.nl; ✆ **020/691-3478**) depart from just outside the Royal Palace on the Dam for traipses through the Old Center, along the canals, and into the Jordaan. Tours operate April to October daily 11am to 6pm (July–Aug to 7pm), and on a limited schedule in winter. Rides are 35€ for 20 minutes, 45€ for 30 minutes, and 65€ for 45 minutes.

It's easy enough to make up your own **walking tour** of Amsterdam and include all the important sights, but if you need guidance, the tourist office has several suggested routes. Brochures (3€) are available at the Visitor Information Center outside Centraal Station and Schiphol airport.

If the canal-boat cruise whets your appetite to ramble the canals on your own, you can rent sturdy **paddleboats called canal bikes** from **Canal** (www.canal.nl; ✆ **020/217-0500**). They seat two or four and come with a guidebook with map and route suggestions. The Canal Bike moorings are at Leidseplein; Westerkerk, near the Anne Frankhuis; and Stadhouderskade, beside the Rijksmuseum. Rental is 8€ per person hourly plus a deposit of 20€.

Finally, like other major Europe cities, Amsterdam has a hop-on, hop-off circular bus tour run by **City Sightseeing** which stops at all the major sights. Buses run every 15 to 20 minutes from 9:15am to 7:20pm (www.citysightseeingamsterdam.nl; ✆ **020/420-4000**). Prices start at 18€ (9€ for children) for 24 hours of access to the service.

**Viator** (www.viator.com; ✆ **888/651-9785** in the U.S.) and **Keytours** (www.keytours.nl; ✆ **020/305-5333**) list bus tours around the city and also across the Netherlands. A favorite trip from March to May is out to the Keukenhof bulb fields at Lisse (p. 320). Rates vary with the particular tour on offer, but typical half-day tours begin around 30€ and full-day tours around 50€.

## Especially for Kids

Amsterdam has a myriad of attractions just for families including modern, interactive museums carefully designed to appeal to youngsters; canal trips; trams to ride; and bikes to hire. With playgrounds in all the parks, kids' shows in several theaters, and pancakes on almost every menu, there's always something to do (or eat). The only downside? Pushing baby strollers across all those cobblestones ain't much fun.

Best options for a happy family day out include **canal cruises;** if you don't think they'll last an hour without getting bored, you might like to blackmail them into behaving by promising a lunchtime treat aboard the ***Pannenkoekenboot*** (**Pancake Boat;** see p. 302). And most families will enjoy spending time in Amsterdam's splendid parks, particularly the **Hortus Botanicus ★★** (Plantage Middenlaan 2A; www.dehortus.nl; ✆ **020/625-9021;** admission 8.50€ adults; 5€ students, 4.50€ seniors and children 5–14; open daily 10am–5pm) which features rare plants from around the world and a live butterfly garden; and the green space in between Amsterdam's top art museums, the **Museumplein ★★★** (free admission) which features and ice skating rink in winter and lively buskers in the summer.

And as for **museums,** there are plenty to choose from. The hands-on **Science Center NEMO ★★★** (p. 301) cleverly unravels the mysteries of science; and all kids will fall in love with the sea lions and penguins at **Artis Royal Zoo ★★** (p. 299). The tales of piratical derring-do aboard the good ship *Amsterdam* at **Het Scheepvaartmuseum** (**National Maritime Museum ★★;** p. 300) will enthrall most kids too.

The heartache of **Anne Frank Huis ★★★** (p. 294) will challenge and interest children 9 and older but can confuse younger kids, and it is not at all stroller-friendly.

## Where to Stay

If you would prefer to have a space to call your own in the city, "self-catering" doesn't come much better than in Amsterdam, where the accommodations stock includes dreamy canal-side townhouses, spacious studios, houseboats out in the IJ, and barges moored up along the Canal Ring. We like locally based agency **www.luxury-apartments-amsterdam.com** for countless smart, fully equipped apartments with all the fluff from Wi-Fi to flowers, while **www.houseboat-rental-amsterdam.com** and **www.houseboathotel.nl** both hire out boats and studios by the water. And, of course, there's always such multinational websites as **www.vrbo.com**, **www.flipkey.com**, and **www.homeaway.com** which have countless listings in Amsterdam, many of which are quite affordable. Make sure you understand, with any of these companies, just what is and isn't included and if there are extra costs (for cleaning, perhaps) involved.

### THE OLD CENTER

#### Expensive

**Hotel de l'Europe ★★** The grande dame of Amsterdam's hotels occupies a prime location overlooking the Binnenamstel and is the last word in ostentatious splendor. The rooms are sumptuous, spacious, and flooded with light, all with barn-size marble bathrooms. In the Dutch Masters Wing, every extravagant apartment has a copy of a famous painting from the Rijksmuseum. On top of a double-Michelin-starred restaurant and spa, l'Europe boasts what might well be Amsterdam's last *fumoir,* where cigars smoking is still very much permitted.

Nieuwe Doelenstraat 2-14. www.leurope.nl. ✆ **020/531-1777.** 111 units. Doubles 450€–720€. **Amenities:** 2 restaurants; 2 bars; sauna; spa; free Wi-Fi.

**Mauro Mansion ★★★** This little gem is a nine-room treasure-trove of quirky design hidden in a 16th-century canal house overlooking Geldersekade. It's run by an equally offbeat couple. Several bedrooms have views over the canal and all are a stylish clash of old and new—wardrobes made of industrial piping, hammocks, beds swathed in net, shiny rubber flooring. Children 11 and under are not allowed and breakfast is optional (5€ per person). You'll need to book here well in advance. The only real drawback? There's no elevator.

Geldersekade 16. www.mauromansion.com. ✆ **061/297-4594.** 9 units. Doubles 130€–250€. **Amenities:** Free Wi-Fi.

### Moderate

**Blue Sheep B&B ★★** This family-run gem is set in a gorgeous canal house on a car-free street in a tranquil backwater of the old city center. Ah! The airy rooms match the setting, filled with a stylish mix of antique and contemporary furnishings. Final perk: The young owners Jan and Novella prepare a standout mega-breakfast each morning. The only downsides to staying here are the lack of an elevator and the fact that some of the bathrooms are shared. But heck that keeps the prices low! In addition to the B&B, the owners rent out a selection of handsomely appointed apartments and suites close by, suitable for couples or families with young kids.

Korsjespoortsteeg 3. www.thebluesheep.net. ✆ **06/2962-3499.** 13 units. Doubles 119€–249€, includes breakfast. **Amenities:** Free Wi-Fi.

## CANAL RING

### Expensive

**The Dylan ★★★** Amsterdam's glossiest boutique hotel—think guest rooms with stripped oak floors, exposed beams, blindingly white bathrooms, and four-poster beds that you could lose a family in—is located in a former 17th-century theater on lively Keizersgracht. Along with standard rooms, the hotel offers dinner cruises in its own boat, a terrace for tea and evening drinks, and light-filled top-floor suites. As if that's not enough, the fabulous Michelin-starred restaurant **Vinkeles ★★★** (p. 314) has its home in the Dylan. For a hotel so upmarket, the ambience is surprisingly chill and informal.

Keizersgracht 384. www.dylanamsterdam.com. ✆ **020/530-2010.** 39 units. Doubles 350€–1,400€, includes breakfast. **Amenities:** 2 restaurants; bar; gym; on-boat catering; free Wi-Fi.

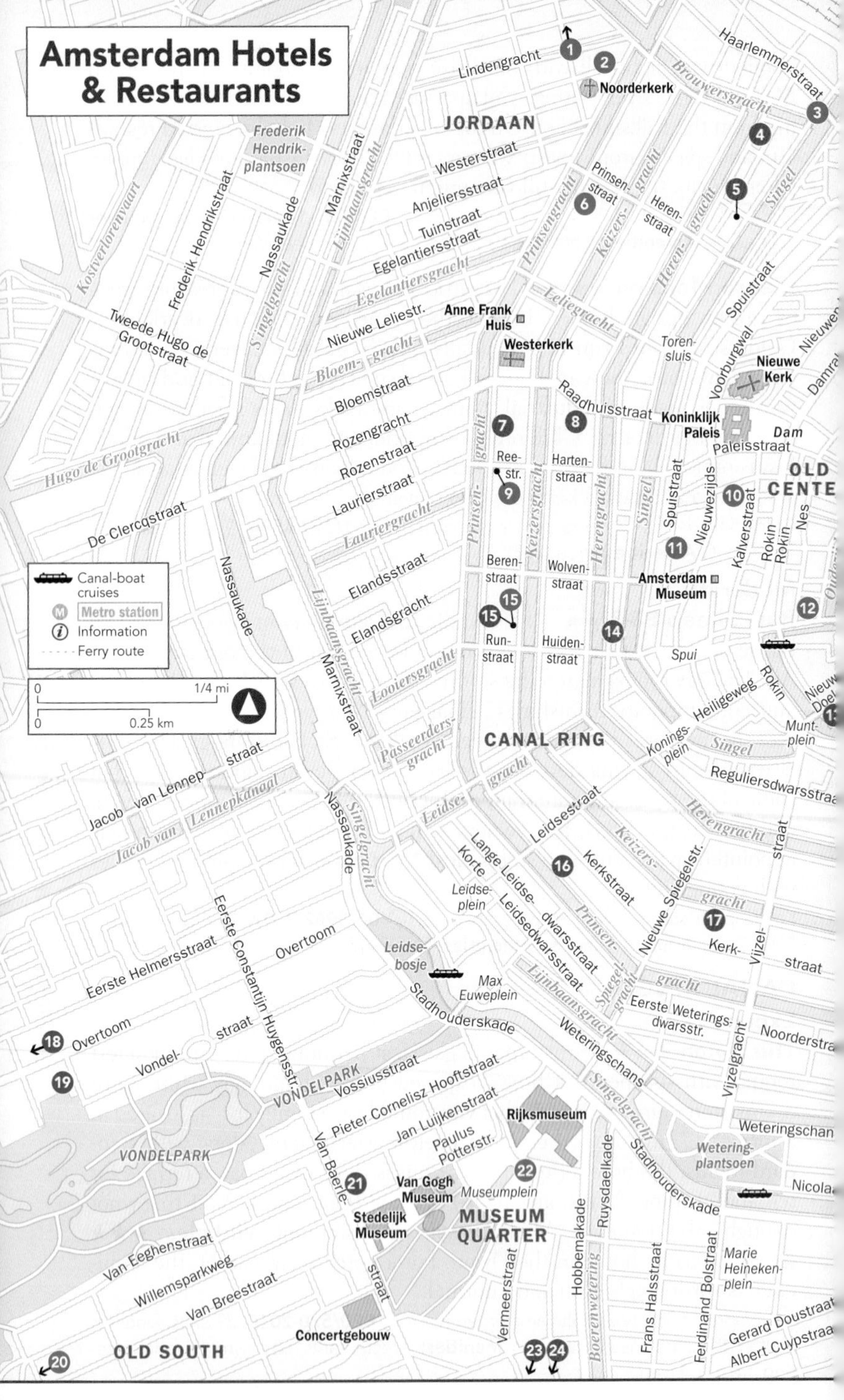
Amsterdam Hotels & Restaurants
JORDAAN
CANAL RING
MUSEUM QUARTER
OLD SOUTH
Noorderkerk
Anne Frank Huis
Westerkerk
Nieuwe Kerk
Koninklijk Paleis
Amsterdam Museum
Rijksmuseum
Van Gogh Museum
Stedelijk Museum
Concertgebouw
VONDELPARK
Canal-boat cruises
Metro station
Information
Ferry route
0 1/4 mi
0 0.25 km

Het IJ
De Ruijterkade
Centraal Station
IJ-Tunnel
Muziekgebouw aan 't IJ/ Bimhuis
Passenger Terminal Amsterdam
JAVA-EILAND
IJhaven
OOSTERDOK
Prins Hendrikkade
Stationsplein
Centraal Station
Piet Heinkade
Oosterdokskade
Dijksgracht
Damrak
Zeedijk
31
Beurs van Berlage
Oude Kerk
RED LIGHT DISTRICT
Geldersekade
Kromme Waal
Scheepvaarthuis
Oosterdok
Science Center NEMO
MARINETERREIN (Former naval complex, under development)
Binnenkant
Oude Waal
Eilandsgracht
Rechtboomssloot
30
Nieuwmarkt
Het Scheepvaart-museum
Kattenburgerstraat
Rapenburg
Kromboomssloot
Sint-Antoniesbreestraat
Oude-schans
Nieuwe Uilenburgerstraat
Uilenburgergracht
Valkenburgerstraat
Kattenburgergracht
Kattenburgervaart
Wittenburgergracht
Nieuwe Vaart
Hoogte Kadijk
Laagte Kadijk
29
Raamgracht
Kloveniersburgwal
Groenburgwal
Zwanenburgwal
Jodenbreestr.
Rapenburgerstr.
Waterlooplein
Mr. Visserplein
Muiderstr.
Wertheimpark
Entrepotdok
28
Plantage Doklaan
Planetarium
National Opera & Ballet
Binnenamstel
Amstel
J.D. Meierplein
Hortus Botanicus
Plantage Kerklaan
Plantage Middenlaan
ARTIS ZOO
Rembrandtplein
Blauwbrug
Waterlooplein
Nieuwe Herengracht
Plantage Muidergracht
27
Hermitage Amsterdam
Herengracht
Nieuwe Keizersgracht
Utrechtsestraat
25
Keizersgracht
Kerkstraat
Magere Brug
Nieuwe Kerkstraat
Weesperstraat
Nieuwe Prinsengracht
Amstelveld
Prinsengracht
Amstelsluizen
Reguliersgracht
Utrechtsedwarsstraat
26
Achtergracht
Weesperplein
Falckstraat
Frederiksplein
Sarphatistraat
Hogesluis
Huidekoperstr.
Westeinde
Oosteinde
Singelgracht
Toronto Brug
Mauritskade
Stadhouderskade
Hemonylaan
Amsteldijk
Weesperzijde
Albert Cuypstraat
Van Woustraat
DE PIJP
SARPHATIPARK
Ceintuurbaan
Nieuwe Amstelbrug
HOTELS
Ambassade Hotel 14
Blue Sheep B&B 5
chic&basic 4
citizenM Amsterdam City 24
Clemens Amsterdam 8
College Hotel 23
Conscious Hotel Vondelpark 18
Conservatorium 21
The Dylan 15
Hampshire Hotel Lancaster Amsterdam 27
Hotel de l'Europe 13
Keizershof 17
Mauro Mansion 31
Pulitzer 7
Sandton Hotel De Filosoof 19
Seven Bridges 25
Seven One Seven 16
RESTAURANTS
Bloesem 1
Bordewijk 2
Brasserie Plancius 28
Café Cobra 22
Café de Sluyswacht 29
Golden Temple 26
Kapitein Zeppos 12
Koffiehuis de Hoek 9
Pancake Bakery 6
Restaurant Blauw 20
Restaurant-Café In de Waag 30
Stubbe's Haring 3
Supperclub Amsterdam 10
Vinkeles 15
Visrestaurant Lucius 11

**Pulitzer ★★★** Awarded a place in the prestigious Condé Nast list of the top-25 hotels in northern Europe, the Pulitzer offers its lucky guests pure luxury without sinking into ostentation. We'd venture to say it has a, er, prize-winning location on the side of Prinsengracht in between the charming Jordaan and the tourist hotspots of the Old Center, and it's right there among the retail delights of the Nine Streets (p. 318). The rooms and suites are smartly furnished and decorated in soothing creams and beiges. There's also a plush spa and restaurant with summer terrace.

Prinsengracht 315-331. www.pulitzeramsterdam.com. ✆ **020/523-5235.** 230 units. Doubles 309€–706€. **Amenities:** Restaurant; 3 bars; on-boat catering; art gallery; pet-friendly; gym; Wi-Fi 19€/day.

**Seven One Seven ★★** Furnished in lavish 19th-century style (yes those are real antiques) and with every possible amenity on tap, this suite-only hotel is a popular honeymoon pick. With views either over the canal or a leafy patio to the rear, there's no bad choice of room here. The public areas, which include an elegant drawing room, a sunny terrace, and a flower-filled breakfast room are just as swoon-worthy. Our only gripe? The extra charge for breakfast over and above an already expensive stay.

Prinsengracht 717. www.717hotel.nl. ✆ **020/427-0717.** 9 units. Doubles 275€–450€. **Amenities:** Free Wi-Fi.





## Moderate

**Ambassade Hotel ★★** Swags of curtains, gilt-edged mirrors, statement color palettes, chandeliers, antiques, fine artworks and en extensive library—this conjoined collection of 17th- and 18th-century gabled townhouses are about as far as you can get from the bland, minimalist chain hotels of the city. Hallelujah! A few doors down at Herengracht 321, you'll find the hotel's blissful Koan Float massage center. Although not all rooms are accessible by elevator, plenty are. Alas, breakfast is not included in the room rate.

Herengracht 341. www.ambassade-hotel.nl. ✆ **020/555-0222.** 58 units. Doubles 186€–225€. **Amenities:** Spa; free Wi-Fi.

**Seven Bridges ★★★** This is quite simply one of the most gorgeous hotels in the city, with individually decorated rooms boasting genuine antique furnishings in a variety of opulent Biedermeier, Art Deco, or rococo styles set on original 17th-century wooden floors. We're particularly fond of the attic rooms, which have sloped ceilings and exposed wood beams and provide the perfect romantic hideaway. Breakfast is served in the guest rooms, as there are no public spaces beyond the entrance lobby and there's no elevator, which may explain the exceptionally reasonable prices for a hotel of such comfort and opulence.

Reguliersgracht 31. www.sevenbridgeshotel.nl. ✆ **020/623-1329.** 11 units. Doubles 95€–205€. **Amenities:** Free Wi-Fi.

The Ambassade Hotel's library.



### Inexpensive

**Keizershof ★** Offering quite exceptional value for your money in the expensive city center, the Keizershof occupies a four-story, narrow canal house that dates back to 1672, so of course there's no elevator. Guest rooms have simple, modern furnishings, and only two have private bathrooms; they either overlook the bustle of the canal or a tranquil pocket-size, flower-filled courtyard (breakfast is served in it in summer). Downstairs, a TV lounge shares its space with a grand piano, but what makes this place memorable is the warm welcome from its owners, the hospitable De Vries family, who go that extra mile for guests.

Singel 301. www.hotelkeizershof.nl. ✆ **020/622-2855.** 6 units. Doubles 95€–130€, includes breakfast. **Amenities:** TV lounge; free Wi-Fi.

## JORDAAN

### Moderate

**chic&basic ★** This newish and ultra-cool boutique hotel is part of a European chain enjoying great success for its hip styling and decent prices. It's tucked away behind a canal-house facade, and the compact bedrooms are gaily decorated with homey touches like patchwork quilts or wackily upholstered comfy chairs (the public spaces in the hotel are all smooth and contemporary). No elevator.

Herengracht 13-19. www.chicandbasic.com. ✆ **020/522-2345.** 28 units. Doubles 135€–190€, includes breakfast. **Amenities:** Coffee bar; free Wi-Fi.

### Inexpensive

**Clemens Amsterdam ★★** A little hotel that packs a big punch, the Clemens is a budget choice that, although not long on amenities, offers updated rooms that are pristine and welcoming. Bear in mind when booking that the Clemens sits on one of the city's main thoroughfares, so while rooms at the front do have the added pull of cute wrought-iron balconies, they can be noisy. Typical for a small hotel in central Amsterdam, it occupies four floors in a narrow townhouse and there's simply no place to put an elevator. But the hotel is fantastically located near the Anne Frank Huis and the Westerkerk.

Raadhuisstraat 39. www.clemenshotel.nl. ✆ **020/624-6089.** 14 units. Doubles 85€–100€, includes breakfast. **Amenities:** Free Wi-Fi.

## MUSEUM QUARTER

### Expensive

**Conservatorium Hotel ★★** It can be difficult to make a large hotel feel welcoming, but the superb staff at the Conservatoriun do just that. Both patient and knowledgeable, they have a knack of making each guest feel special. Of course, the swank and often quirky decor (love the violin chandelier!) go a long way toward pumping up guests. Who wouldn't like to lounge in a bathroom bigger than most guest rooms, and relax in guest rooms that sport such lovely touches as shiny wood floors, a soothing neutral-toned color palettes, and insanely comfortable beds? On-site are two terrific eateries and a swank spa. The hotel occupies the former neo-Gothic Sweelinck Conservatory of Music, hence its name.

Van Baerlestraat 27. www.conservatoriumhotel.com. ✆ **020/570-0000.** 129 units. Doubles 345€–945€. **Amenities:** 2 restaurants; bar; pool; spa; gym; free Wi-Fi.

### Moderate

**College Hotel ★★** This sleek and urbane hotel, set in a former school, is a couple of minutes from Amsterdam's "Big Three" museums. It's also dangerously close to the expensive designer stores on PC Hoofstraat, so you'll spy plenty of glam 30-something professionals mingling in the hotel's luscious, shady courtyard and bar. The guest rooms are the last word in contemporary cool, in soothing beiges and tans, with stacks of pillows, smart fixtures and fittings, and plenty of space.

Roelof Hartstraat 1. www.thecollegehotel.com. ✆ **020/571-1511.** 40 units. Doubles 125€–230€. **Amenities:** Restaurant; bar; free Wi-Fi.

**Sandton Hotel De Filosoof ★★** A staple on the Amsterdam hotel scene for decades, the Filosoof was the city's first theme hotel, decorated to pay homage to various philosophers, which means that a smattering of quotes and portraits adorn the walls. Housed in a graceful 19th-century townhouse in refined residential neighborhood a step away from the Vondelpark, rooms are small and cheerily idiosyncratic, with crooked walls and madly sloping floors. A tiny bar is tucked into the lobby, and a tranquil patio garden lurks behind the hotel.

Anna van den Vondelstraat 6. www.sandton.eu. ✆ **020/683-3013.** 38 units. Doubles 120€–195€, includes breakfast. **Amenities:** Bar; free Wi-Fi.

## OUD ZUID

### Moderate

**citizenM Amsterdam City ★★** One of the new gaggle of no-frills accommodation options that seem to be flooding European cities, citizenM has washed up close to the World Trade Center and caters largely to short-stay business travelers, although it's convenient to the Tram 5 service right into the city center. Check-in is automated, barista-standard coffee is on tap 24/7, and a canteen serves up sushi and salads at lunch. The ultramodern room designs include podlike showers; touch-screen remotes; huge, comfortable beds; and free movies. Breakfast is extra at 11€ if preordered, 3€ more on the day.

Prinses Irenestraat 30. www.citizenm.com. ✆ **020/811-7090.** 215 units. Doubles 89€–150€. **Amenities:** 24/7 snack room; bar; free Wi-Fi.

**Conscious Hotel Vondelpark ★★** By "conscious" they mean "eco-friendly"—living plant walls, eco-roofs, and green energy. This green-house-cum-hotel is run by a young and very cool staff who go all out to please guests. They let their collective hair down on weekends, when every night is party night, with music and dancing in the bar. Bedrooms are compact and wittily adorned with pithy slogans on energy conservation. The breakfast bar is an organic delight. Tram Line 1 (5 min. to the city center) stops right outside the hotel.

Overtoom 519. www.conscioushotels.com. ✆ **020/820-3333.** 81 units. Doubles 90€–175€. **Amenities:** Bar; free Wi-Fi.

## DE PLANTAGE

### Moderate

**Hampshire Hotel Lancaster Amsterdam ★** Located on the eastern, gentrified side of the city, a world away from the sketchy Red Light District, this hotel is perfectly placed for family visits to Artis Zoo and the Hortus Botanicus. Even better, it's just a 10-minute ride on trams 9 or 14 to all the central amenities and action. Prices are reasonable (although Wi-Fi is 13€ per day and breakfast is also extra) with oversized bedrooms furnished in neutral, inoffensive tones and gigantic black-and-white images over the beds. If you're traveling with kids, there are several triple rooms available.

Plantage Middenlaan 48. www.edenlancasterhotel.com. ✆ **020/535-6888.** 91 units. Doubles 138€–188€. **Amenities:** Restaurant; bar.

# Where to Eat

As with most northern European countries—and certainly in comparison with Spain and Italy, where families are still munching away at midnight—Amsterdam eats early. Even the smartest restaurants open around 6pm, which makes dining out a family-friendly experience.

## OLD CENTER

### Expensive

**Bloesem** ★★ MEDITERRANEAN With the money saved from printing menus, rising-star Chef Marco Deegan invests in organic, in-season ingredients which he uses to surprise and delight the lucky few who find this hidden gem (it's just off Haarlemmerdijk). Guests come in, a smiling waiter asks if they have any food allergies or dislikes, and with that info the chef creates an individualized five-course feast, with creative dishes such as beef tenderloin with cocoa sauce and pumpkin, or gazpacho with rose water. The setting is intimate and romantic and the fare topnotch.

Binnen Dommersstraat 13-15. www.restaurant-bloesem.info. ✆ **06/1445-6644.** Fixed-price menus 33€–43€. Tues–Sun 6–10:30pm.

### Moderate

**Kapitein Zeppos** ★ FISH Charming and quirky—the plant-filled cafe looks a bit like a greenhouse—Zeppos serves some of the best mussels in the city, plus feasts of Portuguese *mariscos* (mixed seafood platter), paella, and Coquille St.-Jacques. It's popular with students from the University of Amsterdam across the street and hosts live music most evenings, when folks come in for the craft beers and atmosphere.

Gebed Zonder End 5, Spui. www.zeppos.nl. ✆ **020/624-2057.** Mains 17€–24€. Daily noon–1am (Fri–Sat until 3am).

**Restaurant-Café In de Waag** ★ DUTCH Bang in the middle of vibrant Nieuwmarkt, the historic Waag (set in one of Amsterdam's oldest and most atmospheric buildings) buzzes day and night; its outdoor cafe is filled to bursting all afternoon, and it serves late-night snacks of nachos and Dutch cheeses to soak up any surfeits of alcohol. The restaurant inside features a candlelit dining room and long trestle tables. The menu is short and predictable; you're really here for the ambiance.

Nieuwmarkt 4. www.indewaag.nl. ✆ **020/422-7772.** Mains 19€–25€. Daily 10am–10:30pm.

**Supperclub Amsterdam** ★ FUSION Having been on the list of things to do in Amsterdam for years, Supperclubs now spread across the world, with branches in San Francisco and Dubai. This wildly popular restaurant–cum–cocktail bar has two tricks up its sleeve: Diners lounge on couches to listen, and there is no menu—you're served a five-course feast of whatever is available seasonally. Inform your waiter of any dietary restrictions and sit back to see what arrives. Post-supper sees live music, wild dancing, and sometimes wacky performances. Reservations required.

Jonge Roelensteeg 21. www.supperclub.com. ✆ **020/344-6400.** Mains 20€, fixed-priced menus 69€. Daily 8pm–late.

**Visrestaurant Lucius** ★★ SEAFOOD A top choice for fresh fish in Amsterdam, Lucius is decked out like a traditional fishmonger's, with

Café de Sluyswacht.

tiled walls and marble tabletops, wooden seating, and ceiling fans. It has been going great guns for 40 years. Cooking styles are unfussy, allowing the true taste of the fish to shine on the plate. Reservations are recommended on the weekend.

Spuistraat 247. www.lucius.nl. ✆ **020/624-1831.** Mains 22€–30€, fixed-price menu 40€, seafood platters to share 63€–115€. Daily 5pm–midnight.

### Inexpensive

**Café de Sluyswacht ★★** DUTCH Tilting at a precarious angle over the Oudeschans canal, this former 17th-century lock-keeper's cottage is one of the oldest and most famous pubs in Amsterdam. Inside all is crooked, with wooden bars and uneven stone floors. Sample the *wit bier* (white beer) and a plate of strong Dutch cheese and enjoy the tiny, crowded terraces with spectacular views over the canal.

Jodenbreestraat 1. www.sluyswacht.nl. ✆ **020/625-7611.** Mon–Thurs 12:30pm–1am, Fri–Sat 12:30pm–3am, Sun 12:30–7pm. Mains 7.50€–18€.

**Stubbe's Haring ★★★** FISH Raw herring on a roll with pickles and sweet onions is a Dutch specialty, and there are dozens of *haringhuis* stands in town, but this one is regarded as the best. Tip your head back and try to eat the fish whole for a quintessential Amsterdam experience.

Nieuwe Haarlemmersluis, on a bridge near Centraal Station. ✆ **020/623-3212.** Sandwiches 5.50€. Midday–evening. No credit cards.

## AMSTERDAM'S brown CAFES

Traditional Dutch taverns or "brown cafes" are great places to mix with local Amsterdammers, as they are the very embodiment of *gezellighied*—that particularly Dutch mixture of charm, conviviality, and comfort all wrapped into one welcoming package. Some brown cafes date back to Rembrandt's day; all are warm and cheery, with dark interiors and simple wooden furniture and bars. Some have kitchens where short-order chefs rustle up all manner of moderately priced breakfasts, all-day dishes, *broodjes* (sandwiches), and simple suppers. Opening hours are anywhere between 8 and 10am and 1 and 3am the following day.

**Hoppe ★★** is an ancient brown cafe that dates back to 1670. It has a convivial, English-pub atmosphere, and is standing-room-only in the early evening, when the place fills up with a merry after-work bunch. Things can become a bit rowdy after a couple of samplings of Dutch *jenever*, a gin-like liqueur with recipes dating back to the 18th century. Main dishes are 7.50€ or less. It's open daily 8am to 1am (Sat–Sun until 2am). You'll find it at Spui 18-20 (www.cafe-hoppe.nl; ✆ **020/420-4420**).

**'t Smalle ★★★** is on the edge of the Jordaan area. It's a locals' cafe decked out in wood and glass and offering a small menu of snacks (dishes 3.50€-8.75€). The primary business here is the beer, so grab a glass and join local drinkers at the bar, or sit outside on the decking over the canal. 't Smalle is on Egelantiersgracht 12, and open daily 10am to 1am (www.t-smalle.nl; ✆ **020/623-9617**).

## CANAL RING

### Expensive

**Vinkeles ★★★** FUSION Those celebrating 25th anniversaries or other special events make a beeline for Vinkeles, because it serves, with no exaggeration, some of the most original, tasty food in all of Europe, and does so in a way that makes each guest feel like a VIP. Dennis Kuipers has run the kitchen to much acclaim since 2006, and he's known for whipping up such unusual signature dishes as sea bass with cannabis seed, Iberico ham, and baby squid. He also often plays with Asian ingredients and spicing. The restaurant is set in the converted bakery of a 17th-century almshouse that is now the Dylan (p. 305), one of Amsterdam's top boutique hotels.

Dylan Hotel, Keizersgracht 384. www.vinkeles.com. ✆ **020/530-2010.** Mains 34€–60€, fixed-price menus 105€–135€. Mon–Sat 7–10:30pm.

### Moderate

**Golden Temple ★★** VEGETARIAN And that temple is your body, because the food here is not only delish, it's marvelously healthy, consisting entirely of vegetarian, vegan, and raw-food options. Housed in a narrow, candle-lit dining hall with an open kitchen, low-slung tables, and rugs as decoration, the menu goes one step beyond the normal veggie affairs with its unlikely roster of Indian and Middle Eastern plates, chunky salads (with such items as quinoa and tempeh), and Italian pizza. Sadly it's closed at lunchtime, as this would make a great sightseeing pit stop.

Utrechtsestraat 126. www.restaurantgoldentemple.com. ✆ **020/626-8560.** Mains 14€–21€. Daily 5:30–9:30pm.

### Inexpensive

**Koffiehuis de Hoek ★** DUTCH An old-style cafe on the corner of the Nine Streets shopping enclave and overlooking the canal, this place bursts at the seams with local workers at lunchtime. Grab a table for an all-day breakfast or a Dutch snack of croquettes or *bitterballen* washed down with excellent espresso or local beer. If you don't fancy sharing a table, join the line for takeout sandwiches piled high with salami and salad.

Prinsengracht 341. ✆ **020/625-3872.** Snacks from 5€. Tues–Fri 7:30am–4pm, Sat 9am–3:30pm.

**Pancake Bakery ★** PANCAKES There are many, many pancake houses in Amsterdam, but this is one of the finest, partially because these yummy treats come with a choice of 70 (!) toppings and stuffings, from Indonesian chicken to honey, nuts, and whipped cream. The bakery is set in a 17th-century canal warehouse on Prinsengracht, suitably placed for a treat after a visit to the sobering Anne Frank Huis.

Prinsengracht 191. www.pancake.nl. ✆ **020/625-1333.** Pancakes 6€–17€. Daily 9am–9:30pm.

## JORDAAN

### Moderate

**Bordewijk ★★** MODERN FRENCH Bordewijk is patronized by locals in the know, who appreciate the affordable prices and casual vibe of this minimalist restaurant, which is sparsely but stylishly kitted out with wooden floors and spindly tables. In true French style, there's not much here for vegetarian diners—the menu inhabits the world of suckling pig and tripe, all expertly cooked by Chef Wil Demandt. His fine fare is paired with a superb wine list and service is relaxed, so expect dinner

#### Amsterdam's Fab Fast Food

Must tries include ***bitterballen*** (fried meatballs) available in most bars and bistros and served with cold beer, or ***patat*** (fries) bought from street vendors and eaten dunked in mayonnaise, straight from the paper cone. ***Haring*** (herring) is the most popular fish in Amsterdam, traditionally eaten whole and pickled from street vendors such as the famous **Stubbe's Haring ★★★** (p. 313) in Nieuwe Haarlemmersluis.

For sweet Dutch street food options, see box on the facing page.

here to last all night. There's a terrace for alfresco dining alongside the canal.

Noordermarkt 7. www.bordewijk.nl. ✆ **020/624-3899.** Mains 20€–30€, fixed-price menus 39€–54€. Tues–Sat 6:30–10:30pm.

## MUSEUM QUARTER

### Moderate

**Café Cobra** ★ DUTCH Considering the fact that this is the only real restaurant adjacent to the Rijksmuseum, Stedelijk, and Van Gogh museums, Café Cobra is far better than it needs to be. Sure, it's always heaving with tourists, but those who order the spicy croquettes and *bitterballen* accompanied with fat fries, mayo, and a glass of prosecco come away quite pleased. Perfect for a quick bite while sightseeing.

Hobbemastraat 18. www.cobracafe.nl. ✆ **020/470-0111.** Mains 7€–20€. Daily 10am–7pm.

## OUD ZUID

### Expensive

**Restaurant Blauw** ★★★ INDONESIAN Heading out for a *rijstaffel* meal—a holdover from the days when the Dutch had colonies in Indonesia—is a classic Amsterdam experience, and Blauw is the best place to do it. It serves a first-class version of the traditional Indonesian dishes, and its minimalist decor, and service from the charming wait staff, is thoroughly 21st century. Plus there's a decent wine list—a rarity in Indonesian eateries. The *rijsttafel* consists of an amazing 17 plates, including slow braised beef in coconut sauce, fried and sticky rice, pork balls, plantain, satay, and chili-laden pork, chicken, and fish dishes. Heaven! Remember to book ahead, because it's always jammed.

Amstelveenseweg 158-160. www.restaurantblauw.nl. ✆ **020/675-5000.** Mains 21€–27€, *rijstaffel* 26€–32€. Mon–Thurs 6–10:30pm, Fri 6–11pm, Sat 5–11pm, Sun 5–10:30pm.

### The Dutch Sweet Tooth

The always-slim Dutch happily devour *pannenkoek* (pancakes) and thick, sweet *poffertjes* served with heart-busting butter and sprinkled with sugar at any given opportunity, without ever seeming to gain an ounce! So why not join them? Other calorie-laden treats include *stroopwafels* (treacle wafers oozing with caramel) and deep-fried *oliebollen* (donuts) filled with raisins and dusted with sugar, which can be bought on street stalls all over the city center. Amsterdammers also have a thing for chocolate sprinkles, which you'll find shaken over breakfast rolls as well as all sorts of *broodjes* (sandwiches), sweet and savory; a favorite combination is chocolate sprinkles with salty peanut butter. A final treat: a dollop of thick, syrupy *appelstroop* made from sugar and apple, added to your lunchtime cheese *broodje* (sandwich).

### DE PLANTAGE

#### Moderate

**Brasserie Plancius ★★** BRASSERIE The perfect spot to head after an outing to the Artis Royal Zoo or the Dutch Resistance Museum, the cavernous interior of Plancius fills up quickly with local families and glamorous women loudly treating each other to lunch. Menus offer carefully constructed brasserie-style dishes such as *croque-monsieur,* organic burgers, satay chicken salad, or steak and fries. There's a calorific afternoon tea, plus two sittings for dinner (at 5:30 and 8:10pm). Kids who are impatient to visit the zoo get their own menu (pancakes, fries) and a coloring book to distract them while their parents eat.
Plantage Kerklaan 61. www.brasserieplancius.nl. ✆ **06/2324-4069.** Mains 3€–19€. Daily noon–10:30pm.

## Shopping

Although Amsterdam is no Paris or Milan in the shopping stakes, it's no slouch either. Ignore the tatty souvenir stores selling plastic tulips and mass-produced clogs around Dam Square. **Leidsestraat** and **Koningsplein** are among the most popular shopping spots, with mid-range boutiques and design stores. Upping the ante are young designers changing the face of the retail scene around the **Nine Streets** (see box p. 318) and in the **Museum Quarter,** where independents are giving the international designers a run for their money. The **Spiegelkwartier** at the south end of the Canal Ring is famous for its antiques and art stores, and is the place to head for genuine blue-and-white Delftware. Try Galleria d'Arte Rinascimento (www.delft-art-gallery.com) for new and antique Delftware, or Jorrit Heinin (www.delftsblauwwinkel.nl), which also sells leaded crystal.

Typically Dutch products such as cheese (De Kaaskamer van Amsterdam [www.kaaskamer.nl] is the city's most famous cheese emporium) and flower bulbs are bargains, and diamonds can be bought—carefully—from a reputable dealer such as Gassan (www.gassandiamonds.nl).

## Entertainment & Nightlife

Amsterdam's top orchestra—indeed, one of the world's top orchestras—is the renowned **Royal Concertgebouw Orchestra** (www.concertgebouworkest.nl), whose home is the **Concertgebouw ★★★,** Concertgebouwplein 2-6 (www.concertgebouw.nl; ✆ **0900/671-8345**), which first opened its doors in 1888 and is still touted as one of the most acoustically perfect concert halls in Europe. The **Dutch National Opera** (www.dno.nl) as one of the leading companies in Europe. They perform at the **Dutch National Opera & Ballet,** Waterlooplein 22 (www.operaballet.nl; ✆ **020/625-5455**).

## the negen straatjes—AMSTERDAM'S NINE STREETS

Tucked away between the historic Old Center and the bohemian Jordaan, the Nine Streets are a classy one-stop shopping destination crisscrossing the western side of the 17th-century Canal Ring between Reestraat and Runstraat. The streets provide a welcome relief from the tatty souvenir stores of Dam Square, as they offer chic stores selling designer labels, artisan jewelry, offbeat vintage fashions, and luxury toiletries, all interspersed with plenty of stylish bars and restaurants.

Fashion store **Van Ravenstein** (www.van-ravenstein.nl; ✆ **020/639-0007**) sells on-trend Belgian designers Ann Demeulemeester and Dries van Noten. **L'étoile de Saint Honoré** (Oude Spiegelstraat 1; www.etoile-luxuryvintage.com; ✆ **020/330-2419**) is the best place for vintage handbags, **Anecdote** (Wolvenstraat 15; www.anecdote.nl; ✆ **020/427-9156**) for simple, stylish fashion, and **Spoiled** (Wolvenstraat 19; www.spoiled.nl; ✆ **020/626-3818**) offers arguably the best selection of denim labels in Amsterdam. **United Nude** (125A Spuistraat; www.unitednude.com; ✆ **020/626-0010**) sells cool shoes and boots for women, **Parisienne** (Berenstraat 4; www.nlstreets.nl/EN/shop/parisienne; ✆ **020/428-0834**) offers lovely vintage jewelry, and **MINT Mini Mall** (Runstraat 27; www.mintminimall.nl; ✆ **020/627-2466**) sells cushions, pottery, and furniture in all shades of pastel. **Skins Cosmetic** (Runstraat 11; www.skins.nl; ✆ **020/528-6922**) is the place for organic toiletries, and **La Savonnerie** (Prinsengracht 294; www.savonnerie.nl; ✆ **020/428-1139**) for handmade soaps. For more info about the Nine Streets in English, visit **www.theninestreets.com**.



At the other end of the musical spectrum, lovers of avant-garde and experimental music should head to the **Muziekgebouw aan 't IJ,** Piet Heinkade 1 (www.muziekgebouw.nl; ✆ **020/788-2000**), which opened in 2005 on the ever-expanding IJ waterfront east of Centraal Station. Right next door is the **Bimhuis**, Piet Heinkade 3 (www.bimhuis.com; ✆ **020/788-2188**), Amsterdam's much-loved improvisational jazz and blues club, where ticket prices range from 10€ to 25€.

**Royal Theatre Carré ★★★** is a lovely old theater that hosts a few English-language productions of opera, contemporary dance, and ballet, as well as best-selling big-name shows (www.carre.nl).

Favorite bars and pubs, so central to life in this laidback city, include **Bubbles & Wines ★★,** a sophisticated champagne and wine bar in the Old Center (De Nes 37; www.bubblesandwines.com; ✆ **020/422-3318**). **Café Pollux ★★** is a real treasure in the Dam area, primarily due to the charismatic and slightly bonkers owner Frits and his enigmatically smiling wife (121 Prins Hendrikkade; www.cafepollux.com; ✆ **020/624-9521**). With sawdust on the floor and wooden barrels lining the walls, **De Drie Fleschjes ★★★** (Gravenstraat 18; www.dedriefleschjes.nl; ✆ **020/624-8433**) is a real find and a welcome escape from the Red

### Soft Drugs Tolerance

Amsterdam's reputation as a party town is due in part to its tolerance toward soft drugs. But in fact the practice is technically illegal. Whereas it's fine to carry 5 grams (1/6 oz.) for personal use, it's not fine to buy dope anywhere other than in a **coffee shop.** These are licensed and controlled venues where you can purchase marijuana or hashish, and can sit and smoke all day if you want to. Around 200 coffee shops still exist in Amsterdam (most concentrated around the Red Light District; **The Bulldog** at Oudezijds Voorburgwal 88 is the best known). It is illegal to smoke dope in the streets, to buy drugs in the streets, and to buy drugs at all if you are under 18. And don't be tempted to take any drugs out of the country with you.

Light District hinterland. Although one or two tourists may find their way in here, most of your fellow drinkers will be Dutch. **De Jaren ★★** (Nieuwe Doelenstraat 20-22; www.cafe-de-jaren.nl; ✆ **020/625-5771**) overlooks the Binnenamstel waterfront and has panoramic upper-floor terraces perfect for reading newspapers on sunny Sunday afternoons or meeting up with the girls for lunch. **Vesper ★★★** (Vinkenstraat 57; www.vesperbar.nl) in Jordaan is one of a new breed of super-smooth and super-friendly cocktail bars with some wacky and wonderful concoctions.

For **dancing and live music**, try **Jimmy Woo ★★** (Korte Leidsedwarsstraat 18; www.jimmywoo.com; ✆ **020/626-3150**), an Asian-themed club with a posh clientele who happily sit around quaffing champagne all night. **Paradiso ★** (Weteringschans 6-8; www.paradiso.nl; ✆ **020/626-4521**), an Amsterdam institution, is based in a former church that has converted well into a majestic, multi-purpose club with lofty ceilings and high balconies encircling the dance floor. The **Vondelpark Openluchttheater (Open Air Theater) ★★★** (www.openluchttheater.nl; ✆ **020/428-3360**) in the Museum Quarter hosts Amsterdam's best summer street party, with a series of concerts at the moon-shaped open-air stage. Best of all, everything is free.

### Amsterdam Gay Pride

The summer's biggest street party is the riotous Amsterdam Gay Pride, which normally takes place the last week of July. A celebration of the open-hearted, welcoming, and tolerant culture of the Netherlands, Pride kicks off with a canal parade of lavishly decorated barges around the Canal Ring, and the week that follows is a non-stop round of street parties, concerts, and drag queen Olympics. A schedule of events is at www.amsterdamgaypride.org.

## Day Trips from Amsterdam

The compactness of the Netherlands means that everything is close—even The Hague and Rotterdam are only about 30 miles away from Amsterdam. Here are our favorite excursions from the city:

## THE BULB DISTRICT

A dazzlingly patchwork quilt of vibrant color, Holland's tulip bulb fields contribute millions of euros to the Dutch economy. The greatest concentration lies in the **Bloemenbollenstreek (Bulb District) ★,** a strip of land 16km (10 miles) long and 6km (4 miles) wide between Haarlem and Leiden, about 22 miles west of Amsterdam. In the spring (end of Jan–May), visiting here is a frenzied Dutch rite of passage.

Viewing the flowers is easy. Just follow all or parts of the circular, signposted **Bollenstreek Route** (60km/37 miles) by car or bike—although you could find your way there by the trail of roadside stalls flogging bunches of cut flowers. To get to the bulb fields from Amsterdam, drive to Haarlem, then go south on N206 through De Zilk and Noordwijkerhout, or on N208 through Hillegom, Lisse, and Sassenheim. There are also scores of **bus tours** from all the main cities. Viator (www.viator.com; ✆ **888/651-9785** in the U.S.) provides several, even offering a package including a flight over the fields. Special seasonal buses transport visitors on the direct service no. 858 from Schiphol Airport, and tourists staying over in Leiden can catch bus service no. 854 from Leiden Central train station.

If you're in Holland between March and May, consider a trip to the 32-hectare (79 acre) estate of **Keukenhof ★★★** (www.keukenhof.nl) where every year, more than 800,000 flower fans from all across the world flock to see eight million bulbs explode into life. Keukenhof claims to be the greatest flower show on earth, and certainly it is Holland's annual spring gift to the world.

The Bulb District in bloom.

## LEIDEN

Stately yet bustling, the old heart of Leiden is classic Dutch, filled with handsome, gabled brick houses along canals spanned by graceful bridges. The Pilgrim Fathers lived here for 11 years before sailing to North America from Delfshaven in Rotterdam. Leiden's proudest moment came in 1574, when it became the only Dutch town to withstand a Spanish siege, although William of Orange *was* forced to flood the land around the city to win that battle. The town is the birthplace of Rembrandt (the **Rembrandt Walk** takes in sites from his boyhood), the Dutch tulip trade, and the oldest university in the Netherlands (founded in 1575). The 12th-century citadel of De Burcht stands on a mound in the town center, providing a great view of the surrounding rooftops.

The impressive **Hortus Botanicus der Rijksuniversiteit (University Botanical Garden)** ★★ (Rapenburg 73, 2311 GJ Leiden; www.hortus.leidenuniv.nl; ✆ **071/527-7249;** adults 7€; Apr–Oct 10am–6pm, Nov–Mar 10am–4pm) was established by the University of Leiden in 1590 to cultivate tropical trees and plants, and as such imported the first tulip bulbs that would go on to change Dutch destiny. For works from local-boy-made-good Rembrandt, and his 16th- and 17th-century peers, head to the **Museum De Lakenhal** ★★ (Oude Singel 32 2312 RA Leiden; www.lakenhal.nl; ✆ **071/516-5360;** adults €7.50; Tues–Fri 10am–5pm, Sat–Sun 12–5pm). For a grand tour of Dutch colonial plundering, the **Rijksmuseum van Oudheden (National Museum of Antiquities)** ★★★ (Rapenburg 28, 2311 EW Leiden; www.rmo.nl; ✆ **071/516-3163;** adults €9.50; Tues–Sun 10am–5pm) is, quite simply, one of the best museums in the Netherlands. If you're short of time in Leiden, make this your priority for the collection of Egyptian, Near Eastern, Greek, and Roman treasures.

Up to eight **trains** per hour run from Amsterdam Centraal Station to Leiden Centraal Station. The ride takes around 35 minutes. For more details, visit **www.ns.nl**. By **car,** take A4/E19.

## HAARLEM

Just 18 miles west of Amsterdam, quaint and quiet Haarlem is home to one of Holland's premier art museums: the **Frans Hals Museum** ★★★ (Groot Heiligland 62; www.franshalsmuseum.nl; ✆ **023/511-5775;** adults 13€, Tues–Sat 11am–5pm, Sun noon–5pm). Housed in the elegant former Oudemannenhuis, a home for retired gentlemen dating from 1608, the wonderful paintings by Frans Hals (1580–1686) and other masters of the Haarlem School hang in a setting reminiscent of the 17th-century houses they were intended to adorn.

The old center of Haarlem is a 10-minute walk from the graceful Art Nouveau rail station dating from 1908, most of it via pedestrian-only shopping streets. First-time visitors generally head straight for the **Grote**

**Markt ★★★,** the beautiful central market square adjacent to **Sint-Bavokerk ★★,** a colossal late-Gothic church. The monumental buildings around the tree-lined square date from the 15th to the 19th centuries and are a microcosm of the development of Dutch architecture. The glorious 15th-century **Stadhuis (Town Hall)** has an ornate bell tower, gables, and elaborate balconies. It was once a hunting lodge of the Counts of Holland and is now—rather prosaically—the home of the tourist information office.

**Trains** for Haarlem depart at least every half-hour from Amsterdam Centraal Station; the ride takes 15 minutes. A round-trip ticket is 8€. For more details, visit **www.ns.nl**. By **car** from Amsterdam, take N200/A200 west; parking is around 3€ an hour.

# ROTTERDAM ★★

A mere hour from Amsterdam by train, Rotterdam is an utterly different city. In Rotterdam there are no tangles of old streets, no canals, and no 17th-century town houses; instead, there's an abundance of sleek contemporary architecture, and one of the world's busiest ocean harbors. This bustling metropolis has risen from the ashes of Nazi bombing in 1942, which reduced it to rubble overnight.

But not all of Rotterdam is brand new. Take the Metro to the tiny harbor area known as **Delfshaven (Delft Harbor),** a neighborhood that the German bombers somehow missed when they bombed the city to smithereens. Historically, this is one of the most important places in Europe for U.S. citizens, because it was from here that the Puritan Pilgrim fathers embarked on the first leg of their trip to found Massachusetts in 1620. Wander into the 15th-century **Pelgrimvaderskerk (Pilgrim Fathers Church),** Aelbrechtskolk 20 (www.pilgrimfatherschurch.org/en), in which the pilgrims prayed before departure, and where they are remembered in special services every Thanksgiving Day. The church is open irregularly, but at least admission is free. Then peek into antiques stores and galleries, and check on the progress of this historic area's housing renovations.

Historic Delfshaven.

## Essentials

Rotterdam's tourism portal is **www.rotterdam.info**.

**GETTING THERE** From Amsterdam, two to six **trains** depart each hour around the clock. On **NS Hispeed Fyra** trains, the ride takes 40 minutes; on ordinary InterCity trains, around 70 minutes. The round-trip fare from Amsterdam is 29€. For more details, visit **www.ns.nl**.

By **car** from Amsterdam, take A4/E19, and then A13/E19; expect delays during commuter times—or to be honest, most of the time.

**GETTING AROUND** Once in Rotterdam, you can use the trams and the Metro with the same **OV-chipkaart** public transportation card used in Amsterdam (p. 283) on the extensive **RET** (www.ret.nl) public transportation network of bus, tram, and Metro.

Explore the Maas waterfront using waterbuses operated by **RET Fast Ferry** (see above) and **Watertaxi Rotterdam** (www.watertaxirotterdam.nl).

Taxi stands are sprinkled throughout the city. You can hail cabs on the street, or by calling **Rotterdamse Taxi Centrale** (www.rtcnv.nl; ✆ **010/462-6333**) or **Rotterdam Taxis** (www.rotterdamtaxiservice.nl; ✆ **062/651-9697**).

## Exploring Rotterdam

**Euromast ★★** HISTORIC BUILDING This slender, 185m-tall (607-ft.) tower is indisputably the best vantage point for an overall view of Rotterdam and its environs; on clear days, you can see about 30km (20 miles). You can have lunch or dinner in the **Euromast Brasserie,** 96m (315 ft.) above the harbor park. A rotating elevator departs from here for the **Euroscoop viewing platform** at the top of the spire. From the Brasserie level, for an additional payment (53€), you can abseil or rope slide back to the ground—definitely not for the faint of heart.
Parkhaven 20. www.euromast.nl. ✆ **010/436-4811.** 9€ adults, 6€ children 4–11. Apr–Sept daily 9:30am–11pm, Oct–Mar daily 10am–11pm.

**Museum Boijmans van Beuningen ★★★** MUSEUM Rotterdam's leading art museum showcases the story of Western art from medieval times to the present. The highlights of this wonderful collection of 140,000 works include Pieter Breughel's peerless *The Tower of Babel* (ca. 1553); scores of delicate drawings by Renaissance artist Fra Bartolommeo; Rembrandt's winsome portrait of his son, entitled *Titus at his Desk*; and a collection of Gerrit Rietveld's distinctive colored wooden furniture.
Museumpark 18-20. www.boijmans.nl. ✆ **010/441-9475.** 15€ adults, 7.50€ students, free for children 18 and under. Tues–Sat 11am–5pm.

**Wereldmuseum ★★★** MUSEUM Reflecting the rich maritime heritage of the Netherlands, the World Art Museum has cobbled together thousands of historic artifacts from across the world, many picked up by Dutch sailors as they plundered the planet during the 17th-century Golden Age. The result is a beautiful, vibrant, and unusual series of displays of tribal artwork not seen anywhere else, from Tibetan prayer flags to primitive Australian Aboriginal paintings and beautiful Indonesian

## Rotterdam Harbor ★★★

The Port of Rotterdam handles more ships and more cargo every year than any other port in Europe, and it is the world's third-busiest port after Shanghai and Singapore. A dredged channel, the **Nieuwe Waterweg (New Waterway)** connects Rotterdam with the North Sea and forms a 40km-long (25-mile) deep-water harbor known as **Europoort.** The Netherlands owes a fair piece of its prosperity to the port, which employs 86,000 people. The port authority handles around 35,000 ships, 16 million containers, 160 million tons of crude oil, and 450-million metric tons of cargo annually. Container ships, cargo carriers, tankers, and careworn tramp ships are waited on 24 hours a day by a vast retinue of people and automated machines—trucks, trains, and barges all moving hither and thither in a blur of activity. A trip around the harbor may be one of the more unusual experiences to be had in Europe. The sheer scale of the operation will make your jaw drop.

hand-printed batiks, showcased alongside African carvings and a luscious collection of silk textiles embroidered in gold. The museum is housed in a lovely Art Nouveau building that contains a classy restaurant. Willemskade 25. www.wereldmuseum.nl. ✆ **010/270-7172.** 15€ adults, free for children 12 and under. Tues–Sun 10:30am–5:30pm.



## Organized Tours

An essential part of the Rotterdam experience is taking a **Spido Harbor Tour ★★** (www.spido.nl; ✆ **010/275-9988**) of **Europoort** on board a two-tier boat with open decks. April to September, departures from the dock below Erasmus Bridge run daily every 30 to 45 minutes from 9:30am to 5pm; October to March, departures are limited to two to four times a day. The basic harbor tour is a 75-minute sail along the city's waterfront; between April and September an extended (2¼-hr.) trip also runs daily at 10am and 12:30pm. In July and August, you can make



The Erasmusbrug cable bridge and the Rotterdam skyline.

## contemporary ARCHITECTURE IN ROTTERDAM

The first thing any visitor notices about Rotterdam is its architecture. Nicknamed "Manhattan on the Maas," it's a shiny, new city rising phoenix-like from the ashes of its destruction in one terrible night during World War II. With only wisps of the old gabled townhouses left around Delfshaven and Oude Haven, this is a skyline of innovative buildings, its iconic landmark the elegant lines of the **Erasmusbrug cable bridge,** nicknamed "the Swan" and floodlit at night.

Looking positively old-fashioned these day, a city landmark near Oude Haven is the geometric chaos of quirky, cube-shaped apartments balancing atop tall concrete stalks; the elevated, tree-house-like, and custard-yellow Kubuswoningen (Cube Houses) were designed by Dutch architect Piet Blom in the early 1970s. One of these lopsided little abodes, the **Kijk-Kubus (Show-Cube),** Overblaak 70 (www.kubuswoning.nl; ✆ **010/414-2285;** 11am–5pm daily; 2.50€ for adults, 2€ for seniors/students, 1.50€ for children 4–12), is open for visits.

As the city's heavy industry migrated northwest toward the North Sea, the **old port area** has been revamped with innovative skyscrapers including the Norman Foster–designed **World Port Center,** the Maastoren office block, and the **New Orleans** building, currently the tallest residential structure in the Netherlands at 43 stories; all can be seen on a **boat tour of the harbor** (see facing page).

Rem Koolhaas designed the Museumpark's **Kunsthal Rotterdam** in the 1990s, setting a precedent for stylish public buildings that has been followed by the red-brick **New Luxor Theatre,** the frothy bubbles of the **Drijvend Paviljoen** (Floating Pavilion) in the Rijnhaven, and the dynamic **Red Apple** apartment block.

all-day excursions along Europoort's full length to the Delta Works sluices. Tours start at 11€ for adults, 7€ for children 4 to 11.

If you're traveling with kids, head straight for the bright-yellow **Pannenkoekenboot (Pancake Boat) ★,** Parkhaven (www.pannenkoekenboot.nl; ✆ **010/436-7295**), moored at the foot of the Euromast to get high on sugary treats. Departures on the family cruise are year-round on Saturday and Sunday at 1:30pm. The 2½-hour cruise is 24€ for adults and 20€ per child.

For sheer novelty value, try cruising down the canals aboard the world's first **HotTug** (www.hottug.nl; ✆ **010/412-5449**), a floating, wood-fired hot tub open in all types of weather (the water keeps you warm).

### Where to Stay & Eat

Some of Rotterdam's best beds for the night can be found at the Hotel New York (Koninginnenhoofd 1; www.hotelnewyork.com; ✆ **010/439-0500;** doubles from 99€), perched on the Maas with views downriver. At the other end of the price (and luxury) spectrum, the floating H2otel

## THE windmills OF KINDERDIJK ★★

Kinderdijk (www.kinderdijk.nl), a tiny community between Rotterdam and Dordrecht, on the south bank of the Lek River, has 19 water-pumping windmills; that means 76 mill sails, each with a 13m (42-ft.) span. It's a spectacular sight, and one important enough for Kinderdijk to have been placed on UNESCO's World Heritage list.

By regulating the level of water, Kinderdijk's windmills guarded the fertile polders (reclaimed land) of the Alblasserwaard. The **Windmill Exposition Center** at Kinderdijk gives a detailed explanation of the part they played in the intricate system of water control. It also looks at the culture that developed on the polders.

The mills operate on Saturday afternoons in July and August 2:30 to 5:30pm; the visitors' mill is open April to October Monday to Saturday 9:30am to 5:30pm. The most adrenaline-thumping way to get to Kinderdijk from Rotterdam is by RET high-speed catamaran (www.ret.nl), from the dock adjacent to the Erasmusbrug; this goes to the De Schans dock at Ridderkerk for the local ferry across to Kinderdijk. If you're driving, take N210 east to Krimpen aan de Lek, from where a small car ferry crosses over the Lek River to Kinderdijk.

**A few of Kinderdijk's 19 windmills.**





(Wijnhaven 20a; www.h2otel.nl; ✆ **010/444-5690;** doubles from 59€) combines budget accommodation with a warm welcome and a brilliant location within walking distance of the shopping center, Spido boat dock, and the oddball Kijk-Kubus. Eating options include the cafes around historic Oude Haven, a sunny spot for eating al fresco, or the restaurants of Rotterdam's Chinatown around Kruisplein—where you'll also find Surinamese, Middle Eastern, and Japanese cuisine. A handy pit stop for lunch after taking a Spido tour, Zenne (Willemskade 27; www.zenne.nl; ✆ **010/404-9696;** lunch mains 7€–15€) serves simple dishes (lamb burgers, kebabs, bitterballen) on a terrace overlooking the river and the cute marina at Veerhaven.

## A Side Trip to Delft

Minute Delft is perhaps the prettiest town in all of Holland. The facades of the Renaissance and Gothic houses here reflect age-old beauty, a sense of tranquility pervades the air, and linden trees bend over its gracious canals. Indeed, it's easy to understand why Old Master painter Jan Vermeer chose to live here.

A hefty part of Dutch history is preserved in Delft. William of Orange, who led the Dutch insurrection against Spanish rule, was assassinated in the Prinsenhof and now rests in a magnificent tomb in the Nieuwe Kerk; every member of the Royal House of Oranje-Nassau has since been brought here for burial.

Of course, to many visitors, Delft means only one thing—the prized blue-and-white earthenware still produced by the meticulous methods of yore. Every piece of genuine Delftware is hand-painted by skilled craftspeople; a trip to Delft really should encompass a visit to a porcelain factory. It is produced predominantly, but not exclusively, by three Delft-based firms: **De Koninklijke Porceleyne Fles** (Rotterdamseweg 196; www.royaldelft.com; ✆ **015/251-2030;** showroom free, factory tour 13€; daily 9am–5pm, closed Sun in Nov/Dec); **De Delftse Pauw** (Delftweg 133; www.delftpottery.com; ✆ **015/212-4920;** free factory tours, daily 9am–4:30pm, reduced weekend hours Nov–Mar 15); and **De Candelaer** (Kerkstraat 13; www.candelaer.nl; ✆ **015/213-1848;** call for hours). Genuine Delftware is for sale throughout the Netherlands, but it is fascinating to visit a workshop and see it being made.

Once you've emptied your wallet for that precious porcelain, hit Delft's other highlights, including **Museum Het Prinsenhof ★★** (Sint Agathaplein 1; www.prinsenhof-delft.nl; ✆ **015/260-2358;** adults 13€; Tues–Sun 11am–5pm, Jun–Aug, also Mon). The "Prince's Court" dates from the late 1400s and was originally a convent. William of Orange, the "Father of the Dutch Nation," maintained his battle HQ here during all the years he fought the Spanish to found the Dutch Republic, and also where an assassin's bullets ended his life in 1584. The **Nieuwe Kerk**

The Markt, Delft's main square.

**(New Church)** ★ (Markt 80; www.nieuwekerk-delft.nl; church and tower 6.50€ adults; open Mon–Sat, hours vary) isn't new at all—it was begun in 1383 and completed in 1510. Inside is the magnificent tomb of William of Orange.

Six **trains** an hour to Delft from Amsterdam (one is direct; transfer in Rotterdam for the others) and eight an hour from Rotterdam. By **car,** the town is just off the A13/E19 expressway from The Hague to Rotterdam.

# THE HAGUE

Stately and dignified, The Hague is an easy day trip from Amsterdam or Rotterdam, but some travelers prefer it as a more relaxed sightseeing base. 's-Gravenhage, to give the city its full name, or more commonly Den Haag, is a cosmopolitan town bursting with style and culture, full of parks and elegant homes. Its 18th-century French vibe suits its role as a world-class diplomatic center and the site of the International Court of Justice.

## Essentials

The Hague's tourism website is **www.denhaag.nl**.

**GETTING THERE** Amsterdam's **Schiphol Airport** (p. 303), 40km (25 miles) away, also serves The Hague. Trains run directly from the airport to The Hague, with up to six trains an hour during the day and one an hour at night; the ride takes around 35 minutes, and round-trip fare is 16€. A taxi from Schiphol to The Hague city center takes 40 minutes in reasonable traffic and costs around 100€.

The Hague has excellent **rail** connections from Amsterdam, with fast InterCity **trains** that take around 50 minutes. The city has two main stations, **Den Haag Centraal Station** and **Den Haag HS;** most city sights are closer to Centraal Station, but some trains stop only at HS. The round-trip fare from Amsterdam is 22€. For more details, visit **www.ns.nl**.

**Driving** from Amsterdam and the north, take A4/E19. You'll want to avoid all three *snelwegen* (expressways) during the morning and evening commuter hours, when traffic grinds to a halt. At other times, you should be able to drive to The Hague from Amsterdam in under an hour.

**GETTING AROUND** Public transportation in The Hague is operated by **HTM** (www.htm.net). Centraal Station is the primary interchange point for bus and tram routes, and HS station is the secondary node. Going by **tram** is the quickest way to get around, but some points are served only by **bus.** Tram no. 1 is useful for sightseers as it travels from the North Sea coast at Scheveningen through The Hague and all the way to Delft. For details on using the **OV-chipkaart** stored-value card for public transportation in The Hague (as well as the rest of the Netherlands), see p. 283.

Regulated taxis wait at stands outside both main rail stations and at other strategic points around town; you can also hail them in the streets. A new eco-friendly service is provided by **gCab** (www.gconcepts.eu/gcab/gcab-den-haag), which operates a fleet of electric buggies and charges a flat fee of 5€ throughout the city.

## Exploring The Hague

One of the great pleasures of spending a day or more in The Hague is walking through its genteel streets, matching your pace to the unhurried leisure that pervades the city. Stroll past the mansions that line Lange Voorhout, overlooking a broad avenue of poplar and elm trees, and you'll be struck by how these spacious, restrained mansions differ from Amsterdam's gabled, ornamented canal houses. Take time out in more than 30 sq. km (12 sq. miles) of parks, gardens, and other green spaces within the city limits or head out to The Hague's sophisticated seacoast resort, Scheveningen, on Tram no 1.

**Binnenhof & Ridderzaal (Inner Court & Hall of the Knights) ★★**
HISTORIC BUILDING The imposing Binnenhof is one of the oldest buildings in the Netherlands and was originally the 13th-century hunting lodge of the counts of Holland. When Count Willem II was crowned king of the Romans and emperor-elect of the Holy Roman Empire in 1248, he appointed the Binnenhof as his official royal residence. Today it forms

The Binnenhof.

the hub of Dutch political life in a series of offices and ceremonial halls, including the First and Second Chamber of the Staaten-Generaal (States General), the two houses of the nation's Parliament.

At the courtyard's heart is the beautiful, twin-towered Ridderzaal (Hall of the Knights), which was the last building to be added to the Binnenhof in 1280 by King Floris V, who was the son of Willem II. Soaring 26m (85 ft.) to its oak roof, its immense interior is adorned with provincial flags and leaded-glass windows depicting the coats of arms of Dutch cities.

Binnenhof 8A. www.english.prodemos.nl. ✆ **070/757-0200.** Courtyard free; 8€ guided tours (book in advance online). Mon–Sat 10am–4pm.

**Escher in Het Paleis (Escher at the Palace) ★** MUSEUM Behind its elegant neoclassical 17th-century facade, the palace was formerly the winter residence of Queen Emma of the Netherlands and later the home of Dutch graphic artist **M. C. Escher.** Escher became famous for his perspective-twisting lithographs, woodcuts, engravings, drawings, and prints. These eccentric works, the largest collection in the world, are exhibited throughout his former home.

Lange Voorhout 74. www.escherinhetpaleis.nl. ✆ **070/427-7730.** 9€ adults, 6.50€ children 7–15, free children 6 and under, 25€ family. Tues–Sun 11am–5pm.





**Gemeentemuseum Den Haag (The Hague Municipal Museum) ★★★** MUSEUM Housed in a honey-toned brick building (1935) by architect Hendrik Petrus Berlage, this fine museum has plenty to see. Top billing goes to the world's most comprehensive collection—more than 50 works—by De Stijl artist Piet Mondrian, among them his last painting, the unfinished *Victory Boogie Woogie* (1944), an abstract representation of New York. Other rooms cover 19th-century Dutch Romantic art, the Impressionist Hague School, and 20th-century art, along with a few works by van Gogh, Monet, and Picasso, and prints and drawings by Karel Appel and Toulouse-Lautrec. The prizes in the decorative arts collection are ceramics from Delft, China, and the Middle East; Dutch and Venetian glass; silver; period furniture; and an intricate 1743 dollhouse. The music department has antique instruments from Europe—harpsichords, pianos, and more—and from around the world, and an impressive library of scores, books, and prints. Plan to spend a couple hours here.

Stadhouderslaan 41. www.gemeentemuseum.nl. ✆ **070/338-1111.** 17€ adults, 14€ students, free for children 18 and under. Tues–Sun 11am–5pm.

**Mauritshuis ★★★** MUSEUM Once the residence of Count Johan Maurits van Nassau-Siegen—court dandy, cousin of the ruling Oranje-Nassaus, and governor-general of Dutch Brazil—this small but delightful neoclassical mansion from 1637 houses the **Koninklijk Kabinet van Schilderijen (Royal Cabinet of Paintings),** a stunning collection of 15th- to 18th-century Low Countries art—masterworks by Rembrandt, Frans Hals, Johannes Vermeer, Jan Steen, Peter Paul Rubens, and Hans Holbein the Younger—given to the nation by King Willem I in 1816. The intimate rooms are set on two floors; it almost feels like you're viewing a private collection. It's here that you'll see Rembrandt's *The Anatomy Lesson of Dr. Nicolaes Tulp* (1632); Vermeer's meticulous *View of Delft* (ca. 1660), in which cumulous clouds roil the skies above the neat little town; and his *Girl With a Pearl Earring* (ca. 1660).

Korte Vijverberg 8. www.mauritshuis.nl. ✆ **070/302-3456.** 14€ adults, 11€ students, free for 18 and under. 18€ including entrance to Galerij Prins Willem V. Daily 10am–6pm (Thurs until 8pm).

### The Royal Palace in The Hague

King Willem-Alexander's workplace is the majestic **Paleis Noordeinde** on Noordeinde, just west of Lange Voorhout, which dates from 1553. Dutch super-architect Jacob van Campen created much of what we see today in the 17th century, including the palace's H-shape and serene neoclassical facades, but 200 years later, the palace was almost derelict. An 1815 restoration brought it back to a state suitable for a royal residence, and although it isn't open to visitors, you can view it from the street and surrounding gardens; combine a stroll in the Royal Park with a visit to the **Mauritshuis** ★★★ (see facing page) and the **Dutch Parliament Buildings** (see Binnenhof, p. 329).

**Vredespaleis (Peace Palace)** ★ HISTORIC BUILDING American philanthropist Andrew Carnegie donated over a million dollars toward the construction of this immense mock-Gothic palace, home to the International Court of Justice and the Permanent Court of Arbitration. The building was designed by French architect Louis Cordonnier and completed in 1913. Today it can be visited only by guided tour with reservations made online ahead of time. You'll see most of the ornate apartments and marvel at the grandiose gifts given by each of the participating countries: crystal chandeliers made with real rubies and emeralds and each weighing 1,750kg (3,900 lb.) from Delft; incredible mosaic floors from France; a huge Turkish carpet woven in 1926 in Izmir; and an immense 3,500kg (7,700 lb.) vase from Czar Nicholas of Russia. If the courts aren't in session, your guide will take you inside the International Court of Justice, which handles all of the UN's judicial cases.

Carnegieplein 2. www.vredespaleis.nl. ✆ **070/302-4242.** Tour tickets 9.50€ adults, free for children 10 and under. Visitor Center: Tues–Sun 10am–5pm (mid-Nov to mid-Mar 11am–4pm). Guided tours: Mon–Fri 10 and 11am, and 2, 3, and 4pm (4pm tour not always offered). Tours last 50 min. or 1½ hr.

## Especially for Kids

Like Amsterdam, The Hague is a happily child-friendly city, with plenty of rolling parks and the nearby beaches of Scheveningen. It's also got several attractions aimed at kids, kicking off with Holland's only **IMAX theater at Omniversum** (President Kennedylaan 5. www.omniversum.nl; © **900/666-4837;** films 11€ adults, 9€ children 4–12 years; daily from 10am). Almost next door is **Museon** (Stadhouderslaan 37; www.museon.nl; © **070/338-1338;** 12€ adults, 7€–9€ children; Tues–Sun 11am–5pm), The Hague's hyper-interactive museum of science and nature. Then for a change of pace, head to the top of **Hague Tower** for afternoon tea in The Penthouse and far-reaching views across the city (www.thehaguetower.com; © **070/305-1000**). The Hague's tallest skyscraper reaches an impressive 132m (433 ft.) and is regarded as the city's answer to New York City's Flatiron Building. The observatory is open daily from noon to 10pm; tickets are 6€ and include a drink voucher.

But The Hague's biggest attraction for youngsters lies a short ride on tram 9 away from the city center toward Scheveningen. Here you'll find **Madurodam ★★** (George Maduroplein 1; www.madurodam.nl; © **070/416-2400;** 16€ adults; open daily, hours vary by season), a well-conceived theme park showcasing the Netherlands in miniature. Dutch townscapes and famous landmarks—the Anne Frank Huis and Rijksmuseum in Amsterdam; the Binnenhof and Mauritshuis in The Hague; and Rotterdam's Euromast—act as a brilliant introduction to the wonders of the Netherlands.

## Where to Stay & Eat

The oh-so-refined **Hotel Des Indes** (Lange Voorhout 54-56; www.hoteldesindesthehague.com; © **070/361-2345;** doubles from 240€) comes highly recommended, as does the **Steigenberger Kurhaus Hotel** (Gevers Deynootplein 30; www.kurhaus.nl; © **070/416-2636;** doubles from 119€) in Scheveningen, which has wonderful North Sea views and every possible luxury, too. More moderately priced suggestions include the eco-friendly **Court Garden** (Laan van Meerdervoort 96; www.hotelcourtgarden.nl; © **070/311-4000;** doubles from 75€), a well-located oasis of "green" principles, and the simple but immaculate **Hotel Sebel** (Prins Hendrikplein 20; www.hotelsebel.nl; © **070/345-9200;** doubles from 99€).

**Dining options** abound along Prinsenwaal Straat, and there's lots of **bar action** around the Grote Markt. **Restaurant Café UNO Den Haag** (Grote Markt 1; www.unodenhaag.nl; © **070/220-1117**) in particular serves killer cocktails. In Chinatown, the **Kee Lun Palace** (Wagenstraat 95; © **070/364-9988**) rustles up a decent chow mein and Singapore noodles.

# [FastFACTS] THE NETHERLANDS

## Business Hours

Stores usually open from 9:30am to 6pm Tuesday, Wednesday, Friday, and Saturday. Many are closed on Monday morning, opening at 1pm, and most shops outside the center close all day Sunday. Some stay open until 8 or 9pm on Thursday. Most museums close one day a week (often Mon), but open some holidays, except for Koningsdag (King's Day, on Apr 27; see p. 290), Christmas, and New Year's Day.

## Currency

The Netherlands is a member of the European Union and uses the E.U. common currency, the euro (€). See p. 860 for information on money and costs.

## Embassies & Consulates:

**Australia:** Carnegielaan 4, The Hague; www.netherlands.embassy.gov.au; ✆ **070/310-8200.**

**Canada:** Sophialaan 7, The Hague; www.Netherlands.gc.ca; ✆ **070/311-1600.**

**New Zealand:** Eisenhowerlaan 77N, The Hague; www.nzembassy.com/netherlands; ✆ **070/346-9324.**

**United Kingdom:** Lange Voorhout 10, The Hague; www.gov.uk/government/world/netherlands; ✆ **070/427-0427.**

**United States:** Lange Voorhout 102, The Hague; http://netherlands.us embassy.gov; ✆ **070/310-2209.**

## Emergencies

For any **emergency** (fire, police, ambulance), the number is ✆ **112.** For 24-hour urgent but **nonemergency** medical or dental services, call ✆ **088/0030-600.** To **report a theft,** call ✆ **0900/8844.**

## Pharmacies

In the Netherlands, a pharmacy is called an ***apotheek*** and sells both prescription and nonprescription medicines. Regular open hours are Monday to Saturday from around 9am to 6pm. Pharmacies post details of nearby **all-night and Sunday pharmacies** on their doors.

## Post Office

The city of Amsterdam doesn't have post offices anymore; instead various branches of newsagents, supermarkets, and grocery stores have postal points run by **PostNL** (www.post.nl). Stamps can also be purchased from your hotel and any newsstands that sell postcards.

6

# SCANDINAVIA

John Newcomb & Jason Cochran

In the days when the U.S. dollar was even stronger than it is today (in fact, much stronger), my wife and I furnished our first apartment with the revolutionary, ground-breaking furniture displayed in stores lining Copenhagen's "walking street," the stroget. We fell in love with Arne Jacobson's "swan" (dining rooms chairs resembling the shape of a swan), with his "egg" (a large easy chair looking like a giant, cutaway egg), with stainless steel cutlery looking like something made for a futuristic spaceship. We were overwhelmed by the modernity of Scandinavian design, which we also found on our later trips to Stockholm and Helsinki.

That modernity continues to greet you in buildings and streets all over the Scandinavian capitals other than Oslo (be sure to take a walk along the pedestrian-only *"stroget"*—shopping street—in Copenhagen), and in their many futuristic structures. But the "modernity" of Scandinavia is even more heavily apparent in the social and political policies of these nations. Here was the birth of cradle-to-grave security, where unemployment benefits and old age retirement payments are a large percentage of what you had earned while working. Here are fascinating social experiments, like Sweden's subsidies given to opposition newspapers: if, in a particular community, the newspaper of one political party is dominant, the government subsidizes a newspaper of the opposition political party in order to maintain a balance of political advocacy. Here are countries where poverty scarcely exists. And yet in all these countries, freedom of speech is an absolute (witness Denmark's support of political cartoonists who outrage religious groups). Here, too, are countries where maternity leave is for at least a year (and paternity leave is close behind), and excellent, free-of-charge daycare is universally available.

Here, in sum, are countries whose residents believe that theirs are the most advanced, pleasant, and gratifying nations on earth—a sentiment once voiced to me by a much-traveled, sophisticated Dane, who had experienced life in other countries and came back willingly to spend his retirement in Denmark. Denmark, a nation where fast-food workers enjoy the equivalent of $20 an hour in wages and 5 weeks per year of paid vacation, has one of the world's highest per capita incomes and lowest level of income inequalities, but also a high rate of income taxation. Medical care

FACING PAGE: **Copenhagen's Nyhavn district.**

is free, as are college and university education, and its prime minister is currently a woman. After you have met with the people in these countries, you may well share the opinion of that cosmopolitan Dane I have quoted, who regards these nations as the happiest on earth. As for Sweden, the seventh-richest country in the world, it has universal healthcare and totally free university education, and a thriving industrial base (think of Volvo and IKEA, among others).

On a recent trip to Stockholm, my wife and I resolved that we wanted to hear the opinions of local residents. So we pestered our friends for the names and addresses of Stockholm residents they knew, and we then wrote letters to them, in advance of leaving for Stockholm, inviting them to be our guests for dinner at a good Stockholm restaurant. Of the various Swedish couples who accepted our invitation, one arrived for dinner carrying a large pile of papers bearing economic statistics. Sensing what we would ask, they wanted to be well-prepared for our questions. At one point during a very pleasant dinner, they also told us of their own recent trip to the United States, where they were puzzled by the appearance of numerous American flags outside buildings. Why, they asked, would anyone want to display a national flag? Isn't that a bit backward?

And there you have it, a first contact with Scandinavia. You will also enjoy the marvelous open sandwiches of Copenhagen (*"smørrebrød,"* which you should make a point of having for lunch), the smorgasbord buffets of Stockholm, the superb museums of both countries (especially the 17th-century Swedish warship *Wasa* resurrected from the depths of Stockholm's harbor), the incomparable Tivoli Gardens amusement park of Copenhagen (an inspiration to Walt Disney, who made a point of inspecting it), and countless other attractions of both great cities.

I envy you your trip there. Skål!

***–Arthur Frommer***

# COPENHAGEN

Denmark's capital is the fun capital of Scandinavia—and the most affordable big city in an expensive region. There is an enthusiasm for life here that always sweeps us up in its spell.

Copenhagen got its name from the word *køben-havn,* which means "merchants' harbor." It grew in size and importance because of its position on the Øresund (the Sound), the body of water between Denmark and Sweden, guarding the strategic passage of all maritime traffic heading into or out of the Baltic. Today, it's the largest city in Scandinavia, home to 1.8 million people, and the seat of one of the oldest kingdoms in the world.

There is talk of a Renaissance in Copenhagen, as Denmark moves deeper into the 21st century. A sea of change is sweeping across the city as tired, seedy old buildings are restored—many turned into boutique hotels. At trendy restaurants, young Danes are reinventing the cuisine of their ancestors, too long dominated by the Danish pig.

Yet Copenhagen is still a city long on old-world charms, as reflected in its canals, narrow streets full of cyclists, and old houses.

The summer sun may not set until 11pm, and winters are cold, dark and rainy. "We brood like Hamlet then," said a local. "But winter or summer, we're super friendly and welcoming . . . and in English too."

We'd heartily agree with that assessment.

## Essentials

**VisitCopenhagen** (www.visitcopenhagen.dk) is the city's official tourist portal, and it provides information to help you plan your trip.

**ARRIVING** Flights arrive at **Kastrup Airport** (www.cph.dk; ✆ **32-31-32-31**), 12km (7½ miles) from the center of Copenhagen. Air-rail trains link the airport to the Central Railway Station in the center of Copenhagen. The ride takes 13 minutes and costs DKK 36. The Air Rail Terminal is a short escalator ride from the gates. You can also take a bus to the city terminal; the fare is DKK 36. A taxi to the city center costs DKK 250 to DKK 300.

**Trains** arrive at the **HovedBanegården** (Central Railway Station; ✆ **70-13-14-15** for rail information), in the center of Copenhagen, near Tivoli Gardens. From the Central Railway Station, you can connect with the **S-tog,** a local train; trains depart from platforms in the terminal itself. The information desk is near tracks 5 and 6.

**Buses** from other parts of Denmark and elsewhere pull into the Central Railway Station. For bus info, call ✆ **36-13-14-15** daily 7am to 9:30pm.

If you're **driving** from Germany, a **car ferry** will take you from Travemünde to Gedser in southern Denmark. From Gedser, get on E55 north, an express highway that will deliver you to the southern outskirts of Copenhagen. If you're coming from Sweden via the Øresund Bridge, it will deposit you on the city's eastern outskirts, close to Kastrup airport. From here, it's a short drive into the center.

**CITY LAYOUT** The heart of Old Copenhagen is a warren of pedestrian streets, bounded by Nørreport Station to the north, Rådhuspladsen (Town Hall Square) to the west, and Kongens Nytorv, a busy square that's positioned at the top of the Nyhavn Canal, to the east. **Strøget,** the longest continuous pedestrian-only route in Europe, is lined with shops, bars, restaurants, pizza parlors, and, in summer, sidewalk cafes. **Pistolstræde** contains a maze of galleries, restaurants, and boutiques, housed in restored 18th-century buildings.

At the end of Strøget, you approach **Kongens Nytorv** (King's Square). This is the site of the Royal Theater and Magasin, the largest department store in Copenhagen. This will put you at the beginning of **Nyhavn,** the former seamen's quarter that has been gentrified into an upmarket area of expensive restaurants, apartments, cafes, and boutiques.

The government of Denmark has been centered, for the past 800 years, on the small and very central downtown island of **Slotsholmen,** which is connected to the center by eight different bridges. The island's most immediately visible attraction is the imperial-looking granite mass of Christiansborg Castle, home of the Danish parliament, the prime minister's offices, the country's Supreme Court, and several museums.

The center of Copenhagen is **Rådhuspladsen** (Town Hall Square). From here it's a short walk to the Tivoli Gardens, the major attraction of Copenhagen; the Central Railway Station; and the Bus Station terminus. **Vesterbrogade,** a wide, densely trafficked boulevard, passes by Tivoli en route to the Central Railway Station. **H. C. Andersens Boulevard,** a major avenue named after Denmark's most famous writer, runs beside the Rådhuspladsen and Tivoli Gardens.

**GETTING AROUND** Copenhagen is a walker's paradise, neat and compact. Many of its major attractions are close to one another.

A joint zone fare system covers Copenhagen's **public transport** system (www.rejseplanen.dk): buses, State Railway, Metro, S-tog trains and some private railway routes within a 40km (25-mile) radius of the capital, enabling passengers to transfer from train to bus and vice versa with the same ticket. A *grundbillet* (basic ticket) for **buses and trains** costs DKK 24. Up to two children, age 11 and under, ride for half fare when accompanied by an adult. For DKK 80, travelers can purchase a ticket allowing 24-hour bus and train travel in the city and surrounding areas.

The **Copenhagen Card** (www.copenhagencard.dk) entitles the bearer to free and unlimited travel by bus and rail throughout the metropolitan area, 25% to 50% discounts on crossings to and from Sweden, and free admission to many sights. The card is available for 1 or 4 days and costs DKK 339 to DKK 779 depending on duration. Up to two children under the age of 10 are allowed to go free with each adult card. Otherwise, children ages 10 to 15 pay DKK 179 to DKK 379 for 1 or 4 days. Buy the card at tourist offices, at the airport, at train stations, and at most hotels.

Tourists have little need for a **car** in Copenhagen. Much of the city consists of traffic-free walkways, parks, gardens, and canalside promenades. It's best to park in any of the dozens of city parking lots, then retrieve the car when you're ready to explore the countryside. For more info about parking, go to www.car-parking.eu/denmark.

Watch for the fri (free) sign or green light to hail a **taxi**, and be sure the taxis are metered. **Taxa 4x35** (**© 35-35-35-35**) operates the largest fleet of cabs. Tips are included in the meter price: DKK 37 at the drop of the flag and DKK 14 per kilometer thereafter, Monday to Friday 7am to 4pm. From 6pm to 6am, and all day Saturday and Sunday, the cost is DKK 15 per kilometer. Many drivers speak English.

To reduce pollution from cars (among other reasons), many Copenhageners ride **bicycles**. Join them by grabbing one of the nifty electric bikes of Copenhagen's bike-share system, available around the city. The cost is DKK 25/hour and you're going to need to set up an account in advance, on computer, at www.bycyklen.dk.

## The Neighborhoods in Brief

**TIVOLI GARDENS** Steeped in nostalgia, these amusement gardens were built in 1843 on the site of former fortifications in the heart of Copenhagen, on the south side of Rådhuspladsen. Some 160,000 flowers and 110,000 electric lights set the tone, and a collection of restaurants, dance halls, theaters, beer gardens, and lakes draw many thousands of visitors every year.

**STRØGET** This pedestrian-only urban walkway stretches between Rådhuspladsen and Kongens Nytorv, two of the city's busiest plazas. Along its trajectory are two spectacular squares, Gammeltorv and Nytorv, "old" and "new" squares, which blossom during the summer months with outdoor seating at the many restaurants that line its edges. The "Strøget," which usually doesn't appear on maps, encompasses five interconnected streets: Frederiksberggade, Nygade, Villelskaftet, Amagertorv, and Østergade.

**NYHAVN/KONGENS NYTORV** Nyhavn ("New Harbor") was originally conceived in the 1670s by the Danish king as a shelter from the storms of the North and Baltic Sea, and as a means of hauling building supplies into central Copenhagen. Today it's the site of the densest concentration of restaurants in Copenhagen.

For many generations, Nyhavn was the haunt of sailors looking for tattoos, cheap drinks, and other diversions. In its current, gentrified form, it's filled with outdoor terraces that are mobbed during warm-weather months with chattering, sometimes hard-drinking Danes on holiday.

**INDRE-BY** This is the Old Town, the heart of Copenhagen. Once filled with monasteries, it's a maze of streets, alleyways, and squares. The neighborhood around Gammeltorv and Nørregade, sometimes called "The Latin Quarter," contains many buildings linked with the university. The **Vor Frue Kirke** (Cathedral of Copenhagen) is here, as is the **Rundetårn** (Round Tower).

**SLOTSHOLMEN** This island, site of Christiansborg Palace, was where Bishop Absalon built the city's first fortress in 1167. Today it's the seat of the Danish parliament and home of Thorvaldsen's Museum. Bridges link Slotsholmen to Indre By. You can also visit the Royal Library, the Theater Museum, the Royal Stables, and the 17th-century *Børsen* (stock exchange) here.

# Copenhagen

**ATTRACTIONS**
Amalienborg Palace **33**
Botanisk Have (Botanical Gardens) **27**
Christiansborg Slot (Christiansborg Palace) **18**
Danish Design Centre **13**
Dansk Jødisk Museum (Danish Jewish Museum) **14**
Den Lille Havfrue (The Little Mermaid) **35**
Designmuseum Danmark **34**
Frederikskirke (Marble Church) **32**
Holmens Kirke **19**
Københavns Museum (Museum of Copenhagen) **6**
Kongelige Bibliotek (Royal Library) **15**
Nationalmuseet (National Museum) **12**
Rådhus (Town Hall) and World Clock **11**
Rosenborg Slot (Rosenborg Castle) **28**
Rundetårn (Round Tower) **25**
Statens Museum for Kunst (National Gallery of Denmark) **29**
Tivoli Gardens **10**
Vor Frelsers Kirken (Our Saviour's Church) **17**
Vor Frue Kirke (Copenhagen Cathedral) **24**

**HOTELS**
Andersen Hotel **8**
Hotel d'Angleterre **22**
Hotel Kong Arthur **1**
Hotel SP34 **3**
Ibsens Hotel **2**
Imperial Hotel **5**
Wakeup Copenhagen, Borgergade **30**

**RESTAURANTS**
Cap Horn **21**
Ida Davidsen **31**
No. 2 **16**
Noma **20**
Øl & Brød **7**
Restaurant Kronborg **23**
Restaurant Schønnemann **26**
Restaurant Tårnet **18**
Restaurant Uformel **4**

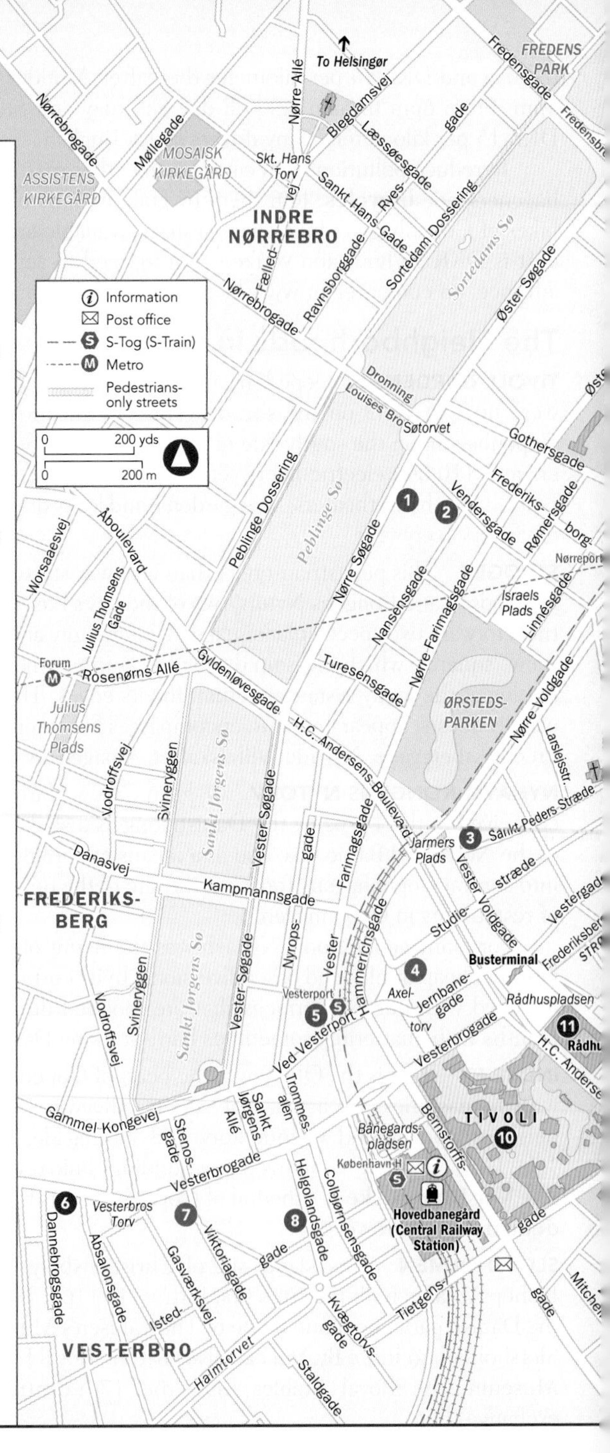

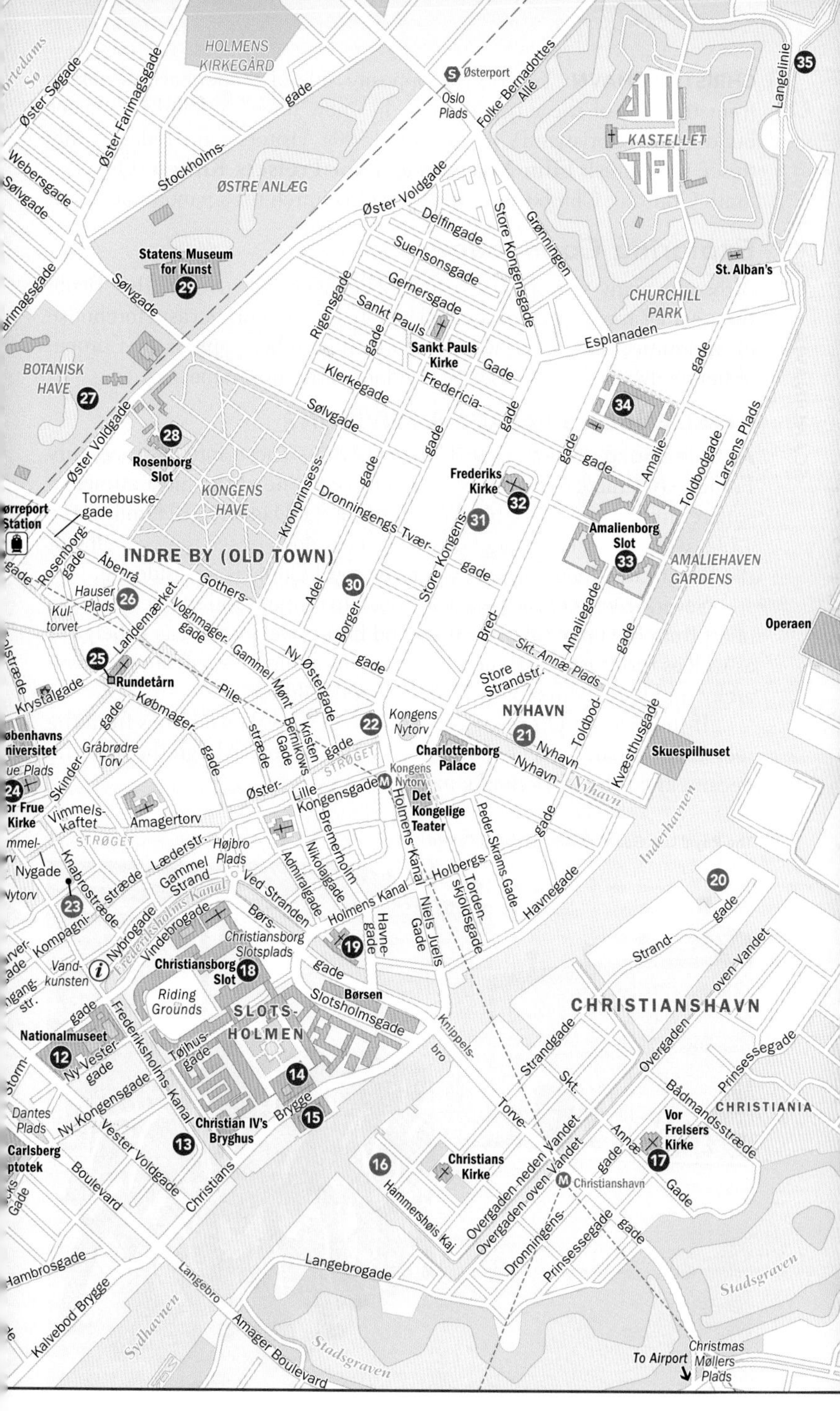
HOLMENS KIRKEGÅRD
Østerport
Oslo Plads
Folke Bernadottes Allé
KASTELLET
Langelinie
ØSTRE ANLÆG
Øster Søgade
Webersgade
Sølvgade
Øster Farimagsgade
Stockholmsgade
Øster Voldgade
Delfingade
Suensonsgade
Gernersgade
Sankt Paulsgade
Sankt Pauls Kirke
Store Kongensgade
Grønningen
St. Alban's
CHURCHILL PARK
Esplanaden
Statens Museum for Kunst
BOTANISK HAVE
Rigensgade
Klerkegade
Fredericiagade
Sølvgade
Rosenborg Slot
KONGENS HAVE
Kronprinsessegade
Dronningens Tværgade
Frederiks Kirke
Amalienborg Slot
AMALIEHAVEN GARDENS
Amaliegade
Toldbodgade
Larsens Plads
Operaen
Nørreport Station
Tornebuskegade
Rosenborggade
INDRE BY (OLD TOWN)
Åbenrå
Gothersgade
Adelgade
Borgergade
Bredgade
Hauser Plads
Kultorvet
Landemærket
Vognmagergade
Gammel Mønt
Ny Østergade
Skt. Annæ Plads
Store Strandstr.
NYHAVN
Rundetårn
Krystalgade
Købmagergade
Pilestræde
Bernikows Gade
Kristen
Kongens Nytorv
Charlottenborg Palace
Nyhavn
Kvæsthusgade
Skuespilhuset
Københavns Universitet
Gråbrødre Torv
Frue Plads
Vor Frue Kirke
Skindergade
Vimmelskaftet
STRØGET
Amagertorv
Østergade
Lille Kongensgade
Det Kongelige Teater
Peder Skrams Gade
Inderhavnen
Nygade
Knabrostræde
Læderstr.
Gammel Strand
Højbro Plads
Ved Stranden
Admiralgade
Nikolajgade
Bremerholm
Holmens Kanal
Holbergsgade
Tordenskjoldsgade
Havnegade
Niels Juels Gade
Havnegade
Kompagnistræde
Nybrogade
Vindebrogade
Frederiksholms Kanal
Børsgade
Christiansborg Slotsplads
Vandkunsten
Christiansborg Slot
Riding Grounds
SLOTSHOLMEN
Børsen
Slotsholmsgade
Knippelsbro
Strandgade
CHRISTIANSHAVN
Overgaden oven Vandet
Prinsessegade
Nationalmuseet
Ny Vestergade
Tøjhusgade
Frederiksholms Kanal
Brygge
Skt. Annæ Gade
Bådmandsstræde
CHRISTIANIA
Vor Frelsers Kirke
Dantes Plads
Ny Kongensgade
Vester Voldgade
Christian IV's Bryghus
Torvegade
Carlsberg Glyptotek
Christians Kirke
Overgaden neden Vandet
Christianshavn
Boulevard
Christians
Hammershøis Kaj
Dronningensgade
Prinsessegade
Hambrosgade
Langebrogade
Langebro
Kalvebod Brygge
Sydhavnen
Amager Boulevard
Stadsgraven
To Airport
Christmas Møllers Plads

**CHRISTIANSHAVN** Set on the opposite side of Copenhagen's harbor from the rest of the city, this was the "new town" ordered by master builder King Christian IV in the early 1500s. Visitors come today mainly to see the Danish **Film Museum** and **Vor Frelsers Kirken** (Our Saviour's Church). Climb the spire of the old church for a panoramic view.

## Exploring Copenhagen

Although many visitors arrive in Copenhagen just to visit the Tivoli, there's a lot more going on here. The city is proud of its vast storehouse of antiquities and holds its own with most other capitals of Europe, although dwarfed, of course, by London, Paris, and Rome.

### AMALIENBORG PALACE & ENVIRONS

**Amalienborg Palace ★★** LANDMARK These four 18th-century French-style rococo mansions—opening onto one of the most attractive squares in Europe—have been the home of the Danish royal family since 1794, when Christiansborg burned. Visitors flock to see the changing of the Royal Life Guard at noon when the royal family is in residence.

Several rooms of the palace are open to visitors, and showcase works of art from the imperial workshops and from jewelers such as Faberge—as well as furniture, costumes, souvenirs, embroideries, gifts to the monarchy, and handicrafts made by royal grandchildren.

If the beloved Dronning is in residence, a swallowtail flies from the roof of this palace. The Dronning is the queen, Margrethe II, who became the ruler of Denmark in 1972.

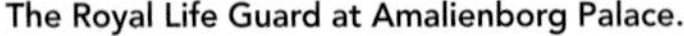

The Royal Life Guard at Amalienborg Palace.

Amalienborg. www.kongernessamling.dk/en/amalienborg. ✆ **33-12-21-86.** DKK 70–DKK 90 adults, DKK 50–DKK 60 students; 17 and under free. Bus: 1A or 20E. May 1–Oct 31 10am–4pm; Nov 1–April 30 Tues–Sun 11am–4pm.

*Den Lille Havfrue.*

**Den Lille Havfrue (The Little Mermaid)** ★ LANDMARK The statue *everybody* wants to see in Copenhagen is the slightly smaller than life-size bronze of *Den Lille Havfrue,* inspired by Hans Christian Andersen's fairy tale *The Little Mermaid*. Unveiled in 1913, it was sculpted by Edvard Eriksen. It rests on rocks off the shoreline of the entrance to Copenhagen's harbor, close to Castellet and the Langelinie cruise piers.

Near *The Little Mermaid* statue is ***Gefionspringvandet*** (Gefion Fountain). This massive art work, largest in Copenhagen, was sculpted by Anders Bundgaard. Toss a coin if you have a wish you'd like to come true.

Also in the area is **Kastellet** at Langelinie (✆ **33-11-22-33**), a pentagonal citadel, replete with moats, constructed by King Frederik III in the virtually impregnable style of the 1660s. The Citadel functioned as the capital's first line of defense from seagoing invasion until the 18th century. During the Nazi occupation of Copenhagen, the Germans made it their headquarters; today the Danish military occupies the buildings. Bus: 15, 26, 1A or anything to Østerport Station. Open 6am–sunset.

**Designmuseum Danmark** ★ MUSEUM One of Denmark's premier museums for the decorative and functional arts is set in a centuries-old former hospital building. You'll find the changing exhibitions to be well-marked in both Danish and English; alas, the permanent collection

### Literary Landmarks

Fans of **Hans Christian Andersen** may want to seek out the various addresses where he lived in Copenhagen, including Nyhavn 18, Nyhavn 20, and Nyhavn 67. He also lived for a time at Vingårdsstræde 6. He's buried at **Assistens Kirkegård,** where Søren Kierkegaard also lies in existential repose. Dating from 1711, and the largest burial ground in Copenhagen, this land is also a public park.

Frederikskirke.

is less thoroughly explained. A few items are worth a look, including Thorvald Bindesbøll's original Carlsberg label, still stuck to an antique bottle; and some lumpy, childish Gauguin ceramics that seem to justify his success in an entirely different artistic area.

Bredgade 68. www.designmuseum.dk. ✆ **33-18-56-56.** Adults DKK 90, seniors DKK 60, students and ages 25 and under free. Bus 1A. Tues, Thurs–Sun 11am–5pm, Weds 11am–9pm.

**Frederikskirke (Marble Church)** ★ RELIGIOUS SITE This landmark church is more richly decorated and impressive than Copenhagen's cathedral, Vor Frue Kirke. Lying just a short walk from Amalienborg Palace, it began construction in 1749, but because the treasury dried up in 1770, work didn't resume until late in the 19th century. The original design was for neoclassical revival, but in the end the church was constructed in the Roman baroque style, opening in 1894. Inspired by Michelangelo's dome for St. Peter's in Rome, the Danish church was crowned with a copper dome, measuring 46m (151 ft.) high, making it one of the largest in the world.

Frederiksgade 4. www.marmorkirken.dk. ✆ **33-15-01-44.** Free; tower tours DKK 25 adults, DKK 10 children. Bus: 15, 26, or 1A. Church Mon–Thurs 10am–5pm; Fri–Sun noon–5pm. Dome June 15–Aug daily 1 and 3pm.

## ROSENBORG CASTLE, THE BOTANICAL GARDENS & ENVIRONS

**Botanisk Have (Botanical Gardens)** ★ PARK/GARDEN Planted from 1871 to 1874, these botanical gardens are on a lake that was once part of the city's defensive moat around Rosenborg Slot, which fronts the gardens. Greenhouses grow both tropical and subtropical plants, none finer than the **Palm House,** an exotic apparition this far north. An alpine garden contains mountain plants from all over the world.

Gothersgade 130. www.botanic-garden.ku.dk. ✆ **35-32-22-22.** S-tog: Nørreport. Bus: 40, 42, 43, 14, 5A, 6A. Daily May–Sept 8:30am–6pm; Oct–Apr 8:30am–4pm.

**Rosenborg Slot (Rosenborg Castle) ★★★** LANDMARK With a facade that hasn't changed since 1633, the Rosenborg is the purest Renaissance structure in Denmark, and has survived both fire and war. Christian IV conceived of the palace in 1606, but it began with **Kongens Have,** the King's Garden, which still surrounds the palace today. The king liked the place so much that he built a summer pavilion here, which led to the creation of this monumental red-brick *slot,* which houses everything from narwhal-tusked and ivory coronation chairs to Frederik VII's baby shoes. Its biggest draws are the dazzling **crown jewels and regalia,** in the Treasury. Try to see the **Knights Hall** in Room 21, with its coronation seat, three silver lions, and relics from the 1700s. Room 3 was used by founding father Christian IV, who died in this bedroom.

Øster Voldgade 4A. www.rosenborgslot.dk. ✆ **33-15-32-86.** DKK 90 adults, DKK 60 students; 17 and under free. Bus: Anything to Nørreport station. Jun–Aug daily 10am–5pm; Sept–Oct, May 10am–4pm; Nov–Dec 21, Jan 2–Apr Tues–Sun 10am–4pm.

**Statens Museum for Kunst (National Gallery of Denmark) ★** MUSEUM Also known as SMK, the National Gallery is the country's most important repository for artwork, and its wide umbrella covers everything from the Middle Ages to today. If you're going chronologically, start upstairs, where the entire floor is given over to European work, mostly paintings—the Dutch and their light, the French and their fruit, the Danes and their old women. Although much of the collection outside of the Danish stuff is of a lesser quality (though you *will* find some Rubens, Titians, and Rembrandts), it's still worth seeing. Particularly striking are *The Judgement of Solomon,* depicting a soldier holding a baby by its ankle and on the cusp of cleaving him in two with a sword; and Joakim Skovaard's skin-crawling *Christ in the Realm of Dead,* depicting Jesus

Rosenborg Slot.

more or less ministering to a horde of zombies. The entire back half of the museum, in a huge modern glass pavilion, is for contemporary art.

Sølvgade 48-50. www.smk.dk. ✆ **33-74-84-94.** Free; special exibitions DKK 95 adults, DKK 75 seniors, DKK 65 students and those 24 and under. Bus: 26, 40, 43, 184,185, 6A, or 150S. Tues, Thurs–Sun 10am–5pm; Wed 10am–8pm.

## CHRISTIANSBORG PALACE & ENVIRONS

**Christiansborg Slot (Christiansborg Palace)** ★★★ LANDMARK

Christiansborg Castle has led a rough life ever since the founding father of Copenhagen, Bishop Absalon, completed the first castle here in 1167. That one burned down—and so did the next two. Rebuilt in 1732 and burned down again in 1794, what is left standing today is a granite-and-copper palace from 1928. It is in Slotsholmen, a small island in the center of Copenhagen that has been the seat of political power in Denmark for 800 years. Today it houses the Danish parliament, the Supreme Court, the prime minister's offices, and the Royal Reception Rooms. A guide will lead you through richly decorated rooms, including the Throne Room, Banqueting Hall, and the Queen's Library.

Under the palace, visit the well-preserved ruins of the 1167 castle of Bishop Absalon. Nearby, you can also see **Kongelige Stalde & Kareter,** the royal stables and coaches. Elegantly clad in riding breeches and jackets, riders exercise the royal horses. Vehicles include regal coaches and "fairy tale" carriages.

Christiansborg Slot. www.christiansborg.dk. ✆ **33-92-64-92.** Guided tour of Royal Reception Rooms DKK 80 adults, DKK 70 students, DKK 40 children 7–14; ruins DKK 50 adult, DKK 25 ($3/£2) students and children 7–14. Free admission to parliament.

**Christiansborg Slot.**

Dansk Jødisk Museum.

Metro: Kongens Nytorv or Nørreport. Bus: 1A, 2A, 26, 40, 66, or 350S. Daily 10am–5pm; closed Mon Oct–Apr; English guided tour daily 3pm.

**Dansk Jødisk Museum (Danish Jewish Museum)** ★ MUSEUM Daniel Libeskind designed this museum in a wing of the Royal Library, and his sloping walls and glass can feel as disorienting as a fun house. Alas, that's the museum's greatest distinction. A critical problem with this institution is that it doesn't really tell the story of the Jews in Denmark. There were never very many, and the museum admits that the Jews who did live here didn't get along; they argued so long about how to rebuild a synagogue that for decades, nothing got constructed. Instead, many of the exhibits are devoted to the general practices of Judaism. The real story that most outsiders want to learn about the Danish Jews—how so many of them were miraculously protected from the Nazis through special laws and then ushered to safety in Sweden—is only given two paltry display windows that don't go into much depth.
Proviantpassagen 6. www.jewmus.dk. ✆ **33-11-22-18.** DKK 50 adults, DKK 40 students, free for children 17 and under. Bus: 15, 26, 29, 40, 66, 1A, or 2A. June–Aug Tues–Sun 10am–5pm; Sept–May Tues–Fri 1–4pm, Sat, Sun noon–5pm.

**Holmens Kirke** ★ RELIGIOUS SITE This royal chapel and naval church lies across the canal from Slotsholmen, next to the National Bank of Denmark. Although the structure was converted into a church for the

Royal Navy in 1619, its nave was built in 1562 as an anchor forge. By 1641, the ever-changing church was renovated to its current, predominantly Dutch Renaissance style. Inside, the extraordinary feature of this church is its ostentatious **baroque altar** of unpainted oak, a carved pulpit that extends right to the roof. In the burial chamber are the tombs of Denmark's most towering naval figures, including Admiral Niels Juel, who successfully fought off a naval attack by Swedes in 1677 in the Battle of Køge Bay. Peder Tordenskjold, who defeated Charles XII of Sweden during the Great Northern War in the early 1700s, is also entombed here.

Holmens Kanal 21. www.holmenskirke.dk. ✆ **33-13-61-78.** Bus: 15, 26, 29, 1A, 11A, or 350S. Mon, Wed, Fri, Sat 10am–4pm; Tues and Thurs Sat 10am–3:30pm

**Kongelige Bibliotek (Royal Library)** ★ LIBRARY/UNIVERSITY The Danish Royal Library, dating from the 1600s and done in the Classical style, is the largest and most impressive in the Norse countries. The library owns original manuscripts by such Danish writers as H. C. Andersen and Karen Blixen (Isak Dinesen). In 1998, a gargantuan and sharply angular granite annex, the Black Diamond, extended the antique structure over the waterfront traffic artery, expanding it in a dazzling study in architectural contrasts. After viewing the interiors of the high-ceilinged library, you can wander through its formal gardens.

Søren Kierkegaard Plads 1. www.kb.dk. ✆ **33-47-47-47.** Bus: 66; harbor bus: 901 or 902. Mon–Fri 9am–9pm, Sat 10am–5pm.

**Nationalmuseet (National Museum)** ★★★ MUSEUM The Nationalmuseet looks and feels like a rambling palace because it has royal origins; it began as Frederik II's "Royal Chamber of Curiosities" in 1650. That collection grew until it became Denmark's top repository of artifacts. Wander a while—and you will wander, because the layout, like

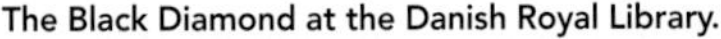
The Black Diamond at the Danish Royal Library.

a multi-level figure eight, can be confusing—and you'll find a few palatial rooms and a lot more random booty that's immensely fascinating. One case contains a tangle of *lur* horns, twisty-necked Bronze Age instruments that can still make music despite the fact they're now 2,500 years old (no, you may not try). Another contains the world-famous *Sun Chariot,* a gorgeous Bronze Age piece that was probably made around 1200 B.C. and was rediscovered by a Zealand farmer as he plowed in 1902.

The museum is subdivided into five areas, beginning with the Prehistoric Wing on street level. In the Runic Stone Hall, don't miss the **Hjortespring Boat,** a plank-built vessel made around 300 B.C. and unearthed not too long ago in a stunning discovery. The **Stone Age** gallery is a must for its spectacular collection of **oak coffins** which were generally preserved in bogs; the bones found within some, plus the clothes and hair of the people they belonged to, are still lying in state for you to behold.

The second floor is the place to be if your goal is to learn about Danish life. Displays take you back in time (things get more interesting the further back you go) and you learn about how Denmark's social support system was created, its reform movements, and the country's shift from an absolute monarchy to a democracy. Not all of the artifacts are very special, but you will see the head of the axe that probably lopped off the head of reformist Johann Friederich Struensee in 1772; he was executed for being too liberal. How times have changed in Denmark! In the same area, you can find a terrific collection of **Doll's Houses.** And if you're searching for that prototypically Viking sight of an animal horn turned into a drinking vessel, you won't come away disappointed. There's a bunch.

The **Peoples of the World** ethnographical collection is one of the oldest in the world, with artifacts ranging from Papua New Guinea to Central America. The **Childrensmuseum,** on the ground floor to the left, contains such novel hands-on features as a *faering* boat with a sail kids can sit in.

Ny Vestergade 10. www.natmus.dk. ✆ **33-13-44-11.** Free. Bus: 14, 15, 26, 29, 40, 1A, 2A, or 11A. Tues–Sun 10am–5pm.

## CHRISTIANSHAVN

**Vor Frelsers Kirken (Our Saviour's Church)** ★★ RELIGIOUS SITE The green-and-gold, spiral-topped tower of this Gothic structure is a Copenhagen landmark, dominating the Christianshavn area. Inside, view an elaborate organ from 1698 and the splendid baroque altar, richly adorned with a romp of cherubs and other figures. The carillon sounds out on Saturdays at 4pm.

Four hundred vertigo-inducing steps, many of them clambering up wooden ladders in the belfry, will take you to the top of the unique spindled tower. You won't be in a good position to see the spectacular gilded figure of Christ standing on a globe—that's better seen from points away from the building—but you will soak up a **panoramic view** of the city. ***Warning:*** Those steps grow narrower as they reach the pinnacle. In fact, you won't be able to officially summit the structure; the path dwindles into a point, like the Yellow Brick Road, while climbers nervously try to turn around and pass each other in a 2-foot-wide space. You may feel as if you're about to make your own plummet from the spire, because it's made of oak that shimmies uncomfortably in stiff winds. It's great fun—and you'll come away feeling like you conquered some fears.

Skt. Annægade 29. www.vorfrelserskirke.dk. ✆ **32-54-68-83.** Sanctuary admission free; tower DKK 40 adults, DKK 30 students/seniors, DKK 10 children 4–14. Bus: 40. 66, 2A, 350S, or anything to Christianshavn Station. Church 11am–5:30pm; Tower Apr to mid-Dec Mon–Sat 10am–4pm, Sun 10:30am–4pm; Tower open until 7pm mid-June to mid-Sept.

## IN & AROUND THE TIVOLI GARDENS

**Danish Design Centre** ★ GALLERY Architect Henning Larsen designed this five-story center, which hides behind a smoked-glass exterior. This is the best place for not only looking at the work of classic Danish designers, but seeing the best young innovators as well.

27 H. C. Andersens Blvd. www.ddc.dk. ✆ **33-69-33-69.** DKK 55 adults, DKK 30 seniors, students, and children 12–18; 11 and under free. Bus: 12, 14, 15, 26, 29, 33, 40, 1A, 2A, or 11A. Mon–Fri 9am–5pm.

**Københavns Museum (Museum of Copenhagen)** ★★ MUSEUM The essential function of the museum is to give a nuanced and yes, somewhat liberalized look at the city's history, so much of the ground floor is dedicated to showing what life in Copenhagen has been like for a range of citizens, from the century-old door of a Jewish tailor to a satellite dish that marks the home of many Asian immigrants. That's interesting, and it will re-shape your preconceived notions of all Danes as slender, blue-eyed blondes, but the real treasure trove is upstairs, under

### CHRISTIANIA: a free city

For an offbeat adventure—though maybe not the safest place at night—you can head for the commune of **Christiania,** a few blocks to the east of Vor Frelsers Kirken. This area once housed Danish soldiers in barracks. When the soldiers moved out, the free spirits of Copenhagen moved in, occupying the little village, even though—technically speaking—they are squatters and in violation of the law. They declared the area a "free city" on September 24, 1971. Copenhagen authorities have not moved in to oust them in all this time, fearing a full-scale riot. The area is a refuge for petty criminals and drug dealers. But there has been success in the community as well, evoking the communes of the 1960s. For example, the villagers have helped hundreds of addicts kick heroin habits. Adventurous visitors enter Christiania to eat at one of the neighborhood's little restaurants, many of which are surprisingly good. Prices here are the cheapest in Copenhagen, because the restaurant managers refuse to pay taxes.

the chandeliers of a former ballroom. There, arranged artfully in a circle of glass cabinets, are relics from one of the city's favorite sons, philosopher Søren Kierkegaard. Each case is themed to a turning point in the writer's life—a five-diamond ring a girlfriend returned to him when they broke up, a lock of his hair taken on his deathbed, his quill, his original gravestone plaque (which broke; the one in Assistens cemetery now is from 1927). On the opposite side of each case, past museum visitors have donated a token that reflects a similar period in their own lives (for example, someone's first apartment key as demonstration of Love of Self), and push-button displays in both Danish and English explain the connection. It's a smart way to bring the eternal tenets of a 19th-century philosopher to life.

Vesterbrogade 59. www.copenhagen.dk/en. ✆ **33-21-07-72.** Adult DKK 40, senior DKK 20, under 18 free; free on Fridays. Bus 26, 6A. Daily 10am–5pm.

**Rådhus (Town Hall) and World Clock ★** LANDMARK Built in 1905, the town hall has impressive statues of Hans Christian Andersen and Niels Bohr, the Nobel Prize–winning physicist. Jens Olsen's **World Clock** is open for viewing Monday to Friday 11am to 2pm and Saturday at noon. Frederik IX set the clock on December 15, 1955. The clock is so exact that it's accurate to within half a second every 300 years. Climb the tower for an impressive view—but its 300 steps are not for the faint of heart.

Rådhus. www.kk.dk. ✆ **33-66-25-82.** World Clock 10DKK adults, 5DKK children; Tower 20DKK. Bus: 10, 12, 14, 26, 29, 40, 2A, 5A, or 6A. Mon–Fri 8:30am–4:30pm, Sat 10am–1pm. Call for tour information.

**Tivoli Gardens ★★★** THEME PARK Created in 1843, Tivoli Gardens occupies an 8-hectare (20-acre) site in the center of Copenhagen.

Tivoli Gardens.

Its greatest admirers call it a pleasure park or flower garden; its critics suggesting that it's one giant beer garden. Michael Jackson tried to buy the complex but was turned down, as were Disney execs. The Tivoli is the virtual symbol of Denmark, and no Dane wants to see it go to foreigners.

Let's face it: The Tivoli is filled with schmaltz, but somehow with its glitz, glamour, and gaiety it manages to win over hardened cynics. Children prefer it during the day, but adults tend to like it better at night, when more than 100,000 specially made soft-glow light bulbs and at least a million regular bulbs are turned on—what an electric bill!

It features thousands of flowers, a merry-go-round of tiny Viking ships, games of chance and skill (pinball arcades, slot machines, shooting galleries), and a Ferris wheel of hot-air balloons and cabin seats. The latest attraction at Tivoli, "The Demon," is the biggest roller coaster in Denmark. Passengers whiz through three loops on the thrill ride, reaching a top speed of 80kmph (50 mph). There's also a playground for children.

An Arabian-style fantasy palace, with towers and arches, houses more than two dozen expensive restaurants, from a lakeside inn to a beer garden. The oldest building at Tivoli, the Chinese-style Pantomime Theater, with its peacock curtain, offers pantomimes in the evening.

Vesterbrogade 3. www.tivoli.dk. ✆ **33-15-10-01.** DKK 99 adults, free for children under 7; combination ticket including admission and all rides DKK 209–DKK 479 adults, DKK 329 children under 7. Bus: 1, 16, or 29. Apr 1–Sept 20; Oct 9–Nov 1; Nov 14–Jan 3. Sun–Thurs 11am–11pm; Fri–Sat, 11am–midnight.

## INDRE-BY (OLD TOWN)

**Rundetårn (Round Tower)** ★ LANDMARK For a panoramic view of the city of Copenhagen, climb the spiral ramp (no steps) leading up to the top of this tower, which was built in 1642. The walk to the top is unique in European architecture, measuring 268m (880 ft.) and winding itself seven times around the hollow core of the tower, forming the only link between the individual parts of the building complex. Rundetårn is also the oldest functioning observatory in Europe; now anyone can observe the night sky through the astronomical telescope.

Købmagergade 52A. www.rundetaarn.dk. ✆ **33-73-03-73**. DKK 25 adults, DKK 5 children 5–15. Bus: 14, 5A, 6A, 11A, 350S, or anything to Nørreport Station.

**The Rundetårn.**

May 21–Sept 20 10am–8pm; Sept 21–May 20 10am–6pm. Mid-Oct to mid-March Tues–Wed 10am–9pm.

**Vor Frue Kirke (Copenhagen Cathedral)** ★ RELIGIOUS SITE This Greek Revival–style church features Bertel Thorvaldsen's white marble neoclassical works, including *Christ and the Apostles*. The funeral of H. C. Andersen took place here in 1875, and that of Søren Kierkegaard in 1855. The interior is a thing of austere beauty. To boot, the surrounding square, Vor Frue Plads, harbors the University of Copenhagen (founded 1479) and is easily one of the most well-preserved and beautiful squares in the Old Town.

Nørregade 8. www.domkirken.dk. ✆ **33-37-65-40.** Free. Bus: 14 or 11A. Mon–Fri 8am–5pm.

## Organized Tours

To see the city the way locals do, head to **Cycling Copenhagen** ★★★ (Westend 4, 1661; www.cycling-copenhagen.dk; ✆ **21-76-28-29;** 3-hr. tours including helmet and bike rental; DKK 299). Their top-of-the-line bikes are sturdy and smooth, and you won't be led into a terrifying river of aggressive commuters—you're guided (often by English-speaking owner Christian) through side streets and along bike-only greenway paths through the scenic parts of town. The most popular tour is the 3-hour "Must See," which scoots past the major monuments, but there are three others, including an evening version.

## Especially for Kids

Copenhagen is a wonderful place for children, and many so-called adult attractions also appeal to kids. **Tivoli** is an obvious choice, as is the statue of ***Den Lille Havfrue (The Little Mermaid).*** Try to see the changing of the Queen's Royal Life Guard at **Amalienborg Palace,** including the entire parade to and from the royal residence. Kids also enjoy **Frilandsmuseet** (natmus.dk/museerne/frilandsmuseet), the open-air museum. The **Zoologisk Have/Copenhagen Zoo** (www.zoo.dk) in Frederiksberg, west of the center of Copenhagen, is home to 3,300 animals and 264 species.

## Where to Stay

Copenhagen's historic center is compact and walkable. Here, we concentrate our accommodations picks in the Indre-By (Old Town), trending Kongens Nytorv/Nyhavn and the hotel-packed area around Tivoli Gardens. Most are within easy walking distance of the major attractions.

High season in Denmark is May to September, which pretty much coincides with the schedule at Tivoli Gardens. Once Tivoli closes for the winter, lots of rooms become available. Make sure to ask if breakfast is included (usually it isn't).

## INDRE-BY/OLD TOWN

### Expensive

**Hotel Kong Arthur ★★** Founded in the 1970s by Arthur Frommer (creator of the Frommer guides), the hotel shifted owners in the 1980s and absorbed additional buildings. But the new owners insisted that the name "King Arthur" (in Danish) remain. (At Frommer's, Arthur will always be king.) Amiably informal, it's ideally situated along the east side of Peblinge Lake, a 10-minute walk to pretty much everything in the city. Ceilings are high, walls and linens are soothingly white. Rooms are comfortable, larger than the city norm, and adequate in every way. Noise is a downside, both in the hallways and from the courtyard, but it's manageable. Wi-Fi is free, and there's even an on-premises spa, unusual in these parts. It's also a carbon-neutral property, if that helps sway you.

Nørre Søgade 11, 1370. www.kongarthur.dk. ✆ **33-11-12-12.** Doubles DKK. Metro: Nørreport. Bus: 5A, 350S, 14, 40. **Amenities:** Restaurant; bar; sauna; car rental; room service; massage; babysitting; laundry service; dry cleaning; free Wi-Fi.

### Moderate

**Ibsens Hotel ★** Although it dates from 1906, this excellent, moderately priced property keeps current by embracing the middle-class bohemianism of the surrounding Nansensgade neighborhood. It's evident the second you step into the lobby, which doubles as the breakfast room and is cozy enough to seduce folks into hanging during the day. Rooms are cozy, too (high-floor rooms have sloped ceilings or rafters). You could say they're comfy in that European way—nothing flashy, but executed with style. Most overlook a quiet street, although some have views of a courtyard. The breakfast buffet is abundant but expensive.

Vendersgade 23. www.ibsenshotel.dk. ✆ **33-13-19-13.** Doubles DKK 900. Metro: Nørreport. Bus: 14, 40, 42, 43, 5A, or 350S. **Amenities:** 2 restaurants; bar; car rentals; babysitting; laundry service; free Wi-Fi.

## KONGENS NYTORV/NYHAVN

### Expensive

**Hotel d'Angleterre ★★★** Although the Hotel d'Angleterre is well into its third century, with all the rich stories and long heritage to accompany such a *grande dame* hotel, the interior is still young and fresh, so those seeking luxury will be well served. This is the upper class escape—fresh flowers, gourmet restaurant, and fawning staff downstairs; soft towels, quilted bedspreads, marbled bathrooms upstairs. One gently African-themed suite is named for Isak Dinesen (Karen Blixen), who stayed here. Another is named for Hans Christian Andersen, who also stayed here—you get the picture. The location on the central Kongens Nytorv puts you within a few minutes' walk of just about everything, but

The Hotel d'Angleterre.

bear in mind that the square will be torn up for Metro construction until 2018.

Kongens Nytorv 34. www.dangleterre.dk. ✆ **33-12-00-95.** Doubles DKK 3,060–DKK 4,300, suites from DKK 5,530. Bus: 15, 25, 1A, 11A, or 350S. **Amenities:** Restaurant; bar; indoor heated pool; gym; spa; sauna; babysitting; laundry service; free Wi-Fi.

### Inexpensive

**Wakeup Copenhagen, Borgergade ★★** You'll get a rack and hangers instead of a wardrobe. The bathroom is a unit slotted into a corner of the room (glass is frosted but not opaque, so platonic couples beware). The shower is in a clear plastic cylinder that'll have you wondering when Scotty is gonna beam you up. But we promise you the rooms, though a small 12 to 15 sq. m (129–161 sq. ft.), are crisp and well-designed. And you'll find that, in a town of pricey hotels, yours has everything you need to be happy. Rooms have air-conditioning, flatscreen TVs, a small desk made of a half-moon of glass, and there's free Wi-Fi. "Standard" rooms are the cheapest and are on lower floors and face the back. The best double rooms, "Heaven," are on the top floors and aren't much bigger than three double mattresses (they also come in "Large," with pull-out beds that fit three). There's another location east and south of the central station, but this one is better-located for the major sights.

Borgergade 9. www.wakeupcopenhagen.com. ✆ **44-80-00-00.** Doubles DKK 700–DKK 900. **Amenities:** Free Wi-Fi.

## TIVOLI GARDENS

### Expensive

**Hotel SP34 ★★★** For its impeccable design (every octagonal Swedish lamp and sled-like scoop headboard is available for purchase) and ideal location amid the nightspots of the Latin Quarter, this 2014 newcomer was an instant smash. The check-in desk doubles as a bar where you can order a draft beer or something from the owner's own wine cellar—which says a lot about the casual-chic clientele the SP34 is shooting for. The hotel interiors (concrete floors, filament bulbs, corridors with a carefully unfinished look) satisfy a yearning for Danish design. Rooms in the front have luxuriously large windows, but they face a street with bars; things are quiet when the windows are closed, but if you want them open, get a room in the rear of the building. Nearly all of the breakfast ingredients are organic, and later in the day, you can choose from a tapas bistro (Bar Moritz) and a casual cocktails-and-burger mashup (Cocks & Cows).

Skt. Pederstræde 34. www.brochner-hotels.dk. ✆ **33-95-77-00.** Doubles DKK 1300, suites from DKK 3500, rates include breakfast. **Amenities:** 2 restaurants; bar; roof terrace; free Wi-Fi.

### Moderate

**Andersen Hotel ★★★** This old five-story hotel building has undergone a funky refresh, and now it's a highly recommended boutique lodging very close to Tivoli and other principal sites. The staff is friendly and helpful, and every afternoon there's a free wine hour in the lobby, where you also get the breakfast buffet (80% organic). Bathrooms are also surprisingly lush, with heated floors, Molton Brown toiletries, and unsparing tile and marbling. Rooms don't have phones, but they're otherwise happily equipped, and even the small rooms have plenty of space compared to the European standard. And here's a handy twist: The hotel says you may stay for 24 hours from whenever you check in. Arrive at 5pm? You don't have to leave until then. Ask for "Concept24" when you book to get that; there's no extra charge, but you do have to reserve it.

Helgolandsgade 12. www.andersen-hotel.dk. ✆ **33-31 46-10.** Doubles DKK 850–DKK 1,145, includes breakfast. Metro: Central Station. Bus: 6A, 26. **Amenities:** Bar; flexible check-out; bike rentals; free Wi-Fi.

**Imperial Hotel ★** Its borderline-bleak black exterior, which seems more appropriate to an office building, is misleading. Inside is a perfectly comfortable, if predictable, hotel whose bones have just a touch of '60s Danish design. Rooms have big windows, good-size writing desks, couches, ample space, and all the usual amenities you'd expect of a respectable hotel that, it must be said, is popular with group tours. The breakfast feels a bit like a tourist-feeding machine, and the lifts are sometimes inadequate for the job of carrying all its guests. But in 5 minutes, you can walk to Tivoli or Rådhuspladsen. Overall, it's not a bad place to stay if you don't expect personalized service.

Vester Farimagsgade 9. www.imperialhotel.dk. ✆ **33-12-80-00.** Doubles DKK 900–1100. Metro: Vesterport. Bus: 9A, 12, 14, 26. **Amenities:** Restaurant; bar; room service; bike and car rental; free Wi-Fi.

## Where to Eat

It's estimated that Copenhagen has more than 2,000 cafes, snack bars, and restaurants, and a high concentration of Michelin-starred restaurants (10 with at least one star), in an area measuring 4 sq. km (about 1½ sq. miles) on each side. The most convenient restaurants are in Tivoli Gardens, around Rådhuspladsen (Town Hall Square), around the Central Railway Station, and in Nyhavn. Others are in the shopping district, on streets off Strøget. Note that you'll pay for the privilege of dining in Tivoli; prices are always higher. Park restaurants are open only May to mid-September.

Reservations are not usually important, but it's best to call in advance. Nearly everyone who answers the phone at restaurants speaks English.

### INDRE-BY-OLD TOWN

#### Expensive

**Restaurant Uformel** ★★★ NORDIC Uformel, a spinoff of Michelin-starred Formel B, is under the command of young chef Frederik Rudkjøbing, and his vitality informs the experience here. Some of the flavors are a bit more adventurous than what most people might normally order—veal sweetbreads won't be for everyone—but there are plenty of

### quick bites IN COPENHAGEN

Copenhagen has many hot dog stands, chicken and fish grills, and *smørrebrød* counters that serve good, fast, inexpensive meals.

**Hot dog stands,** especially those around Rådhuspladsen, offer *polser* (steamed or grilled hot dogs) with shredded onions on top and *pommes frites* (French fries).

***Bageri or konditori* (bakery),** found on almost every block, sell fresh bread, rolls, and Danish pastries.

***Viktualiehandler*** (small food shops), found throughout the city, are the closest thing to a New York deli. The best buy is smoked fish. Ask for a Bornholmer, a large, boneless sardine from the Danish island of Bornholm, or for *røgost*, a popular and inexpensive smoked cheese.

You can picnic in any of the city parks in the town center. Try Kongsgarten near Kongens Nytorv; the Kastellet area near *Den Lille Havfrue*; Botanisk Have (site of the Botanical Gardens); the lakeside promenades in southeastern Copenhagen; and the old moat at Christianshavn. Remember not to litter!

more accessible gourmet choices to please those who aren't so daring, including, at times, ceviche, steak tartare, monkfish, teriyaki Danish duck, and fresh oysters from nearby waters. The browned butter ice cream with crunchy hazelnut is a particular treat.

Studiestræde 69. www.uformel.dk. ✆ **70-99-91-11.** Mains DKK 100, 4-course menu with wine DKK 750. Metro: Vesterport. Mon–Thurs noon–2pm, 5:30pm–midnight (Fri until 2am), Sat–Sun 5:30pm–2am.

### Inexpensive

**Ida Davidsen ★★** NORDIC The Davidsen family has served *smørrebrød* to the hungry of Copenhagen since 1888, and the cook from the current generation, Ida Davidsen, has cannily found ways to set her *smørrebrød* palace apart from others. For one, it's more casual than the stuffier specialists elsewhere, adorned with simple black wood chairs and ink cartoons on the walls, rather than white tablecloths and antique paintings. (The prices, alas, are just as high as the other *smørrebrød* landmarks.) But the real point of difference is the massive lunch-only menu—nearly 180 varieties of sandwiches, making it, Davidsen brags, "more than 140 centimeters long" (4 ft. 7 in.).

Store Kongensgade 70. www.idadavidsen.dk. ✆ **33-91-36-55.** Mains DKK 80–DKK 160. Mon–Fri 10:30am–5pm; last order at 4pm.

**Restaurant Kronborg ★★** NORDIC Named for Hamlet's castle in Elsinore, Kronborg is a modern *smørrebrød* luncheon cellar cast from a traditional mold: a low, bang-your-head doorway, beamed ceilings, tightly packed tables, and, in good weather, outdoor seating. Tucked on a side street off pedestrian Strøget, it's all soothingly conducive to conversation and upscale lunching. Ingredients are fresh, the kitchen blends its own list of distinctive aquavit (in flavors as curious as dill and beech), and the desserts are gorgeously piled high. Menus are available in English. Make a reservation by e-mail (reservation@restaurantkronborg.dk) or you're likely to be declined, because the Danes take their *smørrebrød* seriously.

Brolæggerstræde 12. www.restaurantkronborg.dk. ✆ **33-13-07-08.** Mains DKK 65–DKK 75. Bus: 11A. Mon–Sat 11am–5pm.

**Restaurant Schønnemann ★★★** NORDIC There may be no more iconic choice for *smørrebrød* in Copenhagen. Since 1877, this cellar-level spot has served up the classic Danish dish in a classy setting—green walls with gold-framed paintings, tablecloths, friendly waiters in neckties, sand sprinkled on the floorboards to keep them polished—earning it a beloved station in the minds of city lunchers. Although the recipes are classic to the core, the gastronomy meets modern demands for quality ingredients: the kitchen matures its own herring, the smoked eel comes on a bed of warm scrambled eggs, the calf liver is organic, and the rye bread is baked in-house. Pair your authentic meal with one of more than 130 types of aquavit. Reservations required!

*Hauser* Plads 16-18. www.restaurantschonnemann.dk. ✆ **33-12-07-85.** Most mains DKK 100–DKK 160. Metro: Norreport. Mon–Sat 11:30am–5pm (kitchen closes 3:30pm).



## KONGENS NYTORV & NYHAVN

### Moderate

**Cap Horn** ★ INTERNATIONAL Pretty much everyone who lays eyes on the pretty finger wharf of Nyhavn, lined with masted ships and sidewalk cafes, wants to dine there. And pretty much every one of those cafes is a tourist trap. Cap Horn is the exception, and it also serves food later than most of its competitors. The dark, wooden interior is authentically old, but if you can, opt to sit outside on the water. The menu ranges from hamburgers to pasta to venison—think of an upscale version of a diner menu, but with organic ingredients and perfectly cooked meats. Though nothing qualifies as truly gourmet, everything is reliable. If you want to eat along Nyhavn, this is the place.

Nyhavn 21. www.caphorn.dk. ✆ **33-12-85-04.** Mains DKK 140–DKK 200. Bus: 15, 26, 29, 1A, 11A, or 350S. Daily 10am–midnight.

## CHRISTIANSHAVN

### Expensive

**No. 2** ★★★ NORDIC This scion of acclaimed Copenhagen restaurant AOC is exceptionally delicious, and makes for one of the best

## IN PRAISE OF THE smørrebrød

The favorite Danish dish at midday is the ubiquitous *smørrebrød* (open-faced sandwich)—a national institution. Literally, this means "bread and butter," but the Danes stack this sandwich as if it were the Leaning Tower of Pisa—and then throw in a slice of curled cucumber and bits of parsley, or perhaps sliced peaches or a mushroom for added color.

Though *smørrebrød* is often served as an hors d'oeuvre, two of these sandwiches can make a more-than-filling lunch. They're everywhere—from the grandest dining rooms to the lowliest pushcart. Many restaurants offer a wide selection; guests look over a checklist and then mark the ones they want. Some are made with sliced pork (perhaps a prune on top), roast beef with béarnaise sauce and crispy fried bits of onion, or liver pâté adorned with an olive or cucumber slice and gelatin made with strong beef stock. The "ugly duckling" of the *smørrebrød* family is anything with a cold sunny-side-up egg on top of it.

*Smørrebrød,* **a Copenhagen specialty.**

choices for those who want an authentically Nordic meal in a refined setting. The flavors are spectacular, and there's always an interesting point of provenance to what you're eating: shaved ham from the isle of Fanø, cod pulled from the North Sea outside the windows, nuts flavored with gunpowder. Cocktails, too, are assembled by picky foodies with adventurous ideas, and the wine list is among the top in town. The dining room, a plate-glass box overlooking the water, was designed by longtime Danish style leader Gubi and epitomizes the crisp look of the Danish school—scoop chairs, charcoal greys, plank floor simplicity. It makes for a memorable and distinctly modern Danish meal.

Nicolai Eigtvedsgade 32, Hammershøi Kaj. www.nummer2.dk. ✆ **33-11-11-68.** Mains DKK 85–145; 6-course menu DKK 450. Metro: Christianshavn, Harbour Bus 991, 992. Mon–Fri noon–2pm, Mon–Sat 5:30pm–10pm.

**Noma ★★★** NORDIC Noma, which is short for *nordatlantisk mad,* or North Atlantic cuisine, is routinely voted one of the best restaurants in the world—that's with good reason, and that's a good warning. If you don't make a reservation at least two months ahead, you won't be finding out why. Chef Rene Redzepi starts by importing seafood a few times a week from Greenland, Iceland, the Faroe Islands, and other Nordic locales. He then takes his carefully sourced ingredients and concocts plated artworks. The dazzling result is about a dozen small-plate courses and as many as nine *amuse-bouches,* in parry after parry of novel gastronomy. A "leather" made from sea buckthorn. Pickled rose hips. Radish and asparagus sprouting from malt "soil." Reindeer moss. And famously, honest-to-goodness live ants that are meant to be scooped up and eaten with sour cream and rye bread. Every flavor is a surprise, and by the end, you feel like part of the magic, even if you've had to kill one or two ingredients to get them down. This is a place people book plane tickets for once they snare a reservation.

Strandgade 93. www.noma.dk. ✆ **32-96-32-97.** Set menu of 20 courses DKK 1,600. Bus: 66. Tues–Sat noon–4pm, 7pm–12:30am.

## CHRISTIANSBORG PALACE

### Expensive

**Restaurant Tårnet ★★★** NORDIC It's a dramatic and luxurious way to experience the city: dining two-thirds of the way up the tower that soars above Christiansborg Palace. Until 2014, this huge aerie was just a neglected workshop space, and its look nods to that—surveying diners are colossal plaster models of exterior statuary, plus two monumental stone lions of uncertain provenance. Of more definite origin are the ingredients, which all come from Denmark or very nearby—sirloin steak, sea buckthorn, langoustine, and more. The huge window surveys the royal Riding Ground and the roofs of Copenhagen beyond. With only about 100 diners per night, this is a hard-to-get reservation, so book ahead. It's worth it to experience modern Danish cuisine and that timeless skyline.

Christiansborg Slotsplads, 1218. www.taarnet.dk. ✆ **33-37-31-00.** Mains from DKK 95 (lunch), DKK 235 (dinner). Afternoon tea: 3 cakes with tea DKK 135. Tues–Sun 11:30am–4pm and 6–11pm.

### NEAR TIVOLI GARDENS

#### Moderate

**Øl & Brød ★★** NORDIC Usually, *smørrebrød* places lean toward the old-fashioned and conservative, but this one intentionally modernizes the decor and the local go-to food into something more gastronomic. Even the pickled herring and smoked eel are likely to interest those who normally steer away from the stuff. Booze is also part of the package—Øl & Brød pours intriguing homemade aquavits and will pair most courses with an ideal beer. Reservations are recommended, even for lunch.

Viktoriagade 6, 1655. www.ologbrod.dk. ✆ **33-31-44-22.** Lunch mains DKK 90–DKK 130. Dinner set menu from DKK 320. Bus: 6A, 26. Tues–Thurs and Sun 11:30am.

## Shopping

Copenhagen is in the vanguard of shopping in Europe, and much of the action takes place on **Strøget**, the pedestrian street in the heart of the capital. Strøget begins as Frederiksberggade, north of Rådhuspladsen, and winds to Østergade, which opens onto Kongens Nytorv. It's home to **Illums Bolighusv ★★★** (10, Amagertorv; www.illumsbolighus.com), a multi-level wonderland of cool stuff, from housewares to furniture to kid gear. Another department store, **Magasin du Nord ★★** (Kongens Nytorv 13; www.magasin.dk) on Kongens Nytorv, is in a grand, ancient palace, though its offerings are thoroughly modern.

In two nearby walking areas—**Gråbrødretorv** and **Fiolstræde**—you can browse through antiques shops. **Bredgade**, beginning at Kongens Nytorv, is the antiques district, where prices tend to be very high. The shopping street **Læderstræde** competes with Bredgade in antiques.

### Shipping It Home & Recovering VAT

Denmark imposes a 25% tax on goods and services, a "value-added tax" known in Denmark as **MOMS** (pronounced "mumps," and every bit as painful). Tax-free exports are possible. Many stores will mail goods to your home so you can avoid paying the tax. If you want to take your purchases, look for shops displaying Danish tax-free shopping notices. Such shops offer tourists tax refunds for personal export. This refund applies to purchases of over DKK 300 for visitors from the United States and Canada—spent at the same store, but not necessarily all at once. For answers to tax refund questions, call **Global Refund** (✆ **32-52-55-66**).

In a country famed for its designers and craftspeople, the best buys are in stainless steel, porcelain, china, glassware, toys, functionally designed furniture, textiles, and jewelry.

## Entertainment & Nightlife

Danes know how to party. A good night means a late night, and on warm weekends, hundreds of rowdy revelers crowd Strøget until sunrise. Merrymaking in Copenhagen is not just for the younger crowd; jazz clubs, traditional beer houses, and wine cellars are routinely packed with people of all ages. Of course, the city has a more highbrow cultural side as well, exemplified by excellent theaters, operas, ballets, and one of the best circuses in Europe.

To find out what's happening at the time of your visit, pick up a free copy of *Copenhagen This Week* at the tourist information center. For tickets to most of the musical, cultural, and sports-themed entertainment, use **Billetnet** (www.billetnet.dk; ✆ **70-15-65-65**).

Opened by Queen Margrethe, the 1,700-seat **Copenhagen Opera House** ★★★ (August Bournonvilles Passage 8; www.kglteater.dk) is the luxurious home of the world-renowned **Royal Danish Ballet** and **Royal Danish Opera.** Performances from these venerable troupes are major winter cultural events. Because the arts are state-subsidized in Denmark, ticket prices are comparatively low, and some seats may be available at the box office the day before a performance. The season runs August to June.

You don't have to go to clubs or attend cultural presentations to experience Copenhagen nightlife. Copenhagen's elegant spires and tangle of cobbled one-way streets are best viewed at night, when they take on the aura of the Hans Christian Andersen era. The old buildings have been well preserved, and at night they're floodlit. The city's network of drawbridges and small bridges is also particularly charming at night.

One of the best places for a walk is **Nyhavn** (New Harbor), which, until about 25 years ago, was the haunt of sailors and some of the roughest dives in Copenhagen. Today it has gone upmarket and is the site of numerous restaurants and bars. Another neighborhood that takes on special magic at night is **Christianshavn,** whose principal landmark is **Christiansborg Slot.** This neighborhood, which glows under the light of antique street lamps, is the closest Copenhagen comes to the charm of Paris's Left Bank.

# STOCKHOLM

Stockholm is the most regal, elegant, and intriguing city in Scandinavia, although don't tell our Danish and Norwegian friends that we said that. Presiding over a country the size of California (without the massive population), the city was founded more than seven centuries ago, though it didn't become the capital of Sweden until the mid-17th century. Today Stockholm reigns over one of the world's most progressive and democratic societies, an early adopter of same-sex unions and gender equality.

Because of Sweden's neutrality, Stockholm was saved from aerial bombardment during World War II, so much of what you see today is antique, especially the historical heart, Gamla Stan (the Old Town). Yet Sweden is one of the world's leading exponents of modern architecture, specifically *funkis* (functionalist) architecture and design, and you will find it here as well. Swedish fashion and Swedish design in glassware, furnishings, and industrial products remain at the cutting edge.

In our opinion, Stockholm also enjoys the most dramatic setting of any small capital in Europe. The city was built on 14 islands in Lake Mälaren, which marks the beginning of an archipelago of 24,000 islands, skerries, and islets stretching all the way to the Baltic Sea. A city of bridges and islands, cobblestone squares and broad boulevards, Renaissance splendor and steel-and-glass skyscrapers, Stockholm also has close access to nature. You can even go fishing in the downtown waterways, thanks to a long-standing decree signed by Queen Christina.

## Essentials

For help with trip planning, **www.visitstockholm.com** is the comprehensive website of the Stockholm Visitors Board.

**ARRIVING** If you're flying in, you'll arrive at **Stockholm Arlanda Airport** (www.arlanda.se; ✆ **08/797-60-00**), about 45km (28 miles) north

Stockholm's Gamla Stan.

of the city on the E-4 highway. The fastest, but not necessarily the cheapest, way to go from the airport to the Central Station within Stockholm is on the **Arlanda Express** train (www.arlandaexpress.com), which takes only 20 minutes and is covered by the Eurailpass. Trains run every 15 to 20 minutes daily from 5am to midnight. If you don't have a rail pass, the cost of a one-way ticket is 260 SEK for adults and 130 SEK for seniors and students 8 to 25 (those 7 and under ride free).

A slower (about 40 min.) but cheaper option involves taking a bus from outside the airport terminal building. It will take you to the **City Terminal** (www.flygbussarna.se), on Klarabergsviadukten, for 105 SEK.

A **taxi** to or from the airport is pricey, costing around 500 SEK or more.

**Trains** arrive at Stockholm's **Centralstationen** (**Central Station; © 07/717-57-575** in Sweden) on Vasagatan, in the city center where connections can be made to Stockholm's subway, the T-bana. Follow the tunnelbana sign, which is sometimes abbreviated to merely the capital letter "t" in blue ink on a white background, enclosed in a blue circle.

**Buses** also arrive at the Centralstationen, and from here you can catch the T-bana to your Stockholm destination. For bus information, check with the bus system's **ticket offices** at the station (www.flygbussarna.se; **© 08/588-228-28**). Offices in the station labeled bus stop sell bus tickets.

Parking a **car** in Stockholm is extremely difficult unless your hotel has a garage (most don't). If you're driving into the city, you can often park long enough to unload your luggage; a member of the hotel staff will then direct you to the nearest parking garage.

Large **ferries**, including those of the **Silja Line,** Sveavägen 14 (www.tallinksilja.com; **© 08/22-21-40**), and the **Viking Line,** Centralstationen (**© 08/452-40-00**), arrive near the junction of Södermalm and Gamla Stan. Holders of a valid Eurailpass can ride the Silja ferries to Helsinki and Turku at a reduced rate.

**CITY LAYOUT** As you'd expect of a city spread across 14 major islands in an archipelago, Stockholm has many neighborhoods, but those of concern to the ordinary visitor lie in central Stockholm.

**GETTING AROUND** With Stockholm's extensive **public transportation** network (www.sl.se/en), you can travel throughout Stockholm county by bus, local train, subway (T-bana), and tram, going from Singö in the north to Nynäshamn in the south. The routes are divided into zones, and one ticket is valid for all types of public transportation in the same zone within 1 hour of the time the ticket is stamped. **Tickets** can be purchased from the tollbooth on the subway platform, or from vending machines at most metro and commuter railway stations. Each ticket costs 36 SEK and allows travel to points within most of urban Stockholm.

Your best transportation bet is to purchase a tourist season ticket. A 1-day card costs 115 SEK for adults and 70 SEK for ages 7 to 20 and seniors and is valid for T-bana, buses, and commuter trains within Stockholm. A 3-day card costs SEK230 and SEK 140 for youths/seniors. Both cards are valid for travel on the Djurgården ferries between Slussen and Djurgården.

If you're **driving** around the Swedish capital, you'll find several parking garages in the city center as well as on the outskirts. In general, you can park at marked spaces Monday through Friday from 8am to 6pm. Exceptions or rules for specific areas are indicated on signs in the area.

**Taxis** are expensive—in fact, the most expensive in the world—with the meter starting at 45 SEK, with 10 SEK to 14 SEK for every kilometer, depending on the time of day. Those that display an illuminated dome light can be hailed directly on the street, or you can order one by phone. **Taxi Stockholm** (www.taxistockholm.se; ✆ **08/15-00-00**) is one of the city's larger, more reputable companies. More than any other nation in Scandinavia, in Sweden, it's best to inquire before you get in whether the taxi is metered or what the price will be.

## The Neighborhoods in Brief

**GAMLA STAN (OLD TOWN)** The "cradle" of Stockholm, Gamla Stan lies at the entrance to Lake Mälaren on the Baltic. Along with the excavated wreck of the Vasa, it's the most popular attraction in Stockholm. The buildings here are most evocative of 18th-century Stockholm, built in romantic architectural styles. Though it's our favorite neighborhood for dining and lodging, the downside is that there are few hotels, and they tend to be expensive. Gamla Stan's major shopping street is the narrow Västerlånggatan, and many artisans' galleries, souvenir shops, and antiques stores abound on its small lanes. Its main square, and the heart of the ancient city, is Stortorget.

**NORRMALM** North of Gamla Stan, what was once a city suburb is now the cultural and commercial heart of modern Stockholm. The area is generously endowed with hotels in all price ranges. This is also the most convenient location for most visits, as it encompasses the City Terminal and the Central Station.

The most famous park in Stockholm, **Kungsträdgården** (King's Garden), is in Norrmalm, which also embraces the important squares of Sergels Torg and Hötorget, the latter a modern shopping complex. Normalm's major pedestrian shopping street is Drottninggatan, which starts at the bridge to the Old Town.

**KUNGSHOLMEN** Once known as "Grey Friars Farm," Kungsholmen (King's Island), to the west of Gamla Stan, is the site of City Hall. One of its major arteries is Fleminggatan. Established by Charles XI in the

17th century as a zone for industry and artisans, the island is now gentrified with bars and restaurants.

**ÖSTERMALM** Set in central Stockholm, east of the main artery Birger Jarlsgatan, Östermalm is the site of the Army Museum. The area is home to one of the city's biggest parks, Humlegården, dating from the 17th century.

**DJURGÅRDEN** To the east of Gamla Stan (Old Town) is Djurgården (Deer Park), a forested island in a lake that's the summer recreation area of Stockholm. Here you can visit the open-air folk museums of Skansen, the *Vasa* man-of-war ship, Gröna Lund's Tivoli (Stockholm's own version of the Tivoli), the Waldemarsudde estate and gardens of the "painting prince" Eugen, and the Nordic Museum.

## Exploring Stockholm

Though Stockholm is an expensive city, it's loaded with free or bargain sights and activities. If the *Vasa* Ship Museum doesn't pique your interest (highly unlikely), perhaps the changing of the guard at the Royal Palace? Even window shopping for beautifully designed Swedish crafts can be an enjoyable way to spend an afternoon. And after dark, Stockholm becomes the liveliest city in the north of Europe.

### GAMLA STAN & NEIGHBORING ISLANDS

**Kungliga Slottet (Royal Palace) & Museums ★★** HISTORIC SITE Sweden has been a monarchy for 1,000 years, and this is your best chance to observe official court life. Although the King and Queen prefer to live at Drottningholm, this massive 608-room showcase remains their official address.

Nothing inside the palace is as impressive as the **Royal Apartments** on the second floor of the north wing. Decorated in the 1690s by French artists, they have the oldest interiors in the palace. The ballroom and gallery have been called the most spectacular in the north of Europe.

#### A Good Deal for Seeing Stockholm

**Stockholmskortet** (Stockholm Card; www.visitstockholm.com/en/stockholmcard) is a discount card that allows unlimited travel by public transportation throughout the city and county of Stockholm (except on airport buses). It also includes the hop-on, hop-off by City Sightseeing (available mid-June to mid-Aug). In addition, the card enables bearers to take a boat trip to the Royal Palace of Drottningholm for half-price. Admission to 80 museums and attractions is also included in the package.

You can purchase the card at several places in the city, including in Central Station. Cards are valid for between 1 and 5 days, and cost between 525 SEK to 1095 SEK for adults and 235 SEK to 350 SEK for ages 7 to 20 and seniors.

Stockholm's main square, Stortorget, at Christmas.

Second in importance to the state apartments is the **Skattkammaren,** or Royal Treasury. These vaults contain the greatest collection of royal regalia in Scandinavia. The competition is tough here, but we think the most impressive exhibits are Gustava Vasa's etched sword of state from 1541 and the ornate silver baptismal font of Karl XI.

The original palace, destroyed in a fire in 1697, was called Tre Kronor (Three Kronors). On the ground floor of the palace's northern wing, the **Tre Kronor Museum** features objects rescued from that fire. Finally, the royal armory (**Livrustkammaren,** see below) is hugely impressive; founded in 1633, it's also Sweden's oldest museum.

Outside the palace, military units from all over Sweden take turns at the **Changing of the Royal Guard.** In summer, you can watch the military guard parade daily. In winter, parades take place on Wednesdays and Sundays; on days there are no parades, you can still see the changing of the guard.

Kungliga Husgerådskammaren. www.royalcourt.se. ✆ **08/402-61-30.** Combination ticket to all parts of palace is 150 SEK adults, 75 SEK students/children 7–17. T-bana: Gamla Stan. Bus: 43, 55, 71, or 76. Apartments and Treasury Sept 14–May 15 Tues–Sun 10am–4pm, May15–Sept 13 daily 10am–5pm; closed during government receptions. Royal Armory daily 10am–5pm. Museum of Antiquities May 15–Sept 14 daily 10am–5pm.

**Livrustkammaren ★** MUSEUM The Swedish royal family has taken a beating these last few years (sex scandals, rumors of Nazi membership in the 1940s), but this museum is still a haven of monarchy. All the

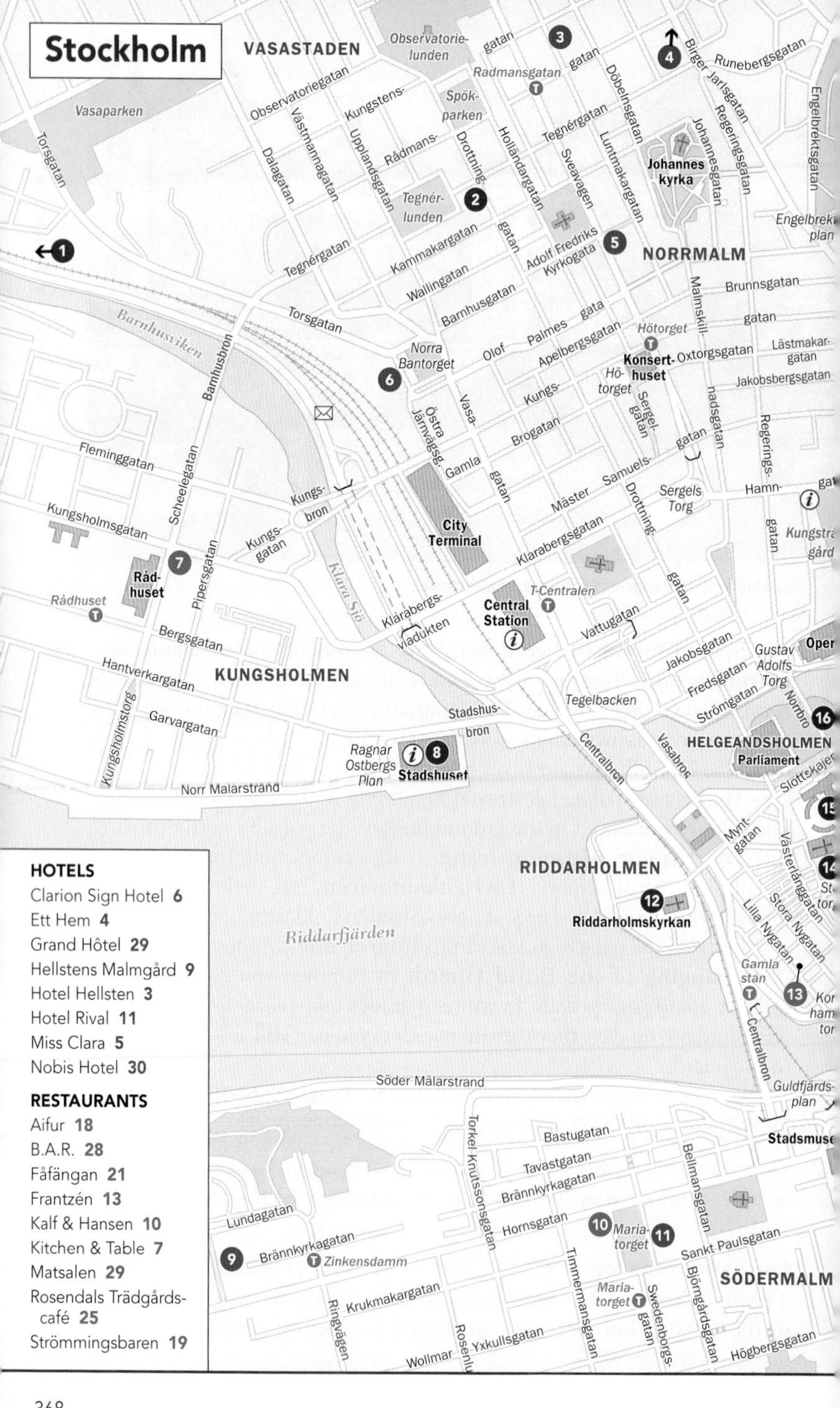

Stockholm
VASASTADEN
Observatorie-lunden
Vasaparken
Torsgatan
Observatoriegatan
Dalagatan
Västmannagatan
Kungstens-
Upplandsgatan
Rådmans-
Spök-parken
Radmansgatan
gatan
Drottning-
gatan
Tegnér-lunden
Holländargatan
Tegnérgatan
Sveavägen
Döbelnsgatan
Luntmakargatan
Johannes kyrka
Johannesgatan
Birger Jarlsgatan
Regeringsgatan
Runebergsgatan
Engelbrektsgatan
Engelbrekt plan
Kammakargatan
Adolf Fredriks Kyrkogata
NORRMALM
Tegnérgatan
Wallingatan
Barnhusgatan
Brunnsgatan
Malmskill-
nadsgatan
Torsgatan
Barnhusviken
Norra Bantorget
Olof
Palmes gata
Apelbergsgatan
Hötorget
Konsert-huset
Oxtorgsgatan
Lästmakar-gatan
Jakobsbergsgatan
Hö-torget
Sergel-gatan
Barnhusbron
Östra Järnvägsg.
Vasa-
gatan
Kungs-
Brogatan
Gamla
Fleminggatan
Scheelegatan
Kungs-bron
Kungsgatan
Samuels-
gatan
Mäster
Regerings-
gatan
Sergels Torg
Hamn-
Kungsträdgården
Kungsholmsgatan
City Terminal
Klarabergsgatan
Drottning-
gatan
Rådhuset
Rådhuset
Pipersgatan
Klara Sjö
Klarabergs-viadukten
Central Station
T-Centralen
Vattugatan
Bergsgatan
Jakobsgatan
Gustav Adolfs Torg
Oper
KUNGSHOLMEN
Hantverkargatan
Fredsgatan
Strömgatan
Norrbro
Tegelbacken
Kungsholmstorg
Garvargatan
Stadshus-bron
Centralbron
Vasabron
HELGEANDSHOLMEN
Parliament
Slottskajen
Ragnar Östbergs Plan
Stadshuset
Norr Mälarstrand
Mynt-gatan
Västerlånggatan
RIDDARHOLMEN
Riddarholmskyrkan
Stora Nygatan
Lilla Nygatan
Riddarfjärden
Gamla stan
Centralbron
HOTELS
Clarion Sign Hotel 6
Ett Hem 4
Grand Hôtel 29
Hellstens Malmgård 9
Hotel Hellsten 3
Hotel Rival 11
Miss Clara 5
Nobis Hotel 30
RESTAURANTS
Aifur 18
B.A.R. 28
Fåfängan 21
Frantzén 13
Kalf & Hansen 10
Kitchen & Table 7
Matsalen 29
Rosendals Trädgårds-café 25
Strömmingsbaren 19
Söder Mälarstrand
Guldfjärds-plan
Stadsmuse
Torkel Knutssonsgatan
Bastugatan
Tavastgatan
Bränkyrkagatan
Bellmansgatan
Lundagatan
Hornsgatan
Maria-torget
Brännkyrkagatan
Zinkensdamm
Timmermansgatan
Sankt Paulsgatan
SÖDERMALM
Maria-torget
Krukmakargatan
Ringvägen
Swedenborgsgatan
Björngårdsgatan
Wollmar Yxkullsgatan
Högbergsgatan

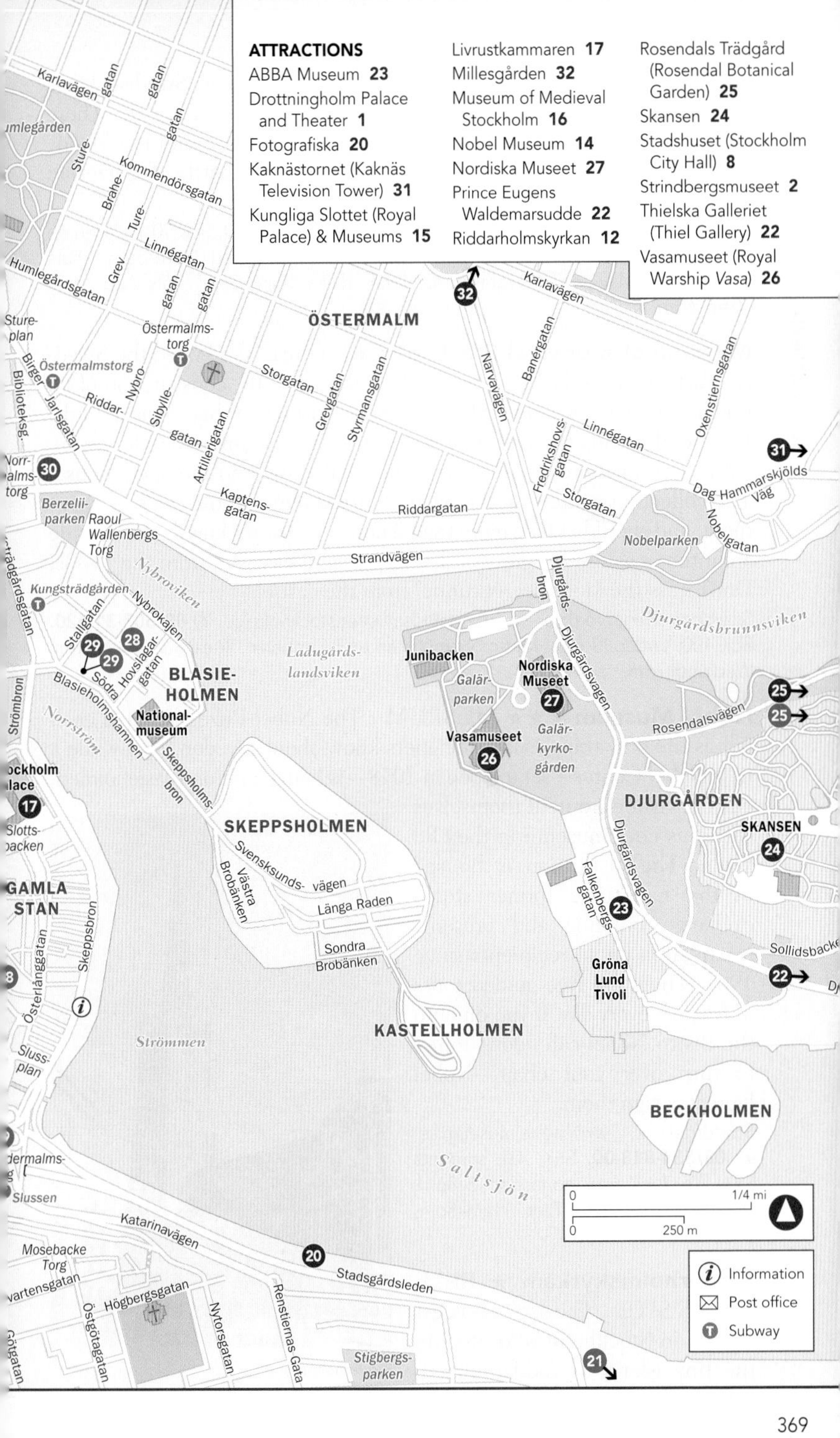
ATTRACTIONS
ABBA Museum 23
Drottningholm Palace and Theater 1
Fotografiska 20
Kaknästornet (Kaknäs Television Tower) 31
Kungliga Slottet (Royal Palace) & Museums 15
Livrustkammaren 17
Millesgården 32
Museum of Medieval Stockholm 16
Nobel Museum 14
Nordiska Museet 27
Prince Eugens Waldemarsudde 22
Riddarholmskyrkan 12
Rosendals Trädgård (Rosendal Botanical Garden) 25
Skansen 24
Stadshuset (Stockholm City Hall) 8
Strindbergsmuseet 2
Thielska Galleriet (Thiel Gallery) 22
Vasamuseet (Royal Warship Vasa) 26
ÖSTERMALM
BLASIE-HOLMEN
SKEPPSHOLMEN
KASTELLHOLMEN
DJURGÅRDEN
BECKHOLMEN
GAMLA STAN
SKANSEN
Junibacken
Nordiska Museet
Vasamuseet
Nationalmuseum
Gröna Lund Tivoli
Galärparken
Galärkyrkogården
Nobelparken
Berzelii-parken
Raoul Wallenbergs Torg
Stigbergs-parken
Mosebacke Torg
Östermalmstorg
Kungsträdgården
Slussen
Nybroviken
Ladugårdslandsviken
Djurgårdsbrunnsviken
Norrström
Strömmen
Saltsjön
Karlavägen
Kommendörsgatan
Linnégatan
Humlegårdsgatan
Storgatan
Riddargatan
Strandvägen
Narvavägen
Banérgatan
Oxenstiernsgatan
Dag Hammarskjölds Väg
Nobelgatan
Djurgårdsbron
Djurgårdsvägen
Rosendalsvägen
Sollidsbacken
Falkenbergsgatan
Skeppsholmsbron
Svensksundsvägen
Västra Brobänken
Långa Raden
Sondra Brobänken
Katarinavägen
Stadsgårdsleden
Högbergsgatan
Renstiernas Gata
Nytorsgatan
Östgötagatan
Birger Jarlsgatan
Nybrokajen
Stallgatan
Hovslagargatan
Södra Blasieholmshamnen
Skeppsbron
Österlånggatan
Strömbron
Artillerigatan
Grevgatan
Styrmansgatan
Fredrikshovsgatan
Kaptensgatan
0 1/4 mi
0 250 m
Information
Post office
Subway

relevant—as well as some irrelevant—paraphernalia of Swedish kings and queens across the ages crams the cellars of the royal castle. There are coronation gowns, orders of merit, whole carriages, and the bloody shirt Gustavus Adolphus was wearing at the fateful battle of Lützen in 1632. Even the horse he rode in on is here.

Slottsbacken 3. www.livrustkammaren.se/en. ✆ **08/402-30-30.** SEK 90, children up to 19 free. Metro: Gamla stan. Sept–Apr Fri–Sun, Tues–Wed 11am–5pm, Thurs 11am–8pm; May daily 11am–5pm; June daily 10am–5pm; July–Aug daily 10am–6pm.

**Museum of Medieval Stockholm** ★MUSEUM When the Swedish Parliament building got a facelift in the late '70s, construction of an underground garage unearthed a whole host of archaeological finds. Instead of carting these off to a warehouse, a museum was built on-site, with its entrance roughly between the royal castle and the opera house. The collection centers on the birth of Stockholm and the city's development, and shouldn't take more than 2 hours to absorb. Highlights include a church, a gallows, a graveyard, and part of a city wall from the 1530s. Don't miss the king's secret tunnel from the castle.

Strömparterren, Norrbro. www.medeltidsmuseet.stockholm.se. ✆ **08/508-31-620.** SEK 100, under 19 free. Metro: Gamla stan or T-Centralen. Tues–Sun noon–5pm, Wed until 7pm.

**Nobel Museum** ★★★ MUSEUM The Nobel Prize, awarded each fall, is the only thing many foreigners know about Sweden. And while a new Nobel Center—set to open in 2018—is being built on Blasieholmen, current visitors content themselves with this cozy museum in the Old Town. The institution is housed in the handsome former stock-exchange building and presents information on all recipients since 1901. There are free guided tours in English every day. If you dip into the Bistro Nobel cafe, don't forget to turn over your chair—Nobel laureates sign them.

Stortorget 2. www.nobelmuseum.se. ✆ **08/534-818-00.** SEK 100, students SEK 70; Tues free admission 5–8pm. Metro: Gamla stan. Tues 11am–8pm, Wed–Sun 11am–5pm.

Riddarholmskyram.

**Riddarholmskyrkam** ★ RELIGIOUS SITE The second-oldest church in Stockholm is located on the tiny island of Riddarholmen,

Costume memorabilia at the ABBA Museum.

next to Gamla Stan. It was founded in the 13th century as a Franciscan monastery, but today it is a virtual pantheon of Swedish kings. The last king buried here was Gustav V in 1950. Before that, some of the greatest monarchs in Swedish history were interred inside, including Gustav III and Gustav II Adolf. Karl XIV Johan, the first king of the present Bernadotte ruling dynasty, is also buried here, in a large marble sarcophagus, as are many Swedish soldiers from the Thirty Years' War.

Riddarholmen. www.royalcourt.se. ✆ **08/402-61-30.** 50 SEK adults, 25 SEK students, free for 18 and under. T-bana: Gamla Stan. May 15–Sept 13 10am–5pm; Closed Sept 15–May 14.

## DJURGÅRDEN

**ABBA Museum** ★ MUSEUM Admit it—you know all the lyrics, you've seen *Mamma Mia!*, and you still have ABBA albums in your basement. Now see the museum. Opened in 2013, it's a kitschy temple to 1970s bad taste. The halls are crammed with gold records, outrageous stage outfits, and even the helicopter from the *Arrival* album cover. Just submit. The museum has a smart policy of letting visitors in at allotted times, so you won't have to wait in lines.

Djurgårdsvägen 68. www.abbathemuseum.com. ✆ **08/121-328-60.** SEK 195, under 7 free. Tram #7 from Sergels Torg to Liljevalchs/Gröna Lund. Mon–Tues 10am–6pm, Wed–Fri 10am–8pm, Sat–Sun 10am–6pm.

**Nordiska Museet ★★** MUSEUM Nordiska Museet, which explores Sweden's cultural heritage, was founded by Artur Hazelius, the man behind zoo/museum Skansen, just down the road. Everyday objects, elements of clothing and fashion, letters, diaries, 250,000 other books and journals, and 7 million photographs can all be found here. It sounds a little dusty—there are no interactive displays or computer monitors—but the 10 to 20 annual exhibits are usually quite compelling, covering such themes as "The Bathroom," "Old People," and "The Guillotine." It's all housed in a magnificent 1907 building with an elaborate Danish-Renaissance design and a glorious, cathedral-like main hall. Block out at least 2 hours.

Djurgårdsvägen 6-16. www.nordiskamuseet.se. ✆ **08/519-546-00.** SEK 100, under 18 free, free Wed 5–8pm (except in summer). Tram #7 to Nordiska Museet/Vasamuseet. Daily 10am–5pm, until 8pm Wed, except summertime.

**Prince Eugens Waldemarsudde ★★** HISTORIC SITE The youngest of Oscar II's four children, Prince Eugen (1865–1947) was more interested in becoming an artist than a king. And he was no Sunday painter; he became one of the great landscape artists of his day, referred to as the "The Painting Prince" by Swedes. His former home and studio—a lovely three-story mansion on the water—serves as an art gallery today, showing not only his work, but those by the Edvard Munch, Carl Larsson, Anders Zorn, and the other great Scandinavian artists he collected. The prince's studio is on the top floor and is used for temporary exhibitions.

The park is filled with sculptures by some of the greatest masters in Europe—Carl Milles to Auguste Rodin—and is also studded with classical Roman and Greek sculptures acquired by the art-loving prince. While at Waldemarsudde, also see the **Old Mill,** a windmill built in the 1780s.

Prins Eugens Väg 6. www.waldemarsudde.se. ✆ **08/545-837-00.** 120 SEK adults, 100 SEK seniors/students, free for 19 and under. Bus: 47. Tues–Sun 11am–5pm, Thurs until 8pm.

**Rosendals Trädgård (Rosendal Botanical Garden) ★★** PARK/GARDEN For anyone who has ever tried to cultivate a plant, this is among the most appealing sites in Sweden. Its origins go back to the early 18th century, when Djurgården was dotted with small farms. Today, the site contains greenhouses and a sweeping mass of meticulously weeded beds for all kinds of plants. Visitors are encouraged to walk along the brick paths, gathering produce and flowers directly from the beds. A caretaker charges by the kilo for whatever is taken.

Rosendalsterrassen 12. www.rosendalstradgard.se. ✆ **08/545-812-70.** Free. Bus: 47. Hours vary with the season, but the best way to see this place is with a visit to its cafe and gift shop, open Mon–Fri 11am–4 or 5pm. Closed Jan.

**Skansen** ★★ MUSEUM The world's first open-air museum (it opened in 1891), Skansen was the brainchild of scholar and folklorist Arthur Hazelius, who thought it would be a good idea to gather a little bit of every Swedish region in one place. To that end, he moved more than 150 reconstructed dwellings here, which are today scattered over some 30 hectares (74 acres) of parkland. Most date from the 18th and 19th centuries, and include windmills, manor houses, blacksmith shops—even a complete town quarter. Folk costumes, culinary customs, animals, houses, workshops—nothing was too insignificant for this intellectual hoarder. It's kept alive by today's staff, who reenact the life and craftmaking of yore. The Solliden stage at the museum is the outdoor venue for Sweden's most popular summertime sing-along, "Allsång på Skansen," which regularly draws around two million viewers. If you get tickets to this Tuesday event, you will be treated to a rare glimpse into the modern Swedish soul.

Djurgården 49-51. www.skansen.se. ✆ **08/442-80-00.** 100 SEK-180 SEK adults (depending on season), 60 SEK children 6-15, free for children 5 and under. Bus: 44, 69, 69K from central Stockholm. Ferry from Slussen. Historic buildings Oct-Apr daily 11am-3pm; May-Sept 11am-5pm.

**Thielska Galleriet (Thiel Gallery)** ★★ GALLERY Ernest Thiel was a wealthy banker and art collector who commissioned this mansion, drawing upon architectural influences from both the Italian Renaissance and the Far East. Over the years, Thiel began to fill his palatial rooms with great art. However, in the wake of World War I, he went bankrupt and the state took over his property in 1924, eventually opening it as a museum. Highlights include Gustav Fjaestad's furniture, a portrait of Nietzsche, whom Thiel greatly admired, and works by Manet, Rodin, Toulouse-Lautrec, Edvard Munch, and Anders Zorn. Thiel is buried on the grounds beneath Rodin's statue *Shadow.*

Sjötullsbacken 6-8, Djurgården. www.thielska-galleriet.se. ✆ **08/662-58-84.** 100 SEK adults, 80 SEK students, free for children 18 and under. Bus: 69. Tues–Sun noon–5pm, Thurs noon–8pm, closed Mon.

**Vasamuseet (Royal Warship *Vasa*)** ★★★ MUSEUM If you can only swing a single museum while in Stockholm, this should be it. The *Vasa* is a 17th-century warship that sank on its maiden voyage in 1628 after a 3 km. journey. (Because of the risk of speaking your mind at the time, nobody had dared to contradict the king when he rushed the ship through production to get it ready for war on Poland.) After the disaster, the *Vasa* spent 333 years at the bottom of Stockholm harbor before it was salvaged in 1961. This museum is today Scandinavia's most visited.

For those who want to walk through the ship—and who doesn't?—a full-scale model of half of the *Vasa*'s upper gun deck has been built, together with the steering compartment and the admiral's cabin. Visitors

The Royal Warship *Vasa*.

stroll past appallingly primitive medical equipment, preserved clothes, and a backgammon board, getting an idea of what life would have been like at sea during this era. Captioned exhibits describe the almost unimaginable hardships the average soldier and sailor would have faced. Galärvarvsvägen 14, Djurgården. www.vasamuseet.se. ✆ **08/519-548-00.** 130 SEK adults, 100 SEK students, free ages 18 and under. Bus: 44,69,76. Ferry from Slussen year-round, from Nybroplan in summer only. Sept–May Thurs–Tues 10am–5pm, Wed 10am–8pm; June–Aug daily 8:30am–6pm. Closed Jan 1, Dec 23–25.

## DROTTNINGHOLM

**Drottningholm Palace and Theater ★★★** LANDMARK No palace in the north of Europe is as grand and spectacular as this regal complex of stately buildings sitting on an island in Lake Mälaren. The royal family still lives here, but don't expect to discover the king walking the corridors in his underwear. The royal apartments are screened off.

The palace is dubbed the "Versailles of Sweden," and so it is. In fact, work began on this masterpiece in 1662 about the same time as Versailles. Nicodemus Tessin the Elder (1615–81), one of the most celebrated architects of the 17th century, was the master builder.

Listed as a UNESCO World Heritage Site, Drottningholm needs about 3 hours of your time to visit it. Must-stops include the palace itself, the theater, the magnificent gardens, and the Chinese Pavilion. One highlight of any tour is the **State Apartments**, with a spectacular staircase decorated by Giovanni Carove, the Italian master.

Drottningholm Palace.

After checking out the grand interior, you should retreat to the **Kina Slott (Chinese Pavilion)**. Built during the European craze for the exotic architecture of Asia, the pavilion was constructed in Stockholm in 1753.

Allow as much time as you can to stroll through **Drottningholm Gardens**, the wonderful creation of Tessin the Younger in 1681. The **Hercules Fountain** here is a famous bronze work, created by Adriaen de Vries and brought by Swedish soldiers from Prague in 1648. Other features of the park include English-style bridges, ornamental pools, canals, and a "water garden" with nearly a dozen water jets.

**Drottningholm Court Theatre** is the grandest theater in all of Scandinavia. The first performance was presented here back in 1766, and the theater reached its apogee under Gustav III. Between June and July, some two dozen performances are staged; seating only 450, the theater offers one of the most unusual entertainment experiences in Sweden. Many performances sell out far in advance to season ticket holders. Theater buffs can visit the **Theatre Museum,** the setting for exhibits tracing the history of European theater since the 1700s, including displays of costumes, stage models, drawings, and paintings.

For tickets to the evening performances, which cost 165 SEK to 610 SEK, call ✆ **08/660-82-25.** For more information about the theater, call ✆ **08/759-04-06** or 08/556-931-07, or visit www.dtm.se.

Ekerö, Drottningholm. www.royalcourt.se. ✆ **08/402-62-80.** Palace 120 SEK adults, 60 SEK students. Theater tour 90 SEK adults, 55 SEK students; Chinese Pavilion 100

Drottningholm Court Theatre.

SEK adults, 50 SEK students. All free for children 17 and under. T-bana: Brommaplan, then bus 301 or 323 to Drottningholm. Ferry from the dock near City Hall. Hours vary according to season and special events; check website to plan your visit.

## SÖDERMALM

**Fotografiska ★★** MUSEUM The most successful Swedish museum launch since Hedenhös (that's a Swedish expression meaning the Stone Age), this private museum dedicated to photography opened in 2010 in a former Customs building. During its brief existence, it has put on exhibitions by world-class photographers such as Annie Leibovitz, Robert Mapplethorpe, and Anton Corbijn, as well as less-renowned shutterbugs. The very generous opening hours make it delightfully accessible, and if the art doesn't float your boat, you can spend an hour at the house's über-cool alfresco bar/restaurant. Celebrity chef Paul Svensson heads the kitchen.

Stadsgårdshamnen 22. www.fotografiska.eu. ✆ **08/509-005-00.** SEK 120, students SEK 90, under 12 free. Metro: Slussen; summertime by boat with Strömma's Hop-on Hop-off Boat. Sun–Wed 9am–9pm, Thurs–Sat 9am–11pm.

## NORRMALM

**Kaknästornet (Kaknäs Television Tower) ★** LANDMARK North of the Djurgården stands the tallest manmade structure in Scandinavia—a 152m-high (499-ft.) radio and television tower. The 1967 tower itself may be ugly, but once you reach the top, the view of greater Stockholm is the best there is. From the observation platform you can see everything from the cobblestone streets of Gamla Stan (Old Town) to the city's modern concrete-and-glass structures and the archipelago beyond. An eatery serves Swedish cuisine on the 28th floor.

Mörka Kroken. www.kaknastornet.se. ✆ **08/667-21-80.** 55 SEK adults, 20 SEK children 7–15, free for children 6 and under. Bus: 69. Hours vary by season; check website for current info.

## LIDINGÖ

**Millesgården ★★** MUSEUM Lidingö is a posh island to the northeast of downtown Stockholm, known for expensive real estate, the world's biggest cross-country footrace, and not much more. An exception: The home of Sweden's greatest sculptor Carl Milles ("mill-less," not "mills," 1875–1955) and the open-air museum he left behind. Works of Milles can be found all around town, but the real stash is here at Millesgården, including his monumental and much-reproduced *Hands of God* sculpture. In Milles's early works, you can see how much he was influenced by the French sculptor Rodin, and also by the Art Nouveau movement. The villa also displays his personal collection of art which spans the ages from ancient Greece to his contemporaries.

Herserudsvägen 32. www.millesgarden.se. ✆ **08/446-75-90.** SEK 100. Metro to Ropsten, then bus #201, 202, 204, 205, 206, or 212 across the bridge to Torsviks torg. May 1–Sept 30, daily 11am–5pm; Oct 1–Apr 30 Tues–Sun 11am–5pm.

## KUNGSHOLMEN

**Stadshuset (Stockholm City Hall) ★★** LANDMARK When you are awarded the Nobel Prize, this is where you'll go to receive your medal. Built in the "National Romantic Style," the Stockholm City Hall on the island of Kungsholmen is one of the finest examples of modern architecture in Europe. Designed by Ragnar Ostberg, it was completed in 1923. A lofty square tower bearing three gilt crowns (the symbol of Sweden) and the national coat of arms dominates the red-brick structure. In summer, you can climb the 100m-high (328-ft.) tower for what we consider the finest panoramic view of Gamla Stan (Old Town) in the area. The Blue Hall is used the Nobel Prize banquet. About 18 million pieces of gold and colored-glass mosaics cover the walls of the Golden Hall.

Hantverksgatan 1. www.stockholm.se/stadshuset. ✆ **08/508-29-05.** 70 SEK-100 SEK adults, 20 SEK–40 SEK ages 12–19, free for children 11 and under. Tower additional 50 SEK, free for children under 11. T-bana: Centralen or Rådhuset. Bus: 3 or 62. Check website for visits and tours timetable.

## NORRMALM

**Strindbergsmuseet ★** MUSEUM August Strindberg, the father of modern Swedish literature, spent his last 5 years here, in "The Blue Tower" at the northern end of Drottninggatan. Today it is a time-warp museum filled with stuff the angry man left behind, both in his apartment and in the sixth floor room he had to rent to house his 3,000-book library. Look for snippets of his writing embedded in the street outside.

Drottninggatan 85. www.strindbergsmuseet.se. ✆ **08/411-53-54.** SEK 60, students SEK 40. Metro: Rådmansgatan. Sept 1–June 30, Tues–Sun noon–4pm; July 1–Aug 31, Tues–Sun 10am–4pm.

## Especially for Kids

The open-air park **Skansen ★★** (see p. 373) offers **Lill-Skansen,** the children's version of the museum, with a popular petting zoo. A miniature train ride through the park is also a must. Lill-Skansen is open daily in summer from 10:30am to 4pm.

Kids can easily spend a day or several at Skansen and not get bored. Before going to Skansen, stop off at the ***Vasa* Museum** (see p. 373), which many youngsters find an epic adventure. Cap the evening with a visit to **Gröna Lunds Tivoli** (www.gronalund.com), which also is on Djurgården.

## Where to Stay

By the standards of many U.S. or Canadian cities, hotels in Stockholm are very expensive. Most of the city's medium-priced hotels are in Norrmalm, north of the Old Town, and many of the least-expensive lodgings are near the Central Station. There are comparably priced inexpensive accommodations within 10 to 20 minutes of the city, easily reached by subway, streetcar, or bus.

### NORRMALM

#### Moderate

**Clarion Sign Hotel ★★** This is a big, hyper-modern design hotel within walking distance of Central Station and the Arlanda Express airport train. Its sign may look like a Federation starship from the outside, but it devotes its inside to classic Scandinavian design, with each floor themed for a different Nordic country. Rooms feature crisp white walls and bold accent colors on throw pillows and curtains. They're quiet, comfortable and feature excellent beds. Celebrity chef Marcus Samuelsson has lent his name to the hotel's American Table restaurant. For a guaranteed surreal experience, slip into the rooftop swimming pool on a snowy evening.

Östra Järnvägsgatan 35. www.clarionsign.se. ✆ **08/676-98-00.** Doubles SEK 1,600–SEK 3,800, includes breakfast. Metro: T-Centralen. **Amenities:** Restaurant; bar; spa; sauna; gym; heated pool; free Wi-Fi.

**Ett Hem ★★★** Built as a private residence in 1910, the Lärkstan manor house still feels like a home. That means arresting pieces of art on the walls, old-fashioned armchairs upholstered in quirky modern fabrics, working fireplaces, guest rooms that can be lit by candles (this is one of the few hotels we've ever seen that encourages the use of candles), shelves of books and plants, plush linens—all the elements in harmony with one another. On-site is a wonderful sauna and hammam, a small but well-equipped gym, and a terrific restaurant.

Sköldungagatan 2. www.etthem.se. ✆ **08/20-05-90.** Doubles SEK 3,800, includes breakfast. Metro: Tekniska högskolan. **Amenities:** Restaurant; gym; sauna; massages; free Wi-Fi.

**Hotel Hellsten** ★★ Per Hellsten may not boast the biggest hotel collection in Stockholm, but he is certainly putting together an intriguing one. This is his namesake, tucked into a 19th-century building on a sleepy street parallel to Sveavägen. The mood and decor is African and Asian, complete with relics that the owner brought home from the overseas trips he undertook as an anthropologist. All of the 78 rooms are individually kitted out—all romantic, personal, odd, and lovely, with jewel-toned walls, four-poster beds in some, wooden beams in others, and lovely balconies in a lucky few. The result is a place that will stick in your memory. Thursday nights feature jazz sessions in the hotel's colonial-style Earth Bar.

Luntmakargatan 68. www.hellsten.se. ✆ **08/661-86-00.** Doubles SEK 790–SEK 2,300, includes breakfast. Metro: Rådmansgatan. **Amenities:** Bar; gym; sauna; free Wi-Fi.

**Miss Clara** ★★★ This vibrant hotel is set in a classic Art Nouveau building that was recently renovated by Gert Wingårdh, Sweden's most renowned architect and interior designer. The result is more tasteful than quirky, with room floors and walls in darker wood and stone than you would expect from Nordic design, balanced by subtle ways of leading natural light into nooks and crannies such as bathrooms. Guest rooms tend to be marvelously insulated both from street noise and from the commotion in surrounding rooms. The original building—you can still see its handsome and well-preserved "bones"—dates to 1920 and used to be an all-girls school, with the property taking its name from former headmistress Clara Strömberg.

Sveavägen 48. www.missclarahotel.com. ✆ **08/440-67-00.** Doubles SEK 1,900–SEK 2,300, includes breakfast. Metro: Hötorget. **Amenities:** Restaurant; bar; gym; sauna; free Wi-Fi.

## ÖSTERMALM

### Expensive

**Grand Hôtel** ★★ This swanky spot is where most superstars and world leaders stay when they come to Stockholm, plus practically every Nobel Prize winner since 1901. And many more come for events at the hotel's ballroom, an exact replica of the Hall of Mirrors at Versailles. The hotel proudly retains the tradition of serving an opulent daily smorgasbord (it's one of the last in Sweden to do so). The Grand Hotel is also home to the three restaurants of celebrity chef Mathias Dahlgren, the first Swedish winner of the Bocuse d'Or (see p. 383). As for the rooms, all 300 are designed in an updated French Empire style—lots of handsome patterned brocades, thick carpets or oriental rugs, chandeliers, and even wall murals and inlaid wood floors in the ritziest of suites.

Södra Blasieholmshamnen 8. www.grandhotel.se. ✆ **08/679-35-00.** Doubles from SEK 2,200. Metro: Kungsträdgården. **Amenities:** 3 restaurants; bar; gym; spa; indoor pool; room service; free Wi-Fi.

**Nobis Hotel ★★★** Come for the lounge, stay for the lounge. Seriously, you could spend an entire afternoon in one of the four "living rooms" here. Its 90 feet of ceiling height is what people talked about when this five-star hotel opened in 2010, and it still pulls in crowds, as do the snacks and the expertly mixed cocktails. Those who decide to stay the night notice that 1) luxury in Scandinavia never gets vulgar; 2) the design group Claesson Koivisto Rune does subdued interiors like nobody else—with stylish contemporary furniture and bathrooms covered floor to ceiling in Carrera marble; and 3) location really does matter, and this one can't be beat. The building used to be a law-firm office, so the 201 rooms come in seven different sizes (from 160 sq. ft. and up), presumably depending on the status of the former occupant.

Norrmalmstorg 2-4. www.nobishotel.se. ✆ **08/614-10-00.** Doubles SEK 1,600–SEK 2,450, includes breakfast. Metro: Östermalmstorg. **Amenities:** 2 restaurants, bar, lounge, gym, free Wi-Fi.

## SÖDERMALM

### Moderate

**Hellstens Malmgård ★★★** This three-star manor, with the feeling of a countryside B&B, is the latest addition to Per Hellsten's hotel mini-empire (see the Hotel Hellsten, above). The house was built in 1770; the chestnut tree in the courtyard was planted when the house was completed. Mr. Hellsten, a former anthropologist with a flair for the dramatic, is not a design minimalist, so be prepared for strong colors and a healthy mix of antiques from around the world. Each unit is different, with sizes and layouts varying, some with four-poster beds, and a dozen with handmade porcelain stoves that are as old as the manor house. Bathrooms tend to be small but are well equipped. Rooms have such mod cons as TVs, Wi-Fi, and very comfortable mattresses. Breakfast in the garden on a summer morning beats anything you will find at more upper-end hotels.

Brännkyrkagatan 110. www.hellstensmalmgard.se. ✆ **08/465-058-00.** Doubles SEK 900–SEK 1,800, includes breakfast. Metro: Zinkensdamm. **Amenities:** Free Wi-Fi.

**Hotel Rival ★★** Who knows what they were thinking in the 1930s, when somebody reckoned that a combination hotel, movie house, restaurant, patisserie, and apartment complex would be a money-maker. Today, that odd mix is known for being owned by Benny Andersson, of ABBA fame. The cinema is still functioning and seats a massive 700. The on-site restaurant earns kudos, as does the buzzy bar area and music club below it (well-insulated from the guest rooms). The hotel is a high-cachet choice in Stockholm, announcing that guests are hip enough to want to stay on Södermalm, but refined enough not to grunge it. Sadly, there's no trace of the '30s in the average-size rooms. Instead, you'll find Nordic minimalism enlivened, a bit, by a massive photo over the bed, different in each room. Baths are unusually large, and the choicer rooms have balconies overlooking lovely Mariatorget. Service is top notch, as is the breakfast buffet (so take it if it's offered as part of the room rate). Mariatorget 3. www.rival.se. ✆ **08/545-789-00.** Doubles SEK 1,400–SEK 3,500. Metro: Mariatorget. **Amenities:** Restaurant; bar; lounge; free Wi-Fi.

## Where to Eat

Split-pea soup, sausages, and boiled potatoes are still around, but in the past decade Stockholm has emerged as a citadel of fine dining. Its improved reputation is due partly to the legendary freshness of Swedish game and produce; and partly to the success of Sweden's culinary teams at cooking contests around the world. These days, some claim that

**A room at the Hotel Rival.**

Sweden's chefs are practically as famous as its national hockey-team players.

There are an estimated 1,500 restaurants and bars in Stockholm alone, so you'll have plenty of choices. At all restaurants other than self-serve cafeterias, a 12% to 15% service charge is added to the bill to cover tipping, and the 21% value-added tax also is included in the bill. Wine and beer can be lethal to your final check, so proceed carefully. For good value, try ordering the *dagens ratt* (daily special), also referred to as dagens lunch or dagens menu, if available.

## GAMLA STAN

### Expensive

**Aifur** ★★★ VIKING In the last thousand years, Sweden hasn't produced anything remotely as exciting to tourists as, well, the Vikings. And so a number of businesses have grown up over the years to sell Viking goods, from horned helmets to commemorative t-shirts to highly inauthentic meals. Aifur is Stockholm's only real Viking eatery contender. The kitchen uses pre-medieval spices like saffron and caraway, and the menu is an approximation of how Viking food could have looked and tasted, based on the archeological record. This includes such dishes as "flap steak," racks of lamb, and an entire "dwarf chicken." As for the interior decoration, it's enough to make you feel like you're in a re-enactment of the bar scene from *The Seventh Seal*. Big fun.

Västerlånggatan 68B. www.aifur.se. ✆ **08/20-10-55.** SEK 200–SEK 350. Metro: Gamla stan. Mon–Thurs 5–11pm, Fri–Sat 5pm–1am.

**Frantzén** ★★★ GOURMET SWEDISH This is one of only two Stockholm restaurants with two Michelin stars, and many consider it to be the finest restaurant in Scandinavia. The menu strives to surprise an exacting clientele, through exotic dishes like oven-baked bone marrow, tomato marmalade, and smoked pork fat; a salad made up of 42 ingredients; and dishes crafted from lichen, ox blood, horse, and other unusual ingredients. Try to get a seat at the bar overlooking the kitchen so you can watch the chefs scurrying around to create your 17-course tasting menu. Frantzén only seats 19, so you must call ahead.

Lilla Nygatan 21. www.restaurantfrantzen.com. ✆ **08/20-85-80.** Tasting menu SEK 2,300. Metro: Gamla stan. Tues–Fri 6.30pm–1am, Sat 3pm–1am.

### Moderate

**Fåfängan** ★★ CAFE Fåfängan is the best place in Stockholm to indulge in the Swedish institution of *fika* ("fee-kah"). What's that? On the face of it, fika is simply a snack of cake and coffee, but for the Swedish psyche, it is what the couch was for Freud—a place where we open up, unload, and define who we are. Fåfängan features the best views in the city, north across the waters toward Djurgården. Set on the hill overlooking the Viking ferry terminal, it's not very convenient to get here, but we think the trek is worth it. ***Note:*** Fåfängan is occasionally booked for weddings, so check the website before commencing the climb.

Klockstapelbacken 3. www.fafangan.se. ✆ **08/642-99-00.** Brunch SEK 315. Metro: Slussen, then bus or 15-minute walk. Sept–Mar, mostly weekend brunch only. Apr–Aug, open daily; check website for hours.

## ÖSTERMALM & NORRMALM

### Expensive

**Matsalen ★★★** MODERN SCANDINAVIAN Chef Mathias Dahlgren has nearly cornered the market on Michelin stars in Stockholm. Of the eleven stars the city's restuarants awarded in 2014, three belong to Dahlgren: two for Matsalen, his signature dining room, and one for the more casual "food bar" Matbaren. These two are housed on the ground floor of the Grand Hôtel (p. 379), in elegantly clean and simple spaces, with cream and charcoal accents and stylish contemporary furnishings. Like many super-exclusive eateries, Matsalen has a chef's table where you can see the food being prepared. Diners are treated to a five-course tasting menu of elegant and purposefully light ingredients. Culinary daredevils prefer the Monday–Tuesday Radical Cooking session, where chefs challenge themselves to serve you something there's no way you ever tasted before.

Södra Blasieholmshamnen 8. www.mathiasdahlgren.com. ✆ **08/679-35-84.** Tasting menu SEK 1,900. Metro: Kungsträdgården. Tues–Sat 7pm–midnight.

### Moderate

**B.A.R. ★★** SEAFOOD This name is a misnomer: It's not a bar, but an acronym for Blasieholmens Akvarium & Restaurant. One of the finest fish restaurants in the city, B.A.R. buys its catch daily at the fish auction in Gothenburg, races it to Stockholm and waits for you to arrive. When you've had a look at the menu, the waiter will bring you over to the fish counter and walk you through the day's catch. (Which is a good thing, because the overly long menu bewilders most guests.) B.A.R. focuses more on food than on trimmings, which means bare walls, a low ceiling, and the odd wobbly table. It more than makes up for the humble setting by generating that great feeling that you're among friends. Fish-eating friends.

Blasieholmsgatan 4A. www.restaurangbar.se/en. ✆ **08/611-53-35.** Mains SEK 165–SEK 255. Metro: Kungsträdgården. Mon–Fri 11:30am–2:30pm and 5pm–1am, Sat 4pm–1am, Sun 5pm–1am.

## SÖDERMALM

### Inexpensive

**Kalf & Hansen ★★★** NORDIC Swedish fast food is improving its reputation considerably thanks to Kalf & Hansen and its visionary owner/chef Rune Kalf-Hansen. Here quick meals are made from a set menu in which the main ingredients, all organic and Nordic in origin, will vary by what's best that day (red deer was a recent option). This daily change makes for a varied and surprising mix even for regulars.

Mariatorget 2. www.kalfochhansen.se. ✆ **08/551-531-51.** SEK 70–SEK 90 for lunch. Metro: Mariatorget. Mon–Fri 9am–7pm, Sat 10am–4pm.

**Strömmingsbaren** ★★★ SWEDISH A classic street food cart, herring-specialist Strömmingsbaren has a cult following. And rightly so, as the food is delish. Most diners get "the classic," a helping of herring on crisp bread (*knäckebröd*) with dill sauce. Others opt for more creative variations like *strömming,* which is mashed potatoes on black rye bread, rolled up in flatbread, or—have they no shame?—tucked into a burger bun. Customers customize their noshes with lingonberries, dill sauce, or pickles. Any which way, you're likely to have a more genuine Stockholm experience than nearby tourist traps can provide, and at a tenth of the cost.

Södermalmstorg 1. SEK 35–SEK 75. Metro: Slussen. Mon–Fri 10am–7pm, Sat–Sun noon–5pm.

## KUNGSHOLMEN

### Moderate

**Kitchen & Table** ★★ FUSION Swedish-raised celebrity chef Marcus Samuelsson cut his culinary teeth as a teenager in New York. Lately Samuelsson has cooked on both sides of the Atlantic, and his latest venture in Sweden is a string of Kitchen & Table restaurants inside Clarion Hotels, this particular one at Amaranten on Kungsholmen. The menu and atmosphere are more bustling neighborhood eatery than haute cuisine, mixing influences from both of the chef's home countries, with a little Asian twist thrown in for good fun. Think forest-mushroom pizza, jerk chicken Caesar salad, or baked Arctic char with ponzu broth. Matching the cuisine, the interiors aim for a clean-but-cluttered living-room. All in all, you get a quality, unpretentious meal in a friendly setting.

### picnic fare & WHERE TO EAT IT

Fast-food eateries and fresh food markets abound in Stockholm, especially in the center of the city, around Hötorget. Here you can visit **Hötorgs Hallen,** a fresh food market where you can buy the makings of an elegant picnic. Recently arrived immigrants sell many Turkish food products here, including stuffed pita bread.

For the most elegant fare of all, however, go to Östermalms Hallen, at the corner of Humlegårdsgatan and Nybrogatan, east of the city center. Stall after stall sells picnic fare, including fresh shrimp and precooked items that will be wrapped carefully for you. With your picnic fixings in hand, head for **Skansen** or the wooded peninsula of **Djurgården.**

Kungsholmsgatan 31. www.kitchenandtable.se. ✆ **08/692-52-00.** Mains SEK 175–SEK 295. Metro: Rådhuset. Mon–Tues 11am–midnight, Wed–Fri 11am–1am, Sat noon–1am, Sun noon–midnight.



### DJURGÅRDEN

#### Moderate

**Rosendals Trädgårdscafé ★★★** SWEDISH A former gardening school from 1861 on the museum island of Djurgården, Rosendals has been a foundation-run gardening center since 1982, with a mission to spread the good word regarding organic farming. To finance this quest, there is a shop, a traditional bakery, and a glorious open-air cafe/restaurant. A maximum of 100 people can fit inside, but there are always the beautiful green fields outside. Picnic aficionados bring a blanket so they don't get their tushes wet on the surrounding grassy knolls.

Rosendalsterrassen 12. www.rosendalstradgard.se. ✆ **08/545-812-70.** Mains SEK 85–SEK 145. Tram #7 to Bellmansro, follow signs to Rosendal. Open for lunch and late afternoon fare. Call or check website for specific days/times.

## Shopping

Stockholm is filled with shop after shop of dazzling merchandise—often at dazzlingly steep prices that reflect the high esteem in which Swedish craftspeople are held. Some good buys do exist, but it takes searching.

Swedish glass, of course, is world famous. Swedish wooden items are works of great craftsmanship, and many people like to acquire Swedish functional furniture in blond pine or birch. Other items to look for include playsuits for children, silver necklaces, reindeer gloves, stainless-steel utensils, hand-woven neckties and skirts, sweaters and mittens in Nordic patterns, Swedish clogs, and colorful handicrafts from the provinces. The most popular souvenir is the Dala horse from Dalarna.

### Avoiding Mr. Taxman

The **value-added tax** in Sweden, called MOMS, is imposed on all products and services, but you can avoid MOMS if you spend a total of at least 1,200 SEK in each shop. Just give the store your name, address, and passport number and ask for a tax-free check. Don't unwrap your purchase until you've left Sweden. The Customs official will want to see both the tax-free check and your purchase; you'll be given a cash refund, minus a small commission, on the spot.

Everybody's favorite shopping area in Stockholm is **Gamla Stan (Old Town).** The main street for browsing is **Västerlånggatan;** many antiques stores are found here, but don't expect low prices.

**Skansen** is most fun to explore in the summer, because many craftspeople display their goods here. In the **Sergels Torg** area, the main shopping street is **Hamngatan,** site of the famous shopping center **Gallerian,** at the corner of Hamngatan and Sergels Torg, and crossing the northern rim of Kungsträdgården at Sweden House. Big department stores, such as NK and Åhléns, are located nearby.

The **Kungsgatan** area is another major shopping district, stretching from Hötorget to the intersection of Kungsgatan and Vasagatan. **Drottninggatan** is one long pedestrian mall. **Hötorget,** home to the PUB department store, is another major shopping district.

**Hornstullstrand Street Market,** often known simply as "Street," is a funky, battered market on the western waterfront of trending Södermalm, often compared to London's Camden Market. Dozens of stalls here sell costume jewelry, secondhand clothing, and budget-conscious products of struggling, up-and-coming designers.

## Entertainment & Nightlife

Pick up a copy of ***What's On,*** distributed at virtually every hotel in town, to see what entertainment and cultural events are scheduled.

**Djurgården** is the city's favorite spot for both indoor and outdoor evening events. Afterward, you can make the rounds of Stockholm's jazz venues and nightclubs, some of which stay open until 3 or 4am.

When it comes to splendid venues for the **performing arts,** Stockholm suffers from an embarrassment of riches. The splendid **Operahauset (Royal Opera House) ★★★** (www.opera.se) was founded in 1773 by Gustav III (who was later assassinated here at a masked ball). It is the home of the **Royal Swedish Opera** and the **Royal Swedish Ballet.**

**The Filharmonikerna i Konserthuset (Concert Hall) ★** (www.konserthuset.se) is home to the Stockholm Philharmonic Orchestra, and is the principal place to hear classical music in Sweden. The Nobel Prizes are also awarded here. Besides local orchestras, the hall features visiting ensembles, such as the Chicago Symphony Orchestra.

Greta Garbo got her start at the **Kungliga Dramatiska Teatern (Royal Dramatic Theater) ★★★** (www.dramaten.se), and Ingmar

### The Capital of Gay Scandinavia

Beginning in the mid-1990s, Stockholm witnessed an eruption of new gay bars, discos, and roaming nightclubs. Today, thanks partly to the huge influence of London's gay subcultures, no other city in Scandinavia offers gay-friendly nightlife options as broad and diverse as Stockholm's. Some of the gay bars and clubs maintain fixed hours and addresses. Others, configured as roving parties, constantly change addresses.

Listings for gay entertainment venues appear regularly in **QX,** a gay magazine published in Swedish and English. It's available at gay bars and news kiosks throughout Stockholm. You can also check out the magazine's website (**www.qx.se**). And don't overlook the comprehensive website **www.rfsl.se** maintained by RSFL, a Swedish organization devoted to equal rights for gays.

Bergman staged two productions a year until his death in 2007. The theater presents the latest experimental plays and the classics—in Swedish only.

**Oscars Teatern ★** (www.oscarsteatern.se) is the flagship of Stockholm's musical entertainment world. Known for its extravagant staging of traditional operettas, it's been the home of classic operetta and musical theater since the turn of the 20th century. The **Regina Theater Company ★** (www.reginateatern.se) presents everything from Victorian thrillers to Dickensian Christmas musicals in a London-style theater pub.

All the major opera, theater, and concert seasons begin in the fall, except for special summer festivals. Most of the major opera and theatrical performances are funded by the state, which keeps ticket prices reasonable.

Stockholm's nightlife scene ranges from the intellectual cafes of yesteryear (witness **Berns ★★★;** Berzelii Park; www.berns.se; ✆ **08/566-322-00;** where August Strindberg once held court) to hipper-than-thou **Debaser Medis ★★★** (Medborgarplatsen 8; www.debaser.se; ✆ **08/694-79-00**), a live music venue where young Swedes go to hear the bands you will love a decade from now.

Dance club **Grand Garbo ★★** (Landsvägen 67; www.grandgarbo.com; ✆ **08/98-45-15**) has a bit of a meat-market reputation, but it's known as a place to have an unpretentious good time. Oldie-but-goodie **SpyBar ★★** (Birger Jarlsgatan 20; www.stureplansgruppen.se; ✆ **08/545-076-00**) is still the granddaddy of Stockholm nightclubs and still a celebrity favorite.

**Gröne Jägaren ★** (Götgatan 64; www.gronejagaren.com; ✆ **08/640-96-00**) is a dive in the best sense of the word—honest, straightforward, and not about to become fancy any time soon, with cheap beer, down-to-earth chow, and unaffected patrons. Beer aficionados should flock to **Nya Carnegiebryggeriet ★** (Ljusslingan 17; www.nyacarnegiebryggeriet.se; ✆ **08/510-650-82**), a Carlsberg-led microbrewery housed just off Södermalm in the former Luma lightbulb factory (built in 1930). The traditional Swedish menu is tailored to go with beer.

## [FastFACTS] SCANDINAVIA

**Business Hours** Most **banks** are open Monday to Friday 10am to 4pm (to 6pm Thurs). **Stores** are generally open Monday to Thursday 9am to 6pm, Friday 9am to 7 or 8pm, and Saturday 9am to 2pm; most are closed Sunday. **Offices** are open Monday to Friday 9 or 10am to 4 or 5pm.

**Currency** Although both Denmark and Sweden are members of the European Union, each has retained its own currency. In Denmark, it's the krone (DKK) and in Sweden, it's the krona (SEK). See p. 860 for information on money and costs.

### Doctors & Dentists
To reach a doctor in Copenhagen call ✆ **38-11-40-00** (www.laegelinien.dk). In Stockholm, check with **Medical Care Information** (✆ **08/320-100**). The doctor's fee is payable in cash. Language is hardly a problem in either country, where virtually all doctors speak English. During regular business hours, ask your hotel to call the nearest English-speaking dentist.

### Embassies & Consulates:
**In Denmark:**

**Australia:** Dampfaergevej 26, 2nd floor, Copenhagen; www.denmark.embassy.gov.au; ✆ **70-26-36-76.**

**Canada:** Kristen Bernikowsgade 1, Copenhagen; www.denmark.gc.ca; ✆ **33-48-32-00.**

**New Zealand:** Store Strandstraede 21, Copenhagen; E-mail: mail@nzconsulate.dk; ✆ **33-37-77-02.**

**United Kingdom:** Kastelsvej 36-40, Copenhagen; www.gov.uk/government/world/denmark; ✆ **35-44-52-00.**

**United States:** Dag Hammarskjölds Allé 24, Copenhagen; http://denmark.usembassy.gov; ✆ **33-41-71-00.**

**In Sweden:**

**Australia:** Klarabergsviadukten 63, Stockholm; www.sweden.embassy.gov.au; ✆ **08/613-2900.**

**Canada:** Klarabergsgatan 23, Stockholm; www.sweden.gc.ca; ✆ **08/453-3000.**

**New Zealand:** Contact the Embassy of New Zealand in Belgium, Avenue des Nerviens 9/31, B-1040 Brussels; www.nzembassy.com/belgium; ✆ **32-2-512-1040.**

**United Kingdom:** Skarpogatan 6-8, Stockholm; www.gov.uk/government/world/sweden; ✆ **08/671-3000.**

**United States:** Dag Hammarskjolds Vag 31 Stockholm; http://stockholm.usembassy.gov; ✆ **08/783-5300.**

### Emergencies
Dial ✆ **112** to report a fire or to call the police or an ambulance. Emergency calls from public telephones are free (no coins needed).

### Pharmacies
In Copenhagen, an *apotek* (pharmacy) open 24 hours a day is **Steno Apotek,** Vesterbrogade 6C (✆ **33-14-82-66;** bus: 6), lying opposite the Central Railway Station. In Stockholm, **Apotek C.W. Scheele**, across from the Central Railway Station (Klarabergsgatan 64; ✆ **0771/450-450**) is open 24 hours.

### Post Offices
Copenhagen's main post office is located at Tietgensgade 37, DK-1704 København (✆ **80-20-70-30;** bus: 10 or 46). It's open Monday to Friday 11am to 6pm and Saturday 10am to 1pm. In Stockholm, the main post office is at Centralstationen 10126 (✆ **08/781-20-42**), open Monday to Friday 8am to 6pm, and Saturday 8am to 2pm.

### Taxes
Throughout Denmark, you'll come across moms on your bills, a government-imposed value-added tax of 25%. It's included in hotel and restaurant bills, service charges, entrance fees, and repair of foreign-registered cars. No refunds are given. In Sweden, you'll pay 25% tax on purchases and 12% on hotel and restaurant bills.

# GERMANY

by Stephen Brewer

7

I self-published my first travel book—a little tome called *The G.I.'s Guide to Traveling in Europe*—at a print shop in Oberammergau, Germany, where it was set in type by a Bavarian who knew no English. He slowly and laboriously spelled out the entire text letter by letter, speaking each letter aloud, and I spent so much time watching that process that I was also able systematically to witness the work habits of his fellow printers.

Each day, they returned from lunch with smiles on their faces, as if they were overjoyed to be back. Each day, they made the rounds of each person in the print shop, wishing "Mahlzeit"—a word that apparently meant "I-hope-you-had-a-good-lunch"—to each one of them, individually. And it gradually dawned on me that they were unlike any commercial staff that I had ever seen.

Unlike other people, who work to live, they lived to work—they enjoyed working. They were eager to produce, to labor, to create the best possible print shop. And although you obviously can't draw larger conclusions from this one group of Germans, I nevertheless thought I had seen something important. I had witnessed the determination, the drive, that had almost permitted them to win the war—and that was now making an economic powerhouse out of their country.

Germany, with its population of 81,000,000 persons, is not simply the largest country in Western Europe but also the most productive. It manufactures more goods, sells more products, and earns more money than any other European country. And from its perch as the number-one economy, it often dictates the policies of others and urges their adoption continent-wide. It also displays its wealth in flawlessly maintained highways and hospitals, rich residential districts, elegant shops and stores, clean downtown streets, and impressive office buildings occupied by world-famous corporations.

**Berlin** is the indispensable visit on a trip to Germany; it is well on its way toward regaining its pre-war position as the third most heavily visited city in Europe (London, Paris, Berlin), ousting Rome from that third place position. It's a dynamic, progressive city with an unusually large youth population resulting, it's rumored, from the fact that young people settling in Berlin in the 1990s were granted exemption from the German military draft. Whatever the reason for their migration to Berlin, youthful Berliners are large in

PREVIOUS PAGE: **Museum Island on the Spree River, with the Fernsehturm TV tower in background.**

number and constantly engaged in defying conventions in art, theater, literature, politics, and just-plain counterculture lifestyles; the cafe scene here is electric, nervous, and fun. Every political conviction is on display, and every venue for concerts, drama, opera, and museum exhibitions is jam-packed with intellectual sorts. That's not to say that the more material aspects are shortchanged: Berlin's shopping options are almost as compelling as its superb museums, and high on your list of activities should be a trip to the food halls of the KaDaWe Department Store, which challenges Harrods in London as having the world's most enticing array of eats. I'll conclude my paean to Berlin with mentions of Checkpoint Charlie, Potsdamer Platz, Kurfürstendamm shopping, and an excursion to the nearby city of Potsdam (summer palace of Frederick the Great), none of which you should miss.

The city of **Munich,** the effective capital of Bavaria, is in some ways the opposite of Berlin, even though it enjoys an almost equally rich cultural life in its many major museums (Alte Pinakothek for art, Deutsches Museum for science—it being perhaps the world's finest science museum), concert halls, and theaters. But, in addition to its conservative political stance, the very opposite of Berlin's socialist politics, it also displays a hokey, countrified life best seen in its unique beerhalls, of which the Hofbräuhaus is the most famous but given tough competition from the similar halls of Lowenbrau, Paulaner and Augustiner beers. There you'll view the lifestyle of the typical Bavarian (lederhosen shorts, dirndls on the women, and boisterous rough humor, at which the Berliners would sneer).

Munich is also the jumping-off point for many of Germany's most stellar attractions, especially the awesome royal palaces and castles associated with the life of mad King Ludwig II of Bavaria (be sure to read about his checkered career): Schloss Neuschwanstein (the building which nearly bankrupted the state of Bavaria) and Schloss Hohenschwangau. Consider, too, the much-visited city of **Regensburg** in Bavaria, whose medieval center is a UNESCO treasure.

**Heidelberg** on the River Neckar (near the Rhine) is another great city-site of Germany that will be discussed in the chapter below; and **Hamburg** is a great port city, second in size (in Germany) only to Berlin. It also resembles Berlin in many ways, in the enormous number of its theatres and museums, which underpin an important cultural life in a city that is also a major media center, housing numerous important publications and book publishing companies. It is also famous (or infamous) for its Reeperbahn, a mile-long street dotted with bars, playhouses, and a number of strip clubs and sex exhibitions; on side streets, prostitution is legally offered.

We at Frommer Media LLC offer a full-sized Easy Guide to Germany discussing that nation in detail. But for the highlights of this important country, please continue reading here. And have a good trip!

**–Arthur Frommer**



# BERLIN

Even in history-rich Europe, few cities are as storied as Berlin, rooted in a past that's both glorious and horrific, and now heading at lightning pace into the future. Bombed to ruin by the end of World War II, the seat of the Nazi regime was then divided by the Berlin Wall, the gruesome concrete barrier that split Berlin—and, symbolically, all of Germany—into communist East and democratic West for more than 40 years. Berlin is these days one of the most exciting cities in Europe (many would say *the* most exciting), it's once again Germany's capital, and its lively avenues are lined with some of the world's finest museums, grandest monuments, and shops and cafes that defy the somber communist days of yore. The nightlife scene is only a bit tamer than it was in the decadent 1920s and '30s, the arts are thriving, and gritty old neighborhoods are quickly becoming chic. Despite the near-total destruction at the end of World War II, the city still evokes its imperial past on a grand scale, with monuments evoking Prussian might and museums filled with treasures amassed by a succession of kings and emperors. The city is also full of memorials and reminders of the Nazi and communist eras, suggesting that as fast-paced and forward-thinking as Berlin can be, the city will be confronting its past for generations to come.

## Essentials

Berlin's excellent tourism portal is at **www.visitberlin.de**. For in-person assistance and bookings, it also runs five walk-in Berlin Infostores, including those at Tegel Airport, Hauptbahnhof train station, and the Brendenberg Gate.

**ARRIVING** Berlin has two **airports,** Tegel and Schönefeld (after many delays, a third airport, **Berlin-Brandenburg International (BBI),** is tentatively scheduled to open in 2018).

**Tegel (TXL)** airport, 8km (5 miles) northwest of the center, currently serves European and long-haul destinations. **Buses** 128, X9, 109, and the **Jet Express TXL** depart for Berlin from stops outside the terminal every 10 or 20 minutes from 6am to 11pm. The journey takes between 15 and 40 minutes; tickets cost 2.60€ and can be purchased at the BVG kiosk close to the airport exit or from the ticket machines at the bus station.

The Berlin skyline, dominated by the Fernsehturm TV tower.

Validate your ticket by stamping it in the machine on the bus. A **taxi** ride costs approximately 35€; taxis depart from ranks outside the terminal.

**Schönefeld (SFX)** airport, 18km (11 miles) southeast of the center, connects with destinations across Europe, Asia, and Africa, and is served by low-cost airlines like **easyJet, Ryanair,** and **Germanwings.** A regular **S-Bahn** service (S45 and S9) departs from the airport and takes about 45 minutes to reach central Berlin. Alternatively take the **Airport Express** train, departing every half-hour from 4:30am to 11pm and taking about 30 minutes to reach Hauptbahnhof (Berlin's main train station), stopping en route at Ostbahnhof, Alexanderplatz, and Friedrichstrasse. Tickets for either service cost 3.20€ and can be purchased from the machines on the platforms. Expect to pay around 40€ for the 45-minute **taxi** journey into town. For information on the airports, go to www.berlin-airport.de.

Long-distance high-speed **trains** arrive at and depart from the **Hauptbahnhof** (main train station), Europaplatz 1 (www.bahn.com; ✆ **0800-15-07-090**). The station is well connected to all public transport in Berlin: the entrance to the S-Bahn (elevated train) is on the second floor of the station; the entrance to the U-Bahn (subway or underground train) is on the first floor; and buses and trams stop outside.

By **car,** four Autobahn (freeway) routes enter Berlin from western Germany; three enter from the east. The drive from Frankfurt or Munich takes about 8 hours, depending on traffic. After you're in Berlin, however, a car is a nuisance. Unless you know this huge city well, getting around by public transportation is far easier.

**CITY LAYOUT** Covering some 300 square miles, Berlin is one of the world's largest cities in area, and for first-time visitors, the sprawl can be daunting. A spin around town on a sightseeing bus at the beginning of a visit is an excellent way to orient yourself (see p. 411). Essentially, Berlin has two city centers. One is the commercial district around Zoo Station, extending west along the Kurfürstendamm, a lively shopping avenue, through the Charlottenburg district (this was the heart of West Berlin when the Wall divided the city). The other is the rapidly developing Mitte, the once-drab heart of the old East Berlin and these days a vibrant shopping and office area that clusters around Potsdamerplatz and Alexanderplatz. Stretching between Charlottenburg and Mitte is the Tiergarten park, laid out in the 16th century as a royal hunting ground. At the western end of the park is the business-residential district near Bahnhof Zoo train station, a major transportation hub named for the nearby zoological park; Charlottenburg extends west from here. At Tiergarten's eastern border is the cultural center known as the Kulturforum, home of the Philharmonie (Philharmonic Hall), the famed Gemäldegalerie (Painting Gallery), and other museums, along with the Brandenburg Gate and the Reichstag (Parliament) building; Mitte extends east from these landmarks.

**GETTING AROUND** An excellent public transportation system makes it easy to get around Berlin. Given the distances between points in this sprawling city—it's an expedition-worthy long trek from the Ku'Damm to Alexanderplatz, for instance—you will want to get to know the public transportation system and use it frequently. Berlin is divided into three **tariff zones:** AB (2.60€ for a single fare), BC (2.90€ for a single fare), and ABC (3.20€ for a single fare). A single AB ticket is good for most of the journeys you'll be making in central Berlin. Buy your tickets at any U-Bahn or S-Bahn station and validate them in the station machines before you board. (The entire system runs on an honor system.) Tickets are good for 2 hours. For information on all forms of Berlin's public transportation, call ✆ **030/19-449** or visit **www.bvg.de**.

## Money-Saving Strategies

If you're planning more than two trips on public transportation in Berlin, you'll save money by buying a **Tageskarte (day pass)** for 6.90€ to 7.20€, and good for unlimited transportation within the zones for which you purchase it. You can save euros on transportation and sightseeing with a **Berlin WelcomeCard,** which covers unlimited public transport in zone AB and discounts for 200 sights and attractions. A 2-day pass costs 19.50€; 3- and 5-day passes cost 26.70€ and 34.50€. Another money-saving option is the 3-day **Berlin Welcome Card Museumsinsel,** which costs 40.50€ and provides entry to all five museums on Museum Island plus unlimited public transportation in Berlin's central fare zone. A 3-day **Museum Pass,** including admission to Museum Island's galleries and the city's other major museums (without transportation option), costs 24€. These passes can be purchased at any Berlin Infostore. For more information, visit www.visitberlin.de.

Speedy and efficient, elevated **S-Bahn** trains (www.s-bahn-berlin.de) ply 15 routes. Purchase and validate your ticket at one of the red or yellow ticket-validation machines on the platform before boarding. The S-Bahn operates from 4am to 12:30am, later at weekends. S-Bahn entrances are marked with an s in a green background. Some S-Bahn lines intersect with U-Bahn lines, so you can transfer from one to the other. The S-Bahn is particularly handy if you are traveling from Bahnhof Zoo in western Berlin to Mitte in eastern Berlin.

**U-Bahn** underground trains (www.bvg.de) run to more than 170 stations from 4am until midnight, later on the weekend. At peak times, trains depart every 3 to 5 minutes. U-Bahn entrances are marked with a u in a blue background. Validate your ticket in one of the validation machines before boarding.

If you're not in a hurry, Berlin's **buses and trams** are a great way to see the city, especially from the upper deck of buses. Bus routes 100 and 200 are particularly scenic and travel east-west between Bahnhof Zoo and stops throughout Mitte, passing many Berlin landmarks along the way. Buy your ticket from machines at U-Bahn and S-Bahn stations before boarding, not on the bus. You can download routes from www.bvg.de.

**Taxis** wait outside major hotels, stations, and airports around the clock. Most drivers speak some English. There's a minimum charge of 3.20€, plus 1.65€ per kilometer. If you're going less than 2km (1¼ miles) and flag down the cab, ask for the *kurzstreckentarif* (short-route fare); the driver should switch off the meter and charge no more than 4€. Reputable companies include **TaxiFunk Berlin GmbH** (✆ **030/44-33-22**) and **Funk Taxi Berlin** (✆ **030/26-10-26**).

As in any large city, ditch the **car** before coming to Berlin; it's cheaper and easier to get around on the excellent public transport network. Pay-and-display parking costs around 2.50€ per hour from 9am to 6pm or 8pm. Clearly display your ticket on the dash.

It's even easier to get around as many Berliners do, by **bike,** on the city's network of cycling trails and bike lanes. Stands installed in front of many hotels rent bikes for about 12€ a day. Most S-Bahn and U-Bahn trains have a dedicated car for bikes, but you need to buy an additional reduced-fare ticket to take the bike on public transportation.

Berlin has plenty of grand avenues, pedestrian-only streets, leafy parks, squares, and riverside and canal-side promenades that are well-suited to **walking.** Even so, distances are great enough that you'll probably want to use public transportation to get from one area to another, and then do your explorations on foot once you get there.

## The Neighborhoods in Brief

**ZOO STATION/CHARLOTTENBURG** This wealthy district extends west along the 4km-long (2½-mile) boulevard known as **Kurfürstendamm,** or **Ku'Damm** for short, lined with expensive shops and department stores.

The train station **Bahnhof Zoologischer Garten** (**Bahnhof Zoo** or just Zoo for short), near the Ku'Damm, is the major transportation hub on this side of the city. The 22-story **Europa Center,** a shopping and entertainment complex (Berlin's first, dating from the 1960s), rises near Banhof Zoo, across the plaza from the **Kaiser-Wilhelm-Gedächtnis Kirche (Memorial Church),** bombed in World War II and left in ruin as a reminder of the horrors of war. Charlottenburg's regal centerpiece is **Schloss Charlottenburg (Charlottenburg Palace),** with its lovely gardens. Charlottenburg also is the home of the **Deutsche Oper Berlin (German Opera House),** one of Berlin's three opera houses.

**MITTE** Before the war and the division of the city, the district known as **Berlin-Mitte, Stadtmitte** (City Center), or just plain **Mitte** (Center), was, in fact, the center of Berlin. The oldest and most historic part of Berlin is quickly regaining its prominence. Mitte symbolically begins at **Potsdamerplatz** and the **Brandenburg Gate,** on the east side of **Tiergarten** park (the **Reichstag** is here, too). The grand boulevard called **Unter den Linden,** which starts at the Brandenburg Gate and extends east to the Spree River, is lined with 18th- and 19th-century palaces and monuments. **Museumsinsel (Museum Island),** where five major museums house Berlin's treasure trove of ancient artifacts and other art, anchors the eastern end of Unter den Linden. Near this end of the avenue also stands the grandiose **Berliner Dom (Berlin Cathedral).**

**Friedrichstrasse,** which intersects Unter den Linden, has regained its pre-war status as one of Berlin's major shopping streets. U-Bahn and S-Bahn lines converge at **Friedrichstrasse train station,** the transportation hub of the eastern end of Berlin. **Hauptbahnhof,** Berlin's main train station, is at the northern edge of Mitte in the Government Quarter.

**Alexanderplatz,** a square named for Russian Czar Alexander I, was the center of East Berlin, and along with Potsdamerplatz, is a major Mitte hub. You will know where Alexanderplatz is from just about anywhere in Berlin because the **Fernsehturm (TV tower),** a Soviet-era landmark, rises from the square to a height of 368m (1,207 ft.), making it the highest structure in Europe. The **Nikolaiviertel (Nicholas Quarter),** just south of Alexanderplatz along the Spree River, has been restored to look as it did (with some contemporary touches) in Berlin's medieval and baroque eras.

## Exploring Berlin

Don't be disappointed to learn that two of the city's top attractions are closed for renovations—the Pergamon Altar in the Pergamon Museum on Museum Island is closed until 2019. The Neue Nationalgalerie (New National Gallery) by famed German architect Ludwig Mies van der Rohe is closed for several years. Don't worry: There's plenty else to see in Germany's fascinating capital. Many Berlin museums are closed on Mondays.

### MITTE

**Brandenburger Tor (Brandenburg Gate) ★★★** LANDMARK/ARCHITECTURAL SITE Berlin's most famous and potent symbol is a neoclassical triumphal arch completed in 1791 and crowned by the famous Quadriga, a four-horse copper chariot drawn by the goddess Victoria. The revolutionary events of 1848 and 1918, like those in 1989, saw the gate used as a symbolic gathering place for Berliners. When the Wall came down, hundreds of thousands of East Germans walked freely through the gate into West Berlin for the first time since 1961. In the Room of Silence, built into one of the guardhouses, visitors still gather to meditate and reflect on Germany's past.

Pariserplatz at Unter den Linden. Free admission. S-Bahn: Unter den Linden. Room of Silence daily 10am–6pm.

**DDR Museum ★★** MUSEUM This is life the way it was in the former East Germany, in 17 themed rooms laid out like a prefab housing estate. Answer the phone in the Soviet-era living room, peek into closets, or rev the engine of a Trabant. While the look into everyday lives of ordinary East Germans shows some friendlier aspects—such as the freedom of *Freikörperkultur* (FKK), or nudism—you also learn about the Stasi spy network and step into an interrogation cell for a reminder that this was, at heart, a police state.

Karl-Liebknecht-Strasse 1. www.ddr-museum.de. ✆ **030/847123731.** 6€ adults, 4€ students. U-/S-Bahn: Alexander-Platz. Sun–Fri 10am–8pm, Sat 10am–10pm.

**Deutsches Historisches Museum (German History Museum) ★★** MUSEUM A walk through the old Zeughaus (Armory) brings you face to face with 2,000 years of German history, brought colorfully to life with artifacts that include Napoléon's bicorn hat and sword, which Prussian soldiers discovered after he ran from the Battle of Waterloo in 1815. Especially sobering are first-floor galleries devoted to World War II (where a globe shows the Nazi plot to take over the world), while

**The Brandenburg Gate.**

7

GERMANY | Berlin

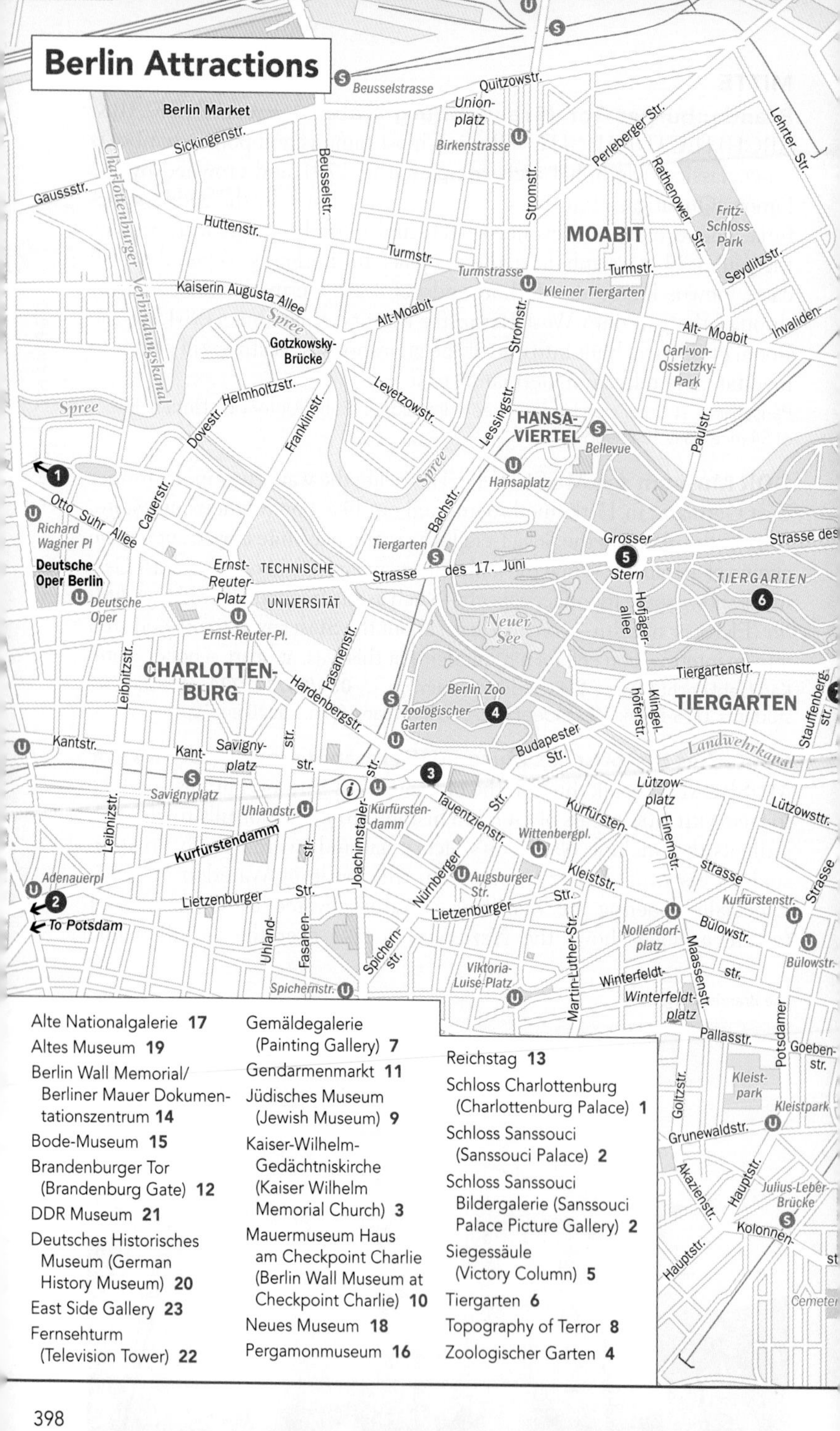
Berlin Attractions
Berlin Market
Beusselstrasse
Quitzowstr.
Union-
platz
Birkenstrasse
Sickingenstr.
Beusselstr.
Perleberger Str.
Lehrter Str.
Rathenower Str.
Stromstr.
Gaussstr.
Charlottenburger Verbindungskanal
Huttenstr.
Turmstr.
MOABIT
Fritz-
Schloss-
Park
Seydlitzstr.
Turmstrasse
Kleiner Tiergarten
Kaiserin Augusta Allee
Spree
Alt-Moabit
Gotzkowsky-
Brücke
Alt- Moabit
Invaliden-
Carl-von-
Ossietzky-
Park
Helmholtzstr.
Levetzowstr.
Lessingstr.
HANSA-
VIERTEL
Bellevue
Paulstr.
Dovestr.
Franklinstr.
Hansaplatz
Otto Suhr Allee
Cauerstr.
Richard
Wagner Pl
Bachstr.
Tiergarten
Grosser
Stern
Strasse des
Deutsche
Oper Berlin
Deutsche
Oper
Ernst-
Reuter-
Platz
TECHNISCHE
UNIVERSITÄT
Strasse des 17. Juni
TIERGARTEN
Ernst-Reuter-Pl.
Neuer
See
Hofjäger-
allee
Fasanenstr.
CHARLOTTEN-
BURG
Leibnitzstr.
Hardenbergstr.
Berlin Zoo
Zoologischer
Garten
Tiergartenstr.
Klingel-
höferstr.
TIERGARTEN
Stauffenberg-
str.
Kantstr.
Kant-
Savigny-
platz
str.
Budapester
Str.
Landwehrkanal
Savignyplatz
Joachimstaler-
str.
Tauentzienstr.
Lützow-
platz
Lützowstr.
Uhlandstr.
Kurfürsten-
damm
Kurfürstendamm
Kurfürsten-
strasse
Wittenbergpl.
Leibnizstr.
Nürnberger
Augsburger
Str.
Kleiststr.
Einemstr.
Adenauerpl
Lietzenburger
Str.
Lietzenburger
Kurfürstenstr.
Strasse
To Potsdam
Uhland-
Fasanen-
Spichern-
str.
Martin-Luther-Str.
Nollendorf-
platz
Bülowstr.
Maassenstr.
Viktoria-
Luise-Platz
Winterfeldt-
Winterfeldt-
platz
Spichernstr.
Pallasstr.
Potsdamer
Goeben-
str.
Goltzstr.
Kleist-
park
Kleistpark
Grunewaldstr.
Akazienstr.
Hauptstr.
Julius-Leber-
Brücke
Kolonnen-
Hauptstr.
Cemeter
Alte Nationalgalerie 17
Altes Museum 19
Berlin Wall Memorial/ Berliner Mauer Dokumentationszentrum 14
Bode-Museum 15
Brandenburger Tor (Brandenburg Gate) 12
DDR Museum 21
Deutsches Historisches Museum (German History Museum) 20
East Side Gallery 23
Fernsehturm (Television Tower) 22
Gemäldegalerie (Painting Gallery) 7
Gendarmenmarkt 11
Jüdisches Museum (Jewish Museum) 9
Kaiser-Wilhelm-Gedächtniskirche (Kaiser Wilhelm Memorial Church) 3
Mauermuseum Haus am Checkpoint Charlie (Berlin Wall Museum at Checkpoint Charlie) 10
Neues Museum 18
Pergamonmuseum 16
Reichstag 13
Schloss Charlottenburg (Charlottenburg Palace) 1
Schloss Sanssouci (Sanssouci Palace) 2
Schloss Sanssouci Bildergalerie (Sanssouci Palace Picture Gallery) 2
Siegessäule (Victory Column) 5
Tiergarten 6
Topography of Terror 8
Zoologischer Garten 4

PRENZLAUER BERG
MITTE
MUSEUMS-INSEL
NIKOLAI-VIERTEL
KREUZBERG
TEMPELHOF
Reichstag
Brandenburger Tor
Fernsehturm
Unter den Linden
Gendarmenmarkt
Information
S-Bahn
U-Bahn
0 1/2 mi
0 0.5 km

galleries covering the post-war period up to reunification are extensive and enlightening. The adjacent glass spiral exhibition space, designed by architect I. M. Pei, houses some provocative exhibitions, such as the work of Jewish caricaturist Arthur Szyk, known for his illustrations mocking Hitler and Mussolini.

Unter den Linden 2. www.dhm.de. ✆ **030/203040.** 8€, free for 17 and under. U-Bahn: Französischestrasse. Daily 10am–6pm.



**Fernsehturm (Television Tower)** ★ VIEW/LANDMARK/ARCHITECTURAL SITE You can't miss this weird-looking television tower, with its metallic glint and revolving silver sphere. The Communists built this symbol of technological advancement in 1968—the tallest structure in Europe (368m/1,208 ft.) is visible from almost everywhere in the city. Berliners call the tower "the speared onion" because of its shape, or the "Pope's Revenge" because what looks like a cross appears on the silvery surface when light is reflected in a certain way. The tower is definitely a presence, and it's the best lookout point in town. Sweeping views over the city extend some 40km (25 miles) on a clear day—plus, as has been said of the Eiffel Tower, the top of this structure is the only place in town where you don't have to look at the damned thing. An elevator zooms you up to the viewing platform in 40. Also up here is "the world's highest bar," where you can order an expensive beer.

Panoramastrasse 1A. www.berlinerfernsehturm.de. ✆ **030/2423333.** 13€ adults, 8€ children under 16. U-/S-Bahn: Alexanderplatz. Mar–Oct 9am–midnight; Nov–Feb 10am–midnight.

**The Jüdisches Museum.**

## REMEMBERING THE berlin wall

The majority of the Berlin Wall was torn down in the early 1990s, but Berliners won't forget this concrete symbol of political division anytime soon, and remaining sections are among the city's most cherished landmarks.

The **East Side Gallery ★★★** (U-Bahn: Warschauerstrasse), a 2km (¾-mile) section of the Wall along the Spree River southeast of Alexanderplatz, is the longest and best-preserved section left standing. It was painted by an international group of artists in the 1990s and is considered an outdoor art gallery.

A portion of the Berlin Wall.

The **Berlin Wall Memorial/Berliner Mauer Dokumentationszentrum ★★★** (Bernauerstrasse 111; www.berliner-mauer-dokumentationszentrum.de; Tues–Sat 10am–6pm, Nov–Mar to 5pm; free admission; U-Bahn: Bernauerstrasse), created by the government as a memorial center, is a 230-ft.-long (70m) reconstructed stretch of the Wall at Bernauerstrasse and Ackerstrasse. The memorial consists of two mirrorlike stainless-steel walls that include fragments of the original wall, and a memorial building with photos of the area pre-1989 and eyewitness testimonies of what it was like when the Wall stood. Part of the memorial is the Chapel of Reconciliation *(Kapelle der Versöhnung)*, a contemporary building set on the site of a church that was blown up in 1985 in order to widen the border strip at this spot.



**Gemäldegalerie (Painting Gallery) ★★★** MUSEUM One of the world's greatest collections of European paintings shows off more than 1,500 canvases—more than you will be able to see even in multiple visits, so you'll want to focus on the highlights. Among these are 16 Rembrandts, including his portrait, *The Mennonite Preacher Anslo and His Wife,* eloquent proof that devotion and prosperity can coexist; and Caravaggio's *Amor Vincit Omnia,* depicting an insolent teenaged cupid with tousled hair, an earthy evocation of "love conquers all." Botticelli's *Portrait of Simonetta Vespucci* and five Madonnas by Raphael are among the many masterpieces of the Italian Renaissance, while two paintings by Vermeer and Peter Paul Rubens's *Perseus Liberating Andromeda* are part of the one of the world's most comprehensive collections of Northern and Netherlandish paintings—these also include a stunning trove of works by Dürer, Cranach, and other 15th- and 16th-century German painters.

Mattäiskirchplatz 4. www.smb.spk-berlin.de/gg. ✆ **030/266423040.** 10€ adults, 5€ students, free for 16 and under. U-/S-Bahn: Potsdamerplatz. Tues–Sun 10am–6pm (Thurs until 8pm).

Checkpoint Charlie.

**Jüdisches Museum (Jewish Museum) ★★★** MUSEUM This tribute to Jewish life in Germany occupies an 18th-century baroque courthouse and an elongated, zinc-clad new wing shaped like a stretched out Star of David, designed by American architect Daniel Libeskind. One section documents the significant role that Jewish inventors, scientists, artists, business people, and bankers played in German society until the terror-filled 1930s, while another presents Jewish culture and way of life—an important undertaking in a country that did its best to annihilate a race. Most effective are sections on the Shoah, reached through dark underground passages and in which a Path of Exile leads past displays of belongings of expelled families, whose grim fates are told on the Street of Extermination. The Holocaust Tower is a black, bare, three-story-high concrete space, where only a little weak light filters in through bars in the ceiling, and a heavy iron door and gives you the terrifying sense of being trapped inside a box car or gas chamber. Other poignant creations include Israeli sculptor Menashe Kadishman's *Shalechet* (Fallen Leaves), a triangular void filled with 10,000 screaming iron faces that clank as you cross them.

Lindenstrasse 9-14. www.jmberlin.de. ✆ **030/25993300.** 5€, free for children 6 and under. U-Bahn: Hallesches Tor or Kochstrasse. Daily 10am–8pm (Mon until 10pm).

**Mauermuseum Haus am Checkpoint Charlie (Berlin Wall Museum at Checkpoint Charlie) ★** MUSEUM Checkpoint Charlie was the most frequently used traffic crossing at the Berlin Wall, used from 1961 to its fall in 1989. Here, the border and the sad era that gave rise to it are commemorated with photographs, newspaper clippings, and other paraphernalia. Most intriguing are the various escape devices, from relatively mundane false passports to chairlifts, hot-air balloons, even a mini-sub; the old "hide in the car trunk" was the most commonly used and costly means of escape, offered by diplomats whose vehicles were not subject to search. The rather gimmicky approach to the exhibits and the too-steep admission charge don't mask the emotional impact of just how desperate those trapped behind the Wall were for a taste of freedom. Friedrichstrasse 43-45. www.mauermuseum.de. ✆ **030/2537250.** 13€ adults, 9.50€ students, free for 16 and under. U-Bahn: Kochstrasse or Stadtmitte. Daily 9am–10pm.



**Reichstag (Parliament) ★★★** LANDMARK/ARCHITECTURAL SITE One of Berlin's most iconic new landmarks is a spectacular glass dome that crowns the seat of the German Parliament. Mirrors reflect light onto the legislators meeting far below, but most eyes are on the city spreading out in all directions. When lit from within like a beacon at night, especially, the spectacle has a Fritz Lang–like quality of a modern metropolis. Views aside, the glittering dome is richly evocative of recent German history. The German Republic was established here at the end of World War I in 1918. A fire that ripped through the building was blamed on a communist, but it was likely set by thugs of Adolf Hitler, who soon swept into power. World War II bombs rendered the landmark a ruined shell, and it languished in a no-man's land between East and

**Interior of the Reichstag dome.**

West until it was restored and reopened in 1999, a symbol of a new, unified Germany. The dome also has an outdoor observation area and a rooftop restaurant. Because this is one of Berlin's most popular attractions, lines can be long.

Platz der Republik 1. www.bundestag.de. ✆ **030/2270.** Free. Tours daily when Parliament is not in session. S-Bahn: Unter den Linden.

**Topography of Terror ★★** MEMORIAL/MUSEUM The location of this modern concrete-and-glass pavilion set amid ruined foundations itself strikes fear, on the site of the former headquarters of the Secret State Police, or SS, and the Gestapo. While the focus is on the nefarious tactics of these terror organizations, the museum takes a broader look, with photographs and other well-presented documentation at how, between 1933 and 1945, the Nazi regime orchestrated the genocide of European Jews, gypsies, homosexuals, and political opponents. The 11-acre, indoor-outdoor site, partially strewn with the remnants of brick torture chambers, is also intended as a chilling memorial to victims of Nazis. Next door rises a remaining section of the Berlin Wall, another haunting reminder of repression.

Niederkirchnerstrasse 8. ✆ **030/254509950.** Free. U-Bahn: Potsdamerplatz. May–Sept daily 10am–8pm; Oct–Apr daily 10am–6pm.

## MUSEUMSINSEL (MUSEUM ISLAND)

Five museums on an island in the River Spree form the oldest museum complex in Berlin, constructed in 1820 after Frederick William III made the privately owned artwork of the royal family accessible to the public. The remarkable neoclassical assemblage of faux-Greek temples and baroque palaces is now listed as a UNESCO World Heritage Site. Do not make the same mistake so many weary travelers have and try to see all five museums in one visit—concentrate on the Pergamon Museum and the Neues Museum to see their ancient treasures, then try to squeeze in a refreshing hour viewing the Impressionist works in the Alte Nationalgalerie. If you are going to visit the museums on Museum Island over a period of several days (and this is the best way to approach them) consider buying a money-saving museum pass, described in "Money-Saving Strategies" box, p. 394, and available for sale from a kiosk on the island.

**Alte Nationalgalerie ★★** MUSEUM This faux-Greek temple atop a high base is a lofty perch for 19th-century paintings. A respectable but small smattering of works by Pissarro, Cezanne, Delacroix, Degas, and van Gogh. Two paintings, Édouard Manet's *In the Conservatory* and Claude Monet's *View of Vétheuil,* were the first Impressionist works ever purchased by a museum. These artists, however, are overshadowed by Germany's own Caspar David Friedrich (1774–1840), a wildly romantic painter of gloomy landscapes and Gothic ruins. His *Abbey in the*

*Oakwood* has been compared to a scene from a horror movie, while *Man and Woman Contemplating the Moon* seems to capture the German sensibility with its appreciation for folklore and nature combined with an over-riding sense of sadness.

Bodestrasse 1-3. www.smb.museum.de. ✆ **030/20905577.** 8€ adults, 4€ students, free for children 16 and under. S-Bahn: Hackescher Markt. Tues–Sun 10am–6pm (Thurs until 10pm).

**Altes Museum ★★★** MUSEUM An 1822 Greek Corinthian temple, with a Pantheon-like rotunda, houses Berlin's treasure trove of antiquities. Greek statuary and amazingly contemporary-looking jewelry and intriguing household objects fill the ground-floor galleries, while the Etruscans and Romans take center stage on the top floor, with a preponderance of tombs and tomb paintings. A Greek bronze of a *Praying Boy* from around 300 B.C., probably the most exquisite bronze statue from antiquity, is the museum's poster child. Most visitors (provided they're 18 years and older) soon find themselves in the quaintly named "Erotic Cabinet," a room filled with statues of satyrs, phalluses, and other Roman pornography.

Am Lustgarten, Museumsinsel. www.smb.museum. ✆ **030/20905577.** 10€ adults, 5€ students, free for 16 and under. S-Bahn: Hackescher Markt. Daily 10am–6pm (Thurs until 10pm).

**Bode-Museum ★★** MUSEUM Museum Island's most romantic architectural presence is this domed palace with a curved and arched facade that seems to rise from the Spree River. The airy, uncluttered galleries house an eon-spanning collection of sculpture, from the Byzantines to the 19th-century Europeans. An hour or so of wandering will provide a glimpse at Donatello's *Pazzi Madonna,* an utterly charming frieze in which the Virgin gazes lovingly into her child's eyes, with just a whiff of sadness as she foresees his death. Among the so-called *Apse Mosaics* from churches in Ravenna is a rich portrayal of a pleasant-looking Archangel Michael in brilliant gold and deep hues of blue and red. The *Mannheim High Altar* is especially poignant, given that so little of it is left after World War II bombings—a youthful Adam and Eve remain, looking a little perplexed by the events they unleashed when they ate the apple.

Monbijoubrücke, Bodestrasse 1-3. www.smb.museum. ✆ **030/20905577.** 10€ adults, 5€ students/children. U-Bahn: Friedrichstrasse. Tues–Sun 10am–6pm (Thurs until 8pm).

**Neues Museum ★★★** MUSEUM Largely destroyed in World War II, the "New Museum" did not reopen until 2009 after a renovation/rebuilding by English architect David Chipperfield. Unless you have a special interest in prehistory (a Neanderthal skull here belongs to one of the world's earliest-known humans), you'll want to focus on the entrancing and enigmatic **bust of Queen Nefertiti** (1350 B.C.), who holds crowds spellbound in her own gallery. As you sweep through the other galleries, linger over the glorious Egyptian collection, which includes some delightfully sensuous statues of royalty of the ancient kingdom carved from wood, a rare substance in vegetation-starved Egypt. The top-floor galleries house a wonderfully whimsical conical gold hat from around 1,000 B.C., probably worn by priests of a cult in what is now southern Germany and engraved with what are believed to be astronomical markings.

Bodestrasse, Museumsinsel. www.neues-museum.de. ✆ **030/266424242.** 12€ adults, 6€ students/children. S-Bahn: Hackescher Markt. Daily 10am–6pm (Thurs until 8pm).

**Pergamon Museum ★★★** MUSEUM You will not be able to see this museum's most lauded treasure, the **Pergamon Altar,** discovered in 1876 in western Turkey and considered one of the Seven Wonders of the Ancient World—that monument is closed for renovation until 2019. What you'll see, though, is hardly a concession. The magnificent two-storied **Market Gate of Miletus,** built during the reign of Hadrian around A.D. 120 for the entrance to the agora in Miletus, a city in what is now Turkey, stretches for almost 30m (100 ft.), richly ornamented with columns and friezes. The **Ishtar Gate** was built in 575 B.C. as one of eight entrances to ancient Babylon and is an astonishing presence, almost 15m (50 ft.) high and incorporating part of a processional way that runs for almost 30m (100 ft.), all in blue-glazed brick embellished with golden lions, dragons, and floral motifs. A third outsized presence is that of the **Mshatta Facade,** from a desert palace outside Amman in Jordan. A huge section, 30m long and 4½m tall (100 x 15 ft.), fills part of the top-floor galleries and is intricately carved with animal motifs. Almost every turn in this remarkable museum turns up another astonishing treasure, such as a fragment of a tablet carved with the Mesopotamian *Epic of Giglamesh,* or a beautifully painted reception room from the mansion of an Ottoman-era banker in the Syrian city of Aleppo.

Am Kupfergraben 5, Museumsinsel. www.smb.spk-berlin.de. ✆ **030/20905577.** 12€ adults, 6€ students, 16 and under free. U-Bahn/S-Bahn: Friedrichstrasse. Daily 10am–6pm (Thurs until 8pm).

Queen Nefertiti at the Neues Museum.

The Ishtar Gate, Pergamon Museum.

## CHARLOTTENBURG & BEYOND

**Kaiser-Wilhelm Gedächtniskirche (Kaiser Wilhelm Memorial Church)** ★★ LANDMARK/MEMORIAL/CHURCH One of Berlin's most famous landmarks, this neo-Romanesque structure from the late 19th century would be rather unremarkable had it not been blown to smithereens in World War II. The ruined shell has been preserved as a haunting symbol of the ravages of war. You can step inside, but no need to—the shell and stub of the shuttered steeple are a moving presence as seen against a backdrop of the snazzy new glass buildings around Zoo Station.

Breitscheidplatz. www.gedaechtniskirche-berlin.de. ✆ **030/2185023.** Free. U-Bahn: Zoologischer Garten. Daily 9am–7pm.

The ruins of Kaiser Wilhelm Memorial Church.

**Schloss Charlottenburg (Charlottenburg Palace)** ★★★ PALACE/CASTLE While the remarkable Sanssouci palace (see

Charlottenburg Palace.

below) is a marvel of royal restraint, this palace built for the queen of Frederick I, Sophie Charlotte, is an extravaganza meant to impress in every nook and cranny. You'll meet the royal line amid the busts and portraits in the Oak Hall, then encounter their tastes in the various chambers in which they left their mark, such as Frederick I's Porcelain Cabinet, quite literally crammed with thousands of pieces of invaluable Chinese and Japanese blue ware; Frederick II's gilded and mirrored Golden Gallery; and the silk-lined boudoirs of Queen Louise (1776–1810). Among the palace's more human-scale corners are the bathroom Frederick I had installed off his baroque bed chamber, and the delightful Orangerie, where thousands of rare plants once flourished, now awash in more mundane greenery. The outbuildings tucked away in the extensive park include the Schinkel Pavilion, an Italian-style summer house from 1825 where King William Frederick III could retreat from the cares of running the Prussian state. You can see the palace only on a tour, given only in German (you can buy an English-language guidebook at the ticket counter).

Luisenplatz. www.spsg.de. ✆ **030/320911.** Day pass for palace and buildings on grounds, 19€ adults, 15€ students and children 13 and under. U-Bahn: Richard-Wagner-Platz. Tues–Sun 10am–6pm (Nov–Mar until 5pm).

**Schloss Sanssouci ★★★** PALACE/CASTLE/PARK/GARDEN This palace set amid gardens and vineyards in the baroque town of Potsdam on the Havel River is one of the greatest and most beautiful examples of European rococo and is often called the German Versailles. But what comes across most vividly is the presence of Frederick II, who had this relatively modest palace built between 1745 and 1747 according to his own designs. The man who became known as Frederick the Great (and "Old Fritz" to his subjects) spent all but the winter months here, escaping court life in Berlin (the name means "without care") and avoiding his wife, the duchess he was forced to marry. One of the most complex of all European rulers, he was abused by his authoritarian father, probably homosexual, a patron of the arts, a brilliant military tactician, and a forceful ruler who shaped Prussia into a powerful European state. The 10 lovely rooms spread out from the elliptical **Marble Hall,** modeled on the Pantheon, are the only lapse into formal pretense. In the rest of the palace, Frederick entertained his esteemed guests in human-scale rooms decorated with birds and flowers. Look for the monkey in the so-called Voltaire room, where the philosopher settled in for long stays. As you wander through the rooms to the accompaniment of an informative English-language audio guide, also notice the portrait of Frederick in the armchair in which he died, unable to lie down because of his pleurisy, and landscapes by Watteau and Canaletto, some of the king's favorite artists; you'll see more of his commendable collection in the Picture Gallery (see below). The **S-Bahn line S7** stops at the **Potsdam Hauptbahnhof (train station).** Hop on **bus no. 695** in front of the station and ride nine stops to the Schloss Sanssouci stop. You can buy a ticket for timed entry to the palace or book online in advance, a good idea during crowded summer months.

at. www.spsg.de. ✆ **0331/9694200.** 8€ adults, 5€ seniors/students. Apr–Oct Tues–Sun 10am–6pm (Nov–Mar to 5pm).

**Schloss Sanssouci Bildergalerie (Picture Gallery)** ★★ GALLERY/MUSEUM Frederick the Great's cultured tastes extended to art, and his collection of works from the Italian Renaissance and baroque eras, housed in marble galleries in a converted gatehouse on the eastern side of the park, is the one other sight on the Sanssouci grounds that you should make time to see. A flyer in English details the most important works, but there are three not to miss: *The Incredulity of St. Thomas* by Caravaggio (1571–1610) is one of the artist's most masterful works, a study in chiaroscuro (contrasting lights and darks) that shows Christ guiding the saint's hands into one of his wounds—"Doubting Thomas" had not witnessed Christ's resurrection and famously said, "Unless I see the nail marks in his hands and put my finger where the nails were, and put my hand into his side, I will not believe it." *Pentecost,* by Anthony van Dyck (1599–1641), shows another divine appearance, this one of the Holy Spirit to the Apostles, a swirl of light and color that is one of the Flemish-born artist's most noted forays into biblical subjects; this canvas was part of a series that was largely destroyed in World War II. Among several works by Peter Paul Rubens (1577–1640) is *St. Jerome in His Hermitage.* It seems fitting that the scholarly Frederick would gravitate to a portrait of this learned saint, and because Rubens was probably the most prolific and most respected painters of his time, it's only natural that his work would find its way to Sanssouci.

Park Sanssouci. 6€ adults, 5€ seniors/students. May–Oct Tues–Sun 10am–6pm.





## BERLIN'S BEST OUTDOOR SPACES

**Gendarmenmarkt ★★★** SQUARE Alexanderplatz and Potsdamerplatz, Berlin's most famous squares, are awash in traffic and surrounded by office towers—those in Potsdamerplatz are glitzy new constructions while the Soviet-era blocks surrounding Alexanderplatz are slated for a redo. You'll encounter an entirely different atmosphere in Gendarmenmarkt, the most beautiful architectural ensemble in Berlin, flanked by twin churches inspired by Rome's Piazza del Popolo. On the north side of the square is the **Französicher Dom (French Cathedral),** built for the influx of French Huguenots (Protestants) who settled in Berlin after being forced to flee Catholic France in 1685. Facing this church like a mirror image on the south side is the **Deutscher Dom (German Cathedral).** The centerpiece is imposing, neoclassical **Schauspielhaus,** or theater, now called the **Konzerthaus am Gendarmenmarkt.** Looking at the square today, it's hard to imagine that by the end of World War II, the Gendarmenmarkt was reduced to a pile of smoldering rubble and remained in ruins until 1977, when the East Berlin government undertook its reconstruction.

U-Bahn: Hausvogteiplatz or Stadmitte.

**Tiergarten ★★★** PARK/GARDEN This private park, laid out in the early 16th century so royalty could hunt wild boar, has been open to all since 1742, when Frederick II decreed the tract a "pleasure garden" for his subjects to enjoy. Berliners' favorite spot to stroll is an urban oasis of lawns, canals, trees, and miles of cycling and walking paths that meander over some 540 acres through the center of the city. You can find furred, feathered, and finned company in The **Zoologischer Garten (Berlin Zoo)** and **Aquarium** in the park's southwestern corner, and you'll never be too far from civilization anywhere in the park. German presidents reside in the dignified **Schloss Bellevue,** while the **Siegessäule (Victory Column),** erected in 1873 to commemorate the Prussian victory in the Prussian-Danish war, is topped by a golden goddess of victory (dubbed "Golden Elsie" by Berliners). The reward for a climb up the 290 steps of the spiral staircase is a monumental view over the park and city and down the Strasse des 17 Juni, a wide boulevard that bisects the Tiergarten, past the Brandenburg Gate and Reichstag to the Unter den Linden.

S-Bahn: Tiergarten or Bellevue; S/U-Bahn: Zoologischer Garten. Observation platform 3€ adults, 2.50€ students/children. Platform open daily (Apr–Oct Mon–Fri 9:30am–6:30pm, Sat–Sun 9:30am–7pm; Nov–Mar Mon–Fri 10am–5pm, Sat–Sun 10am–5:30pm.

The 1873 Victory Column in Tiergarten.



## Organized Tours

For an excellent introduction to Berlin and its history, try one of the themed **walking tours** offered by **Berlin Walks** (www.berlinwalks.de; ✆ **030/3019194**). "Discover Berlin" is a 4-hour introductory tour; "Infamous Third Reich Sites" focuses on the sites of major Nazi buildings in central Berlin; "Jewish Life in Berlin" takes you through the pre-war Jewish community. Reservations are unnecessary—simply meet the guide at the appointed starting point, which will be listed on the website. Tours (in English) cost 12€ for adults, 10€ for 14- to 25-year-olds.

Berlin is a sprawling metropolis, and an organized **bus tour** is the best way to get a good overview of the entire city and its many neighborhoods. **Berlin City Circle,** Kurfürstendamm 216 (www.city-circle.de; ✆ **030/88-04-190;** U-Bahn: Kurfürstendamm), is one of several operators offering frequent hop-on, hop-off service and decent commentary via a taped spiel you listen to on headphones (better than hard-to-hear and just-as-rote live commentary on some tours). You can board at stops along the Kurfürstendamm and more than a dozen other major sites. Opt for the 2-day pass so you can take the full tour one day and hop on and off at various sites the next day; about 24€, but check the website for special offers.

The city's best-known boat operator, **Stern und Kreisschiffahrt,** Pushkinallee 15 (www.sternundkreis.de; ✆ **030/53-63-600**), offers several tours along the Spree and Havel rivers. The most popular cruise, "Historische Stadtfahrt" (Historic City Tour, 13€), is offered daily from March through October, and takes you for a 1-hour ride on the Spree.



## Especially for Kids



Parents will want to use their judgement about what and what not to expose their kids to in Berlin. The city's Nazi past can be traumatic even to adults who are familiar with the gruesome facts. And some exhibits, such as those at the Topography of Terror and the experiential installations at the Jewish Museum might be quite upsetting to youngsters. On the other hand, with a little parental guidance to explain the photographs of Berlin as a bombed-out ruin, young visitors will love the **Reichstag,** with its irresistible ramps inside the glass dome and the wide-ranging views of the city. A climb to the top of the **Victory Column,** with its viewing platform, is another surefire hit. Once in the **Tiergarten,** head over to the **Zoo** in the southwest corner at Hardenbergplatz 8 (www.zoo-berlin.de; ✆ **30/254010**); the pandas steal the show, though other animals, who inhabit the world's first zoo enclosures to mimic natural habitats, put on a good display, too; it's open daily 9am to 5pm, to 6:30pm in summer; 13€ adults, 6.50€ children 5 to 15, under 5 free (S-Bahn/U-Bahn: Zoologischer Garten). Meanwhile, even the crankiest little museumgoers will come to life in the **Pergamon Museum**, with its magnificent installations of walls and gates from ancient civilizations.

## Where to Stay

Good news all around on the Berlin hotel front: Rooms are plentiful, and a lot less expensive than they are in most other European cities. Unless a big event is happening in town, you'll likely get an especially good price on hotel websites. Note, though, that breakfast usually is not included in the lower rates.

### IN & AROUND MITTE

#### Expensive

**Hotel de Rome ★** An ornate stone bank from 1889 is now one of Berlin's most atmospheric getaways, with dramatic, ornately ceilinged, mosaic-floored lounges created from the former banking floor and a swimming pool filling a former vault. Guest quarters are a little less dramatic, but soothingly done in soft hues and handsomely furnished with contemporary flair. Suites occupy the former executive offices and are especially welcoming, with warmly paneled walls and soaring ceilings; the fact that East German politicos once hammered out economic policy in these rooms does not seem to cramp the luxurious aura, while World

War II bullets and shrapnel embellished in the woodwork add a bit of historic cache. A warm-weather rooftop terraces offers sweeping views across the city.

Behrenstrasse 37. www.roccofortehotels.com. ✆ **030/4606090.** 108 units. Doubles 295€–355€. U-Bahn: Franzosischestrasse. **Amenities:** Restaurant; bar; spa; pool; free Wi-Fi.

**The Mandala Hotel ★★★** In this modern tower, candles and splashing water features offer a sense of calm the moment you step through the doors off busy Potsdamerplatz. The large rooms and suites begin on the fifth floor, removing them from street noise, and contemporary decor with natural finishes of wood and stone and comfortable furnishings add a relaxing sheen. All units have kitchenettes, and even the simple doubles are suite size. The opulent breakfast buffet is served in the lovely Facil restaurant, a glass-walled structure surrounded by bamboo and greenery.

Potsdamerstrasse 3. www.themandala.de. ✆ **030/590050000.** 167 units. Doubles 180€–280€. U-Bahn: Potsdamerplatz. **Amenities:** Restaurant; bar; gym; room service; spa; free Wi-Fi.

### Moderate

**Arcotel Velvet ★★★** Floor-to-ceiling, wall-to-wall windows create a sense of openness and light in the contemporarily styled guest rooms, bringing the vibrant neighborhood indoors. Only a sheer silk drapery separates the bathing area and sink from the main room, so you can enjoy the view while soaking in the extra-deep tubs. Upper-floor suites, an especially good value, have sloping walls of glass overlooking the rooftops of Berlin, along with living areas and kitchenettes that will make you feel like you've settled into your own Berlin garret. The ground-floor bar changes its decor every couple of months and serves some of the best cocktails in town.

Oranienburgerstrasse 52. www.arcotel.at. ✆ **030/2787530.** 85 units. Doubles 89€–114€. S-Bahn: Oranienburgerstrasse. **Amenities:** Bar; bikes; free Wi-Fi.

**Honigmond Garden and Honigmond Hotels ★★★** A green bower with lawns and creeping vines delivers on the promise of the name, providing a welcome urban retreat where the only disturbances are birdsong and a splashing fountain. The high-ceilinged, 19th-century guest rooms are no less delightful, filled with period pieces on glistening hardwood floors and oil paintings on handsomely papered walls. The old world charm extends to the Honigmond, just down the street, which remains open in the winter, when the Honigmond Garden closes for a couple of months.

Invalidenstrasse 122. www.honigmond-berlin.de. ✆ **030/284455077.** 16 units Honigmond Garden; 44 units Honigmond. Doubles 125€–230€, includes breakfast. U-Bahn: Berlin-Nordbahnhof Tor. **Amenities:** Restaurant; bar; room service, free Wi-Fi.

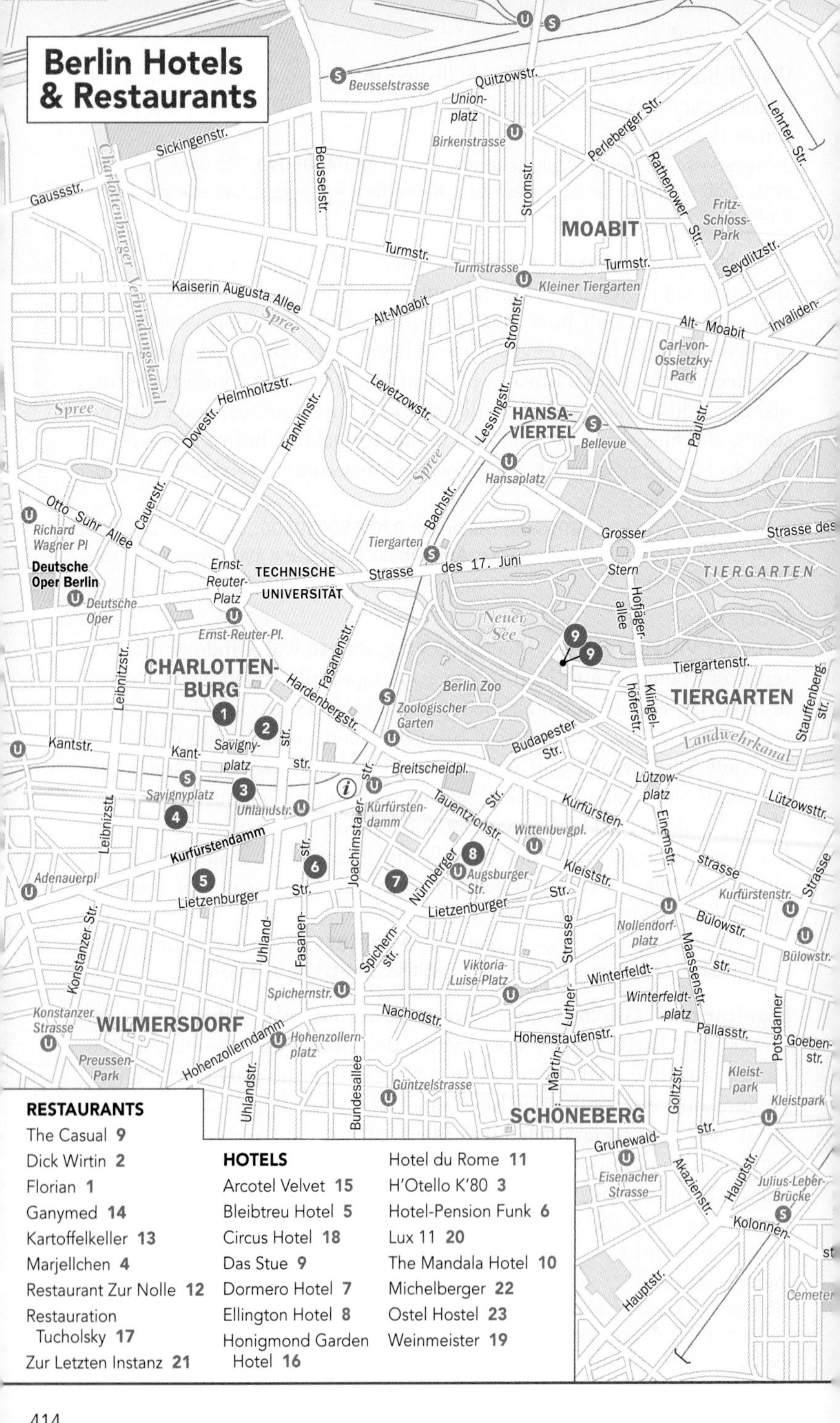

Berlin Hotels & Restaurants
MOABIT
HANSA-VIERTEL
TECHNISCHE UNIVERSITÄT
CHARLOTTEN-BURG
TIERGARTEN
WILMERSDORF
SCHÖNEBERG
Beusselstrasse
Quitzowstr.
Union-platz
Birkenstrasse
Perleberger Str.
Lehrter Str.
Sickingenstr.
Gaussstr.
Charlottenburger Verbindungskanal
Beusselstr.
Stromstr.
Rathenower Str.
Fritz-Schloss-Park
Turmstr.
Turmstrasse
Kleiner Tiergarten
Seydlitzstr.
Kaiserin Augusta Allee
Spree
Alt-Moabit
Invaliden-
Carl-von-Ossietzky-Park
Helmholtzstr.
Levetzowstr.
Lessingstr.
Dovestr.
Franklinstr.
Bellevue
Paulstr.
Hansaplatz
Bachstr.
Otto Suhr Allee
Richard Wagner Pl
Deutsche Oper Berlin
Deutsche Oper
Cauerstr.
Tiergarten
Grosser Stern
Strasse des 17. Juni
Ernst-Reuter-Platz
Ernst-Reuter-Pl.
Hofjägerallee
Neuer See
Fasanenstr.
Hardenbergstr.
Leibnitzstr.
Tiergartenstr.
Berlin Zoo
Zoologischer Garten
Klingelhöferstr.
Stauffenbergstr.
Kantstr.
Kant-str.
Savigny-platz
Savignyplatz
Budapester Str.
Landwehrkanal
Breitscheidpl.
Lützowplatz
Lützowstr.
Uhlandstr.
Kurfürstendamm
Tauentzienstr.
Kurfürstenstrasse
Wittenbergpl.
Einemstr.
Leibnizstr.
Joachimstaler-str.
Nürnberger Str.
Augsburger Str.
Kleiststr.
Adenauerpl
Lietzenburger Str.
Kurfürstenstr.
Nollendorfplatz
Bülowstr.
Konstanzer Str.
Uhland-str.
Fasanen-str.
Spichernstr.
Viktoria-Luise-Platz
Martin-Luther-Strasse
Winterfeldtstr.
Winterfeldtplatz
Maassenstr.
Nachodstr.
Konstanzer Strasse
Hohenzollerndamm
Hohenzollernplatz
Hohenstaufenstr.
Pallasstr.
Potsdamer str.
Goebenstr.
Preussen-Park
Güntzelstrasse
Bundesallee
Goltzstr.
Kleistpark
Grunewaldstr.
Eisenacher Strasse
Akazienstr.
Hauptstr.
Julius-Leber-Brücke
Kolonnenstr.
RESTAURANTS
The Casual 9
Dick Wirtin 2
Florian 1
Ganymed 14
Kartoffelkeller 13
Marjellchen 4
Restaurant Zur Nolle 12
Restauration Tucholsky 17
Zur Letzten Instanz 21
HOTELS
Arcotel Velvet 15
Bleibtreu Hotel 5
Circus Hotel 18
Das Stue 9
Dormero Hotel 7
Ellington Hotel 8
Honigmond Garden Hotel 16
Hotel du Rome 11
H'Otello K'80 3
Hotel-Pension Funk 6
Lux 11 20
The Mandala Hotel 10
Michelberger 22
Ostel Hostel 23
Weinmeister 19

PRENZLAUER BERG
MITTE
MUSEUMS-INSEL
NIKOLAI-VIERTEL
KREUZBERG
TEMPELHOF
Reichstag
Brandenburger Tor
Holocaust Memorial
Berliner Dom
Fernsehturm
Gendarmen-markt
Hauptbahnhof
Friedrich-strasse
Alexander-pl.
Hackescher Markt
Potsdamer Platz
Spree
Landwehrkanal
Tempelhofer Feld
Viktoriapark
Volkspark Hasenheide
Unter den Linden
Karl-Marx-Allee
Information
S-Bahn
U-Bahn
0 1/2 mi
0 0.5 km

**Lux 11** ★★★ Casually redone with just the right amount of contemporary flair, these three interconnected 19th-century buildings offer big, bright spaces with crisp white walls and low-flung furnishings set on neutral flooring. Many units open to balconies, and those in the back face a leafy courtyard. Bathroom vanities backed by rain showers (and deep soaking tubs in some suites) are open to the sleeping quarters (making the arrangements seem even more spacious) and small kitchenettes are niftily tucked into alcoves. A very attractive cafe serves light fare throughout the day, and an Asian-themed restaurant goes into full swing for dinner.

Rosa-Luxemburg-Strasse 9-13. www.lux-eleven.com. ✆ **030/9362800**. 72 units. Doubles 149€–229€. S-Bahn: Alexanderplatz. **Amenities:** Restaurant; bar; free Wi-Fi.

**Michelberger Hotel** ★ Set designers, graphic artists, and furniture designers combined forces to create idiosyncratic spaces out of a former warehouse, where rooms might resemble a mountain chalet, a cozy library, or a funky industrial space. Flea-market finds, mirrors suspended on ropes, and cat-themed wallpaper contribute to the eclectic decor. Some elements—beds suspended dizzyingly from the ceiling and shower windows that open into rooms—are decidedly for the young and young at heart, as is the popular bar and courtyard beer garden.

Warschauerstrasse 39/40. www.michelbergerhotel.com. ✆ **030/29778590**. 119 units. Doubles 85€–145€. U-Bahn: Warschauerstrasse. **Amenities:** Restaurant; bar; free Wi-Fi.

**Weinmeister** ★ Late sleepers find nirvana in this haven of stylish comfort where modular, high-backed, upholstered beds take up most of the floor space in guest rooms soothingly done in darks tones of gray and brown; crawl into one of these sleep capsules after a night in the clubs and you won't want to get out again. Luxurious showers opening directly into the rooms deliver another sort of hedonistic pleasure, while a rooftop terrace offers a breath of fresh air and sweeping views across Mitte. If you are too relaxed to leave the premises, the downstairs lobby/bar is crammed with overstuffed chairs that are as cocooning as the beds upstairs.

Weinmeisterstrasse 2. www.the-weinmeister.com. ✆ **030/7556670.** Doubles 129€–179€. U-Bahn: Weinmeisterstrasse. **Amenities:** Bar; spa; free Wi-Fi.

### Inexpensive

**Circus Hotel** ★★★ Relaxing in the friendly, sofa-filled downstairs cafe is reason enough to seek out this lively corner of Mitte. Rooms upstairs are similarly welcoming, mixing cheerily colorful walls (think orange, aqua, or deep red, offset by white), 1960s-esque furniture created by the hotel's designer, and homey bric-a-brac for an added dash of personality. Ask for a room facing the rear garden and you'll forget that you're only a short walk from Museum Island and other city-center attractions. Circus also operates a hostel right across the street from the hotel at Weinbergsweg 1A (✆ **030/20003939**) with 16 simple bedrooms, costing 29€ to 31€ for a dorm bed, 29€ to 43€ for a double.

Rosenthalerstrasse 1. www.circus-berlin.de. ✆ **030/20003939.** 60 units. Doubles 85€–95€. U-Bahn: Rosenthalerplatz. **Amenities:** Restaurant; bar; free Wi-Fi.

**Ostel Hostel ★** Here's your chance to indulge in what Berliners call *Ostalgia,* a kitschy nostalgia for Soviet culture. In a concrete post-war tower-block, you'll find funky, functional furniture and quirky modern lamps, accented with lurid brown and orange wallpaper and portraits of Soviet officials. Singles and doubles offer shared or private baths, while a few apartments sleep four in two bedrooms with a living room and kitchen. For all the communist inspiration, a definite capitalist vibe prevails in the surrounding Friedrichshain district, one of Berlin's trendiest enclaves.

Wriezener Karree 5. www.ostel.eu. ✆ **030/5768660.** Doubles with private bath 39€–44€. S-Bahn: Ostbahnhof. **Amenities:** Free Wi-Fi.

## HOTELS IN CHARLOTTENBURG

### Expensive

**Das Stue ★★★** Berlin is at its most glamorous in this stylish redo of the 1930s Danish embassy and a stunning new addition that hangs over the adjacent zoo. The name is Danish for "living room," and intimate, sumptuously designed lounges open off the lobby and grand staircase. In the similarly soothing guest rooms, wool carpets on dark-wood floors, rich fabrics, and custom-made furnishings ooze style and comfort, augmented with sliding walls, hidden cabinets, and loads of other clever design touches and the latest electronics. From many rooms, strutting ostriches and hopping kangaroos put on a show just outside the floor-to-ceiling windows. Suites are truly grand, occupying the embassy's former reception rooms, and a delightful swimming pool and spa are tucked into the lower-level.

Drakestrasse 1. www.das-stue.com. ✆ **030/3117220.** 80 units. Doubles 206€–300€. S-Bahn: Zoo. **Amenities:** Restaurant; bar; room service; spa; free Wi-Fi.

**Dormero Hotel ★★** This elegantly converted apartment house is largely Bauhaus in design, and the airy, high-ceilinged accommodations are filled with light and century-old moldings, paneling, and rich oak floors. Rooms are pleasantly sleek and modernist, embellished with museum-worthy contemporary art. The sense of serenity—a gift here in central Berlin—is accented by views into a lovely Japanese garden. Charlottenburg shopping and attractions are just outside the door, but first waste an hour or two over a coffee or drink in the enticing Wintergarten conservatory.

Eislebenerstrasse 14. www.dormero-hotel-brandenburgerhof.de. ✆ **030/214050.** 86 units. Doubles 180€–315€. U-Bahn: Kurfürstendamm or Augsburgerstrasse. **Amenities:** 2 restaurants; bar; spa; gym access; room service; free Wi-Fi.

### Moderate

**Bleibtreu Hotel ★★** High-ceilinged, tall-windowed guest rooms in what was once a patrician townhouse just off the Ku'Damm are coolly and comfortably contemporary. Handsome furnishings custom-made with blonde woods and neutral natural fabrics set a soothing tone that extends to the little side garden littered with glittering blue stones, while clever, remote-controlled lighting includes a "sunlight" setting to combat Berlin's gloomy winters. Also relaxing is the Wellness Center, where an herbal steam bath is a surefire way to erase stress.

Bleibtreustrasse 31. www.bleibtreu.com. ✆ **030/884740.** 59 units. Doubles 120€–180€ e. U-Bahn: Uhlandstrasse. **Amenities:** Restaurant; bar; gym; room service; sauna; free Wi-Fi.

**Ellington Hotel ★** The ground-floor ballroom of Charlottenburg's most distinctive Bauhaus landmark, a 1920s office block, once hosted Duke Ellington and other musicians. The jazz legend has long since departed, but original Art Moderne details stand out against white interiors so crisply stark you won't want to unpack for fear of ruining the effect. Completing the antiseptically airy effect are low-lying beds topped with fluffy white linens, light wood floors, white-framed windows, and white surfaces. If you find the guest quarters to be just a bit too sterile, retreat to the downstairs lounge, where comfy couches and live music carry on the premises' tradition.

Nuernbergerstrasse 50-55. www.ellington-hotel.com. ✆ **030/683150.** 285 units. Doubles 115€-145€. U-Bahn: Wiitenbergerplatz. **Amenities:** Restaurant; 2 bars; free Wi-Fi.

### Inexpensive

**H'Otello K'80 ★★** Handsome furnishings set on gleaming wood floors bring a dash of modern style to elegant Savignyplatz, with its fine shops and restaurants just outside the door—conveniently, so is the S-Bahn stop (double-glazing keeps noise at bay). Top floor rooms come with some extra space and terraces and are excellent value for the tony neighborhood, whose denizens like to relax in the welcoming ground-floor bar.

Knesebeckstraße 80. www.hotello.de. ✆ **030/6807310.** 28 units. Doubles 80€–120€. S-Bahn: Savignyplatz. **Amenities:** Bar; sauna; free Wi-Fi.

**Hotel-Pension Funk ★★** You'd almost expect *Cabaret*'s Sally Bowles to greet you at the door of this 19th-century apartment, the former home of Danish silent-movie star Asta Nielsen and a delightfully atmospheric throwback to the Berlin of yesteryear. The high-ceilinged guest rooms and public spaces are replete with such original features as Art Nouveau windows and plasterwork ceilings, and the sturdy, dark-wood furnishings, Turkish carpets, patterned wallpaper, upholstered divans, and carved headboards are kept at high polish. Modern baths (a few are shared) don't intrude on the glorious old world ambience. The location off Ku'Damm is still a top address, and the hearty buffet breakfast served in the elegant dining room is a stylish way to start a day of exploring. Fasanenstrasse 69. www.hotel-pensionfunk.de. ✆ **030/8827193.** 14 units. Doubles with private bath 82€–129€, includes breakfast. U-Bahn: Kurfürstendamm or Uhlandstrasse.



## Where to Eat

Brace yourself, because Berlin food is stick-to-your-ribs sort of fare, fairly basic and *very* filling: grilled or pickled herring with onions, fried potatoes, and bacon; pickled or roast pork *(Schweinefleisch)* or pork knuckles *(Eisbein)* with red cabbage and dumplings; meatballs *(Buletten)* with boiled potatoes; and pea soup *(Erbsensuppe)*. Berliners also love ethnic food, especially Italian, and two kinds of fast food are ubiqutious: the doner kebab, meat (usually lamb) roasted on a vertical spit, a gift from Turkish workers who have settled in Berlin, and currywurst, a sausage (usually cut into bite-size pieces) sprinkled with curry powder and traditionally served with *pommes frite,* cabbage salad, or a Brötchen (white roll). You'll see kebab and currywurst stands all over Berlin.

### MITTE

#### Expensive

**Ganymed** ★★ FRENCH An air of contentment settles over this wonderfully old-fashioned bistro near the banks of the River Spree. It's been around since 1929, serving French and German classics through the war and the GDR days. The cozy, art-laden rooms—where candlelight flickers on checkered tablecloths and aproned waiters are firmly in command—carry a hefty whiff of Paris, but the brasserie-style fare leans

*Eisbein* **(pork knuckles) with cabbage and potatoes, a classic German dish.**

toward such Berlin classics as green-pea soup and pig knuckles, braised here in Beaujolais and served on broad beans and minced potatoes.
Schiffbauerdamm 5. www.ganymed-brasserie.de. ✆ **030/28599046.** Mains 15€–28€; 3-course fixed-price dinner 33€. Daily noon–midnight. U-Bahn: Friedrichstrasse.



### Moderate

**Restauration Tucholsky** ★★★ GERMAN Kurt Tucholsky was a critic and journalist in the 1920s, and this homey corner pub pays its namesake tribute by providing a welcoming atmosphere suited to lingering and talking. A neighborhood crowd does just that, and though service can be brisk, there's no pressure to rush through such Berlin specialties as lentil soup with chunks of fried knockwurst or *kasseler,* braised roast of pork rump. In summer, the action moves to a front garden, one of the liveliest spots in this quiet corner of Mitte.
Torstrasse. www.restauration-tucholsky.de. ✆ **030/817349.** Mains 10€–20€. Daily noon–midnight. S-Bahn: Oranienburgerstrasse.



**Zur Letzten Instanz** ★★ GERMAN Berlin's oldest restaurant, dating from 1525, occupies two floors of a much-restored baroque building amid a maze of medieval lanes in the Nikolaiviertel (Nicholas Quarter). The wood-paneled dining rooms have hosted everyone from Napoléon, who supposedly warmed his tootsies next to an old-fashioned *Kachelofen* (ceramic stove) still in place, and, a couple of centuries later, Jacques Chirac. These days, appreciative tourists flock in, but the menu is traditional and excellent, with Berlin staples like grilled herring, meatballs, and braised lamb knuckles with green beans and dumplings. The quick-witted waiters who have worked here for decades run a tight Teutonic ship. It's worthwhile to leave room for the house dessert: chocolate-covered pancakes filled with blueberries, vanilla ice cream, and whipped cream.
Waisenstrasse 14-16 (near the Alexanderplatz). www.zurletzteninstanz.de. ✆ **030/2425528.** Mains 12€–20€. Mon–Sat noon–1am. U-Bahn: Klosterstrasse.

### Inexpensive

**Kartoffelkeller** ★ GERMAN The potato *(kartoffel)* is a mainstay of German cuisine, and in this cozy cellar *(keller)* the staple comes into its own and is celebrated as a key and delicious ingredient of more than 100 dishes. Several types of potato soups (one with shrimp and salmon and another with smoked sausage and bacon), ten or so versions of potato pancakes, and a hefty choice of fried potato dishes (such as with fried onions and bacon) are available. In many dishes the potato is relegated to a delicious side, often boiled or mashed and accompanying many variations of pork. It's all washed down with a good choice of beers, and served in a garden in warmer months.
Albrechtstrasse 14b. www.kartoffelkeller.com. ✆ **030/282-85-48.** Mains 9€–14€. Daily 11am–11pm. S-Bahn: Friedrichstrasse.

**Restaurant Zur Nolle** ★★ GERMAN The arched arcades beneath the Friedrichstrasse S-Bahn station are the atmospheric setting of these lively rooms, which were already a hot spot a century ago when the place was a working-class beer hall. The scene is a little tamer and snazzier now, but the inviting 1920s ambience remains, and the menu focuses on filling, unpretentious Berlin favorites served in hearty portions. Jacket potatoes are filled with herring, yogurt, apple, or onions, and homemade *Buletten* (meatballs) may come with fried egg, bacon, onions, or mushrooms. This friendly place is as popular with office workers as it with Mitte nightowls, and joining them provides a good look at a real cross-section of Berliners.

Georgenstrasse, S-Bahnbogen 203 (beneath the arches of Friedrichstrasse S-Bahn station). ✆ **030/2082645.** Mains 7€–13€. Mon–Thurs 11:30am–midnight; Fri–Sat 11:30am–1am; Sun 11:30am–6pm.



## CHARLOTTENBURG

### Expensive

**The Casual** ★★ CONTINENTAL It's a pleasure just sitting in this beautiful and intimate space in **Das Stue** ★★★ hotel (see p. 417), more like the living room of a private home than a hotel dining room, with richly covered banquettes at the widely spaced tables and warmly textured walls and floors. The menu is geared to tasting and sharing, with small plates of cheese, Iberian ham, and pastas, with some forays into spring rolls and ham croquettes and other international fare, including some more substantial lamb, beef, and fish dishes. On a warm summer evening, this is a perfect place to end up after a walk in the Tiergarten.

Drakestrasse 1. www.das-stue.com. ✆ **030/3117220.** Dishes 9€–30€. Daily 7–11:30pm. S-Bahn: Zoo.

### Moderate

**Florian** ★★★ AUSTRIAN Berliners have come to count on these casually chic rooms for beautifully prepared versions of German and Austrian classics, served by a friendly staff intent on providing a satisfying dining experience. The menu changes daily and is presented on handwritten cards (with a few English translations included). You can always find some hearty meat dishes, such as venison goulash in season, or rump steak with a red wine sauce. A few fish choices are always included, and among the pasta dishes are some memorable variations of risotto. The kitchen stays open into the wee hours, making this an excellent choice for a meal after a performance at the nearby Deutsche Oper Berlin.

Grolmanstrasse 52. www.restaurant-florian.de. ✆ **030/3139184.** Mains 12€–24€. Daily 6pm–3am. S-Bahn: Savignyplatz.

**Marjellchen** ★★ EAST PRUSSIAN Old East Prussian recipes prepared by the owner's grandmother inspire dishes served amid a lot of old

Appetizers at Marjellchen.

world charm, with oil lamps lighting the pink tablecloths and vintage prints covering every inch of wall space. Aproned waiters will steer you to some traditional dishes you don't always encounter in modern Berlin: *Beetenbartsch,* a red-beet soup with beef strips and sour cream, is a delicious starter, and you can venture on to pork kidneys in sweet-and sour cream sauce or play it safe with that old Berlin favorite, *Königsburger Klöpse* (meatballs with parsley potatoes and beetroot).

Mommsenstrasse 9. www.marjellchen-berlin.de. ✆ **030/8832676.** Mains 11€–24€. Daily 5pm–midnight. U-Bahn: Adenauerplatz or Uhlandstrasse.

### Inexpensive

**Dicke Wirtin ★** GERMAN It can be surprisingly difficult to find a good German meal in fashionable Charlottenburg, where the preference seems to be for anything foreign, especially of the Italian persuasion. That may explain the popularity of this cozy beer hall, where the home-cooking includes stuffed cabbage, several kinds of sausages and meatballs, and a delicious pork *Weinerschnitzel* served in portions so large that the meat hangs over the side of the plate. The three paneled rooms can be packed to the rafters with neighborhood regulars, but there's usually room at the friendly bar, where hardworking bartenders dispense nine brews on tap.

Carmestrasse 9. www.dicke-wirtin.net. ✆ **030/3124952.** Mains 9€–18€. Daily 11am–1am. S-Bahn: Savignyplatz.

## Shopping

For former East Berliners, shopping for anything but the basics was a dream just a few decades ago. But the now-united city has lost no time in catching up with consumer culture. You can buy just about anything you want in Berlin, in the west or the east—don't expect any great bargains, though the quality of many German-made items is exceptionally fine.

The main shopping boulevard in the western part of Berlin is the famous **Ku'Damm** (short for Kurfürstendamm), where Chanel, Dior, and what seems like every other designer in the world puts in an appearance. For a distinctly Berlin experience, though, head to the adjoining Tauentzienstrasse and **Kaufhaus des Westens (KaDeWe),** Tauentzienstrasse 21 (www.kadewe.de; ✆ **030/21210;** U-Bahn: Witten), a huge department store that has been supplying Berliners with high fashion and housewares for more than a century, and feeding them, too—counters in the sixth-floor food department are piled high with sausage, bread, and thousands of German specialties, much of it on offer at sit-down counters.

**Europa Center** (also on Tauentzienstrasse), is Berlin's first shopping mall, dating back to the 1960s, and houses dozens of shops, restaurants and cafes. **Neues Kranzler Eck,** an upscale, outdoor retail "passage" off the Ku'Damm at Joachimstalerstrasse, is newer and trendier.

The largest shopping mall in Mitte is the **Potsdamerplatz Arkaden** (U-/S-Bahn: Potsdamerplatz), with more than 100 shops on three levels. **Friedrichstrasse,** one of Berlin's main shopping streets before World War II, lost its consumer clout when it became a main avenue of communist East Berlin but is staging a comeback as a glittering Mitte shopping venue.

## Entertainment & Nightlife

The caliber and variety of Berlin's performing arts scene is extraordinary, and enjoying a concert or opera is among the great pleasures of visiting the city. The **Berlin Philharmonic,** one of the world's premier orchestras, performs in the acoustically superb Philharmonie in the Kulturforum, Herbert-von-Karajan-Strasse 1 (www.berlin-philharmonic.com; ✆ **030/25488999;** U-Bahn: Potsdamerplatz). **Deutsche Oper Berlin** performs a full repertoire of classic and contemporary operas, recitals, and ballet in its famous post-war opera house in Charlottenburg at Bismarckstrasse 35 (www.deutscheoperberlin.de; ✆ **030/34384343;** U-Bahn: Deutsche Oper). Another landmark venue for the performing arts is **Konzerthaus Berlin,** on Gendarmenmarkt (www.konzerthaus.de; ✆ **030/203092101;** U-Bahn: Französischestrasse), where the Berlin Symphony Orchestra and Deutsches Sinfonie Orchestr perform in a glittering, pitch-perfect hall. **Komische Oper Berlin,** Behrenstrasse

## BERLIN specialties

Berliners have long appreciated cutting-edge design, and their good taste comes to the fore at **Stilwerk,** spread over four floors at Kantstrasse 17 in Charlottenburg (www.stilwerk.de; ✆ **030/315150;** S-Bahn: Savignyplatz), offering everything from understated jewelry to ultra-sleek home furnishings. More traditional are the designs at KPM (Königliche Porzellan-Manufaktur), a producer of fine porcelain (called "white gold") for 250 years. Pieces are hand-painted and hand-decorated with patterns based on traditional 18th- and 19th-century KPM designs. The best selection is at the KPM flagship store and factory, Wegelystrasse 1 (www.kpm.de; ✆ **030/39009215;** U-Bahn: Tiergarten); you can take a guided tour (12€) on Saturdays at 3pm.

Berliners are real sweet tooths, and any number of enterprises do a brisk business satisfying the cravings. At old-fashioned **Bonbonmacherei,** Oranienburgerstrasse 32 (✆ **03044055243;** S-Bahn: Oranienburgerstrasse) sweets (bonbons, in German) are made by hand in small batches and include Maiblätter, shaped like tiny leaves and flavored with woodruff leaf. **Königsberger,** at Pestalozzistrasse 54a in Charlottenburg (✆ **030/323-82-54;** U-Bahn: Wilmersdorferstrasse), specializes in marzipan, lovingly hand-wrapped in attractive packets.

For those in the know, nothing says Berlin like a gift from **Ampelmann,** Hof V, Hackesche Höfe (www.ampelmann.de; ✆ **030/44726438;** S-Bahn: Hackescher Markt): Ampelmann was the "walk" figure you saw when the traffic lights in the old DDR turned green—a little man in a hurry—and this much-loved symbol of East Germany is emblazoned on retro lamps, T-shirts, and umbrellas. Berlin takes part in the national craze for all things related to Christmas at **Erzgebirgshaus,** at Friedrichstrasse 194-199 (✆ **030/2045097;** U-Bahn: Stadtmitte), stocked year-round with hand-carved wooden ornaments and decorations from the Erzgebirge, a region in Saxony—the incense-smoking carved figures are especially endearing.

55-57 (www.komische-oper-berlin.de; ✆ **030/202600;** U-Bahn: Französischestrasse; S-Bahn: Friedrichstrasse or Unter den Linden) is one of the most highly regarded theater ensembles in Europe, presenting many contemporary productions of operas, operettas, ballets, and musical theater.

The Berlin cabaret scene as it was in the 1920s seems to come back to life at the **Friedrichstadt Palast,** Friedrichstrasse 107 (www.friedrichstadtpalast.de; ✆ **030/23262326;** U-/S-Bahn: Friedrichstrasse), where acts include multilingual comedians and singers, jugglers, acrobats, musicians, plenty of coyly expressed sexuality, and lots of costume changes. Another nostalgic Berlin cabaret, **Wintergarten Varieté,** Potsdamerstrasse 96 (www.wintergarten-variete.de; ✆ **030/588433;** U-Bahn: Kurfürstenstrasse) offers a variety show every night, with magicians, clowns, jugglers, acrobats, and live music. Also a throwback to old Berlin is **Cafe Einstein,** a legendary Viennese-style cafe in an old townhouse at Kurfürstenstrasse 58 (www.cafeeinstein.com; ✆ **030/2615096;**

U-Bahn: Wittenbergplatz) that serves mellow house-roasted kaffee and freshly made *kuchen* (cakes) as well as breakfast, lunch and dinner. There is another branch at Unter den Linden 42. Berliners enjoy a friendly beer garden as much as other Germans do, and the oldest in town is **Prater Garten,** Kastanienallee 7-9 (www.pratergarten.de; ✆ **030/4485688;** U-Bahn: Eberswalderstrasse), a cavernous place where the 600 seats are usually filled to capacity with Berliners from all walks of life. **Golgatha,** in the heart of the Kreuzberg's district's Viktoriapark, Dudenstrasse 40 (www.golgatha-berlin.de; ✆ **030/7852453;** U-Bahn: Platz der Luftbrücke) is a leafy beer garden that becomes an open-air club after 10pm, with DJs spinning electro, rock, and pop.

Berlin has one of the biggest gay and lesbian scenes in Europe, but the twist here is that a lot of bars and clubs are a part of the mainstream. At places like **Kumpelnest 3000,** Lützowstrasse 23 (www.kumpelnest 3000.com; ✆ **030/2616918;** U-Bahn: Kurfürstenstrasse), gay or straight are welcomed to enjoy a good time and dance to disco classics in what used to be a brothel. Down-to-earth **Prinzknecht,** Fuggerstrasse 33 (www.prinzknecht.de; ✆ **030/23627444;** U-Bahn: Viktoria-Luise-Platz), is large, brick-lined, and mobbed with ordinary guys who just happen to be gay. **SO36,** a dance club at Oranienstrasse 190 (www.so36.de; ✆ **030/61401306;** U-Bahn: Kottbusser Tor) caters to a mixed gay-lesbian-straight crowd with a varied musical line-up from Asian house to techno, punk, and funk.

## HAMBURG

Germany's second-largest city after Berlin and Europe's second-largest port after Rotterdam, Hamburg has so many facets that visitors stumble into one fascinating cityscape after another. The copper-roofed tower of old baroque Hauptkirche St. Michael's rises next to glass and steel office buildings. The port, with its wharfs, cranes, dry docks, and a flotilla of ships coming and going day and night rambles along the banks of the Elbe River as far as the eye can see. A maze of canals laces through the old city, lined with sturdy brick warehouses where Hamburg merchants once stashed carpets, tea, and the other lucre of trade.

These days, boldly designed high-rise corporate headquarters—Hamburg is a media capital and industrial center—are the powerhouses of wealth and influence. Elegant 19th-century facades along the shores of the Alster, the shimmering lake at Hamburg's center, and Jugenstil (Art Nouveau) villas scream bourgeois comforts; smart-phone-toting, Armani-clad execs carry on the legacy of well-fed Middle Age burghers who made fortunes after Frederick Barbarossa declared the city a free port in 1193. Then there's Hamburg's underbelly—the infamous Reeperbahn, the sleazy avenue where "Hiya sailor" is the anthem of easy virtue. The stag partiers and other denizens of the night who dip into this slice of lowlife are onto something—Hamburg might be business-minded, even stuffy in places, but it can also be a lot of fun, whatever your notion of a good time is. That might also mean gazing at an Expressionist canvas in the Kunsthalle; or watching Hamburgers haggle over the price of cod at the Fischmarkt; or cruising past architectural stunners in HafenCity, a brand new waterfront quarter. As you get to know Hamburg, you will be surprised at just how easy it is to succumb to this city's many charms.

## Essentials

Try the **tourist-information** website (www.hamburg-tourism.de) for trip planning assistance for Hamburg.

**ARRIVING** **Hamburg-Fuhlsbüttel,** 8km (5 miles) north of the city center, is served by frequent flights to and from major German airports and many European and intercontinental destinations. Lufthansa flies into Hamburg from most major German and European cities, and many national carriers also serve Hamburg, including Air France from Paris and British Airways from London. United Airlines offers nonstop service from the United States (from Newark) but on most carriers a flight from the U.S. requires a change in Frankfurt or another European hub.

During the day, the S-Bahn (suburban rail network) line S1 operates every 10 minutes between the airport and Hamburg's central railway station, Hauptbahnhof (the trip takes 25 min.). The airport (Flughafen) S-Bahn station is directly in front of the air terminals. The one-way fare to the center is 3€, or 1.50€ for ages 11 and under.

There are two major rail stations: the centrally located **Hamburg Hauptbahnhof,** Hachmannplatz 10 (www.bahn.com; ✆ **040/39183046**), and **Hamburg-Altona** (www.bahn.com; ✆ **040/39182387**), at the eastern edge of the Altstadt. Most trains arrive at the Hauptbahnhof, although trains from the north of Germany, including Westerland and Schleswig, arrive at Altona. The two stations are connected by train and S-Bahn. Hamburg has frequent train connections with all major German cities, and is a hub for international routes as well. From Berlin, 15 trains arrive daily (trip time: 2½ hr.). For information, call ✆ **01805/996633** (www.bahn.com).

If you're arriving by **car,** the A1 Autobahn reaches Hamburg from the south and west, the A7 from the north and south, the A23 from the northwest, and the A24 from the east.

**CITY LAYOUT** A couple of things to keep in mind. One, Hamburg is not compact and can't be easily covered on foot; you'll probably have to depend on public transportation or taxis. Two, think water. Hamburg lies on the Elbe River, 109km (68 miles) from the North Sea, and water seems to be everywhere in this city that is centered around a lake (the Alster). Hamburg faces a busy harbor and is laced with canals. (These canals are commercial and industrial waterways, lined with docks and warehouses; don't fall for the touristic mumbo jumbo that Hamburg is the Venice of the North, because busy, business-minded Hamburg in no way resembles that Italian city.)

The **Alster,** often sparkling with white sails, is divided by bridges into the Binnenalster (Inner Alster) and the larger Aussenalster (Outer Alster). Busy avenues, including the elegant, shop-lined Ballindamm, flank the Binnenalster, as do such noteworthy landmarks as the Colonnaden, an arcade of shops and cafes, and the Hamburgische Staatsoper, the opera house.

The **Altstadt (Old Town)** is south of the Binnenalster, tucked between the lakeshore and the Elbe River waterfront. The Hauptbahnhof is on the eastern fringe of the Altstadt, and the Rathaus, the Renaissance-style city hall, and adjacent Rathausmarkt are on the western edge. Two major shopping streets run between the Hauptbanhof and the Rathausmarkt, the Spitalerstrasse (a pedestrian mall), and Mönckebergstrasse to the south.

A new district, **HafenCity,** is growing up south of the Altstadt in former docklands that extend 3km (2 miles) along the Elbe River. At the moment, much of HafenCity looks like a forest of cranes rising above construction sites, but it's predicted that by 2020 or so a concert hall, bars, slick office buildings, and hundreds of waterfront apartments will have transformed the docklands into the city's new pride and joy.

**St. Pauli,** west of the Altstadt, is the Hamburg's famous red light district, where shops and clubs line the lurid Reeperbahn, a street where sex is sold over-the-counter, not under.

**GETTING AROUND** A word to the wise: Park your car and use public transportation to avoid traffic and the hassle and expense of parking. Hamburg's U-Bahn, one of the best subway systems in Germany, connects with the S-Bahn surface trains. This combined network is the fastest means of getting around, though buses are also fast and efficient and travel in special lanes throughout the city center. Single tickets for the U-Bahn, S-Bahn, and the bus cost 2.80€ for citywide service and 1.30€ for trips within the center city. A 3-day pass for 1 person costs 17€. For information, go to www.hvv.de or call ✆ **040/19449.** Tickets are sold at machines in U-Bahn and S-Bahn stations, on buses, and at railroad ticket counters.

### Have Card, Will Travel

The **Hamburg Card** offers unlimited travel on all public transport in Hamburg, as well as discounts to museums, other attractions, and city tours. A 1-day card costs 8.90€ for individuals or 15€ for families (one adult and up to three children 14 years old and under). A 3-day card costs 22€ for individuals and 39€ for families, and a 5-day card costs 38€ for individuals and 64€ for families. You can get these cards at some hotels, major U-Bahn stations, and the tourist office, or go to www.hamburg-travel.com or call ✆ **040/30051300.**

**Taxis** are available at all hours; call ✆ **040/211211** (www.taxi211211.de). Taxi meters begin at 2.70€ and charge 1.70€ per kilometer after that.

## The Neighborhoods in Brief

**CENTRAL HAMBURG** Hamburg's commercial and shopping districts are on the southernmost shores of the **Alster** (the lake at the city center) and in the **Altstadt** (Old City), around the **Rathaus** (City Hall). Don't look for a lot of historic charm—there certainly is some, though World War II laid waste to much of it. Notable survivors include the city's distinctive red-brick warehouses that line canals near the waterfront, and some noble landmarks, such as **St. Petri Church** with its skyline-piercing dome. **St. Georg,** an inner city neighborhood running alongside the lake just north of the Hauptbanhof, is one of many old quarters that have been gentrified in recent years. Parts are still a bit dodgy, but leafy streets near the lake, especially the Langhe Reihe, are lined with cafes and restaurants, and some of the city's most character-filled hotels are in this old neighborhood.

**THE WATERFRONT** The Port of Hamburg is the world's fifth-largest harbor, stretching for nearly 40km (25 miles) along the Elbe River. Hamburg has been one of the busiest centers of trade on the Continent for almost ten centuries and is, largely as a consequence of this maritime trade, one of Germany's wealthiest cities. **HafenCity,** Europe's largest inner-city urban development project, extends for 3km (2 miles) along the Elbe River. The emerging district is expected to double the population of central Hamburg with thousands of waterfront apartments, and includes a concert hall, bars, and slick office buildings.

**ST. PAULI** Hamburg's infamous nightlife and red-light district centers on the **Reeperbahn,** neon-lit, garish, and offering all sorts of pleasures—cafes, sex shows, bars, dance clubs, and music halls. This maritime quarter is a lot less raucous than it once was, and these days many habitués are more intent on drinking and dancing than paying for companionship.

**ALTONI** Once populated mainly by Jews and Portuguese, this western district is the scene of some great dining and nightlife. Those in search of more traditional pursuits can wake at the crack of dawn on Sunday to check out what's happening in the stalls of the historic **Altona Fischmarkt.**

**AROUND THE LAKE** Many villas dating from the 1800s and some stunning Jugendstil buildings line the streets of tree-filled residential districts around the **Aussenalster.** A particularly attractive lakeside enclave is Harveststude; since the 19th century, this was home to Hamburg's wealthy burghers, whose villas are now occupied by many foreign consulates.

## Exploring Hamburg

Hamburg is large and spread out, but geography won't put a damper on your sightseeing. Most of what you'll want to see is in or near the central city, and even if a cold wind off the Baltic Sea deters you from walking, it's easy to get around town on the U-Bahn or bus.

Unless you have a big appetite for ticking off sights, you may be pleased to know that Hamburg has far fewer landmarks and stellar museums than Berlin or Munich do. You can probably see what you want in a full day. Even if your appreciation of art is on the low side, you'll want to step into the **Kunsthalle ★★★** (p. 433), to see the tortured creations of the German expressionists. The facade of the over-the-top, neo-Renaissance-style **Rathaus ★** (p. 434) is a must-see, and so is **Hauptkirche St-Michaelis ★** (below), where you should make the ascent to the dome for a view over the far-flung metropolis at your feet. The city itself is the main attraction. You can't leave town without catching a glimpse of the Alster, the lake in the city center, and you'll want to see the port—best viewed from the deck of a tour boat (p. 436). Two neighborhoods to check out are **HafenCity,** an emerging waterside quarter where some of the world's leading architects are in a contest to see who can create the most stunning glass tower, and, of course, **St. Pauli**—whether you come to this red-light district dedicated to debauchery to partake or observe, you'll never think of Germany as uptight and strictly businesslike again.

### HOLY HAMBURG

For a city that's probably best known for its red light district, Hamburg has a number of notable churches. Hamburgers' favorite, **St. Petri Kirche ★,** Speersort 10 (www.sankt-petri.de; ✆ **040/3257400;** U-Bahn: Rathausmarkt), deserves a quick stop just because it's so venerable, founded in 1192 and in continuous use since. The lion-head knocker on the main door dates from 1342, making it the oldest piece of art in Hamburg, though little else in the church can claim similarly notable provenance or artistic merit. The present structure itself dates from the mid-19th century, when the early church was razed by a fire—a feat World War II bombers attempted to repeat many times but failed to achieve, making St. Peter's one of old Hamburg's proud survivors. The best time to visit is Wednesday afternoon at 5:15, when the organ pumps out a Stunde der Kirchenmusik (Hour of Church Music).

At **Hauptkirche St-Michaelis ★** on Michaeliskirchplatz, Krayenkamp 4C (www.st-michaelis.de; ✆ **040/376780;** U-Bahn: Rodgingsmarkt or St. Pauli), you'll want to soak in the sumptuous baroque interior, admire the pipe organs (maybe playing if you come for a morning service or evensong), and pay homage at the tombs of esteemed Hamburgers in the huge crypt. But save your energy for the climb up the 449 steps of the twisting, narrow staircase (there's also an elevator for the less

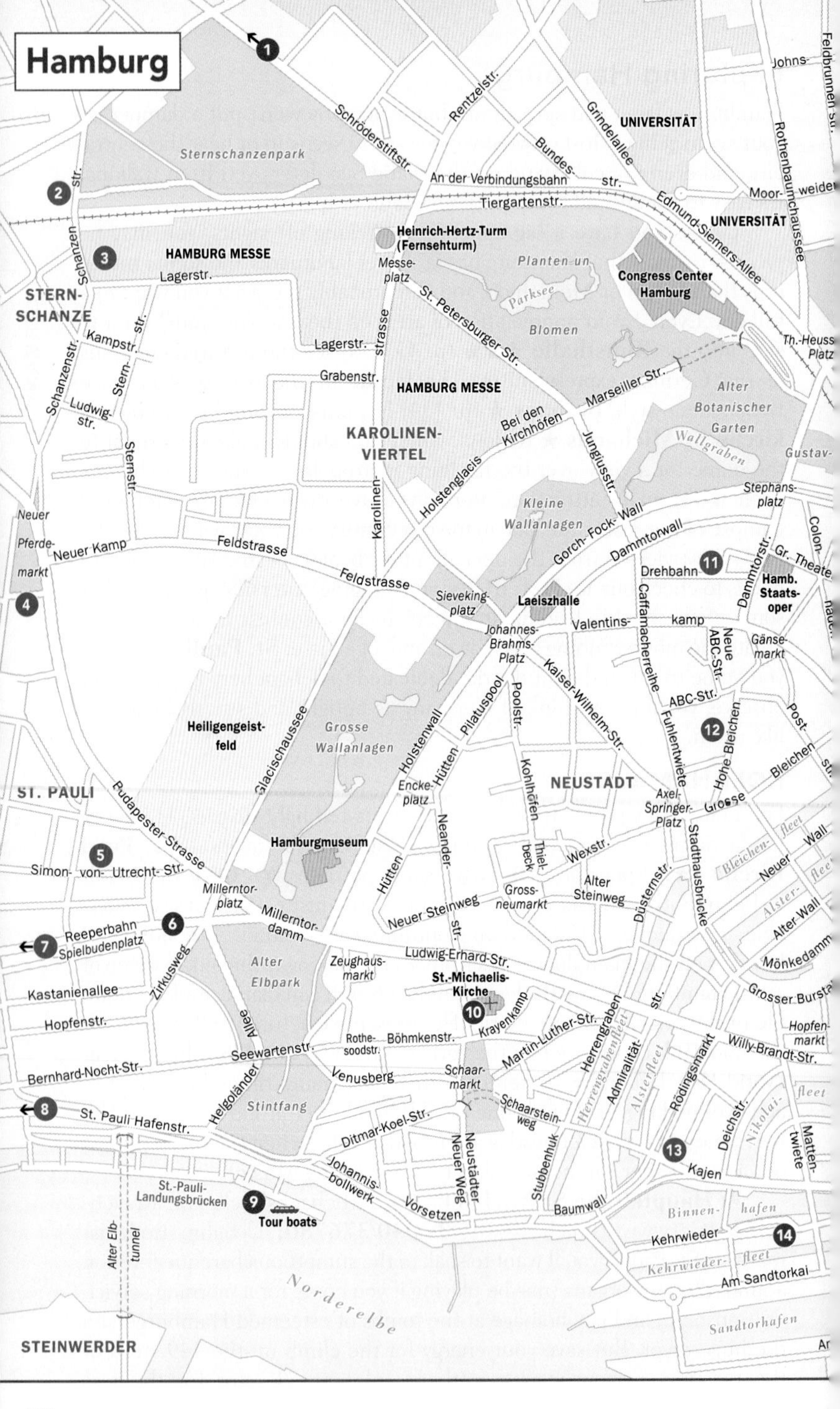

Hamburg
Sternschanzenpark
HAMBURG MESSE
STERN-
SCHANZE
KAROLINEN-
VIERTEL
UNIVERSITÄT
Heinrich-Hertz-Turm
(Fernsehturm)
Planten un Blomen
Congress Center
Hamburg
Alter
Botanischer
Garten
Kleine
Wallanlagen
Laeiszhalle
Hamb.
Staats-
oper
Heiligengeist-
feld
Grosse
Wallanlagen
NEUSTADT
ST. PAULI
Hamburgmuseum
Alter
Elbpark
St.-Michaelis-
Kirche
Stintfang
Tour boats
Norderelbe
STEINWERDER
Binnen-
hafen
Sandtorhafen

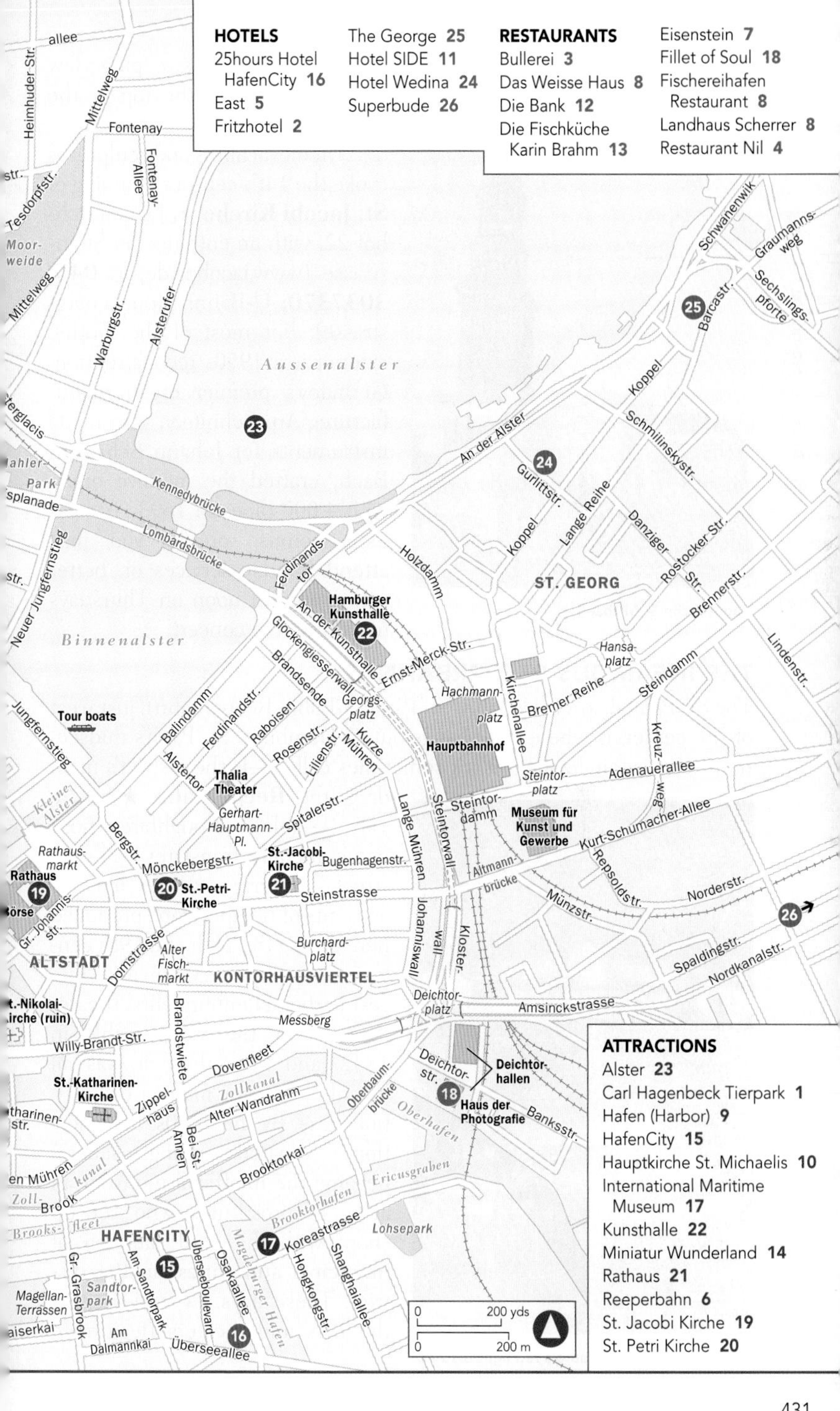
HOTELS
25hours Hotel HafenCity 16
East 5
Fritzhotel 2
The George 25
Hotel SIDE 11
Hotel Wedina 24
Superbude 26
RESTAURANTS
Bullerei 3
Das Weisse Haus 8
Die Bank 12
Die Fischküche Karin Brahm 13
Eisenstein 7
Fillet of Soul 18
Fischereihafen Restaurant 8
Landhaus Scherrer 8
Restaurant Nil 4
Aussenalster
Binnenalster
ST. GEORG
Hamburger Kunsthalle
Hauptbahnhof
Thalia Theater
Museum für Kunst und Gewerbe
Tour boats
Rathaus
St.-Petri-Kirche
St.-Jacobi-Kirche
ALTSTADT
KONTORHAUSVIERTEL
St.-Nikolai-Kirche (ruin)
St.-Katharinen-Kirche
Deichtorhallen
Haus der Photografie
HAFENCITY
Lohsepark
ATTRACTIONS
Alster 23
Carl Hagenbeck Tierpark 1
Hafen (Harbor) 9
HafenCity 15
Hauptkirche St. Michaelis 10
International Maritime Museum 17
Kunsthalle 22
Miniatur Wunderland 14
Rathaus 21
Reeperbahn 6
St. Jacobi Kirche 19
St. Petri Kirche 20
0 200 yds
0 200 m

Hauptkirche St-Michaelis.

adventurous) for a sweeping view of Hamburg from the top of the copper-roofed tower.

Medieval altars and sculptures evoke the 14th-century founding of **St. Jacobi Kirche ★,** Jakobikirchhof 22, with an entrance on Steinstrasse (www.jacobus.de; ✆ **040/3037370;** U-Bahn: Mönckebergstrasse), but most of the Gothic exterior is a 1950s reconstruction. Germany's premier organ manufacturer, Arp Schnitger, who made instruments for Johann Sebastian Bach, crafted the massive organ with 4,000 pipes in 1693. To hear its sonorous sounds, you may attend Sunday services or, better yet, stop in at noon on Thursdays to enjoy a free concert.

## THE INFAMOUS REEPERBAHN

The St. Pauli district (U-Bahn: St. Pauli; S-Bahn: Reeperbahn), just west of the center, is where it all hangs out in Hamburg. St. Pauli's midsection—the "genital zone," as it's sometimes called—is the district's main drag, the **Reeperbahn ★★★,** a 1km (½-mile) thoroughfare whose name literally translates as "rope street," referring to the massive amounts of hempen rope produced here during the 18th and 19th centuries for ships in Germany's biggest harbor. Hamburg's first theater opened on the Reeperbahn in 1842, and from there it was all downhill into any manner of licentiousness. By the 1860s, the question, "Whatcha doing, sailor?" became the unofficial motto of an army of prostitutes who set up shop (with the legal sanction of municipal authorities) in the district. These days, by mid-evening the bars and theaters (legitimate

The Reeperbahn, Hamburg's red light district.

and otherwise) are roaring away, and you'll find thousands of women and men in drag, strutting their stuff along the turf. German enterprise has honored these women by naming one of Hamburg's native beers in their honor—the famous "St. Pauli Girl."

The most exclusive and expensive area is Herbertstrasse, where women display their charms to window-shoppers from behind plate-glass. By city ordinance, this street is open only to men 19 and over (women are officially banned, but this does not seem to be enforced). Less expensive rents can be found on the streets near Herbertstrasse: Gunterstrasse, Erichstrasse, Friedrichstrasse, Davidstrasse, and Gerhardstrasse. If it's erotic theater you're looking for, you'll have to move a few blocks away to Grosse Freiheit, a street whose name appropriately translates as "Great Freedom." Any act of sexual expression, with every conceivable permutation, except those that involve animals (bestiality is one of the few things expressly forbidden), is shown in these theaters. Be it joyful, be it disgusting, it's all here, often performed by artists who can barely conceal their boredom.

### THE ALSTER ★★

Top spot for a jog or power walk is the pedestrian walkway around Hamburg's *other* waterfront, this lake in the city center. It's about 7km (4 miles) all the way around, but you can do a shorter circuit around the smaller, inner lake, the Binnenalster, in about 1½km (1 mile). The **Aussenalster H. Pieper** (www.segelschule-pieper.de; © **040/247578**), a boathouse just off Kennedybrucke, rents rowboats, paddle boats, and one-occupant sailing dinghies; prices begin at 15€ per hour. They're open April to late September, daily 10am to 8pm.

### THE CENTRAL CITY

**Kunsthalle ★★★** GALLERY A walk through one of Germany's outstanding art museums provides a head-spinning look at Western masterpieces. For many Hamburgers, pride of place in the two buildings belongs to the Bertram altarpiece, painted for the St. Petri Church in 1379. The 24 scenes depict the history of humankind as told in the Bible, from creation to the flight into Egypt. Look for some sardonic touches, like the little fox chewing the neck of the lamb next to it, a sad comment perhaps on the fate of the meek. Continue through the Canalettos, Rembrandts, Holbeins, and other old masters to German Romanticism. The new wing houses the Galerie der Gegenwart, Art of the Present, with an impressive collection of canvases by Picasso, Warhol, Beuys, Munch, Kandinsky, Klee, Hockney, and many other leading contemporary artists, among them installation artist Rebecca Horn, photorealist Gerhard Richter, and conceptualist Jenny Holzer. A large showing of German Expressionism is

Interior, Kunsthalle.

a credit to the museum's effort to rebuild a collection of "degenerate" art banned and often destroyed by the Nazis.

Glockengiesser Wall. www.hamburger-kunsthalle.de. ✆ **040/428131200.** 12€ adults, 6€ children 4–12, children 3 and under free, 18€ family ticket. U-Bahn: Hauptbahnhof. Tues–Sun 10am–6pm (Thurs until 9pm).

**Rathaus** ★ LANDMARK It's new by German standards—late 19th century—but the neo-Renaissance City Hall with 647 rooms makes quite an impression nonetheless, a sandstone testimony to Hamburg's wealth and importance. The 49m (161-ft.) clock tower looms high above the Rathausmarkt and the Alster Fleet, the city's largest canal. Tours through grandiose staterooms, but this behemoth is just as satisfyingly admired from the outside—unless you are detail-oriented and might enjoy hearing about the 3,780 pinewood piles upon which the block-long structure rests, or the 8,605 souls who perished in the 1897 cholera epidemic and are commemorated by a gurgling fountain. The 16th-century **Börse** (Stock Exchange), Adolphsplatz 1 (✆ **040/361-3020**), stands back to back with the Rathaus; guides conduct free tours (in German) of the Börse on Tuesday and Thursday at 11am and noon.

Rathausplatz. ✆ **040/428310.** Rathaus tours 3€. U-Bahn: Rathausmarkt. Mon–Fri 10am–3pm and Sat–Sun 10am–1pm (no tours during official functions).

## NEAR THE WATERFRONT

Ever since the emperor Friedrich Barbarossa issued an edict granting free-trading privileges to Hamburg in 1189, the city has earned fame and

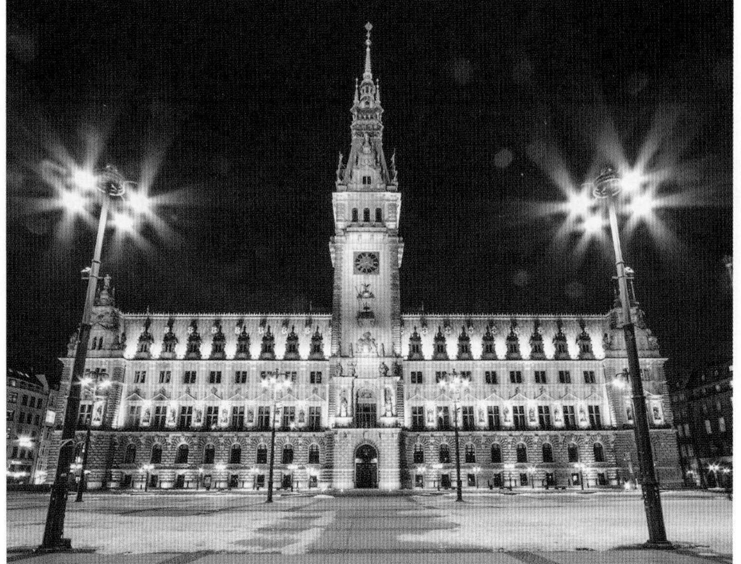

Hamburg's 19th-century Rathaus.



riches from its busy harbor, one of the largest in the world. Hamburg commemorates Frederic's gesture in early May with 3 days of windjammer parades, fireworks, and other celebrations, and these days most of the maritime activity takes place in a vast swath of riverside docks and warehouses just southwest of the city, where the Elbe splits into two arms as it nears the North Sea. The only real way to see the docklands is on a harbor cruise that departs from the city's main passenger landing stage, **St. Pauli-Landungsbrücken.** Don't board the 19th-century clipper ship *Rickmer Rickmers* and expect to get anywhere; docked just east of the landing at Pier 1, the magnificent vessel is now a museum of maritime history (✆ **040/319-5959;** daily 10am–5:30pm; 3€/$4 for adults, 2.50€/$3.50 for children ages 4–12).

## HAFENCITY ★★

More than 400 acres of former docklands along the River Elbe are being transformed in a huge urban-renewal project that will eventually increase the size of the inner city by almost half and double the amount of housing in Hamburg. Although it's estimated that it will be 2020 before finishing touches are put on the streets, plazas, and riverside promenades, some stunning glass towers are already transforming the skyline. Check out the shiplike Unilever building at Strandkai 1, and the Elbphilharmonie, the new philharmonic hall, an undulating wedge of frosted glass that seems to rise from the water like the prow of a ghost ship. You can find out more at the **HafenCity InfoCenter,** Sandtorkai

### A Bit of Beatlemania

John Lennon once said, "I was born in Liverpool, but I grew up in Hamburg." As Beatles fans know, the group got its start here in the early 1960s, when they played gigs at a string of sleazy St. Pauli clubs. When the group returned to Liverpool in 1960, they were billed as "The Beatles: Direct from Hamburg." They soon returned to Germany and introduced such hits as "Love Me Do" in St. Pauli clubs. Though a museum to the Fab Four has been shuttered, the city has not lost interest in the sensation it nurtured. A corner on the Reeperbahn has been designated "Beatles-Platz," where effigies of the five are enshrined in glass (the fifth wheel is bassist Stuart Sutcliffe, who left the group to study art and died soon afterward). The boys stand in the middle of a circle of paving stones blackened to look like a vinyl record.

30 (www.hafencity.de; ✆ **040/3690-1799**), open Tuesday through Sunday from 10am to 6pm (May–Sept until 8pm). To reach the InfoCenter, take the U3 U-Bahn line to Baumwall, Bus 3, or Bus 6.

**International Maritime Museum** ★ MUSEUM In a tribute to Hamburg's longstanding relationship with the sea, ten floors of a formidable old redbrick neo-Gothic warehouse near the waterfront in Hafencity are stacked chockablock with all things nautical. The vast spaces are literally crammed with memorabilia, and eclectic holdings run the nautical gamut from a 3,000-year-old dugout unearthed on the banks of the Elbe; to 47 letters of Lord Horatio Nelson, hero of the Battle of Trafalgar; to photographs and drawings of ships; to uniforms and navigation equipment. If the 15,000 menus from ocean liners seem overwhelming, wait until you get to the top floor and come across the 26,000 model ships, stacked tightly side by side in row after row of glass cases as if they were moored in the world's most impossibly crowded harbor.

Koreastrasse 1. www.internationales-maritimes-museum.de. ✆ **040/3009-3300.** 13€, 15€ family (1 adult/2 children) or 25€ family (2 adults/3 children). U-Bahn: Überseequartier. Tues–Sun 10am–6pm.

## Organized Tours

Guided tours are a good way to see spread-out Hamburg, and plenty of operators are on hand to show you around. To get a sense of the city and see the far-flung landmarks, hop on one of the Top Tour double-decker buses operated by **Hamburger Stadtrundfahrten** (www.top-tour-hamburg.de; ✆ **040/641-3731**) that leave from the main train station, Kirchenallee entrance, every 30 minutes from 9:30am to 5pm (hourly in winter). The 90-minute tours cost 18€ for adults, 15€ for children up to 14.

For a look at Hamburg's port, a fascinating hubbub of maritime activity, climb aboard one of the pleasure craft operated by **HADAG Seetouristik und Fährdienst AG,** Bei den St. Pauli, Fischmarkt 28 (www.hadag.de; ✆ **040/3117070**). The 75-minute tours, in German and English, depart the Landungsbrücken, Pier 3, in St. Pauli at hourly intervals every day April to September 10:30am to 4:30pm, and from October to March 11am to 3:30pm. The fare is 17€ for adults, 8€ for children 13 and under, and 25€ for a family ticket.

Relaxing, but a lot less colorful, are tours of the Inner and Outer Alster operated by **ATG-Alster-Touristik,** Am Anleger Jungfernstieg (www.alstertouristik.de; ✆ **040/3574240**). In good weather, departures are daily about every 30 minutes from 10am to 6pm, with trips lasting 50 minutes—just about the right amount of time to get your fill of pleasant vistas of the tree-lined shores, church spires, and sailing boats. November to March, tours depart daily at 10:30am, noon, 1:30, and 3pm. Boats leave from the Jungfernstieg quayside (U-Bahn: Jungfernstieg). Trips cost 15€ for adults and 7€ for children 15 and under.

## Especially for Kids

Adult-oriented and X-rated as some of Hamburg is, kids will find a lot of amusements. A **harbor tour** (see above) should be on the top of the "to do" list for anyone arriving with young companions in tow. The wonderfully quirky **Miniatur Wunderland,** Kehrwieder 2 (www.miniatur-wunderland.de; U-Bahn: Baumwell), will keep the young and young at heart enchanted for hours—Lilliputian trains (900 in all) chug through snowy Alpine peaks and American deserts, planes descend from the sky and make a smooth landing at Hamburg airport, trucks roar down highways, and fire trucks and police cars race through city streets. Who knows? The tableaux of miniature prostitutes standing alluringly in windows and punks smoking at a rock concert might gently introduce youngsters to the ways of the world. Admission is 13€ adults, 6.50€ children and it's open Sunday 8:30am to 6pm; Monday and Wednesday through Friday 9:30am to 9pm; Tuesday 9:30am to 9pm; Saturday 8am to 9pm.

Hamburg's Zoo, **Carl Hagenbeck's Tierpark,** 5km (3 miles) southwest of the city center at Hagenbeckallee at Steilingen (www.hagenbeck.de; ✆ **040/5300330;** U-Bahn: Hagenbeck's Tierpark), is home to 2,500 animals, who live among some appealing creations that include a Nepalese temple and Japanese garden. Admission is 16€ adults, 11€ children 4 to 16, free for children 3 and under, 49€ family ticket. It's open March to October daily 9am to 5pm (closes later in nice weather); November to February daily 9am to 4:30pm.

## Where to Stay

You'll probably want to stay near the center of this far-flung metropolis—choice locales are the central city in the Altstadt and around the Alster, and near the waterfront, around the port and St. Pauli. A hotel in any of these spots will put you within easy reach of sights, restaurants, and nightlife.

## THE CENTRAL CITY

### Expensive

**Hotel SIDE ★** Offbeat and postmodern, built around an elliptical atrium, this design statement in steel and glass puts you right in the heart of Hamburg while giving you a break from the typical chain-hotel circuit. Neutral-toned bedrooms are not only airy and stylish but also extremely comfortable, with commodious, snazzy bathrooms embellished with glass sinks and big windows. Suites float above the city in special glass-enclosed quarters cantilevered above the main structure.

Drehbahn 49. www.side-hamburg.de. ✆ **040/309990.** 178 units. Doubles 150€–300€. U-Bahn: Gänsemarkt or Stephansplatz. **Amenities:** Restaurant; bar; gym; indoor heated pool; room service; spa; free Wi-Fi.

### Moderate

**The George ★★** A handsome library and some other clubby touches play off the English-sounding name, but for the most part these lodgings at the edge of the St. Georg neighborhood give off a chic, contemporary vibe. More than half of the handsome guest rooms open to balconies, as do most of the corner suites. In all, dark carpeting, subdued lighting, and sleek furnishings enhanced with rich fabrics ensure a nice refuge from the busy city. Especially relaxing are the friendly, ground-floor Ciao bar and the top-floor spa and sauna, where a lounge and terrace overlook the Alster.

Barcastrasse 3. www.thegeorge-hotel.de. ✆ **040/2800300.** 125 units. Doubles 155€–216€, includes buffet breakfast. Parking 16€. U-Bahn: Uhlandstrasse. **Amenities:** Restaurant; bar; bikes; concierge; gym; spa; room service; free Wi-Fi.

**Hotel Wedina ★★★** You can choose from a lot of options at this stylish and low-key retreat near the shores of the Alster: a choice of pillows and bedding, the style of decor (traditional or soothingly minimalist), which of four buildings you prefer (from a 19th-c. villa to a sleek concrete-and-glass modern annex), even where you want to enjoy breakfast—in a conservatory that, like many rooms, overlooks a lovely Italianate garden or, in good weather, the garden itself. Many famous writers like to lay low in these soothing surroundings while in Hamburg, and autographed copies of many modern masterpieces are proudly displayed in the cozy library.

Gurlittstrasse 23. www.wedina.de. ✆ **040/2808900.** 59 units. Doubles 118€–170€, includes buffet breakfast. Bus: 6. **Amenities:** Bar; bikes; free Wi-Fi.

### Inexpensive

**Superbude ★★** It's a little too cool for its own good sometimes—montages made from newspaper clippings on the walls, funky furnishings fashioned from crates, lots of high-tech lighting. But that's the only snarky thing to be said about this incredibly fair-valued hostel. Functional though colorfully stylish lounges and rooms are spotless, fridges are stocked with cheap beer, the optional breakfast is substantial, the beds are super comfortable, and bathrooms are modern and spiffy. A lot of rooms are cozy doubles and can be let as singles, though young backpackers and young-at-hearts on a budget often opt for a bunk in a four-bedded room.

Spaldingstrasse 152. www.superbude.de. ✆ **040/3808780.** 64 units. Doubles with private bathroom 59€–133€. U-Bahn: Berliner Tor. **Amenities:** Cafe; bikes; free Wi-Fi.



## NEAR THE WATERFRONT

### Expensive

**East ★★** Style has soul in this sophisticated redo of a formidable, red-brick, early 20th-century iron foundry where minimalist design is accented with exposed brick, wrought iron, and natural fabrics to create a transporting environment that is surprisingly warm and welcoming and vaguely exotic. Nattily curved headboards separate even the smallest rooms into lounging and sleeping areas, while bathrooms are tucked away behind floating curtains and have separate water closets and shower cabins with rainfall showerheads. A modernistic candlelit bar, soaring Eurasian restaurant, leafy courtyard, rooftop terrace, and gym and spa provide plenty of in-house diversions, and St. Pauli nightlife is just outside the door.

Simon-von-Utrecht-Strasse 31. www.east-hotel.de. ✆ **040/309930.** 78 units. Doubles 155€–290€. U-Bahn: St. Pauli. **Amenities:** Restaurant; bar; babysitting; gym; room service; spa; free Wi-Fi.

### Moderate

**25hours Hotel Hamburg HafenCity ★** If you're smack dab in the middle of Hamburg's new waterfront district, you'd better make the most of your surroundings, and that's exactly what this trendy outpost of a Hamburg-based, design-oriented hotel group does. Shipping crates, old timbers, and stacks of Oriental carpets (a nod to the surrounding warehouses that once stored the bounty of Eastern trade) fill the lounge areas, while bedrooms are cabin style, varying in size from snug to commodious enough for a captain, and carrying out the nautical theme with tattoo-emblazoned wallpaper, crate-like furnishings, portholes, and logbooks in which you can follow the story of seafarers. If all this design gets to be a bit much, head up to the rooftop sauna to chill out while taking in the city below.

Paul-Dessau-Strasse 2. www.25hours-hotel.com. ✆ **040/855070.** 89 units. Doubles 135€–165€, includes breakfast. S-Bahn: Bahrenfeld. **Amenities:** Restaurant; 2 bars; babysitting; bikes; free Wi-Fi.

### Inexpensive

**Fritzhotel ★★** Hamburg doesn't get much more hip than it does in the arty Sternschanze quarter, and here's a hotel that coolly—as in quietly and tastefully—suits the surroundings. Bright, high-ceilinged guest rooms in a 19th-century apartment house are done in soothing neutrals with bold splashes of color. Some open to balconies, but the quieter ones face a leafy courtyard off the street. There are few amenities—and no bar or restaurant—but fresh fruit and coffee are on hand and the neighborhood, at the edge of lively St. Pauli, is chockablock with cafes and bars. Schanzenstrasse 101-103. www.fritzhotel.com. ✆ **040/82222830.** 17 units. Doubles 95€. U-Bahn: Sternschanze. **Amenities:** Free Wi-Fi.



## Where to Eat

Hamburg is married to the sea, and all sorts of denizens of the deep end up on the table: lobster from Helgoland; shrimp from Büsum; turbot, plaice, and sole from the North Sea; and huge quantities of fresh oysters. It's no accident that many of the Hamburg's best and most popular restaurants are seafood houses—and they're reasonably priced, because seafood is not exorbitantly expensive in this port city. But Hamburgers are carnivores, too, hence their eponymous contribution to world cuisine, here known as *stubenküchen* (hamburger steak). A traditional sailor's dish, *labskaus,* is made with beer, onions, cured meat, potatoes, herring, and pickles, but brace yourself for at least a taste of the city's iconic treat, *aalsuppe* (eel soup). Whatever your epicurean appetite, you can probably satisfy it in this city that's long had ties with exotic lands—ethnic restaurants do a brisk business in almost every neighborhood. While dining can be a fine art and a costly pursuit in this expense-account-oriented city, you can also eat well without breaking the bank. No matter how much you spend, in many places your meal will probably be seasoned with an ingredient that Hamburg seems to care a lot about, a generous dash of trendiness.



### CENTRAL CITY

#### Moderate

**Bullerei ★** MEAT An old cattle hall in the Schanze meatpacking district just north of St. Pauli has been transformed into an industrial-looking dining room geared to some serious meat eating (dried beef hangs in a glass display case). Graffiti art, exposed brick walls, and lots of wood furnishings create comfortable surroundings for enjoying pork cheeks, veal knuckles, salty ham, or maybe just some old-fashioned German sausages, even fresh fish—washed down with a selection from the excellent wine list or a wide choice of German beers.

Lagerstrasse 34b. www.bullerei.com. ✆ **040/33442110.** Mains 18€–30€. U-Bahn: Sternschanze. Mon–Sun 11am–11pm.

**Die Bank ★★** NORTHERN GERMAN/CONTINENTAL You'll feel like a robber baron on the marble-columned trading floor of this former bank. Imaginatively backlit photos of money might get you in the mood to part with some yours for the richly satisfying Banker's Plate, an embarrassment of crustacean riches; or foie gras and other traditional French indulgences. You can also dine simply on wurst or steak *frites,* or explore some adventurous Asian-fusion dishes. The lounge-music-infused space is hopping at all times, with diners crowded onto communal tables and a long, long bar, but stick around after dessert and you'll see this former temple of commerce turned into a rather riotous dance club.

Hohebleichen 17. www.diebank-brasserie.de. ✆ **040/2380030.** Mains 14€–25€. U-Bahn: Gasenmarkt. Mon–Sat noon–3pm and 6:30–10:30pm.



### Inexpensive

**Fillet of Soul** ★ INTERNATIONAL The Deichtorhallen is a turn-of-the-20th-century gem, two adjoining steel-and-glass structures near the harbor that once served as market halls and these days house temporary art and photography exhibitions. Tucked into a wing of the vast spaces is an intimate, minimalist dining room where chefs in an open kitchen do nouvelle takes on German standards that are works of art in themselves. Think pink-roasted breast of goose with saffron-flavored rice and pan-fried zanderfish with bacon-studded sauerkraut. Coffee, pastries, and light fare are available in the adjoining cafe, and any daytime visit should include a walk through the galleries, open Tuesday through Sunday from 9 to 6 (admission is 9€).

In the Deichtorhallen Museum, Deichtorstrasse 2. www.fillet-of-soul.de. ✆ **040/70705800.** Mains lunch 8.50€–12€, dinner 14€–24€. No credit cards. U-Bahn: Steinstrasse. Cafe and bar Tues–Sun 11am–midnight; restaurant Tues–Sun noon–3pm and 6–10pm.

**Restaurant Nil** ★ INTERNATIONAL The name is a reference to some innovative spicing in such classics as beef bourguignon, but that's about as exotic as this classic French bistro gets. A regular clientele (many are in publishing and the arts) can count on the kitchen to serve heartier northern-style dishes in the colder months, then dip into the south for inspiration come spring. Any time of year, mirrored walls and lots of brass and plush upholstery will probably transport you to Paris.

Neuer Pferdemarkt 5. www.restaurant-nil.de. ✆ **040/4397823.** Mains 18€–22€; fixed-price menu 41€. No credit cards. U-Bahn: Feldstrasse. Wed–Mon 6pm–midnight.

## NEAR THE WATERFRONT

### Moderate

**Die Fischküche Karin Brahm** ★★ SEAFOOD This unpretentious, brightly lit fish house near the harbor works hard to satisfy Hamburg's unquenchable appetite for seafood, serving the freshest catch in many variations. To get a taste of some local favorites, start with smoked eel and move on to cod served with potatoes and mustard sauce. Nothing that comes out of the kitchen is trendy or haute, service is no-nonsense, and there's nothing stylish, cozy, or otherwise notable about the modern surroundings, but fresh ingredients deftly prepared make this a surefire hit with piscivores.

Kajen 12. www.die-fischkueche.de. ✆ **040/365631.** Mains 15€–40€. U-Bahn: Rödingsmarkt. Mon–Fri noon–midnight; Sat 4pm–midnight.

## IN ALTONA

### Expensive

**Das Weisse Haus ★** GERMAN/SEAFOOD Unlike the Washington landmark with which it shares a name, Hamburg's famous White House is a cramped old fisherman's cottage. That doesn't keep eager diners away, and you'll have to book well in advance for the privilege of submitting yourself to the whims of the kitchen, which, other than catering to allergies and strong dislikes, sends out whatever it wants, based on what looked good in the market that day. A Hamburg classic, *aalsuppe* (eel soup), often makes an appearance, followed by some creative seafood preparations, though the kitchen is just as comfortable with meat and vegetarian meals.

Neumühlen 50. www.das-weisse-haus.de. ✆ **04/309016.** 2-course menu 28€; 3-course menu 34€; 4-course menu 42€. U-Bahn: Altona. Mon–Sat noon–3pm and 6–9pm.

**Landhaus Scherrer ★★** NORTHERN GERMAN/CONTINENTAL A cozy, white-brick converted brewery in Altona soothes at first sight, surrounded as it is by shady lawns. Wood-paneled walls and low lighting do nothing to disrupt the mellow mood. The inventive menu combines northern German and international flavors to satisfying effect, and the kitchen throws in an emphasis on locavore ingredients. Crispy whole north German duck with seasoned vegetables is a feast for two, but you can dine solo on roast goose with rhubarb in cassis sauce and other hearty classics. The adjoining bistro serves lighter fare.

Elbchaussee 130. www.landhausscherrer.de. ✆ **040/8801325.** Mains 28€–39€; fixed-price menu 111€. Bus: 135. Mon–Sat noon–3pm and 6:30–10:30pm.

### Moderate

**Eisenstein ★** INTERNATIONAL/PIZZA The crowd of stylish regulars here doesn't let the clamor deter them from enjoying a fusion of Italian, Mediterranean, and German fare in one of Hamburg's most appealing dining spaces. A restored factory envelops diners in brick walls and rough-hewn timbers. Southern Europe meets the north in dishes like Atlantic cod flavored with Provencal spices and Italian-style thin crust pizza topped with gravlax. An excellent selection of beer and light fare makes this a popular stop on the late-night circuit.

Friedensallee 9. www.restaurant-eisenstein.de. ✆ **040/3904606.** Mains 18€–25€; fixed-price dinners 33€–37€; pizzas 8€–14€. No credit cards. U-Bahn: Altona Bahnhof. Daily 11am–11pm.

**Fischereihafen Restaurant ★★** SEAFOOD A harborside perch near the fish market is a fortuitous locale for this long-standing Hamburg favorite, an institution that's popular with a well-dressed crowd who looks like they're used to fancier surroundings. What matters here is freshness, and fish and shellfish are right out of the market stalls and show up in some simple but memorable renditions, along the lines of

Arctic trout with wild garlic and rare tuna steak with peppercorns and honey-laced soy sauce. A nice view of the Elbe, through large picture windows and from a small terrace in good weather, nicely tops off a memorable meal.

Grosse Elbstrasse 143. www.fischereihafenrestaurant.de. ✆ **040/381816.** Mains 18€–46€; fixed-price menu 60€. S-Bahn: Königstrasse. Sun–Thurs 11:30am–10pm; Fri–Sat 11:30am–10:30pm.



## Shopping

Hamburg is historically a city of merchants and still has a strong commercial bent. Even so, Americans especially will be surprised to learn that most stores close Saturday at 2pm (until 4 or 6pm on *langer Samstag,* the first Saturday of the month) and remain shut until Monday morning. Hamburg has two main shopping zones. In the old center, **Mönckebergstrasse and Spitalerstrasse,** a pedestrian mall (U-Bahn: Hauptbahnhof) run parallel to one another and connect the main train station with the Rathaus; they are lined with big department stores and lots of outlets of midrange international clothing chains. To the north, elegant, shop-lined **Ballindamm and Jungfernstieg** flank the Binnenalster, Hamburg's inner-city lake, and are home to high-end fashion retailers and jewelry stores. Along these two waterside streets you'll come to some especially elegant shopping arcades, most notably the **Colonnaden, Hamburger Hof,** and **Gänsemarkt Passage.** You're never far from the sea in Hamburg, and if you want to take some of the nautical atmosphere home with you, step into **Binikowski,** Lokstedter Weg 68 (✆ **040/462852;** U-Bahn: Eppendorfer Baum) for a Buddelschiff (ship in a bottle). **Captain's Cabin,** St. Pauli Landungsbrücken 3 (www.captains-cabin.de; ✆ **040/316373;** S-Bahn: Landungsbrücken), also sells ship models, telescopes, barometers, figureheads, lamps, nautical clothing, prints, posters, and more.

## Entertainment & Nightlife

Hamburg is famous and infamous for nightlife. You can go highbrow, because the city has excellent opera, dance companies, and symphonies; middlebrow in chic bars and homey rathskellers; or lowbrow on and around the Reeperbahn, in Hamburg's notoriously sex-oriented St. Pauli district.

**Hamburgische Staatsoper** (Hamburg State Opera), Grosstheaterstrasse 25 (www.hamburgische-staatsoper.de; ✆ **040/356868;** U-Bahn: Stephansplatz; S-Bahn: Dammtor), is one of the world's leading opera houses, built after World War II and known for excellent acoustics and advanced technical facilities; it's home to the Hamburg State Opera and the Hamburg Ballet. **Musikhalle,** Johannes-Brahms-Platz 1 (www.laeiszhalle.de; ✆ **040/357666;** U-Bahn: Stephansplatz; S-Bahn: Dammtor) is a survivor of Germany's Romantic age and was painstakingly restored after World War II; the hall hosts concerts by the Hamburg Symphony, the Hamburg Philharmonic, the NDR Symphony, and the Monteverdi-Chor, known for its interpretations of baroque and Renaissance music. The **English Theatre of Hamburg,** Lerchenfeld 14 (www.englishtheatre.de; ✆ **040/2277089;** U-Bahn: Mundsburg), is the only English-speaking theater in northern Germany.





The **Deutsches Schauspielhaus,** Kirchenallee 39 (www.schauspielhaus.de; ✆ **040/248713;** U-Bahn: Hauptbahnhof), is one of the largest and most important theaters in the German-speaking world, performing both classics and modern plays—but you'll need to understand German to fully appreciate the genius of these productions.

Almost as refined as these performing arts houses is **Le Lion,** Rauthaustrasse 3 (www.lelion.net; ✆ **040/334753780;** S-Bahn: Rathaus), a sophisticated bar that's so intimate you might not get in—try though, by ringing the buzzer hidden inside the lion's head on the door to enjoy serious cocktails in a grown-up, subtly lit room. The Beatles performed in the basement **Kaiserkeller** in their earliest days, and Prince and Willie Nelson have been on the bill at the larger **Grosse Freiheit** upstairs; today the venue at Grosse Freiheit 36 (www.grossefreiheit36.de; ✆ **040/31777811;** S-Bahn: Reeperbahn) is best known as a cultural landmark, though some of the pop and rock concerts pull in big crowds. **Cotton Club,** Alter Steinweg 10 (www.cotton-club.de; ✆ **040/343878;** S-Bahn: Stadthausbrücke), is Hamburg's oldest jazz club and hosts jazz and Dixieland bands from throughout Europe and the United States. **Fabrik,** Barnerstrasse 36 (5 min. from Bahnhof Altona; www.fabrik.de; ✆ **040/391070;** U-Bahn: Altona) an old ammunition depot turned factory and now performance space, hosts musician of every stripe almost every night and features club music, classical, African bands, jazz, and blues, along with film and stage events.

**Meanie Bar,** Spielbudenplatz 5 (www.molotowclub.com; ✆ **040/4301110;** S-Bahn: Reeperbahn), one of the few places along the Reeperbahn that caters to locals, attracts a lot of artists and musicians. **Molotow,** a much-beloved venue in the Meanie cellar, is the place to dance to funk and alternative.

Hamburg's gay scene is almost as robust as that in Berlin, and centers in St Georg, just to the east of the Haupthbanhoff, where most of the district's gay venues center around two main streets, Lange Reihe and Steindamm. **Tom's Saloon,** Pulverteich 1 (www.toms-hamburg.de; ✆ **040/25328943;** U-Bahn: Hauptbahnhof) is Hamburg's landmark gay bar, named for gay icon Tom of Finland (once a regular) and has a street-level dance club, a friendly cocktail lounge, and a cellar bar where leather is de rigueur; men of all ages mix here, and women won't feel comfortable anywhere but the crowded dance floor, and even there aren't a terribly welcome presence. More laid-back is **Café Gnosa,** Lange Reihe 93 (www.gnosa.de; ✆ **040/243034;** U-Bahn: Hauptbahnhof) an

## (BAR)ROOMS WITH A view

You can enjoy the spectacle of Hamburg's port while keeping warm and dry and slacking your thirst at 20Up, on the 20th floor of the **Empire Riverside Hotel,** Bernhard-Nocht-Strasse 97 (www.empire-riverside.de; ✆ **40/311190**). A similarly dramatic view is to be had from the 14th-floor **Tower Bar** of the Hafen Hotel, Seewartenstrasse 9 (www.hotel-hafen-hamburg.de; ✆ **040/311130**). The perspective of the maritime activity and sprawling city is eye-catching by day, and downright dazzling at night.

Art Deco inspired, gay-friendly bar and restaurant that's a popular place to sip coffee or wine and enjoy breakfast and a nice selection of salads and more substantial meals.

# MUNICH

Little wonder that Munich (München, pronounced *Mewn*-shin in German) is a favorite city of many Germans, and visitors, too. The handsome capital of Bavaria is a place of welcoming squares, exuberantly decorated baroque and rococo churches and palaces, and beautiful gardens. While the beer-drinking, oom-pah-pah image makes most Germans laugh or

**The Munich skyline, with City Hall in foreground.**

cringe, you'll certainly find a festive atmosphere during the city's acclaimed Oktoberfest—and for that matter, on any day of the week at the Hofbräuhaus and other beer halls, where it's a tradition to share a communal table and enjoy the company of complete strangers. Or walk through the Altstadt (Old City) on a sunny winter's day or a balmy summer evening and you'll see people enjoying life in a city that is rich, cultured, and sophisticated, with a kind of proud, purring prosperity that appreciates the finer things in life (such as the BMWs that are produced here). Munich shows off its remarkable artistic heritage in several collections amassed in part by the kings of Bavaria, who reigned here until 1918. An added thrill to looking at a Rubens or a Rembrandt in the Alte Pinakothek (Old Masters Gallery), or just drinking a beer in the Hofbrauhaus, is that you're doing so in Munich, the capital of *gemütlichkeit*. This not-quite-translatable word means something between cozy and good-natured. Once you visit, you'll understand just why this quality makes Munich so appealing.



## Essentials

Munich's tourist office, Fremdenverkehrsamt München, offers a comprehensive website, **www.muenchen.de**.

As one of Germany's major cities, Munich has no lack of transportation options. Like Frankfurt, Munich has an international airport, so you can fly there directly from the U.S. and the U.K., and it's easily accessible by air from anywhere within Europe.

**ARRIVING** Munich's **Franz Josef Strauss International Airport** (www.munich-airport.com; ✆ **089/9752-1313;**) is located 29km (18 miles) northeast of the city center. The S-8 **S-Bahn light-rail train** connects the airport with the **Hauptbahnhof** (main train station) in downtown Munich. Trains leave from the S-Bahn platform beneath the airport every 20 minutes daily between about 4am and 10:45pm, less frequently through the night. The fare for the 40-minute trip is 10€ adults. (If you are going to be using public transportation once in the city, you'll save money by buying an **All-Zone Tageskarte/Day Ticket** for 11€ and using it to get into the city.) The **Lufthansa Airport Bus** (www.airportbus-muenchen.de; ✆ **0180/583-8426**) runs between the airport and the main train station in Munich every 20 minutes from about 6:30am to 10:30pm. The trip takes about 40 minutes and costs 11€. A **taxi** to the city center costs about 70€ and can take more than an hour if traffic is heavy.

Munich's **Hauptbahnhof,** on Bahnhofplatz near the city center, is one of Europe's largest train stations, with a hotel, restaurants, shopping, and banking facilities. A train information office on the mezzanine level is open daily from 7am to 8pm. Connected to the rail station are the city's extensive **S-Bahn** rapid-transit system and the **U-Bahn** (subway) system.

Think twice about bringing a **car** into Munich. Most of downtown is a pedestrian-only area—wonderful if you're a walker, a nightmare if you're a driver. Traffic jams are frequent, and parking spaces are elusive and costly.

**CITY LAYOUT** The center of Munich is compact and easy to navigate on foot. The rail station, Hauptbahnhof, lies just west of the town center. Follow Schützenstrasse east through **Karlsplatz,** and keep going—you're now in the **Altstadt (Old Town),** and Schützenstrasse becomes the pedestrians-only Neuhauserstrasse then the Kaufingerstrasse and soon reaches **Marienplatz,** the city center. To the northwest of Marienplatz are the cluster of museums on and around **Königplatz;** to the north are **the Nationaltheater** and the former royal palace, the **Residenz;** and due east is the **Platzl quarter,** where the Hofbräuhaus, the most famous beer hall in Europe, anchors a fairly tame nightlife scene.

**GETTING AROUND** Greater Munich is fairly large and sprawling, though most of what you want to see is located in and around the compact Innenstadt (Inner City). This means that, provided you stay in a hotel in this area, you will be able to walk to just about anywhere you want to go. Even the farthest-flung attractions in the Innenstadt, such as the clutch of museums on and around Köngplatz, are only a 10- or 15-minute walk from Marienplatz.

From the train station, it takes about 15 minutes to walk to hotels in and around Marienplatz, and most of the walk is through a pedestrian zone. Should you wish to zoom into the town center from the train station, Marienplatz is just two stops away on the **U-Bahn** (subway) or **S-Bahn** (light-rail), which, along with **Strassenbahn** (trams) and **buses,** run throughout the city. The same ticket entitles you to ride any of these. Purchase tickets from vending machines in U-Bahn and S-Bahn stations; the machines display somewhat confusing instructions in English. You also can buy tickets in the tram or from a bus driver. A **single ticket** (*einzelfahrkarte*) in Zone 1 (which covers the city center) costs 2.70€. Tickets must then be **validated** in the machines found on U-Bahn and S-Bahn platforms and in buses and trams; stick your ticket into the machine, which stamps it with the date and time. A validated ticket is valid for 2 hours. You can transfer as often as you like to any public transportation as long as you travel in the same direction.

At first encounter, it might seem that a degree in engineering would be helpful in figuring out the extensive U-Bahn and S-Bahn systems. In many stations signage is poor, and maps are few and far between and small and hard to read; maps in the cars are displayed on the ceiling, requiring a craned neck and some serious squinting. Take heart: Once you get used to the system, using it is a breeze. For information, go to www.mvv-muenchen.de or call ✆ **089/41424344.**

### Saving Money on Transportation

A **Tageskarte** (day ticket) good for a day of travel within the inner city costs 5.80€ for one adult; a **Partner Tageskarte** costs 11€ and is good for up to 5 people traveling together. A **3-Tageskarte** (3-day ticket) costs 16€; the **Partner 3-Tageskarte,** good for up to 5 people traveling together, costs 27€. You can buy these cards from the ticket vending machines or at station ticket windows.

Taxis are cream-colored, plentiful, and expensive. You can get a taxi at one of the stands located all across the city, or you can hail a cab on the street if its rooftop light is illuminated. Taxi fares begin at 3.30€ and rise by 1.60€ per kilometer; there's an additional 1.20€ charge to order a taxi by phone. Call **Taxizentrale** at ✆ **089/21610** for a radio-dispatched taxi.

Munich is a bike-friendly city. One of the most convenient places to rent a bike is **Radius Bikes** (www.radiustours.com; ✆ **089/5434877740**), at the far end of the Hauptbahnhof at Arnulfstrasse 2. The charge is 3€ per hour, or 15€ to 18€ per day. You can also partake of Deutsche Bahn's popular **Call a Bike** program, but you need to have your phone handy and be prepared for a little prep work. After registering with Deutsche Bahn and providing a credit-card number, locate a bike outside the train station (and many U-Bahn and S-Bahn stations) then call a toll-free number listed on the bike to get an unlock code and start the clock (cost is 8 cents a min., with a maximum of 15€ a day); when you're done, simply lock up the bike at a Call a Bike stand to stop the clock. To register, call ✆ **49-0345/292970** or 07000 522 5522 from within Germany (English speakers available). You can also register and get more info at www.callabike.de (German only). Call a Bike is also available in Berlin and other German cities.

## The Neighborhoods in Brief

**INNENSTADT (INNER CITY)** Most of the sights of interest to visitors, many restaurants and shops, and probably the hotel where you'll choose to stay are in the Innenstadt, encompassing central Munich west of the Isar River. At the center of the Innenstadt is the **Altstadt (Old City),** an oval-shaped pedestrian-only district. Munich's **Hauptbahnhof** (main train station) lies just west of the Altstadt. **Theresienwiese,** where Oktoberfest is held, is located southwest of the Altstadt.

**ON AND AROUND THE MARIENPLATZ** The Altstadt's most important square is **Marienplatz,** dominated by not one but two town halls, the 15th-century **Altes Rathaus** and the 19th-century **Neues Rathaus.** This large pedestrian-only space is the old heart of Munich, and you'll return here again and again, because many of the city's main attractions, along with shops and restaurants, are nearby. **Kaufingerstrasse,** a pedestrian-only shopping street, starts at the west end of Marienplatz, and **Tal,** a retail and restaurant street, begins at the east side of the square. Just to the south of Marienplatz is the **Viktualienmarkt,** a wonderfully lively outdoor market.

The 15th-century Altes Rathaus, or Old City Hall.

**ODEONPLATZ** **Odeonsplatz,** to the north of Marienplatz, is site of the **Residenz** (former royal palace) and the giant **National Theatre,** home of the famed Bavarian State Opera. Between Marienplatz and Odeonsplatz is the **Platzl** quarter, famed for its nightlife, restaurants, and the **Hofbräuhaus,** the iconic beer hall that has fueled enough frivolity to become one of the city's major landmarks.

**KONIGSPLATZ & THE MUSUEM ZONE** Munich's antiquities collections—the **Propyläen,** the **Glyptothek,** and the **Antikensammlungen**—are on Königsplatz (King's Square), a beautiful yet austere assemblage of neoclassical palaces flanking a large expanse of greenery, and another trio of world-famous art museums—the **Alte Pinakothek (Old Masters Gallery),** the **Neue Pinakothek (New Masters Gallery),** and the **Pinakothek Moderne Kunst (Gallery of Modern Art)**—are located in the so-called **Museum Quarter,** just northeast of Königsplatz along Brennerstrasse.

## Exploring Munich

If you've come to Munich just to drink beer, you're in for a pleasant surprise, or a rude jolt, depending on just how much of a plebian you really are. The former turf of Bavarian nobility is crammed with antiquities and art treasures the royal family amassed over the centuries, augmented with a wealth of 19th-century, 20th-century, and contemporary works. You can spend days wandering through some of Europe's best art museums, though there's plenty else to do in this engaging city, too, from visiting royal palaces to pedaling through the Englischer Garten (English Garden) to, yes, hanging out in the Hofbräuhaus and other beer halls.

### THE ALTSTADT

#### Bayerisches Nationalmuseum (Bavarian National Museum) ★

You'll discover everything you've ever wanted to know about Bavaria and then some in this rambling repository of art and artifacts. Even on a fairly

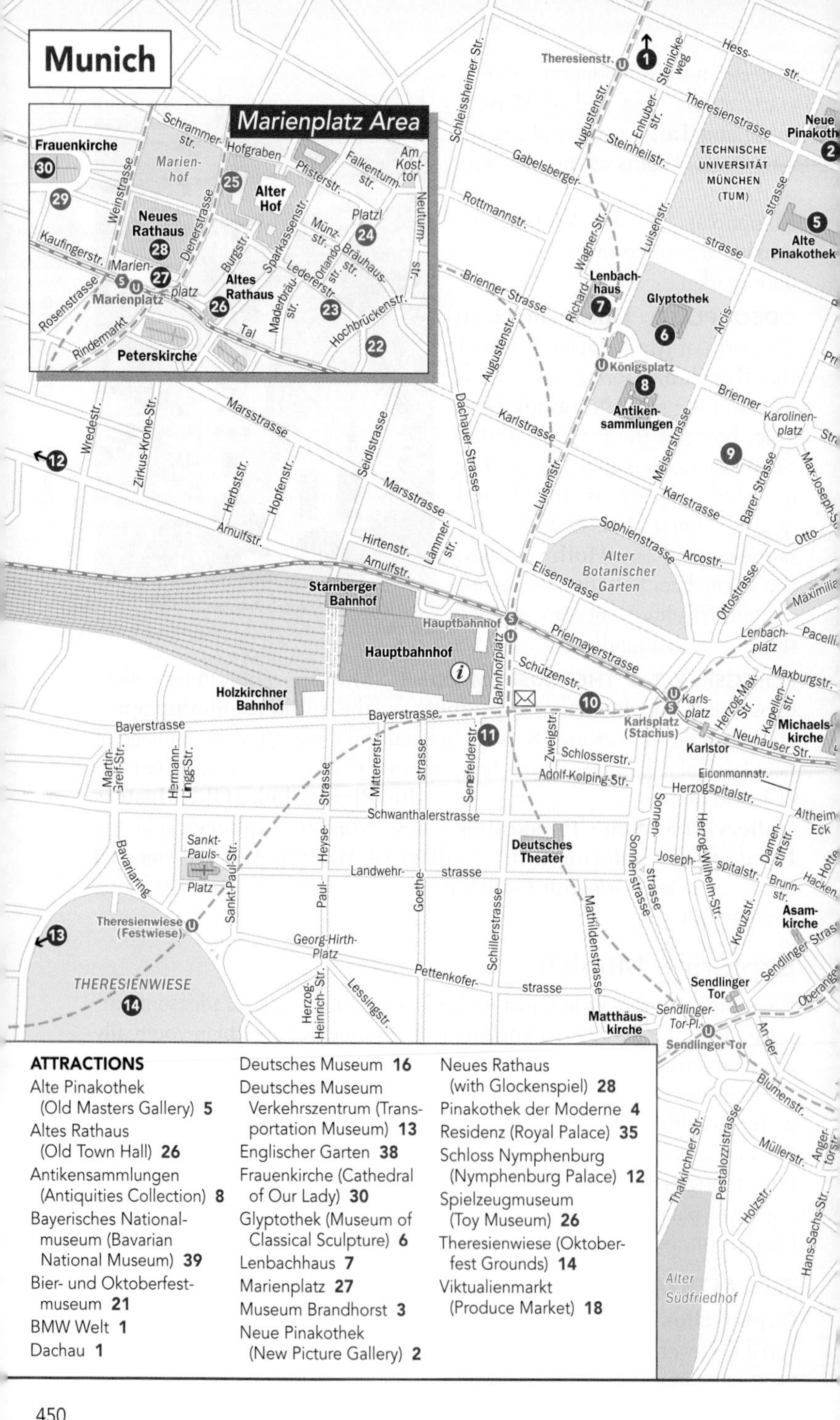
Munich
Marienplatz Area
Frauenkirche
Marienhof
Alter Hof
Neues Rathaus
Altes Rathaus
Marienplatz
Peterskirche
Schrammerstr.
Hofgraben
Pfisterstr.
Falkenturmstr.
Am Kosttor
Neuturmstr.
Platzl
Münzstr.
Orlandostr.
Bräuhausstr.
Sparkassenstr.
Ledererstr.
Maderbräustr.
Hochbrückenstr.
Burgstr.
Dienerstrasse
Weinstrasse
Kaufingerstr.
Rosenstrasse
Rindermarkt
Tal
Theresienstr.
Steinickeweg
Hessstr.
Theresienstrasse
Neue Pinakothek
Technische Universität München (TUM)
Alte Pinakothek
Enhuberstr.
Steinheilstr.
Augustenstr.
Schleissheimer Str.
Gabelsbergerstr.
Rottmannstr.
Luisenstr.
Richard-Wagner-Str.
Lenbachhaus
Glyptothek
Arcisstrasse
Brienner Strasse
Königsplatz
Antikensammlungen
Karolinenplatz
Dachauer Strasse
Karlstrasse
Meiserstrasse
Barer Strasse
Max-Joseph-Str.
Marsstrasse
Seidlstrasse
Wredestr.
Zirkus-Krone-Str.
Herbststr.
Hopfenstr.
Arnulfstr.
Hirtenstr.
Lämmerstr.
Sophienstrasse
Arcostr.
Ottostrasse
Alter Botanischer Garten
Elisenstrasse
Starnberger Bahnhof
Hauptbahnhof
Bahnhofplatz
Prielmayerstrasse
Lenbachplatz
Maxburgstr.
Schützenstr.
Holzkirchner Bahnhof
Bayerstrasse
Karlsplatz (Stachus)
Karlstor
Herzog-Max-Str.
Kapellenstr.
Michaelskirche
Neuhauser Str.
Zweigstr.
Schlosserstr.
Adolf-Kolping-Str.
Senefelderstr.
Mittererstr.
Martin-Greif-Str.
Hermann-Lingg-Str.
Herzogspitalstr.
Schwanthalerstrasse
Sonnenstrasse
Herzog-Wilhelm-Str.
Damenstiftstr.
Altheimer Eck
Deutsches Theater
Sankt-Pauls-Platz
Sankt-Paul-Str.
Paul-Heyse-Strasse
Landwehrstrasse
Goethestrasse
Josephspitalstr.
Brunnstr.
Hackenstr.
Asamkirche
Bavariaring
Theresienwiese (Festwiese)
Georg-Hirth-Platz
Schillerstrasse
Mathildenstrasse
Kreuzstr.
Sendlinger Strasse
Pettenkoferstrasse
Theresienwiese
Herzog-Heinrich-Str.
Lessingstr.
Matthäuskirche
Sendlinger Tor
Sendlinger-Tor-Pl.
Oberanger
An der
Blumenstr.
Thalkirchner Str.
Pestalozzistrasse
Müllerstr.
Angerstr.
Holzstr.
Hans-Sachs-Str.
Alter Südfriedhof
ATTRACTIONS
Alte Pinakothek (Old Masters Gallery) 5
Altes Rathaus (Old Town Hall) 26
Antikensammlungen (Antiquities Collection) 8
Bayerisches Nationalmuseum (Bavarian National Museum) 39
Bier- und Oktoberfestmuseum 21
BMW Welt 1
Dachau 1
Deutsches Museum 16
Deutsches Museum Verkehrszentrum (Transportation Museum) 13
Englischer Garten 38
Frauenkirche (Cathedral of Our Lady) 30
Glyptothek (Museum of Classical Sculpture) 6
Lenbachhaus 7
Marienplatz 27
Museum Brandhorst 3
Neue Pinakothek (New Picture Gallery) 2
Neues Rathaus (with Glockenspiel) 28
Pinakothek der Moderne 4
Residenz (Royal Palace) 35
Schloss Nymphenburg (Nymphenburg Palace) 12
Spielzeugmuseum (Toy Museum) 26
Theresienwiese (Oktoberfest Grounds) 14
Viktualienmarkt (Produce Market) 18

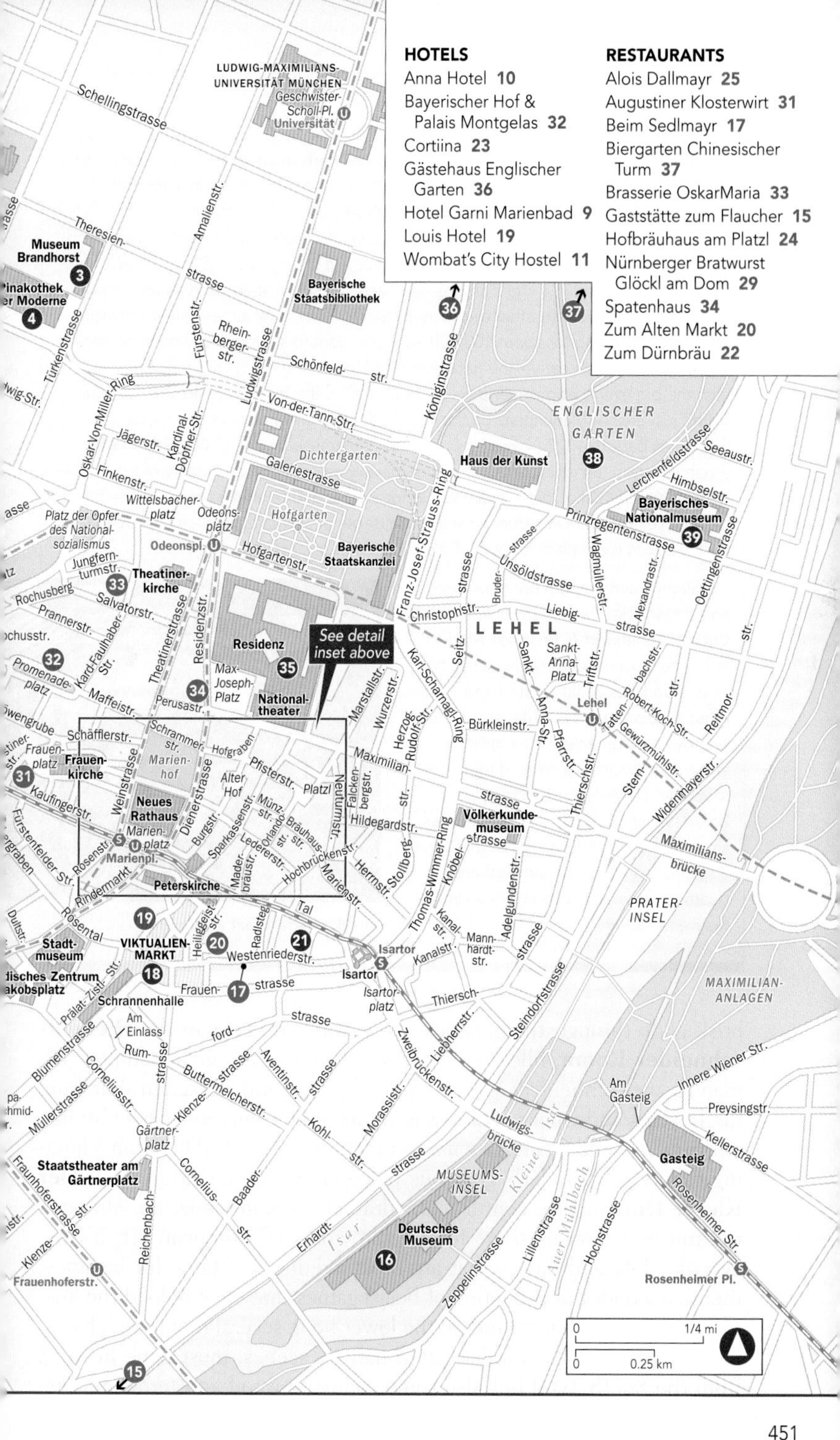
HOTELS
Anna Hotel 10
Bayerischer Hof & Palais Montgelas 32
Cortiina 23
Gästehaus Englischer Garten 36
Hotel Garni Marienbad 9
Louis Hotel 19
Wombat's City Hostel 11
RESTAURANTS
Alois Dallmayr 25
Augustiner Klosterwirt 31
Beim Sedlmayr 17
Biergarten Chinesischer Turm 37
Brasserie OskarMaria 33
Gaststätte zum Flaucher 15
Hofbräuhaus am Platzl 24
Nürnberger Bratwurst Glöckl am Dom 29
Spatenhaus 34
Zum Alten Markt 20
Zum Dürnbräu 22
LUDWIG-MAXIMILIANS-UNIVERSITÄT MÜNCHEN
Museum Brandhorst
Pinakothek der Moderne
Bayerische Staatsbibliothek
ENGLISCHER GARTEN
Haus der Kunst
Bayerisches Nationalmuseum
Dichtergarten
Hofgarten
Bayerische Staatskanzlei
Theatinerkirche
Residenz
See detail inset above
National-theater
LEHEL
Frauenkirche
Neues Rathaus
Peterskirche
Völkerkunde-museum
PRATER-INSEL
Stadt-museum
VIKTUALIEN-MARKT
Schrannenhalle
Isartor
MAXIMILIAN-ANLAGEN
Gasteig
MUSEUMS-INSEL
Deutsches Museum
Staatstheater am Gärtnerplatz
Rosenheimer Pl.
Frauenhoferstr.
0 1/4 mi
0 0.25 km

## festive MUNICH

**Oktoberfest,** the city's famous 16-day beer bash, starts in late September and runs for 2½ weeks to the first Sunday in October. All the *trinken und essen* (drinking and eating) takes place at the traditional **Theresienwiese** ("Wiesn" for short) festival grounds, where each of the 14 different tents offers its own atmosphere and food (sausage and sauerkraut prevail). Oktoberfest beer is delicious but strong, with a 5% to 7% alcohol level, and it's served in 1-liter portions—so pace yourself, lest you find yourself waking up on a sidewalk next to other dazed revelers. The Wiesn welcomes millions of visitors, but only has seating for about 100,000, so if you want to sit, especially on busy weekend evenings, arrive early—the gates open at 10am—and claim your space. If you miss the big event, Augustiner Brewery has installed the **Bier- und Oktoberfestmuseum,** just east of Marienplatz off the Tal, in a former brewhouse at Sterneckstrasse 2 that dates back to 1327 (www.bier-und-oktoberfestmuseum.de; ✆ **089/24243941;** S-Bahn: Isartor). Exhibits explain the beer-making process and the history of the Oktoberfest. Your 4€ ticket includes a voucher for a glass of beer and a snack like the Bavarian cheese Obatzda with *leberwurst* (liver sausage) or *schmaltz* (chicken fat spread over freshly baked rye bread). It's open Tuesday to Saturday 1 to 5pm.

Slightly tamer and more family-oriented than Oktoberfest is Munich's giant **Christkindlemarkt (Christmas Market),** from late November through December, when hundreds of illuminated and decorated outdoor stands fill Marienplatz and sell toys, tree ornaments, handicrafts, and a mouthwatering array of traditional snacks and sweets, including gingerbread, sugarcoated almonds, fruitcakes, smoked meats, and piping hot *glühwein,* a spiced red wine. The atmosphere is guaranteed to put even Scrooges into a festive mood.

**An Oktoberfest tent in Munich.**

brisk glide through the galleries, you'll want to linger in the **Riemenschneider Room,** filled with works in wood by the great sculptor Tilman Riemenschneider (1460–1531), who lived and worked in Wurzburg for 48 years and whose genius was an uncanny ability to capture human empathy in wood, stone, or whatever medium he worked in. In an adjoining gallery is a similarly gorgeous piece of craftsmanship in gold, **Der Kleine Dom,** a 14th-century cathedral rendered in miniature. Although the museum houses some formidable works of European art, it's the everyday bits and pieces that are most riveting. Upstairs, for instance, there's a wonderful collection of board games that once helped the aristocracy pass idle hours, and on the lower floor, several rooms are charmingly filled with elaborately crafted nativity scenes, most done in wood from the South Tyrol but also some elaborate wood and terracotta *presepe* from southern Italy.

Prinzregentenstrasse 3. www.bayerisches-nationalmuseum.de. ✆ **089/2112401.** 5€ adults, 4€ students/seniors, children 14 and under free; Sun 1€ for all. U-Bahn: Lehel. Tram: 17. Bus: 100. Tues–Sun 10am–5pm (Thurs until 8pm).

**Residenz (Royal Palace) ★★** The Wittelsbach family, the rulers of Bavaria from 1385 to 1918, spent centuries embellishing their palace, magnificently restored after World War II bombs laid waste to some of the finest craftsmanship in Europe. You'll meet them all in the Ahnengallery (Ancestors Gallery), where 121 portraits of the rulers of Bavaria, tidily arranged in chronological order, look out from a riot of rococo stucco and gilt. An English-language audioguide is free with your admission and will steer you to the other highlights of the palace. Allow at least half a day to wander through the 90 or so rooms on display, slowing down to admire such showstoppers as the Grottenhof (Grotto Court), where the god Perseus stands in the middle of a fountain holding the dripping head of Medusa and the over-the-top Reich Zimmer (Rich Rooms), the work of an army of stucco and fresco artists given free rein to cover ever inch with elaborate decoration. The Antiquarium, where frescoes set off the royal collection of antiquities and the Steinzimmer (Stone Rooms), the emperor's private quarters paneled in intricately patterned and colored marble, are sedate by comparison. For a breath of fresh air, step into the Italianate **Hofgarten (Court Garden),** laid out between 1613 and 1617.

Max-Joseph-Platz 3. www.residenz-muenchen.de. ✆ **089/290671.** 13€ adults, 11€ seniors, free for students/children. U-Bahn: Odeonsplatz. Daily Apr–Sept 9am–6pm; Oct–Mar 10am–4pm.

## MUSEUMSVIERTEL (MUSEUM QUARTER)

You could spend days exploring the four art museums that make up the Museum Quarter, also called the Kunstareal. All four are worth visiting, but the enormous **Alte Pinakothek,** with its world-class collection of Old Masters, is the must-see.

**Alte Pinakothek (Old Masters Gallery) ★★★** It's largely thanks to a passion for collecting that ran through royal Bavarian blood lines that this remarkable collection of 800 masterpieces is here, and amazingly intact, too, given World War II pillage and bombings. The House of Wittelsbach amassed what are unquestionably some of the world's finest paintings, and Ludwig I brought them together here in this elegant, mid-19th-century neoclassical temple. You'll want to pare

### Museum Savings on Sunday

On Sunday, you can enjoy the treasures in all three Pinakotheks (Alte, Neue, der Moderne), as well as Museum Brandhorst and the Schack-Galerie for 1€. You can also purchase a day pass (available at any of the museums) that gives you admission to all five museums for 12€, or a pass that entitles you to five visits for 29€. Admission to the Antikensammlungen and Glyptohek is also 1€ on Sundays.

The Alte Pinakothek.

down what you have time to see (allow at least two hours here; the free English audio guide will steer you to the highlights in about that amount of time). Any short list should include the Flemish and northern artists whose works are the scene stealers: Rubens's *The Rape of the Daughters of Leucippus* and his *Last Judgement,* which is almost 20-feet tall; Albrecht Durer's *Self Portrait With Fur-Trimmed Robe,* painted in 1500 when he was 29 and allegedly the first self-portrait an artist ever undertook, and Pieter Bruegel the Elder's *Land of Cockaigne* (1567), a wonderfully decadent portrayal of excess. Leave time to wander through the galleries filled with the Italian Renaissance masters (including Raphael and Botticelli), the Spanish masters El Greco and Velazquez, and the French school, especially works by Boucher and Poussin.

Barerstrasse 27. www.pinakothek.de/alte-pinakothek. ✆ **089/23805216.** 4€ adults, 2€ students/seniors; Sat 1€. U-Bahn: Theresienstrasse. Tram: 27. Bus: 100. Tues–Sun 10am–5pm (Tues until 8pm).

**Museum Brandhorst ★★** An array of multicolor ceramic rods comprise the facade of this remarkable pavilion, inside of which handsome, oak-floored galleries house the private collection amassed by detergent heiress Anette Brandhorst and her husband, Udo Fritz-Hermann. From the 1970s until Brandhorst's death in 1999, the wildly wealthy couple purchased no fewer than 100 works by Andy Warhol and at least 60 by Cy Twombly. Warhol's portraits of Marilyn Monroe and Natalie Wood will probably be familiar to you; the stunner is Twombly's *Battle of*

*Lepanto,* his abstract cycle of the 1571 bloodbath in which a coalition of European states routed the Ottomans in the Gulf of Corinth, colorfully depicted on 12 gigantic canvases that hang in their own custom-fitted gallery. Also spend a little time checking out the 112 books illustrated by Pablo Picasso.

Kunstareal, Theresienstrasse 35A. www.museum-brandhorst.de. ✆ **089/238052286.** 7€ adults, 5€ children 5–16; Sat 1€. U-Bahn: Königsplatz or Theresienstrasse. Bus: 100 or 154. Tues–Sun 10am–6pm (Thurs until 8pm).



**Neue Pinakothek (New Picture Gallery) ★★★** Light and airy galleries in a postmodern building from 1981 pick up Munich's formidable artistic heritage where the Alta Pinakothek leaves off: The emphasis here is 19th-century German and European art, starting right around 1800. The museum's most popular works are the ever-pleasing canvases by the Impressionists, including those by Manet, van Gogh (one of his *Sunflowers* from 1888 is one of the museum's star attractions), Monet, Degas, and Renoir. German painters make a formidable showing, too, and the Romantic Casper David Friedrich is an especially powerful presence; his brooding, emotionally charged works in which human presence seems insignificant amid vast landscapes include the wonderfully moody *Riesengebirge with Rising Fog* (1819). A nice companion piece is the similarly atmospheric, mist-shrouded *Ostende* (1844) by Turner, one of several British painters on view. A tour of the highlights takes a couple of hours; an audio tour in English is free with your admission.

Barerstrasse 27 (across Theresienstrasse from the Alte Pinakothek). www.pinakothek.de. ✆ **089/23805195.** 7€ adults, 5€ students/seniors; Sat 1€. U-Bahn: Theresienstrasse. Tram: 27. Bus: 100. Wed–Mon 10am–6pm (Wed until 8pm).

**Pinakothek der Moderne ★★** Proof that Munich's art scene can be as edgy as Berlin's comes to the fore in these stark galleries surrounding a light-filled rotunda, housing four collections of 20th-century work in art, graphic art, architecture, and craft and design. Galleries, though, are small, intimate, and beautifully lit. Most impressive in the modern art collection are works the German *Die Brücke* artists (seek out Kirchner's wonderfully colorful, almost primitive *Bohemian Lake* from 1911) and the *Blaue Reiter* group, including Kandinsky, Franz Marc, and Auguste Macke. They're joined by a long roster of international 20th-century masters, from Picasso and Magritte to Andy Warhol and David Hockney. The **Neue Sammlung (Craft and Design Collection)** houses an array of artifacts from modern life, here elevated to art forms and some dramatically poised on multistory-tall shelves—the VW Beetle, snowmobiles, and aircraft prototypes take their place among laptops, teapots, and Lucite radios, as well as some beautifully crafted 20th-century furniture—the ubiquitous Eames chairs seem much less elegant than a collection of Art Nouveau armoires and buffets. Only a tiny portion of the **Graphische Sammlung (Graphics Collection),** with its light-sensitive works on paper by such masters as Leonardo da Vinci, is open for viewing at any time. An excellent audiovisual guide is free all days except Sunday, when it costs 4€.

Barerstrasse 40. www.pinakothek.de. ✆ **089/23805360.** 10€ adults, 7€ students/seniors; Sat 1€; free on Wed. U-Bahn: Odeonsplatz. Tues–Sun 10am–6pm (Thurs until 8pm).





## KÖNIGSPLATZ

Ludwig I (reigned 1825–48) set out to redo Munich in neoclassical style, a second Athens, an endeavor that was thwarted but is best embodied in the classically inspired architecture of Königsplatz, 2 blocks south of the Museumsviertel. An ardent classicist (as a supporter of Greek independence, he successfully lobbied to have his son, Otto, named king of Greece in 1832) Ludwig collected an impressive array of Greek and Roman artifacts, housed here in the **Antikensammlungen** and **Glyptothek,** flanking the temple-like **Propyläen** monument.

**Antikensammlungen (Antiquities Collections) ★** Five grandiose main-floor halls house the artifacts that Ludwig largely purchased from Italian excavations unearthed in the early 19th century. Most prominent are more than 650 Greek vases, including distinctive black-figure pottery from around 700 B.C., in which gods, goddesses, and other figures were etched in black, and red-figure pottery that supplanted it around 500 B.C. Work of the greatest potter of them all, 6th-century B.C. Exekias, includes a drinking cup in which the wine god Dionysus reclines in a ship, as if he's sleeping off a bender. From about nine centuries later comes another lovely vessel, a fragile-looking, intricately wrought glass Roman goblet.

Königsplatz 1. www.antike-am-koenigsplatz.mwn.de. ✆ **089/59988830.** 6€ adults, 4€ students/seniors (includes Glyptothek); Sun 1€. U-Bahn: Königsplatz. Tues–Sun 10am–5pm (Thurs until 8pm).

**Glyptothek (Museum of Sculpture) ★★** Ludwig amassed what has become Germany's largest collection of ancient Greek and Roman sculpture. Among the almost otherworldly 6th-century-B.C. *kouroi* (statues of youths) and somber busts of Roman emperors, is the museum's most popular piece, the colossal *Sleeping Satyr* (also known as the *Barberini Faun*). Ludwig purchased this work, probably by Greek artisans of the 2nd century B.C., from Rome's Barberini clan of popes and cardinals. The reclining, naked, blatantly virile figure reposes peacefully, unaware of the gawks and titters of modern viewers.

Königsplatz 3. www.antike-am-koenigsplatz.mwn.de. ✆ **089/286100.** 6€ adults, 4€ students/seniors (includes Antikensammiungen); Sun 1€. U-Bahn: Königsplatz. Tues–Sun 10am–5pm (Thurs until 8pm).

**Lenbachhaus ★★★** If you aren't familiar with Munich's *Blaue Reiter* (Blue Rider) school of artists, many of whom were deemed degenerate by the Nazis, this is the place to get to know them. This dazzling collection of late-19th and early-20th-century paintings by Wassily Kandinsky, Paul Klee, Franz Marc and Gabriele Münter hang in modern galleries of the Lenbachhaus, a Tuscan villa built by the painter Franz von Lenbach between 1887 and 1891 to serve as his residence and atelier. The star of the show is the Russian-born Kandinsky, whose bright, colorful canvases morph over the course of his career into pure abstraction. His former mistress donated more than 1,000 pieces of his work to the gallery in 1957, and they now gloriously fill the third-floor galleries.

Luisenstrasse 33. www.lenbachhaus.de. ✆ **089/2333200**. 12€ adults, 6€ students. U-Bahn: Königsplatz. Tues–Sun 10am–6pm (Tues until 9pm).



## OUTSIDE CENTRAL MUNICH

**BMW Welt ★★** Munich-based BMW (Bavarian Motor Works) makes no secret of its success and prestige in headquarters that are an exercise in showiness. Part of the sprawling complex looks like a giant glass funnel cloud, and in it, the latest models are beautifully spotlit like celebrities along a central, hourglass-shaped ramp. For a voyeuristic look at luxury consumerism in action, you can stand in a glass gallery and watch as new owners pick up the keys to their cars just off the assembly lines, which you can also visit on a 2-hour tour. Or, for a Walter Mitty–like experience, you can arrange to rent one of the shiny beauties by the hour or day and take it out for a spin through the nearby Alps. The less adventurous can settle for a gawk at the company's superb collection of vintage

**BMW Welt.**

vehicles from the company's beginning in 1929, in the **BMW Museum,** where racing cars, motorcycles, sporty coupes, and even a hydrogen-powered roadster of the future are displayed as precious treasures; the glitzy Rolls-Royces, part of the BMW family, seem like frumps compared to their sleeker cousins.

Am Olympiapark 1. www.bmw-welt.com. © **0180/1118822.** Museum 10€ adults, 7€ seniors/children; factory tour 6€ adults, 3€ seniors and children. U-Bahn: Olympiazentrum. Showroom daily 7:30am–midnight; museum daily 9am–6pm; factory tours Mon–Fri 8:30am–10pm.



**Dachau Concentration Camp Memorial Site (KZ-Gedenkstatte Dachau)** ★★★ HISTORIC SITE In 1933, shortly after Hitler became chancellor, Himmler and the SS set up the first German concentration camp on the grounds of a former ammunition factory in the small town of Dachau, 10 miles (15km) northwest of Munich. Until American GIs liberated the camp in 1945, more than 206,000 mostly male prisoners from 30 countries were imprisoned at Dachau—communists, Jews, homosexuals, Gypsies, Jehovah's Witnesses, clergymen, political opponents, trade-union members, and others—stripped of all human rights and dignity and turned into slave laborers who were tortured, beaten, shot, hung, starved, lethally injected, and used for medical experiments. Officially, at least 30,000 prisoners died, though Dachau was not a "death camp" per se and was shown off to visitors as a labor camp where political dissidents and "social and sexual deviants" could be "rehabilitated" through work. It's estimated that thousands more were murdered here, even if their deaths weren't officially logged, and many prisoners were transported from Dachau to the gas chambers at camps farther east.

In the large building where prisoners were registered and processed, photographs, text panels (all translated into English), and documents tell the story of the camp, how it was run, who was incarcerated and killed, and who some of the personnel were. The most effective experience is simply walking across the grounds, with their bleak, haunted quality. The rebuilt barracks, once hideously filthy, overcrowded and breeding grounds for typhus and vermin; the roll-call yard, where prisoners were brutally mustered; a bunker that was used as a camp prison and torture area; barbed-wire fences; and the crematorium area all have a sense of remove from the reality of the horrors that transpired here. Even so, Dachau is not an easy place to visit, as important as it is to do so.

KZ-Gedenkstätte Dachau. Alte-Römerstrasse 75. www.kz-gedenkstaette-dachau.de. © **08131/669970.** Free admission; guided tours 3€. S-Bahn train S2 from the Hauptbahnhof to Dachau (direction: Petershausen), then bus no. 726 to the camp (total trip time 45 min.). Open daily 9am–5pm.

**Schloss Nymphenburg** ★★★ If you've toured the Munich Residenz of the Bavarian royal family, you've probably gotten a sense that the family did not go in for restrained decor. They showed the same lack of

Schloss Nymphenburg.



restraint in their summer palace, creating one of the great showcases of royal Europe over the course of 150 years, beginning in 1664. The most beautiful of the grand rooms is the **Great Hall,** with its vibrant flourishes of rococo stuccowork, and by far the most intriguing is a relatively recent addition, the **Gallery of Beauties** that Josef Karl Stieler frescoed between 1827 and 1850; look for the portrait of Lola Montez, the raven-haired dancer whose affair with Ludwig caused a scandal. Even the stables are grand and house a dazzling fleet of ornate, gilded coaches and sleighs, including those used by Ludwig II (the "Mad" King who built Neuschwanstein; see p. 473).

The 500-acre **Schlosspark,** stretching all the way to the so-called **Grand Cascade** at the far end of the formal, French-style gardens, is a refreshing tonic after so much ostentation—though there's plenty of that out here among the quiet meadows and forests. As you wander the paths, and allow a couple of hours to do so, you'll come to the **Badenburg Pavilion,** with an 18th-century swimming pool; the **Pagodenburg,** decorated in the Chinese style that was all the rage in the 18th century; the **Magdalenenklause (Hermitage),** a retreat for prayer and solitude; and the **Amalienburg,** built in 1734 as a hunting lodge for Electress Amalia; the interior salons are a riot of flamboyant colors, swirling stuccowork, and wall paintings.

Schloss Nymphenburg, Schloss Nymphenburg 1. www.schloss-nymphenburg.de. ✆ **089/179080.** Palace grounds free; admission to all attractions Apr to mid-Oct 12€ adults, 9€ seniors; Oct 16–Mar 8.50€ adults, 6.50€ seniors. Badenburg and Magdalenenklause closed Oct 16–Mar. S-Bahn to "Laim" then the bus marked "Schloss Nymphenburg." Apr–Oct 15 daily 9am–6pm; Oct 16–Mar daily 10am–4pm.

## MUNICH'S GREAT OUTDOORS SPACES

### Marienplatz ★★★

A large pedestrian-only square in the heart of the Altstadt is Munich's ground zero and a delightful assemblage of famous landmarks. The **Neues Rathaus (New City Hall),** built in 19th-century Gothic style, anchors the north side of the square with a riot of ornate decoration that swirls and swishes across every inch of the heavy facade. The 280-foot central spire is enlivened with the **Glockenspiel,** from which brightly painted mechanical figures make an appearance twice a day, to the accompaniment of 43 clanging bells and folksy Bavarian chimes. Join the crowds who gather below to watch them at noon and 9pm daily (also at 11am and 5pm during the holiday seasons). There's meaning behind the jaunty antics: the jousting knights on the top level are reenacting a tournament during the 1586 wedding feast of Wilhelm V and Renate of Lorraine, and, just below them, a circle of jolly men are performing the *Schäfflertanz* (Coopers' Dance), expressing gratitude for the end of a 1683 plague outbreak. You can take an elevator to the top of the Rathaus's tower for a good view of the city center (1.50€; Mon–Fri 9am–7pm and Sat–Sun 10am–7pm).

To the east of the Neues Rathaus is the **Altes Rathaus (Old City Hall),** a much more humble and dignified affair with an unembellished facade and a plain, 15th-century Gothic tower. To the west of the Neues Rathaus rises the distinctive twin onion domes of the **Frauenkirche (Cathedral of Our Lady),** Munich's largest church (Frauenplatz 1; www.muenchner-dom.de; ✆ **089/2900820**) These domed towers from 1525 were all that were left standing after World War II bombs leveled the rest of the structure, along with most of central Munich; the strikingly simple and dignified church is a reconstruction.

The Glockenspiel at Neues Rathaus.

### The Viktualienmarkt ★★★

Munich's outdoor food market colorfully and sometimes odiferously fills a square just to the south of Marienplatz (well-marked lanes lead to it). Butchers, bakers, everyone but the candlestick maker occupy stands stocked with dozens of different kinds of Bavarian breads, cheese, fish, produce, cakes and sweets, and lots of wurst and other prepared foods. Most of the permanent stands open at 6am

Fresh produce at the Viktualienmarkt.

and stay open until 6pm on weekdays and until 1pm on Saturday. You can buy food at the market stalls and eat it in the market's own beer garden if you buy a beverage there.

**Englischer Garten (English Garden) ★★★**
In one of the most beautiful city parks in Europe, established in 1789, you can wander over 922 acres, along tree-shaded walks, streams, and lakes, pausing to admire the view of Munich's Altstadt from the round, hilltop Greek temple called the **Monopteros.** You'll come upon plenty of other noteworthy sights, including the exotic **Chinesischer Turm (Chinese Pagoda)** and, in warm weather, lots of nude sunbathers sprawled along the banks of the Eisbach stream and the **Kleinhesseloher See,** the lovely lake at the center of this popular, much-appreciated greensward. The park is just northwest of the Aldstadt, with entrances off Von-der-Tann Strasse and Prinzregentenstrasse; a convenient U-Bahn stop is Odeonplatz.

## Organized Tours

A couple of companies offer hop-on, hop-off bus tours of Munich, but the old city is so compact and easy to explore on foot that you might want to save your money for a round of beers; if you can't resist a spin on the open-air top of a double-decker, sign on for a 1-hour **Stadtrundfahrt (City Tour)** from **CitySightseeing** (www.citysightseeing-munich.com), with a circuit of 13 stops. Tours depart daily (10am–5pm) about every 20 minutes from Bahnhofsplatz in front of the main train station; cost is 17€

adults, 7.90€ children. Buy your ticket onboard or get a discounted price online.

For a more active experience, tour Munich by bicycle with the English-speaking expats at **Mike's Bike Tours** (www.mikesbiketours.com; **© 089/2554-3988**). The 4-hour tour (26€ adults, 13€ children) spins around the sights of central Munich, including an hour in a beer garden (lunch not included).

**Munich Walk Tours** (www.munichwalktours.de; **© 0171/274-0204**), conducted in English, include a daily 10:45am City Walk tour (also 2:45pm high season) and a 2½-hour Hitler's Munich tour (Nov–Mar daily 10:30am). Tours cost 12€ adults, 10€ under 26, free for kids under 14.

## Especially for Kids

Munich's **Altstadt,** with its traffic-free streets and plazas, is like one big playground for young travelers. Parents can give kids a fairly long leash, resting assured they'll be safe from traffic. **Marienplatz** is especially appealing to youngsters, with its handsome, fairy-tale-like landmarks and the twice-daily **Glockenspiel** show in the Neues Rathaus (see p. 460). You may also want to take them into the Altes Rathaus (Old City Hall), where the **Spielzeugmuseum** shows off a huge toy collection (**© 089/294-001;** 3€ adults, 1.50€ children; daily 10am–5pm), but be warned—the cases full of teddy bears may have them eager to head into the nearby Marienplatz shops in search of one to take home. An even bigger hit with kids is **Deutsches Museum Verkehrszentrum** (Transportation Museum), Theresienhohe 14a (www.deutsches-museum.de/verkehrszentrum; **© 089/500806762;** 6€ adults, 3€ children; daily 9am–5pm; U-Bahn: Schwanthalerhöhe), where they can see "Puffing Billy," an early steam-engine locomotive from 1814, step into a passenger train from the late 19th century, and peer inside a modern high-speed ICE train. Adults tend to spend their time ogling the superlative collection of historic automobiles, including Daimlers, Opels, Mercedes, Tatas, Citroens, and Bugattis. When seeing the sights becomes too much, do as world-weary Münchners do and retreat to the **Englischer Garten** (English Garden).

## Where to Stay

Hotels in Munich are more expensive than elsewhere in Germany, and rooms are scarce (and prices higher) during Oktoberfest and when trade fairs are being held. It's a good idea to book your Munich hotel room in advance.

### IN & AROUND THE ALTSTADT

#### Expensive

**Bayerischer Hof and Palais Montgelas ★★★** Built 175 years ago to hosts guests of the Bavarian royal family, Munich's largest and oldest hotel is still the grandest and makes all guests feel a bit like royalty, with attentive service and spacious, glamorous, high-ceilinged guest rooms. All the accommodations are different, but elegant grays and neutral tones set a classically modern norm, with comfy sofas, luxurious beds with tufted headboards, large writing desks, and handsome marble bathrooms with deep soaking tubs and huge walk-in showers. Restaurants include a glass-walled aerie on the sixth floor where a lavish champagne buffet breakfast (included in many rates) is served, and a beautiful indoor pool, sauna, spa, cinema, and a famous nightclub provide plenty of in-house diversions.

Promenadeplatz 2-6. www.bayerischerhof.de. ✆ **089/21200**. 340 units. Doubles 260€–460€, suites 790€–2,000€, most rates include buffet breakfast. U-/S-Bahn: Marienplatz. **Amenities:** 2 restaurants; 2 bar-lounges; nightclub; pool; sauna; gym; cinema; free Wi-Fi.

### Moderate

**Cortiina ★★** Hip contends with homey for a truly soothing effect in these lovely rooms that combine handsome kilim rugs on polished parquet floors, specially designed furnishings with slight 1950s overtones, and lots of eye-pleasing patterns and mellow colors. Some suites have kitchenettes and terraces for an "at home in Munich" feel, and the biggest perk of all is the location a stone's throw from Marienplatz.

Ledererstrasse 8. www.cortiina.com. ✆ **089/2422490.** 75 units. Doubles 159€–259€. U-Bahn: Marienplatz. **Amenities:** Bar; free Wi-Fi.

**Louis Hotel ★★★** Modern European design with a slight Asian overlay is geared to function and style, with some nice touches in the sleek, white-walled, wood-floored rooms that include cabinetry suggestive of old steamer trunks. The travel reference is slightly redundant if you have a room with the most colorful view in town, overlooking the lively Viktualienmarkt from its own little balcony; others face a quiet courtyard. In winter, a lobby lounge is warmed by a stone hearth, and the roof terrace is the perfect place to relax with a cocktail in summer.

Viktualienmarkt 6. www.louis-hotel.com. ✆ **089/41119080.** 72 units. Doubles 179€–320€. U/S-Bahn: Marienplatz. **Amenities:** Restaurant; bar; roof terrace; free Wi-Fi.

## OUTSIDE THE ALTSTADT

### Moderate

**Anna Hotel ★★** You'll discover just what a difference beautiful accents like thoughtful lighting can make in these carefully designed rooms, where luxurious furnishings, from handsome upholstered lounge chairs to sleek blonde cabinets, have been especially crafted for this calm oasis next to the Kastor, one of the entrance gates to the historical part of the city. Creamy upholstered walls and shining teak floors strike a note of drama, as do such nods to comfortable decadence in the suites as deep bathtubs facing flatscreens to encourage long soaks. At night, the dramatically lit towers of the old town steal the show.

Schützenstrasse 1. www.annahotel.de. ✆ **089/599940.** 75 units. Doubles 165€–220€. U/S-Bahn: Hauptbahnhof. **Amenities:** Restaurant; bar; free Wi-Fi.

**Gästehaus Englischer Garten ★★** You'll trade a city-center location for a perch right next to Munich's famous park. The bucolic setting in an ivy-clad villa with a stream darting past the garden is enhanced with a homey mix of antiques, old-fashioned beds, and Oriental rugs. Should all this verdant charm be too much, the U-Bahn station is a short walk away, and the city center is also easy to reach on a trek through the park. This charming guesthouse rents out 15 small apartments in a more modern annex across the street; each has a kitchenette.
Liebergesellstrasse 8. www.hotelenglischergarten.de. ✆ **089/383-9410.** 25 units. Doubles 83€–186€. U-Bahn: Münchener Freiheit. **Amenities:** Free Wi-Fi.

**Hotel Garni Marienbad ★** An old patrician villa where Sigmund Freud, Giacomo Puccini, Rainer Maria Rilke, and their intellectual and artistic ilk used to be entertained over beef and dumplings is now a charmingly atmospheric getaway set back from the street amid a curtain of trees. Munich's museum zone is just around the corner, making this a perfect base for anyone wanting to immerse themselves in the city's bounty of art and antiquities—or just to enjoy the quiet surroundings, woodsy Bavarian furnishings, and all the homey charm.
Barerstrasse 11. www.hotelmarienbad.de. ✆ **089/595585.** 30 units. Doubles 120€–155€, includes breakfast. U-Bahn: Königsplatz. **Amenities:** Free Wi-Fi.

### Inexpensive

**Wombat's City Hostel Munich ★★** Even if you've outgrown sharing a dorm with multiple backpackers, Munich's best hostel can accommodate you in a small but cheerful private room, with a bathroom and (in many) a balcony attached. Wood floors, blonde furnishings, and bright colors give the spartan surroundings a cool, contemporary look, and should the urge to socialize with other travelers strike, there's a ground-floor bar and a glassed-in, plant-filled central atrium. All-you-can-eat continental breakfast is included, and the train station is a short walk away.
Senefelderstrasse 1. www.wombats-hostels.com/munich. ✆ **089/59989180.** 60 units. 20€ dorm bed, 40€ double with bathroom. U-Bahn: Hauptbahnhof. **Amenities:** Bar; laundry room; free Wi-Fi in lobby.

## Where to Eat

Munich is a city that loves to eat—and eat *big*. Homemade dumplings are a specialty, and so are all kinds of sausages (*Weisswurst* in particular) and *Leberkäse,* a large loaf of sausage eaten with freshly baked pretzels and mustard. *Schweinbraten,* a braised loin of pork served with potato dumplings and rich brown gravy, is Bavaria's answer to the north's *sauerbraten* (pot- or oven-roasted marinated beef).

### EXPENSIVE

**Spatenhaus ★★** BAVARIAN/INTERNATIONAL A classy antidote to Munich's boisterous beer halls overlooks the opera house through huge windows and spills out into a patio in warmer months. You won't forgo ambience here, as the beautifully paneled rooms and linen-covered tables set with fine silver are the epitome of Bavarian elegance. Nor will you have to deprive yourself of homey Bavarian cooking, as such specialties as veal sausages with potato salad and grilled calf's liver with roast onions are piled high on the fine china; the *Bayerische Teller* (Bavarian plate) comes loaded with various meats, including pork and sausages. Wash down your meal with the restaurant's own Spaten-Franziskaner-Bier. A more formal restaurant occupies the upper floor, but the ground floor hall delivers the more authentic experience.

Residenzstrasse 12. ✆ **089/290-7060.** Mains 12€–28€. U-Bahn: Marienplatz. Daily 9:30am–12:30am.

## MODERATE

**Alois Dallmayr ★★** GERMAN/CONTINENTAL Germany's most famous gourmet food shop, Munich's version of Paris's Fauchon, has been in business for almost 300 years, through good times and bad—including the World War II years, when the establishment burned to the ground during bombings. The main floor fountain stocked with crayfish tells you that they take freshness seriously here, and even the stacks of sausages are presented like works of art. The house coffee is said to be the best in Europe. You can pick up ready-made sandwiches, but enjoying a meal in the sleek bistro is an affordable treat not to be missed: a very earnest staff proudly presents the house bouillabaisse, perhaps followed by one of the excellent pastas, such as the pappardelle with oxtail ragout. You can also take a seat on the velvet banquettes and simply enjoy *Kaffee und Kuchen* (coffee and cake).

Dienerstrasse 14-15. www.dallmayr.de. ✆ **089/2135100.** Mains 12€–38€. U-Bahn: Marienplatz. Mon–Sat noon–7pm.

**Augustiner Klosterwirt ★** BAVARIAN/GERMAN One of Munich's oldest breweries operates this good-natured beer hall across from the Frauenkirche that manages to be both elegant and genuinely *gemütlich* (comfortable) at the same time. In a series of handsomely paneled rooms on the ground floor and under atmospheric brick vaulting in the cellars, the house beer, Augustiner Brau, flows like water, accompanied by such local specialties as dumpling soup and roast duck with red cabbage.

Augustinerstrasse 1. www.augustiner-klosterwirt.de. ✆ **089/550-54466.** Mains 10€–20€. U-Bahn/S-Bahn: Marienplatz. Daily 11am–midnight.

**Brasserie OskarMaria ★** VEGETARIAN Munich is one of the great publishing capitals of Europe, and this vast, two-story eatery overlooking a pretty square space is attached to the Literature House, a revered institution that sponsors readings and other events. It's named after Munich writer Oskar Maria Graf, who eventually settled in New

York after the Nazis took power. Light as a feather risottos are a perfect accompaniment to bookish discussions, and you can also sample a number of French-inspired fish preparations and some hearty Bavarian meat dishes. This light-filled space is perfect for lingering over morning coffee and pastry.

Salvatorplatz 1. www.oskarmaria.com. ✆ **089/29196029.** Mains 12€–18€. U-Bahn: Josephsplatz. Mon–Sat 10am–midnight.



**Zum Alten Markt ★** BAVARIAN/INTERNATIONAL With the Viktualienmarkt, Munich's big outdoor produce market, just down the lane, it's little wonder the chef makes use of local produce to prepare favorites such as *Tafelspitz* (boiled beef). Fresh vegetables find their way into a delicious cream of carrot soup, and for a few weeks in spring, an entire menu is based on *spargel* (asparagus). You can eat outside in good weather, but that would mean missing the chance to sit back in one of the city's coziest interiors, a richly paneled room with a gorgeous coffered ceiling transported from a 400-year-old Tyrolean castle.

Dreifaltigkeitsplatz 3. www.zumaltenmarkt.de. ✆ **089/299995.** Mains 13€–17€. No credit cards. U-/S-Bahn: Marienplatz. Mon–Sat 11am–midnight.

**Zum Dürnbräu ★** BAVARIAN Munich restaurants don't get any older or more authentic than this one, established in 1487. Regulars settle in with two dozen or so other diners at the central table or in one of the cozy wood alcoves to enjoy generous portions of *Wienerschnitzel*, spaetzle with fried onions, duck with red cabbage, and roast pork marinated in dark beer. The sunny garden is a great spot for lunch on a warm day.

Dürngräugasse 2 (off Tal). www.zumduernbraeu.de. ✆ **089/222-195.** Mains 9€–15€. No credit cards. U-/S-Bahn: Marienplatz. Daily 9am–midnight.

## INEXPENSIVE

**Beim Sedlmayr ★★** GERMAN/BAVARIAN At this local favorite, a bit off the tourist track on a small lane just south of the Victualmarkt, you'll sit at communal tables in a welcoming, stucco-walled room run by an overworked but friendly staff who appears to have been serving the crowd of regulars for decades. A relatively short menu (a sheet with English translations is available) focuses on such Bavarian favorites as roast pork with cracklings and dumplings and grilled *Kalbsbraten*, mushrooms served with dumplings and a creamy herb sauce. It's a good idea to reserve in advance, especially on weekends, because a meal here is one of the city's most authentic dining experiences and popular with Münchners.

Westenriederstrasse 14. www.beim-sedlmayr.com. ✆ **089/226219.** Mains 8€–18€. No credit cards. U-/S-Bahn: Marienplatz. Mon–Fri 10am–11pm; Sat 9am–4pm.

**Hofbräuhaus am Platzl ★★** GERMAN The world's most famous beer hall is Munich's most popular attraction, a revered 200-year-old institution that's filled to the rafters any night of the week with hordes of beer-quaffing regulars and tourists. In the vast and noisy *Schwemme* (tap room) on the ground floor, even the stuff shirts among us can't resist joining in the revelry, joining arms with fellow guests at long communal tables and swaying back and forth as the oom-pah-pah band plays Bavarian golden oldies. The food is good, with favorites like *Weisswürste* and several other sausages, *Schweinbraten* (roasted pork), *Spanferkel* (roast suckling pig), and the big favorite, *Schweineshaxn* (ham hocks). But really, this is not a place to dine—save your appetite for more digestion-conducive places. Instead, order a beer, which is Hofbrau and served by the *mass* (equal to about a liter) and buy one of the giant pretzels dispensed by dirndl'd Frauleins who parade around the room like cigarette girls of yore. Then settle back and enjoy the fun for as long as it takes you to get through that giant glass of beer.

Am Platzl 9. www.hofbraeuhaus.de. ✆ **089/2901360.** Mains 6.50€–18€. No credit cards. U-/S-Bahn: Marienplatz. Daily 9am–midnight.

**Nürnberger Bratwurst Glöckl am Dom** ★ BAVARIAN This cozy, century-old inn across from the Frauenkirche is a local institution, and its wooden chairs at shared tables are filled with an appreciative crowd served by hard-working dirndl-clad Frauleins dispensing specialties from the city of Nürnberg, just to the north. *Nürnberger Schweinwurstl mit Kraut* (pork sausages with cabbage) is the dish to try; hot dogs

## MUNICH beer GARDENS & beer HALLS

It's hard to imagine coming to Munich and not finding yourself in a beer garden at least once or twice, sitting at a communal table with friendly Münchners and swaying to the sound of an oom-pah-pah band or zither player. No one's going to mind if you just drink (expect to pay 5€ to 8€, depending on size, for a glass or mug of the house brew in which each one specializes). After a few beers you'll probably end up ordering some hearty Bavarian grub or at least a homemade *brezeln* (pretzel) or a *radl*, a large white radish that's a beer hall staple.

The **Hofbräuhaus am Platzl** (see "Where to Eat," p. 464) is the Mecca of beer drinkers around the world, but the city has plenty of other convivial and atmospheric places to get a taste of this civic pastime. One of Munich's largest and most pleasant, **Biergarten Chinesischer Turm,** occupies prime real estate in the Englischer Garten at the foot of the Chinese pagoda (Englischer Garten 3; ✆ **089/383-8720;** U-Bahn: Giselastrasse); it's open in warm weather only, daily from May to October from 11am to 1am. The tree shaded garden of **Gaststätte zum Flaucher,** Isarauen 8 (✆ **089/723-2677;** Bus: 52), is also a delightful spot in which to lose an afternoon looking for the answers to life at the bottom of a beer stein as the Isar River flows lazily past; open daily from May to October from 10am to midnight; from November to April, it's open Friday, Saturday, and Sunday from 10am to 9pm.

will never taste the same again after you've tried one of these delectable little treats, grilled over a beechwood fire. Munich Leberkäse, a Bavarian version of meat loaf, is also delicious. The crowd you see loitering around the side door isn't up to trouble—the house dispenses its delicious chilled barrel beers at a discount to those willing to quaff while standing in the little courtyard.



Frauenplatz 9. www.bratwurst-gloeckl.de. ✆ **089/295264.** Mains 6€–14€. No credit cards. U-/S-Bahn: Marienplatz. Daily 10am–1am.



## Shopping

Müncheners are eager consumers, and they demand quality. Accordingly, you'll find a lot of fine goods for sale in Munich, but don't expect bargains—as any Bavarian will tell you, quality does not come cheap. That said, German handmade crafts (such as Christmas ornaments and wood carvings) are a good value here—not that they're inexpensive, but you'll pay less for them here than you will at specialty shops in the United States.

**Marienplatz,** the center of Munich, is the also the city's main shopping district. The square's classy **Ludwig Beck** department store, sometimes called the "Bloomingdale's of Munich," sets the tone for the neighborhood shopping scene with its high-end clothing and designer housewares. An enticing network of shopping streets rays out from Marienplatz and wide, pedestrian-only **Kaufingerstrasse** and **Neuhauserstrasse.** The best streets for elegant boutiques and specialty shops are **Briennerstrasse, Maximilianstrasse, Maffeistrasse,** and **Theatinestrasse.** On these streets, all the top European couturiers and Germany's and Munich's own designers have shops: Jil Sander, Joop, Bogner, Max Dietl, and Rudolph Moshammer. Antiques devotees with deep pockets find what they want on **Ottostrasse.** The biggest concentration of shops selling secondhand goods is on **Westenriederstrasse.**

## Entertainment & Nightlife

As southern Germany's cultural capital, Munich is almost as renowned for its opera and symphony concerts and theater as it is for its beer halls. The **Bavarian State Opera,** one of the world's great opera companies, mounts a full season of grand operas in the beautiful 1830s Nationaltheater on Max-Joseph-Platz, with the world's greatest singers and a superlative orchestra (www.bayerische.staatsoper.de; ✆ **089/21851920;** U-/S-Bahn: Odeonsplatz). The Nationaltheater is also the home of the **Bavarian State Ballet,** and the **Bayerisches Staatsschauspiel,** the Bavarian State Theater, known for its performances of the classics by Goethe, Schiller, Shakespeare, and others. **Münchner Philharmoniker,** one of Europe's great orchestras, performs in Philharmonic Hall in the modern

## MUNICH specialties

Bavarians are known for their craftsmanship. You can experience the local devotion to quality by driving a new BMW out of the automaker's suburban headquarters, but plenty of other finely made and more affordable goods are available as well. A prime showcase for Bavarian artisans is Bayerischer Kunstgewerbe-Verein (The Bavarian Association of Arts and Crafts), Pacellistrasse 6-8 (www.kunsthandwerk-bkv.de; ✆ **089/2901470;** U-Bahn: Karlsplatz), where ceramics, glass, jewelry, woodcarvings, pewter, and Christmas decorations are on sale. For woodcarvings fashioned in workshops throughout the South Tyrol, make the short trip out to Prinoth; it's about 6km (4 miles) west of Munich's tourist zones at Guido Schneblestrasse 9A (www.prinoth.de; ✆ **089/560378;** U-Bahn: Laimerplatz), so prices are a little lower than they are in shops closer to the Marienplatz. This is an especially satisfying stop if you want to expand your cache of Christmas decorations, as shelves are filled with beautifully carved Nativity figurines, angels, and Madonnas. Another holiday shopping venue is Münchner Puppenstuben und Zinnfiguren Kabinette, at Maxburgstrasse 4 (www.minikabi.net; ✆ **089/293797;** U-Bahn: Karlsplatz). Germany's oldest miniature pewter foundry, dating from 1796, creates traditional Christmas decorations and is one of the best sources in Germany for dollhouse furniture and some especially intriguing miniature bird cages, all crafted from pewter or carved wood. Porzellan-Manufaktur-Nymphenburg (www.nymphenburg.com; ✆ **089/1791970**), one of Germany's most famous porcelain factories, is located on the grounds of Schloss Nymphenburg (see p. 458) and there's a branch in the city center at Odeonsplatz 1 (✆ **089/282428;** U-Bahn: Odeonsplatz). We would strongly advise you to resist the urge to buy a dirndl or a pair of lederhosen, especially if the decision is fueled by a few beers at the Hofbräuhaus. But if you must, the place to do it is Dirndl-Eck, "Dirndl Corner," near the famous beer hall at Am Platzl 1 (✆ **089/220163;** U-/S-Bahn: Marienplatz).

Gasteig Cultural Center, Rosenheimerstrasse 5 (www.mphil.de; ✆ **089/480985500;** S-Bahn: Rosenheimerplatz).

Munich also has a small but lively nightclub scene. The most sophisticated night spot in town is the **Bayerischer Hof Night Club,** in the tony Bayerischer Hof hotel (Promenadeplatz 2-6; ✆ **089/21200**), with a piano bar as well as a grand room with a dance band. **Jazzclub Unterfahrt,** the city's leading jazz venue, Einsteinstrasse 42 (www.unterfahrt.de; ✆ **089/4482794;** U-Bahn: Max-Weber-Platz), attracts artists from throughout Europe and North America.

Munich's gay and lesbian scene is centered around the blocks between the Viktualienmarkt and Gärtnerplatz, particularly on Hans-Sachs-Strasse. Bavaria's largest gay bar, **Bau,** Beethovenstrasse 1 (www.bau-munich.de; ✆ **089/269208;** U-Bahn: Sendlinger Tor), covers two floors and draws an international crowd, mostly men. **NY Club,** Sonnenstrasse 25 (www.nyclub.de; ✆ **089/62232152;** U-Bahn: Sendlinger Tor) is currently the most stylish and modern gay dance club in town, with a beautifully designed lounge and a high-tech dance floor.

## Day Trips from Munich

Nothing says Germany like the so-called Romantische Strasse, or Romantic Road, a scenic route that rambles through Bavarian landscape, interspersed with small medieval cities, north and south of Munich. While you'd want to allow yourself at least a week to follow the 350km (220 miles) of specially marked lanes and secondary roads, you can get a taste of Romantic Road on easy day trips to Regensburg, one of Germany's best-preserved medieval cities, and to Neuschwanstein, the fantasy castle that King Ludwig II built in the Alpine foothills in the second half of the 19th century. When making these day trips, you'll save money by buying a Bayern ticket from ticket agents in any train or S-Bahn station; tickets are good for a full day of travel (from 9am to 3am) on trains, the S-Bahn, and regional buses and cost 23€ for one person and 5€ apiece for up to four additional travelers.

### REGENSBURG ★★

Some 1,400 medieval buildings have survived the centuries (Regensburg is the only German city to remain unscathed by World War II bombings) to create a jumble of steep, red-tiled roofs above narrow lanes and lively squares. Strategically poised on the northernmost reaches of the Danube River, Regensburg was a Celtic settlement, then a Roman outpost known as Castra Regina, and the center from which, beginning in the 7th century, Christianity spread throughout Germany and even into central Europe via the river. Regensburg was also a major hub for trade, and by the 12th century the town was pouring its wealth into churches, towers, and some genuinely lovely houses and public buildings. Some of Regensburg's more famous contemporary residents have been Oskar Schindler, Pope Benedict, and the princely Thom und Taxis family.

Regensburg is about 122km (76 miles) northeast of Munich, via the A93 autobahn. More than 20 trains make the 90-minute trip daily from Munich; call ✆ **01805/996633** or visit www.bahn.com for info.

Nearly all places of interest to visitors are in Regensberg's **Altstadt** (Old Town). It's an easy 10-minute stroll from the Hauptbahnhof to the town's medieval core, and the walk takes you through the also-attractive 19th-century commercial district that expanded beyond the now-demolished medieval walls; almost the entire area is closed to car traffic. You can also hop onto one of the bright yellow Altstadt **buses** that line up along Maximilianstrasse, next to the station. One-way fare is 1€, and a day ticket valid for up to five people costs 2€ and must be purchased on the bus. Buses run at 6-minute intervals every Monday to Friday 8:30am to 8:30pm, but there's no service on Saturday and Sunday.

The town's tourism site is **www.tourismus.regensburg.de**.

The Danube River at Regensberg.

## Exploring Regensburg

Start your explorations with a panoramic view of the roofs and spires of the Altstadt (Old Town) from the 12th-century Steinerne Brücke (Stone Bridge), built between 1135 and 1146 and spanning the Danube on 16 arches. A major engineering feat in its day, the bridge opened up land routes between northern Europe and Venice, making Regensburg a major trading center. For a quick trip back to the Middle Ages, stroll down Hinter der Grieb, an ancient alleyway lined with 15th-century houses with high towers.

The town's most majestic edifice, **Dom St. Peter's ★** (www.regensburger-dom.de; ✆ **0941/5865500;** free admission; Mon–Sat 8am–5pm; Sun noon–4pm), has towered over the Domplatz since the 13th century, though its formidable presence is deceiving—constructed with easily eroded limestone and green sandstone, this French Gothic cathedral is continually deteriorating and constantly in need of shoring up. Even the massive spires that tower high above Regensburg's red roofs are 1950s makeovers, fortified with more durable materials. Two little stone gremlins in niches on either side of the main entrance are known as "The Devil" and "The Devil's Grandmother," suggesting that evil in any guise is to be left at the door. Inside, soaring vaulting suggests a protective canopy under which all are welcome, and acres of sumptuous stained glass seems to embrace the faithful in light and color. The most famous panel is of St. Peter holding his telltale key to the kingdom, and is 1 of more than 100 images of the saint in the nave and chapels. The most popular figure, though, is the Archangel Gabriel, a happy-looking fellow affixed to a pillar near the altar with a big grin on his face, suggesting that fire and brimstone aside, divine salvation can be a pretty happy business. The cathedral is home to the world's oldest boys' choir, the 1,000-year-old Chor Domspatzen, which performs every Sunday morning at 10am mass, open to all.





Tucked away near the cathedral is a wealth of ecclesiastical treasures, including gold and textiles in the **Domschatzmuseum ★,** testimony to Regensburg's role as a textile center, and statuary the church has collected since the 11th century in **Diözesanmuseum St. Ulrich ★,** an appropriately early Gothic building to one side of the cathedral. (Domplatz 2; ✆ **0941/51688;** 3€ adults, 1€ for students and children 13 and under.)

The Romans established a garrison town they called Castra Regrina that became their power base on the upper Danube. Though the encampment covered an area of almost 25 hectares (62 acres), not much remains. The ancient **Porta Praetoria,** behind the cathedral, is the most impressive reminder, and through the grille beside the eastern tower you can see the original level of the Roman street, nearly 3m (10 ft.) below—which is why you often have to step down into the churches of Regensburg. Other Roman artifacts are showcased in a former monastery that is now the **Historisches Museum (History Museum) ★** (Dachauplatz 2-4; www.regensburg.de/museumsportal; ✆ **0941/5072448;** 2.20€ adults; 1.10€ students, seniors, and children 8–18; 4.40€ for a family ticket; free for children 7 and under; Tues–Sun 10am–4pm, Thurs to 8pm); artifacts here include a stone tablet noting the establishment of the garrison, an altar to the god Mercury, and several Christian tombstones from the late Roman period.

You can't come to Regensburg without making a stop at the **Historiche Wurstkuchl** (Historic Sausage Kitchen; Thundorferstrasse 3; www.wurstkuchl.de; ✆ **0941/46621**). Opened 900 years ago to feed crews building the adjacent Steinerne Brücke (Stone Bridge), they've been serving the delectable little bratwursts, cooked over beechwood fires in the small kitchen, ever since. These days the place dispenses more than 6,000 sausages a day, serving 6, 8, or 10 to a platter, accompanied by house-made, grainy mustard, sauerkraut or potato salad, and bread and washed down with the house beer. No matter how enamored you are of German cooking and Hofbrauhaus environs, take a quick trip to Paris in the delightful **Restaurant Orphée** (Unterre Bachgasse 8; www.hotel-orphee.de; ✆ **0941/52977**), self-pronounced as the most authentic French bistro east of the Rhine. Wainscoting, watercolors, wicker chairs, and the rest of the 1890s decor make good the claim, as does a big selection of homey bistro classics—from crepes to quiche to cote d'agneau, accompanied by French wines and service that, thankfully, is a lot more Bavarian than Parisian.

## HOHENSCHWANGAU ★ & NEUSCHWANSTEIN ★★★

The two neighboring "Royal Castles" of Hohenschwangau and Neuschwanstein are Germany's most popular attractions, combining fantasy and scenery amid Alpine peaks and valleys. Be prepared for long lines (sometimes up to 3 hr.) in the summer, especially in August. To save yourself time, try to arrive as soon as the castles open in the morning.

The castles are 120km (72 miles) SE of Munich via the A95 and B17. Hourly trains from Munich make the 2-hour trip to Füssen; from there you can catch the number 78 bus right outside the station for the 15-minute trip to the castles.

### Hohenschwangau ★

Ludwig II's father, Crown Prince Maximilian (later Maximilian II) purchased the 12th-century castle of the knights of Schwangau in 1832 and had it completely restored in faux-medieval style. This decorative scheme comes to the fore in the Hall of the Swan Knight, named for the wall paintings depicting the saga of Lohengrin (a Germanic hero associated with the swan; the name of the castle literally translates as High Swan County Palace). Ludwig II spent much of his joyless childhood at Hohenschwangau with his straitlaced father and his mother, Queen Maria of Prussia. As a young man, he received Richard Wagner in the castle's chambers; the music room on the second floor contains copies of letters between Ludwig II and the composer, and the grand piano on which the two played duets.

Although Hohenschwangau has the comfortable air of a home, the heavily Gothic halls and chambers recall knights' castles of the Middle Ages. Maximillian's restorations were part of a 19th-century European craze for re-creating medieval settings—his son would take the concept to new extremes with Neuschwanstein, on an adjoining mountaintop.

Hohenschwangau (www.hohenschwangau.de; © **08362/930830**), is open April to September daily 8am to 5:30pm, and October to March daily 9am to 3:30pm. Admission is 12€ for adults and 8€ for students and children 12 to 15; children 11 and under enter free.

### Neuschwanstein ★★★

Most fanciful of the father-and-son castles is multi-turreted **Neuschwanstein,** perched high on a crag and the ultimate fantasy creation of Ludwig II, the strange, self-obsessed monarch who has become one of the legendary figures in Bavarian history. Neuschwanstein was one of many excesses that eventually threatened to bankrupt the kingdom, and in 1886, at age 41 and before his castle was completed, Ludwig was declared insane. Three days later, he was found drowned in Lake

Neuschwanstein Castle.

Starnberg on the outskirts of Munich, along with the physician who had declared him unfit. It has never been determined if Ludwig was murdered or committed suicide. Enigmatic in life and in death, his dream castle has drawn millions of visitors to this part of Bavaria over the years.

Ludwig II's folly floats in the clouds on a rugged hilltop above little villages and mountain lakes, his romantic homage to the Middle Ages and to the Germanic mythology evoked in the music of Richard Wagner. Just as Ludwig built Neuschwanstein to recreate legend, his ersatz version of a distant past has become the iconic European castle—appropriated most famously by Walt Disney as Cinderella's Castle. It's no accident that one of Ludwig's designers was the Wagnerian set designer Christian Jank, who ensured that almost every room suggested legend and saga. The king's study is decorated with painted scenes from the medieval legend of Tannhäuser. Murals in the king's bedroom portray the doomed lovers Tristan and Isolde (a mood reinforced by scenery—through the balcony window you can see a waterfall in the Pöllat Gorge, with the mountains in the distance). The Sängerhalle (Singer's Hall) takes up almost the entire fourth floor and is modeled after Wartburg castle in Eisenach, the site of song contests in the Middle Ages; frescoes depict the life of Parsifal, a mythical medieval knight. Ludwig's illusions of grandeur come quite forcibly to the fore in the unfinished Throne Rome, designed to resemble a Romanesque basilica, with columns of red porphyry and a mosaic floor and frescoes of Christ looking down on the 12 Apostles and 6 canonized kings of Europe.

Reaching Neuschwanstein involves a steep half-mile climb from the parking lot at Hohenschwangau Castle. You may take a bus to Marienbrücke, a bridge that crosses over the Pöllat Gorge at a height of 90m (300 ft.). If you want to photograph the castle, do it from here instead of at the top of the hill, where you'll be too close for a good shot. It costs 1.80€ for the bus ride up to the bridge or 1€ to return. From Marienbrücke, it's a 10-minute walk to Neuschwanstein castle. This footpath is very steep. The traditional way to reach Neuschwanstein is by horse-drawn carriage; this costs 6€ for the ascent and 3€ for the descent. ***Note:*** Some visitors have complained about the rides being overcrowded and not at all accessible for those with limited mobility. Also note there is no guarantee of arrival time, and if you miss your timed entry, you're out of luck. Our recommendation is to avoid the ride unless you have plenty of time to wait in line and make the ascent before your timed entry into the castle.

The castle is open year-round. The castle can be visited only on one of the guided tours (offered in English), which are given daily year-round, except November 1; December 24, 25, and 31; January 1; and Shrove Tuesday (the day before Ash Wednesday). April to September, tours are given 8am to 5pm, and October to March, times are 9am to 3pm. Tours leave every 45 minutes and last 35 minutes. Admission is 12€ for adults, 8€ for students and seniors over 65, and free for children 14 and under. A combination ticket for both castles is 22€ for adults and 15€ for children 14 and under. For more information, visit www.neuschwanstein.com. ***Note:*** It is imperative to arrive by the time indicated on your ticket; otherwise, you will have to go back to the kiosk at the base and pick up a new ticket and start all over again.

## HEIDELBERG ★★

This ancient university town at the edge of the Black Forest on the Neckar River enjoys a reputation as an enchanted purveyor of wine and romance, song and student life, fun and frivolity. It drew 19th-century German Romantics, who praised and painted it; Mark Twain, who cavorted in its lively streets and made cynical observations in *A Tramp Abroad;* and fans of the 1924 operetta *Student Prince,* set in Heidelberg (and with a rousing chorus, "Drink, drink, drink" that is still an anthem for many young residents and their visitors). A little less poetically, this attractive city of 135,000 inhabits also housed a U.S. army base for many decades after World War II, helping ensure its popularity with Americans. Heidelberg was ravaged by French invaders during the 30 Years War in the 17th century, yet was relatively unscathed in World War II;

## IS THE HEIDELBERG CARD A money saver?

The short answer is: not usually. Yes, the **Heidelberg Card** offers discounts on attractions and free use of public transportation. But since most of what you want to see in Heidelberg is within walking distance and there aren't many attractions you'll be paying to see, the card will probably be a money saver only if you're staying a tram or bus ride away from the Altstadt or will be going back and forth to the Hauptbanhof frequently. Transport-wise, you'd have to make three round trips on the bus or tram within a 2-day period to break even.

If you still would like to purchase it, know that cards valid for any consecutive 2-day period cost 13€ per person; cards valid for any consecutive 4-day period go for 16€ per person. A family card valid for two adults and two children 15 and under for any consecutive 2-day period sells for 28€.

the Altstadt (Old Town) looks much as it did a century or two ago, with a lot of architectural landmarks from the later Middle Ages and early Renaissance still standing. Historically, though, Heidelberg is young at heart; the oldest university in Germany is based here, dating to 1386. Some 28,000 students impart a palpable energy to the narrow lanes and lively inns of the Altstadt. While great monuments and museums are thin on the ground in Heidelberg, this youthful aura and romantically historic ambiance will no doubt make your time here memorable.

## Essentials

The **Heidelberg Tourist Bureau** website, www.heidelberg-marketing.de, can assist with trop-planning.

**ARRIVING** The nearest major airport is Frankfurt, with a direct bus link to Heidelberg. The shuttle bus between Frankfurt and Heidelberg costs 20€ per person. Call ✆ **0621/651620** or visit www.transcontinental-group.com/en/frankfurt-airport-shuttles for shuttle information. Heidelberg's **Hauptbahnhof** is a major railroad station, lying on the Mannheim line, with frequent service to both regional towns and major cities. From Frankfurt, 26 direct trains arrive per day (trip time: 1 hr.); travel time to and from Munich is about 3½ hours. For information, visit www.bahn.de. Motorists should take the A5 Autobahn from the north or south.

**CITY LAYOUT** You'll spend most of your time in Heidelberg on or near the banks of the Neckar River, either in the **Altstadt** (Old Town) that's wedged between the hilltop castle on the south side of the river, or the pleasant hillsides on the north side. The Hauptbahnhof (train station) is in more modern precincts on the western side of town, about 2km (1½ miles) outside the Altstadt. You can get from there into the Altstadt via

Hauptstrasse, a long, pleasant pedestrian street that's the commercial heart of Heidelberg.

**GETTING AROUND** Heidelberg is crisscrossed with a network of trams and buses, many of which intersect at the **Bismarckplatz** in the town center. Probably the only time you'll ever feel the need to hop on one, though, is going to and from the train station. Bus nos. 31 and 32 travel between a plaza in front of the station and the **Universitätsplatz,** in the Altstadt. The Altstadt's lanes run off either side of the **Hauptstrasse,** the long, pedestrian-only thoroughfare that stretches from the Marktplatz all the way to Bismarckplatz in the new town. Bus or tram fares cost 2.20€ for a single ride; you can buy tickets from machines at many stops or pay the driver.

## Exploring Heidelberg

Most of what you'll want to see in Hedielberg is clustered near the **Marktplatz (Marketplace)** at the center of the Altstadt. On market days (Wed and Sat mornings), stalls over-spilling with fresh flowers, fish, and vegetables surround the Rathaus and the **Heiliggeistkirche (Church of the Holy Spirit),** a stark, late-Gothic structure from around 1400. Gone from the nave is the dividing wall that was a sign of

Heidelberg Castle, above the Altstadt.

Heidelberg's conciliatory approach the Reformation: For more than a century both Protestants and Catholics used separate ends of the church. No such compromise tactics spared the Heiliggeistkirche and most of the rest of Heidelburg from the rampaging French troops of King Louis XV, who in 1690 pillaged the interior, along with the graves of the city's prince-electors.



**Heidelberg Castle ★★★** HISTORIC SITE Perched enticingly above the Altstadt, set amid woodlands and terraced gardens, Heidelberg's half-ruined castle has impressed everyone from kings and princes to the poet Goethe, novelists Victor Hugo and Mark Twain, and millions of visitors for whom the red sandstone walls clinging to the green hillside are the epitome of German romanticism. Even in ruin, one of the great Renaissance landmarks of northern Europe suggests beauty, grandeur, and long vanquished empires—in this case a division of the Holy Roman Empire known as the County Palatine of the Rhine, whose prince electors lived here from the 13th century.

Visitors enter through Elizabeth's Gate, named for the teenaged daughter of English King James I who married prince elector Frederick V and came to Heidelberg in 1605. The soulless salons of the heavily restored Friedrichsbau, the early-17th-century palace where the young couple took up residence, are less evocative than the shells of most of the rest of the compound's royal enclaves, laid waste to in 1690 by the French troops of Louis XV and finished off by a disastrous lightning strike. Enough gables and arches remain to suggest the grandeur of the place, and a multi-language audioguide does a good job of filling in the missing pieces.

An especially noteworthy relic is the Great Cask, aka the Heidelberg Turn, a symbol of the exuberant life the prince electors enjoyed. The vulgar vessel was built in 1751 to store more than 208,000 liters (55,000 gal.) of wine but failed to impress Mark Twain, who wrote, "An empty cask the size of a cathedral could excite but little emotion in me." The Chemist's Tower houses the Apothekenmuseum (Pharmaceutical Museum) and the old chambers quite engagingly spotlight the importance of German pharmaceutical research (much of it conducted at Heidelberg University) with utensils, laboratory equipment, and a re-created chemist's shop from the 18th and 19th centuries. The castle's perennial crowd pleasers are the views that stretch across the old town and down the Neckar Valley. You can enjoy them 24 hours day, since the castle courtyard is always open.

You can reach the castle by several routes. The Bergbahn (mountain train) whisks you up from the Kornmarkt. A paved road winds up the Neue Schlossstrasse past old houses perched on the hillside, while the steeper Burgweg walk climbs uphill from Kornmarkt.

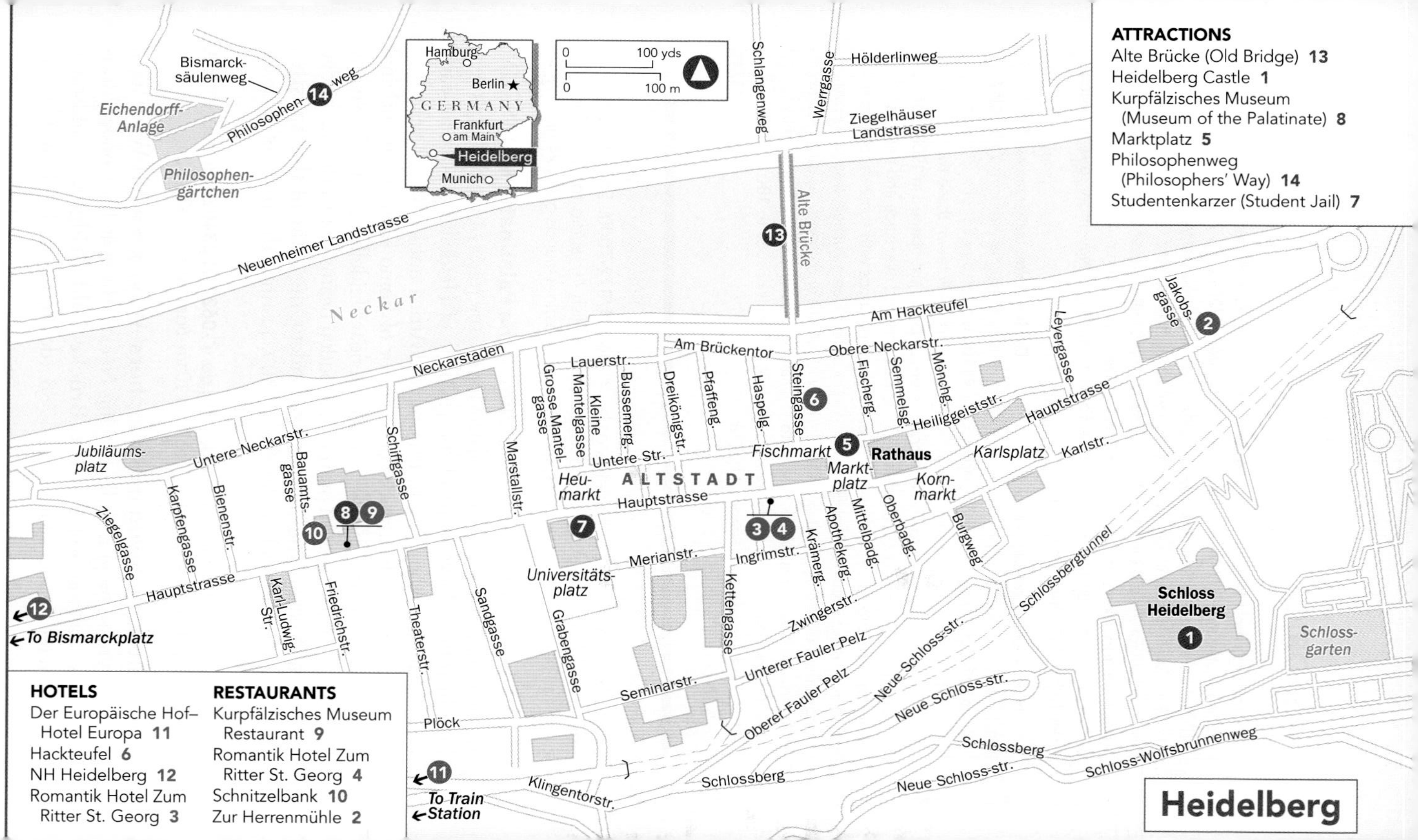
Heidelberg
ATTRACTIONS
Alte Brücke (Old Bridge) 13
Heidelberg Castle 1
Kurpfälzisches Museum (Museum of the Palatinate) 8
Marktplatz 5
Philosophenweg (Philosophers' Way) 14
Studentenkarzer (Student Jail) 7
HOTELS
Der Europäische Hof–Hotel Europa 11
Hackteufel 6
NH Heidelberg 12
Romantik Hotel Zum Ritter St. Georg 3
RESTAURANTS
Kurpfälzisches Museum Restaurant 9
Romantik Hotel Zum Ritter St. Georg 4
Schnitzelbank 10
Zur Herrenmühle 2
Schloss Heidelberg
Schlossgarten
Rathaus
ALTSTADT
Alte Brücke
Neckar
Karlsplatz
Kornmarkt
Marktplatz
Fischmarkt
Heumarkt
Universitätsplatz
Jubiläumsplatz
Philosophengärtchen
Eichendorff-Anlage
Bismarcksäulenweg
Philosophenweg
Hauptstrasse
Neuenheimer Landstrasse
Ziegelhäuser Landstrasse
Schlossbergtunnel
To Train Station
To Bismarckplatz
100 yds
100 m
GERMANY
Hamburg
Berlin
Frankfurt am Main
Heidelberg
Munich

## HISTORIC student drinking clubs

Heidelberg's most famous and revered student tavern, **Zum Roten Ochsen** (Red Ox Inn), Hauptstrasse 217 (www.roterochsen.de; ✆ **06221/20977;** bus: 33), opened in 1703. For six generations, the Spengel family has welcomed everybody from Bismarck to Mark Twain. It seems that every student who has attended the university has left his or her mark (or initials) on the walls, and every tourist in town eventually finds his or her way here, too. Meals go from 9€ to 17€. The tavern is open from April to October Monday to Saturday 11:30am to 2pm and 5pm to midnight, November to March Monday to Saturday 5pm to midnight.

Next door is **Zum Sepp'l,** Hauptstrasse 213 (www.zum-seppl.de; ✆ **06221/23085;** bus: 11 or 33), open since 1634, the second most famous drinking club in Heidelberg and another perennial crowd pleaser. It's filled with photographs and carved initials of former students, along with memorabilia that ranges from old Berlin street signs to Alabama license plates. Meals cost 8€ to 18€. It's open Monday to Friday noon to 11pm, and Saturday and Sunday 11:30am to 3:30pm and 5pm to midnight.

**Dorfschänke,** Lutherstrasse 14 (www.dorfschaenke-hd.com; ✆ **06221/419041;** tram: 5 or 23, bus: 31), doesn't have the pedigree of these two old taverns, having just opened in 1908. But it's been packed ever since and pairs its beer selections with some serious food, including Flammkuchen, a square pizza with onions and cheese—a bit like tarte flambée. It's open daily, 5pm to midnight. Meals cost 8€ to 18€.

Schlossberg. www.schloss-heidelberg.de. ✆ **06221/872-7000.** 5€ (includes tram ride to and from castle). 1-hr. guided tours in English 4€; audio tours 4€. Ticket is good for 24 hrs. Castle open daily 8am–5:30pm; castle grounds open 24 hr.

**Kurpfälzisches Museum (Museum of the Palatinate)** ★ MUSEUM In the salons of the baroque Palais Morass, the relics of Heidelberg's very long history include a cast of the jawbone of Heidelberg Man, an early type of human who lived in Europe and Africa until 250,000 years ago and is thought to be the direct ancestor of homo sapiens; the original (stored at the university) was unearthed near Heidelberg in 1907. Nearby are some remarkably well preserved wooden beams from a Roman bridge across the Neckar. The collection's standout, the **Altar of the Apostles** by Tilman Riemenschneider from 1509, justifies the price of a ticket alone.

Hauptstrasse 97. www.museum-heidelberg.de. ✆ **06221/5834020.** 3€ adults, 1.80€ students/children 17 and under. Tues–Sun 10am–6pm. Bus: 31, 32, or 35.

**The Philosophenweg (Philosophers' Way)** ★★★ VIEWS You'll want to cross the gracefully flowing Neckar River at least once during your stay, walking over the **Alte Brücke (Old Bridge),** a handsome, twin-towered stone span from 1788 (destroyed in 1944 by German troops trying to halt the advance of the Allied army and rebuilt 2 years later). After a stop in front of the raffish **Brückenaffe (Bridge Ape)**—touch the mirror he's holding for wealth, his outstretched fingers to ensure a return to Heidelberg, and the mice that surround him to ensure progeny—continue up the **Schlangenweg (Snake Path)** to the **Philosophenweg (Philosophers' Way).** This winding, 2km (1¼-mile) walking trail above the north bank of the Neckar provides memorable views of the castle, the river, and the Altstadt. The amble ends at the the **Philosophengärtchen (Philosophers' Garden),** where the river valley's mild climate nurtures Japanese cherries, cypresses, lemons, bamboos, rhododendrons, gingkoes, yucca trees, and other warm-weather plants.



**Studentenkarzer (Student Jail)** ★ HISTORIC SITE It's ironic that one of the few parts of the august university—founded in 1386—open to the public are these rough cells where unruly and drunken students were once incarcerated. (If laughter and screaming disrupt your sleep in an Altstadt hotel, you may wish the practice were still in force.) Prisoners bedecked the walls and even the ceilings with graffiti and drawings, including portraits and silhouettes, until the last ones left in 1914. Even the curmudgeonly Mark Twain commented that "idle students are not the rule" in Heidelberg. Germany's oldest university, officially known as the Ruprecht-Karls-Universität Heidelberg and centered around the Universitätsplatz, has produced 55 Nobel Prize winners.

Augustinergasse 2. www.heidelberg-marketing.com. ✆ **06221/543593.** 3€ adults, 2.50€ students/children 14 and under. Includes entry to the University Museum and Old Auditorium. Bus: 31, 32, or 35. Apr–Sept Tues–Sun 10am–6pm; Oct Tues–Sun 10am–4pm; Nov–Mar Tues–Sat 10am–4pm.

## Where to Stay

You'll definitely want to stay in our near the Altstadt. But to make sure you can, book in advance, since Heidelberg is popular with travelers, especially Americans—partly because so many were based at nearby U.S. airbases that have largely shut down in recent years. Rates vary throughout the year, but you can count on them being higher in summer and around Christmas.

### EXPENSIVE

**Der Europäische Hof-Hotel Europa** ★★★ Heidelberg's best, and one of the finest in Germany, seems to do everything right and makes it all seem effortless. Lounges are plush and attractive; guest rooms, ranging over an old wing and a newer extension, are enormous and beautifully furnished with a mix of old-fashioned comfort and contemporary accents, lit by crystal chandeliers and equipped with sumptuous marble baths. Service is unfailingly attentive while still unobtrusive and personable. A rooftop spa includes a large indoor pool and state of the art gym, and the wood-paneled grill room serves sophisticated French fare. You'll pay a bit more to stay here than in other Heidelberg hotels, but you'll be staying in style you're not going to find many other places in the world.

Friedrich-Ebert-Anlage 1. www.europaeischerhof.com. ✆ **06221/5150.** 118 units. Doubles 148€–384€, includes breakfast. Tram: Bismarckplatz. **Amenities:** 2 restaurants; bar; babysitting; concierge; gym and spa; indoor heated pool; room service; Wi-Fi (fee).



## MODERATE

**Hackteufel ★★** A guesthouse right in the heart of the Altstadt, between the Marketplace and Old Bridge, offers some of the most spruced up and comfortable lodgings in town. Each of the 12 rooms is different, but most are extra-large and embellished with wood floors, beams, dormers, and plenty of nice traditional wood furnishings; number 12 is a cross-beamed garret with a castle view, and number 8 is a commodious suite with a terrace. Downstairs is a handsome restaurant and wine bar that serves snacks and drinks throughout the day and traditional specialties at mealtimes, accompanied by lots of cozy ambiance.

Steingasse 7. www.hackteufel.de. ✆ **06221/905380.** 12 units. Doubles 120€–170€, includes buffet breakfast. **Amenities:** Restaurant, bar; free Wi-Fi.

**Romantik Hotel Zum Ritter St. Georg ★** The glorious German Renaissance facade right on the Marktplatz is a Heidelberg landmark, and the old inn behind the welcoming doors is a Heidelberg institution. The large, high-ceilinged rooms and suites in the front do justice to the surroundings, and the others off the rambling back corridors are smaller and perfectly comfortable, done in an unremarkable but pleasing contemporary style. A stay here puts you right in the heart of the Altstadt, and just a flight of stairs away from the Ritter's wonderful in-house restaurant (see p. 484).

Hauptstrasse 178. www.ritter-heidelberg.de. ✆ **06221/1350.** 37 units. Doubles 118€-176€. Bus: 31, 32, or 35. **Amenities:** 3 restaurants; room service; free Wi-Fi.

## INEXPENSIVE

**NH Heidelberg ★** A courtyard that was once filled to the brim with kegs of beer is now the glass-filled atrium of these smart lodgings at the far edge of the Altstadt. Bright, commodious, business-style rooms range through a restored former brewery and modern wing, all nicely done in traditional-meets-modern decor. The Bräustüberl, serving Bavarian specialties, is the most popular of the three in-house restaurants, among many perks that also include a spa and health club. Weekend and summer specials here can make these spiffy rooms some of the best lodging bargains in Heidelberg.

> **WHERE beer drinking IS A RELIGION**
>
> In the Middle Ages, monks were the world's great brewmeisters, making the "liquid [that] does not break the fast"—that is, you could drink all the beer you wanted to. It's pretty well established that beer-drinking is a religion in Heidelberg, so it's only natural that the tradition continues at the brewery **Brauerei zum Klosterhof,** part of Heidelberg's 12th-century Neuburg Abbey, on the banks of the Neckar River about 2km (1 mile) east of the Altstadt. To this day, 15 monks live in the monastery and oversee the production of organic beer, including the popular HeidALEberg Red Summer Ale. You can see the brewery, taste the beer, enjoy some grilled sausages and dumplings, and tour the abbey on tours arranged by **Heidelberg Tourism** (www.heidelberg-marketing.de; ✆ **06221/5840200**); Tours cost from 20€ to 24€, depending on how much you eat.

Bergheimer Strasse 91. www.nh-hotels.com. ✆ **06221/13270.** 174 units. Doubles 82€–175€. Tram: 22. Bus: 35. **Amenities:** 3 restaurants; bar; gym; spa; room service; Wi-Fi (fee).

## Where to Eat

Think homey German fare: *rinderrouladen* (roasted beef rolls stuffed with onions and bacon), served with *knödel* (dumplings) or spätzle and red cabbage, or *kurpfälzer,* liver dumplings and sausages served with potatoes and sauerkraut. If you've come here to lose weight, forget about it—and just wait until the gingerbread and Black Forest cake comes out for dessert.

### EXPENSIVE

**Zur Herrenmühle** ★ GERMAN/INTERNATIONAL A 17th-century grain mill with thick walls, antique paneling, and heavy beams doesn't skimp on atmosphere, and the cuisine does justice to the surroundings. Fresh fish, grass-fed lamb, and homemade pastas appear in classic preparations served with more flair than is the norm in Heidelberg restaurants, and the vine-covered courtyard is the city's most atmospheric setting for summertime meals.

Hauptstrasse 237. www.herrenmuehle-heidelberg.de. ✆ **06221/602909.** Mains 18€–26€; fixed-price menu 29€. Bus: 33. Mon–Sat 6–11pm. Closed last 2 weeks of Mar.

### MODERATE

**Kurpfälzisches Museum Restaurant** ★ GERMAN The baroque Palais Morass not only houses museum exhibits but is also the setting for a pleasant meal, served in a baronial dining hall, some smaller rooms, and a garden next to a splashing fountain in good weather. The cuisine is a bit more pedestrian than the surroundings, with pizzas sharing space on the menu with schnitzels and other traditional fare.

Hauptstrasse 97. www.restaurantkurpfaelzischesmuseumheidelberg.com. ✆ **06221/24050.** Mains 16€–19€. Bus: 31 or 32. June–Sept Sun–Thurs 11am–11pm, Fri–Sat to midnight; off season Sun–Thurs 11am–3pm and 5:30–10pm, Fri–Sat to 11pm.





**Romantik Hotel Zum Ritter St. Georg ★★★** GERMAN/INTERNATIONAL An atmospheric and very grown-up dining room occupies the ground floor of the city's most decorative Renaissance-era landmark, where high-ceilings, paneling, frescoes, and Persian carpets provide lovely old-world surroundings for a menu to match. Rumpsteak with cream sauce, roasted venison, calf's livers with apples and onions, and *Kurpfälzer* are among the many local specialties that seasoned waiters serve on starched linens. One of the advantages of staying in one of the comfortable rooms upstairs (see listing p. 482) is lingering late over a meal in this memorable dining room without worrying about moving on.

Hauptstrasse 178. www.ritter-heidelberg.de. ✆ **06221/1350.** Mains 10€–23€. Bus: 31, 32, or 35. Daily noon–2pm and 6–10pm.

### INEXPENSIVE

**Schnitzelbank ★** GERMAN The well-worn tables here are workbenches from the days when the premises were a barrel factory. These days the business is wine, with an emphasis on local varieties and sold by the glass. You can also dine well on the namesake schnitzels, of course, along with lots of other tavern mainstays.

Bauamtsgasse 7. www.schnitzelbank-heidelberg.de. ✆ **06221/21189.** Mains 8€–12€. Daily noon–11pm.

## [FastFACTS] GERMANY

**Business Hours** Most banks are open Monday through Friday 9am to 3pm. Most other businesses and stores are open Monday through Friday 9 or 10am to 6 or 6:30pm and Saturday 9am to 4pm. Some stores are open late on Thursday (usually 8:30pm). But . . . Germans do *not* shop on Sundays. If you need to buy toiletries or food items, head to a train station, where some shops will be open.

**Currency** Germany is a member of the European Union and uses the E.U. common currency, the euro (€). See p. 860 for information on money and costs.

**Dentists** If you need a dentist, ask your hotel concierge or contact your embassy.

**Doctors & Hospitals** You'll find a list of hospitals in Germany, with contact info and descriptions of services offered, at germany.hospitalsdata.com.

**Embassies & Consulates:**
**Australia:** Wallstrasse 76-79, Berlin; www.germany.embassy.gov.au; ✆ **030/8800880.**

**Canada:** Leipziger Platz 17, Berlin; www.germany.gc.ca; ✆ **030/20312470.**

**New Zealand:** Atrium, Friedrichstrasse 60, Berlin; www.nzembassy.com/germany; ✆ **030/206210.**

**United Kingdom:** Wilhelmstrasse 70/71, Berlin; www.gov.uk/government/world/germany; ✆ **030/204570.**

**United States:** Pariser Platz 2, Berlin; berlin.usembassy.gov; ✆ **030/83050.**

### Emergencies

To call the police, dial ✆ **110.** To summon an ambulance, dial ✆ **112.**

### Pharmacy

Pharmacies *(Apotheken)* operate during normal business hours and post details of the nearest 24-hour pharmacy on their front door. In most German cities, at least one per district stays open all night.

### Post Offices

Most post offices are open Monday through Friday 8am to 6pm and Saturday 8am to 1pm.

# AUSTRIA

by John Newcomb

8

A considerable part of my Army service was spent in a mountain village of Bavaria, just a half-hour by car from the Austrian border. And though I spent the weekdays teaching covert intelligence at a secretive military school, I devoted many weekends to forays into the picturesque and nearby Austrian city of Innsbruck, which resembled—to an uncanny extent—the *Sound of Music* town of Salzburg. I was constantly surrounded by mountains, and it was thrilling to be there.

In fact, nearly three-quarters of the terrain of Austria consists of mountains—it lies squarely in the Alps. As you travel through it, you are only occasionally in flat lands less than 500 meters high. And although those infrequent "plateaus" are occasionally devoted to industries and commerce, the general picture you receive is that of a tourist's paradise. Your memories are of villages occupied by country folk wearing dirndls if they are women and lederhosen (short pants) if they are men, all of them living in the most picturesque, decorated, and colorfully painted alpine-style buildings clustered around the high and narrow pointed spire of a church. Tourism is immensely important in Austria, second only to more general forms of commerce. A huge number of Europeans come here for skiing in the winter and mountain hiking in the warmer months.

The other great tourist draw is culture, especially music. Austria—and especially its capital, Vienna—was the home or second home of Mozart, Schubert, Franz Liszt, Johann Strauss Sr. and Jr., Haydn, Bruckner, and more; and the concerts available to you are world-famous and alone a potent reason for visiting what is universally deemed to be the capital of music.

***Vienna!*** It was the centerpiece of one of the world's most powerful empires named "Austro-Hungarian," and in past times it played a major role in the politics of Europe. It was here, following Napoléon's defeat at Waterloo, that the victorious countries held the Congress of Vienna. Immediately afterward, Austria emerged as one of the superpowers of Europe.

That powerful position later disintegrated, and seldom do we any longer hear of Vienna or Austria as having any especial importance. But a stay in Vienna is like entering a time machine into the

FACING PAGE: **The Salzburg skyline with Hohensalzburg fortress.**

past. The word "stately" could have been coined for that graceful and large city on the Danube. The grand and imposing 19th-century buildings that line the "Ringstrasse" (a wide, major, circular boulevard encasing the central, historic part of the town) were once the commercial and political headquarters of a world giant. And none of them has been altered through removal of a single brick. When you stroll the streets of Vienna, and occasionally stop for a "Sachertorte" (a scrumptious Viennese pastry) with tea, you are in a bygone world of the late 1800s.



And when you gaze over the nearly mile-long grounds that lead to Schőnbrunn Palace, you are looking at a royal residence that rivals Paris's Palace of Versailles in size and splendor. When you go to Vienna's Kunsthistorisches Museum, you are in an institution almost as grand as Paris's Louvre. You attend world-famous operas and operettas, and classic and progressive theater productions in some of Europe's most heralded performing arts venues.

And none of us should forget that this was the home of Sigmund Freud, and therefore the birthplace of psychoanalysis. You can visit his residence, from which he was forced to flee to England after Nazi threats in 1938.

Another touristic highlight of Austria is, of course, the picturesque *Sound of Music* town of **Salzburg,** with its almost-perfectly preserved historic central area of baroque (late 16th century, early 17th century) buildings heavily influenced by church leaders of the time. Add an awesome castle overlooking the city, add the birthplace and early residence of Mozart, and you have some of the reasons why multitudes of tourists head here, especially during almost-continuous music festivals in summer. They—the tourists—seem, as our authors will point out, in a state of near-enchantment by this immersion into ancient times.

So once again, you go to Austria and Vienna and Salzburg to experience either nature at its grandest, world leadership at its 19th-century peak, or the performing arts at their epitome. It all makes for an absorbing, pleasant travel experience. Enjoy it!

***– Arthur Frommer***

## VIENNA

A whirl of gilded Hapsburg palaces and regal parks on the banks of the blue Danube, Vienna is a fine romance of a city. Tradition and innovation walk hand in hand: Strauss waltzes are still hip to 20-something ball-goers, and even the imperial stables were born again in the surprising and vibrant Museum Quarter. The Viennese love *gemütlichkeit* (relaxation), so this city is to be savored not rushed, whether you're indulging in a dark chocolate Sachertorte in a chandelier-lit coffee house or rising gently above the twinkling Prater in the Riesenrad Ferris wheel.

A bit of history: From its place as the Roman Celtic settlement on the Danube River (their most important central European fort), "Vindobona," the city we now know as Vienna, has always been the meeting place of the nations and cultures. Today, the many-peopled city of the Habsburgs is again at the center of a borderless Europe, as its imperial palaces and art museums mingle with modern installations and the challenge of cultural encounter. The result is a creative explosion on the stages and in the streets, in clubs and cabarets, in the open markets and on the menus. Having lived through war, siege, victory, defeat, the death of an empire and the birth of a republic, foreign occupation, independence, and the new internationalism of the European Union, fortunately, the Viennese character—a devotion to the good life—has endured.



## Essentials

**Wien.at** (www.wien.gv.at) is the Vienna Tourist Board's official information portal, but we find **Welcome to Vienna!** (www.wien.info) to be a more user-friendly site for trip-planning.

**ARRIVING** **Flights** arrive at **Vienna International Airport** (**VIE;** www.viennaairport.com), about 20 km (12 miles) southeast of the city center. Many flights from North America require a transfer in another major European city.

There's a regular, high-speed City Airport Train (CAT) service between the airport and the **City Air Terminal,** adjacent to the Vienna Hilton and directly across from the **Wien Mitte/Landstrasse** rail station, where you can easily connect with subway and tram lines. Trains run every 30 minutes from 6:05am to 11:35pm. The trip takes 16 minutes and costs €19. There's also a bus service between the airport and several central city destinations leaving every 30 minutes to an hour. Fares are €12. Tickets are sold on the bus.

Cheapest, at just €4.40, is local train service, the Schnellbahn (S-Bahn), between the airport and the Wien Nord and Wien Mitte rail stations. Trains run every half hour from 5am to 11:40pm and leave from the airport basement. Trip time is 25 to 30 minutes.

Your **train** to Vienna will likely arrive at one of two stations. **Westbahnhof (West Railway Station),** on Europaplatz, with its 19th-century bones and modern facelift, sees mostly trains from Western Europe and has connections to local trains, the U3 and U6 underground lines, and several tram and bus routes.

Most trains from the east and south head to the newly opened **Hauptbahnhof (Main Railway Station),** at Südtirolerplatz. It houses a large shopping center and links to the U1 underground line as well as local rail, tram, and bus routes.

Because of the excellent rail service funneling from all parts of the Continent into Vienna, **bus transit** is limited and not especially popular. **Eurolines,** part of National Express Coach Lines (✆ **0871/781-8181**) is a 21-hour option from London costing €71 one way. The **City Bus Terminal** is at Wien Mitte rail station, Landstrasser Hauptstrasse 1.

By **car,** Vienna can be reached from all directions via *Autobahnen* (major highways) or secondary highways. The main artery from the west is Autobahn A1, coming in from Munich (468km/291 miles), Salzburg (336km/209 miles), and Linz (186km/116 miles). Autobahn A2 arrives from the south, from Graz (200km/124 miles) and Klagenfurt (308km/191 miles). Autobahn A4 comes in from the east, connecting with Route E58, which runs to Bratislava and Prague.



**CITY LAYOUT** Vienna's population numbers about 1.8 million, of whom 32% are foreign born. It's one of the largest capitals of central Europe, with a surface area covering 414 sq. km (160 sq. miles), reputed to have a greater percentage of green space within the city limits than any other city in Europe. That city is divided into 23 *Bezirke* (districts), each with its own character and reputation; for example, the 9th District is known as Vienna's academic quarter, whereas the 10th, 11th, and 12th Districts are home to blue-collar workers and are the most densely populated.

The 1st District, known as the **Innere Stadt (Inner City),** is where most foreign visitors first flock. This compact area is Vienna at its most historic. With St. Stephan's at its core, it boasts the city's astounding array of monuments, churches, palaces, parks, and museums, in addition to its finest hotels and restaurants. Its size and shape roughly correspond to the original borders (then walls) of the medieval city.

The Inner City is surrounded by the **Ring** or **Ringstrasse,** a circular boulevard about 4km (2½ miles) long. Constructed between 1859 and 1888, it's one of the most ambitious examples of urban planning and restoration in European history. Built over the foundations of Vienna's medieval fortifications, the Ring opened new urban vistas for the dozens of monumental 19th-century buildings that line its edges today. The name of this boulevard changes as it moves around the Inner City, which can get confusing. Names that correspond with the boulevard end in *ring:* Schottenring, Universitätsring, Burgring, Opernring, Kärntner Ring, Stubenring, Parkring, and Schubertring.

Ironically, the river for which Vienna is so famous, the **Danube,** doesn't pass through the center of the city at all. Between 1868 and 1877, the river was channeled into its present muddy banks east of town, and was replaced with a small-scale substitute, the **Donaukanal (Danube Canal),** which was dug for shipping food and other supplies to the Viennese and is now lined with cafes, clubs, and restaurants. The canal is set against Ringstrasse's eastern edge.

Surrounding the Ring and the Inner City, in a more or less clockwise direction, are the inner suburban districts (2–9), which contain many hotels and restaurants popular for their proximity to the city center. The 5th District is an exception, as it squeezes in between the 4th and 6th, not touching the Inner City. The villas and palaces of Vienna's 18th-century aristocrats can be found in the first 9 districts. These districts are profiled below under "The Neighborhoods in Brief."

The outer districts (10–23) form another concentric ring of suburbs, comprising a variety of neighborhoods from industrial parks to rural villages. **Schönbrunn,** the Habsburg's vast summer palace, is located in these outlying areas in the 13th District, **Hietzing.** Also noteworthy is the 19th District, **Döbling,** with its grand villas and famous *Heurigen* villages, such as Grinzing and Sievering (see "Into the Woods" box, p. 524), and the 22nd District, **Donau-stadt,** home to the verdant Donauinsel (Danube Island) and the adjoining UNO-City, an impressive modern complex of United Nations' agencies.

Most of the top attractions in the Inner City can be seen by foot, tram, or bus, but the **U-Bahn** is your best bet to get across town quickly or reach the suburbs. It consists of five lines labeled U1, U2, U3, U4, and U6 (there is no U5). Stephansplatz, in the heart of the Inner City, and Karlsplatz are the most important underground stations for visitors, as the U1, U2, U3, and U4 stop at either of them. The U-Bahn runs daily 6am to midnight and all night on Fridays and Saturdays.

Riding the **trams** (*Strassenbahn*) is not only a practical way to get around, but it's also a great way to see the city. Lines 1 and 2 will bring you to all the major sights on the Ringstrasse, but not all the way around. There is also a yellow Ring Tram that circles the Ring and costs €6 for adults and €4 for children.

Vienna maintains a uniform fare that applies to all forms of public transport. A ticket for the bus, subway, or tram costs €2.20 if you buy it in advance at one of the automated machines in U-Bahn stations, or at a *Tabac-Trafik* (a store or kiosk selling tobacco products and newspapers) or €2.30 if you buy it onboard. Smart Viennese buy their tickets in advance, usually in blocks of at least five at a time, from any of the city's thousands of *Tabac-Trafiken* or at any vending machine. Tourists can take save with 24-, 48- or 72-hour travel cards. Even better, the flexible **Vienna Card** (www.wien.info/en/travel-info/vienna-card) allows unlimited travel on all Inner City public transport, plus various discounts at city museums, restaurants, and shops. It's available in 2- or 3-day options (€19 or €22); one child 15 or younger can ride free with a cardholder.

**Taxis** are easy to find within the city center, but be warned that fares can quickly add up. Taxi stands are marked by signs, or you can call **© 01/31300** (additional €2 for ordering by phone). The basic fare is €3.80, plus €1.20 per kilometer. There are extra charges of €1 for luggage in the trunk. For night rides after 11pm, and for trips on Sunday and holidays, there is a surcharge of €2.50. The fare for trips outside the city should be agreed upon in advance; a 10% tip is the norm.

When in Austria, use a **car** only for excursions outside Vienna's city limits; don't try to drive around the city. Parking is a problem; the city is a maze of one-way streets; and the public transportation is terrific. That being said, **underground parking garages** are scattered throughout the city; most of them charge between €3.50 and €6 per hour.

A *Fiaker* **(horse-drawn carriage)** has been used as a form of transportation in the Inner City for some 3 centuries. You can clip-clop along in one for about 20 minutes at a cost of about €55. Prices and the length of the ride must be negotiated in advance. In the 1st District, you'll find *Fiaker* at the following sites: On the north side of St. Stephan's, on Heldenplatz near the Hofburg, and in front of the Albertina.

Vienna has more than 1,000km (620 miles) of marked **bicycle** paths. For nearly free rides, use a **Citybike** (www.citybikewien.at). The kiosks are across city and the bikes can be rented with a credit card for a €1 deposit. After registering, the ride is free for the first hour, so if you return it to a kiosk in that time, you don't pay again. The second hour costs €1, the third €2, and every further hour €4.

**GETTING AROUND** Whether you want to visit the Inner City's historic buildings or the outlying Vienna Woods, ***Wiener Linien*** (**Vienna Public Transport;** www.wienerlinien.at) can take you there. This vast transit network—U-Bahn (subway), Strassenbahn (streetcar/tram), or bus—is safe, clean, and easy to use.

## The Neighborhoods in Brief

Many of Vienna's hotels and restaurants are conveniently located within or just outside the 1st District. In this section, we profile the Inner City, or Innere Stadt, and some adjacent districts.

**INNERE STADT (1ST DISTRICT)** This compact area is the oldest part of Vienna, bounded on all sides by the legendary Ring, the street tracing the former city walls. The Innere Stadt remains at the center of Viennese life, with dozens of streets devoted exclusively to pedestrian traffic, including **Kärntnerstrasse,** which leads from the Vienna State Opera House, to the **Graben,** which it meets at Stephansplatz, home to the famous cathedral. Competing with both the cathedral and the Opera House as the district's most famous building is the **Hofburg,** the Habsburg palace that's now a showcase of attractions, including the National Library, the Spanish Riding School, and six museums. Other significant landmarks include the Rathaus (City Hall), Parlament (Parliament), the Universität Wien (University of Vienna), the Naturhistorisches (Natural History) and Kunsthistorisches (Art History) museums, and Stadtpark.

**LEOPOLDSTADT (2ND DISTRICT)** Once inhabited by Balkan traders and later by Vienna's Jewish community, this area doesn't physically border the Ringstrasse, but lies on the eastern side of the Danube Canal, across from Schwedenplatz or Schottenring. The district boasts lots of green, including the massive **Prater Park,** with an amusement park, miles of tree-lined walking paths, and numerous sports facilities.

**LANDSTRASSE (3RD DISTRICT)** The stately **Stadtpark** spreads into this district, where you'll see more streets dotted with churches, monuments, and palaces. One is the grand **Schwarzenberg Palace** and the looming **Konzerthaus** (concert house). The top attraction remains **Belvedere Palace,** an exquisite example of baroque architecture. The **Wien Mitte rail station** and the **City Air Terminal** are also here.

**WIEDEN (4TH DISTRICT)** This small neighborhood extends south from Opernring and Kärtnering, and is almost as fashionable as the 1st District. Most activity centers on **Karlsplatz,** a historic square with its domed namesake, Karlskirche. Nearby is the **Historical Museum of the City of Vienna.** Kärntnerstrasse, the main boulevard of the city center, turns into **Wiedner-Hauptstrasse** as it enters this district, and the **Südbahnhof,** one of the two main train stations, lies at its southern tip.

**NEUBAU (7TH DISTRICT)** Bordering the expansive Museumsquartier, this is an ideal place to stay, as it's easily accessible by public transportation. The picturesque and once neglected **Spittelberg quarter** lies atop a hill just beyond Vienna's most famous museums. The old Spittelberg houses have been renovated into boutiques, restaurants, theaters, and art galleries.

**ALSERGRUND (9TH DISTRICT)** This area is often referred to as the Academic Quarter, not just because of housing a campus of the University of Vienna, but also because of its many hospitals and clinics. This is Freud territory, and you can visit his home, now the **Freud Museum,** on Berggasse.

## Exploring Vienna

Viennese prosperity under the Habsburgs reached its peak during the long reign of Maria Theresa in the late 18th century. Many of the sights described below originated under the great empress.

### The Vienna PASS

Vienna offers multiday tourist passes that include free or discounted admission to most major sites. If you're planning to hit a lot of attractions in a few days, these passes are almost always a bargain. The Vienna PASS (www.viennapass.com) comes in 2- to 6-day options, costing €69 to €99 for adults and €35 to €50 for kids 18 and under. With the optional travel upgrade, passholders have unlimited free travel on public transport in central Vienna.

21er Haus **20**
Albertina **9**
Augustinerkirche **8**
Beethoven Pasqualatihaus **2**
Burgkapelle **6**
Domkirche St. Stephan **28**
Haus der Musik **26**
Haydns Wohnhaus **16**
Heeresgeschichtliches Museum **21**
Johann Strauss Wohnung **33**
Jüdisches Museum Wien **31**
Kaiserappartements **3**
Kaiserliche Schatzkammer **5**
Kapuzinerkirche **25**
Karlskirche **18**
Kunsthalle **13**
Kunsthistorisches Museum **11**
Leopold Museum **13**
Michaelerkirche **4**
Mozartwohnung **27**
MUMOK (Museum of Modern Art Ludwig Foundation) **13**
Museum für Angewandte Kunst (MAK) **24**
Naturhistorisches Museum **12**
Neue Burg **10**
Österreichische Galerie Belvedere **22**
Österreichische Nationalbibliothek **7**
Peterskirche **30**
The Prater **34**
Ruprechtskirche **32**
Schönbrunn Palace **14**
Schubert Geburtshaus **1**
Secession **17**
Sigmund Freud Museum Wien **1**
Stadtpark **23**
Technisches Museum Wien **15**
Wien Museum **19**

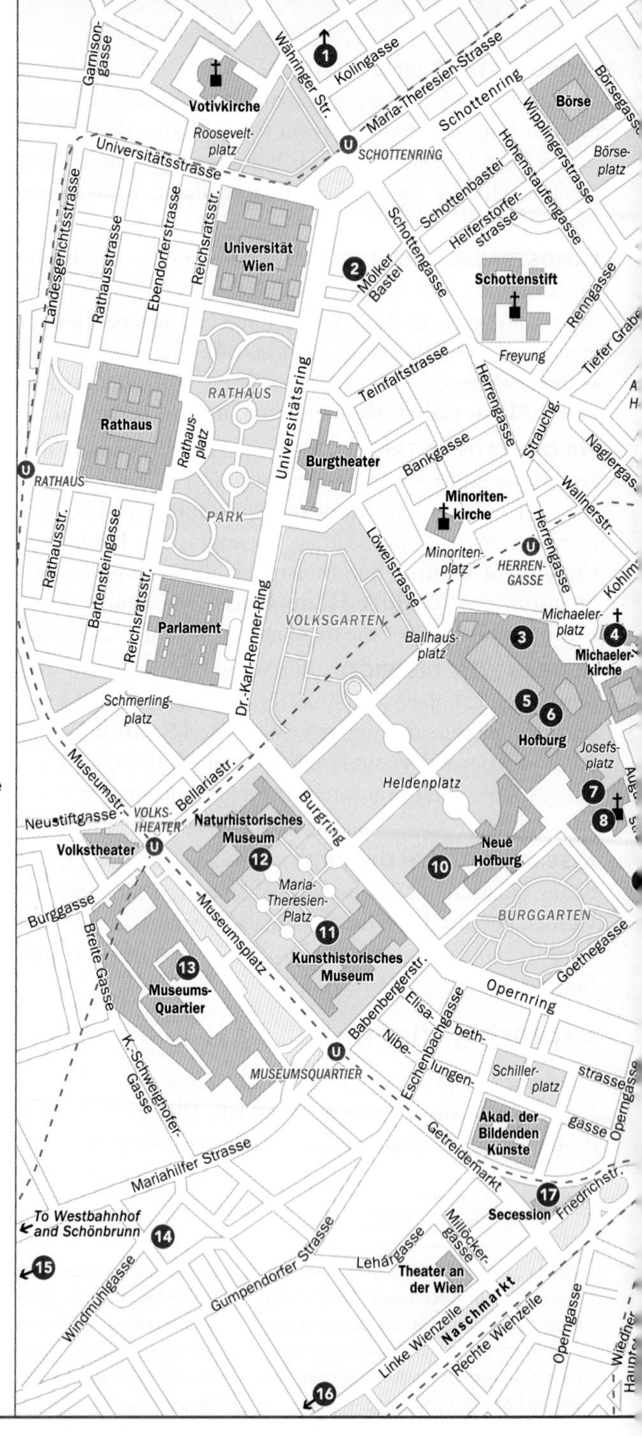

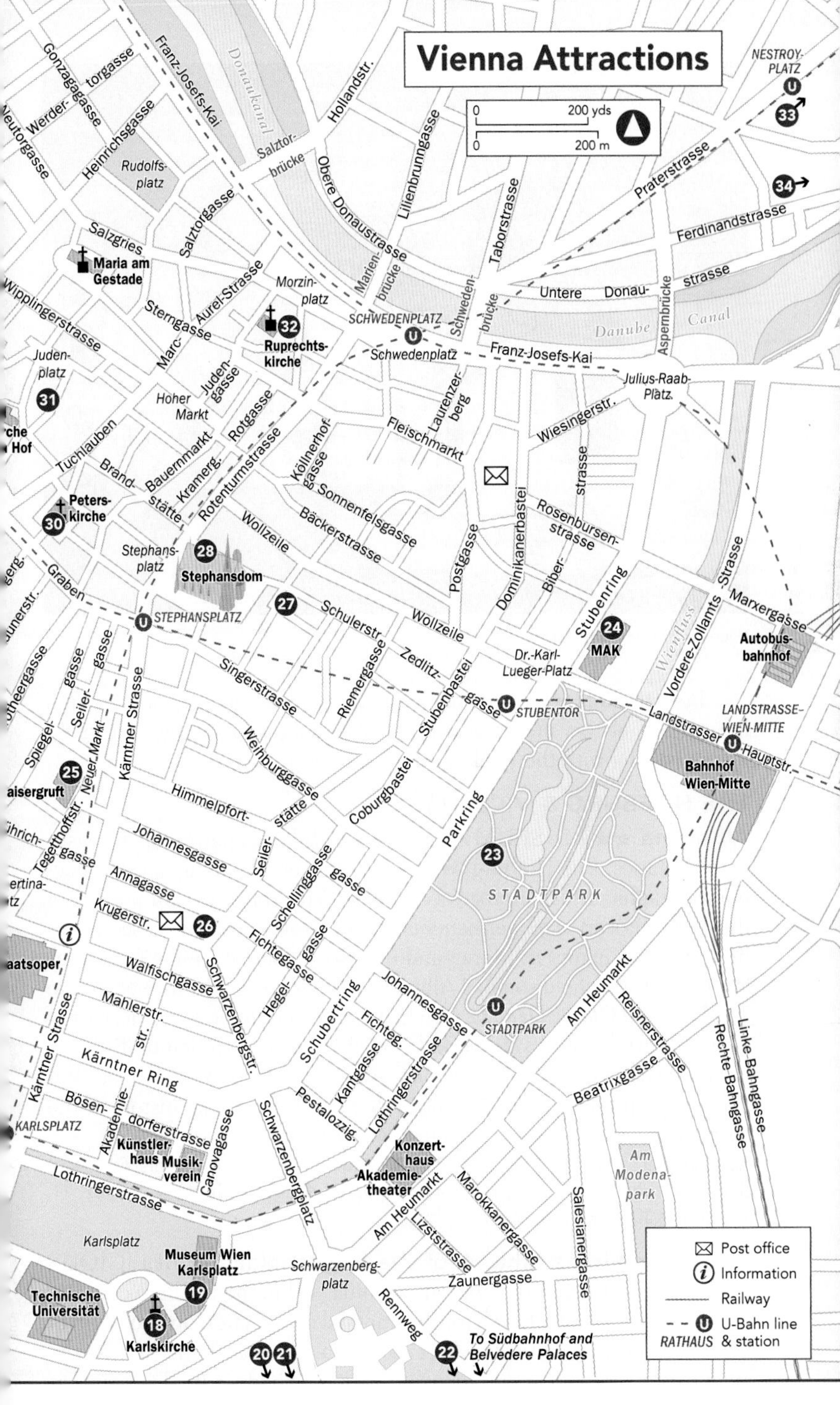

Vienna Attractions
0 200 yds
0 200 m
Donaukanal
Franz-Josefs-Kai
Salztorbrücke
Hollandstr.
Obere Donaustrasse
Lilienbrunngasse
Taborstrasse
Praterstrasse
NESTROY-PLATZ
Ferdinandstrasse
Untere Donau-strasse
Aspernbrücke
Danube Canal
Marienbrücke
Schwedenbrücke
SCHWEDENPLATZ
Schwedenplatz
Julius-Raab-Platz
Gonzagagasse
Werdertorgasse
Neutorgasse
Heinrichsgasse
Rudolfsplatz
Salztorgasse
Salzgries
Maria am Gestade
Wipplingerstrasse
Sterngasse
Marc-Aurel-Strasse
Morzinplatz
Ruprechtskirche
Judenplatz
Judengasse
Hoher Markt
Rotgasse
Laurenzerberg
Fleischmarkt
Wiesingerstr.
Köllnerhofgasse
Tuchlauben
Bauernmarkt
Kramerg.
Rotenturmstrasse
Brandstätte
Peterskirche
Sonnenfelsgasse
Bäckerstrasse
Postgasse
Dominikanerbastei
Rosenbursenstrasse
Biberstrasse
Wollzeile
Stephansplatz
Stephansdom
Graben
STEPHANSPLATZ
Schulerstr.
Stubenring
MAK
Marxergasse
Autobusbahnhof
Vordere-Zollamts Strasse
Wienfluss
Dr.-Karl-Lueger-Platz
Zedlitzgasse
Stubenbastei
STUBENTOR
Singerstrasse
Riemergasse
Seilergasse
Kärntner Strasse
Spiegelgasse
Neuer Markt
Kaisergruft
Tegetthoffstr.
Führichgasse
Albertinaplatz
Weihburggasse
Himmelpfortgasse
Seilerstätte
Coburgbastei
Parkring
Landstrasser Hauptstr.
LANDSTRASSE-WIEN-MITTE
Bahnhof Wien-Mitte
Johannesgasse
Annagasse
Krugerstr.
Schellinggasse
STADTPARK
Staatsoper
Walfischgasse
Fichtegasse
Hegelgasse
Schwarzenbergstr.
Mahlerstr.
Kärntner Ring
Schubertring
Fichteg.
Kantgasse
Lothringerstrasse
Am Heumarkt
Reisnerstrasse
Beatrixgasse
Rechte Bahngasse
Linke-Bahngasse
Bösendorferstrasse
Akademiestr.
KARLSPLATZ
Künstlerhaus
Musikverein
Canovagasse
Pestalozzig.
Konzerthaus
Akademietheater
Schwarzenbergplatz
Marokkanergasse
Am Modenapark
Salesianergasse
Lisztstrasse
Zaunergasse
Karlsplatz
Museum Wien Karlsplatz
Technische Universität
Karlskirche
Rennweg
To Südbahnhof and Belvedere Palaces
Post office
Information
Railway
U-Bahn line & station
RATHAUS

Neue Berg at Hofburg Palace.

Be warned that it's possible to spend a week here and only scratch the surface of this multifaceted city. We'll take you through the highlights, starting with the Hofburg.

## THE HOFBURG & VICINITY

**Albertina ★★** MUSEUM Once the Habsburg apartments for visiting dignitaries, this Hofburg Museum holds the world's greatest collection of graphic art, spanning 6 centuries. While only a small portion of the Albertina's art is on permanent display, visitors can always see works from such big names as Monet and Picasso, making it a must for any art lover. The vaults hold some of Albrecht Dürer's most famous pieces, like *The Hare and Clasped Hands,* which are displayed to the public as part of a rotating exhibit alongside works by Michelangelo, Rembrandt, Rubens, Casper David Friedrich, Kokoschka, and many others. Visits are accompanied by multilingual audio guides that also recount the history of the apartments in which these priceless works reside.

Albertinaplatz. www.albertina.at. ✆ **01/534-830.** €12 adults, €10 seniors, €8.50 students, free ages 18 and under. U-Bahn: U1/U2/U4 Karlsplatz; Tram: D, 1, 2, 62, 71. Thurs–Tues 10am–6pm, Wed 10am–9pm.

**Augustinerkirche (Church of the Augustinians) ★** RELIGIOUS SITE This 14th-century church was built within the Hofburg complex to serve as the parish church for the imperial court. The **Tomb of Maria Christina,** the favorite daughter of Maria Theresa, is housed in the main nave near the rear entrance; but there's no body in it. (The princess was actually buried in the Imperial Crypt, described in the Kapuzinerkirche entry, p. 502.) Still, her richly ornamented empty tomb is one of Canova's masterpieces. A small room in the Loreto Chapel is filled with urns containing the hearts of the imperial Habsburg family (they're visible through a window in an iron door.) The Chapel of St. George and the Loreto Chapel are open to the public by prearranged guided tour.

The Augustinerkirche was the site of many royal weddings: Marie Antoinette to Louis XVI of France in 1770, Marie-Louise of Austria to Napoléon in 1810, and Maria Theresa to François of Lorraine in 1736.

Visit the church on Sunday at 11am, when a high Mass is accompanied by a choir, soloists, and an orchestra.

Augustinerstrasse 3. © **01/533-7099.** Free. U-Bahn: Stephansplatz. Daily 6:30am–6pm.

**Burgkapelle (Home of the Vienna Boys' Choir) ★** RELIGIOUS SITE Construction of this Gothic chapel began in 1447 during the reign of Emperor Frederick III, but it was later massively renovated. Today, the Burgkapelle hosts the Hofmusikkapelle, an ensemble of the Vienna Boys' Choir and the Vienna State Opera chorus and orchestra, which performs works by classical and modern composers. If you failed to reserve in advance, and can find standing room, it's free.

Hofburg-Schweizer Hof. www.hofmusikkapelle.gv.at. © **01/533-9927**. Mass: Seats and concerts €9–€35; standing room free. Masses held Jan–June and mid-Sept to Dec, Sun and holidays 9:15am. Concerts held May–June and Sept–Oct Fri 4pm.

**Kaiserappartements (Imperial Apartments) ★★** HISTORIC SITE The Kaiserappartements, on the first floor, are where the emperors and their wives and children lived. The apartments are richly decorated with tapestries, many from Aubusson in France. (Unfortunately, you can't visit the quarters once occupied by Empress Maria Theresa, because they're now used by the president of Austria.) A highlight: the outrageously ornate court tableware and silver in the **Imperial Silver and Porcelain Collection,** from the household of the 18th and 19th centuries.

The Imperial Apartments are most closely associated with the long reign of Franz Joseph. A famous portrait of his beautiful wife, Elisabeth of Bavaria (Sissi), hangs in one. You'll see the "iron bed" of Franz Joseph, who claimed he slept like his own soldiers. (Maybe that explains why his wife spent so much time traveling.) The **Sissi Museum** is six rooms devoted to the life and complex personality of this famous, tragic empress.

Michaeler Platz 1. www.hofburg-wien.at. © **01/533-7570.** €13 adults, €12 students, €7.50, children 6–18, free for children 5 and under. U-Bahn: U1 or U3 to Stephansplatz. Tram: 1, 2, 3, or J to Burgring. Daily 9am–5:30pm (to 6pm in July/Aug).

**Kaiserliche Schatzkammer ★★★**MUSEUM The Austro-Hungarian Empire was no less decadent than other royal houses in Europe and the Kaiserliche Schatzkammer (Imperial Treasury) holds what is considered the greatest collection of, well, bling in the world. In the Secular Treasury, the baubles and finery span a millennium of European history, most

A jewel-encrusted gold orb at Kaiserliche Schatzkammer.

importantly the massive imperial crown, embellished with emeralds, sapphires, diamonds, and rubies (it dates from 962). It's so large that it probably slipped down the forehead of many a Habsburg at his coronation. The collection also includes one of the world's largest sapphires, a narwhal tusk (long mistaken for a unicorn's horn), and an ancient agate bowl, once thought to be the Holy Grail. The Ecclesiastical Treasury has more dubious treasures, like alleged fragments of Jesus's cross, a nail from the crucifixion, and a table cloth from the Last Supper.

Schweizerhof, 1010. www.kaiserliche-schatzkammer.at. ✆ **01/525-240.** €12 adults, €9 students/seniors, free for 18 and under. U-Bahn: U3 Herrengasse. Wed–Mon 9am–5:30pm.

**Michaelerkirche (Church of St. Michael)** ★ RELIGIOUS SITE Over its long history, this church has felt the hand of many architects and designers, resulting in a medley of styles, not all harmonious. Some of the Romanesque sections date to the early 1200s. The exact date of the chancel is not known, but it's probably from the mid-14th century. The catacombs remain as they were in the Middle Ages. Most of St. Michael's as it appears today dates from 1792, when the facade was redone in neoclassical style; the spire is from the 16th century. The main altar is richly decorated in baroque style, and the altarpiece, entitled *The Collapse of the Angels* (1781), was the last major baroque work completed in Vienna.

Habsburgergasse 12 ✆ **01/533-8000**. Free. U-Bahn: Herrengasse. Bus: 1A, 2A, or 3A. Mon–Sat 7am–10pm; Sun 8am–10pm.

**Neue Burg** ★★ MUSEUM Besides multiple ballrooms and the Austrian National Library, the Neue Burg houses three museums in the southeast wing of the Vienna Hofburg. The Sammlung Alter Musik Instrumente (Collection of Historic Musical Instruments) holds the most important array of Renaissance and baroque instruments in the world, from clavichords to woodwind instruments of the 15th and 16th centuries. At matinee performances visitors can even hear some of the better-kept pieces being played. The Ephesos Museum displays artifacts from Ephesus and Samothrace retrieved (some say lifted) by 19th-century Austrian archaeologists who excavated the ruins of Ephesus in Turkey. Then there's the Hofjagd und Rüstkammer (Collection of Arms and

Interior, Sammlung Alter Musik Instrumente.



Armor), which is among the best of its kind in the world. It has a range of armor dating from the 15th through the early 20th century.

Heldenplatz, 1010. www.khm.at. ✆ **01/525-244-502.** Combined ticket with Kunsthistorisches Museum; €14 adults, €11 students/seniors. U-Bahn: U3 Herrengasse or U2 Museumsquartier/Volkstheater; Tram: 1, 2, D to Burgring. Wed–Sun 10am–6pm.

**Österreichische Nationalbibliothek (Austrian National Library) ★** LIBRARY/UNIVERSITY The royal library of the Habsburgs dates from the 14th century; and the library building, developed on the premises of the court from 1723 on, is still expanding to the Neue Hofburg. The Great Hall of the present-day library was ordered by Karl VI and designed by those masters of the baroque, the von Erlachs. With its manuscripts, rare autographs, globes, maps, and other historic memorabilia, this is among the finest libraries in the world.

Josefplatz 1. www.onb.ac.at. ✆ **01/5341-0202.** €7 for adults. Thurs 10am–9pm; Fri–Sun and Tues–Wed 10am–6pm.

## ST. STEPHEN'S & VICINITY

**Domkirche St. Stephan (St. Stephan's Cathedral) ★★★** RELIGIOUS SITE A basilica built on the site of a Romanesque sanctuary, this cathedral was founded in the 12th century in what was, even in the Middle Ages, the town's center.

A 1258 fire that swept through Vienna virtually destroyed Stephansdom; and toward the dawn of the 14th century, a Gothic building replaced the basilica's ruins. The cathedral suffered terribly during the Turkish siege of 1683, and again from Russian and German bombardments during World War II. Restored and reopened in 1948, the

Interior, Domkirche St. Stephan.

cathedral is one of the greatest Gothic structures in Europe, rich in woodcarvings, altars, sculptures, and paintings. The 135m (450-ft.) steeple has come to symbolize the spirit of Vienna. The 106m-long (352-ft.) cathedral is inextricably entwined with Viennese and Austrian history. Mourners attended Mozart's "pauper's funeral" here in 1791, and Napoléon posted his farewell edict on the door in 1805.

The **pulpit** of St. Stephan's is the enduring masterpiece of stonecarver Anton Pilgrim, but the chief treasure of the cathedral is the carved wooden **Wiener Neustadt altarpiece**, which dates from 1447. The richly painted and gilded altar, in the left chapel of the choir, depicts the Virgin Mary between St. Catherine and St. Barbara. In the Apostles' Choir, look for the curious **tomb of Emperor Frederick III.** Made of pinkish Salzburg marble in the 17th century, the carved tomb depicts hideous hobgoblins trying to wake the emperor from his eternal sleep. You can climb the 343-step South Tower of St. Stephan's for a view of the Vienna Woods. Called **Alter Steffl (Old Steve),** the tower, marked by a

## amadeus SLEPT HERE

Thanks to the patronage of the Hapsburgs, Vienna of the 18th and 19th centuries was a who's who of famous and aspiring composers. You can visit the former homes of many of these musical giants, including **Beethoven Pasqualatihaus** ★ (Mölker Bastei 8; ✆ **01/535-8905**), where the master lived on and off from 1804 to 1814 and composed his Fourth, Fifth, and Seventh symphonies. Mozart spent a few happy years of his otherwise tragic life at **Mozartwohnung** ★ (Domgasse 5; www.mozarthausvienna.at; ✆ **01/512-1791**), where he composed The Marriage of Figaro. **Haydns Wohnhaus** ★ (Haydngasse 19; ✆ **01/596-1307**) is where Franz Joseph Haydn conceived and wrote *The Seasons* and *The Creation.* He lived in this house from 1797 until his death. The **Johann Strauss Memorial Rooms (Johann Strauss Wohnung)** ★ (Praterstrasse 54; ✆ **01/214-0121**) honor "The King of the Waltz," Johann Strauss, Jr., who lived at this address for a number of years and composed "The Blue Danube Waltz" here in 1867. The house where **Franz Schubert** was born is now a museum (**Schubert Geburtshaus ★;** Nussdorferstrasse 54; ✆ **01/317-3601**), and you can also visit Kettenbrückengasse 6, where he died at age 31.

### An Indestructible Legacy of the Third Reich

As you stroll about Vienna, you'll come across six anti-aircraft towers with walls up to 5m (16 ft.) thick, a legacy of the Third Reich. Built during World War II, they were designed to shoot down Allied aircraft. After the war, there was some attempt to rid the city of these horrors, but the citadels remained, their proportions as thick as the Arc de Triomphe in Paris. "We live with them," a local resident told us. "We try our best to ignore them. No one wants to remember what they were. But even dynamite doesn't work against them. They truly have walls of steel."

needlelike spire, dominates the city's skyline. It was originally built between 1350 and 1433, and reconstructed after heavy damage in World War II. The North Tower (Nordturm), reached by elevator, was never finished to match the South Tower, but was crowned in the Renaissance style in 1579. From here you get a panoramic view of the city and the Danube.

Stephansplatz 1. www.stephanskirche.at. ✆ **01/515-523054.** Cathedral free; catacombs €5.50 adults, €3 children 14–18, €2 children under 14. South Tower €4.50 adults, €2 students 15–18, €1.50 children 6–14. Bus: 1A, 2A, or 3A. U-Bahn: Stephansplatz. Cathedral open Mon–Sat 6am–10pm, Sun and holidays 7am–10pm. Catacombs Mon–Sat 10–11:30am and 1:30–4:30pm; Sun 1:30–4:30pm.

**Haus der Musik ★★** MUSEUM This fun music museum is both hands-on and high-tech. Take the time to inspect every niche. Besides all the interactive music making (you can create your own compositions in a number of ways to take home on CD), you also encounter reminders of the great composers who have lived in Vienna—not only Mozart, but also Beethoven, Schubert, Brahms, and others. You can even take to the podium and conduct the Vienna Philharmonic—it responds to your baton. A memorial entitled "Exodus" pays tribute to the Viennese musicians driven into exile or murdered by the Nazis.

Seilerstätte 30, 1010. www.hausdermusik.at. ✆ **01/513-4850.** €12 adults, €9 students/seniors, €5.50 children 3–12, free children 2 and under. U-Bahn: U3/U1 Stephansplatz, U1/U2/U4 Karlsplatz. Daily 10am–10pm.

**Jüdisches Museum Wien ★★** MUSEUM On one of the pedestrian side streets of the Graben, the Jewish Museum's permanent exhibitions trace the major role that Jews played in the history of Vienna from the Middle Ages to the present day. Extraordinary contributions of members of the Jewish community in areas like philosophy, music, and medicine are documented, and of course Freud's psychiatry. The museum's collection includes many objects rescued from Vienna's private synagogues and prayer houses, concealed from the Nazis throughout the war. Seeing the stories of the rich Jewish culture before World War II sheds a different light on the tragedy of the Holocaust for many, as Vienna was home to 185,000 Jews before 1938. By 1946, only 25,000 remained. It has taken a long time for the Jewish community to become established again, as is displayed in the permanent exhibit "Unsere Stadt" (Our City), which opened in 2014, tracing Jewish life and influences on the city from 1945 to today.

Dorotheergasse 11, 1010. www.jmw.at. ✆ **01/535-0431.** €10 adults, €8 seniors, €5 students, free for 17 and under. U-Bahn: U1/U3 Stephansplatz. Sun–Fri 10am–6pm.

**Kapuzinerkirche** ★ RELIGIOUS SITE The Kapuziner Church (just inside the ring behind the Opera) has housed the **Imperial Crypt,** the burial vault of the Habsburgs, for some 3 centuries. Capuchin friars guard the final resting place of 12 emperors, 17 empresses, and dozens of archdukes. Only their bodies are here: Their hearts are in urns in the Loreto Chapel (see p. 497), and their entrails are in St. Stephan's Cathedral (p. 499).

Most outstanding of the imperial tombs is the double sarcophagus of Maria Theresa and her consort, Francis Stephen (François, duke of Lorraine, or, in German, Franz von Lothringen, 1708–65), the parents of Marie Antoinette. The "King of Rome," the ill-fated son of Napoléon and Marie-Louise of Austria, was buried here in a bronze coffin after his death at age 21. Emperor Franz Joseph was interred here in 1916, just before the final collapse of his empire.

Tegetthoffstrasse 2. ✆ **01/512-6853.** €4 adults, €3 children 10–15. U-Bahn: Stephansplatz. Daily 10am–6pm.

**Peterskirche (St. Peter's Church)** ★ RELIGIOUS SITE This is the second-oldest church in Vienna, and the spot on which it stands could well be Vienna's oldest Christian church site (from the 4th century, it's believed). Charlemagne is credited with having founded a church on the site during the late 8th or early 9th century.

The present St. Peter's is the most lavishly decorated baroque church in Vienna. Gabriel Montani designed it in 1702. Hildebrandt, the noted architect of the Belvedere Palace, is believed to have finished the building in 1732. The fresco in the dome, a masterpiece by J. M. Rottmayr, depicts the coronation of the Virgin. The church contains many frescoes and much gilded carved wood, plus altarpieces by well-known artists of the period.

Petersplatz. www.peterskirche.at. ✆ **01/533-6433**. Free. U-Bahn: Stephansplatz. Mon–Fri 7am–8pm, Sat–Sun 9am–9pm.

### ELSEWHERE IN THE INNERE STADT

**Museum für Angewandte Kunst (MAK)** ★★ MUSEUM What better place to house applied art than in this beautiful red brick building with ornate detailing, stunning interiors and painted vaulted ceilings and pillars? Collections of rococo and Biedermeier furniture, as well as other antiques, glassware, crystal, and large collections of lace and textiles are beautifully displayed. An entire hall is devoted to Art Nouveau. There are outstanding objects from the Wiener Werkstätte (Vienna Workshop), founded in 1903 by architect Josef Hoffman.

Stubenring 5, 1010. www.mak.at/aktuell. ✆ **01/711-360.** €8 adults, €5.50 students/seniors, free for 18 and under, free for all Tues 6–10pm. U-Bahn: U3 Stubentor; tram: 2. Tues 10am–10pm, Wed–Sun 10am–6pm (closed Mon).

**Ruprechtskirche (St. Rupert's Church)** ★ RELIGIOUS SITE The oldest church in Vienna, Ruprechtskirche has stood here since 740, although much that you see now, such as the aisle, is from the 11th century. Beautiful new stained-glass windows, the work of Lydia Roppolt, were installed in 1993. Much of the masonry from a Roman shrine on this spot is believed to have been used in the present church. The tower and nave are Romanesque; the rest of the church is Gothic. St. Rupert is the patron saint of the Danube's salt merchants.

Ruprechtsplatz 1. www.ruprechtskirche.at. ✆ **01/535-6003.** Free. U-Bahn: Schwedenplatz. Mon, Wed, Fri 10am–noon; 3–5pm. Tues, Thurs 10am–noon.

### MUSEUMSQUARTIER

**Kunsthalle** ★★ MUSEUM The ever-changing exhibits of the Kunsthalle concentrate on Austrian and international contemporary art with a focus on photography, video, and new media. The Kunsthalle has no permanent collection and uses two exhibition spaces, one in a glass cube on Karlsplatz and the larger exhibition space in the former winter riding hall of the Museumsquartier. Exhibitions range from group and solo shows to well-curated retrospectives. Public tours take place every Sunday and are included in the ticket price.

Museumsplatz 1, 1070. www.kunsthallewien.at. ✆ **01/891-221**. €8 adults, €6 seniors, €2 students, free for children under 10. U-Bahn: U3 Volkstheater/U2 Museumsquartier; Tram: 49 Volkstheater. Fri–Wed 10am–7pm, Thurs 10am–9pm.

**Kunsthistorisches Museum (KHM)** ★★★ MUSEUM Across from Hofburg Palace, this huge building houses many of the fabulous art collections gathered by the Habsburgs as they added new territories to their empire. From a vast coin collection and unforgettable pieces of ancient Egyptian and Greek art, to rooms dedicated to great European masters, it's a treasure trove of art history. You'll find Roger van der Weyden's Crucifixion triptych, a stunning Memling altarpiece, and Jan van Eyck's portrait of Cardinal Albergati. The Kunstkammer (Art Chamber) displays decadent treasures made for the splendor-addicted European royalty, including the famous Saliera of Cellini (an exquisite salt cellar) and 2,200 other unique objects.

Maria-Theresien-Platz, Burgring 5. www.khm.at. ✆ **01/525-2425-00.** €14 adults, €11 students/seniors, free ages 18 and under. U-Bahn: U2/U3Volkstheater, U2 Museumsquartier; tram: 1, 2, or D. Tues–Sun 10am–6pm, Thurs 10am–9pm.

**Leopold Museum** ★★ MUSEUM In a striking, modern building, the focus here is "Fin de siècle Vienna," the artistic era that marked a break from staid tradition and hurled headlong toward Modernism. Its collections include the world's largest trove of the works of Egon Schiele (1890–1918), who has been rediscovered by the art world and now stands alongside Klimt and Kokoschka as one of the preeminent artists of the Wiener Moderne. The Leopold's inventory boasts more than 2,800 Schiele works, as well as those Klimts you've seen reproduced everywhere. Museumsplatz 1, 1070. www.leopoldmuseum.org. ✆ **01/525-700.** €12 adults, €8 students, €9 seniors, €7 children, free 7 and under. U-Bahn: U2 Museumsquartier, U2/U3 Volkstheater; tram: 49. Fri–Wed 10am–6pm, Thurs 10am–9pm (closed Tues).

**MUMOK** ★★ MUSEUM The MUMOK has one of the exceptional collections of contemporary art in Central Europe. It exhibits mainly Nouveau Réalisme, American pop art, and movements such as the hyperrealism of the 1960s and 1970s. In recent years the museum has acquired a collection of pieces from the era of Vienna Actionism, Austria's most substantial contribution to the development of avant-garde in the '60s.
Museumsplatz 1, 1070. www.mumok.at. ✆ **01/525-00.** €10 adults, €8 seniors, €7 students, free for ages 18 and under. U-Bahn: U2 Museumsquartier, U3/U2 Volkstheater; tram: 49. Mon 2–7pm, Tues–Sun 10am–7pm (Thurs until 9pm).

**Naturhistorisches Museum Wien** ★★ MUSEUM This is the third-largest natural history museum in the world (after New York and London), and holds the oldest collections. It was established by Franz Stephan von Lothringe, husband of Maria Theresa, who received a collection of 30,000 natural artifacts in 1750. His personal gift to the Empress, known as Der Juwelen Strauss, is a 60cm-tall (24-in.) bouquet of flowers crafted from more than 2,000 gemstones. The museum also holds an important collection of early Stone Age artifacts, the best-known of which is the Venus of Willendorf, discovered believed to have been carved during the Paleolithic Period, around 30,000 B.C.
Maria-Theresien-Platz, Burgring 7, 1010. www.nhm-wien.ac.at. ✆ **01/521-770.** €10 adults, €8 seniors, €5 students, free for ages 18 and under. U-Bahn: U2/U3 Volkstheater or U2 Museumsquartier; Tram: 1, 2, 46, 49, D. Thurs–Mon 9am–6:30pm, Wed 9am–9pm.

## BEYOND THE INNERE STADT

**Karlskirche (Church of St. Charles)** ★ RELIGIOUS SITE The Black Plague swept Vienna in 1713, and Emperor Charles VI vowed to build this church if the disease abated. Construction began in 1716. The master of the baroque, Johann Bernhard Fischer von Erlach, did the original work from 1716 to 1722; his son, Joseph Emanuel, completed it between 1723 and 1737. The green copper dome is 72m (236 ft.) high, a dramatic landmark on the Viennese skyline. Two columns, spinoffs from Trajan's Column in Rome, flank the front of the church, which opens onto Karlsplatz. There's also a sculpture by Henry Moore in a little pool. Karlsplatz. www.karlskirche.at. ✆ **01/504-6187.** €8 adults, €4 students, free for children under 10. U-Bahn: Karlsplatz. Mon–Fri 9am–6pm; Sun and holidays noon–7pm.

**Praterverband (The Prater)** ★ PARK/GARDEN This extensive tract of woods and meadowland has been Vienna's favorite recreation

The Prater's 1897 Ferris wheel.

area since 1766, when Emperor Joseph II opened it to the public. Before it became a public park, it had been a hunting preserve and riding ground for the aristocracy. Few other spots in Vienna convey such a sense of the decadent end of the Habsburg Empire—it's turn-of-the-century nostalgia, with a touch of 1950s-era tawdriness.

The best-known part of the huge park is the **Riesenrad** (www.wienerriesenrad.com; ✆ **01/729-5430**), the giant Ferris wheel that was constructed in 1897 and reaches 67m (220 ft.) at its highest point. After St. Stephan's Cathedral, it's the most famous landmark in Vienna. Except for World War II damage, the Ferris wheel has been turning since 1897.
Prater 9. ✆ **01/728-0516.** Park free; prices for rides and amusements vary. U-Bahn: Praterstern. May–Sept daily 10am–1am; Oct–Nov 3 daily 10am–10pm; Nov 4–Dec 1 daily 10am–8pm. The park is open 24 hours a day.

**Secession** ★ MUSEUM This artistic statement was constructed in 1898 and is crowned by a magnificent dome once called "outrageous in its useless luxury." It stands south of the Opernring, beside the Academy of Fine Arts. The Secession was the home of the Viennese avant-garde around the turn of the last century. Led by Gustav Klimt, they launched a movement in rebellion against the conservative ideas of the official Academy of Fine Arts. Here you'll see Klimt's *Beethoven Frieze,* a 30m

(100-ft.) visual interpretation of Beethoven's Ninth Symphony. Most other works by the Secessionist artists are on display in the Belvedere Palace, and the Secession building itself is used for contemporary exhibits.

Friedrichstrasse 12, 1010. www.secession.at. ✆ **01/587-5307.** €9 adults, €5.50 students/seniors. U-Bahn: U1/U2/U4 Karlsplatz. Tues–Sun 10am–6pm.

**Sigmund Freud Museum ★★** MUSEUM Entering the museum, you can almost imagine the good doctor ushering you in and telling you to make yourself comfortable on the couch. Antiques and mementos, including his velour hat and dark walking stick with ivory handle, fill the study and waiting room he used during his residence here from 1891 to 1938. There are changing exhibits with topics like the doctor's travels, opening the experience up to a wider view of how and where he developed his theories.

Berggasse 19, 1090. www.freud-museum.at. ✆ **01/319-1596.** €9 adults, €8 seniors, €6.50 students, €4 children 12-18, free 11 and under. Daily 9am–6pm.

**Technisches Museum Wien ★★** MUSEUM Since it opened in 1918, the Technical Museum has been dedicated to advances in the fields of science and technology. Today, it offers plenty of hands-on gadgets for conducting experiments. But the displays from the past are even more fascinating including a Mercedes Silver Arrow from 1950, a Model-T Ford from 1923, a 150-year-old steam engine, and thousands of everyday objects to remind visitors of how far we've come and what steps it took to get us here. Anything imaginable and much that has been forgotten is on display—barrel washing machines, a giant Dictaphone from the 1920s, phonographs, typewriters, and more. Kids will be thrilled at the Das Mini section with loads of activities specifically aimed at 2- to 6-year-olds.

Mariahilfer Strasse 212, 1140. www.technischesmuseum.at. ✆ **01/899-980.** €10 adults, €8.50 students/seniors, free for ages 18 and under. U-Bahn: U4 Schönbrunn; tram: 10, 52, 58. Mon–Fri 9am–6pm, Sat–Sun 10am–6pm.

**Wien Museum ★★** MUSEUM This fascinating but little-visited attraction is a treasure trove for history buffs. The regular exhibits offer a panorama of Old Vienna's unfolding history, beginning with the settlement of prehistoric tribes in the Danube basin and continuing through Roman relics, artifacts from the reign of the dukes of Babenberg, and a wealth of leftovers from the Habsburg sovereignty. The topographical section shows how Vienna has changed over the past 500 years and how urban planning helped shape Vienna into a city that repeatedly wins awards for best quality of life.

Karlsplatz 4, 1040. www.wienmuseum.at. ✆ **01/505-87470.** €8 adults, €6 students/seniors, free for ages 18 and first Sun each month. U-Bahn: U1/U2/U4 Karlsplatz; tram: 2, 71. Tues–Sun 10am–6pm.

## BELVEDERE PALACE & THE SCHWEIZERGARTEN

**21er Haus ★★** MUSEUM This glass-and-steel modernist structure is devoted to 20th- and 21st-century art with a predominantly Austrian focus. The approach is progressive, with an artist-in-residence always in residence and a collection that include such Austrian powerhouses as Erwin Wurm, Lisa Ruyter, Fritz Wotruba, Franz Graf, and Lisl Ponger, alongside international greats. The restaurant and bar downstairs, Dots twenty-one, is the best lunch or dinner choice in a wide radius.
Schweizergarten, Arsenalstrasse 1, 1030. www.21erhaus.at. ✆ **01/795-57770.** €7 adults, €5.50 students/seniors. U-Bahn: U1 Südtirolerplatz; tram: D, 18, O. Wed–Thurs 11am–9pm, Fri–Sun 11am–6pm.

**Heeresgeschichtliches Museum (Museum of Military History) ★★** MUSEUM Their apt slogan is "Wars belong in a museum." It's certainly been the theme of this museum for quite some time. Constructed in the 1850s, it is the oldest state museum in Vienna, its architecture a precursor to the Ringstrasse style, in red brick with towers. Aside from the permanent exhibits that delineate Habsburg military history—defeats as well as triumphs—it offers changing exhibits about recent and current conflicts, like a 2014 exhibit on child soldiers. The fascinating Sarajevo room contains mementos of the assassination of Archduke Franz Ferdinand and his wife on June 28, 1914, the event that sparked World War I. The archduke's bloodstained uniform is displayed, along with the couple's car speckled with bullet holes. Many exhibits focus on the Austro-Hungarian navy, and frescoes depict important battles.
Arsenal Objekt 1, 1030. www.hgm.or.at. ✆ **01/795-610.** €6 adults; €4 students/seniors; free for 18 and under and first Sun each month. U-Bahn: U1 Südtirolerplatz; tram: D, 18, O to Südbahnhof. Daily 9am–5pm.

**Österreichische Galerie Belvedere ★★** HISTORIC SITE Built as a summer home for Prince Eugene of Savoy, the Belvedere is today the ultimate sightseeing combo-pack, a mixture of historic sights and museum-quality artworks. And even the approach to it is glorious: Southeast of Karlsplatz, the Belvedere sits on a slope above Vienna, and visitors enter through a long garden with a huge circular pond that reflects the looming palace buildings. Two great, flowing staircases dominate the interior. The Gold Salon in Lower Belvedere is one of the most beautiful rooms in the Vienna. A regal French-style garden lies between the two buildings that make up the palace that was once the residence of Archduke Franz Ferdinand, whose assassination sparked World War I. In May 1955, the Allied powers signed the peace treaty recognizing Austria as a sovereign state in Upper Belvedere. The treaty is on display in a large salon decorated in red marble.

Lower Belvedere (built 1714–1716) houses the **Barockmuseum (Museum of Baroque Art).** Displayed here are the original sculptures from the Neuer Markt fountain (replaced now by copies), the work of

The Belvedere Palace museum complex and gardens.

Georg Raphael Donner, who died in 1741. **Museum Mittelalterlicher Kunst (Museum of Medieval Art)** is in the Orangery at Lower Belvedere. Here you'll see art from the Gothic period as well as a Tyrolean Romanesque crucifix that dates from the 12th century. Upper Belvedere (built 1721–1723) houses the **Galerie des 19. und 20. Jahrhunderts (Gallery of 19th- and 20th-Century Art).** Here you also find works by the artists of the 1897 Secessionist movement, most outstanding of which are those by Gustav Klimt (1862–1918) and Egon Schiele (1890–1918), whose masterpieces here include *The Wife of an Artist.*
Prinz-Eugen-Strasse 27. www.belvedere.at. ✆ **01/79557134.** €7–€30 adults, €5.50–€26 students, free for 18 and under. Tram: D to Schloss Belvedere. Daily 10am–6pm.

## SCHÖNBRUNNER SCHLOSSSTRASSE

**Schönbrunn Palace ★★★** HISTORIC SITE The 1,441-room Schönbrunn Palace, designed by those masters of the baroque, the von Erlachs, was built between 1696 and 1712 for Emperor Leopold I who envisioned a palace whose grandeur would surpass Versailles. Alas, Austria's treasury, drained by costly wars, would not support the ambitious undertaking, and the original plans were never carried out.

When Maria Theresa became empress, she changed the original plans; and Schönbrunn looks today much as she conceived it. Done in "Maria Theresa ochre," with delicate rococo, the palace is in complete contrast to the grim, forbidding Hofburg. Schönbrunn was the imperial summer palace during Maria Theresa's 40-year reign, and it was the scene of opulent balls, banquets, and fabulous receptions held during the Congress of Vienna. At the age of 6, Mozart performed in the Hall of Mirrors.

The last of the Habsburg rulers, Karl I, signed a document here on November 11, 1918, renouncing his participation in affairs of state—not

Schönbrunn Palace and Imperial Gardens.



quite an abdication, but tantamount to one. Allied bombs damaged the palace during World War II, but restoration has obliterated the scars.

The **Gloriette,** a marble summerhouse topped with an imperial eagle, embellishes the palace's **Imperial Gardens.** The so-called Roman Ruins (a collection of marble statues and fountains) date from the late 18th century, when it was fashionable to simulate the ravaged grandeur of Rome.

The **State Apartments** are the most stunning display in the palace. Much of the interior ornamentation is in the rococo style, with red, white, and 23½-karat gold predominating. Of the 40 rooms that you can visit, particularly fascinating is the Room of Millions, decorated with Indian and Persian miniatures—an outrageously grand rococo salon.

The **Wagenburg (Carriage Museum)** is also worth a visit. It contains a fine display of imperial coaches from the 17th to 20th centuries. Schonbrunner Schlosstrasse 47. www.schoenbrunn.at. ✆ **01/811-132-39**. €15 adults, €10 children 6–15, free for children under 6. Carriage museum and gardens priced separately. U-Bahn: Schönbrunn. Apr–June and Sept–Oct daily 8:30am–5pm; July–Aug to 6pm; Nov–Mar to 4:30pm.

## Especially for Kids

Palaced- and museumed-out kids can cut loose at the Prater, or dive into **Zoom Children's Museum ★,** where they can touch, play with, and ask questions about anything from medieval knights to the life of the oceans. Admission to the museum is free for kids and €4 for adults. Special programs and exhibits are €4 to €6 per child, per exhibit, free for one accompanying adult. Family tickets are €14. (Museumplatz 1; www.kindermuseum.at; ✆ **01/524-7908;** open Tues–Sun 9am–4pm, closed Christmas and school holidays.)

## Cruising the Danube

The Danube is the quintessential European river, where so many nations and peoples, from Passau, Vienna, Budapest and Belgrade, Galati and Selena all encounter each other. It was this river that carried ships and soldiers, courtiers and culture from one end to the other, and by the 19th century, the Austro-Hungarian army marched to commands in 11 languages. Cynics aside, the Danube is really blue, at least on sunny days, and most visitors to Austria view a day cruise as a highlight of their trip. The most professional of the cruises are operated by the **DDSG Blue Danube Shipping Co** (www.ddsg-blue-danube.at; ✆ **01/588800**). Their Grand Danube River Cruise, with hop-on/hop-off options, last a little more than 3 hours and costs €27 round-trip.



Near the palace, **Schönbrunner Tiergarten** ★ is the world's oldest zoo, founded by the husband of Empress Maria Theresa. The baroque buildings in the historic park landscape make a unique setting for modern animal keeping. Adults €17, children and seniors €8; free for children 5 and under. Open daily 9am to 4:30, 5:30 or 6:30pm, depending on the season. Entrance near Hietzinger Tor at Schönbrunner gardens; www.zoovienna.at.

## Where to Stay

Vienna has some of the greatest hotels in Europe, as well as a terrific range of prices, from ultra-expensive palaces of posh to budget hostels. If you're looking to cut costs, staying outside the Inner City will cut a fifth to a quarter off your nightly rate. Still, because most of the sights you'll want to see are in the Ring, that's where we concentrate our hotel picks.

### 7TH DISTRICT, NEAR MUSEUMSQUARTIER

#### Expensive

**Hotel Sans Souci Wien** ★★★ On the cusp of the 7th District, this slick hotel was designed to leave guests without any worries. From the Zen-like lounge, past the swanky cocktail bar, and up to the charismatic rooms and suites, the place is thought through from head to toe. The spa offers treatments with Anne Semonin products and is spattered with elegant touches like the mini-chandeliers above the pool. The rooms are inspired—all those above the petit and superior size have whimsical touches (for example, a sports-car theme in the Jaguar Suite), and designer furniture. There's plenty of art adorning the walls, including originals by Roy Lichtenstein and Steve Kaufman. The hotel's right on the edge of the Inner City and the artsy Neubau district.

Burggasse 2. www.sanssouci-wien.com. ✆ **01/522-2530.** Doubles €215–€251, suites €296–€621, rates include breakfast. U-Bahn: U2 MuseumsQuartier; tram: 49. **Amenities:** Restaurant; bar; gym; spa; pool; free Wi-Fi.

### Moderate

**25 Hours Hotel ★★★** "We are all mad here" is sprawled in neon letters across the front of the 25 Hours Hotel. Whether or not that's true, this former '70s block concrete student-housing project has been converted into a darn fun place, with a circus theme and never-say-never attitude. They do things their own way here, from freestanding bathtubs on the balconies to the quirky mermaid mosaic on the wall of the cave spa. Guests receive the utmost care, and at the restaurant and rooftop bar, you'll see many a local (they enjoy the social scene here). The m and m+ rooms can be tight for space, but starting with the xl rooms you get elbow room and kooky touches like outdoor bathtubs and TV stands made of antique suitcases. Suites have kitchenettes; other swell touches include free loaner bicycles and Mini Cooper car rentals.

Lerchenfelderstrasse 1-3. www.25hours-hotels.com/wien. ✆ **01/521-510.** Doubles €100–€200, suites €150–€200. U-Bahn: U2/U3 Volkstheater; tram: 46. **Amenities:** Restaurant; bar; spa; gym; free Wi-Fi.

**Altstadt Vienna ★★** Creator Otto Ernst Wiesenthal calls this designer hotel "your personal residence in Vienna" and takes pride in offering individual experiences in the stylishly quirky rooms with big windows, parquet floors, vividly colored walls, mismatched fabrics, and original art. Each has a themed selection of books and art magazines, and the hotel boasts the best collection of lamps in Austria. The hotel also offers apartments for longer stays. Not only is a hearty breakfast included but also tea and cakes in the afternoon. The affordability of the classic rooms is a real find for such elegant and central lodgings.

Kirchengasse 41. www.altstadt.at. ✆ **01/522-6666.** Doubles €125–€215, suites €175–€400; rates include breakfast. U-Bahn: U2/U3 Volkstheater; tram: 49. **Amenities:** Bar; room service; babysitting; free Wi-Fi.

## 1ST DISTRICT/INNERE STADT

### Expensive

**DO & CO Hotel ★★** Some find it woefully pretentious, others love it, but you can't beat the location of this quirky, upscale, design-conscious lodging. Rooms are artfully minimalist and very comfortable, done up in soothing tones of toffee and putty. Sybaritic details include in-room clear glass showers. Bedrooms have mahogany, louvered doors, lots of polished travertine, dark-grained hardwoods, and floor plans with curved walls and tucked-away balconies. Views encompass the crowds scurrying around the all-pedestrian Graben and Stephansplatz.

Stephansplatz 12. www.docohotel.com. ✆ **01/241-88.** Doubles €229–€249, suites €960–€1,550. U-Bahn: Stephansplatz. **Amenities:** Restaurant; bar; free Wi-Fi.

**Hotel Imperial ★★** Stroll off the Ringstrasse and into this palatial marble lobby and instantly you'll feel like royalty. Or something close to it: Charlie Chaplin, Queen Elisabeth II, and Michael Jackson all stayed

**HOTELS**

25 Hours Hotel **8**
Altstadt Vienna **10**
DO & CO Hotel **16**
The Guest House **21**
Hollmann Belletage **33**
Hotel Imperial **17**
Hotel Lamee **31**
Hotel Sacher **19**
Hotel Sans Souci Wien **9**
Kärntnerhof **32**
Palais Coburg Hotel Residenz **23**
Palais Hansen Kempinski **1**
Steigenberger Hotel Herrenhof **6**
Topazz **30**

**RESTAURANTS**

Bitzinger bei der Albertina **13**
Café Central **3**
Café Demel **7**
Café Diglas **26**
Café Dommayer **15**
Café Frauenhuber **22**
Café Imperial **17**
Café Landtmann **2**
Café Sperl's **14**
Café Tirolerhof **20**
Esterházykeller **5**
Figlmüller Wollzeile **27**
Gaumenspiel **11**
Glacis Beisl **12**
Harry's Time **25**
Holy Moly **35**
Motto am Fluss **34**
Plachutta Wollzeile **24**
Schweizerhaus **36**
Steirereck **18**
Trzésniewski **28**
Vestibül **4**
Zum Schwarzen Kameel **29**

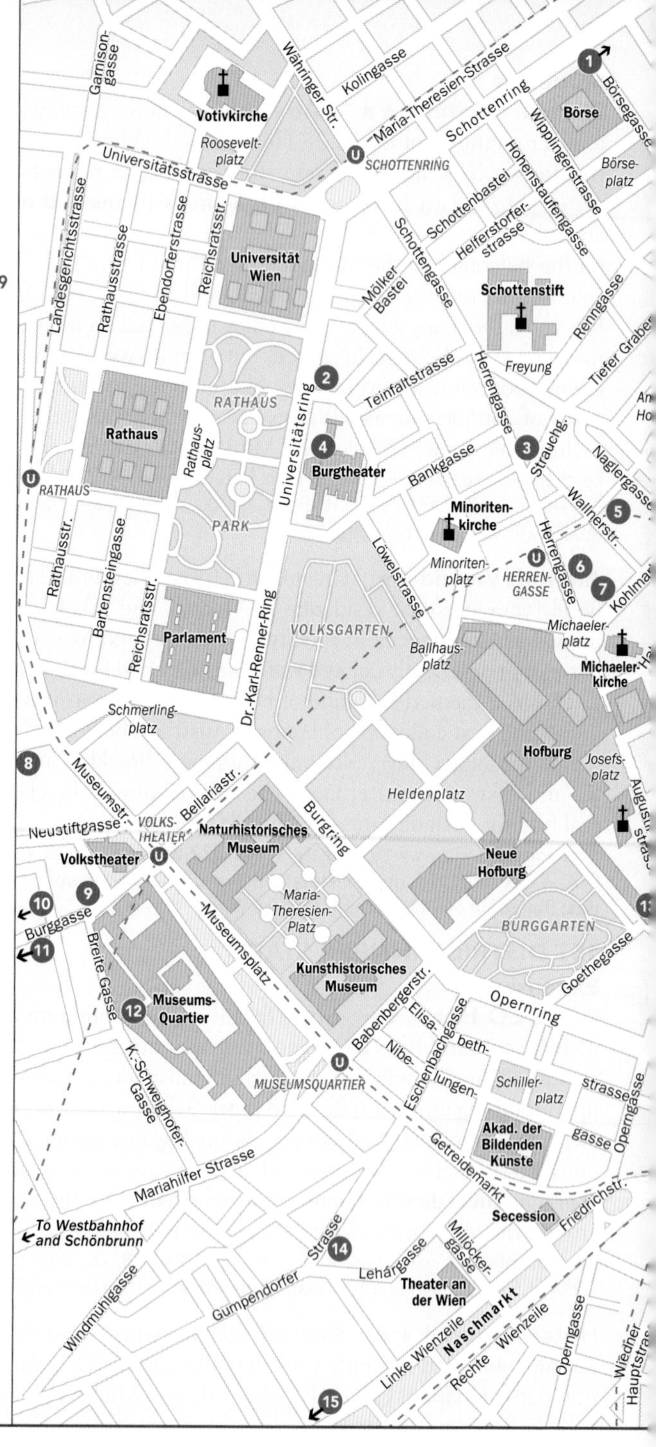

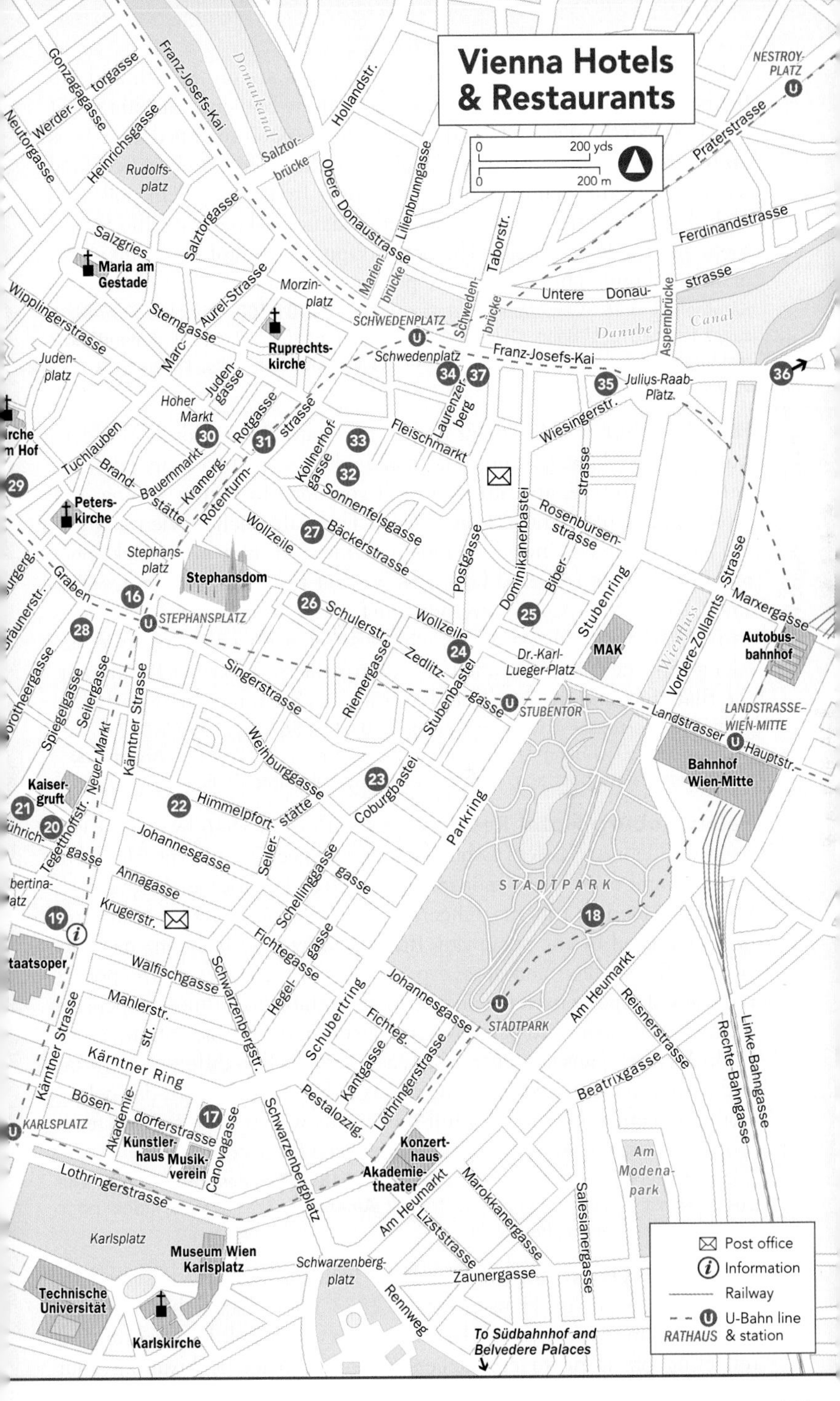

Vienna Hotels & Restaurants
0 200 yds
0 200 m
Post office
Information
Railway
U-Bahn line & station
RATHAUS
Stephansdom
STEPHANSPLATZ
SCHWEDENPLATZ
STUBENTOR
LANDSTRASSE-WIEN-MITTE
NESTROY-PLATZ
STADTPARK
KARLSPLATZ
Maria am Gestade
Ruprechtskirche
Peterskirche
Kaisergruft
Staatsoper
MAK
Autobusbahnhof
Bahnhof Wien-Mitte
Konzerthaus
Akademietheater
Künstlerhaus
Musikverein
Museum Wien Karlsplatz
Technische Universität
Karlskirche
To Südbahnhof and Belvedere Palaces
Donaukanal
Danube Canal
Wienfluss
Am Modena-park

before you after all. The most desirable rooms are on the 4th and 5th floors—they're on a more human scale than the opulent state suites but roomier than the digs on high floors (up there appointments diminish, as do bathroom sizes). The Imperial also has the sweetest period cocktail bar in town, the pianist playing everything from Hungarian polkas to Cole Porter. If this superb 5-star hotel has a weakness, it's the fitness room and the lack of a spa. The hotel's Opus restaurant serves up works of art until midnight; an exquisite post-opera choice.

Kärntner Ring 16. www.imperialvienna.com. ✆ **01/501-100**. Doubles €308–€474, suites from €810. U-Bahn: U1/U2/U4 Karlsplatz; tram: D, 1, 2, 62, 71. **Amenities:** 2 restaurants; bar; gym; sauna; limousine service; butler service; babysitting; free Wi-Fi.



**Hotel Sacher ★★★** Right next to the State Opera House, this central hotel has the silk wallpaper, brocade drapes, 19th-century oils, Biedermeier furniture, and attentive staff you hope to find in Vienna. But most come here for the chocolate cake. The Café Sacher Wien is where the Sachertorte was invented (apricot middle and shiny near-black chocolate—ah!). The attached hotel has been at the heart of Viennese life since 1876. Nine suites have adjoining 23-sq.-m (250 sq.-ft.) terraces with fab views. The spa offers, what else, "hot chocolate treatments." Along with the Confiserie and Café, there's the Anna Sacher Restaurant, the BlaueBar, and the sexy Rote Bar, with its charming winter garden.

Philharmonikerstrasse 4. www.sacher.com. ✆ **01/514-560.** Doubles €395–€765, suites €755–€6,450. U-Bahn: U1/U2/U4 Karlsplatz; tram: 1, 2, 62, 65, D. **Amenities:** 2 restaurants; cafe; 2 bars; spa; room service; babysitting; free Wi-Fi.

**Palais Coburg Hotel Residenz ★★** Built in 1846 by August von Sachsen-Coburg-Saalfeld (whose family managed to sire the House of Windsor and most of the monarchs of western Europe) as the dynasty's Vienna residence, this magnificent, sprawling palace was rebuilt after being wrecked by the occupying Russian army. The Residenz has only suites, the smaller and less expensive of which are contemporary, intensely design-conscious, and very comfortable. The more expensive are high-end posh, with pale satin upholstery and valuable antiques. The Wine Archive spans six cellars with each dedicated to different cultures, and there are breathtaking tasting rooms to boot. No modern-day palace would be complete without a full-service spa with a pool, sauna, steam room, sun terrace, and fitness center reserved for residents.

Coburgbastei 4. www.palais-coburg.com. ✆ **01/518-180.** Suites €695–€2,700, includes breakfast. U-Bahn: U4 Stadtpark; tram: 2. **Amenities:** 2 restaurants; indoor pool; gym; spa, room service; free Wi-Fi.

**Palais Hansen Kempinski ★★★** Inside a building designed by Theophil Edvard von Hansen for the 1873 World Expo, the lobby is a bright atrium, with skylights beaming onto the swank lounge area and reflecting off intricate chandeliers. Yes, this place is luxurious, but

The Sachertorte where it was invented, at the Hotel Sacher.



without the Old-World pomp of some of its Ringstrasse peers. Rooms are ample in size and state-of-the-art, which means true king-size beds, bathrooms clad in marble and Botticino stone, Nespresso machines, and an iPad in each room for ordering room service or making a spa appointment. The fitness area has high-quality equipment, and although the spa is somewhat small, it's spaciously laid out with a decent-size pool for swimming laps. Best perk? The to-die-for breakfast (included in some rates) at Die Küche, with scrumptious fresh bread, pastries, and an omelet bar.

Schottenring 24. www.kempinski.com/wien. ✆ **01/236-1000**. Doubles €255–€448, suites €490–€9,500. U-Bahn: U2 Schottenring; tram: 1. **Amenities:** 2 restaurants; 2 bars; gym; spa; free Wi-Fi.

### Moderate

**The Guest House ★★** Artsy, chic, and central (right next to the Albertina and the Vienna State Opera), The Guest house is a boutique find. Not only is the furniture high-end, but the general feel is that one is the guest of an affluent and generous friend. Suite 802 for instance has an espresso machine, wine refrigerator, and a Bang & Olufsen flatscreen TV. The bathrooms have separate tubs and rain showers, and to top it all off, beer and wine from the minibar are included in the room price. Downstairs is a brasserie and bakery which serve great salads and small meals besides breakfast.

Furichgasse 10. www.theguesthouse.at. ✆ **01/512-1320**. Doubles €170–€250, suites €490–€550. U-Bahn: U1/U3 Stephansplatz or U1/U2/U3 Karlsplatz. **Amenities:** Restaurant; bar; free Wi-Fi.

**Hollmann Belletage ★★★** The Belletage is smack in the heart of town, but it's easy to miss while strolling down the Köllnerhofgasse, perhaps because this charmingly quirky establishment is housed in a fin-de-siècle apartment building. But you don't want to miss this place, because it's one of the most pampering in the city: a six-course breakfast menu is included in the room rate, as is everything in the minibar and showings at the in-house cinema (all the movies are related to Vienna). The public areas are inviting, from the "living room" and spa area with their wood-burning fireplaces, to the peaceful garden terrace in the courtyard. And the rooms are wonderfully comfy, done in a typically modern Austrian style, with rain showers and beautiful baths, some of which are hidden in cupboards or only separated from the bed by a partition. A luxury spa suite has its own Turkish bath, canopy bed, free-standing bathtub, fireplace, kitchen, and a 10-person dining room. Bottom line: Everything about this place is fun, sophisticated, and inspired. Book well ahead as it only has 26 rooms.

Köllnerhofgasse 6. www.hollmann-beletage.at. ✆ **01/961-1960.** Doubles €159–€340, suites €369, rates include breakfast. U-Bahn: U1/U4 Schwedenplatz; tram: 1, 2. **Amenities:** Restaurant; gym; spa; cinema; free Wi-Fi.



**Hotel Lamee ★★** From outside you'll be struck by the Cafe Bar Bloom. It's a real eye catcher, with marble floors, lacquered wood walls, and funky, upholstered stools. Rooms are similarly lavish, with quirky color accents and some with floor-to-ceiling windows and terraces with views of St. Stephen's Cathedral. Other fab touches: a freestanding tub right next to the sleeping area in some rooms, and downright heavenly beds. The Lamee makes up for the lack of a spa with its breathtaking rooftop terrace (it doubles as a cafe and cocktail bar from 2–9pm).

Rotenturmstrasse 15. www.hotellamee.com. ✆ **01/532-2240**. Doubles €181–€208, suites €271–€361. U-Bahn: U3 Stephansplatz. **Amenities**: Rooftop terrace; 2 bar/cafes; free Wi-Fi.

**Kärntnerhof ★★** With a retro sign and charming staff, the "smallest grand hotel in Vienna" lives up to its self-ascribed superlative. It's a boutique hotel with Old-World charm oozing from every oil painting lining the walls. The decor is mostly modern however, and manages to fit seamlessly with the antiques. The rooms are dedicated to different figures from history: The "Madame Rosa" is in honor of the post-war years when the house was a bordello, and the "Christiane Hörbiger Suite" honors one of the greats of German and Austrian cinema. The extra goodie in summer is the adorable rooftop terrace, from which you can view the steeples of the Heiligenkreuzerhof in one of the most historic corners of the Inner City.

Grashofgasse 4. www.karntnerhof.com. ✆ **01/512-1923.** Doubles €109–€245, suites €219–€599, rates include breakfast. U-bahn U1/U4 Schwedenplatz; tram 1, 2. **Amenities:** Rooftop terrace; free Wi-Fi.

**Steigenberger Hotel Herrenhof ★★** Only a few steps from the Hofburg Imperial Palace, the Steigenberger Hotel Herrenhof, built in 1913, occupies an entire corner of the Herrengasse and has retained its stately facade. Most of the interiors have been tastefully modernized to 21st-century interpretations of various historic styles, from baroque to Art Deco. The rooms are spacious and comfortably furnished with violet upholstery and contemporary interpretations of Art Deco. Two suites come with rooftop terraces. The spa covers two floors and has two saunas, a steam room, a small fitness area, and an array of treatments. Herrengasse 10. http://de.steigenberger.com/Wien/Steigenberger-Hotel-Herrenhof. ✆ **01/534-040.** Doubles €144–€170, suites €383–€587. U-Bahn: U3 Herrengasse. **Amenities:** Restaurant; bar; spa; gym; room service; free Wi-Fi.

**Topazz ★★★** The building looks a bit like a space ship, with porthole windows and matte-black metal siding, but the look gets more elegant inside, with touches like designer furnishings and deliciously comfy beds. Rooms are relatively small, but make up for it with cushions in the porthole windows and marble bathrooms. One especially nice touch: the minibar is included in the room price. This is a great place for design lovers who don't need to spend excessive time in the hotel. There are countless restaurants and spas nearby, and because Topazz is across the street from and a sister to Lamee, many amenities and services are shared. Lichtensteg 3. www.hoteltopazz.com. ✆ **01/532-2250**. Doubles €179–€228. U-Bahn: U3 Stephansplatz. **Amenities:** Cafe/bar; free Wi-Fi.



## Where to Eat

In Vienna, dining out is a local pastime. Besides Austrian and French cuisine, you'll find restaurants serving Serbian, Slovenian, Slovakian, Hungarian, and Czech food, along with Asian, Italian, and Russian.

Many are located in Vienna's so-called "Bermuda Triangle," a concentration of restaurants and bars a short walk north of Stephansplatz.

Because Vienna cherishes its theaters, concert halls, and opera houses, many locals choose to dine after a performance, so many restaurants and cafes stay open late to cater to culture vultures.

### The Best of the Würst

On street corners throughout Vienna, you'll find one of the city's most popular snack spots, the **Würstelstand.** These small stands sell beer and soda, plus frankfurters, bratwurst, curry wurst, and other Austrian sausages, usually served on a roll *mit senf* (with mustard). Try the *käsekrainer,* a fat frankfurter with tasty bits of cheese. Conveniently located stands are on Seilergasse (just off Stephansplatz) and Kupferschmiedgasse (just off Kärntnerstrasse).

**Frankfurters and beer at a Würstelstand.**

## 1ST DISTRICT/INNERE STADT

### Expensive

**Harry's Time** ★★★ AUSTRIAN/MEDITERRANEAN Simply meaning "supper," the *abendmahl* tasting menu lets guests choose as many courses as you want from the "surprise menu." After you let them know any dietary restrictions, the decision making is over, and course after course arrives. The fare is mostly Italian, Mediterranean, and Austrian, re-imagined for fine dining. If you're not ready for the main dish you can have three appetizers, and since it's not always easy to get the timing perfect, the staff also brings amuse-bouches between courses to keep guests happy. So don't have lunch and give yourself at least four hours for this feast. The wine accompaniment is optional, but recommended, as the quality in their cellar comes close to that of the kitchen.

Universitätsring Platz 5. www.harrys-time.at. ✆ **01/512-4556.** Abendmahl Menu: €66 plus €43 for wine; small version: €39 plus €28 for wine. U-Bahn: U3 Stubentor; tram: 2. Mon–Fri 11am–1am, Sat 6pm–1am.

**Plachutta Wollzeile** ★★ AUSTRIAN This local institution has become a place of legend for their *Tafelspitz*. They offer 10 variations of the boiled beef dish, which was adored by Emperor Franz Josef. Variations of the dish can be with a *Schulterscherzel* (shoulder of beef) or *Beinfleisch* (shank of beef)—ask the waiters to describe the different tastes and textures. Potatoes, chives, and an enticing mixture of horseradish and chopped apples accompany each order. Other Viennese staples like goulash soup, calf's liver, and braised pork with cabbage are also available. Despite the bustle, the staff is cordial and keeps a healthy sense of humor.

Wollzeile 38. www.plachutta.at. ✆ **01/512-1577.** Mains €18–€32. U-Bahn: U3 Stubentor; Tram: 2. Daily 11:30am–midnight.

**Vestibül** ★★★ INTERNATIONAL This classy eatery at the Vienna Burgtheater comes complete with marble columns and vaulted ceilings. Before or after shows, guests gather in the elegant bar for an aperitif, digestif, or coffee. Tapas are also served, with tables opening on to a view of the City Hall and Ringstrasse; or in the garden when the weather is nice. Prepared by acclaimed Austrian chef Christian Domschitz, the food consists of innovative versions of brasserie classics like fish and chips, here made with regional pike perch and doused in artisan vinegar. A lobster soup might be followed by pheasant with spelt berries, apple, and black salsify. Vegetarian dishes are prepared on a daily basis.

Universitätsring 2. www.vestibuel.at. ✆ **01/532-4999.** Mains €11–€38, fixed-price menus €55–€69. U-Bahn: U2 Schottentor or U3 Herrengasse; Tram: 1, D Rathausplatz/Burgtheater. Mon–Fri noon–midnight, Sat 6pm–midnight.

**Zum Schwarzen Kameel** ★★★ AUSTRIAN Art Deco design, uniformed waiters, and a general feel of decadence make this time machine of a restaurant a place that's popular with both locals and visitors In the same family since 1618 (although its current decor dates from 1902), it's packed with chic locals on Saturday mornings, all trying to recover from a late night by sipping "medicinal" champagne and noshing on open-face sandwiches from the trays on the black countertops (we're partial to the rosy hand-carved *Beinschinken,* boiled ham with fresh horseradish). Beyond the cafe is a perfectly preserved dining room with jeweled copper chandeliers, walls of polished panels and yellowed ceramic tiles, and a dusky plaster ceiling-frieze of grape leaves. The perfect place for a nostalgic meal. The top-notch cuisine features grilled sturgeon with its caviar on a bed of spinach and artichokes in argan oil, or veal filet and sweetbread with truffled peas, celery puree, and mushrooms.

Bognergasse 5. www.kameel.at. ✆ **01/533-8125-11.** Mains €23–€37, fixed-price menus €68–€86. U-Bahn: U1/U3 Stephansplatz, U3 Herrengasse. Mon–Sat noon–3:30pm, 6pm–midnight.

### Moderate

**Figlmüller Wollzeile** ★ AUSTRIAN This century-old tavern, with its vaulted ceilings and warm wooden furnishings, evokes Old Vienna on multiple levels. Although you won't be the only tourist there, it still feels secluded, tucked away in a passageway off the Wollzeile. The waiters are unflappable, and its schnitzels are the kind of plate-filling, golden-brown delicacies that are an obligatory classic to sample when in Vienna. Other house specialties include veal goulash with buttery dumpling noodles and strudels. During mushroom season (autumn and early winter), order the savory fungi in herbed cream sauce over noodles.

Wollzeile 5. www.figlmueller.at. ✆ **01/512-6177.** Mains €10–€17. U-Bahn: U1/U3 Stephansplatz. Daily 11am–10:30pm.

**Holy Moly** ★★★ INTERNATIONAL On the banks of the Danube Canal you'll find a curious boat, always docked between Schwedenplatz and the Urania building. In summer, there's a pool attached and a charming sun deck on the roof. All year round, the "main deck" of the *Badeschiff* (literally, bathing ship) is dedicated to delicious but laid-back and affordable gourmet dining. The decor is weathered and nicked around the edges, just as one would expect on a ship, but what comes out of the kitchen is art: braised lamb shoulder with radish cream on a bed of potato cakes, or black salsify goulash with curd cheese dumplings. The menu changes, but you'll always find the signature spicy Holy Moly fish soup with red curry, which is highly recommended.

On the Danube Canal. www.badeschiff.at. ✆ **01/307-50.** Mains €9–€18, fixed-price menus €31–€46. U-Bahn: U1/U4 Schwedenplatz; tram: 1, 2. Mon–Sat 5pm–1am.

**Motto am Fluss** ★★★ INTERNATIONAL Right on the water, in a boatlike building (which actually function as the docking station for passenger ships along the Danube canal) this ultra-hip cafe/restaurant does both high-end and low-end with style and panache. Upstairs, at the cafe, the breakfast and burgers are spectacular; and the expansive deck is the

perfect place to finish the day with a chilled "sundowner" and good conversation. Downstairs in the more formal dining room, the menu is eclectic (and somewhat confusing, with starters and mains all in one list) but manages to hit just the right festive notes. Our faves are the classic Wienerschnitzel, a bouillabaisse with rouille on a bed of root vegetables, and the chicken supreme with shiitake mushrooms and chard. The lengthy wine list offers a great selection of regional favorites.
Franz-Josefs-Kai 2. www.motto.at/mottoamfluss. ✆ **01/252-5510/5511.** Mains €10–€26. U-Bahn: U1/U4 Schwedenplatz; tram: 1, 2. Open daily, cafe 8am–2am; restaurant 11:30am–2:30pm, 6pm–2am; bar 6pm–4am.



### Inexpensive

**Bitzinger bei der Albertina ★★** SAUSAGE STAND The Würstelstand (sausage stand) is part of Viennese culture, and Bitzinger is perhaps the most famous one. It boasts a sleek modern design and a location right between the opera and the Albertina. On the night of the Opera Ball, it's where the tuxedo–and–ball gown set meet with stagehands, garbage men, and demonstrators to enjoy a chat and a juicy bite of Bitzinger's delectable Käsekrainer, Bratwurst, Burenwurst, Waldviertler, or Bosna. They are served with a kaiser roll or a hot dog bun. Besides ketchup, they'll ask whether you want sweet or spicy mustard, and there are also fries, potato pockets filled with cheese, and 12 different beers and champagne for those who like to munch their Würstel in style.
Augustinerstrasse 1. www.bitzinger.at. ✆ **01/533-1026.** Sausages €3–€5. U-Bahn: U1/U2/U4 Karlsplatz; tram: 1, 2, 62, D. Daily 8am–4am.

**Esterházykeller ★★** AUSTRIAN When this subterranean beer hall opened in 1683, soldiers were given free wine to keep them motivated to guard the city walls. Joseph Haydn tippled here, and often asked to be paid in wine by his boss, Duke Esterházy. Today, Esterházykeller still offers cheap wine (between 4 and 6pm the house wine is reduced to €1 a glass) but the real fun is choosing from the cutlets, spreads, and salads at the bar. The network of caves and long rooms give it a very personal feel despite the vastness of the cellar. No one will mind if kids want to explore the caves, and they'll have fun sampling the finger food and *Almdudler* (herbal lemonade). This is a good Inner City alternative to the more rural Heuriger wine taverns in the outer districts. There's also an upstairs restaurant called the Stüberl, with outdoor seating in summer and a traditional Austrian a la carte menu.
Haarhof 1. www.esterhazykeller.at. ✆ **01/533-3482-33.** Mains €6.50, buffet €15. U-Bahn: U1/U3 Stephansplatz, U3 Herrengasse. Mon–Fri 4–11pm, Sat–Sun 11am–11pm.

**Trzésniewski ★★** SANDWICHES Though most can't pronounce it, everyone in Vienna knows about this spot. It's unlike any buffet you've seen, with six or seven cramped tables and a line of people, all jostling for space next to the glass counters. Most people hurriedly devour the delicious finger sandwiches, which come in 18 different combinations of cream cheese, egg, lox, salami, herring, tomatoes, and many other tasty ingredients. Franz Kafka lived next door and used to come here for sandwiches and beer.

Dorotheergasse 1. www.trzesniewski.at. ✆ **01/512-3291.** Sandwiches €1.20. U-Bahn: U1/U3 Stephansplatz. Mon–Fri 8:30am–7:30pm, Sat 9am–5pm.

## IN STADTPARK

### Expensive

**Steirereck** ★★★ INTERNATIONAL/AUSTRIAN In the historical Meierei building in the Stadtpark, Steirereck has been repeatedly hailed as the best restaurant in Austria. The accolades are deserved. From creations like stewed and roasted veal with cress root, wild broccoli, and mint to Jerusalem artichoke with pea sprouts, collard greens, and Viennese escargots, every dish is a discovery. We were particularly tickled by the amuse bouche that came before our six-course meal: it was composed of fine prosciutto and dried watermelon and served on a mini clothesline, with tiny pins holding each bite. There are small cards accompanying each course that tell diners what they're eating, along with interesting facts about the ingredients. Dining here is a retreat from the ordinary, and while the experience is far from cheap, it's worth every euro.

Am Heumarkt 2A. www.steirereck.at. ✆ **01/713-3168.** Mains €28–€49, 6-course menu €125. U-Bahn: U4 Stadtpark, U3/U4 Landstrasse/Wien Mitte; tram: 2. Mon–Fri 11:30am–2:30pm, 6:30pm–at least 1am.

## IN OR NEAR MUSEUMSQUARTIER

### Expensive

**Gaumenspiel** ★★ AUSTRIAN/INTERNATIONAL Roughly translated, the name means "a game on the palate," and the chefs here do play with your taste buds. Instead of a conventional menu, hosts Martina Kraler and Rodschel Rachnaev offer three menus, with temptations like a risotto with pomelo and octopus, or sea bass and scampi on a hot stone with oysters and clams. Dishes are seasonal, but always provide an explosion of flavor.

Zieglergasse 54. www.gaumenspiel.at. ✆ **01/526-1108.** Fixed-price menus €40–€48. U-Bahn: U3 Zieglergasse; tram: 49. Mon–Sat 6pm–around midnight (kitchen closes 10:30pm).

### Moderate

**Glacis Beisl** ★★ AUSTRIAN First you'll see the garden, its pride and joy in summer, with pea-soup painted wooden furniture, plenty of greenery, and a gravel floor like those in wine taverns in the countryside. The modern interior contrasts nicely with the traditional Austrian fare, which ranges from organic beef goulash to Wienerschnitzel. Dishes are beautifully prepared in classic style. Inside, Museumsquartier Glacis Beisel is a welcome haven from all the tourist bustle.

Museumsplatz 1/Breite Gasse 4. www.glacisbeisl.at. ✆ **01/526-5660.** Mains €7–€18, lunch menu €10. U-Bahn: U2/U3 Volkstheater; U2 Museumsquartier; tram: 49. Daily 11am–2am.

## CAFE kultur

The Viennese might not have invented the idea of elegant coffeehouses which double as luncheries and bars, but they elevated it to a high art. Here are some of our favorite spots for Viennese coffee, light fare, and those legendary pastries:

**Café Central,** Herrengasse 14 (✆ **01/5333764;** U-Bahn: Herrengasse), offers a glimpse into 19th-century Viennese life—it was once the center of Austria's literati. Even Lenin is said to have met his colleagues here. The cafe is open Monday to Saturday from 7:30am to 10pm, Sunday 10am to 10pm.

Café Central.

**Café Demel,** Kohlmarkt 14 (✆ **01/5351717;** U-Bahn: Herrengasse; Bus: 1A or 2A), tempts passersby with windows filled with fanciful spun-sugar creations of characters from folk legends. Inside you'll find a splendidly baroque landmark where dozens of pastries are available daily, and a mammoth variety of tea sandwiches made with smoked salmon, egg salad, caviar, or shrimp. It's open daily from 10am to 7pm.

**Café Diglas,** Wollzeile 10 (www.diglas.at; ✆ **01/5125765;** U-Bahn: Stubentor), evokes prewar Vienna better than many of its competitors. It offers everything from run-of-the-mill caffeine fixes to more elaborate, liqueur-enriched concoctions like the Biedermeier (with apricot schnapps and cream). The cafe is open daily from 7am to 11pm.

**Café Dommayer,** Auhofstrasse 2 (✆ **01/8775465;** U-Bahn: Schönbrunn), boasts a reputation for courtliness that goes back to 1787. In 1844, Johann Strauss, Jr., made his

## 2ND DISTRICT, AT THE FAR END OF THE PRATER

### Inexpensive

**Schweizerhaus ★** AUSTRIAN This place is legendary. Not only does it seat what seems like millions, it has been a beer hall since 1868. The Kolarik family, who now run the place, call it Vienna's biggest beer barrel, and although that may be accurate (endless numbers of *Krügerl,* or large beers, are hauled past on massive trays) the food is very good too. The *Schweinsstelzen* (leg of pork) is served on the bone with a knife and cutting board as the only aid. Other top dishes include schnitzel, goulash, and *Kartoffelpuffer* (fried potato medallions) as well as homemade beer chocolate. A visit is in order after romping through the Prater.

Prater 116. www.schweizerhaus.at. ✆ **01/7280-1520.** Mains €5–€17. U-Bahn: U2 Messe Prater. Daily 11am–11pm (closed Nov to mid-March).

musical debut here. Most patrons come for coffee, tea, and pastries, but if you have a more substantial appetite, try the platters of food, including Wiener schnitzel, *Rostbraten*, and fish. It's open daily from 7am to 10pm.

**Café Frauenhuber,** Himmelpfortgasse 6 (✆ **01/5125353;** U-Bahn: Stephansplatz) is the oldest continuously operating coffeehouse in the city. The ancient decor is a bit battered and more than a bit smoke-stained. Wiener schnitzel, served with potato salad and greens, is a good bet, as are any of the ice cream dishes and pastries. It's open daily Monday to Saturday 8am to 11pm.

**Café Imperial,** Kärntner Ring 16 (www.starwood.com; ✆ **01/50110389;** U-Bahn: Karlsplatz), was a favorite of Gustav Mahler and a host of other celebrities. A daily champagne breakfast/brunch buffet for €41 is served Habsburg-style daily 7am to 11pm. The cafe is open daily from 7am to 11pm.

**Café Landtmann,** Universitätsring 4 (✆ **01/241000;** tram: 1, 2, or D), has a history dating to the 1880s and has long drawn a mix of politicians, journalists, and actors. It was also Freud's favorite. We highly suggest spending an hour or so here, perusing the newspapers, sipping coffee, or planning the day's itinerary. The cafe is open daily from 7:30am to midnight.

**Café Sperl's** (Gumpendorferstrasse 11; www.cafesperl.at; ✆ **01/5864158;** www.cafesperl.at; U-Bahn: Karlsplatz) Gilded Age panels and accessories that were installed in 1880 are still in place. Platters include salads; toast; baked noodles with ham, mushrooms, and cream sauce; omelets; steaks; and Wiener schnitzels. It's open Monday to Saturday 7am to 11pm and Sunday 11am to 8pm (closed Sun July–Aug).

**Café Tirolerhof,** Fürichgasse 8 (✆ **01/5127833;** U-Bahn: Stephansplatz or Karlsplatz), which has been under the same management for decades, makes for a convenient sightseeing break, particularly from a tour of the nearby Hofburg complex. Open Monday to Saturday 7:30am to 10pm.



## Shopping

Visitors can spend many happy hours shopping or just browsing in Vienna's shops, where handicrafts are part of a long-established tradition of skilled workmanship. Popular for their beauty and quality are petit-point items, hand-painted Wiener Augarten porcelain, gold and silver work, ceramics, enamel jewelry, wrought-iron articles, and leather goods.

The main shopping streets are in the city center (1st District). Here you'll find **Kärntnerstrasse,** between the State Opera and Stock-im-Eisen-Platz (U-Bahn: Karlsplatz); the **Graben,** between Stock-im-Eisen-Platz and Kohlmarkt (U-Bahn: Stephansplatz); **Kohlmarkt,** between the Graben and Michaelerplatz (U-Bahn: Herrengasse); and **Rotenturmstrasse,** between Stephansplatz and Kai (U-Bahn: Stephansplatz).

The **Naschmarkt** is a vegetable-and-fruit market with a lively scene every day. To visit it, head south of the opera district. It's at Linke and Rechte Wienzeile (U-Bahn: Karlsplatz.)

## Entertainment & Nightlife

Viennese nightlife offers something for everyone. You can dance into the morning hours, hear a concert, attend an opera or festival, go to the theater, gamble, or simply sit and talk over a drink at a local tavern.

The best source of information about the cultural scene is *Wien Monatsprogramm,* which is distributed free at tourist information offices and at many hotel reception desks.

Music is at the heart of Vienna's cultural life. The city is the home of four major symphony orchestras, including the world-acclaimed Vienna Symphony and the Vienna Philharmonic. In addition to the ÖRF Symphony Orchestra and the Niederöster-reichische Tonkünstler, there are dozens of others, ranging from smaller orchestras to chamber orchestras.

Opera is sacred in Vienna: When World War II was over, the city's top priority was the restoration of the heavily damaged **Weiner Staatsoper (Vienna State Opera) ★★★** (www.staatsoper.at; ✆ **01/5144-42250;** Sept 1–June 30 daily). With the Vienna Philharmonic Orchestra in the pit, globally admired opera stars perform at the legendary venue. In their day, Richard Strauss and Gustav Mahler worked as directors. Tickets are hard to get but worth the effort.

**The Musikverein ★★** (www.musikverein.at; ✆ **01/505-8190**) is where classical musicians aspire to perform. Regarded as one of the four best concert halls in the world, some 600 concerts per season (Sept–June) are presented here. This is also the venue of the legendary New

### Into the Woods

*Heurigen* are traditional Viennese wine taverns in the winemaking villages outside the city; the kind of cozy, woodsy, welcoming inns of travelers' imagination. One of our favorite wine villages is **Grinzing,** at the edge of the Vienna Woods, about 16 km northwest of the city. Much of Grinzing looks the way it did when Beethoven lived nearby. It's a district of crooked old streets and houses, with thick walls surrounding inner courtyards where grape arbors shelter wine drinkers. The sound of zithers and accordions lasts long into the summer night. Plant yourself in a *heurige* for an evening of local wine and homestyle cooking, or sample the fermentations of several of these homey taverns.

Unless you've got a designated driver, don't drive to the *heurigen.* Police patrols are very strict, and you may not drive with more than 0.8% alcohol in your bloodstream. It's much better to take public transportation. Most *heurigen* are within 30 to 40 minutes of downtown. For Grinzing, take tram no. 1 to Schottentor, and change there for tram no. 38 to Grinzing. On summer weekends, a hop-on/hop-off train, the Vienna Heurigen Express (www.cityscenictours.at [German only]; ✆ **01/479-2808**), runs a circuit that includes Grinzing and other stops.

Year's Concert of the Vienna Philharmonic, for which it is nearly impossible to get tickets, but if available they can cost up to €950.

For less cultured (but equally enriching, perhaps?) entertainment, Vienna's blossoming **bar scene** centers on the "**Bermuda Triangle,**" an area roughly bordered by Judengasse, Seitenstättengasse Rabensteig, and Franz-Josefs-Kai. You'll find everything from intimate watering holes to large bars with live music. The closest U-Bahn stop is Schwedenplatz.

# SALZBURG

Salzburg sits astride the Salzach River like a centurion guarding Alpine treasures. Its baroque-studded skyline is set against a pristine mountain backdrop. A city of 17th- and 18th-century buildings, Salzburg is internationally known for its architectural beauty. That beauty lures plenty of visitors but fortunately, Salzburg the city and its surroundings have charm to spare, with splendid architecture, sweeping vistas, and serene pockets of quiet nature.

Once known as the Roman town of Juvavum, the city and river derive their names from the early residents who prospered from the region's salt mines. This "heart of the heart of Europe" is and will likely forever be the city of Mozart, who was born here in 1756. The Old Town lies for the most part on the left bank of the river, where a monastery and bishopric were founded in A.D. 700, becoming an archbishopric in 798. At the height of the prince-archbishop's power, Salzburg was known as the "German Rome."

## Essentials

For trip planning and hotel bookings, the **Salzburg Tourist Information Office** website is www.salzburg.info.

**ARRIVING** The **Salzburg Airport-W. A. Mozart,** Innsbrucker Bundesstrasse 95 (www.salzburg-airport.com; ✆ **0662/8580**), lies 3km (2 miles) southwest of the city center. Bus no. 2 runs between the airport and Salzburg's main rail station, while no. 8 goes to Hanuschplatz and the ***Altstadt* (Old Town).** Departures are every 10 to 20 minutes (Sun and public holidays every 30 min.), and the 20-minute trip costs €2.50 one-way. By taxi it's about 15 minutes, but you'll pay at least €13 to €15.

Salzburg's main **rail station,** the **Salzburg Hauptbahnhof,** Südtirolerplatz (www.oebb.at; ✆ **05/1717**), is on the major rail lines of Europe, with frequent arrivals not only from all the main cities of Austria, but also from other European cities. From the train station, buses depart to various parts of the city, including the Altstadt (Old Town), or you can walk from the rail station to the Old Town in about 20 minutes.

Salzburg is 336km (209 miles) west of Vienna and 153km (95 miles) east of Munich. It's reached from all directions by good roads, including

## The Salzburg Festival

One of the premier music attractions of Europe, the **Salzburg Festival** was founded in 1920 by composer Richard Strauss and takes place every July and August.

Hugo von Hofmannsthal's adaptation of the morality play *Jedermann (Everyman)* is one of the yearly highlights. Performed in German, it is staged outside the cathedral in Domplatz. Concerts are usually conducted in the Rittersaal of the Residenz Palace and in the marble salon of Mirabell Palace. The Salzburger Marionetten Theater also presents performances. Ballet performances are usually given by the Vienna State Opera Ballet with the Vienna State Opera Chorus and the Vienna Philharmonic. International soloists are invited annually, and the London Symphony or the Berlin Philharmonic is also likely to be invited.

Festival tickets are in great demand, and there never are enough of them. Don't arrive expecting to get into any of the major events unless you've already purchased tickets. Hotel concierges, particularly at the deluxe hotels of Salzburg, always have some tickets on hand, but expect to pay outrageous prices for them. At first-night performances of the major productions, evening dress is de rigueur.

For festival details, contact the Salzburg Festival box office at www.salzburgfestival.at; call ✆ **0662/8045.**



Autobahn A8 from the west (Munich), A1 from the east (Vienna), and A10 from the south.

**CITY LAYOUT** Most of what visitors come to see lies on the left bank of the Salzach River in the **Altstadt (Old Town),** although the more modern right bank offers a few old streets and shops leading up to the river. The Old Town is mostly pedestrian-only.

The heart of the Inner City is **Residenzplatz,** which has the largest and finest baroque fountain this side of the Alps. On the western side of the square stands the **Residenz,** palace of the prince-archbishops; and, on the southern side, is the **Salzburg Dom (Salzburg Cathedral).** To the west of the Dom lies **Domplatz,** linked by archways dating from 1658. Squares to the north and south appear totally enclosed.

On the southern side of Max-Reinhardt-Platz and Hofstallgasse, edging toward **Mönchsberg,** stands the **Festspielhaus (Festival Theater),** built on the foundations of the 17th-century court stables.

**GETTING AROUND** The city **buses and trams** provide quick, comfortable service throughout the city center. If bought from a ticket machine, a one-ride ticket is €2.50 for adults and €1.70 for children 6 to 15; those 5 and under travel free. Buses stop running between 11pm and midnight, depending on what part of Salzburg you're in.

The **Salzburg Card** grants unlimited public transportation and admission to the city's most important cultural sites, such as Mozart's birthplace, the Hohensalzburg Fortress, the Residenz gallery, the world-famous water fountain gardens at Hellbrunn, and more. Cards are valid for 24, 48, and 72 hours and cost €24, €32, and €37, respectively, except during festival season (May–Oct), when €3 to €5 are added to the prices. Children up to 15 receive a 50% discount. You can buy the pass from Salzburg travel agencies, hotels, and tobacconists.

Driving a **car** in Salzburg is definitely *not* recommended. In most places it's impossible, because the monumental landmark center is pedestrians only. If you're driving into Salzburg, leave your car on the left bank of the Salzach River. You'll find convenient underground parking areas—designated with a large "P"—like the one at Mönchsberg, from which it's an easy walk to the center and Domplatz.

You'll find **taxi** stands scattered at key points of the city center and in the suburbs. Call ✆ **0662/874400** to order a taxi. Fares start at €3.70.

A "traditional taxi"—a ***Fiaker* (horse-drawn carriage)**—will not only provide you with a ride, but also a bit of history as well. You can rent a *Fiaker* at Residenzplatz. Four people usually pay €44 for 20 to 25 minutes, but all fares are subject to negotiation.

In an effort to keep cars out of the center, Salzburg officials have developed a network of bicycle paths (www.stadt-salzburg.at/radlkarte). Check with your hotel for the nearest bike-rental service.



## The Neighborhoods in Brief

**ALTSTADT** Most visitors head for the Altstadt, or Old Town, on the left bank of the Salzach, tucked beneath the crescent-shaped Mönchsberg. This is a section of narrow streets and slender houses, in complete contrast to the town constructed by the prince-archbishops across the river. The Old Town contains many of Salzburg's top attractions: The **cathedral, Mozart's birthplace,** and **St. Peter's Cemetery.**

**NONNBERG** The eastern hill occupied by the dominating **Hohensalzburg Fortress,** Nonnberg, rises to 455m (1,493 ft.), and provides stunning views of the town and the mountains to the south. Some of the scenes from *The Sound of Music* were shot at the adjacent Stift Nonnberg, a Benedictine nunnery founded in about 700.

**MÖNCHSBERG** To the west of the Hohensalzburg Fortress, this 3-km (2-mile) mountain ridge cradles the Old Town at a height of 542m (1,778 ft.), and provides walking trails with equally stunning views. The fortifications are from the 15th through the 17th centuries.

**RIGHT BANK** The newer part of town is on the right bank of the Salzach, below Kapuzinerberg, the right-bank counterpart of Mönchsberg. This peak rises 637m (2,090 ft.) and offers a lovely woodland area for long walks.

## Exploring Salzburg

The Old Town lies between the left bank of the Salzach River and the ridge known as the Mönchsberg, which rises to a height of 503m (1,650

The Salzburg cityscape.

ft.) and is the site of Salzburg's casino. The main street of the Old Town is Getreidegasse, a narrow thoroughfare lined with five- and six-story burghers' buildings. Most of the houses along the street date from the 17th and 18th centuries. Mozart was born at no. 9.

## LEFT BANK (OLD TOWN)

**Festung Hohensalzburg ★★★** MUSEUM Crowning the Festungsberg and dominating the town of Salzburg, this is the largest completely preserved castle left in central Europe. Besides being the means of defense, the prince-archbishops resided and ruled from here before they moved to the Residenz "downtown." It took 600 years to build the castle, and a visit here reveals the varying tastes and purposes of the builders. The elegant state apartments, once the dwellings of the prince-archbishops and their courts, are on display. Note the coffered ceilings and intricate ironwork, and check out the early-16th-century porcelain stove in the Golden Room. The Burgmuseum has a vast collection of medieval art, as well as plans and prints tracing the growth of Salzburg. From the Reck watchtower there's a panoramic sweep of the Alps and from the Kuenberg bastion, the domes and towers of Salzburg. It's enough to make you wonder why they moved into town! To get here, visitors can hike up one of the paths that lead to the fortress, or they can walk from Kapitelplatz by way of Festungsgasse, or from the Mönchsberg via the Schartentor. There is also a funicular from Festungsgasse, at the station behind the cathedral.

Mönchsberg 34. www.salzburg-burgen.at/en/hohensalzburg. ✆ **0662/8424-3011.** €11 adults, €6.50 children 6–14, family ticket €26. Bus: 3, 5, 6, 7, 8, 20, 25, 28, 840 to Mozartsteg, then the funicular from Festungsgasse. Fortress and museums Jan–Apr, Oct–Dec daily 9:30am–5pm; May–Sept daily 9am–7pm.

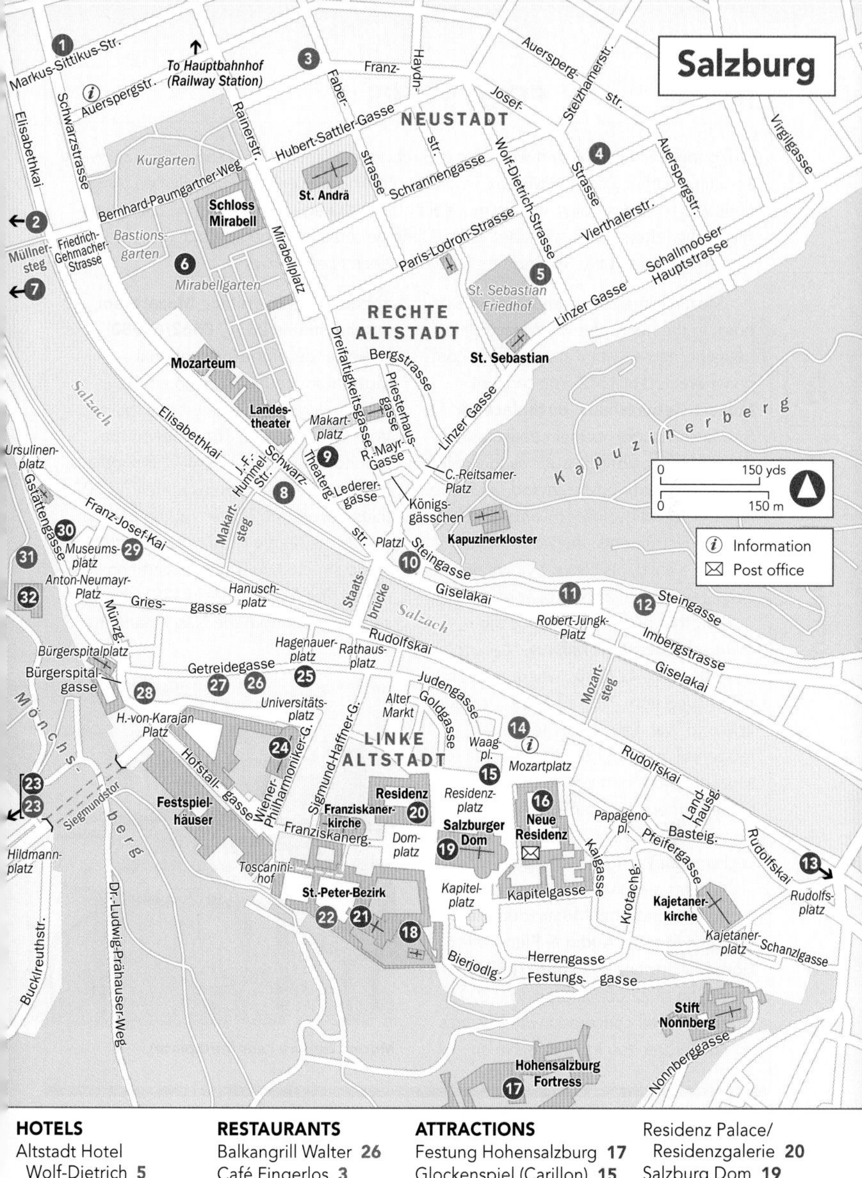


**HOTELS**

Altstadt Hotel Wolf-Dietrich **5**
Arthotel Blaue Gans **28**
Hotel Auersperg **4**
Hotel Goldener Hirsch **27**
Hotel Sacher Salzburg **8**
Hotel Schloss Mönchstein **7**
Hotel Stein **10**
Hotel Villa Carlton **1**

**RESTAURANTS**

Balkangrill Walter **26**
Café Fingerlos **3**
Esszimmer **2**
Flavour **11**
Glüxfall **29**
Ikarus im Hangar-7 **23**
K&K Waagplatz **14**
Kunstgasthaus Blaue Gans **28**
M32 **31**
Maiers **12**
St. Peter Stiftskeller **22**

**ATTRACTIONS**

Festung Hohensalzburg **17**
Glockenspiel (Carillon) **15**
Hangar-7 Flugzeug-museum **23**
Haus der Natur **30**
Kollegienkirche **24**
Mirabell **6**
Mozarts Geburtshaus **25**
Mozart-Wohnhaus **9**
Museum der Moderne **32**
Petersfriedhof **18**
Residenz Palace/ Residenzgalerie **20**
Salzburg Dom **19**
Salzburg Museum Neue Residenz **16**
Schloss Hellbrunn **13**
Stiftskirche St. Peter **21**
Toy Museum **15**

## IN mozart's FOOTSTEPS

Wolfgang Amadeus Mozart was born in Salzburg on January 27, 1756, son of an overly ambitious father, Leopold Mozart, whose controlling power he eventually fled. Amadeus was a child prodigy, writing musical notes at the age of 4, before he could even shape the letters of the alphabet. By the time he'd reached the ripe old age of 6, he was performing at the Schönbrunn Palace in Vienna before royalty.

Mozart's image is everywhere in Salzburg. In the heart of town, Mozartplatz bears his name, with a statue of the composer erected in 1842. You can visit **Mozart Geburtshaus (Birthplace) ★** (see facing page); its main treasures are the valuable paintings (such as the well-known oil painting *Mozart and the Piano,* left unfinished by Joseph Lange) and original instruments: the violin Mozart used as a child, his concert violin, and his viola, fortepiano, and clavichord.

Another pilgrimage stop is the restored **Mozart Wohnhaus,** Makartplatz 8 (✆ **0662/87422740**), where the composer lived from 1773 to 1780. Damaged in World War II air raids, the house reopened in 1996, honoring the year of Mozart's 240th birthday. In the rooms of these former apartments, a museum documents the history of the house, life, and work of Wolfgang Amadeus Mozart.

Mozart aficionados will want to take in the **International Mozarteum Foundation's Mozart Audio & Film Collection,** Makartplatz 8 (✆ **0662/883454**), a collection of 22,000 audio and 2,600 video titles, all concerned with Mozart's compositions. You have to make an appointment to visit the **Mozarteum,** Schwarzstrasse 26 (✆ **0662/61980**). This is the center of the International Mozarteum Foundation, an edifice in Munich Jugendstil architecture, built from 1910 to 1914. The jewel on the second floor is the library—a *Bibliotheca Mozartiana*—with approximately 12,000 titles devoted to Mozart. In the garden stands the Magic Flute House, a little wood structure in which Mozart composed *The Magic Flute* in 1791. It was shipped here from the Naschmarkt in Vienna.

**Mozart Geburtshaus (birthplace).**

**Glockenspiel (Carillon) ★** LANDMARK The celebrated glockenspiel with its 35 bells stands across from the Residenz. The 18th-century carillon tolls at 7 and 11am, and 6pm. Guided tours of the Glockenspiel tower for small groups are held in the spring and through fall, on Thursdays at 5:30pm, and Fridays at 10:30am. However, the ideal way to hear the chimes is from one of the cafes lining the edges of the Mozartplatz while sipping your favorite coffee or drink.
Mozartplatz 1. ✆ **0662/0808-0.** Bus: 1.

**Haus der Natur ★★★** MUSEUM This natural history and science museum is so impressive in size and scope, it seems to belong to a much

Festung Hohensalzburg.



bigger city. Spanning five floors, the "House of Nature" has elaborate dioramas and detailed exhibits on the wildlife and natural phenomena of the alpine region, and a live reptile zoo and aquarium. There are extensive collections of geological findings from all over the world, including giant alpine crystals. The museum devotes half a floor to Christian Andreas Doppler, a Salzburg mathematician and physicist famous for discovering the shift in frequency known as the Doppler effect. The other half of the building has three floors called the "Science Lab," where children and adults can experiment with mechanics, aerodynamics, robotics, and the human body. It's all very hands-on and lots of fun for all ages.
Museumsplatz 5. www.hausdernatur.at. ✆ **0662-842653.** €8 adults, €5.50 ages 4–15, €7.50 seniors. Bus: Any bus to Ferdinand Hanusch Platz. Daily 9am–5pm.

**Kollegienkirche** ★ RELIGIOUS SITE Fronting an open-air marketplace, Collegiate Church was built for the Benedictine university between 1694 and 1707, and was designed by the great baroque architect Fischer von Erlach. This, von Erlach's greatest and largest Salzburg church, is one of the most celebrated baroque churches in all of Austria.
Universitätsplatz. ✆ **0662/8445760.** Free. Bus: 2. Daily 9am–6pm.

**Mozarts Geburtshaus** ★ MUSEUM Even if you're not a Mozart fanatic, his birthplace, on the busy pedestrian shopping street Getreidegasse, is worth a visit. At this museum, you'll see his adorable childhood violin, his clavichord, and rooms decorated to reflect a bourgeois apartment of the time. The rooms are themed around Mozart's relationship to the University of Salzburg, local families, and the church. Upstairs are dioramas and miniature stages that provide an introduction to the Mozart family and tell the story of Mozart's life in the theater.
Getreidegasse 9. www.mozarteum.at/museen/mozarts-geburtshaus. ✆ **0662-844313.** Adults €10, ages 6–14 €3,50, ages 15–18 €4. Bus: 1, 4, 7, 8, or any bus to Ferdinand Hanusch Platz. Daily 9am–5:30pm, July–Aug 9am–8pm.

**Museum der Moderne ★★★** MUSEUM This bastion of contemporary art is built on the side of Mönchsberg, overlooking the city—visitors travel here via an elevator. Atop the mountain, an urban vista and the surrounding natural beauty underline the inherent raison d'etre of contemporary art: To get you out of your comfort zone. The design alone makes this one of the most exceptional museums of Austria. Inside a geometric stone-block structure, large exhibitions of international modern artists rotate in the spacious and beautifully lit galleries. Happily, recent acquisitions have broadened the institution's scope beyond Western art.

Atop the Mönchsberglift, Mönchsberg 32. www.museumdermoderne.at. ✆ **+43-662/842220403.** Adults €8, children 6–18 and students €6. Bus: 1. Tues, Thurs–Sun 10am–6pm, Wed 10am–8pm.

**Petersfriedhof ★★** LANDMARK St. Peter's Cemetery lies at the stone wall that merges into the bottom of the rock called the Mönchsberg. Many of the aristocratic families of Salzburg lie buried here alongside many other noted persons, including Nannerl Mozart, sister of Wolfgang Amadeus (4 years older than her better-known brother, Nannerl was also an exceptionally gifted musician). You can also see the Romanesque Chapel of the Holy Cross and St. Margaret's Chapel, dating from the 15th century. You can also take a self-guided tour through the early Christian catacombs in the rock above the church cemetery.

Sankt-Peter-Bezirk 1. ✆ **0662/8445760.** Cemetery free. Catacombs €1 adults, €0.60 children ages 6–15. Bus: 1. May–Sept daily 10:30am–5pm; Oct–Apr daily 10:30am–3:30pm.

**Residenz Palace/Residenzgalerie ★★** MUSEUM This lavish palace at the center of the old town was the "downtown" home of the Salzburg prince-archbishops after they no longer needed the protection of cheerless Hohensalzburg Fortress. The Residenz dates from 1120, but the baroque rebuilding was ordered by Archbishop Wolfgang (usually called "Wolf") Dietrich at the end of the 16th century. The Residenz fountain, from the 17th century, is one of the largest and most impressive baroque fountains north of the Alps. If these walls could speak, they'd tell of young Mozart, who often played here, and Emperor Franz Josef, who received Napoléon III here in 1867. More than a dozen state rooms, each richly decorated, are open to the public, including the Residenzgalerie Salzburg, which contains European paintings from the 16th to the 19th century.

Residenzplatz 1. www.salzburg-burgen.at/en/residenz. ✆ **0662/8042-2690.** Adults €9.50, children 6–14 €3.50. Bus: 1, 2, 3, 5, 6 to Rathaus or Ferdinand-Hanusch-Platz. Wed–Mon 10am–5pm.

**Salzburg Dom ★★** RELIGIOUS SITE Hailed by some critics as the "most perfect" Renaissance building in the Germanic countries, this cathedral boasts a marble facade and twin symmetrical towers. The interior,

Salzburg Dom.

with its rich baroque style and elaborate frescoes, is *almost* as famous as the cathedral's 4,000 pipe organ. The original 774 building was superseded by a late-Romanesque structure erected from 1181 to 1200. Archbishop Markus Sittikus Count Hohenems commissioned the Italian architect Santino Solari to build the present cathedral, which was consecrated in 1628. Inside you can see the Romanesque font at which Mozart was baptized.

The treasure of the cathedral, and the "arts and wonders" the archbishops collected in the 17th century, are displayed in the **Dom Museum,** entered through the cathedral. The **cathedral excavations** are entered around the corner (left of the Dom entrance). This exhibition of excavation work shows ruins of the original foundation.

Domplatz. ✆ **0662/8047-7950.** Cathedral free; excavations €2.50 adults, €1 children 6–15, free for children 5 and under; museum €10 adults, €4 students, free for under 6. Bus: 1. May–Sept Mon–Sat 8am–7pm Mar–Apr, Oct, Dec Mon–Sat 8am–6pm; Jan–Feb, Nov Mon–Sat 8am–5pm. Sun from 1pm year-round.

Carriage horses in front of the Neue Residenz.

**Salzburg Museum Neue Residenz ★★** MUSEUM In a city of ancient alleys and passageways, this imposing "New Residence" isn't all that new. It was built at the end of the 16th century for the archbishops of Salzburg, who were some of the richest people in the Holy Roman Empire. Much of the museum is based on Salzburg's history, which has been quite colorful, as the region changed hands and nations a number of times over the past four centuries. The tower contains Salzburg's famous 35-bell glockenspiel. Archaeological finds are among the highlights—especially Roman ruins with painting still intact and everyday objects of a Roman dwelling two millennia old. The third floor is dedicated to the myths surrounding the city, and the changing exhibits on the ground and second floors always have some connection to Salzburg's history.

Mozartplatz 1. www.salzburgmuseum.at. ✆ **0662/6208-08700.** Adults €7, ages 16–26 €3, ages 4–15 €3. Bus: 1, 22. Tues–Sun 9am–5pm.

**Stiftskirche St. Peter ★★** RELIGIOUS SITE Founded in A.D. 696 by St. Rupert, whose tomb is here, this is the church of St. Peter's Abbey and Benedictine Monastery. Once a Romanesque basilica, the church was completely overhauled in the 17th and 18th centuries in an elegant baroque style. The west door dates from 1240. The church is richly adorned with art treasures, including altar paintings by Kremser Schmidt. The Salzburg Madonna, in the left chancel, is from the early 15th century.

St.-Peter-Bezirk 1. ✆ **0662/844576.** Free. Bus: 5. Daily 9am–noon.

**Toy Museum ★★** MUSEUM One of the various mini-museums inside the Salzburg Museum, the small and charming Toy Museum runs on a joint ticket with the Museum of Historic Musical Instruments. This is Austria's largest collection of historical European toys, starting with antique dolls and dollhouses, puzzles, optical toys, tin and pewter figures, and whizzing railway sets. Of course there are also soft and furry toys, including an extensive collection of teddy bears. There's a Punch and Judy show every Wednesday at 3 and 3:30pm (€4), except in summer.

Bürgerspitalgasse 2. www.salzburgmuseum.at. ✆ **0662/620808-300.** Adults €4, ages 16–26 €2, ages 4–15 €1.50. Bus: 22. Tues–Sun 9am–5pm.

### RIGHT BANK & OUTSKIRTS OF SALZBURG

**Hangar-7 Flugzeugmuseum ★★** MUSEUM Didi Mateschitz has placed the nucleus of his Red Bull empire in Salzburg, and Hangar-7 at the Salzburg Airport is where his "Flying Bulls" keep their flock of historic aircraft. This architecturally stunning museum resembles a giant wing cross-section encased in glass. In addition to the planes, the Hangar houses Red Bull Formula One racecars, helicopters, motorcycles, and regularly changing art installations. When it isn't out on tour, lucky visitors can catch the Stratos capsule that took Felix Baumgartner to the edges of space for the ultimate skydive in 2013. There are also frequent airshows at Hangar-7, where the Flying Bulls do mind-blowing stunts. For those feeling decadent, the Restaurant **Ikarus ★★★** is a supreme adventure in culinary arts—chefs rotate monthly, working with an in-house team guided by star German chef Eckart Witzigmann (see listing p. 543).

7A Wilhelm-Spazier Strasse. www.hangar-7.com. ✆ **0662-2197.** Free. Bus: 2. Daily 9am–10pm.

**Mirabell ★** HISTORIC SITE/GARDENS On the right bank of the river, the baroque **Mirabell Gardens,** off Makartplatz, laid out by Fischer von Erlach, are the finest in Salzburg. Now a public park, they're studded with statues and reflecting pools. For the best view of the gardens and also of Salzburg, pause at the top of the steps where Julie Andrews and her seven charges showed off their singing in *The Sound of Music*. Be sure to visit Zwerglgarten, a fantasy grove of marble baroque dwarfs and other figures, located by the Pegasus Fountains in the lavish garden west of **Schloss Mirabell.** This palace and its gardens were once a luxurious private residence called Altenau. Prince-Archbishop Wolf Dietrich had it constructed in 1606 for his mistress and the mother of his children, Salome Alt. Unfortunately, not much remains of the original grand structure.

Mirabell. ✆ **0662/8072-2334.** Free. Bus: 1. Palace, Mon, Wed, Thurs 8am–4pm, Tues and Fri 1–4pm. Gardens daily 7am–8pm. In summer, free brass band concerts Wed at 8:30pm and Sun at 10:30am.

**Schloss Hellbrunn ★** HISTORIC SITE A popular spot for outings from Salzburg, this palace dates from the early 17th century and was built as a hunting lodge and summer residence for Prince-Archbishop

**Mirabell palace and gardens.**

Markus Sittikus. The rooms of the palace are furnished and decorated in 18th-century style. See, in particular, the banquet hall with its *trompe l'oeil* painting. There's also a domed octagonal room that was used as a music and reception hall.

The Zoo Hellbrunn, also here, was formerly the palace deer park. The palace **gardens ★,** one of the oldest baroque formal gardens in all Europe, are known for their trick fountains. As you walk through, take care—you might be showered from a surprise source, such as a set of antlers. Set to organ music, some 265 figures in a mechanical theater are set in motion hydraulically. On the grounds, a natural gorge forms the **Stone Theater,** where the first opera in the German-speaking world was presented in 1617. This attraction (signposted) is reached on foot, about a 20-minute walk from the castle.

Fürstenweg 37. www.hellbrunn.at. ✆ **0662/8203720.** €11 adults, €7 students, €5 children. Bus: 25. Tours given daily, July–Aug 9am–9pm; May–June and Sept 9am–5:30pm; Mar–Apr and Oct–Nov 9am–4:30pm.

## Organized Tours

The best organized tours are offered by **Salzburg Panorama Tours,** Mirabellplatz (www.panoramatours.at; ✆ **0662/8832110**), which is the Gray Line company for Salzburg. Their ***Sound of Music* Tour** combines the Salzburg city tour with an excursion to the lake district and other places where the 1965 film was shot. The English-speaking guide shows you not only the highlights from the film, but also historical and architectural landmarks in Salzburg and the Salzkammergut countryside.

You must take your passport along for any of the three trips into Bavaria in Germany. One of these—the **Eagle's Nest Tour**—takes visitors to Berchtesgaden and on to Obersalzburg, where Hitler and his inner circle had a country retreat. The **City & Country Highlights** tour takes in historic castles and the surrounding Land Salzburg landscape.

## Especially for Kids

Salzburg has lots of attractions to appeal to little ones, included the aforementioned **Glockenspiel ★, Hohensalzburg Fortress,** and **Mönchsberg.** At Schloss Hellbrunn (see above). **Zoo Hellbrunn ★** (www.hellbrunn.at; ✆ **0662/820176;** €10 adults, €7 ages 15–19, €4 kids 4–14) provides a wonderful setting for viewing diverse animals such as chamois, otter, white rhinoceros, and antelope. Kids will also enjoy the **Salzburger Marionetten Theater** (see p. 544).

## Where to Stay

Some of the best places to stay, particularly the castle hotels, converted farmhouse pensions, and boardinghouses, lie on the outskirts of Salzburg, within an easy drive of the city. But if you don't have a car, you'll probably want to stay in the city, within walking distance of all the major attractions.

Many hotels in the Old City must be reached on foot because of the pedestrian-only streets, but taxis can drop you at their door. And while most everything you'll want to see in Salzburg lies on the Left Bank, there are many quality hotels on the character-filled streets of the Right Bank, just a stone's throw from the Old City.

## RIGHT BANK

### Expensive

**Hotel Sacher Salzburg ★★★** This elegant choice is owned by the Gürtler family, owners of the Hotel Sacher in Vienna. Private and public spaces here have big windows with panoramic views. Rooms are cheerful and comfortable, with excellent beds and luxurious furniture, seamlessly combining modern and antique styles. Most doubles are large, with spiffy marble bathrooms and separate tubs and showers. Suites are very roomy and polished, with understated color schemes and lots of light. The modest spa offers a sauna, steam bath, and small fitness area, as well as massage service. There is food and drink at every turn: Both the Wintergarden, a banquet room, and the Roter Salon, an opulent dining room facing the river, are great for imbibing. The Zirbelzimmer is a Gault Millau award-winning restaurant. There are also two riverside terraces offering everything from a snack to a steak, and the aforementioned Café Sacher, which is a traditional Austrian cafe. If all that wasn't enough, there's also the Sacher pastry shop, which sells the famous Original Sachertorte.

Schwarzstrasse 5-7. www.sacher.com. ✆ **0662/889770.** Doubles €190–€427, suites €439–€1,023. Bus: 1 or 5. **Amenities:** 3 restaurants; bar; cafe; lounge; gym; room service; sauna; steam room; massages; babysitting; free Wi-Fi.

### Moderate

**Altstadt Hotel Wolf-Dietrich ★★** Two 19th-century townhouses were joined together to make this select little residence. The lobby and ground-floor reception area have a friendly and swank atmosphere, with bright, classical furnishings. The smallish rooms are appealing: cozy and comfortably furnished. The minute spa area includes a sauna, steam room, and massage rooms. This is one of Salzburg's few small hotels with an indoor pool, with walls adorned with mirrors and somewhat unusual murals of Neptune chasing a sea nymph. It's a great choice for families, or couples looking for a romantic getaway that won't break the bank.

Wolf-Dietrich-Strasse 7. www.salzburg-hotel.at. ✆ **0662/871275.** Doubles €125–€230, suites €155–€310. Bus: 1, 2, 51. **Amenities:** Cafe/bar; indoor pool; massages; room service; babysitting; free Wi-Fi.

**Hotel Auersperg ★★** Near the right bank of the Salzach, this family-run hotel is a 5-minute walk from the Old City. It consists of two buildings: a main structure (with ornate molded ceilings and antiques in the common areas) and a less-expensive annex. The inviting rooms are warm, large, and decorated in a tasteful modern style, with large windows, excellent beds, and well-equipped bathrooms. The romantically overgrown garden has tables and chairs for reading, or relaxing at afternoon tea by the gurgling fountain. A rooftop spa offers steam rooms, sauna sessions, and massage treatments, as well as yoga classes. There are nice views of town from this vantage.

Auerspergstrasse 61. www.auersperg.at. ✆ **0662/889440.** Doubles €165–€225, suites €235–€310. Bus: 2 to Stelzhamerstrasse. **Amenities:** Cafe/bar; spa; sauna, garden; bike rental; free Wi-Fi.

**Hotel Stein ★★★** This designer property lies directly on the water, with a panoramic view of the Old Town. Within an 18th-century, six-story building, the Stein was refitted with a contemporary look. The bedrooms, ranging from handsomely furnished doubles to luxurious suites, are well appointed, with state-of-the-art marble bathrooms and extra-large beds. Suites have leather bedspreads and upholsteries, and zebra-skin patterns on some of the fabrics—meow! Other rooms are outfitted in either a "Mozart" motif (that is, vaguely rococo patterns) or the "Stein" design (conservatively modern). The rooftop cafe has accurately been called divine. After a restful sleep, guests are served a breakfast buffet in an atmospheric dining salon.

Giselakai 3. www.hotelstein.at. ✆ **0662/8743460.** Doubles €87–€169, suites €217–€247, rates include breakfast. Bus: 3, 5, or 6. **Amenities:** Bar; room service; free Wi-Fi.

### Inexpensive

**Hotel Villa Carlton ★★** This boutique hotel is exceptional. In a beautiful house right by the Mirabell, Hotel Villa Carlton boasts a funky modern interior and an adorable garden terrace. Each room is unique in layout and style, with elegant, traditional, and pop art options for the decor. The thread that unites them all is the smart bathrooms, nice touches like iPod docking stations, and plenty of sunshine. Superior rooms have a balcony or a lounge area with bay window, and the suites are very spacious. The price is almost unbeatable for the location and design, although it's reflected in the absent minibar and extra cost for buffet. Going for quirky? Book the pop art room with the tub right next to the bed.

Markus-Sittikus-Strasse 3. www.villa-carlton.at. ✆ **0662/882191.** Doubles €91–€181, suites €121–€270. Bus: 1, 2, 3, 5, 6, 25 to Kongresshaus. **Amenities:** Bar/cafe; terrace; free Wi-Fi.

## LEFT BANK (OLD TOWN)

### Expensive

**Hotel Goldener Hirsch ★** This time-honored house has kept its stellar reputation by maintaining a standard of perfect service. Even other hotels' staffs agree the Goldener Hirsch boasts the most able and accommodating team in town. Each room exudes an Alpine-country-house feel, from the carved wood headboards and mounted antlers to the cozy upholstered armchairs. Thankfully, modern luxuries are present in the bathrooms, like the heated mirrors and walk-in showers in some of the rooms. The public spaces have a luxury-hunting-lodge feel. There are two restaurants; we prefer the cozier and more affordable s'Herzl tavern.

Getreidegasse 37. www.goldenerhirsch.com. ✆ **0662/80840.** Doubles €190–€535, suites €420–€970. Bus: 1 or 2. **Amenities:** 2 restaurants; babysitting; free Wi-Fi.

**Hotel Schloss Mönchstein ★★★** This fairytale manor house—really a castle—stands on top of a hill at the center of Salzburg. The building was constructed as a fortified tower in 1350 and wasn't transformed into a hotel until 1950. Rooms come in varying sizes and styles, but are uniformly elegant and comfortable, with bright pastel colors, paneling and antiques. Some rooms are quite luxurious, with king-size beds, marble bathrooms, and oriental rugs on parquet floors. Suites are some of the most spectacularly decorated rooms in Salzburg. The spa boasts an outdoor garden whirlpool and an infinity pool with a view of the city. Restaurant Schloss Mönchstein serves first-rate Austrian and international dishes at elegant, candlelit tables. The hotel also has various terraces for dining, and prepares a charming picnic basket for lazy afternoon lunches on the extensive and romantic castle grounds. For very special occasions, "The Smallest Restaurant in the World" seats up to four in the castle tower, with panoramic views through the petite windows.
Atop the Mönchsberg, Mönchsberg Park 26. www.monchstein.at. ✆ **0662/8485550.** Doubles €345–€620, suites €595–€1,800, rates include breakfast and spa access. Mönchsberglift from downtown. **Amenities:** 2 restaurants; bar; cafe; room service; massages; babysitting; outdoor pool; spa; free Wi-Fi.

### Moderate

**Arthotel Blaue Gans ★★★** The "Blue Goose" gets the prize for the best contemporary makeover of a Salzburger grande dame. At a prime location in the Old Town on Getreidegasse, this guesthouse is over 650 years old but lives very much in the present. No room is like another, but each is decorated in chic, contemporary style, with dark wood paneling and original art. Bathrooms are separate from toilets and not all have tubs, but each is fitted with two sinks on opposite sides, which give a lavishly spacious feel. The doubles are roomy, with beams protruding from the ceiling. The best suite is the City Flat, with antique doors opening up to a minimalist interior. The hotel's Stadtgasthof is a topnotch restaurant. There's a tempting "Wine Archive," where guests descend to a vaulted cellar with 1,600 wines and tastefully modern bar furnishings. It's open to hotel guests on Fridays and Saturdays. An ample breakfast is included.
Getreidegasse 41-43. www.hotel-blaue-gans-salzburg.at. ✆ **0662/8424910.** Doubles €135–€339, suites €269–€499, rates include breakfast. Bus: 1, 4, 7, 8, 10, 22, 24, 27, 28 to Ferdinand-Hanusch-Platz. **Amenities:** Restaurant; wine bar; massages; terrace; bicycle rental; free Wi-Fi.

## Where to Eat

Two special desserts you'll want to sample while in Salzburg are the famous *Salzburger Nockerln,* a light mixture of stiff egg whites, and *Mozart-Kugeln,* with bittersweet chocolate, hazelnut nougat, and marzipan. You should also try a beer in one of the numerous Salzburg breweries.

Although Salzburg is not a late-night dining town, many restaurants stay open late, often to accommodate concert- or theatergoers. But "late" in this sense rarely means beyond 11pm.

## RIGHT BANK

### Moderate

**Flavour** ★★★ AUSTRIAN/INTERNATIONAL Locals frequent this place for the intimate vibe and hidden-in-plain-sight location. Carved into the Kapuzinerberg, there are no more than 10 tables, which are squeezed into the corners of the cave-like space. The menu concentrates on a small number of elegant and ambitious dishes like fettuccine with veal ragout and Manchego. There's not a pretention in sight here.

Imbergstrasse 21. www.flavour.co.at. ✆ **0662/872176.** Mains €13–€30. Bus: 5. Mon–Fri 4pm–1am, Sat–Sun 5pm–1am.

**Maiers** ★★★ AUSTRIAN/MEDITERRANEAN On the legendary Steingasse, at the foot of the Kapuzinerberg on the Right Bank, you'll find what is often called the "best steak in Salzburg." And that steak is put out by a one-man kitchen at this small (read: tight seating), family-run gem. In service and decor, the place goes for understated elegance, with napkin rings made of string, one wall actually the unadorned wall of the cliff, and a handwritten chalkboard menu. The weekly menu always includes a few beefy classics like tartar, carpaccio, rib-eye, and entrecôte. For non-carnivores, there's usually tagliatelle with scallops, and other light specials. Bread is baked daily, and there's a good selection of Austrian wines. It's like dinner in a friend's living room, only with better food.

Steingasse 61. www.maiers-salzburg.at. ✆ **0662/879379.** Mains €10–€30. Bus: 840 to Mozartsteg (Imbergstrasse). Tues–Sat kitchen 6–10pm or later.

### Inexpensive

**Cafe Fingerlos** ★★ AUSTRIAN, DESSERT Generations meet at this Right Bank cafe for the best cakes in town. Everyone from teenagers to grannies can be found enjoying coffee, beer, a lime tart, or a leisurely nibble from the extensive breakfast menu served on an étagère. The cakes are the stuff of legend, with classics like chestnut and Linzer tortes, joined by tempting updates like an aloe-vera cake and a whole list of options for diabetics and those with allergies.

Franz-Josef-Strasse 9. www.cafe-fingerlos.at. ✆ **0662/874213.** Breakfast €4.20–€13. Bus: 260. Tues–Sun 7:30am–7:30pm.

## LEFT BANK (OLD TOWN)

### Expensive

**Esszimmer** ★★★ AUSTRIAN/FRENCH Sometimes cooking is truly art, and here you can watch it from the dining area through a window to the kitchen, where chef Andreas Kaiblinger makes the magic happen. Fine-dining fans will drool at the offerings at this acclaimed establishment, located on the other side of the Mönchsberg from downtown Salzburg. The chef's menu may start with scallops on onions,

## sweet treats & light bites, SALZBURG-STYLE

**Café Bazar,** Schwarzstrasse 3 (www.cafe-bazar.at; ✆ **0662/874278;** bus: 1 or 5), is deeply entrenched in Salzburg's social life and has been since 1906. Housed in a palatial pink-stucco building, it's located across the river from the main section of the Old Town. You can order salads, sandwiches, and omelets. It's open Monday to Saturday 7:30am to 11pm, Sunday 9 to 6pm.

At the **Café-Konditorei Fürst,** Brodgasse 13, at the corner of Getreidegasse (✆ **0662/843759**) the original ***Mozart-Kugeln*** are sold. The owner invented this sweet in 1890 but forgot to patent the recipe. The treat is often duplicated, but here you can sample it from the authentic and original recipe. Open Monday to Saturday 8am to 9pm, Sunday 9am to 9pm.

Established in 1705, **Café Tomaselli,** Alter Markt 9 (www.tomaselli.at; ✆ **0662/844488;** bus: 2 or 5), opens onto one of the most charming cobblestone squares of the Altstadt. Choose from 40 different kinds of cakes or other items, including omelets, wursts, ice cream, and a wide range of drinks. Everything is homemade. Open Monday to Saturday 7am to 9pm; Sunday 8am to 9pm.

At **Hagenauerstuben,** Universitätsplatz 14 (✆ **0662/842657;** tram: 2, 49, or 95), many visitors never get beyond the street-level bar, where snacks and drinks are served in a 14th-century room with stone floors and a vaulted ceiling. The top-floor dining room serves an array of salads and hors d'oeuvres. Open daily 9am to 1am.



speck, and mushrooms, followed by turbot with calf's head, greaves, and muscles; it's all visually stunning, with intense but familiar tastes. While the meals are offered in tasting menu form, guests are also free to order individual courses. The space is modern, with clean lines and subdued lighting. A major highlight is the glass floor, where diners can watch the Almkanal flowing beneath.

Müllner Hauptstrasse 33. www.esszimmer.com. ✆ **0662/870899.** Mains €26–€29, 5–7 course menus €64–€110. Bus: 260, S-Bahn S3. Tues–Sat noon–2pm, 6:30–9:30pm, daily during festival season.

**M32** ★★ AUSTRIAN/INTERNATIONAL You almost feel like a secret agent taking the elevator up through the Mönchsberg to reach M32, a stylish gourmet eatery and bar with a to-die-for view. Truth is, the place is far from secret thanks to the superb, daily-changing menus. A meal could combine variations of tuna (one seared, one smoked) atop an avocado crème, followed by steamed char with bacon, spinach, and sweet potatoes, all well-presented and tasty.

Mönchsberg 32. www.m32.at. ✆ **0662/841000.** Mains €25–€36, fixed-price menus €58–€75. Bus: 1, or take the Mönchsberg elevator from Anton-Neumayr-Platz. Tues–Sun 9–1am, daily during festival season.

**St. Peter Stiftskeller** ★ AUSTRIAN The oldest restaurant in Europe makes no secret of the lore surrounding it. Faust and Mephistopheles are said to have met here, in the same abbey that brought Christianity to Austria. You'll have to reattach your jaw after glimpsing the breathtaking baroque banquet rooms and their ceiling frescoes. Benedictine monks started this tavern, and in addition to wine from the abbey's own vineyards, the kitchen serves hearty homestyle Austrian cooking like roast pork in gravy with parsley and walnut risotto; veal ragout with mushrooms and cognac mousse; or the classic *Tafelspitz* (boiled beef) with spinach. Vegetarian dishes are also featured. And you can't leave without trying the famed soufflé Salzburger Nockerln for dessert. As a tourist you won't be alone here, but the goulash may be the best in Austria.

St.-Peter-Bezirk 1-4. www.stpeter-stiftskeller.at. ✆ **0662/8412680.** Mains €15–€35, fixed-price menus €33–€79. Bus: 29. Daily 11:30am–11:30pm (kitchen noon–10pm).



### Moderate

**K&K Waagplatz** ★★★ AUSTRIAN When the successful Freysauff merchant family bought the place in 1704, the house became renowned for providing meals to the archbishop (legend has it that an underground passageway to the archbishop's residence still exists). One of the Freysauff's daughters is also said to have been a mistress of Mozart, and the event cellar has seen plenty a party since then. The kitchen lives up to the traditions in every way, serving topnotch Austrian classics like a flawless *Frittatensuppe* (clear beef bouillon with crepe strips), a delicious organic *Tafelspitz* (boiled beef), and a juicy duck breast with potato gnocchi and mashed peas. From the sunny rooms upstairs or the bright ground floor terrace, diners can take in the comings and goings on Waagplatz in front of the Salzburg Museum and the cathedral.

Waagplatz 2. www.kkhotels.com. ✆ **0662/842156.** Mains €12–€29. Bus: 3, 5, or 6. Daily 11:30am–2pm and 6pm–midnight.

**Kunstgasthaus Blaue Gans** ★★ AUSTRIAN/INTERNATIONAL For centuries, patrons have satisfied hunger and quenched thirst within these walls, which date back over 600 years. The restaurant got its current face a century ago, with ceiling paintings of the namesake geese, wood paneling, and wrought-iron lamps. An extensive wine archive downstairs means diners can take their pick from over 1,600 vintages, to accompany dishes like pike-perch wrapped in crispy pancetta with steamed pepper and polenta crème, or goose breast with red cabbage, creamy mashed potatoes, and chestnuts. Service is exceptionally attentive. While the prices are definitely old town Salzburg, it's more reasonable here than some neighbors, and the food is worth every penny.

Getreidegasse 41-43. www.hotel-blaue-gans-salzburg.at/en/food-drinks. ✆ **0662/8424910.** Mains €13–€25. Bus: 1, 4, 7, 8, 10, or any to Ferdinand Hanusch Platz. Mon–Sat noon–1am.

### Inexpensive

**Balkangrill Walter** ★★ SALZBURGIAN/SAUSAGES A taste of down-to-earth Salzburg awaits at the Balkan Grill, where the legendary "Bosna" sausage is king. A tiny passageway on Getreidegasse takes you to a small window in the wall where you'll find four variations of the fabled pork sausage, made with chopped onions, parsley, and a secret spice mixture which definitely includes curry and who knows what else. This kiosk has been around since the '50s and seems to have retained signs from that time, with new additions in English, Russian, Italian, and Japanese. The middle-aged woman who works the window doesn't do special orders, so stick to the script. Even though there's usually a line, the wait is worth it for a bite of a true Salzburg tradition.

Down the passageway, Getreidegasse 33. ✆ **0043662 841483.** All variations €3.30. Bus: 1, 4, 7, 8, 10, or any to Freidrich Hanusch Platz. Mon–Fri 11am–7pm, Sat 11am–5pm, July–Dec also Sun 4–8pm.

**Glüxfall ★★★** AUSTRIAN, MEDITERRANEAN This "Stroke of Luck" is run by renowned Salzburg foodies Klaus and Petra Fleischhacker, along with their son and daughter. There are 40 seats in the chic interior and another 40 in the charming courtyard with shade trees and ivy-covered walls. There's a to-die-for breakfast menu, served to 2pm, with mini, midi, and maxi variations of menus like "sweet and sticky" (two marmalades, blood orange panna cotta, waffles, and cheesecake crème), and "colorful and healthy" (fruit salad, warm muesli, parsley root soup, Bloody Mary salmon toast, and a tramezzino with cream cheese) to jump-start the day. In the evening the menu is smaller, offering soups, antipasti, and savory croissants and crepes. Service is charming and attentive.

Franz-Josef-Kai 11. www.gluexfall.at. ✆ **0662/265017.** Breakfast €5.50–€15, dinner mains €6.80–€14. Bus: 1, 4, 7, 8, 10, or any to Ferdinand Hanusch Platz. Wed–Sat 9–2am, Sun 9am–4pm, open Tues and Sun evening during festival season.

## OUTSKIRTS OF SALZBURG

### Expensive

**Ikarus im Hangar-7 ★★★** INTERNATIONAL The one-of-a-kind offerings at Ikarus in Hangar-7, Red Bull's aeronautic showroom, will have you completely rethinking airport food. The patron of the kitchen is the acclaimed Eckart Witzigmann, Germany's first three-Michelin-starred chef, who travels the world in search of guest chefs. Every month a different international culinary superstar is flown in to lead Witzigmann's team. Wealthy foodies come from all over Europe in private jets to "park" and dine in luxury above the Red Bull racecars, propeller planes, and Felix Baumgartner's ultimate-skydive Stratos capsule. Each chef serves three different menus, alongside the Ikarus team's own creations. A menu could include dishes like pommes soufflé, sepia risotto, warm foie gras with Périgord truffle, or pigeon with beet and berries. It's an experience, to put it mildly, to feast on the innovations offered beneath the showroom's futuristic glass canopy.

7A Wilhelm-Spazier Strasse. www.hangar-7.com/de/ikarus/restaurant-ikarus. ✆ **0662/2197.** Mains €32–€50, fixed-price menus €95–€135. Bus: 2. Daily noon–2pm and 6:30–10pm.

## Shopping

Although Salzburg doesn't have Vienna's wide range of merchandise, there's still plenty of shopping here. Good buys in Salzburg include souvenirs of Land Salzburg (dirndls, lederhosen, and petit point) and all types of sports gear. **Getreidegasse** is a main shopping thoroughfare, but you'll also find some intriguing little shops on **Residenzplatz.**

Most stores are open Monday through Friday from 9am to 6pm, but note that many stores, especially smaller shops, take a 1- or 2-hour break for lunch. On weekends, stores are generally open only Saturday mornings.



## Entertainment & Nightlife

It's said that there's a musical event—often a Mozart concert—staged virtually every night in Salzburg. To find out what's playing, visit the **Salzburg tourist office,** Mozartplatz 5 (www.2.salzburg.info; ✆ **0662/889870**), or get a free copy of ***Offizieller Wochenspiegel,*** a monthly pamphlet listing all major and many minor local cultural events;

Christmas Eve in Salzburg is unforgettable. Traditionally, in the little chapel of Oberndorf, north of Salzburg, "Silent Night" is performed. Franz Gruber wrote the melody to that song here when he was an organist in the early 19th century.

The **Salzburger Landestheater** (Schwarzstrasse 22; www.salzburger-landestheater.at; ✆ **0662/8715120**) stages a regular repertoire of operas (not just Mozart) and operettas if you're in Salzburg from September to mid-June. The **Salzburger Marionetten Theater** (Schwarzstrasse 24; www.marionetten.at; ✆ **0662/8724060**) presents shows from Easter to September, as well at Christmas and during Mozart Week, the last week of January. The puppets perform both opera and ballet, to the delight of adults and children alike.

The **Augustiner Bräustübl** ★ (Lindhofstrasse 7; www.augustinerbier.at; ✆ **0662/431246**) is nothing less than Austria's largest beer hall, filling a massive space with vaulted ceilings, wood paneling, and 1,500 extra seats in the outdoor garden come summer. Beer has been brewed here since 1621, and the house seeps traditions from every crevice. Along what looks like a traditional market hall are food and snack stalls. Feel free to bring your own food, though, as it's much less expensive and explicitly allowed. Credit and debit cards are not accepted.

## Side Trips from Salzburg

The environs of Salzburg are wonderfully scenic. The area is a setting of old castles, charming villages, glacial lakes, salt mines, ice caves, and some of the most panoramic alpine scenery in Europe. These attractions are right on the city's doorstep, but you may want a car to reach them.

### HALLEIN & THE DÜRRNBERG SALT MINES ★

The second-largest town in Land Salzburg, Hallein, once a center for processing the salt from the mines of Dürrnberg, was a prize possession of the prince-archbishops of Salzburg. Today you pass through this industrial town on the Salzach River on the way to the Dürrnberg mines.

The **Dürrnberg salt mines** (**Salzbergwerk Hallein;** www.salzwelten.at; ✆ **06245/835110**) are the big draw. This popular attraction is easily visited on a day trip from Salzburg. On guided tours, visitors walk downhill from the ticket office to the mine entrance and then board an electric mine train that goes deep into the caverns. From here, tourists go on foot through galleries, changing levels by sliding down polished wooden slides before exiting the mine on the train that brought them in. An underground museum traces the history of salt mining back to ancient times.

To get to the mines, drive to Hallein from Salzburg or take a train there from Salzburg's main railway station (they depart throughout the day at 20-min intervals). From a point just in front of the railway station at Hallein, you'll then board a bus for the 12-minute ride to Dürnnberg. (Buses depart at 55 min. past the hour, all day.)

Tours of the salt mines are conducted from April to October daily 9am to 5pm, November to March daily 10am to 3pm. Admission is €18 for adults, and €9 for students and children 4 to 15. Children under 4 are not admitted.

## THE ICE CAVES OF EISRIESENWELT ★★

Some 48km (30 miles) south of Salzburg by train is the "World of the Ice Giants," the largest known **ice caves** in the world. The caves, opening at some 1,678m (5,505 ft.), stretch for about 42km (26 miles), although only a portion of that length is open to the public. This underground wonderland is lined with amazing ice figures and frozen waterfalls, ending at the spectacular Ice Palace.

Keep in mind that a visit to this spelunking (cave exploring) oddity is recommended only for those who are quite fit and hardy, and is not suggested for elderly travelers or small children. You'll be walking down narrow, slippery passages.

To reach the **Eisriesenwelt** (www.eisriesenwelt.at; ✆ **06468/5248**), begin by heading for the hamlet of Werfen, which is approximately 40km (24 miles) south of Salzburg. Werfen is also the home of **Castle (Schloss) Hohenwerfen** (✆ **06468/7603**), which was founded in the 11th century. One of the most important castles in Land Salzburg, it's visible for miles around. You can get to Werfen by driving along the main A10 highway (the Tauern motorway), or by taking a train from Salzburg's Hauptbahnhof to Werfen station.

From Werfen, drive up a steep and narrow 6km (3½-mile) access road, following the signs to Eisriesenwelt, which leads to a high-altitude parking area. If you don't have a car, there's a local bus service (the Eisriesenwelt Linie; ✆ **06468/5293;** €3.50 per person). Service is provided only between May and October at 8:20, 10:20am, 12:20 and 2:20pm. It's more convenient to pay around €11 to hire any of the local taxis in lieu of waiting for the bus, and hardy hikers sometimes opt to walk the steep incline.

Once you reach the parking area, expect an additional, relatively easy 20-minute mostly shaded uphill hike to reach the cable car which hauls you vertiginously upward to the entrance to the caves. Then you'll face an additional 20-minute climb from the top of the cable car to the entrance to the ice caves.

There's a cafe and restaurant en route, the Dr.-Friedrich-Oedl-Haus, located at 1,568m (5,144 ft.) above sea level. Supervised tours of the inside of the caves generally last 75 minutes, and cost €8.50 for adults, €7.50 for students, and €4.50 for ages 4 to 14. The caves are open only from May to October, with tours beginning each hour on the half-hour between 9am and 3:30pm (until 4:30pm July–Aug). From Werfen, allow about six hours for the entire trip. Dress warmly and wear shoes appropriate for hiking. Even if you don't want to go underground, consider the trek from Salzburg to the mouth of the cave for the scenery.



## [FastFACTS] AUSTRIA

**Business Hours** Most shops are open Monday to Friday from 9am to 6pm and Saturday from 9am to noon, 12:30, or 1pm, depending on the store. On the first Saturday of every month, shops customarily remain open until 4:30 or 5pm. The tradition is called *langer Samstag.*

**Currency** Austria is a member of the European Union and uses the E.U. common currency, the euro (€). See p. 860 for information on money and costs.

**Dentists** For dental problems, call ✆ **01/5122078** in Vienna, where the staff can tell you about availability of dentists in the area. In Salzburg, call ✆ **0662/873466.**

**Doctors** If you suddenly fall ill, your best source of information on finding a doctor is the reception desk of your hotel. A list of physicians can be found in the telephone directory under "Ärzte." If you have a medical emergency at night, call ✆ **141** daily from 7pm to 7am.

**Embassies & Consulates:**

**Australia:** Mattiellistrasse 2-4, Vienna; www.austria.embassy.gov.au; ✆ **01/506740.**

**Canada:** Laurenzenberg 2, Vienna; www.austria.gc.ca; ✆ **01/531-383000.**

**New Zealand:** Mattiellistrasse 2-4/3, Vienna; www.nzembassy.com/austria; ✆ **01/5053021.**

**United Kingdom:** Jauresgasse 12, Vienna; www.gov.uk/government/world/austria; ✆ **01/716130.**

**United States:** Boltzmanngasse 16, Vienna; http://austria.usembassy.gov; ✆ **01/313390.**

**Emergencies** Call ✆ **122** to report a fire, **133** for the police, or **144** for an ambulance.

**Hospitals** The major hospital in Vienna is **Allgemeines Krankenhaus,** Währinger Gürtel 18-20 (✆ **01/40400**). In Salzburg, there's **Unfallkrankenhaus,** on Dr.-Franz-Rehrl-Platz 5 (✆ **0662/65800**).

**Pharmacies** *Apotheken* (pharmacies) are open Monday to Friday from 8am to noon and 2 to 6pm, and Saturday from 8am to noon. At night and on Sunday, you'll find the names of the nearest open shops on a sign outside every Apotheke.

**Post Offices** Post offices in Vienna can be found in the heart of every district. The *Hauptpostamt* (central post office), Fleischmarkt 19 (✆ **01/5138350**), and most general post offices are open 24 hours a day, 7 days a week. The main post office in Salzburg is at Residenzplatz 9 (✆ **0577/677510**).

# SWITZERLAND

by Teresa Fisher

9

Because of a widespread belief that the Swiss keep themselves aloof from the issues and problems confronting the rest of the world, a vacation in Switzerland can often seem a rather odd experience. It occurs among a people with a reputation—whether justified or not—for strongly isolationist attitudes. One hesitates to query them about their viewpoints on political or other serious matters.

An acquaintance of mine once summed up his understanding of that nation in the following analogy: pose a topic of politics to the average European, he said, and their eyes will light up with interest, their arms and hands will flail about, they will forcefully express an opinion. Pose the same question to most Swiss and, in his experience, their eyes will film over with boredom, and they will switch the subject to something trivial. They simply don't want to burden themselves with the cares afflicting other nations or other peoples.



That widespread belief about the Swiss is based, in part, on recent history, according to the same friend. Switzerland, the richest country on earth, with the highest per capita income, has made an almost religious commitment to neutrality. It refused to go to war, on either side, in both World Wars I and II. It has remained, since then, out of the European Community, it circulates its own currency, it failed even to join the United Nations until 2002, and it has evolved in such a different manner from the rest of us that it did not permit women to vote until 1971.

How much truth is there in the reputation of the Swiss as uninterested in what goes on elsewhere? I can't fully answer that question, because my own contact with Switzerland has been solely as a tourist with little opportunity to engage in personal discussions. But regardless of what others may feel, it is at least undeniable that the Swiss offer a superb touristic experience.

In addition to specializing in confidential commercial transactions (without asking questions), Switzerland has offered remarkable vacations to the hordes of foreigners who descend on it each year to go skiing or mountaineering in its breathtaking Alps. Prior to World War II, it was perhaps the most popular touristic destination in Europe, and although it later lost that position to beachfront

PREVIOUS PAGE: **The Glacier Express in the Swiss Alps.**

resorts that could be reached easily by air, it still counts tourism as one of its most important sources of income.

Now where in Switzerland does the non-European visitor go for vacation pleasures? Many of us confine our stays to four cities: Lucerne, Zurich, Geneva, and Zermatt.

From a strictly touristic standpoint, German-speaking Lucerne (only 80,000 residents) is probably your best choice, for its cog-railway to the top of Mt. Pilatus and Mt. Rigi (commanding awesome views of the Alps), for its remarkable 14th-century wooden bridge, its touching monument of the "Dying Lion" (commemorating Swiss guards killed by Parisian activists during the French Revolution), and for its countless concerts and recitals in a music hall designed by the famous Jean Nouvel. Having myself vacationed there in recent years, I can vouch for its ability to calm and relax even the most stressed-out types.

For a very different stay of urban interest, we go to the much-larger Zurich, the financial, banking, and business capital of Switzerland. On its awesome Bahnhofstrasse, the city's main boulevard, we stroll a world-famous array of glitzy stores and offices. Elsewhere, we encounter a city of cultural riches (big theaters and concert halls, countless important museums) and of vast historical importance (here Zwingli led the Protestant Reformation of the 1500s). We take public transportation out onto the city's lake and river, and then into the heights overlooking it, from which one can view the nearby Alps. I have greatly enjoyed my own stays there, and have devoured more Swiss fondues in the city's excellent cafes than I care to remember.

French-speaking, expensive Geneva is the other largest city of Switzerland (bigger than Berne and Basel, and second in size only to Zurich), the home of numerous international government organizations whose sophisticated staffs patronize its many superb restaurants and theaters. The building and assembly hall of the former League of Nations is now the European headquarters of the United Nations, and numerous UN agencies are located here, as is the headquarters of the international Red Cross. It is no wonder that nearly half its population are resident foreign nationals, who enjoy the countless museums, theaters and concert halls in this graceful and elegant place. It makes for an interesting stop in your European tour.

As for tiny Zermatt (less than 6,000 residents), totally devoted to tourism and skiing, it is famous because it is entirely surrounded by the highest mountain peaks in Switzerland (some 15,000 ft. high), including the renowned Matterhorn, which dozens of adventurers have died attempting to climb (don't try it). The altitude is such that you can ski here year around (with some difficulty in summer). Many visitors claim their travels are complete once they have stayed in Zermatt.

And now you'll read what our Frommer expert says about Switzerland. Enjoy it!

***–Arthur Frommer***

# ZURICH



Zurich is Switzerland's largest and most stylish city, majestically located on the northern shore of Zürichsee (Lake Zurich). It is a dynamic, fun-loving metropolis—a classy, classical city with a contemporary edge, preserving its architectural and cultural heritage yet surprising the world with the latest innovations in art and architecture, music, fashion and design.

Over the decades, the Confederation's long tradition of neutrality has attracted money into Zurich from around the world, and so the Swiss business and finance capital is justifiably famed for its unsurpassed banking prowess.

This generated affluence has also diffused throughout the city to create a self-confident, glossy urban environment. Indeed, today's Zurich

Zurich cityscape.

is far removed from the old, dull, stereotypical image of staid bankers and precision timing, of little more than gold bars and chocolate bars . . . after all, this is the city that saw the birth of Dadaism—the very antithesis of conformity.

Throw in a generous handful of world-class art and music venues; some of the most luxurious shopping in Europe; vibrant, avant-garde nightlife which claims Europe's highest number of nightclubs per capita; and the infections joie de vivre of the Zürcher people, and it's no surprise that Switzerland's "little big city" frequently comes out top of the charts as one of Europe's most popular cities for quality of life—large enough to offer world-class facilities yet small enough to retain its intimate Swiss charm.

## Essentials

The Zurich Tourist Service website, **www.zuerich.com**, provides useful brochures, maps and apps plus a free hotel booking service and city tours.

**ARRIVING** **Kloten Airport** (www.zurich-airport.com; ✆ **043/816 22 11**) is Zurich's international airport, and the biggest airport in Switzerland. From here, it costs around CHF70 by taxi to travel to the city center, approximately 11 km (7 miles) south of the airport. You are better off catching a train from the airport railway station, which adjoins the airport. Direct trains to the city's main railway station, Zürich Hauptbahnhof, take less than 15 minutes and cost CHF11/6.60 (first/second class one-way). Trains run every 15 to 30 minutes between 5:02am and 12:41am. Some hotels near the airport offer a free shuttle-bus or pick-up service.

The main **train station, Zürich Hauptbahnhof,** has good links with many European cities. There are frequent high-speed trains from Munich to Zurich (journey time around 4 hr.) and four direct trains daily from Paris (journey time around 4 hr.); plus good connections from Salzburg (5½ hr.) and Vienna (8½ hr.). The best connection to Italy is via Milan (4 hr.). Within Switzerland, it takes just under one hour to Lucerne; just over one hour to Bern; and around three hours to Geneva. Contact **SBB** (**Swiss Federal Railways;** www.sbb.ch; ✆ **0900/300 300**) for schedules. From the Hauptbahnhof, at the heart of city center, it's easy to walk or to hop on a tram or bus to most Zurich hotels (see "Getting Around," facing page).

If **driving** from Geneva, take A1 northeast, via Bern, and on to Zurich; from Basel, follow the A3 eastward, connecting with the A1 into Zurich.

**Buses** from London, Paris, and other cities arrive at the main bus station at the city-center **Sihlquai terminal** in Limmatstrasse via **Eurolines** (www.eurolines.com; ✆ **227/169 120**).

**CITY LAYOUT** Zurich is situated on Lake Zurich in northeast Switzerland, in a broad valley between the wooded slopes of the Zürichberg,

## the ZÜRICHCARD

If you are planning a short visit to Zurich, the ZürichCARD (**www.zuerich.com/en/visit/your-city-travel-pass**) is an excellent value, especially if you're planning on visiting several museums. It provides free travel from the airport to the city and back; free public transport in the city; a free short round trip on Lake Zurich; free travel to the **Üetliberg** ★★ (see p. 562) and back; free entry to most city museums (including the **Landesmuseum** ★★★ [see p. 558] and the **Kunsthaus** ★★★ [see p. 561]); a 50% discount on guided city tours with Zurich Tourism; plus a host of further discounts. A 24-hour pass costs CHF24 (or CHF16 for children); a 72-hour pass costs CH48/32 (adult/child). The ZurichCARD is available from Zurich Airport, the city tourist office, all railway stations in and around Zurich, various Zurich hotels, and city train and tram automated ticket machines.



Käferberg and Üetliberg hills. The city, and the **Altstadt (Old Town)** at its heart, is bisected into two main areas by the River Limmat. The left or West Bank, generally known as the **City Center,** contains the major slice of the Altstadt (Old Town) plus the legendary **Bahnhofstrasse** luxury shopping boulevard (see p. 572) and the **City** business and banking sector. The right or East Bank is characterized by the cobbled pedestrian district of **Niederdorf** which, with its village-like charm, provides a perfect counterpart to the glitzy, glamorous city center.

**GETTING AROUND** Zurich's city center can be easily explored on foot. To discover the suburbs, there's a comprehensive public transport system that will get you around easily.

Zurich's **public transport** system is operated by the Verkehrsbetriebe Zürich (Zurich Public Transport; www.vbz.ch; ✆ **0848/988 988**), and comprises an easy-to-use, ultra-efficient network of buses, boats, trains, and trams.

There's a bus or tram stop roughly every 300 meters in the city center, and you seldom have to wait longer than 5 minutes for a connection during the day. Most routes pass through the main train station (Hauptbahnhof) at the heart of town, and run daily between the hours of 5:30am and 12:30am.

You can buy tickets from automatic vending machines located at every stop. You must have a ticket and validate it in a ticket-puncher at the stop before you board any vehicle. Tickets are regularly controlled, and if you're caught without one, you'll pay a hefty fine. The basic fare on all buses and trams is CHF4.30 for a trip lasting no more than 1 hour. Better value is a Tageskarte (1-day ticket), which costs CHF8.60 and allows you to travel on all city buses and trams for 24 hours. Children up to age 6 can ride for free with a fare-paying adult. Maps of the transport network and timetables are displayed at all bus and tram stations.

**Taxis** are extremely expensive. Expect to pay CHF6 before you've even gotten into the vehicle, plus a further CHF3.80 per kilometer driven. There are several taxi stands where you can catch a cab, including Bürkliplatz by the lake and at the main railway station, or you can order a taxi by phone on ✆ **044/444 4444.**

I don't recommend attempting to see Zurich **by car.** Once you're installed in your hotel, leave the car at a garage. Zurich can get very congested with traffic, parking is scarce and expensive, and the one-way systems are prevalent and sometimes baffling.

**Cycling** is a terrific way of getting around Zurich (except in winter when the cycle-paths can be icy), especially if you're planning on exploring the lake area beyond the city center. Bicycles can be rented at the baggage counter of the main train station (Hauptbahnhof; www.rentabike.ch; ✆ **051/2222904**) for CHF35/27 per day/half-day. Hours are Monday to Friday, 7:30am to 7:45pm; weekends 8am to 7pm. You can also hire **Züri Rollt** bikes for free (with the presentation of a valid ID and a deposit of CHF20; www.schweizrollt.ch) from various locations, including the Landesmuseum (see p. 558), Bellevue, Enge station and outside Globus City department store in Bahnhofstrasse from May to October.



## The Neighborhoods in Brief

**ALTSTADT (OLD TOWN)** The main Altstadt neighborhood clings to the west bank of the Limmat river. It is a picturesque maze of steeply cobbled streets containing some of the city's most beautiful medieval wooden-framed houses, many adorned with cascading geraniums, as well as a mass of tiny restaurants and boutiques. At its heart, on a small hill near the river bank, the tiny, tranquil **Lindenhof** quarter affords one

### "Zu Reich"

There's no denying the Swiss are an affluent nation, and it's in Zurich that the serious money begins. After all, Zurich is Switzerland's financial engine, and boasts the world's fourth-biggest stock exchange. Most major Swiss banks have their headquarters in or around **Paradeplatz** (Parade Square).

The scene of a medieval market until the 19th century, then the main venue for military processions, nowadays Paradeplatz is better known now as a major tram intersection and the location of **Sprüngli** ★★ (see p. 570), the city's ultimate café experience serving the finest cakes, chocolates, and pâtisseries in the land.

It's ironic to think the vaults of gold that power Switzerland's banking capital lie just beneath the square and also in neighboring **Bahnhofstrasse** (see p. 572) where, at street level, the wealthy, fur-clad locals are happy to splash out on extravagant clothes, watches, jewelry and chocolates in some of Europe's most expensive boutiques. No wonder Zurich is sometimes nicknamed "Zu reich" ("too rich").

of the best panoramas of Zurich from Lindenhofplatz—the original site of the Romans who first settled here in 15 B.C.

**CITY** This neighborhood lies to the west of the Altstadt, and is centered on Zurich's grand tree-lined main thoroughfare, **Bahnhofstrasse**—one of the world's most famous shopping streets (see p. 572)—which runs parallel to the river from the main station at **Bahnhofplatz** down to the lake. The main financial and business district spreads out from **Paradeplatz** westward and toward the lake. The northwest of the City district is fringed by the river Sihl, a small tributary of the Limmat. The predominantly residential neighborhood of **Aussersihl** lies beyond.

**ENGE & WOLLISHOFEN** The western shore of Lake Zurich is dominated by grassy parks, lakeside promenades, and turn-of-the-century mansions. In summer months, when everyone flocks to the lake to swim and relax, you'll find this side less crowded than the eastern Seefeld side. Stroll beyond Mythenquai and, before you know it, you'll be out in the countryside.

**NIEDERDORF** The quaint Niederdorf neighborhood, on the right bank of the River Limmat, forms the eastern half of the city's Altstadt, with its historic guildhall buildings lining the river quaysides. Beyond, a hilly maze of cobbled, pedestrianized lanes hide medieval buildings painted in pretty pastel shades, and shaded fountain-splashed squares full of trendy bars, attractive cafes, and quirky shops. Here too is the red-light district and the Grossmünster church (see p. 560), a veritable city landmark with its enormous twin towers. Above the Niederdorf is the **Hochschulen** district with its grandiose architecture and Switzerland's top gallery, the **Kunsthaus** (see p. 561), and the **University** district beyond.

**SEEFELD** South of the Niederdorf, the Seefeld district, with its grand belle Epoque architecture, is one of the most desirable (and pricey) residential districts of town—on the eastern shore of the lake. This neighborhood boasts the **Operahouse** (see p. 573) and plenty of stylish bars and restaurants, but its main draw is undoubtedly the lake and its attractive promenade, which runs along the grassy shoreline to Zürichhorn Park, past lidos, boat hire venues, an open-air cinema, cafes, museums, and ornamental gardens.

**ZÜRI WEST** The once seedy, former industrial quarter of Zurich, northwest of the railway station, has undergone radical change and is now Zurich's fastest-developing business and residential district. Most striking are its numerous architectural projects, with derelict old factories and industrial buildings converted into trendy housing and cultural and entertainment spaces. With a thriving subculture and a multitude of bars, clubs, and restaurants springing up, Züri West has become the main focus of Zurich's hip party scene.

## Exploring Zurich

Zurich is surprisingly easy to explore on foot, as most of the key sights lie within a compact area on either side of the River Limmat. The quays with their promenades and magnificent buildings are delightful for strolling, or for simply sitting at a cafe terrace, watching the world go by. Where the river opens onto the lake, you'll find Zurich's most impressive churches: **Fraumünster** (see below) and **Peterskirche** ★ (see p. 558) on the west bank, and the **Grossmünster** ★★ (see p. 560) on the east bank. Their spires also come in useful for navigation purposes, should you lose your bearings! From here, it's just a short walk to most of the city museums and galleries.

Many of Switzerland's finest museums are located here, including its premier gallery, the **Kunsthaus** ★★★ (see p. 561), and the **Landesmuseum** ★★★ (Swiss National Museum; see p. 558), which traces the fascinating history of the Confederation from pre-history to the present.

Zurich also claims magnificent **Lake Zurich** for recreation; some of Switzerland's finest restaurants; its best nightlife; and its most sophisticated shopping (famed especially for its haute couture, design, watches, jewelry, and chocolate).



### ALTSTADT

**Fraumünster** ★★★ RELIGIOUS SITE This church, with its slender and distinctive turquoise spire, is well worth a visit. It is on the left bank overlooking Münsterhof, a historic old square on the site of a Benedictine abbey. It was founded here in 853 by Emperor Ludwig, the grandson of Charlemagne. His daughter became the first abbess. The present church dates from the 13th and 14th centuries, and the crypt of the old abbey church is preserved in the undercroft.

Fraumünster and its turquoise spire.

The Fraumünster is also celebrated for its elaborate organ. The basilica has three aisles; the nave is in the Gothic style. The real draw, however, is a set of five **stained-glass windows**—each with its own color theme—designed by Marc Chagall. They are best seen in bright morning light.

Münsterhof. www.fraumuenster.ch. ✆ **044/ 211 41 00.** Free. Tram: 4 to City Hall. May–Sept Mon–Sat 9am–noon, daily 2–6pm; Oct and Mar–Apr Mon–Sat 10am–noon, daily 2–5pm; Nov–Feb Mon–Sat 10am–noon, daily 2–4pm.

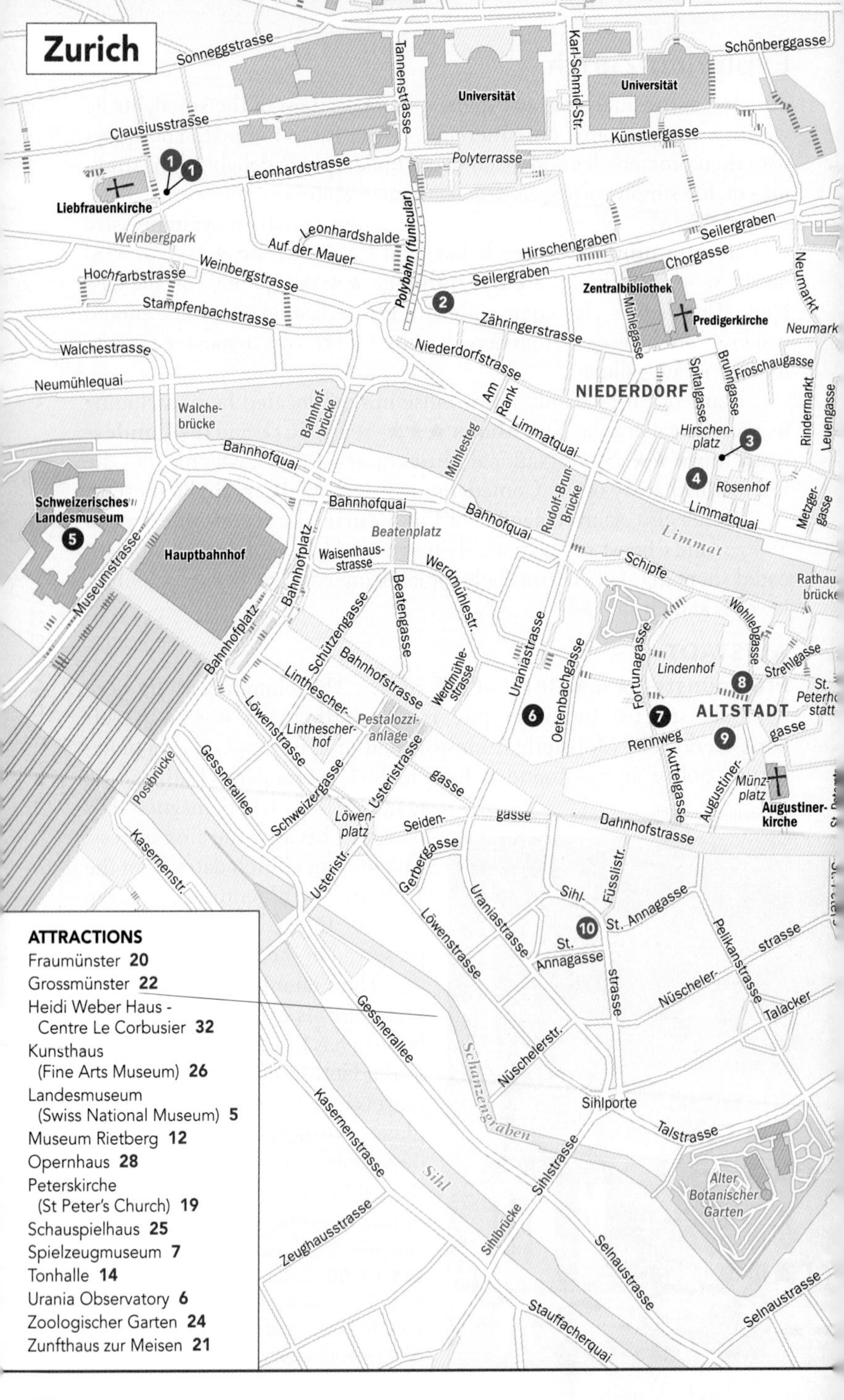
Zurich
Sonneggstrasse
Tannenstrasse
Universität
Karl-Schmid-Str.
Universität
Schönberggasse
Clausiusstrasse
Künstlergasse
Polyterrasse
Leonhardstrasse
Liebfrauenkirche
Weinbergpark
Leonhardshalde
Auf der Mauer
Polybahn (funicular)
Hirschengraben
Seilergraben
Chorgasse
Hochfarbstrasse
Weinbergstrasse
Seilergraben
Zentralbibliothek
Mühlegasse
Predigerkirche
Neumarkt
Stampfenbachstrasse
Zähringerstrasse
Neumarkt
Walchestrasse
Niederdorfstrasse
Spitalgasse
Brunngasse
Froschaugasse
Neumühlequai
Am Rank
NIEDERDORF
Walchebrücke
Bahnhofbrücke
Limmatquai
Hirschenplatz
Rindermarkt
Leuengasse
Mühlesteg
Bahnhofquai
Rudolf-Brun-Brücke
Rosenhof
Schweizerisches Landesmuseum
Bahnhofquai
Limmatquai
Metzgergasse
Bahnhofquai
Beatenplatz
Limmat
Museumstrasse
Hauptbahnhof
Bahnhofplatz
Waisenhausstrasse
Werdmühlestr.
Schipfe
Rathausbrücke
Beatengasse
Wohllebgasse
Schützengasse
Uraniastrasse
Oetenbachgasse
Fortunagasse
Lindenhof
Strehlgasse
Bahnhofplatz
Bahnhofstrasse
Werdmühlestrasse
St. Peterhofstatt
Linthescher-gasse
ALTSTADT
Löwenstrasse
Linthescherhof
Pestalozzianlage
Rennweg
Kuttelgasse
Augustinergasse
Usteristrasse
Münzplatz
Posibrücke
Gessnerallee
Schweizergasse
Augustinerkirche
Löwenplatz
Seidengasse
Bahnhofstrasse
Kasernenstr.
Gerbergasse
Usteristr.
Füsslistr.
Sihlstrasse
Uraniastrasse
St. Annagasse
Löwenstrasse
St. Annagasse
Pelikanstrasse
Nüschelerstrasse
Talacker
Gessnerallee
Schanzengraben
Nüschelerstr.
Sihlporte
Talstrasse
Kasernenstrasse
Sihl
Sihlstrasse
Alter Botanischer Garten
Zeughausstrasse
Sihlbrücke
Selnaustrasse
Selnaustrasse
Stauffacherquai
ATTRACTIONS
Fraumünster 20
Grossmünster 22
Heidi Weber Haus - Centre Le Corbusier 32
Kunsthaus (Fine Arts Museum) 26
Landesmuseum (Swiss National Museum) 5
Museum Rietberg 12
Opernhaus 28
Peterskirche (St Peter's Church) 19
Schauspielhaus 25
Spielzeugmuseum 7
Tonhalle 14
Urania Observatory 6
Zoologischer Garten 24
Zunfthaus zur Meisen 21

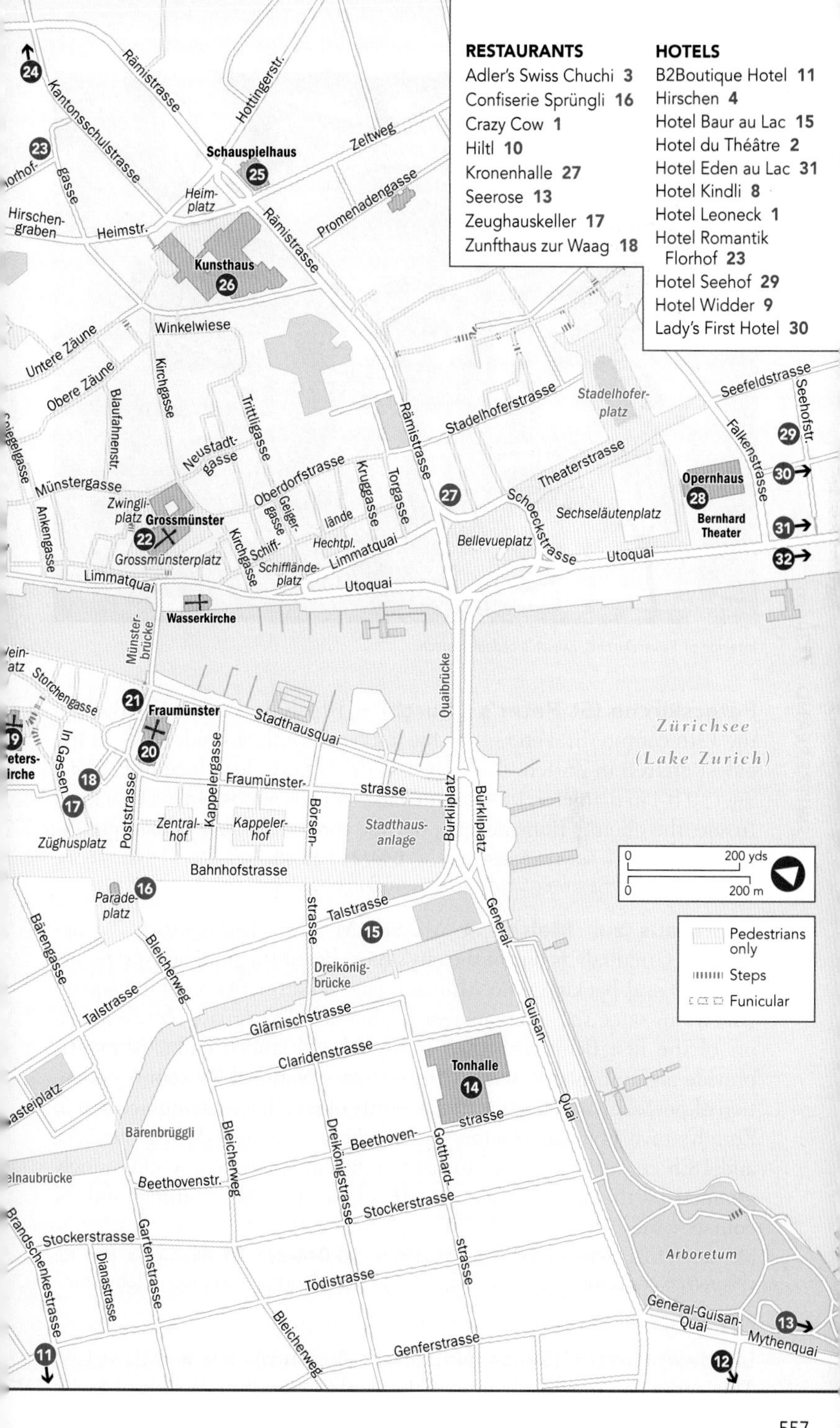
RESTAURANTS
Adler's Swiss Chuchi 3
Confiserie Sprüngli 16
Crazy Cow 1
Hiltl 10
Kronenhalle 27
Seerose 13
Zeughauskeller 17
Zunfthaus zur Waag 18
HOTELS
B2Boutique Hotel 11
Hirschen 4
Hotel Baur au Lac 15
Hotel du Théâtre 2
Hotel Eden au Lac 31
Hotel Kindli 8
Hotel Leoneck 1
Hotel Romantik Florhof 23
Hotel Seehof 29
Hotel Widder 9
Lady's First Hotel 30
Rämistrasse
Hottingerstr.
Kantonsschulstrasse
Schauspielhaus
Zeltweg
Heimplatz
Promenadengasse
Hirschengraben
Heimstr.
Kunsthaus
Winkelwiese
Untere Zäune
Obere Zäune
Kirchgasse
Blaufahnenstr.
Trittligasse
Neustadtgasse
Stadelhoferstrasse
Stadelhoferplatz
Seefeldstrasse
Seehofstr.
Falkenstrasse
Münstergasse
Oberdorfstrasse
Kruggasse
Torgasse
Theaterstrasse
Opernhaus
Schoeckstrasse
Sechseläutenplatz
Bernhard Theater
Zwingliplatz
Grossmünster
Geigergasse
Schifflände
Hechtpl.
Limmatquai
Bellevueplatz
Utoquai
Ankengasse
Grossmünsterplatz
Schiffländeplatz
Wasserkirche
Münsterbrücke
Quaibrücke
Storchengasse
Fraumünster
Stadthausquai
Zürichsee
(Lake Zurich)
In Gassen
Kappelergasse
Fraumünsterstrasse
Bürkliplatz
Zentralhof
Kappelerhof
Börsenstrasse
Stadthausanlage
Züghusplatz
Poststrasse
Bahnhofstrasse
0 200 yds
0 200 m
Paradeplatz
Talstrasse
General-Guisan-Quai
Pedestrians only
Steps
Funicular
Bärengasse
Bleicherweg
Dreikönigbrücke
Glärnischstrasse
Claridenstrasse
Tonhalle
Bärenbrüggli
Beethovenstrasse
Beethovenstr.
Gotthardstrasse
Dreikönigstrasse
Stockerstrasse
Brandschenkestrasse
Gartenstrasse
Dianastrasse
Arboretum
Tödistrasse
Genferstrasse
Mythenquai

Interior of Peterskirche, Zurich's oldest church.

**Peterskirche (St Peter's Church)** ★ RELIGIOUS SITE Built in the 13th century, St. Peter's—on the left bank south of Lindenhof—is the oldest church in Zurich. It also boasts the largest clock face in Europe: 9m (30 ft.) in diameter; the minute hand alone is almost 4m (13 ft.) long. Inside, the choir is Romanesque, but the three-aisle nave is baroque.
St. Peterhofstatt 1. www.st-peter-zh.ch. ✆ **044/211 25 88.** Free. Mon–Fri 8am–6pm; Tram 6, 7, 11, 13 (Rennweg). Sat 10am–4pm; Sun noon–5pm.

**Zunfthaus zur Meisen** ★ MUSEUM The 18th-century "Winegrowers' Guildhall" is one of the city's most beautiful guild houses, facing the river and backing onto Münsterplatz, an attractive cobbled square which was once site of an ancient pig market. The ornate rococo interiors of the first floor, with their rich gold and stucco embellishments, provide an atmospheric setting for the Swiss National Museum's collection of porcelain and faience, the majority of which was manufactured in Zurich's own porcelain factory in Kilchberg-Schooren during the 17th and 18th centuries. Be sure to see the delicate figurines, so charmingly grouped by theme—the seasons, the elements, love, hunting, and, of course, wine.
Münsterhof 20. www.zunfthaus-zur-meisen.ch. ✆ **044/221 21 44.** CHF3; free for children 16 and under. Tram 2, 6, 7, 8, 9, 11, 13 (Paradeplatz). Thurs–Sun 11am–4pm.

### CITY

**Landesmuseum (Swiss National Museum)** ★★★ MUSEUM This sprawling museum contains the world's largest collection of Swiss historical and cultural artifacts, documenting civilization here from prehistory to the modern age. As you enter the museum, one of the first highlights is the gigantic scale model of the Battle of Murten, which most children adore. Beyond, you'll find everything Swiss imaginable from silver to stained glass, and from altarpieces to armor. It's worth getting an iPad tour (available at the entrance with a deposit of a passport or other personal ID) to help you navigate through the high-tech galleries. Highlights include children's toys, Renaissance globes, clock-making, regional costumes, and the characterful collections of artifacts from each of the country's cantons. Don't try to see everything—just pick two or three topics of particular interest, or check out the dynamic temporary exhibitions, and do take a break in the funky museum cafe for a reviving coffee and a scrumptious slice of cake.

Museumstrasse 2. www.musee-suisse.ch. ✆ **044/218 65 11.** CHF10 adults, free for children 16 and under. Tram 4, 11, 13, 14 (Bahnhofquai). Tues, Wed, and Fri–Sun 10am–5pm, Thurs 10am–7pm.

## ENGE & WOLLISHOFEN

**Museum Rietberg** ★★ MUSEUM This is Switzerland's only gallery for non-European cultures, and it's world-renowned for its remarkable collections from Asia, Africa, the Americas, and Oceania—the majority donated to the city by banker and art patron Baron Eduard von der Heydt in 1952. Highlights of the vast collection are housed in Villa Wesendonck (an elegant neoclassical mansion once home to composer Richard Wagner); in the quirky redbrick Park-Villa Rieter; and within a maze of

Interior, Landesmuseum.

underground galleries cleverly built to enlarge the museum without altering its elegant appearance, apart from the addition of a striking "Emerald" glass foyer. Think Native American art, Middle Eastern textiles, Japanese Noh masks, early Buddhist sculptures from China . . . this museum provides a fascinating whistle-stop tour around the cultures of the world.

Gablerstrasse 15. www.rietberg.ch. ✆ **044/415 31 31.** Adults CHF14, free for children 16 and under. Tram 7 (Museum Rietberg). Fri–Tues 10am–5pm, Wed–Thurs 10am–8pm.

## NIEDERDORF

**Grossmünster ★★** RELIGIOUS SITE This Romanesque and Gothic cathedral was, according to legend, founded by Charlemagne, whose horse bowed down on the spot marking the graves of three early Christian martyrs (see box facing page). The edifice has two three-story towers and is situated on a terrace above Limmatquai, on the right bank. Construction began in 1090 and additions were made until the early 14th century.

The choir contains stained-glass windows completed in 1932 by Augusto Giacometti. (Augusto is not to be confused with his more celebrated uncle, Alberto Giacometti, the famous Swiss abstract artist.) In the crypt is a weather-beaten, 15th-century statue of Charlemagne, a copy of which crowns the south tower.

The cathedral was once the parish church of Huldrych Zwingli, one of the great leaders of the Reformation. In accordance with Zwingli's

**The Grossmünster.**

### Headless Saints

The Grossmünster is dedicated to the city's patron saints, Felix, Regula and Exuperantius. In the 3rd century, the three martyrs attempted to convert the citizens of Turicum (the original name for Zurich) to Christianity. According to legend, the governor had them plunged into boiling oil and forced them to drink molten lead. The trio refused to renounce their faith and were beheaded. Miraculously, they still had enough energy to pick up their heads and climb to the top of a hill (the present site of the cathedral), where they dug their own graves and then interred themselves. The seal of Zurich honors these saints, depicting them carrying their heads under their arms. Their remains are said to rest in one of the chapels of the cathedral.

beliefs, Zurich's Grossmünster is austere, stripped of the heavy ornamentation you'll find in the cathedrals of Italy. The view from the towers is impressive.

Grossmünsterplatz. www.grossmuenster.ch. ✆ **044/252-59-49.** Free admission to cathedral; towers 4F. Tram: 4. Cathedral Mar 15–Oct daily 10am–6pm; Nov–Mar 14 daily 10am–5pm. Towers (weather permitting) Mar–Oct daily 10am–5pm; Nov–Feb Sat–Sun 10am–5pm.

**Kunsthaus ★★★** MUSEUM The airy, lofty, glassy galleries of Switzerland's top art museum house art treasures spanning six centuries, from the Middle Ages to the present, but the main focus is on 19th- and 20th-century art, with works by all the greats, including Bonnard, Braque, Cézanne, Chagall, Degas, Mondrian, Monet, and Picasso. There are also some magnificent early Impressionist canvases by lesser-known Swiss artists such as Ferdinand Hodler and Giovanni Segantini, and some key works of Swiss Realism and Zurich Concrete Art. The Kunsthaus also contains the largest collection of works by Edvard Munch outside Scandinavia, and the world's finest collection of works by celebrated Swiss artist, sculptor, and graphic artist Alberto Giacometti. The Kunsthaus is undergoing major redevelopment with the addition of new exhibition spaces and an art garden, so some displays may be closed. If you are interested in a particular collection, call ahead or check the website to make sure it's on view.

Heimplatz 1. www.kunsthaus.ch. ✆ **044/253 84 84.** CHF15 adults (with audioguide), free for kids 16 and under. Tram 3, 5, 8, 9 (Kunsthaus). Tues 10am–6pm, Wed–Fri 10am–8pm, Sat–Sun 10am–6pm.

## SEEFELD

**Heidi Weber Haus—Center Le Corbusier ★** MUSEUM "A house is a machine for living in" once said the renowned Swiss architect and visual artist Le Corbusier. And so he built the Heidi Weber Haus to embody his maxim of ideological formalism, commissioned by the art patron Heidi Weber in the early 1960s but not complete until 2 years after Le Corbusier's death, in 1967.

## ÜETLIBERG—top OF ZURICH

No visit to Zurich would be complete without a trip up the **Üetliberg ★★** (www.uetliberg.ch), dubbed the "top of Zurich" at an elevation of 871m/2,858 ft. In just 20 minutes (catch the S10 Sihltal Zurich-Üetliberg train from the Hauptbahnhof, platform 21 or 22, to Üetliberg station), you can escape from the jet-setting city into the lush meadows, tinkling cowbells, and chocolate-box landscapes which so epitomize Switzerland.

The Üetliberg marks the start of a popular 2-hour hiking route along a forested mountain ridge, with glorious 360-degree views over the city and the lake to the Alps beyond. Simply follow signs to Felsenegg, from where a cable car connects to Adliswil station and trains back to Zurich.

Even if you don't fancy the walk, it's still worth visiting the Üetliberg—there's a restaurant at the top (Gmüetliberg, Hutel Uto Kulm; ✆ **044/463 92 60;** reservations advisable), just 7 minutes' walk from the train station, which serves mouth-watering seasonal fare and Swiss specialties too.



Zurich viewed from the top of the Üetliberg.

Today this extraordinary edifice serves as a quirky museum of his life and works—the culmination of his studies in architecture, interior design, and visual arts. Frustratingly, the interior is seldom open; do go inside if you get the chance. Otherwise, the exterior is also worth admiring if you're strolling by the lake—an eccentric cuboid of brass, concrete, and steel with bold, brightly colored enamel blocks and an oddly elevated, umbrella-like roof, which stands in stark contrast to the gentle parkland of its surrounds.

Höschgasse 8. www.centerlecorbusier.com. ✆ **044/383 64 70.** Bus 912, 916 (Chinagarten). July–Sept Sat–Sun 2–5pm.

## Organized Tours

Forget guided bus tours of Zurich. The best way to discover the city is to get out and about in the fresh air. The Zurich Tourist Service Office offers a number of guided walking tours, as well as tours by bike, Segway, rickshaw, electric-scooter, even paddleboard, so choose your favorite mode of transport and climb aboard.

One of the most appealing **walking tours** in Zurich is a 2-hour guided stroll entitled **Stories of the Old Town,** which costs CHF25 for adults, CHF13 for children. It sets off from the main hall of the Hauptbahnhof at the Tourist Service Office (www.zuerich.com; ✆ **044/215 40 00;** daily Apr–Oct at 3pm, also weekends at 11am; Nov–March Wed, Sat, and Sun at 11am, also Sat at 3pm). For an alternative perspective, the evening **Ghost Walks** (www.ghostwalk.ch) are highly entertaining. They take place Thursdays and Fridays at 8pm, starting at the fountain in Paradeplatz, and cost CH15 per person (not suitable for children under 14).

**Zurich by Bike** offers a weekly **Classic City** tour (www.zurichbybike.ch; CHF25 per person), which explores Züri West as well as the more mainstream sights of the city center, Sundays from May to October, from 10:30am to 1pm. It starts outside the **Züri Rollt** bike hire stand at the main railway station (see p. 553, advance booking is required).

The **Classic Trolley Tour** is a fun way to get your bearings, to learn about the history and lifestyle of the Zürichers, and to sightsee undercover if the weather is inclement. The tour starts at Bus-Parkplatz Sihlquai at 9:45am, midday and 2pm. It costs CHF34 for adults, CHF17 for kids (including multilingual commentary through personal earphones) and lasts 1½ to 2 hours.

The **Zürich Schifffahrtsgesellschaft** (Lake Zurich Navigation Company; www.zsg.ch) operates lake cruises throughout the year, as well as specialty cruises (see box below) and nostalgic paddle-steamer tours in summer months. **Limmatschifffahrt** boats (also operated by ZSG) shuttle up the Limmat river between the Landesmuseum and Bürkliplatz Pier on the lake twice an hour from April to October. The round trip takes approximately one hour and costs CHF4.30.

## Especially for Kids

Zurich is a popular city for kids, with plenty of green spaces, especially around the lake, and over 80 playgrounds—ask your hotel to direct you to the one nearest to you. Children love visiting the **Üetliberg ★★** (see p. 562) and, in summer months, there's swimming and boats for hire on the lake and mini-cruises year-round (see above).

The **Zoologischer Garten (Zoological Gardens) ★★** (Zürichbergstrasse 221; www.zoo.ch; ✆ **044/254 25 00**) is one of the city's big crowd-pleasers for families young and old, with around 2,200 animals of

## ZÜRICHSEE—the city's blue lung

Zürichsee is the city's playground, with beautiful grassy parks, promenades and stately fin de siècle mansions set against a backdrop of snow-clad mountains. During summer, it's where the city's heart beats loudest, popular for strolling, sunbathing, boating, parkour trails, barbecuing, and swimming—the water is very clean and surprisingly warm, so be sure to bring your swimsuit.

No trip here is complete without a **mini-cruise** on the lake. **Zürichsee Schifffahrtsgesellschaft** (Lake Zurich Navigation Company), Mythenquai 333 (www.zsg.ch; ✆ **044/487 13 33**), offers a variety of excursions setting out daily from Bürkliplatz square. They range from 1½-hour mini-tours to romantic sunset cruises, jolly fondue evenings, and full-day outings. During summer, paddle-steamers ply between the towns and villages which dot the shoreline: Küsnacht is especially picturesque, and Rapperswil is also worth a visit for its many rose gardens; Circus Museum; and highly regarded children's zoo, Knies Kinderzoo. The countryside surrounding the lake with its lush, rolling hills, some clad in vineyards, is a hikers' paradise. It's also possible to explore the lake by train (the track runs the length of both shores, offering an easy, scenic journey), or by bicycle.



about 260 species. It also contains a replica of a tropical rainforest, lodged within a state-of-the-art building which successfully replicates the temperatures, light levels, and humidity of Madagascar; while the Zoolino petting area is especially popular with toddlers.

Other family-friendly highlights include the **Landesmuseum ★★★** (Swiss National Museum; p. 558) with its wide variety of hands-on displays; the **Urania Observatory ★★,** Uraniastrasse 9 (www.urania-sternwarte.ch; ✆ **044/211-65-23**) for budding star-gazers; and the tiny **Spielzeug Museum (Toy Museum) ★,** Fortunagasse 15 (www.zuercher-spielzeugmuseum.ch; ✆ **044/211 93 05**), a charming collection of toys dating from the 18th to the 20th centuries.

Urania Observatory.

Several stores are also fun to visit with your kids, especially **Pastorini** (Weinplatz 3; www.pastorini.ch; ✆ **044/284 33 44**) is one of Zurich's biggest toy stores and is charmingly old-fashioned, with five floors brimming with quality toys, puppets, dolls houses, puzzles, board games, arts and crafts; and

**Kinderbuchladen Zürich** (Oberdorfstrasse 32; www.kinderbuchladen.ch; ✆ **044/265 30 00**) is the best-stocked children's bookstore in Switzerland, with many English-language books.

## Where to Stay

Zurich is an ideal city in which to become acquainted with Swiss hospitality. The city has more than 120 hotels to suit all tastes and budgets, from deluxe five-star palace-hotels (with price tags to match) to basic budget hotels. However, it can be difficult to find a room, because the top hotels are often filled with business travelers. So, if possible, make your booking well in advance. All the hotels listed here are within easy walking distance or just a short bus ride or tram-hop from the main Hauptbahnhof train station in the city center.

### ALTSTADT

#### Expensive

**Hotel Kindli ★** This cozy little townhouse hotel has been accommodating guests for more than 500 years. Located on a picturesque cobbled street in the pedestrian-only old town, the hotel manages to be quiet but still central. Every last detail has been considered in its 20 individually designed rooms, each fitted with country-house furnishings, right down to the specially "energized" water in the bathroom (it's like bathing in bottled mineral water and is supposedly very good for you). The superior rooms feature deluxe Swedish Hästens beds. The restaurant has an excellent reputation for its classic Swiss dishes.

Pfalzgasse 1. www.kindli.ch. ✆ **043/888 76 76.** 20 units. Doubles CHF380–CHF440, included breakfast and minibar. Tram 6, 7, 11, 13 or 17 (Rennweg). **Amenities:** Restaurant; free Wi-Fi.

**Hotel Widder ★★★** Old meets new at the luxurious and quirky Widder, made up of eight adjoining medieval houses and named after the 13th-century Augustinian monastery once located here. Thanks to careful restoration, the original stone walls, murals, frescoes, and ceilings have been preserved in the characterful interior. The rooms and suites are individually decorated with furniture and art from such luminaries as Le Corbusier, Mies van der Rohe, Frank Lloyd Wright, Giacometti, and Warhol; the interior schemes match the ice-cream shades of the eight exterior buildings. The restaurant serves top-notch Swiss and vegetarian cuisine; the Widder Bar is a celebrated jazz venue.

Rennweg 7. www.widderhotel.ch. ✆ **044/224 25 26**. 60 units. Doubles CHF650–CHF850, suites CHF1,050–CHF4,000. Tram 6, 7, 11, 13 or 17 (Rennweg). **Amenities:** spa; swimming pool; conference facilities; room service; free Wi-Fi.

### CITY

#### Expensive

**Hotel Baur au Lac ★★★** The Baur au Lac is one of Switzerland's grandest hotels. Set in private parkland on the shores of Lake Zurich, at

## HÜRLIMANN SPA—bathing in beer

Perched on a hill, and a 10-minute ride by tram and bus from the city center, this boldly designed and very happening spa is housed inside the old **Hürlimann Brewery** of 1836—a striking building of whitewashed walls and towering brick chimneys. Within, the original wooden vats have been restored and converted into pools of varying temperatures, heated naturally from a nearby spring. The brewery's former barrel-vaulted stone chambers have been converted into auxiliary pools, steam rooms, and chill-out zones, but the pièce de résistance is undoubtedly the rooftop baths where you can soak up 360-degree city vistas from the vast open-air hot tub.

The adjoining **B2Boutique Hotel** is equally quirky, with its industrial chic bedrooms, its striking library lounge of floor-to-ceiling bookcases boasting 33,000 books, and a theatrical lobby which uses beer crates instead of coffee tables. Hotel guests pay just CHF25 (instead of the regular CHF55 per person) to bathe in the thermal bath complex (Brandschenkestrasse 150; www.thermalbad-zuerich.ch; www.b2boutiquehotels.com; ✆ **044/567 67 67;** tram 5, 8, 13, 17 [Bahnhof Enge/Bederstrasse], then bus 66 [Hürlimannplatz]).



the head of the fashionable Bahnhofstrasse, it has the perfect location for shopping and sightseeing. The hotel has been owned by the same family since it opened in 1844, and it has welcomed royalty, celebrities, and discerning travelers with unequaled hospitality ever since. The beautifully appointed rooms, with sumptuous, classic furnishings, make all guests feel like celebrities, as does the excellent service. In summer months, meals are served in the garden, which overlooks the lake and the Alps beyond.

Talstrasse 1. www.bauraulac.ch. ✆ **044/220 50 20.** 120 units. Doubles CHF870, suites CHF1,200. Tram 2, 8, 9 or 11 (Börsenstrasse or Bürkliplatz). **Amenities:** 3 restaurants; bars; business center; rooftop gym; room service; concierge; free Wi-Fi.

### NIEDERDORF

#### Expensive

**Hotel Romantik Florhof ★★★** Near the Kunsthaus art gallery (see p. 561), this secluded boutique hotel is in a genteel 15th-century merchant's house in a picturesque residential district that twists up from the quaint squares and cobbled alleys of the Niederdorf. The bedrooms are large and airy, and each is individually decorated with traditional English-country-house style furnishings and stylish, modern bathrooms. On the top (fourth) floor, the spacious, air-conditioned deluxe double room and junior suite, with its Jacuzzi, are the pick of the bunch. The elegant restaurant serves upmarket, seasonal Swiss fare and has an extensive list of Swiss wines. And the leafy patio garden here makes a nice break from the bustle of the city center in the summer.

Florhofgasse 4. www.florhof.ch. ✆ **044/250 26 26.** 35 units. Doubles CHF370–CHF430, suites CHF540–CHF670, includes breakfast Tram 3 (Neumarkt). **Amenities:** Restaurant; garden; free Wi-Fi.

### Moderate

**Hirschen ★★★** For location, it's hard to beat the Hirschen, which is at the heart of the fashionable Niederdorf district. It's also well priced and full of character—it's been a guesthouse since the 14th century, making it one of the city's oldest hotels. Today's simple, family-run hotel is kept in good repair, and although the rooms are pint-size, they are bright and functional without being generic, with crisp white bed linens. Some feature exposed ancient stonework, and one of the rooms has its own private roof terrace. In the basement is a wine cellar, the Weinschenke, with an excellent selection of Swiss and international wines.

Niederdorfstrasse 13. www.hirschen-zuerich.ch. ✆ **043/268 33 33.** 27 units. Doubles CHF200, includes breakfast. Tram 4, 9 11, 15 (Rudolf-Brun-Brücke). **Amenities:** Wine bar; roof terrace; free Wi-Fi.

### Inexpensive

**Hotel du Théâtre ★** It's hard to believe that this stylish B&B near the main railway station once housed a German-language theater in the 1950s. The most theatrical element nowadays is its modern glass entrance and lobby. The interior decor is simpler, but still stylish and comfortable. Alongside all the usual amenities, the rooms are furnished with a selection of novels, play scripts, poetry, philosophy, and audio books. The lounge often hosts book readings, harking back to the hotel's dramatic past.

Seilergraben 69. www.hotel-du-theatre.ch. ✆ **044/267 2670.** 50 units. CHF130 single, CHF180 double, breakfast CHF23 extra. Tram 3-7, 10-11 0r 13-15 (Central). **Amenities:** Restaurant; lounge; free Wi-Fi.

**Hotel Leoneck ★★** This adorable and fun hotel, which has been decorated in "Swiss ethnic" style, is a good choice for families. There are cows everywhere: cow ornaments, cowbells, and cow upholstery. The staff is friendly and helpful, and the rooms are bright, simple, and streamlined, with amusing design touches, original wall paintings by local artists, and Toblerone chocolates on your pillow at night. The adjoining **Crazy Cow ★★** restaurant (see p. 572) continues the Swiss-kitsch theme. Situated to the northwest of Niederdorf, Tram 10 will bring you directly from the airport or main train station right to the front door.

Leonhardstrasse 1. www.leoneck.ch. ✆ **044/254 22 22.** 80 units. Doubles CFH160–CHF250, family rooms CHF300–CHF400. Rates include breakfast. Trams 7, 6, 10, 15 (Haldenegg). **Amenities:** Restaurant; free Wi-Fi.

## SEEFELD

### Expensive

**Hotel Eden au Lac ★★★** Set on the shores of Lake Zurich, a few steps from the Opera and a 10-minute walk from Bahnhofstrasse, the five-star Eden au Lac is one of the city's finest hotels. A gem built in 1909, it's got old world charm and elegance—from its bedrooms, furnished in neo-baroque style, to its Art Nouveau banquet halls. The French restaurant here is famed for its hot hors d'oeuvres—one of the earliest tasting menus—which were developed here for the Aga Khan III

Hotel Eden au Lac.



during his stay during World War II. Today's reincarnation comprises six courses and costs CHF145. Our favorite experience is in winter, when the Top of Eden roof terrace provides hot water bottles and blankets with its fondue menu to allow for cold-weather enjoyment of its unsurpassed lake and city views.

Utoquai 45. www.edenaulac.ch. ✆ **044/266 2525.** 56 units. Doubles CHF650. Tram 2, 4, 5, 9, 11 (Kreuzstrasse). **Amenities:** 3 restaurants; bar; conference facilities; room service; concierge; free Wi-Fi.

### Moderate

**Hotel Seehof ★★** Given its close proximity to the opera and the shores of Lake Zurich, this hotel is an excellent value; it's a favorite of in-the-know business travelers—and opera singers. The pink facade of the 1930s townhouse it's in belies a radically modern interior of minimalist white walls, varnished oak floors, trendy furniture, and works by young local artists. The popular bar contains an excellent selection of wines and enhances the generally hip vibe.

Seehofstrasse 11. www.seehof.ch. ✆ **044/254 57 57.** 20 units. Doubles CHF145–CHF370, suites CHF270–CHF430. Tram: 2, 4, 5, 9 or 11 (Opernhaus). **Amenities:** Restaurant; bar; free minibar; free Wi-Fi.

**Lady's First Hotel ★★** This elegant boutique hotel is in a smart residential district, just a stone's throw from the lake and the city center. It's within a 19th-century building that was once a finishing school for young ladies, so it seems fitting that when it first opened in 1994, the hotel was for women only. The spa and the top floors remain that way, although men can get in-room massages in the stylish bedrooms, some of which have balconies overlooking the lake. Expect sleek, contemporary furnishings, high ceilings, parquet floors, and the occasional bold accent of color. A tempting evening menu of Italian dishes is served in the restaurant, garden, or lounge. There's a cozy log fire in winter, and a rose garden in summer, but the crowning glory of the hotel year-round is the roof terrace, which comes with beautiful skyline vistas.

Mainaustrasse 24. www.ladysfirst.ch. ✆ **044/380 80 10.** 28 units. Doubles CHF290, suites CHF325. Rates include breakfast. Tram 4 (Feldeggstrasse). **Amenities:** Spa; roof terrace; free Wi-Fi.

## Where to Eat

Zurich restaurants feature a selection of both international and Swiss specialties. One local favorite is *rösti* (potatoes grated and fried). You should also try *Züri-Gschnätzlets* (shredded veal cooked with mushrooms in a cream sauce laced with white wine) and *Kutteln nach Zürcherart* (tripe with mushrooms, white wine, and caraway seed). Another classic dish is *Leberspiesschen* (liver cubes skewered with bacon and sage and served with potatoes and beans).

Among local wines, the white Riesling Sylvaner is outstanding and great with fish. The light Clevner wines, always chilled, are made from blue Burgundy grapes that grow around the lake. You should be able to order wine by the glass, even in first-class restaurants.

### ALTSTADT

#### Expensive

**Zunfthaus zur Waag ★★★** SWISS The "Weavers' Guildhall" is without a doubt one of the most stylish restaurants in town. Inside a 17th-century hall near the river, its series of wood-paneled Biedermeier-style dining rooms make an intimate, candlelit spot for dining on top-notch local specialties, which are enhanced by the exemplary service. The menu usually includes *Zürcher Geschnetzeltes* (sliced veal in a mushroom cream sauce) with crisp *rösti* (potato cakes); and fried filets of perch straight from the lake, served with almond butter. Reservations are a very good idea.

Markthalle im Viadukt, Münsterhof 8. www.zunfthaus-zur-waag.ch. ✆ **044/216 99 66.** Mains CHF41–CHF56. Tram 2, 6–9, 11, 13 (Paradeplatz). Daily 11:30am–2pm and 6pm–10pm.

### CITY

#### Moderate

**Hiltl ★★★** VEGETARIAN When it opened way back in 1898, Hiltl was Europe's first vegetarian restaurant; more than a hundred years later, it remains Zurich's top vegetarian option, with daily changing seasonal menus. Plan on eating early, or expect to wait in line for the impressive salad bar of 100 homemade dishes (you pay by the weight, per 100g, or about 3.5 oz.). At lunchtime, you can order the dish of the day for CHF20, and add soup or salad to it for an extra CHF3. Or tuck into a copious bowl of pasta, a chili-bean casserole, or one of the daily curry specialties. The spicy Malaysian Rendang and the Paneer Makhani are

two of our favorites, or there's a curry buffet for those who can't decide (pay per 100g at lunchtime, or a fixed price at dinner). Wash it all down with freshly squeezed juices, or homemade iced teas and yogurt-based lassis. There is also a limited wine and beer list. The neighboring Hiltl deli serves great coffees, juices, and vegetarian takeout for those in a hurry.
Sihlstrasse 28. www.hiltl.ch. ✆ **044/227 70 00.** Mains CHF20–CHF36, breakfast buffet (served Mon–Fri 6am–10:30am, Sat 6am–12:30pm) CHF29, Sunday brunch CHF57. Tram 2, 6–9, 11, 13 (Paradeplatz). Mon–Wed 6am–midnight or later, Sun 8am–midnight.

**Zeughauskeller ★★** SWISS Zurich's top beer hall was used to store weapons in the 15th century; these days it's packed instead with wooden tables (and you might be asked to share one with other guests in true, sociable, beer-cellar fashion). Expect a lively atmosphere, old-fashioned Bavarian-style oom-pah music, and massive steins of local beer, all drawn straight from the barrel. The wholesome Swiss fare includes 15 different sausage dishes, all served with a dollop of sauerkraut. The meter-long Kanonenputzer ("Cannon Cleaner") sausage feeds four.
Bahnhofstrasse 28a (main entrance around the corner at In Gassen). www.zeughauskeller.ch. ✆ **044/220 15 15.** Mains CHF19–CHF35, set menu CHF35. Tram 2, 6–9, 11 or 13 to Paradeplatz. Daily 11:30–11pm.



### Inexpensive

**Confiserie Sprüngli ★★** CAFE The extravagant window displays here are good at luring customers into what is Switzerland's top confectionary and chocolate shop, at the hub of its most exclusive shopping boulevard. Less well-known to tourists, however, is the elegant cafe upstairs, where you can sip coffee served on a silver salver while rubbing shoulders with the refined and well-to-do of Zurich. It's like winding the clocks back to the height of the city's Belle Epoque grandeur, with its old-fashioned manners and extravagant mirrors and gilt. The creamy cakes and fruit pastries are each a work of art; the seasonal salads and sandwiches make a perfect light lunch; don't leave without a box of Luxembourgli, Sprüngli's trademark bite-size macaroons.
Bahnhofstrasse 21, above the Sprüngli shop. www.spruengli.ch. ✆ **044/224 46 16.** Sandwiches and salads CHF5.20–CHF14. Tram 2, 6–9, 11, 13 (Paradeplatz). Mon–Fri 7am–6:30pm, Sat 8am–6pm, Sun 9:30am–5:30pm.

## ENGE & WOLLISHOFEN

### Expensive

**Seerose ★★** INTERNATIONAL In summer months, many of the city's fashionable boating crowd head to this chic lakeside hotspot, right on the shores of Lake Zurich. Book well in advance to ensure a table on the attractive lakeside deck, where there are giant nautical-striped parasols. The waiting staff can be a bit snobbish and brusque at times, but the top-notch cuisine more than makes up for any shortfalls in service. The sublime beef tournedos is the signature dish here, although the fish dishes also come highly recommended, especially the grilled sole. The daily two-course lunch menu is a good value at CHF32, or you can opt for the Seerose's latest craze, an "anti-aging menu" for CHF37.

Seestrasse 493. www.dinning.ch. ✆ **044/481 63 83**. Mains at lunch CHF18–CHF59, Mains at dinner CHF24–CHF74. Bus 161, 165 (Seerose). Lake club daily 9am–midnight. Lunch: 11:45am–1:45pm, dinner: 6–9:45pm.

## NIEDERDORF

### Expensive

**Kronenhalle ★★** SWISS Many say Kronenhalle is Zurich's top restaurant, but in fact this former beer hall is more than just a restaurant—it's a culinary landmark, the perfect blend of haute cuisine and fine art. Its intimate, old-world dining areas, with white linen tablecloths, soft candlelight, chandeliers, and dark-wood walls, are also bedecked with a breathtaking collection of paintings by Picasso, Rodin, Matisse, and Bonnard as well as stained glass by Chagall and furnishings by Giacometti. Ever since the restaurant opened in 1921, local politicians, businessmen, musicians, artists, and thinkers (including Sigmund Freud and Albert Einstein) have come here for a traditional menu of exemplary Swiss fare, which is served the old-fashioned way, from silver-domed serving dishes on side tables by elegant, white-frocked waiters. Signature dishes include a salad with Balleron sausage, followed by a chateaubriand steak and the richest of chocolate mousses. Advance reservations are strongly recommended: Ask for the table in the corner of the main dining room, beside a portrait of James Joyce—the author wrote large chunks of *Ulysses* while seated here.

Rämistrasse 4, off Limmatquai. www.kronenhalle.com. ✆ **044/262 99 00.** Mains CHF28–CHF68. Tram 2, 4, 5, 8, 9, 11, 15 (Bellevue). Daily noon–midnight.

### Moderate

**Adler's Swiss Chuchi ★★★** SWISS This simple, bright, chalet-style restaurant with traditional wood-clad walls transports its guests straight

Enjoying fondue at Adler's Swiss Chuchi.

from the city to the Alps. It's an absolute must for all cheese fans. Alongside such popular local staples as Alpine macaroni (baked with lots of potatoes), meat fondues, and crispy rösti potato dishes, there are lots of raclette and fondue options. Our favorite is the "Farmers Fondue," with cheese, bacon, and cherry brandy. The wine menu is exclusively Swiss and broken down by cantons—most are available by the glass as well as by the bottle. In summer months, you can eat outside, on the cobbled pavements of Niederdorf, the city's pedestrian-only medieval quarter. At the end of your meal, as a finishing touch, the bill is presented inside a music box.

Hotel Adler, Rosengasse 10. www.hotel-adler.ch. ✆ **044/266 9696.** Mains CHF21–CHF42. Tram 4, 15 (Rudolf-Brun-Brücke). Daily 11:30am–11:15pm.

### Inexpensive

**Crazy Cow ★★** SWISS There's nothing refined about the Crazy Cow. From the kitschy wall paintings inspired by Swiss stereotypes (snowboarding cows, flying cuckoo clocks, trains, half-eaten Toblerone bars) to the virtually unintelligible menu, written in Swiss dialect, this lively restaurant certainly lives up to the first half of its name. But don't worry, the menu is translated into English, and you can be guaranteed a hearty, rustic meal of such traditional fare as rösti, Swiss-style macaroni casserole (with potatoes, bacon, and cheese), and *raclette* (cheese melted over a fire and then served over potatoes or bread).

Hotel Leoneck, Leonhardstrasse 1. www.crazycow.ch. ✆ **044/261 40 55.** Mains CHF19–CHF40. Trams 7, 6, 10, or 15 (Haldenegg; the tram stop is right outside the restaurant). Daily 6:30am–midnight.

## Shopping

Zurich offers some of the finest shopping in all of Switzerland, and some of the most expensive in the world, with its dazzling selection of boutiques ranging from international haute couture and exclusive Swiss watches to beautifully handcrafted local souvenirs, not to mention more chocolate shops than is good for even the most devoted chocoholics.

The main shopping district occupies a square kilometer (about ⅓ sq. mile) at the heart of the city, centered on glitzy, car-free **Bahnhofstrasse,** one of the world's most celebrated and sophisticated shopping boulevards, stretching from the main train station to the lake. Here renowned confectioners, jewelers, and watchmakers jostle for space alongside haute-couture boutiques in the most overt manifestation of the nation's wealth.

The nearby tiny specialist shops of the hilly, cobbled Altstadt are also worth a browse, as is the tiny artisan quarter beside the river at Schipfe with its quirky antiquities shops. Across the river in the Niederdorf, you'll find a more eclectic, generally cheaper, and certainly quirkier array of boutiques, interior design shops, and galleries.

For that once-in-a-lifetime Swiss timepiece purchase, head to **Beyer,** Bahnhofstrasse 31 (www.beyer-ch.com; ✆ **043/344 63 63**),

## cabaret voltaire—BIRTHPLACE OF THE DADA MOVEMENT

Don't be put off by the somewhat shabby interior of this bar and art gallery—back in 1916, Cabaret Voltaire was the birthplace of the Dada movement. Formed as a "protest against the madness of the times," the venue was frequented by the most avant-garde musicians, thinkers, artists, and literati of the era.

The Dada movement was anti-war, anti-bourgeois, and anarchist in nature, and went on to influence many other genres from surrealism to pop art and punk rock. When World War II came to an end, most Dadaists left Zurich, returning to their home countries. But Cabaret Voltaire lingered on, drawing such painters as Paul Klee and Max Ernst.

Today's "Dadahaus" (as the locals call it) is still patronized by the art-conscious cognoscenti and remains a hip and quirky place for a beer at the heart of the Niederdorf. During the day, the upstairs duDA bar is a place for students to meet for a coffee, or to read or study. By night, the bar is often the venue for art exhibitions, theatrical revues, lectures, and poetry readings. The selection of absinthes here is especially strong. (Spiegelgasse 1; www.cabaretvoltaire.ch; ✆ **043/268 57 20**).

which also contains a small but fascinating **Clock & Watch Museum** in the basement. There's also a more modestly priced **Swatch** shop nearby, at Bahnhofstrasse 94 (www.swatch.ch; ✆ **044/221 28 66**).

Other shopping highlights include Swiss shoe institution **Bally** (Bahnhofstrasse 20; www.bally.ch; ✆ **044/224 39 39**); **Schweizer Heimatwerk** (Uraniastrasse 1; www.heimatwerk.ch; ✆ **044/222 19 55**) for exquisitely made upscale Swiss handicrafts; **einzigart** (Josefstrasse 36; www.einzigart.ch; ✆ **044/440 46 00**) for witty yet practical design items, furnishings, and gift ideas; and **Confiserie Sprüngli,** Bahnhofstrasse 21 (see p. 570) for fantastical displays of chocolates and candies.

## Entertainment & Nightlife

There's more to Swiss entertainment than alphorns and yodeling. Indeed Zurich offers some of Switzerland's best and most sophisticated nightlife, as well as a world-class program of cultural entertainment. Switzerland's finest opera company, the **Zurich Opera,** is located beside the lake in the grandiose neo-baroque **Opernhaus** (Opera House, Falkenstrasse 1; www.opernhaus.ch; ✆ **044/268 66 66**). Placed on the map by such famous composers as Richard Wagner, Richard Strauss, Paul Hindemith, and Arthur Honegger, it is considered among the world's top opera venues and also an important stage for ballet.

The main classical music venue, the grand **Tonhalle** (Claridenstrasse 7; www.tonhalle-orchester.ch; ✆ **044/206 34 34**), hosts a variety of orchestras and chamber ensembles including its own internationally renowned **Zurich Tonhalle Orchestra.**

Opernhaus, home of Opera Zurich.





The **Schauspielhaus** (Rämistrasse 34; www.schauspielhaus.ch; ✆ **044/258 77 77**) enjoys a reputation as the most prestigious theatre in the German-speaking world, known for its ground-breaking productions of classical and contemporary drama. The Playhouse is situated opposite the Kunsthaus in the city center. It also has a second stage in the avant-garde **Schiffbau** arts complex in Züri West, together with **Moods**, the city's top jazz club (Schiffbaustrasse 4; www.moods.ch; ✆ **044/258 77 77**). The **Widder Bar** (Widder Hotel, Rennweg 7; www.widderhotel.ch; ✆ **044/224 25 26**) is another popular venue for live jazz during its international concert seasons (autumn and spring).

Advance online booking is highly recommended for most performing arts venues, although you may be lucky and pick up late-release tickets or returns at short notice too.

Zurich has more than 500 **bars and nightspots** catering to all tastes, as well as a flamboyant club scene. In the city center, cool chill-out bars attract an affluent, sophisticated crowd; you'll find some lively beer cellars and many of the gay bars in the Niederdorf district, while the newly redeveloped industrial quarter of Züri West boasts a host of ultra-trendy bar and clubs, many housed in former factory buildings.

Our favorite watering-holes include the architecturally striking **Nietturm** (Schiffbaustrasse 4; www.nietturm.ch; ✆ **044/258 77 77**) for stylish cocktails and aerial views of the city in Züri West; the jolly **Zeughauskeller** (see p. 570), the city's top beer hall, in a converted 15th-century arsenal in the city center; the tiny candle-lit subterranean wine bar, **Weinschenke** (Hotel Hirschen; see p. 567) in the Niederdorf for wines from around the world; and trendy **Café Bar Odéon** (Limmatquai 2; www.odeon.ch; ✆ **044/251 16 50;** tram 2, 4, 5, 8, 9, 11, 15 [Bellevue]), an ornate Art Nouveau cafe/bar, once frequented by Lenin, Joyce, Einstein, and Mussolini, and now a popular gay and singles bar by night.

### The Zurich Street Parade

In recent years, Zurich's Street Parade has overtaken London's Notting Hill Carnival as the largest street festival in the world. Modelled after Berlin's Love Parade, it began in 1992 as a gigantic techno party with just a thousand revelers. Now, with hundreds of DJs; 30-plus floats known as "love mobiles," each with its own dance theme (embracing house, dubstep, trance, techno, and other electronic music styles); and seven fixed stages around the lake, the street parade draws around a million party-goers all in fancy-dress, and the streets are filled with a crazy, hedonistic party atmosphere one Saturday in August. After the official Street Parade, many of the clubs around town host further techno gigs, including the legendary Lethargy party—a 3-day techno dance festival in a converted factory, the **Rote Fabrik** (Seestrasse 395; ✆ **044/485 58 58;** www.rotefabrik.ch; tram 7 [Post Wallishofen]) on the outskirts of the city beside the lake.

Summer nights are best spent partying in the open-air **Barfuss** bar or chilling with the cool crowd in the riverside bars and open-air cinema zone at **Oberer Letten,** the city's trendiest lido.

Zurich has the highest density of nightclubs in Switzerland, so it's easy to find a place to party late into the night. The city's best-known mainstream nightclub, and still very much the in-place to see and be seen, is **Kaufleuten** (Pelikanstrasse 18; www.kaufleuten.com; ✆ **044/225 33 40;** tram 2, 9 [Sihlstrasse]). Underground dance venue **Zukunft** (Dienerstrasse 33; www.zukunft.cl) is known for its edgy electronic sounds; and **Plaza** (Badenerstrasse 109; www.plaza-zurich.ch; ✆ **044/542 90 90;** tram 2, 3 [Bezirksgebäude]) for high-octane house music and big name DJs. For a grittier nightlife experience, head to the many clubs of Züri West, centered around Escher-Wyss-Platz and Geroldstrasse.

## GENEVA

Geneva is Switzerland's second-largest city, and is probably best known for the major role it plays on the world stage, as home to more than 200 major global organizations including the Red Cross and the United Nations.

Consequently, it is the least Swiss of all Swiss cities. Around 40% of its inhabitants are foreigners. It is a cosmopolitan city with a distinctly French flavor and an almost Mediterranean laidback vibe, sitting astride the Franco-Swiss border at the western corner of expansive Lake Geneva (known to the French as Lac Léman), framed by vineyards and overlooked by Europe's tallest mountain, Mont Blanc.

It is also a city of great contrasts, from the narrow cobbled streets and grey-toned severity of the Vieille Ville (Old Town)—which still somehow conveys some of the strict and unyielding morals of what used to be a stronghold of severely punitive Calvinism amid its lively lanes of

A square in Vieille Ville (Old Town), Geneva.



tiny galleries, boutiques and bistros—to the palatial five-star hotels fringing the vast blue lake, renowned for their extravagance and their fabled Swiss hospitality. The patchwork of parks punctuating the lakeside provide peace and tranquility so rarely found in a city center to the frenetic workings of CERN (the European Center for Nuclear Research), world-leader in particle physics, and the myriad institutions of the International district where, for decades, history has been written.

Elegant and undeniably affluent; dynamic and modern; historic; quirky and characterful—indeed, Geneva radiates a unique atmosphere hard to define although many have tried: "City of Peace," "Smallest of big cities," "Switzerland's international city." The list of ornamental epithets goes on . . .

## Essentials

Geneva's tourist office **(Office du Tourisme de Genève)** website is www.geneve-tourisme.ch.

**ARRIVING** **Geneva International Airport** is situated 4km (2½ miles) northwest of the city center, on the Franco-Swiss border, and can be accessed from both countries. The best way to reach the city center is by train, as taxis are expensive (expect to pay around CHF35 to CHF45 depending on traffic conditions, time of day and number of passengers). By train, it takes just 6 minutes to Geneva-Cornavin (city center). Trains run frequently (every 12 min. in rush hour) from 5:07am to 1:10am, and your transfer from the airport is free: simply take a special UNIRESO ticket from the machine in the baggage collection area of Arrivals and it will entitle you to free public transport in the entire canton of Geneva for a period of up to 80 minutes. This ticket is also valid on any bus: routes 5, 10 and F all operate between the airport and Cornavin station (see below). Some hotels offer a free shuttle bus service.

The main **train station, Gare Cornavin,** has excellent links with European cities. France's high-speed TGV trains from Paris reach Cornavin in just 3 hours (with nine fast trains daily) and there are three express trains to Milan daily (journey time just under four hours). Within Switzerland, it takes 40 minutes to Lausanne (see p. 599), 1 hour to Montreux (see p. 600), less than two hours to Bern, and around three hours to Zurich or Lucerne. Contact **SBB** (**Swiss Federal Railways;** www.sbb.ch; ✆ **0900/300 300**) for rail schedules and prices.

If **driving** from Lausanne, head southwest on the A1 along the northern shore of Lake Geneva, to the very far corner of southwestern Switzerland.

There are frequent daily arrivals into Geneva by **lake steamer** year-round from Montreux, Vevey and Lausanne. For the left bank, disembark at the **Jardin Anglais** stop; for the Right Bank you need **Mont Blanc** or **Pâquis.** Contact the **CGN** (Lake Geneva Navigation Company; www.cgn.ch; ✆ **0848/811 848**) for further details.

International buses come into Switzerland's largest coach station, the **Gare Routière de Genève** (www.gare-routiere.ch; ✆ **022/732 02 30**), near the lake at Place Dorcière. It is also the start-point for sightseeing buses for the city and the region.

**CITY LAYOUT** It's easy to find your bearings in Geneva, because the city has a relaxed, spread-out feel and is conveniently split into two by the lake and the Rhône River: the **Rive Gauche** (Left or South Bank), which contains the Vieille Ville (Old Town), some major shopping streets, the famous Jet d'Eau (see p. 586) and Floral Clock (see p. 588) and some important museums; and the **Rive Droite** (Right or North Bank), characterized by its grandiose hotels; extensive parks and tree-shaded promenades; and, inland from the lake, some important museums and major international organizations. Within the right and left banks, the city is then further divided into a total of eight official districts (quartiers) and many further neighborhoods, each with its own distinctive character.

**GETTING AROUND** Geneva is a sprawling city, and its sights and attractions are quite spread out, especially if you're planning to visit the

## save with the **GENEVA PASS**

Families and avid museum-goers can save by purchasing a Geneva Pass, offering free entry to many top museums and attractions, and free access to the public transport network, plus reductions in some boat trips, tours, shops, and restaurants. The pass is valid for 24, 48, or 72 hours (costing CHF25, CHF35, or CHF45) and is available online in advance at www.geneve-tourisme.ch.

Other savvy travelers plan their visit to Geneva to coincide with the first Sunday of the month, when most museums and galleries are free.

sights of the International District; or CERN (see p. 589) and Carouge (see p. 588) farther afield. Thankfully, in true Swiss style, the public transport system is ultra-efficient, with buses, trams, and boats to whisk you around town with ease—although you can find traffic congestion slows up the procedure at times, especially during rush-hour. The best way to explore the bustling web of streets which forms Geneva's hilly historical core, the Old Town, is on foot: The streets are mostly cobbled and public transport limited. It's also especially pleasant to stroll along the quaysides of the lake—to admire its majestic scenery of the city; and the river, to soak up the downtown vibe.

The city's excellent, fully integrated **public transport system** of buses, trams, some trains, and the yellow taxi-boats of the **Mouettes Genevoises** (see below) is operated by **UNIRESO** and **TPG** (**Transports Publics Genevois;** www.tpg.ch; © **0900/022 021**). Services run daily 6am to midnight.

If you're staying in a hotel, youth hostel, or campsite in Geneva, you'll receive a **Geneva Transport Card** free of charge, enabling you to use the entire TPG network of buses, trams, trains, and yellow taxi-boats for free throughout your stay (including the departure day).

Without a Geneva Transport card, expect to pay CHF3/CHF2.50 per adult/child for a single ticket (valid for one hour); CHF2 for a short trip (3 stops by bus/tram or one boat crossing, valid for adults only); or consider getting a 1-day card—at a cost of CHF10.60/CHF7.60 per adult/child, it's often the most cost-effective option. Maps of the transport network, fares and timetables are displayed at all bus and tram stops.

There are many **taxi** companies in Geneva. A taxi can be ordered by phone (call © **022/331 41 33** or © **033/320 22 02**), hailed in the street, or found at taxi stands all over town, at the airport and at the main station, but it's not the most economical or time-efficient way to travel. The minimum fare is CHF6.30, plus a minimum of CHF3.20 per each additional kilometer (CHF3.80 Sundays, evenings, public holidays, and with more than four passengers).

I don't recommend attempting to see Geneva **by car;** parking is difficult and the many one-way streets make navigation complicated.

**Cycling** is a great way to explore the city, parks, and quays, and ideal if you're planning to venture into the surrounding countryside. From mid-April to mid-October, you can rent bikes from **Genève Roule** for as little as CHF12 a day (CHF8 half-day) or electric bikes from CHF25 a day (CHF17 half-day), from various depots around town, including place de Montbrillant 17 on the right bank, and Ruelle des Templiers 4 on the left bank (www.geneveroule.ch).

No trip to Geneva would be complete without a mini voyage on the lake's **Mouettes Genevoises** (www.mouettesgenevoises.ch; © **022/ 732 29 44**), the quirky little yellow commuter taxis which ply across the lake from one quayside to the other, carrying businessmen, shoppers,

### Events in Geneva

Geneva's calendar is full of festivity year-round, from the fancy-dress parades of February's **Carnival** season, and the world famous **International Motor Show** in March, to the world's largest celebrations outside the USA for **Independence Day;** and the sparkling **Christmas Market,** with its little wooden stalls selling handmade crafts, gingerbread, and mulled wine. But it's most unique event is undoubtedly the historical processions of the **Escalade.**

For centuries, the region of Savoy was a constant threat to Geneva, repeatedly laying siege to the city. One night—11 December 1602—the Genevois victoriously resisted a surprise attack, when the Savoyard troops failed to scale the city walls. Legend has it a housewife, known as the Mère Royaume, tipped a cauldron of scalding vegetable soup over the first soldier's head, then raised the alarm. Ever since, L'Escalade ("The Climbing by Ladder," www.1602.ch) has been celebrated each year, with 3 days and nights of torch-lit costumed processions and festivities, centered on the Old Town. The city's confectioners even sell marmites d'Escalade, chocolate cauldrons filled with marzipan "vegetables."



tourists, and all. There are departures roughly every ten minutes from April to October, less frequently in winter months, from Quai du Mont Blanc and Pâquis on the right bank; and from Quai Gustave Ador and Parc des Eaux Vives on the left bank. There is also a crossing every half-hour from Chateaubriand (in Parc Mon Repos) to Port Noir/Gèneve Plage. The mouettes run from 7:30am until around 9pm weekdays, 10am to 9pm during weekends and public holidays; and you can use the same ticket as for the bus and tram.

## The Neighborhoods in Brief

**VIEILLE VILLE (OLD TOWN)** The Vieille Ville, on the Rive Gauche or Left Bank, is the historic heart of Geneva and one of its most appealing districts, with its picturesque squares, ornamental fountains, and architectural blends of Gothic, Renaissance and 18th-century features. Built on the tallest hill in town, and topped by the **Cathedral of St Pierre** (see p. 585), its quirky narrow streets are full of bistro-style cafes and locals' bars, fascinating antiques shops, boutiques, and galleries. From here, it is a stone's throw to the cultural hub of Place Neuve, just beyond the old town walls.

**RUES BASSES (LOWER TOWN)** Located at the foot of the Vieille Ville on the south bank of the river Rhône (on the Rive Gauche), the Rues Basses literally mean "low streets." These streets form the main commercial and luxury shopping district of Geneva (see **"Shopping,"** p. 597), centered on and around rue du Rhône, rue de la Confédération and rue du Marché. You may also hear locals describe this exclusive shopping area as **Rive.**

**THE QUAIS** The lakeside promenades that hug the water's edge around the lake and at the mouth of the River Rhône almost constitute a "neighborhood" of their own. Flanked by grandiose five-star palace hotels and expansive parks, both sides are worth exploring on foot (or aboard one of their mini tourists trains, see p. 589). One of the most scenic walks is from the **Parc des Eaux-Vives** on the Left Bank round to the **Parc de Mon-Repos** on the Right Bank, with impressive views of the city's **Jet d'Eau** (see p. 586) as you go.

**PÂQUIS** Once used as a wide-open area for grazing cattle, Pâquis (from the Latin pascuum, meaning "pasture") is a tiny, bustling district brimming with bars and nightclubs, ethnic restaurants, ateliers, hipster boutiques, and curio shops, far removed from the luxurious consumerism of the Rues Basses or the genteel hotels lining the Right Bank just a couple of blocks away. One of Geneva's most animated, down-to-earth districts, it appeals mainly to bargain shoppers and party animals.

**INTERNATIONAL DISTRICT** Two kilometers north of the city center, also known as **Pâquis-Nations,** this is a tranquil sector of offices, museums, and neatly manicured parkland. In this district, you'll find the major international organizations, including the impressive European HQ of the United Nations, the World Economic Forum, and the International Red Cross.

## Exploring Geneva

It's hard to get lost in Geneva; not only does the lake provide myriad recreational activities and scenic views, but also—together with the River Rhône—it forms a convenient natural boundary between the right and left banks, the Rive Droite and the Rive Gauche.

The atmospheric Vieille Ville (Old Town) at the heart of town (on the Rive Gauche), with its charming old buildings and historical landmarks, its cozy restaurants and tiny boutiques, is tightly compact and popular with everyone; while the world-class museums and galleries, especially those in the European district (on the Rive Droite), enlighten and entertain and serve as living proof of the major role played over the centuries by Geneva, Switzerland's "international" city.

### RIVE DROITE

**Musée Ariana ★★** MUSEUM This photogenic neoclassical villa—with its domed roof and pastel-pink, heavily ornamented facade, set in gardens overlooking an elegant fountain—is the perfect setting for one of Europe's most important collections of ceramics, and headquarters of the International Academy of Ceramics. It's airy, spacious galleries contain 7 centuries of artifacts (more than 20,000 objects) from the Middle Ages to the present day—and include fine collections of Sévres and Delft, alongside an impressive Islamic collection and some rare treasures from China and Japan. All the main techniques are there: pottery, stoneware, earthenware, porcelain, and china. The museum was built by local arts patron Gustave Revilliod and named after his mother, Ariana de la

Facade of the Musée Ariana.

Rive. The Salon de thé, within the magnificent oval gallery, is a delightful setting to pause for some refreshment.

10 avenue de la Paix. www.ville-ge.ch/ariana. ✆ **022/418 54 50.** Free for permanent collections, CHF8 for temporary exhibitions, free for children under 18. Tues–Sun 10am–6pm.

**Musée International de la Croix-rouge et du Croissant-Rouge ★★**

MUSEUM It's hard not to be moved by this heart-rending museum at the headquarters of the International Committee of the Red Cross. It records the history of the Red Cross and Red Crescent organizations, both of which have provided humanitarian aid around the globe since their foundation in Switzerland by Genevese social activist and first Nobel Peace Prize winner Henry Dunant in 1863. He chose the Swiss flag in reverse (a red cross on a white background) as the symbol of the Red Cross movement, easily visible—even in a war zone—and symbolic of neutrality.

Its permanent displays are divided into three sections: Defending Human Dignity; Restoring Family Links; and Reducing Natural Risks. Their displays—of rare documents and photography, nonstop film footage, and multimedia displays from the 19th-century battlefields of Europe to the 21st-century plains of Africa—portray just some of the many humanitarian missions carried out by these remarkable organizations in times of war and natural disaster.

17 avenue de la Paix. www.redcrossmuseum.ch. ✆ **022/748 95 25.** Adults CHF15, concessions CHF7, free for children younger than 12. Bus 8, 28, F, V or Z (Appia). Apr–Oct Tues–Sun 10am–6pm, Nov–Mar to 5pm. Closed Mon, Christmas, and New Year.

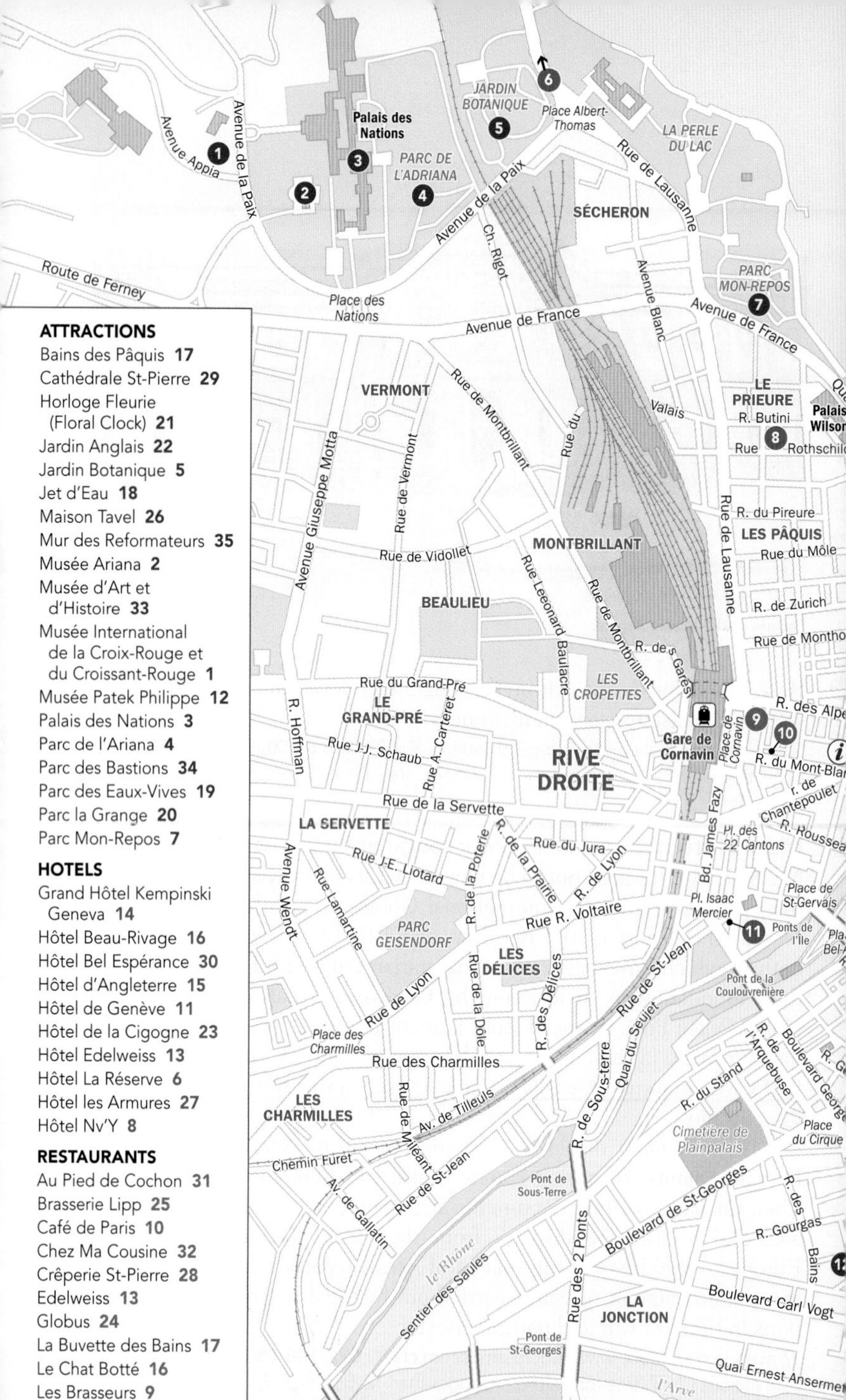
ATTRACTIONS
Bains des Pâquis 17
Cathédrale St-Pierre 29
Horloge Fleurie (Floral Clock) 21
Jardin Anglais 22
Jardin Botanique 5
Jet d'Eau 18
Maison Tavel 26
Mur des Reformateurs 35
Musée Ariana 2
Musée d'Art et d'Histoire 33
Musée International de la Croix-Rouge et du Croissant-Rouge 1
Musée Patek Philippe 12
Palais des Nations 3
Parc de l'Ariana 4
Parc des Bastions 34
Parc des Eaux-Vives 19
Parc la Grange 20
Parc Mon-Repos 7
HOTELS
Grand Hôtel Kempinski Geneva 14
Hôtel Beau-Rivage 16
Hôtel Bel Espérance 30
Hôtel d'Angleterre 15
Hôtel de Genève 11
Hôtel de la Cigogne 23
Hôtel Edelweiss 13
Hôtel La Réserve 6
Hôtel les Armures 27
Hôtel Nv'Y 8
RESTAURANTS
Au Pied de Cochon 31
Brasserie Lipp 25
Café de Paris 10
Chez Ma Cousine 32
Crêperie St-Pierre 28
Edelweiss 13
Globus 24
La Buvette des Bains 17
Le Chat Botté 16
Les Brasseurs 9
Palais des Nations
Avenue Appia
Avenue de la Paix
Jardin Botanique
Place Albert-Thomas
La Perle du Lac
Parc de l'Adriana
Rue de Lausanne
Sécheron
Ch. Rigot
Route de Ferney
Place des Nations
Avenue de France
Parc Mon-Repos
Avenue Blanc
Vermont
Rue de Montbrillant
Le Prieure
Palais Wilson
R. Butini
Rue Rothschild
Valais
Rue du Valais
Avenue Giuseppe Motta
Rue de Vermont
R. du Pireure
Les Pâquis
Rue du Môle
Montbrillant
Rue de Vidollet
Rue Leeonard Baulacre
Beaulieu
R. de Zurich
Rue de Montho
R. des Gares
Les Cropettes
Rue du Grand-Pré
Le Grand-Pré
R. Hoffman
Rue J.-J. Schaub
Rue A. Carteret
Gare de Cornavin
Place de Cornavin
R. des Alpes
R. du Mont-Blanc
Rive Droite
Rue de la Servette
La Servette
r. de Chantepoulet
Bd. James Fazy
Pl. des 22 Cantons
R. Rousseau
Rue du Jura
R. de la Poterie
R. de la Prairie
R. de Lyon
Avenue Wendt
Rue J.-E. Liotard
Rue Lamartine
Place de St-Gervais
Pl. Isaac Mercier
Rue R. Voltaire
Parc Geisendorf
Ponts de l'Île
Les Délices
Rue de St-Jean
Pont de la Coulouvrenière
Rue de Lyon
R. de la Dôle
R. des Délices
Quai du Seujet
R. de l'Arquebuse
Boulevard Georges
Place des Charmilles
Rue des Charmilles
R. du Stand
Les Charmilles
Rue de Miléant
Av. de Tilleuls
R. de Sous-terre
Cimetière de Plainpalais
Place du Cirque
Chemin Furet
Rue de St-Jean
Pont de Sous-Terre
Boulevard de St-Georges
Av. de Gallatin
R. des Bains
R. Gourgas
le Rhône
Sentier des Saules
Rue des 2 Ponts
La Jonction
Boulevard Carl Vogt
Pont de St-Georges
Quai Ernest Ansermet
l'Arve

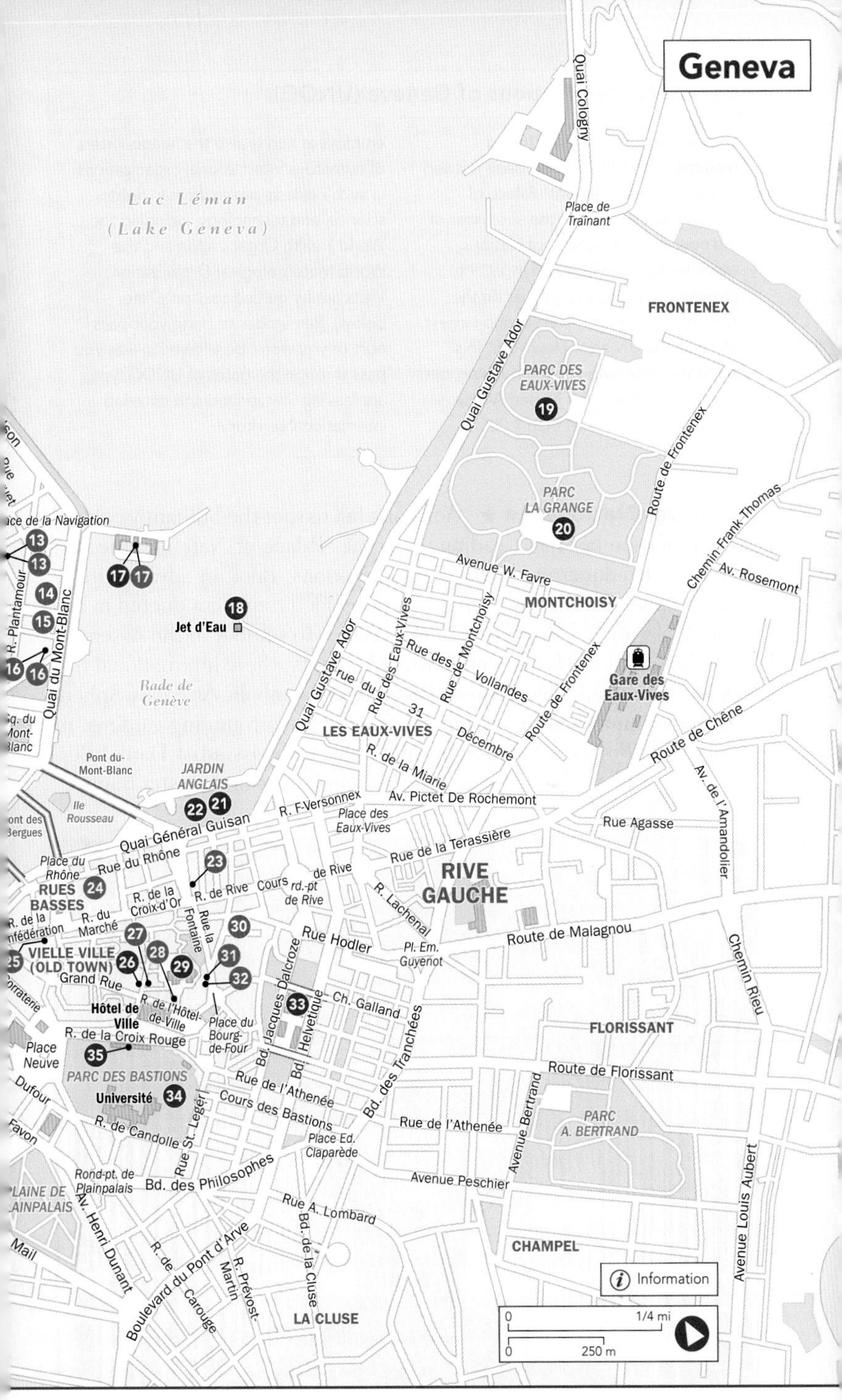
Geneva
Lac Léman
(Lake Geneva)
Quai Cologny
Place de Traînant
FRONTENEX
Quai Gustave Ador
PARC DES EAUX-VIVES
PARC LA GRANGE
Route de Frontenex
Chemin Frank Thomas
Av. Rosemont
Avenue W. Favre
MONTCHOISY
Rue de Montchoisy
Rue des Eaux-Vives
Rue des Vollandes
rue du 31 Décembre
Gare des Eaux-Vives
Route de Chêne
LES EAUX-VIVES
R. de la Miarie
Av. Pictet De Rochemont
Av. de l'Amandolier
Rue Agasse
R. F-Versonnex
Place des Eaux-Vives
Rue de la Terassière
RIVE GAUCHE
R. Lachenal
Route de Malagnou
Chemin Rieu
Jet d'Eau
Rade de Genève
Quai du Mont-Blanc
R. Plantamour
Place de la Navigation
Sq. du Mont-Blanc
Pont du-Mont-Blanc
JARDIN ANGLAIS
Ile Rousseau
Pont des Bergues
Quai Général Guisan
Place du Rhône
Rue du Rhône
RUES BASSES
R. de la Croix-d'Or
R. de Rive
Cours de Rive
rd.-pt de Rive
Rue Hodler
Pl. Em. Guyenot
R. de la Confédération
R. du Marché
Rue la Fontaine
VIELLE VILLE (OLD TOWN)
Grand Rue
Corraterie
Hôtel de Ville
R. de l'Hôtel-de-Ville
Place du Bourg-de-Four
Bd. Jacques Dalcroze
Bd. Helvetique
Ch. Galland
Bd. des Tranchées
FLORISSANT
R. de la Croix Rouge
Place Neuve
PARC DES BASTIONS
Université
Rue de l'Athenée
Cours des Bastions
Route de Florissant
Avenue Bertrand
PARC A. BERTRAND
Dufour
Favon
R. de Candolle
Rue St. Leger
Place Ed. Claparède
Rue de l'Athenée
Rond-pt. de Plainpalais
PLAINE DE PLAINPALAIS
Bd. des Philosophes
Avenue Peschier
Avenue Louis Aubert
Av. Henri Dunant
Mail
Rue A. Lombard
Bd. de la Cluse
R. de Carouge
Boulevard du Pont d'Arve
R. Martin
R. Prévost-
CHAMPEL
LA CLUSE
Information
0
1/4 mi
0
250 m

## The United Nations of Geneva (UNOG)

The Geneva office of the **United Nations**—the UNOG—has been housed in the Palais des Nations (Palace of Nations) since 1966, as the successor of the now-defunct League of Nations, which was originally set up in 1919 to prevent the recurrence of war on the scale of World War I. The second-largest office of the UN after New York, this immense, mile-long (1.6km) building, set in parkland beside the Musée Ariana (see p. 580), contains more than 4,000 employees and is also the headquarters of numerous international organizations in such fields as peace, human rights, science, and technology, including the World Health Organization and the World Meteorological Organization. Visits are by guided tour only (see below). Remember to bring your passport or you won't be allowed in—as you pass through the gates of UNOG, you are leaving Switzerland and entering international territory!



**Palais des Nations ★★★** You can't fail to spot the brilliantly colored avenue of member flags leading up to the "Palace of Nations," the vast European headquarters of the United Nations. Book in advance to be sure of a place on the fascinating 1-hour guided tours (conducted in any of the UN's official languages), and a chance to set foot in the Assembly Hall, the Court of Honour, and other chambers where international history has been made. Don't miss also the UN's symbolic Armillary Sphere and the Conquest of Space monument in the surrounding gardens, or the massive *Broken Chair* sculpture nearby, by Swiss artist Daniel Berset, a powerful symbol of protest against landmines and cluster bombs.

The Palais des Nations, European headquarters of the United Nations.

Interior, Cathédrale St-Pierre.

Parc de l'Ariana, 14 avenue de la Paix. www.unog.ch. ✆ **022/917 48 96.** CHF12 (CHF7 for children). Tours daily Mon–Sat, Apr–Aug; Mon–Fri, Sept–Mar (reservations essential; passport required for entry).

## RIVE GAUCHE

**Cathédrale St-Pierre** ★★ CHURCH A gorgeous fusion of Romanesque, Gothic, and neoclassical styles, St. Peter's Cathedral dominates the Old Town. Built between 1150 and 1232, excavations beneath the edifice have revealed that a Christian sanctuary was sited here as early as A.D. 400 (showcased in the Site Archéologique de Saint-Pierre). The cathedral's austerity dates from the Reformation, when the Genevois gathered in the cloisters in 1536, voted to make St. Peter's Protestant, and stripped all decoration from its once ornate interior. The High Gothic (early 15th-century) Chapelle des Macchabées was used as a storage room during the Reformation. It was restored during World War II. Other highlights of the loft interior include some splendid cross-ribbed vaulting, gigantic rose windows, and an impressive modern organ with 6,000 pipes.

The 145-step climb to the top of the north tower is rewarded by a dramatic bird's-eye view of the city, the lake and beyond—to the Alps to the south, and the Jura Mountains to the north.

Place du Bourg-de-Four 24. www.saintpierre-geneve.ch. ✆ **022/311 75 75.** Cathedral: free (donations welcome); tower, CHF4; archaeological site: CHF8. Bus: 36 (Taconnerie). Daily 10am–5pm.

**Maison Tavel** ★ HISTORIC SITE Maison Tavel is worth a brief visit because it's the oldest house in Geneva (constructed in 1303 and partially rebuilt after a fire in 1334) and it's also home to the **Museum of**

**Ancient Geneva.** The house has undergone several transformations over the centuries, but it retains many traditional elements, including an attractive courtyard, staircase, cellar, and back garden. The museum contains a fascinating albeit small collection of antique furniture, tapestries and silverware, illustrating Genevois lifestyle from the medieval times to the late 19th-century, and don't miss the fascinating model of 19th-century Geneva on the third floor . . . How times have changed!
6, rue du Puits Saint-Pierre. www.ville-ge.ch. ✆ **022/418 37 00.** Free admission to permanent collection, 5F temporary expositions. Bus: 36 (Hôtel de Ville). Tues–Sun 10am–6pm.

**Musée d'Art et d'Histoire ★★** MUSEUM The 100-year-old galleries of Geneva's premier museum are a veritable treasure trove with nearly a million *objets d'art* spanning the centuries. It is an eclectic collection, with something to please everyone: The Archaeology wing houses relics from ancient Egypt, Greece and Rome; the Fine Arts wing contains paintings from the Renaissance to the 20th century; there's medieval furniture, weaponry, stained glass, timepieces, musical instruments, and more in the Applied Arts wing. Don't try to see everything. Art lovers make a beeline for the Impressionist collection, with works by Chagall, Monet, Picasso, Renoir, Rodin, and van Gogh.
rue Charles-Galland 2. www.ville-ge.ch/mah. ✆ **022/418 26 00.** Free; temporary exhibitions CHF5–CHF20. Bus: 1, 8 (Tranchées); Bus: 3, 5, 7, 36 (Athenée). Tues–Sun 11am–6pm.



**Musée Patek Philippe ★★** MUSEUM The world's most extensive and prestigious watch collection is housed in an extravagant museum belonging to the renowned local timepiece-makers and one of the city's most venerated companies, Patek Philippe. Geneva has led the world in watchmaking ever since austere Calvinist times, and on the ground floor, you can see more than 200 machines and tools used by watchmakers, engravers, and goldsmiths over the centuries. The second floor contains the Patek Philippe Collection, and the fourth floor hosts a small but fascinating display devoted to the measurement of time throughout the ages. Devote the majority of your time to the third floor, with its spectacular array of 16th- to 19th-century European and Swiss watches: Star attractions here include the 17th-century astronomical watch and a

## THE jet d'eau

Geneva's best-known landmark, the Water Jet or **Jet d'Eau ★★★** (known affectionately to the Genevois as the *jeddo*), never fails to turn heads as it spurts a staggering 500 liters (132 gallons) of water per second—that's around five bathtubs of water—140 meters (460 ft.) into the air above the lake. This jet was originally a pressure release for a hydro-powered factory, but the locals liked it so much that in 1891 they converted it into a fountain.

A rainbow reflected in the Jet d'Eau.



charming collection of bejeweled animal-shaped timepieces. And don't miss the museum's pride and glory, the Calibre 89, the most complicated watch ever made.

rue des Vieux Grenadiers 7. www.patekmuseum.com. ✆ **022/807 09 10.** Adults CHF10, free for children under 18. Bus: 1 (École-de-Médicine); Tram: 12 (Plainpalais). Tues–Fri 2pm–6pm, Sat 10am–6pm.

## Parks & Gardens

It may be Switzerland's second city, but Geneva is amazingly green nonetheless. Take a pleasant stroll along the quays of the Rive Droite, past the vibrant **Bains des Pâquis lido ★★★,** located on a promontory jutting into the lake, where weather permitting you can take a quick dip, chill on the beach, or drink in views of snow-clad Mount Blanc over a coffee en route. Beyond the lido, you'll arrive at some of the lushest parks in Geneva.

There's tranquil **Parc Mon-Repos ★★** with its first-rate restaurant, **La Perle du Lac ★★** (126 rue de Lausanne; www.laperledulac.ch; ✆ **022/909 10 20**), popular with the well-heeled of Geneva and the local business community for its classic French cuisine, its local fish dishes, and its exemplary list of Swiss wines. Just beyond, Mediterranean blooms, giant cacti, and pink flamingos vie for attention at the luscious lakeside **Jardin Botanique ★★**, while nearby **Parc de l'Ariana ★** shelters **Musée Ariana ★★** (see p. 580) and the iconic United Nations building, the **Palais des Nations ★★★** (see p. 584).

Catch a boat to the other side of the lake and get off at quai Gustave-Ador on the Rive Gauche. From here you can explore two more lakeside parks, **Parc des Eaux-Vives ★,** Geneva's oldest park; and neighboring **Parc la Grange ★,** which boasts the Confederation's most extravagant rose garden.

The Horloge Fleurie (Floral Clock) at Jardin Anglais.





Behind the Vieille Ville, locals congregate to play chess on giant boards in the shady **Parc des Bastions ★,** alongside the **Mur des Reformateurs ★★,** a massive wall of bas-reliefs commemorating Jean Calvin and other key figures of the Reformation.

Downtown, between the main shopping district and the lake, the **Jardin Anglais ★** contains one of the city's biggest tourist draws—the **Horloge Fleurie (Floral Clock) ★★.** Created from 6,500 flowers, and always ticking, it celebrates the Swiss tradition of watch- and clock-making.

## Outlying Attractions

If time permits, the outskirts of Geneva are well worth exploring, in particular the characterful suburb of **Carouge** (just 15 min. from the city center by tram 12 or 13 to Marché) across the L'Arve River on the southwest perimeter of Geneva. Annexed in the 18th century to the Kingdom of Sardinia, this tiny, residential district has a distinctly Mediterranean, village-like feel. You're sure to be captivated by its sunny squares and its attractive Italianate architecture, not to mention its bohemian sidewalk cafes, jazz clubs, artisan markets, and kooky boutiques. It also boasts some top-notch restaurants, including **A L'Olivier de Provence ★★** (rue Jacques-Dalphin 13; www.olivier-de-provence.ch; ✆ **022/342 04 50**) and the more modestly priced **Café des Négociants ★** (rue de la Filature 29; www.negociants.ch; ✆ **022/300 31 30**).

Another excursion, and an absolute must for foodies, is a visit to the **Domaine de Châteauvieux ★★★** (16 Chemin de Châteauvieux, Peney-Dessus; www.chateauvieux.ch; ✆ **022/753 15 11**), a 16th-century luxury country-house hotel and restaurant northwest of the city center at **Peney-Dessus.** This is Geneva's top eatery, thanks to Swiss chef/owner Philippe Chevrier, who uses the finest of seasonal produce from the property's vegetable gardens and vines to create his two-Michelin-starred haute cuisine. Stay the night and even breakfast is a treat, especially in the summer, when it is served alfresco on the floral-filled veranda.

## Organized Tours & Excursions

A number of companies offer city tours and various transport modes. For the most scenic vistas, go by boat.

**Compagnie Générale de Navigation (CGN)** offers a popular hour-long lake cruise (with several departures daily May–Sept) enabling you to see some of key sights of Geneva as well as the beautiful countryside and châteaux bordering the lake beyond the city limits (www.cgn.ch; ✆ **0848/811 848;** 8 quai du Mont-Blanc). **Swiss Boat** offers similar hour-long cruises of the city quaysides but on smaller vessels; plus a 2¾-hour Rhône River tour (www.swissboat.com; ✆ **022/732 47 47;** 4 quai du Mont-Blanc).

On dry land, I like the **STT Trains** tours, especially if you have kids in tow: just hop aboard one of their open-sided mini tourist trains and explore the city (with recorded multilingual commentary) on one of three circuits: the Old Town (35 min., CHF11); the International Tour (exploring the buildings of the UN and other international organizations plus the left bank, 90 min., CHF25); or Parks and Residences, along the right bank (35 min., CHF9). Trains depart at 45-minute intervals from quai du Mont-Blanc (or place du Rhône for the Old Town tour) daily from April to October; weekends only in March, November, and December. You can find further information at www.trains-tours.ch; ✆ **022/781 04 04.**

Explore the Vieille Ville on foot on a 2-hour guided **walking tour** every Saturday at 10am starting at the Tourist Office at Rue du Mont-Blanc 18 (www.geneve-tourisme.ch); or on Segway with **Citywheels,** daily at 10am and 2pm starting at Citywheels' offices beside Cornavin railway station (rue de Lausanne 16-20; www.citywheels.ch; ✆ **022/510 34 56;** 1½ hours; CHF99; minimum age 16, driving license required). If you fancy a Segway tour, but are concerned about negotiating the cobbled streets of the old town, they also offer a 2½-hour Segway tour of the International Quarter and surrounding parkland for CHF129.

There are also some excellent **biking** excursions: Choose from a variety of themes and distances including "Science and Nature," a "Wine

### CERN—the European Center for Nuclear Research

A visit to CERN is a truly a mind-boggling experience, even for scientists. The world-renowned European Center for Nuclear Research (CERN; Route de Meyrin 385, Meyrin; www.cern.c/expoglobe; ✆ **022/767 76 76;** free admission) was built in 1954 near Geneva to analyze the fundamental laws of nature. The Large Hadron Collider is the latest experiment, started in 2010 and comprising a 17-mile-long (27-km) underground accelerator tunnel—the most complex electronic equipment ever built. It recreates the conditions less than a billionth of a second after the Big Bang, helping to explain the origins and structure of the universe. The World Wide Web was developed in CERN in 1990, and you can visit the hands-on Microcosm Museum and the unique Universe of Particles exhibition here to discover more.

Tour," "Famous painters in Geneva," and "Chocolate tasting and famous love letters." Contact **eBike Tour** (www.ebiketour.ch; ✆ **079/623 50 56**) to get the lowdown.

## Where to Stay

As a truly world-class city, it will come as no surprise that Geneva has numerous top-notch hotels to match. But be forewarned—the city frequently hosts a number of international conferences and conventions, so many of its hotels are booked months in advance. And while it does incorporate dozens of expensive hotels in all different architectural styles (from the antique to the super modern), it lacks intimate, family-run inns. The more affordable accommodation—and none of it is cheap—tends to be inland from the lake, clustered around the railway terminal, or on the Rive Gauche. The palatial lakeside hotels which stretch along the Rive Droite count among the nation's top addresses; their fabled Swiss hospitality (which in Geneva comes at times with a particularly high price-tag) is second-to-none.



### ON THE RIVE DROITE

#### Expensive

**Grand Hôtel Kempinski Geneva ★** Don't be put off by the ugly concrete facade of the Kempinsky Geneva. Inside, this sleek, modern hotel offers space, elegance, comfort, and unrivalled views from its waterfront position on the western shore of the lake, just 15 minutes from the airport and 5 minutes from the main financial sector of central Geneva. Expect bright, spacious bedrooms overlooking the lake, decorated in soft, warm hues, with contemporary fittings and marble bathrooms. It is also an excellent, albeit pricey, choice for families: The Kempinski Kids Club provides childcare for children ages 3 to 8, and the hotel boasts the largest private indoor swimming pool in the city.

Quai du Mont-Blanc 19. www.kempinski-geneva.com. ✆ **022/908 90 81.** 398 units. Doubles from CHF460, suites from CHF5,000. Bus: 1, 25 (Monthoux). **Amenities:** 3 restaurants; bar; gym; spa; saltwater swimming pool; shopping arcade; business facilities; babysitting; concierge; chauffeur service; Kids' Club (ages 3–8); free Wi-Fi.

**Hôtel Beau-Rivage ★★** Hotel Beau-Rivage is the oldest hotel in Geneva, operating since 1865 here on the waterfront and still managed by the fifth generation of the founding Mayer family. Its star-studded guest list has included such luminaries as Sarah Bernhardt, the Duke and Duchess of Windsor, and, more recently, Sting and Catherine Deneuve. The hotel also has an illustrious, sometimes-violent, history: Empress Elisabeth of Austria was stabbed near here in 1898 by anarchist Luigi Lucheni, and the birth of Czechoslovakia as an independent nation was signed here in 1918. Today, the Beau-Rivage provides its guests with 21st-century amenities and impeccable service, while retaining a rarified atmosphere that's evident from the moment you step into the elegant five-story open lobby, or into the suites with their wood paneling and Italian frescoes. There's a certain air of decadence here—it feels a bit like staying in a stately home. The rooms are all beautifully decorated with opulent fabrics and antique furnishings. The hotel's Michelin-starred restaurant, **Le Chat-Botté** ★★★ (see p. 593), counts among the top eateries in town.

Quai du Mont-Blanc 13. www.beau-rivage.ch. ✆ **022/716 66 66.** 168 units. Doubles from CHF870, suites from CHF1,620. Bus: 1 (Monthoux). **Amenities:** 2 restaurants; bar; babysitting; concierge; chauffeur; gym; room service; free Wi-Fi.

**Hôtel d'Angleterre** ★★★ Situated on the lakeshore, the palatial Hôtel d'Angleterre is the smaller, more affordable neighbor of the celebrated Beau Rivage (see above) and one of the city's most pleasing hotels. Despite the antiquated lift, this elegant hotel is run to perfecting standards and, as the name implies, the rooms are tastefully outfitted in a style reminiscent of an extravagant English country house, with sumptuous fabrics and fittings and soothing lighting. Most rooms have lake views (the smaller rooms have lake glimpses) and the suites are especially plush, with spacious marble bathrooms. Service is exemplary; the concierge is especially accommodating, and I love the quirky Leopard Room bar, with its safari-inspired decor and extensive whisky selection.

17 Quai de Mont-Blanc. www.dangleterrehotel.com. ✆ **022/906 55 55.** 45 units. Doubles CHF790–1100, suites CHF1,800–6,900. Bus: 1, 25 (Monthoux). **Amenities:** Restaurant; bar; concierge; pet; gym; sauna; limousine service; free Wi-Fi.

**Hôtel La Réserve** ★★★ This contemporary five-star hotel is set in 10 acres of gardens beside the lake on the outskirts of town, with decadent, stylish interiors by maverick Parisian designer Jacques Garcia. Taking inspiration from the style of African lodges, each room offers the ultimate in comfort, with crisp white cotton, velvet, and linen bed-clothing; sleek mosaic and granite bathrooms; and a terrace overlooking the gardens and lake. But La Réserve's real draw is its world-renowned spa. Best-known for its iconic 4- or 7-day Nescens "better-aging" programs (which help you to preserve your youthfulness by analyzing all aspects of your body, lifestyle, and diet), the spa also offers acupuncture, osteopathy, aesthetic angiology for the face and legs, Shiatsu, and reflexology. There's also a swimming pool, tennis courts, endless treatment rooms, and an organic restaurant. For children, there's "La Petite Reserve" club—a supervised play area and parent-free zone—for ages 6 months to 13 years, and a summer camp that offers weeklong multi-sport courses for 6- to 11-year-olds.

301 Route de Lausanne. www.lareserve.ch. ✆ **022/959 59 99.** 102 units. Doubles CHF600–CHF3,100. Train: Tuilleries, then 2-minutes' walk. **Amenities:** Spa; swimming pool; 5 restaurants; bar; DJ; kids' club; tennis courts; gardens; water taxi to city center; free Wi-Fi.

### Moderate

**Hôtel N'vY** ★ This hotel near exudes boho chic, with its flamboyant bars and cafe open round the clock. The minimalist rooms boast state-of-the-art furnishings, with sharp, clean lines in a variety of vibrant colors and textures. The hotel's see-and-be-seen venues include the fashionable

Trilby Restaurant with its arty fusion cuisine, the ultra-sophisticated cocktail bar NVY (with a resident DJ daily 6pm–1am), and cozy Tag's Cafe, which provides iPads for its guests. The price tag for all of this is surprisingly affordable—stay here and you'll be the "envy" of all your friends.

55 rue Rothschild. www.hotelnvygeneva.com. ✆ **022/544 66 66.** 153 units. Doubles from CHF184. Tram: 15 (Butini). **Amenities:** Restaurant; cafe; bar; gym; DJ; free Wi-Fi.

### Inexpensive

**Hôtel de Genève ★** This cheap and cheerful, two-star Belle Époque hotel appeals to budget travelers who don't mind a no-frills atmosphere if it means saving on room costs. The rooms are very basic but spotlessly clean, the bathrooms tiny but adequate. The decor is generally quite quirky, with an abundance of fairy-lights and florid ornaments in public areas, but I especially like the cozy Alpine-chalet atmosphere of the main reception area. The staff is friendly and the buffet breakfasts—with their cold cuts, cereals, and pastries—are big, tasty, and filling. Take note if you need quiet to sleep: Some of the rooms are quite noisy due to the hotel's proximity to the train station.

1 place Isaac-Mercier. www.hotel-de-geneve.ch. ✆ **022/908 54 00.** 39 units. Singles from CHF104, doubles from CHF135. Bus: 10 (Place des 22 Cantons); Tram: 15, 16 (Isaac-Mercier). **Amenities:** Bar; cafeteria/coffee shop; free Internet in lobby.



**Hôtel Edelweiss ★★** Don't be fooled by the modern facade of Hôtel Edelweiss—it's the perfect retreat if you haven't time to stay in the Swiss countryside. Step inside, away from the bustling streets of the lively Pâquis district, and you'll be transported straight to the mountains. Friendly staff dressed in traditional costumes; log fires; fresh flowers; and snug, wood-clad guest rooms with plush fabrics in earthy hues and rustic hand-painted furniture combine to create the atmosphere of an authentic alpine hotel. Book well in advance to clinch one of the roomy family rooms. I love the quirky eponymous restaurant in the basement (**Edelweiss ★★**; see p. 595), which serves a simple menu of Swiss specialties, including some of the best fondues in town.

2 place de la Navigation. www.hoteledelweissgeneva.com. ✆ **022/544 51 51.** 42 units. Doubles from CHF138. Tram: 13, 14 (Place de la Navigation); Bus: 1 (Place de la Navigation). **Amenities:** Restaurant; free Wi-Fi.

## ON THE RIVE GAUCHE

### Moderate

**Hôtel de la Cigogne ★★★** It's easy to spot the Hôtel de la Cigogne, with its smart orange awnings and ornamental gold stork, La Cigogne, above the entrance. Once inside, the ornate interiors instantly conjure up a sense of comforting luxury. Each room is elegant, spacious and refined, exquisitely decorated with antiques from an assortment of periods and styles, and featuring luxurious marble bathrooms. Service is top-notch, and fresh flowers and log fires add the finishing touches to this homey hotel located just off the lakeside and at the foot of the Old Town.

17 place Longemalle. www.cigogne.ch. ✆ **022/818 40 40.** 52 units. Doubles CHF485–CHF620, suites CHF615–CHF2,050. Bus: 6, 8, 9 (Metropole). **Amenities:** Restaurant; concierge, room service; free Wi-Fi.

**Hôtel les Armures ★★★** Hôtel les Armures is an intimate and historic hotel, located at the top of the Old Town, which was converted from four buildings dating from the 13th to 17th centuries. The guest rooms blend modern furnishings with original decorative details, such as painted ceilings, frescoes, wood beams, exposed stonework, and open fireplaces. For the best view, request a room overlooking the quiet, shaded square with its ancient fountain. You may find yourself rubbing shoulders with celebrities here: The hotel's guest list has included luminaries such as Queen Sofia of Spain, Sofia Loren, Paul McCartney, Monica Seles, and George Clooney. There's even a plaque near the front door commemorating Bill and Hillary Rodham Clinton's visit in 1994. And if you're hungry, you won't have to go far: The hotel's eponymous restaurant—a cozy wood-beamed eatery adorned with muskets and armor—is a veritable fondue institution.

1 rue Puits-St Pierre. www.hotel-les-armures.ch. ✆ **022/310 91 72.** 32 units. Doubles from CHF430. Bus: 36 (Cathédrale); Tram: 12 (Rive or Molard). **Amenities:** Restaurant; bar; concierge; room service; babysitting; limousine service; free Wi-Fi.

### Inexpensive

**Hôtel Bel Espérance ★★** On the slopes at the entrance to the Old Town, just a stone's throw from some of the city's most luxurious shopping boulevards, this unpretentious budget hotel is owned and managed by the Salvation Army. Expect simple, functional rooms (including some generously sized family rooms)—not dissimilar to an upmarket hostel—private bathrooms, and fantastic views across the rooftops to the lake.

1 rue de la Vallée. www.hotel-bel-esperance.ch. ✆ **022/818 37 37.** 40 units. Doubles CHF160–CHF190, family rooms CHF235. Bus: 10, 33, A, E, G (Rive). **Amenities:** Kitchen; terrace; laundry room; free Wi-Fi.

## Where to Eat

Thanks to the strong international flavor of the city, eating out in Geneva is a cosmopolitan experience, with restaurants serving food from around the world. Given their proximity to the French border, the Swiss cuisine here has an unmistakably French influence, with cozy Paris-style bistros alongside the plentiful fine-dining options. Meals are often long, drawn-out affairs and, in most cases, more expensive than many travelers are used to. Local delicacies include filets of perch or omble chevalier from the lake; and the local longeole sausage; and traditional Swiss cheese dishes such as fondue and raclette, ideally accompanied by local Geneva wines.

### ON THE RIVE DROITE

### Expensive

**Le Chat-Botté ★★★** FRENCH Situated in the five-star **Hôtel Beau-Rivage ★★** (see p. 590), Le Chat-Botté ("Puss in Boots") is a classical-style restaurant serving some of the finest food in town, and is popular for both pleasurable business lunches and romantic treats, especially during the summer months, when you can dine on the beautiful terrace with a sweeping panorama of the lake. In the capable hands of French Michelin-starred chef Dominique Gauthier, you will be assured of exemplary French cuisine cooked with ingredients sourced from the finest producers, including foie gras from the Landes, snails from Vallorbes, and suckling lamb from the Pyrenees—plus a host of delectable *amuse-bouches* to tickle your taste buds, and some exceptional French wines. Choose from the four-course set menus for the best value—the earth menu, the sea menu, or, for that special occasion, the prestigious (and expensive) set menu that's served to the entire table. Reservations are strongly advised.

Hôtel Beau-Rivage, Quai du Mont-Blanc 13. www.beau-rivage.ch. ✆ **022/716 69 39.** Mains CHF60–CHF105, set 3-course lunch menu CHF70, dinner menus from CHF140. Bus: 1, 25 (Monthoux); Bus: 6, 8, 9, 25, 61 (Mont Blanc). Mon–Fri noon–1:45pm (last order), 7pm–9:45pm (last order); Sat 7–9:45pm (last order).



### Moderate

**Brasserie Lipp ★** SEAFOOD/FRENCH You could be forgiven for thinking you were in the French capital when you visit this stylish restaurant (located on the second floor of a chic shopping mall and named after the renowned Parisian brasserie), with its waiters in black jackets and long white aprons, and a typical old-world brasserie ambience. Fresh oysters are a specialty, and so is fresh lobster, which diners can choose from a tank. Other signature dishes include regional favorites from southwest France, such as charcuterie and *cassoulet*—a flavorful sausage and white bean casserole, slow-cooked the traditional way in a deep earthenware dish. The enormous freshest-of-fresh shellfish platters are not for the faint-hearted; however, they are as every bit as delicious as they are spectacular. Lipp is an especially popular venue for business entertaining, so booking is advisable, even at lunchtime.

Rue de la Confédération 8. www.brasserie-lipp.com. ✆ **022/318 80 30.** Mains CHF23–CHF50, plat du jour CHF19–CHF37. Bus: 1, 2, 3, 5, 7, 9, 10, 19, 20, 29; Tram: 12, 16, 17 (Bel-Air). Mon–Sat 7am–2am, Sun 9am–2am.

**Café de Paris ★★★** FRENCH This lavishly decorated bistro, dubbed "Chez Boubier" by its devoted local clientele, conjures up an atmosphere reminiscent of the Parisian brasseries of the 1930s with its simple wooden tables, wooden wall panels, chandeliers, and its brisk, efficient service. However, it's definitely one to miss if you're vegetarian as it only serves one main course—premium *entrecôte* steak, cooked to perfection to your specifications and served dripping with herb butter (invented here by Monsieur Boubier in the 1930s), three helpings of fries, and a generous, tastily dressed green salad. There's a choice of sorbets, ice cream, fruit salad, or patisseries for dessert. The whole experience is simple but delicious.

Rue du Mont-Blanc 26. www.chezboubier.com. ✆ **022/732 84 50.** Mains from CHF42. Train: Cornavin. Daily 7am–11pm.

**Edelweiss ★★** SWISS Extremely touristy, and especially popular with families, this basement restaurant serves hearty Swiss cuisine in a witty setting reminiscent of a mountain chalet: think red-and-white-checked tablecloths; alphorns, edelweiss, toy St. Bernard dogs, and other kitsch local memorabilia adorning the wood-paneled walls; and an oom-pah band and occasional yodeler in its midst. The fondues (from CHF28 per person) are scrumptious, plus there are plenty of other authentic Swiss specialties for non-cheese-lovers, including rösti potatoes; filets of perch from the lake; and *fondue bourguignonne* (beef fondue served with frites and sauces), all washed down with local wines.

Hôtel Edelweiss, Place de la Navigation (off rue de Berne). www.hoteledelweiss geneva.com. ✆ **022/544 51 51.** Mains: CHF20–CHF54, 3-course menus from CHF48. Tram: 13, 14 (Place de la Navigation); Bus: 1 (Place de la Navigation). 7pm–11pm daily.

**Globus ★★** INTERNATIONAL From breakfast through lunch and dinner to late-night snack, it's fun to eat and drink your way around the world in the massive, modernistic food hall of Globus, Geneva's upscale department store at the heart of a chic shopping neighborhood. Choose from tapas, panini, noodles, crêpes, curries, sushi, salads, caviar, seafood—you name it, they have it here, from light bites to more substantial meals. The fare is essentially high-quality fast food (with a rather elevated price tag), prepared on the spot and served at individual shiny black-and-chrome bars. There are plenty of desserts too, including cakes and pastries, and a wellness bar that serves freshly squeezed juices and smoothies. Even the wine bar offers a choice of wines from around the globe. Unsurprisingly popular with well-heeled shoppers looking for a quick, quality lunch, the whole informal, self-service eating experience makes a pleasant change from the more conventional (and time-consuming) sit-down restaurant.

48 rue du Rhône. www.globus.ch. ✆ **058/578 50 50.** Mains from CHF20. Tram: 16 (Molard). Mon–Fri 7:30am–10pm, Sat 8:30am–10pm.

### Inexpensive

**La Buvette des Bains ★** INTERNATIONAL On first impression, the unprepossessing exterior of this somewhat shabby, ramshackle, white-washed hut—located on a pier in the middle of Lake Geneva—seems an unlikely venue for an lively cafe/bar; a place where locals meet for coffee and cake; simple soups and salads; platters of cold cuts; a wholesome *plat du jour;* or simply just a drink. But perhaps it's best known for its top-notch breakfasts (served 8–11:30am)—the traditionally Swiss Bircher Muesli is especially delicious—and on winter evenings (Sept–Apr), its superb cheese fondues. The shack is located at the far end of the Bains de Pâquis, and is accessed by means of a long wooden board-walk over the lake. Hugely popular year-round, it draws a young, trendy crowd (huddled round wood stoves in winter, and basking on the terraces in summer); and with families who flock to the beaches and lido-style swimming area in sunny weather. Cash only.

Bains de Pâquis, 30 quai du Mont-Blanc. www.buvettedesbains.ch. ✆ **022/738 16 16.** Plat du jour CHF14. Bus: 1 (Pâquis). 7am-10:30pm daily.

**Les Brasseurs ★★** ALSATIAN Centrally located by Cornavin train station, this jolly restaurant draws a young, lively crowd for its menu of tasty German and Alsatian specialties. It's also the only venue in Geneva that brews its own *blanche, blonde,* and *ambrée* beers. These ales provide the perfect accompaniment to the hearty, wholesome cuisine, and you can buy them (or a souvenir glass) to take away—they are sold by the bottle or the barrel. Our favorites here are the thin, crisp *flammeküches,* the Alsatian equivalent of a pizza, made with various toppings that include bacon, onion, cream, cheese, tomatoes, mushrooms, and olives. The salads are generous, and the *choucroute* (braised sauerkraut and sausage) and *carbonnade de boeuf* (a rich beef stew)—both cooked in Les Brasseurs' beer—are standouts. Make a reservation or arrive before 9pm to be sure of a table.

Place de Cornavin 20. www.les-brasseurs.ch. ✆ **022/731 02 06.** Main dishes CHF16–CHF31, plat du jour CHF17–CHF19. Train: Cornavin. Mon–Wed 11am–1am (2am Thurs–Sat), Sun 3pm–1am.

## ON THE RIVE GAUCHE

### Moderate

**Au Pied de Cochon ★★** FRENCH/SWISS Centrally located at the heart of the Old Town, on the lane that leads downhill from the picturesque Place du Bourg-de-Four, Au Pied de Cochon is very much a Genevois institution that appeals to locals as well as tourists for its high-quality, hearty, traditional fare. The setting is classic turn-of-the-century brasserie, with wood paneling, leather banquettes, white linen tablecloths, and mirrors; the first-class service is brisk and efficient. The main draw on the menu, as the name suggests, is a stuffed pig's trotter served with Madeira sauce and market vegetables. But for those with more conservative tastes, the risotto with pan-fried duck liver and local Swiss sausage, or the traditional beef stew are equally delectable. The wine list has a choice of French and Swiss wines, served by the glass or the bottle, with a notable selection of excellent wines from the Geneva region.

4 Place du Bourg-de-Four. www.pied-de-cochon.ch. ✆ **022/310 47 97.** Mains CHF29–CHF65, plat du Jour CHF20. Bus: 3, 5 (Croix-Rouge), 36 (Bourg-de-Four). Mon–Fri 8am–midnight, Sat–Sun 11am–midnight.

### Inexpensive

**Chez Ma Cousine ★★★** SWISS Visit Chez Ma Cousine for delicious Swiss-style fast food. In a happening location at the heart of the Old Town, this cheery, bright-yellow restaurant offers a great value, making it exceptionally family-friendly and popular with students. No airs and graces here, just good-quality, simple home cooking. The full name is actually

"Chez Ma Cousine on y Mange du Poulet" ("At my cousin's house we eat chicken") and accordingly, there's only one dish on the menu: Grilled chicken, served with mountains of crispy sautéed Provençale-style potatoes and a salad, followed by a choice of simple, tempting desserts, such as chocolate mousse or *tarte tatin*. Wines are served by the glass or by the bottle. Service is speedy, so the restaurant doesn't take reservations.
Place du Bourg de Four 6. www.chezmacousine.ch. ✆ **022/310 96 96.** Mains CHF15. Bus: 36 (Bourg-de-Four). Mon–Sat 11am–11:30pm, Sun 11am–12:30pm.

**Crêperie St-Pierre ★★** FRENCH Crêperie St-Pierre, in the heart of Old Town, is the perfect place to tuck into authentic Breton crêpes, washed down the traditional way with cider, or with wine by the glass. This cozy but no-frills cafe crammed full of tiny tables serves an impressive choice of tasty, affordable pancakes (both sweet and savory) plus copious salads. The food is simple, without garnish, but nourishing and a good value for the money/location. I really like the crêpe sarrasin (made with buckwheat) laden with juicy strips of steak and onion, followed by a sweet pancake with sugar, cinnamon and butter—simple but delicious. Warning: Only order a second pancake if you're seriously hungry! In summer, the cobbled pavement terrace is an especially pleasant spot for lunch, in a sunny pedestrian corner right beside the cathedral. The clientele here consists primarily of tourists (plus an occasional smattering of regular locals), and service can be slow and quality variable, especially during high season.
6 Place de la Taconnerie. ✆ **022/310 09 76.** CHF8–CHF20. Bus: 36 (Taconnerie). Daily noon–10pm.

## Shopping

From boutiques to department stores, Geneva is a shopper's dream come true. The city is world-renowned for its watches and jewelry, but it's also a good place to buy embroidered blouses, music boxes from the Jura region, chocolate, Swiss Army knives, and many other items.

Geneva practically invented the wristwatch. In fact, watchmaking in the city dates from the 16th century. Here, more than in any other Swiss city, you should be able to find all the best brands, including Philippe Patek, Tissot, Rolex, Omega, and Blancpain, to name just a few. Be careful not to buy a Swiss watch in one of the souvenir stores; if jewelers are legitimate, they'll display the symbol of the Geneva Association of Watchmakers and Jewelers. **Bucherer,** 45 rue du Rhône (www.bucherer.com; ✆ **022/319 62 66**), one of the nation's leading watch and jewelry retailers, always has a plentiful selection.

An ideal place to start your shopping spree is upscale **place du Molard** on the left bank, and its flanking streets—rue du Rhône and rue du Marché—ogle at the dazzling jewelry, the luxury brands, and the latest in haute couture Genevois, but try not to look at the price tags. Here too are chic department stores **Globus,** 48 rue du Rhône (www.globus.ch; ✆ **058/578 50 50**) and **Bon Genie,** 34 rue du Marché (www.bongenie-grieder.ch; © **022/818 11 11**). Just around the corner, stock up on picnic supplies at **Halle-de-Rive,** 29 boulevard Helvétique (www.halle-de-rive.com), an exclusive indoor market with fine cheeses, cold cuts, bread, fruit, and vegetables.

The cobbled streets of the Old Town contain the quirkier boutiques and fine arts, while bohemian **Carouge** is the place to seek out more whimsical arts and crafts, antiquities, and local designs. There's a charming **Farmers' Market** in Place du Marché on Wednesday and Saturday mornings.

Some of the world's most famous auction houses are also located in the city, including **Sotheby's,** 13 quai du Mont-Blanc; **Christie's,** 8 place de la Taconnerie; and **Antiquorum,** 2 rue du Mont-Blanc, the largest repository of antique timepieces in the world. The tourist office has details of forthcoming sales.

## Entertainment & Nightlife



The grand 19th-century opera house, the **Grand Théâtre ★★★,** has earned international repute for its world-class opera, theatre, ballet, classical concerts, and chamber recitals. Modelled on Paris's acclaimed Opera Garnier, the Grand Théâtre seats 1,500 and is the largest theatre in French-speaking Switzerland. The main opera and ballet season spans September through July, with an ambitious program from its resident companies, as well as performances from such guest troupes as Lausanne's world-renowned Béjart dance troupe.

Also in Place Neuve, Geneva's acclaimed **Orchestre de la Suisse Romande** performs regular classical concerts in the rococo-style **Victoria Hall ★★,** the city's main musical institution.

Don't be fooled by the city's seemingly stately veneer, as Geneva has a surprisingly diverse and varied after-dark scene, which starts to warm up as the sun goes down and neon lights begin to illuminate the lake. In summer, the **outdoor cafes and bars** lining the banks of the river and the lake are always a good starting point for an evening out. You'll find other popular watering holes in and around **place du Bourg-de-Four**—once a 19th-century stagecoach stop, this pebbled square is now one of the nightlife hubs of Geneva's Old Town.

For a listing of nightlife and cultural activities, pick up a copy of the free bilingual monthly *Genève Le Guide* (www.le-guide.ch) from your hotel or tourist information centers.

There's no shortage of bars and pubs in Geneva, and they range from the trendy rooftop hangouts and über-cool cocktail lounges of the five-star lakeside hotels to mellow wine bars and laidback locals' pubs.

**Le Rouge et Le Blanc** wine bar (27 quai des Bergues; www.lerougeblanc.ch; © **022/731 15 50**), as its name suggests, is an ideal place to try out some local wines beside the river, or try fashionable **Arthur's** (7–9 rue du Rhône; www.arthurs.ch; © **022/810 32 60**), at the heart of the shopping district, with its lovely summer terrace overlooking the Rhône and the lake. I also especially like **La Clémence** (20 Place du

Bourg-du-Four; www.laclemence.ch; ✆ **022/312 24 98**), a tiny, wood-paneled watering-hole on the Place du Bourg-du-Four: In winter it serves delicious mulled wine; in summer it boasts ones of the largest sidewalk terraces in the Old Town.

Look no further than **L'Atelier Cocktail Lounge** (rue Henri-Blanvalet 11; ✆ **022/735 22 47.**) or its more casual neighbor, **Yvette de Marseille** (rue Henri-Blanvalet 13; www.yvettedemarseille.ch; ✆ **022/735 15 55**) for creative cocktails; or join the beautiful people in such chic hotel-bar venues as **Le Glow** in Hotel Président Wilson (41 quai Wilson; www.hotelpwilson.com; ✆ **022/906 67 45**) and **Floor Two** (Grand Hotel Kempinski Geneva, Quai du Mont-Blanc 19; www.kempinski.com/en/geneva/grand-hotel-geneva; ✆ **022/908 92 24**) for sophisticated, wallet-walloping cocktails overlooking the lake.

For bars with an after-dark party vibe, it's hard to beat the panoramic outdoor terrace of **Rooftop 42** (42 rue du Rhône; www.rooftop42.com; ✆ **022/346 77 00**) overlooking the lake; or up the beat and head to **Café Cuba** (1 Place du Cirque; www.cafecuba.ch; ✆ **022/328 42 60**), near Pleinpalais, a lively tropical club spread over three floors, where the caipirinhas flow freely and a hip crowd sways to sensual Latin rhythms in a Havana-inspired setting.

Geneva's clubbing scene is vibrant and eclectic. The funky **Au Chat Noir** (13 rue Vautier; www.chatnoir.ch; ✆ **022/307 10 40**) is a veritable institution in the villagey district of Carouge, staging some of Geneva's hottest live music—jazz, funk, hip hop, salsa, and blues performed in a cozy basement club, plus a DJ and a pint-size dance floor.

As most of Geneva sleeps, the chic urban party crowd packs into the Java Club in the basement of the plush Grand Hôtel Kempinski (19 quai du Mont-Blanc; www.javaclub.ch; ✆ **022/908 90 98**) to dance 'til dawn to the hottest house music in town; the atmosphere is hedonistic, the decor deep purple, and the drinks expensive. At the other end of the clubbing spectrum, cult address **L'Usine** (Place des Volontaires 4; www.usine.ch; ✆ **022/781 34 90**), in a former factory, continues to champion the city's alternative clubbing scene with its various concert spaces and varied beats from electro to punk, rock, and metal.

## Day Trips from Geneva

Geneva and its lake make an excellent base for touring the surrounding region, and a perfect springboard into France. The lake fringes two countries, and three Swiss cantons (Geneva, Vaud, and Valais).

Step east to discover the resorts of the northern shore, in particular the "Swiss Riviera" from Lausanne to Montreux, renowned for its spectacular scenery, Mediterranean-style microclimate and long-standing tradition of tourism.

Explore the "Olympic Capital" of **Lausanne,** Switzerland's third largest city, from the Gothic heights of **Notre-Dame Cathedral** (Place de la Cathédrale; www.cathedrale-lausanne.ch; ✆ **021/316 71 60**) to the elegant waterfront promenade at Ouchy, with its exclusive yachting harbor, beautiful Belle Époque architecture, and **Musée Olympique** (**Olympic Museum;** Quai d'Ouchy 1; www.olympic.org/museum; ✆ **021/621 65 11**).

Try to schedule your visit to the gracious spa town of **Montreux** to coincide with the fabled **Montreux Jazz Festival,** which takes place each July (book tickets in advance at www.montreuxjazz.com). The nearby **Château de Chillon** (Avenue de Chillon 21, Veytaux; www.chillon.ch/en; ✆ **021/966 8910**) counts among Switzerland's most visited sights—a beautiful, medieval castle romantically sited on a rock jutting into the lake, immortalized by countless artists and writers, including Lord Byron in "The Prisoner of Chillon." Excursions to Lausanne, Montreux, and Château de Chillon can be made by road, rail (see p. 577), or boat with the Lake Geneva Navigation Company (www.cgn.ch; ✆ **0848/811 848**), who also operate day-long paddle-steamer cruises around the lake.



Hire a bicycle, put it on the train to Lausanne, and follow the 33km (21-mile) Lavaux Wine Trail from there to Chillon, through the celebrated UNESCO Lavaux vineyard terraces which cling precipitously to the slopes of the lake and afford intoxicating alpine vistas. Or stay more local and vine-hop by car, bike, or tram around Geneva's outlying wine villages: Anières, Céligny, Russin, and Satigny.

Cross the Franco-Swiss border to the sedate picture book–pretty town of **Annecy** (40 min. by car from Geneva), set beside a crystal-blue lake and against a backdrop of snowcapped mountains, where flower-lined canals lead to its fairytale red-turreted castle, the medieval **Château d'Annecy** (Place du Château; www.patrimoines.agglo-annecy.fr; ✆ **04/50 33 87 30**). Or visit **Chamonix** (1 hr. by car from Geneva). This French ski-resort ranks among the French Alps' top adventure-sports destinations, and boasts some of Europe's finest mountain hiking.

# LUCERNE

Lucerne (*Luzern* in German) and its magnificent lake represent the very essence of Switzerland, located at the heart of Switzerland not only geographically and historically, but also spiritually. For this is storybook Switzerland, the fabled homeland of William Tell, where the seeds were sown in 1291 that led to the Swiss Confederation (see box p. 608). Little wonder that this historic city, with its world-class museums, rich cultural scene, and fairytale setting—beside a vast, shimmering lake and against a rugged backdrop of dense green forests and snowcapped mountains—is one of Switzerland's most popular tourist destinations.

## Essentials

The **Lucerne Tourist Office** website is www.luzern.com.

**ARRIVING** Lucerne has excellent train connections. Situated at the junction of four major rail lines, it is connected with every other major city in Switzerland by fast train. Allow 50 minutes from Zurich, 1½ hours

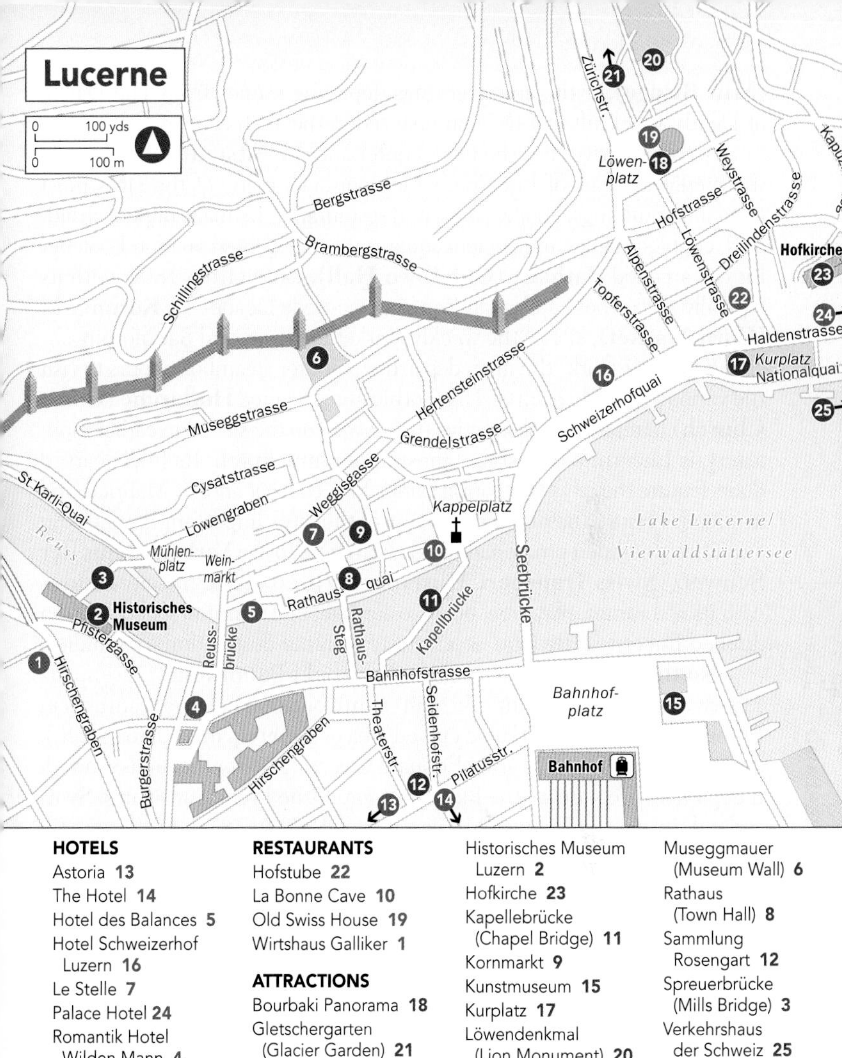


from Bern, and around 3 hours from Geneva. Call ✆ **0900/300 300** (www.sbb.ch) for rail schedules.

If you're driving from the Swiss capital, Bern, take the A1 north then the A2 to Lucerne (allow 1 hr.). From Zurich, head south and west along the A4, which links into the A14 to Lucerne (allow 1 hr.).

**CITY LAYOUT** Most visitors arrive at the train station, on **Bahnhofplatz,** on the left (south) bank of the **River Reuss.** Immediately, you will see the famous covered wooden bridge across the river, the early 14th-century **Kapellbrücke** (**Chapel Bridge;** see p. 605)—the city symbol which adorns so many of the local guidebooks, postcards, and chocolate boxes. Farther downstream, a second wooden bridge—the **Spreuerbrücke**

**(Mill Bridge),** with gable paintings depicting scenes from The Dance of Death, was built in 1407 and restored in the 19th century.

Across the river lies the town center and the **Altstadt (Old Town),** the medieval heart of Lucerne, which contains many of the city's most appealing buildings, shops, cafes, and restaurants. Its maze of pedestrianized, cobbled streets and ancient squares is best explored on foot. Look out for the arcaded **Rathaus (Old Town Hall),** dating from 1602, with its typically Swiss roof and Italian Renaissance–style facade—in **Kornmarkt (Corn Market),** site of the weekly market (on Tues and Sat mornings).

**Kurplatz** marks the main departure point for steamboats tours to visit the various lakeside resorts. The Gothic-Renaissance **Hofkirche (Court Church)** here, with its distinctive twin towers on the site of an earlier monastery, is Lucerne's largest and most important church. Its finely carved doors feature the city's two patron saints, St. Leodegar and St. Maurice, and its arcades house the remains of many of the city's important families. An attractive tree-lined promenade leads from here to the **Verkehrshaus der Schweiz** (**Swiss Transport Museum;** see p. 607), and the city **Lido**—with its restaurant, play area, beach volleyball, and swimming pool—often dubbed Lucerne's "Riviera," is a favorite summer destination for families.

North of the lake, marvel at the **Bourbaki Panorama** (Löwenplatz 11; www.bourbakipanorama.ch; 9am–6pm), one of the largest canvases in Europe, covering a remarkable curved area of 1,009 sq. m. (10,861 sq. ft.), and painted by Genevois artist Edouard Castres. Not for the faint-hearted, it depicts in great detail the bloody retreat of the French army into Switzerland during the Franco-Prussian war of 1870 to 1871—an event still hailed as one of the finest acts of humanitarian courage in Swiss history.

Just around the corner in Denkmalstrasse is the **Löwendenkmal (Lion Monument),** Lucerne's second most visited site (after the Kapellbrücke). This fatally wounded lion, carved into sandstone rocks, is dedicated to the numerous Swiss mercenaries who died in the French Revolution of 1789. Mark Twain described the dying lion as "the saddest and most moving piece of rock in the world." Children are always fascinated by the **Gletschergarten** (**Glacier Garden;** Denkmalstrasse 4;

A view of Lucerne from the Kapellbrücke (Chapel Bridge).

Apr–Oct 9am–6pm, Nov–Mar 10am–5pm), with its 32 extraordinary potholes (measuring up to 9m/30 ft. deep and wide) that were worn into the sandstone bed of an Iron Age glacier during the era when ice covered the surface of Lake Lucerne.

For some of the best city vistas, walk the medieval ramparts (**Museggmauer, Museum Wall**) past the city's nine lookout towers. The most scenic stretch is from Wachtturm to the Zytturm, which contains the city's oldest clock. Bizarrely, since medieval times, it has chimed 1 minute ahead of all the other public clocks in Lucerne.

The Hofkirche, Lucerne.

**GETTING AROUND** You'll soon feel at home in this charming, laid-back city—it's an idyllic town for strolling and lingering, especially on the lakeshore and in the cobbled maze of streets which make up the picturesque Altstadt (Old Town). It's surprisingly compact to explore on foot. However, it's equally easy to explore by **bus** (one ride costs between CHF2–CHF6, depending on the distance you ride). There are route maps and automatic vending machines at the bus stops. A 24-hour ticket costs CHF30.

For outlying attractions, it's hard to resist traveling by **boat** (see p. 603). Lake Lucerne's fleet of beautifully restored steamboats provide links between many small lakeside communities and attractions, some of which are still more easily reached by boat than by any other mode of transport.

**Bikes** can be rented at the railway station for CHF27/CHF35 per half-day/full-day or CHF39/CHF54 per half-day/full-day for an E-bike. See www.rentabike.ch for details and online reservations. The shores of the lake are perfect for bike rides—get a map from the tourist office, and take a picnic! The trail along the southern shore is especially scenic. Set off from the train station toward Tribschen, venue of the **Richard Wagner Museum ★** (see p. 609), St-Niklausen and Kastanienbaum. If you have time, continue on to Winkel-Horw beach for a dip in the lake. Allow a couple of hours for the 18km (11 mile) roundtrip.

## Exploring Lucerne

Thanks to its unique mix of history, culture, folklore, lakes, and mountains, the city of Lucerne is Switzerland at its scenic best. This medieval gem was one of the first Swiss cities to be discovered by 19th-century philosophers, painters, and poets who, wooed by its charm and grandiose

## LUCERNE'S lake

Lucerne's vast, glacial lake is the fourth-largest in Switzerland. It is 38km (24-miles) long and at its broadest 3.3km (2-miles) wide, with numerous fjords and finger-like inlets, flanked by dramatic limestone outcrops, steep forested gorges, and towering mountains. It's known in German as the *Vierwaldstättersee* and in French as the *Lac des Quatre Cantons,* the "lake of the four forest states" (Lucerne, Uri, Unterwalden, and Schwyz), and many consider it Europe's most beautiful and romantic lake. It's hugely popular for walking and watersports, including waterskiing, sailing, and swimming in its popular lidos, and also for its many paddle steamers, which ply between the many small lakeside communities, some of which are more easily reached by boat than by any other means of transport.

Lucerne is the ideal base for nostalgic paddle-steamer excursions into the surrounding "William Tell Country." Some of the resorts hugging the lakeside get very crowded in high season, especially those closest to Lucerne, so I suggest you skip the tourist honeypots of Weggis and Vitznau and head farther afield to explore the narrow inlet of **Urnersee** at the southeastern tip of Lake Lucerne, which not only attracts fewer visitors than other parts of the lake, but also boasts some of its wildest and most majestic scenery. Here also you'll find a giant natural rock obelisk, the **Schillerstein**—dedicated to Friedrich von Schiller, author of *Wilhelm Tell*—which rises some 25 m (82 ft.) out of the lake.

**Schiffahrtsgesellschaft Vierwaldstättersee (Lake Lucerne Navigation Co.;** www.lakelucerne.ch; ✆ **041/367 67 67**) operates Europe's largest flotilla of lake steamers in and out of Lucerne. A return passage to the lake's most distant point, Flüelen (allow 4 hr.), costs CHF72 and departs from the quays opposite the Hauptbahnhof in Lucerne. Tickets for shorter hops are calculated according to their distance (CHF38 to Weggis and back, CHF45 for Vitznau). In midsummer, departures begin at 9:15am and continue every hour or so throughout the day.

Wherever you choose to disembark, be sure to find out the departure time of the last boat back to Lucerne. The last boat from Flüelen usually departs before 4pm. All boats have a restaurant, or at least a cafeteria, onboard. Scheduled cruises are free if you have a Swiss Card or Eurail train pass, and half-price for InterRail pass holders.



scenery, put it on the map of Europe as a stylish resort. Still today, it remains hugely popular, a picturesque city with all the charm and intimacy of a small town, just a stone's throw from Zurich and Bern, at the gateway to the high Alps.

Alongside its top-class museums and cultural venues, take time to explore the Altstadt (Old Town), with its narrow cobbled streets, covered bridges, frescoed houses, historical buildings, and fountains; to stroll beside the clear blue waters of Lake Lucerne; and to walk the medieval ramparts for spectacular views across the rooftops of the town to the majestic, snowcapped mountains beyond.

**Historisches Museum Luzern ★** MUSEUM Kids especially love the eclectic displays of artifacts in this quirky History Museum—lovingly dubbed "The Depot" by locals and housed in a former 16th-century

## Mount Pilatus

Few visitors to the Lucerne area return home without first climbing one of the nearby mountains to see the lake at its finest. Rigi is popular, with dazzling vistas over the lake and Lucerne (accessed via the Rigi Railway from Weggis or Vitznau, www.rigi.ch), but it's hard to beat Pilatus (www.pilatus.ch), 15km (9 miles) south of Lucerne, for the best 360-degree views of central Switzerland. Simply hop aboard a boat to Alpnachstadt (the journey takes around 90 min.) and then the steepest electric **cogwheel railway** in the world—running at a 48% gradient—will whisk you to the top of Mount Pilatus (2,132m/6,994 ft.) in just 30 minutes, where a large sun terrace and two restaurants serve up breathtaking vistas with their traditional Swiss fare. Be forewarned however: The summit is often cloud-covered (hence its name, which is thought to originate from the Latin *pileatus,* meaning "capped"), so try to visit as early as possible in the day for the best chance of a decent view. Many choose to make a circular trip and descent by cable car. If you have family, it's worth pausing at **Fräkmüntegg,** where the **Seilpark Pilatus**—a suspension rope park with aerial cablewalks, log bridges, and ziplines—provides hours of fun, followed by a ride on the **Fräkgaudi Rodelbahn,** a 1,350m (4,429 ft.) toboggan run, the longest summer run in Switzerland. From Fräkmüntegg, another cable car descends to Kriens for a short connecting bus ride back to Lucerne.

arsenal—largely because they get the chance to wave a bar-code-reading hand-held scanner over key items in order to find out information about each object (in English). It is an excellent first port of call, covering every aspect of city life from history and local folklore and fashion to toys and religious relics. Once you have a grasp of Lucerne's colorful history, walks around town are all the more rewarding.

Pfistergasse 24. www.historischesmuseum.lu.ch. ✆ **041/228 54 24.** CHF10 adults, CHF8 seniors, CHF5 children aged 6 to 16, free for children under 6. Bus: 2 or 12. Tues–Sun 10am–5pm.

**Kapellbrücke (Chapel Bridge) ★★★** BRIDGE The Chapel Bridge is Europe's oldest covered wooden footbridge and the most photographed building in Switzerland. The major events which shaped the country over the centuries are portrayed in a series of flamboyant Renaissance wall

The wooden Kapellbrücke (Chapel Bridge).

## **LOCAL** passes

Museum buffs will benefit from the 2-day **Luzern Museum Card** (see www.luzern.com for info), which, for CHF36 per person, gives unlimited access to all the main museums for 2 consecutive days. Even if you're only planning on visiting the Swiss Transport Museum and one other, it's worth your while.

Also, if you stay overnight in Lucerne, you will receive a free **Visitors Card** from your accommodation, which gives you discounts on a number of excursions, museums, boat trips, and cable cars in the region.

If you plan to explore the region, travel around the Vierwaldstättersee is made simple by the **Tell Pass,** which provides unlimited travel on public transport (train, bus, and boat) for a minimum of 2 days (from CHF100). It covers most mountain railways, although some have an additional alpine surcharge.



paintings under the roof of the bridge, together with scenes from the lives of the city's two patron saints, St. Leodegar and St. Maurice. Imagine how upset the locals were when much of their beloved bridge burned down in 1993. It has since been lovingly restored, many of the wall paintings have been reproduced, and the bridge continues to welcome tourists galore. Dominating the bridge, the even older **Wasserturm** (**Water Tower,** closed to the public) dates from around 1300. Over the years, this octagonal structure has been variously used as an archive, treasury, prison, and torture chamber.

Kapellbrücke. Free. Hauptbahnhof. Open 24 hours.

**Kunstmuseum** ★ MUSEUM The Museum of Art is housed in the impressive metal-and-glass KKL Luzern (Lucerne Culture & Convention Center) which dominates the waterfront with its huge overhanging roof, designed by the French architect Jean Nouvel. There is no permanent collection on view here, but rather a rolling program of temporary exhibitions. Depending on the themes, you may get to see some of the museum's own contemporary Swiss art and historic landscape collections—including important works by Swiss artist Ferdinand Hodler.

Europaplatz 1. www.kunstmuseumluzern.ch. ✆ **041/226 78 00.** CHF15 adults, CHF6 children 6–16, free children under 6. Bus: any to the main train station. Tues–Sun 10am–6pm (Wed to 8pm).

**Sammlung Rosengart** ★★★ MUSEUM It's a family affair at Sammlung Rosengart—a stunning collection of 19th- and 20th-century artworks housed in a grand neoclassical former bank building that dates from 1924. Art dealer Siegfried Rosengart, who moved to Lucerne after World War I, was friends with many leading artists including Klee, Chagall, Matisse, and Picasso. Together with his daughter Angela, he amassed and donated to the town an astonishing collection, containing hundreds of works by many of the great modern artists, including Bonnard, Braque, Cézanne, Chagall, Kandinsky, Klee, Matisse, Monet, Pissarro, and Renoir—it is a

## THE TALE OF william tell

The Vierwaldstättersee region is the fabled homeland of Switzerland's national hero, William Tell. Over the centuries, the character of William Tell has become one of the most famous names in Swiss history—symbolizing the struggle for political and individual freedom, and inextricably linked with the founding of the Swiss Confederation, although there is no proof for his actual existence. According to legend, Tell was a simple man from the village of Bürglen, near Urnersee (Lake Uri), one of the inlets of the Vierwaldstättersee. He was arrested by a tyrannical Habsburg bailiff named Gessler, who threatened to execute him unless he could prove his skill as a marksman by shooting an arrow through an apple on his own son's head.

The story goes that Tell successfully split the apple in two but then confessed to having a second arrow, meant for Gessler had his son been injured. Furious, the bailiff refused to free him but took him on a boat ride instead, headed for jail in Küssnacht. During the voyage, a sudden storm blew up and Tell, with his local knowledge of the Vierwaldstättersee, was released to steer the boat to safety. He escaped by jumping ashore near Sisikon, and pushed the boat and its crew back out into the middle of the stormy lake. He later ambushed Gessler, when he finally came ashore, shooting him through the heart with his last arrow. The Tellskapelle (Tell Chapel) stands today on the shore of the Urnersee (Lake Uri), between Sisikon and Flüelen, as a monument to the beloved Swiss hero.



truly remarkable collection. The whole of the ground floor and several of the first-floor rooms are devoted to Picasso and include 32 paintings and 100 drawings, watercolors and sculptural works, including five portraits of Angela who, now in her 80s, still runs the museum. Another highlight is the extensive collection of photographs of Picasso at work and play, taken by American photographer David Douglas Duncan.

Pilatusstrasse 10. www.rosengart.ch. ✆ **041/22016 60.** CHF18 adult, CHF10 children 7–16, free children under 6. Bus: 1. Nov–Mar daily 11am–5pm, Apr–Oct daily 10am–6pm.

**Verkehrshaus der Schweiz (Swiss Transport Museum) ★★★**

MUSEUM Switzerland's most popular museum and the largest of its kind on the continent, the Swiss Transport Museum is really not as geeky as it sounds. It covers every imaginable form of transport from old rolling stock, vintage aircraft and racing cars, ski lifts and spaceships, plus a wonderfully eccentric Road Transport Hall, decorated by 344 road signs. The sections on trains, shipping, and tunnel building are almost entirely Swiss-oriented, but those on air, road, and space travel have a more international flavor. The museum has been considerably expanded since it opened in 1959, with the addition of entire new buildings and an IMAX cinema, and there are lots of hands-on and multimedia exhibits which are fun for young and old: Climb inside an old airliner, or tour Switzerland in just a few steps via the walk-on aerial map, with a gigantic mobile magnifying glass to spot key sights. From train driving to space-travel

Formula One racing cars in the Swiss Transport Museum.



simulation in the planetarium, it's hardly surprising the museum draws over a million visitors annually. However, it never really feels busy—the site is so huge, it even offers bicycles to its public. If you plan to make a day of it, there's a simple cafe as well as a more formal restaurant. It is situated a short bus or boat ride away from the main train station or a 30-minute walk along the quayside from the Old Town.

Lidostrasse 5. www.verkehrshaus.ch. ✆ **041/370 44 44.** CHF30 adults, CHF15 children 6–16, children under 6 free; with IMAX film CHF40 adults, CHF25 children. Bus: 6, 8, or 24 to Verkehrshaus stop; train: S3 or Voralpenexpress to Luzern Verkehrshaus stop; boat: to Verkehrshaus Lido. Apr–Oct daily 10am–6pm, Nov Mar daily 10am–5pm.

## HEADING OUTDOORS

The surrounding countryside yields endless hiking opportunities, and the most famous hike in the region, with exceptional panoramas of the

### Birth of the Swiss Nation

Following the death of the mighty Habsburg ruler, King of Germany and Holy Roman Emperor Rudolph I in 1291, who had heavy-handedly governed much of northern Switzerland, the Swiss people faced an uncertain future, so they decided it was time to secure their own destiny. This led to a series of revolts, which resulted in the forging of new allegiances. The most important partnership made that year was the League of the Three Forest Cantons. It is believed that representatives of three of the nation's most powerful cantons—Uri, Unterwalden, and Schwyz (from which Switzerland derives its name)—met at the Rütli Meadow on the west shore of the Urnersee. Together they secured a historic victory in 1315, defeating the Habsburgs at the Battle of Morgarten. They officially recorded their union of three cantons as the **"Swiss Confederation"**; their land collectively became known as Schwyz and its people became Schwyzers. Support grew over the next 2 centuries, as gradually each canton joined the Swiss Confederation, known in Latin as the *Confoederatio Helvetica.* To this day, the abbreviation CH is used to denote Switzerland.

### Richard Wagner

The German composer came to live near Lucerne in Hauz Tribschen on the southern shore of the lake in 1866, together with Cosima von Bülow, the daughter of Franz Liszt, whom he married 4 years later. His elegant lakeside villa, with its green shutters and verdant sloping lawns, has since been converted into the **Richard Wagner Museum ★** (Wagnerweg 27, Tribschen, CH-6005; www.richard-wagner-museum.ch; ✆ **041/360 23 70**), complete with historic musical instruments, original scores, letters, photos, and various memorabilia belonging to the great maestro. Here, beside the lake, Wagner composed some of his finest opera music, including *Die Meistersinger von Nürnberg* and parts of his epic *Ring Cycle*. Located a short walk from the city center along a scenic lakeside path (allow 30 min. each way), a visit here is a must for all opera buffs.

majestic mountains around the Vierwaldstättersee and beyond, is the **Weg der Schweiz (Swiss Path) ★★★**—an easy 36km (22 miles) walk that loops around the Urnersee (Lake Uri)—which was designed in 1991 to celebrate the 700th anniversary of the Swiss Confederation, which took place in the meadows nearby (see p. 608). Each of the 26 sections of the walk represents a different canton, in the order they joined the Confederation; the length of each stretch is directly proportionate to the number of residents in that canton—every 5mm (⅕ of an inch) represents a Swiss citizen. The trail starts, aptly enough, at Switzerland's birthplace, the Rütli Meadow, although you can join it at any point. The entire path is easily manageable in 2 days, and English-language guide maps of the route are available from local tourist offices.

## Where to Stay

As one of Switzerland's most visited cities, Lucerne offers a wide range of hotels. But they're mostly expensive or, at best, moderately priced; there's a distinct shortage of good budget hotels. Advance reservations are especially important during summer months.

### EXPENSIVE

**The Hotel ★★★** Jean Nouvel, French "starchitect" and designer of the city's landmark KKL (see p. 606) has cleverly converted this old townhouse into an ultra-modern boutique hotel, with minimalist decor and splashy cinematic displays. Every inch of space has been lovingly thought through: Big windows take advantage of the natural light and the hotel's position near a leafy park, while minimalist bathrooms make the most of their dimensions, and each of the 30 rooms has custom-designed furnishings. Choose from four types of accommodation: deluxe studios, corner junior suites, garden and park loft suites (with patios), and penthouse junior suites (roof terrace, great views of the city and mountains). The onsite restaurant **Bam Bou ★,** with its innovative pan-Asian menu and slick decor, makes a pleasant change from Swiss cuisine.

Sempacherstrasse 14. www.the-hotel.ch. ✆ **041/226 86 86.** Doubles CHF370, suites CHF430–CHF750. Bus: 7, 8, 14, or 20. **Amenities:** Restaurant; bar; babysitting; room service; free Wi-Fi.

**Hotel Schweizerhof Luzern** ★★★ The iconic neo-Renaissance-style Schweizerhof stands sentinel over Lucerne's eponymously named Schweizerhofquai, secure in the knowledge that it remains one of the city's best-loved landmarks. Run by the same family for five generations, there's a homespun charm to the service here, despite all the luxury trappings such as the beautifully preserved marble-columned lobby and the snazzy bar; and the rooms artfully combine character with all mod cons. Opera buffs, take note that Richard Wagner wrote *Tristan and Isolde* here in 1859.

Schweizerhofquai 3. www.schweizerhof-luzern.ch. ✆ **041/410 04 10.** 101 units. Doubles CHF360–CHF600, suites CHF600–CHF880. Bus: 1, 6, 8 or 24. **Amenities:** 2 restaurants; bar; babysitting; gym; sauna; room service; free Wi-Fi.



**Palace Hotel** ★★★ The undisputed jewel in the crown, the five-star Palace Hotel is indeed a Belle Epoque beauty—a regal blend of period details and modern refinements, seamlessly held together by sterling service. Think high ceilings, marble columns, warm-hued luxury fabrics, original marble floors, a chic terrace, and dreamy views over the lake. Each room is individually decorated: Some are highly traditional, others boldly modern, and some a mix of the two. There's also a sensational spa, and one of the top restaurants in town, **Jasper** ★★★—where all ingredients are sourced in Switzerland and every plate of perfectly prepared modern Mediterranean cuisine is a culinary marvel, matched by an exemplary wine list.

Haldenstrasse 10. www.palace-luzern.ch. ✆ **041/416 16 16.** 129 units. Low season Doubles CHF352–CHF602, suites CHF552–CHF1,560. Bus: 6, 8, or 24. **Amenities:** 2 restaurants; bar; concierge; spa and fitness; room service; free Wi-Fi.

## MODERATE

**Astoria** ★ From its reception area's icy design ethos to its superior conference facilities, the Astoria targets business travelers. However, its 90 deluxe "Design" rooms, with their minimalist cache and trendy white-on-white decor, are a cut above your average business hotel. Designed by Switzerland's famous Herzog & de Meuron firm, each room features timber flooring, rain showers, and other designer touches. Located close to the Old Town center and a very short stroll to the Sammlung Rosengart, the KKL, and main train station, the Astoria is also ideal for those not looking to travel too far when it comes to dining well. Of several restaurants, our favorite is **La Cucina** ★★, which oozes Italian theatricality and atmosphere, with its exuberant waiters who know that performance is part of the charm; and a delicious menu of homemade pasta and pizzas cooked in a wood-fired oven. At lunchtime, it's very popular with people doing business, and offers a better than average set-price lunch menu. Reservations advised.

Exterior of the Hotel des Balances.

Pilatusstrasse 29. www.astoria-luzern.ch. ✆ **041/226 88 88.** 252 units. Doubles from CHF270. Bus: 1. **Amenities:** 5 restaurants; 2 bars; babysitting; gym; room service; free Wi-Fi.

**Hotel des Balances ★★** This four-star hotel has one of the Altstadt's best locations; its front entrance opens onto a picturesque fountain-splashed square, its buildings adorned with vibrant frescoes, while its back entrance faces the Reuss River, with stunning views over to the Chapel Bridge and Jesuit Church. Inside, the sleek rooms (which face onto either the river or the square) blend modern comforts with high-end contemporary design, gilt-framed mirrors, parquet flooring, and lots of white and neutral tones. Suites are decorated in a similar style, and some have wrought-iron balconies. **Des Balances restaurant ★★** is a firm favorite with locals and a highlight of any stay, especially the five- or seven-course set menu of seasonal European cuisine. Book in advance for a table on the riverside terrace.

Weinmarkt 4. www.balances.ch. ✆ **041/418 28 28.** 56 units. Doubles CHF350–CHF430, suites CHF430–CHF630. Bus: 1, 6, or 8. **Amenities:** Restaurant; bar; babysitting; room service; free Wi-Fi.

**Romantik Hotel Wilden Mann ★★** The oldest building in this intimate complex of seven townhouses dates from 1517, so the much-loved Wilden Mann ("Wild Man"), a warrenlike and character-filled hotel brimming with nostalgic charm, is a must for those looking to revel in Lucerne's old-fashioned charm. The 50 cozy, individually decorated rooms and suites feature original antiques, wooden beams, four-poster beds, warm colors, and embossed fabrics. Its location in the city's Old Town, within walking distance of the city's major sights and historic delights makes it a great choice, and its two very good restaurants only seal the deal. The **Burgerstube ★★** is especially atmospheric, with its wood-paneled dining room, coffered ceiling, coats of arms, and hunting trophies. The menu veers away from the usual formula by presenting regional and traditional ingredients with an imaginative twist; the fixed-price menus are an excellent value for money.

Bahnhofstrasse 30. www.wilden-mann.ch. ✆ **041/210 16 66.** 50 units. Doubles CHF310–CHF425, suites CHF360–CHF490. Bus: 1. **Amenities:** 2 restaurants; babysitting; room service; free Wi-Fi.

### INEXPENSIVE

**Le Stelle ★** Le Stelle brings some much-needed boutique hotel oomph to the historic center of town, although it's a tiny place whose rooms (singles and doubles only) don't leave much space for anything other than guests and their luggage (hence no children can stay at the hotel, because there's no room for a cot). Decor is subtle, modern, and minimal, with gleaming white paint and bedding, plus Moroccan tiling details in the bathrooms, and some rooms even feature period details such as wooden beams. The small on-site restaurant serves Italian food and has a little terrace out front, which is perfect for soaking up the ambience of Old Town. Check-in takes place at the nearby Hotel Krone (Weinmarkt 12).

Hirschenplatz 3. www.lestelle.ch. ✆ **041/412 22 20.** 10 units. Doubles CHF230–CHF320. Bus: 1. **Amenities:** restaurant; free Wi-Fi.



## Where to Eat

Lucerne has some excellent restaurants to suit all budgets, so don't confine yourself to your hotel at mealtimes (although, that said, some of the finest restaurants are situated in the city's hotels, so check out the "Where to Stay" listings, too).

Given the high number of visitors, most restaurants are open all day, and many offer alfresco dining in summer. During your stay, be sure to try the local specialty, the *Lozärner Chügelipastete*—a large puff-pastry filled with veal in a cream and mushroom sauce.

### EXPENSIVE

**Old Swiss House ★★** EUROPEAN Don't be put off by the tour groups galore eating at this landmark half-timbered building near the Lion Monument—it's a veritable culinary institution run by the Buholzer family since 1931, and on many people's must-visit list for its impeccable staff attired in traditional costume, serving a feast of Swiss and European fare. The 40,000-strong wine cellar and such irresistible dishes as Zurich-style veal in a cream sauce served with rösti, or Wienerschnitzel prepared and cooked at your table, should be enough to impress most diners, but the interior decorations that date to the 17th century (hand-carved wall panels, solid oak doors, oil paintings, stained-glass windows, and a porcelain-tiled stove) do their best to distract. Reservations are essential.

Löwenplatz 4. www.oldswisshouse.ch. ✆ **041/410 61 71.** Mains CHF28–CHF69. Bus: 1, 18, 19, 22, or 23. Tues–Sun 9am–12:30am.

### MODERATE

**Hofstube ★** SWISS/FRENCH Join locals and visitors at the popular half-timbered Hotel Zum Rebstock in the Old Town to tuck into an array of food specialties from central Switzerland and France. There are several characterful dining areas to choose from, depending on your mood: the elegant older dining room, or Hofstube, boasts period details and white napery; the newer, more intimate Hofegge is ideal for a quiet tête-à-tête; while the Wirtshuus dining area has a low-key, more casual feel. Wherever you sit, the menu's the same, with a particularly good selection of warming soups and copious salads. In summer, there's a lively terrace and verdant garden for alfresco dining, and on Sundays a popular brunch (CHF30) is served from 7am to 2:30pm. Reservations recommended.
Sankt-Leodegar-Platz 3. www.rebstock-luzern.ch. ✆ **041/417 18 19.** Mains CHF23–CHF58. Bus: 1, 6, 7, or 8. Daily 11:30am–11:30pm, Sun brunch 7:30am–2:30pm.

**Wirtshaus Galliker ★★** SWISS Run by the same family for four generations, this is one of Lucerne's best-loved spots for generous portions of unfussy but delicious local cuisine, heartily served in a traditionally decorated atmosphere that encourages the feeling you've left the modern world and all its travails behind. With all that wood paneling, grandmotherly service, floral curtains, and a talkative local crowd, you'd be mad not to try the Lucerne veal specialty dish, *Chügelipastete,* or something even more substantial, such as calf's head, or local sausages seasoned with caraway seeds. Reservations are advised.
Schützenstrasse 1. ✆ **041/240 10 02.** Mains CHF25–CHF55. Bus: 2, 9, or 12. Tues–Sat 9:30am–midnight.

### INEXPENSIVE

**La Bonne Cave ★** SWISS/ITALIAN Medieval stone vaulting, a stone floor and, as the name suggests, wine wherever your gaze falls sets the scene here, with dozens of vintages from Switzerland and around the world to heighten your mood. Alongside its fine wines, The Good Cellar serves up some good-value midday meals, satisfying pasta dishes, and nice platters of antipasti and Swiss charcuterie (with Bresaola, salami, dried ham, chorizo, olive oil, and pickled vegetables). Menus come with wine suggestions, and bottles from the attached wine shop can be bought to open with your meal. It's a lovely Old Town spot near Reuss River and the Chapel Bridge, with a dash of boho charm and romance come evening, when the candles are lit and the lights are turned low.
Rathausquai 1. www.weinwirtschaft.ch. ✆ **041/410 45 16.** Mains CHF18–CHF38. Bus: 1, 6, or 8. Mon, Wed–Fri 11:30am–10pm; Tues 10am–10pm; Sat 8am–10pm; Sun 8am–8pm.

## Shopping

Shopping in Lucerne relies heavily upon the tourist trade, so expect a mass of touristy boutiques on virtually every street corner. Look closer, however, and you will spot some classic shops selling high-quality goods.

For Swiss timepieces, you won't beat **Bucherer,** Schwanenplatz 5 (www.bucherer.com; ✆ **041/369 77 00**), the biggest jeweler in town, for choice and quality, but also a large price tag.

**Schweizer Heimatwerk,** at Kapellgasse 3 (www.heimatwerk.ch; ✆ **041/266 07 36**), admirably demonstrates that the country has considerably more to offer than cows and edelweiss, with its fine selection of beautiful handicrafts made by Swiss artists and artisans, including pottery, kitchenware, clothing, glassware, and toys. For a quirkier souvenir, **Hofstetter & Berney,** Schweizerhofquai 6 (✆ **041/410 31 06**), have a splendid collection of music boxes. The staff will tell you about the differences in tones and the complexities of sounds produced by the various instruments, all of which are made in Switzerland and which contain varying numbers of musical notes. Also, on the first Saturday of the month, there's a craft fair at the **Weinmarkt,** where you can pick up some unique, locally made gifts.

Foodies will enjoy picnic-shopping at the outdoor fruit and vegetable market on the banks of the river every Tuesday and Saturday (except in winter) from 8am to 1pm; and don't miss a visit to **Confiserie H & M Kurmann,** Bahnhofstrasse 7 (www.art-confiserie-kurmann.ch; ✆ **041/210 19 18**), the most distinguished pastry-and-chocolate shop in Lucerne, with its mouthwatering displays of highly calorific and highly tempting cakes and pastries. Look out also for their masterly chocolate edifices: Just think . . . the city's Watertower, the Old Town Hall, or the Lion Monument made out of chocolate would make a lovely present to take home, if it wasn't just too tempting to eat straight away!

## Entertainment & Nightlife

There's something for everyone after dark in Lucerne. Beer lovers should head straight to **Rathaus Bräuerei** (Unter der Egg 2; www.braui-luzern.ch) near the Chapel Bridge on the riverfront—a tavern that brews its own refreshingly light Pilsner and a rich and malty Bockbier on-site. Our favorite—a blond lager called Rathaus Bier—goes down surprisingly well accompanied by a giant pretzel or one of their hearty platefuls of local sausages and schnitzels.

For an evening of alphorns, cowbells, national costumes, flag-throwing, yodeling, and more, traditionalists will enjoy the folkloric Swiss entertainment at the jolly but undeniably touristy **Stadtkeller** (Sternenplatz 3; www.swissfolkloreshow.com). Both are located in the **Altstadt** (Old Town), together with a clutch of cozy bars and cafes.

You'll find some of the more sophisticated night spots in the hotels: sip cocktails at ultra-cool **Blue** (in the Renaissance Lucerne Hotel, Pilatussstrasse 15) or rub shoulders with Lucerne's beautiful people at **Lounge Bar** (in The Hotel; see p. 609). The **Louis Bar** (in the Art Deco Hotel Montana, Adligenswilerstrasse 22; www.hotel-montana.ch; ✆ **041/419 00 00**), named after the legendary jazz trumpeter Louis Armstrong, boasts over 90 single malt whiskeys and occasional impromptu music sessions.

Party animals will enjoy the hip **Loft** nightclub (Haldenstrasse 2; www.theloft.ch; © **041/410 92 44**); the trendy late-night party vibe and sensational bird's-eye city views at the **Suite Lounge** (at the top of Hotel Monopol—expect to queue at weekends, Pilatusstrasse 1; www.monopolluzern.ch; © **041/226 43 43**) with its open-air terraces; or the more sophisticated atmosphere (and equally splendid aerial views) of the **Penthouse Rooftop Bar** (in the Astoria hotel; see p. 610), which is perfect for early evening sundowners, or for late nights on weekends when DJs get everyone in the party mood.

For something altogether more highbrow, head for the **KKL (Kultur und Kongress Zentrum Luzern/Culture & Convention Center;** Europaplatz 1; www.kkl-luzern.ch; © **041/226 77 77** [box office]; see p. 606). Lucerne's eye-catching postmodern performing arts center on the lake was designed by Parisian architect Jean Nouvel and boasts state-of-the-art acoustics that rank among the best in the world. Its angular glass-and-metal edifice, with a gigantic copper-sheathed roof, sits in stark contrast to the spires and cute alpine architecture of the rest of town; and its year-round entertainment program, spanning from rock and pop to classical music, includes performances from the local resident orchestra, the **Allgemeine Musikgesellschaft,** from October to June. Also by the lake on the railway station side of town, the nearby **Stadttheater** (Theaterstrasse 2; www.luzernertheater.ch; © **041/228 14 14**) stages theater in German and operas in their original language.



## ZERMATT

The picture-postcard mountain village of Zermatt, 1,594m (5,228 ft.) above sea level, is hidden at the top of Switzerland's steepest valley, at the base of the nation's most celebrated mountain—the Matterhorn.

Zermatt Valley and the Matterhorn.

Once a humble farming community, it was put on the map by English mountaineers in the mid-19th century and is now a glamorous resort, especially popular in winter for skiing and snow-sports, but also in summer for mountain hiking—thanks to an impressive ensemble of cable cars, lifts, and cog railways that operates 365 days a year. Zermatt boasts the highest ski area in Europe, with skiing throughout the year on the Theodul glacier at an elevation of up to 3,883 meters (12,740 ft.).

The village itself is a charming jumble of ancient wooden chalets and huts interspersed with glitzy hotels, restaurants, and shops worthy of a capital city. Hardly surprisingly, it attracts more than its fair share of visitors. You can walk from one end of the village to the other in about 15 minutes, which is handy because it is a car-free village.

## Essentials

The **Zermatt Tourist Office** website is www.zermatt.ch.

**ARRIVING** Take a **train** to Visp or Brig, where you can transfer to a narrow-gauge train to Zermatt. Departures are every 20 minutes daily between 6am and 11:30pm. It takes just over 3 hours from Zurich, and around 4 hours from Geneva. For Swiss **rail information,** call © **0900/300-300** or visit www.sbb.ch.

If you're **driving,** head to Täsch, 4.8km (3 miles) from Zermatt. Because Zermatt is a car-free resort, you need to park your car in the large multi-story carpark at Täsch, and jump on the cog rail shuttle (which stops right beside the carpark) up to the resort. Tickets cost CHF16 per person round-trip (half-price for children aged 6–16).

In addition, **buses** run from Visp and Brig to Täsch hourly to connect with the cog train. See the tourist office website (www.zermatt.ch) for more information.

**GETTING AROUND** The best way to discover Zermatt is **on foot,** but take care when crossing the road—although the resort is car-free, there are loads of **electric carts** whizzing around. The village is traversed by the River Vispa, with most of the shops and attractions in the vicinity of the main street (Bahnhofstrasse), and hotels are well sign-posted. The tourist office at Bahnhofplatz 5 can supply you with maps of the resort as well as hiking/skiing routes in the surrounding mountains.

Many sports shops, such as **Bayard Zermatt** (Bahnhofplatz 2; © **027/966-49-50**), rent **bicycles** as well as skiing, hiking, and climbing equipment and clothing, sledges, and even prams. You can even tour the village year-round by **horse and carriage** with local resident **Werner Imboden** (© **079/436-76-12** for a quote).

The comprehensive network of cable cars and the celebrated **Gornergrat** mountain railway (see p. 621) provide easy access to the many ski slopes and hiking trails in the surrounding mountains (see **Mountain Excursions,** p. 620).

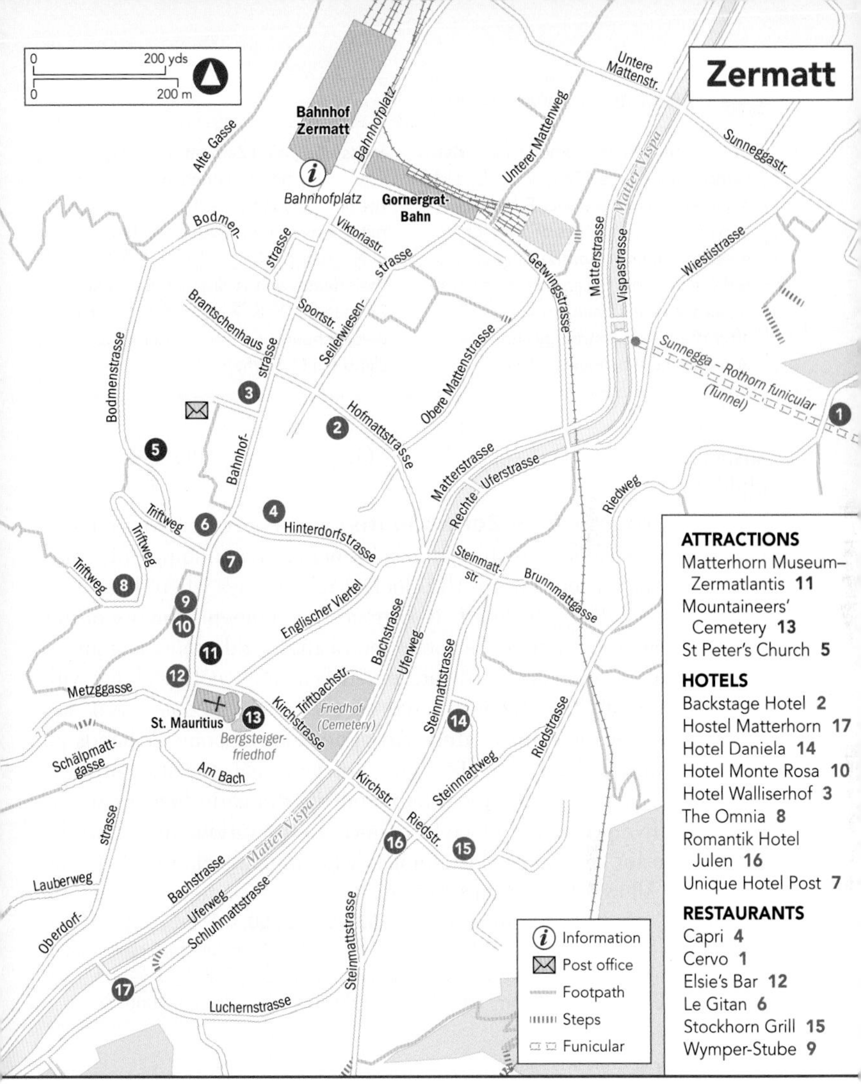


## Exploring Zermatt

Nestled at the foot of Switzerland's landmark mountain—the majestic 4,478m (14,691-ft.) high Matterhorn—and encircled by majestic snow-capped peaks, Zermatt counts among the world's most famous mountain resorts, famed for its skiing, hiking, and mountaineering; its beautiful boutiques; and some of the Alps' most glamorous hotels.

Aside from the mountains, Zermatt village offers many diversions for its visitors, including a variety of specialist shops and an eclectic mix of bars and restaurants. Its sixteen rinks for ice-skating and curling, and its sledging and ski schools in winter, together with a Forest Fun Park (www.zermatt-fun.ch) of ropeways, high wire walkways, and bridges

## Climbing the Matterhorn

World attention first turned to the **Matterhorn** during the 1860s, when English explorer and mountaineer Edward Whymper made a series of attempts to reach the summit. Approaching the Matterhorn from the Italian side, he tried six times and failed. Then, on July 14 1865, after changing his strategy and approaching the mountain from the Swiss side (using Zermatt as his departure point), he succeeded in becoming the first person to reach the elusive summit. It was a fateful expedition however—four climbers in his team fell to their deaths on the descent. Ever since, Zermatt has been a mecca for mountaineers, although only a few attempt to climb the Matterhorn.

suspended in the trees (open Easter–Oct), are especially appealing to children.

**Matterhorn Museum-Zermatlantis ★★★** MUSEUM Hidden beneath the pavement, within an ugly former casino building, this small but ingenious museum winds the clocks back to times when there were no mountain railways or ski lifts in Zermatt. It documents the rise of this tiny farming community to become one of the world's most glamorous resorts. The museum is cleverly presented as an archaeological dig, with entire mountain huts reconstructed to show how people lived and worked here in the 19th century. An appealing selection of hands-on exhibits, multimedia, and ancient film footage reveals the story of Switzerland's most photogenic mountain from its dramatic first ascent by Edward Whymper in 1865 (see box above) to the various routes up the Matterhorn for the 3,000-plus alpinists who annually climb this iconic mountain. Allow 1 to 1½ hours to visit.

Kirchplatz 11. www.matterhornmuseum.ch. ✆ **027/967 41 00.** Adults CHF10, children 10–16 CHF5, free for children 9 and under. Train (Zermatt). Open Jan–May daily 3–7pm (Fri until 8pm); June daily 2–6pm; July–Sept daily 11am–6pm; Oct daily 3–6pm; mid-Nov to mid-Dec Fri–Sun 3–6pm; mid-Dec to end Dec daily 3–7pm (Fri until 8pm).

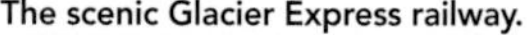

The scenic Glacier Express railway.

### The World's Slowest Express Train

Zermatt is the start-point for one of the grandest and most scenic train rides in Europe. With daily departures, the **Glacier Express ★★★** (www.glacier express.ch) might be the slowest express train in the world, taking 7½ hours to pass through southeastern Switzerland, but it's the most panoramic. A stunning feat of mountain engineering, the train crosses 291 bridges and goes through 91 tunnels as it snakes and loops its way through breath-taking landscapes, through entire mountains and over high alpine passes, arriving in the ritzy resort of St. Moritz in the canton of Graubünden around seven hours later. Windows on the train are designed to take in these stunning mountain panoramas. There's also a dining car on board. It's essential to book well in advance, by calling **Rail Europe** on ✆ **800/622 86 00** (from the U.S.), or see their website at www.rail europe.com.

**Mountaineers' Cemetery ★★** CEMETERY Take time out from the bustling main shopping street of Bahnhofstrasse to hunt down this small sliver of grassy land tucked just behind the Catholic Church of St. Mauritius. Zermatt has been a mecca for mountaineers ever since the dramatic first ascent of the Matterhorn by Edward Whymper in 1865, and many have lost their lives on this iconic peak and its surrounding mountains. The cemetery contains the beautifully tended graves and memorials of a number of those heroic early mountaineers and mountain guides. One grave is poignantly marked *"Hier verloren wir das Leben, dort fanden wir es wieder. Auf dem heiligen Berg des Herrn."* ("We lost our lives here, but found them again there. On the holy mountain of the Lord.")
Behind the walls of the Church of St. Mauritius, off Kirchplatz. Free. Train (Zermatt).

**St. Peter's Church ★** RELIGIOUS SITE The pretty, whitewashed Anglican St. Peter's Church, otherwise known as "The English Church," stands on a rocky ledge overlooking the village and holds a special place in Zermatt's history. During the golden age of alpinism, and the pioneering age of tourism, the majority of the visitors to the village came from England. Initially, Sunday services for English-speaking guests were held in the Monte Rosa and Mont Cervin hotels, but an increasing number of guests expressed the wish to have an Anglican church built. So St. Peter's was founded on donations from wealthy benefactors—some local, some English—including village hoteliers Alexander Seiler and Joseph Clemenz, and the relatives of Lord Douglas and Douglas Robert Hadow, two of the climbers who fell to their deaths during in the first ascent of the Matterhorn. The remains of a third victim, Reverend Charles Hudson, are buried under the high altar. Plaques inside the church recall other mountaineers associated with Zermatt. The church regularly holds services in English.
Just off the main street behind the Alpin Center. www.ics-uk.org/about-ics/seasonal-mission/st-peters-zermatt. ✆ **027/967 55 66.** Free. Train (Zermatt). Open hours vary.

## mountain EXCURSIONS

Zermatt is a giant year-round recreation area for skiers and hikers. Since the first Swiss ski lessons were given here in 1902, it has ranked as one of the world's top ski resorts, offering skiing 365 days a year.

There are three main ski areas: Gornergrat, Rothorn, and Klein Matterhorn. The ski area also links up with Cervinia in Italy, although the best skiing is on the Swiss side. A variety of ski-lift passes are sold in various combinations, but there isn't much saving regardless of the plan you select. A day pass covering all the lifts in the Zermatt area (200km of piste) costs CHF79, while a 2-day pass is CHF146; add the Italian side (360km of piste) and it will cost you CHG170/CHF92 for 1 or 2 days. The one break that ski-pass holders do get is free rides on the ski bus linking all ski areas. To purchase tickets, book online at www.matterhornparadise.ch.

In summer, the high Alpine peaks encircling the resort offer some of Europe's finest hiking, and their waymarked treks are excellent for spotting alpine flora and fauna. Zermatt's Alpin Center (✆ **027/966 24 60**) offers year-round certified instruction and mountain guides for

**Skiing at Gornergrat.**

## Where to Stay

Zermatt has more than 120 hotels and guesthouses to suit all budgets, plus numerous private apartments and condominiums. Most hotels will meet you and your luggage at the cog-railway station by electric cart if you inform them in advance of your arrival time.

visitors wishing to explore Zermatt's mountains in summer and winter.

**Gornergrat ★★★** The Gornergrat is accessed via a spectacular rack railroad, which departs from the village center and zig-zags its way up the mountain to the lofty altitude of 3,099m (10,165 ft.)—it is the highest open-air cogwheel railway in Europe. En route, you'll stop roughly half-way up at **Riffelberg,** which offers a panoramic view of both the Matterhorn and Mount Rosa. The complete ride from Zermatt to Gornergrat is CHF86 round-trip, or CHF43 one-way for ambitious skiers intending to return to the village on skis. At the summit, an observatory looks out on the bleak expanses of the Gorner glacier and over the heights of the Dom, which, at nearly 4,572m (14,996 ft.), is the highest mountain entirely within Switzerland. From here in summer, it is a gentle half-day's hike down past Riffelsee, where on a clear day you can see the Matterhorn perfectly reflected in the lake, to the hotel and restaurant at Riffelalp (see p. 624).

**Blauherd-Unter Rothhorn ★★** To get to Blauherd-Unter Rothorn, take a cog railway through a tunnel from Zermatt to the alpine meadows of Sunegga, and then transfer to a cable car. After changing cable cars at Blauherd (which offers many hiking and skiing options of its own), you'll continue by cable car to the flat, rocky summit of the Unter Rothorn, where possibilities for alpine rambles or ski descents abound.

**Schwarzsee-Theodul ★★**

To reach Zermatt's third major ski area, take a cable car from Zermatt to **Furi-Schweigmatten** (usually abbreviated to Furi), or continue up by cable car to Schwarzsee (Black Lake) for sweeping vistas, more ski pistes and hiking trails and a sunny terrace for lunch and a drink at the **Hotel Schwarzsee** (✆ **0764/61 94 22**) at 2,584m (8,476 ft.). The round-trip excursion from Zermatt to Schwarzsee costs CHF49. One of the most memorable hikes in the region is the climb up from Schwarzsee to the **Hörnli Hut** (3,260 m/10,700 ft.)—basecamp for the Matterhorn, just a few thousand feet below the wind-blasted cliffs that surround the summit.

**Klein Matterhorn ★★★** To reach the "Little Matterhorn" from Furi, you must take two additional cable cars to Trockenersteg, and on to Klein Matterhorn—one of the highest mountain terraces in the world (3,760m/12,333 ft.). From the top, if the sky is clear, you can see the Swiss, French, and Italian Alps and breathe a rarefied air usually reserved for the hardiest of alpine climbers. There's downhill skiing here even in midsummer across the **Théodul Pass.** In winter, you can continue downhill on skis to the Italian ski resort of **Breuil-Cervinia** for lunch, on the opposite side of the Matterhorn from Zermatt. The excursion to Klein Matterhorn from Zermatt costs CHF99 round-trip



## AROUND TOWN

### Expensive

**Hotel Monte Rosa ★★★** It can be hard to resist the opportunity to stay in Zermatt's first hotel. Named after Switzerland's highest mountain, the historic Monte Rosa originated as a simple wooden chalet in the earliest days of mountain tourism in 1839 (its guest list included Edward

Whymper, the first man to summit the Matterhorn). Today's luxury historic hotel at the heart of the village was built on the original foundations in the 19th century. With its distinguished red-shuttered facade and exemplary standards, it seamlessly merges old-world atmosphere and nostalgia for days gone by with modern amenities. Tradition-steeped, timelessly elegant interiors draw a loyal clientele. No two rooms are the same—some are decorated with rich fabrics and antiques, while others have a more contemporary feel. Some of the deluxe suites boast Matterhorn views.

Bahnhofstrasse 80. www.monterosazermatt.ch. ✆ **027/966 03 33.** 41 units. Doubles CHF265–CHF860, suites CHF585–CHF2,320; rates include breakfast. Train (Zermatt). **Amenities:** Restaurant; cafe/bar; use of spa facilities in nearby hotel; ski room; free Wi-Fi.

**The Omnia** ★★★ Perched on a rock high above Zermatt, it's easy to feel at one with the elements here, thanks to the elevated location, a dramatic mountainous backdrop, and lower floors cut right into the rock. It's a bit like staying in the wilderness of the mountains, but with all the amenities at your doorstep—The Omnia is easily accessed via tunnel and lift from the village center. And that's not to mention the amazing views of Zermatt from the bedroom windows. The hotel describes itself as a "contemporary interpretation of the traditional mountain lodge"; to me, it's an upmarket, ultra-modern mountain retreat, with stylish on-trend designer fittings and a gorgeous indoor/outdoor infinity pool.

Auf dem Fels. www.the-omnia.com. ✆ **027/966 71 71.** 30 units. Doubles CHF350–CHF3,500. Train (Zermatt). **Amenities:** Library; lounge bar; club/cinema; wellness center; meeting facilities; ski room; free Wi-Fi.

### Moderate

**Backstage Hotel** ★★★ With its glass floors, floating fireplaces, and eccentric chandeliers made from musical instruments, this trailblazing, über-modern chalet hotel has won a clutch of design awards since its opening in 2010. Think high-tech interiors of walnut, velvet, distressed leather, and brushed stainless steel. For the ultimate design experience, request one of the six split-level, cube-shaped lofts when you book. In the basement, the entertainment space Vernissage contains an art gallery, cinema, and live-music venue. Guests can tuck into highly innovative Michelin-starred gourmet dining at the **After Seven** restaurant, but the real pièce de resistance of the property is the innovative wood, steel, and glass spa. A unique 3-hour experience is offered, comprising seven treatment "cubes" representing the seven days of creation, plus a host of special effects, including whale-song, live streaming from the Hubble Space Telescope, and movement-sensitive music and video installations.

Hofmattstrasse 4. www.backstagehotel.ch. ✆ **027/966 69 70.** 19 units. Doubles CHF190–CHF210, cube lofts CHF390–CHF410; rates include breakfast and spa access. Train (Zermatt). **Amenities:** Restaurant; cafe; lounge-bar; sports shop; spa; Jacuzzi; cinema; art gallery; design shop; nightclub; ski room; free Wi-Fi.

**Hotel Walliserhof ★★** Situated on Zermatt's car-free main street, this characterful, family-owned guesthouse is a charming place to stay. It's unmistakably Swiss with its elegant interiors, friendly staff dressed in traditional *Trachten,* and occasional Matterhorn glimpses from the balconies. Each room is different, although they are all essentially alpine-rustic, with pine-clad walls. The family rooms (some duplex) are practical and spacious. An ideal ski lodge, the walls are hung with wooden skis and vintage photos of mountaineers, and there's a well-heated ski room with boot warmers. There are two restaurants—the **Stübli** serves cheese specialties and rustic Swiss dishes (think röstis, fondues, and raclettes), while the **Restaurant Grill** serves a more international menu. The fitness room and mini wellness area in the basement offer a sauna, solarium, massage shower, steam room, and whirlpool access to soothe aching limbs.

Bahnhofstrasse 30. www.walliserhof-zermatt.ch. ✆ **027/966 65 55.** 34 units (including 4 family rooms). Doubles from CHF270, suites from CHF400; rates include breakfast and use of wellness area).Train (Zermatt). **Amenities:** 2 restaurants; smokers' lounge; fitness; wellness area; ski room; free Wi-Fi.

**Romantik Hotel Julen ★★** Festooned with flowers in summer, this family-run hotel at the center of Zermatt is a stylish option all year-round. Behind the smart red shutters and ornate chalet exterior is a surprisingly bold, modern interior, with warm, strong colors and a cozy fireplace. Bedrooms offer a more traditional chalet ambiance, with spruce paneling and traditional light-pine furnishings. On top of a beautiful pool, sauna area, and caldarium, the spa and fitness center offers such unforgettable treats as indulgent après-ski massages and hay flower and goat-milk butter baths. Ask about the excellent ski packages, too.

Riedstrasse 2. www.julen.ch. ✆ **027/966 76 00.** 27 units. Doubles from CHF300–CHF600; rates include breakfast. Train (Zermatt). **Amenities:** 2 restaurants; 3 bars and clubs; spa; indoor swimming pool; fitness; ski room; free Wi-Fi.

**Unique Hotel Post ★★★** This landmark hotel in the center of Zermatt has long appealed to the jet set for its stylish accommodation and après-ski scene. The hotel has been renovated in an extravagantly chic "mountain lodge style." Think smooth fir wood juxtaposed with exposed stone walls, and sleek lines softened with natural fabrics and furnishings in earthy tones. The spa offers sumptuous treatments in a serene environment. With its funky live music bar, pub, and legendary basement **Broken Bar Disco,** Hotel Post remains one of the hottest nightspots in town.

Bahnhofstrasse 41. www.hotelpost.ch. ✆ **027/967 19 31.** 29 units. Doubles from CHF229, suites from CHF369; rates include breakfast and spa access. Train (Zermatt). **Amenities:** 4 restaurants; 5 bars and clubs; spa; ski room; free Wi-Fi.

### Inexpensive

**Hostel Matterhorn ★** Even by Swiss standards, Zermatt is a very expensive destination. Hostel Matterhorn provides a much-needed in-resort alternative; it's well-located, and although basic, it provides affordable accommodation for budget travelers. At the top of the village, close to the ski slopes, hiking, and biking trails, the hostel occupies a rustic timber chalet built in the '60s. Rooms are clean and no frills, but perfectly adequate, with shared bathroom facilities. Book in advance for weekends during the ski season, and bring your own sleeping bag.

Schluhmattstrasse 32. www.matterhornhostel.com. ✆ **027/968 19 19.** 56 units plus 7 dormitory rooms. Dorm beds from CHF30, private rooms from CHF46. Train (Zermatt). **Amenities:** Bar and restaurant; lounge; in-room lockers; ski room; free Wi-Fi.

**Hotel Daniela ★★** Hotel Daniela holds down a secluded location away from the bustle of the village center, but within easy walking distance of all the shops and boutiques. It's a modern property, built in the classic chalet style. The interior is traditional and elegant, with beautiful, vibrant furnishings and well-appointed bedrooms. Rooms on the third floor have views across village rooftops to the Matterhorn, and the spacious family rooms are especially good values. The Daniela is a sister hotel to the **Romantik Hotel Julen ★★** (they share the same management; see listing above), so guests can enjoy the peace and quiet (and smaller price tag) of these more modest accommodations, yet still have access to the spa, swimming pool, and fine dining of the more deluxe sibling just a stone's throw away.

Steinmattstrasse 39. www.julen.ch/en/hotel-daniela. ✆ **027/966 77 00.** 24 units. Doubles CHF120–CHF350. Train (Zermatt). **Amenities:** Breakfast area; restaurant and spa in nearby hotel; ski room; free Wi-Fi.

## IN THE MOUNTAINS

### Expensive

**Riffelalp Resort ★★★** A 20-minute uphill ride through breathtaking scenery on the Gornergrat cogwheel train brings guests to the Riffelalp plateau where a private tram (summer months only) leads through fragrant pine forests to this deluxe five-star mountain resort, face-to-face with the mighty Matterhorn. A ski-in-ski-out hotel in winter and a trekker's paradise in summer, this beautiful mountain oasis boasts cozy, wood-clad guest rooms with classic furnishings, a sumptuous spa, and Europe's highest outdoor swimming pool. Dining options range from haute cuisine in Restaurant Alexandre to tasty fondues and raclettes at the traditional Walliser-Keller in winter. The hotel's certified ski instructor and mountain guide offers a winter program of skiing, snowshoeing, heli-skiing, Velogemel, tobogganing, and glacier skiing. At 2,222m (7,290 ft.), this is definitely a place where you can enjoy the high life.

Riffelalp Plateau. www.riffelalp.com. ✆ **027/699 05 55.** 72 units. Doubles CHF430–CHF1,200 suites CHF715–CHF2,570; rates include half-board and train fares between Zermatt and Riffelalp. Train (Zermatt) then Gornergrat Railway. **Amenities:** 2 restaurants; bar; smokers' lounge; spa; swimming pool; wine shop; gym; ski instructor/mountain guide; ice skating; tennis court; ski room; free Wi-Fi.

#### Moderate

**Iglu-dorf ★★** For the ultimate romantic experience, stay in one of the highest igloos in the world. "Igloo Village" holds down a spot way up on the mountainside near the Matterhorn at an altitude of 2,727m (8,947 ft.). The full package here includes mulled wine, cheese fondue, a hot tub, nighttime snowshoeing, an ice bar, breakfast in a mountain restaurant, and sleeping bags and liners suitable for as low as -40°C. The range of accommodation goes from special "romantic" igloos for honeymooning couples (with spacious facilities, breathtaking views, and plenty of Prosecco) to the more basic "standard igloo" that sleeps up to six and is ideal for adventurous families. The igloo season runs approximately Christmas to mid-April, depending on snow conditions. Make sure you bring plenty of warm, winter-proof clothing and cash—credit cards are not accepted. There is no Wi-Fi.

Gornergrat. www.iglu-dorf.com. ✆ **041/612 27 28.** 11 units. Package price per person CHF159–CHF499. Train (Zermatt) then Gornergrat railway to Gornergrat. **Amenities:** Hot tub; ice bar.

## Where to Eat

You'll be spoiled for choice of eatery in Zermatt, with its many excellent restaurants serving traditional Swiss dishes and Continental cuisine. Most of the best restaurants are connected with hotels and, given the well-heeled traveler who tends to come to this resort, none of them will hesitate to separate you from your money.

### AROUND TOWN

#### Expensive

**Capri ★★** ITALIAN This Michelin-starred gourmet Italian restaurant right on the Italo-Swiss border is the jewel in the culinary crown of the beautiful five-star Mont Cervin Palace Hotel, serving classic Italian dishes with a contemporary twist. Situated on the fourth floor, the space is accompanied by views of the Matterhorn in an elegant, if unremarkable, dining room. Capri has a reputation as the best Italian restaurant in Switzerland, so advanced booking is essential.

Mont Cervin Palace Hotel, Bahnhofstrasse 31. www.montcervinpalace.ch/en. ✆ **027/966 88 88.** Mains CHF50–CHF60. Train (Zermatt). Late Dec to early Apr, Tues–Sun 7–11pm.

**Cervo ★★** SWISS Part of the boutique Hotel Cervo, the main appeal here is simplicity. Chef Seraina Lauber takes traditional Swiss recipes and reinvigorates them, using the freshest seasonal ingredients, many of which have been grown in the chalet's own vegetable garden, to create a perfect blend of old and new. Try caramelized cheese on a beetroot and leaf salad with smoked pecans; then the black cod with white pine needles, elderflowers, and black rice; followed by meringues and pickled apricots and almonds with lavender cream; or an array of homemade ice creams and sorbets. Combine those scrumptious dishes with crisp, modern-rustic decor and a reliable selection of fine local wines, and you will be guaranteed a meal to remember. Reservations are recommended. Hotel Cervo, Riedweg 156. www.cervo.ch. ✆ **027/968 12 12.** Mains CHF42–CHF72. Train (Zermatt). Dec to late Apr daily noon–10pm.

**Elsie's Bar** ★ OYSTERS Elsie's Bar is where the jet set head at the end of a hard day's skiing to tuck into platters of shucked oysters, washed down with the finest of champagnes. Elsie's oozes tradition and old-world charm, from its cozy wooden interiors to the old-fashioned paintings of Zermatt on its walls. In the '60s it was known for its snails and Irish coffees, in the '70s for its ham and eggs with Berlin-style pancakes. Today it serves a small selection of upmarket delicacies—caviar, snails, oysters, homemade *foie gras,* and beef tartar—along with an outstanding menu of whiskeys and wines. Kirchplatz 16. www.elsiebar.ch. ✆ **027 967 24 31.** Mains CHF46–CHF68. Train (Zermatt). Mid-Nov to Apr daily 4pm–2am; June to mid-Oct, Mon–Sat 2:30pm–midnight, Sun 4–10pm.

**Le Gitan** ★★ INTERNATIONAL There's something rather special about Le Gitan. Perhaps it's the chef preparing roasted meats before your eyes, over a wood fire right in the middle of the candlelit dining room. Maybe it's the cozy, old-fashioned cafe at the front, a perfect place to chill and unwind after an exhilarating day in the mountains. Or it could be the stylish bar, standing by to round off a perfect evening with a classic cocktail. One thing is for certain, this popular, family-run restaurant offers a warm and friendly welcome and delicious, memorable alpine cuisine. Book in advance to avoid disappointment. Hotel Darioli, Bahnhofstrasse 64. www.legitan.ch. ✆ **027/968 19 40.** Mains CHF49–CHF88. Train (Zermatt). Daily noon–2pm, 6:30pm–midnight (kitchen closes at 9:30pm).

### Moderate

**Stockhorn Grill** ★★ SWISS This classic restaurant is something of a local institution. It serves a host of traditional Swiss fare, but the real specialties here are the mouth-wateringly tender grilled meats, cooked over a wood fire. Other staples include the ubiquitous Swiss-cheese fondue, regional raclette and meat fondues, all served in a cozy wood-clad interior, or on the terrace in summer. The restaurant is part of the Hotel Stockhorn, which belongs to the family of the legendary Matterhorn guide Emil Julen, and is hugely popular with both locals and visitors. Hotel Stockhorn, Riedstrasse. www.grill-stockhorn.ch. ✆ **027/967 17 47.** Mains from CHF27. Train (Zermatt). Tues–Sun, 6:30pm–midnight; closed mid-May to mid-June and mid-Oct to mid-Nov.

## MEALS IN THE mountains

Zermatt boasts some excellent mountaintop restaurants, feeding the many hikers, skiers, and mountain-bikers who pass by. High upon a glacier, **Bergrestaurant Fluhalp** ★★ (www.fluhalp-zermatt.ch; ✆ **027/967 25 97**) is the perfect place to go for a leisurely lunch in the sunshine way up on the Rothorn, with unparalleled Matterhorn vistas. The menu comprises delicious soups, pastas, röstis, fondues, copious salads, and steaks, all at reasonable prices. **Restaurant Alexandre** ★ offers gourmet Swiss cuisine with an impressive wine list atop the Riffelalp (see p. 624). But our favorite mountain haunt is the quaint **Bergrestaurant Blatten** ★★★ (www.blatten-zermatt.ch; ✆ **027/967 20 96**), one of Zermatt's oldest eateries, nestled above the ancient wooden hamlet of Blatten, with its unbeatable alpine cuisine (try the glistening fruit tarts and homemade ice creams) accompanied by jaw-dropping views from the sun terrace.

### Inexpensive

**Whymper-Stube** ★★ SWISS Of Zermatt's numerous fondue joints, our favorite is the Whymper-Stube on the lower level of the legendary Hotel Monte Rosa. Perhaps it's for the historic connection—Englishman Edward Whymper allegedly plotted the first ascent of the Matterhorn here in 1865—or perhaps it's simply because you'll find here some of the town's tastiest fondues and raclette. There are meat fondues; and several different types of gooey cheese fondue, including the option to have all three types at once for those who can't decide. The snug dining room is appropriately rustic, with its stone floor, candles, and age-darkened wood-paneled walls.

Hotel Monte Rosa, Bahnhofstrasse 80. www.whymper-stube.ch. ✆ **027/967 22 96.** Raclette CHF9 per person, fondues CHF25–CHF44 and up. Train (Zermatt). Daily 11am–midnight.

## Shopping

Zermatt's critics accuse it of combining a hard-nosed commercialism, shrewdly calculating the value of every snowflake, with a less harsh obsession with Swiss folklore. Consequently, the town's main shopping thoroughfare, **Bahnhofstrasse,** contains branches of stores you might have expected only in much larger cities, with an emphasis on luxury goods, alpine souvenirs, and sporting goods. Ski and mountaineering equipment here tends to be state of the art; sports stores abound, but one worthwhile example is **Slalom Sport,** Kirchstrasse 17 (www.slalom-sport.ch; ✆ **027/966-23-66**), close to the village church. Well-recommended competitors, both on Bahnhofstrasse near the Gornergrat cable car, include **Glacier Sport** (✆ **027/967-27-19**) and **Bayard Sport** (www.bayardzermatt.ch; ✆ **027/966-49-50**).

Local souvenirs in Zermatt include everything from the genuinely artful to the hopelessly kitschy. One such outlet is **WEGA,** on Bahnhofplatz (www.wega-zermatt.ch; ✆ **027/967-21-66**). The cakes, pastries, and mini chocolate Matterhorns at **Fuchs** (Getwingstrasse 24; www.fuchs-zermatt.ch; ✆ **027/967-20-63**) are hard to resist, while **Boîte à Chocolat** (Bahnhofstrasse 7b; www.boiteachocolat.ch; ✆ **027/967-00-25**) is a chocoholic's paradise with its choice selection of Swiss chocolates, plus a bar serving 20 different types of hot chocolate drink.

Snow and ice aren't the only things that sparkle in glitzy Zermatt, so if you're susceptible to impulse purchases of jewelry, one of the best places to browse is **Bijouterie Schindler** (Bahnhofstrasse 5; ✆ **027/967-11-18**), which stockpiles both Swiss watches and gemstones.

## Entertainment & Nightlife

This glamorous resort has been a favorite destination of the jet set for decades, so it's little surprise that Zermatt is as strong on après-ski activities—which include tea dances, bars, nightclubs, and discos—as it is on skiing. It starts with *glühwein* (hot mulled wine) in the slopeside bars and restaurants at **Furi, Blatten,** and **Zum See,** then spills into the bars en route down to Zermatt, including the eternally popular **Hennu Stall,** the terrace bar of **Hotel Cervo,** the **Zermatt Yacht Club,** and **Snowboat.** Other choice venues include any number of tearooms, the legendary **Elsie's Bar** (see p. 626), or **Little Bar** and **Hexenbar** on the main drag.

After dark, **Hotel Post** (www.hotelpost.ch; ✆ **027/967-19-31;** see p. 623), where everybody shows up after recovering from Elsie's Irish coffee, has a virtual monopoly on nightlife in Zermatt. The owner, Karl Ivarsson, an American, has gradually expanded it into one of the most complete entertainment complexes in Zermatt, with a number of restaurants and nightspots under one roof: choose from the **Pink Live Music Bar** for live jazz and soul music (open Dec–Easter); the rustic **Brown Cow** for those with hunger pangs (the menu includes hamburgers, salads, and sandwiches); or join ski bums in the basement **Broken Bar** for some more vigorous partying. Other highly animated venues include **Papperla Pub** (www.papperlapub.ch; ✆ **027/967-40-40**) and **Gram-Pi's** in Bahnhofstrasse (www.grampis.ch; ✆ **027/967-77-88**), frequented by the resort's army of seasonaires and ski instructors.

Other less obvious venues include the ultra-hip **Vernissage Bar** in Backstage Hotel (www.backstagehotel.ch; ✆ **027/966-69-70;** see p. 622) with its art gallery, cinema and live music venue; and the **Kegelstube ("Bowling Alley Bar")** in Hotel Bristol (✆ **027/966-33-80**), which contains the resort's only bowling alley.

# [Fast FACTS] SWITZERLAND

**Business Hours** **Bank** hours vary but are generally Monday to Friday, 8:30am to 4:30pm (closed on public holidays). Most **shops** are open Monday to Friday from 8am to 6:30pm, and on Saturday from 8am to 4pm; in cities, some of the large stores stay open until 9pm on Thursdays.

**Currency** Perpetually neutral and independent Switzerland is not a member of the European Union and as such, uses its own currency, the Swiss franc (CHF). Still, you'll find that many businesses that cater to tourists will accept euros, though they'll likely give you change in CHF. See p. 860 for information on money and costs.

**Doctors & Dentists** Should you become seriously ill, lists of local doctors, dentists, and hospitals can be found in telephone directories or by contacting your consulate, who have lists of English-speaking practitioners. Ask your hotel reception to help, or, in a real medical emergency, dial ✆ **144.**

**Embassies & Consulates:**

**Australia:** Chemins des Fins 2, Geneva; www.geneva.mission.gov.au; ✆ **22/799-9100.**

**Canada:** 5, avenue de l'Ariana, Geneva; www.switzerland.gc.ca; ✆ **22/919-9200.**

**New Zealand:** Grand Saconnex, Geneva; E-mail: mission.nz@bluewin.ch; ✆ **22/929-0350.**

**United Kingdom:** Thunstrasse 50, Berne; www.gov.uk/government/world/switzerland; ✆ **031/359-7700.**

**United States:** 7 rue François-Versonnex, Geneva; www.bern.usembassy.gov; ✆ **22/840-5160.**

**Emergencies** Dial ✆ **117** for police; ✆ **144** for an ambulance; and ✆ **118** to report a fire.

**Pharmacies** Swiss pharmacies dispense over-the-counter and prescription medicines. They are easily identifiable by the sign of a green cross on a white background. Regular hours are Monday to Saturday, from around 9am to 6pm. Major cities have at least one 24-hour pharmacy open. In Zurich, there's one near the lake at Bellevue ✆ **044/266 62 22;** in Geneva, call ✆ **144** to ask which pharmacy is on duty out of hours.

**Post Offices** Switzerland's postal service (Swiss Post; www.post.ch; ✆ **0848-88 88 88**) is fast and reliable. Stamps can be purchased at post offices and some newspaper kiosks. Post office opening times are typically Monday to Friday 8:30am to 6:30pm, Saturday 8:30 to 11am, but main post offices (in Zurich at Europaallee 11, and I Geneva at Cornavin station, rue des Gares 16) are open longer hours.

ITALY
by Donald Strachan
10

I was overwhelmed by my first contact with Italy. I was so affected by its visual sights that in a guidebook designed to deal with dry, dollars-and-cents matters (as my *Europe on $5 a Day* was initially planned to do), I grew lyrical in a chapter dealing with Venice. Arriving there by night, I wrote that "little clusters of candy-striped mooring poles emerge from the dark; the reflection of a slate-grey church bathed in a blue spotlight, shimmers in the water as you pass by." I was literally turned on.

And the people! Unlike the laid-back, reticent, soft-spoken types of northern Europe, here were those who wore emotions on their sleeves. I gloried in the sounds of Italy, in the excitability of shopkeepers, the shouts of merchants and customers, the warm embraces of friends meeting on the street, the happy seniors playing bocce balls in parks and open spaces, the swaggering fashionistas both male and female. I marveled at the giant Roman ruins, the elaborate statuary more numerous than in any other country, the resplendent churches with frescos by artists of genius. I loved the food, the endless varieties of pasta, the Chiantis that accompanied the meals, and the espressos that ended them.

For the first-time visitor to Italy, there is a classic itinerary that can't be equaled, and that forms the heart of our chapter on Italy: Rome, Florence, Venice. While countless other areas, cities, and villages are almost—that's "almost"—as compelling, it is these magical three places that overawe all others, that can be easily reached by inexpensive trains, and that will never fail to excite. From Rome to Florence is only two hours by express train, from Florence to Venice is another two-or-so hours, and each city is an overwhelming touristic experience.

The highlights are, of course, legendary: in Rome, the Roman Forum (best reached by first ascending the Capitoline steps designed by Michelangelo), the Vatican, the Colosseum, the Pantheon and the Piazza Navona, the Via Veneto; in Florence, the original of Michelangelo's *David* in the Accademia Museum, the Uffizi and the Pitti Palace, the Medici Chapels and the Ghiberti Doors; in Venice, the Piazza San Marco, the Ducal Palace, and the Rialto, a ride by vaporetto along the canals.

These and more are colorfully described and appraised in the chapter ahead by a distinguished travel writer in love with Italy.

FACING PAGE: **A gondola on the Grand Canal, Venice.**

Donald Strachan, who spends much of the year in the three cities described in this chapter, has written books and articles about Italy and Italian cities for more than 20 years; we spotted his work at an early time, and immediately enlisted him to prepare a great many of our guidebooks to Italy.

Now, on your return trip to Italy, you may well decide to branch out to Milan and Bologna, Pisa, Siena and Lucca, Naples and the Amalfi Coast, Sicily, Tuscany and Umbria, and you may also decide to use our 700-page *Complete Guide to Italy,* our *Easy Guide to Naples, Sorrento and the Amalfi Coast,* our *Easy Guide to Florence and Tuscany,* our *Venice Day by Day,* our *Florence Day by Day,* our *Rome Day by Day,* our *Shortcut Sicily,* or several other Easy Guides to various Italian locations that will be appearing soon in bookstores. Italy can support a lifetime of travel, and many avid travelers make countless repeat trips there. But for a first introduction to the three leading destinations, we believe the well-thought-out approach in the pages ahead will prove to be just the right thing! From all of us at Frommer's: *Buon Viaggio!*

***–Arthur Frommer***



# ROME

Once it ruled the Western World, and even the partial, scattered ruins of that awesome empire, of which Rome was the capital, are among the most overpowering sights on earth. To walk the **Roman Forum,** to view the **Colosseum** or the **Pantheon**—these are among the most memorable, instructive, and illuminating experiences in all travel. To see evidence of a once-great civilization that no longer exists is a humbling experience. Thrilling, too, are the sights of **Christian Rome,** which speak to the long and complex domination of this city by one of the world's major religions.

But Rome is not just a place of the past; it lives and breathes and buzzes with Vespas in the here and now. So take the time to get away from the hordes to explore the intimate piazzas and lesser basilicas in the backstreets of **Trastevere** or **Monti.** Indulge in eno-gastronomic pursuits and stuff your days with cappuccinos, pizza, trattorias, wine bars, and gelato. Have a picnic in **Villa Borghese** or nap on the grass against a fallen granite column at the **Baths of Caracalla.** Rome is so compact that even without planning too much, you'll end up enjoying both its monuments and its simpler pleasures.

The Roman Forum.



## Essentials

Information, maps, and the Roma Pass (see below) are available at "Tourist Information Points" maintained by **Roma Capitale** (www.turismoroma.it) at various sites around the city.

**ARRIVING** Most flights arrive at Rome's **Leonardo da Vinci International Airport** (www.adr.it; ✆ **06-65951**), popularly known as **Fiumicino,** 30km (19 miles) from the city center. There's a **train station** in the airport. To get into the city, follow the signs marked treni for the 31-minute Leonardo Express shuttle to Rome's main station, **Stazione Termini.** The shuttle runs every 30 minutes (14€ one-way). There's a machine dispensing tickets, or you can buy them in person near the tracks if you do not have small bills.

A **taxi** from da Vinci airport to the city costs a flat-rate 48€ for the 1-hour trip, depending on traffic. That rate is applicable from the airport to central Rome and vice versa, but only if your central Rome location is inside the old Aurelian Walls (most hotels are). Otherwise, standard metered rates apply, which can be 75€ or higher.

If you arrive at **Ciampino Airport** (www.adr.it/ciampino; ✆ **06-65951**), you can take a Terravision bus (www.terravision.eu; ✆ **06-4880086**) to Stazione Termini. Trip time is about 45 minutes; it costs 4€. A **taxi** from here to Rome costs 30€, a flat rate to anywhere within the Aurelian Walls. Otherwise, you'll pay the metered fare, but the trip is shorter than from Fiumicno (about 40 min.).

## ROMA pass

If you plan to do serious sightseeing (and why else would you be here?), the **Roma Pass** (www.romapass.it) is worth considering. For 36€ per card, valid for 3 days, you get free entry to the first two museums or archaeological sites you visit; free admission to Museo della Repubblica Romana, Museo Bilotti, Museo Canonica, Museo delle Mura, Museo Napoleonico, and Villa di Massenzio; discounted entry to all other museums and sites; free use of the public transport network (bus, Metro, tram, and suburban railway lines; airport transfers not included); express entry to the Colosseum; a free map; and free access to a special smartphone app. The shorter-validity **Roma Pass 48 Hours** is less of a value. Buy the passes online and pick them up at one of the Tourist Information Points listed at www.turismoroma.it. Note that the Roma Pass is not valid at the Vatican or in churches and museums operated by the Vatican.

Trains and buses (including from the airport) arrive in the center at **Stazione Termini,** Piazza dei Cinquecento. This is the transportation hub for all Rome. If you're heading for the **Metropolitana** (subway), follow the illuminated red-and-white m signs. You will also find a line of **taxis** parked out front.



By **car** from the north, the main access route is the **Autostrada del Sole (A1).** Called "Motorway of the Sun," the highway links Milan with Naples via Bologna, Florence, and Rome. All the autostrade join with the **Grande Raccordo Anulare,** a ring road encircling Rome, channeling traffic into the congested city. Think twice before driving in Rome—the traffic can be nightmarish. In any case, most of central Rome is a **ZTL (Zone Traffico Limitato),** off limits for nonresidents (hotels can issue temporary permits), and rigorously enforced by cameras.

**CITY LAYOUT** The bulk of what you'll want to visit—ancient, Renaissance, and baroque Rome (as well as the train station)—is on the east side of the **Tiber River (Fiume Tevere),** which meanders through town. However, several important landmarks are on the other side: **St. Peter's Basilica** and the **Vatican,** the **Castel Sant'Angelo,** and the **Trastevere** neighborhood. With the exception of those last sights, it's fair to say that Rome has the most compact and walkable center among Europe's capitals.

### Easter in Rome

In Rome and nationwide, **Holy Week** is marked by processions and age-old ceremonies—some from pagan days, some from the Middle Ages. The most notable procession is led by the pope, passing the Colosseum and the Roman Forum up to Palatine Hill; a torch-lit parade caps the observance. On **Pasqua (Easter Sunday),** in an event broadcast around the world, the pope gives his blessing from the balcony of St. Peter's.

### Two Bus Warnings

Any map of the Roman bus system will likely be outdated before it's printed. Many buses listed on the "latest" map no longer exist, and new buses suddenly appear without warning. There's often talk of renumbering the whole system, so be aware that the route numbers I list might have changed by the time you travel.

Take care when riding Rome's overcrowded buses—pickpockets abound! Bus no. 64, a favorite of visitors because of its route through the historic districts, has earned various nicknames, including "Pickpocket Express" and "Wallet Eater."

That doesn't mean you won't get lost from time to time. Arm yourself with a detailed street map (or a smartphone with a hefty data plan; see p. 859).

**GETTING AROUND** Central Rome is perfect for exploring on foot, with sites of interest often clustered together. Much of the inner core is traffic-free, so you will need to walk whether you like it or not.

The **Metropolitana,** or **Metro** (www.romametropolitane.it; ✆ **06-454640100**), is the fastest means of transportation, operating 5:30am to 11:30pm Sunday to Thursday, and until 1:30am on Friday and Saturday. A big red **m** indicates the entrance to the subway. If your destination is close to a Metro, take it: It will be much faster than a bus. Tickets cost 1.50€ and are available from *tabacchi* (tobacco shops), many newsstands, and vending machines at all stations. You can also buy a **pass** on either a daily or a weekly basis. To open the subway barrier, insert your ticket. If you have a Roma Pass (see p. 634), touch it against the yellow dot and the gates open.

Roman **buses and trams** are operated by **ATAC** (Agenzia del Trasporto Autoferrotranviario del Comune di Roma; www.atac.roma.it; ✆ **06-57003**). For 1.50€ you can ride to most parts of Rome, although it can be slow going in all that traffic, and buses are often crowded. A ticket is valid for 100 minutes, and you can get on many buses and trams during that time (as well as one run on the Metro). Tickets are sold in *tabacchi* and at bus stops.

For all this public transportation, you can buy **special timed passes: BIG** (*biglietto giornaliero* or 1-day ticket) costs 6€, and a **CIS** (*carta settimanale*) is 24€ for 1 week. The **BTI** (*bigiletto turistico,* or "tourist ticket") is 16.50€ for 3 days. If you plan to ride public transportation a lot—and if you are skipping between the *centro storico,* Roman ruins, and Vatican, you likely will—these passes save time and hassle. One-day and weekly tickets are also available at *tabacchi,* many newsstands, and at vending machines at all stations.

Don't count on hailing a **taxi** on the street or getting one at a stand. If you're going out, have your hotel call one. At a restaurant, ask the waiter or cashier to dial for you. The city taxi service is at ✆ **06-0609** (which will redirect to the nearest taxi rank, after you say the name of your location to an automated service), or try one of these radio taxi numbers: ✆ **06-6645,** 06-3570, or 06-4994. Taxis on call incur a surcharge of 3.50€. The meter begins at 3€ (Mon–Fri 6am–10pm) for the first 3km (1¾ miles) and then rises 1.10€ per kilometer.

## The Neighborhoods in Brief

**VATICAN CITY & THE PRATI** **Vatican City** is technically a sovereign state, although in practice it is just another part of Rome. The **Vatican Museums, St. Peter's,** and **Vatican Gardens** take up most of the area. Popes have lived here for 6 centuries. The neighborhood north of the Vatican—called "Borgo Pio"—contains some good hotels (and several bad ones), but is removed from the more happening scene of Rome. **Prati,** just east of the Vatican, is possibly a better choice, thanks to a smattering of affordable hotels and shopping.

**CENTRO STORICO & THE PANTHEON** One of the most desirable (and busiest) areas of Rome, the **Centro Storico** ("Historic Center") is a maze of narrow streets and cobbled alleys dating from the Middle Ages. The only way to explore it is on foot. Its heart is **Piazza Navona,** built over Emperor Domitian's stadium and bustling with cafes, *palazzi,* and street artists.





Rivaling Piazza Navona—in general buzz, the cafe scene, and nightlife—is the area around the **Pantheon,** which remains from ancient Rome and is surrounded by streets built much later. West of Via Arenula lies the old **Jewish Ghetto,** where dining options far outnumber hotels.

**ANCIENT ROME, MONTI & CELIO** Although no longer the heart of the city, this is where Rome began, with the **Colosseum, Palatine Hill, Roman Forum, Imperial Forums,** and **Circus Maximus.** This area offers only a few hotels and not a lot of great restaurants. You will get much more of a neighborhood feel if you stay in **Monti** (Rome's oldest *rione,* or quarter) or **Celio.** Both also have good dining, aimed at locals as well as visitors, and Monti, especially, has plenty of nighttime buzz.

**TRIDENTE & THE SPANISH STEPS** The northern part of Rome's center is sometimes known as the Tridente on account of the trident shape of the roads leading down from the apex of **Piazza del Popolo**—Via di Ripetta, Via del Corso, and Via del Babuino. The star here is **Piazza di Spagna,** which attracts Romans and tourists alike to idly sit on its **Spanish Steps.** Rome's most upscale shopping streets fan out from here.

**VIA VENETO & PIAZZA BARBERINI** In the 1950s and early 1960s, **Via Veneto** was the swinging place to be. The street is still the site of luxe hotels, cafes, and restaurants. To the south, Via Veneto comes to an end at **Piazza Barberini.**

**VILLA BORGHESE & PARIOLI** **Parioli** is Rome's most elegant residential section, a setting for fine restaurants, hotels, and public parks. It is framed by the green spaces of the **Villa Borghese** to the south and the **Villa Glori** and **Villa Ada** to the north. All that being said, Parioli is not central, so it can be a hassle as a base.

**AROUND STAZIONE TERMINI** The main train station, **Stazione Termini,** adjoins **Piazza della Repubblica,** and is for many their first introduction to Rome. Some of the area is slightly seedy. If you stay here, you might not get typical Rome charm, but you'll have several budget options and a convenient location, near a transportation hub and not far from ancient Rome.

**TRASTEVERE** In a Roman adaptation of the Latin "Trans Tiber," Trastevere means "across the Tiber." This former medieval working-class district has been gentrified and is now popular with visitors. As of yet it hasn't burgeoned into a major hotel district, but there are some excellent restaurants and bars. The area centers on the ancient churches of **Santa Cecilia** and **Santa Maria.** It remains one of Rome's most colorful quarters, even if a bit overrun.

## Exploring Rome

Rome's ancient monuments—whether time-blackened or gleaming in the wake of a restoration—are a constant reminder that this was one of the great centers of Western civilization. In the heyday of the Empire, all roads led to Rome, with good reason. It was one of the first cosmopolitan cities, importing slaves, gladiators, great art, and even citizens from the far corners of the world. Alongside carnage, brutality, and corruption, Rome left a legacy of law, and a heritage of art, architecture, and engineering.

But ancient Rome is only part of the spectacle. The **Vatican** has had a tremendous influence on making the city a tourism center. Although Vatican architects stripped down much of the city's ancient glory during the Renaissance, looting ancient ruins (the Forum especially) for the precious marble, they created more treasures in the process. In the years that followed, Bernini adorned the city with the wonders of the baroque, especially his fountains.

### No More Lines

Reservation services can help you avoid long city lines. Buying a **Roma Pass** (p. 634) is a good start: Holders use a special entrance at the Colosseum, and for your first two (free) museums, you can skip the line (so choose busy ones). For the **Vatican Museums,** buy an advance ticket at **www.biglietteria musei.vatican.va**; you pay an extra 4€, but will be able to skip the line at the main entrance (which can be very long). Note that St. Peter's is not included: There is no way to jump the line there. **Coopculture** (www.coopculture.it) operates an online ticket office that allows you to skip the line at several sites, including the Colosseum and the Forum, with a reservation fee of 1.50€ and 2€ to print tickets in advance.

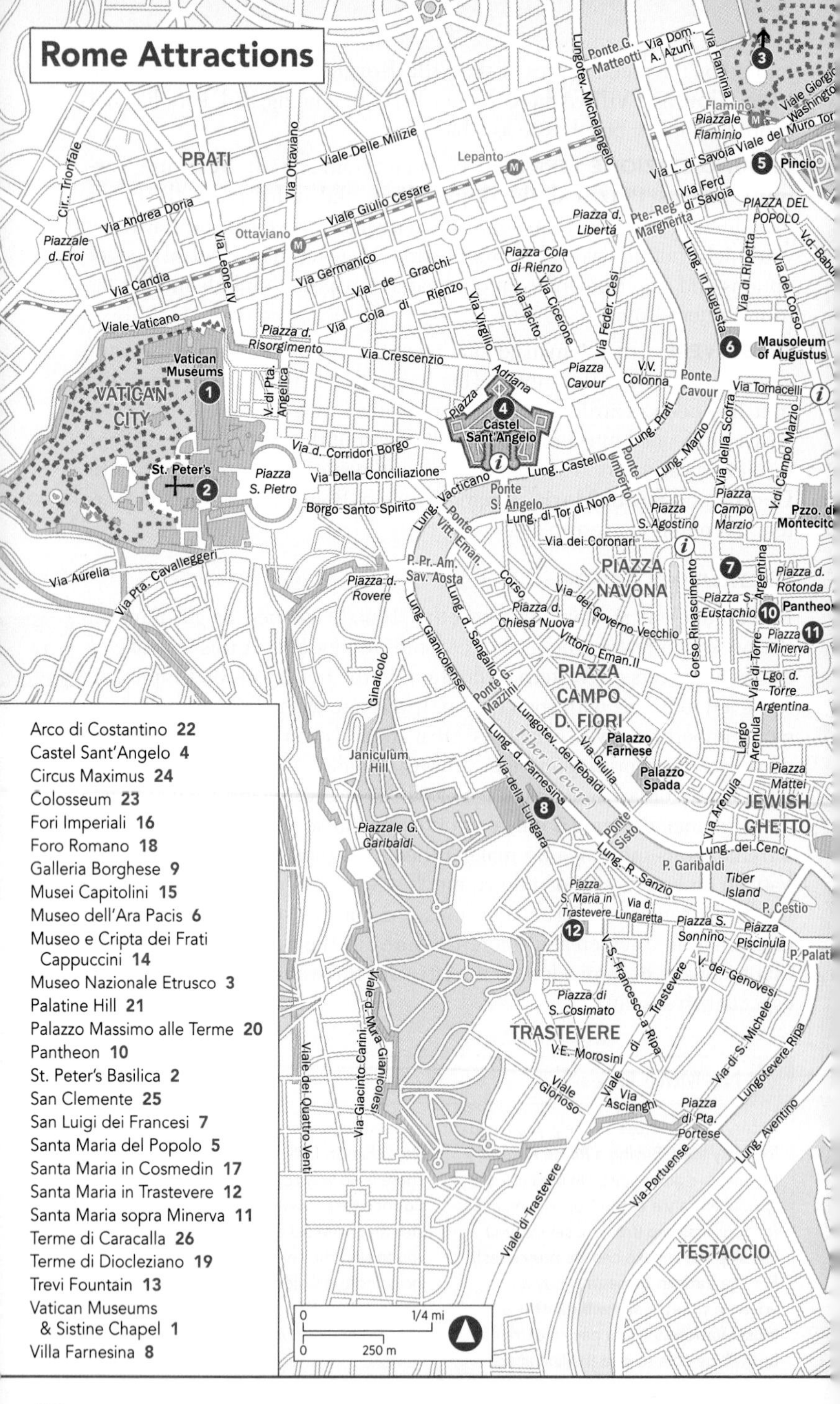
Rome Attractions
PRATI
VATICAN CITY
Vatican Museums
St. Peter's
Castel Sant'Angelo
Mausoleum of Augustus
Pincio
PIAZZA DEL POPOLO
PIAZZA NAVONA
PIAZZA CAMPO D. FIORI
Palazzo Farnese
Palazzo Spada
JEWISH GHETTO
Pantheon
Pzzo. di Montecito
Tiber (Tevere)
Tiber Island
Janiculum Hill
TRASTEVERE
TESTACCIO
Piazza S. Pietro
Piazzale d. Eroi
Piazza d. Risorgimento
Piazza Cola di Rienzo
Piazza d. Libertà
Piazza Cavour
Piazza S. Agostino
Piazza Campo Marzio
Piazza d. Rotonda
Piazza S. Eustachio
Piazza Minerva
Lgo. d. Torre Argentina
Piazza Mattei
Piazza d. Rovere
Piazza d. Chiesa Nuova
Piazzale G. Garibaldi
Piazza S. Maria in Trastevere
Piazza S. Sonnino
Piazza Piscinula
Piazza di S. Cosimato
Piazza di Pta. Portese
Piazzale Flaminio
Flaminio
Lepanto
Ottaviano
Viale Delle Milizie
Viale Giulio Cesare
Via Andrea Doria
Via Candia
Viale Vaticano
Via Germanico
Via de Gracchi
Via Cola di Rienzo
Via Crescenzio
Via Della Conciliazione
Borgo Santo Spirito
Via d. Corridori Borgo
Via Aurelia
Via Pta. Cavalleggeri
Via Leone IV
Via Ottaviano
Cir. Trionfale
V. di Pta. Angelica
Via Virgilio
Via Tacito
Via Cicerone
Via Feder. Cesi
Lungotev. Michelangelo
Ponte G. Matteotti
Via Dom. A. Azuni
Via Flaminia
Viale Giorgio Washington
Viale del Muro Torto
Via L. di Savoia
Via Ferd di Savoia
Pte. Reg. Margherita
Lung. in Augusta
Via di Ripetta
Via del Corso
V.d. Babuino
V.V. Colonna
Ponte Cavour
Via Tomacelli
Lung. Prati
Lung. Marzio
Via della Scrofa
V. di Campo Marzio
Ponte Umberto
Lung. Castello
Ponte S. Angelo
Lung. di Tor di Nona
Lung. Vacticano
Ponte Vitt. Eman.
Via dei Coronari
Corso Vittorio Eman. II
Via del Governo Vecchio
Corso Rinascimento
Via di Torre Argentina
Largo Arenula
Via Arenula
P.-Pr. Am. Sav. Aosta
Lung. Gianicolense
Lung. d. Sangallo
Ponte G. Mazzini
Lungotev. dei Tebaldi
Via Giulia
Lung. d. Farnesina
Via della Lungara
Ponte Sisto
Lung. dei Cenci
Lung. R. Sanzio
P. Garibaldi
P. Cestio
P. Palatino
Ginaicolo
Via d. Lungaretta
V. S. Francesco a Ripa
Via di Trastevere
V. dei Genovesi
Via di S. Michele
Lungotevere Ripa
V.E. Morosini
Viale Glorioso
Via Ascianghi
Viale di Trastevere
Via Portuense
Lung. Aventino
Viale d. Mura Gianicolesi
Via Giacinto Carini
Viale dei Quattro Venti
0 1/4 mi
0 250 m
Arco di Costantino 22
Castel Sant'Angelo 4
Circus Maximus 24
Colosseum 23
Fori Imperiali 16
Foro Romano 18
Galleria Borghese 9
Musei Capitolini 15
Museo dell'Ara Pacis 6
Museo e Cripta dei Frati Cappuccini 14
Museo Nazionale Etrusco 3
Palatine Hill 21
Palazzo Massimo alle Terme 20
Pantheon 10
St. Peter's Basilica 2
San Clemente 25
San Luigi dei Francesi 7
Santa Maria del Popolo 5
Santa Maria in Cosmedin 17
Santa Maria in Trastevere 12
Santa Maria sopra Minerva 11
Terme di Caracalla 26
Terme di Diocleziano 19
Trevi Fountain 13
Vatican Museums & Sistine Chapel 1
Villa Farnesina 8

Galleria
Borghese
National Gallery
of Modern Art
Piazza
di Siena
Viale dei Cavalli Marini
Viale P.Canonica
Vle d. Magnolie
VILLA
BORGHESE/
PARIOLI
Via Pinciana
Via Po
Via Tevere
Via Isonzo
Via Savoia
Venice
Florence
ITALY
Rome
Via Nomentana
Corso D'Italia
Via Campania
Via Sardegna
Via Sicilia
Via Boncompagni
Via Piave
Piazzale di
Porta Pia
Policlinico
Viale del Muro Torto
Via Vittorio Veneto
Via di Porta Pinciana
Spanish
Steps
Spagna
Via Ludovisi
VIA VENETO
Viale Castro Pretorio
Castro
Pretorio
Piazza di Spagna
Via Sistina
Lgo. di
S. Susanna
Via XX Settembre
National
Roman
Museum
Piazza
Indipendenza
Barberini
Via Barberini
Via Fr. Crispi
PIAZZA
BARBERINI
Piazza
Repubblica
Piazza
Cinque-
cento
Staz. Termini
Viale Pretoriano
Via Tritone
Lg. de
Tritone
Palazzo del
Quirinale
Via del Quirinale
Via d. Quattro Fontane
Repubblica
V. d. Viminale
Termini
Station
Trevi
Fountain
Piazza d.
Quirinale
Via Nazionale
Via Milano
Via Torino
Termini
Via Marsala
Teatro
dell'Opera
Piazza
dell'Esquilino
Via Principe Amedeo
Via Giovanni Giolitti
Corso
Palazzo
Colonna
Via XXIV Maggio
Via IV Nov.
Via Cavour
Santa Maria
Maggiore
V. Carlo Alberto
SAN
LORENZO
Via Cavour
Vittorio Emanuele
Monument
Via Leopardi
Vittorio Emanuele
Via Merulana
Piazza
Vittorio
Eman. II
Via Cavour
San Pietro
in Vincoli
Via Dei Fori Imperiali
Capitoline
Museums
Marcello
Golden House
of Nero
Via Macanate
Vle. Manzoni
ANCIENT
ROME
Roman
Forum
Colosseo
Viale d. Domus Aurea
Colosseum
Via Labicana
Manzoni
Piazza d.
Colosseo
Via. di S. Giovanni in Laterano
Vle. Manzoni
Piazza
Bocca
d. Verità
PALATINE
HILL
Via di S. Gregorio
Via Claudia
San Giovanni
in Laterano
Via del Circo Massimo
Circus
Maximus
S. Giovanni
AVENTINE
HILL
Circo
Massimo
Via della Navicella
Via Sannio
Piazza di
Pta.Capena
Piazza di
Pta. Metronia
Via Druso
Via Gallia
Piazza
Albania
Viale Aventino
di S. Anselmo
Via Antonina
Baths of
Caracalla
9
13
14
15
16
17
18
19
20
21
22
23
24
25
26
Information
City Walls
Metro A
Metro B
Railway

## VATICAN CITY & AROUND

### Vatican City ★★★

The world's smallest sovereign state, **Vatican City** is a truly tiny territory, comprising little more than St. Peter's and the walled headquarters of the Roman Catholic Church. There are no border controls, though the city-state's 800 inhabitants (essentially clergymen and Swiss Guards) have their own radio station, daily newspaper, tax-free pharmacy, petrol pumps, postal service, and head of state—the Pope.

The only entrance to **St. Peter's** for tourists is through one of the glories of the Western world: Bernini's 17th-century **St. Peter's Square (Piazza San Pietro).** As you stand in the huge piazza, you are in the arms of an ellipse partly enclosed by a **Doric-pillared colonnade.** Stand in the marked disc embedded in the piazza pavement near the fountains to see the columns all lined up in an impressive optical illusion. Straight ahead is the facade of St. Peter's itself (Sts. Peter and Paul are represented by statues in front, with Peter carrying the keys to the kingdom), and to the right, above the colonnade, are the dark brown buildings of the **papal apartments** and the Vatican Museums. In the center of the square is a 4,000-year-old **Egyptian obelisk,** created in the ancient city of Heliopolis on the Nile Delta and appropriated by the Romans under Emperor Augustus.

St. Peter's Square and Vatican City.

Exterior of St. Peter's Basilica.



**St. Peter's Basilica ★★★** CHURCH The Basilica di San Pietro or simply **St. Peter's,** is the holiest shrine of the Catholic Church, built on the site of St. Peter's tomb by the greatest artists of the 16th and 17th centuries.

In Roman times, the Circus of Nero, where St. Peter is said to have been crucified, was slightly to the left of where the basilica is now located. Peter was allegedly buried here in A.D. 64 near the site of his execution, and in A.D. 324, Emperor Constantine commissioned a church to be built over Peter's tomb. That structure stood for more than 1,000 years. The present basilica, mostly completed in the 1500s and 1600s, is predominantly High Renaissance and baroque. Inside, the massive scale is almost too much to absorb, showcasing some of Italy's greatest artists: Bramante, Raphael, Michelangelo, and Maderno. In a church of such grandeur—overwhelming in gilt, marble, and mosaic—you can't expect much subtlety. It is meant to be overpowering.

Going straight into the basilica, the first thing you see on the right side of the nave (the longest in the world), in the first chapel, is Michelangelo's graceful ***Pietà* ★★★,** one of Rome's great treasures, created in the 1490s when the master was still in his 20s.

### A St. Peter's Warning

St. Peter's has a strict dress code: no shorts, no skirts above the knee, and no bare shoulders and arms. ***Note:*** *You will not be let in if you come dressed inappropriately.* In a pinch, men and women can buy a big, cheap scarf from a nearby souvenir stand and wrap it around their legs as a long skirt or throw it over their shoulders as a shawl. If you're still showing too much skin, a guard hands out blue paper capes similar to what you wear in a doctor's office. Only limited photography is permitted inside.

Farther inside, Michelangelo's dome is a mesmerizing space, rising above the supposed site of St. Peter's tomb. With a diameter of 41.5m (136 ft.) it is Rome's largest, supported by four piers, decorated with reliefs depicting the basilica's key holy relics: St. Veronica's handkerchief (used to wipe the face of Christ); the lance of St. Longinus, which pierced Christ's side; and a piece of the True Cross.

Under the dome is the twisty-columned **baldacchino ★★,** by Bernini, resting over the papal altar. The 29m-high (96-ft.) ornate canopy was created in part, so it is said, from bronze stripped from the Pantheon. Bernini sculpted the face of a woman on the bases of each of the pillars; starting with the face on the left pillar (with your back to the entrance), circle the entire altar to see the progress of expressions from the agony of childbirth through to the fourth pillar, where the woman's face is replaced with that of her newborn baby.

You can head downstairs to the **Vatican grottoes ★★,** with their tombs of the popes, both ancient and modern (Pope John XXIII got the most adulation until the interment of **Pope John Paul II** in 2005). Behind a wall of glass is what is assumed to be the tomb of St. Peter.

Visits to the **Necropolis Vaticana ★★** and St. Peter's tomb itself are restricted to 250 persons per day on guided tours (90 min.) You must send a fax or e-mail 3 weeks beforehand, or apply in advance in person at the Ufficio Scavi (✆/fax **06-69873017;** e-mail: scavi@fsp.va; Mon–Fri 9am–6pm, Sat 9am–5pm), through the arch to the left of the stairs up the basilica. For details, check **www.vatican.va**. Children 14 and under are not admitted to the Necropolis.

After you leave the grottoes, you find yourself in a courtyard and ticket line for the climb to **Michelangelo's dome ★★★,** about 114m (375 ft.) high. The elevator saves you 171 steps, and you *still* have 320 to go after getting off. After you've made it to the top, you'll have a scintillating view over the rooftops of Rome and even the Vatican Gardens and papal apartments.

Piazza San Pietro. www.vatican.va. ✆ **06-69881662.** Basilica (including grottoes) free. Necropolis Vaticana (St. Peter's tomb) 13€. Stairs to the dome 5€; elevator to the dome 7€; sacristy (with Historical Museum) free. Metro: Cipro, Ottaviano/San Pietro.Basilica (including the grottoes and treasury) Oct–Mar daily 7am–6:30pm, Apr–Sept daily 7am–7pm. Dome Oct–Mar daily 8am–5pm; Apr–Sept daily 8am–6pm.

**Vatican Museums & the Sistine Chapel ★★★** MUSEUM Nothing else in Rome quite lives up to the collections of the **Vatican Museums.** It's a vast treasure store of art from antiquity and the Renaissance gathered by the Church throughout the centuries, filling a series of ornate palaces, apartments, and galleries leading to one of the world's most beautiful buildings, the **Sistine Chapel** (considered part of the museums for admission purposes).

Inside the Vatican Museums.



Note that the Vatican dress code also applies to the museums, though it tends to be less rigorously enforced than at St. Peter's. Visitors can, however, take photos (no flash) and even more dubiously, use mobile phones inside (with the exception of the Sistine Chapel). **Guided tours** are a good way to get the best out of a visit, and are the only way to visit the **Vatican Gardens.**

One trip will never be enough to see everything here. Below are the main highlights and masterpieces on display (in alphabetical order).

**APPARTAMENTO BORGIA (BORGIA APARTMENTS) ★:** Created for Pope Alexander VI (the infamous Borgia pope) between 1492 and 1494, these rooms were frescoed with biblical and allegorical scenes by Umbrian painter Pinturicchio and his assistants. Look for what is thought to be the earliest European depiction of Native Americans, painted a year after Columbus had returned from the New World.

**MUSEI DI ANTICHITÀ CLASSICHE (CLASSICAL ANTIQUITIES MUSEUMS):** The Vatican has four classical antiquities museums, the most important being the **Museo Pio Clementino ★★★,** crammed with Greek and Roman sculptures in the small Belvedere Palace of Innocent VIII. At the heart of the complex lies the Octagonal Court, where highlights include the sculpture of Trojan priest ***Laocoön*** **★★★** and his two sons locked in a struggle with sea serpents, dating from around 40 B.C., and the ***Belvedere Apollo*** **★★★** (a 2nd-c. Roman reproduction of a Greek work from the 4th c. B.C.), the symbol of classic male beauty, and a likely inspiration for Michelangelo's *David.*

**MUSEO GREGORIANO ETRUSCO ★:** The core of this collection is a cache of rare Etruscan art treasures dug up in the 19th century, dating from between the 9th and the 1st century B.C. The Romans learned a lot from the Etruscans, as the highly crafted ceramics, bronzes, silver, and gold on display attest. Don't miss the **Regolini-Galassi tomb** (7th c. B.C.), unearthed at Cerveteri.

**PINACOTECA (ART GALLERY) ★★★:** The great painting collections of the popes are displayed within the Pinacoteca, including work from all the big names in Italian art, from Giotto and Fra' Angelico to Perugino, Raphael, Veronese, and Crespi. **Giotto** takes center stage in Room 2, with the *Stefaneschi Triptych* (six panels) painted for the old St. Peter's between 1315 and 1320. **Fra' Angelico** dominates Room 3, with his *Stories of St. Nicholas of Bari* and *Virgin with Child* (check out the Virgin's microscopic eyes in the latter). In the **Raphael salon ★★★** (Room 8) you can view five paintings by the Renaissance master: The best are the *Coronation of the Virgin, Madonna of Foligno,* and vast *Transfiguration* (completed shortly before his death). Room 9 has Leonardo da Vinci's ***St. Jerome with the Lion* ★★,** as well as Giovanni Bellini's *Pietà*. Room 10 showcases Renaissance Venice, with Titian's *Madonna of St. Nicholas of the Frari* and Veronese's *Vision of St. Helen*. Room 12 is all about a particular baroque masterpiece, Caravaggio's ***Deposition from the Cross* ★★.**



**STANZE DI RAFFAELLO (RAPHAEL ROOMS) ★★:** In the early 16th century, Pope Julius II hired the young Raphael and his workshop to decorate his personal apartments, a series of connecting rooms on the second floor of the Pontifical Palace. Completed between 1508 and 1524, the **Raphael Rooms** now represent one of the great artistic spectacles inside the Vatican.

The **Stanza dell'Incendio** served as the pope's high court room and later, under Leo X, a dining room, though most of the fresco work here has been attributed to Raphael's pupils. Leo X himself commissioned much of the artwork, which explains the themes (past popes with the name Leo). Note the intricate ceiling, painted by Umbrian maestro and Raphael's first teacher, Perugino.

Raphael is the main focus in the **Stanza della Segnatura,** originally used as a Papal library and private office and home to the iconic ***School of Athens* ★★★** fresco, depicting primarily Greek classical philosophers such as Aristotle, Plato, and Socrates. Many of the figures are thought to be based on portraits of Renaissance artists, including Bramante (on the right as Euclid, drawing on a chalkboard), Leonardo da Vinci (as Plato, the bearded man in the center), and even Raphael himself (in the lower-right corner with a black hat).

The **Stanza d'Eliodoro** was used for the private audiences of the pope and was painted by Raphael immediately after the Segnatura. His aim here was to flatter his papal patron, Julius II: The depiction of the pope driving Attila from Rome symbolizes the mission of Julius II to drive the French out of Italy. Finally, the **Sala di Constantino,** used for Papal receptions, was completed by Raphael's students after the master's death, based on his designs and drawings. It's a jaw-dropping space, commemorating four major episodes in the life of Emperor Constantine.

**SISTINE CHAPEL ★★★:** Michelangelo labored for 4 years (1508–12) to paint the ceiling of the Sistine Chapel; it is said he spent the entire time on his feet, paint dripping into his eyes. But what a result! The world's most famous fresco is, thanks to a massive restoration in the 1990s, as colorful and filled with roiling life as it was in 1512. And the chapel is still of central importance to the Church: The Papal Conclave meets here to elect popes.

The ceiling **frescoes** are obviously the showstoppers, though staring at them tends to take a heavy toll on the neck. Commissioned by Pope Julius II in 1508 and completed in 1512, they primarily depict nine scenes from the Book of Genesis (including the famed *Creation of Adam*), from the *Separation of Light and Darkness* at the altar end to the *Great Flood* and *Drunkenness of Noah.* Surrounding these main frescoes are paintings of 12 people who prophesied the coming of Christ, from Jonah and Isaiah to the Delphic Sibyl. Once you have admired the ceiling, turn your attention to the wall behind the altar. At the age of 60, Michelangelo was summoned to finish the chapel decor 23 years after he finished the ceiling work. Apparently saddened by leaving Florence, and by the poor, morally bankrupt state of Rome at that time, he painted these dark moods in his *Last Judgment,* where he included his own self-portrait on a sagging human hide held by St. Bartholomew (who was martyred by being flayed alive).

Yet the Sistine Chapel isn't all Michelangelo. On the southern wall is a series of paintings completed in the 1480s: *Moses Leaving to Egypt* by Perugino, the *Trials of Moses* by Botticelli, *The Crossing of the Red Sea* by Cosimo Rosselli (or Domenico Ghirlandaio), *Descent from Mount Sinai* by Cosimo Rosselli (or Piero di Cosimo), Botticelli's *Punishment of the Rebels,* and Signorelli's *Testament and Death of Moses.*

On the right-hand, northern wall are Perugino's *The Baptism of Christ,* Botticelli's *The Temptations of Christ,* Ghirlandaio's *Vocation of the Apostles,* Perugino's *Delivery of the Keys,* and Cosimo Rosselli's *The Sermon on the Mount* and *Last Supper.*

Vatican City, Viale Vaticano (a long walk around the Vatican walls from St. Peter's Sq.). www.museivaticani.va. ✆ **06-69884676.** 16€ adults, 8€ children 6–13, free for children 5 and under. Tours of Vatican Gardens (2hr.) 32€ (Mon, Tues, Thurs–Sat). Metro: Ottaviano or Cipro-Musei Vaticani. Bus: 49. Mon–Sat 9am–6pm (ticket office closes at 4pm); also last Sun of every month 9am–2pm (free admission). Closed Jan 1 and 6, Feb 11, Mar 19, Easter, May 1, June 29, Aug 14–15, Nov 1, and Dec 25–26. Advance tickets (fee 4€) and guided tours through www.bigliettteriamusei.vatican.va.

### Near Vatican City

**Castel Sant'Angelo ★★** CASTLE/PALACE This cylindrical fortress on the Vatican side of the Tiber has a storied, complex history, beginning life as the tomb of Emperor Hadrian in A.D. 138, and later serving as a castle (Pope Clement VII escaped the looting troops of Charles V here in 1527), papal residence in the 14th century, and military prison from the 17th century (Puccini used the prison as the setting for the third act of *Tosca*). The ashes and urns of Hadrian and his family have long since been looted and destroyed, and most of what you see today relates to the conversion of the structure into a fortress and residence from the 14th century.

From the entrance, a stone ramp (*rampa elicoidale*) winds its way to the upper terraces, from which you can see amazing views of the city and enjoy a coffee at the outdoor cafe. The sixth floor features the **Terrazza dell'Angelo** (location of the tragic denouement of *Tosca*), crowned by a florid statue of the Archangel Michael cast in 1752 by the Flemish artist Peter Anton van Verschaffelt.

From here you can walk back down through five floors, including the Renaissance apartments (levels 3–5) used by some of Rome's most infamous popes: Alexander VI (the Borgia pope) hid away in the castle after the murder of his son Giovanni in 1497, overwhelmed with grief.

Below the apartments are the grisly dungeons **("Le Prigioni")** used as torture chambers in the medieval period, and utilized especially enthusiastically by Cesare Borgia. The castle is connected to St. Peter's Basilica by **Il Passetto di Borgo,** a walled 800m (2,635-ft.) passage erected in 1277 by Pope Nicholas III, used by popes who needed to make a quick escape to the fortress in times of danger, which was fairly often. Note that the dungeons, Il Passetto, and the apartments of Clement VII are only usually open on summer evenings (July–Aug Tues–Sun 8:30pm–1am; free 50-min. tours with admission, English tour at 10:30pm).

Lungotevere Castello 50. www.castelsantangelo.com. ✆ **06-6819111.** 11€. Tues–Sun 9am–7:30pm. Bus: 23, 40, 62, 271, 280, or 982. Sun 9am–7:30pm.

## ANCIENT ROME, MONTI & CELIO

The photogenic triumphal arch next to the Colosseum, the **Arco di Costantino (Arch of Constantine) ★★** was erected by the Senate in A.D. 315 to honor Constantine's defeat of the pagan Maxentius at the Battle of the Ponte Milvio (Milvian Bridge) Battle (A.D. 312). Many of the reliefs have nothing whatsoever to do with Constantine or his works, but tell of victories of earlier Antonine rulers.

Today an almost formless ruin, the **Circus Maximus ★** was a grand race track before being pilfered repeatedly by medieval and Renaissance builders in search of marble and stone. But if you squint, and take in its elongated oval proportions and missing tiers of benches, visions of *Ben-Hur* may dance before your eyes. At one time, 250,000 Romans could assemble on its marble seats, while the emperor observed the games from his box high on the Palatine Hill.

**Colosseum (Colosseo)** ★★★ ICON No matter how many pictures you've seen, the first impression you'll have of the Colosseum is amazement at its sheer enormity. It is massive and looks as if it has been plopped down among the surrounding buildings, and not the other way around. Note the different column styles on each level.

Once inside, walk onto the partially reconstructed wooden platform flooring that once covered the *hypogeum*—the place where gladiators and beasts waited their turn in the arena. Vespasian ordered the construction of the elliptical bowl, called the Amphitheatrum Flavium, in A.D. 72; it was inaugurated by Titus in A.D. 80 with a bloody combat, lasting many weeks, between gladiators and wild beasts. The stadium could hold as many as 87,000 spectators, by some counts, and seats were sectioned on three levels, dividing the people by social rank and gender.

The Colosseum was built as a venue for gladiator contests and wild animal fights, but when the Roman Empire fell, it was abandoned and eventually overgrown with vegetation. You'll notice on the top of the "good side," as locals call it, that there are a few remaining supports that once held the canvas awning that covered the stadium during rain or for the summer heat.

**The Colosseum once held 87,000 spectators.**

***Note:*** The same ticket that you buy for the Colosseum includes admission to the Forum and Palatine Hill, and is valid for 2 days.

Piazzale del Colosseo. www.archeoroma.beniculturali.it. ✆ **06-39967700.** 12€ (includes Roman Forum & Palatine Hill). Tours 5€. Metro: Colosseo. Nov–Feb 15 daily 8:30am–4:30pm; Feb 16–Mar 15 daily 8:30am–5pm; Mar 16–27 daily 8:30am–5:30pm; Mar 28–Aug daily 8:30am–7:15pm; Sept daily 8:30am–7pm; Oct daily 8:30am–6:30pm. Last admission 1 hr. before closing. Guided tours (45 min.) in English daily at 10:15, 10:45, 11:15, and 11:45am, 12:30, 1:45, and 3pm.

**Foro Romano (Roman Forum) & Palatino (Palatine Hill) ★★★** RUINS When it came to cremating Caesar, sacrificing a human victim, or just discussing the day's events, the Roman Forum was the place to be. Traversed by the **Via Sacra (Sacred Way) ★,** the main thoroughfare of ancient Rome, the Forum flourished as the center of Roman life in the days of the Republic, before it gradually lost prestige (but never spiritual draw) to the Imperial Forums (see p. 650).

I suggest you enter via the gate on Via dei Fori Imperiali. Turn right at the bottom of the entrance slope to walk west along the old Via Sacra toward the arch. Just before it on your right is the large brick **Curia ★★**, the main seat of the Roman Senate, built by Julius Caesar, rebuilt by Diocletian, and consecrated as a church in A.D. 630.

The triumphal **Arch of Septimius Severus ★★** (A.D. 203) displays time-bitten reliefs of the emperor's victories in what are today Iran and Iraq. During the Middle Ages, Rome became a provincial backwater, and frequent flooding of the nearby river helped bury (and thus preserve) most of the Forum. Some bits did still stick out aboveground, including the top half of this arch. Just to the left, you can make out the remains of a cylindrical lump of rock with some marble steps curving off it. That round stone was the **Umbilicus Urbus,** considered the center of Rome and of the entire Empire; the curving steps are those of the **Imperial Rostra ★,** where orators stood to speak. Nearby is a trio of fluted columns with Corinthian capitals supporting a bit of architrave form the corner of the **Temple of Vespasian and Titus ★★** (emperors were routinely worshipped as gods).

Start heading to your left toward the eight Ionic columns marking the front of the **Temple of Saturn ★★** (rebuilt in 42 B.C.), which housed the first treasury of republican Rome. It was also the site of one of the Roman year's biggest annual blowout festivals, the December 17 feast of Saturnalia, which after a bit of tweaking, Christians now celebrate as Christmas. Turn left to start heading back east, past the stumps of brick pillars outlining the enormous **Basilica Julia ★★,** built by Julius Caesar. Farther along, on the right, are the three Corinthian columns of the **Temple of the Dioscuri ★★★,** dedicated to the Gemini twins, Castor and Pollux. The founding of this temple dates from the 5th century B.C.

Beyond the bit of curving wall that marks the site of the little round **Temple of Vesta** (rebuilt several times after fires), you'll find the reconstructed **House of the Vestal Virgins ★** (A.D. 3rd–4th c.). The temple was the home of the consecrated young women who tended the sacred flame in the Temple of Vesta. Vestals were girls chosen from patrician families to serve a 30-year-long priesthood. During their tenure, they were among Rome's most venerated citizens, with unique powers such as the ability to pardon condemned criminals. The cult was quite serious about the "virgin" part of the job description—if one of Vesta's earthly servants was found to have "misplaced" her virginity, the miscreant Vestal was buried alive, because it was forbidden to shed a Vestal's blood. (Her amorous accomplice was merely flogged to death.)

The path dovetails back to Via Sacra toward the massive brick remains and coffered ceilings of the 4th-century **Basilica of Constantine and Maxentius ★★.** These were Rome's public law courts, with a unique architectural style that was adopted by early Christians for their own houses of worship (the reason so many ancient churches are called "basilicas"). From here, veer right to the Forum's second great triumphal arch, the extensively rebuilt **Arch of Titus ★★** (A.D. 81), on which one relief depicts the carrying off of treasures from Jerusalem's temple.

You can climb the **Palatine Hill ★** (Palatino) on the same ticket. The Palatine, tradition tells us, was the spot on which the first settlers built their huts. In later years, the hill became a patrician residential district that attracted such citizens as Cicero. In time, however, the area was gobbled up by imperial palaces and drew a famous and infamous roster of tenants, such as Livia (some of the frescoes in the House of Livia are in miraculous condition), Tiberius, Caligula (murdered here by members of his Praetorian Guard), Nero, and Domitian.

Via della Salara Vecchia. www.archeoroma.beniculturali.it. ✆ **06-39967700.** 12€ (includes Colosseum). Oct 30–Dec and Jan 2–Feb 15 daily 8:30am–4:30pm; Feb 16–Mar 15 daily 8:30am–5pm; Mar 16–24 daily 8:30am–5:30pm; Mar 25–Aug daily 8:30am–7:15pm; Sept daily 8:30am–7pm; Oct 1–29 daily 8:30am–6:30pm. Last admission 1 hr. before closing. Guided tours daily at 11am, lasting 1 hr.; 4€. Metro: Colosseo.

**Musei Capitolini (Capitoline Museums) ★★** MUSEUM The masterpieces here are considered Rome's most valuable (the Vatican Museums are *not* part of Rome). This is also the oldest public museum *in the world,* with lots to see, so try to schedule adequate time.

On the ground floor of the **Palazzo dei Conservatori,** the unmissable works are in the first series of rooms. These include *Lo Spinario* **(Room III),** a lifelike bronze of a young boy digging a splinter out of his foot that was widely copied during the Renaissance; and the *Lupa Capitolina* **(Room IV),** a bronze statue from 500 B.C. of the famous she-wolf that suckled Romulus and Remus, the mythical founders of Rome. The

## THE FORI IMPERIALI, OR imperial forums

Begun by Julius Caesar as an answer to the overcrowding of Rome's older forums, the Imperial Forums were, at the time of their construction, flashier, bolder, and more impressive than the buildings in the Roman Forum. Alas, Mussolini felt his regime was more important than the ancient one, and issued the controversial order to cut through centuries of debris and buildings to carve out Via dei Fori Imperiali, thereby linking the Colosseum to the grand 19th-century monuments of Piazza Venezia. Excavations under his Fascist regime began at once (ca. 1931), and many archaeological treasures were revealed (and then—argh!—destroyed).

The best view of the Forums is from the railings on the north side of Via dei Fori Imperiali; begin where Via Cavour joins the boulevard. (Visitors are not permitted down into this part of the ruins.) Closest to the junction are the remains of the **Forum of Nerva,** built by the emperor whose 2-year reign (A.D. 96–98) followed the assassination of the paranoid Domitian. You'll be struck by how much the ground level has risen in 19 centuries. The only recognizable remnant is a wall of the Temple of Minerva with two fine Corinthian columns. This forum was once flanked by that of Vespasian, which is now gone.

The next along is the **Forum of Augustus ★★,** built before the birth of Christ to commemorate the emperor's victory over Julius Caesar's assassins, Cassius and Brutus, in the Battle of Philippi (42 B.C.).

Continuing along the railing, you'll see the vast semicircle of **Trajan's Markets ★★** (www.mercatiditraiano.it), whose teeming arcades stocked with merchandise from the far corners of the Roman world collapsed long ago. The shops once covered a multitude of levels. In front of the Markets, the **Forum of Trajan ★★** is the newest and most beautiful of the Imperial Forums, built between A.D. 107 and 113, and designed by Greek architect Apollodorus of Damascus, who also laid out the adjoining market building. There are many statue fragments and pedestals bearing still-legible inscriptions, but more interesting is the great Basilica Ulpia, whose gray marble columns rise roofless into the sky. This forum was once regarded as one of the architectural wonders of the world. Beyond the Basilica Ulpia is **Trajan's Column ★★★,** in magnificent condition, with an intricate bas-relief sculpture depicting Trajan's victorious campaign.

The **Forum of Julius Caesar ★★,** the first of the Imperial Forums to be built, lies on the opposite side of Via dei Fori Imperiali, adjacent to the Roman Forum. This was the site of the stock exchange, as well as the Temple of Venus.

twins were not on the original Etruscan statue; they were added in the 15th century. **Room V** has Bernini's pained portrait of *Medusa,* with its writhing serpent hairdo.

The new wing at the rear, bathed in natural light thanks to an enormous modern skylight, houses the original equestrian **statue of Marcus Aurelius ★★★,** dating to around A.D. 180—the piazza outside, where it stood from 1538, now has a copy. There's a giant bronze head from a statue of Constantine (ca. A.D. 337) and the foundations of the original

Temple of Jupiter that stood on the Capitoline Hill since its inauguration in 509 B.C.

An underground tunnel takes you under the piazza to the other part of the Museums, the **Palazzo Nuovo,** via the **Tabularium ★.** This was built in 78 B.C. to house ancient Rome's city records, and was later used as a salt mine and then as a prison. The atmospheric stone gallery was opened to the public in the late 1990s to exhibit inscriptions, and also to provide access to one of the best balcony **views ★★★** in Rome: along the length of the Forum toward the Palatine Hill.

Much of the Palazzo Nuovo is dedicated to statues that were excavated from the forums below or brought in from outlying areas like Hadrian's Villa in Tivoli. If you're running short on time, head straight for the 1st-century ***Capitoline Venus* ★★,** in Room III, and a chronologically arranged row of busts of Roman emperors and their families (Room IV). Another favorite is the beyond handsome ***Dying Gaul* ★★,** a Roman copy of a lost ancient Greek work.

Piazza del Campidoglio 1. www.museicapitolini.org. ✆ **06-0608.** 13€. Bus: C3, H, 40, 44, 60, 80B, 190, 780, or 781. Tues–Sun 9am–8pm. Last admission 1 hr. before closing.

**San Clemente ★★★** CHURCH This isn't just another Roman church—far from it. In this layered church-upon-a-church, centuries of history peel away. In the 4th century, a church was built on top of a secular house from the 1st century, beside which stood a pagan temple dedicated to Mithras. Down in the eerie grottoes (which you explore on your own) are well-preserved frescoes from the 9th to the 11th centuries. The Normans destroyed this lower church, and a new one was built on top in the 12th century. Its chief attraction is the mosaic adorning the apse, as well as a chapel honoring St. Catherine of Alexandria with 1428 frescoes by Masolino.

Via San Giovanni in Laterano (at Piazza San Clemente). www.basilicasanclemente.com. ✆ **06-7740021.** Basilica free admission; excavations 5€. Bus: 53, 85, or 117. Mon–Sat 9am–12:30pm and 3–6pm; Sun noon–6pm. Last admission 20 min. before closing.

**Santa Maria in Cosmedin ★** CHURCH People come to this little church (indeed, stand in line) not for great art or ancient treasures, but to see the **"Mouth of Truth,"** a large disk under the portico. It is no longer possible to "pull a Gregory Peck" and actually put your hand in the mouth, like the star did, demonstrating to Audrey Hepburn in the film "Roman Holiday," that the mouth is supposed to chomp down on the hands of liars. The purpose of this disk is unclear. One hypothesis suggests it was one of many Roman "talking statues." If you wanted to rat someone out, you could slip an anonymous note inside the open mouth.

Piazza Bocca della Verità 18. ✆ **06-6787759.** Free. Bus: 23, 81, 160, 280, or 628. Summer daily 9:30am–5:50pm; winter daily 9:30am–5pm.

**Terme di Caracalla (Baths of Caracalla)** ★ RUINS Named for the emperor Caracalla, the baths were completed in A.D. 217, after Caracalla's death. The richness of decoration has faded, and the lushness can be judged only from the shell of brick ruins that remain. In their heyday, they sprawled across 11 hectares (27 acres) and could handle 1,600 bathers at one time. Partially opened to the public in 2012, the tunnels below the complex give an idea of the scale of the hydraulic and heating systems needed to serve 8,000 or so Romans per day.

The baths are also a breathtaking setting for summertime outdoor operatic performances in Rome (see p. 674).

Via delle Terme di Caracalla 52. www.archeoroma.beniculturali.it. ✆ **06-39967700**. 7€. Bus: 118 or 628. Oct Mon 8:30am–2pm, Tues–Sun 9am–6:30pm; Nov–Feb 15 Mon 8:30am–2pm, Tues–Sun 9am–4:30pm; Feb 16–Mar 15 Mon 8:30am–2pm, Tues–Sun 9am–5pm; Mar 16–Sept Mon 8:30am–2pm, Tues–Sun 9am–7pm. Last admission 1 hr. before closing.

## CENTRO STORICO & THE PANTHEON

Just across the Tiber from the Vatican and Castel Sant'Angelo lies the true heart of Rome, the **Centro Storico** or "historic center," roughly the triangular wedge of land that bulges into a bend of the river. Alleys are crammed with piazzas, elegant churches, and lavish fountains.



### Piazza Navona & Nearby Attractions

Rome's most famous square, **Piazza Navona** ★★★ is a baroque gem, lined with cafes and restaurants, and often crowded with tourists, street artists, and performers by day and night. Its long, thin shape follows the contours of the old Roman Stadium of Domitian, where chariot races once took place, still a ruin until a mid-17th-century makeover by Pope Innocent X. The twin-towered facade of 17th-century **Sant'Agnese in Agone** lies on the piazza's western side, while the **Fontana dei Quattro Fiumi (Fountain of the Four Rivers)** ★★★ is one of three great fountains in the square, this one a creation of Bernini, topped with an Egyptian obelisk. The four stone personifications below symbolize the world's greatest rivers: the Ganges, Danube, Rio de la Plata, and Nile. It's fun to try to figure out which is which. (***Hint:*** The figure with the shroud on its head is the Nile, so represented

Bernini's Fountain of the Four Rivers, Piazza Navona.

because the river's source was unknown at the time.) At the south end is the **Fontana del Moro (Fountain of the Moor),** also by Bernini; the **Fontana di Nettuno (Fountain of Neptune)** is a 19th-century addition.

**San Luigi dei Francesi ★★** CHURCH For a painter of such stratospheric standards as Caravaggio, it is impossible to be definitive in naming his "masterpiece." However, the ***Calling of St. Matthew ★★,*** in the far-left chapel of Rome's French church, has to be a candidate. The panel dramatizes the moment Jesus and Peter "called" the Customs officer to join them, in Caravaggio's distinct *chiaroscuro* (extreme light and shade) style. Around the same time (1599–1602) Caravaggio painted the other two St. Matthew panels in the Capella Contarelli—including one depicting the saint's martyrdom.

Via di Santa Giovanna d'Arco 5. www.saintlouis-rome.net. ✆ **06-688271.** Free. Bus: C3, 30, 70, 81, 87, 116, 186, 492, or 628. Mon–Wed and Fri–Sat 10am–12:30pm and 3–7pm; Thurs 10am–12:30pm; Sun 3–7pm.

### The Pantheon & Nearby Attractions

The Pantheon stands on **Piazza della Rotonda,** a lively square with cafes, vendors, and plentiful people watching.

**The Pantheon ★★★** HISTORIC SITE Of all ancient Rome's great buildings, only the Pantheon ("Temple to All the Gods") remains intact. It was originally built in wood in 27 B.C. by Marcus Agrippa but was entirely reconstructed by Hadrian in the early A.D. 2nd century after it was destroyed in a fire. This remarkable building, once entirely covered in white marble, 43m (142 ft.) wide and 43m (142 ft.) high (a perfect sphere resting in a cylinder) and laced with white marble statues of Roman gods in its niches, is among the architectural wonders of the world. Hadrian himself is credited with the basic plan, a design that was unique for the time. There are no visible arches or vaults holding up the dome; instead they're sunk into the concrete of the walls of the building, while the ribbed dome outside is a series of almost weightless cantilevered bricks. Animals were once sacrificed and burned in the center, and the smoke escaped through the only means of light, the oculus, an opening at the top 5.5m (18 ft.) in diameter.

The interior now houses the tombs of two Italian kings (Vittorio Emanuele II and his successor, Umberto I), and the resting place of **Raphael** (fans still bring him flowers), between the second and third chapel on the left.

Piazza della Rotonda. ✆ **06-68300230.** Free. Bus: 30, 40, 62, 64, 81, or 492. Mon–Sat 8:30am–7:30pm; Sun 9am–6pm. For Mass attendees only: Sat 5pm, Sun 10:30am.

**Santa Maria sopra Minerva ★** CHURCH Behind the Pantheon, Santa Maria sopra Minerva is Rome's most significant Dominican church, and the only Gothic church in the center. True, the facade is in the Renaissance style (the church was begun in 1280 but worked on until 1725), but inside, the arched vaulting is pure Gothic. The main art treasures here are the *Statua del Redentore* (1521), a statue of Christ by **Michelangelo** (just to the left of the altar) and wonderful fresco cycle in the **Cappella Carafa** (on the right before the altar), created by Filippino Lippi between 1488 and 1493 to honor St. Thomas Aquinas.

Piazza della Minerva 42. www.basilicaminerva.it. ✆ **06-69920384.** Free. Bus: 116. Daily 8am–7pm.

### Campo de' Fiori & the Jewish Ghetto

The southern section of the Centro Storico, **Campo de' Fiori** is another neighborhood of narrow streets, small piazzas, and ancient churches. Its main focus remains the piazza of **Campo de' Fiori ★★** itself, whose produce stalls are a real contrast to the cafes and entertainers of Piazza Navona. The expensive open-air food market runs Monday through Saturday from early in the morning until around 2pm (or whenever food runs out). From the center of the piazza rises a statue of the severe-looking monk **Giordano Bruno,** whose presence is a reminder that heretics were occasionally burned at the stake here: Bruno was executed by the Inquisition in 1600.

The southern part of Campo di Fiori merges into the old **Jewish Ghetto,** established near the River Tiber by a Papal Bull in 1555, which

Produce stalls at Campo de' Fiori.

required all the Jews in Rome to live in one area. Walled in, overcrowded, prone to floods and epidemics, and on some of the worst land in the city, life here was extremely grim. It was only after the Ghetto was abolished in 1882 that its walls were torn down and the area largely reconstructed. Today **Via Portico d'Ottavia** lies at the heart of a flourishing Jewish Quarter, where Romans flock to sample Roman-Jewish and Middle Eastern cuisine.

## THE TRIDENTE & THE SPANISH STEPS

The northern half of central Rome is known as the **Tridente** thanks to the trident shape formed by three roads—Via di Ripetta, Via del Corso, and Via del Babuino—leading down from **Piazza del Popolo.** The area around **Piazza di Spagna** and the **Spanish Steps** was once the artistic quarter of the city, attracting English poets Keats and Shelley, German author Goethe, and Italian film director Federico Fellini (who lived on Via Margutta).

### Piazza del Popolo

Elegant **Piazza del Popolo ★★** is haunted with memories. According to legend, the ashes of Nero were enshrined here, until 11th-century residents began complaining to the pope about his imperial ghost. The **Egyptian obelisk** dates from the 13th century B.C.; it was removed from Heliopolis to Rome during Augustus's reign (and once stood at the Circus Maximus).

The current piazza was designed in the early 19th century by Napoléon's architect, Valadier. The 15th-century **Santa Maria del Popolo ★★** is at its northern curve, its facade modified by the great Bernini between 1655 and 1660 in a baroque style. Raphael's mosaic series the *Creation of the World* adorns the interior of the dome of the **Capella Chigi** inside (second chapel on the left), and **Pinturicchio** decorated the main choir vault with frescoes such as the *Coronation of the Virgin*. The **Capella Cerasi** (to the left of the high altar), contains gorgeous examples of baroque art: an altarpiece painting of *The Assumption of Mary* by Carracci, and on either side two great works by Caravaggio, *Conversion on the Road to Damascus* and *The Crucifixion of Saint Peter.*

**Museo dell'Ara Pacis ★★** MUSEUM Set in a modern glass building (you can walk around the outside for free) and surrounded by more historic structures, the white marble *Altar of Peace* was created in 9 B.C. to honor the achievements of Augustus in subduing tribes north of Alps. Though signs of its existence were discovered in the 16th century, it wasn't until the 1930s that the ancient monument was fully excavated. The current building, finished in 2006 to a design by American architect Richard Meier, is one of the most poignant showcases of Imperial Rome.

The museum provides interactive displays in English and Italian. Note that you get great views of the huge, overgrown ruin of **Augustus's**

**Mausoleum (Mausoleo di Augusto)** from here, but the 1st-century B.C. tomb itself—where the ashes of emperors Augustus, Caligula, Claudius, Nerva, and Tiberius were once stored—is closed to the public, for now.

Lungotevere in Augusta. www.arapacis.it. ✆ **06-060608.** 8.50€. Bus: C3, 70, 81, 87, 186, 492, 628, or 913. Tues–Sun 9am–7pm (last admission 6pm).

### Piazza di Spagna

The undoubted highlight of Tridente is **Piazza di Spagna,** which attracts hordes to lounge on its **Spanish Steps (Scalinata della Trinità dei Monti) ★★,** the largest stairway in Europe, to enjoy the view onto Bernini's *Fontana della Barcaccia,* a fountain shaped like an old boat. The Steps are especially enchanting in early spring, when they're framed by thousands of blooming azaleas.

In an odd twist, the monumental stairway of 135 steps and the square take their names from the Spanish Embassy (it used to be headquartered here), but were actually funded almost entirely by the French. That's because the **Trinità dei Monti** church at the top was under the patronage of the Bourbon kings of France at the time. They were built from 1723 to 1725.



As you elbow your way through the summertime crowds around the nearby **Trevi Fountain ★★,** you'll find it hard to believe that its little

The Spanish Steps and the Fontana della Barcaccia.

piazza was nearly always deserted before the 1950s, when it started appearing in movies, beginning with *Three Coins in the Fountain.* It was also the setting for an iconic scene in Federico Fellini's 1960 masterpiece, *La Dolce Vita,* and it's where Audrey Hepburn's character in *Roman Holiday* gets her signature haircut. To this day, thousands of euros worth of coins are tossed into the fountain every day.

Supplied with water from the Acqua Vergine aqueduct and a triumph of the baroque style, the fountain was based on the design of Nicola Salvi—who's said to have died of illness contracted during his supervision of the project—and was completed in 1762. The design centers on the triumphant figure of Neptune, standing on a shell chariot drawn by winged steeds and led by a pair of tritons.

### Villa Borghese & Parioli

**Villa Borghese ★★,** in the heart of Rome, is not actually a villa but one of Europe's most elegant parks, 6 km (3¾ miles) in circumference and housing outstanding museums. Cardinal Scipione Borghese created the park in the 1600s. Umberto I, King of Italy, acquired it in 1902 and presented it to the city. This heart-shaped greenbelt is crisscrossed by roads, but you can escape from the traffic and seek a shaded area under a tree to enjoy a picnic or relax.

**Galleria Borghese ★★★** ART MUSEUM Occupying the former Villa Borghese Pinciana, the Galleria Borghese was built between 1609 and 1613 for Cardinal Scipione Borghese, who was an early patron of Bernini and an astute collector of work by Caravaggio. Today the gallery is one of Rome's great art treasures.

The ground floor is a **sculpture gallery** par excellence, housing Canova's famously risqué statue of Paolina Borghese, sister of Napoléon and wife of the reigning Prince Camillo Borghese (when asked if she was uncomfortable posing nude, she reportedly replied: "No, the studio was heated."). The genius of Bernini permeates the rooms, with his *David* (the face of which is thought to be a self-portrait), and his ***Apollo and Daphne* ★★,** both seminal works of baroque sculpture. Next to this room, look out also for Bernini's Mannerist sculpture, *The Rape of Persephone.* Caravaggio is represented by the *Madonna of the Grooms,* his shadowy *St. Jerome,* and his frightening ***David Holding the Head of Goliath* ★★.**

Upstairs lies a rich collection of paintings, including Raphael's sinuous *Lady with a Unicorn.* One of Titian's best, ***Sacred and Profane Love* ★,** is in the final rooms. Guided tours of the galleries in English (5€) run 9:10am to 11:10am, but failing that opt for the **audioguides,** as English labeling is minimal.

***Note:*** No more than 360 visitors at a time are allowed on the ground floor, and no more than 90 are allowed on the upper floor, during set, 2-hour windows. **Reservations are essential,** so call ✆ **06-32810**

(Mon–Fri 9am–6pm; Sat 9am–1pm). You can also make reservations by visiting **www.tosc.it**, or by stopping by on your first day in Rome to reserve tickets for a later date.

Piazzale del Museo Borghese 5 (off Via Pinciana). www.galleriaborghese.it. ✆ **06-8413979.** 11€ plus 2€ mandatory "service charge." Audioguides 5€. Bus: 5, 19, 52, 116, 204, 490, or 910. Tues–Sun 8:30am–7:30pm.

**Museo Nazionale Etrusco di Villa Giulia (National Etruscan Museum)** ★★★ MUSEUM The great Etruscan civilization (which gave its name to Tuscany), was one of ancient Italy's most advanced, although it remains relatively mysterious. Once Rome had absorbed the Etruscans in the 3rd century B.C., it set about eradicating all evidence of their achievements.

Today this museum, housed in the Renaissance Villa Giulia, built by Pope Julius III between 1550 and 1555, is the best place in Italy to familiarize with the Etruscans, thanks to a cache of precious artifacts, sculptures, vases, monuments, tools, weapons, and jewels. The most striking attraction is the stunning **Sarcofago degli Sposi (Sarcophagus of the Spouses) ★★,** a late-6th-century B.C. terracotta funerary monument featuring a life-size bride and groom, supposedly lounging at a banquet in the afterlife—there's a similar monument in The Louvre, Paris (p. 121). Equally fascinating are the **Pyrgi Tablets,** gold-leaf inscriptions in both Etruscan and Phoenician from the 5th century B.C., and the **Apollo of Veii,** a huge painted terracotta statue of Apollo dating to the 6th century B.C.

Piazzale di Villa Giulia 9. www.villagiulia.beniculturali.it. ✆ **06-3226571.** 8€. Bus: 926. Tram: 3, 19. Tues–Sun 8:30am–7:30pm.

### Via Veneto & Piazza Barberini

**Piazza Barberini** lies at the foot of several Roman streets, among them Via Barberini, Via Sistina, and Via Vittorio Veneto. It would be a far more pleasant spot were it not for the heavy traffic swarming around its principal feature, Bernini's **Fountain of the Triton (Fontana del Tritone) ★.** For more than three centuries, the strange figure sitting in a vast open clam has been blowing water from his triton.

As you go up **Via Vittorio Veneto,** look for the small fountain on the right corner of Piazza Barberini—it's another Bernini, the **Fountain of the Bees (Fontana delle Api).** At first they look more like flies, but they're the bees of the Barberini crest, complete with the crossed keys of St. Peter. The keys were always added to a family crest when a son was elected pope.

**Museo e Cripta dei Frati Cappuccini (Museum and Crypt of the Capuchin Friars)** ★★ RELIGIOUS SITE/MUSEUM One of the most macabre (and therefore very popular) sights in all Christendom, this otherwise modest museum dedicated to the Capuchin order ends with an eerie series of six chapels in the crypt, adorned with thousands of skulls and bones woven into mosaic "works of art." To make this allegorical dance of death, the bones of more than 3,700 Capuchin brothers were used. Some of the skeletons are intact, draped with Franciscan habits. The tradition of the friars holds that this was the work of a French Capuchin monk, and literature suggests that you should consider the historical context of its origins: a period when Christians had a rich and creative cult of the dead and great spiritual masters meditated and preached with a skull in hand.

Convento dei Frati Cappuccini, Via Veneto 27. www.cappucciniviaveneto.it. ✆ **06-88803695.** 6€, 4€ ages 17 and under. Metro: Barberini. Daily 9am–7pm; last admission 6.30pm.

## AROUND STAZIONE TERMINI

**Palazzo Massimo alle Terme ★★** MUSEUM One third of Rome's ancient art can is conserved at this branch of the Museo Nazionale Romano. Among its treasures are extensive maps of trade routes (with audio and visual exhibits on the network of traders over the centuries) and a vast sculpture collection that includes portrait busts of emperors and their families, as well as mythical figures like the Minotaur and Athena. But the real draw is on the second floor, where you can see some of Rome's oldest **frescoes ★★** depicting an entire garden, complete with plants and birds, from the Villa di Livia in the city's northern Prima Porta. (Livia was the wife of Emperor Augustus and was deified after her death in A.D. 29.)

Largo di Villa Peretti. www.archeoroma.beniculturali.it. ✆ **06-39967700.** 7€; ticket valid for Terme di Diocleziano (see below), Palazzo Altemps, and Crypta Balbi. Metro: Termini or Repubblica. Tues–Sun 9am–7:45pm. Last admission 1 hr. before closing.

**Terme di Diocleziano (Baths of Diocletian) ★** MUSEUM/RUINS Ancient Roman recycling at its finest. This spot once held the largest of Rome's hedonistic baths (dating back to A.D. 298 and the reign of Emperor Diocletian). During the Renaissance, a church, a vast cloister, and a convent were built into the ruins—much of it designed by Michelangelo. Today the entire complex is part of the Museo Nazionale Romano, and this juxtaposition of Christianity, pagan ancient ruins, and exhibit space make for a compelling museum stop that's usually quieter than the city's blockbusters. Only Aula 10 conserves trace of the vast baths, which once accommodated 3,000 bathers at a time.

Viale E. di Nicola 78. www.archeoroma.beniculturali.it. ✆ **06-39967700.** 7€; ticket valid for Palazzo Massimo alle Terme (see above), Palazzo Altemps, and Crypta Balbi. Metro: Termini or Repubblica. Tues–Sun 9am–7:45pm. Last admission 1 hr. before closing.

## TRASTEVERE

**Santa Maria in Trastevere ★** CHURCH This ornate Romanesque church at the heart of Trastevere was founded around A.D. 350 and is one

The piazza and church of Santa Maria in Trastevere.



of the oldest in Rome. Parts of it were added around 1100, and more in the early 1700s. The mosaics on the apse date from around 1140, and below them are the 1293 mosaic scenes depicting the *Life of the Virgin Mary* by Pietro Cavallini. The faded mosaics on the facade are from the 12th or 13th century.

Piazza Santa Maria in Trastevere. ✆ **06-5814802.** Free. Bus: H or 125/Tram: 8. Daily 9:30am–12:30pm and 3–5:30pm.

**Villa Farnesina** ★ HISTORIC HOME Once called Villa Chigi, this was originally built for Sienese banker Agostino Chigi in 1511, but was acquired (and renamed) by the Farnese family in 1579. With two such wealthy Renaissance patrons, it's hardly surprising that the internal decor is stunning. Raphael's ***Loggia of Cupid and Psyche*** ★★ was frescoed to mark Chigi's marriage to Francesca Ordeaschi—though assistants Giulio Romano and Giovanna da Udine did much of the work.

Via della Lungara 230. www.villafarnesina.it. ✆ **06-68077268.** 6€. Bus: 23, 125, 271, or 280. Mon–Sat 9am–2pm; 2nd Sun of month 9am–5pm.

## Organized Tours

Because of the sheer number of sights to see, some first-time visitors like to start out with an organized tour. Although few things can really be covered in any depth on an overview, they're sometimes useful for getting your bearings. One of the leading operators is **Context Travel** ★ (www.contexttravel.com; ✆ **800/691-6036** in the U.S., or 06-96727371), a company that, notably, uses local scholars—historians, art historians, preservationists—to lead their tours. Guides offer small-group walking tours, including visits to monuments, museums, and historic piazzas, as well as culinary walks and meals in neighborhood *trattorie*. Prices of the regular tours are high—beginning at 60€ for 2 hours—but most participants consider them a highlight of their trip. Context also offers an excellent **family program,** which visits the Vatican and the Colosseum, but does so in a way that's appealing to children.

**Walks of Italy** (www.walksofitaly.com; ✆ **06-95583331**) also runs excellent guided **walking tours** of Rome, with their introductory tour (2½ hr.) just 29€, and more in-depth explorations of the Colosseum, Vatican Museums, and Forum ranging 59€ to 99€.

## Especially for Kids

There's a "Jekyll and Hyde" quality to exploring Rome with kids. On the one hand, it's a capital city, big, busy, and hot, and with public transportation that doesn't always work too well. On the other, the best parts of the city for kids—Roman ruins, subterranean worlds, and *gelato*—are aspects you'd want to explore anyway. Seeing Rome with kids doesn't demand an itinerary redesign—at least, away from its museums. Despite what you have heard about its seven hills, much of the center is mercifully flat, and pedestrian.

Food is pretty easy too: Roman **pizzas** are some of the best in the world—see "Where to Eat," p. 667, for my favorites. Ditto the ice cream, or *gelato* (p. 671). The city is shorter on greenery than European cities like London, but the landscaped gardens of the **Villa Borghese ★★** have plenty of space, as well as playgrounds, carousels, and pony rides.

Museums, of course, are trickier. You can probably get kids fired up more easily for the really ancient stuff. The bookshop at the **Colosseum** (p. 647) has a good selection of guides to the city aimed at under-12s, themed on gladiators and featuring funny or cartoon material. Make that an early stop. I have taken a 6-year-old to the **Musei Capitolini** (p. 649), and she loved hunting down the collection's treasures highlighted on the free museum leaflet. It was like a themed treasure hunt, and bought me a couple of hours to admire the exhibits—and the chance to see them from a new and unexpected angle, too. The multiple levels below **San Clemente** (p. 651) are another obvious draw for small visitors.

If kids get really into the gladiator angle, enroll them in the **Scuola Gladiatori Roma (Rome Gladiator School) ★,** where they can spend 2 hours preparing for a duel in a reasonably authentic way. The easiest way to book is through **Viator.com**, but you can find out more about the program at **www.gsr-roma.com**.

Away from the museums, kids will likely enjoy some of the cheesier city sights—at the very least, these will make good family photos to share on Facebook or Instagram. Build in some time to queue for a photo with the Bocca della Verità at **Santa Maria in Cosmedin** (p. 651); to throw a coin into the **Trevi Fountain** (p. 656); and to enjoy watching the feral cats relaxing amid the ruins of **Largo di Torre Argentina ★.** There is a cat sanctuary here that gives basic healthcare to Rome's many strays.

## Where to Stay

Rental apartments and B&Bs are often cheaper and more memorable than standard hotels. Breakfast in all but the highest echelon of hotels is usually a buffet with coffee, fruit, rolls, and cheese. It's not always included in the rate, so check the listing carefully. If you are budgeting and breakfast is a payable extra, skip it and go to a nearby cafe/bar. Nearly all hotels are heated in cooler months, but not all are air-conditioned in summer, which can be vitally important during a stifling July or August. The deluxe and first-class ones are, but after that, it's a toss-up. Be sure to check before you book a stay in the dog days of summer, if you suffer in the heat.

### SELF-CATERING APARTMENTS

Nearly every rental apartment in Rome is owned and maintained by a third party (that is, not the rental agency). That means that the decor and flavor of the apartments, even in the same price range and neighborhood, can vary widely. Every reputable agency, however, posts multiple photos of each property they handle on its website. **Cross Pollinate** (www.cross-pollinate.com; ✆ **06-99369799**) is a multi-destination agency but with a decent roster of apartments and B&Bs in Rome. It was founded by the American owners of The Beehive (see p. 667). **GowithOh** (www.gowithoh.com; ✆ **800/567-2927** in the U.S.) is a hip rental agency that covers several European cities, Rome among them. **Eats & Sheets** (www.eatsandsheets.com; ✆ **06-83515971**) is a small boutique collective comprising two B&Bs (near the Vatican and Colosseum), and 11 beautiful apartments for rent, most in the Centro Storico. Note also that **www.airbnb.com**, the platform that allows individuals to rent their own apartments to guests, covers Rome.

### AROUND VATICAN CITY & PRATI

#### Expensive

**Villa Laetitia ★★★** This elegant hotel overlooking the River Tiber is the work of Anna Fendi, member of the Roman fashion dynasty and a nifty designer. Thanks to Signora Anna the rooms are anything but traditional, although they're set in a 1911 villa surrounded by tranquil gardens. Expect touches like bold, checked patterns on the coverlets and floors, and modern art on the walls. The Stendhal Room is my favorite, with black and white tiles matching the bedspread, chic transparent plastic furniture, a kitchenette painted in red, and a secluded balcony that catches the morning sun.

Lungotevere delle Armi 22–23. www.villalaetitia.com. ✆ **06-3226776.** 14 units. Doubles 155€–250€. Metro: Lepanto. **Amenities:** Bar; babysitting; gym; restaurant; room service; spa; free Wi-Fi.

### Moderate

**QuodLibet ★★★** The name is Latin for "what pleases" and everything is pleasing here. This B&B is a delight, with spacious rooms, gorgeous artwork and furnishings, and generous breakfasts (bread and croissants come from the bakery just next door). All the rooms are set on the fourth floor of an elegant building (with elevator and air-conditioning), so it's quieter than many places. And the location is just a 10-minute walk from the Vatican Museums, and a block from the Metro.

Via Barletta 29. www.quodlibetroma.com. ✆ **06-1222642.** 4 units. Doubles 70€–180€, includes breakfast. Metro: Ottaviano. **Amenities:** Free Wi-Fi.

## ANCIENT ROME, MONTI & CELIO

### Expensive

**The Inn at the Roman Forum ★★★** The name doesn't lie: This small hotel is tucked down a medieval lane, on the edge of Monti and with the forums of several Roman emperors as neighbors. Its midsized rooms are sumptuously decorated, with designs that fuse the contemporary and baroque traditions of the city. The two rooms on the top floor have private gardens, which offer total tranquility, plus there's a shared roof terrace where *aperitivo* is served daily with unforgettable views of the Vittoriano and Palatine Hill.

Via degli Ibernesi 30. www.theinnattheromanforum.com. ✆ **06-69190970.** 12 units. Doubles 210€–960€, includes breakfast. Metro: Cavour. **Amenities:** Bar; concierge; room service; Wi-Fi (10€ per day).

### Moderate

**Duca d'Alba ★★** Monti doesn't have many full-service hotels—at least, not yet. The Duca d'Alba is right on one of the main drags, with all the nightlife and authentic dining you'll need on your doorstep. Rooms in the main building are cozy and contemporary, with modern furniture and gadgetry, but small bathrooms. The annex rooms next door have a *palazzo* character, with terracotta-tiled floors, oak and cherry wood furniture, more space, and street-facing rooms that are soundproofed. Those on the second floor are the brightest.

Via Leonina 14. www.hotelducadalba.com. ✆ **06-484471.** 33 units. Doubles 80€–395€, includes breakfast. Metro: Cavour. **Amenities:** Bar; babysitting; free Wi-Fi.

**Nicolas Inn ★★** This tiny bed-and-breakfast, run by a welcoming American-Lebanese couple, makes the perfect base for those who want to concentrate on Rome's ancient sights—the Colosseum is 1 (long)

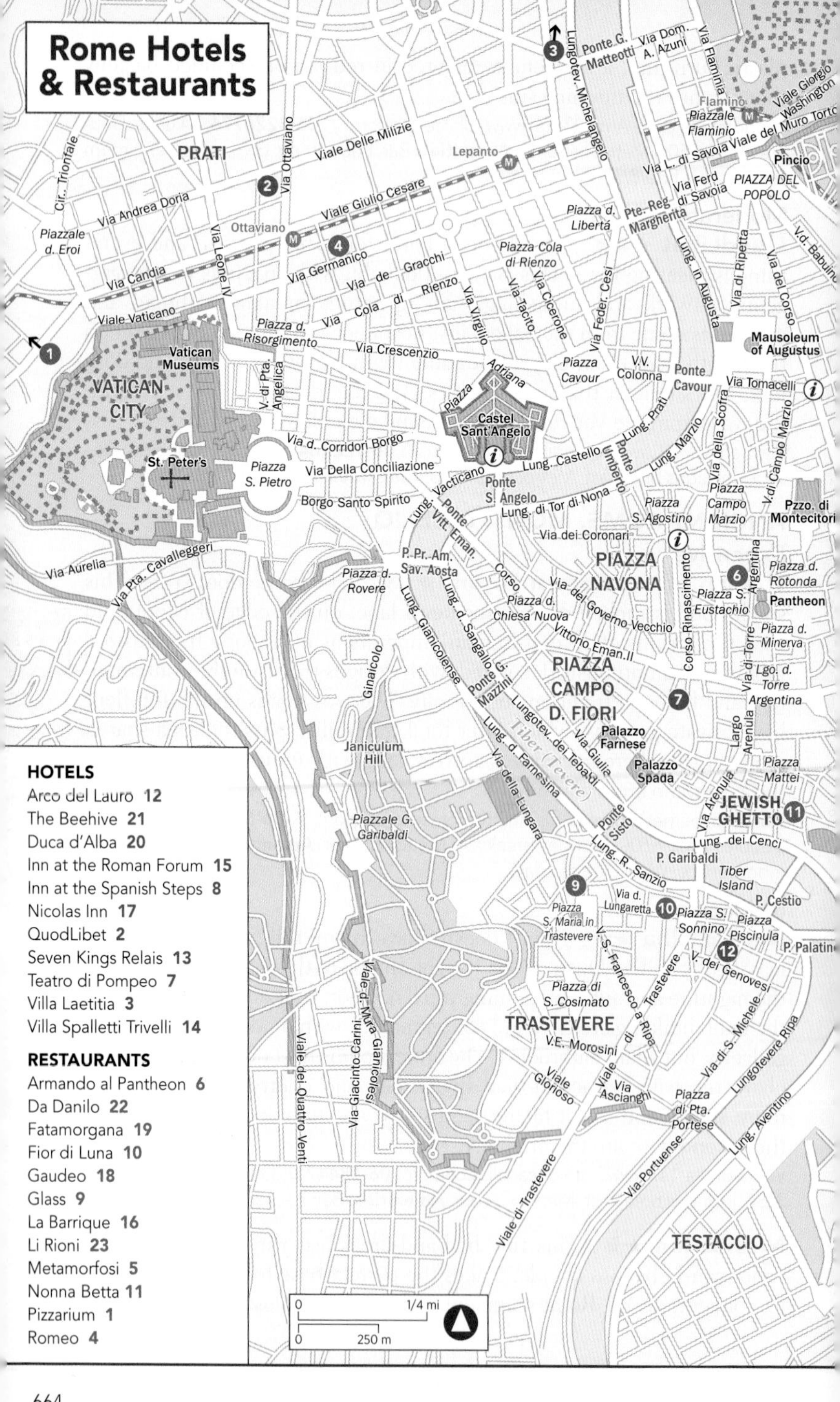

Rome Hotels & Restaurants
HOTELS
Arco del Lauro 12
The Beehive 21
Duca d'Alba 20
Inn at the Roman Forum 15
Inn at the Spanish Steps 8
Nicolas Inn 17
QuodLibet 2
Seven Kings Relais 13
Teatro di Pompeo 7
Villa Laetitia 3
Villa Spalletti Trivelli 14
RESTAURANTS
Armando al Pantheon 6
Da Danilo 22
Fatamorgana 19
Fior di Luna 10
Gaudeo 18
Glass 9
La Barrique 16
Li Rioni 23
Metamorfosi 5
Nonna Betta 11
Pizzarium 1
Romeo 4
PRATI
VATICAN CITY
Vatican Museums
St. Peter's
Piazza S. Pietro
Castel Sant'Angelo
PIAZZA NAVONA
PIAZZA CAMPO D. FIORI
Palazzo Farnese
Palazzo Spada
JEWISH GHETTO
Janiculum Hill
Piazzale G. Garibaldi
TRASTEVERE
TESTACCIO
Tiber (Tevere)
Tiber Island
Pantheon
Mausoleum of Augustus
Pzzo. di Montecitorio
PIAZZA DEL POPOLO
Pincio
Flaminio
Piazzale Flaminio
Lepanto
Ottaviano
Piazzale d. Eroi
Piazza d. Risorgimento
Piazza Cola di Rienzo
Piazza d. Libertà
Piazza Cavour
Piazza d. Rovere
Piazza d. Chiesa Nuova
Piazza S. Agostino
Piazza Campo Marzio
Piazza d. Rotonda
Piazza S. Eustachio
Piazza d. Minerva
Lgo. d. Torre Argentina
Piazza Mattei
P. Garibaldi
P. Cestio
Piazza S. Maria in Trastevere
Piazza S. Sonnino
Piazza Piscinula
P. Palatino
Piazza di S. Cosimato
Piazza di Pta. Portese
Viale Delle Milizie
Viale Giulio Cesare
Via Andrea Doria
Via Candia
Viale Vaticano
Via Germanico
Via de Gracchi
Via Cola di Rienzo
Via Crescenzio
Via Ottaviano
Via Leone IV
Cir. Trionfale
V. di Pta. Angelica
Via Virgilio
Via Tacito
Via Cicerone
Via Feder. Cesi
Lungotev. Michelangelo
Ponte G. Matteotti
Via Dom. A. Azuni
Via Flaminia
Viale Giorgio Washington
Viale del Muro Torto
Via L. di Savoia
Via Ferd di Savoia
Pte. Reg. Margherita
Lung. in Augusta
Via di Ripetta
Via del Corso
V.d. Babuino
Via Tomacelli
V. di Campo Marzio
Via della Scrofa
Ponte Cavour
V.V. Colonna
Lung. Prati
Lung. Marzio
Ponte Umberto
Lung. Castello
Piazza Adriana
Via d. Corridori Borgo
Via Della Conciliazione
Borgo Santo Spirito
Lung. Vacticano
Ponte S. Angelo
Lung. di Tor di Nona
Via dei Coronari
Ponte Vitt. Eman.
P. Pr. Am. Sav. Aosta
Lung. Gianicolense
Lung. d. Sangallo
Corso Vittorio Eman. II
Via del Governo Vecchio
Corso Rinascimento
Via di Torre Argentina
Largo Arenula
Via Arenula
Ponte G. Mazzini
Lungotev. dei Tebaldi
Via Giulia
Lung. d. Farnesina
Via della Lungara
Ponte Sisto
Lung. dei Cenci
Lung. R. Sanzio
Via d. Lungaretta
V.S. Francesco a Ripa
Viale di Trastevere
V. dei Genovesi
Via di S. Michele
Lungotevere Ripa
Lung. Aventino
V.E. Morosini
Viale Glorioso
Via Ascianghi
Via Portuense
Viale di Trastevere
Via Aurelia
Via Pta. Cavalleggeri
Gianicolo
Viale d. Mura Gianicolesi
Via Giacinto Carini
Viale dei Quattro Venti
0 1/4 mi
0 250 m

Galleria Borghese
Villa Borghese/Parioli
Viale P. Canonica
Piazza di Siena
Viale dei Cavalli Marini
Vle d. Magnolie
Viale del Muro Torto
Via Pinciana
Via Po
Via Tevere
Via Isonzo
Via Savoia
Corso D'Italia
Via Campania
Via Sardegna
Via Sicilia
Via Boncompagni
Via Piave
Via Nomentana
Piazzale di Porta Pia
Venice
Florence
Italy
Rome
Policlinico
Viale Castro Pretorio
Castro Pretorio
Spanish Steps
Spagna
Piazza di Spagna
Via di Porta Pinciana
Via Vittorio Veneto
Via Ludovisi
Via Veneto
Lgo. di S. Susanna
Via XX Settembre
National Roman Museum
Piazza Indipendenza
Via Sistina
Via Fr. Crispi
Barberini
Via Barberini
Piazza Barberini
Piazza Repubblica
Piazza Cinquecento
Repubblica
Staz. Termini
Termini Station
Termini
Viale Pretoriano
Via Tritone
Lg. de Tritone
Piazza Colonna
Via del Corso
Palazzo del Quirinale
Via del Quirinale
Via d. Quattro Fontane
V. d. Viminale
Via Torino
Via Marsala
Trevi Fountain
Piazza d. Quirinale
Via Milano
Via Nazionale
Teatro dell'Opera
Piazza dell'Esquilino
Via Principe Amedeo
Via Giovanni Giolitti
Palazzo Colonna
Palazzo Doria Pamphilj
Via IV Nov.
Via XXIV Maggio
Via Cavour
Santa Maria Maggiore
V. Carlo Alberto
San Lorenzo
Palazzo Venezia
Vittorio Emanuele Monument
Via Dei Fori Imperiali
San Pietro in Vincoli
Via Merulana
Via Leopardi
Vittorio Emanuele
Piazza Vittorio Eman. II
Via di Marcello
Capitoline Museums
Golden House of Nero
Via Macanate
Vle. Manzoni
Ancient Rome
Roman Forum
Colosseo
Colosseum
Viale d. Domus Aurea
Via Labicana
Manzoni
Via D. Teatro
Piazza Bocca d. Verità
Piazza d. Colosseo
Via. di S. Giovanni in Laterano
Palatine Hill
Via di S. Gregorio
Via Claudia
San Giovanni in Laterano
S. Giovanni
Via dei Circo Massimo
Circus Maximus
Aventine Hill
Circo Massimo
Piazza di Pta. Capena
Via della Navicella
Via Sannio
Piazza di Pla. Metronia
Via Gallia
Via Druso
Via Antonina
Piazza Albania
Via di S. Anselmo
Viale Aventino
Baths of Caracalla
Information
City Walls
Metro A
Metro B
Railway
5
8
13
14
15
16
17
18
19
20
21
22
23

block in one direction, with the Forum just about 3 blocks in the other. Rooms are spacious, air-conditioned, and decorated with sweet touches like wrought-iron beds, cool tile floors, and wooden furniture. Best of all, light floods in through large windows. Guests take breakfast at a local bar—with unlimited coffee. Downers: no children under 5 years, no pets, and no credit cards.

Via Cavour 295. www.nicolasinn.com. ✆ **06-97618483.** 4 units. Doubles 100€–180€, includes breakfast (at cafe). Metro: Cavour or Colosseo. **Amenities:** Concierge; free Wi-Fi.

### THE CENTRO STORICO & PANTHEON

#### Moderate

**Teatro di Pompeo ★★** History buffs will appreciate this small B&B, literally built on top of the ruins of the 1st-century Theater of Pompey, where Julius Caesar was stabbed to death. The large rooms themselves are not Roman in style, but feel plush, with wood-beam ceilings, cherry-wood furniture, and terracotta-tiled floors. Some rooms feature a view of the internal courtyard while others overlook the small square; all are quiet. The Campo de' Fiori is right behind the hotel, and staff is extremely helpful.

Largo del Pallaro 8. www.hotelteatrodipompeo.it. ✆ **06-68300170.** 13 units. Doubles 65€–220€, includes breakfast. Bus: 46, 62, or 64. **Amenities:** Bar; babysitting; room service; free Wi-Fi.

### TRIDENTE & THE SPANISH STEPS

#### Expensive

**The Inn at the Spanish Steps ★★★** Set in one of Rome's most desirable locations on the Via Condotti shopping strip, this lavish guesthouse is the epitome of luxe. Rooms are fantasias of design, some with parquet floors and cherubim ceiling frescoes, others decked out with wispy fabrics draping plush, canopied beds. Swank amenities include Jacuzzi tubs. Some rooms are located in the annex, and these tend to be larger than those in the main building. The manicured rooftop garden provides beautiful views, to be enjoyed at breakfast—where there's a generous buffet—or at sunset, frosted glass of vino in hand.

Via dei Condotti 85. www.atspanishsteps.com. ✆ **06-69925657.** 24 units. Doubles 250€–750€, includes breakfast. Metro: Spagna. **Amenities:** Bar; babysitting; concierge; room service; free Wi-Fi.

**Villa Spalletti Trivelli ★★★** This really is an experience rather than a hotel, an early-20th-century neoclassical villa revamped into an exclusive 12-room guesthouse, where guests mingle in the gardens or magnificent hall, as if invited by an Italian noble for the weekend. Rooms feature elegant antiques and Fiandra Damask linen sheets on the beds, with sitting area or separate lounge, REN toiletries, and satellite LCD TV.

And the minibar? All free, all day. There's no "nickel-and-diming," here, which makes a relaxing change.

Via Piacenza 4. www.villaspalletti.it. ✆ **06-48907934.** 12 units. Doubles 410€–575€, includes breakfast. Metro: Barberini. **Amenities:** Restaurant; bar; concierge; gym; room service; spa; free Wi-Fi.

### AROUND TERMINI

#### Moderate

**Seven Kings Relais ★★** There's a hipster retro feel to the decor of this striking hotel, kitted out with dark wooden furniture, chocolate-brown bedspreads, and modern tiled floors. Rooms are also unusually large—especially nos. 104, 201, and 205. Despite its location right on one of Rome's busiest thoroughfares, there's no noise: An external court-yard and modern soundproofing see to that.

Via XX Settembre 58A. www.7kings.eu. ✆ **06-42917784.** 11 units. Doubles 90€–220€. Metro: Repubblica. **Amenities:** Babysitting; free Wi-Fi.

#### Inexpensive

**The Beehive ★★** Part hostel, part hotel, The Beehive is a unique lodging experience. Eco-minded American owners have decorated the place with art pieces and flea-market treasures, and rooms cater to a variety of budgets. Some have private bathrooms; others have shared facilities or are six-bed dorms—all are decorated with flair. There's also a walk-in American breakfast, open to all-comers, with fruit, oatmeal or eggs, weekend brunches, and vegan buffets some evenings.

Via Marghera 8. www.the-beehive.com. ✆ **06-44704553.** 12 units. Doubles 70€–80€, dorm beds 25€–35€. Metro: Termini or Castro Pretorio. **Amenities:** Cafe; free Wi-Fi.

### TRASTEVERE

#### Moderate

**Arco del Lauro ★★** Hidden in Trastevere's snaking alleyways, this serene little bed-and-breakfast is divided over two adjacent sites on the ground floor of a shuttered pink *palazzo.* Rooms have parquet floors and simple decor, with a mix of modern and period dressers and tables, and modern plush beds and armchairs. None is large, but they all have a feeling of air and space thanks to original, lofty wood ceilings. Credit cards not accepted.

Via Arco de' Tolomei 29. www.arcodellauro.it. ✆ **06-97840350.** 6 units. Doubles 85€–145€, includes breakfast (at nearby cafe). Bus: 125/Tram: 8. **Amenities:** Babysitting (prebooking essential); free Wi-Fi.

## Where to Eat

Rome remains a top destination for foodies, and has more dining diversity today than ever. Many of its *trattorie* haven't changed their menus in a quarter of a century, but there are an increasing number of creative

Bars and trattorie line an ancient street in Trastevere.

eateries with chefs willing to experiment, and revisit tradition to embrace modernity.

A ***servizio*** (tip or service charge) is almost always added to your bill, or included in the price. Sometimes it is marked on the menu as *pane e servizio* (bread, cover charge and service). You can of course leave extra if you wish—a couple of euros as a token. Don't go overboard on the tipping front.

## VATICAN CITY & PRATI

If you just want a quick, light meal, **Insalata Ricca,** a salad-and-quick-meals chain, is across from the Vatican walls at Piazza del Risorgimento 5 (www.linsalataricca.it; ✆ **06-39730387;** daily noon–3:30pm and 7pm–midnight).

### Moderate

**Pizzarium ★★★** PIZZA Known for good reason as the "Michelangelo of pizza," celebrity chef Gabriele Bonci has always had a cult following in the Eternal City. And because he's been featured on TV shows overseas as well, you can expect long lines at his hole-in-the-wall pizzeria. No matter: It's worth waiting for some of the best pizza you'll ever taste, sold by weight. Ingredients are fresh and organic, the crust is perfect, and the toppings often experimental (try the mortadella and crumbled pistachio). Note that there are only a couple of benches outside to sit on. No reservations.

Via della Meloria 43. www.gabrielebonci.it. ✆ **06-39745416.** Pizza 12€–14€ for large tray. Metro: Cipro. Mon–Sat 11am–10pm, Sun 1–10pm.

**Romeo ★★** MODERN ITALIAN This collaboration between the Roscioli bakery dynasty, and Michelin-starred chef Cristina Bowerman of Glass (see p. 671) offers a refreshing, contemporary detour from traditional Roman cooking, with American-inspired sandwiches, burgers, and creative pasta dishes served in sleek, modern premises. Musts include foie gras sandwiches served with sweet mango mayonnaise, and ravioli stuffed with asparagus and Castelmagno cheese.

Via Silla 26/a. www.romeo.roma.it. ✆ **06-32110120.** Mains 12€–24€. Metro: Ottaviano. Mon–Sat 9am–midnight, Sun 10am–midnight.

### Eat Like a Roman

Authentic local dishes include *saltimbocca alla romana* (literally "jump-in-your-mouth"—thin slices of veal with sage, cured ham, and cheese) and *carciofi alla romana* (artichokes cooked with herbs, such as mint and garlic), and a dish that's become ubiquitous, *spaghetti alla carbonara*—pasta coated in a white sauce made with egg and *pecorino romano* (ewe's milk cheese), with added cured pork (*guanciale*, cheek, if it's authentic). Note authentic Roman pizza is thinner and less doughy than Naples's version.

## ANCIENT ROME, MONTI & CELIO

For a sandwich, there's no beating **Gaudeo,** Via del Boschetto 112 (✆ **06-98183689**). A baked roll loaded with prosciutto, mozzarella, salami, and a whole lot more costs between 4€ and 10€.

### Moderate

**La Barrique ★★** MODERN ROMAN This cozy, contemporary *enoteca* (a wine bar with food) has a kitchen that knocks out farm-to-table fare that complements a well-chosen wine list. The atmosphere is lively and informal, with rustic place settings and friendly service. Dishes come in hearty portions on a daily menu. Expect the likes of *bocconcini di baccalà* (salt-cod morsels), crispy on the outside and served with a rich tomato sauce; or *crostone* (a giant crostino) topped with grilled burrata cheese, chicory, and cherry tomatoes. Wines are available by the glass, quarter-liter, or half-liter.

Via del Boschetto 41B. ✆ **06-47825953.** Mains 10€–18€. Metro: Cavour. Mon–Fri 12:30–2:30pm; Mon–Sat 6:30–11:30pm.

### Inexpensive

**Li Rioni ★★** PIZZA This fab neighborhood pizzeria is close enough to the Colosseum to be convenient, but just distant enough to avoid the dreaded "touristy" label that applies to so much dining in this part of town. Roman-style pizzas baked in the wood-stoked oven are among the best in town, with perfect crisp crusts. There's also a bruschetta list (from around 4€) and salads. Outside tables can be a little cramped, but there's plenty of room inside. If you want to eat late, booking is essential or you'll be fighting for a table with hungry locals.

Via SS. Quattro 24. www.lirioni.it. ✆ **06-70450605.** Pizzas 5.50€–9€. Bus: 53, 85, or 117. Wed–Mon 7:30–11:30pm.

## CENTRO STORICO & THE PANTHEON

### Moderate

**Armando al Pantheon** ★ ROMAN/VEGETARIAN Despite being just a few steps from the Pantheon, this typical Roman trattoria remains an authentic, family-owned business serving as many locals as tourists. Chef Armando Gargioli took over the place in 1961, and his sons now run the business. Roman favorites to look out for include the *pasta e ceci* (pasta and chickpeas, Fri only), the Jewish-influenced *aliciotti all'indivia* (endive and roasted anchovies, Tues only), and the fabulous *abbacchio* (roast lamb). Another bonus: a fairly extensive vegetarian menu.

Salita dei Crescenzi 31. www.armandoalpantheon.it. ✆ **06-68803034.** Mains 10€–24€. Bus: 30, 40, 62, 64, 81, or 492. Mon–Fri noon–3pm and 7–11pm; Sat noon–3pm. Closed Aug.



**Nonna Betta** ★★ ROMAN/JEWISH This Ghetto district mainstay offers two menus: one strictly kosher, and another featuring classic "nonna dishes" like delicious *carciofi alla giudia* (deep fried artichokes), stellar tagliolini with mullet roe and chicory, and homemade baccalà preparations. Leave room for desserts like *pizza ebraica,* a sort of nutty fruit cake, and all manner of Middle Eastern honey and pistachio creations.



Via del Portico d'Ottavia 16. www.nonnabetta.it. ✆ **06-68806263.** Mains 10€. Bus: 23, 63, 280, 630, or 780. Sun–Fri noon–3pm and 7–11pm.

## VILLA BORGHESE & PARIOLI

### Expensive

**Metamorfosi** ★★★ MODERN ITALIAN This Michelin star–awarded restaurant is a feast for eyes and tastebuds. At the helm of the kitchen is Chef Roy Caceres, native of Colombia, who likes to stir his guests' emotions and tell a story with each dish. Caceres shines with risotto, pasta, and elegant game, meat and fish interpretations. Be prepared for creamy soft cheese ravioli mixed with salmon, hazelnut, and smoked pepper; risotto wrapped in a thin saffron film; stellar glazed eel with crumbled farro and sweet onion sorbet; crispy lamb with almonds, eggplant, and gin-juniper ice cream.

Via Giovanni Antonelli 30-32. www.metamorfosiroma.it. ✆ **06-8076839.** Mains 25€–30€. Bus: 168, 223, 910, or 926. Mon–Fri 12:30–3pm, 8–11:30pm; Sat 7:30–midnight.

### Pick Up a Gina "PicNic"

The best place for a picnic in Rome is the Villa Borghese, now made super-easy thanks to **Gina PicNic,** Via San Sebastianello 7a (www.ginaroma.com; ✆ **06-6780251;** daily 11am–8pm) located one downhill block down from the park itself. It's not cheap, but it is certainly elegant. Gina's deli provides a picnic basket complete with a thermos of Italian coffee, glasses, and fine linens for a meal to be enjoyed in the gardens. For 40€, two people get salads, quiches, huge *panini* stuffed with a variety of meats, tomato, eggplant, and mozzarella along with a fruit salad, chocolate dessert, biscotti, water, and even bottles of wine (20€ extra). Order the day before and pick up around noon; you return the basket when you're done.

## AROUND TERMINI

### Moderate

**Da Danilo ★★** ROMAN The general rule is: Don't dine around the train station, but there are a few exceptions. Da Danilo is one of them. Popular with locals on business lunches and *cucina romana* pundits, this intimate trattoria offers authentic Rome fare, made with top-notch local products. Mainstays include one of Rome's best *cacio e pepe,* served out of a massive, scooped-out Pecorino cheese round; the house carbonara, and homemade gnocchi served, as tradition dictates, exclusively on Thursdays. The beef tartare, grilled lamb chops, and lardo-laced rib-eyes are menu strong points, as are any other daily meat special.

Via Petrarca 13. www.trattoriadadanilo.it. ✆ **06-77200111.** Mains 12€–17€. Metro: Vittorio Emanuele or Manzoni. Tues–Sat 12:30–3pm and 7:30–midnight. Closed 2 weeks in Aug.

## TRASTEVERE

### Expensive

**Glass ★★★** CONTEMPORARY ROMAN Sleek modernism rules here, in design as well as cuisine. Walls are stark white and floors are polished, and the menu is a mix of inventive and cosmopolitan flair, with listings that change monthly. Expect the likes of pasta with lemon, black garlic, and wild asparagus, followed by sumac-scented lamb with purple potato chips. Thanks to the rep of Michelin star–awarded chef Cristina Bowerman, this is one of Rome's hottest tables—reservations are essential.

Vicolo del Cinque 58. www.glass-restaurant.it. ✆ **06-58335903.** Mains 28€–45€; fixed-price menus 70€–90€. Bus: 125. Tues–Sun 7:30–11:30pm. Closed 2 weeks in Jan and 2 weeks in July.

## GELATO

Don't leave town without trying one of Rome's outstanding **ice-cream parlors.** However, choose your Italian ice carefully! Gelaterie aimed exclusively at tourists are notorious for poor-quality gelato and sky-high prices. Don't buy close to the main piazzas, and avoid places whose vats display heaped, brightly colored, air-pumped gelato. Most gelaterie keep seasonal hours; the warmer the weather, the later they're open.

**Fatamorgana ★★★** GELATO Creative flavors are the hallmark of this Monti gelateria. Try the *crema di zenzero* (cream of ginger), *cioccolato Lapsang Souchong* (chocolate with smoked black tea), or a surprising basil-walnut-honey combo. Given that the founder has celiac disease, all products—cones included—are gluten-free.
Piazza degli Zingari 5. www.gelateriafatamorgana.it. ✆ **06-86391589.** Cone from 2€. Metro: Cavour. Also at: Via Lago di Lesina 9-11; Via Bettolo 7; Piazza San Cosimato.

**Fior di Luna ★★** GELATO This is Trastevere's best artisan gelato, all made with natural and Fairtrade produce. The range is small, and there are no cones—but you won't care. The stars are the intense chocolate flavors, spiked with fig or orange, or made with single *cru* cocoa.
Via della Lungaretta 96. www.fiordiluna.com. ✆ **06-64561314.** Cup from 1.70€. Bus: H or 780/Tram: 8.



## Shopping

Rome offers temptations of every kind. Below we've summarized streets and areas known for their shops. Note that **sales** usually run twice a year, in January and July.

Most of Rome's haute couture and upscale shopping fans out from the bottom of the **Spanish Steps. Via Condotti** is probably Rome's poshest shopping street, where you'll find Prada, Gucci, Bulgari, and the like. **Via Borgognona** is another street where both the rents and the merchandise are chic and ultra-expensive. **Via Frattina** is the third member of this trio of upscale streets. Here the concentration of shops is denser; chic boutiques rub shoulders with ready-to-wear fashions, high-class chains, and occasional tourist tat vendors.

### A Pause Before Purchasing

Although Rome has many wonderful boutiques, the shopping is generally better in **Florence.** If you're continuing on to there, you may want to hold off, as you're likely to find a better selection and better prices.

The commercial heart of the Prati neighborhood bordering the Vatican, **Via Cola di Rienzo** is a long street known for selling a variety of merchandise at reasonable prices—from jewelry to fashionable clothes, bags and shoes. Among the most interesting is **Bertozzini Profumeria dal 1913,** at no. 192 (✆ **06-6874662**), an historic Roman perfume store.

**Via dei Coronari** is an **antique**-lover's souk. If you're shopping (or even window browsing) for antiques or antique-style souvenir prints, then spend an hour walking the full length of this pretty, pedestrian-only street.

Tranquil Via Marguta is home to art stalls and artists' studios—Federico Fellini used to live here—though the stores tend to offer the same sort of antiques and paintings these days. Highlights include **Bottega del Marmoraro** at no. 53b, the studio of master stonecarver Sandro Fiorentini; and **Valentina Moncada**'s contemporary art gallery at no. 54 (www.valentinamoncada.com; ✆ **06-3207956**).

Rome's most fashion-conscious central neighborhood, **Monti** has a pleasing mix of indie artisan retailers and hip boutiques. There's not a brand name in sight. Roam **Via del Boschetto** for one-off fashions, designer ateliers, and gift-sized homewares. In fact, you can roam in every direction from the spot where it meets **Via Panisperna. Via Urbana** is another to add to the list; **Via Leonina** likewise. Via Urbana hosts the weekly vintage sale, **Mercatomonti** (www.mercatomonti.com).

## Entertainment & Nightlife

Even if you don't speak Italian, you can generally follow the listings of special events and evening entertainment featured in ***La Repubblica,*** a national newspaper published in Rome. See also the "TrovaRoma" section of its city website, **www.roma.repubblica.it**. ***Wanted in Rome*** (www.wantedinrome.com) has listings of opera, rock, English-language cinema showings and such, and gives an insider look at expat Rome.

Unless you're dead set on making the Roman nightclub circuit, try what might be a livelier and less expensive scene—sitting late at night on **Via Veneto, Piazza della Rotonda, Piazza del Popolo,** or one of Rome's other piazzas, all for the (admittedly inflated) cost of an espresso or a Campari and soda. For clubbers, it is almost impossible to predict where the next hot venue will appear, but if you like it loud and late—and have an adventurous streak—jump in a cab to **Monte Testaccio** or **Via del Pigneto** and bar-hop wherever takes your fancy. In Trastevere, there's always a bit of life along **Via Politeana** around the spot where it meets **Piazza Trilussa.** Try your luck there. In the historic center, **No.Au ★,** Piazza di Montevecchio 16 (www.noauroma.wordpress.com; ✆ **06-45652770**), is tricked out a little like a Barcelona cava bar, and sells craft beers from local brewer Birra del Borgo plus a selection of wines (red, white, and sparkling) from around 5€ a glass. For top-class cocktail mixology, visit the **Stravinskij Bar ★★,** inside the Hotel de Russie, Via del Babuino 9 (✆ **06-32888874**). Sit inside for a "designer lounge" feel, or choose terrace seating during warm months.

Although the **music scene** doesn't have the same high-quality opera of Milan's La Scala or **La Fenice** in Venice (p. 733)—classical music fans are still well catered for at the **Teatro dell'Opera di Roma,**

## ROME, illuminated

When the sun goes down, Rome's palaces, ruins, fountains, and monuments are bathed in a theatrical white light. Few evening occupations are as pleasurable as a stroll past the solemn pillars of old temples or the cascading torrents of Renaissance fountains glowing under the blue-black sky. The **Fountain of the Naiads** *(Fontana delle Naiadi)* on Piazza della Repubblica, the **Fountain of the Tortoises** *(Fontana della Tartarughe)* on Piazza Mattei, the **Fountain of Acqua Paola** *(Fontanone)* at the top of Janiculum Hill, and the **Trevi Fountain** are particularly beautiful at night. The **Capitoline Hill** (or *Campidoglio*) is magnificently lit after dark, with its measured Renaissance facades glowing like jewel boxes. The nighttime view of the Roman Forum seen from the rear of Piazza del Campidoglio is perhaps the grandest in Rome. If you're across the Tiber, **Piazza San Pietro** (in front of St. Peter's) is impressive at night without the crowds.

Piazza Beniamino Gigli 7 (www.operaroma.it; ✆ **06-48160255**), where you will find the marquee operas by big names: Think *La Traviata, Carmen,* Puccini's *Tosca,* and the like. In summer, the action moves outdoors for a short season of unforgettable open-air operatic performances at the ruined **Baths of Caracalla** ★ (p. 652).



# FLORENCE

Botticelli, Michelangelo, and Leonardo da Vinci all left their mark on Florence, the cradle of the Renaissance. With Brunelleschi's dome as your backdrop, follow the River Arno to the **Uffizi Gallery** (Florence's foremost museum) and soak in centuries of great painting. Michelangelo's *David* stands tall (literally) behind the doors of the **Accademia,** and nearby are the delicate paintings of Fra' Angelico in the convent of **San Marco.** Works by Donatello, Masaccio, and Ghiberti fill the city's churches and museums. Once home to the Medici, the **Palazzo Pitti** is stuffed with Raphaels and Titians, and backed by the fountains of the regal **Boboli Garden.**

But it's not just about the art. Florentines love to shop, too, and Italy's leather capital strains at the seams with handmade gloves, belts, bags, and shoes sold from workshops, family-run boutiques, and high-toned stores, as well as at tourist-oriented **San Lorenzo Market.** Splurge on designer wear from fashion houses along **Via de' Tornabuoni**—this city is the home of Gucci, Pucci, and Ferragamo, after all.

As for Florentine cuisine, it's increasingly cosmopolitan, but flavors are often still Tuscan at heart—and best washed down with a fine **Chianti Classico.** When you've dined to your fill, retire to a wine bar in the **Oltrarno,** or to one of the edgier joints of **Santo Spirito** or **San Frediano.**

A copy of Michelangelo's *David* at the Piazza Michelangelo.



## Essentials

The official Florence information website, **www.firenzeturismo.it**, contains a wealth of fairly up-to-date information.

**ARRIVING** Several European airlines service Florence's **Amerigo Vespucci Airport** (www.aeroporto.firenze.it; ✆ **055-306-1300** switchboard, 055-306-1700 or 055-306-1702 flight info), also called **Peretola,** just 5km (3 miles) northwest of town. There are no direct flights to or from the United States, but you can make connections through London, Paris, Amsterdam, Frankfurt, and other major European cities. The half-hourly **SITA-ATAF "Vola in bus"** to and from downtown's bus station at Via Santa Caterina 15R (✆ **800-424-500**), beside the train station, costs 6€ one-way or 10€ round-trip. Metered **taxis** line up outside the airport's arrival terminal and charge a flat rate of 20€ to the city center (22€ on holidays, 24€ after 10pm).

The closest major international airport is Pisa's **Galileo Galilei Airport** (www.pisa-airport.com; ✆ **050-849-300**), 97km (60 miles) west of Florence. Two to three **train services** per hour leave the airport for Florence. However, until the **PisaMover** airport transit service opens (scheduled for a Dec 2015 debut), all involve a short bus journey then a change to a rail service at Pisa Centrale (70–90 min.; 9.20€). For early morning departures or anyone with lots of bags, one simpler solution is the regular train from Florence into Pisa Centrale (50–70 min.; 8€), followed by a 10-minute taxi ride (around 10€) from the train station to Pisa Airport. Alternatively, 17 daily buses operated by **Terravision** (www.terravision.eu; ✆ **06-9761-0632**) connect downtown Florence directly with Pisa Airport in 1 hour. One-way tickets are 6€ adults, 4€ children ages 5 to 12; round-trip fares are 10€ and 8€.

Florence is Tuscany's **rail** hub, with regular connections to all of Italy's major cities. To get here from Rome, take the high-speed Frecciarossa or Frecciargento trains (1½ hr.; www.trenitalia.com) or rival high-speed trains operated by private company **Italo** (www.italotreno.it). High-speed trains run to Venice (2 hr.) via Bologna and Padua.

Most trains roll into **Stazione Santa Maria Novella,** Piazza della Stazione, which you'll see abbreviated as **S.M.N.** It lies on the northwestern edge of the city's compact historic center, a brisk 10-minute walk from the Duomo and a 15-minute walk from Piazza della Signoria.

The **A1 autostrada** runs north from Rome past Arezzo to Florence and continues north. To reach Florence from Venice, take the A13 southbound then switch to the A1 at Bologna. **Driving** to Florence is easy; the problems begin once you arrive. Almost all cars are banned from the center—only residents or merchants with permits are allowed into this camera-patrolled *zona a trafico limitato* (the "ZTL"). Have the name and address of you hotel ready and the traffic police wave you through. You can drop off baggage there (the hotel will give you a temporary ZTL permit); then you must relocate to a parking lot (special rates are available through most hotels).

**CITY LAYOUT** Florence is a smallish city, sitting on the Arno River and petering out to olive-planted hills quickly north and south, but extending farther west and east along the Arno valley. It has a compact center that is best navigated on foot. No two major sights are more than a 25-minute walk apart, and most hotels and restaurants in this chapter are in the relatively small ***centro storico*** **(historic center),** a compact tangle of medieval streets and *piazze* (squares). The bulk of Florence, including most of the sights, lies north of the river, with the **Oltrarno,** an old working artisans' neighborhood, hemmed in between the Arno and the hills on the south side.

**GETTING AROUND** Florence is a **walking** city. You can stroll between the two top sights, Piazza del Duomo and the Uffizi, in 5 to 7 minutes. The hike from the most northerly major sights, including Michelangelo's *David,* to the most southerly, the Pitti Palace, should take no more than 30 minutes. From Santa Maria Novella eastward across town to Santa Croce is a flat 20- to 30-minute walk. ***Beware:*** Flagstones, some of them uneven, are everywhere—wear sensible shoes with some padding and foot support.

You'll rarely use Florence's efficient **ATAF bus system** (www.ataf.net; ✆ **800-424-500** in Italy) because the city is so compact. Bus tickets cost 1.20€ and are good for 90 minutes, irrespective of how many changes you make. A 24-hour pass costs 5€, a 3-day pass 12€, and a 7-day pass 18€. Tickets are sold at *tabacchi* (tobacconists), some bars, and most newsstands. Since traffic is limited in most of the historic center, buses make runs on principal streets only, except for four tiny electric buses (*bussini* services C1, C2, C3, and D) that trundle about the *centro storico*. Nos. 12 and 13 serve Piazzale Michelangiolo (p. 691).

**Taxis** aren't cheap, and with the city so small and a one-way system forcing drivers to take convoluted routes, they aren't an economical way to get about. They're useful to get you and your bags between the train station and a hotel. The standard rate is 0.91€ per kilometer, with a minimum fare of 3.30€ to start the meter (that rises to 5.30€ on Sun; 6.60€ 10pm–6am), plus 1€ per bag. There's a taxi stand outside the station and another in Piazza Santa Croce (by Via de' Benci); otherwise, call **Radio Taxi** at ✆ **055-4242** or 055-4798.

Florence is largely flat and increasingly closed to cars, and so is ideal for seeing from the saddle. Many **bike-rental** shops are located just north of Piazza San Marco, such as **Alinari,** Via San Zanobi 38R (www.alinarirental.com; ✆ **055-280-500**), which rents vintage-style city bikes (2.50€ per hour; 12€ per day). Make sure to carry a lock (one will be provided): Bike theft is common.

## The Neighborhoods in Brief

**THE DUOMO** The area surrounding Florence's gargantuan cathedral is as central as you get. This is one of the oldest parts of Florence, and the medieval streets still vaguely follow the grid laid down when the city was a Roman colony. The Duomo neighborhood is, understandably, one of the most hotel-heavy parts of town, offering a range from luxury inns to student dives. However, some places around here rest on the laurels of a sublime location; be choosy. The same goes—even more so—for dining.

**PIAZZA DELLA SIGNORIA** This is the city's civic heart and the best base for museum hounds—the **Uffizi Gallery, Bargello** sculpture collection, and **Ponte Vecchio** are all here. The neighborhood can be crowded in summer—Via Por Santa Maria is one to avoid—but when you catch it empty of tour groups, it remains the romantic heart of Florence.

**SAN LORENZO & THE MERCATO CENTRALE** This wedge of streets between the rail station and the Duomo, centered on the Medici's family church of **San Lorenzo,** is market territory. It's a colorful neighborhood, blessed with a range of budget hotels and affordable restaurants, but not the quietest.

**PIAZZA SANTA TRÍNITA** This piazza sits just north of the river at the south end of Florence's shopping mecca, **Via de' Tornabuoni,** home to Gucci and more. It's a pleasant, well-to-do (but still medieval) neighborhood in which to stay, even if you don't care for couture.

**SANTA MARIA NOVELLA** This neighborhood, bounding the western edge of the *centro storico,* has two characters: an unromantic zone around the station, and a nicer area south of it between the church of **Santa Maria Novella** and the river. The station area does, however, have better budget hotel options than any other quarter, especially along Via Faenza and its tributaries. Piazza Santa Maria Novella has top-priced, stylish boutique hotels.

**SAN MARCO & SANTISSIMA ANNUNZIATA** These two churches are fronted by *piazze*—Piazza San Marco, a busy transport hub, and Piazza Santissima Annunziata, the most architecturally unified square in the city—that together define the northern limits of the *centro storico.* Its quiet streets have hotel gems, but it's not (yet) a great dining or nightlife neighborhood.

**SANTA CROCE** The art-filled church at the eastern edge of the *centro storico* is the focal point of one of the most genuine neighborhoods in the center. The streets around Piazza de' Ciompi have a local feel, and they get lively after dark. The neighborhood boasts some of the best restaurants and bars in the city—*aperitivo* hour is vibrant along Via de' Benci, and there is always something going on along Via Panisperna and Via de' Macci.

**THE OLTRARNO, SAN NICCOLÒ & SAN FREDIANO** "Across the Arno" is the old artisans' neighborhood, still dotted with workshops. Its lively, tree-shaded center, **Piazza Santo Spirito,** is lined with bars and close to some great restaurants. West of here, San Frediano, around the Porta Pisana, becomes ever more fashionable, and San Niccolò at the foot of Florence's southern hills is a lively nightlife spot. You may not choose to stay around here—the hotel range isn't great—but when evening draws nigh, cross one of the bridges to drink and eat better food, at better prices, than you will generally find in the *centro storico.*

## Exploring Florence

Most museums accept only cash at the door. Staff is usually happy to direct you to the nearest ATM *(un bancomat).* Note, too, that the last admission to the museums and monuments listed is usually between 30 and 45 minutes before closing time.

### PIAZZA DEL DUOMO

The cathedral square is filled with tourists and caricature artists during the day, strolling crowds in the early evening, and knots of students strumming guitars on the Duomo's steps at night. It's always crowded, and the piazza's vivacity and the glittering facades of the cathedral and the Baptistery doors keep it an eternal Florentine sight. The square is closed to traffic, making it a welcoming—albeit crowded—pedestrian space.

The Duomo, seen from the top of Giotto's Bell Tower.

**Battistero (Baptistery) ★★★** RELIGIOUS SITE In choosing a date to mark the beginning of the Renaissance, art historians often seize on 1401, the year Florence's powerful wool merchants' guild held a contest to decide who would receive the commission to design the **North Doors ★★** of the Baptistery to match its Gothic **South Doors,** cast 65 years earlier by Andrea Pisano. The era's foremost Tuscan sculptors each cast a bronze panel depicting his own vision of the "Sacrifice of Isaac." Twenty-two-year-old Lorenzo Ghiberti, competing against the likes of Donatello, Jacopo della Quercia, and Filippo Brunelleschi, won. He spent the next 21 years casting 28 bronze panels and building his doors.

The mosaicked dome of the Battistero.

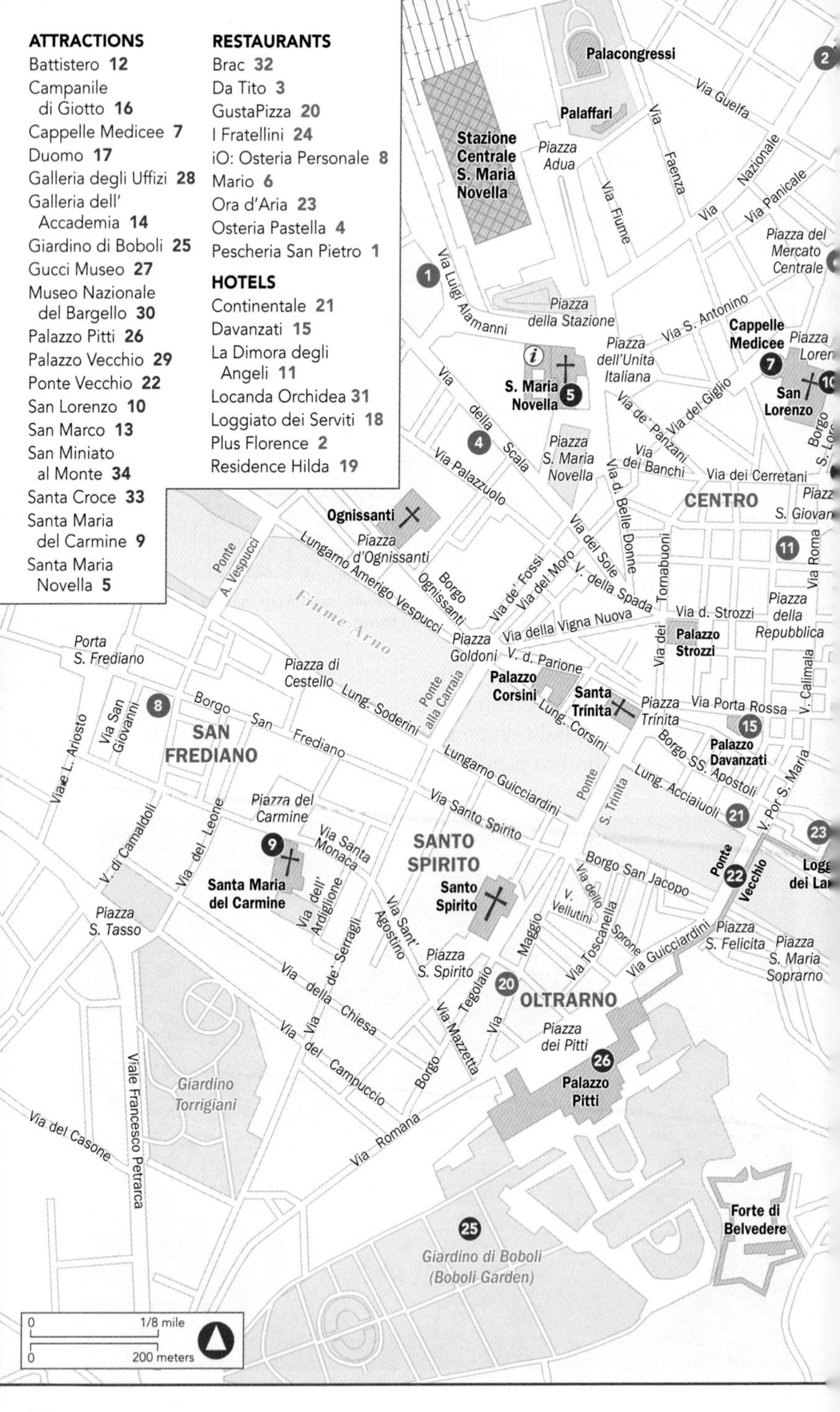
ATTRACTIONS
Battistero 12
Campanile di Giotto 16
Cappelle Medicee 7
Duomo 17
Galleria degli Uffizi 28
Galleria dell' Accademia 14
Giardino di Boboli 25
Gucci Museo 27
Museo Nazionale del Bargello 30
Palazzo Pitti 26
Palazzo Vecchio 29
Ponte Vecchio 22
San Lorenzo 10
San Marco 13
San Miniato al Monte 34
Santa Croce 33
Santa Maria del Carmine 9
Santa Maria Novella 5
RESTAURANTS
Brac 32
Da Tito 3
GustaPizza 20
I Fratellini 24
iO: Osteria Personale 8
Mario 6
Ora d'Aria 23
Osteria Pastella 4
Pescheria San Pietro 1
HOTELS
Continentale 21
Davanzati 15
La Dimora degli Angeli 11
Locanda Orchidea 31
Loggiato dei Serviti 18
Plus Florence 2
Residence Hilda 19
Palacongressi
Palaffari
Stazione Centrale S. Maria Novella
Piazza Adua
Via Guelfa
Via Faenza
Via Nazionale
Via Panicale
Via Fiume
Piazza del Mercato Centrale
Via Luigi Alamanni
Piazza della Stazione
Via S. Antonino
Cappelle Medicee
Piazza dell'Unita Italiana
S. Maria Novella
San Lorenzo
Via della Scala
Via de' Panzani
Via del Giglio
Piazza S. Maria Novella
Via dei Banchi
Via dei Cerretani
Via Palazzuolo
CENTRO
Ognissanti
Piazza d'Ognissanti
Via d. Belle Donne
Via del Sole
Borgo Ognissanti
Lungarno Amerigo Vespucci
Via de' Fossi
Via del Moro
V. della Spada
Via Roma
Piazza della Repubblica
Ponte A. Vespucci
Fiume Arno
Via della Vigna Nuova
Via d. Strozzi
Via dei Tornabuoni
Palazzo Strozzi
Porta S. Frediano
Piazza Goldoni
V. d. Parione
Piazza di Cestello
Palazzo Corsini
Santa Trínita
Piazza Trínita
Via Porta Rossa
V. Calimala
Borgo San Frediano
Lung. Soderini
Ponte alla Carraia
Lung. Corsini
Via San Giovanni
SAN FREDIANO
Borgo SS. Apostoli
Palazzo Davanzati
Viale L. Ariosto
Lungarno Guicciardini
Ponte S. Trinita
Lung. Acciaiuoli
V. Por S. Maria
Piazza del Carmine
Via Santo Spirito
V. di Camaldoli
Via del Leone
Via Santa Monaca
SANTO SPIRITO
Santa Maria del Carmine
Via dell' Ardiglione
Borgo San Jacopo
Ponte Vecchio
Via dello Sprone
V. Vellutini
Santo Spirito
Via Sant' Agostino
Via de' Serragli
Piazza S. Tasso
Maggio
Via Toscanella
Via Guicciardini
Piazza S. Felicita
Piazza S. Maria Soprarno
Piazza S. Spirito
Via della Chiesa
Via Tegolaio
OLTRARNO
Via del Campuccio
Via Mazzetta
Piazza dei Pitti
Palazzo Pitti
Giardino Torrigiani
Viale Francesco Petrarca
Via del Casone
Borgo
Via Romana
Forte di Belvedere
Giardino di Boboli (Boboli Garden)
0 1/8 mile
0 200 meters

Florence
San Marco
Giardino dei Semplici
Giardino della Gherardesca
Piazza Donatello
Santissima Annunziata
Galleria dell' Accademia
Museo Archeologico
Piazza della SS. Annunziata
Ospedale degli Innocenti
Palazzo Medici-Riccardi
Palazzo Pucci
Piazza Brunelleschi
Ospedale S. Maria Nuova
Piazza S. M. Nuova
Teatro d. Pergola
Santa Maria Maddalena dei Pazzi
Piazza d'Azeglio
Sinogoga (Museo Ebraico)
Duomo
Piazza del Duomo
DUOMO
Piazza Sant' Ambrogio
Piazza L. Ghiberti
Piazza Cesare Beccaria
Bargello
Badia
Piazza S. Firenze
SIGNORIA
Palazzo Vecchio
Uffizi
Teatro Verdi
Casa di Buonarroti
Carceri delle Murate
Archivo di Stato
Piazza S. Croce
Santa Croce
SANTA CROCE
Biblioteca Nazionale
Piazza Mentana
Piazza dei Cavalleggeri
Piazza Piave
Fiume Arno
Ponte alle Grazie
Ponte A. Vespucci
SAN NICCOLÒ
Piazza G. Poggi
Piazza F. Ferrucci
Piazzale Michelangelo
Via G. Capponi
Via G. Matteotti
Via degli Artisti
Via P. Cappone
Via G. La Farini
Via Giuseppe Giusti
Via J. Nardi
Via B. Varchi
Viale Antonio Gramsci
Via L. C. Farini
Via G. Carducci
Via della Colonna
Via Laura
Borgo Pinti
Via Cesare Battisti
Via degli Servi
Via della Pergola
Via Alfani
Via Ricasoli
Via Cavour
Via Guelfa
Via de' Ginori
Via S. Zanobi
Via XXVII Aprile
V. degli Arazzieri
Via San Gallo
V. S. Reparata
Via dei Pucci
Via de' Martelli
Via M. Bufalini
Via S. Egidio
Via dell'Oriuolo
Via Fiesolana
Via de' Pepi
Via dei Pilastri
Via di Mezzo
Via Pietrapiana
Via della Mattonaia
Via A. Manzoni
Borgo la Croce
Via F. Paolieri
V. d. Studio
Via del Proconsolo
Via del Corso
Borgo degli Albizi
Via Dante Alighieri
Via de' Pandolfini
Via Ghibellina
V. d. Vigna Vecchia
Via G. Verdi
V. M. Buonarroti
Via Allegri
Via dell' Agnolo
Via de' Macci
Borgo de' Greci
Via dei Neri
Via di San Giuseppe
Via della Giovine Italia
Via Pietro Thouar
Via de' Malcontenti
Viale della Giovine Italia
Viale Giovanni Amendola
Borgo S. Croce
V. Magliabechi
Via de' Benci
Corso dei Tintori
Lung. Gen. Diaz
Lungarno delle Grazie
Via Tripoli
Lung. della Zecca Vecchia
Lung. P. Giraldi
Lungarno Torrigiani
Via de' Bardi
Lungarno Serristori
Via dei Renai
Via di S. Niccolo
Lungarno B. Cellini
Via dei Bastioni
Viale G. Poggi
Via di Belvedere
Via del Monte alle Croci
Viale Michelangiolo

## DISCOUNT tickets FOR THE CITY

The **Firenze Card** (www.firenzecard.it) attractions pass (72€; valid 72 hr.) is a good buy if you are planning a busy, culture-packed break here. If you only expect to see a few museums, skip it.

The card allows entrance to around 60 sites; the list includes a handful that are free anyway, but also the Uffizi, Accademia, Cappella Brancacci, Palazzo Pitti, Brunelleschi's dome, San Marco, and many more. In fact, *everything* I recommend in this section except San Lorenzo and the Gucci Museo is included in the price of the card. It also gets you into much shorter lines, taking ticket prebooking hassles out of the equation—another savings of 3€ to 4€ for busy museums, above all the Uffizi and Accademia. It also includes 3 days' free bus travel (which you probably won't use) and free public Wi-Fi (which you might).

The Opera del Duomo has dispensed with single entry tickets to its sites in favor of a value *biglietto cumulativo*, the **Grande Museo del Duomo** ticket. It covers Brunelleschi's dome, the Baptistery, Campanile di Giotto, Museo Storico dell'Opera, and archaeological excavations of Santa Reparata (inside the cathedral) for 10€, free for accompanied children up to age 14. You have 24 hours from first use to enter them all. Buy it at the ticket office almost opposite the Baptistery, on the north side of Piazza San Giovanni. It includes enough to fill a busy half-day, at least. See www.ilgrandemuseodelduomo.it for more details.



The result so impressed the merchants' guild—not to mention the public and Ghiberti's fellow artists—that they asked him in 1425 to do the **East Doors ★★★,** facing the Duomo, this time giving him the artistic freedom to realize his Renaissance ambitions. Twenty-seven years later, just before his death, Ghiberti finished 10 dramatic lifelike Old Testament scenes in gilded bronze, each a masterpiece of Renaissance sculpture and some of the finest examples of low-relief perspective in Italian art. The panels mounted here are excellent copies; the originals are in the **Museo Storico dell'Opera del Duomo.** Years later, Michelangelo was standing before these doors, and someone asked his opinion. His response sums up Ghiberti's accomplishment as no art historian could: "They are so beautiful that they would grace the entrance to Paradise." They've been nicknamed the Gates of Paradise ever since.

Inside, the ceiling was covered between 1225 and the early 1300s with glittering **mosaics ★★.** Most were crafted by Venetian or Byzantine-style workshops, which worked off designs drawn by the era's best artists.

Piazza San Giovanni. www.ilgrandemuseodelduomo.it. ✆ **055-230-2885.** Included with 10€ Grande Museo del Duomo ticket. Bus: C2, 14, or 23. Mon–Sat 11:15am–6:30pm (Jun–Sept Thurs–Sat until 10:30pm); Sun and 1st Sat of month 8:30am–2pm.

**Campanile di Giotto (Giotto's Bell Tower) ★★** HISTORIC SITE

In 1334, Giotto started the cathedral bell tower but completed only the first two levels before his death in 1337. He was out of his league with the engineering aspects of architecture, and the tower was saved from falling by Andrea Pisano, who doubled the thickness of the walls. Andrea, a master sculptor of the Pisan Gothic school, also changed the design to add statue niches—he even carved a few of the statues himself—before quitting the project in 1348. Francesco Talenti finished the job between 1350 and 1359.

I recommend climbing the 414 steps to the top; the **view ★★** is memorable as you ascend, and offers the best close-up shot in the entire city of Brunelleschi's dome. Queues are also much shorter than the often-epic lines to climb Brunelleschi's dome itself (see below).

Piazza del Duomo. www.ilgrandemuseodelduomo.it. ✆ **055-230-2885.** Included with 10€ Grande Museo del Duomo ticket. Bus: C2. Daily 8:30am–6:50pm.

**Duomo (Cattedrale di Santa Maria del Fiore) ★★** CATHEDRAL
By the late 13th century, Florence was feeling peevish: Its archrivals Siena and Pisa sported huge, flamboyant new cathedrals while it was saddled with the tiny 5th- or 6th-century cathedral of Santa Reparata. So, in 1296, the city hired Arnolfo di Cambio to design a new Duomo, and he raised the facade and the first few bays before his death (probably around 1310). Work continued under architects Giotto di Bondone (who concentrated on the bell tower) and Francesco Talenti (who finished up to the drum of the dome). The facade we see today is a neo-Gothic composite designed by Emilio de Fabris and built from 1871 to 1887.

The Duomo's most distinctive feature is its enormous **dome ★★★** (or *cupola*), which dominates the skyline and is a symbol of Florence itself. The raising of this dome, the largest in the world in its time, was no mean architectural feat, tackled by Filippo Brunelleschi between 1420 and 1436. You can climb up between its double shell for one of the classic panoramas across the city—something that is not recommended for claustrophobes or anyone with no head for heights.

The cathedral is rather Spartan inside, but check out the fake equestrian "statue" of English mercenary soldier Sir John Hawkwood painted on the north wall in 1436, by Paolo Uccello.

Piazza del Duomo. www.ilgrandemuseodelduomo.it. ✆ **055-230-2885.** Admission to church free; Santa Reparata excavations and cupola Included with 10€ Grande Museo del Duomo ticket. Bus: C1, C2, 14, or 23. Church Mon–Wed and Fri 10am–5pm; Thurs 10am–4:30pm (July–Sept until 5pm, May and Oct until 4pm); Sat 10am–4:45pm; Sun 1:30–4:45pm. Cupola Mon–Fri 8:30am–6:20pm; Sat 8:30am–5pm; closed on religious holidays.

## AROUND PIAZZA DELLA SIGNORIA & SANTA TRÍNITA

The oldest and most famous bridge across the Arno, the **Ponte Vecchio ★** was built in 1345 by Taddeo Gaddi to replace an earlier version. The characteristic overhanging shops have lined the bridge since at least the 12th century. In the 16th century, it was home to butchers until Cosimo I

The Ponte Vecchio, Florence's most famous bridge.

moved into the Palazzo Pitti across the river. He couldn't stand the stench, so he evicted the meat cutters and moved in the classier gold- and silversmiths, and jewelers who occupy it to this day.

**Galleria degli Uffizi (Uffizi Gallery) ★★★** ART MUSEUM There is no collection of Renaissance art on the planet that can match the Uffizi. Period. For all its crowds and other inconveniences, the Uffizi remains a must-see.

Start with **Room 2** for a look at the pre-Renaissance, Gothic style of painting. Compare teacher and student as you examine Cimabue's *Santa Trínita Maestà* painted around 1280, and Giotto's ***Ognissanti Madonna*** **★★★** done in 1310. The similar setting for both allows the viewer to see how Giotto transformed Cimabue's iconlike Byzantine style into something more real and human.

**Room 3** showcases the Sienese School at its peak, with Simone Martini's dazzling ***Annunciation*** **★★** (1333) and Ambrogio Lorenzetti's *Presentation at the Temple* (1342). The Black Death of 1348 wiped out this entire generation of Sienese painters, and most of that city's population along with them.

**Room 8** contains the unflattering profiles of the Duke Federico da Montefeltro of Urbino and his duchess, done by **Piero della Francesca** in 1472. The subjects are portrayed in an unflinchingly realistic way. Also here are works by **Filippo Lippi** from the mid-15th century. His most celebrated panel, ***Madonna and Child with Two Angels*** **★★,** dates from around 1465. Lippi's work was a celebrity scandal. The woman who modeled for Mary was said to be Filippo's lover—a would-be nun called Lucrezia Buti whom he had spirited away from her convent before she could take vows.

Courtyard of the Uffizi Gallery.

**Rooms 10 to 14**—still collectively numbered, even though the walls were knocked down to make one large room—are devoted to the works of Sandro Filipepi, better known by his nickname "Little Barrels," or Botticelli. Botticelli's 1485 ***Birth of Venus*** ★★ hangs like a highway billboard you have seen a thousand times. Venus's pose is taken from classical statues, while the winds Zephyr and Aura blowing her to shore, and the muse welcoming her, are from Ovid's "Metamorphoses." Botticelli's 1478 ***Primavera*** ★★★, its dark, bold colors a stark contrast to the pastel *Venus,* defies definitive interpretation (many have tried). But again it features Venus (center), alongside Mercury, with the winged boots, the Three Graces, and the goddess Flora.

Leonardo da Vinci's ***Annunciation*** ★★★ anchors **Room 15.** In this painting, though completed in the early 1470s while he was still a student in Verrocchio's workshop, da Vinci's ability to orchestrate the viewer's focus is masterful.

As soon as you cross to the Uffizi's west wing—past picture windows with views of the Arno River to one side and the Renaissance perspective of the Uffizi piazza to the other—you're walloped with another line of masterpieces. Among the highlights of this "second half" is Michelangelo's 1505–08 ***Holy Family*** ★. The twisting shapes of Mary, Joseph, and Jesus recall those in the Sistine Chapel in Rome for their sculpted nature and the bright colors. The Uffizi has a number of Raphaels, including his often-copied ***Madonna of the Goldfinch*** ★★, with a background landscape lifted from Leonardo and Botticelli. Titian's reclining nude ***Venus of Urbino*** ★★ is another highlight.

Piazzale degli Uffizi 6. www.uffizi.firenze.it. ✆ **055-238-8651.** 6.50€ (11€ during temporary exhibition). Bus: C1, C2, C3, or D. Tues–Sun 8:15am–6:50pm.

### Advance Reservations for the Uffizi, Accademia & More

If you're not buying a Firenze Card (see p. 682), you should bypass the hours-long line at the Uffizi by reserving a ticket and entry time in advance by calling **Firenze Musei** at ✆ **055-294-883** (Mon–Fri 8:30am–6:30pm; Sat until 12:30pm) or visiting **www.firenzemusei.it** (you may need to have patience with their website). You can also reserve for the Accademia Gallery (another interminable line, to see *David*), as well as the Galleria Palatina in the Pitti Palace, the Bargello, and several others. There's a 3€ fee (4€ for the Uffizi or Accademia, where a reservation is strongly advised); you can pay by credit card.

**Gucci Museo** ★ MUSEUM This private museum tells the story of the Gucci empire, from humble beginnings to worldwide megabrand. Guccio Gucci got his flash of inspiration while working as a "lift boy" at London's Savoy Hotel: His first product designs were for travel luggage to suit the lifestyles of the kinds of people he would meet in the elevator every day. The museum places Gucci right at the heart of Florence's artisan tradition—which, of course, is where it belongs.

Piazza della Signoria. www.guccimuseo.com. ✆ **055-7592-3302.** 6€. Bus: C1 or C2. Daily 10am–8pm.

**Museo Nazionale del Bargello (Bargello Museum)** ★★ MUSEUM This is the most important museum anywhere for Renaissance **sculpture**—and often inexplicably quieter than others in the city. In a far cry from its original use as the city's prison, torture chamber, and execution site, the Bargello now stands as a three-story art museum containing some of the best works of Michelangelo, Donatello, and Ghiberti, as well as their most successful Mannerist successor, Giambologna. In the Michelangelo room, you'll witness the variety of his craft, from the whimsical 1497 ***Bacchus*** ★★ to the severe, unfinished *Brutus* of 1540.

Interior, Bargello Museum.

Upstairs, an enormous vaulted hall is filled with some of Donatello's most accomplished sculptures, including his original *Marzocco* (from outside the Palazzo Vecchio; p. 687), and ***St. George*** ★ from a niche on the outside of Orsanmichele. Notable among them is his ***David*** ★★ (which might correctly

## PIAZZA DELLA signoria

When the medieval Guelph party finally came out on top after their political struggle with the Ghibellines, they razed part of the old city center to build a new palace for civic government, the **Palazzo Vecchio.** The space around the *palazzo* became the new civic center of town, L-shaped **Piazza della Signoria ★★,** named after the oligarchic ruling body of the medieval city (the "Signoria").

The statuary on the piazza is particularly beautiful, starting on the far left (as you're facing the Palazzo Vecchio) with Giambologna's equestrian statue of *Grand Duke Cosimo I* (1594). To its right is one of Florence's favorite sculptures to hate, the ***Fontana del Nettuno*** (*Neptune Fountain;* 1560–75), created by Bartolomeo Ammannati as a tribute to Cosimo I's naval ambitions but nicknamed by the Florentines "Il Biancone," or "Big Whitey."

To the right of Neptune is a copy (original in the Bargello; see p. 687) of Donatello's ***Marzocco,*** symbol of the city, with a Florentine lion resting his raised paw on a shield emblazoned with the city's emblem, the *giglio* (lily). To its right is another Donatello replica, ***Judith Beheading Holofernes.*** Farther down is a man who needs little introduction, Michelangelo's ***David,*** a 19th-century copy of the original now in the Accademia. Near enough to David to look truly ugly in comparison is Baccio Bandinelli's ***Hercules*** (1534). Poor Bandinelli was trying to copy Michelangelo's muscular male form but ended up making his Hercules merely lumpy.

At the piazza's south end is one of the square's earliest and prettiest embellishments, the **Loggia dei Lanzi ★★** (1376-82), named after the Swiss guard of lancers *(lanzi)* whom Cosimo de' Medici stationed here. At the front left stands Benvenuto Cellini's masterpiece in bronze, ***Perseus*** **★★★** (1545), holding out the severed head of Medusa. On the far right is Giambologna's ***Rape of the Sabines*** **★★,** a piece you must walk all the way around to appreciate.

be named "Mercury"), done in 1440, the first freestanding nude sculpture since Roman times.

Via del Proconsolo 4. www.polomuseale.firenze.it. ✆ **055-238-8606.** 4€ (7€ during temporary exhibitions). Bus: C1 or C2. Daily 8:15am–1:50pm (until 5pm during exhibitions). Closed 1st, 3rd, and 5th Sun, and 2nd and 4th Mon of each month.

**Palazzo Vecchio ★** PALACE Florence's fortresslike town hall was built from 1299 to 1302 on the designs of Arnolfo di Cambio, Gothic master builder of the city. The palace was home to the various Florentine republican governments (and is today to the municipal government). Cosimo I and his Medici family moved here in 1540 and engaged in massive redecoration.

The grand staircase leads up to the **Sala dei Cinquecento,** named for the 500-man assembly that met here in the pre-Medici days of the Florentine Republic and site of the greatest fresco cycle that ever wasn't. Leonardo da Vinci was commissioned in 1503–05 to paint one long wall with a battle scene celebrating a Florentine victory at the 1440 Battle of Anghiari. He was always trying new methods and materials and decided to mix wax into his pigments. Leonardo had finished part of the wall, but it wasn't drying fast enough, so he brought in braziers stoked with hot coals to hurry the process. As others watched in horror, the wax in the fresco melted and the colors ran down the walls to a puddle on the floor. The search for whatever remains continues, and some hope was provided in 2012 with the discovery of pigments used by Leonardo in a wall cavity.

Michelangelo never even got past making the preparatory drawings for the fresco he was supposed to paint on the opposite wall—Pope Julius II called him to Rome to paint the Sistine Chapel. Eventually, the walls were covered by Vasari and assistants from 1563 to 1565, with subservient frescoes exalting Cosimo I and the military victories of his regime, against Pisa (on the near wall) and Siena (far wall). Opposite the door you enter, is Michelangelo's statue of ***Victory*** **★,** carved from 1533 to 1534 for Julius II's tomb but later donated to the Medici.

The first series of rooms on the second floor is the **Quartiere degli Elementi,** frescoed with allegories and mythological characters, again by Vasari. Crossing the balcony overlooking the Sala dei Cinquecento, you enter the **Apartments of Eleonora di Toledo ★,** decorated for Cosimo's Spanish wife. Her small private chapel is a masterpiece of mid-16th-century painting by Bronzino.

If you can bear the small spaces and 418 steps, the views from **Torre di Arnolfo ★,** the palace's crenellated tower, are grand. The 95m (312-ft.) Torre is closed during bad weather; the minimum age to climb it is 6, and children ages 17 and under must be accompanied by an adult. Piazza della Signoria. www.museicivicifiorentini.comune.fi.it. ✆ **055-276-8325.** Palazzo or Torre 10€; admisson to both 14€. Bus: C1 or C2. Palazzo Fri–Wed 9am–7pm (Apr–Sept until midnight); Thurs 9am–2pm. Torre Fri–Wed 10am–5pm (Apr–Sept 9am–9pm); Thurs 9am–2pm.

## AROUND SAN LORENZO & THE MERCATO CENTRALE

**Cappelle Medicee (Medici Chapels)** ★ MONUMENT/MEMORIAL When Michelangelo built the **New Sacristy ★★** here between 1520 and 1533 (finished by Vasari in 1556), it was to be a tasteful monument to Lorenzo the Magnificent and his generation of relatively pleasant Medici. Michelangelo was supposed to produce three tombs here (perhaps four) but ironically got only the two less important ones done. So Lorenzo de' Medici ("the Magnificent")—wise ruler of his city, poet of note, grand patron of the arts, and moneybags behind much of the Renaissance—ended up with a mere inscription of his name next to his brother Giuliano's on a plain marble slab against the entrance wall. Admittedly, they did get one genuine Michelangelo sculpture to decorate their slab, a not quite finished ***Madonna and Child*** **★.**

On the left wall of the sacristy is Michelangelo's ***Tomb of Lorenzo*** ★, duke of Urbino (and Lorenzo the Magnificent's grandson), whose seated statue symbolizes the contemplative life. Below him on the elongated curves of the tomb stretch "Dawn" (female) and "Dusk" (male), a pair of Michelangelo's most famous sculptures. This pair mirrors the similarly fashioned "Day" (male) and "Night" (female) across the way.

Piazza Madonna degli Aldobrandini (behind San Lorenzo, where Via Faenza and Via del Giglio meet). www.polomuseale.firenze.it. ✆ **055-238-8602.** 6€ (8€ during temporary exhibitions). Bus: C1, C2, 6, 11, or 22. Daily 8:15am–1:50pm (until 4:50pm during exhibition). Closed 1st, 3rd, and 5th Mon, and 2nd and 4th Sun of each month.

**San Lorenzo** ★ CHURCH A rough brick anti-facade hides what is most likely the oldest church in Florence, founded in A.D. 393. It was later the Medici family's parish church, and Cosimo il Vecchio, whose wise behind-the-scenes rule made him popular with the Florentines, is buried in front of the high altar. Off the left transept is the **Sagrestia Vecchia (Old Sacristy)** ★, one of Brunelleschi's purest pieces of early Renaissance architecture.

Piazza San Lorenzo. ✆ **055-214-042.** 4.50€. Bus: C1, 14, or 23. Mon–Sat 10am–5:30pm; Mar–Oct also Sun 1:30–5:30pm.

## NEAR PIAZZA SANTA MARIA NOVELLA

**Santa Maria Novella** ★★ CHURCH Of all Florence's major churches, the home of the Dominicans is the only one with an original **facade** ★★ that matches its era of greatest importance. The lower Romanesque half was started in the 14th century by architect Fra' Jacopo Talenti, who had just finished building the church itself (begun in 1246). Renaissance architect and theorist Leon Battista Alberti finished the facade, adding a classically inspired Renaissance top that not only went seamlessly with the lower half but also created a Cartesian plane of perfect geometry.

Inside, on the left wall, is **Masaccio's *Trinità*** ★★★ (ca. 1425), the first painting ever to use perfect linear mathematical perspective. Florentine citizens and artists flooded in to see the fresco when it was unveiled, many remarking in awe that it seemed to punch a hole back into space, creating a chapel out of a flat wall. The **transept** is filled with frescoed chapels by Filippino Lippi and others.

Out back, the **Chiostro Verde (Green Cloister)** ★★ was partly frescoed between 1431 and 1446 by Paolo Uccello, a Florentine painter who became increasingly obsessed with the mathematics behind perspective. His Old Testament scenes include an "Inundation," which ironically was badly damaged by the Great Arno Flood of 1966. The reopened **Chiostro dei Morti (Cloister of the Dead)** ★ is one of the oldest parts of the convent, dating to the 1200s, and was another area badly damaged in 1966. Its low-slung vaults and chapels were decorated by Andrea Orcagna and others. It is especially atmospheric early in the morning, with the cloister empty and birdsong at full volume.

Piazza Santa Maria Novella/Piazza della Stazione 4. www.chiesasantamarianovella.it. ✆ **055-219-257.** 5€. Bus: C2, D, 6, 11, or 22. Mon–Thurs 9am–5:30pm; Fri 11am–5:30pm; Sat 9am–5pm; Sun 1–5pm (July–Sept opens noon).

## NEAR SAN MARCO

**Galleria dell'Accademia** ★★ ART MUSEUM This museum's most famous resident, ***David*** ★★★—"Il Gigante"—is much larger than most people imagine, looming 4.8m (16 ft.) on top of a 1.8m (6-ft.) pedestal. He hasn't faded with time, either; the marble gleams as if it were his unveiling day in 1504. Viewing the statue is a pleasure in the bright and spacious room custom-designed for him after the icon was moved to the Accademia in 1873, following 300 years of pigeons perched on his head in Piazza della Signoria.

But the Accademia is not only about *David;* you will be delighted to discover he is surrounded by an entire museum stuffed with other notable Renaissance works. Michelangelo's unfinished ***Prisoners*** ★★ statues are a contrast to *David,* with the rough forms struggling to free themselves from the raw stone.

Via Ricasoli 60. www.polomuseale.firenze.it. ✆ **055-238-8609.** 6.50€ (11€ during temporary exhibitions). Bus: C1, 14, or 23. Tues–Sun 8:15am–6:50pm.

**San Marco** ★★★ ART MUSEUM I have never understood why this place is not mobbed; perhaps it's a mix of the unusual opening hours and because it showcases, almost exclusively, the work of Fra' Angelico,

*David* is the star attraction at Galleria dell'Accademia.

Dominican monk and Florentine painter in the style known as "International Gothic." His decorative impulses and the sinuous lines of his figures mark his work as standing right on the cusp of the Renaissance.

The most moving and unusual work is his ***Annunciation*** ★★★ and frescoed scenes from the life of Jesus painted not on one giant wall, but scene by scene, on the individual walls of small monks' cells that honeycomb the upper floor. The idea was that these scenes, painted by Fra' Angelico and his assistants, would aid in the monks' prayer and contemplation; the paintings are intimate and entrancing.

There is much more Fra' Angelico secreted around the cloistered complex, including a ***Crucifixion*** ★ in the Chapter House.

Piazza San Marco 1. www.polomuseale.firenze.it. ✆ **055-238-8608.** 4€ (7€ during temporary exhibitions). Bus: C1, 1, 6, 7, 11, 14, 17, or 19. Mon–Fri 8:30am–1:50pm; Sat–Sun 8:15am–4:50pm. Closed every 1st, 3rd, and 5th Sun and 2nd and 4th Mon.

## AROUND PIAZZA SANTA CROCE

**Santa Croce** ★★ CHURCH The center of the Florentine Franciscan universe was begun in 1294 by Gothic master Arnolfo di Cambio in order to rival the church of Santa Maria Novella being raised by the Dominicans across the city. The church wasn't consecrated until 1442, and even then it remained faceless until a neo-Gothic **facade** was added in 1857.

The Gothic **interior** is vast, and populated with the tombs of rich and famous Florentines. Starting from the main door, immediately on the right is the first tomb of note containing the bones of the most venerated Renaissance master, **Michelangelo Buonarroti,** who died in Rome in 1564 at the ripe age of 89. The tombs of **Galileo** and **Machiavelli** are nearby.

Giotto himself frescoed the two chapels to the right of the high altar. The frescoes were whitewashed over during the 17th century but uncovered from 1841 to 1852 and inexpertly restored. The **Cappella Peruzzi ★,** on the right, is a late work and not in the best shape. More famous, including as the setting for a scene in *A Room with a View,* is the **Cappella Bardi ★★.** In one of Giotto's best-known works, the *Death of St. Francis,* monks weep with convincing pathos.

Outside in the cloister is the **Cappella Pazzi ★,** one of Filippo Brunelleschi's architectural masterpieces (faithfully finished after his death in 1446). It is the defining example of early Renaissance architecture.

Piazza Santa Croce. www.santacroceopera.it. ✆ **055-246-6105.** 6€ adults, 4€ ages 11–17. Bus: C1, C2, or C3. Mon–Sat 9:30am–5pm; Sun 2–5pm.

## THE OLTRARNO, SAN NICCOLÒ & SAN FREDIANO

Panoramic **Piazzale Michelangiolo ★★** is a required stop for every tour bus (or get there solo on bus nos. 12 or 13). The balustraded terrace was laid out in 1869 to give a sweeping vista of the entire city, backed by the green hills of Fiesole beyond. The bronze replica of *David* here points right at his original home, outside the Palazzo Vecchio.

**Giardino di Boboli (Boboli Garden) ★★** PARK/GARDEN The statue-filled park behind the Pitti Palace is one of the earliest and finest Renaissance gardens, laid out mostly between 1549 and 1656 with box hedges in geometric patterns, groves of ilex (holm oak), dozens of statues, and rows of cypress. Just above the entrance through the courtyard of the Palazzo Pitti is an oblong **amphitheater** modeled on Roman circuses, with a **granite basin** from Rome's Baths of Caracalla and an **Ancient Egyptian obelisk** of Ramses II. In 1589, this was the setting for the wedding reception of Ferdinando de' Medici's marriage to Christine of Lorraine. For the occasion, the Medici commissioned entertainment from Jacopo Peri and Ottavio Rinuccini, who decided to set a classical story entirely to music and called it "Dafne"—the world's first opera.

Toward the south end of the park is the **Isolotto ★,** a dreamy island marooned in a pond full of huge goldfish, with Giambologna's *L'Oceano* sculptural composition at its center.

Entrance via Palazzo Pitti, Piazza de' Pitti. www.firenzemusei.it. ✆ **055-238-8791.** 7€ (10€ during temporary exhibitions), includes Giardino Bardini, Museo degli Argenti, and Museo del Costume. Ages 17 and under or 65 and over enter free. Bus: C3, D, 11, 36, or 37. Nov–Feb daily 8:15am–4:30pm; Mar daily 8:15am–5:30pm; Apr–May and Sept–Oct daily 8:15am–6:30pm; June–Aug daily 8:15am–7:30pm. Closed 1st and last Mon of month.



**Palazzo Pitti (Pitti Palace) ★★** MUSEUM/PALACE Although built by and named after a rival of the Medici—merchant Luca Pitti—in the 1450s, this gigantic *palazzo* soon fell into Medici hands. It was the Medici family's principal home from the 1540s, and continued to house Florence's rulers until 1919. The Pitti contains five museums, notably the **Galleria Palatina ★★,** with one of the world's best collections of canvases by Raphael. No gallery comes closer to Mark Twain's description of

Giardino di Boboli and the Palazzo Pitti.

"weary miles" in *Innocents Abroad* than the art-crammed rooms of the Palatina. Paintings are displayed like cars in a parking garage, stacked on walls above each other in the "Enlightenment" method of exhibition.

You will find important treasures here, however. Two giant versions of the *Assumption of the Virgin,* both by Mannerist painter Andrea del Sarto, dominate the **Sala dell'Iliade (Iliad Room).** The **Sala di Saturno (Saturn Room) ★** is stuffed with Raphaels and a giant panel by his teacher, Perugino; next door in the **Sala di Giove (Jupiter Room)** is his sublime, naturalistic portrait of ***La Velata* ★★,** as well as ***The Ages of Man* ★.** The current attribution of the painting is awarded to Venetian Giorgione, although that has been disputed.

Piazza de' Pitti 1. Galleria Palatina, Apartamenti Reali, and Galleria d'Arte Moderna: ✆ **055-238-8614.** 8.50€ (13€ during temporary exhibitions). Bus: D, 11, 36, or 37. Tues–Sun 8:15am–6:50pm. Visitors ages 17 and under or 65 and over enter free.

**San Miniato al Monte ★★** CHURCH High atop a hill, its gleaming white-and-green facade visible from the city below, San Miniato is one of the few ancient churches of Florence to survive the centuries virtually intact. The building began to take shape in 1013, under the auspices of the powerful Arte di Calimala guild, whose symbol, a bronze eagle clutching a bale of wool, perches on the **facade ★★.** Below the choir is an 11th-century **crypt** with frescoes by Taddeo Gaddi. Off to the right of the raised choir is the **sacristy,** which Spinello Aretino covered in 1387 with cartoonish yet elaborate frescoes depicting the ***Life of St. Benedict* ★.** Benedictine monks usually celebrate Mass here in Gregorian Chant at 5:30pm.

Via Monte alle Croci/Viale Galileo Galilei (behind Piazzale Michelangiolo). ✆ **055-234-2731.** Free. Bus: 12 or 13. Daily 8am–1pm and 3:30–dusk (closed some Sun afternoons).

**Santa Maria del Carmine ★★★** CHURCH Following a 1771 fire that destroyed everything but the transept chapels and sacristy, this Carmelite church was almost entirely reconstructed in high baroque style. To see the **Cappella Brancacci ★★★** in the right transept, you have to enter through the cloisters (doorway to the right of the church facade) and pay admission. The frescoes here were commissioned by an enemy of the Medici, Felice Brancacci, who in 1424 hired Masolino and his student Masaccio to decorate it with a cycle on the *Life of St. Peter.* Masolino probably worked out the cycle's scheme and painted a few scenes along with his pupil before taking off for 3 years to Budapest, Hungary, during which time Masaccio kept painting, quietly creating the early Renaissance's greatest frescoes. Masaccio left for Rome in 1428, where he died at age 27. The cycle was completed between 1480 and 1485 by Filippino Lippi.

Piazza del Carmine 14. www.museicivicifiorentini.comune.fi.it/brancacci. ✆ **055-238-2195.** Free admission to church; Cappella Brancacci 6€. Bus: D. Mon and Wed–Sat 10am–5pm; Sun 1–5pm.

## Organized Tours

If you want to get under the surface of the city, **Context Travel ★★** (www.contexttravel.com; ✆ **800/691-6036** in the U.S. or 06-96727371 in Italy) offers insightful culture tours led by academics and other experts in a variety of specialties, from the gastronomic to the artistic. Tours are limited to six people and cost around 75€ per person. **CAF Tours** (www.caftours.com; ✆ **055-283-200**) offers two half-day bus tours of town (48€), including visits to the Uffizi, Accademia, and Piazzale Michelangiolo, as well as several walking tours and cooking classes costing from 27€ to 130€. **ArtViva** (www.italy.artviva.com; ✆ **055-264-5033**) has walking tours and museum guides for every budget, starting at 25€, and including the unique, distinctly dark "Sex, Drugs, and the Renaissance" walking tour (2½ hr.; 39€).

## Especially for Kids

You have to put in a bit of work to reach some of Florence's best views—and the climbs, up claustrophobic, medieval staircases, are a favorite with many kids. The massive ochre dome of **Santa Maria del Fiore ★★** (p. 683), the Palazzo Vecchio's **Torre di Arnolfo ★★** (p. 688), and the **Campanile di Giotto ★★** (p. 682) are perfect for any youngster with a head for heights.

You can also help them to dig a little deeper into the city's history: Probably the best kids' activities with an educational component are run by the **Museo dei Ragazzi ★★** (www.museoragazzi.it; ✆ **055-276-8224**), not a standalone museum but a program that offers daily child's-eye tours around the Palazzo Vecchio's Quartieri Monumentali, led by guides in period costumes and offered in English. Check the program online, or make for the desk next to the Palazzo Vecchio ticket booth.

## Where to Stay

In the past few years, thanks to growing competition, economic crises, and shifting euro-dollar exchange rates, the forces of supply and demand have brought hotel prices in Florence down . . . a little. Peak hotel season is mid-March through early July, September through early November, and December 23 through January 6. May, June, and September are particularly popular; January, February, and August are the months to grab a bargain—never be shy to haggle if you're coming in these months.

### NEAR THE DUOMO

#### Moderate

**La Dimora degli Angeli ★★★** This B&B occupies two levels of a grand apartment building in one of the city's busiest shopping areas. Older rooms are for romantics; bright, modern wallpaper clashes pleasingly with iron-framed beds and traditional furniture. (Corner room Beatrice is the largest, with a view of Brunelleschi's dome—but only just.)

Rooms on a newer floor, added in 2012, are totally different, with the kind of decor you find in an interiors magazine, all sharp lines and bespoke leather or wooden headboards throughout.

Via Brunelleschi 4. www.ladimoradegliangeli.com. ✆ **055-288-478.** 12 units. Doubles 88€–190€, includes breakfast (at nearby cafe). Bus: C2. **Amenities:** Free Wi-Fi.

## NEAR PIAZZA DELLA SIGNORIA

### Expensive

**Continentale ★★★** Everything about the Continentale is cool, and the effect is achieved without a hint of frostiness. Rooms are uncompromisingly modern, decorated in bright-white and bathed in natural light—even the deluxe units built into a medieval riverside tower, which have mighty walls and medieval-sized windows (that is, small). Standard rooms are large for Florence, and there's a 1950s feel to the overall styling. The top-floor **La Terrazza ★★** (p. 702) mixes Florence's best rooftop cocktails.

Vicolo dell'Oro 6R. www.lungarnocollection.com. ✆ **055-27-262.** 43 units. Doubles 220€–730€ double. Bus: C3 or D. **Amenities:** Bar; concierge; gym; spa; free Wi-Fi.

## NEAR PIAZZA SANTA TRÍNITA

### Moderate

**Davanzati ★★** Although installed inside a historic building, the Davanzati never rests on its medieval laurels: There is a laptop in every room and HD movies streamed to your TV. Rooms are simply decorated in the Tuscan style, with color-washed walls; half-canopies over the beds add a little flourish. Room 100 is probably the best family hotel room in Florence, full of nooks, crannies, and split levels that give the adults and the kids a sense of private space.

Via Porta Rossa 5 (at Piazza Davanzati). www.hoteldavanzati.it. ✆ **055-286-666.** 25 units. 122€–199€ double; 152€–229€ superior (sleeping up to 4). Rates include breakfast. Bus: C2. **Amenities:** Bar; babysitting; concierge; free Wi-Fi.

## NEAR SANTA MARIA NOVELLA

### Inexpensive

**Plus Florence ★★** There's quite simply nowhere in Florence with as many services for your buck, including seasonal indoor and outdoor swimming pools, all in a price bracket where you are usually fortunate to get an en suite bathroom (and Plus has those, too). The best rooms in this large, well-equipped hostel are in the new wing, which houses private rooms only. Units here are dressed in taupe and brown, with subtle uplighting and enough space (in some) for up to four beds. The only minuses: an un-picturesque building; and the location, between two busy roads (request a room facing the internal courtyard if you are a light sleeper).

Via Santa Caterina d'Alessandria 15. www.plushotels.com/plusflorence. ✆ **055-462-8934.** 187 units. Doubles 40€–100€ double. Bus: 8, 12, or 20. **Amenities:** Restaurant; bar; concierge; gym; 2 swimming pools; sauna (winter only); free Wi-Fi.

## NEAR SAN MARCO & SANTISSIMA ANNUNZIATA

### Expensive

**Residence Hilda ★★** There's not a hint of the Renaissance here: These mini-apartments are all bright-white decor and designer soft furnishings, with stripped-wood flooring and modern gadgetry. Each is spacious, cool in summer, and totally soundproofed against Florence's permanent background noise. Each apartment also has a mini-kitchen, kitted out just fine for preparing a simple meal—ideal if you have kids in tow. Unusually for apartments, they are bookable by the single night and upward.

Via dei Servi 40 (2 blocks north of the Duomo). www.residencehilda.com. ✆ **055-288-021.** 12 units. 2–4 person apartments 150€–450€ per night. Bus: C1, 6, 19, 31, or 32. **Amenities:** Babysitting; concierge; room service; free Wi-Fi.

### Moderate

**Loggiato dei Serviti ★★** Stay here to experience Florence as the gentlemen and lady visitors of the Grand Tour did. For starters, the building is a genuine Renaissance landmark, built in the 1520s. There is a sense of faded grandeur and unconventional luxury throughout—no gadgetry or chromotherapy showers here, but you will find rooms with writing desks and vintage "occasional tables" dressed with lamps. No unit is small, but most of the standard rooms lack a view of either Brunelleschi's dome or the perfect piazza outside: An upgrade to a Superior represents good value. Air-conditioning is pretty much the only concession to the 21st century—and you will love it that way.

Piazza Santissima Annunziata 3. www.loggiatodeiservitihotel.it. ✆ **055-289-592.** 38 units. Doubles 130€–330€, includes breakfast. Bus: C1, 6, 19, 31, or 32. **Amenities:** Concierge; free Wi-Fi.

## NEAR SANTA CROCE

### Inexpensive

**Locanda Orchidea ★** Over several visits to Florence, this has been a go-to inn for stays on a tight budget. Rooms range over two floors of a historic *palazzo*. The best rooms upstairs face a quiet, leafy rear courtyard. Furniture is a fun mix of mismatched flea-market finds and secondhand pieces; tiled floors and bold-print wallpaper and fabrics keep up the charmingly outdated feel. Note that bathrooms are shared (they have good water pressure), and there is no air-conditioning or onsite breakfast. But the value, character, and welcome are hard to beat in this price bracket.

Borgo degli Albizi 11 (close to Piazza San Pier Maggiore). www.hotelorchideaflorence.it. ✆ **055-248-0346.** 7 units. Doubles 45€–75€. Bus: C1 or C2. **Amenities:** Free Wi-Fi.

## ALTERNATIVE ACCOMMODATIONS

An alternative budget option is to stay in a religious house. A few **monasteries and convents** in the center receive guests for a modest fee,

### Eat Like a Local: Florence

Florence's culinary trademarks are seasonality and simplicity; it's almost the antithesis of "French" cooking, with its multiple processes. The main ingredient for almost any savory dish is Tuscan olive oil, adored for its low acidity. The typical pasta is wide, flat *pappardelle,* generally tossed with a game sauce such as *lepre* (hare) or *cinghiale* (boar). Meat is usually the centerpiece of any *secondo:* A *bistecca alla fiorentina* is the classic main dish, a T-bone–like wedge of meat. An authentic *fiorentina* should be cut only from the white Chianina breed of cattle.

including the **Suore di Santa Elisabetta,** Viale Michelangiolo 46 (near Piazza Ferrucci; www.csse-roma.eu; ✆ **055-681-1884**), in a colonial villa just south of the Ponte San Niccolò. The **Istituto Oblate dell'Assunzione,** Borgo Pinti 15 (✆ **055-2480-582**), has simple rooms in a Medici-era building ranged around a courtyard garden in the lively area east of the center. The easiest way to build an itinerary in Florence and beyond is via U.S.–based agent **MonasteryStays.com**. Remember that most religious houses have a curfew, generally 11pm or midnight.

## Where to Eat

Florence is awash with restaurants, though many in the densely touristy areas (around the Duomo, Piazza della Signoria, Piazza della Repubblica, and Ponte Vecchio) are of low quality, charge high prices, or both. Ipoint out a few that are well worth a visit. The highest concentrations of excellent *ristoranti* and *trattorie* are around Santa Croce and across the river in the Oltrarno and San Frediano. **Reservations** are strongly recommended if you have your heart set on eating anywhere, especially at dinner on weekends.

### NEAR THE DUOMO

#### Inexpensive

**I Fratellini ★** LIGHT FARE This hole-in-the-wall has been serving food to go since 1875. The drill is simple: Choose your sandwich filling, pick a drink, then eat your fast-filled roll on the curb opposite or find a perch in a nearby piazza. There are around 30 fillings to choose from, including the usual Tuscan meats and cheeses—salami, *pecorino* cheese, cured ham—and more flamboyant combos such as goat cheese and Calabrian spicy salami or *bresaola* (air-dried beef) and wild rocket salad. No credit cards.

Via dei Cimatori 38R (at corner of Via Calzaiuoli). ✆ **055-239-6096.** Sandwiches 3€. Bus: C2. Daily 9:30am–dusk (July–Aug often closed Sun). Closed 2 weeks in mid-Aug.

### NEAR PIAZZA DELLA SIGNORIA

#### Expensive

**Ora d'Aria ★★★** CONTEMPORARY TUSCAN If you want to see what the latest generation of Tuscan chefs can do in a kitchen, this place should top your list. Dishes are subtle and creative, and use traditional Tuscan ingredients in an original way. Expect the likes of spaghetti with extract of peppers, capers, and smoked ricotta or beef tartare marinated in beer with black truffle and roasted melon. If you can't stretch the budget for a dinner here, book a table at lunch to taste simpler, cheaper (12€–18€) dishes such as cold salad of salt cod with Pratese vermouth and sweet potato, served in full-size or half-price "tapas" portions. Reservations required.

Via dei Georgofili 11–13R (off Via Lambertesca). www.oradariaristorante.com. ✆ **055-200-1699.** Mains 32€–45€ (at dinner); tasting menu 70€–75€. Bus: C3 or D. Tues–Sat 12:30–2:30pm; Mon–Sat 7:30–10pm. Closed 3 weeks in Aug.

## NEAR SAN LORENZO

### Inexpensive

**Mario ★** FLORENTINE There is no doubt that this traditional market workers' trattoria is now firmly on the tourist trail. But Mario's clings to the traditions and ethos it adopted when it first fired up the burners in its kitchen 60 years ago. Food is simple, hearty, and served at communal benches—"check in" on arrival and you will be offered seats together wherever they come free. Think *zuppa di fagioli* (bean soup) followed by the traditional Tuscan piquant beef stew, *peposo*. No reservations.

Via Rosina 2R (north corner of Piazza Mercato Centrale). www.trattoriamario.com. ✆ **055-218-550.** Mains 7.50€–14€. Closed Aug. Bus: C1. Mon–Sat noon–3:30pm.



## NEAR SANTA MARIA NOVELLA

### Moderate

**Osteria Pastella ★★** TUSCAN There is an air of sophistication about this place that opened near Piazza Santa Maria Novella in 2014. Pasta is handmade in the window, and the offerings includes tortelloni filled with 3 types of ricotta and served with a light seasonal sauce, perhaps butter and sage or artichokes. The *bistecca alla fiorentina* (grilled T-bone–like steak) is up there with the best in the city. Grand, upcycled dining room furniture, a complimentary glass of prosecco while you browse the menu, and a *chanteuse* background soundtrack set the mood for classic Tuscan food.

Via della Scala 17R. www.osteriapastella.it. ✆ **055-267-0240**. Mains 15€–23€. Bus: C2. Daily 11:45am–3pm and 6:30–10:30pm. Closed 2 weeks in Nov.

**Pescheria San Pietro ★★** SEAFOOD It takes a big serving of confidence to open a seafood restaurant—on two floors—in one of Florence's less-fashionable quarters. This place, opened in 2014, has the chops (and the chefs) to pull it off. The fishy focus is unwavering: A route through the menu might take in tuna carpaccio, followed by *tagliatelle* with baby sardines and cherry tomatoes, then a *gran fritto* (mixed fry) of seafood and seasonal vegetables in light tempura batter. Portions are generous.

Via Alamanni 7R. www.pescheriasanpietro.it. ✆ **055-238-2749.** Mains 14€–18€. Bus: C2, D, 2, 13, 28, 29, 30, 35, 36, or 37/Tram: T1. Daily 11am–11pm.

## NEAR SAN MARCO

### Moderate

**Da Tito ★★** TUSCAN/FLORENTINE Sure, they ham it up a little for the tourists, but every night feels like party night at one of central Florence's rare genuine neighborhood trattorias. (And for that reason, it's usually packed—book ahead.) The welcome and the dishes are authentically Florentine, with a few modern Italian curveballs: Start, perhaps, with the *risotto con piselli e guanciale* (rice with fresh peas and cured pork cheek) before going on to a traditional grill such as *lombatina di vitella* (veal chop steak). The neighborhood location, a 10-minute walk north of San Lorenzo, and mixed clientele help keep quality consistent.

Via San Gallo 112R. www.trattoriadatito.it. ✆ **055-472-475.** Mains 12€–18€. Bus: C1, 1, 7, or 25. Mon–Sat 12:30–2pm and 7:30–10:30pm.

## NEAR SANTA CROCE

### Moderate

**Brac ★★** VEGETARIAN An artsy cafe/bookshop for most of the day, at lunch and dinner this place turns into one of Florence's best spots for vegetarian and vegan food. There are plenty of seasonal salads and creative pasta dishes, but a *piatto unico* works out to be the best value for hungry diners: one combo plate loaded with three dishes from the main menu, perhaps a tomato, onion, and oregano salad; potato and broccoli lasagne with ginger and parsley sauce; plus an eggplant and mozzarella *pane carasau* (Sardinian flatbread). Booking at dinner is a must in high season and on weekends.

Via dei Vagellai 18R. www.libreriabrac.net. ✆ **055-094-4877.** Mains 10€–14€. Bus: C1, C3, or 23. Mon–Sat 10am–midnight, Sun noon–midnight.

## IN THE OLTRARNO, SAN NICCOLÒ & SAN FREDIANO

### Expensive

**iO: Osteria Personale ★★** CONTEMPORARY TUSCAN There's a definite hipster vibe, with the stripped brick walls and young staff, but the food ethos is unshakable. Ingredients are staunchly Tuscan and traditional, but combined in a way you may not have seen before, on a menu that rejects pasta. The menu is modular, and diners are free to combine seafood, meat, and vegetarian dishes in any order. Perhaps tempura zucchini flowers stuffed with tomato sorbet followed by guinea-hen "Caesar salad" carbonara.

Borgo San Frediano 167R (at Piazza di Verzaia). www.io-osteriapersonale.it. ✆ **055-933-1341.** Mains 13€–21€; tasting menus 40€ 4 dishes, 55€ 6 dishes. Bus: D or 6. Mon–Sat 7:30–10:30pm. Closed 10 days in Jan and all of Aug.

### Inexpensive

**GustaPizza ★★** PIZZA Florentines aren't known for their pizza-making skills, so I guess it's just as well this place is run by Calabrians. Pizzas are in the Naples style, with fluffy crusts, doughy bases, and just the classic toppings on a menu that you could write on the back of a napkin:

Arugula and Parmesan pizza at GustaPizza.

Margherita (cheese, tomato, basil) and Napoli (cheese, tomatoes, anchovies, oregano, capers) are joined by a couple of simple specials, such as mozzarella and basil pesto. It is self-service, but there are a few tables if you want to eat with a knife and fork (no reservations). On warm evenings, take the pizza out to the steps of Santo Spirito, around the corner.

Via Maggio 46R. ✆ **055-285-068.** Pizzas 4.50€–8€. Tues-Sun 11:30am–3pm and 7–11pm. Closed 3 weeks in Aug. Bus: D, 11, 36, or 37.



## Shopping

After Milan, Florence is **Italy's top shopping city**—beating even the capital. Here's what to buy: leather, fashion, shoes, marbleized paper, hand-embroidered linens, artisan and craft items, Tuscan wines, handmade jewelry, *pietre dure* (known also as "Florentine mosaic," inlaid semiprecious stones), and antiques.

The cream of the crop of Florentine shopping lines both sides of elegant **Via de' Tornabuoni,** with an extension along **Via della Vigna Nuova** and other surrounding streets. Here you'll find the big Florentine fashion names like **Gucci ★** (at no. 73R; www.gucci.com; ✆ **055-264-011**), **Pucci ★** (at no. 22R; www.emiliopucci.com; ✆ **055-265-8082**), and **Ferragamo ★** (at no. 4R; www.ferragamo.com; ✆ **055-292-123**) ensconced in old palaces or minimalist boutiques. A shrine to scents and skincare, **Officina Profumo-Farmaceutica di Santa Maria Novella ★★★,** Via della Scala 16 (www.smnovella.it; ✆ **055-216-276**), is Florence's most historic herbal pharmacy, with roots in the 17th century, when it was founded by Dominicans based in the convent of Santa Maria Novella. Nothing is cheap, but the perfumes, cosmetics,

## THIS CALLS FOR A gelato BREAK!

Florence has a fair claim to being the birthplace of gelato, and has some of the world's best *gelaterie*—but many, many poor imitations, too. Steer clear of spots around the major attractions with air-fluffed mountains of ice cream and flavors so full of artificial colors they glow in the dark.

**Carapina ★★** (Via Lambertesca 18R; www.carapina.it; ✆ **055-291-128**) adheres to militant seasonality, ensuring that the fruit gelato here is the best in the center.

Florence is the birthplace of gelato.

**Gelateria della Passera ★★** (Via Toscanella 15R [at Piazza della Passera]; www.gelaterialapassera.wordpress.com; ✆ **055-291-882**) mixes up milk-free water ices that are some of the most intensely flavored in the city, and relatively low in sugary sweetness. Try the likes of pink grapefruit or jasmine tea gelato.

**Gelateria de' Neri ★** (Via dei Neri 9R; ✆ **055-210-034**) offers a large range of fruit, white, and chocolate flavors here, but nothing overelaborate. If the ricotta and fig flavor is on, you are in luck.



moisturizers, and other products are made from the finest natural ingredients and packaged exquisitely.

**Via Roma** and **Via dei Calzaiuoli** are packed with mainstream stores such as major department stores **Coin,** Via dei Calzaiuoli 56R (www.coin.it; ✆ **055-280-531**) and **La Rinascente,** Piazza della Repubblica (www.rinascente.it; ✆ **055-219-113**) and quality chains such as Geox and Zara. Just across the river is **Madova ★,** Via Guicciardini 1R (www.madova.com; ✆ **055-239-6526**), the best city retailer for handmade leather gloves, lined with silk, cashmere, or lambswool.

Behind Santa Croce is the **Scuola del Cuoio ★★** (www.scuoladelcuoio.com; ✆ **055-244-534**), Florence's leading leather school and also open house for visitors. You can watch trainee artisans at work (Mon–Fri only) then visit the shop to buy items made from the best soft leather. Nearby is the daily flea market, the **Mercato delle Pulci,** in Piazza dei Ciompi. Rifle through the little shacks in search of costume jewelry, Tiffany lamps, vintage postcards, weird objects, and other ephemera. At the center's main food market, the **Mercato Centrale ★,** Piazza del Mercato Centrale, you can browse for and taste cheeses, salamis and cured hams, Tuscan wines, and more. It's picnic-packing heaven. The **Mercato di San Lorenzo ★,** around and along Via dell'Ariento, is the city's tourist street market and a fun place to pick up T-shirts, marbleized paper, or a souvenir. The market runs daily; watch out for pickpockets.

## Entertainment & Nightlife

At tourist offices, pick up free monthly publication ***Informacittà*** (www.informacitta.net), which is strong on theater and other arts events, as well as markets. ***Firenze Spettacolo,*** a 2€ Italian-language monthly sold at most newsstands, is the most detailed and up-to-date listing of nightlife, arts, and entertainment.

Florence has two symphony orchestras and a fine music school in nearby Fiesole. Get tickets to all cultural and musical events online; they will send an e-mail with collection instructions or buy in person at **Box Office,** Via delle Carceri 1 (www.boxofficetoscana.it; ✆ **055-210-804**). The vast new **Teatro dell'Opera ★★,** Viale Fratelli Rosselli 7R (www.operadifirenze.it; ✆ **055-277-9350**), seats up to 1,800 in a daring modernist concert hall.

You will find plenty of tourist-oriented action in **bars** around the city's main squares. **Cantinetta dei Verrazzano ★★,** Via dei Tavolini 18R (www.verrazzano.com; ✆ **055-268-590**), is one of the coziest little wine bars in the center, decked out with antique wooden wine cabinets in genuine *enoteca* style. Wines come from the first-rate Verrazzano estate in Chianti. Rooftop cocktails right by the Ponte Vecchio at **La Terrazza at the Continentale ★★,** Vicolo dell'Oro 6R (✆ **055-27-262**), are unforgettable. For something a little livelier—with a younger and more local focus—check out **Borgo San Frediano, Piazza Santo Spirito,** or the northern end of **Via de' Macci,** close to where it meets Via Pietrapiana. **Via de' Benci** is usually buzzing around *aperitivo* time, and is popular with an expat crowd. Nearby **Beer House Club ★★,** Corso Tintori 34R (www.beerhouseclub.it; ✆ **055-247-6763**), serves the best artisan beers from Italy and farther afield. **Via de' Renai** and the bars of San Niccolò around the **Porta San Miniato** are often lively too, with a mixed crowd of tourists and locals.

## Side Trips from Florence

### SIENA ★★★

Siena is a medieval city of brick. Viewed from the summit of the Palazzo Pubblico's tower, its sea of roof tiles blends into a landscape of steep, twisting stone alleys. This cityscape hides dozens of Gothic palaces and pastry shops galore, longstanding neighborhood rivalries, and painted altarpieces of unsurpassed elegance.

Founded as a Roman colony by Emperor Augustus, the city enjoyed its heyday in the 13th and 14th centuries; in 1270, Sienese merchants established the Council of Nine, an oligarchy that ruled over Siena's greatest republican era, when civic projects and artistic prowess reached their heights. Artists like Duccio, Simone Martini, and the Lorenzetti brothers invented a distinctive Sienese art style, a highly developed Gothicism that was an artistic foil to the emerging Florentine Renaissance. Then in 1348, a plague known as the "Black Death" hit the city, killing perhaps three-quarters of the population, destroying the social fabric, and devastating the economy. Siena never recovered, and much of it has barely changed since.

### Essentials

To get there, the **bus** is much more convenient than the train, because Siena's rail station is way outside of town. Siena Mobilità/SITA (www.tiemmespa.it) runs express (*rapida;* 75 min.) and slower buses (95 min.) from Florence's main bus station to Siena's Piazza Gramsci. There is no need to reserve ahead of time: Buses run at least hourly in the morning; try not to make the trip on a Sunday, when the bus service is much reduced. The last bus back usually departs around 8:45pm (but check ahead).

If you have a rental **car,** there's a fast road direct from Florence (it has no route number; follow the green or blue signs toward Siena), or take the scenic route, down the **Chiantigiana wine road,** the SS222. But the bus makes more sense for a day trip.

### Exploring Siena

Be prepared for one *seriously* busy day (and even then you can't see it all). Several stepped alleys lead down into **Piazza del Campo ("Il Campo") ★★,** arguably the most beautiful piazza in Italy. Crafted like a sloping scallop shell, the Campo was first laid out in the 1100s on the former site of the Roman forum. The herringbone brick pavement is divided by white marble lines into nine sections representing the city's medieval ruling body, the Council of Nine.

Overlooking the Campo, the crenellated town hall, the **Palazzo Pubblico ★★** (built 1297–1310) is the city's finest Gothic palace, and the **Museo Civico** (**✆ 0577-292-226**) inside is home to Siena's best artworks. On the wall of the Sala del Mappamondo is Simone Martini's



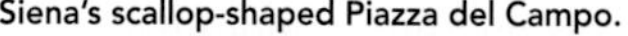
Siena's scallop-shaped Piazza del Campo.

1315 ***Maestà*** **★★,** following the city's tradition of honoring the Virgin Mary (she is Siena's traditional protector). Next door, in the Sala della Pace, Ambrogio Lorenzetti painted his ***Allegories of Good and Bad Government*** **★★★** (1338), full of details of medieval Sienese life, and painted to provide encouragement to the city's governing body, which met inside the room. The museum is open daily from 10am to 6pm (until 7pm Mar 16–Oct). Admission costs 8€, 4.50€ students and seniors ages 65 and over.

Having seen Siena's civic heart, visit the religious monuments of **Piazza del Duomo** (www.operaduomo.siena.it) on a single ticket: The **OPA SI Pass** costs 12€ and is sold from booths in the piazza. Siena's **Duomo ★★** is stuffed with art treasures, including Bernini's **Cappella Chigi ★** (1659) and the **Libreria Piccolomini ★★,** frescoed in 1507 with scenes from the life of Sienese Pope Pius II, by Pinturicchio. If you are visiting between August and October, you will find the cathedral's **floor ★★★** uncovered; it is a mosaic of 59 etched and inlaid marble panels created between 1372 and 1547 by Siena's top artists, including Domenico di Bartolo, Matteo di Giovanni, Pinturicchio, and especially, Domenico Beccafumi. The **Battistero (Baptistery) ★★** has a baptismal font (1417–30) with gilded brass panels cast by the foremost Sienese and Florentine sculptors of the early Renaissance, including Jacopo della Quercia, Lorenzo Ghiberti, and Donatello. Inside the **Museo dell'Opera del Duomo ★** is Duccio di Buoninsegna's 1311 ***Maestà*** **★★★,** Siena's most precious work of art, which used to sit on the cathedral's high altar. It shows the Virgin and Child in majesty, adored by a litany of saints including St. Paul (holding the sword) and St. John the Baptist (pointing at Jesus and wearing animal skins). From inside the museum, climb to the top of the **Facciatone ★★** for the best view in Siena, over the rooftops and down into the Campo. Opening hours for most of the Piazza del Duomo sights are 10:30am to 5:30pm, although it stretches to 6 or 7pm in summer. The cathedral is closed to visitors on Sunday mornings.

You just about have time for **Santa Maria della Scala ★★** (www.santamariadellascala.com; ✆ **0577-534-571**), opposite the cathedral. An "old hospital" might not sound too enticing, but this huge building has treasures hidden away in its eerie corridors. The **Pellegrinaio ★★** was frescoed in the 1440s with sometimes grisly scenes of life in this medieval hospital. The Old Sacristy has an even more gruesome ***Massacre of the Innocents*** **★★,** painted in 1482 by Matteo di Giovanni. Downstairs is the spooky oratory where Sienese St. Catherine used to pray (and stay) during the night; **Bambimus,** where art is displayed at child's-eye height; and the city's **National Archaeological Museum** on the labyrinthine lower floor. Admission costs 9€, 8€ students and seniors ages 65 and over. Opening hours are 10:30am to 6:30pm (closed Tues in winter). It's usually much quieter than other places in the city—and Ihave no idea why.

### Where to Eat

Sienese cooking is rustic and simple, and makes liberal use of sweet meat from the local *Cinta Senese* breed of pig. **L'Osteria ★,** Via de' Rossi 81 (✆ **0577-287-592**) does a mean line in local grilled meats, including veal and *Cinta*. Mains range from 8€ to 21€. It is closed Sundays. At the **Osteria del Gusto ★,** Via dei Fusari 9 (✆ **0577-271-076**), pasta dishes are a great value, and served in filling portions. Think *pici* (hand-rolled, fat spaghetti) served with a *ragù* of *Cinta* and porcini mushrooms for around the 9€ mark.

If you prefer a gourmet sandwich to a sit-down meal, **Gino Cacino di Angelo ★★,** Piazza del Mercato 31 (✆ **0577-223-076**), is the place to head for aged pecorino cheese, Tuscan salami, anchovies, and pretty much everything else. The best gelato in the city is made at **Kopa Kabana ★,** Via de' Rossi 52 (www.gelateriakopakabana.it; ✆ **0577-223-744**).

## SAN GIMIGNANO ★★

The scene that hits you when you pass through the Porta San Giovanni gate, inside the walls of **San Gimignano,** is thoroughly medieval. The center is peppered with the tall towers that have made *San Gimignano delle Belle Torri* ("of the beautiful towers") the poster child for Italian hill towns everywhere. There were at one time around 70 of the things spiking the sky above this little village, yet only a dozen or so remain. The spires started rising in the bad old days of the 1200s, partly to defend against outside invaders but mostly as command centers for San Gimignano's warring families. Several successive waves of the plague that swept through (1348, 1464, and 1631 were especially bad) caused an economy based on textiles and hosting pilgrims traveling the Via Francigena to crumble. San Gimignano slowly became a provincial backwater.

**San Gimignano's skyline framed by vineyards and olive groves.**

By the time tourism began picking up in the 19th century, visitors found a preserved medieval village of decaying towers.

### Essentials

As with Siena, your best bet is the **bus.** From Florence's main bus station, Siena Mobilità/SITA (www.tiemmespa.it) runs buses for most of the day. It is a 50-minute journey to Poggibonsi, and many of the services are timed to meet the connection to San Gimignano (a further 25 min.). Buy through-tickets for the whole journey in Florence. The last bus back to Florence usually departs around 8pm, but check ahead. Try not to make the day trip on a Sunday, when the bus service is much reduced.

Arriving by **car,** take the Poggibonsi Nord exit off the Florence-Siena highway or the SS2. San Gimignano is 12km (7½ miles) from Poggibonsi, through very pretty country. The town is surrounded by well-signposted car parks.

### Exploring San Gimignano

Anchoring the town, at the top of Via San Giovanni, are its two interlocking triangular *piazze:* **Piazza della Cisterna ★★,** centered on a 1237 well, and **Piazza del Duomo,** flanked by the city's main church and civic palace. It is easy to find them: From any direction, just keep walking uphill.

The town's key art site is the **Collegiata ★★,** Piazza del Duomo (www.duomosangimignano.it; ✆ **0577-286-300**). The right wall of this collegiate church was frescoed from 1333 to 1341—most likely by Lippo Memmi—with three levels of **New Testament scenes** (22 in all) on the life and Passion of Christ. In 1367, Bartolo di Fredi frescoed the left wall with 26 scenes from the **Old Testament,** and Taddeo di Bartolo provided a gruesome ***Last Judgment*** just above and left of the main door, in 1410.

In 1468, Giuliano da Maiano built the **Cappella di Santa Fina ★★** off the right aisle, and his brother Benedetto carved the relief panels for the altar. Florentine Renaissance painter Domenico Ghirlandaio decorated the tiny chapel's walls with some of his finest, airiest works: In 1475, he frescoed two scenes summing up the life of Santa Fina, a local girl who, although never officially canonized, is one of San Gimignano's patron saints. Admission to the Collegiata costs 4€, 2€ ages 6 to 17. Hours are April through October Monday to Friday 10am to 7:30pm, Saturday 10am to 5:30pm, and Sunday 12:30 to 7:30pm. From November to March it is open Monday to Saturday 10am to 5pm, Sunday 12:30 to 5pm. It is closed altogether in the second half of November and the second half of January.

The town's small **Museo Civico e Pinacoteca (Civic Art Museum) ★,** Piazza del Duomo 2 (✆ **0577-990-312**), inside the Palazzo del Popolo, houses a ***Maestà*** **★★** (1317) by Sienese painter Lippo Memmi, and some unique, and rather racy medieval "wedding night" frescoes by Lippo's father, Memmo di Filippuccio. Admission costs 6€.

The same ticket gets you up the tallest tower still standing, the **Torre Grossa ★.** From 54m (175 ft.) up, you can see for miles. The museum and tower are open daily 9:30am to 7pm April through September, 11am to 5:30pm otherwise.

At **Sant Agostino,** Piazza Sant'Agostino (✆ **0577-907-012**), Florentine painter Benozzo Gozzoli spent 2 years frescoing the choir behind the main altar floor-to-ceiling with scenes rich in architectural detail from the ***Life of St. Augustine*** **★★.** The church is open daily from 7am to noon and 3 to 7pm (closes 6pm Nov–Mar). Admission is free.

### Where to Eat

The best restaurant for a flying visit is **Chiribiri ★,** Piazzetta della Madonna 1 (www.ristorantechiribiri.it; ✆ **0577-941-948**), because it is open all day so you can dine early before heading for the bus or car parks. It is a small place, with a simple, well-executed menu of Italian and Tuscan classics such as lasagna, *osso buco,* or wild boar stew. Mains are priced fairly—a welcome change from many spots—at 8€ to 12€. No credit cards. For a more snacklike meal try **diVinorum,** Via degli Innocenti 5 (www.divinorumwinebar.com; ✆ **0577-907-192**), for wines by the glass, and *bruschettone* (large bruschettas; 5€–8.50€) loaded with topping combos, such as provolone cheese, ham, and radicchio (bitter purple leaves).

The town's essential foodie stop isn't a restaurant at all, however, but the **Gelateria Dondoli "di Piazza" ★★,** Piazza della Cisterna 4 (www.gelateriadipiazza.com; ✆ **0577-942-244**), for creative combinations like raspberry and rosemary (it works) and the signature *crema di Santa Fina,* made with saffron.

# VENICE

Nothing in the world quite looks like Venice. This vast, floating city of grand palaces, elegant bridges, gondolas, and canals is a magnificent spectacle, truly magical when approached for the first time, when its golden domes and soaring bell towers seem to emerge from the ocean. Although it can sometimes appear that Venice is little more than an open-air museum, where tourists always outnumber—by a large margin—the locals, it is surprisingly easy to lose the crowds. Indeed, the best way to enjoy Venice is to simply get lost in its maze of narrow, enchanting streets, stumbling upon a quiet *campo* (square), market stall or cafe off the beaten track, where even the humblest medieval church might contain a work by Tiepolo, Titian, or Tintoretto.

## Essentials

Venice's tourism office website is www.turismovenezia.it.

**ARRIVING** Flights land at the **Aeroporto di Venezia Marco Polo,** 7km (4¼ miles) north of the city on the mainland (www.veniceairport.it;

© **041-2609260**). The **ATVO airport shuttle bus** (www.atvo.it; © **0421-594672**) connects with Piazzale Roma not far from Venice's Santa Lucia train station (and the closest point to Venice's attractions accessible by car or bus). Buses leave for/from the airport about every 30 minutes, cost 6€ (11€ return), and make the trip in about 20 minutes. The local **ACTV bus no. 5** (© **041-2424**) also costs 6€, also takes 20 minutes, and runs between two and four times an hour depending on the time of day; the best option here is to buy the combined ACTV and "Nave" ticket for 12€, which includes your first *vaporetto* ride at a slight discount (the *vaporetto* is the seagoing streetcar of Venice, which goes to all parts of the city). With either bus, you'll have to walk to or from the final stop at Piazzale Roma to the nearby ***vaporetto*** stop for the final connection to your hotel. It's rare to see porters, so pack light. A **land taxi** from the airport to Piazzale Roma (where you get the *vaporetto*) will run to about 40€.

A more evocative way to arrive in Venice is by sea. For 15€, 14€ if you buy online, the **Cooperative San Marco/Alilaguna** (www.alilaguna.it; © **041-2401701**) operates a large *motoscafo* (shuttle boat) service from the airport (with stops at Murano), arriving after about 1¼ hours in Piazza San Marco. The *Linea Blu* (blue line) runs almost every 30 minutes from about 6am to midnight. The *Linea Arancio* (orange line) has the same frequency, costs the same, and takes the same amount of time to arrive at San Marco, but gets there through the Grand Canal, which is more spectacular and offers the possibility to get off at one of the stops along the way. If you arrive at Piazza San Marco and your hotel isn't in the area, you'll have to make a connection at the *vaporetto* launches.

A good final alternative for airport transfers is the newish **Venice Shuttle** (www.venicelink.com; daily 8am–10pm; 6–8 people), a shared

The Grand Canal at dusk.

water taxi that for just 27€ to 33€ will whisk you directly to many hotels and most of the major locations in the city. You must reserve online.

A **private water taxi** (20–30 min. to/from the airport) is convenient but costly—there is a fixed 100€ fee to arrive in the city, for up to five passengers with one bag each (10€ more for each extra person up to a maximum of 12, and another 10€ for 10pm–7am arrivals). Try **Consorzio Motoscafi Venezia** (www.motoscafivenezia.it; ✆ **041-5222303**) or **Venezia Taxi** (www.veneziataxi.it; ✆ **041-723112**).

**Trains** from Rome (3¾ hr.), Milan (2½ hr.), Florence (2 hr.), and all over Europe arrive at the **Stazione Venezia Santa Lucia.** To get there, all must pass through (although not necessarily stop at) a station marked Venezia-Mestre. Don't be confused: Mestre is a charmless industrial city that's the last stop on the mainland. Occasionally trains end in Mestre, in which case you have to catch one of the frequent 10-minute shuttles connecting with Venice proper.

On exiting, you'll find the Grand Canal immediately in front of you, with the docks for a number of *vaporetto* lines to your left and right. Head to the booths to your left, near the bridge, to catch either of the two lines plying the Grand Canal: the no. 2 express, which stops only at the San Marcuola, Rialto Bridge, San Tomà, San Samuele, and Accademia before hitting San Marco (26 min. total); and the slower no. 1, which makes 13 stops before arriving at San Marco (a 33-min. trip). Both leave every 10 minutes or so.

The only wheels you'll see in Venice are those attached to luggage. Venice is a city of canals and narrow alleys. **No cars are allowed,** or more to the point, no cars could drive through the narrow streets and over the footbridges—even the police, fire department, and ambulance services use boats. Arriving in Venice by car is problematic and expensive—and downright exasperating if it's high season and the parking facilities are full (they often are). You can drive across the Ponte della Libertà from Mestre to Venice, but you can go no farther than Piazzale Roma at the Venice end, where many garages eagerly await your euros. The rates vary; for example, the public **ASM garage** (www.asmvenezia.it; ✆ **041-2727111**) charges 26€ for a 24-hour period, while private outfit **Garage San Marco** (www.garagesanmarco.it; ✆ **041-5232213**) costs 30€ for 24 hours.

**CITY LAYOUT** Even armed with the best map, expect to get a bit lost in Venice. Keep in mind as you wander hopelessly among the *calli* (streets) and *campi* (squares) that the city wasn't built to make sense to people on foot but rather to those plying its canals. Snaking through the city like an inverted S is the **Grand Canal,** the wide main artery of aquatic Venice.

The city is divided into six *sestieri* ("sixths," or districts or wards): **Cannaregio, Castello, San Marco, San Polo, Santa Croce,** and **Dorsoduro.** In addition to the six *sestieri* that cluster around the Grand Canal, there are a host of islands in the Venice lagoon. Opposite Piazza

## CRUISING CANALS BY gondola

A leisurely cruise along the **Grand Canal ★★★** from Piazza San Marco to the train station (Ferrovia)—or the reverse—is one of Venice's must-dos. It's the world's most unusual Main Street, a watery boulevard whose *palazzi* have been converted into condos. Lower water-lapped floors are now deserted, but the higher floors are still coveted by the city's titled families, who have inhabited these residences for centuries.

As much a symbol of Venice as the winged lion of St. Mark, the **gondola ride ★★★** is one of Europe's great traditions, incredibly and inexplicably expensive but truly as romantic as it looks (detractors who write it off as too touristy have likely never tried it). The official, fixed rate is 80€ for a 40-minute tour (100€ 7pm–8am), with up to six passengers, and 40€ for each additional 20 minutes (50€ at night). That's not a typo: 150€ for a 1-hour evening cruise. ***Note:*** Although the price is fixed by the city, a good negotiator at the right time of day (when there is not too much business) can sometimes grab a small discount, for a shorter ride. And at these ridiculously inflated prices, there is no need to tip the gondolier.

Aim for late afternoon before sundown, when light works its magic with the reflections (and bring a bottle of Prosecco and glasses). Though the price is "fixed," establish with the gondolier the cost, time, and route (back canals are preferable to the trafficked Grand Canal). They're regulated by **Ente Gondola** (www.gondolavenezia.it; ✆ **041-5285075**), if you have questions or complaints.

Gondolas near the 16th-century Rialto Bridge.

San Marco and Dorsoduro is **La Giudecca,** a tranquil, mostly residential island that offers phenomenal views of San Marco. The **Lido di Venezia** is the city's sandy beach, a popular summer destination, while **San Michele** is the cemetery island where such celebrities as Stravinsky and

Diaghilev are buried. **Murano, Burano,** and **Torcello** are popular islands northeast of the city, accessible by *vaporetto.*

**GETTING AROUND** Aside from on boats, the only way to explore Venice is by **walking**—and by getting lost, repeatedly. You'll navigate many twisting streets whose names change constantly and don't appear on any map, and streets that may very well simply end in a blind alley or spill abruptly into a canal. As you wander, look for the ubiquitous yellow signs (well, *usually* yellow) whose arrows direct you toward five major landmarks: **Ferrovia** (the train station), **Piazzale Roma** (the parking garage), **Rialto Bridge** (one of four over the Grand Canal), **San Marco** (the main square), and the **Accademia** (the southernmost Grand Canal bridge).

The various *sestieri* are linked by a comprehensive *vaporetto* **(water bus/ferry)** system of about a dozen lines operated by **Azienda del Consorzio Trasporti Veneziano** (**ACTV;** www.actv.it; ✆ **041-5287886**). Transit maps are available at the tourist office and most ACTV stations. It's easier to get around on foot, as the *vaporetti* principally serve the Grand Canal, outskirts, and outer islands.

A ticket valid for 1 hour of travel on a *vaporetto* is a steep 7€; a 24-hour ticket is 20€. Most lines run every 10 to 15 minutes from 7am to midnight, and then hourly until morning. Most *vaporetto* docks (the only place you can buy tickets) post timetables. Note that not all docks sell tickets after dark. If you haven't bought a pass or extra tickets beforehand, you'll have to settle up with the conductor onboard (you'll have to find him—he won't come looking for you) or risk a stiff fine, no excuses accepted. All tickets must be validated in the yellow machines before boarding.

Just four bridges span the Grand Canal, and to fill in the gaps, *traghetti* skiffs (oversize gondolas rowed by two standing *gondolieri*) cross the Grand Canal at seven intermediate points. You'll find a station at the end of any street named Calle del Traghetto on your map and marked by a yellow sign with the black gondola symbol. The fare is 0.70€ for locals and 2€ for visitors.

*Taxi acquei* **(water taxis)** charge high prices and aren't for visitors watching their euros. The meter starts at 15€ and clicks at 2€ per minute. Each trip includes an allowance for 4 to 5 pieces of luggage—beyond that there's a surcharge of 3€ to 5€ per piece (rates differ slightly according to company and how you reserve a trip). Plus there's a 10€ supplement for service from 10pm to 7am, and a 5€ charge for taxis on-call. You can book trips with Consorzio Moscafi Venezia on-line at **www.motoscafivenezia.it** or call ✆ **041-5222303.** Six water-taxi stations serve key points in the city: the Ferrovia, Piazzale Roma, the Rialto Bridge, Piazza San Marco, the Lido, and Marco Polo Airport.

## The Neighborhoods in Brief

**SAN MARCO** The central *sestiere* is anchored by the magnificent **Piazza San Marco** and **St. Mark's Basilica** to the south and the

## carnevale **& OTHER EVENTS**

**Carnevale ★★★** was traditionally the celebration preceding Lent, the period of penitence and abstinence prior to Easter; its name is derived from the Latin *carnem levare*, meaning "to take meat away." Today it builds for 10 days until the big blowout, **Shrove Tuesday** (Fat Tuesday), when fireworks illuminate the Grand Canal, and Piazza San Marco is turned into a giant open-air ballroom for the masses. Book your hotel months ahead, especially for the 2 weekends prior to Shrove Tuesday.

In the 18th-century heyday of Carnevale in La Serenissima Republic, well-heeled revelers came from all over Europe to take part in festivities that began months prior to Lent and reached a raucous climax at midnight on Shrove Tuesday. Masks became ubiquitous, affording anonymity and the pardoning of a thousand sins; they permitted the fishmonger to attend the ball and dance with the baroness, and the properly married to carry on as if they were not. The doges condemned it and the popes denounced it, but nothing could dampen the Venetian Carnevale spirit until Napoléon arrived in 1797 and put an end to the festivities. Resuscitated in 1980 by local tourism powers, Carnevale is calmer nowadays, barely. It is a harlequin patchwork of musical and cultural events, many of them free of charge, which appeals to all ages, tastes, and budgets. Musical events are staged in the city's *piazze*—from reggae and zydeco to jazz and baroque. Special art exhibits are mounted at museums and galleries. Visit **www.carnevalevenezia.com** for details on upcoming events.

Venice also hosts the latest in modern and contemporary painting and sculpture from dozens of countries during the prestigious **Biennale d'Arte** (www.labiennale.org; ✆ **041-5218711**), one of the world's top international modern art shows. It fills the pavilions of the **Giardini** (public gardens) at the east end of Castello (with fringe events in the Arsenale), as well as in other spaces around the city, from June to November every odd-numbered year. The **Venice International Film Festival,** in August and September, is the most respected celebration of celluloid in Europe after Cannes. Films from all over the world are shown in the **Palazzo del Cinema** on the Lido as well as at various venues—and occasionally in some of the *campi*.

**Awaiting the start of a Carnevale parade.**

**Rialto Bridge** to the north; it's the most visited (and, as a result, the most expensive) of the *sestieri*. This area is laced with first-class hotels, but we'll give you some suggestions for staying in the heart of Venice without going broke.

**CASTELLO** This quarter, whose tony waterside esplanade **Riva degli Schiavoni** follows the Bacino di San Marco (St. Mark's Basin), begins just east of Piazza San Marco, skirting Venice's most congested area to the north and east. Riva degli Schiavoni can sometimes get so busy as to seem like Times Square on New Year's Eve, but if you head farther east in the direction of the Arsenale or inland away from the *bacino,* the crowds thin out, despite the presence of such major sights as the **Scuola di San Giorgio.**

**DORSODURO** The residential area of Dorsoduro is on the opposite side of the Accademia Bridge from San Marco. Known for the **Accademia** and **Peggy Guggenheim** museums, it is the largest of the *sestieri* and has been known as an artists' haven until recent escalations of rents forced much of the community to relocate. Good neighborhood restaurants, the lively **Campo Santa Margherita,** and the sunny quay called **le Zattere** (a favorite promenade and gelato stop) all add character and color.

**SAN POLO** This mixed-bag *sestiere* of residential corners and tourist sights stretches northwest of the Rialto Bridge to the church of **Santa Maria dei Frari** and the **Scuola di San Rocco.** The hub of activity at the bridge is due in large part to the **Rialto Market:** Some of the city's best restaurants have flourished in the area for generations, alongside some of its worst tourist traps.

**SANTA CROCE** North and northwest of the San Polo district and across the Grand Canal from the train station, Santa Croce stretches all the way to **Piazzale Roma.** Its eastern section is one of the least-visited areas of Venice, making it all the more desirable for curious visitors. Less lively than San Polo, it feels light-years away from San Marco. The quiet and lovely **Campo San Giacomo dell'Orio** is its heart.

**CANNAREGIO** Sharing the same side of the Grand Canal as San Marco and Castello, Cannaregio stretches north and east from the station to include the old **Jewish Ghetto.** Its outer reaches are quiet, unspoiled, and residential; one-quarter of Venice's ever-shrinking population of 60,000 lives here. Many budget hotels are clustered about the station—not a dangerous neighborhood but not one known for its charm, either.

**LA GIUDECCA** Located across the Giudecca Canal from the Piazza San Marco and Dorsoduro, La Giudecca is a tranquil residential island where you'll find a youth hostel and a handful of hotels.

## Exploring Venice

Venice is notorious for the ever-changing opening hours of its museums and to a lesser degree, its churches. During the peak months, you can

Venice
Stazione Venezia–Santa Lucia
Ferrovia
Ponte Calatrava
Giardino Pápadópoli
Riva da Biásio
Palazzo Giovanelli
Canàl Grande
Fond. d. Turchi
Ca' Tron
S. Stae
Palazzo Donà-Balbi
S. Zan Degolà
S. Simeòn Grande
S. Giacomo dell'Orio
Campo S. Giacomo dell'Orio
Calle d. Tintòr
Pal. Mocenigo
Ca' Pesaro
S. Simeòn Piccolo
Palazzo Gradenigo
Campo N. Sáuro
S. Maria Máter Domini
Palazzo Soranzo-Cappello
Fond. Rio Marin
SANTA CROCE
Pal. Zane
S. Cassiano
Pal. Grioni
Calle d. Chiesa
Rio di S. Agostino
Pal. Muti Baglioni
Scuola Grande di S. Giovanni
Pal. Zane Collalto
Palazzo Albrizzi
Pal. Molin Cappello
Pal. Molin
S. Giovanni Evangelista
Pal. Donà d. Rose
Rio di S. Polo
SAN POLO
S. Nicolò di Tolentino
Ex Convento dei Frari
Pal. Corner
Campo S. Polo
Pal. Soranzo
Palazzo Zen
Palazzo Marcello
S. Rocco
Campo d. Frari
Frari
San Polo
Scuola Grande di San Rocco
Pal. Papadopoli
Palazzo Centani (Museo Goldoni)
Pal. Dona
Pal. Layard
Pal. Grimani
Palazzo Barbarigo
Rio d. Frescada
S. Pantalòn
S. Tomà
Pal. Civràn-Grimani
S. Ángelo
S. Tomà
Rio Ca' Foscari
Calle Foscari
Pal. Balbi
Palazzo Mocenigo
Pal. Cornèr Spinelli
Pal. Fortuny
Campo Santa Margherita
Ca' Foscari
Pal. Contarini d. Figure
Palazzo Foscarini
Palazzo Moro-Lin
Pal. Grassi
Saliz. S. Samuele
C. Crosera
Oratorio d. Annunciata
Campo S. Ángelo
Rio di S. Ángelo
Pal. Nani
Ca' Rezzonico
S. Samuele
San Samuele
S. Stefano
Pal. Zenóbia
Cármini
Ist. Sup. d'Arte Applicata
Campo S. Barnaba
S. Bárnaba
Ca' Rezzonico
Palazzo Malipiero
Campo S. Stefano
S. Maurízio
Rio Malpaga
Pal. Stern
Ca' del Duca
Rio del Duca
C. Vetturi
Rio di S. Vidal
Pal. Morosini
Rio d. Santissimo
Pal. Loredan
Pal. Falier
S. Maria d. Giglio
S. Sebastiano
Pal. Contarini degli Scrigni
Pal. Bárbaro
Pal. Pisani
DORSODURO
Palazzo Cornèr d. Ca' Granda
Ponte dell'Accademia
Accademia
Rio di S. Trovaso
Gallerie dell' Accademia
Palazzo Contarini dal Zaffo
S. Maria d. Giglio
Pal. Molin
Pal. Molin
S. Trovaso
Pal. Centani
S. Basílio
Pal. Nani
Pal. Venièr dei Leoni (Guggenheim)
Pal. Giustiniàn
Rio di S. Vio
S. Maria d. Visitaz.
S. Agnese
Canale della Giudecca
Gesuati
Zàttere
Fond. Bragadin
1
2
4
5
6
7
8
9
10
12
13
14
21

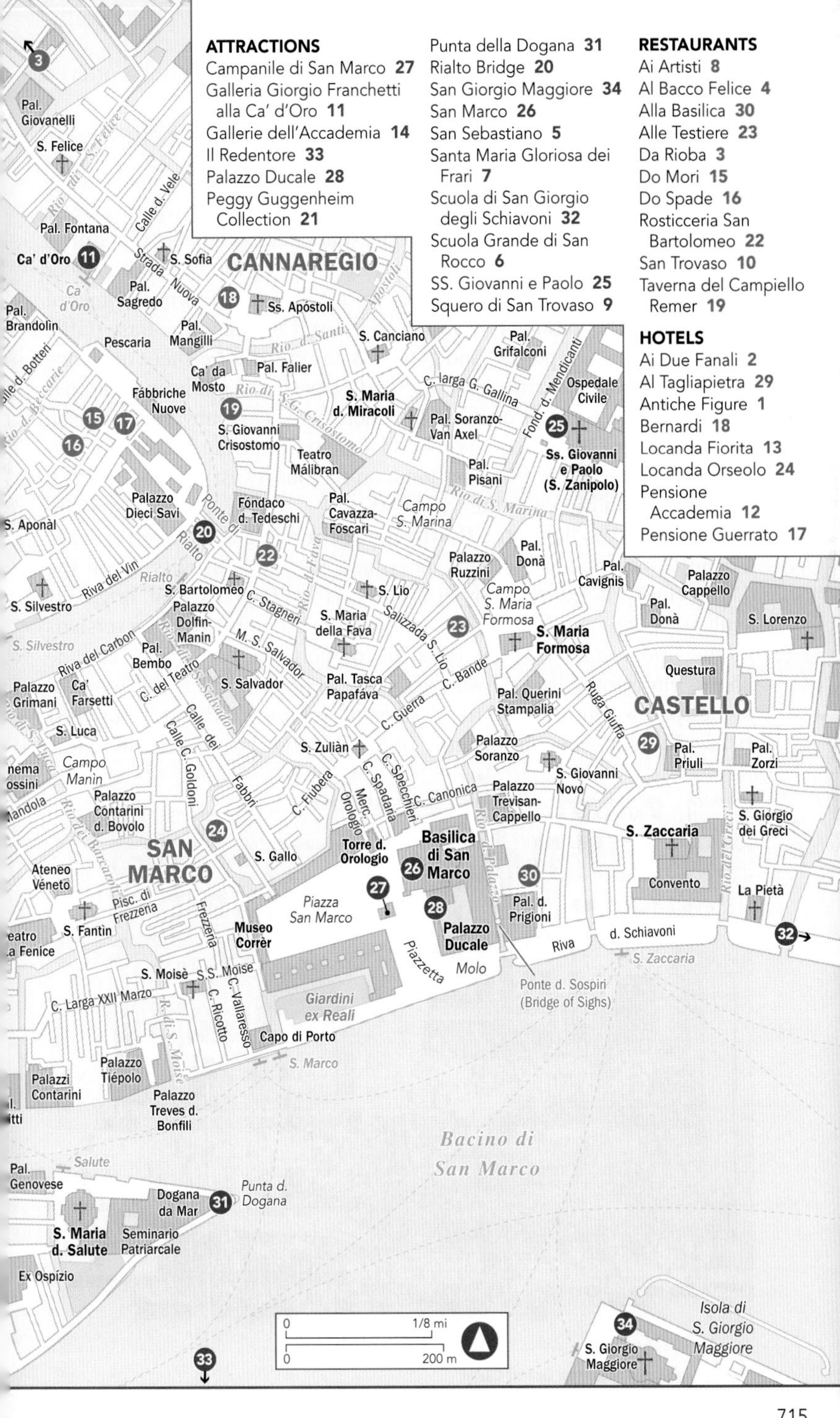
ATTRACTIONS
Campanile di San Marco 27
Galleria Giorgio Franchetti alla Ca' d'Oro 11
Gallerie dell'Accademia 14
Il Redentore 33
Palazzo Ducale 28
Peggy Guggenheim Collection 21
Punta della Dogana 31
Rialto Bridge 20
San Giorgio Maggiore 34
San Marco 26
San Sebastiano 5
Santa Maria Gloriosa dei Frari 7
Scuola di San Giorgio degli Schiavoni 32
Scuola Grande di San Rocco 6
SS. Giovanni e Paolo 25
Squero di San Trovaso 9
RESTAURANTS
Ai Artisti 8
Al Bacco Felice 4
Alla Basilica 30
Alle Testiere 23
Da Rioba 3
Do Mori 15
Do Spade 16
Rosticceria San Bartolomeo 22
San Trovaso 10
Taverna del Campiello Remer 19
HOTELS
Ai Due Fanali 2
Al Tagliapietra 29
Antiche Figure 1
Bernardi 18
Locanda Fiorita 13
Locanda Orseolo 24
Pensione Accademia 12
Pensione Guerrato 17
CANNAREGIO
SAN MARCO
CASTELLO
Pal. Giovanelli
S. Felice
Pal. Fontana
Ca' d'Oro
S. Sofia
Strada Nuova
Calle d. Vele
Pal. Sagredo
Pal. Brandolin
Pescaria
Pal. Mangilli
Ss. Apóstoli
S. Canciano
Pal. Grifalconi
Ca' da Mosto
Pal. Falier
Fábbriche Nuove
S. Maria d. Miracoli
C. larga G. Gallina
Ospedale Civile
Fond. d. Mendicanti
S. Giovanni Crisostomo
Teatro Málibran
Pal. Soranzo-Van Axel
Ss. Giovanni e Paolo (S. Zanipolo)
Pal. Pisani
Rio di S. Marina
Palazzo Dieci Savi
Fóndaco d. Tedeschi
Pal. Cavazza-Foscari
Campo S. Marina
S. Aponàl
Ponte di Rialto
Palazzo Ruzzini
Pal. Donà
Pal. Cavignis
Palazzo Cappello
Riva del Vin
Rialto
S. Bartolomeo
S. Lio
S. Silvestro
Palazzo Dolfin-Manin
C. Stagneri
S. Maria della Fava
Salizzada S. Lio
Campo S. Maria Formosa
S. Maria Formosa
Pal. Donà
S. Lorenzo
Riva del Carbon
Pal. Bembo
M. S. Salvador
S. Salvador
Questura
Palazzo Grimani
Ca' Farsetti
C. del Teatro
Pal. Tasca Papafáva
C. Bande
Pal. Querini Stampalia
Ruga Giuffa
S. Luca
Calle dei Fabbri
Calle C. Goldoni
C. Guerra
S. Zuliàn
Palazzo Soranzo
Pal. Priuli
Pal. Zorzi
Campo Manin
Palazzo Contarini d. Bovolo
C. Fiubera
Merc. Orologio
C. Spadaria
C. Specchieri
C. Canonica
Palazzo Trevisan-Cappello
S. Giovanni Novo
S. Giorgio dei Greci
S. Zaccaria
Torre d. Orologio
Basilica di San Marco
S. Gallo
Ateneo Véneto
Convento
La Pietà
Rio dei Greci
Piazza San Marco
Pal. d. Prigioni
S. Fantin
Frezzeria
Museo Corrèr
Palazzo Ducale
Piazzetta
Riva d. Schiavoni
S. Zaccaria
Teatro La Fenice
S. Moisè
Molo
C. Larga XXII Marzo
C. Vallaresso
C. Ricotto
Giardini ex Reali
Ponte d. Sospiri (Bridge of Sighs)
Capo di Porto
S. Marco
Palazzo Tiépolo
Palazzi Contarini
Palazzo Treves d. Bonfili
Bacino di San Marco
Pal. Genovese
Salute
Punta d. Dogana
Dogana da Mar
S. Maria d. Salute
Seminario Patriarcale
Ex Ospízio
0 1/8 mi
0 200 m
Isola di S. Giorgio Maggiore
S. Giorgio Maggiore

enjoy extended museum hours—some places stay open until 7 or even 10pm.

## SAN MARCO

A leisurely cruise along the **Grand Canal ★★★**—or "Canalazzo"—from Piazza San Marco to the Ferrovia (train station), or the reverse, is one of Venice's (and life's) must-do experiences. Hop on the **no. 1 *vaporetto*** in the late afternoon (try to get one of the coveted outdoor seats in the prow), when the weather-worn colors of the former homes of Venice's merchant elite are warmed by the soft light and the busy traffic of delivery boats, *vaporetti,* and gondolas has eased. The sheer opulence of the 200-odd *palazzi,* churches, and imposing republican buildings from the 14th to 18th centuries is enough to make any visitor's head swim. The best stations to start or end a tour of the Grand Canal are Ferrovia (train station) or Piazzale Roma on the northwest side of the canal and Piazza San Marco in the southeast.

En route you'll pass the **Rialto Bridge ★★,** a graceful arch over the Grand Canal linking the San Marco and San Polo districts. Until the 19th century, it was the only bridge across the Grand Canal, originally built as a pontoon bridge at the canal's narrowest point. Wooden versions of the bridge followed; the 1444 incarnation was the first to include shops, interrupted by a drawbridge in the center. In 1592, this graceful stone span was finished to the designs of Antonio da Ponte (whose last name fittingly enough means "bridge"), who beat out Sansovino,

Piazza San Marco from the Grand Canal.

The Rialto Bridge.

Palladio, and Michelangelo with his plans that called for a single, vast, 28m-wide (92-ft.) arch in the center to allow trading ships to pass.

**Campanile di San Marco (Bell Tower) ★★★** ICON An elevator will whisk you to the top of this 97m (318-ft.) bell tower, where you get an awe-inspiring view of St. Mark's cupolas. It is the highest structure in the city, offering a pigeon's-eye panorama that includes the lagoon, neighboring islands, and the red rooftops, church domes and bell towers of Venice—and, oddly, not a single canal. Originally built in the 9th century, the tower was reconstructed in the 12th, 14th, and 16th centuries, when a pretty marble loggia at its base was added by Jacopo Sansovino. It collapsed unexpectedly in 1902, miraculously hurting no one except a cat. It was rebuilt exactly as before, using most of the same materials, even rescuing one of the five historical bells that it still uses today (each bell was rung for a different purpose, such as war, the death of a doge, religious holidays, and so on).

Piazza San Marco. www.basilicasanmarco.it. ✆ **041-2708311.** 8€. *Vaporetto:* San Marco. Easter–June and Oct daily 9am–7pm; July–Sept daily 9am–9pm; Nov–Easter daily 9:30am–3:45pm.

**Palazzo Ducale and Ponte dei Sospiri (Ducal Palace and Bridge of Sighs) ★★★** PALACE The pink-and-white marble Gothic-Renaissance **Palazzo Ducale,** residence and government center of the doges who ruled Venice for more than 1,000 years, stands between the Basilica di San Marco and the sea. A symbol of prosperity and power, it was destroyed by a succession of fires, with the current building started in 1340, extended in the 1420s, and largely redesigned again after a fire in 1483.

The 15th-century **Porta della Carta (Paper Gate),** the entrance adjacent to the basilica where the doges' proclamations and decrees were posted, opens onto a splendid inner courtyard with a double row of Renaissance arches (visitors enter through a doorway on the lagoon side of the palace). The first major room you'll come to is the spacious **Sala**

**delle Quattro Porte (Hall of the Four Doors),** with a worn ceiling by Tintoretto. The **Sala dell'Anticollegio ★★** is where foreign ambassadors waited to be received by the doge and his council. It is covered in four works by Tintoretto, and Veronese's ***Rape of Europe* ★★,** considered one of the *palazzo*'s finest. It steals some of the thunder of Tintoretto's *Mercury & the Three Graces* and ***Bacchus and Ariadne* ★★**—the latter considered one of his best by some critics. The highlight of the adjacent **Sala del Collegio** (the Council Chamber itself) is the spectacular cycle of **ceiling paintings ★★** by Veronese, completed between 1575 and 1578 and one of his masterpieces. Next door lies the most impressive of the spectacular interior rooms, the richly adorned **Sala del Senato (Senate Chamber),** with Tintoretto's ceiling painting, *The Triumph of Venice.* Here laws were passed by the Senate, a select group of 200 chosen from the Great Council. After passing again through the Sala delle Quattro Porte, you'll come to the Veronese-decorated **Stanza del Consiglio dei Dieci** (**Room of the Council of Ten,** the Republic's dreaded security police), of particular historical interest. It was in this room that justice was dispensed and decapitations ordered. Formed in the 14th century to deal with emergency situations, the Ten were considered more powerful than the Senate and feared by all. Just outside the adjacent chamber, in the **Sala della Bussola (the Compass Chamber),** notice the **Bocca dei Leoni (Lions' Mouth),** a slit in the wall into which secret denunciations of enemies of the state were placed.

The main sight on the next level down—indeed, in the entire palace—is the **Sala del Maggior Consiglio (Great Council Hall).** This enormous space is animated by Tintoretto's huge ***Paradiso* ★** at the far end of the hall above the doge's seat (the painter was in his 70s when he undertook the project with the help of his son). Measuring 7×23m (23×75 ft.), it is said to be the world's largest oil painting; together with Veronese's ***Il Trionfo di Venezia (The Triumph of Venice)* ★★** in the oval panel on the ceiling, it affirms the power emanating from the council sessions held here. Tintoretto also did the portraits of the 76 doges encircling the top of this chamber; note that the picture of the Doge Marin Falier, who was convicted of treason and beheaded in 1355, has been blacked out—Venice has never forgiven him. Although elected for life since sometime in the 7th century, over time *il doge* became just a figurehead; power rested in the Great Council. Tours culminate at the enclosed **Ponte dei Sospiri (Bridge of Sighs),** built in 1600 and which connects the Ducal Palace with the grim **Palazzo delle Prigioni (Prison).** The bridge took its current name only in the 19th century, when visiting northern European poets romantically envisioned the prisoners' final breath of resignation upon viewing the outside world one last time before being locked in their fetid cells.

Piazza San Marco. www.palazzoducale.visitmuve.it. ✆ **041-2715911.** Admission only with San Marco Museum Pass (see "Venice Discounts," p. 722). *Vaporetto:* San Marco. Daily 8:30am–7pm (Nov–Mar until 5:30pm).

**San Marco (St. Mark's) ★★★** CATHEDRAL One of the grandest, most confusing, and certainly the most exotic of all cathedrals in Europe, the **Basilica di San Marco** is a grand treasure-heap of Venetian art and all sorts of lavish booty garnered from the eastern Mediterranean. Legend has it that **St. Mark** was told by an angel his body would rest near the lagoon that would one today become Venice. Centuries later, the city fathers were looking for a patron saint of high stature, more in keeping with their lofty aspirations, and in 828 the prophecy was fulfilled when Venetian merchants stole the body of St. Mark from Alexandria in Egypt (the story goes that the body was packed in pickled pork to avoid the attention of Muslim guards).

Modeled on Constantinople's Church of the Twelve Apostles, the shrine of St. Mark was consecrated in 832, but in 976 the church burned down. The present incarnation was completed in 1094 but extended and embellished over subsequent years, serving as the personal church of the doge. Even today San Marco looks more like a Byzantine cathedral than a Roman Catholic church, with a cavernous interior exquisitely gilded with Byzantine mosaics added over some 7 centuries and covering every inch of both ceiling and pavement. For a closer look at many of the most remarkable ceiling mosaics and a better view of the Oriental carpet–like patterns of the pavement mosaics, pay the admission to go upstairs to the **Museo di San Marco;** this was originally the women's gallery, or *matroneum,* and also includes the outside Loggia dei Cavalli (see below). Here you can mingle with the celebrated ***Triumphal Quadriga*** ★★ of four gilded bronze horses dating from the 2nd or 3rd century A.D.; originally set on the Loggia, the restored originals were moved inside in the 1980s for preservation. (The word *quadriga* actually refers to a car or chariot pulled by four horses though in this case there are only the horses.) The horses were brought to Venice from Constantinople in 1204 along with lots of other loot from the Fourth Crusade

The Basilica di San Marco and Piazza San Marco.

### Know Before You Go

The guards at the cathedral's entrance are serious about forbidding entry to anyone in inappropriate attire—shorts, sleeveless shirts (and shirts too short to hide your bellybutton), and skirts above the knee. Note also that you cannot enter with luggage, and that photos and filming inside are forbidden. Your best bet for avoiding long lines is to come early in the morning.

A visit to the outdoor **Loggia dei Cavalli ★★** (where replicas of the horses now stand) provides a panoramic view of the piazza that Napoléon called "the most beautiful salon in the world" upon his arrival in Venice in 1797. The 500-year-old **Torre dell'Orologio (Clock Tower)** stands to your right; to your left is the **Campanile (Bell Tower)** and, beyond, the glistening waters of the open lagoon and Palladio's **San Giorgio** on its own island. It is a photographer's dream.

The church's greatest treasure is the magnificent altarpiece known as the **Pala d'Oro (Golden Altarpiece),** a Gothic masterpiece encrusted with over 2,000 precious gems and 83 enameled panels. It was created in 10th-century Constantinople and embellished by Venetian and Byzantine artisans between the 12th and 14th centuries. It is located behind the main altar, whose green marble canopy on alabaster columns covers the tomb of St. Mark (skeptics contend that his remains burned in the fire of 976).

Piazza San Marco. www.basilicasanmarco.it. ✆ **041-2708311.** Basilica, free admission; Museo di San Marco (includes Loggia dei Cavalli) 5€, Pala d'Oro 2€, Tesoro (Treasury) 3€. *Vaporetto:* San Marco. Basilica, Tesoro, and Pala d'Oro Mon–Sat 9:45am–5pm, Sun 2–5pm (4pm in winter). Museo di San Marco daily 9:45am–4:45pm.

## CASTELLO

**Scuola di San Giorgio degli Schiavoni ★★** MUSEUM One of the most beautiful spaces in Europe, the main hall of the **Scuola di San Giorgio degli Schiavoni** once served as a meeting house for Venice's Dalmatian community (*schiavoni,* literally "Slavs"), built by the side of their church, San Giovanni di Malta, in the early 16th century. The main reason to visit is to admire the narrative painting cycle that smothers the walls, created by Renaissance master **Vittore Carpaccio** between 1502 and 1509. The paintings depict the lives of the Dalmatian saints George, Tryphon, and Jerome and also feature Carpaccio's masterful *Vision of St. Augustine.*

Calle dei Furlani 3259A. ✆ **041-5228828.** 5€. *Vaporetto:* Rialto. Mon 2:45–6pm, Tues–Sat 9:15am–1pm and 2:45–6pm, Sun 9:15am–1pm.

**SS. Giovanni e Paolo ★** CHURCH This massive Gothic church was built by the Dominican order from the 13th to the 15th century and, together with the Frari Church in San Polo, is second in size only to the Basilica di San Marco. An unofficial Pantheon where 25 doges are buried (a number of tombs are part of the unfinished facade), the church, commonly known as Zanipolo in Venetian dialect, is also home to a number of artistic treasures. Visit the **Cappella del Rosario ★** off the left transept to see the three restored ceiling canvases by Paolo Veronese, particularly *The Assumption of the Madonna*. The brilliantly colored *Polyptych of St. Vincent Ferrer* (ca. 1465), attributed to a young Giovanni Bellini, is in the right aisle.

Anchoring the large and impressive *campo* outside is the **statue of Bartolomeo Colleoni ★★,** the Renaissance condottiere who defended Venice's interests at the height of its power until his death in 1475.

Campo Santi Giovanni e Paolo 6363. www.basilicasantigiovanniepaolo.it. ✆ **041-5235913.** 2.50€. *Vaporetto:* Rialto. Mon–Sat 9am–6pm, Sun noon–6pm.

## DORSODURO

One of the most photographed sights in Venice is the small **Squero di San Trovaso ★★,** a boatyard that first opened in the 17th century. Just north of the Zattere (the sunny walkway that runs alongside the Giudecca Canal), the boatyard lies next to the Church of San Trovaso on the narrow Rio San Trovaso, not far from the Accademia Bridge. It is surrounded by Tyrolean-looking wooden structures—a true rarity in this city of stone built on water—that are home to the multigenerational owners and original workshops for traditional Venetian boats.

### Back to *Scuola*

Founded in the Middle Ages, the Venetian *scuole* (schools) were **guilds** that brought together merchants and craftspeople from certain trades (for example, the dyers of Scuola dei Carmini), as well as those who shared similar religious devotions (Scuola Grande di San Rocco). The guilds were social clubs, credit unions, and sources of spiritual guidance. Many commissioned elaborate headquarters and hired the best artists of the day to decorate them.

**Gallerie dell'Accademia (Academy Gallery) ★★★** MUSEUM

Along with San Marco and the Palazzo Ducale, the **Accademia** is one of the top sights of Venice, a magnificent collection of European art and especially Venetian painting from the 14th to the 18th centuries. Visitors are currently limited to 300 at one time, so lines can be long in high season—advance reservations are essential. The core galleries occupy the old **Scuola della Carità,** dating back to 1343.

Rooms are laid out in rough chronological order, though an ongoing renovation means some rooms may be closed when you visit. The real showstoppers of the collection reside in rooms 4 and 5, with a gorgeous *St. George* by Mantegna and a series of Giovanni Bellini *Madonnas*. Pride of place goes to **Giorgione**'s mystifying ***Tempest* ★★.**

Rooms 6 to 8 feature Venetian heavyweights Tintoretto, Titian and Lorenzo Lotto, while Room 10 is dominated by Paolo Veronese's mammoth ***Feast in the House of Levi* ★★.** The story goes that Veronese wanted to call the painting a "Last Supper" but the Inquisition objected to the dogs, dwarfs, and drunks—Veronese simply changed the name

## VENICE discounts

Venice has a bewildering range of passes and discount cards. The **Museum Pass** (www.visitmuve.it) grants admission to all the city-run museums over a 6-month period. That includes the museums of St. Mark's Square—Palazzo Ducale, Museo Correr, Museo Archeologico Nazionale, and the Biblioteca Nazionale Marciana—as well as the Museo di Palazzo Mocenigo (Costume Museum), the Ca' Rezzonico, the Ca' Pesaro, the Museo del Vetro (Glass Museum) on Murano, and the Museo del Merletto (Lace Museum) on Burano. The Museum Pass is available at any of the participating museums and costs 25€ for adults, and 19€ for students under 30 and kids aged 6 to 14. There is also a **San Marco Museum Pass** (valid for 3 months) that lets you into the four museums of Piazza San Marco for 17€, and 11€ for students under 30 and kids aged 6 to 14.

The **Chorus Pass** (www.chorusvenezia.org) covers every major church in Venice, 16 in all, for 12€ (8€ for students up to 29), from Redentore to Santa Maria dei Miracoli, for up to 1 year.

and all was well. Room 11 contains work by **Tiepolo,** the master of 18th-century Venetian painting, but also Tintoretto's *Madonna dei Tesorieri.*

Room 20 is filled by Gentile Bellini's cycle of ***The Miracles of the Relic of the Cross*** ★, painted around 1500 for the Scuola di San Giovanni Evangelista. The next room contains the monumental cycle of pictures by Carpaccio illustrating the **Story of St. Ursula** ★★. Legend has it that St. Ursula was a British Celtic princess, murdered by the Huns as she was making a pilgrimage to Rome along with her 11,000 virgin attendants.

Campo della Carità 1050, at Ponte dell'Accademia. www.gallerieaccademia.org. ✆ **041-5200345.** 9€ adults (includes Palazzo Grimani). *Vaporetto:* Accademia. Reservations (phone or online) incur a 1.50€ charge. Daily 8:15am–7:15pm (Mon until 2pm).

**Peggy Guggenheim Collection** ★★ MUSEUM Though the **Peggy Guggenheim Collection** is one of the best museums in Italy when it comes to American and European art of the 20th century, you might find the experience a little jarring given its location in a city so heavily associated with the High Renaissance and the baroque. Nevertheless, art aficionados will find fascinating work here, and the galleries occupy Peggy Guggenheim's wonderful former home, the 18th-century Palazzo Venier dei Leoni, right on the Grand Canal. Highlights include Picasso's abstract *Poet,* and his more gentle *On the Beach,* several works by Kandinsky (*Landscape with Red Spots No. 2* and *White Cross*), Miró's expressionistic *Seated Woman II,* Klee's mystical *Magic Garden,* and some unsettling works by Max Ernst (*The Kiss, Attirement of the Bride*), who was briefly married to Guggenheim in the 1940s.

Calle San Cristoforo 701. www.guggenheim-venice.it. ✆ **041-2405411.** 14€ adults; 12€ 65 and over; 8€ students 26 and under and children ages 10–18. *Vaporetto:* Accademia. Wed–Mon 10am–6pm.

**Punta della Dogana** ★★★ MUSEUM The eastern tip (*punta*) of Dorsoduro is crowned by the distinctive triangle of the 17th-century **Dogana di Mare** (Customs house) that once monitored all boats entering the Grand Canal. Transformed by Tadao Ando into a beautiful exhibition space, it's now an engaging showcase for the contemporary art collection of French multi-millionaire François Pinault (officially dubbed the **Centro d'Arte Contemporanea Punta della Dogana**). It's pricey, but you can expect to see quality work from Cindy Sherman, Cy Twombly, Jeff Koons, and Marlene Dumas, among many others.
Fondamenta della Dogana alla Salute 2. www.palazzograssi.it. ✆ **041-2719031.** 15€ adults, 20€ with Palazzo Grassi. *Vaporetto:* Salute. Wed–Mon 10am–7pm.

**San Sebastiano** ★★ CHURCH Lose the crowds as you make a pilgrimage to this monument to **Paolo Veronese,** his parish church and home to some of his finest work. Veronese painted the ceiling of the sacristy with the *Coronation of the Virgin* and the *Four Evangelists,* while he graced the nave ceiling with *Scenes from the Life of St. Esther.*
Campo San Sebastiano. ✆ **041-2750462.** 3€. *Vaporetto:* San Basilio. Mon–Sat 10am–5pm.

## SAN POLO & SANTA CROCE

**Santa Maria Gloriosa dei Frari (Church of the Frari)** ★★ CHURCH Built by the Franciscans (*frari* is a dialectal distortion of *frati,* or "brothers"), this is the largest church in Venice after San Marco. It houses a number of important works, including two Titian masterpieces. The more striking is his ***Assumption of the Virgin*** ★★ over the main altar, painted when the artist was only in his late 20s. Also spy Giovanni Bellini's ***Madonna & Child*** ★★; novelist Henry James was struck dumb by it, writing: "it is as solemn as it is gorgeous."
Campo dei Frari 3072. www.basilicadeifrari.it. ✆ **041-2728611.** 3€. *Vaporetto:* San Tomà. Mon–Sat 9am–6pm; Sun 1–6pm.

**Scuola Grande di San Rocco (Confraternity of St. Roch)** ★★★ MUSEUM Like many medieval saints, French-born San Rocco (St. Roch) died young, but thanks to his work healing the sick in the 14th century, his cult became associated with the power to cure the plague and other serious illnesses. When the saint's body was brought to Venice in 1485, this *scuola* began to reap the benefits, and by 1560 the current complex was completed, work beginning soon after on more than 50 major paintings by Tintoretto. This *scuola* is primarily a shrine to the skills of **Tintoretto,** one of the city's acknowledged grand masters of the paintbrush but an artist who often divides critics. Begin at the upper story, the **Sala dell'Albergo,** where an entire wall is smothered by Tintoretto's mind-blowing *Crucifixion* (as well as his *Glorification of St. Roch,* the painting that actually won him the contract to paint the *scuola*). In the **chapterhouse,** Old Testament scenes adorn the ceiling: *Moses Striking Water from the Rock, The Miracle of the Brazen Serpent,* and *The*

*Miraculous Fall of Manna.* The paintings around the walls, based on the New Testament, are a masterclass of perspective, shadow, and color.

Campo San Rocco 3052, adjacent to Campo dei Frari. www.scuolagrandesanrocco.it. ✆ **041-5234864.** 10€ adults, 8€ ages 18–26; 18 and under free. *Vaporetto:* San Tomà. Daily 9:30am–5:30pm.

## CANNAREGIO

**Galleria Giorgio Franchetti alla Ca' d'Oro ★★** MUSEUM This magnificent palazzo overlooking the Grand Canal, the "golden house" was built between 1428 and 1430 for the noble Contarini family. Baron Giorgio Franchetti bought the place in 1894, and it now serves as an atmospheric art gallery for the exceptional collection he built up throughout his lifetime. The highlight here is ***St. Sebastian*** **★★** by Paduan artist Andrea Mantegna, displayed in its own marble chapel built by the overawed baron. The so-called "St. Sebastian of Venice" was the third and final painting of the saint by Mantegna, created around 1490 and quite different to the other two (in Vienna and Paris respectively); it's a deeply pessimistic work, with none of Mantegna's usual background details to detract from the suffering.

Strada Nuova 3932. www.cadoro.org. ✆ **041-520-0345.** 6€, plus 1.50€ reservation fee (or 12€ during special exhibitions). *Vaporetto:* Ca' d'Oro. Mon 8:15am–2pm; Tues–Sat 8:15am–7:15pm; Sun 10am–6pm.



## GIUDECCA & SAN GIORGIO

**Il Redentore ★★** CHURCH Perhaps the masterpiece among Palladio's churches, Il Redentore was commissioned by Venice to give thanks for being delivered from the great plague (1575–77), which claimed over a quarter of the population (some 46,000 people). The doge established a tradition of visiting this church by crossing a long pontoon bridge made up of boats from the Dorsoduro's Zattere on the third Sunday of July, a tradition that survived the doges' demise and remains one of Venice's most popular festivals.

Campo del Redentore, La Giudecca. ✆ **041-523-1415.** 3€. *Vaporetto:* Redentore. Mon–Sat 10am–5pm.

**San Giorgio Maggiore ★★** CHURCH This church sits on the island of San Giorgio Maggiore across from Piazza San Marco. It is one of the masterpieces of **Andrea Palladio,** the great Renaissance architect from nearby Padua. Most known for his country villas built for Venice's wealthy merchant families, Palladio was commissioned to build two churches (the other is the Redentore on neighboring Giudecca island; see above), beginning with San Giorgio, designed in 1565 and completed in 1610. To impose a classical front on the traditional church structure, Palladio designed two interlocking facades, with repeating triangles, rectangles, and columns that are harmoniously proportioned. To the left of the choir is an elevator that you can take to the top of the campanile—for a charge of 5€—to experience an unforgettable view of the island, the lagoon, and the Palazzo Ducale and Piazza San Marco across the way. San Giorgio Maggiore, across St. Mark's Basin from Piazza San Marco. ✆ **041-5227827.** Free. *Vaporetto:* 82 (to San Giorgio Maggiore). Mon–Sat 9:30am–12:30pm; daily 2:30–6pm (Oct–Apr to 4:30pm).

## Organized Tours

Because of the sheer number of sights to see in Venice, some first-time visitors like to start out with an organized tour. While few things can really be covered in depth on these overview tours, they're useful for getting your bearings. **Avventure Bellissime** (www.tours-italy.com; ✆ **041-970499**) coordinates a plethora of tours (in English), by boat and gondola. The **walking tours** are the best value, covering all the main sights around Piazza San Marco in 2 hours for 25€. For something with a little more bite, try **Urban Adventures** (www.urbanadventures.com; ✆ **348-9808566**), which runs enticing *cicchetti* (tapas-like small plates) tours (3 hr.) for 65€.

For those with more energy, learn to "row like a Venetian" (yes, standing up), at **Row Venice** (www.rowvenice.com; ✆ **347-7250637**), where 1½-hour lessons take place in traditional "shrimp-tail" or *batele coda di gambero* boats for 40€ per person (80€ minimum). Or you could abandon tradition altogether and opt for a guided **Venice Kayak** tour (www.venicekayak.com; ✆ **346-4771327**), an enchanting way to see the city from the water. Day trips are 120€ per person for 2 to 5 persons.

## Especially for Kids

It goes without saying that a **gondola ride** (p. 710) will be a thrill for any child (or adult). If that's too expensive, consider a less expensive alternative, a **ride on the no. 1** ***vaporetto*** (p. 716). They offer two entirely different experiences: The gondola gives you the chance to see Venice through the back door (and ride past Marco Polo's house); the *vaporetto* provides a utilitarian—but no less gorgeous—journey down Venice's aquatic Main Street, the Grand Canal. Look for the ambulance boat, the garbage boat, the firefighters' boat, the funeral boat, even the Coca-Cola delivery boat.

Before you leave town, take the elevator to the **top of the Campanile di San Marco,** the highest structure in the city (p. 717) for a scintillating view of Venice's rooftops and church cupolas, or get up close and personal with the four bronze horses on the facade of the Basilica San Marco. Climbing the bell tower at **San Giorgio Maggiore** (p. 724) is also lots of fun.

## Where to Stay

Few cities boast as long a high season as Venice, beginning with the Easter period. May, June, and September are the best months weather-wise and therefore, the most crowded. July and August are hot (few of the cheapest hotels offer air-conditioning). It's highly advisable to reserve in advance, even in the off-season. If you haven't booked, come as early as you can on your arrival day, definitely before noon. Another alternative upon arrival is to reserve through the **A.V.A.** (Venetian Hoteliers Association), online at www.veneziasi.it or ✆ **041-5222264.** State the price range you want and they'll confirm a hotel while you wait. There are offices at the train station, in Piazzale Roma garages, and at the airport.

## SAN MARCO

### Expensive

**Locanda Orseolo ★★★** An enticing inn made up of three elegant guesthouses right behind Piazza San Marco. This place really oozes character, with exposed wood beams and heavy drapes giving a medieval feel, and rooms lavishly decorated with Venetian-style furniture and tributes to the masks of the Carnevale—it's a cross between an artist's studio and Renaissance palace. Lounge with an aperitif on the terrace overlooking the Orseolo canal, and enjoy eggs and crepes made to order at breakfast.

Corte Zorzi 1083. www.locandaorseolo.com. ✆ **041-5204827.** 15 units. Doubles 150€–240€, includes breakfast. *Vaporetto:* San Marco. **Amenities:** Babysitting; concierge; free Wi-Fi.



### Moderate

**Locanda Fiorita ★★** It's hard to imagine a more picturesque location for this little hotel, a charming, quiet *campiello* draped in vines and blossoms—no wonder it's a favorite among professional photographers. Most standard rooms are small by U.S. standards (bathrooms, too), but all are furnished in an elegant 18th-century style, with wooden floors, shuttered windows, and richly patterned fittings. Air-conditioning is included.

Campiello Novo 3457a. www.locandafiorita.com. ✆ **041-5234754.** 10 units. Doubles 85€–195€, includes breakfast. *Vaporetto:* Sant'Angelo. **Amenities:** Babysitting; concierge; room service; free Wi-Fi.

## CASTELLO

### Inexpensive

**Ai Tagliapietra ★★★** This cozy B&B run by the amicable Lorenzo (who will bend over backward to make your stay a memorable one) is a real bargain in this part of town. Rooms are basic but spotless, modern, and relatively spacious with private showers. Lorenzo will usually meet you at San Zaccaria, will give you a map, print boarding passes, and generally organize your trip (if you desire), making this an especially recommended budget option for first-time visitors.

Salizada Zorzi 4943. www.aitagliapietra.com. ✆ **347-3233166.** 4 units. Doubles 75€–100€, includes breakfast. *Vaporetto:* San Zaccaria. **Amenities:** Free Wi-Fi.

## DORSODURO

### Expensive

**Pensione Accademia ★★** A spellbinding hotel with a tranquil blossom-filled garden and a fascinating history, the Gothic-style Villa Maravege was built in the 17th century as a family residence, but served as the Russian Embassy between two World Wars before becoming a hotel in 1950. If that's not enticing enough, the rooms are fitted with Venetian-style antique reproductions, classical hardwood furniture, handsome tapestries, air-conditioning, and satellite TV, with views over either the Rio San Trovaso or gardens.

Fondamenta Bollani 1058. www.pensioneaccademia.it. ✆ **041-5210188.** 27 units. Doubles 175€–270€, includes breakfast. *Vaporetto:* Accademia. **Amenities:** Bar; babysitting; concierge; room service; Wi-Fi (1€ per day).

## SAN POLO

### Moderate

**Pensione Guerrato ★★★** Dating, incredibly, from 1227, it's tough to find a more historic place to lay your head. The building's long and complicated history—it was once the "Inn of the Monkey," run by nuns, the original mostly destroyed by fire in 1513—is well worth delving into. Rooms are simply but classically furnished, with wood floors, exposed beams, air-conditioning and private bathrooms—some rooms still contain original frescos, possibly leftovers from the medieval inn. Note that some rooms are on the sixth floor, and there's no elevator.

Calle Drio La Scimia 240a (near Rialto Market). www.pensioneguerrato.it. ✆ **041-5227131.** 19 units. Doubles 100€–145€, includes breakfast. Closed Dec 22–26 and Jan 8 to early Feb. *Vaporetto:* Rialto. **Amenities:** Babysitting; concierge; free Wi-Fi.

## SANTA CROCE

### Moderate

**Antiche Figure ★★★** The most convenient upscale hotel in Venice lies directly across the Grand Canal from the train station, a captivating 15th-century *palazzo* adjacent to an ancient gondola workshop (seriously). History aside, this is a very plush choice, with rooms decorated in a neoclassical Venetian style, with gold leaf, antique furniture, red carpets, silk tapestries, and aging Murano glass chandeliers, but also LCD satellite TVs and decent Wi-Fi. With soothing nighttime views across the water, it's certainly a romantic choice, and the staff are definitely worth singling out—friendly and very helpful.

Fondamenta San Simeone Piccolo 687. www.hotelantichefigure.it. ✆ **041-2759486.** 22 units. Doubles 142€–260€, includes breakfast. *Vaporetto:* Ferrovia. **Amenities:** Restaurant; bar; babysitting; concierge; room service; free Wi-Fi.

### Inexpensive

**Ai Due Fanali ★★** Originally a wooden oratory frequented by fishermen and farmers (later rebuilt), this beguiling hotel features small but artsy rooms, even for Venice: Headboards have been handpainted by a local artist, wood beams crisscross the ceiling, and vintage drapes add a cozy feel. Work by Jacopo Palma the Younger, a 16th-century Mannerist painter, adorns public areas. The bathrooms are embellished with terracotta tiles and Carrera marble. The location is excellent for the train station, while the roof terrace on the third floor is the best place to soak up a panorama of the city (breakfast is served up here). It's rightly popular: Book months ahead.

Campo San Simeon Profeta 946. www.aiduefanali.com. ✆ **041-718490.** 16 units. Doubles 76€–135€, includes breakfast. Closed most of Jan. *Vaporetto:* Ferrovia. **Amenities:** Bar; concierge; room service; free Wi-Fi.

### CANNAREGIO

#### Inexpensive

**Bernardi ★★** This hotel is an excellent deal, with small, basic but spotless rooms in a 16th-century *palazzo* (superior rooms are bigger). Most rooms come with one or two classical Venetian touches: Murano glass chandeliers, handpainted furniture, exposed wood beams, or tapestries. The shared showers are kept very clean, and fans are provided in hot summer months for the cheaper rooms (no air-conditioning).

Calle de l'Oca 4366. www.hotelbernardi.com. ✆ **041-5227257.** Hotel 18 units, 11 with private bathroom. Doubles 45€–120€, includes breakfast. *Vaporetto:* Ca' d'Oro. **Amenities:** Babysitting; concierge; room service; free Wi-Fi.

## Where to Eat



**Eating cheaply** in Venice is not easy, but it is by no means impossible. The city's reputation for mass-produced menus and overpriced food can, sadly, be warranted. As a basic rule, value for money tends to increase the farther you travel from Piazza San Marco, and avoid anything described as a *menù turistico.* Note also, that compared with Rome and other points south, Venice is a city of early meals: You should be seated by 7:30 to 8:30pm. Most kitchens close at 10 or 10:30pm, even though the restaurant may stay open until 11:30pm or midnight.

### Eat Like a Venetian

**Venice** is rarely celebrated for its cuisine. Fresh seafood is excellent, however, and figures heavily in the Venetian diet. **Grilled fish** is often served with red **radicchio,** a bitter lettuce that grows best in nearby Treviso. Two typical non-fish dishes are *fegato alla veneziana* (liver and onions) and *risi e bisi* (rice and fresh peas). Perhaps the essential culinary experience here is trawling the neighborhood bars known as ***bacari,*** where you can stand or sit with ***tramezzini*** (small, triangular white-bread half-sandwiches filled with everything from thinly sliced meats and tuna salad to cheeses and vegetables), and ***cicchetti*** (tapas-like finger foods, such as calamari rings, speared fried olives, potato croquettes, or grilled polenta squares), traditionally washed down with a small glass of wine, or *ombra.* All of the above will cost approximately 2€ to 6€ if you stand at the bar, as much as double when seated. Bar food is displayed on the countertop or in glass counters and usually sells out by late afternoon; so although it can make a great lunch, don't rely on it for a light dinner. A concentration of popular, well-stocked bars can be found along the Mercerie shopping strip that connects Piazza San Marco with the Rialto Bridge, the always lively Campo San Luca (look for Bar Torino, Bar Black Jack, or Leon Bianco) and Campo Santa Margherita.

A Venetian fish market.

While most restaurants in Italy include a cover charge (*coperto*) that usually runs 1.50€ to 3€, in Venice they tend to instead tack on 10% to 12% to the bill for "taxes and service." Some places in Venice will charge you the cover and still add on 12%. A menu should state clearly what extras the restaurant charges (sometimes you'll find it in minuscule print at the bottom), and if it doesn't, take your business elsewhere.

## SAN MARCO

### Moderate

**Rosticceria San Bartolomeo ★★** DELI/VENETIAN Also known as Rosticceria Gislon, this no-frills spot has a cheap canteen section popular with locals and a more expensive upstairs sit-down dining room. Don't be fooled by appearances: The downstairs section is just as good, with a range of grilled fish and seafood pastas on offer (lots of scampi, clams, and mussels), and there is a discount if you order takeout. Otherwise, just sit at the counter and soak up the animated scene, as the cooks chop, customers chat, and people come and go.

Calle della Bissa 5424. ✆ **041-5223569.** Mains 10€–22€. *Vaporetto:* Rialto. Daily 9:30am–9:30pm (Mon until 3:30pm).

## CASTELLO

### Expensive

**Alle Testiere ★★★** ITALIAN/VENETIAN This tiny restaurant is the connoisseur's choice for fresh fish and seafood, with a menu that changes frequently and a shrewd selection of wines. Dinner is served at two seatings. You'll choose from appetizers such as scallops with cherry tomatoes and orange, and clams that seem plucked straight from the sea. The John Dory filet with aromatic herbs is always an exceptional main, but the pastas—ravioli with eggplant and pesto, or the ricotta with prawns—are all superb. Finish off with homemade peach pie or chestnut pudding. In peak season, make reservations (which are required) at least 1 month in advance. You'll have a less rushed experience in the second seating.

Calle del Mondo Novo 5801 (off Salizada San Lio). www.osterialletestiere.it. ✆ **041-5227220.** Mains 26€. *Vaporetto:* Rialto or San Marco. Tues–Sat noon–3pm and two seatings at 7 and 9:15pm.

### Inexpensive

**Alla Basilica ★★** VENETIAN Considering this restaurant is just around the corner from the Doge's Palace and St. Mark's, lunch here is a phenomenally good deal. Don't expect romance—it's a large, noisy, canteenlike place—but the simple, freshly prepared meals comprise a pasta course like creamy lasagna or *spaghetti con ragu,* a meat or fish main (think grilled pork chops or *dentice al vapore con zucchini grigliate,* steamed red snapper with grilled zucchini), and mixed vegetables for just 14€, with bread and bottled water. Add a liter of extremely drinkable house wine for just 10€. Basilica is a favorite of local workers, and English is rarely spoken, so you'll need to practice your Italian.

Calle degli Albanesi 4255. www.allabasilicavenezia.it. ✆ **041-5220524.** Lunch set menu 14€. *Vaporetto:* San Marco. Tues–Sun noon–3pm.



## DORSODURO

### Expensive

**Ai Artisti ★★★** VENETIAN This unpretentious, family-owned osteria/enoteca is one of the best dining experiences in Venice, with a menu that changes daily according to what's available at the market (because the fish market is closed on Mondays, no fish is served). Grab a table by the canal and feast on stuffed squid, pan-fried sardines, and an amazing, buttery veal escalope, or opt for one of the truly wonderful pastas.

Fondamenta della Toletta 1169A. ✆ **041-5238944.** Mains 21€–25€. *Vaporetto:* Accademia. Mon–Sat noon–4pm and 6:30–10pm.

### Moderate

**San Trovaso ★** ITALIAN/VENETIAN No-frills tavern perfect for a lunch or dinner of tasty Italian comfort food, with a daily set menu (16€) featuring classics such as spaghetti with pesto, *spaghetti vongole,* and an addictive *gnocchi ai 4 formaggi* (gnocchi with four cheeses). The seafood menu is huge, with *salmone alla griglia* (grilled salmon) and a delightful, finely sliced escalopes with lemon sauce in addition to the usual Venetian line-up of scampi, monkfish, and sea bass. Tends to be touristy, of course, but a good value all the same.

Dorsoduro 1016 (on Fondamenta Priuli). www.tavernasantrovaso.it. ✆ **041-5230835.** Mains 11€–18€. Vaporetto: Accademia. Tues–Sun noon–2:45pm and 7–9:45pm.

## SAN POLO

### Moderate

**Do Spade ★** VENETIAN It's tough to find something so authentic and local this close to the Rialto Bridge these days, but Do Spade has been around since 1415. Most locals come here for the *cicchetti,* typical Venetian small plates such as fried calamari, meatballs, mozzarella, salted cod (mostly 1.50€), and decent wines (3€ a glass). You can sit on benches outside if it's too crowded indoors. The more formal restaurant section is also worth a try, with seafood highlights including a delicately prepared monkfish, scallops served with fresh zucchini, and a rich seafood lasagna.

Sottoportego do Spade 860. www.cantinadospade.com. ✆ **041-5210574.** Mains 12€–21€. *Vaporetto:* Rialto or San Silvestro. Daily 10am–3pm and 6–10pm.

### Inexpensive

**Do Mori ★★** WINE BAR/VENETIAN Serving good wine and *cicchetti* since 1462 (check out the antique copper pots hanging from the ceiling), Do Mori is above all a fun place to have a genuine Venetian experience, a small, dimly lit *bàcari* that can barely accommodate ten people standing up. Sample the baby octopus and ham on mango, lard-smothered *crostini,* and pickled onions speared with salty anchovies, or opt for the *tramezzini* (tiny sandwiches). Local TV (and BBC) star Francesco Da Mosto is a regular, but note that this institution is very much on the tourist trail—plenty of *cicchetti* tours stop by in the early evening.

San Polo 429 (entrances on Calle Galiazza and Calle Do Mori). ✆ **041-5225401.** Tramezzini and cicchetti 1.80€–2.50€ per piece. *Vaporetto:* Rialto. Mon–Sat 8:30am–8pm (Wed until 2pm; June–Aug closed daily 2–4:30pm).



## SANTA CROCE

### Moderate

**Al Bacco Felice ★** ITALIAN This quaint, friendly, neighborhood restaurant is convenient for the train station and popular with locals, with a real buzz most evenings. Stick with the basics and you won't be disappointed: The pizzas, pastas, and fish dishes are always good, with classic standbys *spaghetti alle vongole,* pasta with spicy *arrabbiata,* and *carpaccio* of swordfish especially well done. The meal usually ends with complimentary plates of Venetian cookies, a nice touch.

Santa Croce 197E (on Corte dei Amai). ✆ **041-5287794.** Mains 12€–24€. *Vaporetto:* Piazzale Roma. Mon–Fri noon–3:30pm and 6:30–11pm; Sat–Sun noon–11:30pm.

## CANNAREGIO

### Expensive

**Da Rioba ★★** SEAFOOD/VENETIAN Fresh, creative, and absolutely scrumptious Venetian food served right alongside a serene canal in a lively—but not touristy—area. Plenty of locals eat here, enticed by the beautifully executed seafood: monkfish, sea bass, scampi, turbot, mackerel, tuna, and lots of cod. Top choices include their lightly grilled scampi (massive prawns sliced down the middle), and their "spaghetti noir," an interpretation of a Venetian classic, spaghetti with cuttlefish ink. Note that there are only 35 seats along the canal, so reservations are a must.

Fondamenta della Misericordia 2553. www.darioba.com. ✆ **041-5244379.** Mains 18€–32€. *Vaporetto:* San Marcuola. Tues–Sun 11am–3pm and 6–10pm.

### Inexpensive

**Taverna del Campiello Remer** ★★ VENETIAN Eating on a budget in Venice doesn't have to mean panini and pizza slices. This romantic taverna overlooks the Grand Canal from a small, charming piazza, and the key is to time your visit with the buffets. The 20€ lunch buffet is a fabulous deal, with fish soup, fresh pastas, seasonal vegetables, a choice of two or three quality main dishes (such as Venice-style liver with polenta, or pan-fried squid), a range of desserts, coffee, water, and wine all included. The evening *aperitivo* is an even better deal, just 8€ for as many smoked meats, sausage, salads, seafood risotto, and pasta as you can eat, plus one spritz, vino, or Prosecco—and this is top-notch cuisine, more substantial than your average *cicchetti*. Normal (more expensive) service resumes later, with live music—Latin, soul, jazz—most nights from 8:30pm. As long as you order a few drinks, it's fine to stick around to take in the scene.

Campiello del Remer 5701. www.alremer.com. ✆ **041-5228769.** Lunch buffet 20€; aperitivo (5:30–7:30pm) 8€. *Vaporetto:* San Marcuola. Mon–Tues and Thurs–Sat noon–2:30pm and 5:30pm–midnight; Sun 5:30pm–midnight.

## Shopping



In a city that for centuries has thrived almost exclusively on tourism, remember this: **Where you buy cheap, you get cheap.** Venetians, centuries-old merchants, aren't known for bargaining. You'll stand a better chance of getting a good deal if you pay in cash or buy more than one item.

A mix of low-end trinket stores and middle-market-to-upscale boutiques line the narrow zigzagging **Mercerie** running north between Piazza San Marco and the Rialto Bridge. More expensive clothing and gift boutiques make for great window-shopping on **Calle Larga XXII Marzo,** the wide street that begins west of Piazza San Marco and wends its way to the expansive Campo Santo Stefano near the Accademia. The narrow **Frezzeria,** just west of Piazza San Marco and running north-south, offers a grab bag of bars, souvenir shops, and tony clothing stores like Louis Vuitton and Versace. There are few bargains to be had; the non-produce part of the **Rialto Market** is as good as it gets for basic souvenirs, where you'll find cheap T-shirts, glow-in-the-dark plastic gondolas, and glass trinkets. The **Mercatino dei Miracoli** ★ (✆ **041-2710022**), held only six times a year in Campo Santa Maria Nova (Cannaregio), is a fabulous flea market with all sorts of bric-a-brac and antiques sold by ordinary Venetians—haggling, for once, is acceptable. It usually takes place on the second Saturday or Sunday of March, April, May, September, October, and December.

Venice is famous for some **local crafts** that have been produced here for centuries: the **glassware** from the lagoon island of Murano, the **delicate lace** from Burano, and the ***cartapesta*** **(papier-mâché) Carnevale masks** you'll find in endless *botteghe* (shops), where you can watch artisans paint amid their wares. **La Bottega dei Mascareri** ★★,

Calle dei Saoneri 2720, San Polo (www.mascarer.com; ✆ **041-5242887**), sells high-quality, creative masks—some based on Tiepolo paintings—crafted by the brothers Sergio and Massimo Boldrin since 1984. **Ca' del Sol Maschere ★★**, Fondamenta de l'Osmarin 4964, Castello (www.cadelsolmascherevenezia.com; ✆ **041-5285549**), is another treasure trove of Venetian masks, run by a group of artists since 1986. Convenient, classy, but incredibly expensive, **Venini ★,** Piazzetta Leoncini 314, San Marco (www.venini.it; ✆ **041-5224045**), has been selling quality glass art since 1921, supplying the likes of Versace and many other designer brands. Their **workshop** on Murano is at Fondamenta Vetrai 50 (✆ **041-2737211**).

## Entertainment & Nightlife

If you're looking for serious nocturnal action, you're in the wrong town. Your best bet is to sit in moonlit Piazza San Marco and listen to the cafes' outdoor orchestras, with the illuminated basilica before you, the perfect operatic set—though this pleasure comes with a hefty price tag. **Caffè Centrale ★★,** Piscina Frezzeria 1659, San Marco (www.caffecentralevenezia.com; ✆ **041-2413952**), is a super-hip bar and restaurant, located within the 16th-century Palazzo Cocco Molin, just a short walk from San Marco. There's an intriguing selection of beers, plus a long cocktail list including the city's signature Bellini (sparkling Prosecco wine and fresh peach puree). Other popular spots to hang out include **Campo San Bartolomeo,** at the foot of the Rialto Bridge (although it is a zoo here in high season), and nearby **Campo San Luca.** In late-night hours, for low prices and low pretension, the absolute best place to go is **Campo Santa Margherita,** a huge open *campo* about halfway between the train station and the Accademia Bridge. To get acquainted with all things bubbly, visit **Al Prosecco ★★,** Campo San Giacomo da l'Orio 1503, Santa Croce (www.alprosecco.com; ✆ **041-5240222**), a specialist, as you'd expect, in Prosecco. There are tasty *cicchetti* to wash down the various brands, and a gorgeous terrace. **Paradiso Perduto ★,** Fondamenta della Misericordia 2540, Cannaregio (www.ilparadisoperduto.com; ✆ **041-720581**), is the most happening neighborhood bar in Cannaregio.

Venice has a long and rich tradition of **classical music,** and there's always a concert going on somewhere. Several churches and confraternities (such as San Stae, the Scuola di San Giovanni Evangelista, and the Scuola di San Rocco) regularly host classical music concerts, with an emphasis on the baroque. This was, after all, the home of Vivaldi. **Santa Maria della Pietà ★★,** Riva degli Schiavoni 3701, Castello (www.chiesavivaldi.it; ✆ **041-5221120**), the so-called "Vivaldi Church," built between 1745 and 1760, holds concerts throughout the year. Jewel in the crown for opera fans, however, is **Teatro La Fenice ★★★,** Campo San Fantin 1965, San Marco (www.teatrolafenice.it; ✆ **041-2424**), one of Italy's grandest opera houses. It officially ranks third after La Scala in

Milan and San Carlo in Naples. The opera season runs late November through June, but there are also ballet performances and classical concerts. Tickets cost 70€ to 80€ for the gallery, and 100€ to 220€ for a decent seat ("listening" only seats with no view go for 15€–30€, while obstructed-view seats cost 25€–45€).

## [Fast FACTS] ITALY

**Business Hours** General open hours for **stores, offices,** and **churches** are from 9:30am to noon or 1pm and again from 3 or 3:30pm to 7:30 or 8pm. The early afternoon shutdown is the *riposo*, the Italian siesta (in the downtown area of large cities stores don't close for the *riposo*). **Banks** tend to open Monday through Friday 8:30am to 1:30pm and 2:45 to 4:15pm.

**Currency** Italy is a member of the European Union and uses the E.U. common currency, the euro (€). See p. 860 for information on money and costs.

**Doctors & Dentists** Italy offers universal healthcare to citizens of European Union countries. Others must pay medical bills upfront, though even if you don't have insurance, you will always be treated in an emergency room. Your hotel should have an updated list of general and specialist doctors and dentists.

**Embassies & Consulates:**

**Australia:** Via Antonio Bosio, Rome; www.italy.embassy.gov.au; ✆ **06-852721.**

**Canada:** Via Zara 30, Rome; www.italy.gc.ca; ✆ **06-85444-2911.**

**New Zealand:** Via Clitunno 44, Rome; www.nzembassy.com/italy; ✆ **06-8537501.**

**United Kingdom:** Via XX Settembre 80/a, Rome; www.gov.uk/government/world/organisations/british-embassy-rome; ✆ **06-4220-0001.**

**United States:** Palazzo Margherita, Via Vittorio Veneto 121, Rome; http://italy.usembassy.gov; ✆ **06-46741** Rome, 055-266-951 in Florence.

**Emergencies** The best number to call with a **general emergency** is ✆ **112,** which connects you to the ***carabinieri*** who will transfer your call as needed. For the **police,** dial ✆ **113;** for a **medical emergency** and to call an **ambulance,** the number is ✆ **118;** for the **fire department,** call ✆ **115.**

**Pharmacies** Italian pharmacies offer essentially the same range of generic drugs available in the United States. They are ubiquitous (marked with a green cross) and serve like miniclinics, diagnosing and treating minor ailments with over-the-counter drugs. Pharmacies take turns staying open nights and weekends; if the closest pharmacy is closed, a sign posted on the door will direct you to an open one.

SPAIN
11
by Patricia Harris & David Lyon

It's an awkward adage, but it's often said that Europe brings to you only what you bring to it. If you arrive in Spain without some prior knowledge of its turbulent history—in other words, if you have failed first to read deeply about its unusual past, you will fail to enjoy the best rewards of travel. You will not thrill to the Spanish experience.

Why is that history so unusual, requiring study? Well, would you believe that for seven hundred years, Spain was a Muslim nation occupied by Moorish armies who left distinctive structures in their wake? Would you ever have understood that Spain's awesome power permitted it, in the 1500s, to subjugate such faraway nations as Belgium, The Netherlands and the Philippines? Would you have fully understood how the people of Spain so colonized vast areas of the world that today some 500 million people around the world speak Spanish (the world's second most common language)? Would you have understood how Spain was a violent testing ground for the later military conquests of Adolf Hitler, leaving such relics as a cathedral in honor of Fascist soldiers and Picasso's searing mural of Guernica, both on display at locations outside of and within Madrid?

All of this—and more—is available to be seen in places ranging from the Islamic palaces and gardens of Andalucía to awesome monuments elsewhere to Christopher Columbus. But they require, for full understanding, that you spend a few hours in a library, in advance of your trip, reading of the Spanish story. If you do, you will find that Spain, separated from the rest of Europe by the Pyrenees Mountains, has been shaped by factors much different from those in the rest of Western Europe.

I first came to Spain in the late 1950s during the time of dictator Francisco Franco, who was then in power following his successful rebellion against the democratically elected government of Spain. His reign was so abusive, so ignorant and corrupt, that the atmosphere of Spain was subdued and apprehensive. I recall, for instance, how the only movies in downtown Madrid were second-rate cowboy films from America, chosen because they would not stimulate ordinary citizens to enjoy a higher culture, or to crave a better lot. Spain as a whole was poverty-stricken; its hotels and restaurants were the cheapest in the world; it had bet on the

PREVIOUS PAGE: **Cafes in Madrid's Plaza Mayor.**

wrong horse in World War II, supporting Germany, and it was now barred from membership in the United Nations.

I recall, in my writings, how I decried the economic backwardness of Spain, but also how I paid tribute to its dignified, courteous, and proud people. That population, following Franco's death, quickly transformed the nation into a democracy, and just as soon brought about an economic renaissance that quickly made it—until a bursting of investment bubbles in 2008—one of the richest countries on the continent. Among other things, Spain developed what is probably the world's largest tourism industry, welcoming millions of visitors each year to its stunning beaches, resorts, museums, and cathedrals. There is some reason to believe that the economy of Spain is again on the upswing as this book goes to press, and we can only hope for its revival.

And now you will want to visit stately Madrid, with its elegant squares (don't miss the Plaza Mayor), its remarkable, world-class museums (the Prado and the Reina Sofía displaying Picasso, Velázquez, Goya, El Greco), its famous bull ring (Las Ventas in the Plaza de Toros), its theaters, excellent restaurants, tapas bars, and shops. You will want to spend a lot of time in fast-growing Barcelona, a giant port city which has become one of Europe's most popular touristic capitals, with its sublime architecture of Gaudí (not simply his unique and magnificent cathedral but numerous other masterworks) and its highly regarded museums (including a Picasso museum, and elsewhere the paintings of Joan Miró), its restaurants rated among the best in the world, its opera house and many excellent concert halls, its highly literate and cultured population speaking Catalan, and its surprising beaches.

And you will want to take a high-speed train (Spain has developed a great many high-speed rail routes) to Moorish Andalucía (Sevilla, Granada, Córdoba) on your way to the seaside bathing resorts of the Costa del Sol (on the Mediterranean). You may even want to hop over to Gibraltar at the end of your trip, or to visit the Balearic Islands (like Palma de Mallorca) after your visit to Barcelona. Have a good trip!

***–Arthur Frommer***

# BARCELONA

Perched on the shore of the Mediterranean, Barcelona is an original, with its own fanciful Modernisme architecture to prove it. Two thousand

Les Rambles, Barcelona's main street.

years of Iberian, Roman, Visigothic, Moorish, French, and Aragonese cultures have given the city its own history, language, gastronomy, and sense of style. Today it is the capital of the autonomous region of Catalunya, chafing to leave the federal fold of Spain but enjoying near-country status within the European Union. Having won back its identity from Spain, Barcelona is profoundly Catalan, yet generous about conducting business and pleasure in Castilian Spanish and English—as well as Catalan.

In fact, the local language has a verb that must have been invented for the city. "Badar" means (more or less) to walk around with your mouth wide open in astonishment. You'll be doing a lot of that in Barcelona. The city's artists have always had a fantastical vision—from the gargoyles along the roofline of the cathedral, to Antoni Gaudí's armored warrior chimneys on La Pedrera, to the surreal amoeboid sculptures of Joan Miró (they're on a roof, too). Whether you are rambling the medieval streets of the Barri Gòtic, devouring peel-and-eat shrimp at a beachside cafe, or sipping fresh strawberry-melon juice at La Boqueria, keep your eyes wide open: You never know what will amaze you next.

## Essentials

The **Oficina de Informació de Turisme de Barcelona** website is www.barcelonaturisme.com.

**ARRIVING** Barcelona's international airport (BCN) is **El Prat,** located in El Prat de Llobregat (www.aena.es; ✆ **90-240-47-04**), 12km (7½ miles) southwest of the city center. It has two passenger terminals connected by shuttle buses. Terminal T1 serves the majority of international carriers.

A train runs between the airport and Barcelona's main railway station, **Estació Central de Barcelona-Sants,** every 15 to 30 minutes daily from 5:40am to 11:10pm (from Sants) or 11:40pm (to Sants). The 20-minute trip costs 4.20€. If your hotel is near Plaça d'Espanya or Plaça de Catalunya, take an **Aerobús** (www.aerobusbcn.com; ✆ **93-415-60-20**). It runs every 5 minutes between 6:10am and 1am from the airport, and until 12:30am from Plaça de Catalunya. The fare is 5.90€ single trip, 10€ round-trip. A taxi from the airport costs about 30€.

If you are arriving by **car,** the major access route from France is at the eastern end of the **Pyrenees:** the express highway (E-15) or the more scenic coastal road. If you take the coastal road in July and August, you will often face bumper-to-bumper traffic. You can also approach Barcelona via **Toulouse.** Cross the border at **Puigcerdà** (where there are frontier stations), near the Principality of Andorra. From there, take the N-152 to Barcelona. From **Madrid,** take the N-2 to Zaragoza, and then the A-2 to El Vendrell, followed by the A-7 freeway to Barcelona. From the **Costa Blanca** or **Costa del Sol,** follow the E-15 north from Valencia along the eastern Mediterranean coast.

Barcelona has two major rail stations. Most national and international **trains** arrive at **Estació Central de Barcelona-Sants** (Plaça de Països Catalanes; Metro: Sants-Estació), including high-speed AVE trains from Madrid and the high-speed Trenhotel from Paris. Some slower trains from northern Spain and just over the French border arrive at **Estació de França** (Avenida Marqués de L'Argentera; Metro: Barceloneta, L3). For general RENFE (Spanish Railways) information, visit www.renfe.com or call ✆ **90-232-03-20.**

**Bus travel** to Barcelona is possible, but it's slow and less comfortable than the train. Most buses arrive at **Estació del Nord** (Carrer d'Alí Bei, 80; Metro: Arc de Triomf). **Daily ferries** to and from the Balearic Islands of Mallorca (8 hr.) and Menorca (8 hr.) are operated by **Trasmediterránea** (Muelle de Sant Bertran s/n; www.trasmediterranea.es; ✆ **90-245-46-45**).

**CITY LAYOUT** Barcelona is a port city enclosed by two small mountains (**Montjuïc** on the southwest, **Tibidabo** on the north) that form a natural bowl around the harbor. Although the city sprawls on its east side, the main sections of interest to travelers are the **waterfront, Ciutat Vell** (Old City), **L'Eixample** and **Gràcia** (19th-century extensions inland from the Old City), and **Montjuïc.**

The central artery of the Ciutat Vell is **Les Rambles,** a broad avenue with a pedestrian center strip. It begins at the waterfront at Plaça Portal de la Pau, with its 50m-high (174-ft.) monument to Columbus, and stretches north to Plaça de Catalunya, changing names several times along the way. Along this wide promenade, you'll find bookshops and

## events IN BARCELONA

Barcelona honors the patron saint of Catalunya with **La Diada de Sant Jordi** (St. George) on April 23. Traditionally, men present a red rose to the special women in their lives, while women return the favor with a book. Flower vendors and open-air book stalls give the city a festive air.

The city ushers in summer by celebrating the solstice during the **Verbena de Sant Joan** on June 23 and 24. Dances, bonfires, and other festivities culminate in fireworks.

During the month of July, the **Grec Festival** (http://grec.bcn.cat) presents a stunning array of performances of theater, dance, music, and circus arts in venues throughout the city, including the open-air Teatre Grec on Montjuïc.

In mid-September, Barcelona welcomes fall with the **Festa de la Mercè** in honor of the city's patron Saint Mare de Deu. Spirited activities include parades with giant figures, human towers, and parades of devils with lots of sparklers and firecrackers.

newsstands, stalls selling birds and flowers, and benches or cafe tables where you can sit and watch the passing parade. West of Les Rambles is **El Raval,** while the neighborhood immediately east of Les Rambles is the **Barri Gòtic** (or Gothic Quarter). East of the **Barri Gòtic** are the neighborhoods of **El Born** (where the waterfront transitions into the medieval city) and **La Ribera.**

**Plaça de Catalunya** is crossed by **Gran Via Corts Catalanes,** which is the approximate divider between the old and new cities. Ringed with hotels and restaurants, the plaza is a crossroads of bus and Metro routes. North of Gran Via, the streets of L'Eixample assume an orderly grid. **Passeig de Gràcia** is the most elegant of the north-south boulevards. The exception to the grid is the slash across "new" Barcelona, the **Avinguda Diagonal,** which separates the grid of L'Eixample from the grid of Gràcia.

**GETTING AROUND** You can walk most places in Barcelona's Old City, or through the main districts of interest in L'Eixample. But it's a good idea to use public transport to get to a starting point and then set off on foot to explore.

Barcelona's **public transit system** includes extensive and interlinked networks of buses, subway trains, trams, and "rodalies" (local commuter rail). For a full overview, check the website of **Transports Metropolitans de Barcelona** (www.tmb.cat). This site, available in Catalan, Spanish, and English, has a very useful tool that recommends ways to get from one place to another using any combination of public transit and walking. Individual tickets on subway and buses within the central city cost 2.15€.

Barcelona's **Metro system** consists of six main lines; it crisscrosses the city more frequently and with greater efficiency than the bus network. Service operates Sunday to Thursday from 5am to midnight, and Friday and Saturday from 5am to 2am. Each Metro station entrance is marked with a red diamond. The major station for all subway lines is **Plaça de Catalunya.** About **190 bus lines** traverse the city and, not surprisingly, you don't want to ride them at rush hour. Most buses run daily from 5:30am to 10pm; some night buses go along the principal arteries from 11pm to 4am. You can buy your ticket when boarding. Red buses cut through the city center during the day; yellow ones operate at night.

**The Hola BCN!** card provides 2, 3, 4, or 5 days of unlimited travel on all trains, Metro, buses, and trams for 14€, 20.50€, 26.50€, and 32€, respectively. Consider how many public transit trips per day you expect to take. (We usually find it's between two and four.) Online purchase only, at www.tmb.cat.

Each yellow-and-black **taxi** bears the letters sp *(Servicio Público)* on its front and rear. A lit green light on the roof and a libre sign in the window indicate the taxi is free to pick up passengers. Make sure that the meter is at zero when you enter. The basic rate begins at 2€. Each additional kilometer costs 1€. Supplements might apply—1€ for a large suitcase placed in the trunk, for instance. Rides to the airport carry a supplement of 3.10€. For a taxi, contact **Ràdio Taxi** (www.radiotaxi033.com; ✆ **93-303-30-33**).

To visit the mountains of Tibidabo or Montjuïc, you'll have to use **funiculars or cable cars.** To visit Tibidabo by public transport, take the **Funicular de Tibidabo.** The fare is 7.70€, or 4.10€ if you're also purchasing admission to the Tibidabo amusement park. The funicular operates every 15 to 20 minutes. From mid-April to September, service is daily 10am to 8pm. In the off-season, it usually operates only Saturday and Sunday 10am to 6pm. To get to the funicular, take Metro Line 7 to Avinguda Tibidabo. Exit onto Plaça Kennedy and take either the 1901 tram called **Tramvía Blau** (Blue Streetcar) or **Bus 196** to the funicular. The bus is the usual 2.15€ fare. Tickets on the **Tramvia Blau** are 4€.

Getting to Montjuïc by funicular is a simple ride from the Paral.lel Metro station and is considered part of the Metro network, although you need to change and use a new 2.15€ ticket. Once you're on the mountain, you can ride a cable car to the castle on top. Tickets on **Telefèric de Montjuïc** are 7.30€ one-way, 10€ round-trip (5.50€ or 7.40€ for ages 4-12).

Don't **drive** or try to park in congested Barcelona. Use public transit.

## The Neighborhoods in Brief

**LES RAMBLES & EL RAVAL** **Les Rambles** is the broad, 1.5km-long (1-mile) avenue that runs between the waterfront and Plaça de Catalunya. If you're not jazzed walking up and down **Les Rambles,** check to make sure you still have a pulse. You can spend a day here just exploring the street life, cafes, and shops. But you'll want to take some of that time to wander into El Raval on streets named Nou de la Rambla, Sant Pau, Hospital, Carme, and Elisabets. You'll find both the wonderfully *récherché* world of old Raval, and the modern, hip neighborhood of the arts to the west of Les Rambles. Get to Les Rambles by one of three Metro stops: Drassanes at the waterfront, Liceu halfway up, and Plaça de Catalunya at the top.

**BARRI GÒTIC** East of Les Rambles is Barcelona's main medieval quarter, the **Barri Gòtic.** Built atop the old Roman city of Barcino, it's a tangle of narrow streets that radiate from and connect to slightly larger plazas around the cathedral and a series of other Gothic churches. Buried deep within the Barri Gòtic are the remnants of the **Call,** the medieval Jewish neighborhood. Plan on spending at least a half-day exploring, knowing that you will get a little lost, no matter how good your map. The area assumes a special magic on Sunday mornings, when you can emerge from a warren of small streets onto a square where a musician may be playing for change. Metro stops are Liceu and Jaume I.

**LA RIBERA & EL BORN** With streets a little wider, buildings a little newer, **La Ribera** and **El Born** push the Barri Gòtic eastward. They are still obviously part of the Old City, and can be combined with the Barri Gòtic for a long day or even two of touring. Once working-class districts, both La Ribera and El Born have sprouted gelaterias and tapas bars every few steps. Metro stops include Jaume I, Arc de Triomf, and Urquinaona.

**L'EIXAMPLE** North of Plaça de Catalunya and Gran Via de les Corts Catalanes, **L'Eixample** is the elegant planned "expansion" that unfolded mostly from 1890 to 1910. It contains more than three dozen Modernista landmarks. Don't overlook the small details. Gaudí designed the Modernista light posts and the hexagonal paving tiles that still cover the sidewalks on parts of Passeig de Gràcia. Take a break on the Modernista tile benches on the street corners. The main north-south axis is **Passeig de Gràcia.** At its northern end, it is transected by the broad swath of **Avinguda Diagonal.** Major Metro stops for the neighborhood include Passeig de Gràcia, Diagonal, Provença, Universitat, Girona, and Sagrada Familia.

**LA BARCELONETA & THE WATERFRONT** Redevelopment of the waterfront for the 1992 Olympics turned a sailor's port into a yacht harbor and installed **L'Aquarium Barcelona** and the **Maremagnum** shopping center on an island, the Moll d'Espanya. Another quay was transformed into the **Moll de la Fusta,** a popular walking and cycling path. Its east end intersects **Passeig de Joan de Borbó,** which extends to **La Barceloneta**—the former fishermen's neighborhood that's now a hip bohemian address noted for seafood restaurants and sandy beaches. The beaches flow east to **Port Olimpic,** created for sailing during the Olympics. Three Metro stops provide access to the waterfront: Drassanes, Barceloneta, and Ciutadella/Vila Olimpica.

## WAYS TO save IN BARCELONA

There are several discount programs that may or may not work for you, depending on what you want to see and how you're planning to get around.

A ticket on the **Barcelona Bus Turistic** (p. 759) gets you a coupon book good for the calendar year. Most discounts are modest, and the Museu Picasso is not included, but if you decide to ride the bus, be sure to use the coupons.

The **Barcelona Card** features several free museum admissions (not Picasso) and allows you to skip the lines. It also provides discounts on other admissions and tours, including 15% to 20% on admissions to major Modernista buildings. Unlimited use of Metro, buses, and commuter rail can be a plus. Available at all Barcelona Turisme offices (www.barcelonaturisme.com) and El Corte Inglés department stores, it costs 45€ for 3 days, 55€ for 4 days and 60€ for 5 days. The corresponding prices for children ages 4 to 12 are 21€, 27€, and 32€.

The **ArTicket BCN** is geared to the major art museums, providing priority entry to six museums for 30€: Museu Picasso, Museu Nacional d'Art de Catalunya, Fundació Joan Miró, Fundació Antoni Tàpies, the Centre de Cultura Contemporània de Barcelona (CCCB), and the Museu d'Art Contemporani de Barcelona (MACBA). Tickets to the first three alone will cost more than the pass. The pass also allows you to skip the line—a huge timesaver at the Museu Picasso.

When weighing the options, keep in mind that on the first Sunday of each month, **admission is free** at the Museu Picasso and the Museu Nacional d'Art de Catalunya (MNAC). On the last Tuesday of the month, admission is free at the Museu d'Història de Catalunya. Museu Picasso is also free every Sunday after 2pm, while MNAC is free every Saturday after 3pm.

**MONTJUÏC** **Montjuïc** is a small mountain that seems very tall when you're walking up it in August. It begins at the **Plaça d'Espanya** traffic rotary and goes up to the old Palacio Nacional, now the **Museu Nacional d'Art de Catalunya.** The mountain was used for the 1929 Barcelona International Exposition, which created the roadways, many gardens, and the **Poble Espanyol** area of "typical" architecture from around Spain. It is also the home of the **Fundació Joan Miró.** The 1992 Olympics brought even more structures to Montjuïc. The most useful bus lines are Route 55 from Plaça d'Espanya and Route 150 for circling the Montjuïc roads. You can also take the funicular (mostly underground) from the Paral.lel Metro station, which delivers you to the Telefèric de Montjuïc station. Many visitors prefer the **Bus Turistic** (p. 759) for visiting Montjuïc, because it makes stops at all the attractions.

## Exploring Barcelona

The amazing Modernisme architecture exemplified by the buildings of Antoni Gaudí is what first attracts visitors to Barcelona, but it's the disarming charm of the Mediterranean city that keeps them coming back. Begin by exploring the areas adjacent to slightly madcap Les Rambles,

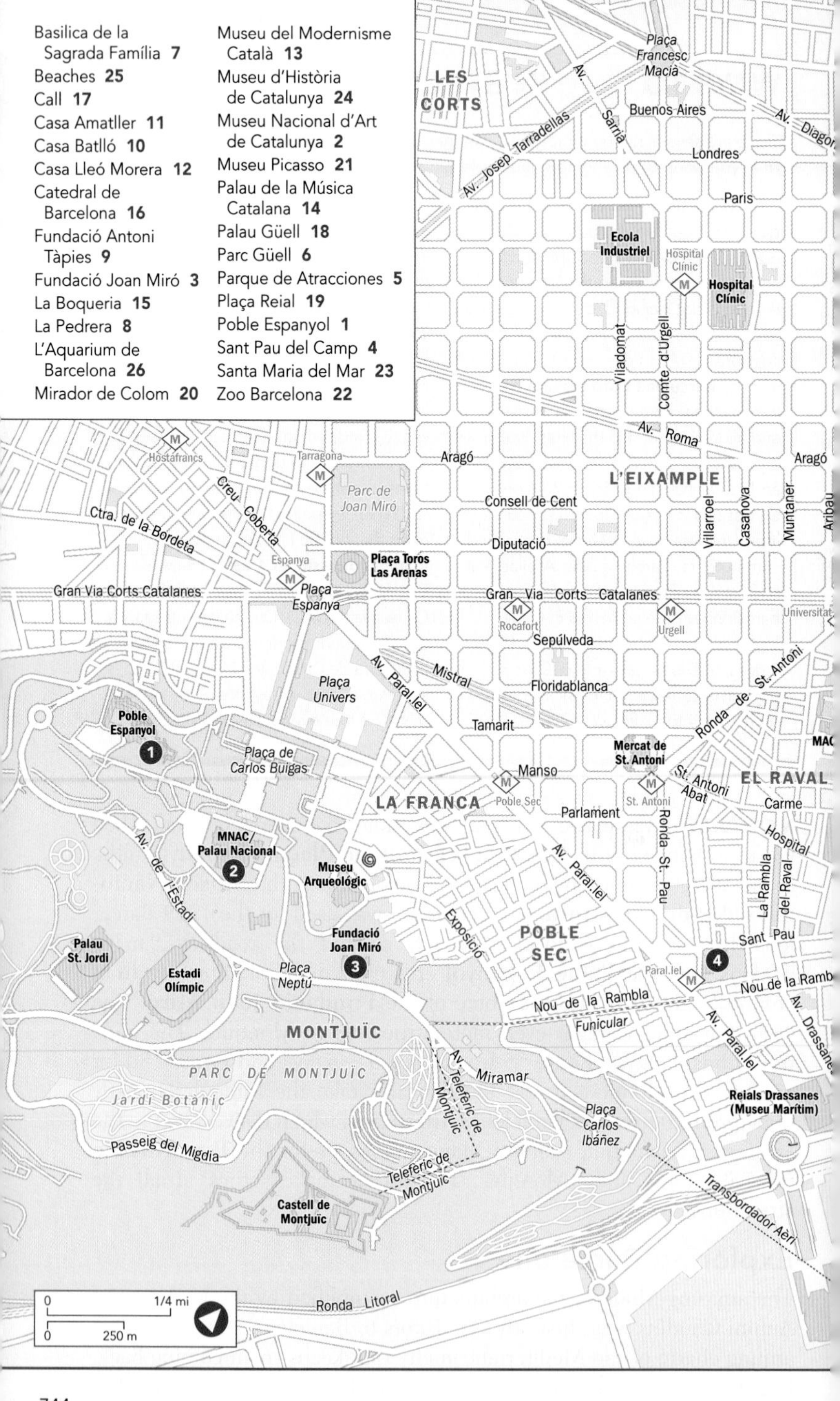

Basilica de la Sagrada Família 7
Beaches 25
Call 17
Casa Amatller 11
Casa Batlló 10
Casa Lleó Morera 12
Catedral de Barcelona 16
Fundació Antoni Tàpies 9
Fundació Joan Miró 3
La Boqueria 15
La Pedrera 8
L'Aquarium de Barcelona 26
Mirador de Colom 20
Museu del Modernisme Català 13
Museu d'Història de Catalunya 24
Museu Nacional d'Art de Catalunya 2
Museu Picasso 21
Palau de la Música Catalana 14
Palau Güell 18
Parc Güell 6
Parque de Atracciones 5
Plaça Reial 19
Poble Espanyol 1
Sant Pau del Camp 4
Santa Maria del Mar 23
Zoo Barcelona 22
LES CORTS
Plaça Francesc Macià
Av. Sarrià
Buenos Aires
Av. Diagonal
Av. Josep Tarradellas
Londres
Paris
Ecola Industriel
Hospital Clínic
Hospital Clínic
Viladomat
Comte d'Urgell
Av. Roma
Aragó
Aragó
L'EIXAMPLE
Villarroel
Casanova
Muntaner
Aribau
Hostafrancs
Tarragona
Parc de Joan Miró
Creu Coberta
Consell de Cent
Diputació
Ctra. de la Bordeta
Espanya
Plaça Toros Las Arenas
Plaça Espanya
Gran Via Corts Catalanes
Gran Via Corts Catalanes
Rocafort
Urgell
Universitat
Sepúlveda
Av. Paral.lel
Mistral
Floridablanca
Plaça Univers
Ronda de St. Antoni
Tamarit
Poble Espanyol
Plaça de Carlos Buigas
Mercat de St. Antoni
Manso
Poble Sec
St. Antoni
St. Antoni Abat
EL RAVAL
LA FRANCA
Parlament
Carme
Av. de l'Estadi
MNAC/ Palau Nacional
Museu Arqueològic
Av. Paral.lel
Ronda St. Pau
Hospital
La Rambla del Raval
Exposició
Palau St. Jordi
Estadi Olímpic
Fundació Joan Miró
Plaça Neptú
POBLE SEC
Sant Pau
Paral.lel
Nou de la Rambla
Nou de la Rambla
Funicular
Av. Drassanes
MONTJUÏC
Av. Paral.lel
PARC DE MONTJUÏC
Av. Miramar
Telefèric de Montjuïc
Jardí Botànic
Plaça Carlos Ibáñez
Reials Drassanes (Museu Marítim)
Passeig del Migdia
Telefèric de Montjuïc
Castell de Montjuïc
Transbordador Aèri
Ronda Litoral
0 1/4 mi
0 250 m

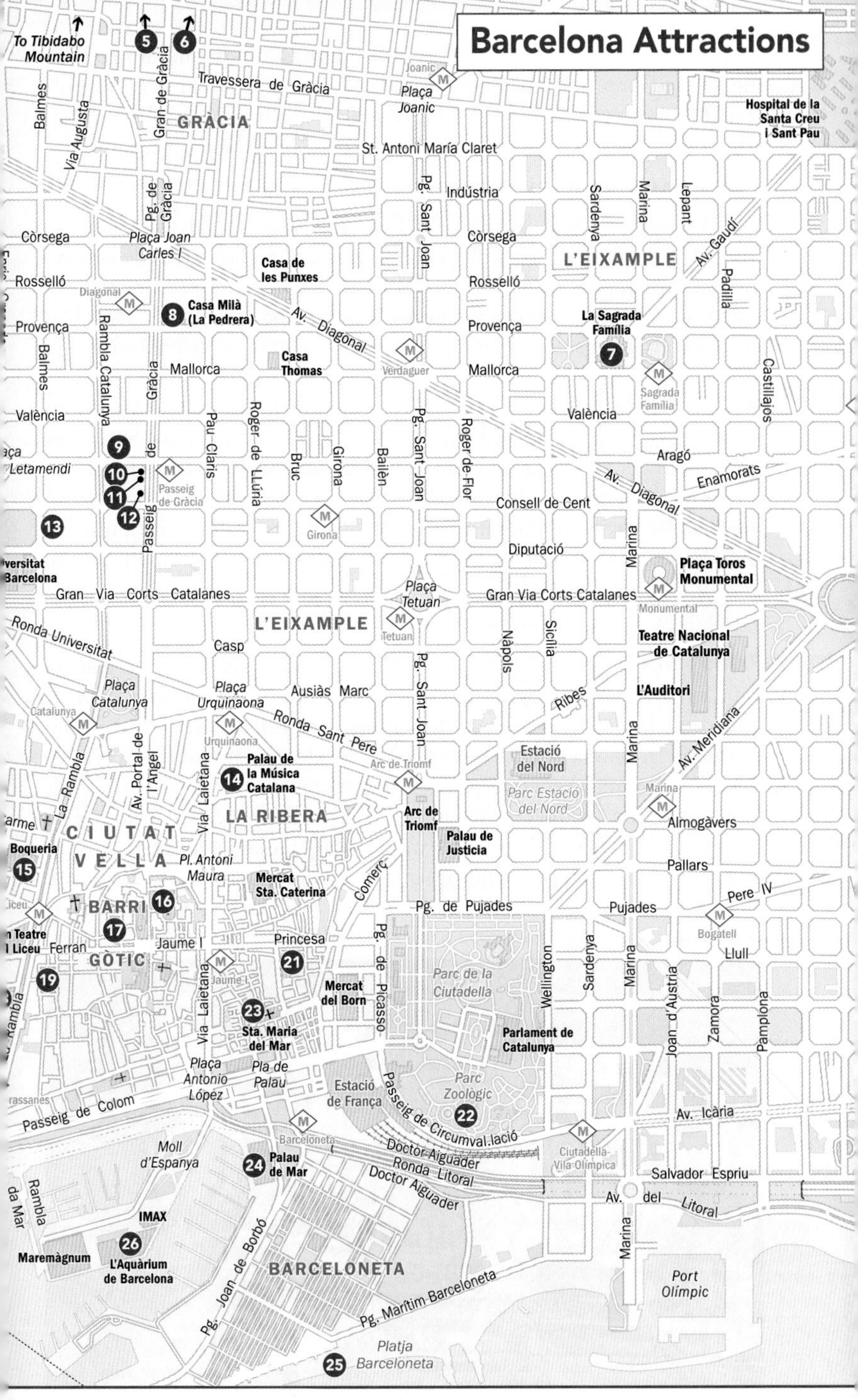

Barcelona Attractions
To Tibidabo Mountain
Travessera de Gràcia
GRÀCIA
Gran de Gràcia
Plaça Joanic
Joanic
Hospital de la Santa Creu i Sant Pau
St. Antoni María Claret
Indústria
Còrsega
Plaça Joan Carles I
Casa de les Punxes
L'EIXAMPLE
Rosselló
Diagonal
Casa Milà (La Pedrera)
Av. Diagonal
Provença
La Sagrada Família
Casa Thomas
Verdaguer
Mallorca
Sagrada Família
València
Aragó
Letamendi
Passeig de Gràcia
Enamorats
Consell de Cent
Girona
Diputació
Plaça Toros Monumental
Universitat Barcelona
Gran Via Corts Catalanes
Plaça Tetuan
Tetuan
Monumental
Ronda Universitat
Casp
Teatre Nacional de Catalunya
Plaça Catalunya
Plaça Urquinaona
Ausiàs Marc
L'Auditori
Catalunya
Urquinaona
Ronda Sant Pere
Ribes
Av. Meridiana
Arc de Triomf
Estació del Nord
Parc Estació del Nord
Palau de la Música Catalana
LA RIBERA
Marina
Almogàvers
Boqueria
CIUTAT VELLA
Pl. Antoni Maura
Palau de Justicia
Pallars
Mercat Sta. Caterina
Comerç
Liceu
BARRI GÒTIC
Pg. de Pujades
Pujades
Pere IV
Bogatell
Teatre Liceu
Ferran
Jaume I
Princesa
Llull
Mercat del Born
Parc de la Ciutadella
Sta. Maria del Mar
Parlament de Catalunya
Plaça Antonio López
Pla de Palau
Estació de França
Parc Zoològic
Passeig de Colom
Passeig de Circumval.lació
Av. Icària
Barceloneta
Doctor Aiguader
Ronda Litoral
Ciutadella-Vila Olímpica
Moll d'Espanya
Palau de Mar
Salvador Espriu
Av. del Litoral
Rambla da Mar
IMAX
Maremàgnum
L'Aquàrium de Barcelona
Pg. Joan de Borbó
BARCELONETA
Pg. Marítim Barceloneta
Port Olímpic
Platja Barceloneta
Balmes
Via Augusta
Rambla Catalunya
Pau Claris
Roger de Llúria
Bruc
Girona
Bailèn
Pg. Sant Joan
Roger de Flor
Sardenya
Lepant
Av. Gaudí
Padilla
Castillejos
Nàpols
Sicília
La Rambla
Av. Portal de l'Àngel
Via Laietana
Pg. de Picasso
Wellington
Joan d'Austria
Zamora
Pamplona
5
6
7
8
9
10
11
12
13
14
15
16
17
19
21
22
23
24
25
26

spend a day or more admiring Gothic churches and medieval plazas in the tangled streets of Barri Gòtic and El Born, and another strolling purposefully in the elegant grid of L'Eixample. And don't miss those Modernisme masterpieces. They are why you came in the first place.

## LES RAMBLES & EL RAVAL

**La Boqueria** ★★★ MARKET Foodies visiting Spain consider the Mercat de Sant Josep de la Boqueria (its official name) a temple deserving reverential pilgrimage. The spot has been a marketplace since medieval days, and the current market is the largest of Barcelona's 35 public markets. It has a sidewalk mosaic in front created by Joan Miró in the 1970s, and the metal-roofed structure is an amalgam of building styles erected between 1840 and 1914. From the outside, it resembles a train station. Inside, it is jammed with stalls selling every imaginable type of fresh produce, fish (segregated to one side), and meat (toward the back). There are bakeries, sandwich stalls, juice bars, and cafes all tucked into the mix. By paying attention to what the stalls are selling, you'll quickly learn what's fresh and in season, and can order accordingly at the restaurants.

Les Rambles, 91. No phone. Mon–Sat 8am–8pm. Metro: Liceu.

**Palau Güell** ★★ HISTORIC SITE Gaudí's second commission appears to have been grown rather than built. Constructed between 1886 and 1890 for aristocrat and industrialist Eusebi Güell, the home shows the architect's budding originality. The family quarters are conventional—"a normal Venetian palace," a guide once sniffed on one of our tours—but the architect's imagination ran wild above and below. The underground brick columns and vaults in 10 musty cellars is a honeycomb of stables and servants' quarters, and functions as much as the

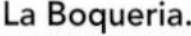
La Boqueria.

Cloister of 13th-century Sant Pau de Camp.

building's root system as its foundation. The rooftop is even more startling. Gaudí wrapped the chimneys with swirling abstract sculptures. They are embedded with mosaics of broken pottery and employ ancient Catalan artistic symbols.

Carrer Nou de la Rambla, 3-5. www.palauguell.cat. ✆ **93-472-57-75.** 12€ adults, 8€ students/seniors. Metro: Liceu. Apr–Oct Tues–Sun 10am–8pm, Nov–Mar Tues–Sun 10am–5:30pm.

**Sant Pau del Camp ★★** RELIGIOUS SITE The antithesis of Gaudí's La Sagrada Familia, the modest ancient church and monastery of Sant Pau del Camp (St. Paul of the Fields) may be the most serene and moving religious space in Barcelona. According to his gravestone, the monastery was founded between 897 and 911 by Guifré Borrell, then count of Barcelona (and son of Wilfred the Hairy). The church was sacked by Al-Mansur's Moorish troops in 985, but the complex was rebuilt during the 13th century—the period of the charming cloister and its stone capitals carved with biblical tales. Centuries of erosion have not dimmed Eve's sudden embarrassment about her nakedness or the ferocity of the reptilian devil being skewered by Archangel Michael. The intimate piety of the church and its small altar are striking. A side chapel holds a beautiful Gothic statue of María del Deu, as well as Borrell's gravestone.

Carrer Sant Pau, 101. ✆ **93-441-00-01.** 3€, Sun morning free. Daily 10am–1:30pm, 4–7:30pm. Metro: Paral.lel. Masses Sat 8pm in Castilian Spanish, Sun noon in Catalan.

## BARRI GÒTIC

**Call** ★ NEIGHBORHOOD Barcelona had one of the most robust Jewish communities in Iberia from the 12th century until 1391, when the community in the heart of the Barri Gòtic came under siege. Six centuries of absence have wiped away most evidence of Jewish presence, but since the 1990s, a concerted effort by scholars and community activists has helped establish the old limits of the Call and has begun to restore the remains of the principal synagogue. The main street of the Call (a Jewish word meaning "small street" related to the Spanish "calle" and Catalan "carrer") was Carrer de Sant Domènc, where the synagogue, the kosher butcher's shop, and the homes of the leading Jewish citizens were located. An information center and display of artifacts recovered through excavations is operated by the Associació Call de Barcelona in a shop above the remains of the **Sinagoga Mayor.**

Carrer Marlet, 5. ✆ **93-317-07-90.** 2.50€. Metro: Jaume I. Mon–Fri 10:30am–6pm, Sat–Sun 10:30am–2:30pm.

**Catedral de Barcelona** ★★ RELIGIOUS SITE A celebrated example of Catalan Gothic architecture, Barcelona's cathedral was begun at the end of the 13th century and more or less completed by the mid-15th century. The western facade dates from the 19th century, when churchgoers felt that the unadorned Gothic surface was somehow inadequate. To get a feel for the cathedral, skip the "tourist visit" and go to Mass, or at least sit silently and reflect. The high naves, which have been cleaned and lit in recent years, are filled with terrific Gothic architectural details, including the elongated columns that blossom into arches in their upper reaches. The separate **cloister** has vaulted galleries that surround a garden of magnolias, medlars, and palm trees and the so-called "well of the geese" (13 geese live in the cloister as a symbol of Barcelona co-patron Santa Eulalia). The cloister also contains the cathedral's museum, of which the most notable piece is a 15th-century *Pieta* by Bartolomé Bermejo. An elevator goes to the roof, which has fanciful gargoyles and terrific views of the Barri Gòtic. At noon on Sundays (sometimes on Sat), folk dancers gather below the cathedral steps to dance the traditional *sardana.* On the feast of Corpus Christi, the cathedral maintains the Catalan tradition of a dancing egg—a decorated hollow egg that "dances" atop a water jet in one of the fountains.

Catedral de Barcelona.

## online INSTEAD OF *IN* LINE

On many summer days, you could wait 2 or more hours to enter the **Museu Picasso.** Or, purchase a timed entry ticket on the museum website for a 1€ surcharge (or buy the ArTicket BCN elsewhere), and you enter via a different door—no line, no hassle. Just proceed to the person scanning entry tickets.

You can also buy ahead and skip the line for **Basilica de la Sagrada Familia** (p. 751) and some of Gaudí's other amazing buildings.

Plaça de la Seu s/n. www.catedralbcn.org. ✆ **93-315-15-54.** Cathedral free; ticket to museum, choir, rooftop terraces, and towers 6€. Metro: Jaume I. Cathedral daily 8am–7:30pm; museum daily 8am–7pm.

**Plaça Reial** ★ PLAZA This harmonious square was built in the early 19th century on the former site of the Santa Madrona Capuchin monastery. It was conceived as a residential square, but these days it's surrounded largely by cafes. Although it attracts many more tourists than locals, it is still a great place to sit beneath an arcade, drink beer, and observe the scene. The fountain of the three graces in the center is flanked by handsome Art Nouveau lampposts that were Antoni Gaudí's first commission. He decorated them with a *caduceus* (a messenger's wand with two snakes entwined around it) and winged helmets—attributes of Hermes, patron of shopkeepers.
Metro: Liceu.

### LA RIBERA & EL BORN

**Museu Picasso** ★★★ MUSEUM This terrific museum was founded on the collections of Jaume Sabartés, a childhood friend who became Picasso's personal secretary in 1935. They include many works made when Picasso was a student in Barcelona or when he retreated before another assault on the art world of Paris. As such, they provide a striking portrait of Barcelona at the end of the 19th century as well as an intriguing look at an evolving artistic genius. Picasso also donated generously to the museum, including 2,400 works in memory of his friend Sabartés. His most significant donation was his entire *Las Meninas* series, which he painted as a tribute to and exploration of the art of Velázquez. The large canvas and dozens of smaller studies are the centerpiece of the collection, which fills five adjoining historic townhouses. *Las Meninas* provides

Interior, Museo Picasso.

a rare opportunity to follow Picasso's thought process and artistic instincts at the height of his mature power. His greatest masterpieces are elsewhere, but you will leave this museum wondering how there could possibly be more.

Carrer Montcada, 15-19. www.museupicasso.bcn.cat. ✆ **93-256-30-00.** 11€ adults (14€ during temporary exhibitions), 7€ students, ages 18–25, and seniors; free under 18; free Sun 2–7pm and all day first Sun of the month. Metro: Jaume I. Tues–Sun 9am–7pm.

**Palau de la Música Catalana** ★★★ LANDMARK One of the most extreme and exciting of the Modernista buildings, this structure is Lluís Domènech i Montaner's masterpiece. Commissioned by the Orfeó Català choral music society, the architect laid the first stone in 1905. The concert hall opened in 1908—a marvel of stained glass, ceramics, ornate wrought iron, and carved stone. In keeping with the architect's signature style, the facade features exposed brick combined with colorful ceramic mosaics. Inside, the vaults of the foyer are lined with Valencian tiles. The concert hall itself is topped with an enormous stained-glass skylight representing a circle of female angels surrounding the sun as a choir—quite appropriate for a choral society. If you want a detailed explanation of the imagery, plan to take a guided tour. The best way to enjoy the hall is to attend a concert. Arrive early and study the rich details from your seat.

Carrer Sant Francesc de Paula, 2. www.palaumusica.org. ✆ **93-295-72-00.** Admission by guided tours 18€, free 10 and under. Metro: Urquinaona. Open daily from 10am–3:30pm. Box office open daily 9:30am–3:30pm.

**Santa Maria del Mar** ★★ RELIGIOUS SITE Built by the trade guilds, this church is the city's most harmonious example of Catalan

**A performance at the Palau de la Música Catalana.**

The soaring interior of Santa Maria del Mar.

Gothic. Construction began in 1329 and was mostly finished in 1383 (bell towers were added in 1496 and 1902). Three soaring naves are supported by wide-spaced columns that bloom like thick stalks as they reach the ceiling. Stained glass windows fill the church with light during the day. Guided tours of the roof terraces are available daily, weather permitting.

Plaça de Santa María. www.santamariadelmarbarcelona.org. ✆ **93-215-74-11.** Free. Tours of terraces: www.itineraplus.com. ✆ **93-343-56-33.** 8€. Metro: Jaume I. Mon–Sat 9am–1pm and 5–8:30pm; Sun 10am–2pm and 5–8pm. Tours on the hour daily 11am–7pm.

## L'EIXAMPLE & GRÀCIA

**Basilica de la Sagrada Familia ★★★** RELIGIOUS SITE Antoni Gaudí (1852–1926) was a profoundly religious man, and from 1912 forward he made the design of this soaring basilica his life's work. If it is not the grandest church in all of Spain, it is certainly the grandest constructed within living memory. Gaudí originally planned to base the church on all the stories of the Bible, but, as a guide once told us, "he decided that was too long, so he settled on the New Testament." The "church of the Holy Family" is, to say the least, a strange and wonderful building that represents the intersection of the imaginative style of Modernisme with the medieval faith that drove construction of the great Gothic cathedrals. The facades are particularly ornate. Every ledge, window, corner, step, or other surface is encrusted with carvings. Fruits of the seasons surround one set of spires, dragons and gargoyles hang off corners, an entire Noah's ark of animals is carved in stone. One facade tells the stories of the birth and childhood of Jesus, another (completed by sculptor Josep Maria Subirachs in 1987) the Passion and crucifixion.

And that's just the exterior. Inside, light streaming through stained-glass windows colors the air. Gaudí conceived the interior as a vast forest, and the columns seem to grow from the floor like powerful trees holding the roof aloft. Construction of the church came to a near halt in 1936 and languished until the late 1980s. The church was consecrated in 2010 by Pope Benedict XVI, and builders hope to complete construction by the 2026 centenary of Gaudí's death. (He's buried in a chapel one

Gaudi's Basilica de Sagrada Familia.

level below the main church.) ***Note:*** Buy tickets online in advance to avoid the wait of an hour or more during high season.

Entrance from Carrer de Sardenya or Carrer de la Marina. www.sagradafamilia.cat. ✆ **93-207-30-31.** 15€ adults, free 10 and under; tower tour 5.50€; audioguide or tour guide 4.50€. Online tickets at http://ow.ly/lqdwr. Metro: Sagrada Família. Apr–Sept daily 9am–8pm, Oct and Mar daily 9am–7pm; Nov–Feb 9am–6pm.

**Casa Amatller** ★ LANDMARK Three of the greatest residential Modernista buildings in Barcelona stand along the single block of Passeig de Gràcia between Carrer del Consell de Cent and Carrer d'Aragó. Architecture critics call it the Mançana de la Discòrdia (Block of Discord), an allusion to the mythical Judgment of Paris over which of three goddesses is the most beautiful. Tourism promoters call the same group the Quadrat d'Or, or "Golden Quarter," which at least points out that they are all wonderful. Casa Amatller is the masterpiece by Josep Puig i Cadalfach. Closed for restoration until at least 2016, this Modernista home designed in 1900 can still be admired from the outside. Inside and out, it reflects the architect's attachment to Northern European Gothic decoration. Puig i Cadalfach made extensive use of ceramics, wrought iron, and fanciful sculptures.

Passeig de Gràcia, 41. www.amatller.org. ✆ **93-487-72-17.** Admission and hours to be announced. Metro: Passeig de Gràcia.

**Casa Batlló** ★★ LANDMARK Next door to Casa Amatller, Casa Batlló was designed by Gaudí in 1905. The facade's sinuous curves in iron and stone give the structure a very lush appeal, and the balconies seem to be sculpted ocean waves. Floral references in the ornament turn more fauna-like as the building rises. The roof evokes the scaly skin of a dragon. Touring means climbing the spiral staircase around the central light shaft and starting with the Batlló family quarters, where Gaudí's architectural flourishes and furniture designs vie for your attention. Sr. Batlló's office has a little nook with two benches and a stove for warmth—perfect for a courting couple to sit on one side and their chaperone on the other. Even this smallest of the rooms has a skylight to let in some natural light. The living room overlooks Passeig de Gràcia. All of the decor, including the eddies of water in the swirling ceiling, alludes to the marine world. The roof terrace has chimneys designed to evoke the backbone of the dragon slain by Sant Jordi (St. George). In the summer, the terrace has live music with cocktails. An audiotour is included with admission, which has the effect of creating bottlenecks at each spot the tour highlights. Lines for admission can get quite long here; buy your ticket online in advance.

Casa Batlló.

Passeig de Gràcia, 43. www.casabatllo.cat. ✆ **93-216-03-06.** 22€ adults; 19€ ages 7–18, students/seniors; free for children under 7. Music and cocktails mid-June to Sept Tues–Sun from 9pm, 22€. Metro: Passeig de Gràcia. Tours daily 9am–9pm.

**Casa Lleó Morera ★** LANDMARK The third member of the Golden Quarter, Casa Lleó Morera was designed by the remaining member of the Modernista triumvirate, Lluís Domènech i Montaner. The 1905 home was revolutionary in its day for its extensive use of different forms of artisanry on the interior (alas, closed to the public) to realize the architect's distinctly floral design. Because it occupies a corner, the house has two beautiful facades that mirror each other with a tower dividing them. Domènech i Montaner's signature floral capitals appear in several variants, and he created a gallery of columns on the top floor that evokes the rhythm of a convent cloister.

Passeig de Gràcia, 35. No phone. Metro: Passeig de Gràcia.

**Fundació Antoni Tàpies ★★** MUSEUM This museum is dedicated to Antoni Tàpies (1923–2012), Catalunya's leading late 20th-century artist. Major holdings consist of gifts from the artist and his wife, and tend to emphasize late works and large-scale pieces. Changing exhibitions show the artist's evolving viewpoints and leave no doubt about his role in bringing unconventional materials (gravel, broken sticks, and chunks of cement) into high art. Seeing so many works by Tàpies in one place shows how, like so many Spanish artists, he returned repeatedly to the motif of the cross for works both secular and sacred. The museum occupies a Modernista landmark, the former home of publishing company Editorial Montaner i Simon built by Montaner scion Lluís Domènech i Montaner from 1880 to 1882. The pioneering structure has a jaunty Moorish cast to it.

Carrer Aragó, 255. www.fundaciotapies.org. ✆ **93-487-03-15.** 7€ adults, 5.60€ students/seniors. Metro: Passeig de Gràcia. Tues–Sun 10am–7pm.

**La Pedrera (Casa Milà) ★★★** LANDMARK When Gaudí's last secular commission, Casa Milà, was finished in 1912, the neighbors took one look at the undulating lines of seemingly wind-eroded rock and dubbed the building La Pedrera ("the stone quarry"). The novelty has faded, but the nickname has stuck. With a sinuous, rippling facade, it is one of the most beloved of Gaudí's works, and is another spot where purchasing an advance ticket online will save you time. The tour includes the patios and the Espai Gaudí (loft and roof), and offers a chance to see Gaudí's innovative domestic designs in the Pedrera Apartment, complete with furniture created by the master. The Espai Gaudí holds period photographs, drawings, and models that elucidate Gaudí's design techniques. Gaudí saved his grandest gestures for the rooftop, transforming chimneys into a sculpture garden of mosaic forms and ominous hooded warriors. The roof was designed as an open-air terrace, and during the summer, there are evening jazz performances. Amid the chimneys, Gaudí

**Gaudí's La Pedrera.**

built a lovely parabolic arch to frame what would become the towering steeples of his masterpiece, La Sagrada Familia. The premium-priced night visits called "The Secret Pedrera" are so popular that they are available all year.

Carrer Provença, 261-265. www.lapedrera.com. ✆ **90-220-21-38.** 21€ adults, 17€ seniors and students, 10€ ages 7–12, free ages 6 and younger; Secret Pedrera 30€ adults, 15€ ages 7–12. Jazz on Rooftop June–Sept Thurs–Sat 22€. Metro: Diagonal. Nov–Feb daily 9am–6:30pm and Wed–Sat 7–10:30pm; Mar–Oct daily 9am–8pm and 8:30pm–11:30pm.

**Museu del Modernisme Català** ★ MUSEUM The first museum dedicated exclusively to Catalan Modernisme occupies two floors of a former textile factory designed by Enric Sagnier and built from 1902 to 1904. The ground level is dominated by a mix of graphic art, wonderful posters, and furniture designed by Antoni Gaudí, Joan Busquets, and Gaspar Homar. The Gaudí displays include some seminal pieces from his collaborations with Josep Maria Jujol. (They worked together on most of the furniture for Casa Batlló, and Jujol assisted with the ornamentation of Casa Mila.) You can't touch the works, let alone sit in the chairs, but nowhere else can you get so close to pieces and study their design and construction. Basement exhibitions include a lot of Modernisme painting and sculpture, including impassioned marbles by Eusebi Arnau, who did some of the major sculpture for the **Palau de la Música Catalana** ★★★ (p. 750).

Carrer Balmes, 48. www.mmcat.cat. ✆ **93-273-28-96.** 10€ adults, 7€ seniors, 5.50€ ages 6–16. Metro: Passeig de Gràcia or Universitat. Tues–Sat 10am–7pm, Sun 10:30am–2pm.

**Parc Güell** ★ PARK Gaudí began this idiosyncratic park in Gràcia (north of L'Eixample) as a real-estate venture for Catalan industrialist Count Eusebi Güell. Although it never came to fruition, Gaudí did complete several public areas, which look like a surrealist Disneyland, complete with a mosaic-encrusted pagoda and a lizard fountain spitting water. A grand central plaza is lined with a long, undulating bench decorated with ceramic fragments. Only two of a planned 60 houses were ever completed. One of them (designed by Ramón Berenguer, not Gaudí) serves as the **Casa-Museu Gaudí.** The architect lived here from 1906 to 1925 while working on La Pedrera and La Sagrada Familia. The museum contains Gaudí models, furniture, drawings, and other memorabilia.

Calle de Olot for park, Carrer del Carmel, 23 for Casa-Museu Gaudí. www.casamuseugaudi.org. ✆ **93-219-38-11.** Free admission to park. Casa-Museu Gaudí: 5.50€ adults, 4.50€ students/seniors. Metro: Lesseps. Park open May–Sept daily 9am–9pm; Oct–Apr daily 9am–7pm; Casa-Museu Gaudí open Apr–Sept 10am–8pm, Oct–Mar 10am–6pm.

## LA BARCELONETA & THE WATERFRONT

Public art along the pedestrian **Moll de la Fusta** captures Barcelona's sense of the absurd. Xavier Mariscal created the giant fiberglass lobster

Barceloneta beach.

for the restaurant Gambrinus, and Roy Lichtenstein's *Barcelona Head* anchors the foot of Via Laietana. In Port Olimpic, Frank O. Gehry's sculpture *Peix* (Fish) is the de facto symbol of Barcelona's rejuvenated waterfront.

**Barcelona Beaches ★★** BEACH You don't have to leave the city to hit the beach. European blue flags (indicators of the highest water quality) fly on all 10 of Barcelona's beaches. Four of the best lie along the strand from the tip of La Barceloneta east to Port Olimpic. Each has showers, bathrooms, snack bars, umbrella and hammock rentals, and lifeguards. They are all free and can be reached from Metro stops Barceloneta or Ciutadella/La Vila Olimpica. Farther east at Metro Poblenou is Platja de Mar Bella, the only beach with a section set off for nude sunbathing and swimming.
Metro: Barceloneta, Ciutadella/Vila Olímpica, or Poblenou. Bus: N6, N8.

**L'Aquarium de Barcelona ★★** AQUARIUM The centerpiece of this contemporary aquarium is the giant ocean tank that wraps around an 80m (262-ft.) corridor with a moving walkway on one side. On the other is a strip where you can step off the path to take photos or simply marvel at the creatures swimming by. Another 21 smaller tanks, which ring the ocean tank, focus on different habitats within the Mediterranean. Some resemble home aquariums full of brightly colored fish, while others are deepwater habitats where eels and anglerfish lie in wait for their prey. The sharks are an enduring attraction, and SCUBA-certified visitors with their own gear can swim with the sharks in the giant tank for a 300€ fee.
Moll d'Espanya, Port Vell. www.aquariumbcn.com. ✆ **93-221-74-74.** 20€ adults, 18€ 65 and older, 15€ ages 5–10, 7€ ages 3–4. Metro: Drassanes or Barceloneta. July–Aug Mon–Fri 9:30am–11pm, Sat–Sun 9:30am–9:30pm; June and Sept daily 9:30am–9:30pm; Oct–May daily 9:30am–9pm.

**Mirador de Colom ★** MONUMENT Les Rambles meets the waterfront at this Columbus monument erected for the Universal Exposition of 1888. Bas-reliefs on the plinth recount the feats of the great navigator. At the top of a 50m (174-ft.) column stands a bronze of Columbus pointing to the New World. His white wig of bird droppings deflates the pomposity of the statue. An elevator ascends to the lookout just below Columbus's feet for a panoramic view of the city and harbor.

Portal de la Pau. ✆ **93-285-38-32.** 4.50€ adults, 3€ children 4–12 and seniors, free for children 3 and under. Metro: Drassanes. June–Sept daily 9am–1:30pm and 4:30–8:30pm; Oct–May daily 9am–2pm and 3:30–7:30pm.

**Museu d'Història de Catalunya ★★** MUSEUM This keeper of "the memory of a country" tells everything you should know about Catalunya. The truly engaging exhibits linger at high points of Catalan history, such as the reigns of Jaume I and II when Catalunya was a major power on the Mediterranean, and the 19th-century industrial revolution that made Catalunya and Barcelona rich and powerful. The 20th-century coverage is almost giddy with depictions of a vibrant Barcelona in the first few decades—and numbing in its accounts of the horrors of the Civil War and the 4 decades the region spent as Franco's whipping boy. The era since Franco's death are less well-digested. The building, the Palau de Mar, is the last survivor of 19th-century Barcelona warehouses. The fourth-floor restaurant has a spectacular terrace with great views of the waterfront.

Plaça de Pau Vila, 3. www.mhcat.cat. ✆ **93-225-47-00.** 4.50€ adults, 3.50€ students/seniors; free last Tues of month; temporary exhibitions 4€ adults, 3€ students/seniors. Metro: Barceloneta. Tues and Thurs–Sat 10am–7pm, Wed 10am–8pm, Sun 10am–2:30pm.

## MONTJUÏC

**Fundació Joan Miró ★★★** MUSEUM Revered as the embodiment of the artistic genius of the Catalan people, Joan Miró (1893–1983)

Fundació Joan Miró.

was born in Barcelona in the Barri Gòtic and trained locally. This marvelous museum assembles 10,000 of his works, including paintings, graphic art, sculpture, and even tapestries. His strong sense of line and tendency to lay in patches of color like a cloisonné jeweler (his father was a goldsmith) gave him a unique style. The original museum building was designed by Miró's close friend, Catalan architect Josep Lluís Sert. A recent extension has made it possible to display a number of pieces donated since the museum opened. The dimly lit **Octagonal Room** contains many of Miró's drawings on paper. Don't miss the amusing rooftop sculptures or the unusually good gift shop.

Plaça de Neptú, Parc de Montjuïc. www.fundaciomiro-bcn.org. ✆ **93-443-94-70.** 11€ adults, 7€ seniors and students. Bus: 50 (at Plaça d'Espanya) or 150. July–Sept Tues–Wed and Fri–Sat 10am–8pm, Thurs 10am–9pm, Sun 10am–2:30pm; Oct–June Tues–Wed and Fri–Sat 10am–7pm, Thurs 10am–9pm, Sun 10am–2:30pm.

**Museu Nacional d'Art de Catalunya (MNAC) ★★★** MUSEUM Some of the greatest Romanesque and early Gothic art in Europe is collected in this stunning museum housed in the Palau Nacional. Most of the Romanesque murals were discovered in crumbling ancient churches in the Pyrenees. MNAC displays more than 100 pieces from these churches, including wall painting panels and polychrome wood carvings. The museum chronicles other eras, but the collections are a little thin until they reach the four Modern galleries on the first floor. The Modernista gallery exhibits have such treasures as the Gaudí-designed furniture from **Casa Lleó Morera ★** (p. 753) and a 1907 fireplace by Lluís Domènech i Montaner. The other three modern galleries blend fine and decorative arts together to give a broader picture of Catalan artistic movements.

Palau Nacional, Parc de Montjuïc. www.mnac.es. ✆ **93-622-03-76.** 12€ adults, 8.40€ ages 15–20, free under 16 and over 65; free to all Sat after 3pm, first Sun of month. Metro: Espanya. May–Sept Tues–Sat 10am–8pm; Sun 10am–2:30pm; Oct–Apr Tues–Sat 10am–6pm, Sun 10am–2:30pm.

Crowds wait for sunset on the steps of the MNAC.

**Poble Espanyol ★** HISTORIC PARK This faux-Spanish village of 117 buildings, streets, and squares was designed in 1929 by Josep Puig i Cadalfach for the International Exposition. Each plaza or street simulates the architecture of parts of Spain from Galicia to Valencia. Buildings are full-scale, and after more than eight decades of patina, some portions are authentic enough to make you do a double-take. The main plaza is ringed with restaurants, cafes, craft workshops, and souvenir shops.

Avinguda Marqués de Comillas, 13, Parc de Montjuïc. www.poble-espanyol.com. ✆ **93-508-63-00.** 12€ adults, 8.40€ seniors, 9.50€ students, 7€ ages 4–12, free for ages 3 and younger. Metro: Espanya. Bus: 55 or 150. Mon 9am–8pm; Tues–Thurs and Sun 9am–midnight; Fri 9am–3am; Sat 9am–4am.

## Organized Tours

Barcelona is best appreciated on foot, and the Barcelona tourist office offers several **Barcelona Walking Tours** in English that cover such highlights as Picasso's Barcelona, Modernisme masterpieces, and gourmet Barcelona. For a full tour listing, visit http://bcnshop.barcelonaturisme.cat, call ✆ **93-285-38-32,** or inquire at the tourist office on Plaça Catalunya. Adult tickets start at 15€; some tours are free for children, others 7€. Online discounts are available.

The double-decker **Barcelona Bus Turistic** (www.barcelonabusturistic.cat) makes three circuits that cover most major tourist attractions, with narration in 11 languages. You can re-board all day, but expect a long wait to get onto a crowded bus during high season. The cost is 27€ for 1 day, 38€ for 2 days, 16€ and 20€ for ages 4 to 12. A bonus discount booklet makes up some of the ticket cost. During summer, inquire about an evening bus to enjoy the city lights at night.

## Especially for Kids

Family-friendly attractions include **L'Aquarium Barcelona** (p. 756), the beaches (p. 756) and the **Zoo Barcelona** ★ (Parc de la Ciutadella; www.zoobarcelona.com; ✆ **90-245-75-45;** admission 20€ adults, 12€ ages 3–12, 10€ 65 and older), home to more than 300 species. When you visit **La Sagrada Familia** (p. 751), reward your children (over age 6) with the tower tour. At **La Pedrera** (p. 754), they'll likely be fascinated by Gaudí's mosaic-crusted rooftop chimneys that evoke *Star Wars'* Darth Vader.

From March to December, the big family excursion is the trip up **Tibidabo Mountain** to **Parc d' Atraccions** ★ (Placa Tibidabo 3-4; www.tibidabo.cat; ✆ **93-211-79-42;** tickets for all rides 29€ adults, 10€ children up to 1.2m [4 ft.] in height, 10€ ages 60 and over). The century-old amusement park, featured in the Woody Allen film *Vicky Cristina Barcelona,* has charming retro rides and modern thrill rides. The trip on the **Funicular de Tibidabo** ★ (7.70€, or 4.10€ with amusement park entries) is a treat in itself. To reach the funicular, take Metro Line 7 to Avinguda Tibidabo, exit onto Plaça Kennedy, and take either the 1901 **Tramvía Blau** (Blue Streetcar; 4€) or **Bus 196** (2.15€) to the funicular.

## Where to Stay

Hotels in Barcelona are among the most expensive in Spain, but that doesn't mean you can't find good values. Many visitors gravitate to hotels

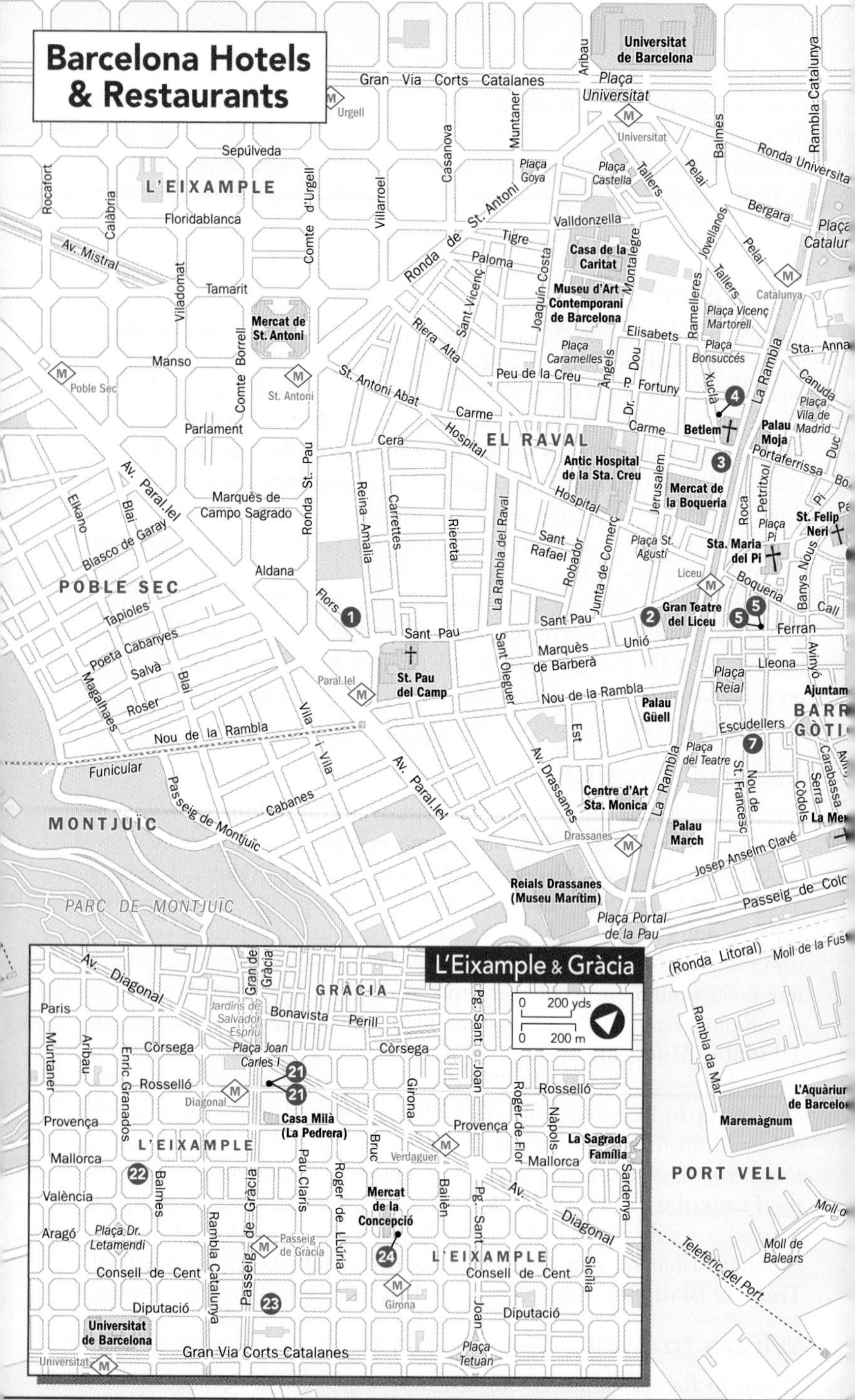

Barcelona Hotels & Restaurants
L'EIXAMPLE
EL RAVAL
POBLE SEC
MONTJUÏC
PARC DE MONTJUÏC
BARRI GÒTIC
PORT VELL
Universitat de Barcelona
Plaça Universitat
Casa de la Caritat
Museu d'Art Contemporani de Barcelona
Mercat de St. Antoni
Antic Hospital de la Sta. Creu
Mercat de la Boqueria
Betlem
Palau Moja
St. Felip Neri
Sta. Maria del Pi
Gran Teatre del Liceu
St. Pau del Camp
Palau Güell
Centre d'Art Sta. Monica
Palau March
Reials Drassanes (Museu Marítim)
Plaça Portal de la Pau
L'Aquàrium de Barcelona
Maremàgnum
Telefèric del Port
Funicular
L'Eixample & Gràcia
GRÀCIA
Casa Milà (La Pedrera)
Mercat de la Concepció
La Sagrada Família
0 200 yds
0 200 m

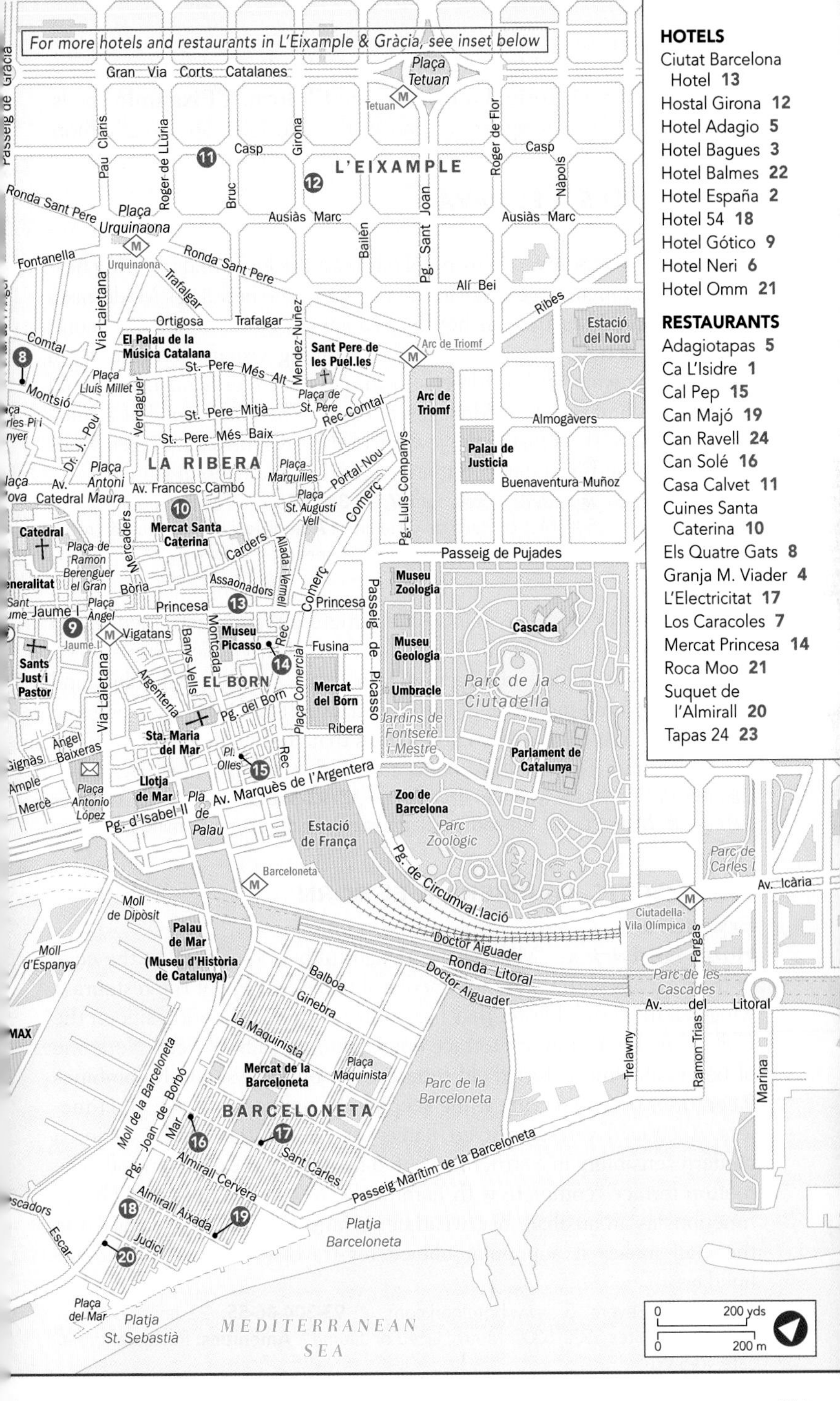
For more hotels and restaurants in L'Eixample & Gràcia, see inset below
HOTELS
Ciutat Barcelona Hotel 13
Hostal Girona 12
Hotel Adagio 5
Hotel Bagues 3
Hotel Balmes 22
Hotel España 2
Hotel 54 18
Hotel Gótico 9
Hotel Neri 6
Hotel Omm 21
RESTAURANTS
Adagiotapas 5
Ca L'Isidre 1
Cal Pep 15
Can Majó 19
Can Ravell 24
Can Solé 16
Casa Calvet 11
Cuines Santa Caterina 10
Els Quatre Gats 8
Granja M. Viader 4
L'Electricitat 17
Los Caracoles 7
Mercat Princesa 14
Roca Moo 21
Suquet de l'Almirall 20
Tapas 24 23
L'EIXAMPLE
LA RIBERA
EL BORN
BARCELONETA
Gran Via Corts Catalanes
Plaça Tetuan
Tetuan
Casp
Girona
Pau Claris
Roger de Llúria
Bruc
Roger de Flor
Nàpols
Ausiàs Marc
Ronda Sant Pere
Plaça Urquinaona
Urquinaona
Fontanella
Trafalgar
Bailèn
Pg. Sant Joan
Alí Bei
Ribes
Estació del Nord
Ortigosa
Via Laietana
Comtal
El Palau de la Música Catalana
Sant Pere de les Puel.les
Mendez Nuñez
Arc de Triomf
St. Pere Més Alt
Plaça Lluís Millet
Montsió
Plaça de St. Pere
Rec Comtal
St. Pere Mitjà
Verdaguer
St. Pere Més Baix
Almogàvers
Palau de Justicia
Dr. J. Pou
Plaça Antoni Maura
Av. Catedral
Av. Francesc Cambó
Plaça Marquilles
Portal Nou
Plaça St. Agustí Vell
Comerç
Pg. Lluís Companys
Buenaventura Muñoz
Mercat Santa Caterina
Catedral
Plaça de Ramon Berenguer el Gran
Mercaders
Carders
Allada i Vermell
Passeig de Pujades
Generalitat
Bòria
Assaonadors
Princesa
Passeig de Picasso
Museu Zoologia
Cascada
Jaume I
Plaça Àngel
Vigatans
Banys Vells
Montcada
Museu Picasso
Rec
Fusina
Museu Geologia
Sants Just i Pastor
Argenteria
Mercat del Born
Umbracle
Parc de la Ciutadella
Pg. del Born
Plaça Comercial
Sta. Maria del Mar
Ribera
Jardins de Fontserè i Mestre
Parlament de Catalunya
Àngel Baixeras
Pl. Olles
Av. Marquès de l'Argentera
Ample
Mercè
Plaça Antonio López
Llotja de Mar
Pla de Palau
Pg. d'Isabel II
Zoo de Barcelona
Estació de França
Parc Zoològic
Parc de Carles I
Barceloneta
Pg. de Circumval.lació
Av. Icària
Moll de Dipòsit
Ciutadella-Vila Olímpica
Palau de Mar (Museu d'Història de Catalunya)
Doctor Aiguader
Ronda Litoral
Moll d'Espanya
Balboa
Fargas
Parc de les Cascades
Av. del Litoral
Ginebra
La Maquinista
Trelawny
Ramon Trias
Marina
IMAX
Moll de la Barceloneta
Mercat de la Barceloneta
Plaça Maquinista
Parc de la Barceloneta
Pg. Joan de Borbó
Mar
Sant Carles
Passeig Marítim de la Barceloneta
Almirall Cervera
Almirall Aixada
Pescadors
Escar
Judici
Platja Barceloneta
Plaça del Mar
Platja St. Sebastià
MEDITERRANEAN SEA
0 200 yds
0 200 m

on or near **Les Rambles** for convenience, but better bargains can are found in the **Barri Gòtic, La Ribera,** and **El Born. L'Eixample** hotels, while typically more expensive than in the Old City, are usually more spacious.

## LES RAMBLES & EL RAVAL

### Expensive

**Hotel Bagues ★★★** This hotel has both the looks and unerring hospitality for a romantic getaway in the Old City. The building's Modernista design is a holdover from its heyday as a jewelry store; the modern comforts don't detract one iota from the stunning visuals of the original designs. The walls and wardrobes in the rooms are enhanced with gold leaf accents and panels of Madagascar ebony. The hotel even has a Masriera Museum, showcasing the jewelry of the Art Nouveau master. Most rooms are called "standard," but are larger than many hotel suites.

Les Rambles, 105. www.derbyhotels.com. ✆ **93-343-50-00.** 31 units. Doubles 165€–380€, suites from 280€. Metro: Plaça de Catalunya. **Amenities:** Bar; restaurant; room service; swimming pool; solarium; spa; gym; limo service; free Wi-Fi.

### Moderate

**Hotel España ★** This handsome structure was transformed into a Modernista hotel in 1903 by Lluís Domènech i Montaner. Guests get a discount on the guided architectural tour. Contemporary technology and up-to-date plumbing augment the Modernista flair. Decor is serene and simple, with dark wood tones and taupes that coordinate nicely with the historic design. The smallest rooms are a little tight, but most are larger.

Carrer Sant Pau, 9-11. www.hotelespanya.com. ✆ **93-550-00-00.** 82 units. Doubles 121€–210€. Metro: Liceu. **Amenities:** Bar; restaurant; terrace; swimming pool; free Wi-Fi.

## BARRI GÒTIC, LA RIBERA & EL BORN

### Expensive

**Hotel Neri ★★★** Most of this delightful boutique hotel at the edge of the Call lies within a rebuilt medieval noble home, but the restaurant wing is a modern addition that harmonizes nicely. Reception sits on the Call, while the restaurant terrace opens onto Plaça Sant Felip Neri, one of Barcelona's most storied old squares. The building skillfully combines 9 centuries of architecture while keeping the rooms open, airy, and timeless. Abstract Expressionist art hangs throughout the hotel, evoking a modern sensibility in a structure rooted in stone and exposed wood. The rooftop terrace (complete with hammocks as well as tables and chairs) functions as an auxiliary bar, weather permitting. The Neri's location in the Call makes it a popular choice for travelers on Jewish heritage holidays.

Carrer Sant Severe, 5. www.hotelneri.com. ✆ **93-304-06-55.** 22 units. Doubles 248€–365€, suites 350€–520€. Metro: Liceu or Jaume I. **Amenities:** Restaurant; bar/cafe; free Wi-Fi.

### Moderate

**Hotel Gótico ★★** This hotel at the crossroads of Jaume I/Princesa and Via Laietana is our favorite among the Gargallo family hotels on the same block. Acres of marble cover the entry foyer (as well as the bathrooms), and golden accents glimmer against wood inlay and exposed brick. Guest rooms are a little snug but are simply decorated with furniture that reinterprets Modernisme via Danish Modern. The location is terrific for walking swiftly to the cathedral in one direction, the Museu Picasso in the other. Friendly and solicitous staff enhance the experience.

Carrer Jaume I, 14. www.hotelgotico.com. ✆ **93-315-21-13.** 81 units. Doubles 68€–224€. Metro: Jaume I. **Amenities:** Bar/cafe; room service; terrace; free Wi-Fi.

### Inexpensive

**Ciutat Barcelona Hotel ★★** A bargain-priced design hotel for grown-ups, the Ciutat Barcelona has a soothing contemporary look to its rooms, including chairs and light fixtures that could have come straight from the showroom at Design Within Reach. Spaces are compact but well-designed, and the rooftop terrace is like having a private oasis in the middle of the city. There is a side entrance for wheelchair users, and some rooms are accessible. The small pool is big enough to make kids happy.

Carrer Princessa, 35. www.ciutatbarcelona.com. ✆ **93-269-74-75.** 78 units. Doubles 80€–150€. Metro: Jaume I. **Amenities:** Rooftop pool; free Wi-Fi.

**Hotel Adagio ★** Barcelona hotels with an official two-star rating can be pretty grim, but Adagio is a delightful exception. About halfway between Plaça Reial and Plaça de Catalunya, Adagio fronts onto Carrer Ferran, one of the broader east-west streets of the Barri Gòtic. The reception area is tiny, but that leaves more room for the excellent tapas restaurant **Adagiotapas ★★** (p. 766) in the front. Rooms are small but very clean. The location is convenient, but it's best to keep windows closed and use the air-conditioning, because the narrow stone streets are noisy at night. Very friendly and eager-to-please staff helps compensate for the lack of luxury.

Carrer Ferran, 21. www.adagiohotel.com. ✆ **93-318-90-61.** 38 units. Doubles 72€–192€. Metro: Liceu or Jaume I. **Amenities:** Free Wi-Fi.

## L'EIXAMPLE

### Expensive

**Hotel Omm ★★★** It's almost worth staying at Omm just for the view from the rooftop bar and swimming pool of La Pedrera's fanciful chimneys across the street. This boutique property is a 21st-century exemplar of style the way Gaudí's Casa Milà (La Pedrera) is the apex of Modernisme. The lobby restaurant **Roca Moo ★★★** (p. 767), and other public areas are all high drama, while the rooms are breezy and relaxing. Guest rooms have parquet wood floors, handwoven rugs, and large windows with views of either the inner courtyard or Passeig de Gràcia.

Carrer Rosselló, 265. www.hotelomm.es. ✆ **93-445-40-00.** 91 units. Doubles 190€–460€, suites 490€–760€. Metro: Diagonal. **Amenities:** Restaurant; bar; babysitting; concierge; rooftop pool; room service; spa; free Wi-Fi.

### Moderate

**Hotel Balmes ★★** The Balmes shares the serene modern style of its Derby hotel group brethren—a cross between a small art museum and a well-appointed gentleman's club. In this case, the art consists of an extensive collection of sub-Saharan African masks and small wooden sculptures in both the public areas and the individual guest rooms. Standard rooms are spacious, and some superior rooms feature small terraces.
Carrer de Mallorca, 216. www.derbyhotels.com. ✆ **93-451-19-14.** 105 units. Doubles 88€–187€. Metro: Diagonal. **Amenities:** Bar; restaurant; sauna; free Wi-Fi.

### Inexpensive

**Hostal Girona ★** Early Modernista architect Ildefons Cerada designed this building in the 1860s, and it retains some significant traces of its heyday. The hostel is located on an upper floor, and only some of the rooms reflect the architectural style. All units have private bathrooms, though some rooms are quite small. Four units have balconies, but for the full Modernista effect, ask for one of the two large rooms with terraces.
Carrer Girona, 24 (piso 1, puerta 1). www.hostalgirona.com. ✆ **93-265-02-59.** 19 units. Doubles 44€–98€. Metro: Girona or Urquinaona. **Amenities:** Free Wi-Fi.

## WATERFRONT

### Moderate

**Hotel 54 ★** If you can't score a room with a view at this pleasant hostelry in the former fishermen's association building, then console yourself by hanging out on the fifth floor terrace to enjoy a 270-degree view of the harbor and city skyline. The location is terrific: You can cut through residential Barceloneta to walk to Platja San Sebastiá, and Les Rambles is a 15-minute walk up the Moll de la Fusta. A major renovation installed nice decorative touches like colored LED mood lights over the beds and cast glass sinks in the bathrooms.
Passeig Joan de Borbó, 54. www.hotel54barceloneta.es. ✆ **93-225-00-54.** 28 units. Doubles 59€–170€. Metro: Barceloneta. **Amenities:** Bar/cafe; room service; rooftop terrace; free Wi-Fi.

## Where to Eat

You can eat fabulously at some of the old-fashioned and casual spots here, but Barcelona is one of the world's great gastronomic destinations, so it's worth splurging a little. It need not break the bank; some top chefs have opened bargain venues to showcase their culinary creativity with less-expensive ingredients. Barcelona dining hours are closer to the European standard than in Madrid. Lunch is usually served 1 to 3pm (and can represent a great bargain), and dinner starts around 8pm, although dining before 9pm is unfashionable. You may see the word *raciones* pop up on menus; that means a plate that's larger than a tapas portion but smaller than an entree.

Seafood paella.



## LES RAMBLES & EL RAVAL

### Moderate

**Ca L'Isidre ★★** CATALAN Isidre Gironés and his wife Montserrat have been serving market cuisine with a seafood emphasis at this El Raval restaurant since 1970. Although the neighborhood used to be rough, gastronomes have always sought them out for hard-to-find old-fashioned dishes like fried salt cod with white beans. You can also order modern preparations like tartare of bream and *cigalas* (the local saltwater crawfish) with parsley oil, or roast kid with baby onions. In summer and early fall, the best available starter is gazpacho with assorted seafood. Carrer Les Flors, 12. www.calisidre.com. ✆ **93-441-11-39.** Reservations required. Mains 18€–50€; weekday lunch menu 40€. Metro: Paral.lel. Mon–Sat 1:30–4pm and 8:30–11pm. Closed 1st 2 weeks in Aug.

### Inexpensive

**Granja M. Viader ★** CATALAN M. Viader invented the drink you see next to the sodas in every cooler: Cacaolat. It's chocolate milk, and Catalans of a certain age gush with nostalgia over it. The founder was instrumental in getting pasteurized milk products out to the public, and this wonderfully old-fashioned cafe, founded in 1870, still serves coffee, pastries, sandwiches, hot chocolate, and (of course!) chocolate milk. In the morning, you can also get hot *churros* to go with the hot chocolate. Carrer Xucla, 4-6. www.granjaviader.cat. ✆ **93-318-34-86.** Sandwiches 3€–5€; pastries 1.80€–4€. Metro: Liceu or Catalunya. Mon–Sat 9am–1:15pm and 5–8:15pm.

## BARRI GÒTIC, LA RIBERA & BORN

### Moderate

**Cal Pep ★★★** CATALAN The only bad thing about Cal Pep is that it closes after lunch on Saturday and doesn't reopen until Monday at dinner. Folks in Barcelona for the weekend miss out on joining the swarm of happy people dining on Pep's small dishes. Plan your time wisely so that you can try what other places call *media raciones,* that is, bigger than a tapa and smaller than a *racion*. There are Catalan classics among the 70 or so dishes available on a given day, but most are the restaurant's own invention—the "atomic" omelet with crumbled sausage, chewy beans, and potent garlic sauce, for example, or baked artichokes stuffed with onions and black olives. Pep himself plays host, making sure everyone is having a good time and recommending what they should try next. There's a small dining room at the back, but most patrons prefer the counter seats up front.

Plaça des les Olles, 8. www.calpep.com. ✆ **93-310-79-61.** Mains 14€–28€. Metro: Barceloneta or Jaume I. Mon–Fri 7:30–11:30pm; Tues–Sat 1–3:45pm. Closed last 3 weeks of Aug.

**Cuines Santa Caterina ★★** ASIAN/MEDITERRANEAN This soaring adjunct to the Mercat Santa Caterina (p. 770) is one of the classiest eating halls in Barcelona. A simple tapas bar stands at the entrance, but the main action is in the dining room of chunky wooden tables surrounded on two sides by open kitchens. That's right, "kitchens" in the plural. Order paella and it comes from the Spanish kitchen; order fried rice and it comes from the Asian kitchen. The restaurant prides itself on total integration with the market, and many of the dishes are suitable for vegetarians. Light vegetable tempuras are offered, as are vegetable sushi rolls and excellent sashimi cut to order. Spanish and Catalan market food—roast duck, monkfish, and clams with romesco sauce—is just as plentiful and just as good. You can't make reservations, so show up early or be ready to wait.

Mercat de Santa Caterina, Avinguda Francesc Cambó, 17. www.grupotragaluz.com. ✆ **93-268-99-18.** Mains 10€–24€. Metro: Jaume I. Sun–Wed 8–11:30pm; Thurs–Sat 8pm–12:30am.

**Els Quatre Gats ★** CATALAN Founded in 1897 as Barcelona's bohemian hangout, the "four cats" (Catalan slang for "just a few people") hit its mark early on. The Modernista crowd hung out here, and the owner gave Picasso one of his first paying art jobs, commissioning the illustration still on the menu cover. The food is hardly revolutionary—cod cooked in ratatouille, roast shoulder of lamb, duck confit with mushrooms—but the midday menu is a good bargain, and the memorabilia on the walls can be engrossing. Note that flip-flops and sloppy attire are banned.

Carrer Montsió, 3. www.4gats.com. ✆ **93-302-41-40.** Reservations required Sat–Sun. Mains 12€–28€. Metro: Plaça de Catalunya. Daily 10am–2am.

### Inexpensive

**Adagiotapas ★★** CATALAN Chef/owner Jordi Herrera is a master of both tradition and innovation. He has a fine-dining restaurant with a Michelin star, but he has more fun at this creative tapas operation. Some dishes are straightforward, like the briny oyster with ginger mignonette, while others are clever reinventions of classics, such as the *tortilla* with caramelized onion that's finished in the oven as a small tart cooked in a cupcake paper.

### The Food Court to End All Food Courts

Tucked into an out-of-the-way corner of El Born, **Mercat Princesa ★★★** features 16 small vendors that offer great food at bargain prices, from the Bravas Mercat stall selling fried potatoes with spicy *bravas* and seven other sauces to a bar that does different rice dishes (Carrer Flassaders, 21; www.mercatprincesa.com; ✆ **93-268-15-18;** main dishes 4€ to 22€; Sun–Wed 9am–midnight, Thurs–Sat 9am–1am; Metro: Jaume I).

Carrer Ferran, 21. www.adagiotapas.com. ✆ **93-318-90-61**. Tapas 2.50€–17€. Metro: Liceu or Jaume I. Daily 1–4pm and 7–11pm.

**Los Caracoles ★** SPANISH You'll probably smell the chickens on a spit in the open window before you see the restaurant. The snails, for which the place was renamed in the mid-20th century, are good and garlicky, but most diners come for the comfort food: chicken and ham croquettes, roast chicken, roast suckling pig, and the expensive lobster paella. The menu has changed little since Los Caracoles was featured in the inaugural edition of *Spain on $5 a Day.* Honest food without subtext never goes out of style.

Carrer Escudellers, 14. www.loscaracoles.es. ✆ **93-301-20-41.** Reservations recommended. Mains 8€–27€. Metro: Liceu or Drassanes. Daily 1:15pm–midnight.

## L'EIXAMPLE

### Expensive

**Casa Calvet ★★** CATALAN Casa Calvet has lovingly preserved the Modernista stained-glass and wood-trim of Antoni Gaudí's 1899 design, matching it with a cuisine that is equally ornamented, essentially Catalan, and tempered by French nouvelle. Sherry-roasted lamb chops, for example, are paired with ratatouille-filled ravioli and a beet-garlic sauce, while bonito tuna is seared and served with fresh green melon, spiced yogurt, and green beans. Vegetarians will find such dishes as a ragout of vegetables with tofu and porcini mushrooms.

Carrer Casp, 48. www.casacalvet.es. ✆ **93-412-40-12.** Reservations required. Mains 27€–31€; tasting menus 49€–70€. Metro: Passeig de Gràcia. Mon–Sat 1–3:30pm and 8:30–11pm.

**Roca Moo ★★★** CATALAN If you're not planning a gastronomic pilgrimage to Girona to eat at Spain's top restaurant, El Celler de Can Roca, you might want to book a dinner here. Chef de cuisine Juan Pretel executes Joan Roca's inspired dishes perfectly, and the design-y decadence of Hotel Omm pumps the otherworldliness up a notch. You might start with *cigalas* (saltwater crayfish) with curry, rose petals, and licorice—a brilliant combination of flavors to give a fairly bland crustacean some real taste. Roca Moo now boasts its own Michelin star and has become more exclusive, trimming back the size of the dining room to expand the adjacent Roca Bar, where the same kitchen serves innovative tapas.

Carrer Rosselló, 265 (in Hotel Omm). www.hotelomm.es. ✆ **93-445-40-00.** Reservations required. Mains 23€–35€; 7-course menu 87€, 125€ with wine; 8-course menu 110€, 154€ with wine. Metro: Diagonal. Mon–Sat 1:30–4pm and 8:30–11pm.

### Moderate

**Can Ravell ★★★** CATALAN There's always been a small area in the back of this gourmet shop that served drinks and a few plates (pork with snails, *tortilla* with sautéed green peppers). But only regular customers know about the full restaurant upstairs. You go through the kitchen and climb a narrow circular stair to reach the airy room filled with solid wooden tables with marble tops. The menu consists of a handful of starters and main dishes selected by the chef after a visit to the market. In the summer, he features one vegetable after another—a feast of green beans one week, tomatoes the next. In the fall, you might find lentils stewed with pig's ear and jowls, a roast quarter lamb (for two or three diners), and the popular side dish of mashed potatoes with foie gras. The cellar here is very extensive, and includes dozens of cava choices in addition to still wines.

Carrer Aragó, 313. www.ravell.com. ✆ **93-457-51-14.** Reservations required. Mains 11€–30€. Metro: Girona. Tues–Sat 10am–9pm; Sun 10am–3pm.

### Inexpensive

**Tapas 24 ★★** TAPAS Tapas in the morning, tapas in the evening, tapas at suppertime. Celebrated chef Carles Abellan set up this basement restaurant in L'Eixample as his personal homage to the tapas lifestyle. It's a treat. Come for breakfast, and you can order *estrellitas*—fried potatoes with a broken fried egg stirred in on top, with or without extra sausage, ham, or foie gras. (Catalan chefs love foie gras, which is local and inexpensive.) The menu changes as the day progresses. Count on always being able to order a bowl of lentils stewed with chorizo, the "McFoie" burger (a hamburger topped with foie gras), or *cap i pota,* which is a gelatinous stew of calf's head and feet beloved by Catalan bar patrons. (It's said to prevent a hangover.) Abellan is also famous for his "bikini" grilled ham and cheese sandwich with black truffle.

Carrer de la Diputació, 269. www.carlesabellan.es. ✆ **93-488-09-77.** Tapas and raciones 2.20€–18€. Metro: Passeig de Gràcia. Mon–Sat 9am–midnight.

## WATERFRONT & LA BARCELONETA

### Moderate

**Can Majó ★** CATALAN/SEAFOOD Steps from the beach, this family restaurant dates from 1968 and is now run by two generations of the Majó family. The dining room resembles a country tavern, but when the weather is good, everyone wants to eat outdoors at the white-linen-clad tables beneath umbrellas. Not all the seafood is local—they fly in amazing oysters from Galicia and France for the raw bar. Many of the shellfish are cooked over a wood-fired grill, which gives them a smoky tang. The restaurant is known, however, for fish soups—both the simple fish and shellfish in a fish broth, and the more elaborate *zarzuela,* a Catalan dish where the mixed fish are more important than the broth.

Almirall Aixada, 23. www.canmajo.es. ✆ **93-221-54-55.** Reservations recommended. Mains 12€–32€. Metro: Barceloneta. Tues–Sat 1–4pm and 8–11:30pm.

**Can Solé ★★** CATALAN/SEAFOOD Proprietor Josep Maria Garcia adheres to the traditional plates of La Barceloneta. That could mean a briny bowl of tiny sweet clams or cabbage hearts stuffed with tuna. Some vanishing dishes make their last stand here, like the fried cod and onions with sweet currants that hint at its North African roots. And there's the *zarzuela,* the priciest dish on the menu because it is an encyclopedia of the Barceloneta catch, jammed with everything including whiting, shrimp, cigalas, bream, mackerel, clams, mussels, and even lobster.
Carrer Sant Carles, 4. www.restaurantcansole.com. ✆ **93-221-50-12.** Reservations suggested. Mains 13€–30€. Metro: Barceloneta. Tues–Sat 1:30–4pm and 8:30–11pm; Sun 1:30–4pm. Closed 2 weeks Aug.

**Suquet de l'Almirall ★★** CATALAN/SEAFOOD Quim Marqués worked at some of Spain's leading restaurants (including elBulli) before taking over this gem from his parents in 1997. He buys all his fish from the auction less than 100 yards away, and supplements the fish with local milk, cheese, eggs, and organically grown vegetables. All the fish dishes here are terrific, but the *suquet* (a traditional Catalan seafood stew) is a classic. Best of all, this is one place on the waterfront where you can order the seafood paella and know it's the real thing.
Passeig Joan Borbo, 65. www.suquetdelalmirall.com. ✆ **93-221-62-33.** Mains 16€–29€. Metro: Barceloneta. Tues–Sat 1:30–4:30pm and 9–11:30pm, Sun 1:30–4:30pm.

### Inexpensive

**L'Electricitat ★★** TAPAS Possibly the favorite neighborhood bar in all of Barceloneta, the atmosphere here at midday matches the name—it's positively electric. It's a great place to have steamed mussels or clams, maybe a bite of fried fish, some anchovies, a finger sandwich with smoked trout, and then perhaps a small crab salad. There's beer on tap and a lot of inexpensive Catalan wines. In cold weather, they also tap the big barrels of house vermouth that are more or less ornamental the rest of the year.
Carrer Sant Carles, 15. ✆ **93-221-50-17.** Tapas and raciones 1.50€–12€. Metro: Barceloneta. Mon–Sat 8am–3pm and 7–10:30pm, Sun 8am–3:45pm.

## Shopping in Barcelona

If you don't want to spend a lot of time looking for unique gifts, head straight for museum shops. The **Museu Picasso** (p. 749) and the **Fundació Joan Miró** (p. 757) have great selections of jewelry, scarves and other accessories, books, posters, and interesting objects for the home at reasonable prices. For items inspired by the Modernisme movement, check the shops at **La Pedrera** (p. 754) and **Casa Batlló** (p. 752), as well as the more modest shop at the **Museu del Modernisme Catalá** (p. 755).

There are two good options for shopping centers. **Centre Comercial Maremagnum** (Moll d' Espanya s/n; www.maremagnum.es; ✆ **93-225-81-00;** Metro: Drassanes or Barceloneta) opened in the early

1990s on the waterfront as a magnet for shopping and nightlife. More interesting is **Arenas de Barcelona** (Gran Via, 373-385; www.arenasdebarcelona.com; ✆ **93-289-02-44;** Metro: Plaça d'Espanya), originally Barcelona's bullring, built 1889 to 1900. Six floors of shops and a movie theater are augmented by an excellent food court. Both complexes have outlets for **FC Barcelona,** the city's wildly popular football club.

Shoppers and window shoppers alike will probably find neighborhood streets more interesting. **Passeig de Gracia** in L'Eixample is Barcelona's most prestigious shopping promenade. For our (more limited) money, the streets of the Barri Gòtic and adjacent Born and La Ribera have more interesting and unpredictable shops. For an overview of regional handcrafts, check out **Artesania Catalunya** (Carrer dels Banys Nous, 11; ✆ **93-467-46-60;** Metro: Liceu or Jaume I). **La Manual Alpargatera** (Carrer Avinyo, 7; www.lamanualalpargatera.es; ✆ **93-301-01-72;** Metro: Jaume I or Barceloneta) has been making espadrilles since the 1940s and claims that Salvador Dalí was an aficionado. Dalí still inspires jewelry designers at **BCN Art Design** (Carrer Argenteria, 76; www.bcnartdesign.es; ✆ **93-295-56-44;** Metro: Jaume I), but you'll also find rings, bracelets, necklaces, and earrings inspired by Gaudí and Picasso. **Krappa** (Carrer Freneria, 1; ✆ **93-442-51-00;** Metro: Jaume I) makes engravings based on historic woodcuts.

Hagglers will enjoy Barcelona's street markets. **El Encants** market of antique, vintage, and more modern goods is held 9am to 8pm (some dealers leave earlier) on Monday, Wednesday, Friday, and Saturday in Plaça de les Glòries (www.encantsbcn.com; Metro: Glòries). One of the best flea markets is held on Thursdays (except Aug) at **Plaça Nova** at the base of the Cathedral of Barcelona (Metro: Jaume 1). If you miss it, there is a smaller flea market Friday to Sunday near the **Mirador de Colom** (Metro: Drassanes). **Plaça Reial** (Metro: Liceu) is the site of a stamp and coin market on Sunday. **Plaça del Pi** (Metro: Liceu) hosts an art fair (www.pintorspibarcelona.com) with dozens of artists on Saturday 11am to 8pm and Sunday 11am to 2pm.

**La Boqueria** (p. 746) and **Mercat Santa Caterina** (Avinguda Francesc Cambó, 16; www.mercatsantacaterina.com; ✆ **93-319-57-40;** Metro: Jaume I) are the best fresh food markets, with good selections of spices and other packaged goods to bring home. For great chocolate, visit **Cacao Sampaka** (Carrer Consell de Cent, 292; www.cacaosampaka.com; ✆ **92-272-08-33;** Metro: Passeig de Gràcia) which was co-founded by Albert Adrià, brother of famed chef Ferran. For gourmet olive oils and other foods from around Spain, check the floor-to-ceiling shelves of **Colmado Quilez** (La Rambla de Catalunya; 63; www.lafuente.es; ✆ **93-215-23-56;** Metro: Passeig de Gràcia).

## Entertainment & Nightlife

Barcelona is as vibrant by night as it is by day. To capture the city's rhythm, take an early evening promenade along Les Rambles, stop in a tapas bar or two, and then enjoy a late dinner sometime after 9pm. Most nights, that will probably be all the entertainment you need.

But Barcelona also has a rich cultural scene, and the landmark venues of **Palau de la Música Catalana** (p. 750) and **Gran Teatre del Liceu** (Les Rambles, 51-59; www.liceubarcelona.com; ✆ **93-485-99-00.** Metro: Liceu) come alive when performers take the stage. The musical performances at the Palau de la Música present no language barriers. The Liceu is known for its opera and theatre, but also presents music and dance. During the summer, the rooftops of **Casa Batlló** (p. 752) and **La Pedrera** (p. 754) host live concerts in the evenings.

The concentration of bars at **Maremagnum** (p. 769) is popular with the college crowd. The somewhat old-fashioned **Poble Espanyol** (p. 758) has a number of night spots, including the open-air disco **La Terrrazza** (www.laterrrazza.com; ✆ **93-272-49-80**) with great city views, the trendy club **The One** (www.poble-espanyol.com), and **El Tablao de Carmen** (www.tablaodecarmen.com; ✆ **93-325-68-95**), a flamenco club named for the Barcelona-born dance legend Carmen Amaya.

Barcelona is not in the forefront of the flamenco revival, but don't miss a show if it is your only opportunity to see Spain's signature art form. **Flamenco Tablao Cordobes** (Les Rambles, 35; www.tablaocordobes.es; ✆ **93-317-57-11;** Metro: Liceu) occupies a Moorish-style performance space with tilework and arched ceilings. Both clubs offer dinner, but you are better off having a drink only and eating elsewhere.

End your evening with a glass of cava at one of the city's classic *xampanyerias* (a bar specializing in sparkling wine), such as **El Xampanyet** (Carrer Montcada, 22; ✆ **93-319-70-03**) or **Xampú Xampany** (Gran Vía de les Corts Catalanes, 702; www.xampuxampany.com; ✆ **93-265-04-83**).

## A Day Trip to Montserrat

Thousands of the faithful flock annually to this mountainside monastery to see and touch the statue of **La Moreneta** (the Black Virgin), a cult with an intense following throughout Catalunya. This mountainside pilgrimage site has geological majesty and drama to accompany the religious fervor. The outline of the serrated mountain range is one of the most recognizable "national" symbols. Many newly married Catalan couples come here for the Virgin's blessing, and many name their daughters "Montserrat" ("Montse" for short). Be prepared for cold weather on the mountain, even during the heat of summer.

Get there on the Catalunyan railway, **Ferrocarrils de la Generalitat de Catalunya** (www.fgc.es; ✆ **93-237-71-56**), with 12 R5-Manresa trains daily from Plaça d'Espanya. The R5 connects with an aerial cableway (Aeri de Montserrat), included in 30€ round-trip fare. An alternative to the Aeri is the **Cremallera de Montserrat,** a 15-minute funicular ride from the village below the mountain. You get off the train a stop sooner at Olesa de Montserrat, and transfer to the funicular. The round-trip fare is also 30€.

Medieval Catalunya espoused a fierce Christian faith that reached its apogee in the cult of the **Virgin of Montserrat,** one of the legendary "dark" virgins of Iberian Catholicism. A polychrome carving of the Virgin and Child (a form known in Catalan as Maria del Deu) was discovered in a grotto on the mountainside in the 12th century, and many miracles have been ascribed to the figure. The **Basilica de Montserrat ★★** and a Benedictine monastery have grown up on the site. To view **La Moreneta,** enter the church through a side door to the right. The meter-high carving sits in a silver altar in a chapel above the main altar. A long line of people parade past the statue, which is mostly encased in bulletproof acrylic to protect it from vandalism. The casing has a cutout that lets the faithful kiss her extended hand. The basilica is open daily from 8 to 10:30am and noon to 6:30pm. Admission is free.

At Plaça de Santa María, you can also visit the **Museu de Montserrat ★** (www.museudemontserrat.com; ✆ **93-877-77-77**), full of art donated by the faithful. Many pieces have religious subjects, some by major artists like Caravaggio and El Greco, but others are purely secular, including an early Picasso (*El Viejo Pescador* from 1895) and some lovely Impressionist works. The museum is open daily 10am to 5:45pm; 7€ adults, 6€ seniors and students, 4€ ages 8 to 16.

You can also visit **Santa Cova (Holy Grotto) ★**, where La Moreneta was discovered. The natural grotto was reworked in the 17th century, and a small church in the shape of a cross was built. You go halfway by funicular, but must complete the trip on foot. The grotto is open daily from 10am to 1pm and 4 to 7pm. The round-trip fare is 4€.

# MADRID

Perched on an arid plateau in the middle of the country, Madrid is the physical and political heart of Spain. Felipe II moved the capital here in 1561, when the Spanish empire was on the ascendancy, and built a city fit for kings. It is a truly royal city, with the monumental architecture, royal palace, and regal art collection to prove it.

The lure of great paintings in the Prado and the spectacle of Bourbon excess in the Palacio Real is undeniable. But Madrid is neither stuck in time nor wed to outmoded formalities. It is the capital of a nationwide flamenco revival, a showcase for new media, and ground zero for annual summits on the state of contemporary cuisine.

Moreover, Madrileños are famous for their capacity to have a good time, so you should follow their lead. You can stand elbow to elbow with them eating tapas in the Plaza Santa Ana bars beneath the sculpted visages of Spain's great playwrights. And you can join them at cafe tables in Plaza Mayor, basking in the sun beneath the visage of Felipe III, forever fixed in bronze on horseback. After all, Madrid is the sunniest capital in Europe. The weather may be hot in summer and often chilly in winter,

Nighttime traffic on Madrid's Gran via.

but the sky is the very definition of cerulean blue. As Madrileños say, *de Madrid al cielo:* from Madrid to heaven.

## Essentials

Madrid's tourist office website, **www.esmadrid.com**, will direct you to locations around the city where you can pick up information and free mp3 audioguides.

**ARRIVING** **Barajas Airport** (www.aena.es; ✆ **90-240-45-04** for general and flight info, +34/91-321-10-00 from outside Spain; airport code MAD) is 15km (9 miles) east of Madrid's city center. Its four terminals are connected by a moving sidewalk and light rail.

Air-conditioned **airport buses** go from the ground floor at Terminal 4 or Level 0 at Terminals 1 and 2 to the Atocha train station a few blocks from the Prado. The fare is 5€, and you can buy tickets on the bus but only with cash. Buses leave every 10 to 15 minutes for the 40-minute trip. The **Metro** subway is another option, but is cumbersome with luggage and not appreciably cheaper than the airport bus. From the airport, take line 8 to Nuevos Ministerios, exit and re-enter the system, and pay a second fare. The airport supplement is 3€ in addition to the usual 1.50€ to 2€ for travel within metropolitan Madrid. By **taxi,** expect to pay 35€ and up, plus surcharges, for the trip from the airport with baggage.

If you are arriving by **car,** all highways within Spain radiate outward from Madrid. The N-I comes from Irun at the French border (507km/315 miles), the N-II from Barcelona (626km/389 miles), the N-III from Valencia (349/km/217 miles), the N-IV from Cádiz (625km/388 miles), the N-V from Badajoz (409km/254 miles), and N-VI from Galicia (602km/374 miles). Once you're in your hotel, leave the car at a parking garage. Madrid is choked with traffic and parking is scarce.

Madrid has two major **railway** stations: **Atocha** (Glorieta Carlos V; Metro: Atocha RENFE), for trains to and from Lisbon, Toledo, Andalucía, Basque Country, Extremadura, Barcelona, and the French frontier via Catalunya; and **Chamartín** (in the northern suburbs at Augustín de Foxá; Metro: Chamartín), for trains to and from Asturias, Cantabria, Castilla y León, the Basque Country, Aragón, Levante (Valencia), Murcia, and the French frontier via Basque Country. For information about connections from any of these stations, call **RENFE (Spanish Railways)** at ✆ **90-232-03-20** (daily 5am–11:50pm), or visit **www.renfe.com**.

Madrid has at least 14 major **bus** terminals, including **Estación Sur de Autobuses** (Calle Méndez Álvaro, 83; www.estaciondeautobuses.com; ✆ **91-468-42-00;** Metro: Méndez Álvaro). Most buses pass through this large station.

**CITY LAYOUT** All roads in Spain ultimately lead to Madrid, which long ago outgrew its early boundaries and continues to sprawl in all directions. But central Madrid can be navigated by its main arteries and squares.

**Puerta del Sol** is the starting point for all road distances within Spain and the crossroads of Madrid's public transit system. The bustling square is the borderland between Madrid's oldest quarters (La Latina, Lavapiés, Las Letras) and the commercial city center. **Calle de Alcalá** begins at Sol and runs northeast for 4km (2½ miles) through Plaza de la Independencia and the entrance to Retiro Park. Follow **Carrera de San Jerónimo** east to reach the Paseo del Prado. Follow **Calle Mayor** west to reach Plaza Mayor.

**Plaza Mayor** lies at the heart of Old Madrid and is an attraction in itself, with its mix of Renaissance and neoclassical architecture. The colonnaded ground level of the plaza is filled with shops and restaurants. The area immediately south of Plaza Mayor—known as *barrios bajos*—is

## events IN MADRID

Food lovers can indulge in **Gastrofestival Madrid** (www.gastrofestivalmadrid.com) from late January until mid-February. The ambitious event features more than 300 gastronomic and cultural activities throughout the city, including specially priced menus at participating restaurants and original tapas in a number of bars.

In mid-May, the **Fiesta de San Isidro** (www.esmadrid.com) honors the city's patron saint with 5 days of street parades, dances, music, bullfights, and fireworks.

In addition to gastronomy, Madrid is also at the forefront of the flamenco revival. For most of the month of June, **Suma Flamenca** (www.esmadrid.com) fills many of the city's performance halls and smaller clubs with singing, dancing, and guitar playing by both established and up-and-coming artists.

a colorful segment of La Latina with cobblestone streets lined with 16th- and 17th-century architecture. Directly west of Plaza Mayor, where Calle Mayor meets Calle Bailén, stands the **Palacio Real** (Royal Palace).

**Gran Vía** cuts a diagonal path across the city from **Plaza de España** to **Plaza de Cibeles,** with its fountain to Cybele, "the mother of the gods." From Cibeles, the wide **Paseo de Recoletos** begins a short run north to Plaza de Colón. North of Colón, the long serpentine central artery of Madrid begins: **Paseo de la Castellana,** flanked by expensive shops, apartment buildings, luxury hotels, and foreign embassies.

Heading south from Cibeles is **Paseo del Prado,** where you'll find the **Museo del Prado** and the striking **Museo Thyssen-Bornemisza.** To the east lies **Parque del Retiro,** a magnificent park once reserved for royalty, with a restaurant, a rose garden, a lake, and two gallery pavilions. (It's best accessed from Plaza de Independencia, north of the Prado.) Paseo del Prado leads south to the Atocha railway station. Just off the roundabout is the third of Madrid's artistic triumvirate, the **Museo Nacional Centro de Arte Reina Sofía.**

**GETTING AROUND** You can walk most places in central Madrid, and it's the best way to experience the city. To save time, it's a good idea to take public transport to a neighborhood and then set off on foot to explore. Madrid has some of the most thorough **public transit** in Europe.

The **Metro** (subway) system (www.metromadrid.es; ✆ **90-244-44-03**) is easy to learn and use. Maps are available free at most ticket booths. The fare is 1.50€ for the first five stations one-way; the price goes up 0.10€ for each additional station up to a 2€ maximum in central Madrid. You have to insert your ticket to exit as well as enter the Metro. A 10-trip **Metrobus** ticket, good on buses and Metro, costs 12€. The Metro operates from 6am to 2am (try to avoid rush hours).

The **public buses,** marked **emt,** are most useful for moving around the circular roads, or *rondas,* such as getting from Atocha to Puerta de Toledo, or for moving quickly up and down the Paseos. They run 6am to 11pm. Tickets for single bus rides are 1.50€, but few people buy just one. Buy a 10-trip Metrobus ticket (see above), or consider one of the special passes designed for tourists. An **Abono Transportes Turístico** for unlimited rides on Madrid's Metro and buses is available at Metro stations and tourist offices. It is sold for 1, 2, 3, 5, and 7 days (for 8.40€, 14€, 18€, 27€, and 35€, respectively). The Abono is valid only for the ticket holder, and you have to show photo ID when you buy it. Unless you'll be a heavy user of public transit, the **Metrobus** ticket is usually a better buy at 12€, especially since two people can share a single ticket.

**Taxi fares** are reasonable. When you flag down a taxi, the meter should register 2.10€ 6am to 9pm or 2.20€ 9pm to 6am; for every kilometer thereafter, the fare increases between 1€ and 1.20€. Supplements are charged for trips to the railway station, the bullring, the football stadiums, or the airport. A 1.20€ supplement is charged on Sundays and holidays. It's customary to tip at least 10% of the fare. Taxis can be hailed on the street or at taxi ranks near attractions and hotels. Call a taxi at ✆ **91-547-82-00** or 91-405-12-13.

Don't **drive** in Madrid. Just don't. Public transit is so good that you should leave the driving to Madrileños. They're the ones who grew up watching bullfights and understand balancing aggression and aversion to navigate Madrid's nonsensical intersections.

## The Neighborhoods in Brief

**ART DISTRICT & PASEOS** Not a real city district, the Paseos form Madrid's north-south axis, and the street name changes along the way. As it approaches Atocha station, the district is suddenly thick with museums and park amenities. The **Museo del Prado** and some of the city's more expensive hotels are found here. Many restaurants and other hotels are located along its side streets. In summer, the large medians of the Paseos become open-air terraces filled with animated crowds. Use Atocha and Banco de España Metro stops.

**PUERTA DEL SOL & LAS LETRAS** Madrid radiated from its eastern gate—**Puerta del Sol** means "Gate of the Sun"—even before Habsburg kings established their capital in the city. Today Sol is the hub of public

### ARE passes A GOOD DEAL?

Don't jump at either of the Madrid discount cards before you have an idea of what you want to see. The offers all sound good, but you may not reap significant savings.

The most clear-cut is the **Tarjeta Paseo del Arte** (26€), which saves 25% off admissions for the Museo Nacional del Prado, Museo Nacional Centro de Arte Reina Sofía, and the Museo Thyssen-Bornemisza, and lets you skip the lines. You can purchase it at any of the museums. The card allows just one entry to each museum.

The big three are among the 50+ museums and monuments included on the **Madrid Card** (www.madridcard.com; 47€ for 24 hr., 60€ for 48 hr., 67€ for 72 hr., 77€ for 120 hr.). The Madrid Card lets you bypass ticket lines, which is a good thing, because you might need to hustle to make the pass worthwhile. Several listed attractions are always free, and the restaurant and shop savings are insignificant. But the card does include free admissions to Bernabéu football stadium and the Plaza de Toros de las Ventas. You also get small discounts on the more tourist-oriented flamenco shows and at El Corte Inglés (p. 799) department store.

You don't need a pass to skip the lines at the Prado, Reina Sofía, and Thyssen-Bornemisza—just buy tickets in advance online. When deciding about discount passes, keep in mind that most Madrid museums have free hours (but are crowded then) and some have no entry fee at all. If you are on a tight budget, it's a better deal to work those free admission hours into your touring plans.

transport. Metro lines 1, 2, and 3 will take you anyplace else you'll want to go. Heading south and uphill from Sol is the barrio known as Las Letras because it was home to writers from the 16th through the 20th centuries. Lope de Vega, Cervantes, and Lorca lived and worked here. Plaza Santa Ana, one of the city's best spots for tapas, is central to Las Letras. It can get rowdy at night, but it oozes Old Madrid charm. Use Sol and Antón Martín Metro stops.

**PLAZA MAYOR & LA LATINA** Madrid (and its visitors) party in this neighborhood. Sometimes called the "Madrid of the Asturias," it is better known as La Latina. From **Plaza Mayor,** the Arco de Cuchilleros leads to Cava de San Miguel, Cava Alta, and Cava Baja, all full of taverns and bars. La Latina continues downhill west to the Manzanares River. In 1617, Plaza Mayor became the hub of Madrid, and it remains a center of activity both day and night. Use Sol and La Latina Metro stops.

**OPERA & PALACIO REAL** Adjacent to Plaza Mayor and La Latina, this section of Madrid revolves around the Teatro Real, the Plaza de Oriente, and the **Palacio Real** with its parks and gardens. It forms a buffer zone between Puerta del Sol and Plaza Mayor, and the district uphill around Gran Vía. Use Opera and Santo Domingo Metro stops.

**SALAMANCA, RETIRO & CHAMBERÍ** Once Madrid's city walls came down in the 1860s, the district of Salamanca to the northeast of Old Madrid became a fashionable address. Calle de Serrano cuts through this neighborhood and is lined with stores and boutiques. The adjacent leafy streets near Parque del Retiro and Chamberí (west of the Paseos and due north of Puerta del Sol) are similar to Salamanca but more residential. This area includes the **Parque del Retiro,** the **Museo Sorolla,** and the **Museo Lázaro Galdiano.** The most useful Metro stops include Retiro, Serrano, Velázquez, and Núñez de Balboa.

## Exploring Madrid

There are three main reasons to visit Madrid: to see the historic royal city; to visit one of the greatest clusters of major art museums anywhere in the world; and to eat, drink, and hang out in its atmospheric public squares. You'll probably want to start at the Prado, Thyssen-Bornemisza, and Reina Sofía museums and take the Metro from Atocha to reach other neighborhoods to continue your explorations.

### ARTS DISTRICT & PASEOS

**CentroCentro ★★** MUSEUM A Baroque Revival palace that once housed the central post office, the Palacio de Cibeles became Madrid's City Hall in 2007. Even city councilors didn't need something this huge, so much of the building was converted to galleries, a concert hall, and other public spaces called CentroCentro. A reading area has daily papers and free computers with Internet access. You'll also find lockers, coat check, public restrooms, an excellent store selling Madrid-oriented books

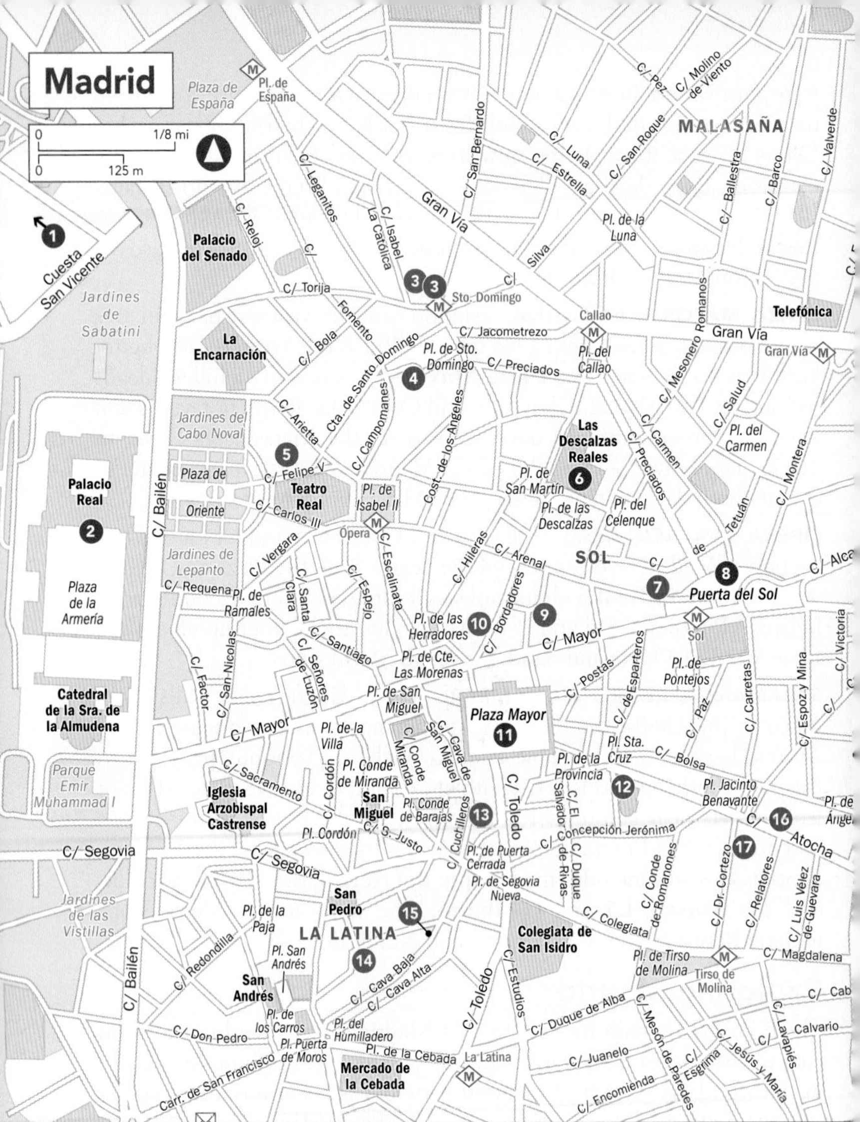


**ATTRACTIONS**

Casa de Campo **1**
Casa de Lope de Vega **31**
CentroCentro **19**
Ermita de San Antonio de Florida – Panteón de Goya **1**
Monasterio de las Descalzas Reales **6**
Museo Arqueológico Nacional **21**
Museo de la Real Academia de Bellas Artes de San Fernando **18**
Museo del Prado **29**
Museo Lázaro Galdiano **20**
Museo Nacional Centro de Arte Reina Sofía **34**
Museo Naval **25**
Museo Sorolla **20**
Museo Thyssen-Bornemisza **26**
Palacio Real **2**
Parque del Retiro **28**
Plaza de Toros Monumental de Las Ventas **24**
Plaza Mayor **11**
Plaza Santa Ana **30**
Puerta del Sol **8**

**RESTAURANTS**

Cerveceria José Luís **23**
Chocolatería San Ginés **9**
El 28 de Larumbe **23**
El Brillante **33**
El Ñeru **10**
Julián de Tolosa **15**
Restaurante Botín **13**
Restaurante Palacio de Cibeles **19**
Restaurante Sandó by Arzak Instruction **3**
Taberna Almendro **14**
Taberna del Alabardero **5**

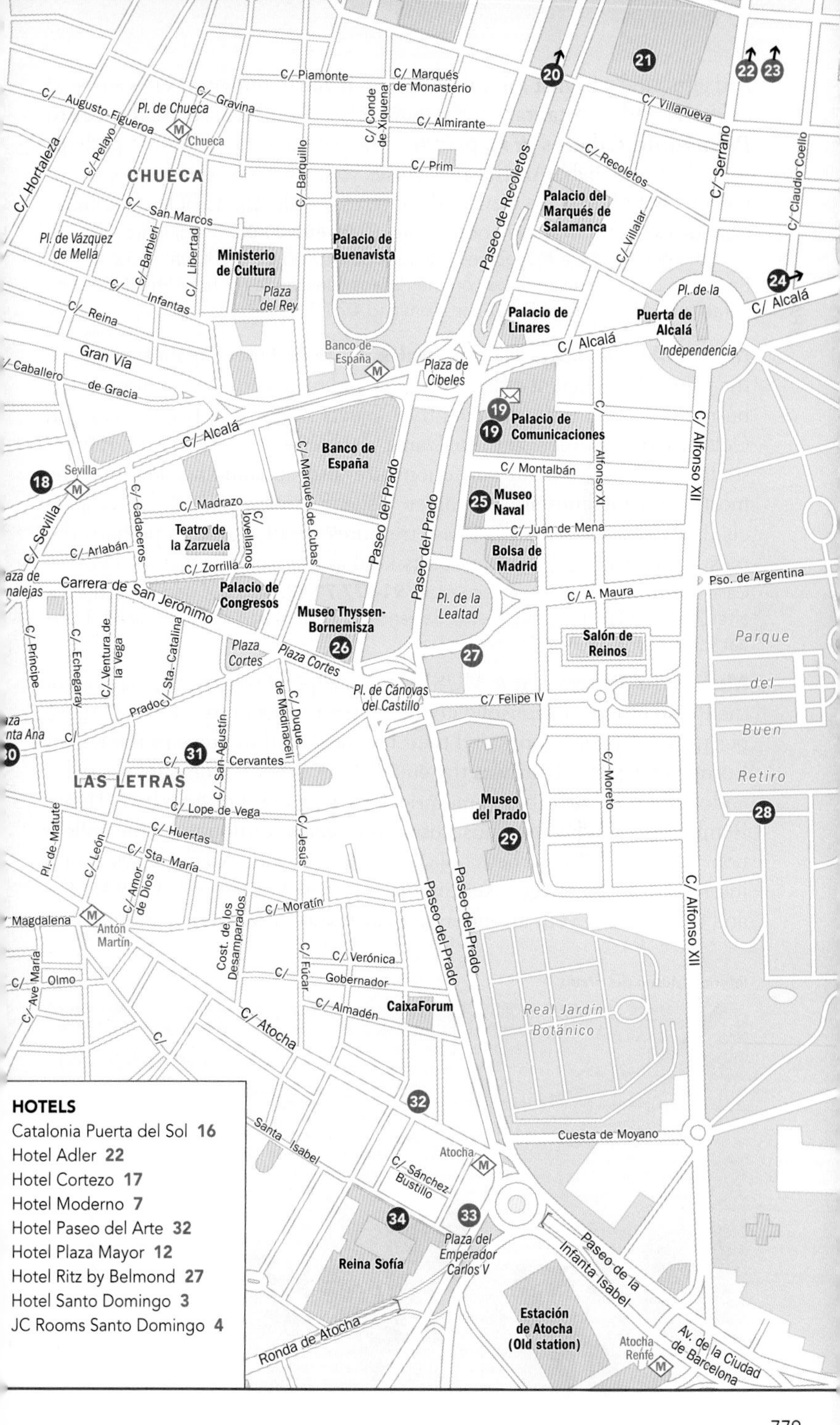
HOTELS
Catalonia Puerta del Sol 16
Hotel Adler 22
Hotel Cortezo 17
Hotel Moderno 7
Hotel Paseo del Arte 32
Hotel Plaza Mayor 12
Hotel Ritz by Belmond 27
Hotel Santo Domingo 3
JC Rooms Santo Domingo 4
CHUECA
LAS LETRAS
Pl. de Chueca
Chueca
C/ Piamonte
C/ Marqués de Monasterio
C/ Gravina
C/ Augusto Figueroa
C/ Conde de Xiquena
C/ Almirante
C/ Prim
C/ Hortaleza
C/ Pelayo
C/ Barquillo
C/ San Marcos
Pl. de Vázquez de Mella
C/ Barbieri
C/ Libertad
Ministerio de Cultura
Plaza del Rey
Palacio de Buenavista
C/ Infantas
C/ Reina
Gran Vía
C/ Caballero de Gracia
Banco de España
Plaza de Cibeles
Paseo de Recoletos
C/ Villanueva
C/ Recoletos
C/ Serrano
C/ Claudio Coello
Palacio del Marqués de Salamanca
C/ Villalar
Pl. de la Independencia
Puerta de Alcalá
C/ Alcalá
Palacio de Linares
Palacio de Comunicaciones
C/ Montalbán
C/ Alfonso XI
C/ Alfonso XII
Museo Naval
C/ Juan de Mena
Bolsa de Madrid
Pso. de Argentina
C/ A. Maura
Pl. de la Lealtad
Salón de Reinos
Parque del Buen Retiro
Sevilla
C/ Sevilla
C/ Madrazo
C/ Cadaceros
Teatro de la Zarzuela
C/ Jovellanos
C/ Marqués de Cubas
Paseo del Prado
C/ Arlabán
C/ Zorrilla
Plaza de Canalejas
Carrera de San Jerónimo
Palacio de Congresos
Museo Thyssen-Bornemisza
Plaza Cortes
Pl. de Cánovas del Castillo
C/ Felipe IV
C/ Príncipe
C/ Echegaray
C/ Ventura de la Vega
C/ Sta. Catalina
C/ Prado
Plaza Santa Ana
C/ Duque de Medinaceli
C/ San Agustín
C/ Cervantes
C/ Moreto
Museo del Prado
C/ Lope de Vega
C/ Huertas
C/ Sta. María
C/ León
C/ Amor de Dios
Pl. de Matute
C/ Jesús
C/ Magdalena
Antón Martín
C/ Moratín
Cost. de los Desamparados
C/ Verónica
C/ Fúcar
C/ Gobernador
C/ Olmo
C/ Ave María
C/ Almadén
CaixaForum
C/ Atocha
Real Jardín Botánico
Santa Isabel
Cuesta de Moyano
Atocha
C/ Sánchez Bustillo
Plaza del Emperador Carlos V
Reina Sofía
Paseo de la Infanta Isabel
Ronda de Atocha
Estación de Atocha (Old station)
Atocha Renfe
Av. de la Ciudad de Barcelona
18
19
20
21
22
23
24
25
26
27
28
29
30
31
32
33
34

and gifts, and a tourist information area. If you're hungry, there's a casual cafeteria and a restaurant for a more leisurely meal (see **Restaurante Palacio de Cibeles ★★**, p. 796). The Mirador de Madrid is perhaps the grandest delight. An elevator whisks you to the seventh floor open-air balcony for a bird's-eye view of the city, especially the Cibeles fountain.

Plaza de Cibeles, 1. www.centrocentro.org. ✆ **91-480-00-08.** Building free; admission charged to some exhibitions. Mirador de Madrid 2€, 0.50€ under 12. Metro: Banco de España. Bus: Any bus on the Paseos lines. Building Tues–Sun 8am–8pm; Mirador de Madrid Tues–Sun 10am–1pm and 4:30–7:30pm.

**Museo Arqueológico Nacional ★★** MUSEUM Spain recognized the value of its ancient culture early on and managed to keep most of the buried heritage inside the country. Objects here range from wonderful Celto-Iberian statues like La Dama de Elche to a wealth of Roman sculpture. The Moorish collections are also outstanding. Possibly the most surprising finds are the golden Visigoth crowns and other royal jewels (the Guarrazar Hoard). These treasures are displayed in perhaps the most state-of-the-art museum of its kind in the world.

Calle Serrano, 13. http://man.mcu.es. ✆ **91-577-79-12.** 3€, 1.50€ under 12, free Sat after 2pm and Sun morning. Metro: Serrano or Colón. Bus: 1, 9, 19, 51, or 74. Tues–Sat 9:30am–8pm, Sun 9:30am–3pm.

**Museo del Prado ★★★** MUSEUM Felipe VI ordered the creation of the Prado in 1819 to consolidate the royal art collections (hence all those portraits of Spanish kings and their families), and to prove to the rest of Europe that Spanish art was the equal of any other nation. He was right, and while the Prado has some priceless works by Fra Angelico, Titian, Rembrandt, and Hieronymus Bosch, the Spaniards dominate the collection. We can't think of a better place to see their work. No matter what else interests you, we suggest starting with **Diego Velázquez** (1599–1660) and then turning your attention to **Francisco de Goya** (1746–1828).

**Interior, Museo del Prado.**

After generations of making Goya the anchor for all Spanish art, the Prado fomented a quiet revolution in 2013 when it rehung the galleries of paintings by Velázquez and made his psychological masterpiece, *Las Meninas,* the sun at the center of its solar system. You have probably seen reproductions of this portrait of Felipe IV's royal family (with a shadowy portrait of the painter himself) a thousand times, but the sheer scope and power of the actual canvas will bowl you over. The focus of the painting is on the young infanta Margarita (daughter of Felipe IV) and her diminutive ladies in waiting, including one of the many royal dwarves whom Velázquez never tired of painting. *Las Meninas* is easily the most popular painting in the Prado. If you want to see *Las Meninas* without crowds, be among the first to enter in the morning—a Madrid Card, Paseo del Arte pass, or printout of an online ticket purchase lets you skip the line.

Velázquez was court painter for 37 years to Felipe IV, a king only a few years his junior. He painted the king as a vacuous-looking young man, as a thoughtful king in middle age, and as an aging ruler weary from grief and depression—a remarkable psychological progression. But Velázquez gets even better as the gallery numbers rise. His religious paintings in **Sala 14** derive amazing intensity from the geometric rigor of their compositions. The dead body on the cross in *Cristo Crucificado* has ceased to be either man or god—he has been transfigured into the devotional icon of Spanish Catholicism.

Most paintings by Velázquez were never seen by anyone but the royal family until they were deposited in the Prado, but Goya did study them when he worked for the crown in the late 1770s. For the rest of his life, he cited Velázquez as one of his most important influences. Goya's mature work, especially after Carlos IV made him court painter in 1799, shows an understanding of character on a par with Velázquez. *The Family of Carlos IV* in **Sala 32,** painted around 1800, shows a burly king uncomfortable in his finery, who would rather hunt than rule. In 1808, Carlos abdicated, and his foolish son invited Napoléon to tidy up Spain.

Goya's brighter side is on display in his paintings of countryside idylls that he made as cartoons for tapestries to cover the walls of a royal hunting palace. It was his first royal commission, and he did his level best to be cheerful and witty. Head to **Salas 90 to 94** to experience this youthful joy.

On the darker side, Goya captured the horrors of the French occupation in *Dos de Mayo,* which shows the popular uprising in Puerta del Sol on May 2, 1808, and *El Tres de Mayo,* which depicts the executions of the Spanish partisans by firing squad on Principe Pío hill the following day. These late paintings that made his modern reputation are found in **Salas 64 and 65** on the ground level. The somber Dark Paintings that he made on the walls of his house in the years after 1819 in fits of depression and madness fill adjacent **Salas 66 and 67.** These nightmarish images became inspirations for German Expressionism and for Surrealism.

Interior, Reina Sofia Museum.

Goya wasn't the first Spaniard with a fantastical imagination. At the opposite end of the Villanueva building, several Gothic and Romanesque rooms radiate from a central rotunda. Visit **Sala 51C** and wait for your eyes to adjust to the dim illumination. The room re-creates a chapel from the A.D. 1125, Iglesia de la Vera Cruz Maderuelo outside Segovia. Animals high on the wall include the artist's conception of a bear and an elephant—a beast he had heard described but had never seen. The creatures are so abstract they could have been painted by Joan Miró.

Paseo del Prado. www.museoprado.es. ✆ **91-330-28-00.** 14€ adults, 7€ seniors, free for students and children 17 and under, free for all Mon–Sat 6–8pm, Sun 5–7pm. Metro: Atocha. Bus: 9, 10, 14, 19, 27, 34, 37, or 45. Mon–Sat 10am–8pm; Sun to 7pm.

**Museo Nacional Centro de Arte Reina Sofía ★★★** MUSEUM

It's about a 3-block walk—and a much larger aesthetic leap—from the Prado to the Reina Sofía, which holds Spain's most significant collection of 20th- and 21st-century works. In fact, that collection has swelled so extensively in recent years that the museum now uses the two 19th-century exhibition palaces in the **Parque del Retiro ★★** (p. 789) as spaces for temporary shows that require large physical spaces. The main museum consists of the neoclassical 18th-century former General Hospital designed by Francisco Sabatini, and the post-modern addition by Jean Nouvel that opened in 2002. Two floors of the Sabatini building contain "permanent" chronological exhibits: Level 2 covers 1900 to 1945, while Level 4 holds work from 1945 to 1968. Level 1 in the Nouvel building addresses more recent art, including work by American pop artists.

Paintings by Picasso, Juan Gris, Joan Miró, and Dalí are surrounded by photographs, posters, and short films that provide context for the world in which the art was created. This approach is particularly effective in the galleries related to the Spanish Civil War, including *Guernica.*

Picasso's response to the unprovoked bombing of a small Basque village remains one of the most powerful antiwar statements ever made.

The sculpture-filled courtyard of the Sabatini building is open during warm weather for light snacks. Admission to temporary exhibitions is usually through the Sabatini entrance. Those interested in the permanent collection only enter through the courtyard of the Nouvel building. Pay attention to signage or you could wait an hour or more in the wrong line. A Paseo del Arte pass, Madrid Card, or advance purchase skips the line.
Sabatini entrance: Calle Santa Isabel, 52. Nouvel entrance: Ronda de Atocha, s/n. www.museoreinasofia.es. ✆ **91-774-10-00.** Permanent exhibitions 8€, free under 18 and over 65; free for all Mon and Wed–Sat 7pm–9pm and Sun 1:30pm–7pm; 4€ for temporary exhibitions. Metro: Atocha. Bus: 6, 10, 14, 19, 26, 27, 32, 34, 36, or 37. Mon & Wed–Sat 11am–9pm, Sun 10am–7pm.

**Museo Naval** ★ MUSEUM We're rarely fans of military museums, but this gem on the ground level of Spanish Navy headquarters is an exception. The museum covers the high points of Spain on the high seas, including the discovery and exploration of the Americas, the exploitation of the Pacific trade routes, the Spanish Armada, and the feared Spanish galleons of the 17th and 18th centuries. A model of Columbus's flagship, the *Santa Maria,* shows what a fat little tub it was. By contrast, the large cutaway models of a circa-1700 galleon bristling with cannons can be seen as the birth of the modern battleship. The detailed coverage of the Battle of Trafalgar could make you forget that the Spanish lost. Marvel over Juan de la Cosa's handwritten map of 1500, said to be the oldest map of Europe that shows the Americas—including such inhabitants as men with faces in their stomachs. Only 300 visitors at a time are allowed inside; on weekends arrive early to avoid a wait. You'll need to show your passport to enter.
Paseo del Prado 5. www.armada.mde.es/museonaval. ✆ **91-523-87-89.** Free. Metro: Banco de España. Bus: 6, 10, 14, 19, 26, 27, 32, 34, 36, or 37. Tues–Sun 10am–7pm (Aug. 10am–3pm).

**Museo Thyssen-Bornemisza** ★★★ MUSEUM With the Prado and the Reina Sofía as neighbors, the Thyssen-Bornemisza has to try harder than it might elsewhere. So the museum has made summer even better for art lovers, keeping its temporary exhibitions open later than normal and the open-air Terrasse bar/restaurant open until 2am so you can discuss the art over drinks. Dominated by the tastes of two strong personalities, this museum prompts plenty of conversation.

The original collection was compiled by the Baron Thyssen-Bornemisza. Covering European art from the 13th through 20th centuries, it was one of the world's great private art collections, which he sold to Spain at a bargain in 1993. Before he sold it, though, he gave some major pieces to his Spanish wife, Carmen, who continued collecting until she donated her collection in 2004. Their collections represent the best art that money could buy in the mid-20th century. Dutch Masters were pretty well picked over by the time they began buying, but a lot of Impressionist art was on the market. The breadth of the collections is astounding. We advise focusing on the strengths—the Baron amassed great works of Italian and German Gothic art and 20th-century German Expressionism. The Baroness bought outstanding German Expressionist works, some beautiful Impressionist paintings, and showed a real affinity for the Spanish Moderns (Picasso, Dalí, and Miró) as well as Abstract Expressionist works by Americans. The museum also mounts blockbuster shows with borrowed works. These temporary exhibitions have a separate ticket.

Palacio de Villahermosa, Paseo del Prado 8. www.museothyssen.org. ✆ **90-276-05-11.** 10€ adults, 7€ students/seniors, free for children 11 and under; free to all Mon noon–4pm. Metro: Banco de España. Bus: Any bus on the Paseos line. Mon noon–4pm; Tues–Sun 10am–7pm (later mid-June to mid-Sept).

## PUERTA DEL SOL & BARRIO DE LAS LETRAS

**Casa de Lope de Vega ★** HISTORIC HOME Félix Lope de Vega may have been a more fascinating character than any that he invented in his plays. He purchased this house in 1610 when he was already an established playwright and lived here—close to the theaters of his day—for the last 25 years of his life. Suspend your disbelief and you may be able to get a sense of the daily life of the author, husband, father, and notorious womanizer who became a priest at age 50. The three-story house is an imagined historic restoration, but the furnishings reflect the contents listed in Lope de Vega's will. It's a good chance to see how a well-off figure lived in Habsburg Madrid. Though he was particularly fond of his little walled garden, the most telling details are the Moroccan-style furnishings in the women's gathering room and the window in his bedroom that overlooks his in-house chapel. All tours are guided, and you're supposed to book in advance, though we've walked in off the street during slow seasons. Call ahead to ask about a tour in English.

Calle Cervantes, 11. www.casamuseolopedevega.org. ✆ **91-429-92-16.** Free. Metro: Antón Martín. Bus: 6, 9, 10, 14, 26, 27, 32, 34, 37, 45, or 57. Tues–Sun 10am–3pm.

**Museo de la Real Academia de Bellas Artes de San Fernando ★★** MUSEUM The intimate galleries of the Royal Academy Museum are a nice change of pace from Madrid's big art museums. Founded in 1752 as a collection to teach art students, the museum has amassed a fine collection of paintings and sculptures from the Renaissance period to the present. Spanish artists, naturally, are the best represented, but in some cases you can compare their work to that of their Italian and Flemish contemporaries. Goya became director of the museum in 1795, and the collection features 13 of his paintings, including an equestrian portrait of Fernando VII and an absorbing scene of the Spanish Inquisition. Most revealing are the two self-portraits, one painted when he was not quite 40 and another painted in 1815, several years before he succumbed to the madness that drove his Dark Paintings. The museum also preserves Goya's paint-covered final palette. But it doesn't ignore other Spanish masters, and you will find works by Zurburán, El Greco, Juan Gris, and Picasso, as well as a striking collection of drawings from the 16th through 20th centuries.

Calle Alcalá, 13. www.realacademiabellasartessanfernando.com/en. ✆ **91-524-08-64.** 6€ adults, 3€ students, free for children 17 and under; free for all on Wed. Metro: Vodafone Sol or Sevilla. Bus: 3, 5, 15, 20, 51, 52, 53, or 150. Tues–Sun 10am–3pm.

**Plaza Santa Ana ★★** SQUARE Sooner or later you'll have a drink or two on Plaza Santa Ana and probably wonder what took you so long to discover the place. The neighborhood has been Madrid's theater district since the late 1500s, when open-air theaters began producing the plays of Lope de Vega (who lived nearby) and other satirists. When the Teatro Español was erected here in the mid-19th century, it made Plaza Santa Ana as hip then as it is now, and bars and cafes popped up all over. They (or their successors) still constitute one of the city's most varied tapas scenes.

Metro: Antón Martín.

**Puerta del Sol ★★** SQUARE Some visitors liken Puerta del Sol to New York's Times Square, but Puerta del Sol is smaller and friendlier. You'll recognize it by the signature neon sign of a Tío Pepe sherry bottle. The square is a central hub for Metro lines and commuter rail. Auto traffic is restricted, and a Louvre-like glass entrance leads to steps down to the trains. The beloved statue of a bear and a *madroña* tree (pictured on the city's coat of arms) sits in the middle of the plaza. Embedded in the pavement in front of the old Casa de Correos building is the **Zero**

**Puerta del Sol.**

### Getting Soaked in Madrid (and Why That's a Good Thing)

Many North Africans have settled in La Latina and adjacent Lavapiés in the last few decades, so it was really only a matter of time before a traditional Arabic bath, a *hammam,* opened in the neighborhood. **Hammam al Andalus** (Calle Atocha, 14; www.hammamalandalus.com; ✆ **90-233-33-34**) is modeled on the baths of Moorish Andalucía, and shares the traditional design of arched brick and tile chambers with grillwork windows to let in light. Alternating hot and cold rooms, a warm room where attendants scrub you with soap, a super-hot steam room, and the option of a massage with aromatic oils round out the sensual experience. Rates vary with services 30€ to 73€.

**Kilometer marker** from which all distances in Spain are calculated. The clock on the former post office displays Spain's official time. When it strikes midnight on New Year's Eve, Spanish revelers eat a dozen grapes—one for each chime.

## PLAZA MAYOR & LA LATINA

**Plaza Mayor ★★★** SQUARE You'd think Plaza Mayor had been custom-built for outdoor dining and arcade souvenir shopping. But the site was originally a food market just outside the city walls, and the current square was constructed in 1619 as the mass gathering spot for the city. People came to Plaza Mayor to see bullfights, attend political rallies, celebrate royal weddings, shop for bread and meat, watch hangings, and witness torture-induced confessions during the Spanish Inquisition. Today, Madrileños come to the plaza for the Sunday morning coin and stamp market and for the annual Christmas market. The plaza's acoustics are excellent, and musicians often perform in the center near the statue of Felipe III. The zodiac murals decorating the Casa de Panadería (originally home to the all-powerful Bakers' Guild) on the north side look ancient, but date only from 1992. The most dramatic of the gates is the Arco de Cuchilleros (Arch of the Knife-Sharpeners), on the southwest corner. Beneath Plaza Mayor are the "cave" restaurants that have lured tourists since the days when Washington Irving commented on the spectacle of roast piglet accompanied by flagons of wine.

Metro: Vodafone Sol, Opera, or Tirso de Molina. Bus: 3, 17, 18, 23, 31, or 35.

## OPERA & PALACIO REAL

**Monasterio de las Descalzas Reales ★★** MUSEUM In the 16th century, the daughters of nobility could either be married off to forge alliances among powerful men or opt for a life behind convent walls. Many of the wealthiest chose this convent, founded by Juana de Austria, the powerful and charismatic sister of Felipe II. As widow of the Prince of Portugal, she took over a palace of the royal treasurer in 1557 to create this Franciscan convent as her retreat. Each noblewoman who took the veil brought a dowry as a bride of Christ, and their treasures still fill the

Plaza de la Armería at Palacio Real.

convent. Ironically, by the mid-20th century, all the nuns came from poor families and were literally starving to death amid a priceless art collection that they were forbidden to sell. The state intervened, and the Pope granted a dispensation to open the convent as a museum. The large hall of the nuns' former dormitory is hung with 20 tapestries woven in Brussels from cartoons by Rubens. (Take a moment to notice the floor tiles that delineate each nun's tiny sleeping area.) About 20 nuns are still cloistered here. Guided tours (about 1 hour; 20 visitors at a time) are in Spanish; French or English tours may be available. One glimpse of the massive staircase with its murals of saints, angels, and Spanish rulers explains the conjunction of art, royalty, and faith that defines Spanish history.
Plaza de las Descalzas Reales s/n. www.patrimonionacional.es. ✆ **91-454-88-00.** 6€; free for children 4 and under. Metro: Opera. Bus: 3, 25, 39, or 148. From Plaza del Callao, off Gran Vía, walk down Postigo de San Martín to Plaza de las Descalzas Reales; the convent is on the left. Tues–Sat 10am–2pm and 4–6:30pm; Sun 10am–3pm.

### Watch Out for Wednesdays

Unless you're a European citizen, you're probably wondering why we are telling you that the **Monasterio de Las Descalzas Reales** and **Palacio Real** are free on Wednesdays for citizens of European Union countries. Free admission swells visitation on those days and can create a real logjam, especially at the monastery.

**Palacio Real ★★★** PALACE Those Bourbons certainly knew how to build a palace! When the old royal palace—a dank, dark, and plain *alcázar* captured from the Moors in 1086—burned down in 1734, Felipe V ordered a new palace designed to rival his French cousins' home at Versailles. Having wrested the throne from the Habsburgs, it was important for this first king of the Bourbon line to eclipse the previous dynasty. He was literally minting money with the gold and silver flowing from the New World colonies, so price was no object, and the finished product is one of the grandest, most heavily decorated palaces in Europe. Construction began in 1738, and Felipe's younger son, Carlos III, finally moved into the 2,000-plus-room complex in 1764. A portion of the palace is open for tours. Although it remains the official residence of the royal family, no monarch has lived here since 1931.

Unless you are a VIP, you'll enter on the south side of the palace complex. When you walk into the blinding sunlight of the Plaza de la Armería, everyone else will make a mad dash for the palace. Ignore them and cross the plaza to start at the Armory. You can take the measure of the Spanish nobility, because the plate and chain armor were individually tailored. Felipe I, the Austrian who married Juana la Loca (daughter of Fernando and Isabel) in 1496, was a medium-slender man nearly 6 feet tall—a giant in his day. Many other royals were almost a foot shorter; generally speaking, the shorter the noble, the larger his metal codpiece.

Once you enter the palace, you're not allowed to backtrack on the rigidly delineated route. Move quickly through the first few ceremonial rooms until you enter the Throne Room (or Hall of Ambassadors), which marks the start of the Carlos III era. Tiepolo took political flattery to new heights in the vault fresco, The *Apotheosis of the Spanish Monarchy.* It's easy to be overwhelmed by the next sequence of rooms, where decor morphs from baroque into rococo, but you also get a sense how the royals lived in such splendor. You see the drawing room where Carlos III had lunch, the over-the-top Gasparini Room where he dressed, and the bedroom where he died. The Yellow Room, which had been Carlos III's study, is rich with avian and floral tapestries. Finally, you'll reach the grand dining hall, first used by Alfonso XII in November 1879 to celebrate his marriage.

Some of the smaller, more intimate rooms are not always open, but they show Alfonso XIII (who left in 1931) as a more domestic king, screening movies with the family on Sunday afternoons. What remains of the royal silver and china is also on display. Unless you have a lot of time, skip the Farmacia Real's collection of apothecary jars in favor of a walk in the **Jardines de Sabatini ★.** Dotted with statues of Spanish kings, the formal gardens were opened to the public by King Juan Carlos I in 1978.
Plaza de Oriente, Calle de Bailén, 2. www.patrimonionacional.es. ✆ **91-454-88-00.** 11€ adults, 6€ students and 16 and under, free to all last 2 hr. of each day. Metro: Opera. Bus: 3, 25, 39, or 148. Oct–Mar daily 10am–6pm; Apr–Sept daily 10am–8pm.

## SALAMANCA, RETIRO & CHAMBERÍ

**Museo Lázaro Galdiano ★★** MUSEUM This highly personalized collection of often extraordinary art ultimately forms a sketch of its collector: José Lázaro Galdiano (1862–1947), a financier, intellectual, collector, and editor. His collections fill the beautiful Palacio Parque Florido. Lazaro championed the works of Spanish masters, including El Greco, Velázquez, Zurbarán, Ribera, Murillo, and Valdés-Leal. He also collected sculpture and decorative arts that he felt spoke to the Spanish spirit, notably ceramics, silverware, and crystal. But he held special affection for Goya, and managed to acquire an important canvas from the "witches' Sabbath" series Goya painted in 1798 for the Duchess of Osuna. Lazáro did not stop at the Pyrenees, though. He managed to buy several important Dutch and Flemish paintings, including an uncharacteristically meditative image of John the Baptist in the desert painted by Hieronymus Bosch. Several English portrait and landscape paintings by Reynolds, Gainsborough, and Constable were an indulgence of his wife's taste. The museum continues on the upper floors with individual cases of swords and daggers, royal seals, Byzantine jewelry, and even some medieval armor.

Calle de Serrano, 122. www.flg.es. ✆ **91-561-60-84.** 8€ adults, 3€ students/seniors, free for ages 12 and under; free for all Mon, Wed–Sat 3:30–4:30pm, Sun 2–3pm. Metro: Rubén Darío. Bus: 9, 12, 16, 19, 27, 45, or 51. Mon, Wed–Sat 10am–4:30pm; Sun 10am–3pm.

**Museo Sorolla ★★** MUSEUM This enchanting house and studio was built between 1910 and 1911 by Joachín Sorolla (1863–1923) and offers a window into the comfortable world of the successful painter, who masterfully balanced his work and his domestic life. The home includes three studios with access to the Andalucían-style garden, as well as large living and dining areas on the main floor, maintained as the family used them. It's easy to imagine Sorolla at work at one of the unfinished paintings on the easels. Galleries on the upper floor display the range of his work from portraits and folkloric paintings to seascapes. But perhaps most telling is the angelic mural of his wife, Clotilde García del Costillo, and children on the dining room ceiling. It was Clotilde who decided to turn the property into a museum as a memorial to her husband. Most visitors fantasize about moving right in.

General Martínez Campos 37. http://museosorolla.mcu.es. ✆ **91-310-15-84.** 3€ adults, 1.50€ students, free for ages 17 and under; free for all Sat 2–8pm and all day Sun. Metro: Iglesia, Gregorio Marañón, or Rubén Darío. Bus: 5, 7, 14, 16, 27, 40, 45, 61, 147, or 150. Tues–Sat 9:30am–8pm; Sun 10am–3pm.

**Parque del Retiro ★★** PARK To meet Madrileños at their most relaxed, spend a Sunday among the families in Parque del Retiro. Originally a royal playground for the Spanish monarchs, the park covers 140 hectares (346 acres), but most main attractions are adjacent to the central pathway, best accessed by the gate at the Puerta de Alcalá traffic circle. The park is big enough to be a playground for much of Madrid—whether they want to rent rowboats on the small lake where Felipe IV used to stage mock naval battles, or watch puppet shows, practice tai chi, play cards or chess, have their fortunes told, or just lounge on the grass. The Reina Sofía museum mounts large-scale exhibitions in the two grand buildings constructed for the 1887 Philippines Exposition. The **Palacio de Cristal** is literally a glass palace, while the **Palacio de Velázquez** is as opaque as the Cristal is transparent. It was constructed of brick and marble with florid tilework in the Mudéjar Revival style. From May through September, there are free concerts in the park on Sunday afternoons. Park and palaces free. Metro: Retiro. Park summer daily 7am–midnight; winter daily 7am–10pm. Palacio de Cristal and Palacio de Velázquez Apr–Sept daily 11am–9pm; Oct–Mar daily 10am–6pm.

### OUTLYING ATTRACTIONS

**Ermita de San Antonio de la Florida-Panteón de Goya ★★** CHURCH Goya rests beneath some of his most charming frescoes in this little hermitage north of the Palacio Real. The paintings on the dome and cupola depict the miracles of St. Anthony. Goya worked on scaffolding in true fresco, applying fresh plaster to the surface, incising his design based on a "cartoon" drawing, and then applying pigment with a sponge instead of a brush. Many early viewers were shocked that Goya painted prostitutes, beggars, and manual laborers. But the patron, Carlos IV, approved, and the work has stood the test of time. The tomb and frescoes are on the right as you enter. Magnifying mirrors on the floor help you see the ceiling without straining your neck.
Glorieta de San Antonio de la Florida, 5. www.munimadrid.es/ermita. ✆ **91-542-07-22.** Free. Metro: Príncipe Pío. Bus: 76, 46, or 41. Tues–Sun 9:30am–8pm.

**Plaza de Toros Monumental de Las Ventas ★** BULLRING This grand Mudéjar-style bullring of red brick, tile, and ornate ironwork is not the largest in the world, but it is arguably the most important. It opened in 1931 and seats 24,000 people. The best bullfighters face the best bulls here—and the fans who pack the stands are among the sport's most passionate and knowledgeable. (Many other Spaniards can't stand the sport.) If you want to try to gain an understanding of the spectacle, audioguide tours begin at the ceremonial Grand Portal and include the stands, the ring itself, and the patio where matadors pause with their admirers before entering the chapel to pray before they enter the ring.
Calle Alcalá, 237. www.lasventastour.com. ✆ **91-356-22-00.** 12€ adults, 8€ children under 12. Metro: Ventas. July–Aug daily 10am–7pm; Sept–June daily 10am–5:30pm. Mar–Oct tours close 4 hr. before corrida. For corrida tickets, expect to pay 10€–40€ for reasonable seats; web sales www.las-ventas.com.

## Organized Tours

Get oriented to Madrid with guided **walking tours** (17€) from the chief tourist information center (Plaza Mayor, 27; www.esmadrid.com/en/official-guided-tours; ✆ **90-222-14-24;** Metro: Vodafone Sol or Opera). Tours are given in several languages. English tours focus on Madrid's history, but other options include historic taverns and a ghost tour. Tours operate all year, but you should book ahead.

**Madrid City Tour** is the city's hop-on, hop-off double-decker sightseeing bus. Recorded commentary is available through headphones in 14 languages, and separate narration is available for children. The buses' two routes cover most of the city's major attractions. Both start at Calle

Felipe IV next to the Museo del Prado. From November to February, buses operate from 10am to 6pm, passing each stop about every 14 minutes, more frequently in peak season (Mar–Oct). Adults pay 21€ for 1 day, 25€ for 2 days; ages 7 to 15 and over 65 pay 10€ for 1 day, 13€ for 2 days. Children 6 and under are free. The City Tour has the advantage of getting you get around without having to deal with public transportation. It is more scenic than the subway, but also more expensive. For information, call ✆ **90-202-47-58,** or visit www.madridcitytour.es.



## Especially for Kids

**Parque del Retiro** (p. 789) is the classic family weekend outing. In addition to other activities, the wide, paved paths are one of the few good places in the city for a family bike ride. Rent bikes at nearby **Rent and Roll** (Calle Salustiano Olozaga, 14; www.rentandroll.es; ✆ **91-576-35-24;** rentals from 5€; Metro: Retiro).

Free admission hours at some of Madrid's best museums can let you work short visits into your day without breaking the bank or taxing your children's attention spans. At the **Museo del Prado** (p. 780), for example, you might want to take your young kids to see the "cartoons" (full-size colored drawings) that Francisco de Goya created for tapestries. Many of them feature children and animals in bucolic settings. Teenagers, on the other hand, are usually engrossed by Pablo Picasso's *Guernica* in the **Museo Nacional Centro de Arte Reina Sofía** (p. 782). Your children might also enjoy seeing the grand fountains of Cibeles and Neptuno as you stroll along the Paseo del Prado. For a grand overview of Cibeles, take them up to the observatory at **CentroCentro** (p. 777) for rooftop views.

A rollercoaster at Parque de Atracciones.

Madrid's other celebrated gathering place, **Plaza Mayor** (p. 786), is also a fine spot for families. Kids will find plenty of entertainment watching artists at work under the arcade and "living statues" posing for change. Since the plaza is enclosed on all sides, you can keep an eye on your children from a cafe table.

**Casa de Campo,** the broad park on the Manzanares River below the Palacio Real, has the **Parque de Atracciones ★** (www.parquedeatracciones.es; ✆ **90-234-50-01;** admission 32€ adults, 25€ children), a 30-ride amusement park that opened in 1969. You'll find mini–fire engines for tykes, graceful "flying chairs," water rides, the "cave of tarantulas," and a twisting roller coaster called "Abismo" that climbs to 200m (656 ft.) and reaches a maximum speed of 105kmph (65 mph). The easiest way to get to Casa de Campo is on the cable car **Teleférico de Madrid** (Paseo del Pintor Rosales; www.teleferico.com; ✆ **91-541-74-50;** fare 4€ one-way, 5.80€ round-trip, free for children under 3). The 11-minute ride starts at Parque del Oeste, not far from the Palacio Real.

The **Zoo Aquarium de Madrid** ★ (Casa de Campo; www.zoomadrid.com; ✆ **90-234-50-14;** admission 23€ adults and children 8 and over, 19€ seniors/children 3–7) was a pioneer in simulated natural habitats for animals, separated from humans by pits or moats. About 6,000 animals from 500 different species roam freely. The zoo also has a tropical marine aquarium.

## Where to Stay

Summer vacationers will be pleased to learn that Madrid hotels consider July and August to be "low" season and price their rooms accordingly. November rates are also typically low. But in all seasons, Madrid hotels generally offer good value for your money.

### ARTS DISTRICT & PASEOS

#### Expensive

**Hotel Ritz by Belmond** ★★★ Many hotels claim to be legendary; this one is. When Alfonso XIII was married in 1908, he was dismayed that Madrid lacked hotels befitting his guests. He wanted a hotel equal to the Ritz in Paris, so he engaged César Ritz to consult on the design and lend his name. Few expenses were spared. The location next to the Museo del Prado by the Neptuno fountain couldn't be much more prestigious. Comfort and luxury are givens, and rooms are fitted with antiques and heavy brocade. The Goya Restaurant is the successor to the original established with the aid of legendary chef Auguste Escoffier.

Plaza de la Lealtad, 5. www.ritz.es. ✆ **800/237-1236** in the U.S. and Canada, or 91-701-67-67. 167 units. Doubles 270€–420€, suites 570€–1010€. Metro: Atocha or Banco de España. **Amenities:** Restaurant; bar; concierge; gym; room service; sauna; spa; free Wi-Fi.

#### Moderate

**Hotel Paseo del Arte** ★★ This large, modern hotel sits across a small plaza from the Reina Sofía and a 5-minute walk down Calle Atocha from Casa Patas. Rates vary, but if you can get them to throw in the buffet breakfast (otherwise a pricey 13€ per person), take the deal. Rooms are modestly sized, so see if you can upgrade to one of the superior rooms with a private terrace. Booking through the website gives less room for haggling, but guarantees a room upgrade, if available, and late check-out.

Calle Atocha, 123. www.hotelpaseodelartemadrid.com. ✆ **91-298-48-00.** 260 units. Doubles 77€–140€. Metro: Atocha. **Amenities:** Restaurant; bar; concierge; gym; room service; spa; free Wi-Fi.

## PUERTA DEL SOL & LAS LETRAS

### Moderate

**Catalonia Puerta del Sol ★★** This hotel near Plaza Santa Ana is the Goldilocks of Madrid hotels—not too big, not too small, just right. It occupies an early-20th-century building, and some of the original carved woodwork is maintained in the top-floor suites. Modest rooms have hardwood floors, marble baths, and low-key brown and gold drapes and bedspreads. Most have large windows opening onto Calle Atocha or the central courtyard with bar and tranquil sitting area.

Calle Atocha, 23. www.hoteles-catalonia.com. ✆ **91-369-71-71.** Doubles 79€–170€. Metro: Vodafone Sol or Tirso de Molina. **Amenities:** Restaurant; bar; cafe; solarium; rooftop terrace; Jacuzzi; free Wi-Fi.

**Hotel Moderno ★★** Family-owned and managed since 1939, the Moderno keeps reinventing itself without losing the charm that makes it one of the best options on Puerta del Sol. Ask for an upper floor for more room to spread out. Rooms with an outdoor terrace might be worth the extra charge during times of year when you want to sit outside. They have the most space as well as fabulous views of Puerta del Sol. A few triple and family rooms are also available.

Calle Arenal, 2. www.hotel-moderno.com. ✆ **91-531-09-00.** 97 units. Doubles 79€–143€. Metro: Sol. **Amenities:** Bar, concierge; free Wi-Fi.

### Inexpensive

**Hotel Cortezo ★★** Decor at this bargain hotel tends toward the gentleman's club boutique look with white linens, dark wooden headboards, and brushed-stainless-steel trim, though rooms are small. The small rooftop terrace has lounge chairs, teak strip decking, and an outdoor shower to cool off and wash off the tanning lotion. Guests are encouraged to bring their own wine to the roof for spectacular sunsets over La Latina. Ready-to-please staff set the Cortezo above other budget hotels.

Calle Doctor Cortezo, 3. www.hotelcortezo.com. ✆ **91-369-01-01.** 92 units. Doubles 55€–105€, suites 70€–125€. Metro: Vodafone Sol, Tirso de Molina. **Amenities:** Bar; room service; free Wi-Fi.

## PLAZA MAYOR & LA LATINA

### Inexpensive

**Hotel Plaza Mayor ★★** This budget boutique hotel was carved out of an old church, and the mass of the stone building keeps the interior cool in summer and warm in winter. Some rooms were constructed around architectural barriers and wound up oddly shaped—long and thin, or not quite rectilinear. They also vary a lot in size, mostly on the small side. But all have solid contemporary furnishings, shiny wood floors, and flatscreen TVs. The single penthouse suite costs 50% more than the standard doubles, but has skylights in the slanted ceiling and an outdoor patio with views across the tiled roofs of La Latina. If the penthouse is booked, opt for a "superior" room on the corner to get views of Plaza Santa Cruz.

## tapas bars AROUND PLAZA SANTA ANA

Tapas are ideally eaten standing at a bar and should be a movable feast: Enjoy the house specialty, and then move on to the next stop. Plaza Santa Ana has one of the best concentrations. Peak hours are usually 6 to 9pm, and a place that was empty at 5pm will have people spilling into the street by 7pm. Tapas-hopping can make for an early dinner. It's also a great way to try food you're not sure you'll like, or specialties too expensive for a full meal. Many tapas bars don't take credit cards, as cash keeps the pace moving. You should do the same.

**Las Bravas ★** Fried potatoes smothered in a spicy red paprika-based sauce are a staple in bars all over Spain. This one invented the dish known as *patatas bravas* and even has a patent on the sauce. At Las Bravas, you can also get a pig's ear, fried baby squid, chicken wings, and even a whole 6-inch *tortilla Española* smothered in it.

Calle Espoz y Mina, 13. www.lasbravas.com. ✆ **91-521-35-07.** Tapas 3€–9€. Daily noon–1am. Cash only. Metro: Sevilla.

**La Casa del Abuelo ★** Grandpa really gets around, as "Grandpa's House" has three separate locations within sight of each other. Choose the original on Calle Victoria to savor the patina of age—it opened in 1906 and has been serving shrimp specialties ever since. Good thing they accept credit cards, because the bill mounts quickly. We like our *gambas* plainly grilled *(gambas a la plancha)* or grilled with garlic *(gambas al ajillo)*, but many customers prefer the smaller plates of breaded shrimp deep-fried in olive oil. The house wine is a bargain.

Calle Atocha, 2. www.h-plazamayor.com. ✆ **91-360-06-06.** 34 units. Doubles 59€–95€. Metro: Vodafone Sol or Tirso de Molina. **Amenities:** Cafeteria; free Wi-Fi.

### OPERA & PALACIO REAL

#### Moderate

**Hotel Santo Domingo ★★** Most rooms at this casual-chic choice are decorated in taupes and tans with dark wood accents and pops of brilliant white in the linens and bathrooms. Budget rooms use lollipop color schemes to make them look bigger than they are; queen-size beds eat up most of the space, but the rooms are well designed and a very good deal. Standard double are larger and superior doubles downright spacious. The few corner rooms (premium priced) are as large as a junior suite and feature two glass walls for panoramic city views. Guests who book directly are loaned a cellular Wi-Fi hot spot that works throughout Madrid.

Calle San Bernardo 1. www.hotelsantodomingo.es. ✆ **91-547-98-00.** 200 units. Doubles (sizes vary widely) 81€–234€ Metro: Santo Domingo. **Amenities:** Restaurant; bar; room service; free Wi-Fi.

#### Inexpensive

**JC Rooms Santo Domingo ★★** This budget boutique hotel offers bright rooms aimed at a young clientele in a strategic spot just off Gran

Calle Victoria, 12. www.lacasadelabuelo.es. ✆ **91-521-23-19.** Daily 1:30pm–1am. Metro: Sevilla.

**Cervezas La Fábrica ★** On a Sunday, everybody here is tossing back draft beer and munching on *montaditos* (tasty bites atop a diagonal slice of baguette). The variety is jaw-dropping. You'll get the most flavor for your euros with the smoked tuna and the blue cheese with salt-packed anchovies.

Calle Jesus, 2. ✆ **91-369-30-67.** *Montaditos* 2€–3€. Daily 10am–2am. Metro: Antón Martín.

**La Trucha ★** The quintessential fish tapas of Madrid belong to La Trucha, off the northeast corner of Plaza Santa Ana. You can order a single slice of smoked trout on toast, but it's so good that most people order a whole plate. To save a few euros, try the salad of mixed smoked fish. All that smoke and salt will make you thirsty, but draft beer is cheap here.

Calle Manuel Fernández y González, 3. ✆ **91-429-58-33.** Tapas 2€–14€. Daily noon–1am. Metro: Antón Martín.

**La Venencia ★** If you're fortunate, you'll score standing room at the bar for the most Andalucían drinking experience in Madrid. La Venencia serves *fino, oloroso,* and *amontillado* sherries straight from the cask—or famous marques from the bottle. Eating is secondary here. We like to nibble some pickled sardines or roasted peppers while savoring the sherries.

Calle Echegaray, 7. ✆ **91-429-62-61.** Tapas 3€–5€. Daily noon–midnight. Cash only. Metro: Sevilla.

Vía. The free minibar is restocked daily, and every room has a computer with Wi-Fi. Rooms are themed to different European countries; some have walls with gigantic photos, others have broad splashes of primary colors. Furnishings are mostly unadorned Scandinavian style.

Cuesta de Santo Domingo, 16. www.jchoteles-santodomingo.com. ✆ **91-547-60-79.** 45 units. Doubles 53€–82€. Metro: Santo Domingo. **Amenities:** Restaurant/brewery; free Wi-Fi.

## SALAMANCA, RETIRO & CHAMBERÍ

### Expensive

**Hotel Adler ★★★** This boutique hotel, constructed inside a 19th century carved limestone facade, is simply glamorous. All rooms have soaring ceilings, and many are equipped with decorative marble fireplaces. While decor varies, many rooms have canopy or four-poster beds—or beds set into alcoves framed by columns. Designer baths include marble shower areas as well as free-standing soaking tubs. No meeting rooms means a leisure clientele. There's an Old World grace—front desk staff wear frock coats, for example—yet the Adler is comfortable, warm, and inviting.

Calle Velázquez, 33. www.adlermadrid.com. ✆ **866/376-7831** in the U.S. and Canada, or 91-426-32-20. 44 units. Doubles 185€–280€, suites from 495€. Metro: Velázquez. **Amenities:** Restaurant; bar; bikes; concierge; room service; Wi-Fi.

## Where to Eat

Madrid has many long-standing gastronomic traditions, the most developed tapas bar scene in the world, and access to everything the country has to offer. If you like regional Spanish food, you'll find good examples here. If you like Spanish seafood, you're in good company. Fresh fish and shellfish are trucked or flown in from the coast daily. Madrid excels at casual dining. Instead of paying for a "restaurant," you can eat very well indeed at a more casual "bar/restaurante" or a "cafe/bar."

### ARTS DISTRICT & PASEOS

#### Expensive

**Restaurante Palacio de Cibeles ★★** SPANISH Adolfo Muñoz presides over this gourmet restaurant on the sixth floor of CentroCentro. When the weather's good, he serves a bar menu on the terrace. But gourmets flock to the elegant indoor dining room for Muñoz's creative twists on La Manchan classics, like partridge stewed with tempranillo red wine sauce or roasted with sherry sauce; or roast leg of lamb with a Spanish version of ratatouille with roasted tomatoes, eggplant, and squash.

Plaza de Cibeles, 1. www.adolfo-palaciodecibeles.com. ✆ **91-523-14-54.** Reservations required. Mains 25€–33€; 4-course menu 50€. Metro: Banco de España. Daily 1–4pm; Mon–Sat 10pm–midnight.

#### Inexpensive

**El Brillante ★★** SPANISH Spaniards snub the nearby Burger King and McDonald's franchises in favor of the equally fast but more varied sandwiches at El Brillante. The finger-sized 4-inch mini-*bocadillos* make a terrific snack, while the 10-inch *bocatas* are a meal. You can get everything from sliced pork with roasted peppers to an omelet sandwich, but El Brillante is acclaimed for its fried calamari rolls. Tables are few, but there's a certain style to eating while standing at the bars as the Spaniards do. Taking half a city block, El Brillante has a door on the Carlos V roundabout and another on the plaza in front of the Museo Reina Sofía.

Calle Atocha, 122. www.barelbrillante.es. ✆ **91-468-05-48.** Sandwiches 3€–9€. Metro: Atocha. Daily 6:30am–midnight or later. No credit cards.

### PUERTA DEL SOL & LAS LETRAS

#### Moderate

**El Ñeru ★** ASTURIAN Skip the upstairs tapas bar in favor of an underground warren of tiled dining rooms. The cuisine of "The Nest" is fish-intensive (including the classic hake braised in hard cider) but the kitchen also makes a hearty *fabada Asturiana* of large white beans stewed with ham and sausage. A Madrileño friend swears that El Ñeru also makes the city's best *arroz con leche,* a creamy rice pudding with a caramelized top. Bread service includes butter blended with Cabrales blue cheese, and the meal ends with a taste of a yellow-green liqueur.

Calle Bordadores, 5. www.restauranteelneru.com. ✆ **91-541-11-40.** Main dishes 12€–22€. Metro: Vodafone Sol or Opera. Tues–Sun 1:30–4:30pm and 8:30–11pm.

## PLAZA MAYOR & LA LATINA

### Moderate

**Julián de Tolosa ★★** BASQUE This Basque *asador* may be the most elegant restaurant along Cava Baja. Almost everything arrives with grill marks, so the house keeps the menu simple. Meat eaters can order a sirloin steak or a thick chop, fish eaters get a choice of hake or monkfish. There are two principal side dishes: grilled sweet and smoky piquillo peppers and fat stalks of asparagus. Large plate-glass windows make the street-level dining room a showcase. Many diners prefer the lower-level dining room with its exposed brick walls and the warmth of the wood grill.
Calle Cava Baja, 18. www.juliandetolosa.com. ✆ **91-365-82-10.** Mains 22€–30€. Metro: La Latina. Daily 1:30–4pm; Mon–Sat 9pm–midnight.

**Restaurante Botín ★** SPANISH Ernest Hemingway really ate at Botín, and he set a scene here at the end of *The Sun Also Rises*. The tavern has been trading on that publicity since 1926, along with the ruling by the Guinness Book of World Records that it is the world's oldest restaurant still in business (since 1725). It's a charming tourist trap worth visiting for the tasty, if pricey food. As you enter, peek into the kitchen to see racks of suckling pigs ready to go into the wood-fired oven. If your party orders a whole pig, it is brought solemnly to the table and then—bam!—smashed on top to break it into parts. The daily menu gets you garlic soup as a starter, a serving of roast suckling pig, a drink, and ice cream. But you can enjoy the atmosphere and eat as well but more cheaply on roast chicken.
Calle de Cuchilleros, 17. www.botin.es. ✆ **91-366-42-17.** Reservations recommended. Mains 15€–32€; fixed-price menu 42€. Metro: Opera or Vodafone Sol. Daily 1–4pm and 8pm–midnight.

### Inexpensive

**Taberna Almendro 13 ★★** ANDALUCÍAN A Hollywood set designer couldn't imagine a more "typical" Spanish bar, from the dark wood and florid 19th-century tiles to the dim lighting and the barrel of manzanilla sold at a pittance per glass. The perfect complement to that mild sherry is an inexpensive plate of sheep's milk cheese with *membrillo* (quince paste). For a meal, it's hard to beat the ratatouille with fried egg. For authenticity's sake, do your eating and drinking while standing.
Calle Almendro, 13. ✆ **91-365-42-52.** Mains 4€–11€. Metro: La Latina. Daily 1:30–4:30pm and 8pm–1am. Cash only.

## OPERA & PALACIO REAL

### Moderate

**Restaurante Sandó by Arzak Instruction ★★★** SPANISH Sandó serves the cuisine of famed chef Juan Mari Arzak with fewer precious ingredients but all the style and panache intact. The dishes draw from the classics that Juan Mari and daughter Elena created in their "laboratory" at San Sebastian. They tend to marry two seemingly incompatible flavors with great success, like white anchovies and sweet strawberries.

## DROP IN FOR A dunk

At some point, all of Madrid comes into **Chocolatería San Ginés ★★** (Pasadizo San Ginés, 5; www.chocolateriasangines.com; ✆ **91-365-65-46**) for a cup of the almost fudgy hot chocolate and the fried dough sticks known as *churros*. When the music stops in the wee hours of the morning, disco queens from Joy Eslava next door pop in for a cup. Later on, before they head to the office, bankers in three-piece suits order breakfast. There's sugar spilled everywhere on the tables, yet the marble counters are an impeccable tableau of cups lined up with the handles all facing at the same angle and a tiny spoon on each saucer. Dipping the sugar-dusted churros into the hot chocolate is de rigeur, and, yes, it's okay to have the snack in the afternoon. Cash only. Metro: Vodafone Sol or Opera.

**Churros and hot chocolate at Chocolatería San Ginés.**

If you consider yourself a foodie (or even if you don't), Sandó is a treat you should not miss.

In Hotel Santo Domingo, Calle Isabel la Católica, 2-4. www.restaurantesando.es. ✆ **91-547-99-11.** Mains 18€–29€; tasting menu 49€. Metro: Santo Domingo. Tues–Sat 1–4pm; Tues–Thurs 8–11pm; Fri–Sat 8pm–midnight. Closed Aug.

**Taberna del Alabardero ★★** SPANISH This handsome restaurant and tapas bar named for the royal guards known as "Beefeaters" opened in 1974 in a historic tavern. The menu represents a light approach to contemporary Spanish cooking, with dishes like bream roasted in a salt crust and served with fresh tomatoes and basil, or oxtail stewed with honey and cinnamon. In the bar, you'll probably have to stand and might have to shout to converse, but the food is even lighter (chilled almond soup with prawns and grapes, "meat" balls of fish and shellfish, brochettes of pork with mushrooms and pineapple). The sherry collection is excellent.

Calle Felipe V, 6. www.grupolezama.es. ✆ **91-547-25-77.** Reservations required for restaurant. Mains 16€–28€; tasting menu 46€. Bar tapas 3€–13€; Metro: Opera. Daily 1–4pm and 9pm–midnight.

### SALAMANCA

#### Moderate

**Cerveceria José Luís ★★** SPANISH This is the original in the group of José Luís restaurants, and it has had a shoeshine man on duty since it opened in 1957. The founder believed that gentlemen should always have clean and shiny shoes, so they can stand at the bar near the door to get their brogues polished. The dining room is elegant, but many patrons favor the bar where you can perch on a stool and have a complete meal of soup, salad, fish, and dessert. The *cervecería* also has a great selection of *pinchos* (tapas on toothpicks), including a signature roll of egg and shrimp salad.

Calle Serrano, 89. www.joseluis.es. ✆ **91-563-09-58.** Mains 13€–22€; tapas 3€–5€. Metro: Gregorio Marañón. Bar daily 9am–1am. Dining room daily noon–4pm and 8pm–midnight.

**El 28 de Larumbe ★★** SPANISH Pedro Larumbe, one of Spain's most celebrated chefs, helms this exquisite fine dining restaurant, with a gastrobar that serves from breakfast to the final gin and tonic of the night. The menu is much the same at lunch and dinner in the restaurant, with elegant choices like hake with goose barnacles, or roast beef with mustard sauce. Gastrobar choices include snacks like ham and beef sliders or fried eggs smothered in roasted peppers as well as whole meals of innovative bar food.

Paseo Castellana, 38. www.pedrolarumbe.com. ✆ **91-575-11-12.** Lunch mains 17€–19€; dinner mains 22€–29€. Gastrobar mains 8€–15€. Metro: Ruben Dario. Tues–Sat 1:30–4pm and 9–11:30pm, gastrobar 8:30am–1am.

## Shopping

There are surprising shopping discoveries to be made throughout Madrid, so keep your schedule flexible enough that you can stop in any shop that catches your eye. Be sure to watch for the sign "Rebajas," which signals that a sale is in progress. (Citywide sales generally take place Jan–Feb and July–Aug.) For serious shopping, two neighborhoods stand out.

**Salamanca** is the more chic, with the boutiques of Spain's top designers as well as international luxury brands. To keep it local, check out the gorgeous leather goods at **Loewe ★★** (Calle Serrano, 26; www.loewe.com; ✆ **91-577-60-56;** Calle Serrano, 47; ✆ **91-200-44-99**. Metro: Serrano), or handle a truly well-made shoe at custom-maker **Gaytan ★** (Calle Jorge Juan, 15; ✆ **91-435-28-24;** Metro: Serrano or Velázquez).

Madrid's nicest shopping mall, **ABC Serrano** (Calle Serrano, 61; www.abcserrano.com; ✆ **91-577-50-31;** Metro: Serrano), is also in Salamanca, as is the city's most beautiful food market, **Mercado de la Paz ★★** (Calle Ayala, 28; www.mercadodelapaz.com; ✆ **91-435-07-43;** Metro: Velázquez), where you can peruse the fresh goods and packaged items to take home. The store at **CentroCentro** (p. 777) may be the best general gift shop in the city, with Spanish cookbooks in English, jewelry by local designers, and clever novelty items such as wind-up *toreadors* and bulls.

The **Puerta del Sol** neighborhood boasts the city's main branch of **El Corte Inglés** (Calle Preciados, 3; www.elcorteingles.es; ✆ **91-379-80-00**; Metro: Vodafone Sol) department store, also a good bet for one-stop souvenir shopping. It carries predictable merchandise such as embroidered shawls and damascene jewelry, as well as the very hip jewelry of Uno de 50. Look also for flamenco CDs or specialty food items like saffron (expensive) and smoked paprika (cheap, but packed in charming tins).

For more choices, follow the streets that radiate out from Puerta del Sol. On Calle Preciados, you'll find **Zara** (Calle Preciados, 18; www.zara.com; ✆ **91-521-09-58**. Metro: Vodafone Sol or Callao), the clothing maker known for on-trend yet affordable styles. Walk uphill to **Capas Seseña ★** (Calle Cruz, 23; www.sesena.com; ✆ **91-531-68-40;** Metro: Vodafone Sol), which has been making investment-quality capes since 1901.

Less costly icons of Spanish style include the constructed Basque caps sold at **La Favorita** (Plaza Mayor, 25; www.lafavoritacb.com; ✆ **91-366-58-77;** Metro: Vodafone Sol or Opera). Right off Plaza Mayor, you can join Spanish women who wait in line to buy hand-sewn espadrilles at **Casa Hernanz** (Calle Toledo, 18; ✆ **91-366-54-50;** Metro: La Latina). Nearby, the long-shuttered **Mercado de San Miguel** (Plaza de San Miguel; www.mercadodesanmiguel.es; ✆ **91-542-49-36;** Metro: Opera, Vodafone Sol, or Tirso de Molina) has assumed a new identity as a lifestyle emporium with specialty food items to eat on premises or take away.

For Spanish ceramics, do not miss **Antigua Casa Talavera ★★** (Calle Isabel La Catolica, 2; ✆ **91-547-34-17;** Metro: Santo Domingo). The beautiful tile facade of the building is only a prelude to the artful ceramics inside.

Madrileños are crazy about football (or soccer to North Americans). **Real Madrid** training jerseys and shorts, scarves, socks, hoodies, and more are sold at official stores, including Tienda Carmen (Calle Carmen, 3; ✆ **91-521-79-50;** Metro: Vodafone Sol or Callao), and Tienda Gran Vía (Gran Vía, 31; ✆ **91-755-45-38;** Metro: Callao or Gran Vía).

Save Sunday morning for the famed flea market **El Rastro ★,** which sprawls across a roughly triangular district of streets and plazas a few minutes' walk south of Plaza Mayor. Its center is Plaza Cascorro and Ribera de Curtidores. It will delight anyone attracted to antiques, bric-a-brac, paintings, and cheap scarves from India.

### Shopping & Clubbing in Chueca & Malasaña

The neighborhoods of Chueca and Malasaña, north of Gran Vía, are off the beaten tourist path. But shoppers make a beeline to **Calle Augusto Figueroa,** where outlets of several top Spanish shoe manufacturers offer good discounts. Up-and-coming designers looking for low rent have set up shop on the side streets. With its hip sense of style, it's no surprise that the area is also the center of gay Madrid. The Malasaña mega-club **Clamores** (Calle Alburquerque, 14; www.clamores.es; ✆ **91-445-54-80;** Metro: Bilbao) features early evening jazz and late-night disco.

Bargains can be had, but you'll need to use your haggling skills. Enjoy the scene, but watch your belongings, because pickpockets work the crowd.

## Entertainment & Nightlife

If you are only going to hit the town for one night, you should see a flamenco show. Madrid is at the forefront of the flamenco revival thanks in great part to **Casa Patas ★★** (Calle Cañizares, 10; www.casapatas.com; ✆ **91-369-04-96**), which presents established artists and rising stars in an atmospheric bar/performance space off Plaza Santa Ana.

For classical music lovers, the richly ornamented **Teatro Real ★** (Plaza Isabel II; www.teatro-real.es; ✆ **91-516-06-60;** Metro: Opera) is known for the fine acoustics that enhance its offerings of opera and classical music. Madrid's largest concentration of theaters is in the vicinity of Plaza Santa Ana. Check **Teatro Monumental** (Calle Atocha, 65; www.rtve.es/orquesta-coro; ✆ **91-429-12-81;** Metro: Antón Martín) or **Teatro Español** (Calle Principe, 25; www.teatroespanol.es; ✆ **91-360-14-84;** Metro: Tirso de Molino or Antón Martín) which schedules dance, orchestral, and chamber music concerts as well as live theater. The **Teatro de la Zarzuela** (Calle Jovellanos, 4; http://teatrodelazarzuela.mcu.es; ✆ **91-524-54-00;** Metro: Banco de España) specializes in *zarzuela,* the Spanish form of musical entertainment that mixes opera, popular song, and spoken narrative. Performances are so expressive that even non-Spanish speakers can enjoy the action.

Madrid dance clubs stay open until the early morning hours. A centrally located option is **Disco-Teatro Joy Eslava** (Calle Arenal, 11; www.joy-eslava.com; ✆ **91-366-37-33;** Metro: Vodafone Sol or Opera) which occupies a 19th-century theater near Puerta del Sol. For late-night chocolate and churros, Joy Eslava is conveniently located near **Chocolatería San Ginés** (p. 798).

## A Day Trip to Toledo

The capital of Iberia under the Romans and the Visigoths, Toledo stands on a high promontory, a walled fortress city surrounded on three sides by the Rio Tagus. Its appearance has barely changed since El Greco, depicted it in *View of Toledo* at the end of the 16th century. Indeed, the painter, who made Toledo his home, is one of the main reasons to visit Toledo. Trains from Madrid's Atocha station and Toledo take only 35 minutes (www.renfe.com; ✆ **90-232-03-20**). To reach the Old City from the rail station, take bus 5 (1€) to Plaza de Zocodover.

To get within inches of several El Greco masterpieces, make your first stop the **Museo de Santa Cruz ★★★** (Calle Miguel de Cervantes, 3; www.turismocastillalamancha.es; ✆ **92-522-10-36;** Permanent collection 5€; Mon–Sat 10am–7pm, Sun 10am–2:30pm). This art museum covers millennia of sculpture, painting, and decorative arts, but

The Toledo cityscape.

with time at a premium, head straight for the El Grecos, including the *Assumption of the Virgin,* painted 1607–13.

It's only a 5-minute walk to **Catedral de Toledo ★★** (Calle Cardenal Cisneros, 1; www.catedralprimada.es; ✆ **92-522-22-41;** free admission to cathedral, admission to Sacristy and Treasure Room 11€; Mon–Sat 10am–6pm; Sun 2–6pm). Skip swiftly through the church to visit the Sacristy, which holds El Greco portraits of each of the 12 apostles, as well as his 1577–79 masterwork, *The Disrobing of Christ.*

If you're hungry, stop off at **Adolfo Colleción Catedral ★★** (Calle Nuncio Viejo, 1; www.grupoadolfo.com; ✆ **92-522-42-44;** main dishes under 10€; daily noon–midnight). Part gourmet store, part deli, part wine bar, this foodie hangout from star chef Adolfo Muñoz serves tapas and light meals in a hip setting. Venison, partridge, and other game figure prominently. The daily menu (two courses and dessert) is around 13€.

A few blocks down Calle Ciudad, the modest 14th century chapel **Santo Tomé ★★** (Plaza del Conde, 4; www.santotome.org; ✆ **92-525-60-98;** 2.30€; daily 10am–6:45pm) displays another El Greco masterpiece, ***The Burial of the Count of Orgaz,*** created in 1586.

The **Museo del Greco ★** (Paseo del Tránsito, s/n; http://museodelgreco.mcu.es; ✆ **92-522-36-65;** 3€ adults; Apr–Sept Tues–Sat

9:30am–8pm, Sun 10am–3pm; Oct–Mar Tues–Sat 9:30am–6:30pm, Sun 10am–3pm) is the only El Greco museum in the world. It mostly owns smaller, later works—except for the magical *View and Plan of Toledo*. Exhibits about El Greco's life and times rival the paintings.

Conclude your visit to Toledo next door at the **Museo Sefardí ★★** (Calle Samuel Leví, s/n; http://museosefardi.mcu.es; ✆ **92-522-36-65;** 3€ adults; Tues–Sat 9:30am–8:30pm, Sun 10am–3pm). The most important part of this museum, which recalls the strong Jewish presence in Toledo before 1492, is the **Sinagoga del Tránsito,** built in 1355 by Samuel Leví with a special dispensation from Pedro I. It was the only Toledo synagogue untouched in the 1391 attacks on the ghetto. The building was Christianized after 1492, so only some of the scrollwork on the walls is original, but restorations have filled in most of the blanks in the original scripts, which include psalms inscribed along the tops of the walls and a poetic description of the Temple on the east wall.

## ANDALUCÍA

Much of what the world imagines as Spain is actually Andalucía. It was the last stronghold of the Moors, who held al-Andalus for over seven centuries, and shines with the medieval Muslim glories of Europe: the world-famous Mezquita (mosque) of Córdoba, the Alhambra Palace of Granada, and atmospheric medieval quarters where the streets twist and turn like Arabic script. The cradle of flamenco, Andalucía is also the heartland of bullfighting and the home of the sherry trade. This section covers them all. It also embraces the Costa del Sol with its long sandy

### events IN ANDALUCÍA

**Sevilla:** Although many of the country's smaller towns stage similar celebrations, the **Semana Santa (Holy Week)** festivities in Seville (www.visitasevilla.es) are by far the most elaborate. From Palm Sunday to Easter Sunday, processions with hooded penitents move to the piercing wail of the *saeta*, a love song to the Virgin or Christ. Ten days before Easter Sunday. Also in Sevilla, the **April Feria** (www.visitasevilla.es) is a week-long festival starting 2 weeks after Easter. Parades and pageantry are grand, but hotel rooms are scarce.

**Córdoba:** The **Córdoba Patio Festival** (www.amigosdelospatioscordobeses.es), in early May offers the rare chance to get inside homeowners' private patios, cool oases replete with central fountains and cascading geraniums.

**Jerez de la Frontera:** The **Jerez Festival** (www.festivaldejerez.es) in late February and early March celebrates Jerez as a birthplace of flamenco with nightly concerts.

**Granada:** Since 1952, the **International Festival of Music and Dance** (www.granadafestival.org) has filled the city with concerts and dance performances in late June through mid-July.

beaches, and the elegant seaside city of Málaga, where Pablo Picasso first saw the world with an artist's eyes.

## Sevilla

Sevilla has been Andalucía's center of power and influence since Fernando III of Castilla tossed out the Moors in 1248. He wisely left Barrio Santa Cruz intact, and the tangled ancient streets of the Judería still make the medieval era palpable. The city is studded with churches and former convents funded by the riches that flowed into the city from its 16th to 18th century trade monopoly with the New World. It may be the most ornately decorated city in Spain. No country does baroque like the Spanish, and no city does Spanish baroque like Sevilla, where the style is the hybrid of Moorish decoration and the Catholic insistence on turning every abstract curlicue of Islam into a Christian angel's wing.

### ESSENTIALS

Sevilla's **Oficina de Información del Turismo** website is www.visitasevilla.es.

**ARRIVING** Sevilla's **Aeropuerto San Pablo** (Calle Almirante Lobo; www.aena-aeropuertos.es; ✆ **90-240-47-04**) lies 9.6km (6 miles) northeast of the city center. **Transportes Urbanos de Sevilla** (✆ **90-245-99-54**) buses offer transport to the city center for 4€.

**Trains** arrive at **Estación Santa Justa** (Av. Kansas City s/n; www.renfe.com; ✆ **90-242-22-42**). The high-speed AVE train has cut travel

Sevilla's grand Plaza de España.

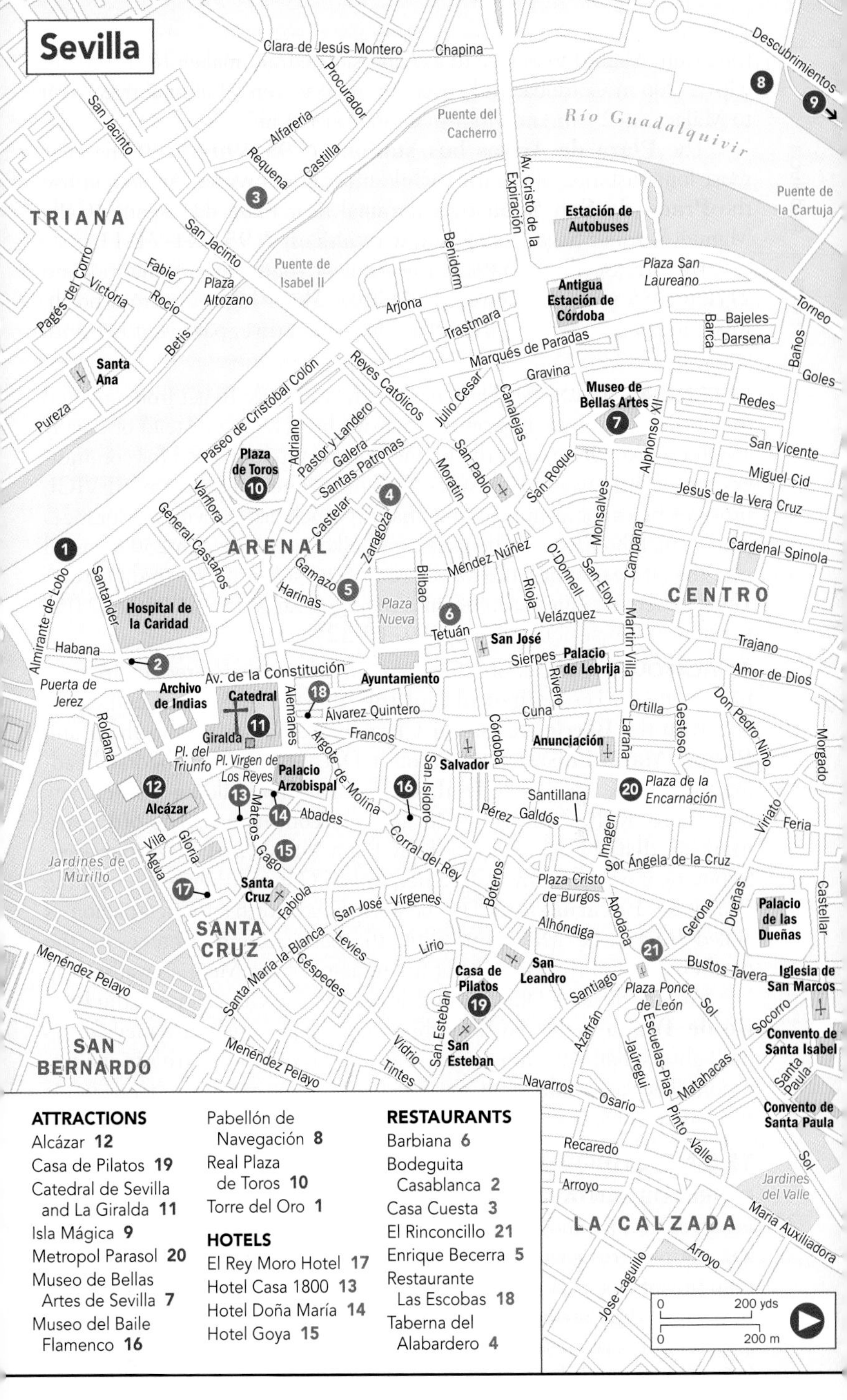
Sevilla
TRIANA
ARENAL
CENTRO
SANTA CRUZ
SAN BERNARDO
LA CALZADA
Río Guadalquivir
Puente del Cacherro
Puente de Isabel II
Puente de la Cartuja
Estación de Autobuses
Antigua Estación de Córdoba
Museo de Bellas Artes
Plaza de Toros
Hospital de la Caridad
Archivo de Indias
Catedral
Giralda
Alcázar
Palacio Arzobispal
Ayuntamiento
Plaza Nueva
San José
Palacio de Lebrija
Salvador
Anunciación
Plaza de la Encarnación
Santa Ana
Santa Cruz
Casa de Pilatos
San Leandro
San Esteban
Palacio de las Dueñas
Iglesia de San Marcos
Convento de Santa Isabel
Convento de Santa Paula
Jardines de Murillo
Jardines del Valle
Plaza Altozano
Plaza San Laureano
Plaza Cristo de Burgos
Plaza Ponce de León
Pl. del Triunfo
Pl. Virgen de Los Reyes
Av. de la Constitución
Paseo de Cristóbal Colón
Av. Cristo de la Expiración
Reyes Católicos
Marqués de Paradas
Menéndez Pelayo
María Auxiliadora
Descubrimientos
Torneo
ATTRACTIONS
Alcázar 12
Casa de Pilatos 19
Catedral de Sevilla and La Giralda 11
Isla Mágica 9
Metropol Parasol 20
Museo de Bellas Artes de Sevilla 7
Museo del Baile Flamenco 16
Pabellón de Navegación 8
Real Plaza de Toros 10
Torre del Oro 1
HOTELS
El Rey Moro Hotel 17
Hotel Casa 1800 13
Hotel Doña María 14
Hotel Goya 15
RESTAURANTS
Barbiana 6
Bodeguita Casablanca 2
Casa Cuesta 3
El Rinconcillo 21
Enrique Becerra 5
Restaurante Las Escobas 18
Taberna del Alabardero 4
0 200 yds
0 200 m

time from Madrid to Sevilla to 2½ hours. The train makes 18 trips daily, with a stop in Córdoba, and costs 55€ to 89€. Ten additional trains run to Málaga (2–2½ hr.) and four to Granada (3–4 hr.).

The **Plaza de Armas bus station** (✆ **95-490-80-40**) handles most long-distance bus traffic, while most buses within Andalucía use the **Prado de San Sebastián** terminal near Plaza de España (Calle Manuel Vazquez Sagastizabal, s/n; www.alsa.es; ✆ **95-441-71-11**).

By **car**, Sevilla is 549km (341 miles) southwest of Madrid and 217km (135 miles) northwest of Málaga. Major highways from north, west, and east converge on Sevilla. Once you arrive, park your car until you leave.

**GETTING AROUND** Sevilla is eminently walkable. To get from one end to another in a hurry, hop an inexpensive bus (1.40€) instead of paying 10€ for a taxi. Otherwise, the public transit system is good for commuters but of little use to sightseers. The bicycle rental program, SEVICI, provides bikes for a subscription charge (which also provides insurance) plus a small hourly fee. The snazzy red bikes are parked in 250 areas all over the city, each with a kiosk where you can subscribe by credit card. A 1-week membership is 13.30€, and time fees range from 1.05€ to 2.05€ per hour (www.sevici.es; ✆ **90-201-10-32**).

**CITY LAYOUT** The city of 1.7 million sprawls in every direction from its historic heart. The **cathedral and the Alcázar** anchor one end of the city, with the **Barrio de Santa Cruz** spreading north from them and **Parque María Luisa** spreading south. Due west of the cathedral, heading toward the river, is **Arenal,** the former ship-building district now dominated by the bullring and its adjacent concert hall. The **old commercial district** expands north of Plaza Nueva and Plaza Santiago. Shopping is anchored by Calles Sierpes and Cuna as they reach north to **Plaza de Encarnación.** The neighborhood north of Encarnación is called **Barrio de Macarena** after the basilica, and stretches to the northern limit of the Old City at the remains of the Moorish walls.

West of Sevilla's Old City and across the Rio Guadalquivír, the **Barrio de Triana** is the old fishermen's and Gypsy quarter, famed for its bullfighters, flamenco musicians, and ceramics in the North African tradition. The large **Isla de Cartuja,** north of Triana in the river, holds some museums, performance centers, and an amusement park.

## THE NEIGHBORHOODS IN BRIEF

**BARRIO DE SANTA CRUZ** The remarkably preserved medieval quarter is one of Sevilla's most colorful districts. Near the old walls of the **Alcázar,** narrow streets with names like Vida (Life) and Muerte (Death) open onto tiny plazas. Part of the essential experience of visiting Sevilla is getting lost in the Barrio de Santa Cruz, only to stumble into a plaza where a waiter offers you a seat and a drink. Flower-filled balconies draped with bougainvillea and dotted with potted geraniums jut over this labyrinth.

To enter the Barrio de Santa Cruz, turn right after leaving the Patio de Banderas exit of the Alcázar. Turn right again at Plaza de la Alianza, going down Calle Rodrigo Caro to Plaza de Doña Elvira. The name "Santa Cruz" is also loosely applied to the dense streets of the **Judería** that lie just west of the main portion of Santa Cruz.

**BARRIO DE LA MACARENA** The district around the **Basilica de La Macarena** is one of the most densely residential parts of the Old City. To see the area at its best, spend a Saturday afternoon watching wedding parties at the basilica. Men in suits or tuxedos escort women resplendent in elegant shawls and flamenco-influenced designer dresses. When the happy couple rides off in their limousine, the Sevillanos pack into a bar across the street. You can also visit the church daily 9am to 2pm and 5 to 9pm. The 17th-century image of the Virgen de Macarena is one of the most venerated in the Holy Week processions.

**BARRIO DE TRIANA** Across the Rio Guadalquivír from the city center, Triana is the traditional quarter of fishermen and gitanos (Roma, or Gypsies) and the birthplace of many famous bullfighters memorialized by commemorative plaques. It is also the neighborhood of alfarerías, makers of the traditional decorative tiles for which Sevilla is world famous. The tile companies are concentrated on **Calle San Jorge** and surrounding streets; most have sales rooms open to the public. The riverfront at the foot of Puente Isabel II is called the **Puerto de Triana,** and it is filled with small tabernas and *marisquerías* (shellfish restaurants) that set up outdoor tables during warm weather. This is a good area for early evening tapas. Farther east along the river, approaching Puente San Telmo, Triana loses its rough edges and gives way to a number of handsome riverfront restaurants. The historic public market, the **Mercado de Triana,** sits at the end of Puente Isabel II. It has become a lively attraction in its own right, with several excellent tapas bars that serve food and drink well after the food stalls have closed. There is even a small theater in the market, which sometimes has lunchtime flamenco performances. The market is adjacent to the historic Moorish fortress known as the **Castillo de San Jorge,** which has archaeological exhibits showing its Almohad origins and an exhibition about the Spanish Inquisition, which was based here from 1481 to 1785. Don't expect thumbscrews and instruments of torture—the exhibits delve sensitively into the causes (and practical political uses) of intolerance and persecution.

**PARQUE MARÍA LUISA & PLAZA DE ESPAÑA** The park dedicated to María Luisa, sister of Isabel II, was once the grounds of the Palacio de San Telmo. In 1929, Sevilla hosted the Exposición Iberoamericana, and many Latin-American countries erected showcase buildings and pavilions in and around the park. Many pavilions still stand, serving as foreign consulates or university buildings. The park is one of the most tranquil areas in the city and attracts Sevillanos who want to row boats on its ponds, walk along flower-bordered paths, jog, or bicycle. The **Plaza de España,** left over from the Exposición Iberoamericana, is a city landmark.

## EXPLORING SEVILLA

**Alcázar ★★★** PALACE Technically the oldest European royal residence still in use (the king and queen stay here when they're in Sevilla), this complex of palaces and fortifications dates from the Almohad rule of Sevilla but was almost entirely rebuilt after the 1248 reconquest. The older, more austere building is the **Palacio Gótico ★,** built by Alfonso X ("the Wise") in the 13th century. Carlos V modified the Great Hall and the Sala de Fiestas to celebrate his 1526 wedding to his Habsburg cousin. The more beautiful and larger **Palacio Mudéjar ★★★** was built in the 14th century by Pedro I ("the Cruel"), likely employing some of the same artisans who worked on the Alhambra in Granada. It's a tour de force of carved plaster and stone, carved wooden ceilings, and splendid decorative tiles. Fernando and Isabel, who at one time lived in the Alcázar, welcomed Columbus here on his return from America. On the top floor, the Oratory of the Catholic Monarchs has a fine altar in polychrome tiles made by Pisano in 1504. The well-kept **gardens ★** are worth the visit.

Plaza del Triunfo s/n. www.patronato-alcazarsevilla.es. ✆ **95-450-23-23.** 9.50€ adults, 2.50€ seniors/students, free under age 17. Oct–Mar daily 9:30am–5pm; Apr–Sept daily 9:30am–7pm.

**Casa de Pilatos ★** HISTORIC HOUSE This 16th-century Andalucían palace of the dukes of Medinaceli recaptures the splendor of the

**A patio in the Alcázar.**

Main altar, Catedral de Sevilla.

past, casually combining Gothic, Mudéjar, and Plateresque styles in its courtyards, fountains, and salons. Legend says that the house is a reproduction of Pilate's House in Jerusalem, but the distinctly Sevillano character of the architecture argues otherwise. The interior includes a collection of Spanish master paintings, as well as some atmospheric if not terribly accomplished Greek and Roman statuary. The lush gardens, however, are the highlight and are worth the entrance fee. The cascading magenta bougainvillea at the entrance is an iconic image of great wealth in Sevilla's desert climate. The palace is about a 7-minute walk northeast of the cathedral on the northern edge of Barrio de Santa Cruz.

Plaza Pilatos, 1. www.fundacionmedinaceli.org. ✆ **95-422-52-98.** Entire house 8€; ground floor, patio, and gardens 6€. Apr–Oct daily 9am–7pm; Nov–Mar daily 9am–6pm.

**Catedral de Sevilla and La Giralda** ★★ CATHEDRAL The largest Gothic building in the world and the third-largest church in Europe (after St. Peter's in Rome and St. Paul's in London), Sevilla's cathedral was designed with the stated goal that "those who come after us will take us for madmen." Construction began in the late 1400s on the site of the Almohad mosque and took centuries to complete. Just inside one portal, the tomb of Columbus is held by four carved pall-bearers.

Works of art abound here, many of them architectural, such as the 15th-century stained-glass windows, the iron screens *(rejas)* closing off the chapels, the elaborate 15th-century choir stalls, and the Gothic reredos above the main altar. On the feasts of Corpus Christi and the Immaculate Conception (and on the 3rd day of Feria), six boys *(Los Seises)* from the choir perform a ceremonial dance on the altar dressed in Renaissance plumed hats and wielding castanets. The treasury has works by Goya, Murillo, and Zurbarán, as well as a display of. You might spot young women praying before the gigantic Murillo painting of the *Vision de San Antonio.* They're asking St. Anthony, patron of the lovelorn, to send them a husband. After touring the dark interior, emerge into the sunlight of the Patio de Naranjas (Orange Trees), with its fresh citrus scents and birdsong.

**La Giralda,** the bell tower of the cathedral, is the city's most emblematic monument. Erected as a minaret in the 12th century, it has seen later additions, such as 16th-century bells. Those who climb to the top get a dazzling view of Sevilla, and ascend on a ramp constructed so that the muezzin could ride up on horseback.

Av. de la Constitución s/n. www.catedraldesevilla.es. ✆ **95-421-49-71.** Cathedral and tower 9€ adults, 4€ students 25 and under, free for ages 14 and under. Mon 11am–3:30pm, Tue–Sat 11am–5pm, Sun 2:30–6pm.

**Metropol Parasol ★★** LANDMARK This sprawling wooden structure overshadows the Plaza de la Encarnación with six parasols in mushroom shapes. Locals simply call it "Las Setas" (Spanish for "mushrooms") and you have to see it to believe it. The plaza had been the site of a public market for more than a century. When excavations began to build a new one, Roman and Moorish ruins were found, delaying the process for years. Now the underground portion is the Antiquarium, a well-interpreted archaeological site, and the sculptural Las Setas, designed by German architect Jürgen Mayer-Hermann, towers above an upscale public market that features tapas bars, delis, and food stalls. Upper levels of Las Setas include an observation deck and restaurant.

Plaza de la Encarnación, s/n. www.setasdesevilla.com. ✆ **60-663-52-14.** Viewing level 3€; Antiquarium 2€. Market Mon–Sat 8am–3pm. Antiquarium Tues–Sat 10am–8pm, Sun 10am–2pm. Viewing level Sun–Thurs 10:30am–11:45pm, Fri–Sat 10:30am–12:45am.

**Museo de Bellas Artes de Sevilla ★★** MUSEUM The convent building that houses this extensive collection of Spanish art nearly upstages the paintings. Built in 1594 for the order of the Merced Calzada de la Asunción, it benefited from Sevilla's golden age of painting and ceramics (the courtyard tiles are enthralling). The galleries hold the greatest works of Bartolomé Esteban Murillo, including a huge *Immaculate Conception* painted for the Convento de San Francisco. Other highlights include works by Sevilla-born Juan Valdés Leal and Francisco de Zurbarán.

Plaza del Museo 9. www.museosdeandalucia.es. ✆ **95-478-65-00.** 1.50€, free to students. Mid-Sept to mid-June Tues–Sat 10am–8:30pm, Sun 10am–5pm; mid-June to mid-Sept Tues–Sat 10am–2:30pm, Sun 10am–5pm.

**Museo del Baile Flamenco ★★** MUSEUM It has been said that there are no schools to create flamenco dancers, just as there are none to

Museo de Bellas Artes de Sevilla.

create poets. Cristina Hoyos, the founder of this museum, drew instead on her depth of feeling to become one of the most celebrated flamenco dancers of the late 20th century. The impressionistic museum is long on film clips and videos that immerse the viewer in the art of the dance. One of the most engrossing exhibits features short videos that demonstrate the seven representative styles (*palos*) of flamenco from the solea to the tangos. In an opening video, Hoyos advises viewers to follow their emotions. It's not necessary to understand flamenco, she asserts. It must be felt. See for yourself at nightly shows, either at the museum or a local club (see p. 801).

Calle Manuel Rojas Marcos, 3. www.museoflamenco.com. ✆ **95-434-03-11.** 10€ adults, 8€ seniors/students, 6€ children. Daily 10am–7pm. Flamenco performances: 24€ adults, 18€ students/seniors, 15€ children. Daily 7pm.

**Real Plaza de Toros ★** LANDMARK The Real Maestranza de Caballería de Sevilla began construction of this slightly oval bullring in 1761 to replace earlier wooden rings. It was completed in stages over the following 120 years and is one of the oldest and loveliest rings in the country. Guided tours begin in the stands, which seat 12,000 people. Although visitors cannot step onto the orange sands of the ring, they can survey the five gates that help orchestrate the *corrida,* including the gates where matadors and bulls enter the ring, the gate where dead bulls are carried out by three mules, and the gate where matadors exit in triumph if they receive the highest honors from the officials. The paintings and sculptures in the museum help trace the history of the spectacle from an aristocratic demonstration of bravery to a more populist sport in which talented bullfighters can achieve the fame of nobility. A number of bullfighters' costumes are on display, along with the red capes (*muletas*) that the bullfighter uses to attract the bull. Bulls, by the way, are colorblind; they respond to the motion, not the traditional color.

Paseo Colón, 12. www.realmaestranza.com. ✆ **95-421-03-15.** 7€ adults, 4€ seniors/students. Nov–Mar daily 9:30am–7pm, Apr–Oct daily 9:30am–9.

**Torre del Oro** ★ MUSEUM The Almohad rulers of Sevilla erected this tower and another just like it across the river in 1220 as a defensive mechanism. A stout chain linked the two to prevent ships from moving in and out of the port without authorization. The system proved fruitless when a Castillian admiral broke the chain in 1248. The other tower vanished centuries ago, but the Torre del Oro has stood for nearly 9 centuries, at various times as administrative offices and a warehouse. Its name derives from the unusual yellow-tinged plaster made of mortar, lime, and straw. These days it serves as the Museo Maritimo and recounts the history of the port from its Almohad era to its heyday of the 16th and 17th centuries.

Paseo de Cristóbal Colón, s/n. ✆ **95-422-24-19.** 3€ adults, 1.50€ seniors and students; free Mon. Mon–Fri 9:30am–6:45pm; Sat–Sun 10:30am–6:45pm.

## ORGANIZED TOURS

Sightseeing buses face a severe limitation in Sevilla, because few medieval streets can handle large vehicles. To compensate, the red **City Sightseeing** bus (every 20–30 min.; 20€ for 24 hr., 24€ for 48 hr.) offers guided **walking tours** of Parque María Luisa and the barrios of Santa Cruz, Macarena, and Triana to everyone who buys a ticket. The bus can be met at the cathedral, the Alcázar, Torre del Oro, the University of Sevilla, and Isla Mágica.

**Sightseeing cruises** on the Río Guadalquivír from **Cruceros Torre del Oro** (www.crucerostorredeloro.com; ✆ **95-456-16-92;** 16€ adults, free under 14) depart from the riverbank below the Torre del Oro at Paseo Muelle Marqués del Contadero. The cruise gives the best perspective on Sevilla's bridges. The most dramatic is the counter-balanced cable-stay Puente Alamillo designed by Santiago Calatrava. The form of the bridge has been variously compared to the prow of a ship or the shape of a harp.

## ESPECIALLY FOR KIDS

**Isla de Cartuja** has several family-friendly destinations. Interactive educational displays at the **Pabellón de la Navegación** (Camino de los

Descubrimientos; www.pabellondelanavegacion.com; ✆ **95-404-31-11;** 4.90€ adults, 3.50€ seniors and ages 5–14) capture the sense of adventure of the early navigators whose discoveries helped make Spain rich. Panoramic views from the 50m (164-ft.) **Torre Mirador** are the highlight of a visit. The Pavilion of Navigation is closed on Mondays.

The amusement park **Isla Mágica** (Rotonda Isla Mágica; www.islamagica.es; ✆ **90-216-17-16**) entertains with rides, shows, and a waterpark. Open April to early November; see website for hours and admission.

## WHERE TO STAY IN SEVILLA

**El Rey Moro Hotel ★★** Created from a 16th-century manor house built around a patio with an 8th-century Moorish fountain, the family-run El Rey Moro spans the centuries with colorful contemporary rooms inspired by historic designs. Colors are warm and intense, and furnishings tend to be quirky, one-of-a-kind pieces. Rooms are on two levels around the central courtyard, and many retain the old plaster walls and exposed ceiling beams of the original house. This corner of Barrio Santa Cruz is about a 4-minute walk from the cathedral.

Calle Lope de Rueda, 14. www.elreymoro.com. ✆ **95-456-34-68.** 19 units. Doubles 89€–189€. **Amenities:** Restaurant; loaner bikes; free Wi-Fi.

**Hotel Casa 1800 ★★** This charming boutique hotel, steps from the cathedral, occupies an 1864 limestone mansion. Many rooms have exposed beams, and the original plaster-on-stone walls were retained wherever possible. The hotel is filled with original art, giving it the gracious air of a private manse. The decor is luxe—tufted ottomans, overhead chandeliers, beds with artistic and elaborate headboards, and parquet wood floors. The rooftop terrace has stunning views of the Alcázar and the cathedral. Three deluxe rooms have private terrace and Jacuzzi tub.

Calle Rodrigo Caro, 6. www.hotelcasa1800.com. ✆ **95-456-18-00.** 24 units. Doubles 145€–240€. **Amenities:** Restaurant; 2 bars; concierge; free Wi-Fi.

**Hotel Doña María ★★** You can never be too close to the center of power. No doubt that's what Samuel Levi thought when he built his 14th-century palace here next to the Alcázar so that he could pop in to advise Pedro the Cruel. Alterations over the years have carved out rooms in many shapes and sizes. Ask to see your room before moving in. The rooftop terrace has a small pool, but most guests gravitate to the bar with its in-your-face views of the cathedral and La Giralda. The hotel has a relaxed, old-fashioned feel complemented by warm, attentive service.

Calle Don Remondo, 19. www.hdmaria.com. ✆ **95-422-49-90.** 64 units. Doubles 97€–224€. **Amenities**: 2 bars; outdoor pool; free Wi-Fi.

**Hotel Goya** ★ With its tiled bathrooms, marble-tile floors, and pale wooden furniture, the Hotel Goya has a lot of hard surfaces, but the staff are warm and welcoming and the rooms are very well-designed to make efficient use of limited space. It's a great bargain lodging, as everything is kept fresh and functional. The hotel sits in the heart of the oldest part of Barrio de Santa Cruz, no more than a 5-minute stroll from the cathedral.

Calle Mateus Gago, 31. www.hostalgoyasevilla.com. ✆ **95-421-11-70.** 19 units. Doubles 45€–85€. **Amenities:** Free Wi-Fi.

## WHERE TO EAT IN SEVILLA

The North African influence on Sevilla cuisine is obvious in the honey-sweetened pastries and the abundant dates, almonds, saffron, and lemons. Gazpacho was made here with almonds and garlic long before tomatoes arrived from the New World, and breads are still baked in ancient ovens.

### Expensive

**Taberna del Alabardero** ★★ ANDALUCIAN Choose the upstairs dining rooms of this elegant townhouse near the Plaza de Toros for some of the finest upscale cuisine in Sevilla. But it's more fun to eat off the bistro menu in the downstairs tile-encrusted dining room. Everything is prepared and served by the faculty and students of the hotel and hospitality school, started here many years ago by a priest looking for a way to give street kids some marketable skills. The dishes are rib-stickers: the hearty potato and sausage stew known as Riojanas; cod *a pil pil* served with ratatouille topped with a poached egg; duck in bitter-orange sauce; and rice pudding with a side of profiteroles. The restored mansion also serves as an inn, with seven spacious and elegant guest rooms.

Calle Zaragoza, 20. www.tabernadelalabardero.es. ✆ **95-450-27-21.** Reservations recommended. Mains 19€–32€; 3-course bistro menu 14€–19€. Daily 1:30–4:30pm and 8:30pm–midnight. Restaurant closed Aug.

### Moderate

**Barbiana** ★★ ANDALUCIAN/SEAFOOD If you've ever tasted the Manzanilla Barbiana from Sanlúcar de Barrameda, you already know what kind to expect at this related restaurant next to Plaza Nueva. Tangy and yeasty, with a hint of green almonds, the sherry is a perfect complement to fish from the Huelva coast and crustaceans from Sanlúcar itself. The kitchen offers mixed seafood with rice (*not* paella) at midday but not in the evening, when the volume of diners steers the menu toward quicker preparations like *tortillitas de camarones,* a fried batter of chickpea flour with tiny whole shrimp.

Calle Albareda, 11. www.restaurantebarbiana.com. ✆ **95-422-44-02.** Reservations recommended. Mains 10€–28€. Mon–Sat noon–5pm and 8pm–midnight.

**Enrique Becerra ★** ANDALUCIAN The upstairs dining room at this establishment just one street off Plaza Nueva serves excellent grilled meat and fish, but it's frankly too quiet. Everyone prefers to crowd into the bar and adjacent dining room on the ground floor to enjoy creative tapas—soft-cooked foie gras on toast, finger rolls stuffed with spicy steamed mussels, lamb meatballs in mint sauce, or cod in a pasta sack with almond-garlic sauce. The 35 sherries by the glass are very reasonably priced.

Calle Gamazo, 2. www.enriquebecerra.com. ✆ **95-421-30-49.** Tapas 3€–4€; *raciones* 6€–13€; Mains 12€–22€. Mon–Sat 1–4:30pm and 8pm–midnight (closed Sat July–Aug).

### Inexpensive

**Bodeguita Casablanca ★★★** ANDALUCIAN This little corner bar near the Puerta de Jerez run by Tomás and Antonio Casablanca is justly acclaimed for the kitchen's deft riffs on traditional dishes. The Casablancas convert the humble *tortilla Española* into the noble Tortilla al Whisky, copied by chefs all over Spain. In deference to the burger craze, the brothers created a radically Spanish version: two salt cod sliders served on a puddle of melted cheese. Most diners graze on tapas, but Casablanca also offers full plates, including a huge roast leg of lamb.

Calle Adolfo Rodríguez Jurado, 12. www.bodeguitacasablanca.com. ✆ **95-422-41-14.** Tapas 2.50€–4.50€; plates 12€–20€. Mon–Fri 7am–5pm and 8:15pm–12:30am, Sat 12:30–5:30pm (closed Sat in July). Closed August.

**Casa Cuesta ★** ANDALUCIAN Across from the Mercado de Triana, this historic tapas bar of fishermen and bullfighters still boasts the checkerboard marble floors and ornate polished bar of its late 19th-century origins. Known for classics such as *jamón serrano,* triangles of Manchego cheese, and potato salad with lots of garlic, Casa Cuesta is also acclaimed for its *flamequines:* pork sirloin wrapped in *jamón serrano,* battered, and deep-fried. They make you thirsty for another beer, which is the point.

Calle Castilla 1, Triana. www.casacuesta.net. ✆ **95-433-33-35.** Tapas 3€–5€; larger plates 7€–19€. Daily noon–midnight.

**El Rinconcillo ★** ANDALUCIAN El Rinconcillo was established in 1670. The latest additions to the decor were the Art Nouveau tile murals installed sometime in the late 19th or early 20th century. The lights are dim, and hams and sausage dangle from the heavily beamed ceilings. Good luck scoring one of the marble-topped tables. We usually stand at the bar where the bartender runs our tab in chalk. Some of the most famous tapas are the house *croquetas* and the casserole of chickpeas and spinach.

Calle Gerona, 42. www.elrinconcillo.es. ✆ **95-422-31-83.** Tapas 2.50€–3.50€; plates 9€–18€; set menus 26€–39€. Thurs–Tues 1pm–1:30am

**Restaurante Las Escobas** ★ ANDALUCIAN/CASTILIAN When Cervantes ate here in the late 16th century, he called Las Escobas a *taberna antigua,* since it had already been around since 1386. It might be the oldest eating establishment in Europe. Las Escobas has been in the hands of its current owners for more than 40 years. Of all the restaurants near the cathedral square, this spot gives the best value for the money and serves the best traditional cuisine.

Calle Alvarez Quintero, 62. www.lasescobas.com. ✆ **95-456-04-16.** Tapas 2.80€–4.50€; Mains 11€–17€; daily menu 16€; tasting menu 47€. Daily noon–midnight.

## SHOPPING

Calle Sierpes is the main pedestrian shopping promenade in Sevilla. Shops tend to be local rather than outlets of international brands. To see the evolution of Sevillana style, stroll Calle Cuna, which runs parallel to Sierpes. The shop windows are a fashion show of flamenco wear and flamenco-inspired contemporary fashion.

It's almost impossible to leave Sevilla without buying a piece of pottery. Visit Triana to see the tile-encrusted facade of **Cerámica Santa Ana,** Calle San Jorge, 31 (✆ **95-433-39-90**). The 1870 factory and showroom has a broad selection of painted tiles, pots, tableware, and decorative items in the *azulejo* tradition.

If you want a bullfight poster, skip the tourist shops that offer to print your name on a generic poster and visit the shop at the Plaza de Toros (p. 811), where artist-designed posters from previous seasons are for sale.

## ENTERTAINMENT & NIGHTLIFE

Sevilla is a cradle of flamenco, and you'll have more opportunities to see a performance here than anywhere else in Andalucía. Two centers offer nightly performances of very pure flamenco that are as educational as they are entertaining: **Museo del Baile Flamenco** (Calle Manuel Rojas Marcos, 13; www.museoflamenco.com; ✆ **95-434-03-11;** 24€ adults) and **Casa de la Memoria de Al Andalus** (Calle Cuna, 6; www.casadelamemoria.es; ✆ **95-456-06-70;** 18€ adults). The museum performances are dance-oriented, while the Casa de la Memoría shows accentuate the ensemble.

The flamenco nightclub spectacle, or *tablao,* of choreographed flamenco performances is an honored tradition in Sevilla. Most *tablaos* give you a drink with basic admission and try to sell you a dinner for an extra 20€ to 40€. The dinner is rarely worth the price, but it is convenient and you may get better seats. The three main companies are **El Patio Sevillano** (Paseo de Cristóbal Colón, 11; www.elpatiosevillano.com; ✆ **95-421-41-20;** 38€), **El Arenal** (Calle Rodó, 7; www.tablaoelarenal.com; ✆ **95-421-64-92;** 38€), and **Los Gallos** (Plaza de Santa Cruz, 11; www.tablaolosgallos.com; ✆ **95-421-69-81;** 35€).

Flamenco dancers in Sevilla.



Though often the setting for operas, Sevilla didn't get its own opera house until the 1990s. The **Teatro de la Maestranza** (Paseo de Colón, 22; www.teatromaestranza.com; ✆ **95-422-33-44**) quickly became one of the world's premier opera venues. The season often includes works inspired by the city, including Verdi's *La Forza del Destino* and Mozart's *Marriage of Figaro*.

## A Side Trip to Jerez de la Frontera

Like Kentucky, with its thoroughbreds and its bourbon, Jerez is defined by its Andalucían horses and its sherry. Just take a walk down pedestrian Calle Larga, and you'll see fashionable young women wearing knee-high black boots with tight pants as a nod to the city's equestrian tradition. And the umbrellas on the cafe tables are emblazoned with the logos of Tío Pepe, Don Patricio, or El Gallo sherries instead of Cruzcampo beer.

There are more than a dozen trains per day from Sevilla. The 1-hour trip costs 11€ to 26€ one-way and arrives at the Mudejar Revival train station (Plaza de la Estación s/n; www.renfe.com; ✆ **90-232-03-20**) at the eastern end of Calle Medina. The **tourist office** (Plaza del Arenal, s/n; www.turismojerez.com; ✆ **95-633-88-74**) is open daily. You will want to visit on a weekday because some sherry bodegas close on weekends (and during Aug), and because the facility of the famous Andalucian horses is only open on selected weekdays.

For best use of your time, start at the **Fundación Real Escuela Andaluza del Arte Ecuestre ★★** (Avenida Duque de Abrantes, s/n. www.realescuela.org; ✆ **95-631-80-15**), which was founded in 1973 to train horses and riders and operate a breeding farm of the Pura Raza Española, or Andalucian horse. Performances of the "dancing horses" (21€–27€ adults, 13€–17€ ages 4–13 and seniors) are held on Thursdays at noon (and other days depending on season). On performance days, short tours of the facility are offered (6.50€ adults, 4.50€ ages 4–13 and seniors; Thurs 10am–2pm). Tours include the saddlery, several museums, and the outdoor practice ring. On Mondays and Wednesdays (11€ adults, 6.50€ ages 4–13 and seniors; 10am–2pm), you can take in the same sights and also watch a training session in the indoor arena, which we prefer for its revealing glimpse at the hard work and patience behind the dazzling artistry.

To delve into the sherry tradition, Jerez is filled with bodegas where you can tour and taste. A typical visit includes a walk through several buildings in which sherry and brandy are manufactured. You'll see grapes being pressed and sorted (in the fall), the bottling process, and thousands of large oak casks. Tours end with a tasting of various sherries. Start with the lightest and driest, either a *fino* or a *manzanilla,* and remember that sherry is higher in alcohol than table wine.

One of the most famous names is **González Byass ★★**, the maker of Tío Pepe (Calle Manuel María González, 12; www.bodegastiopepe.com; ✆ **95-635-70-16;** tours from 13€ adults).

Not surprisingly, a number of Jerez restaurants feature sherry in their cuisine. **Bar Juanito ★** (Calle Pescadería Viejo, 8; www.bar-juanito.com; ✆ **95-633-48-38;** tapas and raciones 4.50€–8€) serves fresh tuna loin salad in sherry vinegar or meatballs in oloroso sauce. **La Carboná Restaurante ★★** (Calle San Francisco de Paula, 2; www.lacarbona.com; ✆ **95-634-74-75;** mains 14€–32€) occupies what appears to be an old sherry warehouse. House specialties include big cuts of Cantabrian beef roasted over charcoal; starters include prawns or spicy sausage in oloroso sauce.

If time allows, stop at the **Alcazár ★** (Alameda Vieja, s/n; www.jerez.es; ✆ **95-614-99-55;** 5€ adults, 1.80€ students/seniors) so that you can compare this frontier outpost with the more refined fortress palaces in Sevilla and Granada. It was built in the 12th century and its highlights include an austerely beautiful mosque, lovely gardens, and well-preserved Moorish baths.

## A Side Trip to Córdoba

A millennium ago, Muslims, Christians, and Jews lived and worked together to create Western Europe's greatest city—a cosmopolitan center of the arts, philosophy, and science. Until the late 11th century, Córdoba was also the capital of western Islam. La Mezquita, the largest medieval mosque in Europe, remains its star attraction. The streets and whitewashed buildings of Andalucía's most intact Moorish city endure, and visiting Córdoba is ultimately less about monuments and more about getting lost in the maze of streets that bore witness to an ancient, harmonious world.

The best way to get here is on a high-speed train from Sevilla (www.renfe.es). The AVE costs 31€ each way, while AVANT trains (21€) and MD trains (14€) take only minutes longer. Trains arrive north of the Old City at Glorieta de las Tres Culturas, off Avenida de América. Bus 3 (1.20€) runs between the rail station and the historic core. Otherwise, it is about a 15-minute walk south on Avenida de Cervantes or Avenida del Gran Capitán. For rail information, call ✆ **90-242-22-42.**

Start your visit at the **Mezquita Catedral de Cordoba ★★★** (Calles Torrijos and Cardenal Herrero s/n; www.mezquitadecordoba.org; ✆ **95-822-52-26;** 8€ adults, 4€ ages 10–14). Enter the mosque through the Patio de los Naranjos (Courtyard of the Orange Trees) where worshippers performed their ablutions before prayer. Even this serene oasis will not prepare you for the interior, with its fantastic forest of arches painted with red and white stripes—a realization in stone of a billowing

**Interior, Mezquita Catedral de Cordoba.**

desert tent. A Roman Catholic cathedral interrupts the vistas, as it sits awkwardly in the middle of the mosque as an enduring symbol of Christian hubris.

You will probably want to spend most of your remaining time exploring the winding streets of the medieval walled city, or **Judería ★★**, that radiate out from the mosque. But before you plunge in, detour 2 blocks west to the **Alcázar de los Reyes Cristianos ★★** (Calle Caballerizas Reales, s/n; ✆ **95-742-01-51;** 4.50€ adults). Commissioned in 1328, it is a fine piece of military architecture. Though not as inspiring as La Mezquita, the Alcázar was backdrop to a number of important historical events. It was the base for Fernando and Isabel as they prepared to reconquer Granada, and Columbus journeyed here to seek Isabel's support for his voyages of discovery.

Retrace your steps to the Judería. Even though many of the old whitewashed buildings have been converted to shops, the winding streets maintain their air of antiquity. For a peek at daily life, watch for **Casa Sefarad ★** (Corner of calles Judíos and Averroes; www.casadesefarad.es; ✆ **95-742-14-04;** 4€ adults) which focuses on 11th- and 12th-century daily Jewish life in Córdoba, the de facto capital of Sephardic Jewry. Córdoba also boasts one of Spain's three remaining pre-Inquisition synagogues. The **Sinagoga ★** (Calle de los Judíos 20; ✆ **95-720-29-28;** 0.30€) was built in 1315 and is noted particularly for its stuccowork.

It's worth a detour to the **Museo Arqueológico de Córdoba ★** (Plaza Jerónimo Páez, 7; www.museosdeandalucia.es; ✆ **95-735-55-17;** 1.50€) which occupies a stunning building on the site of a Roman amphitheater. Intact portions of the theater have been revealed in the basement and help to tell the story of life in and around Córdoba since the first Neanderthals came to the area 300,000 years ago.

With only a day in Córdoba, stick to casual eateries or you'll lose several hours at the table. Two places close to La Mezquita offer different approaches to Córdoban cuisine. **Bodegas Mezquita ★** (Calle Céspedes, 12; www.bodegasmezquita.com; ✆ **95-749-00-04**) started as a deli but has expanded to a full-blown bar and restaurant. The bar opens first; as more customers arrive, the waiters open other rooms until the whole place is packed. Most dishes are offered in a choice of sizes, making it easy to order tapas and taste several. For a local specialty, try the Córdoban rice pot with stewed Iberian pork and mushrooms, or the Sephardic lamb stew with nuts and raisins and a side of couscous. Arabic influences also lend interesting flavors to the grilled meats at **El Churrasco ★** (Calle Romero, 16; www.elchurrasco.com; ✆ **95-729-08-19**). It is a good place to sample *rabo de toro* (stewed oxtail), especially satisfying for hearty eaters. Several fish options are also available.

## Granada

When Boabdil, the last king of Moorish Granada, was exiled to North Africa in 1492, he took the bones of his ancestors with him. But he left behind their fortress-palace, the Alhambra, and a legacy of nearly eight centuries of Islamic culture. Fernando and Isabel may have won the war and completed the reconquest of al-Andalus, but in Granada they lost the history. Few people come to this beautiful city to see the solemn tombs of Los Reyes Católicos. They come for the joyous ornamentation of the Alhambra and the inextinguishably Arabic face of the Albaícin.

### ESSENTIALS

Granada's tourist office website is www.turgranada.es.

**ARRIVING** Granada's **Federico García Lorca Airport** (Carretera Málaga; www.aena-aeropuertos.es; ✆ **90-240-47-04**) is 16km (10 miles) west of town. A bus route links the airport with the center of Granada. The one-way fare is 3€. (Daily 5:30am to 8pm; trip time is 45 minutes.)

Most travelers arrive by **train** to **Estación de RENFE de Granada** (Av. Andaluces s/n; www.renfe.es; ✆ **90-232-03-20**). Four trains daily arrive from Sevilla, taking 3 to 4 hours, depending on the train, and costing 25€ one-way. Granada has **bus** links to virtually all the major towns and cities in Andalucía, and even to Madrid. The main bus terminal is **Estación de Autobuses de Granada** (Carretera de Jaén, s/n; ✆ **95-818-54-80**). For bus information, contact **Alsa** (www.alsa.es; ✆ **95-818-54-80**).

**GETTING AROUND** Just a few buses will take you pretty much anywhere you want to go in Granada. The 30 and 32 city buses (1.20€) run continuously from Plaza Isabel la Catolica to the ticket office of the Alhambra, and the 31 and 32 buses leave from the same spot for Sacromonte.

## The Neighborhoods in Brief

**MODERN GRANADA** Modern is a relative term in Granada, but refers to the city between the cathedral and university and Plaza Nueva, the oldest extant square in Granada. The **Puerta de Elvira** is the gate through which Fernando and Isabel made their triumphant entry into Granada in 1492 after the last Moorish ruler, Boabdil, fled. The street leading from it to the center of Granada is the colorful **Calle de Elvira,** which also marks the eastern edge of the Albaicín.

**ALBAICÍN** This atmospheric old quarter on one of Granada's two main hills stands apart from the city of 19th-century buildings and wide boulevards. A holdover from the Nasrid Empire, it even predates the

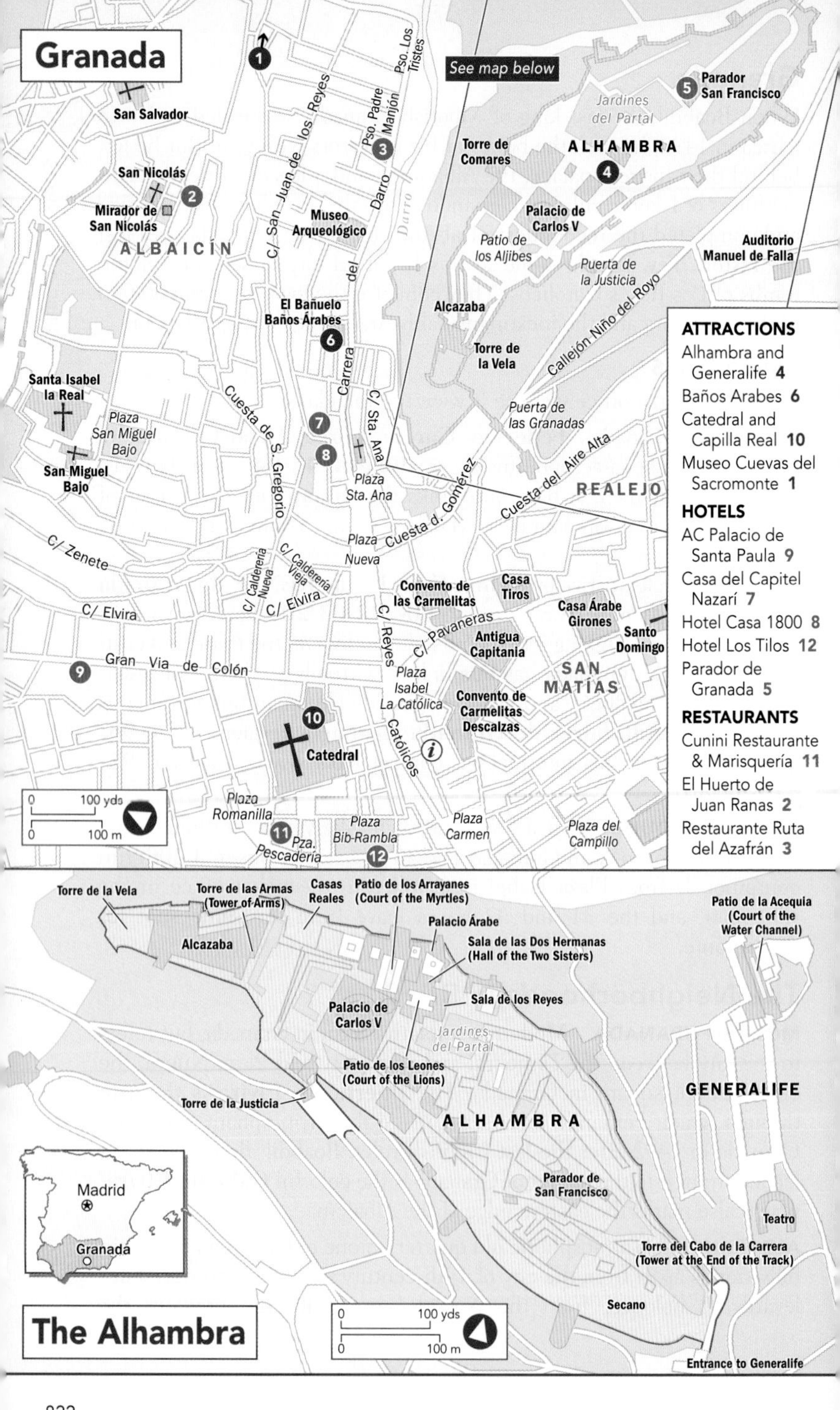
Granada
See map below
San Salvador
San Nicolás
Mirador de San Nicolás
ALBAICÍN
Pso. Los Tristes
Pso. Padre Manjón
C/ San Juan de los Reyes
Carrera del Darro
Darro
Museo Arqueológico
El Bañuelo Baños Árabes
Santa Isabel la Real
Plaza San Miguel Bajo
San Miguel Bajo
Cuesta de S. Gregorio
C/ Sta. Ana
Plaza Sta. Ana
Plaza Nueva
Cuesta d. Goméréz
C/ Zenete
C/ Calderería Nueva
C/ Calderería Vieja
C/ Elvira
C/ Reyes Católicos
C/ Pavaneras
Gran Via de Colón
Plaza Isabel La Católica
Catedral
Plaza Romanilla
Pza. Pescadería
Plaza Bib-Rambla
Plaza Carmen
Plaza del Campillo
Convento de las Carmelitas
Casa Tiros
Antigua Capitania
Convento de Carmelitas Descalzas
Casa Árabe Girones
Santo Domingo
SAN MATÍAS
REALEJO
Cuesta del Aire Alta
Puerta de las Granadas
Torre de la Vela
Alcazaba
Callejón Niño del Royo
Puerta de la Justicia
Patio de los Aljibes
Palacio de Carlos V
Torre de Comares
ALHAMBRA
Jardines del Partal
Parador San Francisco
Auditorio Manuel de Falla
0 100 yds
0 100 m
ATTRACTIONS
Alhambra and Generalife 4
Baños Arabes 6
Catedral and Capilla Real 10
Museo Cuevas del Sacromonte 1
HOTELS
AC Palacio de Santa Paula 9
Casa del Capitel Nazarí 7
Hotel Casa 1800 8
Hotel Los Tilos 12
Parador de Granada 5
RESTAURANTS
Cunini Restaurante & Marisquería 11
El Huerto de Juan Ranas 2
Restaurante Ruta del Azafrán 3
Torre de la Vela
Torre de las Armas (Tower of Arms)
Casas Reales
Patio de los Arrayanes (Court of the Myrtles)
Palacio Árabe
Sala de las Dos Hermanas (Hall of the Two Sisters)
Sala de los Reyes
Alcazaba
Palacio de Carlos V
Jardines del Partal
Patio de los Leones (Court of the Lions)
Torre de la Justicia
ALHAMBRA
Patio de la Acequia (Court of the Water Channel)
GENERALIFE
Parador de San Francisco
Teatro
Torre del Cabo de la Carrera (Tower at the End of the Track)
Secano
Entrance to Generalife
Madrid
Granada
The Alhambra
0 100 yds
0 100 m

Renaissance city that sprung up around the cathedral. The Albaicín and Gypsy caves of Sacromonte farther up the hill (see below) were the homes of marginalized Muslims and Gypsies declared beyond the pale by the Christian conquerors. The narrow labyrinth of crooked streets in the Albaicín was too hilly to tear down in the name of progress; ironically, it is now some of the most desirable real estate in Granada. Its alleyways, cisterns, fountains, plazas, whitewashed houses, villas, and the decaying remnants of the Old City gate have all been preserved. Here and there you can catch a glimpse of a private patio filled with fountains and plants, a traditional, elegant way of life that continues. The plaza known as Mirador San Nicolás is a delightful spot to enjoy a drink at a cafe. It becomes especially romantic at sunset, when the reflected color makes the Alhambra seem to glow on the opposite hill. During the winter and spring, you may even see snow on the peaks of the Sierra Nevada Mountains.

**SACROMONTE** Hundreds of Roma once lived on the "Holy Mountain" on the outskirts of Granada above the Albaicín. The mountain was named for the Christians martyred here, which made it a pilgrimage site. Many of the caves were heavily damaged by rain in 1962, forcing most occupants to seek shelter elsewhere. Nearly all the Roma remaining are in one way or another involved with tourism.

## EXPLORING GRANADA

**Alhambra and Generalife ★★★** PALACE One of Europe's greatest attractions, the stunningly beautiful and celebrated **Calat Alhambra (Red Castle)** is perhaps the most remarkable fortress ever constructed. Islamic architecture in Spain reached its apogee at this palace once occupied by Nasrid princes, their families, and their political and personal functionaries. Although the Alhambra was converted into a lavish palace in the 13th and 14th centuries, it was first built for defensive purposes on an outcropping above the Darro River. The modern city

### Reserving for the Alhambra

The Alhambra is so popular that the government has limited the number of people who can enter each day and has limited the number of tickets purchased by one individual to 10 per day. The best way to enjoy the Alhambra is to arrive first thing in the morning and proceed to the Nasrid Palace as soon as possible (you must enter the palace at the specific time on your ticket). To avoid long ticket lines, buy your tickets in advance. The easiest way is to order online at www.alhambra-tickets.es, or by calling ✆ **95-892-60-31.** Tickets can also be purchased (or picked up) in the city center at the Tienda de la Alhambra, Calle Reyes Católicos, 40. They may also be picked up at the vending machines at the Alhambra entrance. You will need identification to secure your tickets, but once you have them in hand, you can bypass the lines and proceed to the entrance.

The massive fortress of Alhambra, Granada.

of Granada was built across the river from the Alhambra, about 0.8km (½ mile) from its western foundations.

When you first see the Alhambra, its somewhat somber exterior may surprise you. The true delights lie within. Enter through the incongruous 14th-century **Puerta de la Justicia (Gateway of Justice) ★.** Most visitors do not need an expensive guide but will be content to stroll by themselves to see the richly ornamented open-air rooms, the lace-like walls, and the beautiful courtyards built around fountains. Many of the Arabic inscriptions translate to "Only Allah is conqueror."

The strictly defined pathway of the tour begins in the **Mexuar ★★★,** also known as Palacio Nazaríes (Palace of the Nasrids), which is the first of three palaces that compose the Alhambra. This was the main council chamber where the chief ministers met. The largest of these chambers was the Hall of the Mexuar, which Spanish rulers converted to a Catholic chapel in the 1600s. From this chapel, there's a panoramic view over the rooftops of the Albaicín.

Pass through another chamber of the sultan's ministers, the Cuarto Dorado (Golden Room), and you'll find yourself in the small but beautiful **Patio del Mexuar ★★.** Constructed in 1365, this is where the emir sat on giant cushions and listened to the petitions of his subjects, or met privately with his chief ministers. The windows are surrounded by panels and richly decorated with tiles and stucco.

The Palace of the Nasrids was constructed around two courtyards, the **Patio de los Arrayanes (Court of the Myrtles) ★★** and the

**Patio de los Leones (Court of the Lions) ★★★.** The latter was the royal residence.

The Court of the Myrtles contains a narrow reflecting pool banked by myrtle trees. Note the decorative and rather rare tiles, which are arguably the finest in the Alhambra. Behind it is the **Salón de Embajadores (Hall of the Ambassadors) ★★,** with an elaborately carved throne room that was built between 1334 and 1354. The crowning cedar wood dome of this salon evokes the seven heavens of the Muslim cosmos. Here bay windows open onto **panoramic vistas** of the enveloping countryside.

An opening off the Court of the Myrtles leads to the greatest architectural achievement of the Alhambra, the Patio de los Leones (Court of Lions), constructed by Muhammad V. At its center is Andalucía's grandest fountain, which rests on 12 marble lions. The lions represent the hours of the day, the months of the year, and the signs of the zodiac. Legend claims that water flowed from the mouth of a different lion each hour of the day. This courtyard is lined with arcades supported by 124 (count them) slender marble columns. This was the heart of the palace, the private section where the emir and his family retreated.

Opening onto the Court of Lions are other salons of intrigue, notably the Hall of the Two Sisters, **Sala de las Dos Hermanas ★★,** which is named for the two identical large white marble slabs in the pavement. This salon has a stunning dome of carved plaster and is often cited as one of the finest examples of Spanish Islamic architecture.

The nearby **Sala de los Reyes (Hall of Kings) ★** was the great banquet hall of the Alhambra. Its ceiling paintings are on leather and date from the 1300s. A gallery leads to the **Patio de la Reja (Court of the Window Grille) ★,** where Washington Irving lived in furnished rooms and where he began to write *Tales of the Alhambra.*

Before you proceed to the Emperor Carlos V's palace, look at some other gems around the Court of Lions, including the **Baños Reales (Royal Baths) ★,** with their lavish, multicolored decorations. Light enters through star-shaped apertures. To the immediate east of the baths lies the **Daraxa Garden ★,** and to its immediate south the lovely and resplendent **Mirador de Daraxa ★★,** the sultana's private balcony onto Granada.

Move to **Emperor Carlos V's Palace (Palacio de Carlos V) ★★ .** Carlos might have been horrified when he saw a cathedral placed in the middle of the great mosque at Córdoba, but he's also responsible for some architectural confusion in Granada. He did not consider the Nasrid palace grand enough, so in 1526 he ordered Pedro Machuca, a student of Michelangelo, to design him a fitting royal residence. It's quite beautiful, but out of place. Despite its incongruous location, the final

Gardens of the Generalife, Alhambra.

result is one of the purest examples of classical Renaissance architecture in Spain.

Exit the Alhambra via the Puerta de la Justicia, and then circumnavigate the Alhambra's southern foundations until you reach the gardens of the summer palace, where Paseo de los Cipreses quickly leads you to the main building of the **Generalife ★★,** built in the 13th century to overlook the Alhambra and set on 30 lush hectares (74 acres). The sultans used to spend their summers in this palace (pronounced Heh-neh-rah-*lee*-feh), safely locked away with their harems. Don't expect an Alhambra in miniature: The Generalife was always meant to be a retreat, even from the splendors of the Alhambra.

The highlight of the Generalife is its **gardens ★★★.** Of special note is **Escalera del Agua (the Water Staircase) ★,** with water flowing gently down. An enclosed Oriental garden, **Patio de la Acequía ★,** was constructed around a long pool, with rows of water jets making graceful arches above it. The **Patio de la Sultana ★** was the secret rendezvous point for Zoraxda, wife of Sultan Abu Hasan, and her lover, the chief of the Abencerrajes.

Palacio de Carlos V. http://alhambra-patronato.es. ✆ **90-244-12-21.** Combined ticket for Alhambra and Generalife, 15€ adults, 10€ seniors/students, free under 12; Museo de la Alhambra free; garden and Generalife visits 8.40€; illuminated visits

18€. Oct 15–Mar 14 daily 8:30am–6pm, floodlit visits Fri–Sat 8–9:30pm; Mar 15–Oct 14 daily 8:30am–8pm, floodlit visits Fri–Sat 10–11:30pm.

**Baños Arabes** ★ LANDMARK It's remarkable that these 11th-century "baths of the walnut tree," as they were known by the Moors, escaped destruction during the reign of Fernando and Isabel. Among the oldest buildings still standing in Granada, and among the best-preserved Muslim baths in Spain, they predate the Alhambra. Many of the stones used in their construction show the signs of Visigothic and Roman carving.

Carrera del Darro 31. ✆ **95-802-78-00.** Free. Tues–Sat 9am–2:30pm.

**Catedral and Capilla Real** ★★ CATHEDRAL In any other city, this cathedral would be the architectural star. The richly ornate Renaissance building with its spectacular altar is justly celebrated for its beautiful facade and gold-and-white interior. It was begun in 1521 and completed in 1714. Behind the cathedral is the Flamboyant Gothic **Royal Chapel** ★★, where the remains of Isabel and Fernando lie. The coffins are remarkably tiny—a reminder of how short they must have been. The sacristy displays Isabel's personal **art collection** ★★, including works by Rogier van der Weyden and various Spanish and Italian masters.

Plaza de la Lonja, Gran Via de Colón, 5. Catedral ✆ **95-822-29-59.** 4€. Mon–Sat 10:45am–1:15pm/4–7:45pm; winter to 6:45pm. Capilla Real ✆ **95-822-78-48.** 4€. Summer Daily 10:15am–1:30pm/4–7:30pm, Sun from 11am; winter daily 10:15am–1:30pm/3:30–6:30pm, Sun from 11am.

**Museo Cuevas del Sacromonte** ★ MUSEUM The best way to see some of the Sacromonte caves and to learn a bit about Gypsy Granada is to visit this interpretation center, which is a great source of Roma (Gypsy) pride. Several caves are shown as lodgings while others are set up as studios for traditional weaving, pottery, basketry, and metalwork.

Barranco de los Negros. www.sacromontegranada.com. ✆ **95-821-51-20.** 5€. Mid-Mar to mid-Oct daily 10am–8pm, mid-Oct to mid-March daily 10am–6pm. Bus: 35.

## WHERE TO STAY IN GRANADA

**AC Palacio de Santa Paula** ★★★ This adaptation of the 16th-century Convento de Santa Paula and a 12th-century Moorish palace bridges the historic structures with an ultra-modern steel and glass shell. The ambiance of the earlier buildings is maintained in some of the public areas, including the beautiful courtyard of the cloister. Rooms are cool and modern, with ample space. Superior rooms overlook the Moorish courtyard and some deluxe rooms look up at the Alhambra. The Palacio de Santa Paula is Granada's most luxurious hotel, rivaled only by the *parador* on the Alhambra grounds (see box p. 828).

Gran Vía de Colón, 31. www.palaciodesantapaula.com. ✆ **95-880-57-40.** 75 units. Doubles 129€–225€, suites 193€–240€. **Amenities:** Restaurant; bar; gym; sauna; free Wi-Fi.

### Staying at the Alhambra

The **Parador de Granada ★★★** (Real de Alhambra, s/n; www.parador.es; ✆ **95-822-14-40**) has 36 rooms that reflect the architectural and decorative style of the Alhambra. It is one of the most luxurious stays in Spain. It's not quite the same as staying in one of the rooms of the Nasrid Palace, but it's as close as you'll get. If you'd like to wander the grounds after the other tourists have gone home, plan to reserve a room far in advance, but keep in mind that the hotel is inconvenient for visiting the rest of Granada. Double room rates begin at 265€ per night, suites at 631€. For those prices you do get free Wi-Fi.

**Casa del Capitel Nazarí ★** Skip the supplement for a room with a view of the Alhambra, because the view is seriously obstructed and the hotel is worth enjoying in its own right. The lodging takes its name from the original Nasrid capital that helps support the 16th-century building. Historic preservation precluded an elevator, but ground-floor rooms are available. The rooms have carved wooden ceilings in the Nasrid style, and minibars—a luxury that even the emirs didn't enjoy.

Cuesta Aceituneros, 6. www.hotelcasacapitel.com. ✆ **95-821-52-60.** 18 units. Doubles 75€–140€. **Amenities:** Free Wi-Fi.

**Hotel Casa 1800 ★★** Sister to the property by the same name in Sevilla (p. 813), this pretty and welcoming hotel is tucked into a small cul-de-sac off Plaza Nueva, making the location both convenient yet surprisingly quiet. The decorative style nods to baroque revival, with curlicue flourishes in the decorative painting and a palette of browns, tans, and golds. Standard rooms are quite snug but feature queen-size beds. Superior and deluxe rooms have either two twins or a king. Several rooms have exposed brick walls and exposed beams on the ceilings.

Calle Benalúa, 11. www.hotelcasa1800.com. ✆ **95-821-08-00.** 25 units. Doubles 85€–230€, suites 155€–310€. **Amenities:** Afternoon tea; free Wi-Fi.

**Hotel Los Tilos ★** This good-value property has large rooms for the price, with brightly painted walls and modest furnishings. Many rooms have views of the plaza filled with good tapas bars and cafes. The location in the heart of city and the availability of triple rooms (good for families) are big pluses, as is the top-floor balcony where guests often gather in the evening with a bottle of wine.

Plaza Bib-Rambla, 4. www.hotellostilos.com. ✆ **95-826-67-12.** 30 units. Doubles 42€–75€. **Amenities:** Free Wi-Fi in public areas.

## WHERE TO EAT IN GRANADA

**Cunini Restaurante & Marisquería ★★★** SEAFOOD Eating seafood tapas at Cunini is a quintessential Grenadino experience. Granada restaurants are extraordinarily generous with free tapas, and Cunini is more generous than most. You can sample much of the menu here by standing at the bar and ordering drink after drink. (The tapas get better with each drink, and that's not the alcohol talking.) If you want to enjoy the best seafood in Granada, have a seat in the restaurant or on the plaza for the likes of monkfish in white wine or a heaping plate of fried red mullet.

Plaza de Pescadería, 14. ✆ **95-826-75-87.** Mains 13€–33€. Mon–Sat noon–2am. Bus: 23, 30, 31, 32.

**El Huerto de Juan Ranas ★** ANDALUCIAN Chef-owner Juan Ranas is a romantic when it comes to dining, and his "garden" at one corner of the Mirador San Nicolás assumes a magic elegance once the candles are lit. He serves an excellent tapas menu in the garden terrace upstairs, including his creamy croquettes. The downstairs dining room with linen-clad tables and a profusion of glassware features an updated version of Andalucían classics. The roast lamb shoulder, for example, is cooked slowly at a very low temperature until it falls apart, and the Moorish savory pastries are filled with fork-tender meat and chunks of eggplant.

Calle de Atarazana, 8 (Mirador de San Nicolás). www.elhuertodejuanranas.com. ✆ **95-828-69-25.** Mains 20€–42€. Fixed-price menus 48€–60€. Bus: 31. Daily 8–11:30pm.

**Restaurante Ruta del Azafrán ★** ANDALUCIAN Contemporary Spanish cooking with a decidedly North African accent is only half the attraction here. There are also great views of the Alhambra. Choices range from inexpensive couscous to a grilled sirloin steak, with a number of salad entrees at lunch. The wine list is strong on local whites and wines from such emerging regions as Jumilla.

Paseo del Padre Manjón, 1. www.rutadelazafran.com. ✆ **95-822-68-82.** Mains 12€–18€. Bus: 31. Sun–Thurs 1–4pm, 8–11pm; Fri–Sat 1–4pm, 8pm–midnight.

### SHOPPING

**Alcaicería,** once the Moorish silk market, is next to the cathedral in the lower city. The narrow streets of this rebuilt village of shops are filled with vendors selling the arts and crafts of Granada province. Alcaicería offers a good assortment of tiles, castanets, and wire figures of Don Quijote chasing windmills. A more interesting shopping experience is found in the souk of the alleyways of **Calderería Vieja** and **Calderería Nueva,** where wall hangings, pillows, silk tassels, and silver teapots abound. The area is a low-key version of what you'd find in North Africa, and a certain amount of bargaining is not only permitted—it's expected.

### ENTERTAINMENT & NIGHTLIFE

Watching the sun set from the **Mirador San Nicolás** is one of the special experiences in this city. But once you have seen the Alhambra glow from the reflected light, the night will still be young. If you enjoy tapas-hopping, Granada is your city. Its bars usually offer the most generous tapas we have encountered anywhere in Spain. One of the most popular tapas bars is **El Agua Casa de Vinos** (Placeta de Algibe de Trillo, 7; ✆ **95-822-43-46**), a lively place with an adjoining restaurant. Another historic spot with a lovely patio is **Pilar del Toro** (Calle Hospital de Santa Ana, 12; www.pilardeltoro.es; ✆ **95-822-54-70**), near the cathedral and Plaza Nueva. After a few stops, you may find that you don't need dinner.

## Málaga

Málaga seems to prove the adage that flamenco styles reflect their birthplace. Andalucía's second-largest city is as deeply nuanced and improvisational as the *malagueña*. Yet travelers often give it short shrift as they rush from the airport or train station to the Costa del Sol resorts, not realizing that Málaga has superb beaches of its own, historic sites, and a strong identity with native son Pablo Picasso. To have it all, base yourself in Málaga, use the train to spend a few hours a day on a Costa del Sol beach, and return to the vibes of a real Spanish city by nightfall. The redeveloped port district has a striking yacht marina, a romantic walkway by the water, and a new district of shopping, restaurants, and nightlife stretching from the Parque de Málaga to the harbor lighthouse.

### ESSENTIALS

Málaga's tourist office website, **www.malagaturismo.com**, features five themed audiotours in English, as well as a free downloadable app with extensive detail on 85 sites around the city

Calle Larios in Málaga.

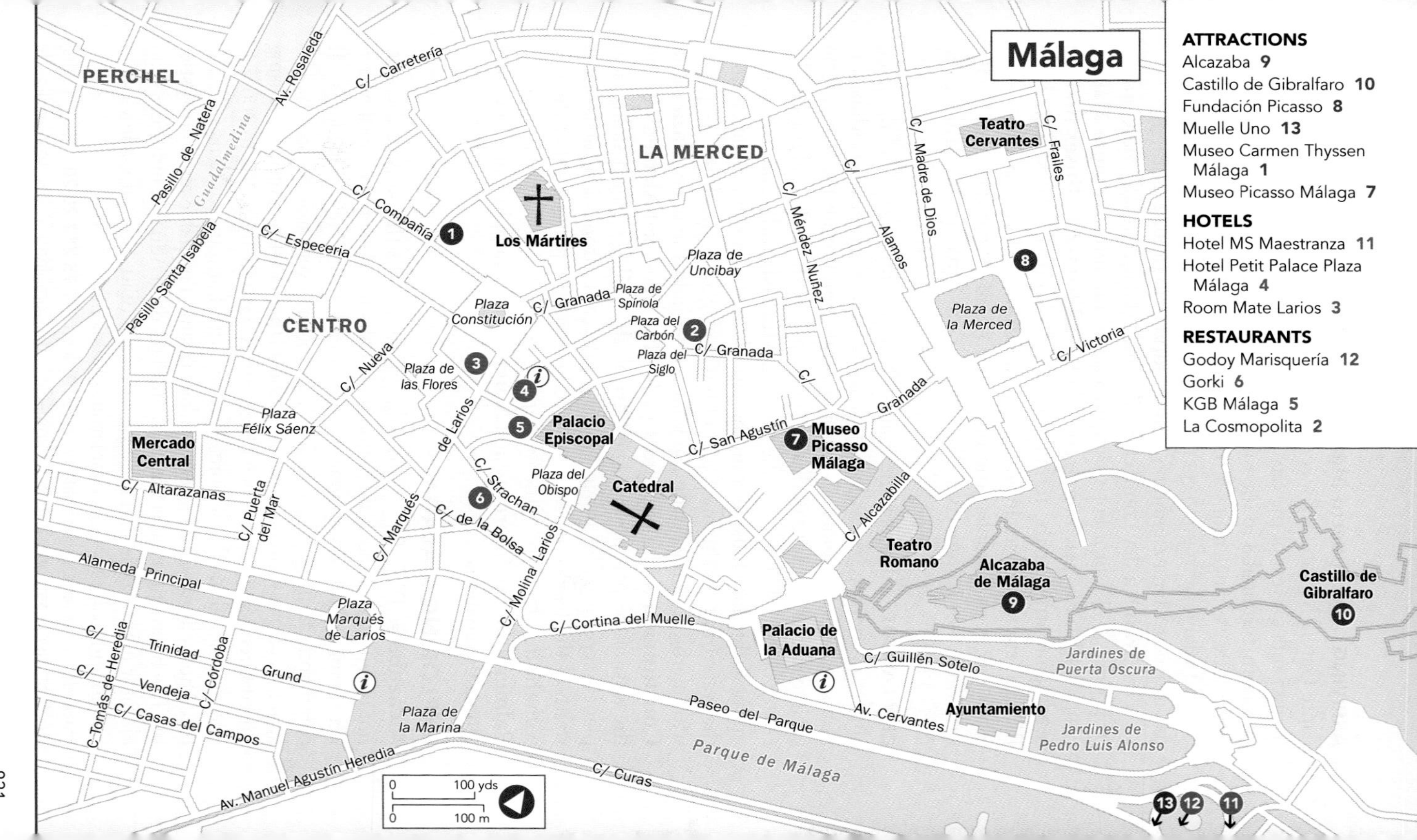
Málaga
ATTRACTIONS
Alcazaba 9
Castillo de Gibralfaro 10
Fundación Picasso 8
Muelle Uno 13
Museo Carmen Thyssen Málaga 1
Museo Picasso Málaga 7
HOTELS
Hotel MS Maestranza 11
Hotel Petit Palace Plaza Málaga 4
Room Mate Larios 3
RESTAURANTS
Godoy Marisquería 12
Gorki 6
KGB Málaga 5
La Cosmopolita 2
PERCHEL
LA MERCED
CENTRO
Los Mártires
Teatro Cervantes
Plaza de la Merced
Plaza de Uncibay
Plaza de Spínola
Plaza del Carbón
Plaza del Siglo
Plaza Constitución
Plaza de las Flores
Plaza Félix Sáenz
Plaza del Obispo
Palacio Episcopal
Catedral
Museo Picasso Málaga
Mercado Central
Teatro Romano
Alcazaba de Málaga
Castillo de Gibralfaro
Palacio de la Aduana
Ayuntamiento
Jardines de Puerta Oscura
Jardines de Pedro Luis Alonso
Plaza Marqués de Larios
Plaza de la Marina
Parque de Málaga
Paseo del Parque
C/ Carretería
Av. Rosaleda
Pasillo de Natera
Guadalmedina
Pasillo Santa Isabela
C/ Compañía
C/ Especeria
C/ Granada
C/ Méndez Nuñez
C/ Alamos
C/ Madre de Dios
C/ Frailes
C/ Victoria
C/ Nueva
de Larios
C/ San Agustín
C/ Strachan
C/ de la Bolsa
C/ Marqués
C/ Molina Larios
C/ Alcazabilla
C/ Altarazanas
C/ Puerta del Mar
Alameda Principal
C/ Cortina del Muelle
C/ Guillén Sotelo
Av. Cervantes
C/ Trinidad
Grund
C/ Córdoba
C/ Vendeja
C. Tomás de Heredia
C/ Casas del Campos
Av. Manuel Agustín Heredia
C/ Curas
0 100 yds
0 100 m

**ARRIVING** **Aeropuerto Málaga-Costa del Sol (AGP)** (Av. Comandante García Morato; www.aena-aeropuertos.es; ✆ **91-321-10-00**) lies 8km (5 miles) west of the city center. There's an 8-minute train connection from Terminal 3 to the main rail station on the western edge of the city (2.10€); change trains at **Estación María Zambrano** for a "Centro Ciudad-Alameda" train to get to the town center. Twelve AVE **trains** per day arrive at María Zambrano from Madrid (trip time: 2½ hr.).

Ten **trains** a day connect Sevilla and Málaga, usually via Córdoba (trip time: 2–2½ hr.). For ticket prices and rail information in Málaga, contact RENFE (www.renfe.com; ✆ **90-232-03-20**). **Buses** from all over Spain arrive at the terminal on the Paseo de los Tilos behind the RENFE station. Buses include 8 per day from Madrid (trip time: 7 hr.), 5 per day from Córdoba (trip time: 3 hr.), and 10 per day from Sevilla (trip time: 3 hr.). From coastal resorts, you can **drive** to Málaga along the N-340/E-15.

**CITY LAYOUT** Although the train and bus stations are west of the river, almost everything you will want to see is located to the east. Málaga is primarily a strolling city progressing gently uphill from the ocean. The skyline makes it easy to navigate, as the spire of the cathedral rises in the center of the Old City, and the restored **Moorish walls** stitch their way up the Gibralfaro hillside from the old **Alcazaba**, a short distance from the waterfront. In the main part of town, elegant **Calle Larios**—paved with marble and lined with top boutiques—links the main **Plaza de la Constitución** to the waterfront parks. The tree-lined **Alameda** lies to the west of the port proper. The **Parque de Málaga,** full of subtropical plants, separates the urban city from the waterfront. The dock areas south of the Parque de Málaga have become the playground of the city with the development of the former port as the delightful walkways of **El Palmeral de las Sopresas** and **Muelle Uno** shopping, nightlife, and dining destinations.

## EXPLORING MÁLAGA

**Alcazaba ★** PALACE This palace-fortress tells the story of the warrior potentates of the Taifa period in Andalucía, when the central Moorish empire had disintegrated into small squabbling kingdoms. It commands an irregular rocky spur that towers over most of the city. The largest sections were built between the 11th and 14th centuries, reusing fluted Greek-style columns with acanthus capitals from 200 to 300 B.C. and occasional blocks of Roman stones with Latin inscriptions still visible. The well-preserved interior palace retains a palpable air of domesticity. The main entrance is via steps on Plaza de la Aduana, but there is an elevator entrance behind the Ayuntamiento (City Hall) at Calle Guillén Sotelo and Calle Francisco Bejarrano Robles.

Plaza de la Aduana, Alcazabilla. www.malaga.eu. ✆ **95-212-20-20.** 2.20€ adults, 0.60€ students/seniors; free Sun 2pm–closing. Combined ticket to Castillo de

Gibralfaro 3.55€. Bus: 4, 18, 19, 24, or 135. Apr–Sept 9am–8pm (Mon until 6pm); Oct–Mar daily 9am–6pm.





**Castillo de Gibralfaro ★** CASTLE The ruins of this Moorish castle-fortress crown a hill overlooking Málaga and the Mediterranean. The walls are crumbling and the keep is overgrown with weeds, but views are spectacular. Walking to the castle from town is fairly strenuous, and muggings have been reported over the years. Still, the walk can be atmospheric if it's not too hot. Otherwise, take the bus from the cathedral.
Castllo del Gibralfaro. 2.20€ adults, 0.60€ students/seniors; free Sun 2pm–closing. Combined ticket to Alcazaba 3.55€. Microbus: 35. Daylight hours.

**Fundación Picasso ★** MUSEUM Picasso was born in Málaga in 1881 in a rented apartment at Plaza de la Merced, 15, and moved two doors down in 1883. He lived there until the family moved to Galicia in 1891. Picasso never really worked in Málaga, but the city was a profound influence. The Fundación Picasso preserves his birth home as a small museum, showing artifacts ranging from baby Pablo's umbilical band and christening dress to some paintings by his father, José Ruiz Blasco. Other exhibits explore Picasso's insistence on his Spanish identity, especially his love of bullfighting and flamenco. When you leave the Casa Natal, look for blue-and-white tile plaques around the Plaza de la Merced that indicate the second family home, the place where his father used to hang out with other artists, and the Iglesia Santiago where Pablo was baptized.
Plaza de la Merced, 15. www.fundacionpicasso.es. ✆ **95-206-02-15.** 2€; admission to Casa Natal and temporary exhibition hall 3€; free for seniors, students, and under age 17; free for all on Sun. Bus: 36, 1, 37. Daily 9:30am–8pm.

**Muelle Uno ★★** LANDMARK This stretch of waterfront from Plaza de General Torrijos to the 1817 Malagueta lighthouse is Málaga's newest dining, shopping, and nightlife district. Broad walkways line the waterfront, and glass cubes containing boutiques, bars, and restaurants stretch the entire distance. Walking along the waterfront at night provides a romantic vantage back on the lighted Moorish walls that zigzag up the hill from the city below. Doglegging off Muelle Uno is El Palmeral de las Sopresas, an elegant palm-lined walkway along the harbor. Where the two meet is "El Cubo," a large glass box where the Centre Pompidou Málaga opened in 2015 as the first satellite museum of the Paris contemporary art institution outside France. At the same junction at the docks are a number of boats that offer site-seeing cruises of the bay.
Centre Pompidou Málaga. www.centrepompidoumalaga.com. ✆ **95-192-60-60.** Call or visit website for admissions and hours.

**Museo Carmen Thyssen Málaga ★★** MUSEUM Located just off the Plaza de la Constitución in a Renaissance palace, this museum displays Spanish paintings circa 1825 to 1925 collected by Carmen

Thyssen of the Museo Thyssen-Bornemisza in Madrid. By concentrating on this narrow slice of European art, the baroness acquired the very best work of the era. Ground-floor galleries feature the romantic paintings of the early and mid-19th century that made Spain into one of the most popular artistic clichés of the day. They include colorful landscapes with even more colorful inhabitants: Roma, flamenco dancers, bullfighters, and ladies clad in mantillas demurely fluttering their fans. One floor up, galleries showcase a more naturalistic, moody style, as well as the parallel "précieux" style in which every flower petal and costume ruffle is articulated. The second-floor gallery shows Italian and Spanish sculpture and painting from 13th-century Gothic through the museum's sole Velázquez portrait. The third floor hosts temporary exhibitions.

Plaza Carmen Thyssen, Calle Compañía, 10. www.carmenthyssenmalaga.org. ✆ **90-230-31-31.** Main collection 6€, 3.50€ seniors/students, free under age 12; temporary exhibitions 6€, 2.50€ seniors/students; combined tickets 9€, 5€ seniors/students. Tues–Sun 10am–8pm.

**Museo Picasso Málaga ★★★** MUSEUM Picasso last visited Málaga at the age of 19, but toward the end of his life expressed the wish that his work be displayed in the city of his birth. Continued gifts by Picasso's daughter-in-law and grandson have brought this collection to 285 works, most of which are unfamiliar since they came from the artist's private collection. Because Picasso's greatest hits are elsewhere, this museum focuses on teasing out the artist's multifaceted genius and showing his different styles. During the same period that he was making abstract Cubist portraits, for example, he also drew delicate portraits of his son so realistic that they could be photographs.

Calle San Agustín, 8. www.museopicassomalaga.org. ✆ **90-244-33-77.** 7€; temporary exhibitions 5.50€; seniors/students half price; free under age 18. Free to all Sun 6–8pm. Daily 10am–8pm.

## ORGANIZED TOURS

For an old, congested city, Málaga has convenient and well-marked bicycle paths. For a two-wheel overview of the city, connect with **Bike 2 Málaga** (Calle Vendeja, 6; www.biketoursmalaga.com; ✆ **65-067-70-63**). Of the company's several tours, the general "City Bike Tour" takes 3 hours and costs 22€ adults, 17€ students, and 12€ children.

## WHERE TO STAY IN MÁLAGA

**Hotel MS Maestranza ★** The hotel is so close to its namesake bullring that guests in rooms on the Calle Maestranza side can see bullfights from the balconies on floors 9 to 12. The other views are maybe more scenic, taking in the beautifully reconstructed yachting port and the lighted Moorish walls rising from the seaside city to the Gibralfaro. Regular rooms are a little tight but well-designed, and the location is perfect

## BEACHES IN THE 'burbs

Starting in the 1950s, tour packagers jammed Northern European bargain seekers into concrete high-rise hotels on Spain's Costa del Sol, which is really a developer's name for the beach villages west of Málaga. About 15km (10 miles) of sandy beaches stretch from Málaga's western city limits through **Torremolinos, Benalmadena,** and **Fuengirola.** The towns are very crowded in high season, but the beaches are free and the water is clear and blue. Beat the crush by staying in Málaga and riding the commuter train to the beach for the day. Trains run every 20 to 30 minutes from Málaga's Estación María Zambrano, taking 18 minutes to Torremolinos or 43 minutes to Fuengirola. Tickets are 2.65€ or 3.55€ one way. The best swimming and sunbathing beaches are in Torremolinos: El Bajondillo and La Carihuela, which borders an old fishing village with good restaurants.

**Kite flying on a Málaga beach.**

for enjoying the nightlife and restaurants of Muelle Uno across the street or walking to the swimming beaches of Málaga.

Av. Canóvas del Castillo, 1. www.mshoteles.com. ✆ **95-221-36-10.** 90 units. Doubles 81€–190€, suites 114€–220€. **Amenities:** Bar; spa; Jacuzzi; sauna, gym; free Wi-Fi.

**Hotel Petit Palace Plaza Málaga ★** Tucked into a small street just a few paces off Plaza de la Constitución, this high-tech hotel offers the usual amenities of the chain, including a laptop in every room. Furnishings are smoothly contemporary and the bathrooms have new porcelain fixtures and high-tech hydromassage showers. Big beds make the small double rooms a little tight, but they are quite functional once you figure out what to do with the luggage. Triple and quad rooms are also available.

Calle Nicasio, 3. www.petitpalace.com. ✆ **95-222-21-32.** 66 units. Doubles 81€–149€. **Amenities:** Restaurant; concierge; gym; free Wi-Fi.

**Room Mate Larios ★★** A striking Art Deco era building near the head of Calle Larios, this Room Mate is set up with several self-sufficient apartments ranging from studios with a cooking corner to units with a separate bedroom and upstairs loft sleeping area. Expanses of contrasting marble and high-sheen black paint make the public areas look as if they had traveled in time from Paris circa 1930. Standard rooms are tight but well-designed, and apartments are spacious. The Picasso Museum is about a 5-minute walk away, and the city's best shopping is just outside the front door. If Larios is full, Room Mate may suggest its other hotel, Lola, in a less convenient neighborhood.

Calle Marqués de Larios, 2. www.room-matehotels.com. ✆ **95-222-22-00.** 41 units. Doubles 75€–139€, suites 130€–195€, apartments 124€–211€. **Amenities:** Restaurant; bar; free Wi-Fi.

## WHERE TO EAT IN MÁLAGA

**Godoy Marisquería ★★** SEAFOOD A pioneer on Muelle Uno, this glittering glass jewel box offers a menu primarily of shellfish—augmented by some fin fish, a couple of steaks, and a few ham-based appetizers. The house specialty is a Málagan version of *zarzuela* consisting of large pieces of monkfish with clams and cockles in a tomato-fish broth. For more casual munching, order a good white wine and an assortment of fried anchovies, red mullet, tiny squid, and pieces of flounder.

Muelle Uno, 34-35. www.marisqueriagodoy.com. ✆ **95-229-03-12.** Mains 12€–25€; shellfish tasting menu 59€. Bus: 251. Tues–Sat 1:30–3:30pm and 8:30–11pm.

**Gorki ★★** SPANISH Just off Calle Larios, this handsome dining room with an equally attractive group of street tables can serve you everything from a single oyster with a sip of Manzanilla to a full-blown multi-course meal accompanied by a flight of wines. For the full meal, order a seared tuna steak or black rice with sautéed cuttlefish and saffron aioli. Or dine lighter on burgers, finger sandwiches of smoked salmon or curried chicken, and plates of goat cheese melted over fresh tomatoes.

Calle Strachan, 6. www.gorki.es. ✆ **95-222-14-66.** Tapas 1.50€–4€; Mains 9€–16€. Daily noon–midnight.

**KGB Málaga ★★** CONTEMPORARY TAPAS KGB offers fun dining on fanciful finger food. Like many star chefs, Kisco García of Córdoba gets a kick out of serving *tapas creativas*. His small plates show a playful sensibility and a willingness to adapt world cuisine flavors to Spanish dishes—sushi-like small strips of butterfish, or barely seared

### A Perfect Málaga Beach Evening

It takes about an hour to stroll along Playa de la Malagueta from the port to Playa Pedregalejo. You'll pass surfcasters, colonies of feral cats living in the rocks, and on a Saturday afternoon, barefoot brides having their pictures taken on the beach. Fish-house restaurants line the beach at Pedregalejo. One of the best is Manuel Cabra's **Restaurante El Cabra ★★** (Paseo Maritimo Pedregal, 17; www.restauranteelcabra.es; ✆ **95-225-15-95**). Specialties include grilled sardines on a wooden stake and a *fritura Malagueña* of mixed fried fish. Linger as long as you want and then walk 2 blocks up from the beach to Avenida Juan Sebastian Elcano to catch the 11, 33, or 34 bus back to Alameda Principal.

cubes of shark. Russian flavors inform his "dishes from the steppes" (in honor of the Cold War name of the bar). KGB also pays homage to other chefs with dishes like Paco Roncero's version of *patatas bravas,* and Angels Serra's version of the Malgueña crispy shrimp omelet. Drinks are as reasonable as the plates of food.

Calle Fresca, 12. www.facebook.com/kgbmalaga. ✆ **95-222-68-51.** Tapas 3.50€–7.50€. Mon–Sat 12:30–4:30pm and 8:30pm–12:30am.

**La Cosmopolita ★** SPANISH A few paces off Plaza del Siglo, this breezy little spot is a midday favorite for Malagueños. Many show up just for the big sandwiches made on baguettes from Las Garrochas bakery. The signature sandwich is the Don José (aka Pepito) with sliced veal, roasted peppers, and grilled octopus. Other highlights include a creamy baby squid risotto, veal steak in mustard sauce, and fried eggs with baby fava beans. On weekdays, La Cosmopolita also serves breakfast.

Calle José Denis Belgrano, 3. ✆ **95-221-58-27.** Tapas 2.50€–3.50€. Mains 12€–19€. Mon–Fri 8:30am–midnight, Sat–Sun noon–12:30am.

## SHOPPING

**Calle Larios** has most of the city's top boutiques, though many are familiar international brands. For quirkier boutiques, check the side streets. **Muelle Uno** is also lined with shops, including **reunión creadores,** Local 1.B (✆ **62-960-94-04**), a collaborative of contemporary craftspeople. Their jewelry and bags are particularly striking. Many craftspeople set up outdoor booths along the Muelle on Sundays.

## ENTERTAINMENT & NIGHTLIFE

Nightlife in Málaga is like nightlife in most big Spanish cities. Spaniards gather to drink, snack, and talk. You'll find tapas scenes on the side streets from Calle Larios, along Calle Granada, and along Muelle Uno.

For music and dancing, try the live band venue **ZZ Pub** (Calle Tejón y Rodríguez, 6; www.zzpub.es; ✆ **95-244-15-95**), which is big with university students. Performances start around 10:30pm and end around 4 to 5am.

Two beautifully restored theaters—**Teatro Echegaray** (Calle Echegaray, 6; www.teatroechegaray.es; ✆ **95-222-41-00**), and **Teatro Cervantes de Málaga** (Ramos Marin, s/n; www.teatrocervantes.es; ✆ **95-222-41-00**), present musical concerts, flamenco, dance, and Spanish-language theater.

# [Fast FACTS] SPAIN

### Business Hours

Banks open Monday to Friday 9:30am to 2pm and Saturday 9:30am to 1pm. Most other offices are open Monday to Friday 9am to 5 or 5:30pm; the longtime practice of early closings in summer seems to be dying out. In restaurants, lunch is usually 1 to 4pm and dinner 9 or 10pm to 11:30pm or midnight. Many bars and taverns open at 8am, others at noon. Most stay open until 1:30am or later. Major stores are open Monday to Saturday from 9:30am to 8pm; smaller shops often take a siesta, doing business 9:30am to 1:30pm and 4:30 to 8pm. Hours often vary from store to store.

### Currency

Spain is a member of the European Union and uses the E.U. common currency, the euro (€). See p. 860 for information on money and costs.

### Doctors & Dentists

All hotel front desks keep a list of doctors available in their area; most of them are fluent in English.

### Embassies & Consulates:

**Australia:** Torre Espacio, Paseo de la Castellana, Madrid; www.spain.embassy.gov.au; ✆ **91-353-66-00,** or 93-362-37-92 in Barcelona.

**Canada:** Nuñez de Balboa, 35, Madrid; www.espana.gc.ca; ✆ **91-423-32-50** Madrid, 93-412-72-36 in Barcelona.

**New Zealand:** Travesera de Gracia 64, Barcelona; www.nzembassy.com/spain; ✆ **93-209-03-99.**

**United Kingdom:** Torre Espacio, Paseo de la Castellana, Madrid; www.gov.uk/government/world/spain; ✆ **91-714-63-00** Madrid, or 90-210-93-56 in Barcelona.

**United States:** Serrano 75, Madrid. http://madrid.usembassy.gov; ✆ **91-587-22-00.**

### Emergencies

Dial ✆ **112** for police, ambulance, paramedics, and the fire department.

### Pharmacies

To find an open pharmacy *(farmacia)* outside normal business hours, check the list of stores posted on the door of any drugstore. The law requires drugstores to operate on a rotating system of hours so that there's always a drugstore open somewhere, even Sunday at midnight.

### Post Offices

Sending a postcard or letter to the U.S. starts at 1€. To calculate the prices, visit http://correos.es. You can also buy stamps at any place that sells tobacco. Most post offices are open Monday to Friday 9am to 5pm.

# PLANNING YOUR TRIP TO EUROPE

12

by Donald Strachan

A little planning goes a long way, especially when you are traveling to and through a continent with several different languages, transport systems, airlines, festivals, and sights to see. This chapter provides a variety of invaluable aids, including information on how to get there from the U.S. and Canada, the U.K., and Australia or New Zealand; the most efficient and budget-friendly ways of getting around; tips on where to stay; and quick, on-the-ground resources for savvy travel around Europe.

## GETTING THERE

### By Plane

Pretty much every major world airline offers competitive fares to a variety of European cities. Price wars break out regularly, deals come on- and off-stream, and tariffs can change overnight. The key factor determining what you'll pay is **season:** Tickets tend to be cheaper if you fly off season. **High season** on most routes is usually from June to mid-September and around Christmas and New Year—the most expensive and most crowded time to travel. **Shoulder season** in most countries is from April to May and mid-September to October. **Low season**—usually with the cheapest fares and regular aggressive offers—is from November to mid-December and January to March. You can sometimes save money by flying midweek, too, or by spending at least a Saturday night in your destination.

Begin thinking about flying plans at least 6 months ahead of time. Consider exchange rate movements: Fares may be calculated in U.S. dollars, British pounds, or euros, depending on the airline. The key window for finding a **deal** is usually between 5 and 6 months ahead of your departure according to a massive study of some 21 million fare transactions by the Airline Reporting Corporation (a middleman between travel agencies and the airlines). They also found that those who booked on a Sunday statistically found the best rates (on average they paid 19% less than those who booked midweek).

The glory days of generous **frequent flyer programs** and bucket-loads of free miles are no more, but those who collect miles via credit cards (rather than trying to fly to get them) are having better luck getting free trips nowadays. The key strategy is to get a card that will work with a number of airlines, rather than one branded by a particular airline (as

PREVIOUS PAGE: **Gare du Nord railway station, Paris.**

those usually have less generous rates of return and more draconian fees). The forum **Flyertalk.com** is a handy resource for learning how to get the most out of your miles (both for airlines and hotels); such companies as AwardMagic.com and IFlyWithMiles.com can help stressed travelers redeem miles for flights for a flat fee that's usually far less than a ticket from the United States to Europe would have cost.

If you're not using miles, remember that the cheapest way between two points may not always be a straight line. Flying into a major European hub, particularly Milan, Dublin, or Reykjavik (currently) is often cheaper than flying direct to your final destination. If you're heading to the U.K., consider entering via Dublin, Ireland to save on Air Passenger Duty (APD, the British flight tax). Such newish airlines as **XL, WOW Airlines,** and **Norwegian** have been offering particularly good values for travel from the United States to Europe. Run searches through the regular online agents such as Expedia, as well as metasearch engines like **DoHop.com**, **Kayak.com**, **Skyscanner.net**, and **Momondo.com**. For complex journeys, with multiple departures, doing multiple searches (so such affordable intra-European airlines Germanwings, EasyJet and Ryanair show up on the search) is a good way to find deals; a specialist flight agent such as **RoundtheWorld Flights.com** or **AirTreks.com** will also likely save you money.

### Don't Stow It—Ship It

Though pricey, it's sometimes worthwhile for North Americans heading to Europe to travel luggage-free. Specialists in door-to-door luggage delivery include **Virtual Bellhop** (www.virtualbellhop.com; **866/416-7447** in the U.S. and Canada) and **Luggage Express** (www.myluggageexpress.com; ✆ **866/416-7447** in the U.S. and Canada).

## Arriving from the United Kingdom

Travelers heading to the Continent from the United Kingdom have a range of options. High-speed **rail services** connect London's **St. Pancras International Station** with Paris and Brussels, via the **Channel Tunnel.** There are also direct trains to Lille and Disneyland Paris all year, and seasonal direct trains to Avignon, Provence, and the French Alps, terminating at Bourg St. Maurice (the so-called "Snow Train"). In the U.K., make reservations for the train by calling **Eurostar** on ✆ **03432/186-186;** in North America, book online at **www.eurostar.com**, or contact **Rail Europe** (www.raileurope.com; ✆ **800/622-8600** in the U.S. or **800/361-7245** in Canada).

A number of **ferry** companies link England's southern coast with the Channel ports of northern **France** and **Spain.** Ferry route search and booking site **Aferry.co.uk** is invaluable for any traveler planning to use ferries anywhere in Europe.

The quickest way for drivers to cross the English Channel is via a car-transporting train that connects Folkestone, southern England, and Calais via the **Channel Tunnel.** Prices tend to be higher than for the ferry (see above), but crossing time is only around 35 minutes. Book online at **www.eurotunnel.com**. Many car-rental companies won't let you rent a car in Britain and take it to the Continent, so always check ahead if you're considering that option.

Although travel by long-distance bus is slower and less comfortable than travel by train, if you're on a tight budget you could opt for one of **Eurolines'** (www.eurolines.com; ✆ **44-8717-8177**) regular departures from London's Victoria Coach Station to destinations across Europe. **Megabus** (www.megabus.com; ✆ **44-141/352-4444,** or 44-141/332-9644 from outside the U.K.) offers budget fares between London and Paris, Amsterdam, Brussels, or Boulogne, France.

# GETTING AROUND

## By Train

In Europe, the shortest—and often cheapest—distance between two points is usually lined with rail tracks. Compared to the United States, for example, European trains are less expensive, far more advanced in many ways, and the rail systems are certainly more extensive. Although it doesn't rival modern Asian rail networks such as Japan's, the European rail system still ranks as one of the best in the world: Not always integrated, and with occasional ticketing frustrations that vary from country to country, but a fine way to travel nonetheless.

Modern **high-speed trains** (traveling up to around 180 mph) make the rails faster than the plane for short journeys; airlines have gone into rapid decline on routes such as London–Brussels, Barcelona–Madrid, and Milan–Rome that have efficient high-speed links. **Overnight trains** get you where you're going without wasting valuable daylight hours—and you save money on lodging to boot.

### SOME IMPORTANT TRAIN NOTES

Many European high-speed trains require you to pay a **supplement** in addition to the regular ticket fare. It's included when you buy tickets, but not usually in any prepaid rail pass, so check at the ticket window before boarding; otherwise, the conductor will sell you the supplement on the train—along with a fine. **Seat reservations** (from 10€ up) are required on some high-speed runs, too. You can usually reserve a seat within a few hours of departure, but be on the safe side and book your seat a few days in advance for any key connections you're building into an itinerary. You need to reserve any sleeping couchette or sleeping berth too.

With some exceptions, there's usually no need to buy individual train tickets or make seat reservations many months before you leave home. However, it's always wise to reserve a seat on the **Eurostar,** as England's **bank holidays** (long weekends with holiday Mondays) book the train solid with Londoners taking a short vacation to Paris or Brussels. Tickets go on sale 120 days before departure, and you'll usually bag the best prices if you book early and avoid Fridays and Sundays. The overnight **Thello** train (www.thello.com; Paris to Milan, Rome, and Venice) is another service worth reserving well ahead of time. You won't save any money, because tariffs are fixed, but because there's only one service each way per day, booking early will help with itinerary planning.

The difference between **first class** and **second class** on European trains is often minor—a matter of 1 or 2 inches of extra padding and maybe a bit more elbowroom. However, upgrades can sometimes be fairly cheap (for first-class seats booked in advance on weekends in the U.K., for example). There's sometimes a complimentary snack thrown in, along with free Wi-Fi. So, our general advice is: Upgrade if it doesn't cost very much to do so, but don't break the bank. Overnight trains can provide more for your upgrade, in terms of space and privacy, but you'll pay for the privilege.

European **train stations** are usually as clean and efficient as the trains, if a bit chaotic at times. In stations you'll find departures boards showing the track number and timetables for regularly scheduled runs (departures are sometimes on a yellow poster, too). Many stations also have tourist offices, banks with ATMs, and newsstands where you can buy phone cards, bus and metro tickets, maps, and local English-language event magazines. Some have shopping malls and hotels, or even public showers.

You can get more details about train travel in Europe by contacting **Rail Europe** (www.raileurope.com; also ✆ **0871/231-0790** in the U.K.) Other excellent agents worth consulting for planning assistance and advance ticket or pass sales include **International Rail** (www.internationalrail.com; ✆ **0871/231-0790** in the U.K.) and **TrainsEurope** (www.trainseurope.co.uk; ✆ **0871/700-7722** in the U.K.). Note that schedules are confirmed and tickets released between 60 and 90 days from travel dates. The most valuable bookmark for planning complex European rail journeys is **The Man in Seat Sixty-One** (www.seat61.com).

## RAIL PASSES

The greatest value in European travel has traditionally been the **rail pass,** a single ticket allowing you unlimited travel (or travel on a certain number of days) within a set time period. If you plan on going all over Europe by train, buying a rail pass will end up being less expensive than buying individual tickets. Plus, a rail pass gives you the freedom to hop on a train whenever you feel like it, and there's no waiting in ticket lines. For more focused trips, look into single-country or regional passes. If you're only planning a few point-to-point journeys plus the odd local excursion, individual tickets will be the cheapest way to go. As well, it's important nowadays to compare the cost of rail with those of the low-cost airlines. Travelers have limited time, so if you're planning on heading from, say, Paris to Berlin, booking a cheap flight might be the most time-effective way of going, and could end up being less expensive. See p. 849 for complete information on flying the low-cost carriers of Europe.

### Countries Honoring Eurail Passes

At the time of writing there were 28: Austria, Belgium, Bosnia-Herzegovina, Bulgaria, Croatia, Czech Republic, Denmark, Finland, France, Germany, Greece, Hungary, Ireland, Italy, Luxembourg, Montenegro, Netherlands, Norway, Poland, Portugal, Romania, Serbia, Slovakia, Slovenia, Spain, Sweden, Switzerland, and Turkey.

**IF YOU LIVE OUTSIDE EUROPE** The granddaddy of passes is the **Eurail Global Pass,** covering some 28 countries (most of Western Europe except Britain, alongside chunks of eastern Europe).

It's best to buy these passes before you leave home. You can get them from most travel agents, but the biggest supplier is **Rail Europe** (www.raileurope.com), which also sells most national passes via its comprehensive website.

The most popular pass is the **Eurail Global Pass,** which offers unlimited first-class travel for adults 26 and older. Options cost an average of US$660 for 15 days, US$850 for 21 days, US$1,045 for 1 month, US$1,470 for 2 months, or US$1,810 for 3 months.

You can also consider a **Eurail Select Pass,** allowing travel in three, four, or five bordering European countries connected by train or ferry. With this pass, you can customize your own trip, traveling by train from 5 to 15 days within a 2-month period.

A **Eurail Regional Pass** is for those who want to see only a small part of Europe in a short time frame. Several different combination regional passes are offered, granting train travel on various numbers of days within periods up to 2 months. Such a pass, for example, might grant you unlimited travel in both France and Switzerland (Eurail France–Switzerland Pass), or a Scandinavia Pass granting travel in four countries. Most European countries, including Austria and Italy, also participate in the **Eurail One Country Pass.** This pass grants unlimited train travel from 3 to 10 days within a 1- or 2-month period in a single participating European country of your choice. For example, eight days of travel in Austria within a 1-month period, costs US$360 first-class, US$290 second-class. In Italy, 8 days' rail travel within a 1-month window costs US$410 first-class, US$290 second-class.

You have to study these passes carefully to see which one would be ideal for you or if an airline ticket would be better (see above). You can

### TRAIN trip tips

To make your train travels as pleasant as possible, remember a few general rules:

- **Hold on to your train ticket** after it's been marked or punched by the conductor. Some European rail networks require that you present your ticket when you leave the station platform at your destination.
- While you sleep—or even nap—**be sure your valuables are in a safe place.** You might temporarily attach a small bell to each bag to warn you if someone attempts to take it. If you've left bags on a rack in the front or back of the car, consider securing them with a small bicycle chain and lock to deter thieves, who consider trains happy hunting grounds.
- Few European trains have drinking fountains, and the dining car may be closed just when you're at your thirstiest, so **take along a bottle of mineral water.** As you'll soon discover, the experienced rail traveler comes loaded with hampers of food and drink and munches away throughout the trip—buying food onboard can be very expensive.
- If you want to leave bags in a train station locker, **don't let anyone help you store them in it.** An old trick among thieves is feigned helpfulness, and then pocketing the key to your locker while passing you the key to an empty one.



check online or call for the latest prices and offerings, which are always subject to changes. Many countries also offer rail passes with add-ons of a few days' car rental, but be sure to cross check the value against standalone deals.

If you plan on traveling in Great Britain, then **BritRail** (www.britrail.com; ✆ **866/938-RAIL [7245]** in the U.S. and Canada), which specializes in rail passes for use in Great Britain, is your best bet.

## By Car

Most rental companies offer their best prices to customers who **reserve in advance** from their home country. Weekly rentals are almost always less expensive than day rentals. Three or more people traveling together can often get around cheaper by car than by train, depending on the distances traveled and the size and efficiency of the engine—compared to most other parts of the world, fuel is very expensive almost everywhere in Europe. You should also factor in **road tolls** that many countries charge. Also keep in mind that the vast majority of available rental cars have **manual transmissions** (stick shifts). Automatics are available, but for a premium.

When you reserve a car, be sure to ask if the price includes: all taxes including value-added tax (VAT); breakdown assistance; unlimited mileage; personal accident or liability insurance (PAI); collision-damage

## the rules of the road: **DRIVING IN EUROPE**

- First, know that European drivers tend to be more **aggressive** than their counterparts from other parts of the world.
- **Drive on the right** except in England, Scotland, and Ireland, where you drive on the left. And *do not drive* in the left lane on a four-lane highway; it is only for passing.
- If someone comes up from behind and flashes his lights at you, it's a signal for you to slow down and either move to the right lane or drive more on the shoulder so that he can pass you more easily (two-lane roads here sometimes become three cars wide).
- Except for the German Autobahn, most highways do indeed have **speed limits** of around 100 to 130kmph (62–81 mph).
- Remember that outside the U.K., everything's measured in **kilometers** (distance and speed limits). For a rough conversion, 1km = 0.6 miles.
- Be aware that fuel is *very* expensive, so you should **rent the smallest, most fuel-efficient car** you think you can manage. Prices at the pumps are quoted in liters (1 U.S. gallon = 3.78 liters).
- Never leave anything of value in a car overnight, and don't leave anything visible when you leave the car.

waiver (CDW); theft waiver; and any other insurance options. If not, ask what these extras cost, because they can make a big dent in your bottom line. The CDW and other insurance might be covered by your credit card if you use the card to pay for the rental; check with your card issuer to be sure. Some travelers like to live dangerously and waive optional insurance. But when no CDW is purchased, many rental agencies will make you pay for any damages on the spot when you return the car—making even the smallest dent or scratch a potentially costly experience. To avoid any issues, take cellphone photos of your car with a time stamp, so that you have any dents and dings recorded and won't be charged for them.

If your credit card doesn't cover the CDW, consider buying Car Rental Collision Coverage from a third party. **Travel Guard** (www.travelguard.com; ✆ **800/826-1300** in the U.S. and Canada), which will insure you for around US$7 to US$9 per day. In the U.K., **Insurance 4 Car Hire** (www.insurance4carhire.com; ✆ **0844/892-1770**) offers similar cover. An annual policy covering unlimited car rental for a maximum of 31 consecutive days on any one trip costs £49. That being said, these are just two players and others may have better rates. To see side-by-side comparisons of CDW rentals, go to the marketplace site www.tripinsurancestore.com.

The main international companies all have rental points across Europe: **Avis** (www.avis.com; ✆ **800/633-3469** in the U.S. and **800/879-2847** in Canada), **Budget** (www.budget.com; ✆ **800/218-7992** in the U.S. and **800/268-8900** in Canada), **Dollar** (www.dollar.com; ✆ **800/800-5252** in the U.S. and Canada), **Hertz** (www.hertz.com; ✆ **800/654-3131** in the U.S. and Canada), and **National** (www.nationalcar.com; ✆ **877/222-9058** in the U.S. and Canada). U.S.-based companies specializing in European rentals include **Auto Europe** (www.autoeurope.com; ✆ **888/223-5555** in the U.S. and Canada), **Europcar** (www.europcar.com), **Europe by Car** (www.europebycar.com; ✆ **800/223-1516** in the U.S. and Canada), **Kemwel** (www.kemwel.com; ✆ **877/820-0668** in the U.S. and Canada) and **Sixt** (www.sixt.com). It's also worth checking prices offered by U.K.–based rental agents such as **Holiday Autos** (www.holidayautos.co.uk; ✆ **44/203-740-9859** in the U.K.). Europe by Car, Kemwel, and **Renault USA** (www.renaultusa.com; ✆ **888/532-1221** in the U.S. and Canada) also offer a competitive alternative to renting for longer than 15 days: **short-term leases** in which you technically buy a fresh-from-the-factory car and then sell it back when you return it. All insurance is included, from liability and theft to personal injury and CDW, with no deductible. And unlike at many rental agencies, who won't rent to anyone 24 and under, the minimum age for a lease is 18. You should also always check your quote against quotes from general travel search sites like **Kayak.com**, as

## IMPORTANT rental-car TIPS

**Check what type of fuel your car takes:** If you damage the car's engine by pumping gasoline rather than diesel, most European car insurance policies won't protect you.

**Choose a smart size for your car:** In many of Europe's cities and villages, the streets were formed well before cars were invented. So having too large a car can limit where you can drive.

**Pack light:** Even the larger European cars will have smaller trunks than we're used to in the United States. If you must bring a large suitcase, inquire whether your car will have a roof rack.

**Take two credit cards:** Often, rental companies will freeze and amount equal to the CDW coverage deductible on the credit card that you use to rent the car. So you're going to want to have a second card handy so that you don't go over your limit with the first.

**See if there are any special regulations for the country you're visiting:** This is particularly important if you're crossing borders in your rental car. In Italy, for example, it's the law that you must buy insurance through your rental company; credit card insurance isn't accepted on the Boot.

**Don't rent a car for city stays:** Every city in Europe, every single one, has terrific public transportation options. You'll ONLY need a car if you're traveling in the European countryside. Having a car in a European city is usually an expensive hassle.

well as car-rental search specialists such as **RhinoCarHire.com** and **CarHireSearch.co.uk**.

For visitors coming from North America, the **AAA** supplies good maps to its members. **Michelin maps** (www.viamichelin.co.uk) are made with the tourist in mind, and are widely available in shops and fuel stations across Europe. There's also a handy route planner online. Be aware that, if you are planning to navigate using your mobile phone, data costs for roaming can be very expensive.

## By Plane

Although trains remain the greenest way to get around in Europe, air-transport networks have improved drastically in the past decade. Intense competition—and the mushrooming of low-cost airlines serving destinations that even few Europeans had heard of 15 years ago—has forced airfares into the bargain basement. Routes such as London–Paris, Milan–Rome, and London–Brussels have also come under sustained competitive pressure from high-speed trains. While the political climate in Europe's higher echelons very much favors the environmental credentials of trains over planes, for journeys longer than a few hundred miles, you'll likely find flying to be the cheapest option.

The predictable airline news in Europe is the continued dominance of the **no-frills airline,** originally modeled on American upstarts like Southwest. By keeping their overhead down through electronic ticketing, forgoing meal service, charging for every "extra," and flying only point-to-point, often to and from less popular airports, these airlines are able to offer very low fares. This means now you can save lots of time (and usually, money) over transcontinental train hauls, especially from, say, London to Venice or from Paris to Spain. You should still compare low-cost carrier flights against the mainstream airlines; many budget airline fares have extra fees such as luggage or credit-card charges buried in their small print.

Most of these airlines do not fly transatlantic, so if you're hopping around Europe by air, we recommend that you book your transatlantic flight as a separate ticket. Then (but still before you depart for your European vacation), book your intra-European country-hopping flights separately. Often, the further out you can book (say, 6 months), the less you'll pay with these cheaper airlines. Keep in mind that the airport you arrive in on your long haul flight might not be the same one you depart from for your flight within Europe; plan ahead for airport transfers and time allowances.

## By Bus

Bus transportation is readily available throughout Europe; it often is less expensive than train travel and covers a more extensive area, but is slower

## FLYING WITH EUROPE'S budget airlines

Europe's skies are awash with budget, low-cost, and no-frills airlines. The names can change, because these small airlines are sometimes at the mercy of a fickle market. They can fail or merge with a bigger airline or smaller competitor. Still, as quickly as one disappears, another takes off, perhaps even another two. You should note that some popular flight search engines do not compare fares from budget airlines: You should either check websites individually, or consult a specialist low-cost website such as **www.whichbudget.com**.

At the time of writing, the following airlines were among the established European no-frills players, offering a selection of useful routes for visitors to Europe:

**Air One** (www.flyairone.com; ✆ **894-444** in Italy) has hubs in Milan, Pisa, and Venice with a good domestic Italian network, as well as key links with the likes of London, Prague, and Athens.

**Blu-Express** (www.blu-express.com; ✆ **06/9895-6666** in Italy) has a route map focused on Italian domestic and Mediterranean island destinations, served mostly from Rome.

**easyJet** (www.easyjet.com) connects airports across Britain with much of Europe, including Switzerland.

**FlyBe** (www.flybe.com) serves more of Britain's regional airports than any other airline, joining them particularly well with France and Germany.

**Germanwings** (www.germanwings.com; ✆ **44/330-365-1918**) serves over 90 destinations from hubs in Germany, Switzerland, Italy, and London. Despite its tragic 2015 crash, its overall safety record is the equivalent of any airline in Europe.

**Niki** (www.flyniki.com) has a wide network centered on Austria, linking it with destinations in central and Eastern Europe, Spain, Italy, and the United Kingdom.

**Norwegian** (www.norwegian.com; ✆ **020/8099-7254** in the U.K.) offers cheap flights from across Europe to cities in Scandinavia including Oslo, Stockholm, and Copenhagen. In 2015, it also started flying to several cities in the United States at jaw-dropping rates, so if you're searching for a good transatlantic fare, don't skip its website.

**Ryanair** (www.ryanair.com; ✆ **0871/246-0003** in the U.K., 01/248-0858 in Ireland) is Europe's busiest point-to-point airline, with hubs in the United Kingdom, Germany, Ireland, and Italy, among others.

**SmartWings** (www.smartwings.com; ✆ **420/220-116-686** in the Czech Republic) offers flights to Prague from cities across southern Europe, as well as from Paris.

**Transavia** (www.transavia.com) has hubs in France and the Netherlands, and routes focused on southern Europe.

**Vueling** (www.vueling.com) is Spain's leading low-cost carrier, with all the country's major cities well served from around Europe.

**Wizz Air** (www.wizzair.com; ✆ **0907/292-0102** in the U.K., or 01/903-6876 in Ireland) has the best range of destinations in Eastern Europe, including Budapest and Prague.

and can be much less comfortable. European buses, like the trains, outshine their American counterparts, but they're perhaps best used only to pick up where the extensive train network leaves off. One major long-haul bus company serves almost all the countries of western, northern, and eastern Europe: **Eurolines** (www.eurolines.com; © **0871/781-8178** in the U.K., **0861/1991 900** in Italy, **6196/2078-501** in Germany). The staff at Eurolines can check schedules, make reservations, and quote prices for travel between cities Europe-wide.



# WHEN TO GO



Europe has a continental climate with distinct seasons, but there are great variations in temperature from one part to another. Northern Norway is plunged into arctic darkness in winter, but in sunny Sicily the climate is usually temperate—although snow can fall even on the Greek islands in winter, and winter nights are cold (or at least, cool) pretty much anywhere. Europe is north of most of the United States, but along the Mediterranean there are weather patterns more along the lines of the U.S. southern states. In general, however, seasonal changes are less extreme than in most of the United States. In Southern Hemisphere terms, Seville, in southern Spain, is at 37° N, about the same distance from the Equator as Auckland, New Zealand (36° S).

The **high season** almost everywhere lasts from mid-May to mid-September, with the most tourists hitting the Continent between mid-June and late August. In general, this is the most expensive time to travel, except in Austria and Switzerland, where prices are a little higher in winter during the ski season. Because Scandinavian city hotels depend mostly on business clients instead of tourists, you can often find lower prices in the fleeting summer.

You'll find smaller crowds, relatively fair weather, and often lower prices at hotels in the **shoulder seasons,** from Easter to mid-May and mid-September to October. **Off season** (except at ski resorts in the Alps, Dolomites, Tyrol, Pyrenees, and elsewhere) is from November to Easter, with the exception of the Christmas period. While prices plunge in the city in low season, tourist facilities in some smaller towns shut down altogether, so do advance research if you're planning on going out into the European countryside during the late-fall, early spring, and winter months. Much of Europe, Italy especially, takes August off, and August 15 to August 30 is vacation time for many locals, so expect the cities to be devoid of natives and many restaurants and shops to be closed—but the beaches and lakes packed.

## Weather

**AUSTRIA** In **Vienna** and along the **Danube Valley,** the climate is moderate. Summer daytime temperatures average in the low 70s Fahrenheit (low 20s Celsius), falling at night to the low 50s (low teens Celsius). Winter temperatures are usually in the 30s Fahrenheit (btw. -1 and +4 degrees Celsius) and 40s (4–9 degrees Celsius) during the day.

**ENGLAND & SCOTLAND** It rains a lot in England and Scotland, especially in the west of both countries, but winters are rainier than summers, and in fact **London** receives less annual rainfall than Rome or Sydney. The sunniest period in the British Isles is usually from June to mid-September. Average summer daytime temperatures average from the low 60s Fahrenheit (mid-teens Celsius) to the mid-60s (upper teens Celsius), with daily highs in summer hovering around the low 70s (low-20s Celsius). Average temperatures drop to the 40s (single digits Celsius) on winter nights, with many nights dropping below freezing inland. The **Scottish Lowlands** have a climate similar to England's, but the Highlands are much colder, with storms and snow in winter.

**FRANCE & GERMANY** The weather in Paris is approximately the same as in the U.S. mid-Atlantic states, but as in most of Europe, there's usually less extreme variation. In summer, the temperature doesn't linger for long above the mid-70s Fahrenheit (mid-20s Celsius). Winters tend to be mild, in the 40s Fahrenheit (4–9 degrees Celsius). It's warmer along the Riviera year-round, and wetter than elsewhere on the western, Atlantic coast. Germany's climate ranges from moderate summers and chilly, damp winters in the north to warm summers and very cold, sunny winters in the alpine south. Away from the coasts, however, both France and Germany can experience sustained periods of summer heat or winter cold, too.

**NORTHERN EUROPE** In the **Netherlands,** the weather is rarely extreme at any time of year. Summer temperatures average around 67°F (19°C) and the winter average is about 40°F (4°C). The climate is rainy, with the driest months April and May—from mid-April to mid-May, the tulip fields burst into color. The climate of **northern Germany** is very similar, as is **Belgium's** climate: moderate, varying from daytime highs of 73°F (23°C) in July and August to an average of 40°F (4°C) in December and January. It can rain at almost any time, but the weather is at its finest in July and August.

**SCANDINAVIA** Summer temperatures in Southern Scandinavia hit highs of around 70°F (21°C), dropping to the 20s Fahrenheit (below 0 Celsius) in winter. Fjords and even the ocean are often warm enough for summer swimming, but rain is frequent. The sun shines 24 hours in midsummer above the Arctic Circle; winter brings semi-permanent twilight. **Denmark's** climate is relatively mild by comparison. It has moderate summer temperatures and winters that can be damp and foggy, with average daytime high temperatures around the mid-30s Fahrenheit (single digits Celsius).

**SOUTHERN EUROPE** Summers are hot in **Italy** and **Spain,** with daytime temperatures around the high 80s Fahrenheit (low 30s Celsius) or higher. Along the Italian coast, winter temperatures are usually mild; and except in the mountains, Italian winter temperatures rarely drop below freezing for long. The area around Madrid is dry and arid, and much colder than you'd expect in the winter (average daily lows of 32°F/0°C). Summers in Spain are coolest along the Atlantic coast, with mild temperatures year-round on the coast of Galicia, much hotter along the Mediterranean Costa del Sol.



**SWITZERLAND** The Alpine climate means winters are cold and bright, and spring comes late, with snow falls well into April. Summers are mild and sunny, with delightfully fresh air, though the alpine regions can experience dramatic changes in weather any time of year. Summer storms aren't uncommon.



# TIPS ON WHERE TO STAY

Traditional European hotels tend to be **simpler** than North American ones, and rooms are on average significantly **smaller.** Hoteliers tend to emphasize character and friendliness over amenities. For example, even in the cheapest American chain motel, free cable is as standard as indoor plumbing. In Europe, however, some independent hotels below the moderate level don't even have in-room TVs. But then, you're probably not over here to watch *The X-Factor.*

Make advance reservations for the popular months of travel. Travel to most places in Europe peaks between May and October, and during that period, it's hard to come by a moderate or inexpensive hotel room. In a trendy spot such as Cornwall in England, Tuscany, or the Dordogne, France, it's nigh impossible to find an excellent hotel room, apartment, or cottage to rent at short notice in the summer. And many smaller, boutique hotels can fill up year-round, especially at weekends and in popular city-break or weekend bolthole destinations. For off-season, you'll often find the best lodging deals by waiting until the last minute, particularly if you use the web. Such websites as **Priceline.com** and **Hotwire.com** can be gold for last-minute deals, as can the popular app **HotelTonight** (which books weeklong stays, despite the name, but only at the last minute).

You'll find hotels and other accommodations inside every conceivable kind of building, from 21st-century concrete cubes to medieval coaching inns. In older hotels, guest rooms can be smaller than you might expect (if you base your expectation on a modern U.S. Radisson, for example), and each room is usually different, sometimes quirkily so. But this is part of the charm. Some rooms may only have a shower, not a bathtub, so if you feel you can't survive without a tub, make that clear when booking.

Most European countries rate hotels by **stars,** ranging from five stars (luxe) to one star (modest). A four- or five-star hotel offers first-class accommodations, a three-star hotel is usually moderately priced, and a one- or two-star hotel is inexpensively priced. Governments grant stars based on rigid, often bizarre, criteria, evaluating such amenities as elevators, private bathrooms, pools, and air-conditioning. In the U.K., a hotel will get another star if it has a bar, which is why you'll often see a collection of dusty bottles sitting in one corner of the lobby! The hotel with the most stars is not necessarily the most elegant or charming. For example, a five-star hotel might be an ugly, modern building, whereas a one-star hotel might be a townhouse but with no elevator, bar, or restaurant. Plenty of fashionable boutique accommodations have no stars at all. Unless otherwise noted, all hotel rooms in this book have **private en suite bathrooms.** And the stars you'll see in this book are based on the assessments of our authors, not on the government criteria. We have no "no" star hotels. Instead, a one-star is a place we think gives good value for the money, a two-star is highly recommended, and a three-star property would be appropriate for a honeymoon or some other type of special-event travel. It will be a very unique and wonderful place (and we're proud to say, some of our three-star properties are budget ones).

You probably don't want to stay in a chain hotel (unless you're trying to help your budget by using hotel award points). If that's the case, know that you'll find all of the large, multinational chains in Europe's capitals, and they'll usually be well-maintained and well-located. For car-tourers, **Ibis** (www.ibishotel.com) are reliable, clean, well-equipped, and value overnight motel-style stops close to many major highways. There are over 700 in Europe, about half in France. In fact, Ibis's parent **Accor** group (www.accorhotels.com) has hotel offerings at just about every level of comfort in several European countries—brands include Mercure, Sofitel, and Novotel. **B&B Hotels** (www.hotel-bb.com) are cheaper, simpler, and also concentrated close to major routes in France. **Louvre Hotels** (www.louvrehotels.com) has a number of affordable brands, including Campanile. **Logis de France** (www.logishotels.com) is a marketing group, not a chain. Properties tend to be more characterful than the chains, but also more variable. If you're winding your way around the French backroads, their website is worth investigating. Reliable, mid-range brands and chains like **Best Western** (www.bestwestern.com) and **Holiday Inn** (www.holidayinn.com) are here too. **Radisson Blu** (www.radissonblu.com) has a strong presence in Europe's cities. You'll find our favorite hotels by consulting the individual chapters in this book.

A **villa** or **rental property** can be great for getting up-close to a European destination, if you're lingering in one spot for more than a couple of nights. **Untours** (www.untours.com; ✆ **888/868-6871** in the U.S. and Canada) provides apartment, farmhouse, or cottage stays of 2 weeks or more in many destinations for a reasonable price, and with the on-the-ground support of a host. **HomeAway.com** is the largest rental property broker on the planet, and offers properties of every kind all over Europe. It owns VRBO.com, which has a similarly wide array of villas and apartments. Other large web-based rental specialists include FlipKey.com and Rentalo.com. **Holidaylettings.co.uk** and **Homelidays** (www.homelidays.co.uk) both have vast rental property portfolios, including villas with private or shared outdoor pools. The simplicity of a French *gîte* (self-catering holiday home) is another to consider this category, especially for cost-conscious visitors: Check **www.gites-de-france.com**. In Great Britain, search cottage rental agents such as **English Country Cottages** (www.english-country-cottages.co.uk) and **Cottages 4 You** (www.cottages4you.co.uk). In Spain, **Rustical Travel** (www.rusticaltravel.com) has an excellent portfolio in Andalusia and across the North. **Ionian & Aegean Island Holidays** (www.ionianislandholidays.com) rents villas on several Greek islands.

**HomeLink International** (www.homelink.org; ✆ **800/638-3841** in the U.S, or ✆ **01962/886882** in the U.K.), which costs $119/£115 for a year's membership, is the oldest, largest, and best home-exchange holiday group in the world. An alternative is is **Intervac International** (www.intervac-homeexchange.com; ✆ **866/844-7567** in the U.S., ✆ **353-41-9837969** in the U.K.), which costs $100 annually. Both have members spread around Europe.

Many European cities are also well represented in online peer-to-peer accommodation networks, including international giants like **AirBnB.com**; **9flats.com** and **Wimdu.com** are other peer-to-peer site worth checking out. **OneFineStay.com** has a small, but special portfolio of apartments in London, serviced in a hotel style.

**Agritourism** is increasingly popular for visitors to rural areas looking to "get away from it all." Most places in this category offer rooms or small apartments on a working agricultural property—which could be anything from an olive oil farm to a wine estate. Many make and sell their own produce (salami, preserves, wine, and the like) to guests. Accommodations aren't always rough and ready: Plenty of Italian *agriturismi,* for example, offer amenities, luxury, and outdoor swimming pools. **Farm Stay UK** (www.farmstay.co.uk; ✆ **024/7669-6909**), set up in part by the Royal Agricultural Society of England, and still owned by a consortium of farmers, features more than 1,200 rural retreats including farms, B&Bs, and campsites in Britain. The best Italian *agriturismo* websites are **www.terranostra.it** and **ww.agriturismo.it**. One U.S.–based agency worth contacting is **Italy Farm Holidays** (www.italyfarmholidays.com). In Spain, you'll find rural properties *(casas rurales)* at excellent prices listed at **www.toprural.com**.

There are still more off-the-wall options for truly "alternative" European accommodations. One of our favorites is **Monastery Stays** (www.monasterystays.com), which represents hundreds of religious institutions in Italy. Rooms range from basic to spacious and comfortable, and staying in a monastery or convent provides an experience you're unlikely to forget. Only married couples or blood relatives can share the same room.

# ORGANIZED TOURS

## Active Tours

### CYCLING

Cycling tours are a great way to see Europe at your own pace. In cycling-mad countries such as Italy and France, you'll be getting the same view as many locals do—from the saddle. Some of the best are conducted by the **CTC (Cyclists' Tourist Club) Cycling Holidays** (www.cyclingholidays.org). **Hindriks European Bicycle Tours** (www.hindrikstours.com) leads 10-day bicycle tours throughout Europe. **ExperiencePlus** (www.experienceplus.com; ✆ **800/685-4565** or 970/484-8489 in the U.S. and Canada), runs bike tours in France, Spain, Italy, and elsewhere. **Ciclismo Classico** (www.ciclismoclassico.com; ✆ **800/866-7314** or 781/646-3377 in the U.S. and Canada) is an excellent outfit running tours of Italy and elsewhere in Europe. Florence-based **I Bike Italy** (www.ibikeitaly.com; ✆ **+39-342/935-2395**), offers guided single-day rides around the city and into the Chianti winelands. And for those interested in less-expensive, self-guided bike tours (which include luggage transport from site to site), we recommend **Cyclomundo** (www.cyclomundo.com; ✆ **+ 33 450 872109**) which is based in France, but also provides itineraries and support for Switzerland, Spain, and Italy.

### HIKING & WALKING

**Wilderness Travel** (www.wildernesstravel.com; ✆ **800/368-2794** or 510/558-2488 in the U.S. and Canada), specializes in walking tours, treks, and inn-to-inn hiking tours of almost 20 European countries, as well as less strenuous walking tours. **Sherpa Expeditions** (www.sherpaexpeditions.com; ✆ **020/8577-2717** in the U.K.), offers both self-guided and group treks through off-the-beaten-track regions. Two somewhat upscale walking-tour companies are **Butterfield & Robinson** (www.butterfield.com; ✆ **866/551-9090** in the U.S. and Canada); and **Country Walkers** (www.countrywalkers.com; ✆ **800/234-6900** in the U.S. and Canada, or 1300/663-206 in Australia). **Macs Adventure** (www.macsadventure.com; ✆ **844/896-6799** in the U.S. and Canada, ✆ **0141/530-3712** in the U.K.) has an impressive portfolio of serviced active holidays, including walking Scotland's Highlands or Italy's Amalfi Coast. **Exodus** (www.exodus.co.uk; ✆ **0845/287-3789** in the U.K.) has walks and hikes for all ability levels all over Europe, from Croatia's Dalmatian coast to the frozen Scandinavian north.

Most European countries have associations geared toward aiding hikers and walkers. In Britain, it's the **Ramblers** (www.ramblers.org.uk; ✆ **020/7339-8500** in the U.K.). In Italy, contact the **Club Alpino**

**Italiano** (www.cai.it; ✆ **02/205-7231** in Italy). For Austria, try the Österreichischer **Alpenverein** (**Austrian Alpine Club;** www.alpenverein.at or www.facebook.com/alpenverein; ✆ **0512/59547** in Austria).

### HORSEBACK RIDING

One of the best companies is **Equitour** (www.ridingtours.com; ✆ **800/545-0019** or 307/455-3363 in the U.S. and Canada), which offers 5- to 7-day rides through many of Europe's most beautiful areas, such as the Scottish Highlands and France's Loire Valley. **FlorenceTown** (www.florencetown.com; ✆ **055/281-103** in Italy) runs easy 1-day rides around the Chianti region of Tuscany.

## Educational Travel

The best (and one of the most expensive) of the escorted group tour companies is **Group IST** (**International Specialty Travel;** www.groupist.com; ✆ **800/833-2111** in the U.S. and Canada), whose offerings are first class all the way and accompanied by a certified expert in whatever field the trip focuses on. If you missed out on study abroad in college, the brainy **Smithsonian Journeys** (www.smithsonianjourneys.org; ✆ **855/330-1542** in the U.S. and Canada) may be just the ticket, albeit a pricey one. Study leaders are often world-renowned experts in their field. Journeys are carefully crafted and go to some of the most compelling places in Europe, avoiding tourist traps. For a smaller, more personalized educational day- and week-long tours, turn to Context Travel (www.contexttravel.com; ✆ **215/392-0303**), which uses local curators, art historians, and art restorers as guides across France and in the major cities of Italy and Spain, as well as Berlin, London, and Vienna.

**Andante Travels** (www.barebonestours.co.uk; ✆ **01722/713-800** in the U.K.) specialists lead guided tours of the most exciting archaeological areas in the world, including Sicilian temples, the ruins of Pompeii, Provence in France, and Ireland's megalithic sites. Butterflies of the Dolomites, Norway's Arctic wilderness, and other flora and fauna throughout Europe are the focus of trips from **Naturetrek** (www.naturetrek.co.uk; ✆ **01962/733-051** in the U.K.), whose naturalists lead walks through some of the continent's most spectacular scenery. A clearinghouse for information on Europe-based language schools is **Lingua Service Worldwide** (www.linguaserviceworldwide.com; ✆ **800/394-LEARN** [394-53276] or 203/938-7406 in the U.S. and Canada).

## Cooking Schools

If you're staying in **agritourism** accommodations (see "Tips on Where to Stay," p. 852) anywhere in Europe, inquire about cookery courses. Many offer half- and full-day tuition in traditional methods and dishes for very reasonable rates. From May to October, the **International Cooking School of Italian Food and Wine** (www.internationalcookingschool.

com), offers courses in Bologna, the "gastronomic capital of Italy," Piedmont (Italy's truffle capital), and Tuscany. Chef Judy Francini of **Divina Cucina** (www.divinacucina.com) leads students through Florence's central market to buy the ingredients to prepare a meal, and also spices up the menu with wine tastings; cooking tours of Chianti, Apulia, and Sicily; and visits to makers of balsamic vinegar and other Italian specialties. **Le Cordon Bleu** (www.cordonbleu.edu; ✆ **01/53-68-22-50** in France), was established in 1895 as a means of spreading the tenets of French cuisine to the world at large. It offers many programs outside its flagship Paris school. And for food-based tours in France, Italy, and Spain—over 90 of them!—consider the long-established, highly respected tour company **The International Kitchen** (www.theinternationalkitchen.com; ✆ **312-467-0560**.)

## Escorted General-Interest Tours

Escorted tours are structured group tours, with a group leader. The price usually includes everything from airfare to hotels, meals, tours, admission costs, and local transportation. Group tours are best for people who want to have the company of other travelers as they tour about and who are nervous about planning their own itinerary. They will not save you money on travel, nor do they offer experiences that most travelers, with this book in hand, can't replicate on their own. That includes guided tours, which can be picked up, on a day-trip basis, in every tourist destination in Europe. But if you want the social aspects of a tour, we highly recommend that you get one that does NOT include meals, as you'll eat much better, and eating well is an integral part of the European experience. With a group tour, you'll be dining at the places that can handle 40 people emerging from a bus all at once (meaning the places the locals have long ago abandoned).

The two largest tour operators conducting escorted tours of Europe are various brands under the umbrella of **Globus/Cosmos** (www.globusandcosmos.com; ✆ **866/755-8581** in the U.S. and Canada, or ✆ **0800/223-0179** in the U.K.) and **Trafalgar** (www.trafalgartours.com; ✆ **0800/533-5619** in the U.K.). Both have tours in all price ranges, the differences consisting of hotel location and the number of activities. (With the cheaper tours, you'll often find yourself stuck out in a suburban hotel, rather than near to sights and restaurants you might want to explore on your own.) There's little difference in the companies' services, so choose your tour based on the itinerary and preferred date of departure. Brochures are available at travel agencies, and there's plenty of itinerary information and ideas online. Other well-respected group tour operators include GoAhead Tours (www.goaheadtours.com; ✆ **877/264-1348**); Perillo Tours (www.perillotours.com; ✆ **800/431-1515**); Gate 1 Travel (www.gate1travel.com; ✆ **800/682-3333**); and YMT Vacations (www.ymtvacations.com; ✆ **855/804-4725**). On the luxury end of the spectrum are **Adventures By Disney** (for luxury family travel, www.adventuresbydisney.com; ✆ **800/543-0865**); **Abercrombie & Kent** (www.abercrombiekent.com; ✆ **888/785-5379**); and **Tauck Tours** (www.tauck.com; ✆ **800/788-7885**).



## Packages for Independent Travelers

Package tours are simply a way to buy the airfare, accommodations, and other elements of your trip (such as car rentals, airport transfers, and sometimes even activities) at the same time and often at discounted prices.

All major airlines flying from North America to Europe sell vacation packages, but the price-leaders tend to be such specialists as **GoToday** (www.gotoday.com; ✆ **800/227-3235**); **smarTours** (www.smartours.com; ✆ **800/337-7773**) and **Friendly Planet** (www.friendlyplanet.com; ✆ **800/555-5765**). Several big **online travel agencies**—Expedia, Travelocity, Orbitz, and Lastminute.com—also do a brisk business in packages for visitors flying from just about anywhere to pretty much anywhere else. Pretty much every European short-haul airline these days—including British Airways, Ryanair, and others—offers flight plus hotel plus car rental deals. Keep an eye on their websites.

For all kinds of packages with a sustainable or eco-friendly ethos, check the listings at **Responsible Travel** (www.responsibletravel.com or www.responsiblevacation.com).

Deals on packages come and go, and the latest are often listed at Frommers.com, so please do search our "Deals" section.



# [Fast FACTS] EUROPE

**Car Rental** See "Getting Around by Car," earlier in this chapter.

**Cellphones** See "Mobile Phones," later in this section.

**Customs** Individual countries usually have their own Customs regulations (see the individual chapters in this book). However, members of the European Union (E.U.) share many guidelines for arrivals. **Non-E.U. nationals aged 17 and over** can bring in 4 liters of wine and 16 liters of beer plus either 1 liter of alcohol more than 22% ("spirits") or 2 liters of "fortified" wine at less than 22%. Visitors may also bring in other goods, including perfume, gifts, and souvenirs, totaling 430€ in value. (Customs officials tend to be lenient about these general merchandise regulations, realizing the limits are unrealistically low.) Tobacco regulations vary by country, although an import limit of 200 cigarettes and 50 cigars is typical. For **arrivals from within the E.U.,** there are no limits as long as goods are for your own personal use, or are gifts. You can find details on Customs and excise rules for anyone entering the E.U. at **www.ec.europa.eu/taxation_customs/common/travellers**.

For specifics on what you can take home and the corresponding fees, U.S. citizens should download the free pamphlet *Know Before You Go* at

**www.cbp.gov**. Alternatively, contact the **U.S. Customs & Border Protection (CBP),** 1300 Pennsylvania Ave. N.W., Washington, D.C. 20229 (✆ **877/CBP-5511**), and request the pamphlet. For a clear summary of their own rules, Canadians should consult the booklet *I Declare,* issued by the **Canada Border Services Agency** (www.cbsa-asfc.gc.ca; ✆ **800/461-9999** in Canada, or 204/983-3500). Australians need to read *Guide for Travellers: Know Before You Go.* For more information, call the **Australian Customs Service** at ✆ **1300/363-263,** or check **www.customs.gov.au/individuals**. For New Zealanders, most questions are answered under "Coming into NZ" at **www.customs.govt.nz**. For more information, contact the **New Zealand Customs Service** (✆ **0800/428-786,** or 09/927-8036).

### Electricity

Not all European electrical systems are the same. Most of continental Europe uses the 220-volt system (two round prongs). However, British electricity operates at 240 volts AC (50 cycles), and almost all overseas plugs don't fit British three-hole wall outlets. Always bring suitable transformers and/or adapters, such as world multiplugs—if you plug some American appliances directly into an electrical outlet without a transformer, for example, you'll destroy your appliance and possibly start a fire. Portable electronic devices such as iPods and mobile phones, however, recharge without problems via USB or using a multiplug. Many long-distance European trains have plugs, for the charging of laptops and mobile phones.

### Embassies & Consulates

If your passport is stolen or lost, or if you are robbed, arrested, or become seriously ill while on vacation, your embassy or nearest consulate should be your first point of contact. While an embassy won't replace lost items (other than passports or national identity cards), bail you out of jail, or pay your plane fare home, it can refer you to English-speaking attorneys, doctors, or others who can assist in a crisis. See "Fast Facts" in each country chapter for contact info for the embassies of Australia, Canada, New Zealand, the United Kingdom, and the United States. For questions about American citizens who are arrested abroad, including ways of getting money to them, telephone the **Citizens Emergency Center** of the Office of Special Consular Services in Washington, D.C. (✆ **202/647-5225**).

### Emergencies

See individual chapters for local police, fire, and ambulance numbers. Dialing ✆ **112** will summon the emergency services wherever you are in the E.U.

### Internet & Wi-Fi

**Wi-Fi** is available at all but the most bare-bones of hotels (and usually at those, too). It's usually free, though oddly, some of the more expensive hotels charge needless daily fees for Wi-Fi. You'll find free or fee-based Wi-Fi hotspots in most cities' downtown areas, as well as at airports and train stations. If you're not connecting with your own laptop, tablet, or smartphone and need to find a local internet cafe, start by checking **www.cybercafes.com**. Although such places have suffered due to the spread of smartphones and free Wi-Fi (see below), they do tend to be prevalent close to popular tourist spots, especially ones frequented by backpackers.

To locate free Wi-Fi hotspots, it's try using the hotspot locator at **www.hotspot-locations.com**. It's worth asking the local tourist office, too. They will likely be able to point you toward local providers where you can surf for free, or for the price of a cup of coffee at most. Many **long-distance trains,** especially on high-speed networks, have onboard Wi-Fi.

### Medical Requirements

Unless you're arriving from an area known to be suffering from an epidemic (particularly cholera or yellow fever), inoculations or vaccinations are not required for entry into Europe.

### Mobile Phones

The three letters that define much of the world's wireless

capabilities are **GSM** (Global System for Mobiles), a satellite network that makes for easy cross-border mobile phone use throughout most of the planet, including all of Europe. Check with your home-based provider to see what it will cost you to use your phone and access data from overseas; many companies will let you purchase an **international calling/data plan** for 1 month (or longer, depending on your length of stay), then cancel it when you return home.

Another alternative if you own an unlocked GSM phone: buy a contract-free **SIM-only tariff** when you arrive. The SIM card will cost very little, but you will need to load it up with credit to make calls. A few familiar names (Vodafone, T-Mobile, and Orange among them) have local network operators in a number of European countries; some operators appear in just one. Tariffs change constantly in response to the market and by country. There are phone and SIM card retailers on practically every high-street in every country, and pretty much whichever operator you go with, you will make substantial savings over roaming with your home SIM.

There are other options if you're visiting from overseas but don't own an unlocked GSM phone. For a short visit, **renting** a phone may be a good idea, and we suggest renting the handset before you leave home. North Americans can rent from **InTouch USA** (www.intouchusa.us; ✆ **800/872-7626** or 703/222-7161) or **iRoam** (www.iroam.com; ✆ **888/454-7626**). However, handset prices have fallen to a level where you can often buy a basic local **pay-as-you-go (PAYG) phone** for less than 1 week's handset rental. Prices at many European cellphone retailers start from under US$50 for a cheap model, and you can often find an entry-level Android smartphone for around US$100. Buy one, use it while you're here, and recycle it on the way home. Unfortunately, per-minute charges for international calls to your home country can be high, so if you plan to do a lot of calling home, use a VoIP service such as **Skype** (www.skype.com) in conjunction with a Web connection. See "Internet & Wi-Fi," above.

## Money & Costs

Frommer's lists exact prices in the local currency. Exchange rates can fluctuate wildly in the space of just a few weeks, so before departing consult a currency exchange website such as **www.xe.com** to check up-to-the-minute rates.

When it comes to obtaining foreign currency, please, **skip the currency exchange kiosks** in airports, train stations, and elsewhere. They give the poorest rates and charge exorbitant fees. Instead, order a small amount of foreign currency from your bank before leaving home, and then figure on using your debit card for the duration of your trip. ATMs will give you a favorable rate, and you can withdraw however much cash you need for a day or so, as opposed to carrying around wads of money.

**ATMs** are everywhere in Europe—depending on the country, you'll find them at banks, city squares, some fuel stations, highway rest stops, supermarkets, post offices, or all of the above. The **Cirrus** (www.mastercard.com) and **PLUS** (www.visa.com) networks span the globe; look at the back of your bank card to see which network you're on, and then check online for ATM locations at your destination if you want to be ultra-organized. Be sure you know your personal identification number (PIN) and daily withdrawal limit before you depart. Confirm with your bank that your PIN will work in Europe, and be sure to let them know the dates and destinations to which you're traveling—you don't want to find your card frozen while you're abroad! Credit cards are accepted just about everywhere, exept street markets, small independent retailers, street-food vendors, and occasional small or family-owned businesses. However, North American visitors should note that American Express is accepted far less widely than at home, and Diners Club Card only at the very highest of highflying establishments. To be sure of your credit line, bring a Visa or MasterCard as well.

Most retailers ask for your 4-digit PIN to be entered into a keypad near the cash register. In restaurants, a server might bring a hand-held device to your table to authorize payment. If you're visiting from a country where Chip and PIN is less prevalent (such as the U.S.), it's possible that some retailers will be reluctant to accept your swipe cards. Be prepared to argue your case: Swipe cards are still valid, and the same machines that read the smartcard chips can also read your magnetic strip. However, do carry some cash with you too, just in case.

## Passports & Visas

To travel throughout Europe, all U.S. and British citizens, Canadians, Australians, and New Zealanders must have a passport valid through their length of stay. No visa is required. The immigration officer may also want to see proof of your intention to return to your point of origin (usually a round-trip ticket) and of visible means of support while you're in Europe. If you're planning to fly from the United States or Canada to Europe and then on to a country that requires a visa (India, for example), you should secure that visa before you depart.

## Taxes

All European countries charge a **value-added tax (VAT)** of between 8% and 25% on goods and services, with most hovering on the high side of 20%. Unlike a U.S. sales tax, it is already included in any store price you see quoted. Rates vary from country to country (as does the name—it's called IVA in Italy and Spain, TVA in France, and so on), though in E.U. countries the minimum rate is 15% for most goods. Usually, some items in each country (books, food, and children's clothes in the U.K., for example) are exempt.

Citizens of non-E.U. countries can, as they leave the country, get back most of the tax on purchases (not services) if they spend above a designated amount (usually around $250) in a single store. Regulations vary from country to country, so inquire at the tourist office when you arrive to find out the procedure; ask what percentage of the tax is refunded, and whether the refund is given to you at the airport or mailed to you later. Look for a **tax free shopping for tourists** sign posted in participating stores. Always ask the storekeeper for the necessary forms, and keep the purchases in their original packages if you want them to be valid for a VAT refund. Save your receipts and VAT forms from each E.U. country to process all of them at your final exit point from the E.U. (allow an extra 30 min. or so at an airport to process forms).

To avoid VAT refund hassles, when leaving an E.U. country for the last leg of your trip, take your goods, receipts, and passport to have the form stamped by Customs. Then take all your documentation to the VAT Refund counter you'll find at hundreds of airports and border crossings. Your money is refunded on the spot. For more information, contact **Global Blue** (www.global-blue.com).

## Time

England and Scotland are 5 hours ahead of New York City (U.S. Eastern Standard Time). The rest of the countries in this book observe CET (Central European Time), and are 6 hours ahead of New York. For instance, when it's noon in New York, it's 5pm in London and Edinburgh; and 6pm in Paris, Copenhagen, and Rome. London is 10 hours behind Sydney; Paris and other CET cities are 9 hours behind. European countries all observe daylight saving time, but the time change doesn't usually occur on the same day as in North America or the Southern Hemisphere countries. There's plenty of extra guidance at **www.timeanddate.com**.

## Tipping

The cultural ins-and-outs of tipping vary widely across Europe. And indeed, the whole concept of tipping isn't without controversy: Some Europeans, for example, resent a "tipping culture being imported" from North America and elsewhere—the practice, where it exists, is nowhere near as ingrained as it is in the U.S.

There are, however, a few instances when a tip is appreciated, no matter where you are. In grand hotels, tip **bellhops** around 1€ per bag and tip the **chamber staff,** too, if you like—though it's not expected in most establishments. In family-run hotels, it's not always considered polite to leave anything at all. Tip the **doorman** or **concierge** of a grand hotel only if he or she has provided you with some specific service (for example, obtaining difficult-to-get theater tickets). If you come across **valet-parking,** tip the attendant 1€ when your car arrives.

In restaurants, tip **service staff** 10% of the check if you feel the service has warranted it, though again this is by no means standard practice among locals in most European countries. Be sure to check if a **service charge** has already been applied; if it has, there's no need to leave more. **Bar staff** expect nothing, unless you're in a very high-toned nightspot, when you should round up and add a euro or two. **Cab drivers** may expect a euro or two on top of the fare, especially if they have helped with your luggage—though luggage fees often apply anyway, so don't feel obliged. **Hairdressers** and **barbers** also appreciate an extra euro or so for a job well done.

VAT See "Taxes," earlier in this section.

Wi-Fi See "Internet & Wi-Fi," earlier in this section.

# Index

See also Accommodations index, below.

## C

## G

## H

## L

## M

## N



## O

## S

## T

## U



## V

## W



## X



## Y



## Z

## Accommodations

# PHOTO CREDITS



Front cover: Thorsten Frisch

Aksenya / Shutterstock.com: p. 675. alarico / Shutterstock.com: p. 348. Alessandro Colle: p. 547. Alex Guerrero: p. 751. Alexander Chaikin: p. 564. Alexander Demyanenko: p. 164. Allie_Caulfield: p. 454, p. 568. Alterna2 http://www.alterna2.com: p. 750. Alxcrs / Shutterstock.com: p. 253. andersphoto / Shutterstock.com: p. 401. Andrey Bayda / Shutterstock.com: p. 746. Andrjuss: p. 206. Anibal Trejo / Shutterstock.com: p. 530. Anilah: p. 641. anshar / Shutterstock.com: p. 144, p. 615. Anton_Ivanov / Shutterstock.com: p. 370, p. 785. Antonio: p. 835. anyaivanova: p. 459. artjazz: p. 320. Artur Bogacki: p. 819. astudio / Shutterstock.com: p. 782. beboy: p. 107, p. 113. Benjamin: p. 434. benjgibbs: p. 309. b-hide the scene: p. 587. Bikeworldtravel / Shutterstock.com: p. 73, p. 839. Bill Perry: p. 679, top. Bokic Bojan / Shutterstock.com: p. 71. Boris Stroujko: p. 329, p. 389, p. 602. Boris-B / Shutterstock.com: p. 588, p. 576. Botond Horvath: p. 239. Brendan Howard / Shutterstock.com: p. 83, bottom, p. 84. Brian Kinney: p. 133, p. 753. Bucchi Francesco: p. 334, back cover. Caminoel / Shutterstock.com: p. 710. canadastock / Shutterstock.com: p. iii, p. 486, p. 509, p. 531, p. 535, p. 630, p. 509. Carles Fortuny / Shutterstock.com: p. 37. Catarina Belova: p. 668, p. 701. catedoty: p. 142. Chalermchai Chamnanyon: p. 376. ChameleonsEye / Shutterstock.com: p. 643. Christine McIntosh: p. 522. Courtesy of Landesmuseum Zürich: p. 559. cyclonebill: p. 359. D.Bond: p. 435. Dan Breckwoldt / Shutterstock.com: p. 24. DAVID HOLT: p. 53. degreezero2000: p. 757. Denise Chan: p. 145. Dennis Jarvis: p. 228. Dmitry Brizhatyuk / Shutterstock.com: p. 120. DOPhoto: p. 1. eFesenko / Shutterstock.com: p. 217. Elena Shchipkova / Shutterstock.com: p. 236, p. 824, p. 826. Emanuele: p. 289. Emi Cristea / Shutterstock.com: p. 224, p. 244, p. 245, p. 254, p. 269. Erik Wilde: p. 515. Ethan Prater: p. 558. Evikka: p. 342. ezpic: p. 716. FloridaStock: p. 197. Gary Bembridge: p. 49. George Grinsted: p. 700. gevision: p. 326. grafalex: p. 660. graphia / Shutterstock.com: p. 496. Grzegorz_Pakula: p. 408. Gurgen Bakhshetsyan: p. 173. gurmit singh: p. 749. hanmon / Shutterstock.com: p. 620. hans engbers / Shutterstock.com: p. 283. HLPhoto: p. 765. Ihor Pasternak: p. 528. Ilona Ignatova: p. 127. In Green / Shutterstock.com: p. 585. IR Stone / Shutterstock.com: p. 40. ISchmidt: p. 152. Ivica Drusany / Shutterstock.com: p. 292. J B: p. 758. jan kranendonk: p. 271. javarman: p. 808. jay8085: p. 611. Jeremy Thompson: p. 791. Jessica Spengler: p. 422. Jim Linwood: p. 70. Jitchanamont: p. 251. JoffreyM / Shutterstock.com: p. 85. John W. Schulze: p. 498. Jon Parise: p. 381. Jordan Tan / Shutterstock.com: p. 322. jorisvo / Shutterstock.com: p. 449. Justin Black: p. 46. Kalin Eftimov: p. 375. Kamira / Shutterstock.com: p. 28. kan_khampanya / Shutterstock.com: p. 117. Katherine Price: p. 747. Kemal Taner / Shutterstock.com: p. 104. Kiev.Victor / Shutterstock.com: p. 261, p. 288, p. 327. Konstantin Yolshin: p. 155. kuhnmi: p. 574. Laborant / Shutterstock.com: p. 190, p. 729. lapas77: p. 719. leoks: p. 7. leoks: p. 802. Leonid Andronov: p. 432, top. lexan / Shutterstock.com: p. 402. Lilu2005: p. 345. Lipskiy / Shutterstock.com: p. 505. Lisa-Lisa / Shutterstock.com: p. 300. lornet / Shutterstock.com: p. 690, p. 738, p. 754. Luciano Mortula / Shutterstock.com: p. 752. Luftphilia: p. 432, bottom. lumen-digital: p. 411. Lynn F: p. 371. MaRap: p. 220. Marcin Wichary: p. 608. Mariia Golovianko / Shutterstock.com: p. 533, bottom. Marina99: p. 748. Marques / Shutterstock.com: p. 809. Martin Good / Shutterstock.com: p. 584. Matthew Hine: p. 798. matthi / Shutterstock.com: p. 75. Matyas Rehak: p. 562. Mediagram / Shutterstock.com: p. 298. meunierd / Shutterstock.com: p. 457. Michael Button: p. 355. Mihai-Bogdan Lazar / Shutterstock.com: p. 273. mihaiulia: p. 324. Mikadun: p. 705. Mirelle: p. 717. mkos83 / Shutterstock.com: p. 47. Nadezhda1906: p. 352. Nataliya Hora / Shutterstock.com: p. 101. Neirfy / Shutterstock.com: p. 282. Nessluop / Shutterstock.com: p. 290. Nikita Gusakov: p. 33. Nikolay Dimitrov - ecobo: p. 168. nito / Shutterstock.com: p. 129, p. 830. np: p. 461. Oleg Znamenskiy: p. 161. Oleksiy Mark: p. 363, p. 367. Olgysha: p. 605. Olivier Bruchez: p. 811. Olliesammons: p. 679, bottom. Pascal Subtil: p. 232. pashamba: p. 804. Paul Arps: p. 313. paul prescott: p. 407, bottom. Pavel L Photo and Video/ Shutterstock: p. 452, p. 735. pcruciatti / Shutterstock.com: p. 12, p. 69. Pe3k / Shutterstock.com: p. 297. Pedro Rufo / Shutterstock.com: p. 654. Peter Fuchs / Shutterstock.com: p. 252. Phant: p. 652. Philip Bird LRPS CPAGB / Shutterstock.com: p. 460. Philip Pilosian / Shutterstock.com: p. 581. photo.ua / Shutterstock.com: p. 150, p. 500. photogearch: p. 555. photogolfer / Shutterstock.com: p. 246. pinggr: p. 618. pio3 / Shutterstock.com: p. 130. pio3 / Shutterstock.com: p. 407, top. pisaphotography / Shutterstock.com: p. 403. Pocholo Calapre: p. 787. posztos / Shutterstock.com: p. 122. r.nagy: p. 29, p. 35. Renata Sedmakova /

Shutterstock.com: p. 248. Richard, enjoy my life!: p. 686. Rrrainbow / Shutterstock.com: p. 143. rubiphoto / Shutterstock.com: p. 780. Rudy Balasko: p. 471. S.Borisov: p. 278, p. 397, p. 477, p. 550. Samo Trebizan: p. 708. Samot: p. 118. SandiMako / Shutterstock.com: p. 817. SASIMOTO / Shutterstock.com: p. 517. Sean Pavone / Shutterstock.com: p. 346, p. 347, p. 351, p. 393, p. 445, p. 773. Sergio Gutierrez Getino: p. 221. S-F / Shutterstock.com: p. 343, p. 344, p. 640. Shebeko: p. 419. Simon: p. 603. skyfish / Shutterstock.com: p. 213. snig: p. 83, top. StevanZZ: p. 82. Steve Allen: p. 180. Steve Cadman: p. 20. Stocksnapper / Shutterstock.com: p. 374. Stuart Monk: p. 9. T photography / Shutterstock.com: p. 685. Thomas La Mela / Shutterstock.com: p. 218. Tiberiu Stan: p. 474. Tobik: p. 684. Ttatty / Shutterstock.com: p. 38. TTstudio: p. 508, p. 560, p. 633. Tupungato / Shutterstock.com: p. 499. Valeri Potapova: p. 756. VanderWolf Images / Shutterstock.com: p. 265. Veniamin Kraskov / Shutterstock.com: p. 183. Ventura / Shutterstock.com: p. 703. Viacheslav Lopatin / Shutterstock.com: p. 5, p. 647, p. 656. vichie81: p. 44. Vladimir Wrangel / Shutterstock.com: p. 406. volkova natalia / Shutterstock.com: p. 692. william casey: p. 712. Wittaya Leelachaisakul / Shutterstock.com: p. 533, top. WorldWide: p. 400. Yusuke Kawasaki: p. 571.
Back cover: Bucchi Francesco.